The Complete

BIBLICAL LIBRARY

THE OLD TESTAMENT STUDY BIBLE

PROVERBS
ECCLESIASTES
SONG OF SONGS

The Complete
BIBLICAL
LIBRARY

The Complete Biblical Library: The Old Testament. Volume 11: STUDY BIBLE, PROVERBS, ECCLESIASTES, SONG OF SONGS. Copyright © 1998 by World Library Press, Inc. Published by World Library Press Inc., Springfield, Missouri, U.S.A.

International Standard Book Number
1-884642-35-7—vol. 11
1-884642-49-7—Set

Library of Congress Cataloging in Publication Data
The Old Testament Study Bible.
   The Complete Biblical Library.
The Old Testament; volumes 1–15.
   Includes Bibliographic references.
Contents: [1] Genesis—[2] Exodus—[3] Leviticus, Numbers—[4] Deuteronomy—[5] Joshua, Judges, Ruth—[6] 1 & 2 Samuel—[7] 1 & 2 Kings—[8] 1 & 2 Chronicles—[9] Ezra, Nehemiah, Esther, Job—[10] Psalms—[11] Proverbs, Ecclesiastes, Song of Songs—[12] Isaiah—[13] Jeremiah, Lamentations—[14] Ezekiel, Daniel—[15] Hosea–Malachi
ISBN: 1-884642-35-7
1. Bible. O.T.—Study and Teaching.
I. Series: Complete Biblical Library (Series). Old Testament; 15 volumes
BS1193.05   1995
221.6'1—dc20   95-49455 CIP

THE NEW TESTAMENT
Study Bible, Greek-English Dictionary,
Harmony of the Gospels

THE OLD TESTAMENT
Study Bible, Hebrew-English Dictionary,
Harmony of the Historical Accounts

THE BIBLE ENCYCLOPEDIA

INTERNATIONAL EDITOR
THORALF GILBRANT

EXECUTIVE EDITOR
Gregory A. Lint, M.Div.

NATIONAL EDITORS

U.S.A.
Stanley M. Horton, Th.D.
Mark A. Phelps, M.T.S.

NORWAY
Erling Utnem, Bishop
Arthur Berg, B.D.

DENMARK
Jorgen Glenthoj, Th.M.

SWEDEN
Hugo Odeberg, Ph.D., D.D.
Bertil E. Gartner, D.D.
Thorsten Kjall, M.A.
Stig Wikstrom, D.Th.M.

FINLAND
Aapelii Saarisalo, Ph.D.
Valter Luoto, Pastor
Matti Liljequist, B.D.

HOLLAND
Herman ter Welle, Pastor
Henk Courtz, Drs.

INTERNATIONAL AND
INTERDENOMINATIONAL
BIBLE STUDY SYSTEM

THE OLD TESTAMENT STUDY BIBLE

PROVERBS
ECCLESIASTES
SONG OF SONGS

WORLD LIBRARY PRESS INC.
Springfield, Missouri, U.S.A.

VERSE-BY-VERSE COMMENTARY

Proverbs—Frederic Clarke Putnam, Ph.D.
Ecclesiastes—Charles Bridges, M.A.
Song of Songs—Gleason L. Archer, Jr., Ph.D.

VARIOUS VERSIONS

Kirk D. Sherman, A.A.
Todd C. Harder, B.A.
Rev. Paul D. Sherman
Lonnie B. Smith, M.S.

John E. Veazey, B.A.
Rev. Gary L. Sherman
Verna M. Sherman, A.S.
Robert D. Grant, M.S.

REVIEW BOARD

Gleason L. Archer, Jr., Ph.D.
Stanley M. Horton, Th.D.

Roger D. Cotton, Th.D.
W. E. Nunnally, Ph.D.

Samuel J. Schultz, Th.D.

ASSISTANT EDITOR

Brian D. Rogers, M.Div.

TECHNICAL ASSISTANCE

Editorial Team: Faye Faucett (editorial assistant); Jess L. Leeper, B.A., James E. Talkington, M.A., Dennis E. Waldrop, M.Div., James R. Wright, B.A. (Hebrew assistance); David D. Ayres, B.S., Pamela S. Behling, B.S., Tiffany Bowman-Rogers, B.S., Jill M. Canaday, B.A., LeAnn Carpenter, M.S., Craig M. Froman, M.A., Chuck J. Goldberg, M.Div., Rachel Hammar, B.A., Kathleen J. Johns, B.A., Scott A. Kirby, B.S., Kary G. McKinley, Wade W. Pettenger, B.S.

Computer Consultant: Martin D. Crossland, Ph.D.

Art Director: Terry Van Someren, B.F.A.

Table of Contents

Introduction

This volume of the *Old Testament Study Bible* is part of a set entitled *The Complete Biblical Library: Old Testament.* It is designed to provide the information needed for a basic understanding of the Old Testament—useful for scholars but also for students and laypeople.

The Complete Biblical Library: Old Testament series consists of a fifteen-volume *Study Bible* and a seven-volume *Hebrew-English Dictionary,* which are closely linked. Information about the *Study Bible's* features are found below. The *Hebrew-English Dictionary* (HED) lists all the Hebrew words of the Old Testament in alphabetical order, with an article explaining the background, significance and meaning of the words. The HED also provides a concordance showing each place the words appear in the Old Testament, a list of synonyms and related words, and many other features for a full understanding of each word.

FEATURES OF THE STUDY BIBLE

The *Study Bible* is a combination of study materials which will help both scholar and layperson achieve a better understanding of the Old Testament and its language. Most of these helps are available in various forms elsewhere, but bringing them together in combination will save many hours of research. Many scholars do not have in their personal libraries all the volumes necessary to provide the information so readily available here.

The Complete Biblical Library accomplishes an unusual task: to help scholars in their research and to make available to laypersons the tools to acquire knowledge which, up to this time, has been available only to scholars. Following are the major divisions of the *Study Bible:*

Overview

Each volume contains an encyclopedic survey of the Old Testament Book. It provides a general outline, discusses matters about which there may be a difference of opinion and provides background information regarding the history, cultures, literature and philosophy of the era covered by the Book.

Interlinear

Following the principle of providing help for both the scholar and layperson, a unique interlinear has been supplied. Most interlinears, if not all, give the Hebrew text and meanings of the words. This interlinear contains five parts:

1. *Hebrew Text.* This is the original language of the Old Testament as we have it today.

2. *Grammatical Forms.* These are shown above each Hebrew word, beneath its assigned number. Each word's part of speech is identified (constructs being italicized). This information is repeated, along with the Hebrew word, in the *Hebrew-English Dictionary* where more details may be found.

3. *Transliteration.* No other interlinears provide this. Its purpose is to familiarize laypersons with the proper pronunciation of Hebrew words so they will feel comfortable when using them in teaching situations. Information on pronunciation is found on page 10, which shows the Hebrew alphabet.

4. *Translation.* The basic meaning of each Hebrew word is found beneath it. Rather than merely compiling past interlinears, a fresh translation has been made.

5. *Assigned Numbers.* The unique numbering system of *The Complete Biblical Library* makes cross-reference study between the *Study Bible* and the *Hebrew-English Dictionary* the ultimate in simplicity. Each Hebrew word has been assigned a number.

The *Hebrew-English Dictionary* then follows the same cross-referencing plan with each word listed in alphabetical sequence and labeled with the proper number. If further study on a certain word is desired, information can be found by locating its number in the *Dictionary.*

Various Versions

The various versions section contains a vast comparison of the Old Testament versions. The King James Version is shown in boldface type; then from more than thirty other versions, various ways the Hebrew phrase may be translated can be found. The Hebrew language of ancient times is such a rich language that, to obtain the full meaning of words, several synonyms may be needed.

Verse-by-Verse Commentary

Many scholars have combined their knowledge and skills to provide a reliable commentary. Providing a basic understanding of every verse in the Old Testament, the commentary opens up the nuances of the Hebrew Old Testament.

HEBREW TRANSLATION

No word-for-word translation can be fully "literal" and still express all the nuances of the original language. Rather, the purpose is to help the reader find the English word which most correctly expresses the original Hebrew word in that particular context. The Hebrew language is so rich in meaning that the same word may have a slightly different meaning in another context.

Language idioms offer a special translation problem. Idioms are expressions that have a meaning which cannot be derived from the conjoined meanings of its elements. The Hebrew language abounds in such phrases which, when translated literally, provide insight, and even humor, to the English reader of the pictorial nature of Hebrew.

LITERARY AND BIBLICAL STANDARDS

Hundreds of qualified scholars and specialists in particular fields have participated in producing *The Complete Biblical Library*. Great care has been taken to maintain high standards of scholarship and ethics, involving scholars in Review Boards for the *Study Bible* and the *Hebrew-English Dictionary*. There has been particular concern about giving proper credit for citations from other works, and writers have been instructed to show care in this regard. Any deviation from this principle has been inadvertent and unintentional.

Obviously, with writers coming from widely differing backgrounds, there are differences of opinion as to how to interpret certain passages. But, the focus of *The Complete Biblical Library* is always from a conservative and evangelical standpoint, upholding Scripture as the inspired Word of God. When there are strong differences in the interpretations of a particular passage, we have felt it best to present the contrasting viewpoints.

STUDY HELPS

As you come to the Scripture section of this volume, you will find correlated pages for your study. The facing pages are designed to complement each other, so you will have a better understanding of the Word of God. Each two-page spread will deal with a group of verses.

First is the interlinear with its fivefold helps: (1) the Hebrew text in which the Old Testament was written; (2) the transliteration, showing how to pronounce each word; (3) the translation of each word; (4) an assigned number (you will need this number to learn more about the word in the *Hebrew-English Dictionary*, companion to the *Study Bible*); and (5) the grammatical form.

The second part of each two-page spread contains two features. The various versions section provides an expanded understanding of the various ways Hebrew words or phrases can be translated. The phrase from the King James Version appears in boldface print, then other meaningful ways the Hebrew language has been translated follow. This feature will bring you the riches of the language of the Old Testament.

The verse-by-verse commentary refers to each verse giving a sufficient basic explanation. Significant viewpoints are discussed in addition to the author's.

THE HEBREW ALPHABET

א	aleph	' (glottal stop)
ב	beth	b, v
ג	gimel	g, gh
ד	daleth	d, dh
ה	he	h
ו	waw	w, v
ז	zayin	z
ח	heth	ch
ט	teth	t̲ (hardened)
י	yodh	y
כ, ך, ך	kaph	k, kh
ל	lamedh	l
מ, ם	mem	m
נ, ן	nun	n
ס	samekh	s̲ (hardened)
ע	ayin	' (aspiration)
פ, ף	pe	p, ph
צ, ץ	tsade	ts
ק	qoph	q
ר	resh	r
שׂ	sin	s
שׁ	shin	sh
ת	taw	t, th

INTERLINEAR COMPONENTS

A & B: Number

The first line of each record of the interlinear is a numeral which refers to the *Hebrew-English Dictionary*. The numbers should be referenced *only* by the digits before the decimal. Most words have an ordinary numeral. Only the verbs have the extended system.

The digits after the decimal refer to the standard verb chart found in Hebrew grammars. The first digit after the decimal refers to the "mood" of the verb (simple, passive, causative, intensive, reflexive); the second refers to the "tense" (perfect, imperfect, jussive, imperative, infinitive or participle); the third refers to the person, gender and number (such as 3rd masculine singular).

C: Location or Grammar

The second line of the interlinear is the description of the grammatical construction of the Hebrew word. Describing a Hebrew word in this manner is called locating the word. You will notice there is often more than one word written as a single Hebrew word. This is because related words are often joined. A full listing of abbreviations and a brief explanation may be found at the end of the book.

D: Hebrew

This is the original language of the Old Testament as we have it today. The Hebrew text of the interlinear is a comparative text, provided by The Original Word Publishers of Roswell, Georgia.

E: Transliteration

This is the key to pronouncing the word. The transliteration matches that which is found in the Septuagint research of the *New Testament Greek-English Dictionary* of *The Complete Biblical Library*.

F: Translation

This is a fresh translation prepared by the executive editor and the commentary writer.

THE FIRST BOOK OF MOSES CALLED
GENESIS בְּרֵאשִׁית

A

1:1

904, 7519	1282.111	435	881	8452	881	800
prep, art, n fs	v Qal pf 3ms	n mp	do	art, n md	cj, do	art, n fs
בְּרֵאשִׁית	בָּרָא	אֱלֹהִים	אֵת	הַשָּׁמַיִם	וְאֵת	הָאָרֶץ
berē'shîth	bārā'	'ĕlōhîm	'ēth	hashshāmayim	weēth	hā'ārets
in the beginning	created	God		the heavens	and	the earth

B

2.

800	2030.112	8744	958	2932	6142, 6686
cj, art, n fs	v Qal pf 3fs	n ms	cj, n ms	cj, n ms	prep, n mp
וְהָאָרֶץ	הָיְתָה	תֹהוּ	וָבֹהוּ	וְחֹשֶׁךְ	עַל־פְּנֵי
wehā'ārets	hāyethāh	thōhû	wāvōhû	wechōshekh	'al-penê
and the earth	it was	formless	and empty	and darkness	over the surface of

8745	7593	435	7646.353	6142, 6686	4448
n fs	cj, n fs	n mp	v Piel ptc fs	prep, n mp	art, n md
תְהוֹם	וְרוּחַ	אֱלֹהִים	מְרַחֶפֶת	עַל־פְּנֵי	הַמָּיִם
thehôm	werûach	'ĕlōhîm	merachepheth	'al-penê	hammāyim
the deep	and the Spirit of	God	hovering	over the surface of	the waters

C

3. / **4.**

569.121	435	2030.121	214	2030.121, 214	7495.121
cj, v Qal impf 3ms	n mp	v Qal juss 3ms	n ms	cj, v Qal impf 3ms, n ms	cj, v Qal impf 3ms
וַיֹּאמֶר	אֱלֹהִים	יְהִי	אוֹר	וַיְהִי־אוֹר	וַיַּרְא
wayyō'mer	'ĕlōhîm	yehî	'ôr	wayhî-'ôr	wayyare'
and He said	God	let there be	light	and there was light	and He saw

435	881, 214	3706, 3005	950.521	435	1033	214
n mp	do, art, n ms	prep, adj	cj, v Hiphil impf 3ms	n mp	prep	art, n ms
אֱלֹהִים	אֶת־הָאוֹר	כִּי־טוֹב	וַיַּבְדֵּל	אֱלֹהִים	בֵּין	הָאוֹר
'ĕlōhîm	'eth-hā'ôr	kî-ṭôv	wayyavdēl	'ĕlōhîm	bên	hā'ôr
God	the light	that good	and He separated	God	between	the light

D

5.

1033	2932	7410.121	435	3937, 214	3219	3937, 2932
cj, prep	art, n ms	cj, v Qal impf 3ms	n mp	prep, art, n ms	n ms	cj, prep, art, n ms
וּבֵין	הַחֹשֶׁךְ	וַיִּקְרָא	אֱלֹהִים	לָאוֹר	יוֹם	וְלַחֹשֶׁךְ
ûvên	hachōshekh	wayyiqrā'	'ĕlōhîm	lā'ôr	yôm	welachōshekh
and between	the darkness	and He named	God	the light	day	and the darkness

E

7410.111	4050	2030.121, 6394	2030.121, 1269	3219	259
v Qal pf 3ms	n ms	cj, v Qal impf 3ms, n ms	cj, v Qal impf 3ms, n ms	n ms	num
קָרָא	לָיְלָה	וַיְהִי־עֶרֶב	וַיְהִי־בֹקֶר	יוֹם	אֶחָד
qārā'	lāyelāh	wayhî-'erev	wayhî-vōqer	yôm	'echādh
He named	night	and it was evening	and it was morning	day	one

6.

569.121	435	2030.121	7842	904, 8761	4448
cj, v Qal impf 3ms	n mp	v Qal juss 3ms	n ms	prep, n ms	art, n md
וַיֹּאמֶר	אֱלֹהִים	יְהִי	רָקִיעַ	בְּתוֹךְ	הַמָּיִם
wayyō'mer	'ĕlōhîm	yehî	rāqîa'	bethôkh	hammāyim
and He said	God	let there be	expanse	in the middle of	the waters

F

7.

2030.121	950.551	1033	4448	3937, 4448	6449.121
cj, v Qal juss 3ms	v Hiphil ptc ms	prep	n md	prep, art, n md	cj, v Qal impf 3ms
וִיהִי	מַבְדִּיל	בֵּין	מַיִם	לָמָּיִם	וַיַּעַשׂ
wîhî	mavdîl	bên	mayim	lāmmāyim	wayya'as
and let it be	what separates	between	waters	from the waters	and He made

THE BOOK OF

PROVERBS

Expanded Interlinear
Various Versions
Verse-by-Verse Commentary

THE BOOK OF
PROVERBS מִשְׁלֵי

1:1 5091 n mp מִשְׁלֵי mishlê the proverbs of	8406 pn שְׁלֹמֹה shelōmōh Solomon	1158, 1784 n ms, pn בֶּן־דָּוִד ven-dāwidh the son of David	4567 n ms מֶלֶךְ melekh the king of	3547 pn יִשְׂרָאֵל yisrā'ēl Israel	**2.** 3937, 3156.141 prep, v Qal inf con לָדַעַת lādha'ath for knowing
2551 n fs חָכְמָה chokhmāh wisdom	4284 cj, n ms וּמוּסָר ûmûsār and discipline	1032.541 prep, v Hiphil inf con לְהָבִין lehāvîn for discerning	571 n mp אִמְרֵי 'imrê sayings of	1035 n fs **3.** בִּינָה vînāh insight	4089.141 prep, v Qal inf con לָקַחַת lāqachath for getting	4284 n ms מוּסַר mûsar the discipline of
7959.542 v Hiphil inf abs הַשְׂכֵּל haskēl understanding	6928 n ms צֶדֶק tsedheq righteousness	5122 cj, n ms וּמִשְׁפָּט ûmishpāt and justice	4478 cj, n mp **4.** וּמֵישָׁרִים ûmêshārîm and equity	3937, 5598.141 prep, v Qal inf con לָתֵת lātheth for giving	3937, 6848 prep, n mp לִפְתָאיִם liphthā'yim to the simple	6430 n fs עָרְמָה 'āremāh shrewdness
3937, 5470 prep, n ms לְנַעַר lena'ar to the young man	1907 n fs דַּעַת da'ath knowledge	4343 cj, n fs וּמְזִמָּה ûmezimmāh and prudence	**5.** 8471.121 v Qal juss 3ms יִשְׁמַע yishma' let him hear	2550 n ms חָכָם chākhām the wise man	3362.521 cj, v Hiphil juss 3ms וְיוֹסֶף weyôseph and let him add
4090 n ms לֶקַח leqach teaching	1032.255 cj, v Niphal ptc ms וְנָבוֹן wenāvôn and the discerning one	8790 n fp תַּחְבֻּלוֹת tachbulôth guidance	7353.121 v Qal juss 3ms יִקְנֶה yiqneh let him acquire	**6.** 1032.541 prep, v Hiphil inf con לְהָבִין lehāvîn for discerning	5091 n ms מָשָׁל māshāl a proverb

1:1. The proverbs of Solomon the son of David, king of Israel: … wise sayings, *Anchor* … Parables of Salomon, *Geneva* … Maxims of Solomon, *Moffatt*.

2. To know wisdom and instruction; to perceive the words of understanding: … education in wisdom and moral discipline, *Anchor* … discern the words, *ASV* … to be clear about the words of reason, *BB* … understand words of intelligence, *Goodspeed* … true wisdom, and self-command, *Knox* … comprehend the words, *MAST*.

3. To receive the instruction: … training in discernment, *Anchor* … instruction of prudence, *Berkeley*.

of wisdom, justice, and judgment, and equity: … right, justice, and uprightness, *Berkeley* … duty, goodness, and integrity, *Moffatt* … the lesson of insight, the dictates of duty and right and honour, *Knox* … instruction, skill, righteousness, justice, and rectitude, *Fenton*.

4. To give subtlety to the simple, to the young man knowledge and discretion: … prudence to the simple, *ASV* … make the uneducated smarter, *NCV* … sharpen the wits of the ignorant, *Anchor* … resourcefulness may be imparted, *NAB* … and serious purpose, *BB*.

5. A wise man will hear, and will increase learning: … the scholar too may give heed, *Anchor* … The

Philosopher can listen, and add to his acquisitions, *Fenton*.

and a man of understanding shall attain unto wise counsels: … will attain to leadership, *Berkeley* … acquire sound principles, *Goodspeed* … an intelligent man will gain sound guidance, *Douay*.

6. To understand a proverb, and the interpretation: … perceiving the meaning of proverbs and obscure sayings, *JB* … a proverb and an allegory, *Darby* … comprehension of proverb and metaphor, *Anchor*.

the words of the wise, and their dark sayings: … teachings of wise men and difficult sayings, *Beck* … and their epigrams, *Goodspeed* …

The title of the entire Book is contained in the first verse, but it was originally the title of the first Solomonic collection (Prov. 1–24). It identifies Solomon as the source of the proverbs contained in this collection. His unequaled wisdom was a direct gift from God himself, given in response to Solomon's prayer (1 Ki. 3:9–14) when, as a relatively young man (2 Sam. 5:4f; cf. 12:24), he became king over Israel in place of David his father (1 Ki. 1:38ff; 2:12).

1:1. David reigned in Jerusalem for thirty-three years (2 Sam. 5:5; 1 Ki. 2:11), and Solomon became king shortly before David died (1 Ki. 1:32–40). Solomon, the son of Bathsheba (2 Sam. 12:24), could not therefore have been more than about thirty years old when he became king—young, indeed, to rule over an empire.

God demonstrated his gift of wisdom to Solomon in two incidents involving women. The apparently insoluble case of the two mothers (1 Ki. 3:16–27) demonstrated his concern to establish justice and righteousness in the land, as well as his ability to judge wisely. It also confirmed what God had said to Solomon, that he would be wise so that he might discern good from evil, and so judge equitably (1 Ki. 3:11f). The nation's response to his decision was to fear the king, recognizing that the "wisdom of God was in him" (1 Ki. 3:28).

The second demonstration of his wisdom was the visit of the queen of Sheba, who "came to test him with difficult questions" (1 Ki. 10:1–10), and who also recognized his ability as a gift from the LORD his God (1 Ki. 10:9).

Between these instances are his wise sayings and songs (1 Ki. 4:32f), and his work to build the Temple (1 Ki. 6–8), both of which demonstrated his ability and wisdom. The narrator concluded that God had carried out his promise to make Solomon wise beyond Solomon's hopes (1 Ki. 4:29ff; cf. 3:11f; 10:23ff).

1:2–6. Introducing the Book of Proverbs is this poem, which outlines why Solomon authored it. These purposes are twofold. The Book will give the young and naive the benefit of Solomon's wisdom and the experience of their elders (v. 4), so that they learn how to live lives which are pleasing to God (vv. 2a, 3ff). It will also give those who study its maxims greater understanding and insight (vv. 2b, 6). This will foster greater ability to understand the proverbs and to discern the true nature of the choices they face, so that they can make right decisions.

This dual purpose (intellectual and moral) is discernible in nearly every verse of the Book.

1:2. Verse 2 summarizes the poem by mentioning both purposes: knowledge and discernment. Wisdom, one of the main themes of Proverbs, is the ability to understand a situation so as to know how to respond in a way that pleases God. Discipline, then, is the internal strength to act on that understanding.

Discernment is an aspect of wisdom—the ability to see to the heart of something or to understand its true nature. Thus, many proverbs contrast two things so that we can better understand the real, or underlying, issue (18:9, for example, says that laziness is destructive, not merely a lack of productivity).

1:3. The proverbs themselves are teachers, pointing their students (those who study them) to whatever is righteous, just and honest (or upright). In other words, the wisdom of v. 2 is not merely cleverness or the ability to understand something. Biblical wisdom yields fruit in the wise, because it transforms their lives so that they live according to the standards of God himself. As king, Solomon was responsible to see that justice was upheld by rulers who were righteous and honest; these were special concerns of every ancient Near Eastern monarch (as the claims of the Assyrian and Babylonian kings demonstrate).

1:4. Verses 2f look at the benefits of studying Proverbs from the standpoint of the student ("to know," "to discern," "to receive"). Verse 3, however, describes those benefits from the standpoint of the proverbs themselves: they will give young and naive students of Proverbs knowledge so that they become increasingly astute and discreet. Unlike the fool, for whom Proverbs offers little hope, the naive are gullible, and do not understand situations because they have not had enough experience. One reason for studying history and literature is to learn from the experiences of others. According to this verse, studying Proverbs has the same benefit. Passages such as 7:6–27 are clearly written with this end in view, but every proverb sets forth a situation, comparison or command based on someone's experience, often compressing many experiences into a few words. These pithy sayings, designed to stick in the heart of the naive, will come back to their minds as they face situations. Thus, if they obey what they know, even if they do not yet understand, they will act wisely.

1:5. Growth in wisdom and understanding is not limited to the young and naive. Whoever is wise will read this Book and accept its counsel. When the

4565	1745	2550	2512	7. 3488	3176
cj, n fs	*n mp*	n mp	cj, n fp, ps 3mp	*n fs*	pn
וּמְלִיצָה	דִּבְרֵי	חֲכָמִים	וְחִידֹתָם	יִרְאַת	יְהוָה
ûmelîtsāh	divrê	chăkhāmîm	wechîdhōthām	yir'ath	yehwāh
and an allegory	the words of	the wise	and their difficult sayings	the fear of	Yahweh

7519	1907	2551	4284	188	995.116	8. 8471.131
n fs	n fs	n fs	cj, n ms	n mp	v Qal pf 3cp	v Qal impv 2ms
רֵאשִׁית	דָּעַת	חָכְמָה	וּמוּסָר	אֱוִילִים	בָּזוּ	שְׁמַע
rē'shîth	dā'ath	chokhmāh	ûmûsār	'ěwîlîm	bāzû	shema'
the beginning of	knowledge	wisdom	and discipline	fools	they despise	listen to

1158	4284	1	414, 5389.123	8784	525
n ms, ps 1cs	*n ms*	n ms, ps 2ms	cj, adv, v Qal juss 2ms	*n fs*	n fs, ps 2ms
בְּנִי	מוּסַר	אָבִיךָ	וְאַל־תִּטֹּשׁ	תּוֹרַת	אִמֶּךָ
benî	mûsar	'āvîkhā	we'al-tittōsh	tôrath	'immekhā
O my son	the discipline of	your father	and do not disregard	the instruction of	your mother

9. 3706	4017	2682	2062	3937, 7513	6291	3937, 1664
cj	*n fs*	n ms	pers pron	prep, n ms, ps 2ms	cj, n mp	prep, n fp, ps 2ms
כִּי	לִוְיַת	חֵן	הֵם	לְרֹאשֶׁךָ	וַעֲנָקִים	לְגַרְגְּרֹתֶיךָ
kî	liwyath	chēn	hēm	lerō'shekhā	wa'ănāqîm	legharg erōthêkhā
because	a garland of	favor	they	for your head	and necklaces	for your neck

10. 1158	524, 6853.326	2492	414, 13.123	11. 524, 569.126
n ms, ps 1cs	cj, v Piel impf 3mp, ps 2ms	n mp	adv, v Qal juss 2ms	cj, v Qal impf 3mp
בְּנִי	אִם־יְפַתּוּךָ	חַטָּאִים	אַל־תֹּבֵא	אִם־יֹאמְרוּ
benî	'im-yephattûkhā	chattā'îm	'al-tōvē'	'im-yō'merû
O my son	if they try to persuade you	sinners	do not be willing	if they say

2050.131	882	717.120	3937, 1879	7121.120	3937, 5538
v Qal impv 2ms	prep, ps 1cp	v Qal juss 1cp	prep, n ms	v Qal juss 1cp	prep, n ms
לְכָה	אִתָּנוּ	נֶאֶרְבָה	לְדָם	נִצְפְּנָה	לְנָקִי
lekhāh	'ittānû	ne'ervāh	ledhām	nitspenāh	lenāqî
go	with us	let us lie in wait	for blood	let us conceal ourselves	for the innocent

2703	12. 1142.120	3626, 8061	2522	8879
adv	v Qal juss 1cp, ps 3mp	prep, n fs	adj	cj, n mp
חִנָּם	נִבְלָעֵם	כִּשְׁאוֹל	חַיִּים	וּתְמִימִים
chinnām	nivlā'ēm	kish'ôl	chayyîm	ûthemîmîm
without cause	let us swallow them	like Sheol	alive	and the blameless

their enigmas, *Berkeley* ... and their riddles, *Anchor.*

7. The fear of the LORD is the beginning of knowledge: ... Respect for the Lord is the first-fruit of Wisdom, *Fenton* ... reverence of Yahweh, *Rotherham* ... Reverence of the LORD, *Berkeley.*

but fools despise wisdom and instruction: ... only fools despise correction, *Fenton* ... wisdom and training, *Beck* ... hate wisdom and self-control, *NCV.*

8. My son, hear the instruction of thy father: ... Heed well, my son, thy father's warnings, *Knox* ... the training of your father, *BB* ... listen to your father's criticism, *Beck.*

and forsake not the law of thy mother: ... reject not your mother's directions, *Moffatt* ... do not forget your mother's advice, *NCV* ... teaching of, *MAST.*

9. For they shall be an ornament of grace unto thy head: ... chaplet of grace, *ASV* ... a crown of grace, *BB* ... fair garland, *Berkeley* ... they are a graceful wreath, *NASB.*

and chains about thy neck: ... ornamental necklace, *Anchor* ... adornments, *Berkeley* ... pendants for your neck, *NRSV.*

10. My son, if sinners entice thee, consent thou not: ... vicious men, *Anchor* ... sinners try to seduce you, *JB* ... take you out of the right way, *BB* ... if scoundrels would lead you astray, never agree to it, *Moffatt.*

11. If they say, Come with us, let us lay wait for blood: ... make designs against the good, *BB* ... trap honest folk, *Moffatt.*

let us lurk privily for the innocent without cause: ... for sport waylay

some innocent!, *Anchor* ... lurk for the careless and fools, *Fenton* ... we'll hide to get the innocent just for fun, *Beck.*

12. Let us swallow them up alive as the grave; and whole, as those that

go down into the pit: ... fortunes to be swallowed up, *Knox* ... like Sheol, *Anchor* ... like the dead-realm, *Berkeley* ... overcome them living, like the underworld, and in their strength, as those who go down to death, *BB.*

---

wise do so, they will strengthen their ability to understand and use proverbs and find that they have gained counselors (the individual proverbs) who will guide their decisions. Wisdom is therefore not static. We do not become wise and then remain wise. This verse implies that if we do not continually exercise our minds by studying the proverbs, so that we increase our learning, we will lose whatever wisdom we may possess (cf. 19:27).

1:6. Not all proverbs are created equal. Some are fairly easy to understand (10:1); others are more difficult (18:1); and some are intentionally enigmatic (30:18f). Even to understand a proverb's meaning is not necessarily to know all of its implications. Solomon here encourages students to persevere in studying, since he wrote this Book so they would grow in their ability to understand even proverbs that are dark sayings and riddles.

1:7. Often called the "theme" of Proverbs, this verse contains both warning and promise. It warns against approaching or using this Book with an improper attitude. The "fear of the LORD" is not terror, but an attitude of obedience, as the contrast with "despise wisdom and discipline" in the second line shows. Fools despise wisdom and discipline (cf. v. 2a), preferring to go their own way (cf. 15:33; 29:1). This attitude underlies the warning that although "a man's ways are right in his own eyes," he may cause his own destruction (cf. 16:2, 25). In order to benefit from this Book as God intends, it must be approached with the conviction that it will be obeyed (cf. commentary on 3:5f).

1:8–9. The first of many times that a "son" is commanded to heed his parents' counsel, this verse contrasts paying attention to instruction with abandoning it. Its second half is identical to 6:20b, which makes virtually the same contrast ("watch" or "keep" for "listen"), again at the beginning of a poem. Contrasting two aspects of a situation in order to make a point is a frequent form of parallelism. The contrast here lies between heeding his parents' advice and abandoning it by listening to the counsel of wicked companions (1:11–14), which reflects another

main theme of Proverbs—the "two ways." To obey halfheartedly is to disobey, since it usually means that we will be following some other authority.

Solomon rarely states a command without adding a reason for obeying it, the motive clause (cf. 3:1–10). The motivation given in v. 9 is that the benefits of obeying instructors are better than the rewards offered by bad companions. Obedience adorns the obedient so that they receive a crown and necklace, precious ornaments that portray wisdom's rewards (cf. Judg. 8:25f). Throughout Prov. 1–9, Solomon portrays wisdom's benefits tangibly in order to make the pursuit of wisdom attractive, and thus encourage his readers to persevere in their study.

1:10–19. The exhortation to follow wisdom (1:9) is immediately contrasted with a negative command, a prohibition, against seduction by the wicked, which introduces this poem. These verses are not about wisdom, as we might expect at the beginning of a Book concerned with wisdom, but they warn against following false and dangerous advice, and especially against harmful companions, which is a recurring theme in Proverbs. The young are always prone to peer pressure, a problem that Solomon attacks immediately. These verses also need to be seen against Wisdom's warning (not invitation) in the following poem, which echoes the disaster proclaimed as the fate of these dangerous companions (1:18f; cf. 1:31f). The choice lies between following the instructions of wisdom (1:8f) and the allurements of the violent (1:10ff).

1:10. The nature of the enticement is not spelled out in this verse, which may imply that the student needs to know the true nature of those who try to persuade him to a particular course of action. If he recognizes them as people who generally do wrong, then he should not let them persuade him to go with them. Since, however, the best way to discern someone's nature is by what they say and do, we must listen and watch. Before accepting any offer, we must reflect carefully on the qualities of the person issuing the invitation.

1:11–12. After inviting him to go along (v. 11a), they describe what they are going to do

13.

4527.320	4834.120	3479	3725, 2019	988	3626, 3495.152
v Piel impf 1cp	v Qal impf 1cp	adj	adj, n ms	n ms	prep, v Qal act ptc mp
נְמַלֵּא	נִמְצָא	יָקָר	כָּל-הוֹן	בּוֹר	כְּיוֹרְדֵי
nᵉmallē'	nimtsā'	yāqār	kol-hôn	vôr	kᵉyôrdhê
we will fill with	we will find	precious	all goods	the Pit	like those going down to

14.

1041	8395	1518	5489.523	904, 8761	3719	259
n mp, ps 1cp	n ms	n ms, ps 2ms	v Hiphil impf 2ms	prep, n ms, ps 1cp	n ms	num
בָּתֵּינוּ	שָׁלָל	גּוֹרָלְךָ	תַּפִּיל	בְּתוֹכֵנוּ	כִּיס	אֶחָד
vāttênû	shālāl	gôrālᵉkhā	tappîl	bᵉthôkhēnû	kîs	'echādh
our houses	booty	your lot	you will cause to fall	in our midst	a bag	one

15.

2030.121	3937, 3725	1158	414, 2050.123	904, 1932	882	4661.131
v Qal impf 3ms	prep, adj, ps 1cp	n ms, ps 1cs	adv, v Qal juss 2ms	prep, n ms	prep, ps 3mp	v Qal impv 2ms
יִהְיֶה	לְכֻלָּנוּ	בְּנִי	אַל-תֵּלֵךְ	בְּדֶרֶךְ	אִתָּם	מְנַע
yihyeh	lᵉkhullānû	bᵉnî	'al-tēlēkh	bᵉdherekh	'ittām	mᵉna'
it will be	to all of us	O my son	do not walk	on a path	with them	withhold

16.

7559	4623, 5594	3706	7559	3937, 7737	7608.126
n fs, ps 2ms	prep, n fs, ps 3mp	cj	n fd, ps 3mp	prep, art, adj	v Qal impf 3mp
רַגְלֶךָ	מִנְּתִיבָתָם	כִּי	רַגְלֵיהֶם	לָרַע	יָרוּצוּ
raghlᵉkhā	minnᵉthîvāthām	kî	raghlêhem	lāra'	yārûtsû
your foot	from their path	because	their feet	to what is evil	they will run

17.

4257.126	3937, 8581.141, 1879	3706, 2703	2306.455	7862
cj, v Qal impf 3mp	prep, v Qal inf con, n ms	cj, adv	v Pual ptc ms	art, n fs
וִימַהֲרוּ	לִשְׁפָּךְ-דָּם	כִּי-חִנָּם	מְזֹרָה	הָרָשֶׁת
wîmahᵃrû	lishpākh-dām	kî-chinnām	mᵉzōrāh	hārāsheth
and they will hurry	to shed blood	because without cause	being spread out	the net

18.

904, 6084	3725, 1196	3796	2062	3937, 1879	717.126
prep, n fd	adj, n ms	n fs	cj, pers pron	prep, n ms, ps 3mp	v Qal impf 3mp
בְּעֵינֵי	כָּל-בַּעַל	כָּנָף	וְהֵם	לְדָמָם	יֶאֱרֹבוּ
bᵉ'ênê	khol-ba'al	kānāph	wᵉhēm	lᵉdhāmām	ye'ᵉrōvû
in the eyes of	all the owners of	wings	but they	for their blood	they will lie in wait

19.

7121.126	3937, 5497	3772	758	3725, 1239.151	1240
v Qal impf 3mp	prep, n fp, ps 3mp	adv	n mp	adj, v Qal act ptc ms	n ms
יִצְפֵּנוּ	לְנַפְשֹׁתָם	כֵּן	אָרְחוֹת	כָּל-בֹּצֵעַ	בָּצַע
yitspᵉnû	lᵉnaphshōthām	kēn	'ārᵉchôth	kol-bōtsēa'	bātsa'
they will conceal themselves	for their lives	thus	the paths of	all those cutting off	a profit

20.

881, 5497	1196	4089.121	2554	904, 2445	7728.127
do, n fs	n mp, ps 3ms	v Qal impf 3ms	n fp	prep, art, n ms	v Qal impf 3fp
אֶת-נֶפֶשׁ	בְּעָלָיו	יִקָּח	חָכְמוֹת	בַּחוּץ	תָּרֹנָּה
'eth-nephesh	bᵉ'ālâv	yiqqāch	chokhmôth	bachûts	tārōnnāh
the life of	it owners	it will take	wisdoms	in the street	they cry out loudly

---

13. We shall find all precious substance: … valuable possessions, *Beck* … take rich treasure, *REB* … all kinds of costly things, *NRSV* … all precious goods, *RSV*.

we shall fill our houses with spoil: … fill our houses with stolen goods, *NCV* … with booty, *NRSV* … with plunder, *REB*.

14. Cast in thy lot among us; let us all have one purse: … we will share with you stolen goods, *NCV* … all have one money-bag, *BB*.

15. My son, walk not thou in the way with them: … never join them, *Moffatt* … keep your steps out of their path, *JB*.

16. For their feet run to evil, and make haste to shed blood: … to mischief do run, *Rotherham* … hasten hotfoot into crime, *REB* … feet rush into sin, *NIV*.

refrain thy foot from their path: … Withhold thy foot, *Young* … hold back thy foot, *RSV* … stay clear of their ways, *REB*.

17. Surely in vain the net is spread in the sight of any bird: ... without cause, *Geneva* ... is the net baited while the bird is looking on, *NRSV.*

18. And they lay wait for their own blood; they lurk privily for their

own lives: ... set an ambush, *RSV* ... watch secretly, *Young* ... they set a trap, *Douay* ... fall into their own traps; they will only catch themselves!, *NCV.*

19. So are the ways of every one that is greedy of gain; which

taketh away the life of the owners thereof: ... everyone who gains by violence, *NASB* ... Such is the end of all who go after ill-gotten gain; it takes away the lives of those who get it, *NIV* ... greed kills selfish people, *NCV.*

(vv. 11b–12). They will set up a deadly ambush ("for blood") against someone who has done them no wrong. This is violence for the sake of gain, carried out with callous arrogance (v. 12). Just as certainly as Sheol devours all flesh (cf. 30:15f), they will send the healthy down to the pit. If they can overpower even the healthy (and therefore strong), how certain they can be of success! This ambush could be any type of plot: political, physical, financial, even religious (cf. 1 Ki. 21; Ezek. 22:25–29), not just lying in wait beside a road.

1:13. Like the parents (1:9), these companions also proffer a motive for following them. Their motive is quite simple: wealth. This is not a condemnation of wealth, but of the greed that pursues wealth unconcerned about morality; it warns against the "love of money" that is a root of any manner of evil (1 Tim. 6:10). To be able to discern this siren call beneath the initial invitation is a mark of the wisdom that Proverbs was written to cultivate.

1:14. They then strengthen their invitation by a suggestion designed to appeal to the heart of a youth, who by nature wants to be accepted. What could signify acceptance more than making him an equal partner in their venture? This does not lower his risk (although it may seem to lower the initial investment), since equal partners will be found equally culpable when caught. Ironically, by placing his funds in their hands (they, after all, outnumber him), he has become their first "victim"; his property is now theirs. Thinking to gain, he has lost.

1:15. The father now reiterates his warning, this time backing up his prohibition with a negative motive statement that uncovers the true nature of the situation (vv. 15b–16) and its inevitable end (vv. 17ff). His prohibition is again both negative and positive: obeying either half fulfills the whole. Both together describe the scope of wisdom.

1:16. His first reason is that they are wicked. Although this seems obvious, he is actually unmasking their desire for wealth for what it really is: a headlong plunge into murder. Their invitation has already

made this clear, but the teacher reiterates it. Why? Because this is the inevitable end of their greed. Even if the initial invitation is merely to "come along," at the end of that seemingly innocent road is violence.

1:17. His second reason is a parable that shows that the thugs may not be as clever as they think. If birds see the snare being set, they will avoid it. Their plan to set up an ambush works only if they truly are clever. They may find that their prey has flown before they can spring their trap. This prey, however, can bite back, as the next verse shows.

1:18–19. Using the same words that they used in their invitation (v. 11), he warns that those who live by the sword die by the sword. He states this quite emphatically, saying in essence that those who think they are lying in wait for this or that person have in fact set themselves up for destruction.

Death is the primary negative motivation in Prov. 1–9. As in God's covenant with his people, the basic choice is life or death (Deut. 30:15–20). Whoever rejects Solomon's counsel, and thereby rejects wisdom, loves death (8:36). Those who attempt to master violence will find themselves its victims.

1:20–33. After Solomon warns the reader to avoid bad companions (1:8–19), Wisdom herself warns those who reject her (vv. 22, 24f, 29f) by describing the consequences of their decision. Faced with disaster, they may realize wisdom's value, but it will be too late, for they will not be able to find her (vv. 26ff) and will suffer the consequences of their naive and foolish behavior (v. 31), and die (v. 32). Unlike the first poem, therefore, these verses address those who are confirmed in their rebellion.

Wisdom speaks as a prophet, warning scoffers of the consequences of their attitude. As the prophets repeatedly warned the nations that their sin would lead them into destruction, so Wisdom warns fools that their sin would lead to their death. Wisdom thus stands, not as a teacher, but as a prophet, a teacher spurned.

1:20–21. Job describes wisdom as being more hidden than precious minerals deep in the earth (Job

21.

904, 7624	5598.122	7249		904, 7513	2064.154	7410.122
prep, art, n fp	v Qal impf 3fs	n ms, ps 3fs	**21.**	prep, *n ms*	v Qal act ptc fp	v Qal impf 3fs
בָּרְחֹבוֹת	תִּתֵּן	קוֹלָהּ		בְּרֹאשׁ	הֹמִיּוֹת	תִּקְרָא
bārechōvōth	tittēn	qōlāhh		berō'sh	hōmîyôth	tiqōrā'
in the plazas	she gives	her voice		on the top of	those making an uproar	she calls out

22.

904, 6860	8554	904, 6111	571	569.122	5912, 5146	6864
prep, *n mp*	n mp	prep, art, n fs	n mp, ps 3fs	v Qal impf 3fs	adv, intrg	n mp
בְּפִתְחֵי	שְׁעָרִים	בָעִיר	אֲמָרֶיהָ	תֹאמַר	עַד־מָתַי	פְּתָיִם
bephithchê	she'ārîm	bā'îr	'ămārêāh	thō'mēr	'adh-māthay	pethāyim
in the entrances of	gates	in the city	her sayings	she says	until when	O simple ones

154.128	6865	4086	4087	2629.116	3937
v Qal impf 2mp	n ms	cj, n mp	n ms	v Qal pf 3cp	prep, ps 3mp
תְּאֵהֲבוּ	פֶתִי	וְלֵצִים	לָצוֹן	חָמְדוּ	לָהֶם
te'ēhăvû	phethî	welētsîm	lātsōn	chāmedhû	lāhem
will you love	simplicity	and mockers	mocking	they have taken pleasure in	for themselves

23.

3809	7983.126, 1907		8178.128	3937, 8763	2079
cj, n mp	v Qal impf 3mp, n fs	**23.**	v Qal impf 2mp	prep, n fs, ps 1cs	intrj
וּכְסִילִים	יִשְׂנְאוּ־דָעַת		תָּשׁוּבוּ	לְתוֹכַחְתִּי	הִנֵּה
ûkhesîlîm	yisne'û-dhā'ath		tāshûvû	lethôkhachtî	hinnēh
and fools	they hate knowledge		you will return	to my correction	behold

5218.525	3937	7593	3156.525	1745	881
v Hiphil juss 1cs	prep, ps 2mp	n fs, ps 1cs	v Hiphil juss 1cs	n mp, ps 1cs	do, ps 2mp
אַבִּיעָה	לָכֶם	רוּחִי	אוֹדִיעָה	דְבָרַי	אֶתְכֶם
'abbî'āh	lākhem	rûchî	'ôdhî'āh	dhevāray	'ethkhem
let me cause to gush forth	to you	my spirit	let me make known to	my words	you

24.

3391	7410.115	4126.327	5371.115	3135	375
cj	v Qal pf 1cs	cj, v Piel impf 2mp	v Qal pf 1cs	n fs, ps 1cs	cj, *sub*
יַעַן	קָרָאתִי	וַתְּמָאֵנוּ	נָטִיתִי	יָדִי	וְאֵין
ya'an	qārā'thî	wattemā'ēnû	nāṭîthî	yādhî	we'ên
because	I have called	but you refused	I have stretched out	my hand	but there is not

25.

7477.551		6797.128	3725, 6332	8763
v Hiphil ptc ms	**25.**	cj, v Qal impf 2mp	adj, n fs, ps 1cs	cj, n fs, ps 1cs
מַקְשִׁיב		וַתִּפְרְעוּ	כָל־עֲצָתִי	וְתוֹכַחְתִּי
maqŏshîv		wattiphre'û	khol-'ătsāthî	wethôkhachtî
one who pays attention		and you have left unattended	all my counsel	and my corrections

26.

3940	13.117		1612, 603	904, 344	7925.125	4074.125
neg part	v Qal pf 2mp	**26.**	cj, pers pron	prep, n ms, ps 2mp	v Qal impf 1cs	v Qal impf 1cs
לֹא	אֲבִיתֶם		גַּם־אֲנִי	בְּאֵידְכֶם	אֶשְׂחָק	אֶלְעַג
lō'	'ăvîthem		gam-'ănî	be'êdhekhem	eschāq	el'agh
not	you were willing		even I	when your calamity	I will laugh	I will scoff

27.

904, 971.141	6586		904, 971.141	3626, 8060	6586	344
prep, v Qal inf con	n ms, ps 2mp	**27.**	prep, v Qal inf con	prep, n fs	n ms, ps 2mp	cj, n ms, ps 2ms
בְּבֹא	פַחְדְּכֶם		בְּבֹא	כְשׁוֹאָה	פַּחְדְּכֶם	וְאֵידְכֶם
bevō'	phachdekhem		bevō'	khesha'ăwāh	pachdekhem	we'êdhekhem
when the coming of	your terror		when coming	like a storm	your terror	and your calamity

28.

3626, 5679	885.121	904, 971.141	6142	7150	6960		226
prep, n fs	v Qal impf 3ms	prep, v Qal inf con	prep, ps 2mp	n fs	cj, n fs	**28.**	adv
כְּסוּפָה	יֶאֱתֶה	בְּבֹא	עֲלֵיכֶם	צָרָה	וְצוּקָה		אָז
kesûphāh	ye'ĕtheh	bevō'	'ălêkhem	tsārāh	wetsûqāh		'āz
like a whirlwind	it will come	when coming	upon you	adversity	and oppression		then

20. Wisdom crieth without; she uttereth her voice in the streets: … raises her voice in public places, *REB* … calls aloud outside; She raises her voice in the open squares, *NKJV*.

21. She crieth in the chief place of concourse, in the openings of the gates: in the city she uttereth her words, saying: … calls at the top of the bustling streets, *REB* … at the noisy intersections she calls, *Berkeley*.

22. How long, ye simple ones, will ye love simplicity?: … how long will you be foolish?, *NCV* … naive ones, *NASB*.

and the scorners delight in their scorning, and fools hate knowledge?: … mockers delight in mockery, *NIV* … scoffers delight themselves in scoffing, *NASB* … and you ignorant hate to be taught?, *Fenton*.

23. Turn you at my reproof: behold, I will pour out my spirit unto you, I will make known my words unto you: … listened when I corrected you, *NCV* … heed my warning, *Anchor* … turned again by my sharp words, *BB*.

24. Because I have called, and ye refused; I have stretched out my hand, and no man regarded: … I extended my hand and no one took notice, *Douay* … and no one heeded, *NRSV* … no one attended, *NEB* … but you paid no attention, *NCV*.

25. But ye have set at nought all my counsel, and would none of my reproof: … rejected all my advice, *REB* … ignored all my advice, *NIV* … despised all my advice, and would have none of my warning, *KJVII*.

26. I also will laugh at your calamity: … laugh at your doom, *REB* … laugh at your disaster, *NIV* … laugh when you are in trouble, *NCV*.

I will mock when your fear cometh: … mock when panic strikes, *RSV* … when terror comes, *REB* … make fun when disaster strikes, *NCV*.

27. When your fear cometh as desolation: … panic strikes you like a storm, *RSV* … terror comes upon you like a hurricane, *NEB* … dread comes like a storm, *NASB*.

and your destruction cometh as a whirlwind; when distress and anguish cometh upon you: … calamity as a hurricane, *Young* … pain and sorrow, *BB*.

28. Then shall they call upon me, but I will not answer; they shall

28). Solomon, however, says that wisdom is freely available to all who respond to its invitation. It is not secret, nor is it limited to initiates or an "inner circle." What is needed is not obscure knowledge, but an ear and heart willing to hear what Wisdom offers, as the contrast with v. 22 clearly shows. Like the prophets who would preach in public places (cf. 1 Ki. 13:1ff; Jer. 26:2), Wisdom delivers her discourse in the streets, squares and gates of the city.

1:22. This reproof is the first sign that this particular poem does not contain an invitation, but an indictment. The naive and scoffers are varieties of fools. Their naiveté blinds them to wisdom's value, and they are too busy mocking all knowledge but their own to recognize the truth when it appears. Fools hate knowledge (cf. 1:7) because they prefer the folly that they know to anything else.

1:23. Probably this verse continues the indictment, "You rebel against my reproof" ("rebellion" in v. 32 is formed from the same verb; HED #8178). They reject what Wisdom makes freely available ("pour out," "make known," HED #5218), the correction that she has offered specifically to them (cf. vv. 29f).

1:24–25. Their refusal to listen implies that they heard Wisdom's call, but chose deliberately to reject it. Not one of them paid attention to any of her counsel, whether positive advice or a nega-

tive rebuke. Not simply a continuation of the accusation of vv. 22f, these verses introduce the central portion of the poem, which shows that attitudes have consequences.

1:26–27. As they have mocked and rejected her counsel, so she will laugh at and deride them when they face disaster. This may seem petty, but it simply means that they will reap what they have sown; that is, by rejecting Wisdom's teaching they cut themselves off from her help. Even if they were to hear her words at that point, they would sound like mockery, like most good advice given too late. Similarly, God's mockery of the mutinous nations (Ps. 2:4ff) does not indicate personal spite or malice, but his judgment upon their sin of rebellion.

Disaster is inevitable, as Wisdom's fivefold list of terrors and pressures shows. It is not that the foolish face more troubles than the wise. They will not, however, have the resources of Wisdom to help them. The opportunity to learn is not open-ended. They cannot reap what they have not sown. They will, however, reap what they have sown (1:31). They have preferred their own wisdom, which often appears successful as long as life goes well. Disaster reveals the inadequacy of their own resources, but that will be all that they have.

1:28. Reflecting v. 26, Wisdom here recognizes that even if they "repent," they will not be able to

7410.126	3940	6257.125	8264.326	3940
v Qal impf 3mp, ps 1cs	cj, neg part	v Qal impf 1cs	v Piel impf 3mp, ps 1cs	cj, neg part
יִקְרָאֻנְנִי	וְלֹא	אֶעֱנֶה	יְשַׁחֲרֻנְנִי	וְלֹא
yiqŏrā'unᵉnî	wᵉlō'	'e'ĕneh	yᵉshachărunᵉnî	wᵉlō'
they will call me	but not	I will answer	they will look intently for me	but not

4834.126	**29.** 8809	3706, 7983.116	1907	3488	3176	3940
v Qal impf 3mp, ps 1cs	cj	cj, v Qal pf 3cp	n fs	cj, n fs	pn	neg part
יִמְצָאֻנְנִי	תַּחַת	כִּי־שָׂנְאוּ	דָעַת	וְיִרְאַת	יְהוָה	לֹא
yimtsā'unᵉnî	tachath	kî-sānᵉ'û	dhā'ath	wᵉyir'ath	yᵉhōwäh	lō'
they will find me	because	that they hated	knowledge	and the fear of	Yahweh	not

1013.116	**30.** 3940, 13.116	3937, 6332	5180.116	3725, 8763
v Qal pf 3cp	neg part, v Qal pf 3cp	prep, n fs, ps 1cs	v Qal pf 3cp	adj, n fs, ps 1cs
בָחֲרוּ	לֹא־אָבוּ	לַעֲצָתִי	נָאֲצוּ	כָּל־תּוֹכַחְתִּי
vächărû	lō'-'āvû	la'ătsāthî	nā'ătsû	kol-tôkhachtî
they chose	they were not willing	for my counsel	they rejected	all my correction

31. 404.126	4623, 6780	1932	4623, 4292	7881.126
cj, v Qal impf 3mp	prep, n ms	n ms, ps 3mp	cj, prep, n fp, ps 3mp	v Qal impf 3mp
וְיֹאכְלוּ	מִפְּרִי	דַּרְכָּם	וּמִמֹּעֲצֹתֵיהֶם	יִשְׂבָּעוּ
wᵉyō'khᵉlû	mippᵉrî	dharkām	ûmimmō'ătsōthêhem	yisbā'û
so they will eat	from the fruit of	their way	and from their counsels	they will be satiated

32. 3706	5050	6864	2103.122	8358	3809
cj	n fs	n mp	v Qal impf 3fs, ps 3mp	cj, n fs	n mp
כִּי	מְשׁוּבַת	פְּתָיִם	תַּהַרְגֵם	וְשַׁלְוַת	כְּסִילִים
kî	mᵉshûvath	pethāyim	taharghēm	wᵉshalwath	kᵉsîlîm
because	the turning aside of	the simple	it will kill them	and the ease of	fools

6.322	**33.** 8471.151	3937	8331.121, 1020
v Piel impf 3fs, ps 3mp	cj, v Qal act ptc ms	prep, ps 1cs	v Qal impf 3ms, n ms
תְּאַבְּדֵם	וְשֹׁמֵעַ	לִי	יִשְׁכָּן־בֶּטַח
tᵉ'abbᵉdhēm	wᵉshōmēa'	lî	yishkān-betach
it will destroy them	but one who listens	to me	he will abide in security

8076.311	4623, 6586	7750	**2:1** 1158	524, 4089.123	571
cj, v Palel pf 3ms	prep, n ms	n fs	n ms, ps 1cs	cj, v Qal impf 2ms	n mp, ps 1cs
וְשַׁאֲנַן	מִפַּחַד	רָעָה	בְּנִי	אִם־תִּקַּח	אֲמָרָי
wᵉsha'ănan	mippachadh	rā'āh	bᵉnî	'im-tiqqach	'ămārāy
and he will be untroubled	from the terror of	evil	O my son	if you receive	my sayings

4851	7121.123	882	**2.** 3937, 7477.541	3937, 2551
cj, n fp, ps 1cs	v Qal impf 2ms	prep, ps 2ms	prep, v Hiphil inf con	prep, art, n fs
וּמִצְוֺתַי	תִּצְפֹּן	אִתָּךְ	לְהַקְשִׁיב	לַחָכְמָה
ûmitswōthay	titspōn	'ittākh	lᵉhaqŏshîv	lachokhmāh
and my commandments	you will store	with you	for making attentive	to the wisdom

---

seek me early, but they shall not find me: ... seek me diligently, *RSV* ... seek me earnestly, *MAST.*

29. For that they hated knowledge, and did not choose the fear of the LORD: ... have not chosen, *Young* ... the reverence of Yahweh, *Rotherham.*

30. They would none of my counsel: they despised all my reproof: ... Consented not ... Disdained all my rebuke, *Rotherham* ... taken no notice of my advice, they have spurned all my warnings, *JB* ... despised every warning of mine, *Moffatt.*

31. Therefore shall they eat of the fruit of their own way: ... fruits of their behaviour, *NEB* ... get what you deserve, *NCV.*

and be filled with their own devices: ... satisfied with your own plans, *Fenton* ... choke themselves with their own scheming, *JB* ... full with their own fancies, *NKJV* ... filled with the fruit of their schemes, *NIV.*

32. For the turning away of the simple shall slay them, and the prosperity of fools shall destroy them: ... the stupid are ruined by their own complacency, *REB* ... the self-will of the simple kills them, the smugness of fools destroys them, *Douay* ... complacency of fools destroys them, *NRSV* ... security of the foolish, *Young*.

33. But whoso hearkeneth unto me shall dwell safely, and shall be quiet from fear of evil: ... be at ease, without fear of harm, *NIV* ... those who listen to me will be secure, *NRSV* ... shall live without a care, *NEB* ... he who obeys me dwells in security, in peace, *NAB*.

2:1. My son, if thou wilt receive my words, and hide my commandments with thee: ... take my words to heart, if you set store by my commandments, *JB* ... accept what I say and keep my instructions close to you, *Beck* ... treasure my commandments within you, *NASB*.

2. So that thou incline thine ear unto wisdom, and apply thine heart to understanding: ... listen to wisdom, *Beck* ... thy heart incline to discernment, *MAST*.

3. Yea, if thou criest after knowledge, and liftest up thy voice for

---

find her, since they had distanced themselves from her. Even if they heard wise words, they would not be helped, because they would not recognize wisdom when they heard it.

1:29–30. These verses repeat the indictment of vv. 22–25, using many of the same terms, but combining them differently. Here, however, Solomon lists the generic charge first, "They hated knowledge" (cf. v. 22c). He then identifies their fundamental sin as not choosing the fear of the LORD, precisely the situation that 1:7 outlines, since "the fear of the LORD is the beginning of knowledge."

Wisdom says "my counsel" and "my reproof" to warn them that they have not merely rejected generic advice from some anonymous source, but the counsel of Wisdom herself. Their peril is all the greater because they have despised their only source of real help, and now have only themselves as guides. They are also on an undisciplined course, having rejected her correction ("reproof," HED #8763), since they will not rebuke or correct themselves (cf. 9:7f).

1:31–32. The consequences of the actions described in vv. 29f are far more severe in this second statement of the judgment (cf. vv. 26ff), which goes far beyond terror in the face of disaster. Every course of action has an outcome; the consequence of rejecting the way of wisdom is death (cf. 29:1). This anticipates the many individual proverbs that warn that a person's own way leads inevitably to death, since it is a way uncounseled by Wisdom (e.g., Prov. 16:2, 18, 25).

Rebellion and complacency are both rooted in arrogance. The rebellious deliberately reject someone else's dominion over them, whereas the self-satisfied cannot be troubled to consider anything other than what they already know. Both are doomed. Such people will come to the same end as the violent (v. 18), since all of these actions arise out of the pride that rejects, either actively or by neglect, the wisdom that they need.

1:33. The consequences of rejecting Wisdom's counsel are dreadful. The only antidote is to listen and then to obey what is heard (1:7). Obedience yields not merely life (as opposed to death), but a life unthreatened by the terror that accompanies disaster, a life lived in peace without fear.

Like the discourses of the prophets, this poem warns of judgment in order to provoke repentance. It lies at the beginning of the Book in order to awaken the smugly self-confident, those who see no need to trouble themselves to seek Wisdom, and who therefore face death if they do not listen. If they turn from their folly, they will live and be blessed.

2:1–22. Proverbs 2, one of the longest poems in Proverbs, aims to motivate students to seek wisdom. To accomplish that goal, it lists some desirable results of studying this Book. To find wisdom is to find God himself (v. 6) and to gain his protection (vv. 7–11) from the temptation to follow the perverse (vv. 12–15) or the adulteress (vv. 16–19). Those who find wisdom also find life (vv. 20f), whereas the wicked perish (vv. 20ff). This knowledge and protection, however, only come through the deliberate and passionate pursuit of wisdom (1:1–4).

2:1–2. The search for wisdom begins by learning from someone else and remembering their teaching against the time when it is needed. To "treasure" may imply that we do not understand the implications of that teaching when we first hear it. Solomon thus implicitly cautions his readers against rejecting advice based on their initial impression of its worth. Learning well requires paying attention with our entire being, our inner selves as well as our senses.

3.

238	5371.523	3949	3937, 8722	3706	524	3937, 1035
n fs, ps 2ms	v Hiphil impf 2ms	n ms, ps 2ms	prep, art, n fs	cj	cj	prep, art, n fs
אָזְנֶךָ	תַּטֶּה	לִבְּךָ	לַתְּבוּנָה	כִּי	אִם	לַבִּינָה
'āzᵉnekhā	tatteh	libbᵉkhā	lattᵉvûnāh	kî	'im	labbînāh
your ear	you will incline	your heart	to the understanding	indeed	if	for the discernment

4.

7410.123	3937, 8722	5598.123	7249	524, 1272.323
v Qal impf 2ms	prep, art, n fs	v Qal impf 2ms	n ms, ps 2ms	cj, v Piel impf 2ms, ps 3fs
תִקְרָא	לַתְּבוּנָה	תִּתֵּן	קוֹלֶךָ	אִם־תְּבַקְשֶׁנָּה
thiqŏrā'	lattᵉvûnāh	tittēn	qôlekhā	'im-tᵉvaqŏshennāh
you will call	for the understanding	you will give	your voice	if you will seek for it

5.

3626, 3826B	3626, 4438	2769.123	226	1032.123
prep, art, n ms	cj, prep, art, n mp	v Qal impf 2ms, ps 3fs	adv	v Qal impf 2ms
כַּכָּסֶף	וְכַמַּטְמוֹנִים	תַּחְפְּשֶׂנָּה	אָז	תָּבִין
khakkāseph	wᵉkhammaṭmônîm	tachpᵉsennāh	'āz	tāvin
like the silver	and like the hidden treasures	you will search for it	then	you will understand

6.

3488	3176	1907	435	4834.123	3706, 3176
n fs	pn	cj, n fs	n mp	v Qal impf 2ms	cj, pn
יִרְאַת	יְהוָה	וְדַעַת	אֱלֹהִים	תִּמְצָא	כִּי־יְהוָה
yir'ath	yᵉhwāh	wᵉdha'ath	'ĕlōhîm	timtsā'	kî-yᵉhwāh
the fear of	Yahweh	and the knowledge of	God	you will find	because Yahweh

7.

5598.121	2551	4623, 6552	1907	8722	7121.111
v Qal impf 3ms	n fs	prep, n ms, ps 3ms	n fs	cj, n fs	cj, v Qal pf 3ms
יִתֵּן	חָכְמָה	מִפִּיו	דַּעַת	וּתְבוּנָה	וְצָפַן
yittēn	chokhmāh	mippîw	da'ath	ûthᵉvûnāh	wᵉtsāphan
He gives	wisdom	from his mouth	knowledge	and understanding	and He stores

8.

3937, 3596	8786	4182	3937, 2050.152	8866	3937, 5526.141
prep, n mp	n fs	n ms	prep, v Qal act ptc mp	n ms	prep, v Qal inf con
לַיְשָׁרִים	תּוּשִׁיָּה	מָגֵן	לְהֹלְכֵי	תֹּם	לִנְצֹר
layshārîm	tûshîyāh	māghēn	lᵉhōlᵉkhê	thōm	lintsōr
for the upright	sound wisdom	a shield	to those who walk with	integrity	to watch over

9.

758	5122	1932	2728	8490.121	226	1032.123
n mp	n ms	cj, n ms	n ms, ps 3ms	v Qal impf 3ms	adv	v Qal impf 2ms
אָרְחוֹת	מִשְׁפָּט	וְדֶרֶךְ	חֲסִידוֹ	יִשְׁמֹר	אָז	תָּבִין
'ārᵉchôth	mishpāṭ	wᵉdherekh	chăsîdhô	yishmōr	'āz	tāvin
the paths of	justice	and the way of	his godly ones	He will guard	then	you will understand

10.

6928	5122	4478	3725, 4724, 3004	3706, 971.122
n ms	cj, n ms	cj, n mp	adj, n ms, n ms	cj, v Qal impf 3fs
צֶדֶק	וּמִשְׁפָּט	וּמֵישָׁרִים	כָּל־מַעְגַּל־טוֹב	כִּי־תָבוֹא
tsedheq	ûmishpāṭ	ûmêshārîm	kol-ma'ăggal-ṭôv	kî-thāvô'
righteousness	and justice	and equity	all the tracks of goodness	because it will come

understanding: ... cry aloud for insight, *Anchor* ... criest after discernment, *Darby* ... you appeal to intelligence, *Goodspeed* ... And to Thoughtfulness lift up your voice, *Fenton* ... your plea is for clear perception, *JB*.

4. If thou seekest her as silver, and searchest for her as for hid trea- sures: ... Search for wisdom as you would search for silver, *CEV* ... as though for buried treasure, *JB*.

5. Then shalt thou understand the fear of the LORD, and find the knowledge of God: ... reverence for the LORD, *Goodspeed* ... respect for, *NCV*.

6. For the LORD giveth wisdom: out of his mouth cometh knowledge and understanding: ... teaches knowledge and discernment, *Anchor* ... come knowledge and reason, *BB*.

7. He layeth up sound wisdom for the righteous: ... Salvation He stores for the upright, *Fenton* ... reserves his advice for the honest, *JB*

... has counsel in store, *Douay* ... reserved success for upright people, *Beck* ... wisdom for the upright, *ASV.*

he is a buckler to them that walk uprightly: ... shield of virtuous lives, *Anchor* ... shield to them that walk in integrity, *ASV* ... those who walk honestly, *Goodspeed* ... those who live blameless lives, *NEB.*

8. He keepeth the paths of judgment, and preserveth the way of his saints: ... guards the paths of justice, And protects the way of his pious ones, *Goodspeed* ... protects those who are loyal to him, *NCV.*

9. Then shalt thou understand righteousness, and judgment, and equity; yea, every good path: ... uprightness, equity and fair dealing, *JB* ... judgment and honesty, *KJVII.*

10. When wisdom entereth into thine heart, and knowledge is pleasant unto thy soul: ... will enter your mind And knowledge will be a joy to your spirit, *Anchor* ... knowledge fills your soul with delight, *JB* ... to thy soul is sweet, *Rotherham.*

11. Discretion shall preserve thee: ... good sense will take charge of you, *Moffatt* ... watch over you, *NAB* ... prudence will watch over you, *NRSV* ... Thoughtfulness doth watch over, *Young.*

2:3–4. In contrast to Wisdom's warning in the previous poem (1:20–33), we are to invite or summon Wisdom to come to us (v. 3). This means that rather than wait for Wisdom to happen along, we pursue it. The search for it (v. 3) begins with accepting the teaching that we receive (v. 1), since our response to what we already know reveals how we will respond to new teaching. We therefore study as intensively as we would search a field if we knew that it contained buried treasure (v. 4). This is the second hint of wisdom's immense value (cf. 1:9), a major motivating theme of Prov. 1–9.

2:5–6. The first four verses portray a relentless, aggressive search for wisdom. The rest of the poem (vv. 5–22) reveals the rewards that come from this search ("then," HED #226, vv. 5, 9). The first result of diligence is the discovery that the search for wisdom leads to the ultimate source of all wisdom, God himself. As we persevere, our understanding and wisdom increase until we begin to understand the fear of the LORD (v. 5a). Even this, however, is not the result of our efforts, but it is the gift of God, found out by all who seek Him diligently.

Wisdom is thus the confluence of two movements: our search and God's gift. As we grow in wisdom, we increasingly understand that that growth itself is the gift of God. Further, since God is the source of wisdom (v. 6), the counsel of the proverbs is not merely human advice. They are the Word of God, and they come with the same authority as the Covenant through Moses, or the word of the LORD through the prophets.

2:7–8. Verse 7 extends the benefits of v. 6 to the upright, those who live lives of integrity. The LORD "treasures" or "stores up" wisdom (the same verb occurs in v. 1) so that He can give it to the upright as they grow in their knowledge and understanding. He also uses that wisdom to shield the upright, those who live in the fear of the LORD, following the wisdom that they have already discovered.

The LORD protects those who walk in integrity, guarding even the processes of justice so that their honor will be upheld. This theme of protection dominates the second section of the poem (vv. 11–20), which describes the further benefit of finding wisdom as deliverance from two destructive ways of life (cf. vv. 12ff, 16ff).

2:9–10. The second result of this pursuit of wisdom is the ability to distinguish and choose what is best (vv. 5 and 9 begin with the same words in Hebrew [HED #226], "then you will understand"). This discernment is possible because wisdom fills the heart of the seeker, informing every aspect of his or her life (cf. v. 5). The final clause of v. 10 implies that the more we grow in wisdom, knowledge and understanding, the more precious ("pleasant," HED 5459) these things become to us.

The first three objects in v. 9 occur in the same order in Prov. 1:3, probably to connect this result with the purposes of the Book. The list is not exhaustive, as the summary phrase "every good path" shows. It points to moral excellence as successful living, rather than to the temporal values touted by those who lack this understanding (cf. 1:13). They also reflect the expectations of the Covenant (Deut. 6:16–25).

2:11. The second major section of the poem (vv. 11–19) is introduced, in which Solomon explains his promise of protection by describing two temptations from which discretion delivers the wise. He does not outline a plan of defense, nor does he narrate either process of deliverance. He describes the wicked and the adulteress so that the insightful can recognize them and avoid them. He goes beyond mere description, however, to reveal their true natures and (in the case of the adulteress)

11.

4343	5459.121	3937, 5497	1907	904, 3949	2551
n fs	v Qal impf 3ms	prep, n fs, ps 2ms	cj, n fs	prep, n ms, ps 2ms	n fs
מְזִמָּה	יִנְעָם	לְנַפְשֶׁךָ	וְדַעַת	בְלִבֶּךָ	חָכְמָה
mᵉzimmāh	yin'ām	lᵉnaphshᵉkhā	wᵉdha'ath	vᵉlibbekhā	chokhmāh
prudence	it will be pleasant	to your soul	and knowledge	into your heart	wisdom

12.

3937, 5522.541	5526.122	8722	6142	8490.123
prep, v Hiphil inf con, ps 2ms	v Qal impf 3fs, ps 2ms	n fs	prep, ps 2ms	v Qal impf 2ms
לְהַצִּילְךָ	תִּנְצְרֶכָּה	תְּבוּנָה	עָלֶיךָ	תִּשְׁמֹר
lᵉhatstsîlᵉkhā	thintsᵉrekkāh	tᵉvûnāh	'ālêkhā	tishmōr
to rescue you	it will keep you	understanding	over you	you will observe

13.

758	6013.152	8749	1744.351	4623, 382	7737	4623, 1932
n mp	art, v Qal act ptc mp	n fp	v Piel ptc ms	prep, n ms	n ms	prep, n ms
אָרְחוֹת	הָעֹזְבִים	תַּהְפֻּכוֹת	מְדַבֵּר	מֵאִישׁ	רָע	מִדֶּרֶךְ
'ārᵉchôth	hā'ōzᵉvîm	tahpukhôth	mᵉdhabbēr	mē'îsh	rā'	midderekh
the paths of	those who abandon	perversity	speaking	from men	evil	from the way of

14.

7737	3937, 6449.141	7975.152	904, 1932, 2932	3937, 2050.141	3598
n ms	prep, v Qal inf con	art, v Qal act ptc mp	prep, n mp, n ms	prep, v Qal inf con	n ms
רָע	לַעֲשׂוֹת	הַשְּׂמֵחִים	בְּדַרְכֵי־חֹשֶׁךְ	לָלֶכֶת	יֹשֶׁר
rā'	la'ăsôth	hassᵉmēchîm	bᵉdharkhê-chōshekh	lālekheth	yōsher
evil	to do	those who are glad	in the ways of darkness	to walk	uprightness

15.

6379	758	866	7737	904, 8749	1559.126
adj	n mp, ps 3mp	rel pron	n ms	prep, n fp	v Qal impf 3mp
עִקְּשִׁים	אָרְחֹתֵיהֶם	אֲשֶׁר	רָע	בְּתַהְפֻּכוֹת	יָגִילוּ
'iqqᵉshîm	'ārᵉchōthêhem	'ăsher	rā'	bᵉthahpukhôth	yāghîlû
crooked	their paths	who	evil	in the perversity of	they will rejoice

16.

2299	4623, 828	3937, 5522.541	904, 4724	4005.256
adj	prep, n fs	prep, v Hiphil inf con, ps 2ms	prep, n mp, ps 3mp	cj, v Niphal ptc mp
זָרָה	מֵאִשָּׁה	לְהַצִּילְךָ	בְּמַעְגְּלוֹתָם	וּנְלוֹזִים
zārāh	mē'ishshāh	lᵉhatstsîlᵉkhā	bᵉma'ăggᵉlôthām	ûnᵉlôzîm
the strange	from the woman	to rescue you	in their tracks	and those who deviate

17.

6013.153	2606.512	571	4623, 5425
art, v Qal act ptc fs	v Hiphil pf 3fs	n mp, ps 3fs	prep, n fs
הַעֹזֶבֶת	הֶחֱלִיקָה	אֲמָרֶיהָ	מִנְּכֻרְיָה
ha'ōzeveth	hechĕlîqāh	'ămārêāh	minnᵉkhᵉrîyāh
the one who abandons	she has caused to be smooth	her sayings	from the foreign woman

---

understanding shall keep thee: ... Reason will guard you, *Goodspeed* ... sound judgment will keep you right, *Moffatt*.

12. To deliver thee from the way of the evil man, from the man that speaketh froward things: ... save thee from the false counsellor, *Knox* ... men who use perverse speech, *Goodspeed* ... speaks wicked things, *KJVII*.

13. Who leave the paths of uprightness, to walk in the ways of darkness: ... paths of honesty, *Anchor* ... who forsake the right road to walk in murky ways, *REB*.

14. Who rejoice to do evil, and delight in the frowardness of the wicked: ... Who delight in the practice of wrong, And rejoice in perversion to vice, *Fenton* ... They enjoy doing wrong, *NCV*.

15. Whose ways are crooked, and they froward in their paths: ... and who are perverted in their course, *Darby* ... tortuous in their paths, *Goodspeed* ... devious in their ways, *NASB*.

16. To deliver thee from the strange woman: ... alien woman, *Berkeley* ... prostitutes, *LIVB* ... Saving you from the wife of another, *Goodspeed* ... from the immoral woman, *NKJV*.

even from the stranger which flattereth with her words: ... her words so smooth, *Moffatt* ... adulteress with her smooth words, *NAB* ... loose woman with her seductive words, *NEB*.

17. Which forsaketh the guide of her youth: ... husband of her youth, the consequences of failing to flee her temptation (cf. 1 Cor. 6:18; 2 Tim. 2:22).

These verses do not imply that deliverance is automatic or miraculous. The promised deliverance comes through exercising the discretion and understanding that God gives to those who truly seek his wisdom. Being wise does not mean to possess a certain quantity of understanding, since knowledge does no good unless it is used, applied correctly. These verses must be understood in light of the continued pursuit of wisdom encouraged by such passages as Prov. 1:5 and 2:1–4.

The rescue in each instance begins by being able to see through the words of temptation, whether the tempter is enticing us to wickedness (2:12–15) or to sexual immorality (vv. 16–19). The need to listen carefully and so to understand the true intent of the words of those around us is reiterated throughout the Book (cf. e.g., 18:4; 20:5).

2:12. Deliverance from wicked companions (cf. 1:10–19) is a result of recognizing the true nature of their ways and deliberately eschewing them in favor of that righteous, just and honest life (v. 9) that is to live in the fear of the LORD (v. 5). Discretion is the dominant theme of the first section of this poem (cf. "understanding," "discernment," "discretion" in vv. 2–9), because we develop the perspicacity required to understand a situation as we grow in wisdom and understanding.

Perverse speech is the fruit of a heart inclined to evil; the ability to recognize its true nature lives in a heart steeped in wisdom and the fear of the LORD.

2:13. The relationship between the lines of this verse is ambiguous, which is probably deliberate, given the terse nature of poetry. Either these would-be companions abandoned upright living in order to walk in darkness, or else they abandoned it by walking in a certain way. The first possibility means that they knew what was right, but deliberately rejected it in order to pursue their own sinful purposes. They may, on the other hand, have strayed from the Covenant only gradually, as they made increasingly sinful choices.

A major theme of Proverbs, the doctrine of the "two ways," teaches that it is impossible to pursue both sin and righteousness, light and darkness. They are mutually exclusive, so that to follow one is to abandon the other. Those whose words encourage others to sin are already walking in darkness. It is from such as these that discretion exercised rescues us.

2:14. The wicked have gone so far into darkness that they delight to plan and pursue evil (cf. Prov. 4:14–17; 6:14). Their happiness, their pleasure in life, comes from pursuing those things that are vile. None of this condemnation (vv. 12ff), however, need mean that their lives are filled with what is illicit, since business, social and personal activities can be within the letter of the Law but far from its spirit (cf. Matt. 5:21–48; 23:23–28).

2:15. Since they themselves are twisted, their paths will also be devious. Hearts shape lives. The result of abandoning an honest way of life in order to walk in darkness (v. 13) and of rejoicing in evil rather than good (v. 14) is that their entire lives are perverted. Their wickedness may not be immediately recognizable as such. The course of their lives, however, is downward, turning in on itself until they are trapped and destroyed by the folly of their persistent rebellion (cf. 5:22f). Well might the students of Proverbs be thankful to escape such a fate.

2:16. Wisdom also delivers from enticement to sexual sin, a major theme of Prov. 1–9 (cf. 5:1–23; 6:20–7:27). "Strange" and "foreign" (HED #2299; 5425) might mean that this warns against marriage to non-Israelites (cf. Exo. 34:16; Deut. 7:3, etc.), but more probably mean simply that she was not one's wife (cf. the "close friend" of the next verse). Unlike the wicked (vv. 12–15), she does not speak perversely (v. 12b), but uses flattery to gain her ends. Flattery, i.e., lying in order to manipulate someone, is routinely condemned in Proverbs (Prov. 26:23–28; 29:5; cf. Ps. 5:9).

Exercising the ability to discern the true meaning of her pleasant words, an ability that is a fruit of the pursuit of wisdom (2:1–11), is the first step of escape.

2:17. Like the perverse, this woman has also abandoned something. In this case, it is the companion of her youth. Since marriage took place at a relatively young age, this "close friend" (HED #443) is probably her husband. This sin is not fornication (which might lead to marriage, cf. Exo. 22:16f; Deut. 22:28f), but adultery (for which the penalty was death; cf. Exo. 20:14; Lev. 20:10; Deut. 22:22).

Just as their abandonment of the paths of uprightness led to, or included, further sin (v. 13b), her rejection of her husband reveals her rejection of the Covenant. The second half of this verse supports the interpretation that this is warning against adultery between Israelites, rather than

18.

3706 cj	8319.153 v Qal act ptc fs	435 n mp, ps 3fs	881, 1311 cj, do, n fs	5454 n mp, ps 3fs	443 n ms
כִּי	שֹׁכְחָה	אֱלֹהֶיהָ	וְאֶת־בְּרִית	נְעוּרֶיהָ	אַלּוּף
kî	shākhēchāh	'ĕlōhêāh	we'eth-berîth	ne'ûrêāh	'allûph
because	one who forgets	her God	and the covenant of	her youth	the close friend of

4724 n mp, ps 3fs	420, 7787 cj, prep, n mp	1041 n ms, ps 3fs	420, 4323 prep, n ms	8190.112 v Qal pf 3fs
מַעְגְּלֹתֶיהָ	וְאֶל־רְפָאִים	בֵּיתָהּ	אֶל־מָוֶת	שָׁחָה
ma'aggelōthêāh	we'el-rephā'îm	bêthāhh	'el-māweth	shāchāh
her tracks	and to the shadows of the dead	her household	unto death	it will sink down

19.

758 n mp	3940, 5560.526 cj, neg part, v Hiphil impf 3mp	8178.126 v Qal impf 3mp	3940 neg part	3725, 971.152 adj, v Qal act ptc mp, ps 3fs
אָרְחוֹת	וְלֹא־יַשִּׂיגוּ	יְשׁוּבוּן	לֹא	כָּל־בָּאֶיהָ
'ārechôth	welō'-yassîghû	yeshûvûn	lō'	kol-bā'êāh
the paths of	and they will not attain	they will return	not	all those who go in to her

20.

6926 n mp	758 cj, n mp	3005 n mp	904, 1932 prep, n ms	2050.123 v Qal impf 2ms	3937, 4775 prep, prep	2522 n mp
צַדִּיקִים	וְאָרְחוֹת	טוֹבִים	בְּדֶרֶךְ	תֵּלֵךְ	לְמַעַן	חַיִּים
tsaddîqîm	we'ārechôth	tôvîm	bedherekh	tēlēkh	lema'an	chayyîm
the righteous	and the paths of	the good	on the way of	you will proceed	so that	life

21.

8879 cj, n mp	8331.126, 800 v Qal impf 3mp, n fs	3706, 3596 cj, n mp	8490.123 v Qal impf 2ms
וּתְמִימִים	יִשְׁכְּנוּ־אָרֶץ	כִּי־יְשָׁרִים	תִּשְׁמֹר
ûthemîmîm	yishkenû-'ārets	kî-yeshārîm	tishmōr
and the blameless	they will stay in the land	because the upright	you will observe

22.

3901.226 v Niphal impf 3mp	4623, 800 prep, n fs	7857 cj, n mp	904 prep, ps 3fs	3613.226 v Niphal impf 3mp
יִכָּרֵתוּ	מֵאֶרֶץ	וּרְשָׁעִים	בָּהּ	יִנָּתְרוּ
yikkārēthû	mē'erets	ûreshā'îm	vāhh	yiwwātherû
they will be cut off	from the land	but the wicked	in it	they will remain

3:1

8784 n fs, ps 1cs	1158 n ms, ps 1cs	4623 prep, ps 3fs	5442.126 v Qal impf 3mp	931.152 cj, v Qal act ptc mp
תּוֹרָתִי	בְּנִי	מִמֶּנָּה	יִסְּחוּ	וּבוֹגְדִים
tôrāthî	benî	mimmennāh	yissechû	ûvōghdhîm
my instruction	O my son	from it	they will tear away	and those who act with deceit

---

Berkeley ... has forsaken the love of her youth, *Knox* ... companion of her youth, *Douay*.

and forgetteth the covenant of her God: ... does not keep the agreement, *BB* ... forgets the pact with her God, *NAB*.

18. For her house inclineth unto death, and her paths unto the dead: ... sinks down to death, And her tracks lead to the dead, *NASB* ... she hath appointed unto death her house, And unto the shades her

courses, *Rotherham* ... paths unto the shades, *MAST* ... unto Rephaim her paths, *Young*.

19. None that go unto her return again, neither take they hold of the paths of life: ... have sexual intercourse with her come back or ever reach the paths of life, *Beck* ... not one returns, they never regain the paths ... attain unto the paths, *ASV*.

20. That thou mayest walk in the way of good men, and keep the paths of the righteous: ... thou dost

go in the way of the good, *Young* ... keep to the paths of the just, *Douay* ... paths of the righteous that thou observe, *Rotherham*.

21. For the upright shall dwell in the land, and the perfect shall remain in it: ... the land will be for the honest to live in, the innocent will have it for their home, *JB* ... shall survive in it, *Anchor* ... the good will have it for their heritage, *BB*.

22. But the wicked shall be cut off from the earth, and the transgres-

a condemnation of intermarriage, since adultery stands condemned throughout the Covenant. As the proverbs constantly remind us, behavior reveals the true state of the heart. If the adulteress (or adulterer) has already defied God by breaking the standards of his covenant, it is a small thing to break a human contract.

This verse further demonstrates that marriage is not merely a social contract, undertaken for the good of society or the protection of women and children. Instead, marriage falls within the standards of the covenant community, because it is one of the Creator's purposes for his creatures (Gen. 2:18–25). The temptation, therefore, to see adultery as somehow less serious than the warped behavior described in vv. 12–15 arises from a misunderstanding of the global (all-encompassing) nature of the Covenant. To depart from the Covenant by committing adultery is no different in essence than rejecting it by any other type of sin.

2:18–19. Not only does adultery violate the Covenant, but as this and other passages demonstrate, it leads to death (2:18, 22; 5:5, 23; 7:22f, 26f). This death is the moral ruin and spiritual chaos of a life that has strayed from the paths of righteousness (cf. 5:23). A path is being followed, because every life always moves in some direction. The end of this road, however, is death and ruin. Those who succumb to the flatterer and so become involved in adultery will not find their way back, because their foolish (and therefore sinful) choices move them constantly away from the path of life.

2:20. The result of being delivered from these temptations (vv. 12, 16) is a life that consistently chooses what is good, and thereby walks in righteousness (cf. v. 9). This contrasts with the fates of the perverse (v. 15) and adulterer (vv. 18f). The life of the one who has sought and exercised it, and thus recognized and rejected both wickedness and adultery in favor of what is right, is the goal of this Book, a life lived in the fear of the Lord.

2:21–22. Solomon strengthens the contrast between the fates of the upright and wicked by choosing terms that create a pun, "upright" (yᵉshārîm; HED #3596), "wicked" (rᵉshā'îm; HED #7857).

These verses demonstrate God's primary concern for his people, that they might choose life and so live (cf. Deut. 30:15–20; Prov. 8:32–36; John 6:47–50; 10:10). Their promises, the blessing (v. 21) of life in the land and the curse (v. 22) of

removal from it, grow out of the Covenant, beginning as far back as God's original promise of a land to Abram (Gen. 12:1ff), but especially the first statutes given at Mount Sinai (Exo. 20:1–17; cf. especially v. 12). The same concerns, longevity and productivity in the land versus defeat and exile, are also the focus of the covenantal blessings and curses of Deut. 28.

This poem thus reiterates the warning of Prov. 1:18f that to pursue folly rather than wisdom leads only to destruction. This is the ultimate motivation offered in Prov. 1–9 as a reason to persevere in the study of this Book. The pursuit of wisdom preserves the student's life.

3:1–12. This poem has six two-verse stanzas, each with the same basic structure (command-motive clause). Within the context of Prov. 1–9, these references to teaching and commandments (v. 1), faithfulness and truth (v. 3), trust and understanding (v. 5), wisdom and the fear of the Lord (v. 7) and discipline and correction (v. 11) reinforce the purpose of these chapters, which is to demonstrate wisdom's worth, and thus motivate Solomon's readers to pursue wisdom by obeying what he has written. They must not be removed from their context and made into abstract laws and promises, since their primary point of reference is the Book of Proverbs.

The combination of the covenantal terms that describe the father's teaching ("my laws," "my commandments") and the benefits that only God himself can give, shows that this passage is closely and intentionally tied to the Covenant. The motive clauses, which expound the benefits of obedience, must also be understood in light of the Covenant. The assurance of the Covenant was that blessing would follow obedience (Lev. 26:1–13; Deut. 28:1–14), as surely as judgment would fall upon covenant-breakers (Lev. 26:14–39; Deut. 28:15–68).

The motive clauses are positive statements that do not necessarily imply the negative. Disobedience does not imply a short, ugly life, nor does a life of grief imply guilt. Even understood within this framework, however, these verses, like many proverbs, may seem unrealistic. Does everyone who obeys the commandments live a long and peaceful life, respected by all who know them, blessed by good health and financial security?

There are many approaches to answering this question. One immediately unacceptable response, propounded by those who deny biblical authority

414, 8319.123	4851	5526.121	3949		3706	775	3219
adv, v Qal juss 2ms	cj, n fp, ps 1cs	v Qal juss 3ms	n ms, ps 2ms	**2.**	cj	n ms	n mp
אַל־תִּשְׁכָּח	וּמִצְוֹתַי	יִצֹּר	לִבֶּךָ		כִּי	אֹרֶךְ	יָמִים
'al-tishkāch	ûmitswōthay	yitstsōr	libbekhā		kî	'ōrekh	yāmîm
do not forget	and my commandments	may it keep	your heart		because	length of	days

8523	2522	8361	3362.526	3937		2721	583
cj, n fp	n mp	cj, n ms	v Hiphil impf 3mp	prep, ps 2ms	**3.**	n ms	cj, n fs
וּשְׁנוֹת	חַיִּים	וְשָׁלוֹם	יוֹסִיפוּ	לָךְ		חֶסֶד	וֶאֱמֶת
ûshenôth	chayyîm	weshālôm	yôsîphû	lākh		chesedh	we'ēmeth
and years of	life	and peace	they will add	to you		faithfulness	and truth

414, 6013.126	7489.131	6142, 1664	3918.131
adv, Qal juss 3mp, ps 2ms	v Qal impv 2ms, ps 3mp	prep, n fp, ps 2fs	v Qal impv 2ms, ps 3ms
אַל־יַעַזְבֻךָ	קָשְׁרֵם	עַל־גַּרְגְּרוֹתֶיךָ	כָּתְבֵם
'al-ya'azuvkhā	qāshrēm	'al-gargerōthêkhā	kāthevēm
do not let them leave you	bind them	around your neck	write them

6142, 4008	3949		4834.131, 2682	7961, 3005	904, 6084
prep, n ms	n ms, ps 2ms	**4.**	cj, v Qal impv 2ms	cj, n ms, adj	prep, n fd
עַל־לוּחַ	לִבֶּךָ		וּמְצָא־חֵן	וְשֵׂכֶל־טוֹב	בְּעֵינֵי
'al-lûach	libbekhā		ûmetsā'-chēn	wesēkhel-tōv	be'ênê
on the tablet of	your heart		and find favor	and good approval	in the eyes of

sors shall be rooted out of it: ... will be cut short, *Anchor* ... unfaithful shall be plucked up out of it, *Darby*.

3:1. My son, forget not my law; but let thine heart keep my commandments: ... do not forget my teaching, *RSV* ... my directions, keep in mind what I command, *Moffatt* ... my rules in your heart, *BB*.

2. For length of days, and long life, and peace, shall they add to thee: ... abundant welfare will they give,

RSV ... a long and healthy life, with abundant prosperity, will they bring, *Goodspeed*.

3. Let not mercy and truth forsake thee: bind them about thy neck; write them upon the table of thine heart: ... Let your loyalty and good faith never fail, *REB* ... kindness and truth, *Young* ... Write them on the tablet of your mind, *Goodspeed*.

4. So shalt thou find favour and good understanding in the sight of

God and man: ... win favour and success, *NEB* ... win favor and a good name in the sight, *NIV* ... you will see how kind and sympathetic God and man will be to you, *Beck*.

5. Trust in the LORD with all thine heart: ... Put all thy heart's confidence in, *Knox* ... Put all your hope in God, *BB*.

and lean not unto thine own understanding: ... do not rely on your own insight, *RSV* ... put no

and integrity, is that these "promises" are false. Another is that Solomon's theology blinded his eyes to "real life," so that he described an ideal life, not understanding that he was insulated from the vicissitudes of life.

The statements could describe tendencies, the law of averages. Some who live by the Covenant are happy, their lives are peaceful, they enjoy respect of others, etc. This interpretation does not seem very motivational. Since obedience would be a lottery, no one would know whether or not their obedience would in fact reap the promised rewards. In favor of this approach, however, is proverbial compactness. By nature, proverbs are short (rarely more than eight words in Hebrew). This makes them sound like absolute statements, though they were never intend-

ed to be understood this way (nor would the wise understand them to be such).

Closely connected to this approach is one that interprets the verses in Proverbs that speak of the prosperity or power of the wicked (cf. 28:15; 29:2, 12) as being in tension with these verses. The motive clauses, however, are positive statements. They do not mention the fate of the disobedient, nor can their fate be deduced as the opposite of the promises given to the righteous.

The promises could be relative. The obedient may indeed live longer or be more prosperous than they would if they (in particular) had been disobedient. Regardless of appearances, therefore, an obedient person who dies of a debilitating disease at a relatively young age has in fact enjoyed a *longer life, better health, greater peace and a better reputation than he would have if he had flouted the Covenant. There is no way to know what might have been, and so in such cases we must trust the promise, not the appearance, and recognize that God's wisdom in every aspect of existence is far beyond human reckoning (Prov. 25:2; cf. Isa. 55:8f; Hab. 1:2–17; Rom. 11:33ff).*

Another approach to these promises, which, given the suffering of the righteous, seems to clash with history, is to combine the first two approaches mentioned above with a perspective that is implied by several verses in Proverbs, but is not fully revealed until the ministry of Christ. Jesus warned his followers not to be surprised if they were persecuted for obeying Him (Matt. 5:10ff; John 15:18–21). Jesus' own obedience brought a torturous death at a relatively young age, abandoned by God (Matt. 27:46) and mocked by those who had at one point wanted to make Him king (Matt. 27:47; cf. John 6:15).

The best solution is to read these promises, and many proverbial promises, as covenantal statements that find their perfect or complete fulfillment after death. The overall thrust of Proverbs is that the wise life is the life of the Covenant, which says at its most basic, "You shall be my people, and I will be your God" (Exo. 6:7; cf. Pss. 100:3; 144:15). Proverbs 12:28 explicitly affirms this by equating "life" (v. 28a) with "no death" (v. 28b); other verses promise life (cf. 2:19; 10:16; 11:19) or deliverance from death (cf. 10:2; 11:4).

Solomon's promise is that obedience is always blessed, whether or not we understand the nature of that blessing. At the same time, the promises come in their fullness only after this life, so that not to see them fulfilled is not a cause to question the faithfulness of God. It instead encourages believers not to set their hearts too fully upon this earth and its circumstances, but to obey in hope of the world to come. If they were true in the life of Christ, they could only have been fulfilled after his death and subsequent exaltation (cf. Phil. 2:6–11).

The poem uses the command-promise pattern consistently, but not rigidly. Couplets may have two or three commands, some negative and some positive, and one or two motive clauses. The last couplet signals the poem's end by changing this pattern (v. 12). This is a common feature of biblical poetry, which often marks the end of a section or entire poem with a longer or shorter verse, or a different pattern (cf. many Psalms, e.g., Ps. 2:12).

3:1–2. As often in Prov. 1–9, this poem begins with an exhortation for the son to hear, remember and obey the teaching that follows (cf. 1:8; 2:1; 3:21; 4:1f; etc.; a poem is occasionally concluded, referring back to the preceding instruction; cf. 7:24). The high value placed upon education reflects its importance in the Covenant itself (cf. Deut. 4:9; 6:4–9), where it occurs primarily in the parent-child relationship, as here.

The word translated "keep" (HED #5526) in v. 1 often refers to observing or obeying the Covenant (Deut. 33:9; Ps. 25:10) or the Word of God (Pss. 78:7; 105:45; 119 (ten times); cf. also Prov. 3:21; 4:13; 5:2; 6:20; 28:7), which extends to "do not forget" (HED #414, 8319) far beyond merely retaining the teaching in memory. "My commandments" refers primarily to the Book of Proverbs. Solomon's sayings are short precisely so they can be remembered. They are to be remembered so they may be followed. Proverbs does not refer explicitly to meditation. Remembering and keeping are its equivalent.

Just as the sixth commandment promises "length of days" for children who honor their parents (Exo. 20:12; Deut. 5:16), so this motive clause promises long life and peace for those who honor their parent(s) by obedience (v. 2). When Paul refers to this commandment, he also links its blessing to obedience (Eph. 6:1ff; Col. 3:20). A long life filled with turmoil would hardly be a blessing, so Solomon adds the promise of peace (cf. Prov. 16:7).

3:3–4. Solomon's mention of "faithfulness" (HED #2721) and "truth" (HED #583) shows that these instructions are to be understood within the Covenant, where they are key concepts. The result of memorizing and obeying the teachings (v. 1) is a life characterized by these qualities; "binding" and "writing" thus refer to the statutes that bring forth these fruit.

The first mention of ornamenting oneself with non-physical entities is in Moses' instructions regarding Passover (Exo. 13; cf. Prov. 1:9, where the teaching is called a "garland" and "necklaces"). The Passover lamb and unleavened bread were to be a sign on the Israelites' hands and foreheads (Exo. 13:9, 16), reminding them of their deliverance from Egypt. The second and third lines of this verse, with the exchange of "fingers" (HED #697) for "neck" (HED #1664) are repeated in Prov. 7:3, where they refer explicitly to the teacher's words and commandments (7:1f).

435	119	**5.** 1019.131	420, 3176	904, 3725, 3949
n mp	cj, n ms	v Qal impv 2ms	prep, pn	prep, adj, n ms, ps 2ms
אֱלֹהִים	וְאָדָם	בְּטַח	אֶל־יְהוָה	בְּכָל־לִבֶּךָ
'ĕlōhîm	we'ādhām	beṭach	'el-yehwāh	bekhol-libbekhā
God	and humankind	trust	toward Yahweh	with all your heart

420, 1035	414, 8550.223	**6.** 904, 3725, 1932	3156.131
cj, prep, n fs, ps 2ms	adv, v Niphal juss 2ms	prep, adj, n mp, ps 2ms	v Qal impv 2ms, ps 3ms
וְאֶל־בִּינָתְךָ	אַל־תִּשָּׁעֵן	בְּכָל־דְּרָכֶיךָ	דָעֵהוּ
we'el-bînāthekhā	'al-tishshā'ēn	bekhol-derākhêkhā	dhā'ēhû
but toward your understanding	do not lean	in all your ways	acknowledge Him

2000	3595.321	758	**7.** 414, 2030.123	2550	904, 6084
cj, pers pron	v Piel impf 3ms	n mp, ps 2ms	adv, v Qal juss 2ms	adj	prep, n fd, ps 2ms
וְהוּא	יְיַשֵּׁר	אֹרְחֹתֶיךָ	אַל־תְּהִי	חָכָם	בְּעֵינֶיךָ
wehû'	yeyashshēr	'ōrechōthêkhā	'al-tehî	chākhām	be'ênêkhā
and He	He will make straight	your paths	do not be	wise	in your eyes

3486.131	881, 3176	5681.131	4623, 7737	**8.** 7786	2030.122	3937, 8634
v Qal impv 2ms	do, pn	cj, v Qal impv 2ms	prep, n ms	n fs	v Qal juss 3fs	prep, n ms, ps 2ms
יְרָא	אֶת־יְהוָה	וְסוּר	מֵרָע	רִפְאוּת	תְּהִי	לְשָׁרֶךָ
yerā	'eth-yehwāh	wesûr	mērā'	riph'ûth	tehî	leshārekhā
fear	Yahweh	and turn away	from evil	healing	may it be	to your naval

8616	3937, 6344	**9.** 3632.331	881, 3176	4623, 2019
cj, n ms	prep, n fp, ps 2ms	v Piel impv 2ms	do, pn	prep, n ms, ps 2ms
וְשִׁקּוּי	לְעַצְמוֹתֶיךָ	כַּבֵּד	אֶת־יְהוָה	מֵהוֹנֶךָ
weshiqqûy	le'atsmôthêkhā	kabbēdh	'eth-yehwāh	mēhônekhā
and refreshment	to your bones	glorify	Yahweh	from your goods

4623, 7519	3725, 8721	**10.** 4527.226	632	7882
cj, prep, n fs	adj, n fs, ps 2ms	cj, v Niphal impf 3mp	n mp, ps 2ms	n ms
וּמֵרֵאשִׁית	כָּל־תְּבוּאָתֶךָ	וְיִמָּלְאוּ	אֲסָמֶיךָ	שָׂבָע
ûmērē'shîth	kol-tevû'āthekhā	weyimmāle'û	'ăsāmêkhā	sāvā'
and from the first of	all your produce	and they will be filled with	your barns	abundance

8822	3449	6805.126	**11.** 4284	3176	1158
cj, n ms	n mp, ps 2ms	v Qal impf 3mp	n ms	pn	n ms, ps 1cs
וְתִירוֹשׁ	יְקָבֶיךָ	יִפְרֹצוּ	מוּסַר	יְהוָה	בְּנִי
wethîrôsh	yeqāvêkhā	yiphrōtsû	mûsar	yehwāh	benî
and grape juice	your vats	they will burst	the discipline of	Yahweh	O my son

faith in your own perception, *JB* ... not looking to your reason for support, *BB*.

6. In all thy ways acknowledge him: ... be mindful of him, *Douay* ... Recognize him in whatever you do, *Anchor*.

and he shall direct thy paths: ... he will clear the road for you, *Moffatt* ... make your paths smooth, *Beck*.

7. Be not wise in thine own eyes: fear the LORD, and depart from evil: ... Do not congratulate yourself, *JB* ... Respect the LORD and refuse to do wrong, *NCV*.

8. It shall be health to thy navel, and marrow to thy bones: ... healing to your flesh, *RSV* ... Healing ... to thy body, And refreshing to thy bones, *Rotherham* ... moistening to thy bones, *Young*.

9. Honour the LORD with thy substance: ... with your wealth, *NIV* ... Pay the Lord his due with what goods thou hast, *Knox*.

and with the firstfruits of all thine increase: ... first of all your produce, *NASB* ... with the best of all you make, *Moffatt*.

10. So shall thy barns be filled with plenty, and thy presses shall burst out with new wine: ... thy storehouses be filled, *Rotherham* ... your barns be filled with grain, with new wine your vats will overflow, *NAB*.

11. My son, despise not the chastening of the LORD: ... do not spurn

Obedience yields a life of kindness and truth that will be approved by all who see it, both human and divine. This verse appeals directly to the very human desire for approval, a powerful attraction, encouraging the student to persevere in obeying the proverbs, even when that obedience might seem to damage his chances for approval.

This description is applied to only two persons in the Bible: Samuel (1 Sam. 2:26) and Jesus (Luke 2:52). This suggests that obedience to those in authority, whether wise (Joseph and Mary) or foolish (Eli), yields fruits that could not otherwise have been foreseen: Samuel as the last judge and first prophet after Moses (Acts 3:24; 13:20) and Jesus as the Christ.

3:5–6. The commands of vv. 1 and 3 are now more pointed. As in both of the first two pairs of verses, the command is both positive ("acknowledge," HED #3156) and negative ("do not lean," HED #8550). This time, however, the divine origin of the words is unmistakable. To trust the LORD is to obey Solomon's counsel in Proverbs, whether or not it makes sense.

After his urgent exhortation to strive for discernment and insight (2:1–11, esp. vv. 5, 9), it may seem incongruous that Solomon warns his readers not to trust that knowledge, but that is precisely the point. Those who gained the understanding promised by Solomon in ch. 2 might be tempted to trust that insight as though it were a skill they had developed on their own, forgetting Prov. 2:6. They might especially be tempted to question the warnings or directions of some of the proverbs, especially when their own insight tells them of a better way. The choice is whether to trust the LORD and his word (specifically, as it is found in Proverbs), or to trust their own understanding, forgetting that any insight they may possess came originally from the same LORD. The proverbs are trustworthy, but only because they come from the trustworthy LORD.

The motive clause says that the LORD blesses obedience by enabling all who trust and obey Him to live upright lives. In Prov. 9:15, 11:5 and 15:21, the same verb that occurs in 3:6b (HED #3595) describes the wise person who lives a righteous life. Obedience thus brings the blessing of walking within the bounds of the Covenant, free from its curses and the fear of divine wrath and condemnation. And this obedience, even without understanding, enables the obedient to trust increasingly the LORD, who will prove faithful each time that trust is exercised, thus completing and strengthening the circle.

3:7–8. Although these verses resemble the preceding couplet, they actually address a different situation. In vv. 5f, the temptation is to act "wisely" in contrast to the requirements of the proverbs. Here, however, the summons is to fear the LORD and shun evil. The basic temptation is the same, to trust one's own understanding (v. 7a), but now that understanding is directing one toward sin, not toward righteousness.

The unexamined life is a grave danger in Proverbs (cf. 12:15; 14:12; 22:3; contrast 14:15f; 16:17). To trust one's own understanding rather than deliberately live in the fear of the LORD by studying and obeying his Word (and, in this context, the proverbs) is to think oneself wise, but to be a fool with regard to righteousness, justice and truth.

This motive clause must also be seen in light of the covenantal blessings (cf. Lev. 26:4–13; Deut. 28:1–14) that promise God's presence among and blessing upon his people. It is well-known today that a tranquil life tends to be more healthful. These verses and others in Proverbs suggest that Solomon observed that a life free from the inevitable worries and problems that accompany sin is a life of emotional and physical well-being that are the fruits of a clean conscience.

3:9–10. The law of firstfruits required all Israelites to present a sample of their first crop to the LORD in token of their redemption from Egypt (Exo. 23:19; 34:26; Lev. 23:9–14; Deut. 26:1–11). Their failure to do this would, centuries after Solomon, lead Isaiah to condemn them (Isa. 43:23). Firstfruits was a reminder to Israel that the produce that they reaped was the gift of God, and that the land itself was his, and they were merely tenants upon it.

The motive (v. 10) appears to appeal to greed, but in an agrarian economy, survival depends upon one's crops. This is not so much a promise of wealth, as it is of provision (although it does promise bounty; cf. Mal. 3:7–12). The LORD Who had promised to be among his people would also provide for them. Faithful observance of this commandment would yield the same blessing promised under the Covenant as noted above (cf. 3:8). The promised provision is not miraculous, as was the manna (cf. Exo. 16:4–35; Josh. 5:11f) and the ravens that fed Elijah (1 Ki. 17:1–7), but the result of work in field, orchard or vineyard. In other words, the normal routines of life would be blessed so that the righteous would not go hungry (cf. 10:3).

Verse 12

Strong's	Parsing	Hebrew	Translit.	Gloss
866	rel pron	אֲשֶׁר	'ăsher	whom
881	do	אֵת	'eth	
3706	cj	כִּי	kî	because
904, 8763	prep, n fs, ps 3ms	בְּתוֹכַחְתּוֹ	bethôkhachtô	at his correction
414, 7258.123	cj, adv, v Qal juss 2ms	וְאַל־תָּקֹץ	we'al-tāqōts	and do not feel disgusted
414, 4128.123	adv, v Qal juss 2ms	אַל־תִּמְאָס	'al-tim'ās	do not despise

Verse 13

Strong's	Parsing	Hebrew	Translit.	Gloss
869	n ms	אַשְׁרֵי	'ashrê	blessed
7813.121	v Qal impf 3ms	יִרְצֶה	yirtseh	He accepts
881, 1158	do, n ms	אֶת־בֵּן	'eth-bēn	a son
3626, 1	cj, prep, n ms	וּכְאָב	ûkhe'āv	even as a father
3306.521	v Hiphil impf 3ms	יוֹכִיחַ	yôkhîach	He reproves
3176	pn	יְהוָה	yehwāh	Yahweh
154.121	v Qal impf 3ms	יֶאֱהַב	ye'ĕhav	He loves

Verse 14

Strong's	Parsing	Hebrew	Translit.	Gloss
3005	adj	טוֹב	tôv	better
3706	cj	כִּי	kî	because
8722	n fs	תְּבוּנָה	tevûnāh	understanding
6572.521	v Hiphil impf 3ms	יָפִיק	yāphîq	he has obtained
119	cj, n ms	וְאָדָם	we'ādhām	and a man
2551	n fs	חָכְמָה	chokhmāh	wisdom
4834.111	v Qal pf 3ms	מָצָא	mātsā'	he has found
119	n ms	אָדָם	'ādhām	a man

Verse 15

Strong's	Parsing	Hebrew	Translit.	Gloss
2026	pers pron	הִיא	hî'	it
3479	adj	יְקָרָה	yeqārāh	more precious
8721	n fs, ps 3fs	תְּבוּאָתָהּ	tevû'āthāhh	its produce
4623, 2843	cj, prep, n ms	וּמֵחָרוּץ	ûmēchārûts	and more than gold
4623, 5693, 3826B	prep, n ms, n ms	מִסְּחַר־כָּסֶף	missechar-kāseph	than the gain of silver
5693	n ms, ps 3fs	סַחְרָהּ	sachrāhh	its gain

Verse 16

Strong's	Parsing	Hebrew	Translit.	Gloss
3219	n mp	יָמִים	yāmîm	days
775	n ms	אֹרֶךְ	'ōrekh	length of
8187.126, 904	v Qal impf 3mp, prep, ps 3fs	יִשְׁווּ־בָהּ	yishwû-vāhh	they can be like it
3940	neg part	לֹא	lō'	not
3725, 2761	cj, adj, n mp, ps 2ms	וְכָל־חֲפָצֶיךָ	wekhol-chăphātsêkhā	and all your desires
4623, 6685	prep, n fp	מִפְּנִיִּים	mippenîyîm	than pearls of coral

---

the LORD's correction, *REB* ... do not undervalue the correction, *Knox*.

neither be weary of his correction: ... resent not his correction, *Goodspeed* ... do not be made angry by his training, *BB*.

12. For whom the LORD loveth he correcteth; even as a father the son in whom he delighteth: ... chastises the son he favors, *Douay* ... father whose son is dear to him, *Knox* ... his own darling child, *Fenton*.

13. Happy is the man that findeth wisdom, and the man that getteth understanding: ... Blessed is ... the man who obtains understanding, *Berkeley* ... the man who Reflection attains!, *Fenton*.

14. For the merchandise of it is better than the merchandise of silver, and the gain thereof than fine gold: ... than the gaining of silver, *ASV* ... it brings more profit than gold, *NCV*.

15. She is more precious than rubies: and all the things thou canst desire are not to be compared unto her: ... beyond the price of pearls, *JB* ... more precious than red coral, and none of your jewels can compare, *REB* ... nothing you could want is equal to it, *NCV*.

16. Length of days is in her right hand; and in her left hand riches and honour: ... With her right hand wisdom offers you a long life, *NCV* ... wealth and honour, *Young*.

3:11–12. These verses return the poem to its beginning. The first and last couplets are the only ones to repeat both "my son" and "for" (HED #3706 in the second verse). Typical of biblical poetry, the couplet also marks the ending of the poem by differing slightly from the preceding lines. The "motive clause" (v. 12) does not describe the benefits of obedience, but explains the command. The previous five sets of commands and motives have already covered the gamut of life (its length, conduct, well-being), so that the explanation found in v. 12 applies to the entire poem, not merely to the preceding verse. The last verse is thus equivalent to another command, "Recognize that the LORD rebukes."

The analogy shows the underlying motive of the commands (vv. 1, 3, 5, 7, 9) as the father's love for his son, wanting him to enjoy a long life (v. 2) lived in the fear of the LORD (v. 6), a good reputation (v. 4) and financial security (v. 8). Hebrews 12:5f quotes these verses to encourage Christians facing persecution. The author of Hebrews expands Prov. 3:12 by explaining that although the analogy seems to be imperfect, human parents can only discipline according to their human understanding. This is all the more reason to respond positively to God's discipline, since it is based on his perfect knowledge and understanding (Heb. 12:10). If they respect their earthly fathers, how much more should they obey their heavenly Father?

Although Prov. 3:11f are applied by the author of Hebrews to the circumstances of life, their primary reference in context is to unpleasant or apparently disastrous events, but to the contents of this Book. In these verses, as in 3:5f, Solomon is primarily concerned with his readers' response to his teaching. Students who are confronted with unpleasant truths about their conduct or choices, i.e., who are reproved by a proverb, may be tempted to respond by rejecting Solomon's advice. Solomon reminds them, however, that his counsel is divine, not human. He further reminds them that this God is a God of love, Who desires only the best for those who are his.

3:13–26. Carefully structured, this poem encourages learners to seek wisdom by promising not only the benefits already mentioned in 3:1–12 (cf. 3:14–18, 22–25), but the presence and protection of the LORD as both a part and reward of that search. The structure of this poem is:

A Exclamation: How blessed is the wise man! (v. 13)
B Reason: Wisdom is incomparable; it offers life, wealth, honor, peace (vv. 14–18)
C The LORD created and rules all things (vv. 19f)
A' Exhortation: Be[come] wise! (v. 21)
B' Reason: Wisdom is valuable; it offers life, security, freedom from fear (vv. 22–25)
C' The LORD is your guardian (v. 26)

The first two sections (vv. 13–18) are tied together by two devices. Forms of the same word ("blessed"; HED #869) begin and end these verses. Wisdom and insight are named only in v. 13. The other references to these qualities in these verses are pronouns, a cohesive device that binds the verses closely to their main topic and each other.

Verses 19f, which relate the LORD's work of creation to his wisdom, understanding and knowledge (cf. 8:22–31), parallel v. 26, which describes the

LORD's role as the student's guardian (cf. Ps. 121). The organization of the poem thus links his ability to protect his people to his work of creation. The motive clauses, therefore, rest on the person and character of God.

3:13. Some of wisdom's blessings are mentioned in vv. 1–12 (long life, peace, good reputation, etc.). Solomon now continues describing wisdom's value (cf. 2:4) with another reference to the dual nature to wisdom as the object of a search and a gift (cf. 2:4, 6). It is not possible to discover wisdom without seeking it diligently (cf. 2:1–4; Matt. 7:7f), but, according to the second line of this verse, wisdom is also a gift (cf. 2:6). The other three occurrences of the verb translated "gains" in Proverbs all refer to receiving favor from the LORD (cf. 8:35; 12:2; 18:22; Prov. 8:35 also refers to finding wisdom).

Being wise is a result of pursuing wisdom, but it is not a terminus. Wisdom is gained as it is pursued, not after it is found. It is an ongoing fruit of the search. This growth, however, is not a mechanical result of the search, however diligent. As Solomon said earlier, wisdom is not a static condition to be attained and held, but a discipline to be strengthened by study and use (cf. 1:5). Apart from the gracious gift of God, however, there is no true wisdom, knowledge or understanding, another encouragement to pursue this goal in the fear of the LORD.

3:14–15. Images from both commerce ("gain"; HED #5693) and agriculture ("produce"; HED #8721) reveal that wisdom is uniquely precious. Nothing, whether the profits of trade or the produce of the soil, can compare to her. Successful commerce and farming require enormous amounts of energy and devotion to the task at hand. Wisdom is worth the same investment of time, effort and energy, since it is more valuable than silver, gold, food, corals, etc. If people spend their lives working to gain these perishable things, therefore, how much more should they pursue wisdom, since it is more valuable than anything that the human heart can imagine or desire?

Wisdom's value does not fluctuate based on circumstances, as does that of precious metals and gems. Wisdom does not tarnish, it cannot be stolen and it is not used up, unlike the valuables to which it is compared (cf. 1 John 2:15ff). These verses do not condemn wealth or property. They do, however, warn human beings not to be misled into thinking the pursuit of these things more important than the pursuit of wisdom. If a choice must be made, choose wisdom (cf. 4:5, 7; 8:10f, 19; 16:16).

17.

1932, 5461	1932	3638	6484	904, 7972	904, 3332
n mp, n ms	n mp, ps 3fs	cj, n ms	n ms	prep, n ms, ps 3fs	prep, n fs, ps 3fs
דַרְכֵי־נֹעַם	דְּרָכֶיהָ	וְכָבוֹד	עֹשֶׁר	בִּשְׂמֹאולָהּ	בִּימִינָהּ
dharkhê-nō'am	derākheāh	wekhāvôdh	'ōsher	bismō'wlāhh	bîmînāhh
ways of pleasantness	her ways	and honor	riches	in her left hand	in her right hand

18.

904	3937, 2480.552	2026	6320, 2522	8361	3725, 5594
prep, ps 3fs	prep, art, v Hiphil ptc mp	pers pron	*n ms*, n mp	n ms	cj, *adj*, n fp, ps 3fs
בָּהּ	לַמַּחֲזִיקִים	הִיא	עֵץ־חַיִּים	שָׁלוֹם	וְכָל־נְתִיבוֹתֶיהָ
bāhh	lammachăzîqîm	hî'	'ēts-chayyîm	shālôm	wekhol-nethîvôthêāh
on her	to those who take hold	she	a tree of life	peace	and all her paths

19.

904, 2551	3176	861.455	8773.152
prep, n fs	pn	v Pual ptc ms	cj, v Qal act ptc mp, ps 3fs
בְּחָכְמָה	יְהוָה	מְאֻשָּׁר	וְתֹמְכֶיהָ
bechokhmāh	yehwāh	me'ushshār	wethōmekhêāh
with wisdom	Yahweh	being declared blessed	and those who hold it securely

20.

8745	904, 1907	904, 8722	8452	3679.311	3354.111, 800
n fp	prep, n fs, ps 3ms	prep, n fs	n md	v Polel pf 3ms	v Qal pf 3ms, n fs
תְּהוֹמוֹת	בְּדַעְתּוֹ	בִּתְבוּנָה	שָׁמַיִם	כּוֹנֵן	יָסַד־אָרֶץ
tehômôth	bedha'attô	bithvûnāh	shāmayim	kônēn	yāsadh-'ārets
the depths	with his knowledge	with skill	the heavens	He established	He founded the earth

21.

414, 4005.126	1158	7780.126, 3030	8263	1260.216
adv, v Qal juss 3mp	n ms, ps 1cs	v Qal impf 3mp, n ms	cj, n mp	v Niphal pf 3cp
אַל־יָלֻזוּ	בְּנִי	יִרְעֲפוּ־טָל	וּשְׁחָקִים	נִבְקָעוּ
'al-yāluzû	benî	yir'ăphû-ṭāl	ûshechāqîm	nivqā'û
may they not deviate	O my son	they drip dew	and clouds	they were broken

22.

2522	2030.126	4343	8786	5526.131	4623, 6084
n mp	cj, v Qal impf 3mp	cj, n fs	n fs	v Qal impv 2ms	prep, n fd, ps 2ms
חַיִּים	וְיִהְיוּ	וּמְזִמָּה	תֻשִׁיָּה	נְצֹר	מֵעֵינֶיךָ
chayyîm	weyihyû	ûmezimmāh	tushîyāh	netsōr	mē'ênêkhā
life	and they will be	and prudence	sound wisdom	keep	from your eyes

23.

1932	3937, 1020	2050.123	226	3937, 1664	2682	3937, 5497
n ms, ps 2ms	prep, art, n ms	v Qal impf 2ms	adv	prep, n fp, ps 2ms	cj, n ms	prep, n fs, ps 2ms
דַּרְכֶּךָ	לָבֶטַח	תֵּלֵךְ	אָז	לְגַרְגְּרֹתֶיךָ	וְחֵן	לְנַפְשֶׁךָ
darkekhā	lāveṭach	tēlēkh	'āz	leghargerōthêkhā	wechēn	lenaphshekhā
your way	with the safety	you will proceed	then	for your neck	and favor	for your soul

24.

3940, 6585.123	524, 8311.123	5238.122	3940	7559
neg part, v Qal impf 2ms	cj, v Qal impf 2ms	v Qal impf 3fs	neg part	cj, n fs, ps 2ms
לֹא־תִפְחָד	אִם־תִּשְׁכַּב	תִגּוֹף	לֹא	וְרַגְלֶךָ
lō'-thiphchādh	'im-tishkav	thiggôph	lō'	weraghlekhā
you will not tremble	if you lie down	it will strike	not	and your foot

25.

4623, 6586	414, 3486.123	8524	6386.112	8311.113
prep, *n ms*	adv, Qal juss 2ms	n fs, ps 2ms	v Qal pf 3fs	cj, v Qal pf 2ms
מִפַּחַד	אַל־תִּירָא	שְׁנָתֶךָ	וְעָרְבָה	וְשָׁכַבְתָּ
mippachadh	'al-tîrā'	shenāthekhā	we'ārevāh	weshākhavtā
of the terror of	do not be afraid	your sleep	it will be pleasant	but you will lie down

26.

3706, 3176	971.122	3706	7857	4623, 8177	6849
cj, pn	v Qal impf 3fs	cj	n mp	cj, prep, *n fs*	sub
כִּי־יְהוָה	תָבֹא	כִּי	רְשָׁעִים	וּמִשֹּׁאַת	פִּתְאֹם
kî-yehwāh	thāvō'	kî	reshā'îm	ûmishshō'ath	pith'ōm
rather Yahweh	it will come	because	the wicked	or of the ruin of	something sudden

17. Her ways are ways of pleasantness, and all her paths are peace: ... way of tranquil ease ... paths are bliss, *Moffatt* ... lead to happiness, *Beck*.

18. She is a tree of life to them that lay hold upon her: and happy is every one that retaineth her: ... to them who secure her,—And they who hold her fast are every one to be pronounced happy, *Rotherham* ... she makes happy those who cling to her, *Beck*.

19. The Lord by wisdom hath founded the earth; by understanding hath he established the heavens: ... laid the earth's foundations, in understanding, he spread out the heavens, *JB* ... He prepared the heavens by understanding, *Young* ... set the heavens in place, *NIV*.

20. By his knowledge the depths are broken up, and the clouds drop down the dew: ... the deep was parted, *BB* ... he made springs flow into rivers, *NCV* ... drop down the showers, *Fenton*.

21. My son, let not them depart from thine eyes: keep sound wisdom and discretion: ... wisdom and thoughtfulness, *Young* ... Seek Enterprise joined with Good-sense, *Fenton*.

22. So shall they be life unto thy soul, and grace to thy neck: ... life of your spirit, *Anchor* ... a charm hung about your neck, *NEB*.

23. Then shalt thou walk in thy way safely, and thy foot shall not stumble: ... walk your way confi-dently, *Berkeley* ... go on your way without a care, *REB*.

24. When thou liest down, thou shalt not be afraid: yea, thou shalt lie down, and thy sleep shall be sweet: ... When you rest, *Goodspeed* ... enjoy untroubled sleep, *Knox*.

25. Be not afraid of sudden fear, neither of the desolation of the wicked, when it cometh: ... blows, *Moffatt* ... don't be afraid of sudden disasters or storms that strike those who are evil, *CEV*.

26. For the Lord shall be thy confidence: ... will be at your side, *NEB* ... the Eternal will be your protection, *Moffatt*.

3:16–18. Wisdom holds in her hands long life and well-being, two rewards mentioned in the previous poem (cf. 3:2, 10). The distinction between her right and left hands is a common feature of biblical poetry (where the right hand is always mentioned first); it does not imply that one reward is superior to the other. The ways of wisdom are pleasant, characterized by peace, life and blessing.

These rewards are not enjoyed by the dilettante, however. They belong to those who seize wisdom and hold it tightly, another view of the intensity of the pursuit of understanding and knowledge described in 2:1–4. In these introductory poems, Solomon rarely lets pass an opportunity to remind his students of the need to pursue, acquire and hold onto wisdom.

3:19–20. According to the structure of this poem, these verses are a reminder that the Lord is the Creator and Ruler of all things, and that He both created and rules by wisdom. Since He is the implicit Source of wisdom in this poem (v. 13b; He is the explicit source in 2:6), these verses reassure the learner. Earth and heaven (v. 19) and the lower and upper waters (v. 20) testify to the greatness of his wisdom.

The reference to the "depths" (HED #8745) may glance back to "the deep" which was present at the very beginning of creation (cf. Gen. 1:2). God's dominion is reinforced later in the great poem about creation (Prov. 8:22–31), where the same word occurs three more times (8:24, 27f). God's control of this vast primordial chaotic mass demonstrates his sovereignty over all things. If He rules the deep, nothing is beyond the wisdom that He offers.

3:21. In most of the poems in Prov. 1–9, the first verse addresses the "son." Here, however, the learner is addressed in the middle of the poem. Solomon, having demonstrated the value of wisdom, now encourages his students to keep fast what they have attained, not allowing it to escape. As the structure shows, this verse looks back to v. 13 as though Solomon were saying, "I have described the blessing. Now, my son, get that blessing for yourself by holding onto the wisdom that you have attained!"

3:22. The main result ("so") of holding onto wisdom and discretion is life (cf. v. 18; 1:9). Merely to get wisdom is not enough. Wisdom must be used. When it consistently guides one's decisions, the result is a life adorned with grace. To "keep" wisdom is therefore to live according to its precepts. In order for a person to live this way, he or she must pursue wisdom by studying and learning (cf. 1:2–6). Only when known and understood can wisdom's teachings guide one's choices.

3:23–25. The life that is the product of obedience is a life filled with peace and security, so that the wise need fear neither disaster (striking their foot against a rock; cf. Ps. 121:3) nor the judgment that will overwhelm the wicked (cf. Ps. 1:5f).

3:26. Their confidence and security come from trusting that the Lord is with them and that He will

4623, 4059	7559	8490.111	904, 3815	2030.121
prep, n ms	n fs, ps 2ms	cj, v Qal pf 3ms	prep, n ms, ps 2ms	v Qal impf 3ms
מִלָּכֶד	רַגְלֶךָ	וְשָׁמַר	בְכִסְלֶךָ	יִהְיֶה
millākhed	raghlekhā	weshāmar	vekhislekhā	yihyeh
from capture	your foot	and He will keep	in your confidence	He will be

3135	3937, 417	904, 2030.141	4623, 1196	414, 4661.123, 3005	27.
n fd, ps 2ms	prep, n ms	prep, v Qal inf con	prep, n mp, ps 3ms	adv, v Qal juss 2ms, adj	
יָדֶךָ	לְאֵל	בִּהְיוֹת	מִבְּעָלָיו	אַל־תִּמְנַע־טוֹב	
yādhekhā	le'ēl	bihyôth	mibbe'ālâv	'al-timna'-ṭôv	
your hands	of the power of	when being	from its owners	do not withhold good	

8178.131	2050.131	3937, 7739	414, 569.123	28.	3937, 6449.141
cj, v Qal impv 2ms	v Qal impv 2ms	prep, n mp, ps 2ms	adv, v Qal juss 2ms		prep, v Qal inf con
וָשׁוּב	לֵךְ	לְרֵעֶיךָ	אַל־תֹּאמַר		לַעֲשׂוֹת
wāshûv	lēkh	lerē'êkhā	'al-tō'mar		la'ăsôth
and return	go	to your fellows	do not say		to do

6142, 7739	414, 2896.123	29.	882	3552	5598.125	4417
prep, n ms, ps 2ms	adv, v Qal juss 2ms		prep, ps 2ms	cj, sub	v Qal impf 1cs	cj, adv
עַל־רֵעֶךָ	אַל־תַּחֲרֹשׁ		אִתָּךְ	וְיֵשׁ	אֶתֵּן	וּמָחָר
'al-rē'ăkhā	'al-tachărōsh		'ittāk	weyēsh	'ettēn	ûmāchār
against your fellow	do not devise		with you	when there is	I will give	and tomorrow

6196, 124	414, 7662.123	30.	882	3937, 1020	2000, 3553.151	7750
prep, n ms	adv, v Qal juss 2ms		prep, ps 2ms	prep, art, n ms	cj, pers pron, v Qal act ptc ms	n fs
עִם־אָדָם	אַל־תָּרִוב		אִתָּךְ	לָבֶטַח	וְהוּא־יוֹשֵׁב	רָעָה
'im-'ādhām	'al-tāriwv		'ittāk	lāvetach	wehû'-yôshēv	rā'āh
with a man	do not contend		with you	with the safety	when he dwelling	evil

2660	904, 382	414, 7349.323	31.	7750	1621.111	524, 3940	2703
n ms	prep, n ms	adv, v Piel juss 2ms		n fs	v Qal pf 3ms, ps 2ms	cj, neg part	adv
חָמָס	בְּאִישׁ	אַל־תְּקַנֵּא		רָעָה	גְּמָלֶךָ	אִם־לֹא	חִנָּם
chāmās	be'îsh	'al-teqannē'		rā'āh	ghemālekhā	'im-lō'	chinnām
violence	a man of	do not be envious of		evil	he has done to you	when not	without cause

3176	8774	3706	32.	904, 3725, 1932	414, 1013.123
pn	n fs	cj		prep, adj, n mp, ps 3ms	cj, adv, v Qal juss 2ms
יְהוָה	תוֹעֲבַת	כִּי		בְּכָל־דְּרָכָיו	וְאַל־תִּבְחַר
yehwāh	thô'ăvath	kî		bekhol-derākhâv	we'al-tivchar
Yahweh	something detestable to	because		any of his ways	and do not choose

and shall keep thy foot from being taken: ... keep your foot from being caught, *RSV* ... keep you from being trapped, *NCV*.

27. Withhold not good from them to whom it is due, when it is in the power of thine hand to do it: ... Withhold not your help from the needy, *Fenton* ... a favour due to him, *REB* ... Do all you can for everyone who deserves your help, *CEV*.

28. Say not unto thy neighbour, Go, and come again, and tomorrow I will give; when thou hast it by thee: ... when you now have it with you, *NIV* ... when you can give at once, *NAB*.

29. Devise not evil against thy neighbour, seeing he dwelleth securely by thee: ... Never plot mischief against your neighbour as he lives near you unsuspecting, *Moffatt* ... him who lives at peace with you, *Douay*.

30. Strive not with a man without cause, if he have done thee no harm: ... Do not pick a quarrel with a man for no reason, *REB* ... Don't accuse a person for no good reason, *NCV*.

31. Envy thou not the oppressor, and choose none of his ways: ... Do not envy the violent, *NRSV* ... the man of violence, *ASV*.

32. For the froward is abomination to the LORD: but his secret is with the righteous: ... the perverse are an abomination, *NRSV* ... the Eternal loathes a bad man, the honest are the Eternal's friends, *Moffatt* ... upright are in his confidence, *RSV* ... He is intimate with the upright, *NASB*.

guard their feet from being trapped. The prudent look ahead, weigh the implications of their decisions and choose wisely, so that they avoid the trouble that plagues the fool (cf. 19:3; 22:3), but their security does not rest in their cleverness or insight. It rests instead in the LORD, Who guides their steps. If He is keeping their feet, then their feet will not be trapped, since the LORD does not tempt anyone with evil (such behavior is abominable; cf. 6:14, 18; Jam. 1:13ff; Matt. 6:13). He instead protects them every step of their lives, and if every step is right, then there will be no misstep. At the same time, He is Master not only of wisdom, and the vagaries of life, but Creator and Master of the world (vv. 19f). They can therefore put their trust in Him, because He is able to care for his own forever.

3:27–35. Using the same pattern as the first poem in this chapter (3:1–12), Solomon lays down a series of negative commands (vv. 27–31) and follows them with an extended motive statement (vv. 32–35). Unlike the beginning of this chapter, however, these prohibitions address interpersonal relationships, rather than one's attitude toward the LORD and his Word. This pattern implies that relationships grow out of and therefore reflect one's attitude toward Scripture, so that those who are the LORD's friends (v. 32b) do what is right and are blessed (v. 33b) and helped (v. 34b) by Him.

By confining himself to negative statements, Solomon encourages his readers to ask what they should do. The only effective way to rid oneself of a bad pattern of behavior, or habit, is to replace it with a good one. The positive corollary to the prohibition is clearly implied by vv. 27f, not as clear in vv. 29f, and much more difficult to see in v. 31.

3:27–28. These verses espouse a general principle (v. 27) and a specific application of that principle (v. 28). To refuse to do good when it is in one's power is to sin by omission. Withholding good from the person who needs it is keeping something that belongs to someone else. It belongs to that person by virtue of his or her need and the ability to meet that need. In a word, the refusal or failure to do good to someone in need is theft. This implies in turn the need to be alert to the needs of others and quick to ask how one can help them. It is to fulfill the commandment to "love your neighbor as yourself" (Lev. 19:18, 34; Matt. 22:39).

The Covenant also describes the refusal to fulfill an obligation, paying a worker on time, as sin (Deut. 24:14f). If it is wrong to withhold good from

"strangers" (Lev. 19:34), how much more wicked is it to break an agreement (cf. Ps. 15:4c), merely because one is in the position of power in the relationship.

The person who delays fulfilling a need or obligation illustrates this principle. This delaying tactic, putting off till tomorrow what should be done today, is even more heinous because it refuses to acknowledge that God has so provided for people that they can meet the needs of others as well. It also assumes that we know the future (cf. Prov. 27:1), an arrogant boast that James calls sin (Jam. 4:13–17).

3:29–30. These verses invert the "Golden Rule" (Matt. 7:12) in a form of what has been called the "Platinum Rule": "Do not do to others what you would not want done to you." As earlier, the first prohibition is general, and the second specific. Plotting against or attacking someone without cause breaks the commandment (Lev. 19:18, 34), and is foolish. Fools spread strife and trouble, but the wise avoid quarrels (15:1, 18; 16:28; 26:20f).

The wise are concerned for the well-being of others (cf. Rom. 12:3–21; Eph. 5:21; Phil. 2:3–16). A society in which no one knows when he or she may be the target of a gratuitous attack (physical, legal or financial) lacks trust. A nation or people characterized by distrust is inherently unstable, given to violence and demagoguery, ready to follow anyone who promises peace and safety. As king, Solomon was concerned for the well-being of his people (cf. his prayer for the discernment to judge wisely; 1 Ki. 3:9), and so here again warns his readers against harming their neighbors (cf. 1:11–14).

3:31. The third main prohibition of the poem, this verse reflects the Book's opening warning against violent companions (1:8–19) and sharpens the "plots" of the previous couplet to violence. Envy often leads to admiration, which can then bring about imitation. Even someone who does not admire violence per se may covet its apparent rewards (1:13f), and be drawn into its net. This rarely begins with copying their lifestyle wholesale. Instead, another pattern of behavior is adopted, until "all of his ways" have been chosen (cf. the contrast with "all its ways," v. 17). Solomon warns against indulging in this sin by anticipating it and forbidding it before it begins (cf. 23:17f; 24:1f).

Another common response to the apparent fortune of the wicked is anger (cf. Pss. 37:1; 73:3–9). The righteous who sees only the tangible "rewards" of sin may be greatly troubled at the disparity between his own situation and theirs (cf. Ps. 73:1f). Even if the

3176	4134	5660	882, 3596	4005.255
pn	*n fs*	n ms, ps 3ms	cj, prep, n mp	v Niphal ptc ms
יְהוָה	**33.** מְאֵרַת	סוֹדוֹ	וְאֶת־יְשָׁרִים	נָלוֹז
yᵉhwāh	mᵉʿērath	sôdhô	wᵉʾeth-yᵉshārîm	nālôz
Yahweh	the curse of	his consultation	but with the upright	one who deviates

1313.321	6926	5297	7857	904, 1041
v Piel impf 3ms	n mp	cj, n ms	n ms	prep, *n ms*
יְבָרֵךְ	צַדִּיקִים	וּנְוֵה	רֶשַׁע	בְּבֵית
yᵉvārēkh	tsaddîqîm	ûnᵉwēh	rāshāʿ	bᵉvêth
He blesses	the righteous	but the abode of	the wicked	on the household of

3638	5598.121, 2682	3937, 6270	2000, 4054.121	524, 3937, 4086
n ms	v Qal impf 3ms, n ms	cj, prep, art, n mp	pers pron, v Qal impf 3ms	cj, prep, art, n mp
35. כָּבוֹד	יִתֶּן־חֵן	וְלַעֲנִיִּים	הוּא־יָלִיץ	אִם־לַלֵּצִים **34.**
kāvôdh	yitten-chēn	wᵉlaʿănîyîm	hûʾ-yālîts	ʾim-lallētsîm
honor	He gives favor	then to the humble	He He will boast	if to one who boasts

1158	8471.133	7320	7597.551	3809	5336.126	2550
n mp	v Qal impv 2mp	n ms	v Hiphil ptc ms	cj, n mp	v Qal impf 3mp	n mp
בָּנִים	**4:1** שִׁמְעוּ	קָלוֹן	מֵרִים	וּכְסִילִים	יִנְחָלוּ	חֲכָמִים
vānîm	shimʿû	qālôn	mērîm	ûkhᵉsîlîm	yinchālû	chăkhāmîm
O sons	listen to	shame	causing to rise	but fools	they will inherit	the wise

4090	3706	1035	3937, 3156.141	7477.533	1	4284
n ms	cj	n fs	prep, v Qal inf con	cj, v Hiphil impv 2mp	n ms	*n ms*
לֶקַח	כִּי	**2.** בִּינָה	לָדַעַת	וְהַקְשִׁיבוּ	אָב	מוּסַר
leqach	kî	bînāh	lādhaʿath	wᵉhaqōshîvû	ʾāv	mûsar
teaching	because	understanding	to know	and be attentive	a father	the discipline of

3005	5598.115	3937	8784	414, 6013.123	3706, 1158	2030.115
adj	v Qal pf 1cs	prep, ps 2mp	n fs, ps 1cs	adv, v Qal juss 2mp	cj, n ms	v Qal pf 1cs
טוֹב	נָתַתִּי	לָכֶם	תּוֹרָתִי	אַל־תַּעֲזֹבוּ	**3.** כִּי־בֵן	הָיִיתִי
ṭôv	nāthattî	lākhem	tôrāthî	ʾal-taʿăzōvû	kî-vēn	hāyîthî
good	I have given	to you	my instruction	do not abandon	when a son	I was

3937, 1	7679	3279	3937, 6686	525	3498.521	569.121
prep, n ms, ps 1cs	adj	cj, adj	prep, *n mp*	n fs, ps 1cs	cj, v Hiphil impf 3ms, ps 1cs	cj, v Qal impf 3ms
לְאָבִי	רַךְ	וְיָחִיד	לִפְנֵי	אִמִּי	**4.** וַיֹּרֵנִי	וַיֹּאמֶר
lᵉʾāvî	rakh	wᵉyāchîdh	liphnê	ʾimmî	wayyōrēnî	wayyōʾmer
to my father	tender	and only	before	my mother	then he taught me	and he said

---

33. The curse of the LORD is in the house of the wicked: but he blesseth the habitation of the just: … the dwelling of the righteous He blesses, *Berkeley* … home of the righteous, *REB*.

34. Surely he scorneth the scorners: … meets the arrogant with arrogance, *NEB* … makes sport of the men of pride, *BB*.

but he giveth grace unto the lowly: … grace to the humble, *NIV* … favours the devout, *Moffatt* … but he gives grace to the gentle-hearted, *BB*.

35. The wise shall inherit glory: but shame shall be the promotion of fools: … will inherit respect, *Fenton* … The wise will have glory for their heritage, *BB* … will inherit honor but fools get disgrace, *RSV*.

4:1. Hear, ye children, the instruction of a father, and attend to know understanding: … Listen, sons, *Fenton* … listen carefully to gain insight, *Berkeley* … attend to know intelligence, *Darby*.

2. For I give you good doctrine, forsake ye not my law: … excellent advice I give you, *NAB* … good advice, *Anchor* … good counsel, *Moffatt* … I give you sound learning, Forsake not my teaching!, *Goodspeed*.

3. For I was my father's son, tender and only beloved in the sight of my mother: … once a son with my father, *Berkeley* … Who because of my mother he loved, *Fenton*.

4. He taught me also, and said unto me, Let thine heart retain my words: keep my commandments, and live: … cling to my

38

only visible difference is a carefree attitude toward life, casual disdain for the LORD and his Word (Ps. 73:10f), the impunity with which they pursue their sinful desires can grate the soul of the righteous.

This disgruntlement may be "righteous indignation." More often it is rage because disobedience seems to be rewarded more than living in the fear of the LORD, an anger that is actually directed at the LORD (Ps. 73:15, 21f). Such anger, being selfish at heart, leads only to sin (Ps. 37:8). Its only cure is to recognize that their judgment is both sure and just (Pss. 37:2, 9f; 73:18ff). This understanding comes from reflecting on the person and nature of God and thereby understanding the truth of their situation (Pss. 37:3–7; 73:16f; cf. Prov. 3:32ff).

If envy leads to emulation, it leads to a life of sin based on the ways of the wicked. If it leads instead to anger, that response is also sinful, even if it poses as righteous indignation.

3:32–34. "Because" (HED #3706) introduces the extended motive statement (vv. 32–35) that supports the prohibitions of vv. 27–31. Each verse contrasts the wicked and righteous; v. 35 ends the poem by reversing their order (see also 3:1–12).

The perverted, those who have "turned aside," withhold good, attack their neighbors without cause, and seek to gain by violence. As a result, they lie under the judgment of God (v. 33a), Who condemns (v. 32a) and pronounces the curse upon them (v. 33a). To fail to seek out and obey the positive side of these prohibitions is to call down this curse and judgment on oneself. On the other hand, the LORD guides those who are honest (v. 32b) and blesses them (v. 33b), even when they are oppressed (v. 34b). The motive statement therefore sets the choice of whether to be for God or against Him. This "for-ness" or "against-ness" is revealed, according to this poem, by the character and quality of one's personal relationships.

3:35. The consequence of acting wisely (in accord with the teaching of these verses) will be honor, just as an inheritance is the natural consequence of being a son or daughter. Fools, on the other hand, are so blind that they cannot recognize what is or is not worthy of honor. In fact, they choose to exalt things that are despicable, things that bring shame and a curse. What someone considers worthy of praise thus indicates the true state of their heart.

4:1–27. Chapter 4 can be viewed as a single poem of three parts (vv. 1–9, 10–19, 20–27), or as three originally independent poems (cf. the differ- *ences in content and tone, below). If they are a single poem, they are all part of the counsel that is being passed from son to grandson (4:3f).*

Each section is addressed to "sons" (v. 1) or "my son" (vv. 10, 20). Although they seem to have different foci, extolling wisdom's rewards (vv. 1–9), contrasting the ways of the upright and the wicked (vv. 10–19) and encouraging watchful self-control (vv. 20–27), also under the image of life as a journey, they are unified by their common assumption (and explicit assertions) that wisdom is the source of life (vv. 4, 10, 13, 22, 23); the word "life" (HED #2522) or "your life" ends the fourth verse of each section. They are also connected by the repetition of the verbs of v. 1 in the opening verse of the second and third sections ("hear," vv. 1a and 10; "pay attention," vv. 1b and 20), the same verbs in the same order in which they appear in v. 1. (Since these verbs are common throughout the hortatory sections of Prov. 1–9, this last point should not be pressed; cf. 5:1.)

They differ further in the proportion of command and statement. Imperatives dominate the first and third poems (only vv. 9 and 22 lack a command or prohibition), whereas the second is much more descriptive (six of nine verses are indicative: vv. 11f, 16–19). The sections thus form a stylistic chiasm (A-B-A') that, by returning to the style of the opening exhortations, strengthens their urgency.

Whereas the first poem is only positive, praising wisdom without mentioning the wicked or foolish, the second contrasts the ways of the righteous (wise) and wicked (foolish) and the third both commends the father's teaching and warns against the ways of wickedness.

4:1–2. The initial call to diligence, positive (v. 1) and negative (v. 2b), identifies the father's discipline and teaching as leading to the knowledge that is necessary for discernment (v. 1b). Calls to discipleship begin most of the poems in Prov. 1–9, where they tend to consist of a command or prohibition followed by an argument or motive clause that promises benefits to the student. Here, however, the motive is the value of the father's teaching (v. 2a). The plural address to "sons" (4:1) is not as frequent in Prov. 1–9 as the singular "my son" (but cf. 5:7; 7:24).

4:3. This verse and the first line of v. 4 provide a narrative framework for vv. 4b–9 and support the claim that the father's instruction is good (v. 2) by noting its age (v. 3). This reflects the biblical assumption that the aged are wiser than the young

3937	8881.123,1745	3949	8490.131	4851	2513.131
prep, ps 1cs	v Qal juss 3ms, n mp, ps 1cs	n ms, ps 2ms	v Qal impv 2ms	n fp, ps 1cs	cj, v Qal impv 2ms
לִי	יִתְמָךְ־דְּבָרַי	לִבֶּךָ	שְׁמֹר	מִצְוֹתַי	וֶחֲיֵה
lî	yithmākh-devāray	libbekhā	shemōr	mitswōthay	wechăyēh
to me	let my words hold fast	your heart	observe	my commandments	and live

5.

7353.131	2551	7353.131	1035	414, 8319.123	414, 5731.123
v Qal impv 2ms	n fs	v Qal impv 2ms	n fs	adv, v Qal juss 2ms	cj, adv v Qal juss 2ms
קְנֵה	חָכְמָה	קְנֵה	בִינָה	אַל־תִּשְׁכַּח	וְאַל־תֵּט
qenēh	chokhmāh	qenēh	vînāh	'al-tishkach	we'al-tēt
acquire	wisdom	acquire	insight	do not forget	and do not turn

6.

4623, 571, 6552	414, 6013	8490.122	154.131
prep, n mp, n ms, ps 1cs	adv, v Qal juss 2ms, ps 3fs	cj, v Qal impf 3fs, ps 2ms	v Qal impv 2ms, ps 3fs
מֵאִמְרֵי־פִי	אַל־תַּעַזְבֶהָ	וְתִשְׁמְרֶךָּ	אֱהָבֶהָ
mē'imrê-phî	'al-ta'azveāh	wethishmerekkā	'ĕhāveāh
from the sayings of my mouth	do not abandon her	and she will keep you	love her

7.

5526.122	7519	2551	7353.131	2551
cj, v Qal impf 3fs, ps 2ms	n fs	n fs	v Qal impv 2ms	n fs
וְתִצְּרֶךָ	רֵאשִׁית	חָכְמָה	קְנֵה	חָכְמָה
wethitsterekkā	rē'shîth	chokhmāh	qenēh	chokhmāh
and she will preserve you	the beginning of	wisdom	acquire	wisdom

8.

904, 3725, 7359	7353.131	1035	5744.331	7597.322
cj, prep, adj, n ms, ps 2ms	v Qal impv 2ms	n fs	v Pilpel impv 2ms, ps 3fs	cj, v Polel impf 3fs, ps 2ms
וּבְכָל־קִנְיָנֶךָ	קְנֵה	בִינָה	סַלְסְלֶהָ	וּתְרוֹמְמֶךָ
ûvekhol-qinyānekhā	qenēh	vînāh	salseleāh	ûtherômemekkā
and with all your acquiring	acquire	insight	prize her	and she will exalt you

9.

3632.322	3706	2354.323	5598.122	3937, 7513
v Piel impf 3fs, ps 2ms	cj	v Piel impf 2ms, ps 3fs	v Qal impf 3fs	prep, n ms, ps 2ms
תְּכַבֵּדְךָ	כִּי	תְּחַבְּקֶנָּה	תִּתֵּן	לְרֹאשֶׁךָ
tekhabbēdhekhā	kî	thechabbeqennāh	tittēn	lerō'shekhā
she will honor you	because	you will embrace her	she will give	for your head

10.

4017, 2682	6065	8930	4181.322	8471.131	1158
n fs, n ms	n fs	n fs	v Piel impf 3fs, ps 2ms	v Qal impv 2ms	n ms, ps 1cs
לִוְיַת־חֵן	עֲטֶרֶת	תִּפְאֶרֶת	תְּמַגְּנֶךָ	שְׁמַע	בְּנִי
liwyath-chēn	'ătereth	tiph'ereth	temaggenekkā	shema'	benî
a garland of favor	a crown of	splendor	she will offer you	listen	O my son

4089.131	571	7528.126	3937	8523	2522
cj, v Qal impv 2ms	n mp, ps 1cs	cj, v Qal juss 3mp	prep, ps 2ms	n fp	n mp
וְקַח	אֲמָרַי	וְיִרְבּוּ	לְךָ	שְׁנוֹת	חַיִּים
weqach	'ămāray	weyirbû	lekhā	shenôth	chayyîm
and receive	my sayings	so they may be numerous	for you	years of	a lifetime

words.   Regard my instructions, *Fenton* ... Hold fast my words in your mind, *Goodspeed* ... keep my principles, *JB*.

5. Get wisdom, get understanding: forget it not: ... Wisdom be thy quest, *Knox* ... turn a deaf ear, *REB*.

neither decline from the words of my mouth: ... swerve not from the words, *Goodspeed* ... turned away from, *BB*.

6. Forsake her not, and she shall preserve thee: love her, and she shall keep thee: ... Don't leave wisdom, *Beck* ... she will safeguard you, *Goodspeed*.

7. Wisdom is the principal thing; therefore get wisdom: ... As the first of your wealth, *Anchor* ... Let Wisdom be first; purchase wisdom, *Fenton* ... Wisdom is the most important thing, *NCV* ... Wisedome is the beginning, *Geneva*.

and with all thy getting get understanding: ... Purchase understanding, *Beck* ... at the cost of all you have, *JB*.

8. Exalt her, and she shall promote thee: ... Cherish her and she'll raise you up, *Beck* ... set thee on high, *Rotherham* ... Prize her, *KJVII* ... Treasure wisdom, and it will make you great, *NCV*.

she shall bring thee to honour, when thou dost embrace her: ... honour you, when you salute, *Fenton* ... she will be your pride, *JB*.

9. She shall give to thine head an ornament of grace: a crown of glory shall she deliver to thee: ... graceful garland, *Anchor* ... adorn

you with charm, *Moffat* ... ... like flowers in your hair, *NCV* ... graceful diadem; a glorious crown will she bestow, *NAB* ... to thy head a wreath of grace, A crown of beauty she doth give thee freely, *Young*.

10. Hear, O my son, and receive my sayings; and the years of thy life

---

because they have had more experience at life. They and their counsel are therefore to be listened to with respect and obeyed. The following verses thus contain not merely a father's personal advice, but wisdom that has been handed down for generations. Its permanence proves its worth.

4:4–6. Together with the preceding verse, the first line (v. 4a) provides a narrative framework and shows that his father's counsel was not casual or implicit, but that the father is teaching his own son as he was taught. There is also the implication that just as he submitted to his father's teaching, the proof of which is his ability to pass it on to his son, so his son should accept what he says. The second line (v. 4b) begins the grandfather's quotation, which probably extends through v. 9.

The call to embrace wisdom is both negative and positive, which is a favorite device of the introductory chapters (cf. 4:1f). It contains commands and prohibitions both with and without supporting arguments (motive clauses). Holding onto wisdom, moreover, has real benefits, life (v. 4b) and protection (v. 6), as these chapters often assert (e.g., 2:11–22; 8:32–35).

Loving wisdom is not primarily emotional, but describes the obedience that rises out of love. This attitude toward instruction and correction ensures protection, since it encourages personal reflection (4:23–27), as well as the prudence that guards one's way (cf. 14:16; 16:17; 22:3, 5; 27:12).

4:7. The bald statement of the primacy of wisdom in getting more wisdom would be quite an abrupt shift of topic, except for its close connection to v. 5 (the commands are identical to those in v. 5a). Because the syntax of the first line is difficult (there is no conjunction in the Hebrew text), English versions add various explanatory phrases, generally equating the "beginning of wisdom" with the command to "get wisdom."

The second line could mean to remember to get discernment along with all the other acquiring that one is doing, or more probably, that discernment (as

a synonym for wisdom) is so valuable it would be wise to sell everything that one has ("all your acquisition") in order to buy it. Of course, neither wisdom nor the kingdom of heaven is for sale (17:16; cf. Matt. 13:44ff), nor could they be bought if they were; they are far too valuable.

4:8–9. As in v. 6, wisdom benefits those who demonstrate that they understand its value. Living wisely by obeying wisdom's precepts and instructions, they will find the success that tends to accompany; e.g., diligence and prudence, honesty and generosity. Success then brings its own rewards (cf. 16:13; 22:11, 29), which are thus the rewards of wisdom.

The closing verse expands on this list of benefits, without command or prohibition (which are nonetheless implied by the preceding verses; cf. 1:9). These benefits are signs of celebration and honor (cf. the use of a crown at weddings, S.S. 3:11; Ezek. 16:12). The crown may also be mentioned here because of its association with old age and grandchildren (Prov. 16:31; 17:6).

4:10–19. Whereas the preceding poem (4:1–9) emphasizes wisdom's permanence and value, these verses focus on life as a journey, using twelve different words that refer to life as a "path" or "way," and to progress along it as "walking," "running," or "(not) turning aside." After a brief exhortation and motivation (v. 10b), the poem commends the way of obedience (wisdom; vv. 11ff), warns against the way of the wicked (vv. 14–17), and concludes by directly contrasting the two paths (vv. 18f; cf. 2:21f). Although these verses point to life as the reward of wisdom (vv. 10b, 13b), they focus on the quality of that life, its length (v. 10b) and ease (vv. 12, 18), in contrast with the troubled life of the wicked (vv. 15b–17, 19).

4:10. These verses begin by holding out life as the reward of obedience as often in chs. 1–9 (cf. 2:21; 3:1; 8:32–36). This is reiterated in 4:13b (as in 4:4, 22f), as the teacher implicitly equates his own "sayings" (v. 10) with the "way of wis-

Proverbs 4:11–19

11.

904, 1932	2551	3498.525	1931.525	904, 4724, 3598
prep, n ms	n fs	v Hiphil impf 1cs, ps 2ms	v Hiphil impf 1cs, ps 2ms	prep, n mp, n ms
בְּדֶרֶךְ	חָכְמָה	הֹרֵתִיךָ	הִדְרַכְתִּיךָ	בְּמַעְגְּלֵי־יֹשֶׁר
bedherekh	chokhmāh	hōrēthîkhā	hidhrakhtîkhā	bema'aggelê-yōsher
in the way of	wisdom	I have taught you	I have led you	in tracks of uprightness

12.

904, 2050.141	3940, 7173.121	7082	524, 7608.123	3940
prep, v Qal inf con, ps 2ms	neg part, v Qal impf 3ms	n ms, ps 2ms	cj, part, v Qal impf 2ms	neg part
בְּלֶכְתְּךָ	לֹא־יֵצַר	צַעֲדֶךָ	וְאִם־תָּרוּץ	לֹא
belekhtekhā	lō'-yētsar	tsa'ădhekhā	we'im-tārûts	lō'
when your walking	it will not be hindered	your step	and if you run	not

13.

3911.223	2480.531	904, 4284	414, 7791.123	5526.131
v Niphal impf 2ms	v Hiphil impv 2ms	prep, art, n ms	adv, v Qal juss 2ms	v Qal impv 2ms, ps 3fs
תִּכָּשֵׁל	הַחֲזֵק	בַּמּוּסָר	אַל־תֶּרֶף	נִצְּרֶהָ
thikkāshēl	hachăzēq	bammûsār	'al-tereph	nitstserēāh
you will stumble	take hold	on the discipline	do not relax	guard her

14.

3706, 2026	2522	904, 758	7857	414, 971.123	414, 861.323
cj, pers pron	n mp, ps 2ms	prep, n ms	n mp	adv, v Qal juss 2ms	cj, adv, v Piel juss 2ms
כִּי־הִיא	חַיֶּיךָ	בְּאֹרַח	רְשָׁעִים	אַל־תָּבֹא	וְאַל־תְּאַשֵּׁר
kî-hî'	chayyêkhā	be'ōrach	reshā'îm	'al-tāvō'	we'al-te'ashshēr
because she	your life	on the path of	the wicked	do not go	and do not walk

15.

904, 1932	7737	6797.131	414, 5882.123, 904	7928.131
prep, n ms	n mp	v Qal impv 2ms, ps 3ms	adv, v Qal juss 2ms, prep, ps 3ms	v Qal impv 2ms
בְּדֶרֶךְ	רָעִים	פְּרָעֵהוּ	אַל־תַּעֲבָר־בּוֹ	שְׂטֵה
bedherekh	rā'îm	perā'ēhû	'al-ta'ăvār-bô	setēh
on the way of	evildoers	ignore it	do not pass over on it	depart

16.

4623, 6142	5882.131	3706	3940	3583.126	524, 3940	7778.526
prep, prep, ps 3ms	cj, v Qal impv 2ms	cj	neg part	v Qal impf 3mp	cj, neg part	v Hiphil impf 3mp
מֵעָלָיו	וַעֲבוֹר	כִּי	לֹא	יִשְׁנוּ	אִם־לֹא	יָרֵעוּ
mē'ālâv	wa'ăvôr	kî	lō'	yishnû	'im-lō'	yārē'û
from on it	and pass on	because	not	they will sleep	if not	they act wickedly

17.

1528.212	8535	524, 3940	3911.526	3706	4033.116
cj, v Niphal pf 3fs	n fs, ps 3mp	cj, neg part	v Hiphil impf 3mp	cj	v Qal pf 3cp
וְנִגְזֵלָה	שְׁנָתָם	אִם־לֹא	יִכְשׁוֹלוּ	כִּי	לָחֲמוּ
wenighzelāh	shenāthām	'im-lō'	yikhshiwlû	kî	lāchāmû
and it is stolen	their sleep	if not	they have caused to stumble	because	they eat

18.

4035	7856	3302	2660	8685.126	758
n ms	n ms	cj, n ms	n mp	v Qal impf 3mp	cj, n ms
לֶחֶם	רֶשַׁע	וְיֵין	חֲמָסִים	יִשְׁתּוּ	וְאֹרַח
lechem	resha'	weyên	chămāsîm	yishtû	we'ōrach
the food of	wickedness	and the wine of	violent deeds	they drink	but the path of

6926	3626, 214	5227	2050.151	213.151
n mp	prep, n ms	n fs	v Qal act ptc ms	cj, v Qal act ptc ms
צַדִּיקִים	כְּאוֹר	נֹגַהּ	הוֹלֵךְ	וָאוֹר
tsaddîqîm	ke'ôr	nōghahh	hôlēkh	wā'ôr
the righteous	like a light of	brightness	proceeding	and becoming brighter

19.

5912, 3679.255	3219	1932	7857	3626, 671	3940	3156.116
adv, v Niphal ptc ms	art, n ms	n ms	n mp	prep, art, n fs	neg part	v Qal pf 3cp
עַד־נְכוֹן	הַיּוֹם	דֶּרֶךְ	רְשָׁעִים	כָּאֲפֵלָה	לֹא	יָדְעוּ
'adh-nekhôn	hayyōm	derekh	reshā'îm	kā'ăphēlāh	lō'	yādhe'û
until the establishing of	the day	the way of	the wicked	like the darkness	not	they know

shall be many: ... master the charge I give thee, *Knox* ... accept what I say, *NIV*.

11. I have taught thee in the way of wisdom; I have led thee in right paths: ... I am giving you wise directions and leading you aright, *Moffatt* ... guided you along the path of honesty, *JB* ... Here lies the road to wisdom, here is the path that will bring thee straight to thy goal, *Knox* ... paths of uprightness, *Darby* ... straightforward paths, *Douay*.

12. When thou goest, thy steps shall not be straitened: ... pace will not be retarded, *Anchor* ... your way will not be narrow, *BB*.

and when thou runnest, thou shalt not stumble: ... you will not have a fall, *BB* ... you will not be overwhelmed, *NCV*.

13. Take fast hold of instruction; let her not go: keep her; for she is

thy life: ... Seize Instruction, *Fenton* ... guard her, *Berkeley*.

14. Enter not into the path of the wicked, and go not in the way of evil men: ... Upon the path of the lawless do not thou enter, And do not advance in the way of the wicked, *Rotherham* ... don't do what evil people do, *NCV* ... do not proceed in the way of, *NASB* ... be not happy in a way of evil doers, *Young*.

15. Avoid it, pass not by it, turn from it, and pass away: ... do not take it, turn your back on it, pass it by, *JB* ... Make a detour and keep on your way, *Anchor* ... Turn aside from it, *Young*.

16. For they sleep not, except they have done mischief: ... evil men can't sleep until they've done their evil deed for the day, *LIVB* ... unless they have first done wrong, *JB* ... except they have done evil, *MAST*.

and their sleep is taken away, unless they cause some to fall: ... robbed of their sleep unless they bring people down, *Beck* ... to have made no one stumble steals away their sleep, *NAB*.

17. For they eat the bread of wickedness, and drink the wine of violence: ... their bread, is the eating of Crime, And outrage the wine that they drink!, *Fenton* ... won by lawlessness, *Goodspeed*.

18. But the path of the just is as the shining light, that shineth more and more unto the perfect day: ... of the righteous is as the dawning light, *ASV* ... going on and brightening until the day be fully come, *Darby* ... growing brighter till it is broad day, *NEB* ... fullness of day, *JB*.

19. The way of the wicked is as darkness: they know not at what they stumble: ... dark as pitch, *Goodspeed* ... dark as night, *JB* ... they can't even see what makes them stumble, *NCV*.

dom" (v. 11) and "discipline" (v. 13). These sayings begin in v. 13.

4:11–13. The teacher's words are trustworthy (v. 11), and because they are founded on wisdom, they will guide the student safely through life (cf. 3:5f, 23). The wise are protected by prudence and understanding (14:16; 22:3; 27:12; cf. 4:6). Every step, which pictures the smallest action of life, is secure when taken in obedience to this teaching. Stumbling, whether due to one's own foolish decisions or the wickedness of others, typifies the fate of the wicked (vv. 16, 19).

The final positive exhortation of this section of the poem (v. 13) reflects the opening verse by repeating "your life" (v. 10), forming an inclusion that closes the first portion of these verses. The masculine suffix and pronoun in the second line ("Guard it") refer to "instruction" (v. 13a; literally "discipline"), even though mûsār (HED #4284) is masculine. This could be due to scribal error (misreading the vowel, a scribe may have written nitsts‹reah for nitstseroh), which might have encouraged a scribe to make the pronoun feminine (a change of "yodh" for "waw"), or it could refer to wisdom under the rubric of discipline (v. 11a; chokhmāh is feminine; HED #2551). It could be

merely a grammatical anomaly (cf. 12:25, where the same type of non-agreement occurs).

4:14–15. The repeated warning to avoid the wicked choices that grow out of a foolish heart contrasts sharply with the preceding promises to lead the student in wise and upright ways (v. 11), but depends for its force on the following description of the consequences of walking in those ways (vv. 16f). The same verb ends both lines of v. 15, which the translations may obscure; it says, in essence, "do not pass by on it," but "pass it by."

4:16–17. The wicked, "eating" what they love (v. 17; cf. Ps. 109:17f), become what they eat, to the extent that wickedness has become more precious to them than sleep. Their choices have led to their dissolution, so that their sin is hypnotic. This hyperbole is designed to frighten the reader so that he or she reflects the danger of even the first step on that path (v. 14).

4:18–19. The last two verses of this section form a conclusion by contrasting the nature of the two ways of life and what it is like to travel on them. Since obedience leads to understanding (cf. 3:5f), continued obedience leads to increased understanding, or light, so that even the naive, who walk in the "gloom" of inexperience, will

20.

904, 4242	3911.226	1158	3937, 1745	7477.531	3937, 571
prep, art, intrg	v Niphal impf 3mp	n ms, ps 1cs	prep, n mp, ps 1cs	v Hiphil impv 2ms	prep, n mp, ps 1cs
בַּמֶּה	יִכָּשֵׁלוּ	בְּנִי	לִדְבָרַי	הַקְשִׁיבָה	לַאֲמָרַי
bammeh	yikkāshēlû	benî	lidhvāray	haqŏshîvāh	la'ămāray
over what	they are stumbling	my son	to my words	be attentive	to my sayings

21.

5371.531, 238	414, 4005.526	4623, 6084	8490.131
v Hiphil impv 2ms, n fs, ps 2ms	adv, v Hiphil juss 3mp	prep, n fd, ps 2ms	v Qal impv 2ms, ps 3mp
הַט־אָזְנֶךָ	אַל־יַלִּיזוּ	מֵעֵינֶיךָ	שָׁמְרֵם
haṭ-'āzenekhā	'al-yallîzû	mē'ênêkhā	shāmerēm
incline your ear	do not let them deviate	from your eyes	keep them

22.

904, 8761	3949	3706, 2522	2062	3937, 4834.152
prep, n ms	n ms, ps 2ms	cj, n mp	pers pron	prep, v Qal act ptc mp, ps 3mp
בְּתוֹךְ	לְבָבֶךָ	כִּי־חַיִּים	הֵם	לְמֹצְאֵיהֶם
bethôkh	levāvekhā	kî-chayyîm	hēm	lemōtse'êhem
in the middle of	your heart	because life	they	to those who find them

23.

3937, 3725, 1340	4995	4623, 3725, 5110	5526.131	3949	3706, 4623
cj, prep, adj, n ms, ps 3ms	n ms	prep, adj, n ms	v Qal impv 2ms	n ms, ps 2ms	cj, prep, ps 3ms
וּלְכָל־בְּשָׂרוֹ	מַרְפֵּא	מִכָּל־מִשְׁמָר	נְצֹר	לִבֶּךָ	כִּי־מִמֶּנּוּ
ûlăkhol-besārô	marpē'	mikkol-mishmār	netsōr	libbekhā	kî-mimmennû
and to all his body	healing	of all guarding	guard	your heart	because from it

24.

8777	2522	5681.531	4623	6381	6552
n fp	n mp	v Hiphil impv 2ms	prep, ps 2ms	n fs	n ms
תּוֹצָאוֹת	חַיִּים	הָסֵר	מִמְּךָ	עִקְּשׁוּת	פֶּה
tôts'ôth	chayyîm	hāsēr	mimmekhā	'iqqeshûth	peh
emanations of	life	remove	from you	perversity of	the mouth

25.

4025	8004	7651.531	4623	6084	3937, 5415
cj, n fs	n fd	v Hiphil impv 2ms	prep, ps 2ms	n fd, ps 2ms	prep, prep
וּלְזוּת	שְׂפָתַיִם	הַרְחֵק	מִמֶּךָ	עֵינֶיךָ	לְנֹכַח
ûlăzûth	sephāthayim	harchēq	mimmekkā	'ênêkhā	lenōkhach
and crookedness of	lips	remove	from you	your eyes	frontward

26.

5202.526	6310	3595.526	5224	6668.331	4724
v Hiphil juss 3mp	cj, n md, ps 2ms	v Hiphil juss 3mp	prep, ps 2ms	v Piel impv 2ms	n ms
יַבִּיטוּ	וְעַפְעַפֶּיךָ	יַישִׁרוּ	נֶגְדֶּךָ	פַּלֵּס	מַעְגַּל
yabbîṭû	we'aph'appêkhā	yayshirû	neghdekhā	palēs	ma'ăggal
may they look	and your eyelids	let them be straight	before you	make level	the track of

---

20. My son, attend to my words; incline thine ear unto my sayings: ... pay attention to what I am telling you, *JB* ... let your ear be turned to, *BB*.

21. Let them not depart from thine eyes; keep them in the midst of thine heart: ... Don't ever forget my words; keep them always in mind, *NCV* ... in the center of your heart, *Beck*.

22. For they are life unto those that find them, and health to all their flesh: ... strength to all his flesh, *BB* ... and health to all humanity, *JB*.

23. Keep thy heart with all diligence: ... More than anything else watch your heart, *Beck* ... guard your inner self, *Moffatt*.

for out of it are the issues of life: ... springs of life, *Anchor* ... because your thoughts run your life, *NCV* ... it is the wellspring of life, *NIV*.

24. Put away from thee a froward mouth: ... Expel from yourself a false mouth, *Fenton* ... an evil tongue, *BB*.

and perverse lips put far from thee: ... put wicked lips, *Geneva* ... cast from yourself a loose life, *Fenton* ... put devious talk far from you, *RSV*.

25. Let thine eyes look right on, and let thine eyelids look straight before thee: ... your gaze straight ahead of you, *Berkeley* ... your eyes look directly ahead, And let your gaze be fixed straight in front, *NASB* ... thine eyelashes point straight, *Rotherham*.

26. Ponder the path of thy feet: ... Make level the path of thy feet, *ASV* ... Keep level the track for your foot, *Goodspeed* ... ever make your footing firm, *Moffatt*.

find their paths increasingly bright, characterized by insight and wisdom, as they seize and obey the instruction that they receive. The full implications of this verse are created by its contrast with the following.

Since the wicked (foolish) have chosen to go their own way, rejecting wisdom (1:20–32), and not obeying whatever instruction they may receive, they are doomed to a life of difficulty (13:21; 22:5). Choosing to walk in darkness, they cannot see the real nature of their road, and so stumble, not realizing that it is their own folly that blinds them (Luke 11:33–36).

4:20–27. Life is portrayed as a journey (vv. 26f), much like the preceding section, but whereas vv. 10–19 use synonyms for "path," vv. 20–27 use the imagery of the body to strengthen its exhortation, referring to the ears (v. 20b), eyes (vv. 21a, 25a), eyelids (v. 25b), heart (vv. 21b, 23), flesh (v. 22b), mouth and lips (v. 24) and feet (vv. 26a, 27b). These terms concretize the exhortations, allowing the student of Proverbs to visualize the actions described in this poem. The opening call to attention (v. 20) is nearly identical to 5:1 (and is identical in tone to all of the opening exhortations of chs. 1–9).

These verses also resemble vv. 1–9 and differ from vv. 10–19 in that they do not describe or discuss the wicked. They warn against particular sins (especially lying, v. 24), but focus on the person's internal life, without contrasting the righteous and the wicked.

4:20–22. The words of the teacher can escape unless they are guarded. Wisdom is not a static entity that, once gained, is a permanent possession. Learning needs to be used, just as minds and muscles need to be exercised, in order to continue to be available when need arises. Solomon warns elsewhere that to stop learning is to begin to sink into folly (19:27; the first half of 4:21 is nearly identical to Prov. 3:21a).

Wise teaching is a source of life and health (v. 22; cf. 3:1f, 7f), which reiterates earlier statements about the life-giving quality of instruction (4:4, 13). This chiastic verse closes the first section of the poem.

4:23. The syntax of 4:23a is nearly identical to that of 4:7b. The two verses emphasize that some things are more important than others, whether continuing to grow in wisdom and understanding (v. 7), or to guard the repository of wisdom

(vv. 21, 23). Since all of the actions of life (literally "the outgoings of life") originate in the heart, its condition determines whether or not one will live wisely (and continue to live) or foolishly (and die). It must therefore be guarded more carefully than anything else. This guarding may have a twofold purpose: to keep and maintain the teaching that one has already received and to protect it from false or misleading teaching. These dual aspects are addressed in the next two verses.

Tying these last four verses together is the repeated "remove" (HED #5681; obscured in most translations), the first referring to ridding oneself of twisted words and speaking the truth (v. 24a), and the second to returning to the right path by removing one's feet from a wrong one (v. 27b).

4:24. Since what comes out of the mouth merely reflects what is already in the heart, guarding one's heart is a means to guarding one's words and rejecting the temptation to twist the truth. This implies the importance of telling the truth to oneself, in one's own heart. Lying and cleverly twisted words are condemned throughout Proverbs (e.g., 6:12, 19), as they are in the Covenant (e.g., Exo. 20:16; 23:1f). This verse thus considers the matter of keeping one's heart based on the evidence that comes out of it.

4:25. Another way to guard one's heart is to choose and act carefully (16:1ff), since the feet follow the eyes. This image anticipates the command of v. 27a. It also assumes that the path being followed is correct, since anyone who is on the wrong way needs to return immediately to the right way (v. 27b).

4:26. The penultimate verse of each of the second and third poetic sections uses different images to make the same point. Just as a path is easier to follow as night turns to day (v. 18), so it is easier to walk on one that is smooth and well-tended. To obey is to smooth one's path, since obedience leads to understanding and insight, both of which enable one to make increasingly wise choices and decisions.

4:27. To walk straight ahead, without deviation, primarily describes faithfulness in keeping the Covenant (e.g., Deut. 5:32; 17:11, 20; 28:14; Josh. 1:7; 23:6). To walk according to the Covenant is to follow the path laid out by God for his people; turning aside to either side is equally perilous. Whoever realizes that he or she has left that path must return to it as quickly as possible, lest they be drawn fur-

7972	414, 5371.123, 3332	27.	3679.226	3725, 1932	7559
cj, n ms	adv, v Qal juss 2ms, n fs		v Niphal impf 3mp	cj, adj, n mp, ps 2ms	n fs, ps 2ms
וּשְׂמֹאול	אַל־תֵּט־יָמִין		יִכֹּנוּ	וְכָל־דְּרָכֶיךָ	רַגְלֶךָ
ûsemō'wl	'al-tēt-yāmîn		yikkōnû	wekhol-derākhêkhā	raghlekhā
nor the left	do not lean toward the right		they will be established	and all your ways	your foot

5681.531	7559	4623, 7737	5:1	1158	3937, 2551	7477.531
v Hiphil impv 2ms	n fs, ps 2ms	prep, n ms		n ms, ps 1cs	prep, n fs, ps 1cs	v Hiphil impv 2ms
הָסֵר	רַגְלֶךָ	מֵרָע		בְּנִי	לְחָכְמָתִי	הַקְשִׁיבָה
hāsēr	raghlekhā	mērā'		benî	lechokhmāthî	haqŏshîvāh
withdraw	your foot	from evil		O my son	to my wisdom	be attentive

3937, 1035	5371.531, 238	2.	3937, 8490.141	4343	1907
prep, n fs, ps 1cs	v Hiphil impv 2ms, n fs, ps 2ms		prep, v Qal inf con	n fp	cj, n fs
לִתְבוּנָתִי	הַט־אָזְנֶךָ		לִשְׁמֹר	מְזִמּוֹת	וְדַעַת
lithvûnāthî	hat-'āzenekhā		lishmōr	mezimmôth	wedha'ath
to my understanding	incline your ear		for observing	discretion	and knowledge

8004	5526.126	3.	3706	5499	5382.127	8004	2299	2607
n fd, ps 2ms	v Qal impf 3mp		cj	n ms	v Qal impf 3fp	n fd	n fs	cj, adj
שְׂפָתֶיךָ	יִנְצֹרוּ		כִּי	נֹפֶת	תִּטֹּפְנָה	שִׂפְתֵי	זָרָה	וְחָלָק
sephāthêkhā	yintsōrû		kî	nōpheth	tittōphenāh	siphthê	zārāh	wechālāq
your lips	they will keep		because	honey	they drip	lips of	an adulteress	and smoother

4623, 8467	2541	4.	321	4914	3626, 4081	2392	3626, 2820
prep, n ms	n ms, ps 3fs		cj, n fs, ps 3fs	adj	prep, n fs	adj	prep, n fs
מִשָּׁמֶן	חִכָּהּ		וְאַחֲרִיתָהּ	מָרָה	כַלַּעֲנָה	חַדָּה	כְּחֶרֶב
mishshemen	chikkāhh		we'achărîthāhh	mārāh	khalla'ănāh	chaddāh	kecherev
than olive oil	her mouth		but the result of her	bitter	like wormwood	sharp	like a sword of

6610	5.	7559	3495.154	4323	8061	7082	8881.126
n mp		n fd, ps 3fs	v Qal act ptc fp	n ms	pn	n mp, ps 3fs	v Qal impf 3mp
פִּיוֹת		רַגְלֶיהָ	יֹרְדוֹת	מָוֶת	שְׁאוֹל	צְעָדֶיהָ	יִתְמֹכוּ
pîyôth		raghlêāh	yōredhôth	māweth	she'ôl	tse'ādhêāh	yithmōkhû
double edges		her feet	going down to	death	Sheol	her steps	they lay hold of

6.	758	2522	6678, 6668.321	5309.116	4724	3940
	n ms	n mp	cj, v Piel impf 3ms	v Qal pf 3mp	n mp, ps 3fs	neg part
	אֹרַח	חַיִּים	פֶּן־תְּפַלֵּס	נָעוּ	מַעְגְּלֹתֶיהָ	לֹא
	'ōrach	chayyîm	pen-tephallēs	nā'û	ma'ggelōthêāh	lō'
	the path of	life	so that she will not make level	they have roamed	her tracks	not

and let all thy ways be established: ... be well-ordered, *Darby* ... let all your courses be firm, *Fenton*.

27. Turn not to the right hand nor to the left: remove thy foot from evil: ... Walk away from evil, *Anchor* ... keep clear of every evil thing, *NEB*.

5:1. My son, attend unto my wisdom: ... Listen to me, my son! I know what I am saying, *LIVB* ... pay attention and listen to my wisdom and insight, *Good News*.

and bow thine ear to my understanding: ... Incline your ear to reason, *Goodspeed* ... bend down your ear to my thoughts, *Fenton* ... listen to my good counsel, *NEB*.

2. That thou mayest regard discretion, and that thy lips may keep knowledge: ... conduct yourself wisely and talk intelligently, *Beck* ... protect discretion; that your lips may guard knowledge, *Berkeley*.

3. For the lips of a strange woman drop as an honeycomb, and her mouth is smoother than oil: ...

loose-living woman, *JB* ... The words of another man's wife, *NCV* ... honey-sweet words the temptress may use, *Knox* ... her palate is smoother than oil, *Berkeley*.

4. But her end is bitter as wormwood, sharp as a twoedged sword: ... in the end she is bitter as gall, *NIV* ... bitter as poison, *Moffatt* ... as a poisonous plant, *Beck* ... she will bring you sorrow, *NCV* ... More sharp than a double-edged sword!, *Fenton*.

5. Her feet go down to death; her steps take hold on hell: ... to the

ther into the way(s) of sin (vv. 14f). The two halves of the verse are thus complementary: "Don't leave the path; if you have, return immediately!"

This is not a hypothetical or unspecified path, however. The repetition of the verb found in 4:5c, "Do not turn aside from the words of my mouth!" implicitly identifies the "words" of both poems.

5:1–23. Appearing in this chapter is a single poem that extols marital fidelity by warning about the nature of the adulteress (vv. 3–6) and the consequences of adultery (vv. 7–14). The poem then exhorts faithfulness (vv. 15–20) and closes with the ubiquitous warning of Prov. 1–9 that to choose folly is to choose death (vv. 21ff).

Adultery is condemned repeatedly in the Covenant (e.g., Exo. 20:14; Lev. 20:10), as well as in three lengthy poems in Proverbs (2:16–19; 6:20–35; 7:1–27). An important point in all of these poems is that companions, and the choices that they encourage by their words and example, tend to affect the course of one another's lives, which is also a theme throughout Proverbs (cf. 1:8–19). Those who are motivated by rebellion and wickedness inevitably lead their associates into the same paths—paths that end in death. This is true whether the course is violence (1:8–19), anger (20:24f) or adultery. Adultery may be a sin to which naive young men are especially prone, but it is only one of many sinful activities that reveal the fatal flaw (folly) that leads to destruction.

Note on translation: *Although many translations use the term "adulteress" (vv. 3, 20; cf. 2:16; 6:24, 26b; 7:5), the Hebrew text does not refer to a woman especially prone to sexual sin or marital infidelity. It uses substantive feminine adjectives ("strange woman" in vv. 3, 20a) and "foreign woman" in v. 20b) to refer to any woman other than one's wife; i.e., any woman who is outside the bond of a particular marital covenant is "strange" or "foreign." An intimate relationship with someone other than one's spouse is inappropriate because of the marital bond that it violates, not due to the nature or predilections of the person(s) involved.*

NRSV, for example, is therefore misleading when it uses "loose woman" instead of "strange woman" (5:3; even the footnote "strange" may be misleading, since "strange" in English rarely connotes "stranger," which is the force of the Hebrew term). Its reference to an "adulteress" (5:20b; literally "foreign woman") is also problematic, although "another woman" (5:20a) clearly points to a woman other than

one's wife. NIV's use of "adulteress" is similarly lacking (5:3, 20a), while "another man's wife" (v. 20b) is overly specific and out of place in this chapter. The phrase "his neighbor's wife" occurs in 6:29 (cf. 7:19), and is followed by an explicit reference to the cuckold's jealous rage (6:34f).

The warning of this chapter (and the poems in 6:20–35 and 7:1–27) should not be limited to a husband's infidelity, since either spouse who commits adultery violates the covenantal union of that marriage. This needs to be kept in mind during the discussion which follows; the comments reflect the masculine orientation of the text.

5:1–2. The opening call to attend the words of the teacher (v. 1) closely parallels those in earlier poems (2:2; 4:20), using terms found throughout the prologue. The result of this attention to his teaching, careful planning and speech must be seen in light of the overall thrust of the poem, especially as it is revealed in the next verses (vv. 3–6), which contrast the character of the "strange woman" with these results in the student's life.

5:3–4. These verses contrast the appearance and reality, the beginning and the consequences, of adulterous relationships. Honey's proverbial sweetness (cf. Judg. 14:18; Prov. 24:13), an image of the sweetness of love (cf. S.S. 4:11), combined with flattery ("smooth"; cf. Prov. 7:21) lead the naive to think that this is true love. Blind to the corruption below the surface, the bitter consequence of tasting forbidden sweets, he does not know that this honey is really gall, and that these flattering words will turn deadly. (This sword has "mouths," more than one cutting edge.)

5:5–6. The end of adultery is misery (v. 4) and death, because to participate in it is to put oneself on the same path as the adulterous woman (cf. Ps. 1:1 and, e.g., Prov. 2:18ff; 7:27). Placing the two key terms, "death" and "Sheol," in the center of the verse focuses on this outcome. Their parallel use also shows that both refer to death (i.e., "death" and "Sheol" should not be interpreted as though they referred to separate entities).

The verbs in v. 6 could be either feminine singular ("she") or masculine ("you"); "you" might fit the meaning of "lest" (HED #6678) better, "lest you ponder (literally "weigh"; HED #6668) the path of her life." Under this interpretation (followed by NKJV) the last line would supply the reason for the exhortation (v. 1) and explain the urgency of the reason (v. 2). The flow of the section would then circle back to the learner with whom it

Proverbs 5:7–15

3156.122 v Qal impf 3fs תֵּדַע thēdha' she knows	**7.** 6498 cj, adv וְעַתָּה we'attāh so now	1158 n mp בָנִים vānîm O sons	8471.133, 3937 v Qal impv 2mp, prep, ps 1cs שִׁמְעוּ־לִי shim'û-lî listen to me	414, 5681.128 cj, adv, v Qal juss 2mp וְאַל־תָּסוּרוּ we'al-tāsûrû and do not turn away

4623, 571, 6552 prep, *n mp*, n ms, ps 1cs מֵאִמְרֵי־פִי mē'imrê-phî from the sayings of my mouth	**8.** 7651.531 v Hiphil impv 2ms הַרְחֵק harchēq distance yourself	4623, 6142 prep, prep, ps 3fs מֵעָלֶיהָ mē'āleāh from her	1932 n ms, ps 2ms דַרְכֶּךָ dharkekhā your way

414, 7414.123 cj, adv, v Qal juss 2ms וְאַל־תִּקְרַב we'al-tiqŏrav and do not come near	420, 6860 prep, *n ms* אֶל־פֶּתַח 'el-pethach to the entrance of	1041 n ms, ps 3fs בֵּיתָהּ bêthāhh her house	**9.** 6678, 5598.123 cj, v Qal impf 2ms פֶּן־תִּתֵּן pen-tittēn so you will not give	3937, 311 prep, adj לַאֲחֵרִים la'ăchērîm to others

2003 n ms, ps 2ms הוֹדֶךָ hôdhekhā your splendor	8523 cj, n fp, ps 2ms וּשְׁנֹתֶיךָ ûshenōthêkhā and your years	3937, 400 prep, adj לְאַכְזָרִי le'akhzārî to the cruel	**10.** 6678, 7781.126 cj, v Qal impf 3mp פֶּן־יִשְׂבְּעוּ pen-yisbe'û so they will not be satisfied by	2299 n mp זָרִים zārîm strangers

3699 n ms, ps 2ms כֹּחֶךָ kōchekhā your strength	6325 cj, n mp, ps 2ms וַעֲצָבֶיךָ wa'ătsāvêkhā and your works	904, 1041 prep, *n ms* בְּבֵית bevêth in the household of	5425 n ms נָכְרִי nākherî a foreigner	**11.** 5277.113 cj, v Qal pf 2ms וְנָהַמְתָּ wenāhamtā then you will groan

904, 321 prep, n fs, ps 2ms בְּאַחֲרִיתֶךָ ve'achărîthekhā at your end	3735.141 prep, v Qal inf con בִּכְלוֹת bikhlôth when coming to an end	1340 n ms, ps 2ms בְּשָׂרֶךָ besārekhā your flesh	8083 cj, n ms ps 2ms וּשְׁאֵרֶךָ ûshe'ērekhā and your body	**12.** 569.113 cj, v Qal pf 2ms וְאָמַרְתָּ we'āmartā and you will say	351 intrg אֵיךְ 'êkh how

7983.115 v Qal pf 1cs שָׂנֵאתִי sānē'thî I hated	4284 n ms מוּסָר mûsār discipline	8673 cj, n fs וְתוֹכַחַת wethôkhachath and correction	5180.111 v Qal pf 3ms נָאַץ nā'ats it has contemned	3949 n ms, ps 1cs לִבִּי libbî my heart	**13.** 3940, 8471.115 cj, neg part, v Qal pf 1cs וְלֹא־שָׁמַעְתִּי welō'-shāma'ttî and I did not listen

904, 7249 prep, *n ms* בְּקוֹל beqôl by the voice of	4310 n mp, ps 1cs מוֹרָי môrāy my teachers	3937, 4064.352 cj, prep, v Piel ptc mp, ps 1cs וְלִמְלַמְּדַי welimlammedhay and to my teachers	3940, 5371.515 neg part, v Hiphil pf 1cs לֹא־הִטִּיתִי lō'-hittîthî I did not incline	238 n fs, ps 1cs אָזְנִי 'āzenî my ear

14. 3626, 4746 prep, sub כִּמְעַט kim'at when a little	2030.115 v Qal pf 1cs הָיִיתִי hāyîthî I was	904, 3725, 7737 prep, *adj*, n ms בְכָל־רָע vekhol-rā' in every evil	904, 8761 prep, *n ms* בְּתוֹךְ bethôkh in the midst of	7235 n ms קָהָל qāhāl the assembly	5920 cj, n fs וְעֵדָה we'ēdhāh and the congregation

15. 8685.131, 4448 v Qal impv 2ms, n md שְׁתֵה־מַיִם shethēh-mayim drink water	3937, 988 prep, n ms, ps 2ms מִבּוֹרֶךָ mibbôrekhā from your cistern	5320.152 cj, v Qal act ptc mp וְנֹזְלִים wenōzelîm and what flows	4623, 8761 prep, *n ms* מִתּוֹךְ mittôkh from the middle of	908 n fs, ps 2ms בְּאֵרֶךָ be'ērekhā your well

nether world her steps attain, *NAB* ... take hold on Sheol, *MRB* ... steps lead straight to the grave, *Moffatt*.

6. Lest thou shouldest ponder the path of life: ... meditate, *KJVII* ... she does not take heed, *RSV*.

her ways are moveable, that thou canst not know them: ... Her ways wander, but she knoweth it not, *MAST* ... her course is uncertain and she does not know it, *JB* ... Her ways are unstable, *NASB* ... but she is unconcerned, *REB*.

7. Hear me now therefore, O ye children, and depart not from the words of my mouth: ... my sons, *NASB* ... turn not away, *Fenton* ... do not ignore what I say, *NEB*.

8. Remove thy way far from her, and come not nigh the door of her house: ... shun her company, *Knox* ... Keep your feet far from her, *Berkeley* ... Don't even go near the door, *CEV*.

9. Lest thou give thine honour unto others, and thy years unto the cruel: ... vigour unto others, *MAST* ... Wouldst thou squander the pride of thy manhood, *Knox* ... and your dignity to some cruel person, *Beck*.

10. Lest strangers be filled with thy wealth: ... thy strength, *MRB* ... spend all thy hopes, bestow all thy pains, *Knox* ... will batten on your property, *JB*.

and thy labours be in the house of a stranger: ... hard-won earnings go to an alien's house, *NAB* ... what you worked so hard for will go to someone else, *NCV*.

11. And thou mourn at the last, when thy flesh and thy body are consumed: ... And you will be full of grief, *BB* ... And you groan at results to yourself, With your body and manhood destroyed, *Fenton* ... When you shrink to skin and bone, *REB*.

12. And say, How have I hated instruction, and my heart despised reproof: ... why did I hate guidance, why did I despise all warning?, *Moffatt* ... I hated discipline, *Beck* ... and scorned admonition, *Goodspeed* ... despised correction!, *Geneva* ... my heart put no value on training, *BB*.

13. And have not obeyed the voice of my teachers, nor inclined mine ear to them that instructed me!: ... not hearkened to the voice of my directors, *Young* ... Nor pay attention to my instructors, *Anchor* ... listen, *NIV*.

14. I was almost in all evil in the midst of the congregation and assembly: ... nearly sentenced to death by the community, *Moffatt* ... come to nearly every kind of misery, *JB* ... I soon earned a bad name, *NEB* ... I am at the point of utter ruin in the public assembly, *NRSV*.

15. Drink waters out of thine own cistern, and running waters out of

---

begins: "pay attention so that you learn discretion, because the strange woman is deceitful; you may be tempted to consider her ways because you do not yet realize just how dangerous her paths are."

The primary difficulty with the third person interpretation ("she") is that if pen (HED #6678), which introduces negative purposes (i.e., "in order that X will not happen" or "in order that I/you/he/she will not do X") refers here to the woman, it is used in a way not found in any other biblical text, perhaps introducing the consequence of v. 5. The ancient versions interpreted this as a simple negative statement, the approach that is followed by most English translations, "She does not" (e.g., NASB, NRSV, NIV). In this case, the strange woman is nearly a tragic figure, ignorant of her own character and the consequences of her actions.

5:7. The term translated "therefore" (HED #6498) always introduces commands or exhortations that are the appropriate response to what has just been said. With this verse, the teacher returns to his opening exhortation (5:1), although here he addresses more than one "son" (cf. 4:1; 7:24; 8:32).

5:8. Stated both negatively and positively, this is the central command of the first main part of the poem (vv. 1–14). Those who cannot yet discern the

real issues involved should avoid situations in which they may be tempted.

5:9–10. An adulterous relationship can destroy one's well-being and threaten financial ruin, especially if the relationship is ongoing (as these verses may imply), or discovered by the woman's husband (6:34f). Often a partner in adultery must be supported, and even if not, gifts are part of every close personal relationship. The youth, whose naiveté may well include ignorance about the costs of supporting and running a household, may not realize this implication, especially when blinded by emotion, but its eventual price could be enormous. A more sinister possibility is blackmail, especially if the adulterer has gained a certain degree of social standing (cf. 22:6), but this probably refers to a situation in which the adulterer(s) attempt to placate a husband's jealousy by gifts or bribes, which will, however, inflame jealousy rather than subdue it (6:34f).

5:11–12. In addition to personal ruin (5:9f), the choices that steer one into an adulterous relationship may lead to self-recrimination (vv. 11–14), but it is clear from these verses that this awareness comes too late. The groaning of the adulterer (v. 11) is contained in the next three verses. The first two

16.

6571.126 v Qal impf 3mp	4754 n mp, ps 2ms	2445 n ms	904, 7624 prep, art, n fp	6631, 4448 n mp, n'md
יָפוּצוּ	מַעְיְנֹתֶיךָ	חוּצָה	בָּרְחֹבוֹת	פַּלְגֵי־מָיִם
yāphûtsû	ma'aynōthêkhā	chûtsāh	bārechōvôth	palghê-māyim
they spread out	your springs	to the outside	in the plazas	streams of water

17.

2030.126, 3937 v Qal juss 3mp, prep, ps 2ms	3937, 940 prep, n ms, ps 2ms	375 cj, sub	3937, 2299 prep, n mp	882 prep, ps 2ms
יִהְיוּ־לְךָ	לְבַדֶּךָ	וְאֵין	לְזָרִים	אִתָּךְ
yihyû-lekhā	levaddekhā	we'ên	lezārîm	'ittākh
let them be for you	only you	and there is not	for strangers	with you

18.

2030.121, 4888 v Qal juss 3ms, n ms, ps 2ms	1313.155 v Qal pass ptc ms	7975.131 cj, v Qal impv 2ms	4623, 828 prep, n fs	5454 n ms, ps 2ms
יְהִי־מְקוֹרְךָ	בָרוּךְ	וּשְׂמַח	מֵאֵשֶׁת	נְעוּרֶךָ
yehî-meqôrkhā	vārûkh	ûsemach	mē'ēsheth	ne'ûrekhā
let your spring be	blessed	and rejoice	because of the wife of	your youth

19.

370 n fs	156 n mp	3389, 2682 cj, n fs, n ms	1767 n md, ps 3fs	7588.326 v Piel juss 3mp, ps 2ms	904, 3725, 6496 prep, adj, n fs
אַיֶּלֶת	אֲהָבִים	וְיַעֲלַת־חֵן	דַּדֶּיהָ	יְרַוֻּךָ	בְכָל־עֵת
'ayyeleth	'ăhāvîm	weya'ălath-chēn	daddêāh	yerawwukhā	vekhol-'ēth
a doe of	loving	and a she-goat of grace	her breasts	let them satisfy you	at all times

904, 157 prep, n fs, ps 3fs	8146.123 v Qal impf 2ms	8878 adv	**20.**	4066 cj, intrg	8146.123 v Qal impf 2ms	1158 n ms, ps 1cs
בְּאַהֲבָתָהּ	תִּשְׁגֶּה	תָמִיד		וְלָמָּה	תִשְׁגֶּה	בְנִי
be'ahvāthāhh	tishgeh	thāmîdh		welāmmāh	thishgeh	venî
with her love	you will go astray	continually		and why	will you stray	O my son

904, 2299 prep, n fs	2354.323 cj, v Piel impf 2ms	2536 n ms	5425 n fs	**21.**	3706 cj	5415 prep
בְזָרָה	וּתְחַבֵּק	חֵק	נָכְרִיָּה		כִּי	נֹכַח
vezārāh	ûthechabbēq	chēq	nākheriyāh		kî	nōkhach
with a stranger	and will you embrace	the bosom of	a foreign woman		because	in front of

thine own well: ... your own storage-well, *JB* ... Be faithful to your own wife, *NCV* ... just as you take water from your own well, *CEV*.

16. Let thy fountains be dispersed abroad, and rivers of waters in the streets: ... Should thy springs be dispersed, *MRB* ... don't be like a stream from which just any woman may take a drink, *CEV* ... don't give your love to just any woman, *NCV*.

17. Let them be only thine own: ... And reserved for your own use alone, *Fenton* ... These things are yours alone, *NCV*.

and not strangers' with thee: ... don't share them with strangers, *Beck* ... never to be shared with strangers, *NIV*.

18. Let thy fountain be blessed: and rejoice with the wife of thy youth: ... Be happy with the wife you married, *CEV* ... derive delight from, *Berkeley*.

19. Let her be as the loving hind and pleasant roe: ... pleasant doe, *MRB* ... graceful as a fawn, *JB* ... a lovely wild goat, *Beck* ... with the lovely gazelles, *Fenton*.

let her breasts satisfy thee at all times: ... be it her bosom that steals away thy senses, *Knox* ... Let her breasts intoxicate you always, *Goodspeed*.

and be thou ravished always with her love: ... the love that ever holds you captive, *JB* ... be always infatuated with her love, *Berkeley*.

20. And why wilt thou, my son, be ravished with a strange woman: ... Why be seduced, my son, by someone else's wife, *JB* ... Why should you ... fall for an adulterous woman, *Beck* ... are you wrapped up in the love of an adulteress?, *NEB*.

and embrace the bosom of a stranger?: ... bosom of an alien?, *MAST* ... an outsider, *Berkeley* ... woman who belongs to another?, *JB* ... an adventuress?, *RSV* ... in the arms of a seductress?, *NKJV* ... Don't hug another man's wife, *NCV*.

21. For the ways of man are before the eyes of the LORD, and he pondereth all his goings: ... Man's goings are observed by the Eternal, he takes account of all his ways, *Moffatt* ... And he maketh level all

50

(vv. 12f) describe his attitude toward instruction, and the third shows the consequence (v. 14).

His "end" refers not to the end of his life, but to the outcome of his chosen way of life. Parallel to "her end" (5:4), it shows that both partners face equally disastrous fates. His "flesh" and "body" may stand for the work that the adulterer did, all of which is lost to him (5:9f), or this verse may mean that he is starving, having lost all that he had. Now that he has worn himself out meeting his lover's demands, he comes to his senses.

5:13–14. The ruined adulterer gives the "moral" of the poem, which is a much more effective means of instruction than a direct speech from the teacher. (The teacher's speech comes in 5:15–23.) The adulterer explains that his refusal to obey his teachers and their instruction was his undoing. He refused to do the very things that the teacher commends to his students in the opening verses of the chapter ("incline your ear"; 5:1b). Instead of merely not listening (5:13), he deliberately rejected their teaching (5:12).

The final consequence of this rejection (5:12) was his near ruin and public disgrace (5:14), although the text is vague about the nature of that ruin. It might have been death by stoning, in fulfillment of the Law (Lev. 20:10; Deut. 22:22), a lawsuit (cf. 6:34f) or some other form of public disgrace. He does not explain how he escaped this fate, but his narrow escape heightens the warning. If he feels this miserable and sees himself in such a state, how much more should the student understand that he needs to obey his teacher in order to avoid a similar fate.

5:15. In images reminiscent of his greatest song (S.S. 1:1), Solomon exhorts young men to find their joy and delight in their own wives, not in another woman's arms. Drinking from one's own cistern is a picture of domestic bliss (Isa. 36:16), and the images of water, cistern, well, fountain, refer to the wife's sexual relationship with her husband (S.S. 4:15; cf. Prov. 22:14; 23:27). Although there is no direct Hebrew equivalent for "your own," that is implied by the context of this verse.

5:16–17. Some have interpreted this verse as a positive statement that marital fidelity yields children, who will then spread beyond the home ("your springs will be dispersed"), others that it warns against the wife's adultery, since the water source images of the surrounding verses (5:15–18) describe the wife (cf. S.S. 4:12, 15). It seems best

to fit the context, however, as an implicit question warning that the man's semen should be kept within his marital relationship, not "spread abroad" or "in the streets" (both images for relationships outside his marriage).

Verse 17 shares some of the same ambiguity, although its import is clearly that the water sources, as images for sexual favors, mentioned in the previous two verses are the exclusive property of the marriage partners, and are not to be shared with anyone else. The "strangers," however, are masculine, not feminine, perhaps referring back to strangers who will gain his wealth if he commits adultery (5:10), or perhaps referring to both them and his sexual partners. Although this masculine form might seem to support the second interpretation of v. 16, that the wife's adultery is condemned, the poem's focus on the husband's role rules this out.

5:18. The parallelism of "wife of your youth" (i.e., whom you married when you were young) with "your source" shows that this water image, like those of v. 15, is his wife. The preposition min (HED #4623) is causal, "on account of," "because of" (cf. Ecc. 2:10).

5:19–20. The first line could go with either this verse or the preceding, and may well be placed here so that it can refer to both. The imagery again reflects that of Song of Songs, where the beloved's breasts are compared to fawns (S.S. 4:5; 7:3), the lover to a stag (S.S. 2:17; 8:14) and the imagery of deer and gazelles occurs in erotic contexts (S.S. 2:7; 3:5). The contrast, however, is between being intoxicated with (or staggering because of) her breasts and her love (v. 19) and being intoxicated with the love of another woman (v. 20), a "stranger" to their marriage covenant.

The explicit rhetorical question balances the implicit question of v. 16, both asserting that the intimacy of sexual union belongs only within marriage. It encompasses, however, not only the blessings of marriage and the delight of the marital relationship, but the dreadful consequences of infidelity (5:9–14) as well, and anticipates the closing statement of the poem (5:21ff). Adultery has immediate personal consequences, as well as covenantal implications that will not be apparent to the naive.

5:21–23. The conclusion of this poem reveals that the negative consequences of adultery are not merely personal or temporal, but that to commit adultery brings one under the condemnation of God, a warning that is missing from the other two

Proverbs 5:22–6:3

6084 — n fd	3176 — pn	1932, 382 — n mp, n ms	3725, 4724 — cj, adj, n mp, ps 3ms	6668.351 — v Piel ptc ms	**22.**	5988 — n mp, ps 3ms
עֵינֵי	יְהוָה	דַּרְכֵי־אִישׁ	וְכָל־מַעְגְּלֹתָיו	מְכַלֵּם		עֲוֹנוֹתָיו
'ênê	yᵉhwāh	darkhê-'îsh	wᵉkhol-ma'aggᵉlōthâv	mᵉphallēs		'awônôthâv
the eyes of	Yahweh	the ways of a man	and all his tracks	He weighs		his transgressions

4058.126 — v Qal impf 3mp, ps 3ms	881, 7857 — do, art, n ms	904, 2346 — cj, prep, n mp	2496 — n fs, ps 3ms	8881.221 — v Niphal impf 3ms	**23.**	2000 — pers pron
יִלְכְּדֻנוֹ	אֶת־הָרָשָׁע	וּבְחַבְלֵי	חַטָּאתוֹ	יִתָּמֵךְ		הוּא
yilkᵉdhunô	'eth-hārāshā'	ûvᵉchavlê	chattā'thô	yittāmēkh		hû'
they ensnare him	the evildoer	also in the ropes of	his sin	he is held		he

4322.121 — v Qal impf 3ms	904, 375 — prep, sub	4284 — n ms	904, 7524 — cj, prep, n ms	198 — n fs, ps 3ms	8146.121 — v Qal impf 3ms
יָמוּת	בְּאֵין	מוּסָר	וּבְרֹב	אִוַּלְתּוֹ	יִשְׁגֶּה
yāmûth	bᵉ'ên	mûsār	ûvᵉrōv	'iwwaltô	yishgeh
he will die	without	discipline	and in the abundance of	his foolishness	he will go astray

6:1 1158 — n ms, ps 1cs	524, 6386.113 — cj, v Qal pf 2ms	3937, 7739 — prep, n ms, ps 2ms	8965.113 — v Qal pf 3ms	3937, 2299 — prep, art, n ms
בְּנִי	אִם־עָרַבְתָּ	לְרֵעֶךָ	תָּקַעְתָּ	לַזָּר
bᵉnî	'im-'āravtā	lᵉrē'ekhā	tāqa'âthā	lazzār
O my son	if you have given security	for your fellow	you have struck	for the stranger

3834 — n fd, ps 2ms	**2.**	3483.213 — v Niphal pf 2ms	904, 571, 6552 — prep, n mp, n ms, ps 2ms	4058.213 — v Niphal pf 2ms
כַּפֶּיךָ		נוֹקַשְׁתָּ	בְּאִמְרֵי־פִיךָ	נִלְכַּדְתָּ
kappêkhā		nôqashtā	vᵉ'imrê-phîkhā	nilkadhtā
your palms		you have been ensnared	by the sayings of your mouth	your have been caught

904, 571, 6552 — prep, n mp, n ms, ps 2ms	**3.**	6449.131 — v Qal impv 2ms	2148 — dem pron	660 — adv	1158 — n ms, ps 1cs	5522.231 — cj, v Niphal impv 2ms
בְּאִמְרֵי־פִיךָ		עֲשֵׂה	זֹאת	אֵפוֹא	בְּנִי	וְהִנָּצֵל
bᵉ'imrê-phîkhā		'asēh	zō'th	'ēphô	bᵉnî	wᵉhinnātsēl
by the words of your mouth		do	this	then	O my son	and save yourself

3706 — cj	971.113 — v Qal pf 2ms	904, 3834, 7739 — prep, n fs, n ms, ps 2ms	2050.131 — v Qal impv 2ms	7806.731 — v Hithpael impv 2ms
כִּי	בָאתָ	בְכַף־רֵעֶךָ	לֵךְ	הִתְרַפֵּס
kî	vā'thā	vᵉkhaph-rē'ekhā	lēkh	hithrappēs
because	you have entered	into the hand of your fellow	go	humble yourself

his paths, *MRB* ... observes all his paths, *Beck*.

22. His own iniquities shall take the wicked himself: ... A wicked person is trapped by his wrongs, *Beck* ... ensnared by his own guilt, *Knox* ... snared in his own misdeeds, *JB*.

and he shall be holden with the cords of his sins: ... held, *KJVII* ... caught in the ropes of his sin, *Beck* ... hold him enchained in his sins, *Fenton* ... and prisoned in the cords of his sin, *BB*.

23. He shall die without instruction: ... He dies because he has no self-control, *Good News* ... He dies for lack of discipline, *Berkeley*.

and in the greatness of his folly he shall go astray: ... the greatness of his foolishness, *KJVII* ... he will go wandering from the right way, *BB* ... he shall reel, *MAST*.

6:1. My son, if thou be surety for thy friend: ... gone bail for your fellow, *Moffatt* ... mortgaged yourself for your neighbor, *Anchor* ... guarantee for somebody else's loan, *NCV*

... given your pledge to your neighbor, *NRSV*.

if thou hast stricken thy hand with a stranger: ... guaranteed the bond of a stranger, *JB* ... pledged thyself for a bond, *Knox* ... given your hand in pledge to another, *NAB*.

2. Thou art snared with the words of thy mouth, thou art taken with the words of thy mouth: ... words of your mouth you have been caught, *Berkeley* ... trapped yourself by promises, *Moffatt*.

3. Do this now, my son, and deliver thyself, when thou art come into the hand of thy friend; go, humble thyself, and make sure thy friend: ... you are now in your neighbor's power, *Anchor* ... go and pester the man, *NEB* ... Go in hot haste, and lay siege to your neighbor, *Goodspeed*

... Go, trample yourself; beg of your neighbor desperately, *Berkeley* ... make your friend strong, *KJVII*.

4. Give not sleep to thine eyes, nor slumber to thine eyelids: ... give yourself no rest, allow yourself no sleep, *NEB* ... your eyelids no rest, *JB*.

5. Deliver thyself as a roe from the hand of the hunter, and as a bird from the hand of the fowler: ... break free like a gazelle from the trap, *JB* ... a deer from captivity ... so swift to escape!, *Knox* ... flying away from a trapper, *NCV*.

---

poems that warn against adultery (6:20–35; 7:1–27). The troubles described in 5:9–14 are thus one aspect of God's judgment against the adulterer. This warning is based on God's evaluation of one's ways, the various verbs used (e.g., "watches," "ponders," "examines") all representing the idea that God "weighs" one's path as in a balance. Repeating the verb from 5:6a, where it describes what the "strange woman" fails to do, reinforces the idea, first seen in 5:11, that the poet compares the fates of both the adulterer and adulteress.

The wicked is not only trapped by his sin (v. 22), he is trapped by it because he chose to leave the path of wisdom. An apparently insignificant step off the path often leads to catastrophe. The only possible outcome of this choice is death, as Solomon warns throughout the prologue (e.g., 1:18f; 2:18f, 22; 8:36; 9:18). The implicit identification of wickedness (v. 22) with folly (v. 23) emphasizes the underlying moral dimension of wisdom and folly.

The problem is not that he was untaught (v. 23), but that he rejected the instruction that he was offered. This is the real warning to the student, who must pay attention to the teaching that he is being offered (5:1) so that he can avoid the same snare. Just as putting the confession in the adulterer's mouth is an indirect lecture to the student, so v. 23 cautions him against imitating his folly and sin. The chiastic structure of the verse both emphasizes the wages of sin and closes the poem. Contrast this warning with the positive injunctions in 4:25ff, which contain many of the same words.

6:1–5. The first poem of this chapter warns against "giving surety" (HED #6386) for someone else. Rather than forbid this folly outright, as he does elsewhere (e.g., 22:26f), Solomon here urges his student to do whatever it takes to get out of that situation (6:1–5). He describes the underlying reality (v. 2) and the urgency of his exhortation to escape the situation by any means (vv. 3ff). Like the "command" proverbs (e.g., 22:22–23:14), this is a warning, not an absolute prohibition. There may be circumstances in which

guaranteeing someone else's loan is wise. Solomon's point is that the guarantor needs to realize how dangerous such help can be to his or her own well being before making that commitment.

"Going surety," as it is often translated, is the ancient equivalent of co-signing a loan or pledging one's own property as collateral for someone else's obligation. The pledge was apparently sealed by clasping hands (6:1b). In the first biblical occurrence of this word, Judah pledged himself as the guarantee that Benjamin would return from Egypt (Gen. 43:9; 44:32). If he failed to bring Benjamin back to Israel their father, Judah would bear his guilt for the rest of his life. Judah then demonstrates how seriously he understood his promise when he offered to become a slave in Egypt rather than forfeit his pledge and bear his guilt (Gen. 44:33).

Solomon reveals the true nature of co-signing in v. 2 when he uses terms from hunting ("snared") and warfare ("taken" or "captured"). To endanger one's property by pledging it as collateral for someone else's loan is to be a wild animal caught in a trap or a prisoner of war. This is largely because whoever shakes hands in pledge gives his or her belongings to another person, without really knowing whether or not that person will fulfill his or her obligation. Moreover, the guarantor has no control over that person's fulfillment. His property is, in essence, lost until the loan is paid off. He has assumed someone else's risk. The verse further focuses on the verbs by making the rest of the lines identical ("by the words of his mouth").

Having described the situation in which the guarantor is entrapped in his neighbor's power, Solomon urges him or her to do whatever is necessary to escape from the contract (vv. 3ff). He must deliver himself, since the person with the obligation is under no pressure, the guarantor having assumed it all for him.

When he says that they should not sleep until they are free (v. 4), this is anticipatory, rather than hyperbolic. The same two words occur, in the same order, in the description of the sluggard (v. 10). Just

7580.131 v Qal impv 2ms	7739 n mp, ps 2ms	**4.** 414, 5598.123 adv, v Qal juss 2ms	8524 n fs	3937, 6084 prep, n fd, ps 2ms	8900 cj, n fs
וּרְהַב	רֵעֶיךָ	אַל־תִּתֵּן	שֵׁנָה	לְעֵינֶיךָ	וּתְנוּמָה
ûrᵉhav	rēʿêkhā	ʾal-tittēn	shēnāh	lᵉʿênêkhā	ûthᵉnûmāh
and importune	your fellows	do not allow	sleep	to your eyes	nor slumber

6310 prep, n mp, ps 2ms	**5.** 5522.231 v Niphal impv 2ms	3626, 6906 prep, n ms	4623, 3135 prep, n fs	3626, 7109 cj, prep, n fs	4623, 3135 prep, n fs
לְעַפְעַפֶּיךָ	הִנָּצֵל	כִּצְבִי	מִיָּד	וּכְצִפּוֹר	מִיַּד
lᵉʿaphʿappêkhā	hinnātsēl	kitsvî	mîyādh	ûkhᵉtsippôr	mîyadh
to your eyelids	save yourself	like a gazelle	from a hand	and like a bird	from the hand of

3463 n ms	**6.** 2050.131, 420, 5431 v Qal impv 2ms, prep, n fs	6339 n ms	7495.131 v Qal impv 2ms	1932 n mp, ps 3fs	2549.131 cj, v Qal impv 2ms	**7.** 866 rel part
יָקוּשׁ	לֵךְ־אֶל־נְמָלָה	עָצֵל	רְאֵה	דְּרָכֶיהָ	וַחֲכָם	אֲשֶׁר
yāqûsh	lēkh-ʾel-nᵉmālāh	ʿātsēl	rᵉʾēh	dhᵉrākhêāh	wachăkhām	ʾăsher
a fowler	go to an ant	O sluggard	watch	its ways	and be wise	which

375, 3937 sub, prep, ps 3fs	7389 n ms	8280.151 v Qal act ptc ms	5090.151 cj, v Qal act ptc ms	**8.** 3679.522 v Hiphil impf 3fs	904, 7302 prep, art, n ms
אֵין־לָהּ	קָצִין	שֹׁטֵר	וּמֹשֵׁל	תָּכִין	בַּקַּיִץ
ʾên-lāhh	qātsîn	shōtēr	ûmōshēl	tākhîn	baqqayits
there is not to it	a leader	an overseer	or a ruler	it prepares	during the summer

4035 n ms, ps 3fs	100.112 v Qal pf 3fs	904, 7392 prep, art, n ms	4120 n ms, ps 3fs	**9.** 5912, 5146 adv, intrg	6339 n ms	8311.123 v Qal impf 2ms
לַחְמָהּ	אָגְרָה	בַּקָּצִיר	מַאֲכָלָהּ	עַד־מָתַי	עָצֵל	תִּשְׁכָּב
lachmāhh	ʾāgᵉrāh	vaqqātsîr	maʾăkhālāhh	ʿadh-māthay	ʿātsēl	tishkāv
its food	it gathers	during the harvest	its food	until when	O sluggard	will you lie down

5146 intrg	7251.123 v Qal impf 2ms	4623, 8535 prep, n fs, ps 2ms	**10.** 4746 sub	8535 n fp	4746 sub	8900 n fp	4746 sub	2355 n ms
מָתַי	תָּקוּם	מִשְּׁנָתֶךָ	מְעַט	שֵׁנוֹת	מְעַט	תְּנוּמוֹת	מְעַט	חִבֻּק
māthay	tāqûm	mishshᵉnāthekhā	mᵉʿat	shēnôth	mᵉʿat	tᵉnûmôth	mᵉʿat	chibbuq
when	will you arise	from your sleep	a little	sleep	a little	slumber	a little	folding of

6. Go to the ant, thou sluggard; consider her ways, and be wise: ... Idler, go to the ant, *JB* ... Go watch the ants, you lazy person, *NCV* ... O slothful one, See her ways, *Young* ... you lazybones, *NRSV* ... you hater of work, *BB*.

7. Which having no guide, overseer, or ruler: ... She had no judge, ...

overseer, or governor, *Beck* ... any chief or officer, *NRSV*.

8. Provideth her meat in the summer, and gathereth her food in the harvest: ... Prepares her food, *NASB* ... her bread, *MAST* ... it stores its provisions in summer, *NIV* ... they store up food during harvest season, *CEV*.

9. How long wilt thou sleep, O sluggard? when wilt thou arise out of thy sleep?: ... How long, you loafer, will you lie there?, *Anchor* ... lie there doing nothing at all? When are you going to get up, *CEV*.

10. Yet a little sleep, a little slumber: ... you take a nap, *NCV* ... yawn a little longer, *Knox*.

as a wild animal would not wait to struggle free, but struggle at once upon being snared (v. 5), they must not delay, because now is the right time to escape (just as now is the right time for the sluggard to get to work).

6:6–11. The second poem of this chapter (vv. 6–11) encourages the sluggard to change his ways before he starves (v. 11). Some of Solomon's 3000 proverbs described plants, animals, birds,

"creeping things" and fish. This is an "animal saying" that has survived (cf. 26:2f, 11; 27:8; 28:15; 30:15, 19, 24–28, 31). About this poem Blaise Pascal wrote, "Scripture sends man to the ant; a clear indication of the corruption of his [man's] nature. How splendid it is to see the master of the world sent off to the animals as though to the masters of wisdom!" Laziness, the characteristic of the sluggard, is a frequent theme in Proverbs (e.g., 21:25f; 24:30–34;

26:13–16). The warning is both positive ("Consider the ant") and negative ("poverty and need").

These verses send the sluggard to the ant because ants never stop gathering food whenever and wherever food is available. Their diligence shames the lazy, who refuse even to exert the energy to feed themselves (cf. 19:24). The timing of their labor, "in harvest," implies, like many proverbs about laziness, that mere work is not enough. Wisdom is not merely self-discipline. It is first the insight that enables the prudent to identify what is most important at that time, and then, having discerned what is most necessary, the discipline to pursue it until the task is finished. If leaderless ants (v. 7), preserve their lives by doing what needs to be done (gather food) at the right time (during harvest), how much more diligently should human beings pursue their tasks at the appropriate time?

The warning for the sluggard is that this is not merely a matter of convenience, but one of life and death (vv. 9ff). Laziness is rarely blatant; the Israelites valued work no less than any other people. Sluggardness usually entails the attitude of "not right now." This is possible because fools (including sluggards) do not consider the implications of their decisions. They lack prudence, and so are unable to examine their ways. Many responsibilities, even those that are vital, can be put off or delayed, often with little short-term damage. Eventually, however, the bill comes due, and when it does, the sluggard has no resources with which to pay. Although the precise meaning of the terms "vagabond" or "highwayman" (HED #2050; literally "one who walks") and "insolent" or "armed" man (HED #4182; literally "a man of a shield") is not certain, their overall meaning, that by his laziness the sluggard endangers his life, is quite clear (6:10f are identical to 24:33f).

Solomon is not saying that one should never rest or sleep, but he is warning his readers to examine their lives to be sure that what is most needful is being done. He is also warning them that, although rest in itself is not bad, too much of it is harmful. They should thus check their inclination to rest against the need of the moment.

6:12–19. The third and fourth poems of this chapter (vv. 12–15, 16–19) warn the reader against those who cause dissension and strife. Both poems describe the end of the wicked in order to warn students of wisdom against becoming this sort of person, and are combined to strengthen this warning. The afflicted may also be comforted by knowing that those who attack relationships (vv. 14b, 19b) lie under and face the judgment of God, a warning that is explicit in the first poem (v. 15) and implicit in the second (v. 16).

By referring to the same elements, the second poem reveals the true significance of the outward behavior described in the first. That behavior is often enigmatic or puzzling (e.g., v. 13a, what is wrong with winking at someone?). In fact, one-half of the acts mentioned in the first poem are enigmatic to us; we must assume that the original readers knew precisely what was being described. The second poem shows, for example, that winking, regardless of its literal meaning, reveals arrogance.

Thus, the "perverted mouth" (v. 12b) lies (v. 17a), even in court (v. 19a); "winking eyes" (v. 13a) signal arrogance (v. 17a); "scraping feet" (v. 13a) run rapidly to evil (v. 18b); "pointing fingers" (v. 13b) belong to hands that shed innocent blood (v. 17b); this person's heart constantly devises wicked schemes against its neighbors (vv. 14a, 18a), and spreads strife (v. 14b), even between close friends and relatives (v. 19b).

The combined poems have an overall pattern of topic (v. 12a; general indictment), description (vv. 12b–14), judgment (v. 15), second general indictment (v. 16) and description (vv. 17ff). Centering the combined poems around judgment (v. 15) and the LORD's assessment (v. 16) focuses the cumulative description of their behavior on what is most important: the LORD's evaluation (v. 16) and response (v. 15).

These poems reveal the value that the Bible places on community and fellowship. Anyone who undermines them lies under the covenantal curse (vv. 12a, 15) and judgment of God (v. 16). This theme is addressed throughout Proverbs under the topics of gossip, flattery and strife (cf. 26:20–28). The clear implication is that the wise life is one lived in friendship and communion with other human beings (and with God), not in isolation (cf. the warning in 18:1).

6:12–15. Anyone, or anything, "of Belial" (probably literally "worthless") lies under the condemnation of the Covenant (v. 12a). This describes Eli's sons (1 Sam. 2:12), those who entice Israelites to worship other gods (Deut. 13:13), the rapists of Gibeah (Judg. 19:22; 20:13) and many others (a total of twenty-seven times in the Bible).

11.

3135	3937, 8311.141	971, 3626, 2050.351	7511	4408
n fd	prep, v Qal inf con	cj, v Qal pf 3ms, prep, v Piel ptc ms	n ms, ps 2ms	cj, n ms, ps 2ms
יָדַיִם	לִשְׁכָּב	וּבָא־כִמְהַלֵּךְ	רֵאשֶׁךָ	וּמַחְסֹרְךָ
yādhayim	lishkāv	ûvā'-khimhallēkh	rē'shekhā	ûmachṣōrekhā
hands	to rest	then it will come like a traveler	your poverty	and your lack

12.

3626, 382	4182	119	1139	382	201	2050.151	6381
prep, n ms	n ms	n ms	n ms	n ms	n ms	v Qal act ptc ms	n fs
כְּאִישׁ	מָגֵן	אָדָם	בְּלִיַּעַל	אִישׁ	אָוֶן	הֹלֵךְ	עִקְּשׁוּת
ke'îsh	māghēn	'ādhām	belîya'al	'îsh	'āwen	hōlēkh	'iqqeshûth
like a man with	a shield	a man of	corruption	a man of	iniquity	proceeding	perversity of

13.

6552	7460.151	904, 6084	4589.151	904, 7559	3498.551
n ms	v Qal act ptc ms	prep, n fs, ps 3ms	v Qal act ptc ms	prep, n fs, ps 3ms	v Hiphil ptc ms
פֶּה	קֹרֵץ	בְּעֵינוֹ	מֹלֵל	בְּרַגְלָו	מֹרֶה
peh	qōrēts	be'ênô	mōlēl	beraghlāv	mōreh
mouth	he winks	with his eye	circling	with his foot	pointing

14.

904, 697	8749	904, 3949	2896.151	7737	904, 3725, 6496	4209
prep, n fp, ps 3ms	n fp	prep, n ms, ps 3ms	v Qal act ptc ms	n ms	prep, adj, n fs	n mp
בְּאֶצְבְּעֹתָיו	תַּהְפֻּכוֹת	בְּלִבּוֹ	חֹרֵשׁ	רָע	בְּכָל־עֵת	מְדָנִים
be'etsbe'ōthāv	tahpukhôth	belibbô	chōrēsh	rā'	bekhol-'ēth	medhānîm
with his fingers	perversity	in his heart	devising	evil	during all times	contentions

15.

8365.321	6142, 3772	6849	971.121	344	6875	8132.221
v Piel impf 3ms	prep, adv	adv	v Qal impf 3ms	n ms, ps 3ms	adv	v Niphal impf 3ms
יְשַׁלֵּחַ	עַל־כֵּן	פִּתְאֹם	יָבוֹא	אֵידוֹ	פֶּתַע	יִשָּׁבֵר
yeshallēach	'al-kēn	pith'ōm	yāvô'	'êdhô	petha'	yishshāvēr
he will send out	therefore	suddenly	it will come	his calamity	suddenly	he will be broken

16.

375	4995	8666, 2079	7983.111	3176	8124	8774
cj, sub	n ms	num, intrj	v Qal pf 3ms	pn	cj, num	n fp
וְאֵין	מַרְפֵּא	שֵׁשׁ־הֵנָּה	שָׂנֵא	יְהוָה	וְשֶׁבַע	תּוֹעֵבוֹת
we'ên	marpē'	shesh-hēnnāh	sānē'	yehwāh	wesheva'	tô'ēvôth
and there is not	healing	behold six	He hates	Yahweh	even seven	abominable things to

17.

5497	6084	7597.154	4098	8632	3135	8581.154	1879, 5538
n fs, ps 3ms	n fd	v Qal act ptc fp	n ms	n ms	cj, n fd	v Qal act ptc fp	n ms, adj
נַפְשׁוֹ	עֵינַיִם	רָמוֹת	לְשׁוֹן	שָׁקֶר	וְיָדַיִם	שֹׁפְכוֹת	דָּם־נָקִי
naphshô	'ênayim	rāmôth	leshôn	shāqer	weyādhayim	shōphekhôth	dām-nāqî
his soul	eyes	being high	a tongue of	lies	and hands	shedding	innocent blood

18.

3949	2896.151	4422	201	7559	4257.354	3937, 7608.141	3937, 7750
n ms	v Qal act ptc ms	n fp	n ms	n fd	v Piel ptc fp	prep, v Qal inf con	prep, art, n fs
לֵב	חֹרֵשׁ	מַחְשְׁבוֹת	אָוֶן	רַגְלַיִם	מְמַהֲרוֹת	לָרוּץ	לָרָעָה
lēv	chōrēsh	machshevôth	'āwen	raghlayim	memahrôth	lārûts	lārā'āh
a heart	devising	plans of	iniquity	feet	being quick	to run	to evil

a little folding of the hands to sleep: ... with hands folded in repose, *Anchor* ... fold your hands and lie down to rest, *NCV* ... thou must pillow head on hand?, *Knox.*

11. So shall thy poverty come as one that travelleth, and thy want as an armed man: ... come upon you like a footpad, *Goodspeed* ... come like a vagabond, *Beck* ... poverty comes like a robber, And your want like a man with a shield, *Fenton* ... poverty will pounce on you, *Moffatt* ... as a bandit, your want like an unyielding warrior, *Berkeley.*

12. A naughty person, a wicked man: ... A knave, a villain, *Goodspeed* ... a good-for-nothing man is an evildoer, *BB* ... A worthless person, *RSV.*

walketh with a froward mouth: ... deals in crooked speech, *Goodspeed* ... goes about with a corrupt mouth, *NIV.*

13. He winketh with his eyes, he speaketh with his feet: ... shuffles with his feet, *Goodspeed* … scrapes with his feet, *RSV* … nudge with the foot, *REB*.

he teacheth with his fingers: … Signs with his fingers, *Goodspeed* … giving news with his fingers, *BB* … points with his finger, *RSV*.

14. Frowardness is in his heart: … Lewd things are in his hearts, *Geneva* … plots evil with deceit in his heart, *NIV* … Trickery in his heart, *JB*.

he deviseth mischief continually; he soweth discord: … Deviseth mischief on every occasion, Strifes he

sendeth forth, *Rotherham* … always starting arguments, *NCV*.

15. Therefore shall his calamity come suddenly: … his doom will come, *Goodspeed* … disaster will come on him, *Beck* … cause his downfall, *BB*.

suddenly shall he be broken without remedy: … In an instant he will be crushed beyond recovery, *Goodspeed* … Instantly he is broken—and no healing, *Young* … so hurt no one can help them, *NCV*.

16. These six things doth the Lord hate: yea, seven are an abomina-

tion unto him: … disgusting to him, *BB* … seven are detestable to him, *REB*.

17. A proud look, a lying tongue, and hands that shed innocent blood: … Haughty eyes, *Goodspeed* … a proud eye, *NEB* … hands that kill innocent people, *NCV*.

18. An heart that deviseth wicked imaginations, feet that be swift in running to mischief: … a mind making wicked plans, *Beck* … A mind full of evil schemes, *Anchor* … forges thoughts of mischief, *NEB* … devising wicked schemes, feet quick to run to evil, *Berkeley*.

The next six lines and half lines describe their activities, although the significance of some are no longer clear. They come from a heart so intent on wickedness that it plans how most effectively to spread trouble and turmoil (v. 14a), and that is perfectly willing to lie (v. 12b) as long as it furthers the goal of disrupting and destroying relationships (v. 14b).

The result, "therefore," is their sudden downfall. This could be the result of one lie too many, causing everyone, especially those who had believed or trusted the lies, to turn against them. Those who have been deceived, especially when their eyes are suddenly cleared to see the extent and depth of the deception, as well as its destructive effects, are most apt to be enraged at the deceiver. If they effectively set everyone at odds, there will be no one left to help when their lies are no longer an effectual defense.

6:16–19. The end of the previous verses correlates with the beginning of this poem. This sort of person not only damages human relationships, but thereby reveals his hatred of God and his covenant, especially of the basic covenantal obligation to love one's neighbor (Lev. 19:18, 33f) that underlies more than half of the basic commandments (cf. Deut. 5:16–21). Those who seek to destroy others are therefore not only condemned by those whose lives they attack, but by God himself (v. 16), Who hates their way of life (vv. 17ff) and the attitudes that underlie it (v. 14).

After describing the arrogance that leads them to use any means, even violence, Solomon warns that the real problem is not behavior (damaging as

that is), but the attitude of the heart. Their hatred grows out of self-centered arrogance that sees others as tools to be used or discarded, and cannot bear to see happiness or love in those whom it despises. A heart that seeks the misery of others will do anything at all to accomplish its ends, as these poems show.

The warning is thus twofold. Explicitly, it warns the student neither to think nor act like this, for such people incur the condemnation of God. Implicitly, it warns against companions who exhibit these qualities, since they will, inevitably, turn against you.

6:20–35. This poem contains the second of three extended warnings against adultery (cf. 5:1–23; 7:1–27), focusing on the danger of material loss (6:27–35), one of the cautions of the preceding poem (5:9ff). In these verses, however, it is the only danger described, rather than one among several. The following poem (7:1–27) does not mention it at all, emphasizing instead the behavior that leads to adultery (7:7–21) and the consequent destruction of the foolish adulterer.

Adultery is mentioned only rarely in Prov. 10–31, unlike the other topics addressed in this chapter, pledging surety, laziness, wickedness, violence. Sexual immorality and adultery are addressed only four times in the body of the Book (22:14; 23:26ff; 29:3; 30:20), which probably means that this theme was rarely the subject of individual proverbs. Such a lack of available sayings could explain why adultery is so dominant in the preface. (More than one-quarter of the verses of these nine chapters address adultery or sexual immorality.)

19.

250 n mp	1033 prep	4209 n mp	8365.351 cj, v Piel ptc ms	8632 n ms	5915 n ms	3695 n mp	6558.521 v Hiphil impf 3ms
אַחִים	בֵּין	מְדָנִים	וּמְשַׁלֵּחַ	שָׁקֶר	עֵד	כְּזָבִים	יָפִיחַ
'achîm	bên	medhānîm	ûmeshallēach	shāqer	'ēdh	kezāvîm	yāphîach
brothers	between	contentions	and sowing	falsehood	a witness of	lies	he breathes out

20.

414, 5389.123 cj, adv, v Qal juss 2ms	1 n ms, ps 2ms	4851 n fs	1158 n ms, ps 1cs	5526.131 v Qal impv 2ms
וְאַל־תִּטֹּשׁ	אָבִיךָ	מִצְוַת	בְּנִי	נְצֹר
we'al-tittōsh	'āvîkhā	mitswath	benî	netsōr
and do not disregard	your father	the commandment of	O my son	keep

21.

8878 adv	6142, 3949 prep, n ms, ps 2ms	7489.131 v Qal impv 2ms, ps 3mp	525 n fs, ps 2ms	8784 n fs
תָמִיד	עַל־לִבְּךָ	קָשְׁרֵם	אִמֶּךָ	תּוֹרַת
thāmîdh	'al-libbekhā	qāsherēm	'immekhā	tôrath
continually	upon your heart	bind them	your mother	the instruction of

22.

881 do, ps 2ms	5328.521 v Hiphil impf 3ms	904, 2050.741 prep, v Hithpael inf con, ps 2ms	6142, 1664 prep, n fp, ps 2ms	6256.131 v Qal impv 2ms, ps 3mp
אֹתָךְ	תַּנְחֶה	בְּהִתְהַלֶּכְךָ	עַל־גַּרְגְּרֹתֶךָ	עָנְדֵם
'ōthākh	tancheh	behithhallekhekhā	'al-gargerōthekhā	'ānedhēm
you	it will guide	when your going	upon your neck	tie them

7943.122 v Qal impf 3fs, ps 2ms	2026 pers pron	7301.513 cj, v Hiphil pf 2ms	6142 prep, ps 2ms	8490.122 v Qal impf 3fs	904, 8311.141 prep, v Qal inf con, ps 2ms
תְשִׂיחֶךָ	הִיא	וַהֲקִיצוֹתָ	עָלֶיךָ	תִּשְׁמֹר	בְּשָׁכְבְּךָ
thesîchekhā	hî'	wahqîtsôthā	'ālêkhā	tishmōr	beshokhbekhā
it will talk to you	it	and you will awaken	over you	it will watch	when you lie down

23.

2522 n mp	1932 cj, n ms	214 n ms	8784 cj, n fs	4851 n fs	5552 n ms	3706 cj
חַיִּים	וְדֶרֶךְ	אוֹר	וְתוֹרָה	מִצְוָה	נֵר	כִּי
chayyîm	wedherekh	'ôr	wethôrāh	mitswāh	nēr	kî
life	and the way of	a light	and instruction	the commandment	a lamp	because

24.

4623, 2613 prep, n fs	7737 n ms	4623, 828 prep, n fs	3937, 8490.141 prep, v Qal inf con, ps 2ms	4284 n ms	8762 n fp
מֵחֶלְקַת	רָע	מֵאֵשֶׁת	לִשְׁמָרְךָ	מוּסָר	תוֹכְחוֹת
mēchelqath	rā'	mē'ēsheth	lishmārekhā	mûsār	tôkhchôth
from smoothness of	evil	from a woman of	to guard you	correction	reproofs of

25.

904, 3949 prep, n ms, ps 2ms	3418 n ms, ps 3fs	414, 2629.131 adv, v Qal juss 2ms	5425 n fs	4098 n fs
בִּלְבָבֶךָ	יָפְיָהּ	אַל־תַּחְמֹד	נָכְרִיָּה	לָשׁוֹן
bilvāvekhā	yāpheyāhh	'al-tachmōdh	nākheriyāh	lāshôn
in your heart	her beauty	do not desire	a foreign woman	the tongue of

26.

2193 n fs	1185, 828 prep, n fs	3706 cj	904, 6310 prep, n mp, ps 3fs	414, 4089 cj, adv, v Qal juss 3fs, ps 2ms
זוֹנָה	בְעַד־אִשָּׁה	כִּי	בְּעַפְעַפֶּיהָ	וְאַל־תִּקָּחֲךָ
zônāh	ve'adh-'ishshāh	kî	be'aph'appêāh	we'al-tiqqāchākhā
a prostitute	on account of a woman	because	with her eyelids	and do not let her capture you

6942.122 v Qal impf 3fs	3479 adj	5497 n fs	382 n ms	828 cj, n fs	4035 n ms	5912, 3724 prep, n fs
תָצוּד	יְקָרָה	נֶפֶשׁ	אִישׁ	וְאֵשֶׁת	לָחֶם	עַד־כִּכַּר
thātsûdh	yeqārāh	nephesh	'îsh	we'ēsheth	lāchem	'adh-kikkar
she hunts	precious	the soul	a man	but the wife of	bread	to a loaf of

58

19. A false witness that speaketh lies, and he that soweth discord among brethren: ... a dishonest witness telling lies, and the man who stirs up quarrels between brothers, *Beck* ... A breather of lies for defrauding; And the sender of strife among friends!, *Fenton*.

20. My son, keep thy father's commandment, and forsake not the law of thy mother: ... your father's precepts, *Anchor* ... nor make light of, *Knox* ... your mother's teaching, *Anchor*.

21. Bind them continually upon thine heart, and tie them about thy neck: ... ever to your heart, *JB* ... on your heart forever, *KJVII*.

22. When thou goest, it shall lead thee; when thou sleepest, it shall keep thee; and when thou awakest, it shall talk with thee: ... when you are walking about, *Berkeley* ... Wisdom, when you walk, will guide you, *Moffatt* ... when you lie down, she will watch over you, *REB* ... talk to you when you are awake, *CEV*.

23. For the commandment is a lamp; and the law is light: ... their advice is a beam of light, *LIVB* ... this teaching is a light, *NIV*.

and reproofs of instruction are the way of life: ... admonitions of discipline, *Goodspeed* ... their bidding will throw light upon your life, *Moffatt*.

24. To keep thee from the evil woman, from the flattery of the tongue of a strange woman: ... from the wife of another man, *REB* ... smooth tongue of the adulteress, *NRSV* ... smoothness of the alien tongue, *MAST*.

25. Lust not after her beauty in thine heart; neither let her take thee with her eyelids: ... let not her eyes take you prisoner, *BB* ... capture you with her eyelashes, *NRSV* ... captivate you with her glance!, *Douay*.

26. For by means of a whorish woman a man is brought to a piece of bread: ... the price of a harlot is but a piece of bread, *Goodspeed* ... A prostitute will treat you like a loaf of bread, *NCV* ... for a prostitute's fee is only a loaf of bread, *NRSV*.

and the adulteress will hunt for the precious life: ... but a married

---

6:20–22. The call to attention is closely related to others in Prov. 1–9 (6:20a reflects 3:1b; 6:20b is identical to 1:8b). Observing and not forsaking are two sides of the same coin; to fail to observe the commandment is to abandon it. The language of "binding" (HED #7489) is also found in the Covenant (Deut. 6:8f, in which Moses exhorted Israel to be sure that they observed the Covenant by keeping it in mind at all times and by having its words and precepts as readily available as their own hands. The same passage urges the Israelites to teach "these words" to their children at all times (Deut. 6:7), the very thing which the father or teacher is doing in this passage of Proverbs.

Verse 22 continues the covenantal imagery by talking of the role of the teaching (traditionally "law") in the student's life. The Israelites were commanded to know the Covenant so that they could discuss it at any time (6:21). Here, however, the roles are reversed. Knowing the commandments, the student is guided and kept by them and continually instructed in them (6:22c).

The plural of the English versions includes both the father's commandment and the mother's teaching (6:20; both are repeated in v. 23). The feminine singular of the Hebrew text may also encompass both (since both are feminine), but this does not explain the masculine plural pronominal suffixes of 6:21. The differences in all three verses (6:20ff) are probably best interpreted as examples of grammatical parallelism, in which gender and number are often contrasted. The feminine singular does not, however, point to one of the components of the parental teaching as more (or less) important than the other.

6:23–24. These verses explain the preceding ("for"), and introduce the main topic of the poem ("to guard you"; HED #8490). Here, the theme of light and darkness seen earlier (2:13; 4:18f) is explained, and anticipates those proverbs which teach that the wise observe their way and act according to what they see, whereas fools blunder ignorantly on, to their hurt and eventual destruction (e.g., 22:3; 27:12). Disciplinary reproofs and teaching are complementary; correction delimits the path that is lit by the teaching (cf. Ps. 119:105).

In this passage, however, the "path of life" is not general, but refers specifically to adultery, from which the student is protected insofar as he attends carefully to the instruction that he is about to receive (6:20f). The "wicked woman" is someone outside the marital covenant who uses flattery to obtain the intimacy that she desires. (See the introductory "note on translation" on 5:1–23.) Her guilt lies in her willful violation of someone else's covenantal relationship.

6:25–26. The state of the heart is the primary concern (4:23), so the first warning is to guard one's

27.

2954.121	382	813	904, 2536	933	3940
intrg part, v Qal impf 3ms	n ms	n fs	prep, n ms, ps 3ms	cj, n mp, ps 3ms	neg part
הֲיַחְתֶּה	אִישׁ	אֵשׁ	בְּחֵיקוֹ	וּבְגָדָיו	לֹא
hăyachteh	'îsh	'ēsh	bechêqô	ûveghādhâv	lō'
does he snatch	a man	fire	into his bosom	and his garments	not

28.

8041.227	524, 2050.321	382	6142, 1544	7559	3940
v Niphal impf 3fp	cj, v Piel impf 3ms	n ms	prep, art, n fp	cj, n fd, ps 3ms	neg part
תִּשָּׂרַפְנָה	אִם־יְהַלֵּךְ	אִישׁ	עַל־הַגֶּחָלִים	וְרַגְלָיו	לֹא
thissāraphnāh	'im-yehallēkh	'îsh	'al-haggechālîm	weraghlâv	lō'
they will be burned	if he will walk	a man	on the hot coals	and his feet	not

29.

3673.227	3772	971.151	420, 828	7739	3940
v Niphal impf 3fp	adv	art, v Qal act ptc ms	prep, n fs	n ms, ps 3ms	neg part
תִּכָּוֶינָה	כֵּן	הַבָּא	אֶל־אֵשֶׁת	רֵעֵהוּ	לֹא
thikkāwênāh	kēn	habbā'	'el-'ēsheth	rē'ēhû	lō'
they will be seared	so	the one entering	to the wife of	his fellow	not

30.

5536.221	3725, 5236.151	904	3940, 972	3937, 1631	3706
v Niphal impf 3ms	adj, art, v Qal act ptc ms	prep, ps 3fs	neg part, v Qal impf 3mp	prep, art, n ms	cj
יִנָּקֶה	כָּל־הַנֹּגֵעַ	בָּהּ	לֹא־יָבוּזוּ	לַגַּנָּב	כִּי
yinnāqeh	kol-hannōghēa'	bāhh	lō'-yāvûzû	laggannāv	kî
he will be innocent	anyone touching	her	they will not despise	the thief	if

31.

1630.121	3937, 4527.341	5497	3706	7742.121	4834.211
v Qal impf 3ms	prep, v Piel inf con	n fs, ps 3ms	cj	v Qal impf 3ms	cj, v Niphal pf 3ms
יִגְנוֹב	לְמַלֵּא	נַפְשׁוֹ	כִּי	יִרְעָב	וְנִמְצָא
yighnôv	lemallē'	naphshô	kî	yir'āv	wenimtsā'
he steals	to fill	his soul	when	he is hungry	when he is discovered

32.

8396.321	8124	881, 3725, 2019	1041	5598.121	5178.151
v Piel impf 3ms	n fd	do, adj, n ms	n ms, ps 3ms	v Qal impf 3ms	v Qal act ptc ms
יְשַׁלֵּם	שִׁבְעָתָיִם	אֶת־כָּל־הוֹן	בֵּיתוֹ	יִתֵּן	נֹאֵף
yeshallēm	shiv'āthāyim	'eth-kol-hôn	bêthô	yittēn	nō'ēph
he will repay	seven times	all the goods of	his household	he will give	an adulterer

828	2742, 3949	8271.551	5497	2000	6449.121
n fs	adj, n ms	v Hiphil ptc ms	n fs, ps 3ms	pers pron	v Qal impf 3ms, ps 3fs
אִשָּׁה	חֲסַר־לֵב	מַשְׁחִית	נַפְשׁוֹ	הוּא	יַעֲשֶׂנָּה
'ishshāh	chăsar-lēv	mashchîth	naphshô	hû'	ya'ăsennāh
a woman	lacking in heart	destroying	his life	he	he does it

33.

5237, 7320	4834.121	2887	3940	4364.222	
n ms, cj, n ms	v Qal impf 3ms	cj, n fs, ps 3ms	neg part	v Niphal impf 3fs	
נֶגַע־וְקָלוֹן	יִמְצָא	וְחֶרְפָּתוֹ	לֹא	תִּמָּחֶה	
negha'-weqālôn	yimtsā'	wecherpāthô	lō'	thimmācheh	
a blow and shame	he will find	and his disgrace	not	it will be blotted out	

woman hunts with a costly appetite, *Beck* ... another man's wife stalks a priceless soul, *Berkeley* ... stalks a man's very life, *NRSV* ... a woman who takes part in adultery may cost you your life, *NCV*.

27. Can a man take fire in his bosom, and his clothes not be burned?: ... scoop fire into his lap,

NIV ... carry fire inside his shirt, *JB* ... kindle a fire in his bosom without setting his clothes alight?, *REB*.

28. Can one go upon hot coals, and his feet not be burned?: ... walk on hot coals, *Berkeley* ... feet not be scorched?, *RSV*.

29. So he that goeth in to his neigh-

bour's wife; whosoever toucheth her shall not be innocent: ... intercourse with his neighbor's wife, *Anchor* ... none who touches her will go unpunished, *RSV* ... will not escape punishment, *Beck*.

30. Men do not despise a thief, if he steal to satisfy his soul when he is hungry: ... Men do not have a low opinion of a thief who takes food when he is in need of it, *BB* ... To satisfy his appetite because he is famished, *Rotherham* ... he stealeth to fill his soul, *Young.*

31. But if he be found, he shall restore sevenfold; he shall give all the substance of his house: ... hand over all his family resources,

JB ... all the wealth of his house, *NAB* ... give up all the goods, *Goodspeed* ... it may cost him everything he owns, *NCV.*

32. But whoso committeth adultery with a woman lacketh understanding: he that doeth it destroyeth his own soul: ... an adulterer is devoid of sense, *Moffatt* ... Only he who

would bring ruin on himself does such a thing, *Goodspeed* ... When he violates her he destroys himself, *Beck.*

33. A wound and dishonour shall he get: ... A stroke and shame he doth find, *Young* ... A degrading beating will he get, *Douay.*

heart against coveting another woman's beauty. The verse does not deny that the other woman may well be more attractive than one's wife. The desire for the beautiful does not, however, justify sin. Since no portraits exist of Israelite women, we do not know the extent to which they were covered from the sight of men outside their families. Their eyes may have been the only visible part of their faces.

Verse 26 is difficult, and most translations depend upon the ancient versions for their renderings of the first line. They read the Hebrew be'adh (HED #1185), normally a preposition meaning "for," as "price" or "hire." If this is the correct meaning, this is the only occurrence of this noun in the Bible. The difficulty in the second line is that nephesh yeqārāh (HED #5497, 3479) means "rare or precious life, soul or person." This may refer to her demand for her lover's entire person (i.e., she will not be satisfied with a crass financial arrangement, as is the prostitute in the first line), or as some have suggested, her requirement that her partner be wealthy (a "person of value"). In either case, the verse points out the difference in cost between a prostitute, who accepts a "loaf of bread," and an adulteress, who is far more costly (cf. 6:34f). This is not condoning the use of prostitutes; it is merely pointing out a danger of adultery. In the long run, an adulteress is infinitely more costly than a prostitute. (A loaf of bread might be a day's wage.)

6:27–29. Two rhetorical questions, both expecting the answer "of course not," describe the inevitability of the adulterer's situation. When he "touches" another man's wife (a euphemism for sexual relations) he becomes guilty, and will be punished, as certainly as fire burns; that is, the negative consequences of sexual immorality are as much a part of the created order as the consequences of playing with fire. The ludicrous nature of the examples should give the reader pause. There are no exceptions to either of these situations (apart from special fireproof materials and fire-walkers,

both of which are exceptions to that test, but do not disprove the rule).

6:30–31. By another example, Solomon illustrates the difference between adultery and another crime condemned by the Covenant: theft (Exo. 20:15; Lev. 19:11; Deut. 5:19). A thief who steals in order to stay alive is just as guilty as one who steals out of greed or for his own self-aggrandizement. Where there may be sympathy for the starving, there is rarely anything but scorn for the latter. Restitution was twofold, fourfold or fivefold (Exo. 22:1–4, 7; cf. 2 Sam. 12:6), not sevenfold, which may be hyperbolic, a way of saying that he will restore completely what was taken (cf. Ps. 79:12), or it may refer to a custom not recorded in Scripture. (We need not assume that the Mosaic legislation was Israel's entire law.)

These verses imply that the desire for sexual relations is not an appetite on the same level as the body's need for food. Nor should it be satisfied outside marriage. This oblique warning points out the social consequence of adultery: a ruined reputation and, perhaps, public ostracization.

Verse 31 also anticipates the thrust of the final verses and reflects the earlier poem on adultery (5:9ff). Adultery bears a cost, whether this is a fine or a bribe (6:34f), and this cost is far greater than a sevenfold restitution, since there is no way to restore what has been stolen.

6:32–33. The root cause of adultery is failure to guard one's heart (cf. 4:23; 6:25), as his lack of heart shows ("sense" [NASB, NRSV], "understanding" [NKJV]). His failure to anticipate the consequences of his actions has set him on a path of self-destruction that leads to physical and social punishment ("wounds," "disgrace"). The word translated "wound" or "blow" (HED #5237) has the same root as the verb "touches" (HED #5236; 6:29). His actions return upon his own head. As he "touched," so he will be "touched"; as the thief was "found," he will find. (In another ironic twist, the

34.

3706, 7352	2635, 1429	3940, 2654.121	904, 3219	5542
cj, n fs	n fs, n ms	cj, neg part, v Qal impf 3ms	prep, n ms	n ms
כִּי־קִנְאָה	חֲמַת־גָּבֶר	וְלֹא־יַחְמוֹל	בְּיוֹם	נָקָם
kî-qin'āh	chămath-gāver	welō'-yachmôl	beyôm	nāqām
because jealousy	wrath of a man	and he will not spare	on the day of	vengeance

35.

3940, 5558.121	6686	3725, 3853	3940, 13.121	3706
neg part, v Qal impf 3ms	n mp	adj, n ms	cj, neg part, v Qal impf 3ms	cj
לֹא־יִשָּׂא	פְּנֵי	כָל־כֹּפֶר	וְלֹא־יֹאבֶה	כִּי
lō'-yissā'	penê	khol-kōpher	welō'-yō'veh	kî
he will not forgive	the presence of	any bribe	and he will not be willing	although

7:1

7528.523, 8245	1158	8490.131	571	4851
v Hiphil impf 2ms, n ms	n ms, ps 1cs	v Qal impv 2ms	n mp, ps 1cs	cj, n fp, ps 1cs
תַּרְבֶּה־שֹׁחַד	בְּנִי	שְׁמֹר	אֲמָרַי	וּמִצְוֹתַי
tharbeh-shōchadh	benî	shemōr	'ămārāy	ûmitswōthay
you will multiply gifts	O my son	observe	my sayings	and my commandments

2.

7121.123	882	8490.131	4851	2513.131
v Qal impf 2ms	prep, ps 2ms	v Qal impv 2ms	n fp, ps 1cs	cj, v Qal impv 2ms
תִּצְפֹּן	אִתָּךְ	שְׁמֹר	מִצְוֹתַי	וֶחְיֵה
titspōn	'ittākh	shemōr	mitswōthay	wechăyēh
you will store	with you	observe	my commandments	and live

3.

8784	3626, 385	6084	7489.131	6142, 697
cj, n fs, ps 1cs	prep, n ms	n fd, ps 2ms	v Qal impv 2ms, ps 3mp	prep, n fp, ps 2ms
וְתוֹרָתִי	כְּאִישׁוֹן	עֵינֶיךָ	קָשְׁרֵם	עַל־אֶצְבְּעֹתֶיךָ
wethôrāthî	ke'îshôn	'ênêkhā	qāsherēm	'al-'etsbe'ōthêkhā
and my instruction	like the pupil of	your eyes	bind them	on your fingers

4.

3918.131	6142, 4008	3949	569.131	3937, 2551	269	879
v Qal impv 2ms, ps 3mp	prep, n ms	n ms, ps 2ms	v Qal impv 2ms	prep, art, n fs	n fs, ps 1cs	pers pron
כָּתְבֵם	עַל־לוּחַ	לִבֶּךָ	אֱמֹר	לַחָכְמָה	אֲחֹתִי	אָתְּ
kāthevēm	'al-lûach	libbekhā	'ĕmōr	lachokhmāh	'ăchōthî	'ātte
write them	on the tablet of	your heart	say	to wisdom	my sister	you

5.

4235	3937, 1035	7410.123	3937, 8490.141	4623, 828	2299
cj, n ms	prep, art, n fs	v Qal impf 2ms	prep, v Qal inf con, ps 2ms	prep, n fs	adj
וּמֹדָע	לַבִּינָה	תִקְרָא	לִשְׁמָרְךָ	מֵאִשָּׁה	זָרָה
ûmōdā'	labbînāh	thiqrā'	lishmārekhā	mē'ishshāh	zārāh
and a relative	to discernment	you will call	to guard you	from a woman	strange

6.

4623, 5425	571	2606.512	3706	904, 5274
prep, n fs	n mp, ps 3fs	v Hiphil pf 3fs	cj	prep, n ms
מִנָּכְרִיָּה	אֲמָרֶיהָ	הֶחֱלִיקָה	כִּי	בְּחַלּוֹן
minnākherîyāh	'ămārêāh	hechĕlîqāh	kî	bechallôn
from the foreign woman	her sayings	she has caused to be smooth	because	at the window of

and his reproach shall not be wiped away: ... disgrace will not be, *NRSV* ... never live down the disgrace, *REB*.

34. For jealousy is the rage of a man: therefore he will not spare in the day of vengeance: ... makes a man furious, *RSV* ... for vindictive is the husband's wrath, he will have no pity, *Douay* ... jealousy inflames the husband who will show no mercy, *JB*.

35. He will not regard any ransom: ... no money buys him off, *Moffatt* ... he will not consider any restitution, *Douay*.

neither will he rest content, though thou givest many gifts: ...

though thou increase the bribe, *Rotherham* ... he will take no amount of money, *NCV*.

7:1. My son, keep my words, and lay up my commandments with thee: ... don't forget what I tell you to do, *CEV* ... store up my precepts within you, *Berkeley*.

2. Keep my commandments, and live; and my law as the apple of thine eye: ... Keep my rules and you will have life, *BB* ... mine instruction as the pupil of, *Rotherham*.

3. Bind them upon thy fingers, write them upon the table of thine heart: ... Wear them like a ring on your finger, *NEB* ... tablet of your heart, *NRSV* ... the tablet of your mind, *Moffatt* ... Inscribe on the book of your heart, *Fenton*.

4. Say unto wisdom, Thou art my sister; and call understanding thy kinswoman: ... You are my darling, *Moffatt* ... nearest kin, *NKJV* ... call insight your intimate friend, *NRSV*

... greet Understanding as a familiar friend, *NEB*.

5. That they may keep thee from the strange woman: ... from the immoral woman, *NKJV* ... keep you from the loose woman, *NRSV*.

from the stranger which flattereth with her words: ... the stranger with

---

same verb occurs in 6:31 and 6:33.) Neither scourging nor public ignomiy, however, can remove the stain of his sin.

6:34–35. Jealousy is more powerful than any gift or bribe (27:4). Nor is there a fine that can restore either the violated marital relationship or the husband's trust in his wife. Indeed, the greater the bribe, the more suspicious it might appear. The person who lightheartedly allows himself to "fall in love" with another man's wife destroys personal and communal relationships and will never rid himself of his tainted reputation. In ancient Israel, where marriage was usually within tribes and people appear to have been relatively sedentary (cf. the law created in response to the situation of Zelophehad's daughters; Num. 27:1–11; 36:1–12), it was probably uncommon to move to another town, city or tribal territory.

The Covenant stipulates death for both adulterous partners (Lev. 20:10; Deut. 22:22; cf. Gen. 38:24), which may be the punishment envisaged in v. 29. On the other hand, the rest of this poem seems to assume a legal situation in which the partners were allowed to live. It may thus reflect a situation in which the male partner tries to bribe the woman's husband into not pressing charges to the extent required by the Law, or perhaps the law that allowed the owner of an ox to redeem his life by paying whatever fine was settled upon him by the victim's family (Exo. 21:30) was extended to other situations, including adultery, so that a fine could serve as punishment.

7:1–27. This chapter comprises the final warning against adultery in the prologue (cf. 2:16–19; 5:1–23; 6:20–35). Addressed to the inexperienced youth (cf. 7:7), it consists of an opening exhortation (vv. 1–5), a lengthy narrative poem (vv. 6–23) and a closing exhortation (vv. 24–27). The commands and prohibitions in the introduction and conclusion enclose the poem, focusing on the teacher's words (vv. 1–5) and warning against the adulteress' ways (vv. 24–27).

7:1–3. The opening verses are typical of these chapters (7:1b, 2a, 3b are identical to 2:1b, 4:4c, 3:3c, respectively). The expression "apple of your eye" refers to something precious (cf. Deut. 32:10; Ps. 17:8). It seems to have originally meant the "small man of your eye," perhaps because a person is reflected in someone else's pupil, and so looks like a miniature person looking out (albeit upside-down). As in other places, the idea of binding and writing (v. 3) reflects the image of knowing the Covenant so well that it is an integral part of one's life (cf. e.g., Deut. 6:8f; 11:18, 20; Prov. 3:3; 6:21).

7:4. This verse implicitly identifies the teacher's words as wisdom. It also personifies wisdom as one's beloved, since "sister" (HED #269) is a term of endearment in the Bible (S.S. 4:9f, 12; 5:1f) and the ancient Near East, especially in Egyptian love poetry. The parallel (HED #4235, which occurs only elsewhere in Ruth 2:1) is a term of familial relationship (cf. e.g., NKJV, NIV) that may refer to a close friendship (cf. e.g., NASB, NRSV). This personification compares the young man's relationship with wisdom, i.e., the words and commandments of the preceding verses, to marriage, and contrasts this with an adulterous relationship, which is, by implication, foolish.

7:5. As in Prov. 6:20–24, the introductory commands of 7:1–4 conclude with a purpose clause ("that they may keep you") that introduces the main subject, and section, of the poem (7:6–23). Obeying his father's teaching and loving wisdom will protect him from the temptation to indulge in extramarital immorality and inoculate him against the flattery that smooths the slide into sin. This woman is a "stranger" and a "foreigner" to his marriage.

7:6–7. These two verses are structurally similar, which binds them together, underlining their joint function as the story's "frame." They are similar because an element lacking in the first line is supplied in the second (the verb [v. 6]; the direct object [v. 7]).

7.

904, 6848	7495.125		8625.215	850	1185	1041
prep, art, n mp	cj, v Qal impf 1cs		v Niphal pf 1cs	n ms, ps 1cs	prep	n ms, ps 1cs
בַּפְּתָאיִם	וָאֵרֶא		נִשְׁקָפְתִּי	אֶשְׁנַבִּי	בְּעַד	בֵּיתִי
vappethā'yim	wā'ēre'		nishqāphettî	'eshnabbî	be'adh	bêthî
among the simple	and I have observed		I have looked down	my lattice	through	my house

8.

904, 8226	5882.151	2742, 3949	5470	904, 1158	1032.125
prep, art, n ms	v Qal act ptc ms	adj, n ms	n ms	prep, art, n ms	v Qal juss 1cs
בַּשּׁוּק	עֹבֵר	חֲסַר־לֵב	נַעַר	בַּבָּנִים	אָבִינָה
bashshûq	'ōvēr	chăsar-lēv	na'ar	vabbānîm	'āvînāh
in the street	passing through	lacking in heart	a young man	among the sons	let me understand

9.

904, 5582, 904, 6394	7081.121	1041	1932	6682	703
prep, n ms, prep, n ms	v Qal impf 3ms	n ms, ps 3fs	cj, n ms	n fs, ps 3fs	prep
בְנֶשֶׁף־בְּעֶרֶב	יִצְעָד	בֵּיתָהּ	וְדֶרֶךְ	פִּנָּהּ	אֵצֶל
benesheph-be'erev	yits'ādh	bêthāhh	wedherekh	pinnāhh	'ētsel
at twilight in the evening of	he takes steps on	her house	and the way of	her corner	near

10.

3937, 7410.141	828	2079	671	4050	904, 385	3219
prep, v Qal inf con, ps 3ms	n fs	cj, intrj	cj, n fs	n ms	prep, n ms	n ms
לִקְרָאתוֹ	אִשָּׁה	וְהִנֵּה	וַאֲפֵלָה	לַיְלָה	בְּאִישׁוֹן	יוֹם
liqŏrā'thô	'ishshāh	wehinnēh	wa'ăphēlāh	laylāh	be'îshôn	yôm
to meet him	a woman	and behold	and darkness	night	in the black of	a day

11.

2026	2064.153	3949	5526.157	2193	8309
pers pron	v Qal act ptc fs	n ms	cj, v Qal pass ptc fs	n fs	n ms
הִיא	הֹמִיָּה	לֵב	וּנְצֻרַת	זוֹנָה	שִׁית
hî'	hōmîyāh	lēv	ûnetsurath	zônāh	shîth
she	being boisterous	heart	and being reserved in	a prostitute	clothing of

12.

904, 2445	6718	7559	3940, 8331.126	904, 1041	5842.153
prep, art, n ms	n fs	n fd, ps 3fs	neg part, v Qal impf 3mp	prep, n ms, ps 3fs	cj, v Qal act ptc fs
בַּחוּץ	פַּעַם	רַגְלֶיהָ	לֹא־יִשְׁכְּנוּ	בְּבֵיתָהּ	וְסֹרָרֶת
bachûts	pa'am	raghlêāh	lō'-yishkenû	bevêthāhh	wesōrāreth
in the street	one time	her feet	they do not remain	at her house	and being rebellious

13.

904	2480.512	717.122	3725, 6682	703	904, 7624	6718
prep, ps 3ms	cj, v Hiphil pf 3fs	v Qal impf 3fs	adj, n fs	cj, prep	prep, art, n fp	n fs
בּוֹ	וְהֶחֱזִיקָה	תֶּאֱרֹב	כָּל־פִּנָּה	וְאֵצֶל	בָּרְחֹבוֹת	פַּעַם
bô	wehechĕzîqāh	the'ěrōv	kol-pinnāh	we'ētsel	bārechōvôth	pa'am
on him	and she seizes	she lies in wait	every corner	and near	in the plazas	another time

---

slippery tongue, *Fenton* ... her words so smooth, *Moffatt*.

6. For at the window of my house I looked through my casement: ... looked out through my lattice, *NRSV* ... through the shutters, *NCV* ... watching through the window, *BB*.

7. And beheld among the simple ones: ... Watching the fools [below], *Anchor* ... naive, *NASB* ... Looking at the silly fellows, *Beck*.

I discerned among the youths, a young man void of understanding:

... a brainless youth, *Moffatt* ... I noticed a lad, a foolish lad, *NEB*.

8. Passing through the street near her corner; and he went the way to her house: ... One of these young men turned the corner, *CEV* ... the way to her house he doth step, *Young* ... he sauntered along, *Rotherham*.

9. In the twilight, in the evening, in the black and dark night: ... in darkness of the night, *Beck* ... middle of the night, *Berkeley*.

10. And, behold, there met him a woman with the attire of an harlot: ... a woman came to meet him, *Beck* ... in the dress of a loose woman, *BB*.

and subtle of heart: ... with secret plans in mind, *Beck* ... crafty of heart, *Fenton* ... heavily veiled, *Anchor* ... wily of heart, *RSV*.

11. (She is loud and stubborn: ... lusty and rebellious, *Beck* ... clamorous and unmanageable, ... boisterous and fickle, *Goodspeed*.

her feet abide not in her house: … their feet never rest in the house, *Fenton* … a woman never content to stay at home, *NEB*.

12. Now is she without, now in the streets, and lieth in wait at every corner): … haunting every corner)!, *Moffatt* … Lurking at every corner, *Anchor*.

13. So she caught him, and kissed him, and with an impudent face said unto him: … seizes him and kisses him, *NRSV* … with a hardened face, *Berkeley*.

The teacher uses a story, one of the longest poetic narratives in the Bible (cf. Judg. 5), to teach a moral lesson. As in other passages, this description is drawn from his own experience (cf. 6:6–11; 22:29; 24:30–34; 26:12). The "for" or "because" (HED #3706) that begins these verses shows that the following narrative, far from being an unrelated story, is the teaching mentioned in vv. 1ff, and shows the consequences of not properly responding to that teaching.

Although the teacher says that he saw these events from his window, he quickly assumes the role of "omniscient" narrator, since he watches the youth walking through the town (v. 8), witnesses their meeting (vv. 10, 13), overhears her words (vv. 14–20) and sees the denouement (vv. 21ff)—all in the dark (v. 9). Not only this, but he knows that the young man is naive (v. 7), that he is intentionally going to her house (v. 8) and that she is there in order to meet him (v. 10). Even if she lived next to or across from the watcher, and even if his window were on a second floor (as the lattice may imply), he could not have seen or known all of this, nor is it probable that the woman would have attempted seduction by shouting! It is possible that the observer was acquainted with the young man and the woman, but previous acquaintance cannot explain all of the details listed above. He writes from an omniscient point of view in order to be able to include whatever information he needs in order to make his point.

The object of his attention is a naive young man, one without the experience to help him make wise decisions. Education means that every generation does not need to discover everything for itself, but can "stand on the shoulders" of previous generations by learning from those who in their turn learned from others before them. This story is told, therefore, not to titillate or entertain, but in order to instruct those who are naive, those who have not yet learned these lessons. To "lack heart"(HED #2742; 3949) is condemned and warned against throughout Proverbs (cf. 6:32; 9:4, 16; 10:13, 21; 11:20; 12:11; 15:21; 17:18; 24:30). The expression is unique to Proverbs), and its precise meaning depends on the context. Here, its comparison with "naive" (HED #6864) shows that it means a lack of sense or discernment (cf. v. 4b).

7:8–9. The scene takes place outside, "in the street" (although a curtain is drawn on the actual events as soon as he follows her, vv. 22f), and at night. Four words progress from twilight to darkness, which may be an attempt to show how long he was wandering about, but are more likely combined to emphasize that all of this took place in the dark of night. The third temporal expression (literally "in the pupil of the night"; cf. v. 2b) is often emended to "time" (a word that occurs only in Prov. 20:20), so that the phrase refers to the moment when darkness falls. This is not necessary, though, since it can also be understood in the sense of the black (i.e., as the pupil is black) of night, an expression which is parallel to "deep darkness."

Verse 8 may imply that he was intentionally seeking this particular woman ("her corner," "he steps the way to her house"). It is also possible, however, that he, being naive, was ignorant of his peril. "Her" both anticipates the subject of the next verses and looks back to v. 5.

7:10. A better translation of v. 10a is "And there was a woman to meet him!"; wᵉhinnēh (HED #2079) usually points to the next event or situation noticed or narrated (cf. Gen. 41:1ff, 5f). The text does not imply that she traveled across the town to meet him: it simply says that he put himself in her neighborhood, then she responded. Nor does the poem directly call her a prostitute. It merely describes her wearing clothing that would have identified her as a prostitute to anyone in that culture (cf. Gen. 38:14–19).

Her outward appearance, however, did not match the state of her heart, which she kept to herself. This may mean that she concealed her illicit activities from her husband (vv. 19f), but may also refer to the non-emotional nature of this relationship, from her point of view.

7:11–12. Although the precise meanings of the adjectives in v. 11a are not certain, they probably mean that she is aggressively (thus "boisterous," "loud"; HED #2064) set on her course of behavior (hence "rebellious," "defiant," "wayward"; HED #5842). Although there are not many biblical examples, women who went out at night

14.

2160	3937	569.122	6686	6006.512	5583.112, 3937
n mp	prep, ps 3ms	cj, v Qal impf 3fs	n mp, ps 3fs	v Hiphil pf 3fs	cj, v Qal pf 3fs, prep, ps 3ms
זִבְחֵי	לוֹ	וַתֹּאמַר	פָּנֶיהָ	הֵעֵזָה	וְנָשְׁקָה-לּוֹ
zivchê	lô	wattō'mar	phānêāh	hē'ēzāh	wenāsheqāh-lô
sacrifices of	to him	and she says	her face	she strengthens	and she kisses him

15.

3428.115	6142, 3772	8369	5266	3219	6142	8399
v Qal pf 1cs	prep, adv	v Piel pf 1cs	n mp, ps 1cs	art, n ms	prep, ps 1cs	n mp
יָצָאתִי	עַל-כֵּן	שִׁלַּמְתִּי	נְדָרַי	הַיּוֹם	עָלָי	שְׁלָמִים
yātsā'thî	'al-kēn	shillamtî	nedhāray	hayyôm	'ālāy	shelāmîm
I have come out	therefore	I have paid	my vows	today	on behalf of me	peace offerings

16.

4926	4834.125	6686	3937, 8264.341	3937, 7410.141
n mp	cj, v Qal impf 1cs, ps 2ms	n mp, ps 2ms	prep, v Piel inf con	prep, v Qal inf con, ps 2ms
מַרְבַדִּים	וָאֶמְצָאֵךְ	פָּנֶיךָ	לְשַׁחֵר	לִקְרָאתֶךָ
marvaddîm	wā'emtsā'ekkā	pānêkhā	leshachēr	liqŏrā'thekhā
coverings	and I have found you	your face	to seek	to meet you

17.

5311.115	4875	332	2497B	6446	7527.115
v Qal pf 1cs	pn	n ms	n fp	n fs, ps 1cs	v Qal pf 1cs
נַפְתִּי	מִצְרַיִם	אֵטוּן	חֲטֻבוֹת	עַרְשִׂי	רָבַדְתִּי
naphtî	mitsrayim	'ētûn	chătuvôth	'arsî	rāvadhtî
I have sprinkled	Egypt	fine linen of	colorful spreads of	my couch	I have covered

18.

1782	7588.120	2050.131	7360	167	4915	5085
n mp	v Qal juss 1cp	v Qal impv 2ms	cj, n ms	n mp	n ms	n ms, ps 1cs
דֹּדִים	נִרְוֶה	לְכָה	וְקִנָּמוֹן	אֲהָלִים	מֹר	מִשְׁכָּבִי
dhōdhîm	nirweh	lekhāh	weqinnāmôn	'ăhālîm	mōr	mishkāvî
love	let us drink our fill of	come	and cinnamon	aloes	myrrh	my bed

19.

382	375	3706	904, 155	6187.720	5912, 1269
art, n ms	sub	cj	prep, art, n mp	v Hithpael juss 1cp	adv, art, n ms
הָאִישׁ	אֵין	כִּי	בָּאֳהָבִים	נִתְעַלְּסָה	עַד-הַבֹּקֶר
hā'îsh	'ên	kî	bā'ăhāvîm	nith'allesāh	'adh-habbōqer
the husband	he is not	because	with love	let us enjoy ourselves	until the morning

20.

4089.111	7154, 3826B	4623, 7632	904, 1932	2050.111	904, 1041
v Qal pf 3ms	n ms, art, n ms	prep, adv	prep, n ms	v Qal pf 3ms	prep, n ms, ps 3ms
לָקַח	צְרוֹר-הַכֶּסֶף	מֵרָחוֹק	בְּדֶרֶךְ	הָלַךְ	בְּבֵיתוֹ
lāqach	tserôr-hakkeseph	mērāchôq	bedherekh	hālakh	bevêthô
he took	the bag of the money	from far away	on a journey	he has gone	in his house

21.

5371.512	1041	971.121	3801	3937, 3219	904, 3135
v Hiphil pf 3fs, ps 3ms	n ms, ps 3ms	v Qal impf 3ms	art, n ms	prep, n ms	prep, n fs, ps 3ms
הִטַּתּוּ	בֵּיתוֹ	יָבֹא	הַכֵּסֵא	לְיוֹם	בְּיָדוֹ
hittattû	vêthô	yāvō'	hakkēse'	leyôm	beyādhô
she enticed him	his house	he will enter	the full moon	at the day of	in his hand

---

14. I have peace offerings with me; this day have I paid my vows: ... I am holding a thanksgiving feast, *Moffatt* ... had to offer a communion sacrifice, *JB* ... peace offerings I owed, *Berkeley* ... Today I have kept my special promises, *NCV*.

15. Therefore came I forth to meet thee, diligently to seek thy face, and

I have found thee: ... to seek you eagerly, *NRSV* ... So I came out in the hope of meeting you, looking for you with care, and now I have you, *BB*.

16. I have decked my bed with coverings of tapestry, with carved works, with fine linen of Egypt: ... couch of pleasure, *Rotherham* ... spread pretty rugs on my couch,—Of

Egypt the bright-coloured chintz, *Fenton* ... with carpets of tapestry, With striped cloths of the yarn of Egypt, *ASV*.

17. I have perfumed my bed with myrrh, aloes, and cinnamon: ... charmingly scented my chamber, With cinnamon, sandal, and myrrh!, *Fenton* ... with aloes and cassia, *NEB*.

18. Come, let us take our fill of love until the morning: ... Let us drown ourselves in pleasure, *NEB* ... let's drink deep of love, *NIV.*

let us solace ourselves with loves: ... delight ourselves with loves, *Darby* ... revel in caresses!, *Goodspeed* ... let us feast on love!, *NAB.*

19. For the goodman is not at home, he is gone a long journey: ...

the master is not in my home, *Fenton* ... husband is not at home, *Darby* ... My husband is traveling, and he's far away, *CEV.*

20. He hath taken a bag of money with him, and will come home at the day appointed: ... won't come home until the full moon, *Beck* ... won't be home for weeks, *NCV* ... no fear of his returning till the moon is full, *Knox.*

21. With her much fair speech she caused him to yield: ... Persuasively she led him on, *NEB* ... She wins him over by her repeated urging, *Douay* ... her persistant coaxing, *JB.*

with the flattering of her lips she forced him: ... with her smooth lips she misleads him, *Beck* ... with the smoothness of her lips she constrained him, *Darby* ... entices him, *Berkeley.*

---

were abused (cf. Gen. 19:5–8; Judg. 19:24–28; the exception is Ruth [ch. 3]). This is not, however, an implicit injunction against women leaving, or working outside, the home (cf. 1:20f).

This woman lies in ambush ('ārav, HED #717, cf. 1:11, 18) wherever she can—street, open square, house or street corner. This verse complicates the interpretation of "her corner/house" (v. 8), since the whole town is her territory. The discretion needed to avoid her does not depend on knowing where she lives, but lies in recognizing her for what she is when one encounters her. Since she waits to ambush the naive passerby, she is truly an enemy, which also explains why she must hide her feelings (v. 10): young men would hardly accompany her if they knew what she truly felt about them.

7:13. Once they meet, she seduces him by physical touch (v. 13), flattery (v. 15), erotic language (vv. 16ff) and reassurance (vv. 19f). The combination is effective, and deadly. Although she begins by seizing and kissing him, most of the space in the text is given to recording her words, since they are her main weapon, alongside her touch. Like the wicked man, she has a bold look (cf. 21:29).

7:14. Peace or fellowship offerings, described in Lev. 3, were given in thanks for God's goodness, or as freewill offerings, and worshipers were allowed to eat some of the meat of the sacrificed animal (Lev. 7:11–18; cf. 1 Sam. 9:11ff). Her invitation thus includes a festive meal; her true purpose shows her low regard for the Covenant. The text is silent about the nature or content of her vows.

7:15. She now flatters him by saying that he was why she was there; she had been looking for him in particular, as the repeated "you" shows. The verse also revolves around the repeated "to meet you" and "to seek you"; in Hebrew the middle syllables of "I went out" (yātsā'thî) and "I have found you" (wā'emtsā'ekhā) are alliterative, a signal that

this speech is a well-polished weapon, ready at a moment's notice.

7:16–18. These three verses, the heart of her appeal, are filled with erotic imagery similar to that found in the Song of Songs, and carefully calculated to arouse his passion until he could no longer resist. Her bed was expensively prepared with imported goods. Since, however, spices were a metaphor for sensual delight (cf. S.S. 1:13; 3:6; 4:6, 14; 5:1, 13), v. 17 probably refers not to her bed, but to her body, which she thus boldly offers to him.

She saves her most explicit invitation, however, for last (v. 18), saying that together they will drink their fill (cf. the same word in 5:19) of love all night and delight in each other with their lovemaking. Her language could hardly be more explicit, since the word translated "love" (HED #1782) in v. 18a is always in a sexual context when plural, as it is here (cf. Ezek. 16:8; 23:17; S.S. 1:2, 4; 4:10; 5:1; 7:13), and usually in a sexual context when singular (cf. S.S. 1:13f, 16; 5:9).

7:19–20. Whether he begins to worry, or expresses his concern, she meets his potential objection by reassuring him that they will not be discovered, since her husband, the one most likely to cause trouble, is on a long journey. If the darkness of the night (v. 9) implies a new moon (which might also explain the peace offering), then her husband will not return for about two weeks. She, however, calls him "the," not "my," husband, which probably shows her disdain for him. (Hebrew usually uses the same word for either "man" or "husband.") Her reference to his bag of silver may express resentment, or hint at her expectations from this relationship (cf. 5:9–14).

7:21. She says more than the teacher reports—flattering, enticing and reassuring until he can resist no longer. She is "persuasive" (HED #4090), a word used elsewhere in Proverbs only for good or wise speech or teaching (1:5; 4:2; 9:9; 16:21, 23).

904, 7524	4090	904, 2609	8004	5258.522
prep, *n ms*	n ms, ps 3fs	prep, *n ms*	n fd, ps 3fs	v Hiphil impf 3fs, ps 3ms
בְּרֹב	לִקְחָהּ	בְּחֵלֶק	שְׂפָתֶיהָ	תַּדִּיחֶנּוּ
berōv	liqōchāhh	bechēleq	sephāthêāh	taddîchennû
with the abundance of	her teaching	with the smoothness of	her lips	she seduced him

22.

2050.151	313	6849	3626, 8228	420, 2984	971.121	3626, 6136
v Qal act ptc ms	prep, ps 3fs	adv	prep, n ms	prep, n ms	v Qal impf 3ms	cj, prep, n ms
הוֹלֵךְ	אַחֲרֶיהָ	פִּתְאֹם	כְּשׁוֹר	אֶל־טָבַח	יָבוֹא	וּכְעֶכֶס
hôlēkh	ʾachărêāh	pithʾōm	keshôr	ʾel-ṭāvach	yāvôʾ	ûkheʾekhes
going	after her	quickly	like an ox	to a slaughter	he entered	and like an anklet

23.

420, 4284	188	5912	6642.321	2777	3634	3626, 4257.341
prep, *n ms*	n ms	adv	v Piel impf 3ms	n ms	n ms, ps 3ms	prep, v Piel inf con
אֶל־מוּסָר	אֱוִיל	עַד	יְפַלַּח	חֵץ	כְּבֵדוֹ	כְּמַהֵר
ʾel-mûsār	ʾĕwîl	ʿadh	yephallach	chēts	kevēdhô	kemahēr
unto the chastisement of	a fool	until	it pierces	an arrow	his liver	when hastening

24.

7109	420, 6583	3940, 3156.111	3706, 904, 5497	2000	6498	1158
n ms	prep, n ms	cj, neg part, v Qal pf 3ms	cj, prep, n fs, ps 3fs	pers pron	cj, adv	n mp
צִפּוֹר	אֶל־פָּח	וְלֹא־יָדַע	כִּי־בְנַפְשׁוֹ	הוּא	וְעַתָּה	בָּנִים
tsippôr	ʾel-pāch	welōʾ-yādhaʿ	kî-venaphshô	hûʾ	weʿattāh	vānîm
a bird	into a snare	and he does not know	that with its life	it	but now	O sons

25.

8471.133, 3937	7477.533	3937, 571, 6552	414, 7928.121
v Qal impv 2mp, prep, ps 1cs	cj, v Hiphil impv 2mp	prep, n mp, n ms, ps 1cs	adv, v Qal juss 3ms
שִׁמְעוּ־לִי	וְהַקְשִׁיבוּ	לְאִמְרֵי־פִי	אַל־יֵשְׁטְ
shimʿû-lî	wehaqshîvû	leʾimrê-phî	ʾal-yēsṭ
listen to me	and be attentive	to the sayings of my mouth	do not let it depart

26.

420, 1932	3949	414, 8912.123	904, 5594	3706, 7521	2592
prep, n mp, ps 3fs	n ms, ps 2ms	adv, v Qal juss 2ms	prep, n fp, ps 3fs	cj, adj	n mp
אֶל־דְּרָכֶיהָ	לִבֶּךָ	אַל־תֵּתַע	בִּנְתִיבוֹתֶיהָ	כִּי־רַבִּים	חֲלָלִים
ʾel-derākhêāh	libbekhā	ʾal-tētaʿ	binthîvôthêāh	kî-rabbîm	chălālîm
to her ways	your heart	do not stray	on her paths	because many	the slain

27.

6640.512	6335	3725, 2103.156	1932	8061
v Hiphil pf 3fs	cj, adj	adj, v Qal pass ptc mp, ps 3fs	n mp	pn
הִפִּילָה	וַעֲצֻמִים	כָּל־הֲרֻגֶיהָ	דַּרְכֵי	שְׁאוֹל
hippîlāh	waʿătsumîm	kol-hărughêāh	darkhê	sheʾôl
she has caused to fall	and vast	all her slain	the pathways of	Sheol

---

22. He goeth after her straightway, as an ox goeth to the slaughter, or as a fool to the correction of the stocks: ... He follows her stupidly, *NAB* ... like an antelope bounding into the noose, *NEB* ... like a deer caught in a trap, *NCV* ... like a dog cajoled to the muzzle, *Moffatt.*

23. Till a dart strike through his liver; as a bird hasteth to the snare, and knoweth not that it is for his life: ... Until the arrow pierced his vitals, *NEB* ... it will cost him his life, *NRSV.*

24. Hearken unto me now therefore, O ye children, and attend to the words of my mouth: ... listen to me, *NKJV* ... give attention to sayings of my mouth, *Young.*

25. Let not thine heart decline to her ways, go not astray in her paths: ... Swerve not toward her ways, *Goodspeed* ... Do not toy with the thought of meeting her, *Anchor* ... Do not let desire entice you into her ways, *REB* ... or let yourself be misled by someone like her, *CEV.*

26. For she hath cast down many wounded: ... For many are the dead she has laid low, *Goodspeed* ... for many wounded hath she caused to fall, *Rotherham.*

yea, many strong men have been slain by her: ... her victims are without number, *NEB* ... a vast host of men have been her victims, *LIVB.*

27. Her house is the way to hell, going down to the chambers of death: ... the way to the underworld, *BB* ... the entrance to Sheol, *NEB* ... made up of ways to the

But flattery is most prominent (vv. 5, 15, 21; cf. 29:5), compelling him until he yields.

7:22–23. When he does yield, it is a sudden decision to follow (v. 22a). Lacking both the resources to resist and the wisdom simply to run away, he is helpless like an animal being led to slaughter (v. 22b) or a bird once it touches the snare (v. 23b).

The great variety of translation of v. 22 reveals the difficulty of the text. The NASB's translation is fairly literal ("or as one in fetters to the discipline of a fool"), but requires the added words, and does not match either vv. 22b or 23b, both of which follow the pattern "as [an animal] to [its fate]." The ancient versions do not agree with the Hebrew text or with each other; it is impossible to know whether they were trying to make sense of the current Hebrew text or had a different text before them. The best conjecture thus far (changing only one letter of the consonantal text) is "as a stag skipping into a noose" (S. R. Driver, *Vetus Testamentum* 1 [1951], 241), but even this is only a well-reasoned guess.

The difficulty of the text does not, however, obscure the point. Once he decides to go with her, he is no better than a brute, led on by his appetites, and not guided by wisdom or instruction.

In addition, just as the animal is trapped so that it may be killed, the young man will suffer for his immorality (v. 23a). Whether this refers to a physical punishment, or is merely an extension of the slaughter/hunting metaphor, this image of a mortal wound (a liver that has been split by an arrow), reveals how serious a crime adultery is. Adultery was a capital crime (Lev. 20:10; Deut. 22:22; cf. Gen. 38:24), the punishment of which may be in view here, although it may also refer to the financial ruin that an unbridled life can bring upon one (cf. 5:9–14).

The preposition beᵉ (HED #904) should not be translated here; the *beth essentiae*, as this use of the preposition is known, introduces "the essence" of the thing, thus equating "it" and "his life" (cf. 3:26; 8:8; 1 Ki. 19:11f; Ps. 29:4).

7:24. The "therefore" (HED #6498) that opens the conclusion represents a different conjunction than that found in v. 15. This "therefore" is followed by a command, prohibition or injunction that is based on the previous passage. In this case, the teacher applies the moral of the story after first calling the student's attention away from the story and back to his words (7:1–4).

7:25. What appears to be a twofold warning is actually one: to turn aside from the ways of wisdom to the path of an adulteress is to wander about lost in her ways. This prohibition stands in direct contrast to walking and living in obedience to the ways taught by the teacher (7:1–5, 24). Since behavior reveals what is, or is not, in the heart (v. 7), the heart must be guarded and kept at all times (4:23). Successful resistance is therefore not a matter of willpower, but of submission and obedience.

7:26–27. Whereas the commands of the introduction of this poem end in a statement of purpose, the motive clauses in these verses reflect the warning of v. 23. These verses universalize the narrative by expanding it beyond the particular relationship described in vv. 6–22. Those whom she has destroyed are nearly countless. The warning is then quite simple: if she has destroyed many in this way, she can also destroy you. The only antidote is to learn well what the teacher is saying (7:1–5, 24). At the same time, this is more than a question of objectionable behavior (v. 25). The major theme throughout the opening chapters, the prologue (Prov. 1–9), is the alternative ways that lead to life or to death. This chapter has explained and warned against wandering lost in her ways, since her house is a house of death, not of life. Her promised "love" is an invitation to a bed in the grave (cf. 2:18f).

8:1–36. The teacher puts most of this chapter in Wisdom's mouth, speaking in her behalf (vv. 4–36). The change from the constant exhortation to listen to human teachers (e.g., 4:1–5; 7:1ff, 24), to listening to Wisdom herself, demonstrates this chapter's function in the prologue. The climax of chs. 1–9 demonstrates that Wisdom is unique and unrivaled, more desirable than anything (8:4–21; especially v. 11) and more necessary than anything (v. 36). Even the final verses are addressed by Wisdom to her "sons" (v. 32), as the rest of her peroration shows; a human father or teacher could hardly claim to be the source of life (v. 35).

This chapter is superficially similar to Wisdom's first speech (1:20–33), since they both begin with descriptions of her public location (1:20f; 8:1ff) and end by the fundamental contrast of the prologue (1:32f; 8:35f). Her invitations, however, introduce quite disparate speeches. In Prov. 1, Wisdom speaks primarily as a prophet, warning those who reject her of the disaster that will attend their rebellion. The worth of her teaching is there implied in largely negative terms. If they had responded, they would have been saved; however, in ch. 8, Wisdom emphasizes her blessings and bene-

8:1

Strong's	Parse	Hebrew	Translit.	English
7410.122	v Qal impf 3fs	תִּקְרָא	thiqŏrā'	is she calling
3940, 2551	intrg part, neg part, n fs	הֲלֹא־חָכְמָה	hălō'-chokhmāh	is not wisdom
420, 2410, 4323	prep, n mp, n ms	אֶל־חַדְרֵי־מָוֶת	'el-chadhrê-māweth	to the chambers of death
3495.154	v Qal act ptc fp	יְרֵדוֹת	yōrᵉdhôth	going down
1041	n ms, ps 3fs	בֵּיתָהּ	bêthāhh	her house

2.

Strong's	Parse	Hebrew	Translit.	English
6142, 1932	prep, n ms	עֲלֵי־דָרֶךְ	'ălê-dhārekh	on the way
904, 7513, 4953	prep, n ms, n mp	בְּרֹאשׁ־מְרוֹמִים	bᵉrō'sh-mᵉrômîm	upon the top of the heights
7249	n ms, ps 3fs	קוֹלָהּ	qôlāhh	her voice
5598.122	v Qal impf 3fs	תִּתֵּן	tittēn	is she giving
8722	cj, n fs	וּתְבוּנָה	ûthᵉvûnāh	and understanding

3.

Strong's	Parse	Hebrew	Translit.	English
3937, 3135, 8554	prep, n fs, n mp	לְיַד־שְׁעָרִים	lᵉyadh-shᵉ'ārîm	by the side of the gates
8807.212	v Niphal pf 3fs	נִצָּבָה	nitstsāvāh	she has taken her stand
5594	n fp	נְתִיבוֹת	nᵉthîvôth	the paths
1041	n ms	בֵּית	bêth	the structure of

4.

Strong's	Parse	Hebrew	Translit.	English
382	n mp	אִישִׁים	'ishîm	O men
420, ps 2mp	prep, ps 2mp	אֲלֵיכֶם	'ălêkhem	to you
7728.127	v Qal impf 3fp	תָּרֹנָּה	tārōnnāh	she cries out loudly
6860	n mp	פְּתָחִים	phᵉthāchîm	the doors
4136	n ms	מְבוֹא	mᵉvô'	the entrance of
3937, 6552, 7469	prep, n ms, n fs	לְפִי־קָרֶת	lᵉphî-qāreth	at the opening of the town

5.

Strong's	Parse	Hebrew	Translit.	English
6848	adj	פְּתָאִים	phᵉthā'yim	O simple ones
1032.533	v Hiphil impv 2mp	הָבִינוּ	hāvînû	learn
119	n ms	אָדָם	'ādhām	humankind
420, 1158	prep, n mp	אֶל־בְּנֵי	'el-bᵉnê	to the sons of
7249	cj, n ms, ps 1cs	וְקוֹלִי	wᵉqôlî	and my voice
7410.125	v Qal impf 1cs	אֶקְרָא	'eqŏrā'	I am calling

6.

Strong's	Parse	Hebrew	Translit.	English
3706, 5233	cj, n mp	כִּי־נְגִידִים	kî-nᵉghîdhîm	because noble things
8471.133	v Qal impv 2mp	שִׁמְעוּ	shim'û	listen
3949	n ms	לֵב	lēv	heart
1032.533	v Hiphil impv 2mp	הָבִינוּ	hāvînû	learn
3809	cj, n mp	וּכְסִילִים	ûkhᵉsîlîm	and O fools
6430	n fs	עָרְמָה	'ārᵉmāh	shrewdness

nether world, *NAB* ... a highway to the grave, *NIV* ... leads down to the halls of death, *NEB*.

8:1. Doth not wisdom cry? and understanding put forth her voice?: ... Hear how Wisdom lifts her voice and Understanding cries out, *NEB* ... Wisdom calls to you like someone shouting, *NCV* ... And then does not Wisdom invite? And Intellect utter her voice?, *Fenton* ... discernment utter her voice?, *Berkeley* ... And, all the while, the wisdom that grants discernment is crying aloud, is never silent, *Knox*.

2. She standeth in the top of high places, by the way in the places of the paths: ... She takes her stand at the ascent to the citadel, *Beck* ... Ascending the road to the acropolis, *Anchor* ... At the top of the highways, at the meeting of the roads, she takes her place, *BB* ... She stands at the junction of streets, *Fenton*.

3. She crieth at the gates, at the entry of the city, at the coming in at the doors: ... at the city's approach, close beside the gates, making proclamation, *Knox* ... where people enter the doors, she's calling loud, *Beck* ... from the portals' entrance she cries out, *Berkeley* ... at the doorways her voice is loud, *BB*.

4. Unto you, O men, I call; and my voice is to the sons of man: ... Listen, everyone, I'm calling out to you; I am shouting to all people, *NCV* ... and my cry is to all that live, *NRSV* ... my appeal is to the children of men, *NAB* ... my words are addressed to all humanity, *JB* ... and talking to you, O human beings, *Beck*.

5. O ye simple, understand wisdom: ... O heedless souls, learn insight, *Moffatt* ... You foolish,—reflect and have sense, *Fenton* ... You who are uneducated, be smarter, *NCV* ... Become expert in reason, *BB* ... Here is better counsel for the simpleton, *Knox*.

and, ye fools, be ye of an understanding heart: ... acquire intelligence, you who lack it, *NRSV* ... O foolish hearts, take warning!, *Knox* ... You stupid,—reflect in your heart!, *Fenton*.

6. Hear; for I will speak of excellent things; and the opening of my lips shall be right things: ... I have

fits in order to encourage those whom she calls to listen to and learn from her.

This chapter's general structure, opening appeal, narrative or descriptive motivation and closing appeal are identical to ch. 7. Both chapters begin by describing wisdom's benefits and value (7:1–5; 8:4–21) and conclude with an appeal and warning (7:24–27; 8:32–36). Proverbs 8, however, focuses on wisdom's value, mentioned in twenty-eight verses in this chapter. It is valuable because it is true (8:6b–9), because it offers many valuable benefits (8:15–21) and because of its divine origin, antiquity and role in creation (8:22–31).

Introduction: Wisdom's availability (8:1–3)

A *Exhortation: Discern and listen! (8:4–6a)*

B *Reasons: Wisdom is trustworthy (8:6b–9)*

A' *Exhortation: Choose Wisdom above all else (8:10)*

B' *Reasons: Wisdom is most valuable (8:11)*

B'' *Reasons: Wisdom has immediate benefits (8:12–21)*

B''' *Reasons: Wisdom's origin, antiquity and work (8:22–31)*

A''' *Exhortation: Listen and heed! (8:32–33)*

B'''' *Reasons: A matter of life or death (8:34–36)*

Previous poems begin with exhortations to listen, learn and obey (cf. 2:1–4; 3:1; 4:1, 10, 20f; 5:1ff; etc.), and then support or strengthen the exhortation by outlining or describing the benefits of a proper response. In Prov. 8, two extensive statements of motivation (vv. 6b–9, 11–21) follow brief exhortations (vv. 5f, 10), before the pattern is reversed with a similarly proportioned motivation (vv. 22–31) and closing call to heed (vv. 32–36). Thus, vv. 32–36 both conclude the entire chapter and respond specifically to the poem in vv. 22–31. Another difference between this poem and the preceding chapters is that it lacks the motif of protection (e.g., 2:12–19; 3:22–26; 4:6; 6:24; 7:5), focusing on wisdom's enabling gifts, rather than on what it prevents or protects people from doing.

A question raised by this chapter is the nature of Wisdom herself—is she an entity separate from God, or a poetic personification of a divine quality? In light of the larger context (e.g., 3:19f), the latter interpretation seems correct. Paul may have had this passage in mind when he described Jesus Christ as the wisdom of God (Col. 1:15ff; 2:3; cf. John 1:1–4; 1 Cor. 1:24, 30).

8:1–3. The opening verses describe the public nature of Wisdom's invitation (8:1ff). They contrast with the secrecy of the previous chapter (7:9) and unite the prologue by returning to the beginning of wisdom's first speech (1:20f). The locations (vv. 2f), all familiar, easily accessible public places, emphasize her availability and encourage students to attend her. Wisdom is not difficult to find for those who respond to her invitation; the places listed in these verses could hardly be avoided by anyone making a thorough search.

Since the city gate was the location of courts of law (cf. Ruth 4:1, 11; Job 29:7; 31:21; Prov. 24:7; 31:23), the appeal is multifaceted. Wisdom was especially needed in legal decisions (cf. 1 Ki. 3:16–28; Prov. 8:15f; cf. 17:15, 23, 26; 18:5; 19:28), and those who were considered wise would be found there, so that from listening to them the naive could learn wisdom (cf. 10:13, 31). The specific reference to the gates (as well as to the other locations) thus reinforces Wisdom's accessibility.

8:4–5. Wisdom clarifies her general invitation (v. 4) by calling the simple or naive, who are one of the primary groups addressed in the Book (1:4). Extending her invitation to "fools" (HED #3809), however, flies in the face of the rest of Proverbs, where the "insolent" are without hope, since they cannot and will not change (the only exceptions, 26:12 and 29:20, are apparent, not real). This parallel may show Wisdom's openness to all, even to those who will spurn her offer, but since the two terms are also parallel in 1:22, they probably refer generally to all who need her teaching.

Verse 5 is oxymoronic. Wisdom calls upon those without insight to discern; they can learn discernment only by attending to Wisdom's "noble" and "upright" teaching (v. 6). The noun "nobles" or "leaders" (HED #5233), is an abstract plural, "noble things" (cf. NASB, NKJV).

8:6–9. In this extended motive clause, Wisdom extols her teaching as truthful and just and denies that any of her words are evil or perverse, bracketing the contrasting central verses (vv. 7f) with statements (vv. 6, 9) that emphasize their complete trustworthiness ("all," v. 9):

v. 6	A	noble things (v. 6a)
	A'	right things (v. 6b)
v. 7	A"	truth (v. 7a)
	B	not wickedness (v. 7b)

7.

2541 n ms, ps 1cs	1965.121 v Qal impf 3ms	3706, 583 cj, n fs	4478 n mp	8004 n fd, ps 1cs	4829 cj, n ms	1744.325 v Piel impf 1cs
חִכִּי	יֶהְגֶּה	כִּי־אֱמֶת	מֵישָׁרִים	שְׂפָתָי	וּמִפְתַּח	אֲדַבֵּר
chikkî	yehgeh	kî-'ĕmeth	mêshārîm	sephāthay	ûmiphtach	'ădhabbēr
my mouth	it will utter	because truth	uprightness	my lips	and the opening of	I will speak

8.

3725, 571, 6552 adj, n mp, n ms, ps 1cs	904, 6928 prep, n ms	7856 n ms	8004 n fd, ps 1cs	8774 cj, n fs
כָּל־אִמְרֵי־פִי	בְּצֶדֶק	רֶשַׁע	שְׂפָתָי	וְתוֹעֵבַת
kol-'imrê-phî	betsedheq	resha'	sephāthay	wethô'ăvath
all the words of my mouth	with righteousness	wickedness	my lips	and the abomination of

9.

5416 adj	3725 adj, ps 3mp	6379 cj, adj	6871. 255 v Niphal ptc ms	904 prep, ps 3mp	375 sub
נְכֹחִים	כֻּלָּם	וְעִקֵּשׁ	נִפְתָּל	בָּהֶם	אֵין
nekhōchîm	kullām	we'iqqēsh	niphtāl	bāhem	'ên
straight	all of them	or perverted	what is twisted	in them	there is not

1907 n fs	3937, 4834.152 prep, v Qal act ptc mp	3596 cj, adj	3937, 1032.551 prep, art, v Hiphil ptc ms
דָעַת	לְמֹצְאֵי	וִישָׁרִים	לַמֵּבִין
dhā'ath	lemōtse'ê	wîshārîm	lammēvîn
knowledge	to those who find	and upright	to the one who understands

10.

1013.255 v Niphal ptc ms	4623, 2843 prep, n ms	1907 cj, n fs	414, 3826B cj, neg part, n ms	4089.133, 4284 v Qal impv 2mp, n ms, ps 1cs
נִבְחָר	מֵחָרוּץ	וְדַעַת	וְאַל־כָּסֶף	קְחוּ־מוּסָרִי
nivchār	mēchārûts	wedha'ath	we'al-kāseph	qōchû-mûsārî
what is chosen	rather than gold	and knowledge	and not silver	receive my discipline

11.

3940 neg part	3725, 2761 cj, adj, n mp	4623, 6689 prep, n fp	2551 n fs	3706, 3009B cj, adj
לֹא	וְכָל־חֲפָצִים	מִפְּנִינִים	חָכְמָה	כִּי־טוֹבָה
lō'	wekhol-chăphātsîm	mippenînîm	chokhmāh	kî-tôvāh
not	and all delights	than pearls of coral	wisdom	because better

12.

4343 n fp	1907 cj, n fs	6430 n fs	8331.115 v Qal pf 1cs	603, 2551 pers pron, n fs	8187.126, 904 v Qal impf 3mp, prep, ps 3fs
מְזִמּוֹת	וְדַעַת	עָרְמָה	שָׁכַנְתִּי	אֲנִי־חָכְמָה	יִשְׁווּ־בָהּ
mezimmôth	wedha'ath	'ārmāh	shākhantî	'ănî-chokhmāh	yishwû-vāhh
discretion	and knowledge	shrewdness	I dwell	I wisdom	they can compare with it

13.

1932 cj, n ms	1377 cj, n ms	1372 n fs	7737 n ms	7985.141 v Qal inf con	3176 pn	3488 n fs	4834.125 v Qal impf 1cs
וְדֶרֶךְ	וְגָאוֹן	גֵּאָה	רָע	שְׂנֹאת	יְהוָה	יִרְאַת	אֶמְצָא
wedherekh	wegha'ôn	gē'āh	rā'	senō'th	yehwāh	yir'ath	'emtsā'
and the way of	and arrogance	pride	evil	to hate	Yahweh	the fear of	I find

---

worthy things to say, *NIV* ... Give heed! for noble things I speak; honesty opens my lips, *Douay* ... Give ear, for my words are true, *BB* ... Hear for princely things will I speak, *Rotherham*.

7. For my mouth shall speak truth; and wickedness is an abomination to my lips: ... What I say is true, I

refuse to speak evil, *NCV* ... Whatever I say is said honestly, To utter wickedness would be abhorrent to me *Anchor* ... For good faith goes out of my mouth, and false lips are disgusting to me, *BB*.

8. All the words of my mouth are in righteousness; there is nothing froward or perverse in them: ...

Sincere are all the words of my mouth, no one of them is wily or crooked, *NAB* ... All the words from my mouth are upright, nothing false there, nothing crooked, *JB* ... Everything I say is honest; nothing I say is crooked or false, *NCV*.

9. They are all plain to him that understandeth, and right to them

that find knowledge: ... To intellect, they are all straight, And plain to the seeker of fact, *Fenton* ... it is all plain to the man of sense, and true to those who are intelligent, *Moffatt* ... People with good sense know what I say is true, *NCV*.

10. Receive my instruction, and not silver; and knowledge rather than choice gold: ... Receive my correction, *Rotherham* ... Accept my discipline in preference to silver, *Anchor* ... Seize my instructions,—not money, *Fenton*.

11. For wisdom is better than rubies: ... than ornaments of coral, *Rotherham* ... fairer than pearls, *Fenton*.

and all the things that may be desired are not to be compared to it: ... no jewels can match her, *NEB* ... And all pleasures equal not hers!, *Fenton* ... no choice possessions, *NAB*.

12. I wisdom dwell with prudence, and find out knowledge of witty inventions: ... I bestow shrewdness, *NEB* ... dwell with experience, and judicious knowledge, *NAB* ... dwelling with skill, And know the discoveries of thought, *Fenton*.

13. The fear of the LORD is to hate evil: pride, and arrogancy: ... Reverence of the LORD is, *Berkeley* ... (Fear of Yahweh means hatred of evil), *JB* ... a high opinion of oneself, *BB* ... love of self, *KJVII*.

and the evil way, and the froward mouth, do I hate: ... wicked behaviour and a lying mouth, *JB* ... the false tongue, are unpleasing to me, *BB* ... perverted speech, *NRSV*.

---

v. 8   A'''   righteousness (v. 8a)
     B'   nothing crooked/perverse (v. 8b)
v. 9   A''''   all are true (v. 9a)
     A'''''   right (v. 9b)

Since these words are spoken by a truthful teacher, and in light of the unity of Prov. 1–24 and the climactic function of this chapter in the prologue, these verses implicitly claim that the proverbs that follow in chs. 10–24 are true, just and upright. The student can thus study them without fear of being led into error or wickedness. (On the preposition that begins in 8:8, see the commentary at 7:23 regarding *beth essentiae*.)

8:10–11. These verses form the second command-motive sequence in this chapter. Although v. 10 does not begin with the word "therefore," it is implicit in the organization of the chapter, closing the first main section (vv. 1–11). Wisdom and knowledge are better than gold in all four occurrences of this word for "gold" (HED #2843) in Proverbs (3:14; 8:19; 16:16). Like the numerous "better than" proverbs (e.g., 15:16f), these verses recommend the less obvious of two options. Unlike the individual sayings, in which the balance is usually tipped by a word or two, this poem gives an extensive basis for this valuation. Wisdom is the path to success (8:12–21).

Proverbs 8:11 is nearly identical to 3:15. Both texts distill a catalog of wisdom's benefits into a statement of her value, beyond thought or desire. Whereas the earlier poem is in the father's mouth, this verse represents Wisdom's own estimate of her worth.

8:12–21. These verses are tied together and connected to the opening poem of the chapter by repeated vocabulary and imagery. Proverbs 8:17 combines the terminology of the opening and closing verses (vv. 12b, 21a), showing its structural and thematic centrality to the entire poem: Wisdom loves those whose love compels them to seek her. As this section shows, she blesses most bountifully those whom she loves.

A   *the knowledge of discretion I find v. 12b*
B   *I love those who love me; v. 17*
A'   *and those who seek me early shall find me. v.17b*
B'   *to cause those who love me to inherit wealth v. 21*

Verse 17 reverses the order of the terms. A chiastic arrangement (i.e., by reversing v. 17a and b) would divide the poem into two sections. The reversal binds the entire poem together into a description of the benefits of finding and loving wisdom in order to encourage that love and search.

8:12. Wherever wisdom is, prudence, knowledge and the ability to plan wisely are also found (8:12). According to Prov. 1:4, these are the specific qualities which the young and naive gain by studying Solomon's proverbs (cf. 8:5). This verse also anticipates the end of the chapter, where Wisdom encourages her students to seek her dwelling (v. 34), where the other qualities are also found. The main terms of vv. 12ff also occur together in Isa. 11:2 and Job 12:13, which shows how closely they were associated in Israel.

8:13. The main terms in the previous verse, prudence and discretion, could be either positive or negative. Although the word translated "prudence"

7737	6552	8749	7983.115	14.	3937, 6332	8786	603
n ms	cj, n ms	n fp	v Qal pf 1cs		prep, ps 1cs, n fs	cj, n fs	pers pron
רָע	וּפִי	תַּהְפֻּכוֹת	שָׁנֵאתִי		לִי־עֵצָה	וְתוּשִׁיָּה	אֲנִי
rā'	ûphî	thahpukhôth	sānē'thî		lî-'ētsāh	wᵉthûshîyāh	'ănî
evil	but the mouth of	perversity	I hate		to me counsel	and sound wisdom	I

1035	3937	1400	15.	904	4567	4566.126	7619.152	2809.326
n fs	prep, ps 1cs	n fs		prep, ps 1cs	n mp	v Qal impf 3mp	cj, v Qal act ptc mp	v Poel impf 3mp
בִּינָה	לִי	גְּבוּרָה		בִּי	מְלָכִים	יִמְלֹכוּ	וְרוֹזְנִים	יְחֹקְקוּ
vînāh	lî	ghᵉvûrāh		bî	mᵉlākhîm	yimlōkhû	wᵉrôznîm	yᵉchōqᵉqû
insight	to me	strength		by me	kings	they reign	and rulers	they decree

6928	16.	904	8015	8049.126	5259	3725, 8570.152
n ms		prep, ps 1cs	n mp	v Qal impf 3mp	cj, n mp	adj, v Qal act ptc mp
צֶדֶק		בִּי	שָׂרִים	יָשֹׂרוּ	וּנְדִיבִים	כָּל־שֹׁפְטֵי
tsedheq		bî	sārîm	yāsrû	ûnᵉdhîvîm	kol-shōphᵉṭê
righteousness		by me	officials	rule	and nobles	all judges of

6928	17.	603	154.152	154.125	8264.352
n ms		pers pron	v Qal act ptc mp, ps 3fs	v Qal impf 1cs	cj, v Piel ptc mp, ps 1cs
צֶדֶק		אֲנִי	אֹהֲבֶיהָ	אֵהָב	וּמְשַׁחֲרַי
tsedheq		'ănî	'ōhăvêāh	'ēhāv	ûmᵉshachăray
righteousness		I	those who love her	I love	and those who diligently seek me

4834.126	18.	6484, 3638	882	2019	6516	6930
v Qal impf 3mp, ps 1cs		n ms, cj, n ms	prep, ps 1cs	n ms	adj	cj, n fs
יִמְצָאֻנְנִי		עֹשֶׁר־וְכָבוֹד	אִתִּי	הוֹן	עָתֵק	וּצְדָקָה
yimtsā'unᵉnî		'ōsher-wᵉkhāvôdh	'ittî	hôn	'āthēq	ûtsᵉdhāqāh
they will find me		riches and honor	with me	wealth	enduring	and righteousness

19.	3005	6780	4623, 2843	4623, 6580	8721	4623, 3826B	1013.255
	adj	n ms, ps 1cs	prep, n ms	cj, prep, n ms	cj, n fs, ps 1cs	prep, n ms	v Niphal ptc ms
	טוֹב	פִּרְיִי	מֵחָרוּץ	וּמִפָּז	וּתְבוּאָתִי	מִכֶּסֶף	נִבְחָר
	tôv	piryî	mēchārûts	ûmippāz	ûthᵉvû'āthî	mikkeseph	nivchār
	better	my fruit	than gold	even than pure gold	and my produce	than silver	what is chosen

20.	904, 758, 6930	2050.325	904, 8761	5594	5122
	prep, n fs, n fs	v Piel impf 1cs	prep, n ms	n fp	n ms
	בְּאֹרַח־צְדָקָה	אֲהַלֵּךְ	בְּתוֹךְ	נְתִיבוֹת	מִשְׁפָּט
	bᵉ'ōrach-tsᵉdhāqāh	'ăhallēkh	bᵉthôkh	nᵉthîvôth	mishpāṭ
	on the path of righteousness	I will walk	on the middle of	paths of	justice

14. Counsel is mine, and sound wisdom: I am understanding; I have strength: ... power of achievement, I am discernment, *Anchor* ... advice and ability, *REB* ... I am intelligent and I have strength, *Beck* ... sound knowledge: I have might, *ASV*.

15. By me kings reign, and princes decree justice: ... Through me kings have their power, and rulers give right decisions, *BB* ... monarchs rule, *JB* ... decree righteousness, *Young* ... lawgivers ... lay down just decrees, *Knox*.

16. By me princes rule, and nobles, even all the judges of the earth: ... great men govern, and magnates rule the earth, *Moffatt* ... Princes use me to lead, and so do all important people who judge fairly, *NCV* ... rulers on earth derive their rank, *REB*.

17. I love them that love me; and those that seek me early shall find me: ... seek me diligently, *NKJV* ... look for me eagerly and you'll find me, *Beck* ... Love me, and thou shalt earn my love; wait early at my doors, and thou shalt gain access to me, *Knox*.

18. Riches and honour are with me; yea, durable riches and righteousness: ... I hold wealth and honour, grandeur and good fortune, *Moffatt* ... In my hands are riches and honour, boundless wealth and the rewards of virtue, *NEB* ... enduring goods with righteousness, *Beck* ... durable wealth and, *Darby*.

19. My fruit is better than gold, yea, than fine gold; and my revenue than choice silver: ... and what I give is better than the best silver, *KJVII* ... what I yield surpasses choice silver, *NIV* ... and my

(HED #6430) is always positive in Proverbs (1:4; 8:5), a related adjective describes the snake (Gen. 3:1). A more literal translation might be "shrewdness," which is also a neutral term. The word translated "discretion" (HED #4343) is ambiguous even in Proverbs, referring both to the ability to plan wisely (1:4; 2:11; 3:21; 5:2), and to wicked plans (12:2; 14:17; 24:8).

This verse removes any potential ambiguity from Wisdom's self-description in v. 12, being written as an incomplete syllogism in order to force the reader to infer the conclusion:

Major premise:	The fear of the LORD is to hate evil (v. 13a)
Minor premise:	Wisdom hates evil (v. 13b–c)
Conclusion:	Wisdom is the fear of the LORD (implied)

Since the fear of the LORD is the primary quality required by this Book (1:7; 9:10), Wisdom both distances herself from all three types of evil (arrogance, wicked deeds, wicked speech) and identifies herself explicitly with the positive sense of the terms of v. 12.

8:14–16. Wisdom now presents proof of her value: she is indispensable to good government since she is the source of all good advice, fruitful planning, insight and strength. Since the Book of Proverbs is addressed to the young men who may someday rule, govern and judge their fellow Israelites, these verses encourage them to heed closely Wisdom's teaching, especially to the extent that they want to rule well. The repeated "to me" (v. 14a, c) and "by me" (vv. 15f) emphasize her role.

In some Hebrew manuscripts and the Septuagint, v. 16 ends with "judges of the earth" (RSV, NKJV), rather than "judges of righteousness" (i.e., "who judge/govern rightly"; NASB, NRSV). The latter reading provides an exact parallel with "justice" at the end of v. 15, and reinforces the theme of just government, which is a major theme of the Book of Proverbs (e.g., 17:15, 26; 19:28; 24:23–26; 29:2, 4, 26; 31:4–9). The former text also makes the same point, but without duplicating the previous verse. There is not enough evidence to choose between the two, although the latter text might have been changed to "judges of the earth" by analogy with the same phrase elsewhere (Pss. 2:10; 148:11; Isa. 48:23).

8:17. In this, the thematic verse of vv. 12–21 (cf. 8:12–21), Wisdom promises her availability and

fidelity to all who love and seek her. The first line reflects the exhortation to view Wisdom as one's lover (7:4); the second may mirror the theme of lovers seeking one another (S.S. 3:3f; 5:6). The language of love and finding also closes the chapter (8:35f), contrasting those who find Wisdom (and thereby find life) and those who hate Wisdom (and thus love death).

8:18–19. The essence of 8:10f, these verses use Wisdom's inestimable value (3:14; 16:16) to show that the search (8:17) is worthwhile. Like the "better than" proverbs [cf. 22:1; 25:7, 24], these verses claim that something intangible is better than what can be held and spent. Like gold and silver, wisdom can be used; unlike precious metals, its user's supply increases even as it is "spent." Although there were certainly differences between the types of gold (HED #2843, 6850) listed in v. 19a, we do not know what these words refer to. (The most common word for gold [HED #2174] is not used in this verse.)

8:20–21. Still building on the image of the search (8:17b), Wisdom tells her students that they should always choose the road that leads to righteousness and justice, because that is the road that she travels upon. Verse 20 also inverts v. 13, which uses the imagery of a negative road or way (cf. 8:2f). Her paths are characterized by righteousness and justice (cf. v. 14), which are the foundation of good government (e.g., 18:5; 19:28; 20:8, 26, 28), another reminder that this Book was originally intended for those who would one day rule over Israel. The treasures mentioned in vv. 18f now reward those who have persevered in their search for Wisdom. (This is the only passage in which yēsh, HED #3552, functions as a noun; it usually means "there is/are," a meaning which cannot fit here.)

8:22–31. *Discussion of these verses usually focuses on the words translated "acquired" or "possessed" (v. 22) or "workman" or "child" (v. 30). These points, important though they are in themselves, do not affect the main point of the passage, which primarily commends Wisdom based on her antiquity, as the many temporal terms show (e.g., "before," "not yet," "beginning"). In Israel, old age deserved honor and respect (Prov. 16:31; 20:29). Wisdom, older than creation itself, is therefore worthy of utmost respect, and her students should attend most carefully all of her teaching.*

In addition, as an eyewitness of the creation of all things, Wisdom understands the secrets of existence, so that her counsel is in line with the way

21.

3937, 5273.541	154.152	3552	212	4527.325
prep, v Hiphil inf con	v Qal act ptc mp, ps 1cs	sub	cj, n mp, ps 3mp	v Piel impf 1cs
לְהַנְחִיל	אֹהֲבַי	יֵשׁ	וְאֹצְרֹתֵיהֶם	אֲמַלֵּא
lehanchîl	'ōhevay	yēsh	we'ōtserōthêhem	'ămallē'
to cause to possess	those who love me	what is	and their treasuries	I will fill

22.

3176	7353.111	7519	1932	7208	4821	4623, 226
pn	v Qal pf 3ms, ps 1cs	n fs	n ms, ps 3ms	n ms	n mp, ps 3ms	prep, adv
יְהוָה	קָנָנִי	רֵאשִׁית	דַּרְכּוֹ	קֶדֶם	מִפְעָלָיו	מֵאָז
yehwāh	qānānî	rē'shîth	darkô	qedhem	miph'ālâv	mē'āz
Yahweh	He created me	the beginning of	his way	the first of	his works	from then

23.

4623, 5986	5445.215	4623, 7513	4623, 7208, 800
prep, n ms	v Niphal pf 1cs	prep, n ms	prep, n mp, n fs
מֵעוֹלָם	נִסַּכְתִּי	מֵרֹאשׁ	מִקַּדְמֵי־אָרֶץ
mē'ôlām	nissakhtî	mērō'sh	miqqadhmê-'ārets
from eternity	I was woven	from the first	from the beginnings of the earth

24.

904, 375, 8745	2523.415	904, 375	4754	3632.256, 4448
prep, sub, n fp	v Polal pf 1cs	prep, sub	n mp	v Niphal ptc mp, n md
בְּאֵין־תְּהֹמוֹת	חוֹלָלְתִּי	בְּאֵין	מַעְיָנוֹת	נִכְבַּדֵּי־מָיִם
be'ên-tehōmôth	chôlāletî	be'ên	ma'ăyānôth	nikhbaddê-māyim
without depths	I was given birth to	without	springs	waters having become heavy

25.

904, 3071	2098	2993.616	3937, 6686	1421	2523.415
prep, adv	n mp	v Hophal pf 3cp	prep, n mp	n fp	v Polal pf 1cs
בְּטֶרֶם	הָרִים	הָטְבָּעוּ	לִפְנֵי	גְבָעוֹת	חוֹלָלְתִּי
beterem	hārîm	hātebbā'û	liphnê	ghevā'ôth	chôlāletî
before	the mountains	they were planted	before	the hills	I was given birth to

26.

5912, 3940	6449.111	800	2445	7513	6312	8725
adv, neg part	v Qal pf 3ms	n fs	cj, n fp	cj, n ms	n mp	n fs
עַד־לֹא	עָשָׂה	אֶרֶץ	וְחוּצוֹת	וְרֹאשׁ	עַפְרוֹת	תֵּבֵל
'adh-lō'	'āsāh	'erets	wechûtsôth	werō'sh	'āpherôth	tēvēl
when not	He had made	the earth	and the open places	or the first of	the dust of	the world

27.

904, 3679.541	8452	8427	603	904, 2809.141	2423
prep, v Hiphil inf con, ps 3ms	n md	adv	pers pron	prep, v Qal inf con, ps 3ms	n ms
בַּהֲכִינוֹ	שָׁמַיִם	שָׁם	אָנִי	בְּחוּקוֹ	חוּג
bahkhînô	shāmayim	shām	'ānî	bechûqô	chûgh
when his establishing	the heavens	there	I	when his inscribing	a circle

increase, *Berkeley* … and my yield, *NRSV*.

20. I lead in the way of righteousness, in the midst of the paths of judgment: … On the way of duty I walk, along the paths of justice, *NAB* … I do what is right, *NCV* … I walk firmly the way of right, Where the paths of justice meet, *Anchor*.

21. That I may cause those that love me to inherit substance; and I will fill their treasures: … endowing with wealth those who love me, *RSV* … giving integrity to those who love me, and filling their storerooms, *Beck* … failing never to enrich the souls that love me with abundant store, *Knox* … enriching those who love me, and filling their stores full, *Moffatt*.

22. The LORD possessed me in the beginning of his way, before his works of old: … The Eternal formed me first of his creation, *Moffatt* … at the birth of time, before his creation began, *Knox*.

23. I was set up from everlasting, from the beginning, or ever the

earth was: … I was appointed from eternity, from the beginning, *NIV* … Ages ago I was set up, at the first, *NRSV* … At the outset of the ages had I been established In advance of the antiquities of the earth, *Rotherham* … I was created in the very beginning, even before the world began, *NCV*.

24. When there were no depths, I was brought forth; when there were no fountains abounding with water: … When there was no deep I was given birth, when there were no fountains flowing, *BB* … Before there was any ocean, I was born,

76

before there were springs, or sources of, *Beck* … when there were no mountains filled with water, *KJVII*.

25. Before the mountains were settled, before the hills was I brought forth: … Before the mountains were sunk, *Goodspeed* … I came to birth, *JB*.

26. While as yet he had not made the earth, nor the fields, nor the highest part of the dust of the world: … When he had not yet made the wide world, Nor the first morsels of the earth's soil, *Anchor* … nor the first clods of the world, *Douay*.

27. When he prepared the heavens, I was there: when he set a compass upon the face of the depth: … When He formed the suns I was there, *Fenton* … when he ordained the circle upon the face of the deep, *Darby* … when he girdled the ocean with the horizon, *NEB* … when he marked out the vault over the face of the deep, *NAB*.

---

things really are. This parallels the earlier statement that Wisdom was part of the process of creation (Prov. 3:19f).

These verses are highly structured:

Wisdom's existence "before" (vv. 22–26)
Wisdom's existence "when" (vv. 27–30a)
Wisdom's delight and joy during and after (vv. 30b–31)

The first two sections are also marked off by the variety of temporal expressions in vv. 22–26, and the syntactical unity of vv. 27–30a; the chiastic arrangement of vv. 30b–31 separates them from the preceding sections. None of these divisions are as neat as a diagram, since, for example, the form at the beginning of v. 30b ties the last section (vv. 30f) closely to v. 30a, where the same form is repeated. The entire poem is thus tightly woven, as repeated words and forms show, although there is clear movement through its parts.

8:22. Although this verse begins with Yahweh (HED #3176), "the LORD," wisdom is the central point of the passage. Each of the fourteen temporal clauses (vv. 23–29) mentions some facet of creation, but the point is that Wisdom existed before any of God's creative acts. "Beginning" (HED #7519) seems to reflect other statements in Prov. 1–9; just as "the fear of Yahweh is the beginning of wisdom" (9:10; cf. 1:7), so wisdom is the beginning of his way (works).

Even the question of whether the LORD "created" (NRSV), "possessed" (NASB, NKJV) or "brought forth" (NIV) Wisdom does not affect this central message. Although the verb (HED #7353) has several meanings, it usually means "to possess," often by virtue of having acquired (always in Proverbs; e.g., 1:5; 4:5, 7). In several places it means "to create" (Deut. 32:6; Ps. 139:13; probably also Gen. 14:19, 22), and once it may mean "to give birth" (Gen. 4:1; it could mean "to possess" here). The birth metaphors (vv. 24f) are also said to demonstrate that this poem teaches that Wisdom

came into being by God's first creative act. There is no reason, however, to reject the usual meaning of qānāh (HED #7353). The verse states that wisdom was a characteristic of God from the beginning.

8:23–26. These verses list foundational events in the history of creation. This is not intended to be an exhaustive list, nor is it designed to correspond directly with other biblical statements of creation (e.g., Gen. 1:1–2:3; Ps. 104:5–9). The emphasis is on the elements of the physical world (earth, water, sea) so that plants and animals are not mentioned (although the creation of humanity is implied in v. 31b).

The poet heaps up synonymous temporal adverbs ("from of old," "from the beginning," "from earliest times," "when there was not," "not yet," "before," "while not yet," "first") in order to clarify his point that Wisdom precedes all things, including the earth (v. 23) and its components (vv. 25f; cf. v. 29c) and the sea and other waters (v. 24; cf. vv. 28b–29). (The heavens and sky are mentioned in the second part of the poem in vv. 27f.)

Wisdom's role is entirely passive, having already been established (HED #5445; v. 23; cf. the same verb in Ps. 2:6), and "brought forth" (HED #2523; vv. 24a, 25b), which, like being "possessed" or "acquired" (v. 22), are figurative means of describing her existence. According to these verses, Wisdom existed before creation began.

8:27–30a. These verses differ from the preceding by describing some of the creative acts of God, which are only anticipated in vv. 23–26. Wisdom, which existed before anything else (vv. 22–26), was also present at the moment(s) of creation (v. 27a, "I was there").

The two catalogs are tied together by two devices. First, they are not identical; that is, these verses do not simply change "before" to "when" and repeat the preceding list. The combination of the lists implies that Wisdom was also present when the events of the first list finally took place. Both are also incomplete: the sky is not mentioned in

28.

904, 6022.141	4623, 4762	8263	904, 563.341	8745	6142, 6686
prep, v Qal inf con	prep, prep	n mp	prep, v Piel inf con, ps 3ms	n fs	prep, n mp
בַּעֲזוֹז	מִמָּֽעַל	שְׁחָקִים	בְּאַמְּצוֹ	תְּהוֹם	עַל־פְּנֵי
ba'ăzoz	mimmā'al	shechāqîm	be'ammetsô	thehôm	'al-penê
when strengthening	from above	clouds	when his making firm	the deep	on the face of

29.

4448	2805	3937, 3328	904, 7947.141	8745	6084
cj, n md	n ms, ps 3ms	prep, art, n ms	prep, v Qal inf con, ps 3ms	n fs	n fp
וּמַיִם	חֻקּוֹ	לַיָּם	בְּשׂוּמוֹ	תְּהוֹם	עִינוֹת
ûmayim	chuqqô	layyām	besûmô	tehôm	'înôth
and the waters	its limit	for the sea	when his setting	the deep	the fountains of

800	4280	904, 2809.141	5882.126, 6552	3940
n fs	n mp	prep, v Qal inf con, ps 3ms	v Qal impf 3mp, n ms, ps 3ms	neg part
אָרֶץ	מוֹסְדֵי	בְּחוּקוֹ	יַעַבְרוּ־פִיו	לֹא
'ārets	môsdhê	bechûqô	ya'avrû-phîw	lō'
the earth	the foundations of	when his inscribing	they will pass by its mouth	not

30.

7925.353	3219	3219	8562	2030.125	533	703	2030.125
v Piel ptc fs	n ms	n ms	n mp	cj, v Qal impf 1cs	n ms	prep, ps 3ms	cj, v Qal impf 1cs
מְשַׂחֶקֶת	יוֹם	יוֹם	שַׁעֲשֻׁעִים	וָאֶהְיֶה	אָמוֹן	אֶצְלוֹ	וָאֶהְיֶה
mesacheqeth	yôm	yôm	sha'ăshu'îm	wā'ehyeh	'āmôn	'etslô	wā'ehyeh
rejoicing	a day	a day	delight	and I was	a craftsman	beside Him	then I was

31.

8562	800	904, 8725	7925.353	904, 3725, 6496	3937, 6686
cj, n mp, ps 1cs	n fs, ps 3ms	prep, n fs	v Piel ptc fs	prep, adj, n fs	prep, n mp, ps 3ms
וְשַׁעֲשֻׁעַי	אַרְצוֹ	בְּתֵבֵל	מְשַׂחֶקֶת	בְּכָל־עֵת	לְפָנָיו
wesha'ăshu'ay	'artsô	bethēvēl	mesacheqeth	bekhol-'ēth	lephānâv
and my delight	his earth	in the world of	rejoicing	during all times	before Him

32.

1932	869	8471.133, 3937	1158	6498	119	881, 1158
n mp, ps 1cs	cj, n ms	v Qal impv 2mp, prep, ps 1cs	n mp	cj, adv	n ms	do, n mp
דְּרָכַי	וְאַשְׁרֵי	שִׁמְעוּ־לִי	בָנִים	וְעַתָּה	אָדָם	אֶת־בְּנֵי
derākhay	we'ashrê	shim'û-lî	vānîm	we'attāh	'ādhām	'eth-benê
my ways	and blessed	listen to me	O sons	so now	humankind	the sons of

33.

8490.126	8471.133	4284	2549.133	414, 6797.128	869
v Qal impf 3mp	v Qal impv 2mp	n ms	cj, v Qal impv 2mp	cj, adv, v Qal juss 2mp	n ms
יִשְׁמֹרוּ	שִׁמְעוּ	מוּסָר	וַחֲכָמוּ	וְאַל־תִּפְרָעוּ	אַשְׁרֵי
yishmōrû	shim'û	mûsār	wachăkhāmû	we'al-tiphrā'û	'ashrê
they will observe	listen	correction	and be wise	and do not neglect	blessed

34.

28. **When he established the clouds above: when he strengthened the fountains of the deep:** ... he fixed the canopy of clouds overhead, *REB* ... made firm the skies above, *ASV* ... and set the springs of ocean firm in their place, *NEB*.

29. **When he gave to the sea his decree, that the waters should not pass his commandment:** ... I was there when he enclosed the sea within its confines, forbidding the waters to transgress their assigned limits, *Knox* ... In His setting for the sea its limit, *Young*.

when he appointed the foundations of the earth: ... when he poised, *Knox* ... fixed fast the foundations, *Douay*.

30. **Then I was by him, as one brought up with him:** ... I was beside him as a ward of his, *Goodspeed* ... then was I beside him as his craftsman, *Douay* ... beside him a firm and sure worker, *Rotherham*.

and I was daily his delight, rejoicing always before him: ... Playing always before Him, *MAST* ... As I sported before him all the time, *Goodspeed*.

31. **Rejoicing in the habitable part of his earth; and my delights were with the sons of men:** ... enjoying the whole world, and delighted with all its people, *NCV* ... delighting in the human race, *NRSV* ... Exulting in the fruitful land of his earth, Yea my fulness of delight was with the sons of men, *Rotherham*.

32. **Now therefore hearken unto me, O ye children: for blessed are they that keep my ways:** ... Now listen to me, children, *Moffatt* ... Give ear to me then, my sons: for happy are those, *BB*.

vv. 22–26; the earth's foundations, but not the earth itself, are noted in v. 29c. This means that both are required to describe the entirety of creation.

The "circle" (v. 27b) refers to the horizon (cf. Job 22:14; Isa. 40:22), which appears circular in flat terrain or at sea. This verse also reflects the creation account, the only other occurrence of "the face of the deep" (Gen. 1:2). The strengthening of the clouds and the springs of the deep (v. 28b) is probably a poetic way of describing their creation. Three lines describe the creation of the sea (vv. 28b–29), which was a fearful element to the Israelites (cf. Ps. 46:2). This fear may reflect the myths of their neighbors (especially as they are seen in texts from Ugarit), but may also be the result of the geography of Canaan, which has few natural harbors, so that Israelites were not sailors, but they hired others to sail their vessels for them (cf. 1 Ki. 5:9; 9:26f; 10:11; Jon. 1:2f). Other descriptions of the sea's creation also delineate the limits that God set upon it (Job 38:10f; Ps. 104:7ff; Jer. 5:22); these are all probably oblique references to the covenant with Noah (Gen. 9:9–16).

Another structural device that ties together these verses is the question implied by v. 27: "Where was Wisdom?" It is answered in v. 30a, the last line of this section: "I was beside [or 'near'] him."

In this line is also the second major interpretive difficulty in this passage, the meaning of 'āmôn (HED #533), the last word in v. 30a. This word occurs only here in Biblical Hebrew (the identical form in Jer. 52:15 is usually read as "multitude"), and so most ancient translations and modern versions change it slightly so that it reads either "master workman" (cf. S.S. 7:1) or "beloved child," based on this root's occasional meaning of "nurse," "foster parent" (Lam. 4:5).

A contextual objection to Wisdom as workman or craftsman is that the poem does not assign Wisdom any creative role. She is merely present (v. 30a, c). The idea of wisdom as a nursing child is also difficult, since it occurs in only one passage (Lam. 4:5), which, however, is a passive participle, not a noun (which is what is in 8:30). A third suggested interpretation is that it was originally "master craftsman" (cf. the form in S.S. 7:1), but that it refers to the LORD rather than to Wisdom. This would explain why it is masculine rather than feminine; the noun would stand in apposition to the suffix: "I was beside him, i.e., the master craftsman." Although all three of these suggestions require different vowel

points, this third interpretation seems to fit the context, both conceptually and grammatically.

8:30b–31. As mentioned above, these verses are tightly connected to the preceding by the repeated verb ("I was"; v. 30a and b), but are also set off by the chiastic arrangement of their primary elements:

v. 30b	delight
v. 30b	rejoicing
v. 31a	rejoicing
v. 31b	delight

Wisdom's response to God's work of creation mirrors that of the morning stars, which sang for joy (Job 38:7). The word translated "delight" (HED #8562; vv. 30f) refers to something that gives one pleasure, such as Yahweh's delight in his vineyard (Isa. 5:7) or the word of the LORD (Ps. 119:24, 77, 92, 143, 174), whereas that rendered "rejoicing" (HED #7925; vv. 30b–31) can describe joking (Prov. 26:19), a hero's welcome (1 Sam. 18:7), merrymaking in general (Jer. 15:17; 30:19; 31:4) and even holy dancing before the LORD (2 Sam. 6:5, 21). Here it describes a response to his work that brings pleasure and delight to Yahweh. Its first occurrence describes Wisdom herself as the LORD's delight (v. 30b), whereas the second refers to Wisdom's delight in the human beings whom God has created.

8:32–36. These verses climax not only this chapter, but the entire prologue. (Wisdom's last words, in ch. 9, are a denouement rather than a climax.) They return to the themes of Wisdom's first speech (1:20–33), utter the last explicit call to listen (vv. 32ff) and set the consequence of following or rejecting wisdom in its starkest terms, life or death (vv. 35f).

8:32–34. "Therefore" (HED #6498) refers to the preceding poems. In light of Wisdom's preexistence, her role in creation (vv. 22–31) and all the benefits that she freely bestows upon those who seek her (vv. 1–21), her students should listen. But she gives further reasons for paying attention to her. The structure of vv. 32ff is fairly complex, climaxing in vv. 35f:

v. 32a	exhortation (1 line)
v. 32b	motive (1 line)
v. 33	exhortation (2 lines)
v. 34	motive (3 lines)
vv. 35–36	motive (4 lines)

The first two motives (vv. 32b, 34) are the same, "how blessed" or "happy," and show the

119	8471.151	3937	3937, 8613.141	6142, 1878	3219	3219	3937, 8490.141
n ms	v Qal act ptc ms	prep, ps 1cs	prep, v Qal inf con	prep, n fp, ps 1cs	n ms	n ms	prep, v Qal inf con
אָדָם	שֹׁמֵעַ	לִי	לִשְׁקֹד	עַל־דַּלְתֹתַי	יוֹם	יוֹם	לִשְׁמֹר
'ādhām	shōmēa'	lî	lishqōdh	'al-dalthōthay	yôm	yôm	lishmōr
a man	one who listens	to me	watching	at my doors	a day	a day	observing

4331	6860	35.	3706	4834.151	4834.152	2522
n fp	n mp, ps 1cs		cj	v Qal act ptc ms, ps 1cs	v Qal act ptc mp	n mp
מְזוּזֹת	פְּתָחָי		כִּי	מֹצְאִי	מֹצְאֵי	חַיִּים
mezûzōth	pethāchāy		kî	mōtse'î	mōtse'ê	chayyîm
the posts of	my doors		because	one who finds me	finding	life

6572.521	7814	4623, 3176	36.	2490.151	2659.151	5497
cj, v Hiphil impf 3ms	n ms	prep, pn		cj, v Qal act ptc ms, ps 1cs	v Qal act ptc ms	n fs, ps 3ms
וַיָּפֶק	רָצוֹן	מֵיְהוָה		וְחֹטְאִי	חֹמֵס	נַפְשׁוֹ
wayyāpheq	rātsôn	mēyehwāh		wechōte'î	chōmēs	naphshô
and he will obtain	favor	from Yahweh		but one who offends me	doing violence to	his soul

3725, 7983.352	154.116	4323	9:1	2554	1161.112	1041	2778.112
adj, v Piel ptc mp, ps 1cs	v Qal pf 3cp	n ms		n fp	-v Qal pf 3fs	n ms, ps 3fs	v Qal pf 3fs
כָּל־מְשַׂנְאַי	אָהֵבוּ	מָוֶת		חָכְמוֹת	בָּנְתָה	בֵּיתָהּ	חָצְבָה
kol-mesan'ay	'āhēvû	māweth		chokhmôth	bānethāh	vêthāhh	chātsevāh
all who hate me	they love	death		wisdom	she has built	her house	she has hewn

33. Hear instruction, and be wise, and refuse it not: … Listen to instruction and don't reject wisdom, *Beck* … grow wise; do not ignore it, *REB*.

34. Blessed is the man that heareth me, watching daily at my gates, waiting at the posts of my doors: … The man who hears me will succeed, Who stands at my gate day by day, Who waits till I open its doors, *Fenton* … watching daily at my threshold with his eyes on the doorway, *NEB* … Blessed are they who listen to me, keep vigil, day by day, at my threshold, watching till I open my doors, *Knox*.

35. For whoso findeth me findeth life, and shall obtain favour of the LORD: … wins favour from the Eternal, *Moffatt* … the LORD will be pleased with them, *NCV* … shall obtain favor of, *ASV*.

36. But he that sinneth against me wrongeth his own soul: all they

close connection between observing or "keeping" Wisdom's ways (v. 32) and listening to her (v. 34).

Listening to (learning from) Wisdom cannot be pursued halfheartedly (v. 34; cf. 2:1–4). "Keeping watch" and "observing" explain that "listening" (v. 34a) entails diligence. In a development of the image used in the preceding chapters, the learners are not here exhorted to pursue or seek wisdom. By searching diligently (v. 17), they have discovered where she lives, and are to be attentive, watching over the entrance to her house lest they miss her or any of her instruction.

Between these two statements of blessing, v. 33 adds that listening to Wisdom's disciplinary instruction makes one wise, but only if he is diligent. (The repeated "listen" identifies Wisdom's teaching with discipline.)

8:35–36. The theme of life as one of wisdom's blessings crops up throughout the prologue (3:2, 18, 22; 4:4, 10, 13, 22f; 6:23; 7:2; cf. 9:11). These two verses show that life is not merely one among the many benefits of finding Wisdom—life is the fundamental motivation to seek Wisdom. To search for Wisdom is to search for life and to discover that life is both the reward at the end of the search and a benefit of the process. Since there are only two ways that one can go, the path that leads to life and that which leads to death, to be on the path leading to life is also to be on the way of life—the path that is itself life. Wisdom and the proverbs thus offer much more than the prosperity, popularity, success or avoidance of sin with which they are usually associated. They offer the underlying reality that gives meaning to these things.

This contrast of life and death lies also at the heart of the Covenant. Moses exhorted Israel to be faithful to the Covenant because, he said, "I have set before you today life and good, blessing and disaster. Life and death have I set before you, the blessing and the curse. So choose life, that you may live" (Deut. 30:15–20).

Just as a father's reproof is for his child's good (3:11f; cf. 13:24), so the corrections and rebukes found in this Book are for the good of its serious readers. Wisdom is not found casually or by accident. Those who love her find her (cf. vv. 35a–36), whereas those who ignore the guidelines that she has set thereby reveal their arrogant hatred of Wisdom and all that she represents (cf. 1:29–32; 2:19; 7:23–27; 9:18).

9:1–18. If Prov. 8 is the climax of the prologue, this chapter is the necessary anticlimax, presenting the choice described in 8:35f as sharply as possible. It might seem that Prov. 8 would make a better conclusion to the prologue, especially given its dramatic close (vv. 35f). To move from that fundamental opposition to the largely antithetical proverbs of chs. 10–15 would seem to be a natural progression.

Proverbs 9, however, serves an important function, placing for the first time the two figures of Wisdom and Folly side by side, describing them in similar ways (vv. 1ff, 13ff), quoting their invitations, which begin identically (vv. 4, 16), but dramatically diverge (vv. 5f, 17). The structural, though not numerical, center of the chapter, v. 10 reflects the beginning of the prologue (1:7) and forms an envelope that encloses all nine chapters within the theme of the fear of the LORD.

Although Prov. 9 appears to have three sections (vv. 1–6, 7–12, 13–18), the second set of verses are actually the focus of the chapter, concluding Wisdom's invitation and introducing Folly's:

> *Wisdom's Invitation (9:1–6)*
> *Evaluation/Consequence (9:7–12)*
> *Folly's Invitation (9:13–17)*
> *Evaluation/Consequence (9:18)*

Proverbs 1–8 warn against various forms of folly (wicked companions, adultery, pledging surety, laziness) and exhort the student to seek Wisdom, often with vivid descriptions of the benefits of obedience (e.g., 3:13–17; 8:10f, 18–21, 35) and consequences of rejecting her counsel (e.g., 1:26–32; 2:19; 3:33f; 7:26f; 8:36). When the general contents of the earlier chapters are analyzed, warnings precede exhortations. Proverbs 9 reverses this order, capping the entire prologue, and setting the emphasis squarely on the consequences of the choice (9:18; cf. 8:36):

Warning(s)	*Exhortation(s)*
ch. 1b–c	*ch. 2–4a*
ch. 4b	*ch. 4c*
ch. 5–7	*ch. 8*
ch. 9b	*ch. 9a*

The sections of this chapter also reverse the order of the contents of the previous chapters:

A	*Prov. 7*	*warning against adultery*
B	*Prov. 8*	*exhortation to love and seek Wisdom*
B′	*Prov. 9:1–12*	*invitation of Wisdom*
A′	*Prov. 9:13–18*	*invitation of Folly (cf. 9:17; 5:15)*

Biblical poetry often indicates the end of a section, whether of a poem or section of a poem, by changing the order of the contents or words, or by using a different type of poetical structure, e.g., parallelism. Reversals of the type found in Prov. 9 are thus a standard device of biblical poetry, including many of the poems in the prologue. Whether this emphasizes the middle or the ends of the chiasm is not known. What is certain is that the structure, found throughout Proverbs, reflects the author's focus on the choice entailed in this opposition, the choice common to the entire prologue, i.e., the choice of life or death.

9:1–2. The closing poem of the prologue begins with a picture of vigorous action respresented by five verbs in five lines. This action, startling because of wisdom's passivity in 8:22–31, describes Wisdom strenuously preparing for the guests whom she is about to invite into the house which she has built (cf. 14:1). This contrasts sharply with Folly's lack of preparation (no activity is mentioned in vv. 13f).

The meaning of the seven pillars (v. 1b) has been long debated. Suggestions include the pillars of a temple, the "seven heavens" or the seven pillars that support the world, or a feature of domestic architecture. Pillars were used in larger houses to support a second-floor portico around the central courtyard. Most houses with pillars had only four. More pillars were used in larger houses. Here, "seven" probably refers to completion or perfection. Since Wisdom has boasted of her wealth (e.g., 8:18–21), it is fitting that she live in a house that reflects her status.

That animal(s) were slaughtered and wine prepared (probably by flavoring it with spices or diluting it with water; but cf. Isa. 1:22) shows that this

6204	**8124**		**2983.112**	**2984**	**4687.112**	**3302**	**652**
n mp, ps 3fs	num	**2.**	v Qal pf 3fs	n fs, ps 3fs	v Qal pf 3fs	n ms, ps 3fs	cj
עַמּוּדֶיהָ	שִׁבְעָה		טָבְחָה	טִבְחָהּ	מָסְכָה	יֵינָהּ	אַף
'ammûdhêāh	shiv'āh		ṯāvechāh	ṯivchāhh	māṣekhāh	yênāhh	'aph
her pillars	seven		she has slaughtered	her slaughter	she has mixed	her wine	also

6424.112	**8374**		**8365.112**	**5472**	**7410.122**
v Qal pf 3fs	n ms, ps 3fs	**3.**	v Qal pf 3fs	n fp, ps 3fs	v Qal impf 3fs
עָרְכָה	שֻׁלְחָנָהּ		שָׁלְחָה	נַעֲרֹתֶיהָ	תִקְרָא
'ārekhāh	shulchānāhh		shālechāh	na'ărōthêāh	thiqrā'
she has prepared	her table		she has sent out	her maidservants	she calls

6142, 1652	**4953**	**7469**		**4449, 6864**	**5681.121**	**2077**
prep, *n mp*	*n mp*	n fs	**4.**	intrg, n ms	v Qal juss 3ms	adv
עַל־גַּפֵּי	מְרֹמֵי	קָרֶת		מִי־פֶתִי	יָסֻר	הֵנָּה
'al-gappê	merōmê	qāreth		mî-phethî	yāṣur	hēnnāh
on the back sides of	the high places of	the town		who simple	let him turn aside	here

2742, 3949	**569.112**	**3937**		**2050.133**	**4033.133**	**904, 4035**
adj, n ms	v Qal pf 3fs	prep, ps 3ms	**5.**	v Qal impv 2mp	v Qal impv 2mp	prep, n ms, ps 1cs
חֲסַר־לֵב	אָמְרָה	לוֹ		לְכוּ	לַחֲמוּ	בְלַחֲמִי
chăṣar-lēv	'āmerāh	lô		lekhû	lachămû	velachămî
lacking in heart	she said	to him		come	eat	with my bread

8685.133	**904, 3302**	**4687.115**		**6013.133**	**6848**	**2513.133**
cj, v Qal impv 2mp	prep, n ms	v Qal pf 1cs	**6.**	v Qal impv 2mp	adj	cj, v Qal impv 2mp
וּשְׁתוּ	בְּיַיִן	מָסָכְתִּי		עִזְבוּ	פְתָאיִם	וִחְיוּ
ûshethû	beyayin	māṣākhettî		'izvû	phethā'yim	wichăyû
and drink	with wine	I have mixed		leave	O simple ones	and live

861.133	**904, 1932**	**1035**		**3364.151**	**4086**	**4089.151**
cj, v Qal impv 2mp	prep, *n ms*	n fs	**7.**	v Qal act ptc ms	n ms	v Qal act ptc ms
וְאִשְׁרוּ	בְּדֶרֶךְ	בִּינָה		יֹסֵר	לֵץ	לֹקֵחַ
we'ishrû	bedherekh	bînāh		yōṣēr	lēts	lōqēach
and walk	on the way of	understanding		one who instructs	a mocker	taking

3937	**7320**	**3306.551**	**3937, 7856**	**4113**		**414, 3306.523**
prep, ps 3ms	n ms	cj, v Hiphil ptc ms	prep, n ms	n ms, ps 3ms	**8.**	adv, v Hiphil juss 2ms
לוֹ	קָלוֹן	וּמוֹכִיחַ	לְרָשָׁע	מוּמוֹ		אַל־תּוֹכַח
lô	qālôn	ûmôkhîach	lerāshā'	mûmô		'al-tôkhach
for himself	shame	and one who chastises	a wicked person	his blemish		do not chastise

that hate me love death: ... he who misses me harms himself, *Douay* ... doeth violence to his own soul, *Darby* ... all my haters are in love with death, *BB* ... those who miss me injure themselves, *NRSV.*

9:1. Wisdom hath builded her house, she hath hewn out her seven pillars: ... made her house, putting up her seven pillars, *BB* ... See, where wisdom has built herself a house, carved out for herself those seven pillars of hers!, *Knox* ... built her mansion, *Moffatt.*

2. She hath killed her beasts; she hath mingled her wine: ... slaughtered her sacrifice, *Anchor* ... slaughtered her meat, *NKJV* ... dressed her meat, mixed her wine, *NAB.*

she hath also furnished her table: ... spread her table, *NAB* ... laid her table, *JB* ... her table is ready, *BB.*

3. She hath sent forth her maidens; she crieth upon the highest places of the city: ... sent out her servant girls, *NCV* ... sent forth her damsels, *Young* ... sent her maidens to proclaim from the highest point of the town, *REB* ... On the heights of the city highways, *Goodspeed.*

4. Whoso is simple, let him turn in hither: ... If you're untaught, turn in here, *Beck* ... Whoever is naive, let him turn in here!, *NASB* ... Who is ignorant, let him turn back, *Fenton.*

as for him that wanteth understanding, she saith to him: ... To him who is without sense she says, *RSV* ... that is void of understanding, *MRB* ... Whoso lacketh heart, *Young* ... While to him who is senseless she says, *Goodspeed.*

5. Come, eat of my bread, and drink of the wine which I have mingled: ... Come, dine with me and taste the wine that I have spiced, *NEB* ... Come, feast on my food, And drink of the wine I have poured out, *Anchor* ... drink of the wine I have brewed, *Knox* ... drink wines that I have blended, *Moffatt*.

6. Forsake the foolish, and live; and go in the way of understanding: ... Give up the simple ones and have life, and go in the way of knowledge, *BB* ... Quit the company of the simple and live, *Berkeley* ... Leave off, ye simple ones, and live, *ASV* ... advance in the way of understanding, *Rotherham* ... walk the road that leads to, *Beck* ... advance on the road of good sense, *Fenton*.

7. He that reproveth a scorner getteth to himself shame: ... He that instructeth a scorner, *Darby* ... Whoever corrects a scoffer wins abuse, *NRSV* ... Who corrects a derider, gets insult, *Fenton*.

and he that rebuketh a wicked man getteth himself a blot: ... if you criticize a wicked person, you get hurt, *Beck* ... he who says sharp words to a sinner gets a bad name, *BB* ... he that reproveth a lawless man getteth to himself his shame, *Rotherham*.

8. Reprove not a scorner, lest he hate thee: ... Reproach a scoffer,

---

was an important meal, given in honor of special guests (cf. Gen. 18:1–8; 43:16). The words for "slaughter" (HED #2983, 2984) refer to butchery, not sacrifice, which probably shows that this is not a religious feast. The particle that begins v. 2b (HED #652) may mean "even," as in "she has even arranged her table" (cf. Ps. 23:5), which may indicate that her preparation went beyond the usual meal.

9:3. The grammatical parallel with vv. 1f shows that sending out her maidens is the final stage of her preparation, but the second line reveals that they are the extension of her invitation beyond the sound of her voice. As in other passages that describe her invitation, it is public, in a prominent part of the city (1:20f; 8:1ff), again in contrast to Folly's invitation, given from her seat by her doorway (v. 14). Wisdom's invitation is open to all who hear, not secret or private, not limited to initiates.

9:4. Wisdom's invitation, addressed to the naive and those who lack "heart" (i.e., discernment, understanding), calls them to "turn aside" from whatever they are pursuing. Since she is not at home (v. 3b), she is not inviting them to "turn in here" (NASB), but to come to her so that she can take them to the feast which she has prepared. The call assumes that the naive will recognize that they need instruction.

9:5. The second part of her invitation deals specifically with the meal that she has prepared (v. 2). Although it mentions "food" (literally "bread") instead of slaughtered animals, lechem (HED #4035), the staple of life, refers to any kind of food in the Bible (cf. "meat" in Elizabethan English). Bread would be part of nearly any meal; the surprise in these verses is the meat that accompanies it. The repeated "my" is probably intended to contrast with Folly's "stolen water" and "secret bread" (v. 17). Because changes in grammatical form, such as the change in number from singular (v. 4) to plural (v. 6), are a regular part of biblical poetry, they need not imply that though the first part of Wisdom's invitation was addressed to individuals (v. 4), the second part was addressed to a crowd.

9:6. The end of Wisdom's invitation is also its heart. Those who identified themselves as naive are to leave gullibility behind by learning from her (i.e., attending her banquet). The plural is used for the abstract noun (cf. "folly," NASB, "immaturity," NRSV), instead of "naive ones."

The reward of responding to Wisdom's invitation is the promise of life, which is set between the negative ("leave") and positive ("walk") commands. The implication is that Wisdom is about to teach them how to live a life characterized by insight, since they have not ceased to be naive by their initial response. Some of this instruction follows (vv. 7–12). Most of it is contained in the rest of the Book of Proverbs.

9:7–12. These verses appear to be a misplaced list of proverbs that look more like those in chs. 10–29 than like the poems in the prologue. They are in fact a carefully composed section of the larger poem, linking the descriptions and invitations of Wisdom and Folly and focusing on the foundational theme of the Book (9:10; cf. 1:7).

The references to the scoffer/wicked and the wise/righteous in vv. 7ff and 12 are carefully balanced between a threefold repetition (vv. 7ff) and their single mention in v. 12:

A	*scoffer - wicked - scoffer (vv. 7–8a)*
B	*wise - wise - righteous (vv. 8b–9)*
C	*the fear of Yahweh leads to wisdom, which gives life (vv. 10–11)*
B	*wise (v. 12a)*
A	*scoff (v. 12b)*

4086	6678, 7983.121	3306.531	3937, 2550	154.121
n ms	cj, v Qal impf 3ms, ps 2ms	v Hiphil impv 2ms	prep, n ms	cj, v Qal juss 3ms, ps 2ms
לֵץ	פֶּן־יִשְׂנָאֶךָ	הוֹכַח	לְחָכָם	וְיֶאֱהָבֶךָ
lēts	pen-yisnā'ekkā	hôkhach	lechākhām	weye'ĕhāvekkā
a mocker	so he will not hate you	chastise	a wise man	that he may love you

5598.131	3937, 2550	2549.121, 5968	3156.531	3937, 6926
v Qal impv 2ms	prep, n ms	cj, v Qal juss 3ms, adv	v Hiphil impv 2ms	prep, n ms
תֵּן	לְחָכָם	וְיֶחְכַּם־עוֹד	הוֹדַע	לְצַדִּיק
tēn	lechākhām	weyechkkam-'ôdh	hôdha'	letsaddîq
give	to a wise man	that he may become wise again	teach	a righteous man

9.

3362.521	4090	8795	2551	3488	3176
cj, v Hiphil juss 3ms	n ms	n fs	n fs	n fs	pn
וְיוֹסֶף	לֶקַח	תְּחִלַּת	חָכְמָה	יִרְאַת	יְהוָה
weyôseph	leqach	techillath	chokhmāh	yir'ath	yehwāh
that may he increase	insight	the beginning of	wisdom	the fear of	Yahweh

10.

1907	7202	1035	3706, 904	7528.126
cj, n fs	n mp	n fs	cj, prep, ps 1cs	v Qal impf 3mp
וְדַעַת	קְדֹשִׁים	בִּינָה	כִּי־בִי	יִרְבּוּ
wedha'ath	qŏdhōshîm	bînāh	kî-vî	yirbû
and the knowledge of	holy things	understanding	because by me	they will multiply

11.

3219	3362.526	3937	8523	2522	524, 2549.113	2549.113
n mp, ps 2ms	cj, v Hiphil impf 3mp	prep, ps 2ms	n fp	n mp	cj, v Qal pf 2ms	v Qal pf 2ms
יָמֶיךָ	וְיוֹסִיפוּ	לָךְ	שְׁנוֹת	חַיִּים	אִם־חָכַמְתָּ	חָכַמְתָּ
yāmêkhā	weyôsîphû	lekhā	shenôth	chayyîm	'im-chākhamtā	chākhamtā
your days	and they will increase	to you	years of	life	if you are wise	you are wise

12.

Anchor … Do not say sharp words to a man of pride, BB … With a rash fool never remonstrate; it will make him thy enemy, Knox … Correct a derider, he hates you, Fenton.

rebuke a wise man, and he will love thee: … make them clear to a wise man, and you will be dear to him, *BB* … reprove a man of sense, and he will love you, *Moffatt* … only the wise are grateful for a remonstrance, *Knox.*

9. Give instruction to a wise man, and he will be yet wiser: … Give advice to a wise person, *Beck* … Be open with the wise, he grows wiser

still, *JB* … Instruct a man of sense, and he will gain more sense, *Moffatt.*

teach a just man, and he will increase in learning: … teach the upright, he will gain yet more, *JB* … teach a righteous man and he will add to his grasp of things, *Berkeley.*

10. The fear of the LORD is the beginning of wisdom: … the reverence of Yahweh, *Rotherham* … Wisdom begins with respect for the LORD, *NCV* … The first step to wisdom is the fear of the LORD, *NEB.*

and the knowledge of the holy is understanding: … he best discerns,

who has knowledge of holy things, *Knox* … to know the Deity is what knowledge means, *Moffatt* … What God's holy ones know—this is understanding, *JB* … knowledge of the Holy One gives a wise mind, *BB.*

11. For by me thy days shall be multiplied, and the years of thy life shall be increased: … days will be many, and years will be added to your life, *NIV* … years be adjoined to your life, *Fenton* … Long life I bring thee, and a full tale of years, *Knox.*

12. If thou be wise, thou shalt be wise for thyself: but if thou

Nor is the order of the elements incidental. The negative traits bracket the positive, and both surround the theme of the Book, demonstrating that the fear of the LORD, and the wisdom that begins with it, is necessary in order to choose wisely between the conflicting invitations. They are tied closely to the first and third sections by their contents, but also by the chiasm of the letters in the last word in v. 12 and the first word in v. 13: "taw," "shin" and "aleph" (cf. the close connection of the end of the second poem of ch. 8 to the preceding verses by the repeated verb form in 8:30a and b). Verses 10f are thus the final summation of the essence of the prologue, set in the middle of the only "face-to-face" encounter of the two women.

9:7–9. The first three lines (vv. 7f) describe the response of the wicked to correction: they will curse and hate whoever dares reprove them. This response contrasts sharply with that of the wise and righteous (vv. 8b–9), or contextually, those who have forsaken their folly (v. 6). The wise know their need and appreciate both instruction and rebuke (cf. 10:8; 25:12; 27:5f; 28:23), knowing how to benefit by them. Since they are open to being taught, they continue to grow in wisdom and insight (1:5; 19:27).

These verses, part of Wisdom's speech ("by me," v. 11), reveal her insight in addressing those who can benefit from her instruction, but they also call for self-evaluation on the part of the reader. A person's response to the content of this Book reveals the state of his or her heart (cf. 3:11f). These contrasting pictures lead naturally to the question of whether or not one fears the LORD.

9:10–11. Verses 10ff call for a response from the reader and identify the only appropriate response as obedience (the "fear of Yahweh"; cf. 1:7), which is where and how wisdom begins. Since v. 10 returns to the thematic statement of these opening chapters (cf. 1:7, 29; 2:5; 3:7; 8:13; 9:10; and often in chs. 10–31), and since v. 11 reemphasizes life as the primary benefit of a positive response to Wisdom's invitation (1:33; 2:21f; 3:2, 16, 18, 22; 4:10, 13, 22; 8:35f; 9:6), these verses climax Wisdom's invitation and contrast sharply with the consequences of choosing to learn from the woman of folly (9:18). Like the words of the teacher throughout the prologue, Wisdom's instruction lengthens one's life.

The root qādhôsh (HED #7202) refers to Yahweh ("the Holy One") only twice in Proverbs (here and in 30:3, in the words of Agur), which suggests that holiness is integral to this portion of the poem. Holiness is neither defined nor described in Proverbs, although it is a major theme in Scripture in general (cf. Lev. 19:2; Isa. 6:3; 1 Pet. 1:13–16). Its occurrence here, in close proximity to Wisdom (v. 11), suggests that there is a close connection between holiness and the content of this Book. This further implies that holiness is not limited to "religious" areas of life, but like the proverbs themselves, affects every area of life (cf. 31:10–31). Although the noun translated "Holy One" is plural, which usually refers to heavenly beings or holy persons, plural forms do refer to Israel's God (e.g., "Holy One," Prov. 30:3; Hos.

11:12; "Creator," Ecc. 12:1; "husband maker," Isa. 54:5; and, especially, "God"), perhaps as a so-called "plural of majesty."

9:12. The introspection called for by vv. 7–10 is here made more pointed. The choice of Wisdom or folly in the form of scornful rejection of Wisdom sets one course from the beginning (v. 10). The Book of Proverbs does not hold out hope for fools. By choosing to reject Wisdom (cf. 1:24–32), they have chosen to embrace rebellion (1:7b), and the inevitable destruction that it entails. This verse is the strongest statement of personal responsibility in the Bible (although cf. Ezek. 18; Gal. 6:4f), but it does not mean that personal choices do not affect others. The proverbs warn against entangling one's affairs with those of a fool (cf. 17:12; 22:24f), but those who are foolish (and wise) affect the lives of many others (cf. 13:22; 14:1).

9:13–18. The outline of this portrait of Folly reflects that of Wisdom (vv. 1–6):

preparation	*vv. 1–2*	*v. 13*
location	*v. 3*	*v. 14*
invitation	*vv. 4–6*	*vv. 16–17*
outcome	*vv. 6–12*	*v. 18*

There are important differences between the two women. Whereas wisdom is diligent (vv. 1f), folly is noisy and ignorant (v. 13). Though wisdom seeks learners (v. 3), folly waits for them to come to her (vv. 14f). Their invitations are initially identical (vv. 4, 16), but their moral overtones are diametrically opposed (vv. 5f, cf. v. 17). Finally, Wisdom offers life (v. 6), whereas Folly leads only to death (v. 18). Without explicitly referring to any specific passage, this image of Folly summarizes all of the negative female references of the prologue. Her invitation should thus be viewed as no different than the flattery of the adulteress (7:14–20); her charms are those of the illicit lover (5:20).

9:13. Despite the difficulties of translation, this verse clearly presents the "woman Folly" as an ignorant and undisciplined person (on "loud," cf. 7:11), without moral scruples. The great irony of this section of the poem is that she offers to teach others with the same need (the root is the same as the word "naive" in v. 16).

9:14. Folly apparently stays at the door to her own house, although she is also said to be in the same heights of the city that are occupied by

3812	828		5558.123	3937, 940	4054.113	3937
n fs	n fs	**13.**	v Qal impf 2ms	prep, n ms, ps 2ms	cj, v Qal pf 2ms	prep, ps 2ms
כְּסִילוּת	אֵשֶׁת		תִשָּׂא	לְבַדֶּךְ	וְלַצְתָּ	לָךְ
keşîlûth	'ēsheth		thissā'	levaddekhā	welatstā	lākh
foolishness	a woman of		you will bear	only you	but you will scoff	for yourself

3937, 6860	3553.112	4242	1118, 3156.112	6868	2064.153
prep, n ms	cj, v Qal pf 3fs	intrg	cj, neg part, v Qal pf 3fs	n fs	v Qal act ptc fs
לְפֶתַח	**14.** וְיָשְׁבָה	מָה	וּבַל־יָדְעָה	פְּתַיּוּת	הֹמִיָּה
lephethach	weyāshevāh	māh	ûval-yādhe'āh	pethayyûth	hōmîyāh
at the door of	and she sits	what	and she does not know	simplicity	acting boisterous

3937, 7410.141	7469	4953	6142, 3802	1041
prep, v Qal inf con	n fs	n mp	prep, n ms	n ms, ps 3fs
15. לִקְרֹא	קָרֶת	מְרֹמֵי	עַל־כִּסֵּא	בֵּיתָהּ
liqrō'	qāreth	merōmê	'al-kissē'	bêthāhh
to call	the town	the high places of	on the seat of	her house

4449, 6864	758	3595.352	3937, 5882.152, 1932
intrg, n ms	n mp, ps 3mp	art, v Piel ptc mp	prep, v Qal act ptc mp, n ms
16. מִי־פֶתִי	אֹרְחוֹתָם	הַמְיַשְּׁרִים	לְעֹבְרֵי־דָרֶךְ
mî-phethî	'ōrechôthām	hamyashsherîm	le'ōverê-dhārekh
who simple	their paths	the ones making straight	to those passing on the way

3937	569.112	2743, 3949	2077	5681.121
prep, ps 3ms	cj, v Qal pf 3fs	cj, n ms, n ms	adv	v Qal juss 3ms
לוֹ	וְאָמְרָה	וַחֲסַר־לֵב	הֵנָּה	יָסֻר
lô	we'āmerāh	wachăsar-lēv	hēnnāh	yāşur
to him	and she says	and the lacking of heart	here	let him turn aside

5459.121	5848	4035	5159.126	4448, 1630.156
v Qal impf 3ms	n mp	cj, n ms	v Qal impf 3mp	n md, v Qal pass ptc mp
יִנְעָם	סְתָרִים	וְלֶחֶם	יִמְתָּקוּ	**17.** מַיִם־גְּנוּבִים
yin'ām	sethārîm	welechem	yimtāqû	mayim-genûvîm
it will be pleasant	secrecy	and bread of	they will be sweet	waters having been stolen

8061	904, 6232	8427	3706, 7787	3940, 3156.111
pn	prep, n mp	adv	cj, n mp	cj, neg part, v Qal pf 3ms
שְׁאוֹל	בְּעִמְקֵי	שָׁם	כִּי־רְפָאִים	**18.** וְלֹא־יָדַע
she'ôl	be'imqê	shām	kî-rephā'îm	welō-yādha'
Sheol	in the depths of	there	that dead spirits	and he does not know

2550	1158	8406	5091		7410.156
adj	n ms	pn	n mp	**10:1**	v Qal pass ptc mp, ps 3fs
חָכָם	בֵּן	שְׁלֹמֹה	מִשְׁלֵי		קְרֻאֶיהָ
chākhām	bēn	shelōmōh	mishlê		qōru'êāh
wise	a son	Solomon	the proverbs of		those being called to by her

scornest, thou alone shalt bear it: … if your heart is full of pride, you only will have the pain of it, *BB* … if you are a scoffer, *Moffatt* … A mocker? The burden is yours alone, *JB* … if you are haughty, you alone are to blame, *NEB*.

13. A foolish woman is clamorous: she is simple, and knoweth noth-

ing: … Folly is boisterous and wanton, She has no sense of shame, *Goodspeed* … A foolish woman is noisy, *RSV* … The Lady Stupidity is a flighty creature; a fool, she cares for nothing, *REB* … She is naive, *NASB* … silly woman acts on impulse, *JB*.

14. For she sitteth at the door of her house, on a seat in the high places of

the city: … sits at the door of her mansion, *Moffatt* … her chair commanding the city's height, *Knox* … On a seat by the city highways, *Goodspeed*.

15. To call passengers who go right on their ways: … who are going along, minding their own business, *NCV* … going straight on their way, *BB* … to them that pass by, *MRB*.

16. Whoso is simple, let him turn in hither: and as for him that wanteth understanding, she saith to him: … And to the weak-hearted, she says, *Fenton* … If you're untaught, turn in here, *Beck* … for him that is void of understanding, *ASV* … Whoso is thoughtless, *MAST.*

17. Stolen waters are sweet, and bread eaten in secret is pleasant: … Stolen waters are sweetest, and bread is better eating when there is none to

see, *Knox* … Food eaten secretly is delightful, *Anchor* … and bread got by stealth tastes good, *NEB.*

18. But he knoweth not that the dead are there; and that her guests are in the depths of hell: … Little he knows that dead men are within, the guests of Death!, *Moffatt* … In the depths of hades are her guests, *Rotherham* … But the fool does not know that this is where the Shades are and that her

guests are already in the vales of Sheol, *JB.*

10:1. The proverbs of Solomon. A wise son maketh a glad father: but a foolish son is the heaviness of his mother: … A wise son makes his father glad, A foolish son his mother grieves, *Fenton* … A sensible son is a joy to his father, but a senseless son is a grief to his mother, *Moffatt* … A father's smile, a mother's tears, tell of a son well schooled or ill, *Knox.*

Wisdom (v. 3b). This puzzle resembles ch. 7, in which the youth seeks out her house (7:8; where presumably he expects to find her), but she is "now in the streets, now in the squares, lurking by every corner" (7:12), since "her feet do not remain at home" (7:11). This may be an intentional device to identify Folly as not merely a foolish teacher, but an unfaithful wife, as well as to strengthen the parallel with Wisdom's description.

9:15. Folly's invitation seems indiscriminate, addressed to all passersby (v. 15a), but it is actually to malign, aimed specifically at those who are trying to live uprightly. Anyone who is not trying to do so is already living foolishly; they have already visited Folly's house and tasted her "delights." She has no further interest in them, and they, now bent on their own devices, are no longer dependent on her continued teaching. Folly, once begun, unlike wisdom and knowledge, feeds itself.

9:16–17. Folly's invitation begins in deliberate imitation of Wisdom's. Like her choice of location, she aims to confuse those who lack the discretion that will enable them to distinguish true from false. Her "feast," however, is poor fare in comparison to Wisdom's (water instead of wine, no mention of meat), and even what she offers is illicit ("stolen," "secret"), just as her "counsel" is much poorer fare.

9:18. Like many poems and sections of the prologue, this chapter ends by warning that folly leads to death (1:18f, 32; 2:22; 5:23; 6:15; 7:23, 26f; 8:36; especially 2:18; 5:5; 7:27). Although this may seem an unnecessarily somber ending, the importance of the issue, life or death, merits sober reflection. Proverbs as a whole is a serious Book, warning of destruction, treachery, infidelity and a host of other troubles, ultimately death, as the natural penalties of disobedience and rebellion. Ending with the warning of death underlines the motif of

the prologue, the choice between life and death, and prepares the reader for the stark choices presented in the following chapters.

10:1–15:33. Proverbs 10:1 begins the format usually associated with Proverbs—short capsules of wisdom that address a particular behavior or attitude. The content and style of the first verse in this section set the stage for the next six chapters (Prov. 10–15), in which most of the proverbs contrast wise and foolish, or righteous and wicked, behavior. In Proverbs, wisdom and righteousness, and foolishness and wickedness, are interrelated: the righteous are those who learn from and obey wisdom, subordinating their understanding to God's (3:5f); and the foolish are those who reject and rebel against the counsel and correction of wisdom (1:7; 9:7f). Trusting in their own "wisdom," fools destroy themselves by their increasingly wicked decisions, just as the wise find themselves on a path that is increasingly clear (4:18f).

The sin of the wicked is thus the same as the original sin of Adam and Eve, who rejected the standard of God, preferring to follow their own (Gen. 3:1–6). The result of that sin was the same as the contumacy of the fool.

10:1. Children's effects on their parents may seem obvious—who needs wisdom to know that this is true? However, since Solomon's intent is not merely to point out wise and foolish behavior, but to enable even the naive to learn to discern the potential consequences of their choices (1:4), the point of this verse—and other "obvious" sayings—is not merely what it says, but what it signifies. (On obvious, or apparently tautological, proverbs, see 14:5.)

Decisions affect other people, and the closer those people are, the more drastically they will be affected. No one acts—wisely or foolishly—for himself or alone. Since every life intersects other

2.

3940, 3385.526	525	8755	3809	1158	7975.321, 1
neg part, v Hiphil impf 3mp	n fs, ps 3ms	n fs	adj	cj, n ms	v Piel impf 3ms, n ms
לֹא־יוֹעִ֗ילוּ	אִמּֽוֹ	תּוּגַ֥ת	כְּסִ֗יל	וּבֵ֥ן	יְשַׂמַּח־אָ֑ב
lō'-yôʻîlû	'immô	tûghath	kesîl	ûvēn	yesammach-'āv
they do not profit	his mother	the grief of	foolish	but a son	he makes a father glad

4623, 4323	5522.522	6930	7856	212
prep, n ms	v Hiphil impf 3fs	cj, n fs	n ms	n mp
מִמָּ֑וֶת	תַּצִּ֥יל	וּצְדָקָ֗ה	רֶשַׁע	אוֹצְר֥וֹת
mimmāweth	tatstsîl	ûtsedhāqāh	resha'	'ôtsrôth
from death	it delivers	but righteousness	wickedness	treasures of

3.

3940, 7742.521	3176	5497	6926	2010	7857
neg part, v Hiphil impf 3ms	pn	n fs	n ms	cj, n fs	n mp
לֹא־יַרְעִ֣יב	יְהוָ֣ה	נֶ֣פֶשׁ	צַדִּ֑יק	וְהַוַּ֥ת	רְשָׁעִ֥ים
lō'-yar'îv	yehwāh	nephesh	tsaddîq	wehawwath	reshā'îm
He will not allow to hunger	Yahweh	the soul of	the righteous	but the desire of	the wicked

4.

1990.121	7511	6449.151	3834, 7711	3135
v Qal impf 3ms	n ms	v Qal act ptc ms	n fs, n fs	cj, n fs
יֶהְדֹּ֑ף	רָ֑אשׁ	עֹשֶׂ֣ה	כַּף־רְמִיָּ֑ה	וְיַ֥ד
yehdōph	rā'sh	'ōseh	khaph-remîyāh	weyadh
He will drive away	poverty	something which makes	a hand of laziness	but the hand of

5.

2845	6483.522	100.151	904, 7302	1158	7959.551
n mp	v Hiphil impf 3fs	v Qal act ptc ms	prep, art, n ms	n ms	v Hiphil ptc ms
חָרוּצִ֑ים	תַּעֲשִׁ֑יר	אֹגֵ֣ר	בַּקַּ֑יִץ	בֵּ֥ן	מַשְׂכִּ֑יל
chārûtsîm	ta'ashîr	'ōghēr	baqqayits	bēn	maskîl
the diligent	it causes to be rich	one who gathers	in the summer	a son	being wise

6.

7578.255	904, 7392	1158	991.551	1318	3937, 7513
v Niphal ptc ms	prep, art, n ms	n ms	v Hiphil ptc ms	n fp	prep, n ms
נִרְדָּֽם	בַּקָּצִ֑יר	בֵּ֥ן	מֵבִ֣ישׁ	בְּרָכ֣וֹת	לְרֹ֣אשׁ
nirdām	baqqātsîr	bēn	mēvîsh	berākhôth	lerō'sh
one who sleeps deeply	during the harvest	a son	causing shame	blessings	to the head of

7.

6926	6552	7857	3803.321	2660	2228
n ms	cj, n ms	n mp	v Piel impf 3ms	n ms	n ms
צַדִּ֑יק	וּפִ֥י	רְשָׁעִ֥ים	יְכַסֶּ֑ה	חָמָ֥ס	זֵ֣כֶר
tsaddîq	ûphî	reshā'îm	yekhasseh	chāmās	zēkher
the righteous	but the mouth of	the wicked	it conceals	violence	the remembrance of

---

2. Treasures of wickedness profit nothing: ... Wealth gained through wickedness will prove of no advantage, *Anchor* ... treasures of lawlessness do not profit, *Rotherham* ... Ill-gotten treasures are of no value, *NIV*.

but righteousness delivereth from death: ... honesty will save a man in mortal danger, *Anchor* ... honest living is death's avoiding, *Knox* ... uprightness is a safeguard against death, *REB*.

3. The LORD will not suffer the soul of the righteous to famish: ...

Yahweh, *JB* ... The LORD does not let the righteous go hungry, *NEB* ... The Lord permits not the just to hunger, *Douay* ... Still the Lord gives honesty a full belly, *Knox* ... The Eternal never stints an honest man, *Moffatt*.

but he casteth away the substance of the wicked: ... but he keeps evil people from getting what they want, *NCV* ... but he thwarts the greed of the wicked, *JB* ... But he rebuffs the craving of the wicked, *Anchor* ... and on the knave's scheming shuts his door, *Knox*.

4. He becometh poor that dealeth with a slack hand: but the hand of the diligent maketh rich: ... Lazy hands make a man poor, *NIV* ... Poor is he who works with a negligent hand, But the hand of the diligent makes rich, *NASB* ... A slack hand causes poverty, *RSV* ... If you do things carelessly, you'll be poor, but the hands of busy people make them rich, *Beck* ... diligent effort brings wealth, *Anchor*.

5. He that gathereth in summer is a wise son: ... is a prudent son, *Berkeley* ... A son who fills the granaries in summer is a credit, *NAB* … A son who gathers [fruit] in summer shows intelligence, *Anchor* … He who reaps in summer is a man of sense, *Moffatt* … Wilt thou gather in harvest time, a son well schooled?, *Knox*.

but he that sleepeth in harvest is a son that causeth shame: … is a source of disappointment, *REB* … acts shamefully, *Berkeley* … is a disgrace, *NEB, Anchor*.

6. Blessings are upon the head of the just: but violence covereth the mouth of the wicked: … crown the head of the righteous, but violence overwhelms the mouth of the wicked, *NIV* … the bad man's face shall be darkened with disaster, *Moffatt* … face of sinners will be covered with sorrow, *BB* … the sinner's lips are silenced by his own ill-doing, *Knox*.

7. The memory of the just is blessed: … of the upright, *BB* … righteous are remembered in blessings, *NEB* … Good people will be remembered as a blessing, *NCV*.

but the name of the wicked shall rot: … reputation of evil men will rot away, *Anchor* … it is the sinner's name that rusts, *Knox* … name of the wicked falls into decay, *REB* … will be turned to dust, *BB*.

---

lives, every seemingly personal action, word and attitude brings joy or sorrow into those lives. Parents are perhaps most affected, since their children and grandchildren are their hope for the future, and since they usually expect great things from their children.

This verse refers to the effect of grown children upon their parents, as do its parallels (cf. 15:20; 17:21, 25; 23:24f; 29:3). As adults, they are making consequential choices that indicate the general bent of their lives (the verse does not describe the effect of the silly or amusing acts of childhood). Their poor choices can cause despair, but to see them living righteously brings joy. Parents need to realize their responsibility for raising their children (cf. 19:18; 22:15), just as children, who are by nature self-centered, need to realize that their decisions affect everyone touched by their lives (cf. 19:13). (On the subtitle [10:1a], see "Overview." The first line of the proverb itself [10:1b] is identical to 15:20a.)

10:2. Possessions gained by fraud, deceit, treachery or any other wickedness often appear substantial, whereas righteousness may seem unrewarded (cf. 19:1). The ultimate ends of these two ways of life, however, do not lie in material prosperity or security: to do what is right is always better, regardless of appearances. The rewards of living wisely, and therefore righteously, are eternal, whereas unlimited wealth cannot buy life. This does not, on the other hand, mean that wealth is wicked, only that wealth gained through sin reveals the state of the heart (cf. 4:23).

This verse implies that some proverbs need to be understood from an eternal perspective, not as mere earthly promises (cf. the discussion of 3:1–12).

10:3. On its surface, this verse contrasts God's provision (cf. Pss. 34:9f; 37:25f; Matt. 6:33) and judgment, reflecting the covenantal blessings (Lev. 26:4f, 10; Deut. 28:4f, 8, 11f) and curses (Lev. 26:19f, 26; Deut. 28:18, 23f, 30–33, 38–42), but it also speaks

beyond the physical level. Wisdom, which leads to righteousness, is precious far beyond the value of any tangible thing (cf. 3:14ff; 8:10f, 18–21; 10:20); it is the possession of the righteous, not of the wicked. Since the wicked have replaced the standards of the Covenant with their own desires, they can justify anything that they desire, but they are doomed to frustration. Those who trust in the LORD as the giver of every good and perfect gift (cf. 18:22; Matt. 6:33; Jam. 1:17) find their satisfaction in his gifts.

10:4. Half-hearted work gains little reward, if any. It is better, therefore, to work carefully and well—no matter how unwelcome or unloved the task—since only work well done is appreciated and rewarded in the long run. The careless worker is more concerned about the immediate circumstance than about the long-term effects of his actions. One aspect of diligence is considering consequences, something which the fool consistently fails to do.

10:5. One aspect of wisdom is the ability to discern what is most important at a given time, and then the diligence to work at it until it is done. For example, the activity appropriate to harvest is gathering. There is nothing wrong with sleep (the word implies a deep sleep), but harvest is the time to work. Prudence considers the future when determining what to pursue (21:5). The lazy would rather indulge their vice than work, and so come to poverty (cf. 10:4; 20:4), bringing shame upon themselves and those who depend upon them. This verse thus addresses the general topic of v. 4.

10:6. By contrasting cause ("words") and effect ("blessings"), the verse warns that words reveal the true condition of the individual, and that others will respond to his behavior (speech and deeds). The righteous, who seek the welfare of those around them, will be thanked and honored, whereas the wicked, who study how to trouble their neighbors, will be cursed (10:6b; cf. 10:11b).

8.

2550, 3949	7830.121	7857	8428	3937, 1318	6926
n ms, n ms	v Qal impf 3ms	n mp	cj, n ms	prep, n fs	n ms
חֲכַם־לֵב	יִרְקַב	רְשָׁעִים	וְשֵׁם	לִבְרָכָה	צַדִּיק
chăkham-lēv	yirqāv	reshā'îm	weshēm	livrākhāh	tsaddîq
the wise of heart	it will rot	the wicked	but the name of	for a blessing	the righteous

4089.121	4851	188	8004	3964.221
v Qal impf 3ms	n fp	cj, n ms	n fd	v Niphal impf 3ms
יִקַּח	מִצְוֹת	וֶאֱוִיל	שְׂפָתַיִם	יִלָּבֵט
yiqqach	mitswōth	we'ĕwîl	sephāthayim	yillāvēt
he will receive	commandments	but the foolish of	lips	he will become ruined

9.

2050.151	904, 8866	2050.121	1020	6378.351	1932
v Qal act ptc ms	prep, art, n ms	v Qal impf 3ms	n ms	cj, v Piel ptc ms	n mp, ps 3ms
הוֹלֵךְ	בַּתֹּם	יֵלֶךְ	בֶּטַח	וּמְעַקֵּשׁ	דְּרָכָיו
hôlēkh	battōm	yēlekh	betach	ûme'aqqēsh	derākhâv
one who walks	in integrity	he will walk	security	but one perverting	his ways

10.

3156.221	7460.151	6084	5598.121	6329	188
v Niphal impf 3ms	v Qal act ptc ms	n fs	v Qal impf 3ms	n fs	cj, n ms
יִוָּדֵעַ	קֹרֵץ	עַיִן	יִתֵּן	עַצֶּבֶת	וֶאֱוִיל
yiwwādhēa'	qōrēts	'ayin	yittēn	'atstsāveth	we'ĕwîl
he will become known	one winking	the eye	he will give	pain	and the foolish of

11.

8004	3964.221	4888	2522	6552	6926
n fd	v Niphal impf 3ms	n ms	n mp	n ms	n ms
שְׂפָתַיִם	יִלָּבֵט	מְקוֹר	חַיִּים	פִּי	צַדִּיק
sephāthayim	yillāvēt	meqôr	chayyîm	pî	tsaddîq
lips	he will become ruined	a fountain of	life	the mouth of	the righteous

12.

6552	7857	3803.321	2660	7985	6445.321	4209
cj, n ms	n mp	v Piel impf 3ms	n ms	n fs	v Polel impf 3ms	n mp
וּפִי	רְשָׁעִים	יְכַסֶּה	חָמָס	שִׂנְאָה	תְּעוֹרֵר	מְדָנִים
ûphî	reshā'îm	yekhasseh	chāmās	sin'āh	te'ôrēr	medhānîm
but the mouth of	the wicked	it conceals	violence	hatred	it stirs up	contentions

13.

6142	3725, 6840	3803.312	157	904, 8004	1032.255	4834.221
cj, prep	adj, n mp	v Piel pf 3fs	n fs	prep, n fd	v Niphal ptc ms	v Niphal impf 3ms
וְעַל	כָּל־פְּשָׁעִים	תְּכַסֶּה	אַהֲבָה	בְּשִׂפְתֵי	נָבוֹן	תִּמָּצֵא
we'al	kol-peshā'îm	tekhasseh	'ahăvāh	besiphthê	nāvôn	timmātsē'
but over	all offenses	it covers	love	on the lips of	the discerning one	it is found

8. The wise in heart will receive commandments: but a prating fool shall fall: ... will accept commandments, But he that is foolish with his lips shall be thrust away, *Rotherham* ... accepteth commands, And a talkative fool kicketh, *Young* ... will heed commandments, but a babbling fool will come to ruin, *NRSV* ... A sensible man will take orders, But the fool who talks back will be crushed, *Anchor*.

9. He that walketh uprightly walketh surely: ... Honest people are safe and secure, *Good News* ... He who walks honestly walks safely, *Goodspeed* ... He that walketh in integrity walketh securely, *Darby* ... A blameless life makes for security, *NEB*.

but he that perverteth his ways shall be known: ... Who twists his ways, will be shunned!, *Fenton* ... whoever follows crooked ways is soon unmasked, *JB* ... crooked courses shall fare badly, *Moffatt* ... whose ways are twisted will be made low, *BB*.

10. He that winketh with the eye causeth sorrow: but a prating fool shall fall: ... A wink of the eye brings trouble, a bold rebuke brings peace, *JB* ... It needs no more than a wink of the eye to bring trouble; what wonder if the fool who talks earns a beating?, *Knox* ... Who winks his eye will give offence; And the jabbering fool repels, *Fenton* ... one who rebukes boldly makes peace, *NRSV*.

11. The mouth of a righteous man is a well of life: ... The talk of good men is a lifegiving fountain, *Moffatt* ... speech of a good man, *Anchor* ... mouth of the Good is a living spring, *Fenton*.

but violence covereth the mouth of the wicked: ... mouth of the godless is a cover for violence, *JB* ... mouth of the evildoer is a bitter cup, *BB* ... talk of bad men overflows with harm, *Moffatt* ... mouth of the wicked uncovers [his] violence, *Anchor*.

12. Hatred stirreth up strifes: ... Hatred awaketh contentions, *Young*

... is ever ready to pick a quarrel, *Knox* ... stirs up dissension, *NIV* ... Hate is a cause of violent acts, *BB*.

but love covereth all sins: ... love covers all offenses, *RSV* ... covers every wrong, *Beck* ... love draws a veil over all transgressions, *Goodspeed* ... passes over all kinds of offence, *Knox*.

13. In the lips of him that hath understanding wisdom is found: ... A discerning man talks sense, *Anchor* ... Wisdom finds the lips of Reflection, *Fenton*.

but a rod is for the back of him that is void of understanding: ... people without wisdom should be punished, *NCV* ... the senseless needs a stick to his back, *Anchor*.

Furthermore, this blessing and curse are both human (the primary point of the verse) and divine (as the prologue emphasizes; cf. 2:8, 22).

This is the first of thirteen verses in this chapter that contrast the speech of the wise or righteous and the wicked or foolish (vv. 8, 10–14, 18–21, 31f).

10:7. Reputations outlive their owners. As time passes, the reputations of persons tend to become more honest, revealing how others view them. The righteous enjoy a good reputation even after death, whereas the reputation of the wicked eventually rots, like wood or meat. When Boaz bargained for Ruth to become his wife, the women of Bethlehem invoked the names of Rachel, Leah and Perez, asking the LORD to bless Ruth as He had Rachel and Leah (Ruth 4:11) and to make Boaz like Perez (Ruth 4:12). Sinners may accomplish many things, but a reputation that brings with it the favor of others is a greater treasure (cf. 22:1).

10:8. The wise realize how much there is to know and understand. They also understand that wisdom is not a state into which one enters permanently, but that it must be nurtured in order to be maintained (cf. 19:27). They therefore seek constantly to learn and grow in their understanding, and thus are open to being taught. The fool, however, is much too busy talking to learn from anyone else, and so, persisting in folly, comes to destruction. (Verse 8b is identical to v. 10b.)

10:9. Crookedness will be found out. Once discovered, it will bring shame and, perhaps, ruin, especially for a life built on trust; after death it destroys the reputation (cf. 10:7). In addition, the coming judgment will reveal all things (cf. Rev. 11f). So, Solomon says, peace with yourself, others and God (freedom from the fear that comes from living a lie) grows out of integrity, not success, especially not success gained at a high price (cf. 28:1, 18).

10:10. The cultural significance of winking (HED #7460) is no longer clear, but it is consis-

tently condemned in Scripture (Ps. 35:19; Prov. 6:13; cf. 16:30b, where the same verb describes "squeezing the lips"). In a section comprised mainly of antithetical proverbs (chs. 10–15), this verse equates winking with talking foolishly. The first line describes the effect on others (pain or injury), whereas the second describes the fool's words as self-destructive.

Some authorities translate the second half of this verse (which is identical to v. 8b) as "but whoever rebukes boldly makes peace" (cf. RSV, NRSV), following the Septuagint (which cannot be related to the Hebrew of this line). That this reading is not supported by the Vulgate suggests that the Septuagint was supplying a line for one that was either lacking or obscure. The main reason for following this reading seems to be the assumption that the proverbs in this section of the Book should be antithetical (see "Overview").

10:11. The second line of this verse is identical to v. 6b, but the two sayings emphasize slightly different concerns. The focus of the earlier verse is on the response to one's words, whereas this verse focuses on the words' effect. The righteous (i.e., the wise) use their words to strengthen and encourage others—to give them life; the wicked use their words as a cover for their own base designs (26:23–28). The effect of someone's words reveals both the condition and intent of his or her heart; the wise can distinguish the difference.

Both "well" (NKJV) and "fountain" (NRSV, NIV, NASB) are too specific. "Fountain," the traditional rendering, is used in its older sense of "source," which is a better translation (cf. 16:22, where NKJV has "wellspring"). Although they are separate sayings, this verse and the next are closely related by their topics (cf. also 13:14; 14:27).

10:12. Both the prominence of the theme of speech in the surrounding verses and the parallelism show that "covereth" does not mean to ignore, but

14.

2550	7121.126, 1907
n mp	v Qal impf 3mp, n fs
חֲכָמִים	יִצְפְּנוּ־דָעַת
chăkhāmîm	yitspᵉnû-dhā'ath
the wise	they store up knowledge

2551	8101	3937, 1490	2742, 3949
n fs	cj, n ms	prep, n ms	adj, n ms
חָכְמָה	וְשֵׁבֶט	לִגְוֵ	חֲסַר־לֵב
chokhmāh	wᵉshēvet	lᵉghēw	chăsar-lēv
wisdom	but a rod	for the back of	lacking in heart

15.

6010	7439	6474	2019
n ms, ps 3ms	n fs	n ms	n ms
עֻזּוֹ	קִרְיַת	עָשִׁיר	הוֹן
'uzzô	qiryath	'āshîr	hôn
his strength	the city of	the rich	the wealth of

6552, 188	4425	7427
cj, n ms, n ms	n fs	adj
וּפִי־אֱוִיל	מְחִתָּה	קְרֻבָּה
ûphî-'ĕwîl	mᵉchittāh	qŏrōvāh
but the mouth of the fool	destruction	near

16.

4425	1859	7677	6715	6926	3937, 2522	8721
n fs	n mp	n ms, ps 3mp	n fs	n ms	prep, n mp	n fs
מְחִתַּת	דַּלִּים	רֵישָׁם	פְּעֻלַּת	צַדִּיק	לְחַיִּים	תְּבוּאַת
mᵉchittath	dallîm	rêshām	pe'ullath	tsaddîq	lᵉchayyîm	tᵉvû'ath
the destruction of	the poor	their poverty	the work of	the righteous	for life	the produce of

17.

7857	3937, 2496	758	3937, 2522	8490.151	4284	6013.151
n ms	prep, n fs	n ms	prep, n mp	v Qal act ptc ms	n ms	cj, v Qal act ptc ms
רָשָׁע	לְחַטָּאת	אֹרַח	לְחַיִּים	שׁוֹמֵר	מוּסָר	וְעוֹזֵב
rāshā'	lᵉchattā'th	'ōrach	lᵉchayyîm	shômēr	mûsār	wᵉ'ôzēv
the wicked	for sin	a path	to life	one observing	discipline	but one who abandons

18.

8763	8912.551	3803.351	7985	8004, 8632
n fs	v Hiphil ptc ms	v Piel ptc ms	n fs	n fd, n ms
תּוֹכַחַת	מַתְעֶה	מְכַסֶּה	שִׂנְאָה	שִׂפְתֵי־שָׁקֶר
tôkhachath	math'eh	mᵉkhasseh	sin'āh	siphthê-shāqer
correction	going astray	one who conceals	hatred	lips of falsehood

19.

3428.551	1730	2000	3809	904, 7524	1745	3940
cj, v Hiphil ptc ms	n fs	pers pron	n ms	prep, n ms	n mp	neg part
וּמוֹצֵא	דִּבָּה	הוּא	כְּסִיל	בְּרֹב	דְּבָרִים	לֹא
ûmôtsi'	dhibbāh	hû'	khᵉsîl	bᵉrōv	dᵉvārîm	lō'
and one who causes to go out	slander	he	a fool	in the abundance of	words	not

14. Wise men lay up knowledge: ... Sensible men are reticent, *Moffatt* ... store up knowledge, *Beck, NIV.*

but the mouth of the foolish is near destruction: ... mouth of a fool is imminent ruin, *NAB, Douay* ... is a terror near at hand, *Rotherham* ... is a present destruction, *MRB* ... When a fool talks, trouble is brewing, *Anchor.*

15. The rich man's wealth is his strong city: ... substance of the rich, *Rotherham* ... is his fortress, *NASB, Goodspeed* ... wealth is his protection, *Moffatt.*

the destruction of the poor is their poverty: ... the undoing of the helpless, *NEB* ... poverty spells disaster for the helpless, *REB* ... and the poor man's need his peril, *Knox.*

16. The labour of the righteous tendeth to life: ... wages of Virtue are Life, *Fenton* ... good man's earnings, *Moffatt* ... advance the cause of righteousness, *LIVB* ... is his livelihood, *NEB.*

the fruit of the wicked to sin: ... harvest of a wicked man, *Beck* ... revenue of a wicked [man], *Darby* ... income of the wicked, *Goodspeed* ... wages of the wicked, *NKJV.*

17. He is in the way of life that keepeth instruction: ... who takes note of teaching, *BB* ... lives by the lessons he has learned, *Knox* ... Whoever abides by discipline, walks towards life, *JB.*

but he that refuseth reproof erreth: ... rejects a rebuke goes astray, *NRSV* ... neglect reproof, *REB* ... the way is lost when warnings go unheeded, *Knox.*

18. He that hideth hatred with lying lips, and he that uttereth a slander, is a fool: ... who reveals hatred ... tells lies is a fool, *NCV* ... conceals hatred, *RSV* ... spreads accusations, *Douay* ... who spreads slander, is a rogue, *Anchor.*

19. In the multitude of words there wanteth not sin: ... When words are many, transgression is not lacking, *NRSV* ... Danger lurks in many words, *Fenton* ... A flood of words is never without fault, *JB* ... sin is not absent, *NIV.*

to avoid reviewing or discussing someone else's faults, mistakes or sinful deeds (cf. 1 Pet. 4:8). Refusing to speak ill of someone else builds and strengthens relationships (17:9; contrast 26:20ff). In the same way, confessing and abandoning one's own sins is a source of great blessing and encouragement (28:13).

10:13. Where can seekers find wisdom? From those who are already wise. The contrast is oblique, but the fool's lack of wisdom, recognized by the quality of his life and words, results in rebuke, discipline and punishment. The wise, also recognized by their life and words, are honored by being sought out as teachers. Even students who are not discerning enough to distinguish wise from foolish words (v. 13a) should be able to distinguish disgrace and honor.

10:14. The wise know that there is nothing to be gained by displaying their understanding (17:27), but fools cannot keep their folly to themselves, and freely reveal their ignorance and rebelliousness (e.g., 14:33; 15:2; 18:2). The result for the fool is correction or rebuke, humiliation and possibly ruin. Since the word translated (HED #4425) "ruin" also means "terror," this could be an intentional pun (there are plenty of unambiguous words for either that Solomon could have used). A fool with any degree of understanding ought to be afraid of what might come out of his mouth, knowing that his words will only bring him trouble. The wise, whose words are a source of life (10:11) and a blessing to both others and themselves (e.g., 10:6f), need fear neither rebuke nor ruin.

10:15. Wealth often insulates the rich from circumstances that terrify the poor, since they have the resources that enable them to survive. The great danger for the rich is that they may begin to trust their riches—or their own cleverness in gaining them—rather than the God Who gave them the wealth (cf. Deut. 6:10ff; 8:10–14; Hos. 2:5–13). The first line of Prov. 18:11, which also makes this point, is identical to the first line of this verse. The Bible does not consider poverty as good or desirable in itself, but it may be preferable to wealth under certain circumstances (cf. 15:16f; 19:1, 22; Ps. 26:9ff).

10:16. Neither righteousness nor wickedness can be hidden—both yield fruit. Even this is not the end, since each type of fruit has its own result. The contrast of this verse is also the main contrast of the prologue—life or death. Wickedness feeds

itself, leading nearer and nearer to death, whereas righteousness (the result of obedience) leads to life (cf. 10:2b). The saying thus encourages the righteous to persevere and rebukes the wicked by warning them of the eventual outcome of their ways.

10:17. The goal of discipline and correction is to keep one on the right path, but rebukes alone cannot accomplish this. Instead, the response determines the result. Those who insist on going their own way, refusing to listen or respond to correction, will soon find themselves wandering lost, whereas those who respond in obedience will find themselves back on the path that they had left. This does not imply that every criticism is equally valid, for every rebuke needs to be weighed in order to see whether or not it is in accord with wisdom's way. To abandon correction, however, is to guarantee eventual abandonment by correction, which means death (cf. 1:22–32).

10:18. Hatred often underlies hypocrisy ("lying lips") in Proverbs, so that those who hate often invent or pass on bad news in order to destroy someone's reputation, opportunities, or both. To the person's face, however, the words are friendly (cf. 26:24, 26), which may give them even more opportunity for harm, since they can present themselves as sympathetic listeners or advisors. The prohibition against false testimony underlies this proverb (Exo. 20:16), since the people of God are to demonstrate his truthfulness in their dealings with one another. This verse also shows that the fool of Proverbs is morally wicked, not mentally deficient.

10:19. Fools talk too much (cf. 17:27f), whereas the prudent know the value of silence. The more words a person says (or writes), the less able he is to weigh each word, and the greater the probability that he will offend someone. The prudent speak but little, knowing the power and worth of words (cf. 12:18; 18:21). Because they anticipate the outcome of a decision or action, the prudent know that words too quickly get out of control, offending God and others.

10:20. Like wisdom's yield (8:19), the words of the righteous are better than choice silver, whereas the wicked are rotten at the core, and thus nearly worthless. Similar to other sayings in this chapter about speech (cf. 10:6, 21), this proverb encourages its readers to consider the lives of those who offer advice, counsel or teaching, and to learn from those who exhibit the righteousness that

20.

1013.255	3826B		7959.551	8004	2910.151	2403.121, 6840
v Niphal ptc ms	n ms		v Hiphil ptc ms	n fd, ps 3ms	cj, v Qal act ptc ms	v Qal impf 3ms, n ms
נִבְחָר	כֶּסֶף	20.	מַשְׂכִּיל	שְׂפָתָיו	וְחֹשֵׂךְ	יֶחְדַּל־פָּשַׁע
nivchār	keseph		maskîl	sephāthâv	wechōsēkh	yechăddal-pāsha'
what is chosen	silver		being wise	his lips	but one who restrains	transgression ceases

21.

6926	8004		3626, 4746	7857	3949	6926	4098
n ms	n fd		prep, adj	n mp	n ms	n ms	n ms
צַדִּיק	שִׂפְתֵי	21.	כִּמְעָט	רְשָׁעִים	לֵב	צַדִּיק	לְשׁוֹן
tsaddîq	siphthê		kim'āt	reshā'îm	lēv	tsaddîq	leshôn
the righteous	the lips of		like a little	the wicked	the heart of	the righteous	the tongue of

22.

1318	4322.126	904, 2742, 3949	188	7521	7749.126
n fs	v Qal impf 3mp	prep, art, adj, n ms	cj, n mp	adj	v Qal impf 3mp
בִּרְכַת	יָמוּתוּ	בַּחֲסַר־לֵב	וֶאֱוִילִים	רַבִּים	יִרְעוּ
birkath	yāmûthû	bachăsar-lēv	we'ěwîlîm	rabbîm	yir'û
the blessing of	they will die	because of lacking of heart	but fools	many	they feed

23.

3626, 7926	6196	6325	3940, 3362.521	6483.522	2026	3176
prep, n ms	prep, ps 3fs	n ms	cj, neg part, v Hiphil impf 3ms	v Hiphil impf 3fs	pers pron	pn
כִּשְׂחוֹק	עִמָּהּ	עֶצֶב	וְלֹא־יוֹסִף	תַּעֲשִׁיר	הִיא	יְהוָה
kischôq	'immāh	'etsev	welō-yôsiph	tha'ăshîr	hî'	yehwāh
like a joke	with it	sorrow	and He does not add	it makes rich	it	Yahweh

24.

4173	8722	3937, 382	2551	2239	6449.141	3937, 3809
n fs	n fs	prep, n ms	cj, n fs	n fs	v Qal inf con	prep, n ms
מְגוֹרַת	תְּבוּנָה	לְאִישׁ	וְחָכְמָה	זִמָּה	עֲשׂוֹת	לִכְסִיל
meghôrath	tevûnāh	le'îsh	wechokhmāh	zimmāh	'ăsôth	likhsîl
the fear of	understanding	to a man of	but wisdom	a shameful deed	to do	to a fool

5598.121	6926	8707	971.122	2026	7857
v Qal impf 3ms	n mp	cj, n fs	v Qal impf 3fs, ps 3ms	pers pron	n ms
יִתֵּן	צַדִּיקִים	וְתַאֲוַת	תְּבוֹאֶנּוּ	הִיא	רָשָׁע
yittēn	tsaddîqîm	wetha'ăwath	thevô'ennû	hî'	rāshā'
He will give	the righteous	but the desire of	it will come upon him	it	the wicked

25.

3356	3626, 5882.141	5679	375	7857	6926	3356
	prep, v Qal inf con	n fs	cj, sub	n ms	cj, n ms	n ms
25.	כַּעֲבוֹר	סוּפָה	וְאֵין	רָשָׁע	וְצַדִּיק	יְסוֹד
	ka'ăvôr	sûphāh	we'ên	rāshā'	wetsaddîq	yesôdh
	when passing	a storm	then there is not	the wicked	but the righteous	a foundation

26.

5986	3626, 2663	3937, 8514	3626, 6476	3937, 6084	3772	6339
n ms	prep, art, n ms	prep, art, n fd	cj, prep, n ms	prep, art, n fd	adv	art, n ms
עוֹלָם	כַּחֹמֶץ	לַשִּׁנַּיִם	וְכֶעָשָׁן	לָעֵינַיִם	כֵּן	הֶעָצֵל
'ôlām	kachōmets	lashshinnayim	wekhe'āshān	lā'ênayim	kēn	he'ātsēl
everlasting	like vinegar	to the teeth	and like smoke	to the eyes	so	the sluggard

---

but he that refraineth his lips is wise: ... controls the lips, *JB* ... shrewd man holds his tongue, *Anchor* ... common sense holds its tongue, *NEB* ... prudent are restrained in speech, *NRSV*.

20. The tongue of the just is as choice silver: the heart of the wicked is little worth: ... of the upright man is like tested silver, *BB* ... Silver refined is the just man's every word, and trash the sinner's every thought, *Knox* ... sense of the lawless is very small, *Rotherham* ... mind of the wicked, *RSV* ... what the wicked thinks, *Beck*.

21. The lips of the righteous feed many: but fools die for want of wis- **dom:** ... teaching of the righteous guides many, *REB* ... are a sustenance to many, *Goodspeed* ... fools perish from their own stupidity, *Anchor* ... die for lack of understanding, *ASV*.

22. The blessing of the LORD, it maketh rich, and he addeth no sorrow with it: ... 'Tis the Eternal's

94

blessing, *Moffatt* ... blessing of Yahweh is what brings riches, to this, hard toil has nothing to add, *JB* ... Toil yields no increase like it, *Goodspeed* ... no effort can substitute for it, *Douay* ... never does it bring trouble as well, *Moffatt*.

23. It is as sport to a fool to do mischief: but a man of understanding hath wisdom: ... Lewdness is entertainment for the stupid, *REB* ... To execute schemes is the play of a fool, *KJVII* ... fool finds pleasure in evil conduct, *NIV* ... the intelligent in cultivating wisdom, *JB* ... wise conduct is pleasure to a man of understanding, *RSV*.

24. The fear of the wicked, it shall come upon him: but the desire of the righteous shall be granted: ... will overtake them, *NEB* ... terrors of the wicked catch him, but the wish of the good will be done, *Fenton* ... comes to him as a present, *JB*.

25. As the whirlwind passeth, so is the wicked no more: but the right- eous is an everlasting foundation: ... passing by of a hurricane, *Young* ... the just man is established forever, *Douay* ... good person will always be safe, *NCV*.

26. As vinegar to the teeth, and as smoke to the eyes, so is the sluggard to them that send him: ... Like acid to teeth, *Fenton* ... is a lazy person to him who sends him, *Beck* ... are the lazy to their employers, *NRSV* ... so is the hater of work, *BB*.

---

comes from wisdom, since they can lead their students along the path of great blessing.

10:21. This is the first proverb that directly compares the righteous to fools. This comparison shows that "wise" and "foolish" are interchangeable with "righteous" and "wicked" (cf. 14:9), and thus are moral evaluations—they do not merely describe mental ability or capacity.

The words of the righteous bless ("feed") those around them, including themselves, whereas fools, who lack understanding ("heart"), can sustain neither themselves nor anyone else. To seek nourishment from a fool is a waste of time, and may even lead to disaster; only wisdom can stave off moral starvation (10:13; cf. 10:20).

10:22. Diligence is necessary to success (e.g., 10:4), but well-being is the work of God. The noun translated "sorrow" may also mean "labor" (cf. 5:10; 14:23); it is probably the subject of the verb—"and toil he does not add [increase] to it"—so that the verse corrects the notion that human effort alone ultimately determines well-being (cf. Ps. 127:1f; Ecc. 5:18ff). A humble and thankful heart shows that one understands this truth. Although this is a somewhat unusual use of the preposition "with" (HED #6196), it both suits the parallelism and context.

10:23. What a person chooses to spend time and energy on reveals his true nature, because people receive pleasure from, and therefore seek, what is most in accord with their inner nature. Fools, who are self-centered, naturally enjoy making and enacting wicked plans; the discerning love and pursue wisdom (8:17–21). Solomon warns that what a person most enjoys reveals the state of his heart.

10:24. The wicked will be overtaken by the disaster that they fear (cf. the same expression in 28:22; Job 15:21; 20:22; Ps. 36:12; Ezek. 32:11); the righteous are confident because their obedience has placed them in the path of life (10:17), where they are not only protected, but blessed. A later proverb says that the hope and desire of the wicked are destroyed (10:28). All that is left them is their fear.

Together with Prov. 28:1, this saying suggests that the wicked are miserable, regardless of their apparent prosperity or "happiness," because they live their lives in fear of what may happen, and because they know what happens to those upon whom fortune frowns (e.g., 19:4, 6f). Those who entrust themselves to the LORD, on the other hand, and who submit to his wisdom, live without fear.

10:25. Sin may prevail for a moment, but it cannot endure, because it opposes the standards of God, the final Judge. Proverbs that contrast the relative permanence of wickedness and righteousness warn that however attractive sin's activities or rewards may appear, they will perish, because every standard but one will survive the ultimate judgment (e.g, 10:28; 12:7; 29:16). In all but one of its occurrences (Job 37:9), the word translated "whirlwind" refers to the judgment of God (cf. 1:27; Isa. 5:28; 17:13; 21:1; 29:6; 66:15).

10:26. This proverb is a single comparison, using two emblems (see "Overview") to illustrate how a lazy person's failure to fulfill an obligation affects those who entrusted him with it (cf. 25:13). Those with a need, such as a job to be done, should know the character of the person to whom they assign it, lest they be irritated by his failure to fulfill his responsibility. The lazy should also be warned that their poor or lacking performance may bring punishment (if a slave) or loss

27.

3488 n fs	3176 pn	3362.522 v Hiphil impf 3fs	3219 n mp	8523 cj, n fp
יִרְאַת	יְהוָה	תּוֹסִיף	יָמִים	וּשְׁנוֹת
yir'ath	yᵉhwāh	tôsîph	yāmîm	ûshᵉnôth
the fear of	Yahweh	it will add	days	but the years of

3937, 8365.152 prep, v Qal act ptc mp, ps 3ms
לִשְׁלְחָיו
lᵉshōlᵉchâv
to those who send him

28.

8760 n fs	6926 n mp	7977 n fs	8951 cj, n fs
תּוֹחֶלֶת	צַדִּיקִים	שִׂמְחָה	וְתִקְוַת
tôcheleth	tsaddîqîm	simchāh	wᵉthiqōwath
the hope of	the righteous	rejoicing	but the expectation of

7857 n mp	7403.127 v Qal impf 3fp
רְשָׁעִים	תִּקְצֹרֶנָה
rᵉshā'îm	tiqōtsōrᵉnāh
the wicked	they will become short

29.

4735 n ms	3937, 8866 prep, art, n ms	1932 n ms	3176 pn	4425 cj, n fs
מָעוֹז	לַתֹּם	דֶּרֶךְ	יְהוָה	וּמְחִתָּה
mā'ôz	lattōm	derekh	yᵉhwāh	ûmᵉchittāh
a stronghold	to the upright	the way of	Yahweh	but destruction

7857 n mp	6.122 v Qal impf 3fs
רְשָׁעִים	תֹּאבֵד
rᵉshā'îm	tō'vēdh
the wicked	it will perish

30.

201 n ms	6926 n ms	3937, 5986 prep, n ms	1118, 4267.221 neg part, v Niphal impf 3ms
אָוֶן	צַדִּיק	לְעוֹלָם	בַּל־יִמּוֹט
'āwen	tsaddîq	lᵉ'ôlām	bal-yimmôt
iniquity	the righteous	unto eternity	he will not totter

3937, 6713.152 prep, v Qal act ptc mp
לְפֹעֲלֵי
lᵉphō'ălê
to those practicing

31.

6552, 6926 n ms, n ms	5286.121 v Qal impf 3ms
פִּי־צַדִּיק	יָנוּב
pî-tsaddîq	yānûv
the mouth of the righteous	it yields

7857 cj, n mp	3940 neg part	8331.126, 800 v Qal impf 3mp, n fs
וּרְשָׁעִים	לֹא	יִשְׁכְּנוּ־אָרֶץ
ûrᵉshā'îm	lō'	yishkᵉnû-'ārets
but the wicked	not	they will stay in the land

32.

8749 n fp	3901.222 v Niphal impf 3fs	8004 n fd	6926 n ms
תַּהְפֻּכוֹת	תִּכָּרֵת	שִׂפְתֵי	צַדִּיק
tahpukhôth	tikkārēth	siphthê	tsaddîq
perversities	it will be cut off	the lips of	the righteous

2551 n fs	4098 cj, n fs
חָכְמָה	וּלָשׁוֹן
chokhmāh	ûlāshôn
wisdom	but the tongue of

11:1

7814 n ms	6552 cj, n ms	7857 n mp	8749 n fp	4118 n md
רָצוֹן	וּפִי	רְשָׁעִים	תַּהְפֻּכוֹת	מֹאזְנֵי
rātsôn	ûphî	rᵉshā'îm	tahpukhôth	mō'zᵉnê
what is acceptable	but the mouth of	the wicked	perversities	scales of

3156.126 v Qal impf 3mp
יֵדְעוּן
yēdhᵉ'ûn
they will know

2.

3176 pn	63 cj, n fs	8400 adj	7814 n ms, ps 3ms	971.111, 2171 v Qal pf 3ms, n ms
יְהוָה	וְאֶבֶן	שְׁלֵמָה	רְצוֹנוֹ	בָּא־זָדוֹן
yᵉhwāh	wᵉ'even	shelēmāh	rᵉtsônô	bā'-zādhôn
Yahweh	but a weight	just	his delight	pride comes

4983 n fs	8774 n fs
מִרְמָה	תּוֹעֲבַת
mirmāh	tô'ăvath
deceit	an abomination to

---

27. The fear of the LORD prolongeth days: but the years of the wicked shall be shortened: ... The reverence of Yahweh addeth days, *Rotherham* ... Whoever respects the LORD, *NCV* ... will add to your life, *Beck* ... years of the wicked are brief, *NAB*.

28. The hope of the righteous shall be gladness: ... The hope of the just brings them joy, *Douay* ... hope of the righteous blossoms, *NEB* ... expectation of good men flourishes, *Anchor*.

but the expectation of the wicked shall perish: ... comes to nothing, *Berkeley* ... withers away, *NEB*.

29. The way of the LORD is strength to the upright: ... is a strong hold, *MRB* ... a strong tower for the upright man, *BB* ... is a rampart for the honest, *JB* ... LORD's way is a fortress for the innocent, *Beck*.

but destruction shall be to the workers of iniquity: ... he is the terror of evildoers, *Anchor* ... but ruin to those who do wrong, *Beck*.

30. **The righteous shall never be removed: but the wicked shall not inhabit the earth:** ... never be shaken, *REB* ... just man will never be disturbed, *NAB* ... never be uprooted, *NIV* ... wicked have no permanence in the land, *Anchor*.

31. **The mouth of the just bringeth forth wisdom: but the froward tongue shall be cut out:** ... mouth of the Good utters wisdom, *Fenton* ... of the righteous buddeth with wis-

dom, *MAST* ... the subversive tongue will be torn out, *REB* ... liar's tongue will be stopped, *NCV* ... tongue that deceives, *JB*.

32. **The lips of the righteous know what is acceptable:** ... suit words to the occasion, *REB* ... know what is fitting, *NIV* ... pour out good will, *Beck*.

but the mouth of the wicked speaketh frowardness: ... but the perverted tongue destruction, *Fenton*

... drips with malice, *Anchor* ... is perverse, *Beck*.

11:1. **A false balance is abomination to the LORD: but a just weight is his delight:** ... LORD hates dishonest scales, *NCV* ... Balances of deceit are an abomination, *Young* ... A false balance the Lord hates; nothing but full weight will content him, *Knox*.

2. **When pride cometh, then cometh shame: but with the lowly**

(if a hireling). Work is part of the creation of God, and is therefore not only good, but necessary to life.

10:27. This verse reflects the prologue's teaching that obedience to the precepts of wisdom is blessed (e.g., 3:1f) because it avoids the ways that lead to death (e.g., 12:28). The careful inversion of lengthened days and shortened years heightens the contrast, as do vv. 28ff.

10:28. Righteousness and wickedness, the two basic ways of life described throughout Proverbs, are here contrasted by comparing their results—joy for the righteous and death for the wicked. The righteous can be sure that truth and justice will ultimately prevail, and thus look beyond their circumstances with confidence (cf. 10:25; 29:16), whereas wickedness looks forward to the doom of coming judgment (cf. 11:7, 23).

This does not teach that the rebellious realize their fate, but warns that their plans and desires will not succeed in the long run (cf. 10:3). Though the heart of the fool despises the wisdom of God (1:7), establishing itself as the measure of righteousness, it cannot prevail against the only true God. The warning is thus the same as that of 10:25—act only after considering both the nature of the choice (wickedness or righteousness) and its outcome (joy or death).

10:29. The security of the upright reminds the wicked of their inevitable judgment, so that the way of the LORD spells their ruin and strikes terror into their hearts (mᵉchittah [HED #4425] can mean either "ruin" or "terror"). Since righteousness will eventually triumph, evil will eventually be destroyed. There is therefore ultimately safety only in obedience, as the prologue emphasizes (cf. the contrast between 1:20–32 and 1:33; also 3:21–26), because ruin lurks off the path on every side.

10:30. Like the preceding verses (10:27ff), this saying promises security to the obedient and warns the wise that the wicked will not endure. Although this is a common theme in Proverbs, several later sayings imply that the wicked may indeed dominate the righteous, albeit temporarily (28:15f, 28; 29:2, 16). The wise can indeed take comfort, but must not misread this verse as an absolute promise of well-being (cf. 16:7).

10:31. The verb in 10:31a (nûv; HED #5286) may mean either "be fruitful" or "thrive," perhaps because healthy plants tend to be fruitful (cf. its other occurrences: Pss. 62:10; 92:14; Zech. 9:17). Its "object," however, must be an adverbial accusative, "[with respect to] wisdom," so that this verse is closely related to others in this chapter (e.g., vv. 11, 13f, 32).

The agricultural metaphor contrasts a lush or fruitful plant with one that has either been cut off, and is therefore unfruitful, or one that was cut off because it was not fruitful (cf. Isa. 5:1–6; John 15:1–6). The righteous are fruitful because they pass on wisdom, which increases in the lives of its hearers. Those who use the gift of speech for their own perverse ends may flourish, but not for long (cf. 10:24).

10:32. Because the wise think long before speaking (e.g., 10:19), they know how to make their teaching and counsel acceptable and pleasing. The wicked, who speak from themselves, and are careless of their words (10:19) offer nothing but their own twisted thoughts. As in other proverbs in this chapter, and especially v. 31, a person's words reveal the nature of his or her heart. This verse contrasts the inherent beauty of wise words (25:11f) with the ugliness of wickedness.

11:1. The call for honesty rises out of, and is linked to, the command to love one's neighbor,

3.

3596	8870		2551	882, 7067	7320	971.121
n mp	n fs	**3.**	n fs	cj, prep, n mp	n ms	cj, v Qal impf 3ms
יְשָׁרִים	תֻּמַּת		חָכְמָה	וְאֶת־צְנוּעִים	קָלוֹן	וַיָּבֹא
yesharim	tummath		chokhmah	we'eth-tsenu'im	qalon	wayyavo'
the upright	the integrity of		wisdom	but with the humble	shame	then it will come in

8161.121	931.152	5752	5341.522
v Qal impf 3ms, ps 3mp	v Qal act ptc mp	cj, n ms	v Hiphil impf 3fs, ps 3mp
וְשַׁדָּם	בּוֹגְדִים	וְסֶלֶף	תַּנְחֵם
weshaddam	boghdhim	weseleph	tanchem
it will devastate them	the treacherous	but the crookedness of	it will guide them

4.

5522.522	6930	5887	904, 3219	2019	3940, 3385.521	
v Hiphil impf 3fs	cj, n fs	n fs	prep, n ms	n ms	neg part, v Hiphil impf 3ms	**4.**
תַּצִּיל	וּצְדָקָה	עֶבְרָה	בְּיוֹם	הוֹן	לֹא־יוֹעִיל	
tatstsil	utsedhaqah	'evrah	beyom	hon	lo-yo'il	
it delivers	but righteousness	wrath	in the day of	wealth	it does not profit	

5.

1932	3595.322	8879	6930		4623, 4323
n ms, ps 3ms	v Piel impf 3fs	n ms	n fs	**5.**	prep, n ms
דַּרְכּוֹ	תְּיַשֵּׁר	תָּמִים	צִדְקַת		מִמָּוֶת
darko	teyashsher	tamim	tsidhqath		mimmaweth
his way	it will make straight	the blameless	the righteousness of		from death

6.

3596	6930		7857	5489.121	904, 7858
n mp	n fs	**6.**	n ms	v Qal impf 3ms	cj, prep, n fs, ps 3ms
יְשָׁרִים	צִדְקַת		רֶשַׁע	יִפֹּל	וּבְרִשְׁעָתוֹ
yesharim	tsidhqath		rasha'	yippol	uverish'atho
the upright	the righteousness of		the wicked	he will fall	but by his wickedness

7.

904, 4322.141		4058.226	931.152	904, 2010	5522.522
prep, v Qal inf con	**7.**	v Niphal impf 3mp	v Qal act ptc mp	cj, prep, n fs	v Hiphil impf 3fs, ps 3mp
בְּמוֹת		יִלָּכֵדוּ	בֹּגְדִים	וּבְהַוַּת	תַּצִּילֵם
bemoth		yillakhedhu	boghedhim	uvehawwath	tatstsilem
when dying		they will be caught	deceitful ones	but by the desire of	it will deliver them

8.

6926		6.112	202	8760	8951	6.122	7857	119
n ms	**8.**	v Qal pf 3fs	n mp	cj, n fs	n fs	v Qal impf 3fs	adj	n ms
צַדִּיק		אָבְדָה	אוֹנִים	וְתוֹחֶלֶת	תִּקְוָה	תֹּאבַד	רֶשַׁע	אָדָם
tsaddiq		'avadhah	'onim	wethocheleth	tiqowah	to'vadh	rasha'	'adham
the righteous		it is lost	strength	and hope of	expectation	it will be lost	wicked	a man

---

is wisdom: ... Insolence comes, *Fenton* ... disgrace soon follows, *JB* ... wisdom goes hand in hand with modesty, *REB* ... modest men show good sense, *Moffatt*.

3. The integrity of the upright shall guide them: ... Upright men are guided by their honesty, *Goodspeed* ... righteousness of the upright will be their guide, *BB* ... The Just are guided by Right, *Fenton*.

but the perverseness of transgressors shall destroy them: ... hypocrisy of unfaithful people leads them to ruin, *Beck* ... crookedness of the treacherous destroys them, *RSV* ... the perfidious are ruined by their own duplicity, *REB*.

4. Riches profit not in the day of wrath: but righteousness delivereth from death: ... When the time for reckoning comes, little shall wealth avail, *Knox* ... In the day of retribution riches will be useless, *JB*.

5. The righteousness of the perfect shall direct his way: but the wicked shall fall by his own wickedness: ... honest man's path is kept straight, *Goodspeed* ... By uprightness the blameless keep their course, *NEB* ... virtue of good men keeps them on the right road, *Anchor*.

6. The righteousness of the upright shall deliver them: ... Doing right brings freedom to honest people, *NCV* ... Good people are saved by their righteousness, *Beck* ... For his honesty, the upright man shall go free, *Knox* ... virtue of the upright is their salvation, *Anchor*.

but transgressors shall be taken in their own naughtiness: ... deceivers shall be taken in their own mischief, *KJVII* … unfaithful are trapped by evil desires, *NIV* … rascals are caught by their crimes, *Fenton* … treacherous are taken captive by their schemes, *NRSV*.

7. When a wicked man dieth, his expectation shall perish: and the hope of unjust men perisheth: … the lawless man dieth, *Rotherham* … expectation of the godless comes to nought, *RSV* … yes, the hope of his strength dies out, *Berkeley*.

8. The righteous is delivered out of trouble, and the wicked cometh in his stead: … are rescued from disaster, *REB* … brought safe out of adversity, *Moffatt* … in his place comes the sinner, *BB* … wicked man succeeds him in it, *Beck*.

---

including the non-Israelite (cf. Lev. 19:18, 33–37, where honesty is explicitly commanded in judgment, weights and measures). Modern precision was unknown in the biblical world. Dozens of stone weights inscribed with the word "shekels," for example, have been found and vary from 11.08–12.25 grams, although the distribution of fairly uniform weights across the ancient Near East shows that the standards were widely recognized and fell within tolerable limits. Both scales and weights might be made by the individual seller (or buyer); the strict covenantal warnings show that dishonesty was a problem (Deut. 25:13–16, where the same language occurs; cf. Prov. 16:11; 20:10, 14, 23).

11:2. The inevitable consequences of insolence are disgrace and shame, since the arrogant inevitably falls prey to his own pride (16:18). When the arrogant comes, therefore, dishonor is sure to follow. The humble, or "lowly" (the word occurs only here and in Mic. 6:8), on the other hand, are accompanied by wisdom. They realize the limits of their own understanding, and, far from being proud, are quick to admit their need, benefit from the counsel of others and avoid disgrace. The consequences of these attitudes commend humility, since wisdom is much more attractive than the embarrassment that accompanies the failure that follows after pride (cf. 15:32f).

11:3. Integrity preserves the wise because it enables them to choose the paths that lead to life (cf. 3:18; 8:35; see also the prologue). The wickedness of the treacherous blinds them so that they cannot choose wisely. Both ways are progressive—every choice paving the way for the next, whether toward life or death. Several proverbs in ch. 11 contrast the consequences of wickedness and righteousness (11:3, 5–8, 18f, 21, 23, 27, 29, 31).

11:4. Verses 4ff contrast the fates of the righteous and wicked. They warn the wealthy that although they may feel safe because of their riches (18:11), a test will come from which their riches cannot save them. Their wealth, therefore, must not be the ultimate source of their confidence. It is their attitude toward and relationship with the Lord

rather than the state of their bank account, that will determine their fate. At the same time, the righteous, those who trust in the Lord, should be encouraged to know that their circumstances do not indicate God's favor (or lack thereof) toward them.

11:5. No external force is required to ensure the outcome of righteousness and wickedness. The righteous do not fall, because their integrity directs them into the wise decisions that lead to life (11:3; cf. the same verb in 3:6; 15:21). Wickedness sows its own destruction by pursuing its own course, despising instruction and correction (1:22–32; 8:36; cf. 26:27). Like all of the "obvious" proverbs, this verse encourages students of wisdom to consider which end they are pursuing (cf. 11:6ff).

11:6. Closely linked to the preceding verse both topically and formally, the second line specifically addresses the wicked desires that entrap the treacherous. Treachery is not simply betraying someone's trust, but betraying someone for personal gain. Their shortsighted view of life makes the wicked willing to destroy relationships and reputations for some temporary gain. When the betrayal is discovered (10:9), however, the traitor's reputation is destroyed.

Treason ranges from the apparently innocuous (feigning personal support, but actually withholding it from, or undermining, those to whom it is due) to military or political betrayal, just as the anticipated gain can range from one's personal reputation to financial or political enrichment. The scope of the sin does not affect the outcome.

The righteous, who are characterized by integrity, are not only free from the fear of being found out (cf. 10:9; 28:1), but may even be rescued from difficult circumstances by their honesty (11:8f).

11:7. Unlike most proverbs that contrast the ends of the righteous and wicked (e.g., 10:25, 28; 11:23; 29:16), this verse focuses solely on the fate of the wicked, whose hope lasts only until death. It is thus one of the group of proverbs that look beyond this life to the eventual vindication of the righteous (e.g., 12:28).

904, 6552 prep, n ms בְּפֶה bᵉpheh by the mouth	**9.**	8809 prep, ps 3ms תַּחְתָּיו tachtâv instead of him	7857 n ms רָשָׁע rāshā' the wicked	971.121 cj, v Qal impf 3ms וַיָּבֹא wayyāvō' but he will enter	2603.211 v Niphal pf 3ms נֶחֱלָץ nechĕlāts he will be set apart	4623, 7150 prep, n fs מִצָּרָה mitstsārāh from adversity

2603.226 v Niphal impf 3mp יֵחָלֵצוּ yēchālētsû they will be set apart	6926 n mp צַדִּיקִים tsaddîqîm the righteous	904, 1907 cj, prep, n fs וּבְדַעַת ûvᵉdha'ath but by knowledge	7739 n ms, ps 3ms רֵעֵהוּ rē'ēhû his fellow	8271.521 v Hiphil impf 3ms יַשְׁחִת yashchith he will destroy	2715 n ms חָנֵף chāneph the godless

10.	904, 3008 prep, n ms בְּטוּב bᵉtûv because of the good of	6926 n mp צַדִּיקִים tsaddîqîm the righteous	6192.122 v Qal impf 3fs תַּעֲלֹץ ta'ălōts it rejoices	7439 n fs קִרְיָה qiryāh a city	904, 6.141 cj, prep, v Qal inf con וּבַאֲבֹד ûva'ăvōdh but when perishing	7857 n mp רְשָׁעִים rᵉshā'îm the wicked

7726 n fs רִנָּה rinnāh shout of joy	**11.**	904, 1318 prep, n fs בְּבִרְכַּת bᵉvirkath by the blessing of	3596 n mp יְשָׁרִים yᵉshārîm the upright	7597.122 v Qal impf 3fs תָּרוּם tārûm it will be exalted	7469 n fs קָרֶת qāreth a town	904, 6552 cj, prep, n ms וּבְפִי ûvᵉphî but by the mouth of

7857 n mp רְשָׁעִים rᵉshā'îm the wicked	2117.222 v Niphal impf 3fs תֵּהָרֵס tēhārēs it will be overthrown	**12.**	972.151, 3937, 7739 v Qal act ptc ms, prep, n ms, ps 3ms בָּז־לְרֵעֵהוּ bāz-lᵉrē'ēhû one who despises his fellow	2742, 3949 adj, n ms חֲסַר־לֵב chăsar-lēv lacking in heart	382 cj, n ms וְאִישׁ wᵉ'îsh but a man of

8722 n fp תְּבוּנוֹת tᵉvûnôth understanding	2896.521 v Hiphil impf 3ms יַחֲרִישׁ yachărîsh he keeps silent	**13.**	2050.151 v Qal act ptc ms הוֹלֵךְ hôlēkh going	7689 n ms רָכִיל rākhîl a slanderer	1580.351, 5660 v Piel ptc ms, n ms מְגַלֶּה־סּוֹד mᵉghalleh-sôd revealing a secret

548.255, 7593 cj, v Niphal ptc ms, n fs וְנֶאֱמַן־רוּחַ wᵉne'ĕman-rûach but one who is faithful of spirit	3803.351 v Piel ptc ms מְכַסֶּה mᵉkhasseh concealing	1745 n ms דָּבָר dhāvār a matter	**14.**	904, 375 prep, sub בְּאֵין bᵉ'ên without	8790 n fp תַּחְבֻּלוֹת tachbulôth guidance	5498.121, 6194 v Qal impf 3ms, n ms יִפָּל־עָם yippāl-'ām a people will fall

---

9. An hypocrite with his mouth destroyeth his neighbour: but through knowledge shall the just be delivered: ... With their mouths the godless would destroy their neighbors, *NRSV* ... A traitor wrecks his friend by his mouth, *Fenton* ... A godless man would ruin his neighbour with slander, *Moffatt* ... the upright are safeguarded, *JB* ... sagacity of good men will save them, *Anchor*.

10. When it goeth well with the righteous, the city rejoiceth: and when the wicked perish, there is shouting: ... When good people suc-ceed, the city is happy, *NCV* ... things go well for the upright man, all the town is glad, *BB* ... wicked are destroyed, there is singing, *KJVII* ... wicked are overthrown there is jubilation, *Anchor*.

11. By the blessing of the upright the city is exalted: but it is overthrown by the mouth of the wicked: ... city is raised on the blessing of the honest, *JB* ... city is advanced, *Berkeley* ... Good people bless and build up their city, *NCV* ... words of the wicked tear it down, *NEB* ... overthrown by the policy of knaves, *Moffatt*.

12. He that is void of wisdom despiseth his neighbour: ... who belittles his neighbor lacks sense, *RSV* ... who reviles his neighbor, *Douay* ... man who lacks judgment derides his neighbor, *NIV*.

but a man of understanding holdeth his peace: ... intelligent keeps a check on the tongue, *JB* ... farsighted man keeps his opinions to himself, *Anchor* ... observeth silence, *Rotherham*.

13. A talebearer revealeth secrets: but he that is of a faithful spirit

The different renderings of the second line—e.g., "the wicked" (NKJV, NRSV), "the strong men" (NASB), "all that he expected from his power" (NIV)—reflect different, but equally possible, interpretations of the noun. If it means power or might (cf. Job 18:7, 12; Hos. 12:4), then the proverb teaches that not even strength guarantees success, any more than the apparent success of the wicked. If, however, it means wealth (as in Job 20:10 and Hos 12:8), then financial security is also vain. The direct comparison is reinforced by the use of the same verb in both lines, which is concealed in some translations (e.g., NIV).

11:8. Earlier proverbs contrast the consequences of righteousness and wickedness (11:3, 5f, 27); this verse asserts that the trouble that the wise escape is inherited by the wicked (11:18f, 21; cf. 13:22). The wise understand that most choices have ramifications far beyond the immediate result, and so ponder each move carefully—the more momentous the choice, the more carefully it must be made. The foolish, on the other hand, act on the basis of their own wisdom, and so fall into problems that the wise avoid (14:16; 22:3; 27:12f).

11:9. As in the preceding verses, this proverb contrasts wisdom and folly by comparing the consequences of righteousness and godlessness (11:3, 5f, 8); it is closely linked to 11:8 by the repetition of "are delivered" (the only times that this verb occurs in Proverbs). Solomon explains that the righteous are delivered (11:8) because they have chosen to submit to and learn from wisdom (11:9).

The asymmetry between the deliverance of the righteous and the violence of the wicked may imply that the righteous may escape even when attacked, and so encourage diligence in the pursuit of knowledge. It also warns that the wicked may indeed prevail over others, but, as the preceding verse shows, any such success will be only temporary.

11:10. Closely related to several other proverbs on justice (28:12, 28; 29:2) and to the general theme of leadership (cf. 29:12, 14), this verse links the strength and glory of a nation or people to the character of its justice. The populace rejoices when the just prosper, because that shows that justice prevails. Their response to the conviction and eradication of the guilty is even stronger: they shout in triumph, as if over a vanquished foe. The people of any land know that if justice prevails, it will go well with them. As the standards of the Covenant are upheld, so goes the nation and everyone in it (Lev. 26; Deut. 28).

11:11. Like the previous verse, this proverb links the welfare of a people to their moral values. Words reveal the heart (cf. 11:12). A nation blessed by the presence of upright and just citizens will be honored, whereas the words and lives of wicked citizens eventuate in the nation's destruction. The first line may also mean that a city that blesses the upright—that pursues justice by exonerating the innocent—will be established (cf. 25:4f; 29:14). The point is then nearly the same as the preceding verse (and other verses cited there).

11:12. A primary mark of wisdom, according to Proverbs, is knowing when to be silent (cf. 17:27f; 26:4f). Verbally expressing a hypercritical opinion of someone else ("despising" them), as the contrast with silence implies, marks the fool. This is not, however, the only warning of the verse. Since the mouth reveals the state of the heart, it warns against looking down at others, even in silence. Audible silence is an external mark of wisdom, but it grows out of a self-disciplined inner life which rejects the simplistic approach which condemns others' thoughts, opinions and persons out of hand, without weighing their value.

Holding people in contempt reduces them from objects of potential compassion to those of scorn. The discernment that seeks to understand people and their situations realizes how difficult that knowledge is (cf. 14:10, 13) and also understands the discretion of silence.

11:13. It is foolish to trust or confide in people who reveal other people's secrets—they will continue to gossip and bear tales, because that is their pattern of life (cf. 20:19). Those who know far more than they tell, however, have demonstrated their trustworthiness—they understand that wisdom entails respect for confidences and conceal their knowledge. The first line of this proverb is nearly identical to 20:19a.

Like 20:19, this is next to a proverb that deals with the importance of obtaining advice when working toward a decision (11:13f; 20:18f). This juxtaposition warns that it is dangerous to seek personal advice or counsel from someone who is likely to reveal the situation to others.

11:14. The willingness to seek and accept advice demonstrates wisdom. Although too much advice or over-analysis can hinder the planning process, more advice is usually better than less. This is not just a truism, but a reminder that humility is a sign of wisdom and that the wise therefore seek advice from as wide a circle as is practical, including those who may not agree with them, or who are

15.

7737, 7778.221 n ms, v Niphal impf 3ms רַע־יֵרוֹעַ ra'-yērōa' disaster disaster will happen	3398.151 v Qal act ptc ms יוֹעֵץ yô'ēts counselors	904, 7524 prep, n ms בְּרֹב berōv in the abundance of	9009 cj, n fs וּתְשׁוּעָה ûtheshû'āh but salvation

1019.151 v Qal act ptc ms בּוֹטֵחַ bôṭēach being secure	8965.152 v Qal act ptc mp תֹקְעִים thōqe'îm striking a pledge	7983.151 cj, v Qal act ptc ms וְשֹׂנֵא wesōnē' but one who hates	2299 n ms זָר zār a foreigner	3706, 6386.111 cj, v Qal pf 3ms כִּי־עָרַב kî-'ārav because he has given security for

16.

8881.126, 6464 v Qal impf 3mp, n ms יִתְמְכוּ־עֹשֶׁר yithmekhû-'ōsher they will attain wealth	6422 cj, n mp וְעָרִיצִים we'ārîtsîm and tyrants	3638 n ms כָּבוֹד kāvôdh honor	8881.122 v Qal impf 3fs תִּתְמֹךְ tithmōkh she will attain	828, 2682 n fs, n ms אֵשֶׁת־חֵן 'ēsheth-chēn a woman of favor

17.

400 n ms אַכְזָרִי 'akhzārî a cruel man	8083 n ms, ps 3ms שְׁאֵרוֹ she'ērô his body	6138.151 cj, v Qal act ptc ms וְעֹכֵר we'ōkhēr but troubling	2721 n ms חָסֶד chāsedh kindness	382 n ms אִישׁ 'îsh a man of	5497 n fs, ps 3ms נַפְשׁוֹ naphshô his soul	1621.151 v Qal act ptc ms גֹּמֵל gōmēl benefiting

18.

7966 n ms שֶׂכֶר sekher a wage of	6930 n fs צְדָקָה tsedhāqāh righteousness	2319.151 cj, v Qal act ptc ms וְזֹרֵעַ wezōrēa' but one who sows	6715, 8632 n fs, n ms פְּעֻלַּת־שָׁקֶר phe'ullath-shāqer a wage of deceit	6449.151 v Qal act ptc ms עֹשֶׂה 'ōseh making	7857 n ms רָשָׁע rāshā' the wicked

19.

3937, 4323 prep, n ms, ps 3ms לְמוֹתוֹ lemôthô to his death	7750 n fs רָעָה rā'āh evil	7579.351 cj, v Piel ptc ms וּמְרַדֵּף ûmeraddēph so one who pursues	3937, 2522 prep, n mp לְחַיִּים lechayyîm to life	3772, 6930 adv, n fs כֵּן־צְדָקָה kēn-tsedhāqāh as righteousness	583 n fs אֱמֶת 'ēmeth truth

20.

1932 n ms דָּרֶךְ dhārekh way	8879 n mp תְּמִימֵי temîmê the blameless of	7814 cj, n ms, ps 3ms וּרְצוֹנוֹ ûretsônô but his delight	6379, 3949 n mp, n ms עִקְּשֵׁי־לֵב 'iqqeshê-lēv those perverse of heart	3176 pn יְהוָה yehwāh Yahweh	8774 n fs תּוֹעֲבַת tô'ăvath an abomination to

concealeth the matter: ... He who is a habitual talebearer betrays confidence, *Berkeley* ... Who bears ill tales, keeps no secrets, *Knox* ... true-hearted man keeps things covered, *BB* ... keeps the matter hidden, *KJVII*.

14. Where no counsel is, the people fall: ... For want of skilful strategy an army is lost, *NEB* ... For want of leadership a people perishes, *JB* ... Where no wise guidance is, *MRB*.

but in the multitude of counsellors there is safety: ... in an abundance of, *RSV* ... deliverance is in a multitude, *Young* ... safety reigns where counsel abounds, *Knox*.

15. He that is surety for a stranger shall smart for it: ... A man who guarantees a stranger's loan will get into real trouble, *Beck* ... He is in a bad way who becomes surety for another, *NAB* ... Give a pledge for a stranger and know no peace, *NEB*.

and he that hateth suretyship is sure: ... whoever refuses to strike hands in pledge is safe, *NIV* ... To be free from anxiety one should avoid rash bargains, *Anchor* ... It is safer to avoid such promises, *NCV*.

16. A gracious woman retaineth honour: and strong men retain riches: ... wins respect, *Goodspeed* ... kind woman gets respect, *NCV* ... aggressive gain riches, *NRSV* ... ruthless men retain riches, *NKJV* ... the diligent shall obtain wealth, *Rotherham*.

17. The merciful man doeth good to his own soul: but he that is cruel troubleth his own flesh: ... A man who is kind benefits himself, *RSV* ...

kindly man is the friend of his own well-being, *Knox* ... trouble maker hurts himself, *Beck* ... torments himself, *Fenton.*

18. The wicked worketh a deceitful work: but to him that soweth righteousness shall be a sure reward: ... wicked man earns illusive wages, *Goodspeed* ... lawless man earneth the wages of falsehood, *Rotherham* ... makes empty profits, *NAB* ... whoever sows uprightness reaps a solid reward, *JB* ... goodness yields a lasting profit, *Moffatt.*

19. As righteousness tendeth to life: so he that pursueth evil pursueth it to his own death: ... He who is steadfast in righteousness will live, *RSV* ... Virtue directs toward life, *Douay* ... Whoever establishes uprightness is on the way to life, *JB.*

"inferior" to them (cf. Ecc. 9:13ff). Each person has a different perspective, so the truth, and therefore the best course of action, often lies between many different suggestions (cf. 15:22; 20:18; 24:5f; the second half of this verse is identical to 24:6b).

11:15. Solomon consistently warns against the destructive folly of co-signing loans (cf. 6:1–5; 17:18; 20:16). Anyone who makes a practice of it will eventually co-sign a bad loan, and have to pay the debt himself. There are very few things more certain in Proverbs than the disaster that follows foolish behavior. The causal relationship is much stronger in the original text: "He will suffer harm *because* he pledged himself for another."

Those who avoid this practice live without the fear that their property or persons will be seized in payment of someone else's debt. Solomon does not intend to imply that avoiding co-signing loans is the way to a peaceful life. Co-signing, on the other hand, is sure to bring trouble.

Although there is no biblical record of co-signing leading to such disaster, Eliphaz accused Job of using pledges to oppress others (Job 22:6–9). Failure to pay a loan could result in literal bondage, as the covenantal laws of redemption show (Lev. 25:47–55). Nehemiah (more than five centuries after Solomon) was approached by those who had mortgaged their fields, vineyards and houses. Having lost their real estate to pay their debts, they were allowing their children to be enslaved in order to raise the money (Neh. 5:1–5).

11:16. Two basic interpretations to this verse are possible. First, the proverb may advise young men about the kind of wife that they should seek (cf. 12:4; 14:1; 19:13f; 21:9; 25:24; 27:15). However, because other verses warn against choosing a wife simply because she seems "gracious" (11:22; 31:30), a second interpretation is necessary. Secondly, therefore, if "honor" is better than wealth, then the verse contrasts the honor that comes to a gracious woman with the mere wealth gained by violence and commends gracious speech and habits rather than force (cf. 25:15).

11:17. A person's behavior affects others (cf. 10:11) as well as himself (on nephesh [HED #5497] as "self," see "Overview"; the parallelism shows that "flesh" has the same connotation here). Cruelty, like all expressions of wickedness, ultimately harms those who are cruel (cf. 1:18f; 26:26f). The parallelism also suggests that cruelty and faithfulness are incompatible. The wise thus know better than to expect or seek trustworthy friends among the cruel. These three verses (11:17ff) all describe how a person's behavior directly brings consequences according to his actions (cf. also 11:3, 6ff).

11:18. Wickedness is often an object of envy, especially when it prospers (3:31; 23:17f; 24:1f, 19f), whereas those who pursue righteousness in their lives may not appear successful (cf. 19:1, 22). The former see only what their own strength can gain and, being the source of their own "wisdom," pursue their ends without regard for either the standards of the Covenant or the consequences of their behavior. The contrast between "earning" and "sowing" also reflects the difference between the self-centered impatience of the wicked and those who diligently pursue righteousness and wait upon the LORD for the harvest (cf. Pss. 37; 73).

11:19. Closely related to the preceding verse, this proverb describes the long-term consequences of choices. At the heart of Proverbs lies the contrast between death and life, opposed fates which are determined by the response to wisdom (cf. 1:32f; 2:19–22; 8:35f). Just as the pattern of a person's life is created by his choices, those choices are based on, and reflect, that prior response. The contrast between the adjective and participle also suggests the difference between the firm and secure and the activity ("those who pursue") of those whose only concern is their own desire(s). The adjective kēn (HED #3772) may be either substantive, "one who is upright [in] righteousness," or adjectival, "true righteousness." The force is the same.

11:20. The contrast between men and women of integrity and the deceitful is not merely one of appearances. The difference between them is far more seri-

21.

3135	3937, 3135	3940, 5536.221	7737	2320
n fs	prep, n fs	neg part, v Niphal impf 3ms	n ms	cj, n ms
יָד	לְיָד	לֹא־יִנָּקֶה	רָע	וְזֶרַע
yādh	leyādh	lō'-yinnāqeh	rā'	wezera'
a hand	to a hand	he will not go unpunished	an evil person	but the descendant of

22.

6926	4561.211		5321	2174	904, 653	2478	828
n mp	v Niphal pf 3ms		n ms	n ms	prep, n ms	n ms	n fs
צַדִּיקִים	נִמְלָט		נֶזֶם	זָהָב	בְּאַף	חֲזִיר	אִשָּׁה
tsaddîqim	nimlāt		nezem	zāhāv	be'aph	chāzîr	'ishshāh
the righteous	he will be delivered		a ring of	gold	in the nose of	a wild boar	a woman

23.

3413	5681.153	3051		8707	6926	395, 3005
adj	cj, v Qal act ptc fs	n ms		n fs	n mp	adv, adj
יָפָה	וְסָרַת	טַעַם		תַּאֲוַת	צַדִּיקִים	אַךְ־טוֹב
yāphāh	wesārath	tā'am		ta'ăwath	tsaddîqim	'akh-ṭov
beautiful	yet a woman departing from	discretion		the longing of	the righteous	only good

24.

8951	7857	5887		3552	6582.351	3362.255
n fs	n mp	n fs		sub	v Piel ptc ms	cj, v Niphal ptc ms
תִּקְוַת	רְשָׁעִים	עֶבְרָה		יֵשׁ	מְפַזֵּר	וְנוֹסָף
tiqōwath	reshā'îm	'evrāh		yēsh	mephazzēr	wenôsāph
the expectation of	the wicked	wrath		there is	one who scatters freely	but being increased

25.

5968	2910.151	4623, 3598	395, 3937, 4408		5497, 1318
adv	v Qal act ptc ms	prep, n ms	adv, prep, n ms		n fs, n fs
עוֹד	וְחוֹשֵׂךְ	מִיֹּשֶׁר	אַךְ־לְמַחְסוֹר		נֶפֶשׁ־בְּרָכָה
'ôdh	wechôsēkh	mîyosher	'akh-lemachsôr		nephesh-berākhāh
yet	but one who holds back	more than what is upright	only to poverty		a person of blessing

26.

1941.421	7588.551	1612, 2000	7588.621		4661.151
v Pual impf 3ms	cj, v Hiphil ptc ms	cj, pers pron	v Hophal impf 3ms		v Qal act ptc ms
תְּדֻשָּׁן	וּמַרְוֶה	גַּם־הוּא	יוֹרָא		מֹנֵעַ
thedhushshān	ûmarweh	gam-hû'	yôre'		mōnēa'
he will be made fat	and one who waters	he also	he will be watered		one who withholds

1277	7181.126	3947	1318	3937, 7513	8132.551
n ms	v Qal impf 3mp, ps 3ms	n ms	cj, n fs	prep, n ms	v Hiphil ptc ms
בָּר	יִקְּבֻהוּ	לְאֹם	וּבְרָכָה	לְרֹאשׁ	מַשְׁבִּיר
bār	yiqqevuhû	le'ôm	ûverākhāh	lerō'sh	mashbîr
grain	they will curse him	people	but a blessing	for the head of	one who sells grain

20. They that are of a froward heart are abomination to the LORD: ... LORD hates those with evil hearts, *NCV* ... LORD detests the crooked heart, *NEB* ... who are evil-minded, *Berkeley* ... Crooked minds are an abomination, *NRSV*.

but such as are upright in their way are his delight: ... honesty wins his favour, *REB* ... those who are whole-hearted in their ways, *Berkeley*.

21. Though hand join in hand, the wicked shall not be unpunished: ... wicked man shall not be held inno-cent, *Rotherham* ... evil man shall not go free, *Anchor* ... wicked is not acquitted, *Young*.

but the seed of the righteous shall be delivered: ... righteous and all their offspring will go free, *REB* ... race of the righteous will escape, *Goodspeed* ... race of the upright will come to no harm, *JB*.

22. As a jewel of gold in a swine's snout, so is a fair woman which is without discretion: ... A beautiful woman without good sense is like a gold ring in a pig's snout, *NCV* ... who perversely turns aside from good, *KJVII* ... with a rebellious disposition, *NAB*.

23. The desire of the righteous is only good: but the expectation of the wicked is wrath: ... hope of the wicked brings about fury, *Beck* ... wrath is waiting for the evil-doer, *BB* ... expectation ... is retribution, *JB*.

24. There is that scattereth, and yet increaseth: ... Some give freely, yet grow all the richer, *NRSV* ... One scatters money around, yet only adds to his wealth, *JB*.

and there is that withholdeth more than is meet, but it tendeth to poverty: ... another withholds what he should give, and only suffers want, *RSV* ... another is excessively mean, but only grows the poorer, *JB*.

25. The liberal soul shall be made fat: and he that watereth shall be

watered also himself: ... The generous man will be enriched, *Goodspeed* ... Be generous to others and you'll grow prosperous; refresh others and you'll be refreshed, *Beck*.

26. He that withholdeth corn, the people shall curse him: ... who

hoards grain, *NIV* ... Him who monopolizes grain, *NAB*.

but blessing shall be upon the head of him that selleth it: ... who sells it earns their blessing, *REB* ... blessings upon the head of him who distributes it, *NAB*.

---

ous, since their external choices reveal whether their hearts are aligned with God's purposes and standards. This in turn leads to divine approbation or condemnation. An "abomination" is an object of loathing, whether divine (as here) or human (cf. 29:27).

11:21. Although originally separate from the preceding verse, this proverb shows the outcome of the choices made by the deceitful and honest described in 11:20 ("deceitful" and "just" are subtypes of "wicked" and "righteous"). The origin of the idiom "hand for [to] hand" is lost to us, but in its only other occurrence it also precedes the phrase "will not be free [exempt]" (Prov. 16:5). In both cases, it follows the phrase "abomination to the LORD"—here in the preceding verse, in 16:5 in the first line of the proverb. (This is not the expression "hand for hand" that is found in the covenantal *lex talionis* [e.g., Exo. 21:23ff].)

11:22. A piece of jewelry (a nose ring), no matter how precious its substance, cannot change the nature of its wearer. Beauty is no substitute for wisdom, especially when it conceals a rebellious heart (11:22b says that she "turns aside [from] discretion" [lit., "taste"]). Since people can, and do, manipulate their appearance for their own purposes, appearances often deceive. Those who reject instruction, correction and discipline are fit to be neither life partners (cf. 12:4; 14:1) nor companions, and should be avoided (cf. 14:7; 19:19; 22:24). To the Israelites, pigs represented the utmost in disgusting creatures—even to touch a pig made a person unclean (Lev. 11:7f). To modern readers, a metaphor comparing a fair woman without discretion to a cockroach or tapeworm might produce the same shock value the original metaphor did for the Israelites.

Since the heart determines the direction of a person's life (4:23), what is unseen is always more important than what is seen (cf. 1 Sam. 16:7). This proverb encourages the wise to choose companions based on their words and lives, not on their appearance.

11:23. Since the righteous desire what is good, their hopes and plans do not lead to wrath—whether

it is their own reaction (19:3), the response of others (14:17) or the opposition and judgment of God (15:9). Since the plans of the wicked are themselves evil, their best hopes are certain to arouse anger, condemnation and judgment (cf. 11:27). This common proverbial theme—that reaping follows sowing (cf. 12:13f)—reiterates the covenantal themes of blessing and cursing (Lev. 26; Deut. 28), even though this verse may refer primarily to the human response. That which characterizes a person determines the result of his planning so that the wise seek righteousness, submitting their plans and desires to the LORD (16:1ff).

11:24. A good example of a topical cluster, Prov. 11:24ff address generosity (cf. 14:31; 21:13; 22:9; 31:20). These verses are arranged to contrast the effects of generosity and miserliness, while emphasizing the benefits of generosity, which are both divine (vv. 24a, 25) and human (v. 26b):

A	generosity blessed (v. 24a)
B	miserliness cursed (v. 24b)
A'	generosity blessed (v. 25)
B'	miserliness cursed (v. 26a)
A"	generosity blessed (v. 26b)

As Solomon warns in the introduction (cf, 3:5f), many proverbs contradict human expectations. Proverbs 11:24 is a good example of this principle, echoing the gospel statement that "whoever will save his life shall lose it: and whoever will lose his life for [Christ's] sake shall find it" (Matt. 16:25). Generosity to the poor grows out of faith in God, since it honors the LORD (Prov. 14:31; 19:17). Other proverbs (e.g., 22:16; 23:4f; 28:27) also warn of (or promise) the same consequence.

11:25. Being fat was a sign of the LORD's blessing, and this was promised to the generous, the diligent (13:4) and the trusting (28:25). The gift blesses both the giver and the receiver so that this verse parallels the first line of the preceding verse, reiterating the principle of sowing and reaping (cf. Gal. 6:7).

27.

8264.151	3005	1272.321	7814	1938.151	7750	971.122
v Qal act ptc ms	adj	v Piel impf 3ms	n ms	cj, v Qal act ptc ms	n fs	v Qal impf 3fs, ps 3ms
שֹׁחֵר	טוֹב	יְבַקֵּשׁ	רָצוֹן	וְדֹרֵשׁ	רָעָה	תְבוֹאֶנּוּ
shōchēr	tôv	yevaqqēsh	rātsôn	wedhōrēsh	rā'āh	thevô'ennû
one who seeks	good	he searches for	favor	but one who seeks	evil	it will come to him

28.

1019.151	904, 6484	2000	5489.121	3626, 6149	6926
v Qal act ptc ms	prep, n ms ps 3ms	pers pron	v Qal impf 3ms	cj, prep, n ms	n mp
בֹּטֵחַ	בְּעָשְׁרוֹ	הוּא	יִפֹּל	וְכֶעָלֶה	צַדִּיקִים
bōṭēach	be'āsherô	hû'	yippōl	wekhe'āleh	tsaddîqîm
one who trusts	in his riches	he	he will fall	but like a leaf	the righteous

29.

6775.126	6138.151	1041	5336.121, 7593	5860
v Qal impf 3mp	v Qal act ptc ms	n ms, ps 3ms	v Qal impf 3ms, n fs	cj, n ms
יִפְרָחוּ	עוֹכֵר	בֵּיתוֹ	יִנְחַל־רוּחַ	וְעֶבֶד
yiphrāchû	'ôkhēr	bêthô	yinchal-rûach	we'evedh
they will flourish	one who troubles	his household	he will inherit the wind	and a servant

30.

188	3937, 2550, 3949	6780, 6926	6320	2522	4089.151
n ms	prep, art, n ms, n ms	n ms, n ms	n ms	n mp	cj, v Qal act ptc ms
אֱוִיל	לַחֲכַם־לֵב	פְּרִי־צַדִּיק	עֵץ	חַיִּים	וְלֹקֵחַ
'ĕwîl	lachăkham-lēv	peri-tsaddîq	'ēts	chayyîm	welōqēach
a fool	to the wise of heart	the fruit of the righteous	a tree of	life	and one who receives

31.

5497	2550	2075	6926	904, 800	8396.421	652
n fp	adj	intrj	n ms	prep, art, n fs	v Pual impf 3ms	cj
נְפָשׁוֹת	חָכָם	הֵן	צַדִּיק	בָּאָרֶץ	יְשֻׁלָּם	אַף
nephāsôth	chākhām	hēn	tsaddîq	bā'ārets	yeshullām	'aph
lives	wise	behold	the righteous	on the earth	he will be recompensed	surely

12:1

3706, 7857	2490.151	154.151	4284	154.151	1907
cj, n ms	cj, v Qal act ptc ms	v Qal act ptc ms	n ms	v Qal act ptc ms	n fs
כִּי־רָשָׁע	וְחוֹטֵא	אֹהֵב	מוּסָר	אֹהֵב	דָּעַת
kî-rāshā'	wechôṭē'	'ōhēv	mûsār	'ōhēv	dā'ath
indeed the wicked	and a sinner	one who loves	discipline	one who loves	knowledge

2.

7983.151	8763	1221	3005	6572.521	7814	4623, 3176
cj, v Qal act ptc ms	n fs	adj	n ms	v Hiphil impf 3ms	n ms	prep, pn
וְשֹׂנֵא	תּוֹכַחַת	בָּעַר	טוֹב	יָפִיק	רָצוֹן	מֵיְהוָה
wesōnē'	thôkhachath	bā'ar	ṭôv	yāphîq	rātsôn	mêyehwāh
but one who hates	correction	stupid	a good man	he will obtain	favor	from Yahweh

---

27. He that diligently seeketh good procureth favour: ... He who, with all his heart, goes after what is good is searching for grace, *BB* ... He whose aims are good wins the goodwill of God, *Moffatt* ... Plan thou good, thou canst not be afoot too early, *Knox*.

but he that seeketh mischief, it shall come unto him: ... it shall recoil, *Knox* ... he whose aims are evil, evil shall befall him, *Moffatt* ... but he who is looking for trouble will get it, *BB*.

28. He that trusteth in his riches shall fall: but the righteous shall flourish as a branch: ... Trust in your money and down you go! Trust in God and flourish as a tree!, *LIVB* ... the righteous will flourish like the green leaf, *NASB* ... A man who trusts in his riches withers While good men burgeon like green leaves, *Anchor*.

29. He that troubleth his own house shall inherit the wind: ... The man who brings trouble on his family will have nothing at the end, *Good News* ... will be left with nothing but the wind, *NCV*.

and the fool shall be servant to the wise of heart: ... fool becomes slave to a wise man, *NEB*.

30. The fruit of the righteous is a tree of life; and he that winneth souls is wise: ... and a wise man wins friends, *Berkeley* ... whoso is taking souls is wise, *Young*.

31. Behold, the righteous shall be recompensed in the earth: much more the wicked and the sinner: ... If a righteous person is paid back, *Beck* ... shall be rewarded, *KJVII* ... shall be requited, *MAST*.

12:1. Whoso loveth instruction loveth knowledge: … A lover of training, *BB* … Whoever loves discipline, *JB, NRSV* … Anyone who loves learning accepts correction, *NCV.*

but he that hateth reproof is brutish: … is stupid, *RSV* … a hater of teaching is like a beast, *BB* … who hates correction is stupid, *NIV* … who hates reproof is like a cow, *Berkeley.*

2. A good man obtaineth favour of the LORD: … The honest obtains Yahweh's favour, *JB* … good man has grace in the eyes of, *BB.*

but a man of wicked devices will he condemn: … will punish the

---

The image of watering may even reflect the covenantal imagery of Ps. 65:10, which uses this language of rain upon the fields in reference to the blessings of the Covenant (Deut. 28:12). Whoever is generous to the poor (who cannot "water" anyone) will be watered by the One Who is most generous, and Who waters, or withholds water from, all (cf. Matt. 5:45). The basic issue, applied here to property, is thus whether someone will trust the principles of God or those of "common sense."

11:26. Like 11:24, this verse contrasts the effects of generosity and parsimony, this time from the perspective of the needy, whose lives are directly affected by the response to their situation. Respect and affection naturally flow to those who do what they can to address the needs of their fellow human beings, whereas greed is reviled. This also expresses a fundamental value of the Covenant (cf. Deut. 15:7–11), which warns that the LORD judges the response to the situations of others (cf. Prov. 23:10ff; 24:11f).

11:27. One who diligently seeks the good of others will find himself blessed with favor (cf. 16:13). Since this fulfills the second great commandment (Lev. 19:18; Matt. 22:39), such a person is also blessed by the favor of God. The second line could refer either to those who seek wicked deeds in order to participate in them or to those who work to bring trouble and disaster into the lives of others. In either case, what they seek will come upon them (1:18f; 26:27).

11:28. The object of trust determines a person's fate (cf. 11:4). The righteous—those who trust the LORD, not their circumstances (11:28b; cf. 10:2b)—are delivered by the object of their trust. Those who count on material possessions will come to realize that these things cannot provide ultimate security. The parallelism does not contrast righteousness with wealth, but with *trusting* wealth, nor does it suggest that the righteous will be wealthy, merely that they will be fruitful.

Although these verses (11:4, 28) do not condemn wealth outright, the contrast of wealth with righteousness hints at the difficulty of resisting the

temptation proffered by wealth—to gain it immorally (1:11ff) and, when it is the reward of diligence (10:4), to trust the gift rather than the Giver (cf. Deut. 6:10ff; 8:10–14).

11:29. Sin affects more than the sinner. If the gain is illicit (cf. 15:27, which begins with the same two words), it will ultimately destroy the wicked and those around them. But the verse may simply describe those whose foolish decisions ruin their property (cf. 14:1), enslaving them to those who are wise and manage their households well (cf. 17:2; 31:10–31).

11:30. "Fruit" is a metonymy for what characterizes everything that results from the words and lives of the righteous, in both their own lives and the lives of those who are affected by them. The verb translated "wins" (HED #4089; NASB, NKJV, NIV) can also mean "lead" (cf. Gen. 48:1; Exo. 12:32; 14:6f), even in the sense of a rescue (Prov. 24:11). The verse probably describes the value of good teachers so that students will search for and learn from them (they can be recognized by their words; cf. 10:11a).

11:31. If the phrase "on earth" is interpreted as describing the righteous who are "in the land," this verse warns the wicked that the suffering of the innocent (as the word translated "righteous" [HED #6926] often means in Proverbs) is a signal that their own fate will be much worse. Conversely, the proverb could also mean that covenant-breakers should infer their own condemnation when the righteous are blessed (i.e., rewarded for their righteousness). The verb means simply to "be [re]paid" (NRSV) or to be "rewarded" (NASB); the contrast between the types of people gives it the flavor of judgment (as 1 Pet. 4:18, quoting the Septuagint—"If the righteous scarcely be saved"—also interprets it).

This verse thus caps the many proverbs in this chapter that describe the consequences of wisdom and folly under the rubrics of the wicked and righteous (11:3, 6ff, 17ff, 29).

12:1. A necessary condition of learning is having a teachable spirit—the desire to learn. Those who love knowledge are willing, even eager, to be corrected, since they know that learning has at least

382 cj, *n ms* וְאִישׁ wᵉ'îsh but a man of	4343 n fp מְזִמּוֹת mᵉzimmôth evil schemes	7855.521 v Hiphil impf 3ms יַרְשִׁיעַ yarshîa' He will condemn	**3.**	3940, 3679.221 neg part, v Niphal impf 3ms לֹא־יִכּוֹן lō'-yikkôn he will not be established	119 n ms אָדָם 'ādhām a man	904, 7856 prep, n ms בְּרֶשַׁע bᵉresha' by wickedness
8659 cj, *n ms* וְשֹׁרֶשׁ wᵉshōresh and the root of	6926 n mp צַדִּיקִים tsaddîqîm the righteous	1118, 4267.221 neg part, v Niphal impf 3ms בַּל־יִמּוֹט bal-yimmôt it will not be moved	**4.**	828, 2524 *n fs* אֵשֶׁת־חַיִל 'ēsheth-chayil a wife of valor	6065 *n fs* עֲטֶרֶת 'ătereth the crown of	1197 n ms, ps 3fs בַּעְלָהּ ba'ălāhh her husband
3626, 8731 cj, prep, n ms וּכְרָקָב ûkhᵉrāqāv but like rot	904, 6344 prep, n fp, ps 3ms בְּעַצְמוֹתָיו bᵉ'atsmôthâv in his bones	991.553 v Hiphil ptc fs מְבִישָׁה mᵉvîshāh one who brings shame	**5.**	4422 *n fp* מַחְשְׁבוֹת machshᵉvôth the plans of	6926 n mp צַדִּיקִים tsaddîqîm the righteous	5122 n ms מִשְׁפָּט mishpāt justice
8790 *n fp* תַּחְבֻּלוֹת tachbulôth the guidance of	7857 n mp רְשָׁעִים rᵉshā'îm the wicked	4983 n fs מִרְמָה mirmāh deceit	**6.**	1745 *n mp* דִּבְרֵי divrê the words of	7857 n mp רְשָׁעִים rᵉshā'îm the wicked	718.141, 1879 v Qal inf con, n ms אֱרָב־דָּם 'ĕrāv-dām lying in wait for blood
6552 cj, *n ms* וּפִי ûphî but the mouth of	3596 n mp יְשָׁרִים yᵉshārîm the upright	5522.521 v Hiphil impf 3ms, ps 3mp יַצִּילֵם yatstsîlēm it will deliver them	**7.**	2089.142 v Qal inf abs הָפוֹךְ hāphôkh being overthrown		7857 n mp רְשָׁעִים rᵉshā'îm the wicked
375 cj, *sub*, ps 3mp וְאֵינָם wᵉ'ênām and they are no more		1041 cj, *n ms* וּבֵית ûvêth but the household of	6926 n mp צַדִּיקִים tsaddîqîm the righteous		6198.121 v Qal impf 3ms יַעֲמֹד ya'ămōdh it will stand
8.	3937, 6552, 7961 prep, *n ms*, n ms, ps 3ms לְפִי־שִׂכְלוֹ lᵉphî-sikhlô at the mouth of his insight		2054.421, 382 v Pual impf 3ms, n ms יְהֻלַּל־אִישׁ yᵉhullal-'îsh a man will be praised	5971.255, 3949 cj, v Niphal ptc ms, n ms וְנַעֲוֵה־לֵב wᵉna'ăwēh-lēv but one who is perverse of heart	2030.121 v Qal impf 3ms יִהְיֶה yihyeh he will be

mischievous man, *Fenton* … the schemer is condemned, *NAB* … condemns a malicious schemer, *Beck.*

3. A man shall not be established by wickedness: … No man can hold his own by doing wrong, *Moffatt* … Doing evil brings no safety at all, *NCV* … man can't stand firm on a wicked basis, *Beck* … A man cannot build upon wrong, *Fenton.*

but the root of the righteous shall not be moved: … But the foot of the good has a sure base, *Fenton* … good

men have roots that cannot be dislodged, *NEB.*

4. A virtuous woman is a crown to her husband: … A good wife, *RSV* … A wife of noble character, *NIV* … A worthy woman is the crown of, *ASV.*

but she that maketh ashamed is as rottenness in his bones: … corruption in his bones, *Geneva* … is like a wasting disease, *BB* … a veritable decay, *Rotherham* … shameless wife rots all his strength away, *Moffatt* … But the vicious, a rot in his bones, *Fenton.*

5. The thoughts of the righteous are right: but the counsels of the wicked are deceit: … purposes of the righteous are just, *REB* … plans of the just are legitimate, *NAB* … plans of the righteous are honest; The designs of the wicked are treacherous, *Goodspeed.*

6. The words of the wicked are to lie in wait for blood: but the mouth of the upright shall deliver them: … brings about bloodshed, *Beck* … wicked talk about killing people, *NCV* … lay a fatal snare, *Knox* … words … are a deadly ambush, but the speech of the upright, *NRSV*.

Fenton ... line of the righteous continues, *REB* ... good person's family continues, *NCV*.

wisdom of the wise wins praise, *NCV*.

7. The wicked are overthrown, and are not: but the house of the righteous shall stand: ... Evil-doers are overturned and never seen again, *BB* ... The wicked fall, and vanish,

8. A man shall be commended according to his wisdom: ... person is praised for prudence, *JB* ... according to his good sense, *RSV* ...

but he that is of a perverse heart shall be despised: ... he who is of a crooked heart, *KJVII* ... brainless creature, *Moffatt* ... wrong-minded man will be looked down on, *BB* ...

---

two aspects: gaining new material and having wrong information, interpretations or practices corrected. Whoever despises correction, however, is little better than a brute, since their attitude renders them unwilling and unable to learn. It also makes them vulnerable, since they cannot benefit from the wisdom of others (cf. 1:25, 30; 13:18).

This verse is closely related to the many proverbs dealing with arrogance (cf. 15:32f; 16:18f; 18:12), since those verses imply or explicitly equate pride with unwillingness to receive instruction or correction.

12:2. "Good" (HED #3005) here is not abstract, nor is it a static quality, but is someone who plans to do good, or to act well, as its contrast with "a man who devises evil" shows. The second verb (HED #7855) can mean either "to condemn as guilty" (NASB, NRSV, NKJV, NIV; cf. 17:15) or "to act wickedly" (cf. Neh. 9:33; Job 34:12; Dan 9:5; 12:10), and the verse may be intentionally ambiguous. If it is the former, then the verse warns that judgment is coming. If the latter, then it suggests that a life of plotting increases in wickedness and promotes sin in others. Their lives—again, by the poetic contrast—come under increasing condemnation.

This verse and the next were undoubtedly separate sayings, but are closely linked; v. 2 explains the righteous' and the wicked's contrasting fates on the basis of divine activity, and v. 3 contrasts the two from a human perspective.

12:3. Although sin may seem to pay quite well, as the warnings against envying the wicked imply (e.g., 23:17f; 24:1f, 19f; cf. Pss. 37; 73), it does not provide a firm foundation for life. A righteous life, which grows out of a heart of wisdom, has a permanent and secure foundation. The phrase "it shall not be moved" (bal [HED #1118] with the Niphal of môṭ [HED #4267]) usually describes the permanence of something, a stability that is the result of a deliberate work of creation or preservation (10:30; cf. 12:12; see also Pss. 16:8; 17:5; 30:6; 121:3).

12:4. Not only are the "excellent" respected, their honor also reflects upon their spouses. The

crown is a highly visible sign of honor, unlike the emotional distress caused by a shameful (rather than merely embarassing) husband or wife. Solomon's physiology is impeccable; as modern medicine has discovered, emotions are an important factor in physical health. The contrasting effects of one spouse upon the other highlight the importance of choosing wisely (cf. 11:22; 18:22; 19:14).

12:5. This proverb reveals the close relationship between a person's thoughts and words (cf. 10:20; 12:6). The thoughts and plans of the righteous are just, so that their advice is trustworthy, whereas the wicked counsel only what is in their own best interest. Advice is only as good as its source, which must be evaluated before acting on counsel. Further, since the state of the heart determines the quality of counsel, the proverb encourages regular self-examination.

12:6. As in the previous verse, the wicked offer counsel that serves their own ends, careless of its effects on others (cf. 26:23–28; 29:5). The righteous, however, who follow wisdom's counsel, act in a way that frees them from the snares of the wicked (cf. 12:12; 14:16; 22:3). Furthermore, they cannot be trapped or harmed by their words, since they say only what is right.

12:7. Like many of the preceding verses, this proverb warns that the consequences of wickedness and righteousness are diametrically opposed (cf. 11:3–6, 8, 18f, 21, 23, 27f, 31; 12:2f). In this case, the wicked are overthrown (NASB, *et al.*) or "overturned," so that they become like nothing (lit., "they are not"). The household (or dynasty) of the righteous, in contrast, is enduring, since it is built on a firm foundation.

All of the proverbs on this topic imply a judgment that overtakes everyone, and that is based on internal character, not external accomplishments or "worth." They thus encourage the student to live so that he or she will stand in that day.

12:8. People who offer suggestions, advice and counsel are honored or praised according to its value, since it reveals the depth of their understand-

9.

3937, 973	3005	7319.255	5860	3937
prep, n ms	adj	v Niphal ptc ms	cj, n ms	prep, ps 3ms
לָבוּז	טוֹב	נִקְלֶה	וְעֶבֶד	לוֹ
lāvûz	ṭôv	niqǒleh	weʿevedh	lô
for contempt	better	one who is lightly esteemed	and a servant	to him

10.

4623, 3632.751	2742, 4035	3156.151	6926	5497
prep, v Hithpael ptc ms	cj, adj, n ms	v Qal act ptc ms	n ms	n fs
מִמְּתַכַּבֵּד	וַחֲסַר־לָחֶם	יוֹדֵעַ	צַדִּיק	נֶפֶשׁ
mimmethakkabbēdh	wachăsar-lāchem	yôdhēaʿ	tsaddîq	nephesh
than one who honors himself	but lacking bread	regarding	the righteous	the life of

11.

966	7641	7857	400	5856.151	124
n fs, ps 3ms	cj, n mp	n mp	adj	v Qal act ptc ms	n fs, ps 3ms
בְּהֶמְתּוֹ	וְרַחֲמֵי	רְשָׁעִים	אַכְזָרִי	עֹבֵד	אַדְמָתוֹ
behemtô	werachămê	reshāʿîm	'akhzārî	ʿōvēdh	'adhmāthô
his animal	but the compassion of	the wicked	cruel	one who cultivates	his soil

7881.121, 4035	7579.351	7673	2742, 3949
v Qal impf 3ms, n ms	cj, v Piel ptc ms	n mp	adj, n ms
יִשְׂבַּע־לָחֶם	וּמְרַדֵּף	רֵיקִים	חֲסַר־לֵב
yisbaʿ-lāchem	ûmeraddēph	rêqîm	chăsar-lēv
he will have plenty of bread	but one who pursues	worthless things	lacking in heart

12.

2629.111	7857	4847	7737	8659	6926	5598.121
v Qal pf 3ms	n ms	n ms	adj	cj, n ms	n mp	v Qal impf 3ms
חָמַד	רָשָׁע	מְצוֹד	רָעִים	וְשֹׁרֶשׁ	צַדִּיקִים	יִתֵּן
chāmadh	rāshāʿ	metsôdh	rāʿîm	weshōresh	tsaddîqîm	yittēn
he desires	the wicked	a net of	evil	but the root of	the righteous	it will yield

13.

904, 6840	8004	4305	7737	3428.121	4623, 7150	6926
prep, n ms	n fd	n ms	n ms	cj, v Qal impf 3ms	prep, n fs	n ms
בְּפֶשַׁע	שְׂפָתַיִם	מוֹקֵשׁ	רַע	וַיֵּצֵא	מִצָּרָה	צַדִּיק
bepheshaʿ	sephāthayim	môqēsh	rāʿ	wayyētsēʾ	mitstsārāh	tsaddîq
in transgression of	lips	the snare of	evil	but he gets out	of adversity	the righteous

14.

4623, 6780	6552, 382	7881.121, 3005	1618
prep, n ms	n ms, n ms	v Qal impf 3ms, n ms	cj, n ms
מִפְּרִי	פִי־אִישׁ	יִשְׂבַּע־טוֹב	וּגְמוּל
mippʿrî	phî-'îsh	yisbaʿ-ṭôv	ûghemûl
from the fruit of	the mouth of a man	he will be satisfied with good	and the work of

shall be an object of contempt, *Rotherham*.

9. He that is despised, and hath a servant: ... Better to be a nobody and yet have a servant, *NIV* ... Better a common fellow who has a slave, *JB* ... Better is a man of humble standing who works for himself, *RSV*.

is better than he that honoureth himself, and lacketh bread: ... than to be self-important and lack food, *NRSV* ... someone who gives himself airs and has nothing to eat, *JB* ... one who makes a show, *Moffatt*.

10. A righteous man regardeth the life of his beast: but the tender mercies of the wicked are cruel: ... A right-minded person, *REB* ... understands the needs of his livestock, *Berkeley* ... hearts of evildoers are cruel, *BB* ... wicked are heartless through and through, *Knox*.

11. He that tilleth his land shall be satisfied with bread: but he that followeth vain persons is void of understanding: ... He who tills his land has enough to eat, *NEB* ... who chases fantasies lacks judgment, *NIV* ... one who chases empty dreams is not wise, *NCV* ... But who follows a demagogue is senseless, *Fenton*.

12. The wicked desireth the net of evil men: ... covet the catch of evil men, *NKJV* ... lawless man craveth the prey of the wicked, *Rotherham* ... wicked wish for wrongful plunder, *Fenton*.

but the root of the righteous yieldeth fruit: ... good man's root remains untouched, *Moffatt* ... it is honesty that strikes deep root, *Knox*.

13. The wicked is snared by the transgression of his lips: ... trapped by his own falsehoods, *NEB* ... trapped by their evil talk, *NCV* ... bad are caught by rebellious lips, *Fenton* ... By the sin of his lips is the guilty man ensnared, *Goodspeed*.

but the just shall come out of trouble: ... righteous goeth out from distress, *Young* ... comes safe through trouble, *NEB* ... while honest men find acquittal, *Knox*.

People will be rewarded for what they say, *NCV* ... From the fruit of his words a man has his fill of good things, *Douay* ... One man wins success by his words, *NEB*.

14. A man shall be satisfied with good by the fruit of his mouth: ...

and the recompence of a man's hands shall be rendered unto him:

---

ing. Insight, however, is a moral quality in Proverbs. Those who possess the insight that counsels righteous actions are honored, whereas those whose counsel is perverse are despised for the wickedness that that counsel reveals.

This verse assumes, of course, that the ones seeking advice are themselves righteous, since fools delight in sin (10:23; 26:11). Proverbs asserts repeatedly that the wicked (or foolish) will neither seek nor accept advice, preferring their own "wisdom" (e.g., 1:7). This proverb also warns the reader that his or her counsel will be weighed against an external standard, not merely by its pragmatic value.

12:9. This is the first example in this section of Proverbs of a "better than" proverb. Three of the examples of this type of statement in Prov. 1–9 assert that wisdom is more valuable than gold, silver and corals (3:14; 8:11, 19). The other nineteen point out which of two options is to be preferred, based on the circumstances. In each case except this verse, the option commended by the proverb—the "better" choice—is not what people would naturally prefer (salad rather than steak, poverty rather than wealth, etc.). Here, however, Solomon notes that it is better to have a servant and be despised by him than to go hungry: his opinion cannot be eaten! The fool puts on airs, hoping to disguise his poverty, but little realizing that this costs him respect in the long run.

12:10. In an agrarian society like ancient Israel, everyone who could afford them would have had sheep, goats, donkeys and cattle; they represented wealth (cf. Gen. 12:16 and 13:2, which list Abraham's cattle alongside his silver and gold). Once Israel had settled in the land, such beasts of burden also provided some of the power for agriculture (cf. Deut. 25:4).

This verse argues implicitly from lesser to greater. How people treat their animals reveals how they will treat people. The wise ("righteous"), who understand what their flocks and herds require, give them compassionate care. The attitude and actions of the wicked reveal that they are willing to manipulate and destroy other people in order to gain their own ends. It is as futile to hope for compassion and understanding from the wicked as to expect good advice from them (12:5f, 8). In a non-agrarian society, a person's treatment of his or her subordinates (e.g., employees, students) yields the same insight.

12:11. This verse differs from 28:19 only in the last two Hebrew words: "lacks sense." Whereas 28:19 contrasts the results of their different goals, 12:11, by using a different conclusion, points out why they chose different goals in the first place. The choice of goals reveals the true nature of the heart. The discerning, who are able to determine and pursue proper goals, succeed; the empty-hearted, who by their very nature cannot, fail.

12:12. Although this verse is usually called "difficult" by commentators, the text is straightforward, with the exception of the last word, which usually occurs with an object: "The wicked covets the net of the wicked, but the root of the righteous gives [yields]." The verb *nāthan* (HED #5598) has the meaning "yields" or "produces" (13:15; cf. 29:15, 25; Gen. 4:12), but in each case the object is named.

The basic contrast of the verse probably lies between "coveting" and "producing." The wicked are concerned only with gaining their own desires, by any means, including the tools of sin. Wickedness is thus a negative or parasitic force that cannot produce anything of itself, whereas righteousness, like a plant, naturally produces what is good (implied by the contrast). It is therefore foolish to expect the wicked to produce good results, so that both may be known by their fruit.

12:13. Words affect others (cf. 10:11f, 14), but they also rebound on the speaker. Fools, who speak wickedly, arrogantly and without concern for the consequences of their words, entrap themselves, since their words, however clever, will eventually reveal their true nature. Because the righteous, on the other hand, weigh their words before speaking, and are careful to say what is true, good and helpful, they need not fear being ensnared by them (12:6; 21:23).

12:14. Resembling 13:2 (their first lines are identical but for "be satisfied"/"eats"; cf. also

3135, 119	8178.121	3937	15.	1932	188	3596	904, 6084
n fd, n ms	v Qal impf 3ms	prep, ps 3ms		n ms	n ms	adj	prep, n fd, ps 3ms
יְדֵי־אָדָם	יָשׁוּב	לוֹ		דֶּרֶךְ	אֱוִיל	יָשָׁר	בְּעֵינָיו
yᵉdhê-'ādhām	yāshûv	lô		derekh	'ĕwîl	yāshār	bᵉ'ênâv
the hands of a man	it will return	to him		the way of	a fool	upright	in his eyes

8471.151	3937, 6332	2550	16.	188	904, 3219	3156.221	3833
cj, v Qal act ptc ms	prep, n fs	adj		n ms	prep, art, n ms	v Niphal impf 3ms	n ms, ps 3ms
וְשֹׁמֵעַ	לְעֵצָה	חָכָם		אֱוִיל	בַּיּוֹם	יִוָּדַע	כַּעֲסוֹ
wᵉshōmēa'	lᵉ'ētsāh	chākhām		'ĕwîl	bayyôm	yiwwādha'	ka'ăṣô
but one who listens	to counsel	wise		a fool	in the day	it is known	his anger

3803.151	7320	6415	17.	6558.521	536	5222.521	6928
cj, v Qal act ptc ms	n ms	adj		v Hiphil impf 3ms	n fs	v Hiphil impf 3ms	n ms
וְכֹסֶה	קָלוֹן	עָרוּם		יָפִיחַ	אֱמוּנָה	יַגִּיד	צֶדֶק
wᵉkhōseh	qālôn	'ārûm		yāphîach	'ĕmûnāh	yaggîdh	tsedheq
but one who covers	shame	prudent		he will utter	truth	he will tell	righteousness

5915	8632	4983	18.	3552	1017.151	3626, 4237	2820
cj, n ms	n mp	n fs		sub	v Qal act ptc ms	prep, n fp	n fs
וְעֵד	שְׁקָרִים	מִרְמָה		יֵשׁ	בּוֹטֶה	כְּמַדְקְרוֹת	חָרֶב
wᵉ'ēdh	shᵉqārîm	mirmāh		yēsh	bôṭeh	kᵉmadhqǒrôth	chārev
but a witness of	lies	deceit		there is	one who speaks rashly	like the stabs of	a sword

4098	2550	4995	19.	8004, 583	3679.222
cj, n ms	n mp	n ms		n fs, n ms	v Niphal impf 3fs
וּלְשׁוֹן	חֲכָמִים	מַרְפֵּא		שְׂפַת־אֱמֶת	תִּכּוֹן
ûlāshôn	chăkhāmîm	marpē'		sᵉphath-'ĕmeth	tikkôn
but the tongue of	the wise	healing		a lip of truth	it will endure

3937, 5911	5912, 7567.125	4098	8632	20.	4983
prep, n ms	cj, adv, v Hiphil juss 1cs	n ms	n ms		n fs
לָעַד	וְעַד־אַרְגִּיעָה	לְשׁוֹן	שֶׁקֶר		מִרְמָה
lā'adh	wᵉ'adh-'argî'āh	lᵉshôn	shāqer		mirmāh
unto eternity	but as long as I may allow to rest	a tongue of	deception		deceit

904, 3949, 2896.152	7737	3937, 3389.152	8361	7977
prep, n ms, v Qal act ptc mp	n ms	cj, prep, v Qal act ptc mp	n ms	n fs
בְּלֶב־חֹרְשֵׁי	רָע	וּלְיֹעֲצֵי	שָׁלוֹם	שִׂמְחָה
bᵉlev-chōrᵉshê	rā'	ûlᵉyō'ătsê	shālôm	simchāh
in the heart of those who devise	evil	but to those who plan	peace	rejoicing

... he will be paid according to what his hands have accomplished, *Beck* ... comes back to reward him, *Douay* ... manual labor has its reward, *NRSV*.

15. The way of a fool is right in his own eyes: but he that hearkeneth unto counsel is wise: ... Fools think the way they go is straight, *JB* ... the wise listens to advice, *Berkeley* ... gives ear to suggestions, *BB*.

16. A fool's wrath is presently known: ... immediately shows his anger, *Douay* ... vexation is presently known, *MRB* ... The fool—in a day is his anger known, *Young* ... shows his annoyance at once, *NIV* ... Fools quickly show that they are upset, *NCV*.

but a prudent man covereth shame: ... sensible man ignores an affront, *Goodspeed* ... shrewd man hides the offence, *Beck* ... clever person who is slighted conceals his feelings, *REB* ... wise man stays cool when insulted, *LIVB*.

17. He that speaketh truth showeth forth righteousness: ... honest witness comes out with the truth, *REB* ... tells what is right, *NASB* ... He who speaks truth gives correct evidence, *Berkeley* ... He tells the truth who states what he is sure of, *NAB* ... truthful witness gives honest testimony, *NIV*.

but a false witness deceit: ... lying witness that which will bring disappointment, *Goodspeed* ... dishonest witness furthers injustice, *Moffatt*.

18. There is that speaketh like the piercings of a sword: ... Careless words stab like a sword, *NCV* ... There is one who speaks rashly,

NASB … Loose talk is a stabbing sword, *Fenton* … Reckless words pierce like a sword, *NIV*.

but the tongue of the wise is health: … wise words bring healing, *Knox* … tongue of the wise heals, *NEB*.

19. The lip of truth shall be established for ever: … Truthful speech

stands firm for ever, *REB* … Truth told endures, *Moffatt* … Sincere lips endure for ever, *JB*.

but a lying tongue is but for a moment: … false tongue is only for a minute, *BB* … a lying tongue only as long as it takes to wink an eye, *Beck*.

20. Deceit is in the heart of them that imagine evil: but to the counsellors of peace is joy: … Those who plan evil are full of lies, *NCV* … The heart contriving evil deceives, *Fenton* … The schemer's thoughts dwell ever on treachery, *Knox* … those who plan for people's welfare are happy, *Beck*.

18:20a), this saying may mean that both labor and words are rewarded. It seems more likely, however, that it commends words and work by comparing their potential effect. In the life of the wise and upright, words and deeds will be consistent with each other—both will be equally valued and rewarded.

12:15. One difference between wisdom and folly is that the wise realize that they need counsel, because they understand the benefit of gaining a variety of viewpoints. Fools, on the other hand, convinced of the accuracy of their own understanding (28:26), do not seek advice, but assume that their choices and decisions are good because they are their own (cf. 3:5f).

Other verses that refer to humans' natural self-satisfaction with their own plans also warn that since everyone's ways are right "in his own eyes" (cf. 16:2, 25), counsel is vital to a wise life (19:20). That counsel includes the standards of the God Who will judge the ways and motives of all (16:2; 21:2).

12:16. A major difference between the wise and the fool is that fools have no patience, thus freely and constantly exhibit their vexation (cf. 17:27; 19:11; 29:11). The perennially angry person is therefore a dangerous companion (cf. 22:24f), because he is a fool. The wise, however, realizing that offense may be more often taken than intended and that there is little profit in mentioning them (especially if the offense was intentional) have disciplined themselves to ignore the slights, snubs and insults of life in a fallen world.

12:17. The syntax of the first line is unusual—two asyndetic independent clauses—but similar sayings (cf. 14:5) support interpreting the first as the subject of the second: "He [who] breathes truth reports justly." The worth of a witness's verbal testimony is directly related to his character—the testimony of his life. The principle is not reserved for the law courts, since the wise weigh everyone's

words in light of what they know about his character. In court, however, the implications can be far more serious, since a perjurer can destroy someone else's life with only a few words. Several of the surrounding verses also address the nature and effect of speech (e.g., 12:6, 13f, 18, 22f; cf. especially the warning in v. 19).

12:18. Not understanding the power of words (cf. 18:21), and therefore not valuing them highly enough, fools often injure those around them. Careless speech can be no less damaging than premeditated gossip, slander or lies (cf. 26:20–28; 29:5). Properly used, words delight, heal and restore (16:24), but this requires knowing how to say the right thing at the right time (25:11f). Since other proverbs condemn lying (cf. those cited under 12:17), healing words are truthful, but not rash. They may wound, but only as a surgeon's scalpel wounds to heal (27:5; 28:23), never out of clumsiness or carelessness. The power of words revealed here probably underlies Jesus' statement about judgment upon "idle" words (cf. 12:36).

12:19. Liars are safe until they are caught, which is inevitable, since lies eventually break down. Those who tell the truth, on the other hand, have built on what is firm and secure. The Hebrew pun in the middle of this verse focuses the contrast between durability ("for ever") and transience ("for a moment"). This verse is one of several that discuss speech in this chapter (12:17f, 25).

12:20. Not only must those who plot evil deceive others about their true intent (cf. 26:23–28), but their hypocrisy is the outgrowth of hearts laden with deceit. In contrast, those who are sincerely concerned for the welfare of others give them advice that leads to their good; they then rejoice to see them blessed. One test of someone's motivation is thus the nature of his counsel as well as his response to what happens to others. "Deception" and "joy" contrast the source of one behavior with the outcome of the other.

21.

3940, 589.421	3937, 6926	3725, 201	7857	4527.116
neg part, v Pual impf 3ms	prep, art, n ms	adj, n ms	cj, n mp	v Qal pf 3cp
לֹא־יְאֻנֶּה	לַצַּדִּיק	כָּל־אָוֶן	וּרְשָׁעִים	מָלְאוּ
lō'-yeʿunneh	latstsaddîq	kol-'āwen	ûreshā'îm	māle'û
it will not happen	to the righteous	every sorrow	but the wicked	they will be filled with

22.

7737	8774	3176	8004, 8632	6449.152	536	7814
n ms	n fs	pn	n fd, n ms	cj, v Qal act ptc mp	n fs	n ms, ps 3ms
רָע	תּוֹעֲבַת	יְהוָה	שִׂפְתֵי־שָׁקֶר	וְעֹשֵׂי	אֱמוּנָה	רְצוֹנוֹ
rāʿ	tôʿăvath	yehwāh	siphthê-shāqer	weʿōsê	'ĕmûnāh	retsônô
evil	an abomination of	Yahweh	lips of deceit	but workers of	truth	his delight

23.

119	6415	3803.151	1907	3949	3809	7410.121
n ms	adj	v Qal act ptc ms	n fs	cj, n ms	n mp	v Qal impf 3ms
אָדָם	עָרוּם	כֹּסֶה	דָּעַת	וְלֵב	כְּסִילִים	יִקְרָא
'ādhām	'ārûm	kōṣeh	dāʿath	welēv	kesîlîm	yiqŏrā'
a man	prudent	concealing	knowledge	but the heart of	fools	it proclaims

24.

198	3135, 2845	5090.122	7711	2030.122	3937, 4671
n fs	n fs, n mp	v Qal impf 3fs	cj, n fs	v Qal impf 3fs	prep, n ms
אוֶּלֶת	יַד־חָרוּצִים	תִּמְשׁוֹל	וּרְמִיָּה	תִּהְיֶה	לָמַס
'iwweleth	yadh-chărûtsîm	timshôl	ûremîyāh	tihyeh	lāmaṣ
foolishness	the hand of the diligent	it will rule	but the slothful	it will be	for forced labor

25.

1722	904, 3949, 382	8246.521	1745	3005	7975.321
n fs	prep, n ms, n ms	v Hiphil impf 3ms, ps 3fs	cj, n ms	adj	v Piel impf 3ms, ps 3fs
דְּאָגָה	בְלֶב־אִישׁ	יַשְׁחֶנָּה	וְדָבָר	טוֹב	יְשַׂמְּחֶנָּה
de'āghāh	velev-'îsh	yashchennāh	wedhāvār	ṭôv	yesamme chennāh
worry	in the heart of a man	it weighs it down	but a word	good	it causes it to rejoice

26.

8780.521	4623, 7739	6926	1932	7857
v Hiphil juss 3ms	prep, n ms, ps 3ms	n ms	cj, n fs	n mp
יָתֵר	מֵרֵעֵהוּ	צַדִּיק	וְדֶרֶךְ	רְשָׁעִים
yāthēr	mērē'ēhû	tsaddîq	wedherekh	reshā'îm
let him search out	from his fellow	the righteous	but the way of	the wicked

27.

8912.522	3940, 2865.121	7711	6987	2019, 119
v Hiphil impf 3fs, ps 3mp	neg part, v Qal impf 3ms	n fs	n ms, ps 3ms	cj, n ms, n ms
תַּתְעֵם	לֹא־יַחֲרֹךְ	רְמִיָּה	צֵידוֹ	וְהוֹן־אָדָם
tath'ēm	lō'-yachărōkh	remîyāh	tsêdhô	wehôn-'ādhām
it leads them astray	he does not roast	the lazy	his prey	but the wealth of a man

21. There shall no evil happen to the just: ... No mischief, *REB* ... No grave trouble will overtake, *NKJV* ... No harm befalls, *NIV*.

but the wicked shall be filled with mischief: ... are overwhelmed with misfortune, *NAB, Douay* ... lawless are full of misfortune, *Rotherham*.

22. Lying lips are abomination to the LORD: ... are abhorrent to Yahweh, *JB* ... are loathsome to the Eternal, *Moffatt* ... The LORD detests a liar, *NEB* ... The LORD hates lips that lie, *Beck*.

but they that deal truly are his delight: ... is pleased with those who keep their promises, *NCV* ... stedfast doers are his delight, *Young* ... those who act faithfully, *NRSV*.

23. A prudent man concealeth knowledge: ... A sensible man doesn't display what he knows, *Beck* ... clever person conceals, *REB* ... No cautious man blurts out all, *Moffatt* ... shrewd man, *NAB*.

but the heart of fools proclaimeth foolishness: ... mind of a fool broadcasts folly, *NRSV* ... stupid one blurts out, *REB* ... fools gush forth folly, *Douay*.

24. The hand of the diligent shall bear rule: ... Hard workers will become leaders, *NCV* ... Diligence brings a man to power, *NEB* ... hand of the ready worker will have authority, *BB*.

but the slothful shall be under tribute: ... slack hand will be forced to serve, *Berkeley* ... lazy shall be under service, *KJVII* ... slothfulness becometh tributary, *Young* ... laziness ends in slave labor, *NIV*.

25. Heaviness in the heart of man maketh it stoop: ... Care in the heart of a man boweth it down, *MAST* ... Grief depresses the heart, *Fenton* ... Worry weighs a man down, *Moffatt* ... anxious heart is dispiriting, *REB*.

but a good word maketh it glad: ... gentle word can cheer it, *Fenton* ... kindly word, *JB* ... good word cheers it up, *NRSV*.

26. The righteous is more excellent than his neighbour: but the way of the wicked seduceth them: ... is a guide to his neighbor, *NASB* ... should choose his friends carefully, *NKJV* ... gives good advice to friends, *NRSV* ... evil person is easily led to do wrong, *NCV*.

27. The slothful man roasteth not that which he took in hunting: ... idle has no game to roast, *JB* ... will not catch his prey, *RSV* ... lazy catch no food to cook, *NCV*.

but the substance of a diligent man is precious: ... industrious man reaps a rich harvest, *NEB* ... diligence is anyone's most precious possession, *JB* ... diligent man will get wealthy, *Beck*.

12:21. The contrast between "meeting" and "being filled" reveals both the extent to which the righteous are protected from trouble or harm (12:6, 13, 28; cf. the same verb in Ps. 91:10) and the fact that wickedness increases until it fills the sinful, leaving room for nothing else.

12:22. Several proverbs condemn violence and deceit (6:16–19), dishonest business (11:1; 20:23) and fraudulent worship (15:8f; 21:27; 28:9) as equally abominable to the LORD. The parallel between "lying lips" and "those who practice righteousness" reveals the close connection between words and deeds; that is, lies are condemned, but they are merely symptomatic. The fundamental issue is the heart, since its state is revealed in words and deeds. Although this verse may refer primarily to legal testimony, its application—like that of the commandment which it reflects (Exo. 20:16)—should extend to every aspect of human relationships.

12:23. Because the wise understand the value of words, they use them carefully. Because they know that wisdom comes by listening and learning, they speak sparingly and well (10:19; 17:27). Fools, ignorant of words' value, are so busy demonstrating their "wisdom" that they speak without thought (18:2).

12:24. Just as the diligent will stand before kings (cf. 22:29), they will also rule over others (although this is not the word that means specifically "to reign as king"). Specifically, the diligent will rule over the indolent, since the refusal of such people to work means that they will fail to produce and to earn. The slothful are therefore at the mercy of those to whom they owe money or property. They cannot pay their debts, and are forced to work in order to pay off their creditors. They are thus put to forced labor just as surely as if they had been conscripted (cf. 1 Ki. 5:13–16; 12:18). The irony is that sluggards tend to view themselves as free (from work, at least) and may even view the diligent as enslaved to their occupations.

12:25. Anxiety can break a person's heart, but the point of this verse lies in the second line, not the psychology of stress. Words are so potent (18:21) that the right word at the right time can change the entire outlook (12:18; 15:4, 23, 30; 25:25). Words that heal rather than wound (12:17) reflect the forethought and compassion that characterize the wise.

12:26. The antonyms "righteous" and "wicked" indicate that this proverb contrasts these two groups, but the obscurity of the first line makes the verse difficult to interpret. The first word tûr (HED #8780) means "he searches out," but its occurrence with the preposition min (HED #4623) "from" is anomalous. None of the many suggested emendations is compelling; the interpretative rendering of the NIV ("The righteous is cautious in friendship" [i.e., studies people before making friends]; cf. NKJV) is as good as any, and provides an oblique parallel with the second line. The friends whom the wicked choose carelessly will lead them astray (cf. 19:19; 24:24f).

12:27. The first line of this verse is extremely difficult to translate, mostly because this is the only biblical occurrence of the verb. Some suggest that it means "to catch prey," but the etymologies used to support this interpretation seem forced. The traditional rabbinic interpretation is that it means that the slothful does not "roast" what he has caught (so NIV, NASB, NKJV). If this is an accurate translation, this line parallels other verses that describe the sluggard as beginning a task, but failing to complete it (19:24; 26:24). The second line commends diligence without using the image of preparing food (on diligence, cf. 12:11; 13:4; 22:29).

28.

3479	2845	904, 758, 6930	2522	1932	5594	414, 4323
adj	n ms	prep, n fs, n fs	n mp	cj, n ms	n fs	neg part, n ms
יָקָר	חָרוּץ	בְּאֹרַח־צְדָקָה	חַיִּים	וְדֶרֶךְ	נְתִיבָה	אַל־מָוֶת
yāqār	chārûts	be'ōrach-tsedhāqāh	chayyîm	wedherekh	nethîvāh	'al-māweth
precious	diligence	on the path of righteousness	life	and the way of	the path	no death

13:1

1158	2550	4284	1	4086	3940, 8471.111	1648
n ms	adj	n ms	n ms	cj, n ms	neg part, v Qal pf 3ms	n fs
בֵּן	חָכָם	מוּסַר	אָב	וְלֵץ	לֹא־שָׁמַע	גְּעָרָה
bēn	chākhām	mûsar	'āv	welēts	lō'-shāma'	ge'ārāh
a son	wise	the discipline of	a father	but a scoffer	he does not heed	a rebuke

2.

4623, 6780	6552, 382	404.121	3005	5497	931.152
prep, n ms	n ms, n ms	v Qal impf 3ms	adj	cj, n fs	v Qal act ptc mp
מִפְּרִי	פִּי־אִישׁ	יֹאכַל	טוֹב	וְנֶפֶשׁ	בֹּגְדִים
mipperî	phî-'îsh	yō'khal	tôv	wenephesh	bōghedhîm
from the fruit of	the mouth of a man	he will eat	what is good	but the soul of	deceitful ones

3.

2660	5526.151	6552	8490.151	5497	6834.151	8004
n ms	v Qal act ptc ms	n ms, ps 3ms	v Qal act ptc ms	n fs, ps 3ms	v Qal act ptc ms	n fd, ps 3ms
חָמָס	נֹצֵר	פִּיו	שֹׁמֵר	נַפְשׁוֹ	פֹּשֵׂק	שְׂפָתָיו
chāmās	nōtsēr	pîw	shōmēr	naphshô	pōsēq	sephāthâv
violence	one who keeps	his mouth	guarding	his life	one who opens	his lips

4.

4425, 3937	181.753	375	5497	6339	5497
n fs, prep, ps 3ms	v Hithpael ptc fs	cj, sub	n fs, ps 3ms	n ms	cj, n fs
מְחַתָּה־לוֹ	מִתְאַוָּה	וָאַיִן	נַפְשׁוֹ	עָצֵל	וְנֶפֶשׁ
mechittāh-lô	mith'awwāh	wā'ayin	naphshô	'ātsēl	wenephesh
destruction to himself	desiring	but there is not	his soul	a sluggard	but the soul of

5.

2845	1941.422	1745, 8632	7983.121	6926	7857
n mp	v Pual impf 3fs	n ms, n ms	v Qal impf 3ms	n ms	cj, n ms
חָרוּצִים	תְּדֻשָּׁן	דְּבַר־שֶׁקֶר	יִשְׂנָא	צַדִּיק	וְרָשָׁע
chārutsîm	tedhushshān	devar-sheqer	yisnā'	tsaddîq	werāshā'
the diligent	it will be made fat	a word of deception	he hates	the righteous	but the wicked

6.

919.521	2763.521	6930	5526.122
v Hiphil impf 3ms	cj, v Hiphil impf 3ms	n fs	v Qal impf 3fs
יַבְאִישׁ	וְיַחְפִּיר	צְדָקָה	תִּצֹּר
yav'îsh	weyachpîr	tsedhāqāh	titstsōr
he causes to be loathsome	and he causes to be shameful	righteousness	it keeps

---

28. In the way of righteousness is life; and in the pathway thereof there is no death: ... Wouldst thou attain life, honesty is the high road, *Knox* ... the abominable way leads to death, *Douay* ... way of error leads to death, *RSV*.

13:1. A wise son heareth his father's instruction: ... is a lover of teaching, *BB* ... loves discipline, *NRSV* ... sensible son heeds what his father tells him, *Moffatt*.

but a scorner heareth not rebuke: ... cynic will not listen to reproof, *JB*

... mocker does not listen to rebuke, *NIV* ... senseless one heeds no rebuke, *NAB*.

2. A man shall eat good by the fruit of his mouth: ... People will be rewarded for what they say, *NCV* ... From the fruit of his mouth will the good man enjoy what is good, *Goodspeed*.

but the soul of the transgressors shall eat violence: ... those who can't be trusted want only violence, *NCV* ... evil souls come to an untimely end, *Moffatt* ... desire of

the treacherous is for violence, *RSV* ... desire of the false is for, *BB*.

3. He that keepeth his mouth keepeth his life: ... He who guards his mouth controls himself, *Berkeley* ... preserves his life, *NASB* ... is keeping his soul, *Young*.

but he that openeth wide his lips shall have destruction: ... to open wide one's lips brings downfall, *NAB* ... there shall be ruin, *MAST*.

4. The soul of the sluggard desireth, and hath nothing: ... idler longs, while his body starves, *Fenton* ... lazy man longs, but he gets nothing, *Moffatt* ... hater of work does not get his desires, *BB* ... appetite of the lazy craves, *NRSV*.

but the soul of the diligent shall be made fat: ... soul of the hard worker, *KJVII* ... shall be abundantly gratified, *MAST* ... is richly supplied, *NRSV*.

5. A righteous man hateth lying: ... upright hates a lying word, *JB* ... Good people hate what is false, *NCV* ... Anything deceitful the just man hates, *NAB*.

but a wicked man is loathsome, and cometh to shame: ... acts shamefully and disgracefully, *RSV* ... lawless causeth shame and disgrace, *Rotherham* ... wicked revile and libel, *Fenton*.

6. Righteousness keepeth him that is upright in the way: but wickedness overthroweth the sinner: ... guards him who is blameless in the way, *Berkeley* ... keeps a straight-on course, *Fenton* ... Goodness safeguards men of integrity, but vice is the downfall of sinful men, *Moffatt*.

7. There is that maketh himself rich, yet hath nothing: there is that

---

12:28. This verse stands out not only because its lines are synonymous (the verses in chs. 10–15 are nearly all antithetical), but because it returns to the deep concern of the prologue (Prov. 1–9): wisdom as the source of life. Although the second line ("the pathway thereof") is difficult, the saying seems to present the positive side of the contrast that typifies these early chapters of the actual proverbs—the consequences of wisdom and folly, or righteousness and wickedness (e.g., 10:11f; 11:3–6; 12:2f, 6f). Wisdom is the source of life (cf. 1:33; 2:20f; 3:18; 8:35); a righteous life is the result of attending to wisdom's teaching.

13:1. Although the lack of a verb in the first line leads some translations to supply "accepts" (NASB) or "loves" (NRSV), the parallel with the scoffer who rejects correction suggests that the son who is wise accepts his father's instruction. Such wisdom is both cause and result—whoever is wise enough to respond correctly to a rebuke will thereby grow more wise (cf. 19:27). Scoffers, by refusing to listen, increasingly confirm their own opinion (cf. 9:7f; 26:12) and face destruction (29:1).

13:2. The wise know how to speak so that their words strengthen, heal and calm others (cf. 12:18; 15:2), or to rebuke them appropriately and at the right time (25:11f; 28:23), all of which are a source of great blessing to their hearers, and reflect on them as well. They thus "eat" the good fruit of their lips (cf. 10:6, 11). Treachery (the opposite of integrity) hates those with whom it deals, looking only for some means by which to entrap or destroy them (cf. 26:23–28; 29:5). The essence of treachery is violence against others, so that the treacherous engender no good fruit for anyone, including themselves. Recognizing treachery and wisdom, avoiding the one and seeking out the other, characterize the wise.

13:3. Reticence is so much a mark of wisdom (cf. 10:14; cf. 10:12), that even a fool seems wise if he will but keep quiet (17:27f). The only requirement for avoiding trouble is often silence (21:23). This is possible because the prudent anticipate the consequences of their words and avoid saying things that injure or inflame (15:1; cf. 14:16; 22:3). Fools, however, who delight only in displaying the paltry sum of their knowledge, constantly trouble themselves and everyone else.

13:4. Because he refuses to work, the sluggard's desires remain unfulfilled (21:25f). Diligence (discerning and setting goals and then working to achieve them) is the path to successfully fulfilling one's desires (cf. 10:4; 12:24; 21:5). To be fat was not only a sign of blessing in biblical times (cf. 11:25; 15:30; 28:25; Ps. 23:5), it also stood in direct contrast to the self-afflicted starvation of the lazy (19:15; 20:4).

13:5. Since they tell the truth, the righteous do not need to fear that their reputations will suffer (10:7). Since even the cleverest lies are eventually uncovered (10:9), liars who are caught in their lies become objects of reproach, and their counsel is despised. The only way to avoid this fate is to hate lies—to refuse to lie, or to be party to deception. This begins when individuals submit to wisdom's rebuke and instruction, refusing to deceive themselves about their own wisdom, or to consider themselves more wise. When there is truth in the heart, then both words and deeds are true, and there is no fear of shame (cf. 13:6).

13:6. Choices have consequences (among many verses, cf. 11:3, 5f, 8). Those who, by attending to wisdom, obey and fulfill the Covenant, will find that their integrity has guarded and protected them at each step. Wickedness, on the other hand, perverts and distorts sinners ("sin," as the result, stands for "the sinner," the agent), so that they become increasingly characterized by sin (cf. 12:21).

8866, 1932	7858	5751.322	2496		3552	6483.755
n ms, n ms	n fs	v Piel impf 3fs	n fs	**7.**	sub	v Hithpael ptc ms
תָּם־דָּרֶךְ	וְרִשְׁעָה	תְּסַלֵּף	חַטָּאת		יֵשׁ	מִתְעַשֵּׁר
tām-dārekh	werish'āh	tesallēph	chattā'th		yēsh	mith'ashshēr
integrity of a way	but wickedness	it perverts	the sinner		there is	one who pretends to be rich

375	3725	7609.755	2019	7521		3853
cj, sub	n ms	v Hithpolel ptc ms	cj, n ms	adj	**8.**	n ms
וְאֵין	כֹּל	מִתְרוֹשֵׁשׁ	וְהוֹן	רָב		כֹּפֶר
we'ên	kōl	mithrôshēsh	wehôn	rāv		kōpher
and there is not	anything	one who pretends to be poor	yet wealth	abundant		the ransom of

5497, 382	6484	7851	3940, 8471.111	1648
n fs, n ms	n ms, ps 3ms	cj, n ms	neg part, v Qal pf 3ms	n fs
נֶפֶשׁ־אִישׁ	עָשְׁרוֹ	וְרָשׁ	לֹא־שָׁמַע	גְּעָרָה
nephesh-'îsh	'āsherô	werāsh	lō'-shāma'	ge'ārāh
the life of a man	his riches	but a poor man	he does not listen to	a rebuke

	214, 6926	7975.121	5552	7857	1906.121
9.	n ms, n mp	v Qal impf 3ms	cj, n ms	n mp	v Qal impf 3ms
	אוֹר־צַדִּיקִים	יִשְׂמָח	וְנֵר	רְשָׁעִים	יִדְעָךְ
	'ôr-tsaddîqîm	yismāch	wenēr	reshā'îm	yidh'ākh
	the light of the righteous	it will be glad	but the lamp of	the wicked	it will be extinguished

	7828, 904, 2171	5598.121	4844	881, 3398.256	2551
10.	adv, prep, n ms	v Qal impf 3ms	n fs	cj, do, v Niphal ptc mp	n fs
	רַק־בְּזָדוֹן	יִתֵּן	מַצָּה	וְאֶת־נוֹעָצִים	חָכְמָה
	raq-bezādhôn	yittēn	matstsāh	we'eth-nô'ātsîm	chokhmāh
	only with presumptuousness	he will give	strife	but those who are advised	wisdom

2019	4623, 1961	4745.121	7192.151	6142, 3135	7528.521
n ms	prep, n ms	v Qal impf 3ms	v Qal act ptc ms	prep, n fs	v Hiphil impf 3ms
11. הוֹן	מֵהֶבֶל	יִמְעָט	וְקֹבֵץ	עַל־יָד	יַרְבֶּה
hôn	mēhevel	yim'āt	weqōvēts	'al-yādh	yarbeh
wealth	from vanity	it will diminish	but one who gathers	beside a hand	it will increase

8760	5082.457	2571.557, 3949	6320	2522	8707
n fs	v Pual ptc fs	v Hiphil ptc fs, n ms	cj, n ms	n mp	n fs
12. תּוֹחֶלֶת	מְמֻשָּׁכָה	מַחֲלָה־לֵב	וְעֵץ	חַיִּים	תַּאֲוָה
tôcheleth	memushshākhāh	machālāh-lēv	we'ēts	chayyîm	ta'āwāh
hope	having been dragged	making the heart sick	but a tree of	life	a desire

971.153	972.151	3937, 1745	2341.221	3937	3486.151
v Qal act ptc fs	v Qal act ptc ms	prep, n ms	v Niphal impf 3ms	prep, ps 3ms	cj, v Qal act ptc ms
בָּאָה	**13.** בָּז	לְדָבָר	יֵחָבֶל	לוֹ	וִירֵא
vā'āh	bāz	ledhāvār	yēchāvel	lô	wîrē'
coming	one who despises	a word	he will destroy	himself	but one who fears

maketh himself poor, yet hath great riches: ... pretendeth himself rich, *MAST* ... another pretends to be poor, though he has plenty, *Moffatt*.

8. The ransom of a man's life are his riches: but the poor heareth not rebuke: ... A man will give his wealth in exchange for his life, *BB* ... poor will face no such danger, *NCV*

... poor man finds no means of redemption, *Goodspeed*.

9. The light of the righteous rejoiceth: but the lamp of the wicked shall be put out: ... light of the righteous dances, *Berkeley* ... of the just shines gaily, *NAB* ... the wicked is snuffed out, *NIV* ... is extinguished, *Young*.

10. Only by pride cometh contention: ... causes nothing but strife, *Goodspeed* ... only effect of pride is fighting, *BB* ... vanity of pride makes strife, *Fenton*.

but with the well advised is wisdom: ... with those who take counsel is, *NAB* .... wisdom lies with those who take advice, *JB* ... with the modest there is wisdom, *Goodspeed*.

11. Wealth gotten by vanity shall be diminished: ... hastily gotten will dwindle, *RSV* ... gained by dishonesty, *NKJV* ... got by scheming, *Goodspeed*.

but he that gathereth by labour shall increase: ... whoso is gathering by the hand becometh great, *Young* ... who gathers little by little will increase it, *RSV* ... gathered gradually, it will grow, *Moffatt*.

12. Hope deferred maketh the heart sick: but when the desire

cometh, it is a tree of life: ... Hope put off is a weariness to the heart, *BB* ... but a wish fulfilled, *NAB* ... a longing fulfilled, *NIV*.

13. Whoso despiseth the word shall be destroyed: ... brings destruction on himself, *RSV* ... Contempt for the word is self-

---

13:7. This verse has several possible interpretations. Most versions (e.g., NASB, NRSV, NIV) and many commentaries assume that the proverb addresses (and implicitly condemns) deceit, or that it warns against judging others by their appearance (cf. 12:9). Another interpretation is that some people enrich or impoverish themselves in some way, but that their actual condition is the opposite. This would imply that the wise understand that there may be a gap between someone's external, material condition and their internal, spiritual state (cf. 19:1).

Since this verse contains the only occurrence of these verbs in this stem, we cannot define their nuance as "deceptive" or "real." And, since the verse merely presents an observation without any "code words" (e.g., "righteous," "wicked," "foolish," "wise"), it is difficult to say what, if anything, is being condemned. The proverbial emphasis on honesty and truth implicitly condemns this type of deception, but that is only implicit here (if it is even present).

13:8. Although other proverbs warn that wealth is not a source of true security (e.g., 10:2; 11:4, 28; 18:11), it may be able to save someone's life. Those who are poor do not have the resources of the wealthy (10:15), but neither do they face the same kinds of threats. As many verses illustrate (including, perhaps, 13:7), the value of wealth and poverty is relative; neither estate is honorable or desirable in itself. Proverbs thus counsels diligence (another word for faithfulness) without thought of reward (although diligence is rewarded; cf. 13:11; 22:29), as well as contentment, since every situation has its own rewards and dangers.

13:9. This proverb echoes the warning of the prologue (e.g., 8:32-36): wisdom, which yields a righteous life, is the source of life, but the rebellious attitude of the fool, leads only to death. The warning of the verse is certainly external (choose friends, teachers, companions, etc. wisely, since they are on one of these two paths, and whoever accompanies them will end up like them, sharing their fate). It is also internal, encouraging students of Proverbs to check their own attitude (and destiny).

13:10. Not only is there wisdom in a multitude of counselors (11:14; 15:22), there is also the peace that accompanies humility (11:2). Only the truly wise recognize that they need advice, and are willing to accept it. The insolent presume the superiority of their own understanding and reject the insights of others. Their arrogance inevitably causes strife, since their plans often fail and since they despise those around them. The Book of Proverbs values life and planning in communion with others, gaining from their wisdom and insights. The lone thinker (or actor) is not a biblical hero (cf. verses cited above).

13:11. Diligence (gathering "by hand") requires the patience that comes from understanding that long-term benefits outweigh quick gains. In a society in which virtually all work was done by directing muscle power, whether human or animal, to the task, this verse may have implied a contrast between working and trying to gain wealth without working for it. "Vanity" may refer to fraud, thievery or some other type of illicit activity. Wealth gained in this way is deceptive and impermanent (11:18). Better to work diligently, for diligence is always rewarded—first, by a task well done, and sometimes, by the regard of others (22:29).

13:12. Those who are wise understand how deadly delay can be to the soul (13:19; 25:13). Because they also understand the virtue of diligence and of fulfilling their obligations, and because they wish others well, they strive to encourage and strengthen them by meeting their responsibilities as quickly and as well as they can. Those who think only or primarily of themselves, of course, feel no such obligation, and so are a constant source of irritation to those who entrust them with responsibilities (10:26; 26:6). Knowing the truth of this verse in one's own life becomes a motivation to do good to others (cf. Luke 6:31).

13:13. Although some translations (e.g., NASB, NIV) interpret the main verb in the first line (HED #2341) as "become pledged," it is probably from another verbal root meaning "be corrupted

4851	2000	8396.421		8784	2550	4888
n fs	pers pron	v Pual impf 3ms	**14.**	n fs	n ms	n ms
מִצְוָה	הוּא	יְשֻׁלָּם		תּוֹרַת	חָכָם	מְקוֹר
mitswāh	hû'	yeshullām		tôrath	chākhām	meqôr
a commandment	he	he will be recompensed		the instruction of	the wise	a fountain of

2522	3937, 5681.141	4623, 4305	4323		7961, 3005	5598.121, 2682
n mp	prep, v Qal inf con	prep, n mp	n ms	**15.**	n ms, adj	v Qal impf 3ms, n ms
חַיִּים	לָסוּר	מִמֹּקְשֵׁי	מָוֶת		שֵׂכֶל־טוֹב	יִתֶּן־חֵן
chayyîm	lāsûr	mimmōqōshê	māweth		sēkhel-ṭôv	yitten-chēn
life	to turn	from the snares of	death		good understanding	it produces favor

1932	931.152	393		3725, 6415	6449.121	904, 1907
cj, n ms	v Qal act ptc mp	adj	**16.**	adj, n ms	v Qal impf 3ms	prep, n fs
וְדֶרֶךְ	בֹּגְדִים	אֵיתָן		כָּל־עָרוּם	יַעֲשֶׂה	בְדָעַת
wedherekh	bōghedhîm	'êthān		kol-'ārûm	ya'aseh	vedhā'ath
but the way of	deceitful ones	ever flowing		all the prudent	he will act	with knowledge

3811	6816.121	198		4534	7857	5489.121	904, 7737
cj, n ms	v Qal impf 3ms	n fs	**17.**	n ms	adj	v Qal impf 3ms	prep, n ms
וּכְסִיל	יִפְרֹשׂ	אִוֶּלֶת		מַלְאָךְ	רָשָׁע	יִפֹּל	בְּרָע
ûkhesîl	yiphrōs	'iwweleth		mal'ākh	rāshā'	yippōl	berā'
but the fool	he spreads	foolishness		a messenger	wicked	he will fall	into evil

7005	551	4995	7677		7320	6797.151	4284
n ms	n mp	n ms	n ms	**18.**	cj, n ms	v Qal act ptc ms	n ms
וְצִיר	אֱמוּנִים	מַרְפֵּא	רֵישׁ		וְקָלוֹן	פּוֹרֵעַ	מוּסָר
wetsîr	'emûnîm	marpē'	rêsh		weqālôn	pôrēa'	mûsār
but an envoy of	faithfulness	healing	poverty		and disgrace	one who abandons	discipline

8490.151	8763	3632.421		8707	2030.257	6386.122
cj, v Qal act ptc ms	n fs	v Pual impf 3ms	**19.**	n fs	v Niphal ptc fs	v Qal impf 3fs
וְשׁוֹמֵר	תּוֹכַחַת	יְכֻבָּד		תַּאֲוָה	נִהְיָה	תֶּעֱרַב
weshômēr	tôkhachath	yekhubbādh		ta'awāh	nihyāh	te'erav
but one who observes	correction	he will be honored		a desire	being fulfilled	it is pleasant

3937, 5497	8774	3809	5681.141	4623, 7737		2050.142
prep, n fs	cj, n fs	n mp	v Qal inf con	prep, n ms	**20.**	v Qal inf abs
לְנָפֶשׁ	וְתוֹעֲבַת	כְּסִילִים	סוּר	מֵרָע		הָלוֹךְ
lenāphesh	wethô'avath	kesîlîm	sûr	mērā'		hālôkh
to the soul	but the abomination of	fools	to turn aside	from evil		walk

destructive, JB ... who despises God's decree shall perish, Moffatt.

but he that feareth the commandment shall be rewarded: ... those who respect, NRSV ... who attends to the law has peace, Fenton ... respect for the commandment wins salvation, JB.

14. The law of the wise is a fountain of life, to depart from the snares of death: ... teaching of the wise, RSV, MAST ... is a wellspring of life, Rotherham ... shows how to evade the nets of Death,

Moffatt ... To turn one away from, NKJV.

15. Good understanding giveth favour: but the way of transgressors is hard: ... Sound discretion yieldeth favour, But the way of the treacherous is rugged, Rotherham ... way of the faithless is their ruin, NAB, NRSV.

16. Every prudent man dealeth with knowledge: ... sensible man acts with intelligence, Goodspeed ... sharp man does everything with, BB ... clever do all things intelligently, NRSV.

but a fool layeth open his folly: ... fool is quick to show annoyance, Anchor ... displays folly, NRSV ... flaunteth his folly, ASV ... makes clear his foolish thoughts, BB.

17. A wicked messenger falleth into mischief: ... bad messenger brings trouble, NRSV ... unreliable messenger precipitates trouble, Berkeley.

but a faithful ambassador is health: ... with a reliable envoy, all is well, Moffatt ... trustworthy envoy is a healing remedy, NAB.

18. Poverty and shame shall be to him that refuseth instruction: ... will come to him who neglects discipline, *NASB* ... Instruction scorned, brings want and shame, *Fenton* ... Need and shame will be the fate of him who is uncontrolled by training, *BB.*

but he that regardeth reproof shall be honoured: ... who takes note of teaching, *BB* ... who listens to correction, *KJVII* ... one listening to reproof, *Berkeley.*

19. The desire accomplished is sweet to the soul: ... To attain our wish is sweet to the mind, *Fenton* ... Longing fulfilled, *Berkeley* ... It is so good when wishes come true, *NCV.*

but it is abomination to fools to depart from evil: ... fools hate to abandon sin, *Fenton* ... hate to give up evildoing, *Moffatt* ... to give up evil is disgusting to the foolish, *BB.*

20. He that walketh with wise men shall be wise: but a companion of fools shall be destroyed: ... will fare badly, *NAB* ... suffers

[destroyed]" (cf. KJV, NKJV, NRSV). Since the universe was created with wisdom (3:19f; 8:22–31), to ignore or reject wisdom's teaching (as the parallel "command" implies) is to put oneself at odds with the nature of creation (cf. 8:35f), whereas the "reward" of obedience is life. Attitude toward wisdom may seem a trivial matter, but its repercussions are remorseless—for good or ill.

13:14. Except for the first two words, this verse is identical to 14:27, so that between them they identify the fear of the LORD with the teaching of the wise. It is not the content of their teaching, however, that is the source of life, but the attitude of obedience that characterizes the fear of the LORD (1:7). Wisdom is only found among the wise (10:11, 13; 17:24), who themselves have been taught (4:1–4). Life, the goal of the Book of Proverbs, is the fruit of wisdom (8:35).

13:15. Good advice that flows from insight and prudence is welcomed, and gains favor and respect (cf. a similar phrase used to describe Abigail in 1 Sam. 25:3). The last word of the second line (HED #393) is difficult. It usually means "ever-flowing" or "perennial" when applied to streams of water (e.g., Exo. 14:27; Amos 5:24), and "permanent" when used to describe a nation (Jer. 5:15) or abode (Num. 24:21; Jer 49:19; 50:44). Since this meaning would contradict the unanimous teaching of Proverbs, it is often interpreted as "hard" in the sense of "difficult" (e.g., NASB, NIV, NKJV); the RSV's reading, "their ruin," requires a change of two letters. The word may have a meaning that is unattested in the rest of Scripture, or this verse may contain an irrecoverable textual error.

The contrast between "good insight" and the "treacherous" suggests, apart from the textual problem, that this is another proverb that describes the consequences of wisdom and folly (cf. 11:3, 5f; 12:2; 13:2, 6).

13:16. Since people act out what is in their hearts, the shrewd act according to true knowledge, but fools, who have rejected wisdom and understanding in favor of their own "knowledge," increase their folly. Words and actions reveal the inner person. Someone whose advice is constantly causing trouble for him and others is best avoided; his advice, if offered, should be rejected. Good counsel is found only among the wise (cf. 10:11, 13, 31).

13:17. A task entrusted to someone who is untrustworthy guarantees a self-inflicted wound. Although the message may get through, or the task be accomplished, some of the time, their wickedness will eventually afflict both them and the person who trusted them (10:26; 26:6). A trustworthy messenger, on the other hand, is good medicine (25:13).

13:18. Response to correction is an important condition in determining relative success or failure in life, as the prologue's warnings and exhortations show (1:23, 25, 30; 3:11f; 5:9–14). The human heart in its folly ignores or rejects the suggestions and counsel of others, having already determined for itself what is right (16:2, 25; 21:2). Solomon wrote this proverb cleverly, so that the last word can mean "is honored" or "is made wealthy [or heavy]," the opposite of "poverty," which begins the verse. This is the true contrast—the outcome reveals the true reaction to the insights of others (cf. 6:23; 10:17; 12:1; 15:5, 10, 31f; 29:1).

13:19. Cutting off their nose to spite their face, fools would rather live with unrealized hopes and dreams than to admit and leave their wickedness. Along with other proverbs, this shows that neither carrots nor sticks turn the rebellious to the truth (cf. 17:10; 27:22), since they differ from the wise as does a dog from a person (cf. 26:11). The wise, on the other hand, understanding the benefit of accomplishing their goals, work diligently to realize them (cf. 13:12) and to fulfill any obligations that they have to others.

13:20. A person's companions affect his or her behavior and basic outlook on life, for better or worse. Like other proverbs, this verse also warns of the need to choose friends and companions carefully,

21.

2492	7778.221	3809	7749.151	2549.131	882, 2550
n mp	v Niphal impf 3ms	n mp	cj, v Qal act ptc ms	cj, v Qal impv 2ms	prep, n mp
חַטָּאִים	יְרוֹעַ	כְּסִילִים	וְרֹעֶה	וַחֲכָם	אֶת־חֲכָמִים
chaṭṭā'îm	yērôa'	khesîlîm	werō'eh	wachkhām	'eth-chăkhāmîm
sinners	disaster will happen	fools	but a companion of	and be wise	with the wise

22.

7579.322	7750	881, 6926	8396.321, 3008	3005	5336.521
v Piel impf 3fs	n fs	cj, do n mp	v Piel impf 3ms, n ms	adj	v Hiphil impf 3ms
תִּרְדֹּף	רָעָה	וְאֶת־צַדִּיקִים	יְשַׁלֶּם־טוֹב	טוֹב	יַנְחִיל
teraddēph	rā'āh	we'eth-tsaddîqîm	yeshallem-ṭôv	ṭôv	yanchîl
it pursues	evil	but the righteous	good will reward	good	he causes to inherit

23.

1158, 1158	7121.155	3937, 6926	2524	2490.151	7521, 406
n mp, n mp	v Qal pass ptc ms	prep, art, n ms	n ms	v Qal act ptc ms	adj, n ms
בְּנֵי־בָנִים	וְצָפוּן	לַצַּדִּיק	חֵיל	חוֹטֵא	רָב־אֹכֶל
benê-vānîm	wetsāphûn	latstsaddîq	chêl	chôṭē'	rāv-'ōkhel
sons of sons	and being laid up	for the righteous	the wealth of	a sinner	much food

5403	7511	3552	5793.255	904, 3940	5122
n ms	n mp	cj, sub	v Niphal ptc ms	prep, neg part	n ms
נִיר	רָאשִׁים	וְיֵשׁ	נִסְפֶּה	בְּלֹא	מִשְׁפָּט
nîr	rā'shîm	weyēsh	nispeh	belō'	mishpāṭ
the newly tilled ground of	poor people	but it is	what is carried away	without	justice

24.

2910.151	8101	7983.151	1158	154.151
v Qal act ptc ms	n ms, ps 3ms	v Qal act ptc ms	n ms, ps 3ms	v Qal act ptc ms, ps 3ms
חוֹשֵׂךְ	שִׁבְטוֹ	שׂוֹנֵא	בְּנוֹ	וְאֹהֲבוֹ
chôsēkh	shivṭô	sônē'	venô	we'ōhevô
one who withholds	his rod	hating	his son	but one who loves him

25.

8264.311	4284	6926	404.151	3937, 7883	5497
v Piel pf 3ms, ps 3ms	n ms	n ms	v Qal act ptc ms	prep, n ms	n fs, ps 3ms
שִׁחֲרוֹ	מוּסָר	צַדִּיק	אֹכֵל	לְשֹׂבַע	נַפְשׁוֹ
shichărô	mûsār	tsaddîq	'ōkhēl	lesōva'	naphshô
he will seek him	discipline	the righteous	eating	to the satisfaction of	his soul

14:1

1027	7857	2741.122	2554	5571	1161.112	1041
cj, n fs	n mp	v Qal impf 3fs	n fp	n fp	v Qal pf 3fs	n ms, ps 3fs
וּבְטֶן	רְשָׁעִים	תֶּחֱסָר	חַכְמוֹת	נָשִׁים	בָּנְתָה	בֵּיתָהּ
ûveṭen	reshā'îm	techĕsār	chakhmôth	nāshîm	bānethāh	vêthāhh
but the belly of	the wicked	it will lack	the wisdom of	women	she will build	her house

---

harm, *NIV* ... will smart for it, *Goodspeed*.

21. Evil pursueth sinners: ... Misfortune pursues, *RSV* ... Ill fortune will dog sinners, *Goodspeed* ... Suffering follows the wicked, *Fenton*.

but to the righteous good shall be repaid: ... just shall be recompensed with good, *NAB* ... prosperity rewards the righteous, *RSV* ... good fortune will overtake the righteous, *Goodspeed*.

22. A good man leaveth an inheritance to his children's children: ... causeth sons' sons to inherit, *Young* ... Grandchildren succeed the good, *Fenton* ... heritage of the good man is handed down to, *BB*.

and the wealth of the sinner is laid up for the just: ... sinner lays up treasure—to enrich the good!, *Moffatt* ... is stored up for the upright man, *BB* ... laid up for the righteous is the sinner's wealth, *Young*.

23. Much food is in the tillage of the poor: ... fallow ground of the poor yields much food, *RSV* ... is in the plowed ground, *KJVII* ... fallow land of the proud yields food in abundance, *Goodspeed*.

but there is that is destroyed for want of judgment: ... is swept away for want of justice, *Rotherham* ... some men perish for lack of a law court, *NAB*.

24. He that spareth his rod hateth his son: but he that loveth him chasteneth him betimes: ... He who keeps back his rod is unkind to his son, *BB* ... are diligent to discipline them, *NRSV* … he who loves him chastens him early, *KJVII* … affection corrects him early, *Fenton*.

25. The righteous eateth to the satisfying of his soul: … eats to his heart's content, *Goodspeed* … When the just man eats, his hunger is appeased, *NAB* … upright man has food to the full measure of his desire, *BB*.

but the belly of the wicked shall want: … is empty, *NRSV* … appetite of the wicked is never satisfied, *Goodspeed* … there will be no food for the stomach of evil-doers, *BB*.

14:1. Every wise woman buildeth her house: … Wisdom builds the house of life, *Moffatt* … Wisdom is building her house, *BB*.

but the foolish plucketh it down with her hands: … foolish pull down, *Fenton* … Folly tears hers down, *NAB* … frivolity pulls it down, *Moffatt*.

2. He that walketh in his uprightness feareth the LORD: … person whose conduct is upright, *REB* … man who lives right, *Beck* … To do right honors God, *LIVB*.

since those with whom a person spends time are a powerful force for good or disaster in life (14:7; 27:5f, 17; 28:7). To become wise, someone must choose wise companions (an ability that implies a certain amount of insight) and avoid those who have rejected the fear of the LORD. The second line uses similar roots for both subject and verb (HED #7749; 7778), a pun typical of Biblical Hebrew.

13:21. The translations (e.g., NASB) make the second line passive because of the unusual personification of "good" ("prosperity"), but the parallel with "disaster" supports the text as it stands. Because they leave the path of wisdom, sinners fall into all sorts of adversity (13:17), so that it seems to pursue them. This verse does not mean that the condition of a person's heart can be determined by his or her circumstances. It is instead a warning to consider how choices affect life and an encouragement to decide wisely. The next verse gives a specific example of this principle.

13:22. Other proverbs assert that the treasures of wickedness do not endure (11:29; 13:11; 15:27); this one warns that that wealth will not be passed on to their descendants (cf. 28:8). A pointed application of the general principle contained in the preceding verse, this warns that the righteous will in fact receive a double portion (their own and that of the wicked), the portion of the firstborn. How this happens is not clear. One possible scenario is that the wicked would have to pay a fine if they were convicted of perjury (Deut. 19:15–21), but this verse is far more general than that specific judicial action.

13:23. Although it is difficult to see how fallow (unplanted) fields could contain "much food," Proverbs clearly teaches that the LORD provides for and watches over the poor and righteous (cf. 10:3; 22:22f; 23:10ff). The word "much" (HED #7521) may mean that they would have enough food to survive if they were left alone to gather it. The condemnation of the miscarriage of justice is especially prominent in the later chapters of Proverbs (e.g.,

17:15, 23, 26; 18:5; 19:28; 24:23–26; 28:21; 29:7, 12, 14; 31:4–9). The second line, "But there is that which is swept away without justice," is often smoothed in translation to "But it is swept away," which may be possible, but is syntactically unusual.

13:24. "Love" that refuses to correct someone ensures long-term damage for the sake of short-term peace or harmony, because only a love that views life as a process of growth in wisdom and grace or devolution into corruption and self-destruction (cf. 13:1) understands the need to imbue self-discipline before foolish behaviors become bad habits. The need for discipline (cf. 13:1; 19:18; 20:20) is never outgrown (3:11f), so that even this Book's teachings become God's means of addressing foolish behavior and attitudes. The "rod" in this and other proverbs represents any type of discipline, not merely corporal punishment.

13:25. The contrast in circumstances is intended to encourage righteousness. Since the righteous are protected and provided for by the LORD (10:3, a close parallel), they are provided for. The close connection between wisdom (righteousness) and diligence also means that those who understand the value of hard work and apply themselves will also provide for their households, whereas those who chase "easy," or illicit, wealth are doomed to eventual frustration (cf. 13:11).

14:1. Slightly different vowels and the specifying word "woman" differentiate the first line from 9:1a, which describes personified Wisdom. The abstract noun "folly" (not "the foolish woman"; cf. the Hebrew text of 9:13) in the second line also suggests that this verse probably refers to qualities rather than individuals: "The wisdom of women builds her house; folly with her own hands destroys it." Fools do not realize that even their *con*struction is *de*structive. This proverb is thus not primarily addressing the choice of a spouse (cf. 11:22; 18:22; 19:14), but the need to pay attention to the true consequences of actions.

198	904, 3135	2117.122		2050.151	904, 3598
cj, n fs	prep, n fd, ps 3fs	v Qal impf 3fs, ps 3ms	**2.**	v Qal act ptc ms	prep, n ms, ps 3ms
וְאִוֶּלֶת	בְּיָדֶיהָ	תֶּהֶרְסֶנּוּ		הֹלֵךְ	בְּיָשְׁרוֹ
we'iwweleth	beyādhêāh	thehersennû		hōlēkh	beyāsherô
but folly	with her hands	she will tear it down		proceeding	in his uprightness

3486.151	3176	4005.255	1932	972.151
v Qal act ptc ms	pn	cj, v Niphal ptc ms	n mp, ps 3ms	v Qal act ptc ms, ps 3ms
יְרֵא	יְהוָה	וּנְלוֹז	דְּרָכָיו	בּוֹזֵהוּ
yerē'	yehwāh	ûnelôz	derākhāv	bôzēhû
one who fears	Yahweh	one who deviates from	his ways	one who despises Him

	904, 6552, 188	2507	1375	8004	2550	8490.122
3.	prep, n ms, n ms	n ms	n fs	cj, n fd	n mp	v Qal impf 3fs, ps 3mp
	בְּפִי־אֱוִיל	חֹטֶר	גַּאֲוָה	וְשִׂפְתֵי	חֲכָמִים	תִּשְׁמוּרֵם
	bephî-'ĕwîl	chōter	ga'ăwāh	wesiphthê	chăkhāmîm	tishmûrēm
	with the mouth of a fool	a shoot of	pride	but the lips of	the wise	they will keep them

	904, 375	511	16	1276	7521, 8721	904, 3699	8228
4.	prep, sub	n mp	n ms	adj	cj, adj, n fp	prep, n ms	n ms
	בְּאֵין	אֲלָפִים	אֵבוּס	בַּר	וְרָב־תְּבוּאוֹת	בְּכֹחַ	שׁוֹר
	be'ên	'ălāphîm	'ēvûs	bār	werāv-tevû'ôth	bekhōach	shôr
	when there is not	oxen	a trough	clean	but abundant produce	when the strength of	an ox

	5915	551	3940	3695.321	6558.521	3695	5915
5.	n ms	n mp	neg part	v Piel impf 3ms	cj, v Hiphil impf 3ms	n mp	n ms
	עֵד	אֱמוּנִים	לֹא	יְכַזֵּב	וְיָפִיחַ	כְּזָבִים	עֵד
	'ēdh	'ĕmûnîm	lō'	yekhazzēv	weyāphîach	kezāvîm	'ēdh
	a witness of	faithfulness	not	he will lie	but he blows out	lies	a witness of

8632		1272.311, 4086	2551	375	1907	3937, 1032.255
n ms	**6.**	v Piel pf 3ms, n ms	n fs	cj, sub	cj, n fs	prep, v Niphal ptc ms
שֶׁקֶר		בִּקֶּשׁ־לֵץ	חָכְמָה	וָאָיִן	וְדַעַת	לְנָבוֹן
shāqer		biqqesh-lēts	chokhmāh	wā'āyin	wedha'ath	lenāvôn
deception		a mocker will seek	wisdom	but there is not	but knowledge	to a discerning one

7327.211		2050.131	4623, 5224	3937, 382	3809	1118, 3156.113
v Niphal pf 3ms	**7.**	v Qal impv 2ms	prep, prep	prep, n ms	n ms	cj, neg part, v Qal pf 2ms
נָקָל		לֵךְ	מִנֶּגֶד	לְאִישׁ	כְּסִיל	וּבַל־יָדַעְתָּ
nāqāl		lēkh	minneghedh	le'îsh	kesîl	ûval-yādha'ättā
it is easy		go	from before	to a man	a fool	and you will not know

8004, 1907		2551	6415	1032.541	1932
n fd, n fs	**8.**	n fs	n ms	v Hiphil inf con	n ms, ps 3ms
שִׂפְתֵי־דָעַת		חָכְמַת	עָרוּם	הָבִין	דַּרְכּוֹ
siphthê-dhā'ath		chokhmath	'ārûm	hāvîn	darkô
lips of knowledge		the wisdom of	a prudent man	one who understands	his way

but he that is perverse in his ways despiseth him: ... is crooked in his ways, NASB ... one who is devious in conduct despises him, NRSV ... hee that is lewd in his wayes, despiseth him, Geneva ... the double-dealer scorns him, REB.

3. In the mouth of the foolish is a rod of pride: ... speech of a fool is a rod for his back, NEB ... fool's talk brings a rod to his back, NIV ... In the mouth of the foolish is a haughty rod, Rotherham.

but the lips of the wise shall preserve them: ... lips of the wise protect them, NIV ... wise man's words are his safeguard, NEB.

4. Where no oxen are, the crib is clean: ... trough is clean, NKJV ... stable is clean, Berkeley ... no food is in the barn, NCV ... there is no grain, RSV, Goodspeed.

but much increase is by the strength of the ox: ... with a strong ox, much grain can be grown, NCV ... great is the increase by the power of the ox, *Young* … abundant crops come by, *RSV*.

5. A faithful witness will not lie: … truthful witness, *Goodspeed* … reliable witness always tells the truth, *Good News* … does not deceive, *NIV*.

but a false witness will utter lies: … false witness breathes out falsehoods, *Berkeley* … false witness uttereth deceitful things, *Rotherham*.

6. A scorner seeketh wisdom, and findeth it not: … conceited man, *NEB* … scoffer searches, *Beck* … scoffer tries to be sagacious but cannot, *Anchor* … arrogant aspire in vain to wisdom, *REB*.

but knowledge is easy unto him that understandeth: … is easy to the man of intelligence, *Douay* … comes readily to the open-minded man, *BB* … comes easily to the perceptive, *Anchor*.

7. Go from the presence of a foolish man, when thou perceivest not in him the lips of knowledge: … Keep well clear of the fool, you will not find wise lips there, *JB* … Go thy way, and let the fool go his, *Knox* … Withdraw from an impatient man; you will not find one word of sense in him, *Moffatt*.

8. The wisdom of the prudent is to understand his way: but the folly of fools is deceit: … is the wisdom of the clever to understand where they go, but the folly of fools misleads, *NRSV* … is to discern his way, but the folly of fools is deceiving, *RSV*.

14:2. Since words and actions reveal the heart, this proverb commends both self-examination and careful evaluation of others. Honest lives are the fruit of obedience (cf. 1:7), just as dishonesty (the "crookedness" implied by the parallelism) reveals contempt for correction and instruction, as well as for the LORD's standards of truth and righteousness. Such a person ought not be trusted.

14:3. The fool's arrogance, displayed in his words, often gets him into trouble (cf. 13:3; 18:6f), because he neither considers the effect of his words before speaking (cf. 12:18; 15:1), nor attempts to control his mouth (18:2; 20:3). The wise understand the power of words (18:21), and so speak cautiously and appropriately (25:11), matching their words to the occasion and the needs of their hearers (25:12). Knowing how (and when) to speak, they guard themselves by their relative silence (17:27f; 21:23).

14:4. The "feed trough" probably stands for the entire area where animals were kept. Filled with cattle, that area would require a good deal of cleaning. The trade-off, however, is lack of food, since animal power was essential to the harvest cycle (cf. Deut. 25:4). Like other proverbs that reflect Israel's agrarian economy, its application is not limited to the family farm (cf. 12:11; 27:23–27; 28:19). The wise understand that any enterprise involves costs and benefits and weigh the relative value of each. (NRSV and NEB unnecessarily revise the word "trough" to read "there is no.")

14:5. Character is a primary issue when weighing witnesses' testimony (12:17). Those to whom lying comes as naturally as breath are false witnesses, and their testimony should be discounted, whereas those whose deeds and lives have proved the worth of their words are trustworthy. Since integrity and justice are proverbial and covenantal themes (Exo. 20:16; 23:1–7; Prov. 17:15, 23), judges must be certain that they know the witnesses well, so that they can properly judge their testimony and uphold justice. (The second line is nearly identical to 6:19a.)

14:6. Proverbs 14:6ff are connected topically (they all concern finding or possessing and using wisdom) and by their vocabulary ("wisdom" [vv. 6, 8], "knowledge" [vv. 6f], "fool" [vv. 7f].) Wisdom cannot be leisurely found, and especially not when the heart is essentially opposed to its counsel (cf. 1:24–28). Scoffers are bent on rebellion against wisdom. This is not an attitude that can be put on and off at will, nor does it allow them even to recognize wisdom when they see it. Like the prologue, then, this proverb urges the reader to pursue wisdom, and not to assume that they will be able to do this later, after a period of rebellion.

14:7. Not only do people become like those with whom they associate (c.f. 13:20; 22:24f), their folly infects each other to such an extent that they do not even know that they have begun to listen to (and spout) folly (cf. 19:27). Wisdom and discretion are not changeless, since we are always on one path or the other, growing in insight or becoming increasingly foolish (cf. 12:21; 14:6). The wise choose their friends carefully.

14:8. Because the wise are patient to ponder decisions, they understand and anticipate the consequences of their choices. They are thus able to avoid trouble (cf. 14:15f; 22:3). Fools deceive themselves into thinking that they understand, and thus they walk blithely into the troubles that the wise avoid.

9.

Strong's	Parsing	Hebrew	Translit.	English
1033	cj, prep	וּבֵין	ûvên	and between
844	n ms	אָשָׁם	'āshām	guilt
4054.121	v Qal impf 3ms	יָלִיץ	yālîts	they will scoff at
188	n mp	אֱוִלִים	'ĕwilîm	fools
4983	n fs	מִרְמָה	mirmāh	deceit
3809	n mp	כְּסִילִים	kesîlîm	fools
198	cj, n fs	וְאֻוֶּלֶת	we'iwweleth	but the foolishness of

10.

Strong's	Parsing	Hebrew	Translit.	English
3949	n ms	לֵב	lēv	the heart
3156.151	v Qal act ptc ms	יוֹדֵעַ	yôdhēa'	knowing
4948	n fs	מָרַּת	mārrath	the bitterness of
5497	n fs, ps 3ms	נַפְשׁוֹ	naphshô	its soul
904, 7977	cj, prep, n fs, ps 3ms	וּבְשִׂמְחָתוֹ	ûvesimchāthô	and in its joy
3596	n mp	יְשָׁרִים	yesharîm	the upright
7814	n ms	רָצוֹן	rātsôn	favor

11.

Strong's	Parsing	Hebrew	Translit.	English
1041	n ms	בֵּית	bêth	the house of
7857	n mp	רְשָׁעִים	resha'îm	the wicked
8436.221	v Niphal impf 3ms	יִשָּׁמֵד	yishshāmēdh	it will be destroyed
3940, 6386.721	neg part, v Hithpael impf 3ms	לֹא־יִתְעָרַב	lō'-yith'ārav	it will not give security to
2299	n ms	זָר	zār	a foreigner

12.

Strong's	Parsing	Hebrew	Translit.	English
3552	sub	יֵשׁ	yēsh	there is
1932	n ms	דֶּרֶךְ	derekh	a way
3596	n ms	יָשָׁר	yāshār	uprightness
3937, 6686, 382	prep, n mp, n ms	לִפְנֵי־אִישׁ	liphnê-'îsh	before a man
164	cj, n ms	וְאֹהֶל	we'ōhel	but the tent of
3596	n mp	יְשָׁרִים	yesharîm	the upright
6775.521	v Hiphil impf 3ms	יַפְרִיחַ	yaphrîach	it will blossom

13.

Strong's	Parsing	Hebrew	Translit.	English
1612, 904, 7926	cj, prep, n ms	גַּם־בִּשְׂחוֹק	gam-bischôq	also with laughter
3628.121, 3949	v Qal impf 3ms, n ms	יִכְאַב־לֵב	yikh'av-lēv	the heart suffers pain
321	cj, n fs, ps 3fs	וְאַחֲרִיתָהּ	we'achărîthāhh	and its end
7977	n fs	שִׂמְחָה	simchāh	rejoicing
321	cj, n fs, ps 3fs	וְאַחֲרִיתָהּ	we'achărîthāhh	but its end
1932, 4323	n mp, n ms	דַּרְכֵי־מָוֶת	darkhê-māweth	ways of death

14.

Strong's	Parsing	Hebrew	Translit.	English
5657.151	v Qal act ptc ms	סוּג	sûgh	one who deviates in
3949	n ms	לֵב	lēv	the heart
8755	n fs	תּוּגָה	thûghāh	grief
4623, 1932, ps 3ms	prep, n mp, ps 3ms	מִדְּרָכָיו	midderākhâv	from his ways
7881.121	v Qal impf 3ms	יִשְׂבַּע	yisba'	he will be satiated

15.

Strong's	Parsing	Hebrew	Translit.	English
6864	n ms	פֶּתִי	pethî	the simple
548.521	v Hiphil impf 3ms	יַאֲמִין	ya'ămîn	he believes
3937, 3725, 1745	prep, adj, n ms	לְכָל־דָּבָר	lekhol-dāvār	every word
4623, 6142	cj, prep, prep, ps 3ms	וּמֵעָלָיו	ûmē'ālâv	but from beside him
382	n ms	אִישׁ	'îsh	a man
3005	adj	טוֹב	tôv	good

16.

Strong's	Parsing	Hebrew	Translit.	English
2550	adj	חָכָם	chākhām	wise
3486.151	v Qal act ptc ms	יָרֵא	yārē'	one who fears
6415	cj, adj	וְעָרוּם	we'ārûm	but a prudent man
1032.121	v Qal impf 3ms	יָבִין	yāvîn	he discerns
3937, 864	prep, n fs, ps 3ms	לַאֲשֻׁרוֹ	la'ashurô	his step

---

9. Fools make a mock at sin: ... make a mock at guilt, *MRB* ... A trespass-offering mocketh fools, *ASV* ... mock at the guilt offering, *NRSV*.

but among the righteous there is favour: ... among the upright there is good will, *ASV, MRB* ... upright enjoy God's favor, *NRSV*.

10. The heart knoweth his own bitterness: ... knows its own grief best, *JB* ... distress, *Fenton* ... No one has knowledge of a man's grief but himself, *BB*.

and a stranger doth not intermeddle with his joy: ... share its joy, *JB* ... prevents, *Fenton* ... no prying stranger can tell when it finds relief, *Knox*.

11. The house of the wicked shall be overthrown: ... shall be torn down, *REB* ... house of the lawless shall be destroyed, *Rotherham*.

but the tabernacle of the upright shall flourish: ... tent of honest men shall flourish, *Anchor* ... tent of good people will prosper, *Beck* ... home of the upright, *NEB*.

12. There is a way which seemeth right unto a man, but the end thereof are the ways of death: … Some people think they are doing right, *NCV* … that seems straight to a man, *Goodspeed* … What man thinks a right course, may end upon the road to death, *Moffatt.*

13. Even in laughter the heart is sorrowful; and the end of that mirth is heaviness: … the heart acheth, *MAST* … may be sad and joy

may eventuate in grief, *Berkeley* … heart may ache, and joy may end in grief, *NIV.*

14. The backslider in heart shall be filled with his own ways: … The heart that declineth, shall be satiate with his owne wayes, *Geneva* … He who goes wrong must take the consequences, *Moffatt.*

and a good man shall be satisfied from himself: … from what is in

himself, *Darby* … his fruits, *Young* … reaps the harvest of his deeds, *Moffatt.*

15. The simple believeth every word: … simpleton believes everything, *NAB* … thoughtless believeth every word, *MAST.*

but the prudent man looketh well to his going: … considers well his steps, *NKJV* … man of insight makes sure where he is going, *Berkeley* … gives thought to his steps, *NIV.*

14:9. This verse is difficult to interpret because the grammar of the first line requires that "guilt" or "guilt-offering" be the subject: "Guilt [or a guilt-offering] mocks fools." The contrasts between "fools" and the "upright" and "mockery" and "goodwill" (cf. NIV, NASB) suggest that the proverb focuses on differences in the social relationships between those who reject and accept the strictures of wisdom.

Since the word translated "guilt" means "guilt-offering" in three-fifths of its occurrences (e.g., Lev. 5:15f, 18f, 25; 19:21f; Num. 6:12; 18:9), the saying may address their different attitudes toward injury. Fools mock at restitution, whereas those who are honest strive to honor their covenantal obligations.

14:10. It is impossible to communicate fully the depth of our emotion or experience with anyone else (cf. 14:13). "Stranger" (as in some translations) is much too strong here—the point is that everyone is a stranger to everyone else's heart (cf. Ecc. 7:3). This warns us to guard ourselves against thinking (or saying) that we understand someone else's situation or feelings. That depth of understanding is reserved for God alone, which is why the psalmists ask him to search and know them (cf. Pss. 7:9; 26:2; 139:23f).

14:11. Comparing the instability of a house with the fruitfulness of a tent gives this proverb an ironic tone. That which is temporary outlasts that which appears solid and enduring. One of the constant refrains of Proverbs is the relative value of wisdom and wickedness in light of the stability of the righteous and the impermanence of the fool (e.g., 10:25; 11:3–6; 12:7). This contrast reflects the warnings of the prologue (cf. 2:29–33; 8:32–36) and the covenantal blessings and curses (Lev. 26; Deut. 28).

14:12. This verse is identical to 16:25. In both passages, it is closely related to nearby verses (here, to, e.g., 8, 11, 15f).

14:13. Closely related to 14:10, this verse warns that no one can understand someone else based on his appearance or words, since the outside appearance often masks the true state of the heart. The second line may mean that public joy turns to grief once the person is no longer in public, or that joy today is no guarantee of happiness in the future. It is thus also important to be cautious about interpreting someone's present feelings or situation based on his past circumstance. These words may also reflect the uncertainties of life (cf. 16:1; 27:1).

14:14. The verb "is satisfied" (implicit in the second line) is used in two senses, one ironic, one positive. Both types of behavior have consequences; both are "satiated." Those who have turned away from wisdom will be filled with the disaster that results from their folly (cf. 12:21; 14:12), whereas the wise, who are also therefore righteous, are blessed (cf. 12:3; 14:11). The state of the heart determines not only words and choices (cf. 4:23), but also the consequences of those words and choices.

14:15. The naive ("simple") lack the discernment that comes through experience, and so tend to be too trusting. Unable to distinguish good counsel from bad, they also fail to learn from their experience, and so repeat their errors. The prudent, however, have learned to weigh carefully every decision, no matter how insignificant it may appear (in Proverbs, a "step" represents the smallest unit of one's life). This self-discipline is progressive. At first, every decision is weighed, but experience reveals which deserve more attention than others. This verse and the next three contrast types of decisions and their consequences, forming a small thematic unit (not a poem) closed by another verse describing the prudent and naive (14:18).

14:16. Because the wise are neither arrogant nor blinded by anger, they are able to count the cost

Strong's	Parsing	Hebrew	Translit.	Gloss
5681.151	cj, v Qal act ptc ms	וְסָר	wesār	and one who turns aside
4623, 7737	prep, n ms	מֵרָע	mērā'	from evil
3811	cj, n ms	וּכְסִיל	ûkhesîl	but a fool
5882.751	v Hithpael ptc ms	מִתְעַבֵּר	mith'abbēr	keeps passing on
1019.151	cj, v Qal act ptc ms	וּבֹטֵחַ	ûvôtēach	and being confident

17.

Strong's	Parsing	Hebrew	Translit.	Gloss
7405, 653	adj, n md	קְצַר־אַפִּים	qōtsar-'appayim	quick tempered of nostrils
6449.121	v Qal impf 3ms	יַעֲשֶׂה	ya'aseh	he will act with
198	n fs	אִוֶּלֶת	'iwweleth	foolishness
382	cj, n ms	וְאִישׁ	we'îsh	and a man of
4343	n fp	מְזִמּוֹת	mezimmôth	plans
7983.221	v Niphal impf 3ms	יִשָּׂנֵא	yissānē'	he will be hated

18.

Strong's	Parsing	Hebrew	Translit.	Gloss
5336.116	v Qal pf 3cp	נָחֲלוּ	nāchalû	they have inherited
6848	adj	פְּתָאיִם	phethā'yim	the simple
198	n fs	אִוֶּלֶת	'iwweleth	foolishness
6415	cj, adj	וַעֲרוּמִים	wa'arûmîm	but the prudent
3932.526	v Hiphil impf 3mp	יַכְתִּרוּ	yakhtirû	they will wear a headdress
1907	n fs	דָעַת	dhā'ath	knowledge

19.

Strong's	Parsing	Hebrew	Translit.	Gloss
8249.116	v Qal pf 3cp	שַׁחוּ	shachû	they will be brought low
7737	n mp	רָעִים	rā'îm	the evil
3937, 6686	prep, n mp	לִפְנֵי	liphnê	before
3005	n mp	טוֹבִים	tôvîm	the good
7857	cj, n mp	וּרְשָׁעִים	ûreshā'îm	and the wicked
6142, 8554	prep, n mp	עַל־שַׁעֲרֵי	'al-sha'arê	beside the gates of
6926	n ms	צַדִּיק	tsaddîq	the righteous

20.

Strong's	Parsing	Hebrew	Translit.	Gloss
1612, 3937, 7739	cj, prep, n ms, ps 3ms	גַּם־לְרֵעֵהוּ	gam-lerē'ēhû	even to his fellow
7983.221	v Niphal impf 3ms	יִשָּׂנֵא	yissānē'	he will be hated
7851	n ms	רָשׁ	rāsh	a poor man
154.152	cj, v Qal act ptc mp	וְאֹהֲבֵי	we'ōhevê	but those who love
6474	n ms	עָשִׁיר	'āshîr	the rich
7521	adj	רַבִּים	rabbîm	many

21.

Strong's	Parsing	Hebrew	Translit.	Gloss
972.151, 3937, 7739	v Qal act ptc ms, prep, n ms, ps 3ms	בָּז־לְרֵעֵהוּ	bāz-lerē'ēhû	one who despises his fellow
2490.151	v Qal act ptc ms	חוֹטֵא	chôtē'	a sinner
2706.351	cj, v Poel ptc ms	וּמְחוֹנֵן	ûmechônēn	but having compassion on
6270	n mp	עֲנָיִים	'ănāyîm	the afflicted
869	n ms, ps 3ms	אַשְׁרָיו	'ashrâv	his happiness

22.

Strong's	Parsing	Hebrew	Translit.	Gloss
1950B, 3940, 8912.126	intrg part, neg part, v Qal impf 3mp	הֲלוֹא־יִתְעוּ	hălô'-yith'û	will they not go astray

---

16. A wise man feareth, and departeth from evil: ... is cautious and turns his back on evil, *NEB* ... shuns evil, *Douay* ... Wise people are careful and stay out of trouble, *NCV*.

but the fool rageth, and is confident: ... a dullard is haughty and confident, *Rotherham* ... fool is reckless and sure of himself, *Douay* ... fools are careless and quick to act, *NCV* ... stupid is heedless and falls headlong, *NEB*.

17. He that is soon angry dealeth foolishly: ... quick-tempered acts like a fool, *Fenton* ... who is quickly angry will do what is foolish, *BB* ... short-tempered man commits folly, *Anchor*.

and a man of wicked devices is hated: ... schemer makes enemies, *Knox* ... a man plotting evil is hated, *Beck* ... mischievous fellow is hateful, *Fenton*.

18. The simple inherit folly: ... naive inherit, *NASB* ... Simpletons wear the trappings of folly, *REB* ... Simpletons have folly for their portion, *JB*.

but the prudent are crowned with knowledge: ... the clever, *REB* ... wise are crowned, *KJVII* ... people of discretion knowledge for their crown, *JB*.

19. The evil bow before the good: ... Evildoers cringe before the good, *REB* ... Vile men will be made to bow before the righteous, *Anchor* ... knees of the evil are bent before the good, *BB* ... Vice lies prostrate before virtue, *Knox*.

and the wicked at the gates of the righteous: ... gates of the upright,

JB ... sinner at the gates of the just, *Knox* ... sinners go down in the dust at the doors of the upright, *BB*.

20. The poor is hated even of his own neighbour: ... poor are disliked, *NRSV* ... poor are rejected, *NCV* ... His brother hates the poor, *Fenton*.

but the rich hath many friends: ... many love a rich man, *Beck* ... lovers of the rich man are many, *Rotherham*.

21. He that despiseth his neighbour sinneth: but he that hath mercy on the poor, happy is he: ... He who despises a hungry man does wrong,

but he who is generous to the poor is happy, *NEB* ... he that is gracious unto the humble, happy is he, *MAST* ... blessed is he who is kind to the needy, *NIV*.

22. Do they not err that devise evil?: ... Do not those who think evil go astray?, *KJVII* ... those who plot

---

of various courses of action, and thus avoid making disastrous decisions. Careful, considered action is always the best course. The second line is difficult, since the meaning of the first verb is uncertain. It may mean to become so angry that one throws off all restraint. Decisions made when enraged, or when blinded by arrogance, tend to lead to trouble. Those who make decisions hastily or in a highly emotional state are not to be trusted to choose wisely.

14:17. This proverb contrasts the short-tempered fool with one who acts deliberately (cf. 29:22). The fool, who cannot control his temper, lashes out (cf. 15:18; 19:3), and is routinely condemned in Proverbs (cf. 19:19; 22:24). He accomplishes nothing, since hasty words and actions are not based on prudence or planning. Folly begets only more folly, which is typified by the rage and fruitlessness that characterize the fool's life.

The person described in the second line is not at all impetuous. Rather than striking out impulsively, he plans both words and actions for maximum effect. Someone who lives this way may conceal his wicked intent (cf. 10:18; 26:23–28), but when his plots are discovered (10:9), he will be hated by others (cf. 12:2; 24:8f), just as he is an abomination to the LORD (6:18). The hot-tempered fool may be pitied for his lack of self-control or avoided because of his behavior, but the plotter is despised for his wickedness. Wisdom avoids both.

14:18. Due to their naiveté, the simple accumulate and "store up" the consequences of their many foolish decisions, which will, at some point in their lives, come back to haunt them. The discerning, by contrast, are known and honored by the wisdom that characterizes their lives. They, in essence, crown themselves by their knowledge, which is evident to all. The NRSV's "are adorned with" (marg., "Or inherit") changes the vowels of the first verb to provide a better parallel with the second line, although the verb in that line is used in an unusual way (only here and in Ps. 142:7).

14:19. Although the wicked may prevail (e.g., 28:28; 29:16), making sin appear beneficial, the proverbs unanimously warn the wicked and encourage the righteous by describing their contrasting fates (e.g., 11:31; 12:7; 13:13, 21; 14:11). Nor is this reversal simply a "natural" process. Their folly is self-destructive (14:1), since their decisions and choices will inevitably be characterized by the myopia of the impatient and self-assured.

14:20. Since fools weigh people's worth by their ability to help the wicked accomplish their goals, they value the wealthy (19:4), especially those who are "generous" (19:6), and despise or oppress the poor (14:21, 31; 17:5; 18:23; 19:4, 7), who are powerless. The proverbs counsel creation (no one is "self-made") as the basis of mutual respect and encouragement (14:31; 22:2).

14:21. Looking down on someone because of his poverty is sinful because it bases the person's worth upon his situation. Graciousness is never wrong, regardless of the situation, but it is especially upright when it rises out of a sense of the innate worth and dignity of every human being without considering his station in life. Since this attitude reveals the fear of the LORD and the understanding that He is the Maker of all (cf. 22:2; 29:13), it is blessed, whereas the arrogance that credits itself for its "superior" situation reveals a heart at enmity with God, and therefore with its neighbor.

14:22. The rhetorical question pulls the reader into the proverb, asking, in essence, "Don't you agree?" The contrast between those who wander about lost and those who by seeking good find faithfulness and truth reflects the frequent teaching that behavior has consequences (cf. 11:23, 27; 12:13f) or that what is reaped grows only from what was sown (cf. Gal. 6:7–10). Because they have rejected the way of wisdom, the wicked are already lost. Seeking to further their wickedness, they only remove themselves further from the path (12:21; cf. 28:19).

2896.152	7737	2721	583	2896.152	3005		904, 3725, 6325
v Qal act ptc mp	n ms	cj, n ms	cj, n fs	v Qal act ptc mp	adj	**23.**	prep, *adj*, n ms
חֹרְשֵׁי	רָע	וְחֶסֶד	וֶאֱמֶת	חֹרְשֵׁי	טוֹב		בְּכָל־עֶצֶב
chōreshê	rā'	wecheṣedh	we'ĕmeth	chōreshê	ṭôv		bekhol-'etsev
those who devise	evil	but loyalty	and faithfulness	those who devise	good		with all toil

2030.121	4325	1745, 8004	395, 3937, 4408		6065	2550
v Qal impf 3ms	n ms	cj, *n ms*, n fd	adv, prep, n ms	**24.**	*n fs*	n mp
יִהְיֶה	מוֹתָר	וּדְבַר־שְׂפָתַיִם	אַךְ־לְמַחְסוֹר		עֲטֶרֶת	חֲכָמִים
yihyeh	môthār	ûdhevar-sephāthayim	'akh-lemachṣôr		'ătereth	chăkhāmîm
it will be	profit	but a word of the lips	only to poverty		a crown of	the wise

6484	198	3809	198		5522.551	5497	5915
n ms, ps 3mp	*n fs*	n mp	n fs	**25.**	v Hiphil ptc ms	n fp	*n ms*
עָשְׁרָם	אִוֶּלֶת	כְּסִילִים	אִוֶּלֶת		מַצִּיל	נְפָשׁוֹת	עֵד
'āsherām	'iwweleth	kesîlîm	'iwweleth		matstsîl	nephāshôth	'ēdh
their riches	foolishness of	fools	foolishness		rescuing	lives	a witness of

583	6558.521	3695	4983		904, 3488	3176
n fs	cj, v Hiphil impf 3ms	n mp	n fs	**26.**	prep, *n fs*	pn
אֱמֶת	וְיָפִחַ	כְּזָבִים	מִרְמָה		בְּיִרְאַת	יְהוָה
'ĕmeth	weyāphiach	kezāvîm	mirmāh		beyir'ath	yehwāh
truthfulness	but someone blows out	lies	deceit		with the fear of	Yahweh

4148, 6007	3937, 1158	2030.121	4406		3488	3176
n ms, n ms	cj, prep, n mp, ps 3ms	v Qal impf 3ms	n ms	**27.**	*n fs*	pn
מִבְטַח־עֹז	וּלְבָנָיו	יִהְיֶה	מַחְסֶה		יִרְאַת	יְהוָה
mivtach-'ōz	ûlevānâv	yihyeh	machseh		yir'ath	yehwāh
security of strength	and to his children	it will be	a hiding place		the fear of	Yahweh

4888	2522	3937, 5681.141	4623, 4305	4323		904, 7524, 6194
n ms	n mp	prep, v Qal inf con	prep, *n mp*	n ms	**28.**	prep, *n ms*, n ms
מְקוֹר	חַיִּים	לָסוּר	מִמֹּקְשֵׁי	מָוֶת		בְּרָב־עָם
meqôr	chayyîm	lāṣûr	mimmōqeshê	māweth		berāv-'ām
a fountain of	life	to turn aside	from the snares of	death		in an abundance of people

1997, 4567	904, 675	3947	4425	7615		774
n fs, n ms	cj, prep, *n ms*	n ms	*n fs*	n ms	**29.**	*adj*
הֲדְרַת־מֶלֶךְ	וּבְאֶפֶס	לְאֹם	מְחִתַּת	רָזוֹן		אֶרֶךְ
hadhrath-melekh	ûve'ephes	le'ōm	mechittath	rāzôn		'erekh
an adornment for a king	but with the end of	people	destruction of	a dignitary		long of

---

evil, *NAB* ... that imagine evil, *Geneva*.

but mercy and truth shall be to them that devise good: ... those intent on good gain kindness and constancy, *NAB* ... Those who devise good meet loyalty and faithfulness, *RSV* ... loving-kindness and truth are for those that devise good, *Darby*.

23. In all labour there is profit: but the talk of the lips tendeth only to penury: ... In all hard work, *BB* ... pains of toil bring gain; mere talk yields nothing but need, *REB* ...

Hard work is sure wealth; of chattering comes only poverty, *Knox*.

24. The crown of the wise is their riches: ... The crown wise people wear is their wealth, *Beck* ... Made rich, the wise are crowned, *Knox* ... is their virtue, *Anchor*.

but the foolishness of fools is folly: ... folly the chief ornament of the stupid, *REB* ... foolish behaviour is round the head of the unwise, *BB* ... folly crowns the Perverse!, *Fenton*.

25. A true witness delivereth souls: ... saves lives, *NASB, Douay* ... deliverer of souls is a faithful witness, *Rotherham*.

but a deceitful witness speaketh lies: ... liar breathes out danger, *Fenton* ... who speaks lies is treacherous, *NASB* ... false witness is a traitor, *NCV* ... one who utters lies is a betrayer, *NRSV*.

26. In the fear of the LORD is strong confidence: and his children shall have a place of refuge: ... In reverence for the LORD, *Berkeley* ... He who reveres the LORD has a strong ground of confidence, *Goodspeed* ... who fears the LORD has a secure fortress, *NIV*.

27. The fear of the LORD is a fountain of life, to depart from the snares of death: ... Reverence for the Eternal is a fount of life, it shows how to evade the nets of Death, *Moffatt* ... to help us avoid the snares, *Beck*.

28. In the multitude of people is the king's honour: ... A king's majesty is derived from a populous nation, *Anchor* ... When a nation swarms, it is the monarch's glory, *Moffatt*.

but in the want of people is the destruction of the prince: ... in the lack of people is the downfall of a prince, *NKJV* ... commeth the destruction of the Prince, *Geneva* ... Without [his] people, a prince is nothing, *Anchor*.

29. He that is slow to wrath is of great understanding: ... To be forbearing is to show great sense, *Moffatt* ... To be patient shows, *REB* ... Patience comes of sovereign prudence, *Knox*.

but he that is hasty of spirit exalteth folly: ... he who is impulsive exalts folly, *NKJV* ... he whose spirit is over-quick gives support to what is foolish, *BB* ... hot temper is the height of folly, *Beck*.

14:23. Though Solomon often mentions the power of words (e.g., 11:9, 11; 12:18, 25; 18:21), this proverb points out their weakness. Without action, talk is like the sluggard's daydreams (13:4; 21:25f), which accomplish nothing. There is a time for discussion and planning (15:22; 19:2), but wise counsel does no good unless it is followed. The wise recognize when it is time for talk to turn to work. Fools, who love to hear themselves speak, talk endlessly (18:2, 13) and destroy their own lives because they reject advice, preferring their own "wisdom" (cf. the next verse).

14:24. The internal qualities of wisdom and folly are ultimately as visible as an external crown (NIV changes the syntax of the first line). The parallelism shows that the point of this verse is the moral condition, more than material well-being or poverty (cf. 14:18). There is thus no hope of concealing the true nature, and by the same token the wisdom or folly of others can be weighed by their words and actions. This saying may have been placed after the preceding so that it would reflect the proverbial emphasis on the rewards of diligence.

14:25. An honest witness actually saves lives—either the lives of the innocent who are falsely accused, or of others who might be threatened or endangered by the guilty. Perjurers, on the other hand, endanger the lives of the innocent by their deceit and endanger others by seeking to free the guilty. Liars are treacherous by definition. Their testimony cannot be trusted; but the wise, who understand the value of truth, are trustworthy.

14:26. The obedience that characterizes "the fear of the LORD" (1:7) engenders confidence as the righteous continually witness the LORD's goodness and protection. Although the syntax is difficult, "his" apparently refers to the person characterized in the first line, perhaps reflecting the covenantal

promise (Exo. 34:6f). This verse and the next are closely related, describing the fear of the LORD as a source of confidence that provides a refuge and a source of life that protects from death.

14:27. The second line explains the first. The fear of the LORD is a source of life (on the meaning of the word translated "fountain" or "well," see 10:11) because it turns away from the snares that lead to death (or "deadly snares"). This verse is closely related to 14:26, and only differs in two words from 13:14, which calls the teaching of the wise the source of life.

In the prologue, the fear of the LORD is identified with wisdom (1:7; 9:10), which is life (8:35). This obedience (see on 1:7) turns away from folly's deadly snares because it sees and recognizes them (14:16; 22:3) and because those who obey never leave the path of life (10:29), off which lie the snares. As in the prologue, obedience yields life, rebellion death (1:20–32; 8:36). (On the "source of life" cf. 10:11; 13:14; 16:22.)

14:28. A king may be called "king" without a kingdom, but there is no reality to his kingship. Even if he has an army, if it is not large enough for defense, he will be destroyed. The first line seems too obvious to be worth stating, but the second counsels leaders to consider carefully their resources before engaging an enemy (cf. Luke 14:31f; 2 Ki. 14:9f) or, by implication, engaging upon any great project, lest they be defeated or the project fail, and they become a laughingstock (cf. Luke 14:28ff).

14:29. Patience is a sign of discernment and understanding (cf. 12:16; 17:27), but the short-tempered act and speak foolishly, provoked by life in general and everyone and everything in particular. A short temper is not a virtue, nor should it ever be used to "excuse" unacceptable behavior. This proverb reveals why the quickly angered are so dan-

30. 2522 / n mp — חַיֵּי chayyê "life for" | 198 / n fs — אִוֶּלֶת 'iwweleth "foolishness" | 7597.551 / v Hiphil ptc ms — מְרִים mērîm "uplifting" | 7405, 7593 / cj, adj, n fs — וּקְצַר־רוּחַ ûqŏtsar-rûach "but short tempered of spirit" | 7521, 8722 / adj, n fs — רַב־תְּבוּנָה rav-tevûnāh "abundant in insight" | 653 / n md — אַפָּיִם 'appayim "nostrils"

7352 / n fs — קִנְאָה qin'āh "jealousy" | 6344 / n fp — עֲצָמוֹת 'ătsāmôth "the bones" | 7831 / cj, n ms — וּרְקַב ûreqav "but rottenness of" | 4996 / n ms — מַרְפֵּא marpē' "healing" | 3949 / n ms — לֵב lēv "a heart of" | 1340 / n mp — בְּשָׂרִים vesārîm "the body"

31. 6479.151, 1859 / v Qal act ptc ms, n ms — עֹשֵׁק־דָּל 'ōshēq-dāl "one who oppresses the poor" | 2884.311 / v Piel pf 3ms — חֵרֵף chērēph "he has scoffed at" | 6449.151 / v Qal act ptc ms, ps 3ms — עֹשֵׂהוּ 'ōsēhû "his Maker" | 3632.351 / cj, v Piel ptc ms, ps 3ms — וּמְכַבְּדוֹ ûmekhabbedhô "but honoring Him"

2706.151 / v Qal act ptc ms — חֹנֵן chônēn "one who has compassion for" | 33 / n ms — אֶבְיוֹן 'evyôn "the needy" | **32.** 904, 7750 / prep, n fs, ps 3ms — בְּרָעָתוֹ berā'āthô "by his evil" | 1815.221 / v Niphal impf 3ms — יִדָּחֶה yiddācheh "he will be pushed down" | 7857 / n ms — רָשָׁע rāshā' "a wicked man"

2725.151 / cj, v Qal act ptc ms — וְחֹסֶה wechōseh "but being secure" | 904, 4323 / prep, n ms, ps 3ms — בְּמֹתוֹ vemôthô "during his death" | 6926 / n ms — צַדִּיק tsaddîq "the righteous" | **33.** 904, 3949 / prep, n ms — בְּלֵב belēv "in the heart of" | 1032.255 / v Niphal ptc ms — נָבוֹן nāvôn "the discerning one"

5299.122 / v Qal impf 3fs — תָּנוּחַ tānûach "it will come to rest" | 2551 / n fs — חָכְמָה chokhmāh "wisdom" | 904, 7419 / cj, prep, n ms — וּבְקֶרֶב ûveqerev "but in the inmost parts of" | 3809 / n mp — כְּסִילִים kesîlîm "fools" | 3156.222 / v Niphal impf 3fs — תִּוָּדֵעַ tiwwādhēa' "it will be known"

34. 6930 / n fs — צְדָקָה tsedhāqāh "righteousness" | 7597.322, 1504 / v Polel impf 3fs, n ms — תְּרוֹמֵם־גּוֹי therômēm-gôy "it will exalt a nation" | 2722 / cj, n ms — וְחֶסֶד wechesedh "but a shameful thing" | 3947 / n mp — לְאֻמִּים le'ummîm "peoples" | 2496 / n fs — חַטָּאת chattā'th "sin"

35. 7814, 4567 / n ms, n ms — רְצוֹן־מֶלֶךְ retsôn-melekh "the favor of the king" | 3937, 5860 / prep, n ms — לְעֶבֶד le'evedh "to a slave" | 7959.551 / v Hiphil ptc ms — מַשְׂכִּיל maskîl "being wise" | 5887 / cj, n fs, ps 3ms — וְעֶבְרָתוֹ we'evrāthô "but his rage" | 2030.122 / v Qal impf 3fs — תִּהְיֶה tihyeh "it will be"

---

30. A sound heart is the life of the flesh: ... tranquil heart is life to the body, *NASB* ... Peace of mind means a healthy body, *NCV* ... contented heart strengthens the frame, *Fenton.*

but envy the rottenness of the bones: ... passion makes the bones rot, *NRSV* ... jealousy rots the bones, *Douay* ... decay of the bones is jealousy, *Rotherham.*

31. He that oppresseth the poor reproacheth his Maker: ... blasphemeth his Maker, *MAST* ... insults his Maker, *Berkeley* ... curses his Maker, *KJVII* ... shows contempt for their Maker, *NIV.*

but he that honoureth him hath mercy on the poor: ... who is kind to the needy honors Him, *Berkeley* ... he that is gracious unto the needy, *MAST.*

32. The wicked is driven away in his wickedness: ... thrust down, *ASV* ... by his evil-doing, *Darby* ... in his calamity, *MRB* ... brought down by his wrongdoing, *Goodspeed*.

but the righteous hath hope in his death: … hath a refuge, *ASV* … in integrity the upright will find refuge, *JB* … upright man is secure in his own honesty, *NEB*.

33. Wisdom resteth in the heart of him that hath understanding: … abides in the mind of, *RSV* … reposes in the heart of the discerning,

NIV … In the heart of the intelligent wisdom abides, *NAB*.

but that which is in the midst of fools is made known: … in the bosom of fools it is unknown, *NAB* … in the inward part of fools, *MAST*.

34. Righteousness exalteth a nation: … Uprightness makes a nation great, *JB* … Doing what is right makes a nation great, *NCV* … Virtue exalts a nation, *Douay*.

but sin is a reproach to any people: … is a disgrace, *NIV* … a shame, *KJVII* … a people's disgrace, *Douay*.

35. The king's favour is toward a wise servant: … is toward the servant who deals wisely, *Berkeley* … shows favour to a wise minister, *JB* … king is pleased with, *NCV* … favors the intelligent servant, *Douay*.

---

gerous: they have foolish hearts and would rather talk than listen or learn (cf. 18:2), which inevitably leads them into trouble (18:6f).

14:30. One consequence of a peaceful spirit (cf. the preceding verse) is a healthful life. The contrast between "envy" (NASB) and a healthy attitude suggests the commandment against covetousness, although the word can also mean "zeal" or nonsexual "passion." The wise person asks whether his choices (thoughts, ambitions, etc.) tend toward one or the other of these poles.

14:31. This proverb deepens the thought of 14:21. "His" Maker could refer to the poor, which would imply that the oppressor (who is not necessarily wealthy; cf. Lev. 6:2; Hos. 12:7) does not recognize that the poor are also the special creation of God. It could also refer to oppressors, which would imply their refusal to recognize an authority beyond their own power. The pronoun in the second line is equally ambiguous: the contrast could either be with those who recognize that the poverty of the poor does not change their innate dignity and worth as image-bearers of God, or with those who act out of true humility, knowing that they live before the divinely imposed standards of the Covenant (cf. 22:2).

14:32. It is common to follow the Septuagint in the second line ("in his integrity" rather than "in his death"), as do NRSV and many commentaries, which yields the common teaching of Proverbs that the wicked are punished and the righteous blessed. This is a possible reading, but it is not necessary. The proverb may refer to the eternal hope of the righteous after death, so that the wise can face death calmly, knowing that their true refuge does not lie in anything in this life.

The pronoun "his," however, is ambiguous, so that it could also refer to the death of the wicked (described in the first line). The verse then parallels

other proverbs that describe how judgment upon the wicked affects the righteous (e.g., 28:12, 28) and could be translated "in the death [of the wicked] the righteous have a refuge," or "whoever takes refuge in the death [of the wicked] is righteous."

The two lines seem to contrast the insecurity of the wicked with the safety of the righteous. The wicked have no refuge (since a righteous judge, for example, would condemn them), whereas when the wicked are not in power the righteous (or innocent) are safe.

14:33. Most translations follow the Septuagint and Vulgate in the second line, "But within fools it is not known" (cf. NRSV, NIV). Although it is difficult to imagine a scribe dropping such an important word as "not" from the text, this creates a strong parallelism and makes good sense. The image of the first line—wisdom "resting" in those who have insight—may be the point of the contrast. In that case, the second line may well mean that even fools may have flashes of understanding. That is, however, all that they have. There is no steady, constant presence to guide them, so that even that which whey do "understand" leads them astray.

14:34. This verse is related to the next (cf. 16:12f for a similar sequence), and reflects the covenantal blessings and curses (Lev. 26; Deut. 4:5f; 28), as well as the general message of the proverbs that the righteous will be blessed and the wicked destroyed (e.g., 12:7; 14:11).

14:35. A king who understands the principle of the preceding verse (cf. 16:12; 29:4, 12, 14) also knows the value of good counselors, and seeks them out. Those who would rise in the government (or, more generally, in any organization or corporation) should therefore seek to become wise, that they may succeed and not cause themselves or anyone else shame (14:34). Since success

15:1

1745, 6325	2635	8178.521	4776, 7679	991.551
cj, n ms, n ms	n fs	v Hiphil impf 3ms	n ms, adj	v Hiphil ptc ms
וּדְבַר־עֶצֶב	חֵמָה	יָשִׁיב	מַעֲנֶה־רַּךְ	מֵבִישׁ
ûdhevar-'etsev	chēmāh	yāshîv	ma'ăneh-rakh	mēvîsh
but a word of offense	wrath	it will turn back	a soft answer	one who causes shame

2.

1907	3296.522	2550	4098	6148.521, 653
n fs	v Hiphil impf 3fs	n mp	n ms	v Hiphil impf 3ms, n ms
דָּעַת	תֵּיטִיב	חֲכָמִים	לְשׁוֹן	יַעֲלֶה־אָף
dā'ath	têṭîv	chăkhāmîm	leshôn	ya'ăleh-'āph
knowledge	it causes to be good	the wise	the tongue of	it will cause anger to go up

3.

3176	6084	904, 3725, 4887	198	5218.521	3809	6552
pn	n fd	prep, adj, n ms	n fs	v Hiphil impf 3ms	n mp	cj, n ms
יְהוָה	עֵינֵי	בְּכָל־מָקוֹם	אִוֶּלֶת	יַבִּיעַ	כְּסִילִים	וּפִי
yehwāh	'ênê	bekhol-māqôm	'iwweleth	yabbîa'	khesîlîm	ûphî
Yahweh	the eyes of	in every place	foolishness	it pours out	fools	but the mouth of

4.

5752	2522	6320	4098	4996	3005	7737	7099.154
cj, n ms	n mp	n ms	n ms	n ms	cj, adj	adj	v Qal act ptc fp
וְסֶלֶף	חַיִּים	עֵץ	לָשׁוֹן	מַרְפֵּא	וְטוֹבִים	רָעִים	צְפוֹת
weseleph	chayyîm	'ēts	lāshôn	marpē'	ûṭôvîm	rā'îm	tsōphôth
but crookedness	life	a tree of	tongue	calm of	and good	evil	keeping watch

5.

1	4284	5180.121	188	904, 7593	8133	904
n ms, ps 3ms	n ms	v Qal impf 3ms	n ms	prep, n fs	n ms	prep, ps 3fs
אָבִיו	מוּסַר	יִנְאַץ	אֱוִיל	בְּרוּחַ	שֶׁבֶר	בָּהּ
'āviw	mûsar	yin'ats	'ewîl	berûach	shever	bāhh
his father	the discipline of	he will despise	a fool	in the spirit	brokenness	in it

6.

2738	6926	1041	6429.121	8763	8490.151
n ms	n ms	n ms	v Qal impf 3ms	n fs	cj, v Qal act ptc ms
חֹסֶן	צַדִּיק	בֵּית	יַעְרִם	תּוֹכַחַת	וְשֹׁמֵר
chōsen	tsaddîq	bêth	ya'ărim	tôkhachath	weshōmēr
storage	the righteous	the household of	he is prudent	correction	but one who observes

7.

2550	8004	6138.255	7857	904, 8721	7521
n mp	n fd	v Niphal ptc fs	n ms	cj, prep, n fs	adj
חֲכָמִים	שִׂפְתֵי	נֶעְכָּרֶת	רֶשַׁע	וּבִתְבוּאַת	רָב
chăkhāmîm	siphthê	ne'ăkkāreth	rāshā'	ûvithvû'ath	rāv
the wise	the lips of	happening trouble	the wicked	but with the produce of	abundant

8.

2306.326	1907	3949	3809	3940, 3772	2160	7857
v Piel impf 3mp	n fs	cj, n ms	n mp	neg part, adv	n ms	n mp
יְזָרוּ	דָּעַת	וְלֵב	כְּסִילִים	לֹא־כֵן	זֶבַח	רְשָׁעִים
yezārû	dhā'ath	welēv	kesîlîm	lō'-khēn	zevach	reshā'îm
widely disperse	knowledge	but the heart of	fools	not so	a sacrifice of	the wicked

---

but his wrath is against him that causeth shame: ... shameful servant incurs his wrath, *NIV* ... but anger to one who shames him, *JB* ... worthless one incurs his wrath, *Douay*.

15:1. A soft answer turneth away wrath: ... gentle answer will calm a person's anger, *NCV* ... A mild answer calms wrath, *Douay*.

but grievous words stir up anger: ... a harsh word arouses anger, *Berkeley* ... unkind answer will cause more, *NCV*.

2. The tongue of the wise useth knowledge aright: but the mouth of fools poureth out foolishness: ... makes knowledge welcome, *JB* ... commends knowledge, *NIV* ... makes knowledge attractive, but the mouth of fools gushes forth with folly, *Berkeley*.

3. The eyes of the LORD are in every place, beholding the evil and the good: ... eyes of Yahweh are everywhere, *JB* ... The LORD sees what happens everywhere; he is watching us, *Good News* ... keeping watch upon, *MAST*.

4. A wholesome tongue is a tree of life: ... tongue that brings healing, *NIV* ... As a tree gives fruit, healing words give life, *NCV* ... Gentleness of tongue, *Darby*.

but perverseness therein is a breach in the spirit: ... is a wound to the spirit, *MAST* ... crushes the spirit, *NAB* ... a deceitful tongue crushes, *NIV* ... dishonest words crush, *NCV*.

5. A fool despiseth his father's instruction: but he that regardeth reproof is prudent: ... spurns his father's discipline, *NIV* ... Fools reject their parents' correction, but anyone who accepts correction is wise, *NCV*.

6. In the house of the righteous is much treasure: ... the upright there is no lack of treasure, *JB* ... the just there are ample resources, *Douay*.

but in the revenues of the wicked is trouble: ... income of the wicked, *NIV* ... earnings of the wicked are fraught with anxiety, *JB* ... earnings of the wicked are in turmoil, *Douay*.

7. The lips of the wise disperse knowledge: ... disseminate knowledge, *NAB* ... Wise people use their words to spread knowledge, *NCV*.

---

and shame are the results of the decisions that reveal moral character (cf. 10:5), a king will pay special attention to the reputation and history of those who aspire to his ear.

15:1. Many proverbs may seem tautologous—too obvious to mention. The proverbs, however, are given in order to increase insight, as well as to give moral guidance. Non-directive verses like this one require reflection in order to discern their intent, figuring out the "ought" from their description (although this is a fairly obvious example, others are not).

Since anger is always condemned in Proverbs, the wise person will seek to deflect it by answering gently. Knowing the wise course of action is relatively easy in this case. Answering calmly in the face of anger or aggression, however, is not as easy. It requires a person to have his own emotions under control, so that he does not respond in kind. It also urges the wise to listen carefully, in order to be able to discern the particular words that will be "soft" in that case.

15:2. As the contrast with "spouts" (NASB) or "gushes" (NIV) shows, the care with which the wise choose their words makes their knowledge attractive (17:27; for this use of the verb, cf. Exo. 30:7; 2 Ki. 9:30; Prov. 17:22; Hos. 10:1). The wise are reticent to speak because they understand the power of words (18:21), whereas fools refuse to benefit from the wisdom and insight of others because they prefer their own "understanding." They are too busy speaking to learn (18:2). Their words are drivel (10:32), often wicked (10:19), because they flow from foolish hearts.

15:3. A major theme of Prov. 10–20 is that the LORD judges every person's motives (15:11; 16:2; 17:3; 21:2). His judgment underlies his treatment of the righteous and wicked and explains that their circumstances represent his valuation of their hearts and

deeds (cf. 3:32f; 10:3; 11:20; 12:2, 22; 17:15). This proverb finds it sufficient to note the LORD's implicit judgment, without describing the consequences. It thus encourages students of wisdom to consider, and live in accord with, the LORD's character.

15:4. Both wisdom and healing words are equated with a "tree of life" (cf. 3:18; 10:11), because words that heal, strengthen and restore come from thoughtful hearts (12:18). Those who would be a source of encouragement must exercise both forethought and insight. The contrast of healing with "treachery" or "deceit" discourages "white" lies by warning that they ultimately do not heal; indeed, healing may be better accomplished by a wise rebuke (27:5f; 28:23). Affable or pleasant words that mask motives rather than exhibit concern for the hearer's welfare are not only deceitful, but destructive, a point emphasized by the many verses that address flattery (e.g., 29:5) and deceit (e.g., 26:23–28).

15:5. Fools do not understand that only by being corrected can they become wise. Prudence comes through being willing to listen and learn, something that does not characterize fools. Those who accept rather than despise correction grow in their ability to plan and act wisely (cf. 13:16; 14:8; 22:3; 27:12).

15:6. One of the blessings that attend wisdom is protection from various sorts of trouble (cf. 2:12–15, 16–19), whereas the lives of the wicked produce little but trouble for themselves and others. In this version of the frequent assertion of inevitable consequences (cf. 10:2f, 25; 12:7, 21), the ear of the ancient Israelites could hardly have missed the pun on the verbal root that gives its name to the Valley of Achor, "Trouble" (Josh. 7:24, 26; 15:7; cf. Isa. 65:10; Hos. 2:15).

15:7. Since the wise are able to distinguish good from evil, they are careful to say only that which is true and helpful to others. They "winnow" their words before speaking. Fools, whose hearts are filled

Verse 9

8774	3176	8940	3596	7814	9.	8774	3176
n fs	pn	cj, n fs	n mp	n ms, ps 3ms		n fs	pn
תּוֹעֲבַת	יְהוָה	וּתְפִלַּת	יְשָׁרִים	רְצוֹנוֹ		תּוֹעֲבַת	יְהוָה
tô'ăvath	yᵉhwāh	ûthᵉphillath	yᵉshārîm	rᵉtsônô		tô'ăvath	yᵉhwāh
an abomination to	Yahweh	but a prayer of	the upright	his delight		an abomination to	Yahweh

Verse 10

1932	7857	7579.351	6930	154.121	10.	4284	7737
n ms	n ms	cj, v Piel ptc ms	n fs	v Qal impf 3ms		n ms	n ms
דֶּרֶךְ	רָשָׁע	וּמְרַדֵּף	צְדָקָה	יֶאֱהָב		מוּסָר	רָע
derekh	rāshā'	ûmᵉraddēph	tsᵉdhāqāh	ye'ĕhāv		mûsār	rā'
the way of	the wicked	but one who pursues	righteousness	He loves		chastisement	evil

Verse 11

3937, 6013.151	758	7983.151	8763	4322.121	11.	8061	11
prep, v Qal act ptc ms	n ms	v Qal act ptc ms	n fs	v Qal impf 3ms		pn	cj, pn
לְעֹזֵב	אֹרַח	שׂוֹנֵא	תּוֹכַחַת	יָמוּת		שְׁאוֹל	וַאֲבַדּוֹן
lᵉ'ōzēv	'ōrach	sônē'	thôkhachath	yāmûth		shᵉ'ôl	wa'ăvaddôn
to one who abandons	a path	one who hates	correction	he will die		Sheol	and Abaddon

Verse 12

5224	3176	652	3706, 3949	1158, 119	12.	3940
prep	pn	cj	cj, n mp	n mp, n ms		neg part
נֶגֶד	יְהוָה	אַף	כִּי־לִבּוֹת	בְּנֵי־אָדָם		לֹא
neghedh	yᵉhwāh	'aph	kî-libbôth	bᵉnê-'ādhām		lō'
before	Yahweh	also	indeed the hearts of	the children of humankind		not

Verse 13

154.121, 4086	3306.542	3937	420, 2550	3940	2050.121	13.	3949
v Qal impf 3ms, n ms	v Hiphil inf abs	prep, ps 3ms	prep, n mp	neg part	v Qal impf 3ms		n ms
יֶאֱהַב־לֵץ	הוֹכֵחַ	לוֹ	אֶל־חֲכָמִים	לֹא	יֵלֵךְ		לֵב
ye'ĕhav-lēts	hôkhēach	lô	'el-chăkhāmîm	lō'	yēlēkh		lēv
a scoffer loves	chastising	of him	to the wise	not	he will go		a heart

Verse 14

7976	3296.521	6686	904, 6329, 3949	7593	5405	14.	3949
adj	v Hiphil impf 3ms	n mp	cj, prep, n fs, n ms	n fs	adj		n ms
שָׂמֵחַ	יֵיטִב	פָּנִים	וּבְעַצֶּבֶת־לֵב	רוּחַ	נְכֵאָה		לֵב
sāmēach	yêṭiv	pānîm	ûvᵉ'atstsᵉvath-lēv	rûach	nᵉkhē'āh		lēv
joyful	it causes to be good	the face	but with the pain of the heart	a spirit	dejected		a heart

(continuation of Verse 14)

1032.255	1272.321, 1907	6686	3809	7749.121	198
v Niphal ptc ms	v Piel impf 3ms, n fs	cj, n mp	n mp	v Qal impf 3ms	n fs
נָבוֹן	יְבַקֶּשׁ־דָּעַת	וּפְנֵי	כְּסִילִים	יִרְעֶה	אִוֶּלֶת
nāvôn	yᵉvaqqesh-dā'ath	ûphᵉnê	khᵉsîlîm	yir'eh	'iwweleth
discerning	it will seek knowledge	but the face of	fools	it will feed on	foolishness

---

but the heart of the foolish doeth not so: ... heart of fools is perverted, *Douay* ... not so the minds of fools, *NRSV.*

8. The sacrifice of the wicked is an abomination to the LORD: but the prayer of the upright is his delight: ... is a hateful thing, *KJVII* ... is abhorrent to Yahweh, dear to him is the prayer of the honest, *JB* ... pleases him, *NIV.*

9. The way of the wicked is an abomination unto the LORD: ... LORD hates what evil people do, *NCV*

... road of Sin disgusts the LORD, *Fenton* ... conduct of the wicked is abhorrent to Yahweh, *JB.*

but he loveth him that followeth after righteousness: ... he loves the man who pursues virtue, *Douay* ... the person whose goal is uprightness, *JB* ... loves those who do what is right, *NCV.*

10. Correction is grievous unto him that forsaketh the way: and he that hateth reproof shall die: ... Stern discipline awaits him who leaves the path, *NIV* ... Severe punishment is in

store for the man who goes astray, *Douay* ... Who leaves that way will suffer grief, Who hates His reproof will die, *Fenton.*

11. Hell and destruction are before the LORD: how much more then the hearts of the children of men?: ... Sheol and destruction, *Darby* ... Sheol and Perdition lie open to Yahweh, *JB* ... The Grave and the Lost are before, *Fenton* ... Sheol and Abaddon lie open, *NASB* ... he surely knows the thoughts of the living, *NCV.*

12. A scorner loveth not one that reproveth him: neither will he go unto the wise: ... doesn't like to be corrected, *Beck* ... Scoffers do not like to be rebuked, *NRSV* ... mocker resents correction, *NIV* ... senseless man loves not to be reproved, *Douay*.

13. A merry heart maketh a cheerful countenance: ... A glad heart lights up the face, *NAB* ... A joyful heart makes a cheerful face, *NASB* ... Happinesss makes a person smile, *NCV*.

but by sorrow of the heart the spirit is broken: ... heartache crushes the spirit, *NIV* ... by mental anguish the spirit is broken, *NAB* ... where the heart is sad, *JB*.

14. The heart of him that hath understanding seeketh knowledge: but the mouth of fools feedeth on foolishness: ... discerning heart seeks, *NIV* ... mind of the intelligent

---

with their own "knowledge," neither understand nor care about wisdom and so speak without regard for the quality or effect of their words (12:18; 15:1).

15:8–9. These two proverbs have been set together in a lesser-to-greater (*a fortiori*) pattern. Not only are the religious deeds of the wicked an abomination, but their entire way of life is rejected by the LORD. On the other hand, He loves and delights in those who follow the teaching of this Book and the rest of the Covenant—righteousness is the pattern of their way of life. The verses warn that external sacrifice does not atone for unrepentant rebellion (21:27; 28:9), as psalmists and prophets emphasize (Ps. 51:16f; Isa. 1:10–15; Mic. 6:7).

These verses do not compare or contrast the acceptability of sacrifice with that of prayer, as though one were better than the other. Rather, the contrast focuses on the attitude of the heart (15:26).

15:10. The first line can be interpreted in two ways: "Stern discipline is for him who forsakes the way" or "Discipline is evil to him who forsakes the way." The first interpretation implies that after a certain point, only unusually harsh discipline, like death, holds out any hope; thus it is harsh for the wicked (though not for the righteous).

The other translation means that to a person who has chosen to leave the path, the discipline that would turn him back is not only loathsome, but his values have become so perverted that the teachings of righteousness are now "wicked" (cf. 28:4; Isa. 5:18–23). Having determined that he will not be turned, he hates the rebukes which he knows have his correction as their end (cf. 9:7f). The second line then means that such a person, by rejecting the path of life, has chosen death (cf. 6:23; 29:1). Both interpretations are possible, and both may be intended, given the description of some of these sayings as "figures" and "riddles" (1:6).

15:11. An argument from the greater to the lesser, this proverb says, in effect, if the greater is true, how much more is the lesser true! Whether Sheol is viewed as the abode of the dead after death,

or merely the grave, Abaddon ("destruction") apparently refers to a place or condition within Sheol (27:20; Job 26:6; 28:22; 31:12; Ps. 88:12). If these places, utterly unknown to the living, are open before the LORD, how much more are human hearts and motives (cf. 15:3; 16:2).

15:12. Since scoffers are unwilling to be corrected, they avoid the wise when they are looking for "advice." They seek not advice, but mere confirmation of their opinions or plans, and they know that the wise offer whatever is truly needed, whether rebuke, correction or praise. Solomon thus warns that avoiding sound counsel indicates a rebellious and sinful heart. The wise are marked by humility, and understand their own need to be corrected and rebuked (cf. 29:1).

15:13. True happiness can rarely be concealed, but some circumstances overwhelm even the most resilient. People crushed by emotional injury or distress often manage to hide their despair (cf. 14:10, 13). Sensitivity and discernment are crucial to good relationships, so that the right words may be spoken and the right help offered (cf. 25:11f).

15:14. The discerning know the importance and value of wisdom and knowledge, and so continually seek to increase their understanding (1:5; 14:7; 19:27). Fools, however, who lack understanding and wisdom, continue in their folly. The second verb has nuances. If it means "to pasture," then this verse parallels others which warn that whatever a fool says (i.e., that with which he attempts to "feed" others [10:11, 21]) endangers himself and his hearers. If, on the other hand, it means "to feed on," then fools, unable to distinguish wisdom from folly, accept whatever they are told.

Given the reluctance of fools to accept advice, and their insatiable desire to hear their own words (cf. 18:2), the first interpretation may be more likely, although both are possible, and the ambiguity may well be a deliberate aspect of the proverb to encourage Solomon's readers to ponder both images. Three of these four proverbs (15:14f, 17)

15.

3725, 3219	6270	7737	3005, 3949	5136	8878
adj, n mp	n ms	adj	cj, adj, n ms	n ms	adv
כָּל־יְמֵי	עָנִי	רָעִים	וְטוֹב־לֵב	מִשְׁתֶּה	תָמִיד
kol-yemê	'ānî	rā'îm	wetôv-lēv	mishteh	thāmîdh
all the days of	the afflicted	disastrous	but a good heart	a feast	continually

16.

3005, 4746	904, 3488	3176	4623, 212	7521	4245	904
adj, sub	prep, n fs	pn	prep, n ms	adj	cj, n fs	prep, ps 3ms
טוֹב־מְעַט	בְּיִרְאַת	יְהוָה	מֵאוֹצָר	רָב	וּמְהוּמָה	בּוֹ
tôv-me'aṭ	beyir'ath	yehwāh	mē'ôtsār	rāv	ûmehûmāh	vô
better a little	with the fear of	Yahweh	than a storehouse	abundant	and dismay	with it

17.

3005	760	3536	157, 8427	4623, 8228	70.155
adj	n fs	n ms	cj, n fs, adv	prep, n ms	v Qal pass ptc ms
טוֹב	אֲרֻחַת	יָרָק	וְאַהֲבָה־שָׁם	מִשּׁוֹר	אָבוּס
tôv	'ăruchath	yārāq	we'ahvāh-shām	mishshôr	'āvûs
better	a portion of	vegetables	and love there	than an ox	having been fattened

18.

7985, 904	382	2635	1667.321	4209	774	653
cj, n fs, prep, ps 3ms	n ms	n fs	v Piel impf 3ms	n ms	cj, adj	n md
וְשִׂנְאָה־בּוֹ	אִישׁ	חֵמָה	יְגָרֶה	מָדוֹן	וְאֶרֶךְ	אַפַּיִם
wesin'āh-vô	'îsh	chēmāh	yeghāreh	mādhôn	we'erekh	'appayim
but hatred with it	a man of	wrath	he will contend	strife	but long of	nostrils

19.

8618.521	7663	1932	6339	3626, 5029	2407
v Hiphil impf 3ms	n ms	n ms	n ms	prep, n fs	n ms
יַשְׁקִיט	רִיב	דֶּרֶךְ	עָצֵל	כִּמְשֻׂכַת	חָדֶק
yashqîṭ	rîv	derekh	'ātsēl	kimsukhath	chādheq
he will quiet	contention	the way of	a sluggard	like a thorn hedge of	a thornbush

20.

758	3596	5744.157	1158	2550	7975.321, 1	3811
cj, n ms	n mp	v Qal pass ptc fs	n ms	adj	v Piel impf 3ms, n ms	cj, n ms
וְאֹרַח	יְשָׁרִים	סְלֻלָה	בֵּן	חָכָם	יְשַׂמַּח־אָב	וּכְסִיל
we'ōrach	yeshārîm	selulāh	bēn	chākhām	yesammach-'āv	ûkhesîl
but the path of	the upright	is built up	a son	wise	he makes a father glad	but a fool

man, *NAB* ... People with understanding want more knowledge, *NCV*.

15. All the days of the afflicted are evil: ... Every day is hard for those who suffer, *NCV* ... All the days of the coward are griefs, *Fenton* ... Those who suffer are always miserable, *Beck*.

but he that is of a merry heart hath a continual feast: ... for the joyous heart it is always festival time, *JB* ... bold heart always feasts, *Fenton* ... cheerful mind is always feasting, *Beck*.

16. Better is little with the fear of the LORD than great treasure and trouble therewith: ... Better a humble lot, and the fear of the Lord present, than great riches that leave a man unsatisfied, *Knox* ... Better a lit-

tle, with reverence for the Eternal, than large wealth with worry, *Moffatt*.

17. Better is a dinner of herbs where love is: ... Better sit down to a dish of herbs seasoned with charity, *Knox* ... a dish of vegetables if love goes with it, *REB*.

than a stalled ox and hatred therewith: ... than to eat meat with those who hate you, *NCV* ... fatted calf with hatred, *NKJV* ... fat ox eaten in hatred, *NEB*.

18. A wrathful man stirreth up strife: ... Bad temper provokes quarrels, *REB* ... An ill-tempered man stirs up disputes, *Moffatt* ... man of fury stirreth up contention, *Young* ... passionate man stirs up discord, *Goodspeed*.

but he that is slow to anger appeaseth strife: ... allays contention, *NKJV* ... patience heals discords, *NEB* ... forbearing man smoothes strife away, *Moffatt*.

19. The way of the slothful man is as an hedge of thorns: ... Thorns are round the way of the hater of work, *BB* ... Idleness finds ever a hedge of thorns in its path, *Knox* ... lazy man finds life beset with thorns, *Moffatt*.

but the way of the righteous is made plain: ... path of the upright is paved like a highway, *Goodspeed* ... road of the hard worker becomes a highway, *BB* ... diligent find it a well-paved road, *Moffatt*.

20. A wise son maketh a glad father: ... brings joy, *NEB* ... wise

mention eating (this verse metaphorically), which may explain their proximity.

15:15. Affliction, for whatever cause, is disastrous, but a person's inner resources can enable him to persevere and even triumph. This verse is related to the following verses (15:16f), which are in turn the specific application (v. 17) of a general principle (v. 16). All three of these proverbs (15:15ff) thus encourage the wise to distinguish physical or tangible circumstances from the underlying realities that give them their true value.

15:16. Those who have set their hearts to obey the LORD live at peace with themselves and others. Their irenicism grows out of their concern to serve God and other individuals rather than to forward themselves or their goals. The result is a calm that outweighs all outward success.

This does not mean that it is better to be poor than wealthy. The value of relative poverty depends on the circumstances through which the wealth or poverty comes (cf. 15:17; 16:8; 17:1; 19:1; 28:6). The contrast between the "fear of the LORD" and "turmoil" implies that if the choice lies between obedience and disobedience, obedience (with its accompanying blessing) is always the best choice, regardless of the consequences. If a less successful, but peaceful, life is the price of that loyalty to the Covenant, it is still far better to live under the covenantal blessings than under its curses. It also implies that fortunes gained immorally tend to be accompanied by trouble, because sin has consequences for the sinner and others, consequences that include the judgment of God.

This reflects the "better than" statements in the prologue (e.g., 3:14; 8:11, 19), all of which assert that wisdom is far more valuable than gold, silver or jewels (cf. also 16:16). The fear of the LORD that leads to wisdom (1:7) often leads away from fame and fortune. Wisdom is, however, far more valuable because it leads to the knowledge of God (2:5f) and to a life of peace (1:33).

15:17. An "obvious" choice may not be obvious, since choices always have unseen consequences. The real choice may not lie between a roast ox and a salad, but between the decisions that lead to a peaceful life (even though poor) and those that lead to wealth (and strife). The best beef loses its flavor if the meal is filled with hatred and turmoil, whereas kindness and true affection season even the simplest fare. An Israelite who could afford to kill a fattened ox was obviously finan-

cially secure; however, even the best fare is not worth peace of heart.

This "better than" proverb is a specific application of the preceding verse, illustrating a particular consequence of choosing wealth rather than the fear of the LORD. It does not condemn eating meat, nor does it commend poverty per se (cf. 15:16; 17:1). These verses also do not imply that choosing wealth necessarily entails disobedience. They do, however, warn that when these paths (and all that they lead to) diverge, only one way is right. Both this verse and 15:15 mention feasting, which may account for their proximity.

15:18. Resolving a quarrel depends on patience and tact (cf. 15:1). This implies the need to know someone well before asking him or her to undertake such a task. Those, for example, who have a reputation for being angry are not good mediators. They lack the patience that characterizes the wise and that enables them to speak thoughtfully (15:28) and in a way that quiets tempers. Peacemakers are doubly blessed—by being at peace with themselves (14:29f), by those whom they restore, and by God (Matt. 5:9). (The first line is similar to 29:22a; that verse, however, is synonymous, not antithetical.)

15:19. An obvious characteristic of sluggards is their inactivity. If they finally decide to do something, they find that their laziness has trapped them. While the upright (those who work at the opportune time) travel on a road that is built up (cf. Isa. 57:14; 62:10; Jer. 18:15 for the same word), the lethargy of the lazy has planted and nourished thorn hedges. By contrasting the "sluggard" and the "upright" (cf. 21:25f), Solomon points out that laziness is a moral failure and that a quality common to the righteous is diligence.

15:20. Whereas 10:1 considers the effect of children's behavior on their parents, this verse (which begins in the same way as 10:1) reveals why its effect can be so devastating (cf. 30:11–14, 17). Children's words and behavior reveal that they either accept or despise their parents' wisdom and discipline. Although disobedience may not seem significant, it signals an antagonistic attitude toward discipline and the wisdom that it seeks to inculcate.

15:21. People enjoy what is most important to them, so what a person delights in is an important clue to his inner nature. Those who delight in folly lack discernment and prefer their own

21.

382	3937, 2742, 3949	7977	198	525	995.151
cj, *n ms*	prep, *adj*, n ms	n fs	n fs	n fs, ps 3ms	v Qal act ptc ms
וְאִישׁ	לַחֲסַר־לֵב	שִׂמְחָה	אִוֶּלֶת	אִמּוֹ	בּוֹזֶה
we'îsh	lachăsar-lēv	simchāh	'iwweleth	'immô	bôzeh
but a man of	to one lacking in heart	rejoicing	foolishness	his mother	despising

(119 — *n ms* — אָדָם — 'ādhām — a man)

22.

5660	904, 375	4422	6815.542	3595.321, 2050.141	8722
n ms	prep, *sub*	n fp	v Hiphil inf abs	v Piel impf 3ms, v Qal inf con	n fs
סוֹד	בְּאֵין	מַחֲשָׁבוֹת	הָפֵר	יְיַשֶּׁר־לָכֶת	תְּבוּנָה
sôdh	be'ên	machăshāvôth	hāphēr	yeyashsher-lākheth	tevûnāh
consultation	without	plans	being thwarted	he will walk uprightly	understanding

23.

3937, 382	7977	7251.123	3398.152	904, 7524
prep, art, n ms	n fs	v Qal impf 2ms	v Qal act ptc mp	cj, prep, *n ms*
לָאִישׁ	שִׂמְחָה	תָּקוּם	יוֹעֲצִים	וּבְרֹב
lā'îsh	simchāh	tāqûm	yô'ătsîm	ûverōv
to the man	rejoicing	you will rise up	advisors	but with an abundance of

24.

2522	758	4242, 3005	904, 6496	1745	904, 4776, 6552
n mp	*n ms*	intrg, adj	prep, n fs, ps 3ms	cj, n ms	prep, *n ms, n ms, ps 3ms*
חַיִּים	אֹרַח	מַה־טּוֹב	בְּעִתּוֹ	וְדָבָר	בְּמַעֲנֵה־פִיו
chayyîm	'ōrach	mah-tôv	be'ittô	wedhāvār	bema'ănēh-phîw
life	a path to	how good	in its time	and a word	with an answer in his mouth

25.

1041	4432	4623, 8061	5681.141	3937, 4775	3937, 7959.551	3937, 4767
n ms	prep	prep, pn	v Qal inf con	prep, prep	prep, v Hiphil ptc ms	prep, prep
בֵּית	מַטָּה	מִשְּׁאוֹל	סוּר	לְמַעַן	לְמַשְׂכִּיל	לְמַעֲלָה
bêth	māṭṭāh	mishshe'ôl	sûr	lema'an	lemaskîl	lema'ălāh
the household of	beneath	from Sheol	to turn aside	so that	to one who is wise	upward

496	1397	5507.521	3176	5442.121	1373
n fs	*n ms*	cj, v Hiphil impf 3ms	pn	v Qal impf 3ms	adj
אַלְמָנָה	גְּבוּל	וְיַצֵּב	יְהוָה	יִסַּח	גֵּאִים
'almānāh	gevûl	weyatstsēv	yehwāh	yissach	gē'îm
a widow	the boundary of	but He will station	Yahweh	He will tear down	the proud

26.

571, 5461	2999	7737	4422	3176	8774
n mp, n ms	cj, adj	n ms	n fp	pn	*n fs*
אִמְרֵי־נֹעַם	וּטְהֹרִים	רָע	מַחְשְׁבוֹת	יְהוָה	תּוֹעֲבַת
'imrê-nō'am	ûtehōrîm	rā'	machshevôth	yehwāh	tô'ăvath
sayings of pleasantness	but pure	evil	plans of	Yahweh	an abomination to

27.

5152	7983.151	1240	1239.151	1041	6138.151
n fp	cj, v Qal act ptc ms	n ms	v Qal act ptc ms	n ms, ps 3ms	v Qal act ptc ms
מַתָּנֹת	וְשׂוֹנֵא	בָּצַע	בּוֹצֵעַ	בֵּיתוֹ	עֹכֵר
mattānōth	wesônē'	bātsa'	bôtsēa'	bêthô	'ōkhēr
bribes	but one who hates	a profit	one who cuts off	his household	one who troubles

---

child is a father's joy, *JB* ... A father well content, *Knox*.

but a foolish man despiseth his mother: ... a dullard despiseth, *Rotherham* ... foolish son disrespects, *NCV* ... only a brute despises, *JB*.

21. Folly is joy to him that is destitute of wisdom: ... may amuse the empty-headed, *REB* ... is a delight to senseless men, *Moffatt* ... joy to a man without sense, *Goodspeed*.

but a man of understanding walketh uprightly: ... man of intelligence directeth his going, *Young* ... keeps a straightforward course, *Goodspeed* ... taketh a straight course, *Rotherham*.

22. Without counsel purposes are disappointed: ... plans go awry, *NKJV* ... Schemes lightly made come to nothing, *NEB* ... When no one is consulted, plans are foiled, *Moffatt*.

but in the multitude of counsellors they are established: ... with the advice of many, they should have thriven, *Knox* … when there are many advisers, they succeed, *Goodspeed.*

23. A man hath joy by the answer of his mouth: and a word spoken in due season, how good is it!: … An apt utterance is a joy, *Goodspeed* … A man can please by the word of his mouth, *Fenton* … how good is a timely word!, *NIV.*

24. The way of life is above to the wise, that he may depart from hell beneath: … For men of intelligence the path of life leads upwards and keeps them clear of Sheol below, *NEB* … A mind well schooled sees the way of life stretching upwards, leading away

from the pit beneath, *Knox* … wise man's road winds upward into life; he shuns the downward path to death, *Moffatt.*

25. The LORD will destroy the house of the proud: … will pull down, *REB* … Eternal overthrows, *Moffatt* … LORD will uproot, *Goodspeed.*

but he will establish the border of the widow: … keeps the widow's boundaries intact, *NIV* … will establish the widow's landmark, *Goodspeed* … maintain the widow's boundary stones, *REB.*

26. The thoughts of the wicked are an abomination to the LORD: … Evil designs are disgusting, *BB* …

Evil devices, *ASV* … schemes of wickedness he abhors, *Knox.*

but the words of the pure are pleasant words: … of the clean-hearted are pleasing, *BB* … a delight, *NEB* … pleasing in his sight, *Goodspeed.*

27. He that is greedy of gain troubleth his own house: … A dishonest gainer is troubling his house, *Young* … A grasping man brings trouble, *NEB* … He who traffics in ill-gotten gain wrecks his own household, *Goodspeed.*

but he that hateth gifts shall live: … who spurns a bribe will enjoy long life, *REB* … who has no desire for offerings, *BB.*

"insight" to that of anyone else. Because the wise pursue wisdom and eschew folly, they walk uprightly, following the paths of wisdom (cf. the same verb in 3:6f). Their different views of the basic issue of life (obedience to the LORD; 1:7) lead to very different ends.

15:22. Plans made without advice are more easily frustrated or made ineffectual because they are based on only one point of view (self-advised is ill-advised). The Hebrew word translated "consultation" (sôdh; HED #5660) is not that found in the other proverbs that encourage seeking advice. In its other uses in Proverbs, it refers to private counsel that should not be made public (cf. 11:13; 20:19; 25:9).

15:23. This proverb can be interpreted in two different ways. If the lines are synonymous, then "the answer of his mouth" is the right word at the right time. If, however, they present a contrast, then the verse means that everyone (i.e., any fool) delights in hearing himself speak, but only the right word at the right time is truly good. Both interpretations are possible, and the verse may be intentionally ambiguous. In either case, it commends care in speech (cf. 25:11).

15:24. Since Sheol is the fate of everyone who rejects wisdom (5:5; 7:27; 9:18), those who grow and flourish in wisdom are on a path that leads away from it. In fact, the two paths lead in opposite directions. The contrast in destinations (Sheol or life) may hint at existence beyond death, but it primarily reflects the equation of wisdom with life

and folly with death that is found throughout Proverbs (e.g., 8:32–36; 12:28).

15:25. The contrast between the lines reveals that the "proud" in this verse are those who attempt to take advantage of the weakness of the poor. Since the LORD defends the helpless (22:22f; 23:10f), their plots set them against Him. This verse warns the arrogant and encourages the afflicted, but it may also entail oblique advice for future judges, who need to align their sense of justice with the LORD's, so that they allow themselves neither to be led astray by the power of the proud, nor to despise the poverty of the widow. (Cf. "justice" in the topical index.)

15:26. Like the earlier proverbial pair in this chapter (15:8f), this verse warns that since the plans of the wicked are impure, they are rejected; if their plans are rejected, how much more their lives. The contrast with pure words that are pleasing (cf. 15:1, 23, 28) shows that the plans of the wicked inevitably yield words and deeds that do not please the LORD (cf. 23:7a).

15:27. Bribes are a form of violence (implied by bātsaʻ; HED #1240), since they pervert justice (17:23; 29:4). Those who hate bribery (and therefore the violence perpetrated by injustice) are safe; they are innocent of anything that might cause them scandal (10:9) or trouble. Under the Covenant, false witnesses were punished by the sentence that would have been meted out if the accusation had been true (Deut. 19:15–21). This verse may imply that someone who bought or forced false testimony would be

28.

6552 cj, n ms	3937, 6257.141 prep, v Qal inf con	1965.121 v Qal impf 3ms	6926 n ms	3949 n ms	2513.121 v Qal impf 3ms
וּפִי	לַעֲנוֹת	יֶהְגֶּה	צַדִּיק	לֵב	יִחְיֶה
ûphî	laʿănôth	yehgeh	tsaddîq	lēv	yichăyeh
but the mouth of	to answer	it will mediate	the righteous	the heart of	he will live

29.

8940 cj, n fs	4623, 7857 prep, n mp	3176 pn	7632 adj	7750 n fp	5218.521 v Hiphil impf 3ms	7857 n mp
וּתְפִלַּת	מֵרְשָׁעִים	יְהוָה	רָחוֹק	רָעוֹת	יַבִּיעַ	רְשָׁעִים
ûthephillath	mērəshāʿîm	yehwāh	rāchôq	rāʿôth	yabbîaʿ	reshāʿîm
but a prayer of	from the wicked	Yahweh	far	evil things	it pours out	the wicked

30.

3009B adj	8444 n fs	7975.321, 3949 v Piel impf 3ms, n ms	4115, 6084 n ms, n fd	8471.121 v Qal impf 3ms	6926 n mp
טוֹבָה	שְׁמוּעָה	יְשַׂמַּח־לֵב	מְאוֹר־עֵינַיִם	יִשְׁמַע	צַדִּיקִים
ṭôvāh	shemûʿāh	yesammach-lēv	meʾôr-ʿênayim	yishmaʿ	tsaddîqîm
good	news	the heart will rejoice about	a lamp for the eyes	He hears	the righteous

31.

904, 7419 prep, n ms	2522 n mp	8763 n fs	8471.153 v Qal act ptc fs	238 n fs	1941.322, 6344 v Piel impf 3fs, n fs
בְּקֶרֶב	חַיִּים	תּוֹכַחַת	שֹׁמַעַת	אֹזֶן	תְּדַשֶּׁן־עָצֶם
beqerev	chayyîm	tôkhachath	shōmaʿath	ʾōzen	tedhashshen-ʿātsem
in the midst of	life	a correction of	listening to	the ear	it will make the bones fat

32.

5497 n fs, ps 3ms	4128.151 v Qal act ptc ms	4284 n ms	6797.151 v Qal act ptc ms	4053.122 v Qal impf 3fs	2550 n mp
נַפְשׁוֹ	מוֹאֵס	מוּסָר	פּוֹרֵעַ	תָּלִין	חֲכָמִים
naphshô	môʾēs	mûsār	pôrēaʿ	tālîn	chăkhāmîm
his life	one who abhors	correction	one who abandons	it will lodge	the wise

33.

4284 n ms	3176 pn	3488 n fs	3949 n ms	7353.151 v Qal act ptc ms	8763 n fs	8471.151 cj, v Qal act ptc ms
מוּסָר	יְהוָה	יִרְאַת	לֵב	קוֹנֶה	תּוֹכַחַת	וְשׁוֹמֵעַ
mûsar	yehwāh	yirʾath	lēv	qôneh	tôkhachath	weshômēaʿ
correction with	Yahweh	the fear of	the heart	acquiring	correction	but one who listens to

16:1

4623, 3176 cj, prep, pn	4795, 3949 n mp, n ms	3937, 119 prep, n ms	6265 n fs	3638 n ms	3937, 6686 cj, prep, n mp	2551 n fs
וּמֵיְהוָה	מַעַרְכֵי־לֵב	לְאָדָם	עֲנָוָה	כָּבוֹד	וְלִפְנֵי	חָכְמָה
ûmēyehwāh	maʿarkhê-lēv	leʾādhām	ʿănāwāh	khāvôdh	weliphnê	chokhmāh
but from Yahweh	the plans of the heart	to a man	humility	honor	and before	wisdom

28. The heart of the righteous studieth to answer: ... ponders before answering, *Berkeley* ... just man weighs well his utterance, *NAB, Douay* ... think before they answer, *NEB.*

but the mouth of the wicked poureth out evil things: ... from the lips of the wicked comes mischief in full flood, *Knox* ... bad men let out a flood of evil talk, *Moffatt* ... gushes evil, *NIV.*

29. The LORD is far from the wicked: but he heareth the prayer of the righteous: ... does not listen to, *NCV* ... stands aloof from, *REB* ... far from sinners but his ear is open to the prayer of the upright, *BB.*

30. The light of the eyes rejoiceth the heart: and a good report maketh the bones fat: ... A bright look brings joy to the heart, and good news warms a man's marrow, *NEB* ... it lends vigour to a man's frame!, *Knox* ... cheerful look brings joy to the heart, and good news gives health to the bones, *NIV.*

31. The ear that heareth the reproof of life abideth among the wise: ... A man who listens to healthy reproof will rank among wise men, *Moffatt* ... who listens to wholesome admonition, *Goodspeed* ... whose ear is open to the teaching, *BB.*

32. He that refuseth instruction despiseth his own soul: ... who ignores discipline despises himself, *NIV* ... who ignores correction, *Berkeley* ... who disdains instruction, *NKJV* ... He holds his life cheap, that will not listen to a warning, *Knox.*

but he that heareth reproof getteth understanding: ... who listens to admonition gains, *Goodspeed* ... who listens to reproof acquires intelligence, *Berkeley*.

33. The fear of the LORD is the instruction of wisdom: ... Respect for the LORD will teach you wisdom, *NCV* ... Reverence for the Eternal trains men to be wise, *Moffatt* ...

teaches the lessons of, *Knox* ... is the basis of, *Goodspeed*.

and before honour is humility: ... a low opinion of oneself goes before honour, *BB* ... If you want to be honored, you must be humble, *NCV*.

16:1. The preparations of the heart in man, and the answer of the tongue, is from the LORD: ...

plans of the heart belong to man, *ASV* ... designs of the heart are man's, *BB* ... Orderly thinking belongs to man, *Berkeley* ... A man may plan what he's going to say, but what he says comes from the LORD, *Beck* ... A man may arrange his thoughts; But the utterance of the tongue is from the LORD, *Goodspeed*.

---

equally culpable—their violence rebounds on their own heads (cf. 26:27).

15:28. Those who are wise are slow to speak (cf. Jam. 1:19). They know the power and value of words, and they want to speak in ways that are good, healing (12:18) and peaceful (15:18)—in essence, to offer words of beauty (25:11f). This type of speech is the fruit of insight grown out of reflection and thought. Fools, careless of the effect that their words might have (cf. 12:18), speak without thinking, bubbling forth with counsel that leads themselves and others to disaster (cf. 10:19; 15:2, 7).

15:29. The LORD helps those who call upon Him if their prayer comes from a heart that is aligned with his standards. But a wicked heart cannot offer righteous words (cf. 15:28). This addresses prayers in general, not prayers of repentance, which, by definition, correspond to a situation in which someone has acted wickedly. The truly penitent has already turned from his or her rebellion, which is the beginning of the fear of the LORD (1:7). The many proverbs that contrast the righteous and wicked are actually calls to self-examination and exhortations to righteousness in light of the consequences of the two ways of life.

15:30. Other verses that relate a person's outer and inner condition merely contrast the negative and positive (15:13; 17:22). This proverb, however, prescribes a remedy—good news that refreshes and encourages its hearers (25:25), putting "fat on their bones." Knowing the importance and power of words, the wise refrain from speaking until they have carefully weighed their words in order to assess their effect (15:28). This verse, especially the first line, may underlie Jesus' reference in Matt. 6:22f.

15:31. As occurs several times in Proverbs, a sub-section ends with more than one verse on the same or a closely related topic (cf. 24:30–34). Verses 31ff, which end the section of largely antithetic proverbs (chs. 10–15), address one's attitude toward instruction or correction.

Wisdom is able to recognize which rebukes lead to life and should therefore be followed. The second line could mean that someone who is willing to be corrected will, as a result of his humble response, be counted among the wise. In the context of Proverbs, however, it probably means that his attitude demonstrates his wisdom. The translations unfortunately conceal the central image of this verse, which literally says, "An ear that listens to the rebukes of life lodges among the wise."

15:32. This verse recalls the end of Wisdom's peroration in 8:32–36. The subject and predicate of the first line are not clearly distinguished in the Hebrew text, so that the first line could read, "Whoever neglects discipline despises himself," or, "Whoever despises himself neglects discipline." The second line more clearly distinguishes "Whoever listens" as the subject of "acquires understanding."

Either way, the point is clear: refusing or failing to respond properly to instruction and discipline demonstrates failure to consider the consequences. On the other hand, learning comes from responding appropriately to rebuke (cf. 15:33).

15:33. The connection between the fear of the LORD and humility that is insinuated in Prov. 1:7 is here made explicit. To obey the LORD means to accept the discipline that He tenders (3:11f). That acceptance (obeying his word) yields wisdom and insight (cf. 1:2–7). In turn, these form a life that will be honored (cf. 31:28–31). The second line is identical to the second line of 18:12, which contrasts the blessing that comes from meekness with the disastrous consequences of pride.

16:1. Prov. 16:1–4 and several other verses in this chapter (vv. 9, 23, 33) address the relationship of a person's intentions and the LORD's standards or purposes. Although this may explain the motivation behind marking these verses as the beginning and end of the chapter (on chapter divisions, cf. 21:30f), it does not mean that the entire chapter revolves

4776	4098		3725, 1932, 382	2217	904, 6084	8834.151
n ms	n fs	**2.**	adj, n mp, n ms	adj	prep, n fd, ps 3ms	cj, v Qal act ptc ms
מַעֲנֵה	לָשׁוֹן		כָּל־דַּרְכֵי־אִישׁ	זַךְ	בְּעֵינָיו	וְתֹכֵן
ma'ănēh	lāshôn		kol-darkhê-'îsh	zakh	be'ênâv	wethōkhēn
the answer of	the tongue		all the ways of a man	pure	in his eyes	but One Who examines

7593	3176		1597.131	420, 3176	4801	3679.226
n fp	pn	**3.**	v Qal impv 2ms	prep, pn	n mp, ps 2ms	cj, v Niphal impf 3mp
רוּחוֹת	יְהוָה		גֹּל	אֶל־יְהוָה	מַעֲשֶׂיךָ	וְיִכֹּנוּ
rûchôth	yehwāh		gōl	'el-yehwāh	ma'ăsêkhā	weyikkōnû
spirits	Yahweh		roll	to Yahweh	your works	and they will be established

4422		3725	6713.111	3176	3937, 4777	1612, 7857
n fp, ps 2ms	**4.**	n ms	v Qal pf 3ms	pn	prep, n ms, ps 3ms	cj, cj, n ms
מַחְשְׁבֹתֶיךָ		כֹּל	פָּעַל	יְהוָה	לַמַּעֲנֵהוּ	וְגַם־רָשָׁע
machshevōthêkhā		kōl	pā'al	yehwāh	lamma'ănēhû	wegham-rāshā'
your thoughts		everything	He has made	Yahweh	for his purpose	even also the wicked

3937, 3219	7750		8774	3176	3725, 1392, 3949	3135	3937, 3135
prep, n ms	n fs	**5.**	n fs	pn	adj, adj, n ms	n fs	prep, n fs
לְיוֹם	רָעָה		תּוֹעֲבַת	יְהוָה	כָּל־גְּבַהּ־לֵב	יָד	לְיָד
leyôm	rā'āh		tô'ăvath	yehwāh	kol-gevahh-lēv	yādh	leyādh
for a day of	evil		an abomination to	Yahweh	everyone proud of heart	a hand	to a hand

3940	5536.221		904, 2721	583	3848.421	5988
neg part	v Niphal impf 3ms	**6.**	prep, n ms	cj, n fs	v Pual impf 3ms	n ms
לֹא	יִנָּקֶה		בְּחֶסֶד	וֶאֱמֶת	יְכֻפַּר	עָוֹן
lō'	yinnāqeh		bechesedh	we'ěmeth	yekhuppar	'āwōn
not	he will be innocent		by loyalty	and faithfulness	it will be atoned for	a transgression

904, 3488	3176	5681.141	4623, 7737		904, 7813.141	3176
cj, prep, n fs	pn	v Qal inf con	prep, n ms	**7.**	prep, v Qal inf con	pn
וּבְיִרְאַת	יְהוָה	סוּר	מֵרָע		בִּרְצוֹת	יְהוָה
ûveyir'ath	yehwāh	sûr	mērā'		birtsôth	yehwāh
but with the fear of	Yahweh	turning aside	from evil		when being pleasing to	Yahweh

1932, 382	1612, 342.152	8396.521	882		3005, 4746
n mp, n ms	cj, v Qal act ptc mp, ps 3ms	v Hiphil impf 3ms	prep, ps 3ms	**8.**	adj, sub
דַּרְכֵי־אִישׁ	גַּם־אוֹיְבָיו	יַשְׁלִם	אִתּוֹ		טוֹב־מְעַט
darkhê-'îsh	gam-'ôyvâv	yashlim	'ittô		tôv-me'at
the ways of a man	also his enemies	He causes to be peaceful	with him		better a little

---

2. All the ways of a man are clean in his own eyes; but the LORD weigheth the spirits: ... A man's ways seem all right to himself, but the Eternal has the verdict on his life, *Moffatt* ... All the ways of a man may be pure in his own eyes, but it is the LORD who proves the spirit, *NAB* ... You may believe you are doing right, but the LORD will judge your reasons, *NCV* ... But the LORD weighs the motives, *NASB*.

3. Commit thy works unto the LORD, and thy thoughts shall be established: ... Commit to the LORD all that you do, and your plans will be fulfilled, *NEB* ... Put your works into the hands of the Lord, and your purposes will be made certain, *BB* ... your plans will succeed, *NIV* ... plans will be successful, *REB*.

4. The LORD hath made all things for himself: yea, even the wicked for the day of evil: ... Lord has made everything for his purpose, even the sinner for the day of, *BB* ... LORD made all for his purpose, Yes, the bad for the day of distress!, *Fenton* ... and also the wicked for the day of trouble, *Beck* ... even the wicked for the day of calamity, *Berkeley*.

5. Every one that is proud in heart is an abomination to the LORD: though hand join in hand, he shall not be unpunished: ... Every proud-minded man is an abomination, *Goodspeed* ... Every arrogant heart is abhorrent to Yahweh: be sure this will not go unpunished, *JB* ... A proud man the Lord holds in abhorrence; depend upon it, no acquittal shall he find, *Knox* ... The LORD hates those who are proud. They will surely be punished, *NCV*.

6. By mercy and truth iniquity is purged: and by the fear of the

LORD **men depart from evil:** ... Guilt is wiped out by faith and loyalty, and the fear of the LORD makes men turn from evil, *NEB* ... Through love and faithfulness sin is atoned for; through the fear of the LORD a man avoids evil, *NIV* ... In mercy and truth Atonement is provided for iniquity, *NKJV* ... By loyalty and integrity guilt is atoned for, By rever-

ence for the Lord and turning from wrong, *Anchor*.

7. When a man's ways please the LORD, he maketh even his enemies to be at peace with him: ... When the LORD is pleased with anyone's ways, he makes even his enemies become his friends, *Beck* ... Let Yahweh be pleased with someone's

way of life and he makes that person's very enemies into friends, *JB* ... he makes even his haters be at peace, *BB* ... Even his foes are at peace, *Fenton*.

8. Better is a little with righteousness than great revenues without right: ... Better a little with honesty, than a large income with injustice,

---

around this theme. The verses that address the relationship of a person's intentions and the LORD's purposes remind careful readers that everything is subject to the dominion and purposes of God (cf. 19:21; 21:1f, and the verses cited above).

Solomon consistently encourages planning and denigrates careless, half-hearted or impulsive activity (cf. 21:5). Here, however, he warns that the most careful and thorough plan will not necessarily be carried out. If the tongue is under the LORD's control plans will be also. Nothing is more personal than words. This verse is most closely related to 16:9 and 20:24, although it also leads into the next two verses.

16:2. Every course of action (individually and in total) chosen by a person seems not only right, but "pure" (human beings have an infinite capacity for self-deception). Nevertheless, the LORD knows what underlies those choices. Since the other biblical occurrences of zakh (HED #2217) refer to pure (i.e., unmixed) oil (e.g., Exo. 27:20; Lev. 24:2) and incense (Exo. 30:34; Lev. 24:7), and its uses in Proverbs are positive (Prov. 20:11; 21:8), this may imply that these choices are indeed outwardly "pure." The proverb suggests, however, that far more is entailed in their evaluation than their appearance. This leads naturally to the counsel of the next verse.

16:3. Since every action is governed by the LORD (16:1), and since motives are notoriously difficult to establish (cf. 16:2), plans need to be committed to (lit., "roll[ed] upon") the only One Who can "establish" the thoughts underlying those plans by directing them into right paths (the same verb occurs in 4:26, 16:9 and Ps. 119:5). The verb portrays the image of rolling all of our business upon God like a weight (cf. Pss. 22:8; 37:5), just as the verb is used literally of rolling a stone (cf. 26:27; Gen. 29:3, 8, 10; Josh. 10:18; 1 Sam. 14:33).

16:4. Divine sovereignty extends to all things, not only to words (v. 1) and plans (vv. 2f). Nothing happens, for good or ill, apart from the rule of God, Who has a purpose for everything that He creates.

Like earlier passages on creation (8:22–31; cf. Gen. 1; Ps. 104; Job 38–40), this verse begins by asserting that God creates everything in order to fulfill his own design and intentions ("for himself" [KJV, NKJV] is literally "for its *or* his answer"). His work of creation is not, however, limited to what is obviously "very good" (Gen. 1:31), but encompasses all things, including what is created in order to "have fun" (Ps. 104:26) and those created either to inflict or to suffer disaster.

This aspect of his sovereignty is perhaps most obvious in the prophetic announcements concerning nations. God raises up one nation in order to punish another and will judge even the nation used to judge others (cf. Hab. 1:2–2:19). It is no less true in the vicissitudes of personal life, whatever their scale or scope (cf. Ps. 139:1–6).

16:5. The arrogant are not only condemned, but they will not escape their due penalty, since the LORD is the One Who judges them. The expression "hand to hand" (v. 5b) also occurs in a nearly identical clause in 11:21a, where the subject is "the wicked." The idiom appears to mean "assuredly" or "most certainly," perhaps based on clasping hands to seal an agreement (6:1, 3; 11:15; 17:18), or because the word yādh (HED #3135) can mean "strength" or "power" (cf. Josh. 8:20; Ps. 76:5), so that the idiom was originally "strength to strength."

16:6. This proverb may address the need for a proper attitude in offering sacrifice. It is not the sacrifice itself, but the offerer's faithfulness to the Covenant and honesty that lead to his forgiveness (cf. 1 Sam. 15:22). These attitudes characterize those who fear the LORD and avoid wickedness (cf. 15:24; 16:17). Token righteousness is not acceptable (15:8, 29).

16:7. The many verses that hold out peace, well-being and long life as rewards of wisdom and obedience reflect the covenantal blessings (e.g., Exo. 20:12; Lev. 26:3–13; Deut. 28:1–14; cf. Prov. 10:30). This saying probably refers to the situation

904, 6930	4623, 7524	8721	904, 3940	5122	9.	3949	119
prep, n fs	prep, n ms	n fp	prep, neg part	n ms		n ms	n ms
בִּצְדָקָה	מֵרֹב	תְּבוּאוֹת	בְּלֹא	מִשְׁפָּט		לֵב	אָדָם
bitsdhāqāh	mērōv	tevû'ôth	belō'	mishpāṭ		lēv	'ādhām
with righteousness	than an abundance of	produce	not with	justice		the heart of	a man

2913.321	1932	3176	3679.521	7082	10.	7365
v Piel impf 3ms	n ms, ps 3ms	cj, pn	v Hiphil impf 3ms	n ms, ps 3ms		n ms
יְחַשֵּׁב	דַּרְכּוֹ	וַיהוָה	יָכִין	צַעֲדוֹ		קֶסֶם
yechashshēv	darkô	wayhwāh	yākhîn	tsa'ădhô		qesem
it devises	its way	but Yahweh	He establishes	his steps		a decision

6142, 8004, 4567	904, 5122	3940	4760.121, 6552	11.	6669
prep, n fd, n ms	prep, n ms	neg part	v Qal impf 3ms, n ms, ps 3ms		n ms
עַל־שִׂפְתֵי־מֶלֶךְ	בְּמִשְׁפָּט	לֹא	יִמְעַל־פִּיו		פֶּלֶס
'al-siphthê-melekh	bemishpāṭ	lō'	yim'al-pîw		peles
on the lips of the king	in a judgment	not	his mouth should act disloyally		scales

4118	5122	3937, 3176	4801	3725, 63, 3719	12.	8774
cj, n md	n ms	prep, pn	n ms, ps 3ms	adj, n fp, n ms		n fs
וּמֹאזְנֵי	מִשְׁפָּט	לַיהוָה	מַעֲשֵׂהוּ	כָּל־אַבְנֵי־כִיס		תּוֹעֲבַת
ûmō'zenê	mishpāṭ	layhwāh	ma'ăsēhû	kol-'avnê-khîs		tô'ăvath
and balances of	justice	to Yahweh	his work	all the stones of the bag		an abomination of

4567	6449.141	7856	3706	904, 6930	3679.221	3802
n mp	v Qal inf con	n ms	cj	prep, n fs	v Niphal impf 3ms	n ms
מְלָכִים	עֲשׂוֹת	רֶשַׁע	כִּי	בִּצְדָקָה	יִכּוֹן	כִּסֵּא
melākhîm	'ăsôth	resha'	kî	vitsdhāqāh	yikkôn	kissē'
kings	to act with	wickedness	because	by righteousness	it will be established	a throne

13.	7814	4567	8004, 6928	1744.151	3596	154.121
	n ms	n mp	n fd, n ms	cj, v Qal act ptc ms	n mp	v Qal impf 3ms
	רְצוֹן	מְלָכִים	שִׂפְתֵי־צֶדֶק	וְדֹבֵר	יְשָׁרִים	יֶאֱהָב
	retsôn	melākhîm	siphthê-tsedheq	wedhōvēr	yeshārîm	ye'ĕhāv
	the delight of	kings	lips of righteousness	and one who speaks	uprightness	he loves

14.	2635, 4567	4534, 4323	382	2550	3848.321
	n fs, n ms	n mp, n ms	cj, n ms	adj	v Piel impf 3ms, ps 3fs
	חֲמַת־מֶלֶךְ	מַלְאֲכֵי־מָוֶת	וְאִישׁ	חָכָם	יְכַפְּרֶנָּה
	chămath-melekh	mal'ăkhê-māweth	we'îsh	chākhām	yekhapperennāh
	the wrath of a king	messengers of death	and a man	wise	he will cover over it

Moffatt ... Better a little with virtue, than a large income with injustice, *NAB* ... It is better to be poor and right than to be wealthy and dishonest, *NCV* ... A little, gained honestly, is better than great wealth gotten by dishonest means, *LIVB*.

9. A man's heart deviseth his way: but the LORD directeth his steps: ... People may make plans in their minds, but the LORD decides what they will do, *NCV* ... Man plans his journey by his own wit, but it is the LORD who guides, *NEB* ... In his heart a man plans his course, but the LORD determines his steps, *NIV* ... The human mind plans the way, *NRSV*.

10. A divine sentence is in the lips of the king: his mouth transgresseth not in judgment: ... Inspired words are on the lips of a king, When he renders judgment he does not err, *Anchor* ... Decision is in the lips of the king: his mouth will not go wrong in judging, *BB* ... When an oracle is on a king's lips, he cannot speak wrong in a legal decision, *Beck* ... The king speaks with divine authority; his decisions are always right, *Good News*.

11. A just weight and balance are the LORD's: all the weights of the bag are his work: ... A true balance and scales are the Lord's [concern], He has to do with all the weights in the bag, *Anchor* ... True measures and scales are the Lord's, *BB* ... The LORD wants honest balances and scales; all the weights are his work, *NCV* ... all the weights in the bag are his business, *NEB*.

12. It is an abomination to kings to commit wickedness: for the throne is established by righteousness: ... Wrongdoing is hateful to kings, For through the right the throne stands secure, *Anchor* … Evil-doing is disgusting to kings: for the seat of the ruler is based on righteousness, *BB* … Kings detest wrongdoing, *NIV* … for a throne rests firmly on righteousness, *REB* … For to do right supports the throne, *Fenton*.

13. Righteous lips are the delight of kings; and they love him that speaketh right: … Kings delight in honest words, anyone telling the truth is loved, *Beck* … A king wants to hear the truth and will favor those who speak it, *Good News* … Upright lips are welcome to a king,

he loves someone of honest words, *JB* … Kings are for honest talk; free-spoken is well loved, *Knox* … Kings like honest people; they value someone who speaks the truth, *NCV.*

14. The wrath of a king is as messengers of death: but a wise man

described in 3:1f (cf. 1 Sam. 2:26; Luke 2:52)—whoever has peace with God has the fundamental requirement of life, that which is most important. This assurance puts human conflict in perspective. At the same time, this is not merely a relative statement. Though the LORD watches over and keeps his own, guarding and protecting them, He does not promise a trouble-free life or a life without enemies.

16:8. Justice is better than injustice, which is fundamentally wicked and violates the Covenant (cf. Exo. 23:1ff, 6–9). Its sinful nature is not altered by the consequences. The contrast shows that "righteousness" (v. 8a) is better understood as "justice"—acting uprightly, refusing bribes, seeking the truth without regard for the status of the claimants. Wealth can be obtained legally (and in morally upright ways), but if the choice is between wealth through wrongdoing or doing what is right despite the consequences, the pursuit of justice is always wiser, since justice is demanded by the Covenant and therefore blessed (Deut. 28:1–13). This "better than" proverb makes the contrast explicit.

Like many other proverbs, this verse implies a standard beyond human senses. Although the proverbs focus on this life, some hint at a final reckoning of deeds and words beyond present life.

16:9. This verse, a more active form of 16:1, also changes the image slightly from "the tongue's answer" to "his step," the smallest part of the "way" of his life (cf. 20:24). This proverb, however, uses the same verb as 16:3b, confirming that every detail is made firm by the LORD.

16:10. The king was obliged to uphold justice because, as the court of final appeal, he determined the standard of justice for the land (29:4, 12). Kings across the ancient Near East claimed to speak and determine justice as they had received the laws from their gods (cf. 1 Ki. 3:3–28; Hammurabi), and this view even colored the popular Israelite understanding. Hebrew has relatively few modal verbs (e.g., "may," "should"), but the logic of this proverb (since A, then B) requires a modal verb in the second line: "*must* not act treacherously" (so NASB, NKJV, NIV;

but a stative verb [not necessarily implying contingency to the first part of the verse] in the NRSV); in 16:12, this is explicit. This is the first of six verses that are mainly concerned with kingship (16:10–15).

16:11. The other verses that address honesty (11:1; 20:10, 23) reveal that God is concerned with the details of life, even business. Verse 11 strengthens this picture, since the stones (which were carried around in a bag so that they were available to balance scales) are identified as "his work," just as the scale and balance with which they were used belonged to Him. This verse fits well among the other verses in this chapter which describe the LORD's judgment of good and evil (16:2, 5, 7).

16:12. The king was God's vice-regent, ruling under the Covenant (Deut. 17:18ff). His primary responsibility, therefore, was to administer justice by condemning the wicked (cf. 20:8, 26; 2 Sam. 23:3f). To join in their wickedness, whether it was physical, financial or legal, was to deny his role and break the Covenant (cf. 25:5; 29:4, 12, 14). Thus Israel and Judah languished under many kings, who not only promoted or permitted paganism, but failed to rule justly (cf. Jer. 22:3, 13–17; Ezek. 22:25–29; 45:8f; Amos 2:6ff; 5:24; Mic. 6:8). As a proverb, this verse implicitly compares the role and standards of the successful king to those of the LORD, Who considers the wicked an abomination (15:9, 26; 16:5; 17:15). It is also closely linked to 16:10 and the following verse (cf. 14:34f).

16:13. Kings who would do what is right (16:12) must be surrounded by counselors who will give them wise advice (cf. 14:7, 35; 29:12), not merely that which is expedient, or which they may want to hear. This proverb warns kings that they ought to prefer truthful, thoughtful advice, and counsels those who want to be advisors to consider their words. Since Proverbs views everyone as needing counsel, this verse is a general warning about the source of any advice or counsel.

16:14. Since kings exercised the power of life and death, a wise courtier would either be careful not to provoke it, or be able to appease it (20:2;

15.

4597	3626, 5854	7814	2522	904, 214, 6686, 4567
n ms	prep, *n ms*	cj, n ms, ps 3ms	n mp	prep, *n ms, n mp*, n ms
מַלְקוֹשׁ	כְּעָב	וּרְצוֹנוֹ	חַיִּים	בְּאוֹר־פְּנֵי־מֶלֶךְ
malqôsh	keʿāv	ûretsônô	chayyim	beʾôr-penê-melekh
a late rain	like a cloud of	and his delight	life	with the light of the face of the king

16.

1013.255	1035	7353.141	4623, 2843	4242, 3005	7353.141, 2551
v Niphal ptc ms	n fs	cj, v Qal inf con	prep, n ms	intrg, adj	v Qal inf con, n fs
נִבְחָר	בִּינָה	וּקְנוֹת	מֵחָרוּץ	מַה־טּוֹב	קְנֹה־חָכְמָה
nivchār	bînāh	ûqĕnôth	mēchārûts	mah-ṭôv	qĕnōh-chokhmāh
what is more chosen	understanding	and to acquire	than gold	how better	to acquire wisdom

17.

5497	8490.151	4623, 7737	5681.141	3596	4697	4623, 3826B
n fs, ps 3ms	v Qal act ptc ms	prep, n ms	v Qal inf con	n mp	*n fs*	prep, n ms
נַפְשׁוֹ	שֹׁמֵר	מֵרָע	סוּר	יְשָׁרִים	מְסִלַּת	מִכֶּסֶף
naphshô	shōmēr	mērāʿ	sûr	yĕshārîm	mĕsillath	mikkāṣeph
his life	one who guards	from evil	turning aside	the upright	the highway of	than silver

18.

1394	3912	3937, 6686	1377	3937, 6686, 8133	1932	5526.151
n fs	n ms	cj, prep, *n mp*	n ms	prep, *n mp*, n ms	n ms, ps 3ms	v Qal act ptc ms
גֹּבַהּ	כִּשָּׁלוֹן	וְלִפְנֵי	גָּאוֹן	לִפְנֵי־שֶׁבֶר	דַּרְכּוֹ	נֹצֵר
gōvahh	khishshālôn	wĕliphnê	gāʾôn	liphnê-shever	darkô	nōtsēr
haughtiness of	a stumbling	and before	pride	before ruin	his way	one who keeps

19.

882, 1373	8395	4623, 2606.341	882, 6270	8587, 7593	3005	7593
prep, n mp	n ms	prep, v Piel inf con	prep, n mp	*adj*, n fs	adj	n fs
אֶת־גֵּאִים	שָׁלָל	מֵחַלֵּק	אֶת־עֲנָיִים	שְׁפַל־רוּחַ	טוֹב	רוּחַ
ʾeth-gēʾîm	shālāl	mēchallēq	ʾeth-ʿănîyîm	shĕphal-rûach	ṭôv	rûach
with the proud	booty	than the dividing of	with the afflicted	lowly in spirit	better	spirit

20.

869	904, 3176	1019.151	4834.121, 3008	6142, 1745	7959.551
n mp, ps 3ms	prep, pn	cj, v Qal act ptc ms	v Qal impf 3ms, n ms	prep, n ms	v Hiphil ptc ms
אַשְׁרָיו	בַּיהוָה	וּבוֹטֵחַ	יִמְצָא־טוֹב	עַל־דָּבָר	מַשְׂכִּיל
ʾashrâv	bayhwāh	ûvôṭēach	yimtsā-ṭôv	ʿal-dāvār	maskîl
his happiness	in Yahweh	and being confident	he will find good	about the word	being wise

21.

3362.521	8004	5161	1032.255	7410.221	3937, 2550, 3949
v Hiphil impf 3ms	n fd	cj, n ms	v Niphal ptc ms	v Niphal impf 3ms	prep, *n ms*, n ms
יֹסִיף	שְׂפָתַיִם	וּמֶתֶק	נָבוֹן	יִקָּרֵא	לַחֲכַם־לֵב
yōṣîph	sĕphāthayim	ûmetheq	nāvôn	yiqqārēʾ	lachăkham-lēv
he will add	lips	and sweetness of	discerning	he will be called	the wise of heart

will pacify it: … The wrath of the king is like those who give news of death, but a wise man will put peace in place of it, *BB* … A king's wrath is a herald of death, *Fenton* … king's wrath is a forerunner of death, *Goodspeed* … a wise man will appease it, *NEB*.

15. In the light of the king's countenance is life; and his favour is as a cloud of the latter rain: … When the king's face brightens it spells life, his favour is like the rain in spring, *JB* … his smile is life; not more welcome the spring rains, than royal favour, *Knox*

… A smiling king can give people life; his kindness is like a spring shower, *NCV* … In the light of the king's face there is life; and his approval is like a cloud of spring rain, *BB*.

16. How much better is it to get wisdom than gold! and to get understanding rather to be chosen than silver!: … To obtain wisdom is better than to obtain gold, And to possess insight than to possess silver, *Anchor* … It is better—much better—to have wisdom and knowledge than gold and silver, *Good News* … and to get knowledge is more to be desired than

silver, *BB* … and the getting of intelligence to be preferred to silver!, *Darby* … and to gain discernment is better than pure silver, *NEB*.

17. The highway of the upright is to depart from evil: he that keepeth his way preserveth his soul: … To turn from evil is the highway of the upright; watch your step and save your life, *NEB* … The highway of the upright avoids evil; he who guards his way guards his life, *NIV* … The highway of good people turns away from evil; if you watch your step, you can preserve your life, *Beck* …

Those who are good travel a road that avoids evil; so watch where you are going—it may save your life, *Good News.*

18. Pride goeth before destruction, and an haughty spirit before a fall: ... Presumption comes first, and ruin closes behind it; pride ever goes before a fall, *Knox* ... Pride ends in disaster; haughtiness means a downfall, *Moffatt* ... Pride will destroy a person; a proud attitude leads to ruin,

NCV ... And a haughty spirit before stumbling, *NASB.*

19. Better it is to be of an humble spirit with the lowly, than to divide the spoil with the proud: ... Better to be lowly in spirit and among the oppressed than to share plunder with the proud, *NIV* ... Better it is to have a gentle spirit with the poor, than to take part in the rewards of war with men of pride, *BB* ... Better sit humbly with those in need than

divide the spoil with, *NEB* ... Better is it to be of a humble spirit with the meek, than to divide, *Darby.*

20. He that handleth a matter wisely shall find good: and whoso trusteth in the LORD, happy is he: ... The skilful in business find success; But who trusts in the LORD is happy, *Fenton* ... Whoever listens to what is taught will succeed, and whoever trusts the LORD will be happy, *NCV* ... He who plans a thing will be

Dan. 2:12–16 and 3:19–23 describe a pagan king centuries after Solomon). The wise, therefore, who understand human nature, study peacemaking (cf. 15:1) so that they may be able to save their lives. This verse and the following were undoubtedly set together because of their contrasting situations.

16:15. The "spring rain" (the last showers at the end of the rainy season) was critical because it would not rain again for four or five months. This was the rain that sustained life through the dry summer. Comparably, a happy king would be a source of blessing to those around him (cf. 19:12). A wise counselor would therefore seek to speak and act righteously (14:34; 16:13) in a winsome way (25:11), rather than to provoke his wrath (16:14).

16:16. This proverb parallels three verses in the prologue that extol wisdom as far more valuable than earthly riches (3:14; 8:11, 19; cf. Ecc. 9:16, 18). The choices that lead to one or the other may not be obvious at first, since there is no necessary conflict between wealth and wisdom. It may even be possible to pursue both at the same time. The warning of Proverbs, however, is that when these goals conflict, it is better to choose the path that leads to wisdom, unconcerned for the consequences (financial, social, etc.), rather than to reject wisdom for mere things. In such a situation, to reject wisdom is to choose death, since only wisdom leads to life (3:35).

16:17. Although the verb translated "turn aside" (HED #5681) usually refers to turning aside *from* the road, here it is right, turning away from those things that would lead away from the path of life. Staying on the path of wisdom requires diligence (cf. 21:16), constant attention to the nature of the choices and decisions made—being careful to avoid (to turn away from) every decision that leads off the path.

16:18. Arrogance entails disaster. Since the proud will not listen to others, they bring destruction on themselves (cf. 1:25, 30; 29:1). The only antidote is a humble and meek spirit that fears the LORD (15:33; 18:12), but this verse, by not mentioning that or any alternative, strengthens its warning. The first three Hebrew words also begin 18:12. The end of 18:12a and 16:18b use the same root, tying together the verses and their message.

16:19. Although they are separate proverbs, this verse is closely related to the preceding. Like all "better than" proverbs, it weighs a situation's value by considering it in its entirety, rather than by evaluating it based on its appearance. The proud may be wealthy and the humble poor, but humility is better than pride because the proud face only disaster (16:18). Nor do they understand that "the last shall be first, and the first last" (Matt. 20:16). The verse also hints at another proverbial theme: the wealthy tend to be arrogant, exalted in their own minds by their riches (cf. 18:11).

16:20. Trust in the LORD is a primary requirement of wisdom and its consequent righteousness (3:5f) and blessing. Those who would be blessed must first cultivate a spirit of obedience (1:7), so that they will attend to the wisdom they find. Their trust also means that they will obey, since they believe that the ways which the LORD reveals to them through his word (especially Proverbs, given this context) are right and good.

16:21. Because they give thought to their words, the wise know how to make wisdom winsome (16:23f). The benefits of wisdom are thus twofold: words that make others wise (second line) are recognized (and, presumably, valued), so that the speaker is called "discerning" (the idiom is that of naming a person or place, as in, e.g., 1 Sam. 9:9; 2 Sam. 18:18; Isa. 1:26).

22.

4090 n ms	4888 n ms	2522 n mp	7961 n ms	1196 n mp, ps 3ms	4284 cj, n ms	188 n mp	198 n fs
לֶקַח	מְקוֹר	חַיִּים	שֵׂכֶל	בְּעָלָיו	וּמוּסַר	אֱוִלִים	אִוֶּלֶת
leqach	meqôr	chayyîm	sēkhel	beʿālâv	ûmûsar	ʾĕwilîm	ʾiwweleth
teaching	a fountain of	life	insight	it owners	but correction to	fools	foolishness

23.

3949 n ms	2550 n ms	7959.521 v Hiphil impf 3ms	6552 n ms, ps 3ms	6142, 8004 cj, prep, n fd, ps 3ms	3362.521 v Hiphil impf 3ms
לֵב	חָכָם	יַשְׂכִּיל	פִּיהוּ	וְעַל־שְׂפָתָיו	יֹסִיף
lēv	chākhām	yaskîl	pîhû	weʿal-sephāthâv	yōsîph
the heart of	the wise	he will act wisely with	his mouth	and on his lips	he will add

24.

4090 n ms	6951, 1756 n ms, n ms	571, 5461 n mp, n ms	5142 adj	3937, 5497 prep, art, n fs	4995 cj, n ms
לֶקַח	צוּף־דְּבַשׁ	אִמְרֵי־נֹעַם	מָתוֹק	לַנֶּפֶשׁ	וּמַרְפֵּא
leqach	tsûph-devash	ʾimrê-nōʿam	māthôq	lannephesh	ûmarpē
teaching	flowing of honey	sayings of pleasantness	sweet	to the soul	and healing

25.

3937, 6344 prep, art, n fs	3552 sub	1932 n ms	3596 n ms	3937, 6686, 382 prep, n mp, n ms	321 cj, n fs, ps 3fs	1932, 4323 n mp, n ms
לָעֶצֶם	יֵשׁ	דֶּרֶךְ	יָשָׁר	לִפְנֵי־אִישׁ	וְאַחֲרִיתָהּ	דַּרְכֵי־מָוֶת
lāʿātsem	yēsh	derekh	yāshār	liphnê-ʾîsh	weʾachărîthāhh	darkhê-māweth
to the bones	there is	a way	upright	before a man	but its end	ways of death

26.

5497 n fs	6221 n ms	6219.112 v Qal pf 3fs	3937 prep, ps 3ms	3706, 410.112 cj, v Qal pf 3fs	6142 prep, ps 3ms	6552 n ms, ps 3ms
נֶפֶשׁ	עָמֵל	עָמְלָה	לּוֹ	כִּי־אָכַף	עָלָיו	פִּיהוּ
nephesh	ʿāmēl	ʿāmelāh	lô	kî-ʾākhaph	ʿālâv	pîhû
the soul of	a workman	it toils	for him	because it compels	on him	his mouth

27.

382 n ms	1139 n ms	3868.151 v Qal act ptc ms	7750 n fs	6142, 8004 cj, prep, n fd, ps 3ms	3626, 813 prep, n fs	7148 n fs
אִישׁ	בְּלִיַּעַל	כֹּרֶה	רָעָה	וְעַל־שְׂפָתָיו	כְּאֵשׁ	צָרָבֶת
ʾîsh	belîyaʿal	kōreh	rāʿāh	weʿal-sephāthâv	keʾēsh	tsārāveth
a man of	corruption	digging up	evil	and on his lips	like a fire of	scorching

successful, *NAB* … The shrewd man of business will succeed well, *NEB*.

21. The wise in heart shall be called prudent: and the sweetness of the lips increaseth learning: … The sensible man seeks advice from the wise, he drinks it in and increases his knowledge, *NEB* … The wise in heart are called discerning, and pleasant words promote instruction, *NIV* … The wise-hearted will be named men of good sense: and by pleasing words learning is increased, *BB* … The wise man is counted intelligent; And sweetness of speech adds persuasiveness to his teaching, *Goodspeed*.

22. Understanding is a wellspring of life unto him that hath it: but the instruction of fools is folly: …

Wisdom is a fountain of life to him who has it; but the punishment of the foolish is their foolish behaviour, *BB* … Prudence is a fountain of life to its possessor, but folly is the chastisement of fools, *Berkeley* … To those who possess understanding, it is a fountain of life, but fools punish themselves with their foolishness, *Beck* … The prudent man drinks from a living fountain; fools only learn the lessons of their folly, *Knox*.

23. The heart of the wise teacheth his mouth, and addeth learning to his lips: … Wise people's minds tell them what to say, and that helps them be better teachers, *NCV* … wise man's mind guides his speech, and what his lips impart increases learning, *NEB* … heart guides his mouth, and his lips

promote instruction, *NIV* … adds persuasiveness to his lips, *NASB*.

24. Pleasant words are as an honeycomb, sweet to the soul, and health to the bones: … Kind words are like dripping honey: sweetness to the palate and health for the body, *REB* … Sweet to one's taste and refreshing to one's being, *Anchor* … sweet to the soul and new life to the bones, *BB* … sweet to the spirit and healthy for the body, *Beck* … and healing to the bones, *Berkeley*.

25. There is a way that seemeth right unto a man, but the end thereof are the ways of death: … There's a way that a man thinks is right, but it ends up as the way to death, *Beck* … a way that seems straight to a man; But the end of it leads to death, *Goodspeed* ... The right road in a man's thinking may be the one whose goal is death, *Knox* ... What you think is the right road may lead to death, *Good News*.

26. He that laboureth laboureth for himself; for his mouth craveth it of him: ... The laborer's appetite labors for him, for his mouth urges him on, *NAB* ... The workers' hunger helps them, because their desire to eat makes them work, *NCV*

... The labourer's appetite is always plaguing him, his hunger spurs him on, *NEB* ... For his hunger drives him, *Anchor*.

27. An ungodly man diggeth up evil: and in his lips there is as a burning fire: ... A worthless man deviseth mischief; And in his lips there is as a scorching fire, *ASV* ... A worthless man plots harm, and his speech is like a searing flame, *Berkeley* ... A good-for-nothing man is a designer of evil,

BB ... A worthless person concocts trouble, *Beck*.

28. A froward man soweth strife: and a whisperer separateth chief friends: ... A malicious man starts quarrels, and a slanderer can break up a friendship, *Beck* ... Gossip is spread by wicked people; they stir up trouble and break up friendships, *Good News* ... A perverse man causes fighting; and a whisperer separates, *KJVII* ... And a

---

"The discerning calls upon [summons] the wise of heart" (NEB) involves repointing the verb in the first line (but not changing the consonantal text) to mean that the discerning know they need to seek wisdom from the wise (cf. 10:13). This and other renderings seem to reflect a desire to avoid the apparent tautology of calling a wise person "discerning," since that also means "wise." This point of the verse, however, is that wisdom is eventually recognized by its words and honored.

16:22. The English versions follow the Septuagint in supplying a letter that apparently dropped out of the Hebrew text by being written once rather than twice. By protecting those who have it from foolish words or actions, prudence preserves their lives (cf. 10:11; 13:14). The second line is less clear, meaning either that the discipline practiced by fools is itself foolish (and thus not discipline) or that the attempt to discipline fools is worthless. On either interpretation, certain death awaits fools. They have no source of life (on the word translated "fountain," see 10:11).

16:23. Because the wise understand the importance of their words, they weigh them before speaking (15:28). They are thus able to speak in a way that makes their counsel attractive, desirable and timely (cf. 15:23; 25:11f). Anyone who wants to be heard, therefore, needs to consider his or her words, weighing their possible effects and choosing those that will gain the best hearing (cf. 16:21, 24).

16:24. Since words have the power of life and death (12:18), the wise use them carefully and thoughtfully (15:28). Those who want to strengthen, delight or comfort others must think first about the needs of the individuals (contrast 25:20) and then decide how to address them in an acceptable way (16:21, 23). Good news is a tonic with which to bless others (25:25). Well-spoken words delight and

heal (12:18) because they are motivated by a desire to help.

16:25. Every decision seems right when it is made, especially in absence of thinking through the consequences. Some courses of action, being foolish or sinful, lead to destruction, even though they seem upright at the moment. This verse is identical to 14:12. Here it fits the general theme of the context—that wise planning is that which is done in the light of God's sovereign judgeship over human affairs (cf. 16:2, 9, 16ff, 33).

16:26. A self-motivated person works more diligently than one who has to be cajoled, browbeaten or coerced into working. Hunger is only one of many reasons to work; it is, however, probably the most universal (cf. Ecc. 4:7f, where greed drives a man). Not even hunger motivates everyone, as the proverbs about the sluggard show (cf. 12:27; 19:15, 24; 26:15), so this verse may encourage an employer or supervisor to consider what will best motivate those under him or her.

16:27. Someone who searches out bad reports in order to trap others is despicable. (The word translated "dig" [HED #3868] occurs only here and in 26:27 in Proverbs.) The usual translations, "worthless" (NASB), "ungodly" (NKJV) and "scoundrel" (NIV), are not nearly strong enough (cf. 1 Sam. 2:12; 25:17, 25). This term is, if possible, even stronger than "fool" (cf. Prov. 6:12; 19:28, its other occurrences in Proverbs).

Such people cannot hold in what they have discovered. Their "news" burns their lips in their eagerness to share it. Once they have sent it out, it also sets others afire with strife and distress of all sorts, as it destroys reputations and lives. There is no defense against calumniators, since they never confront one publicly or personally. The entire attack is invisible, but no less felt! Indeed, the only

28.

Strong's	Parsing	Hebrew	Translit.	Gloss
382	n ms	אִישׁ	'îsh	a man of
8749	n fp	תַּהְפֻּכוֹת	tahpukhôth	perversity
8365.321	v Piel impf 3ms	יְשַׁלַּח	yeshallach	he will send out
4209	n ms	מָדוֹן	mādhôn	strife
7566.255	cj, v Niphal ptc ms	וְנִרְגָּן	wenirgān	and a slanderer
6754.551	v Hiphil ptc ms	מַפְרִיד	maphrîdh	causing division
443	n ms	אַלּוּף	'allûph	close friends

29.

Strong's	Parsing	Hebrew	Translit.	Gloss
382	n ms	אִישׁ	'îsh	a man of
2660	n ms	חָמָס	chāmās	violence
6853.321	v Piel impf 3ms	יְפַתֶּה	yephatteh	he will entice
7739	n ms, ps 3ms	רֵעֵהוּ	rē'ēhû	his fellow
2050.511	cj, v Hiphil pf 3ms, ps 3ms	וְהוֹלִיכוֹ	wehôlîkhô	and he will cause him to go
904, 1932	prep, n ms	בְּדֶרֶךְ	bedherekh	in a way

30.

Strong's	Parsing	Hebrew	Translit.	Gloss
3940, 3005	neg part, adj	לֹא־טוֹב	lō'-ṭôv	not good
6330.151	v Qal act ptc ms	עֹצֶה	'ōtseh	one who makes a sign with
6084	n fd, ps 3ms	עֵינָיו	'ênâv	his eyes
3937, 2913.141	prep, v Qal inf con	לַחְשֹׁב	lachshōv	to devise
8749	n fp	תַּהְפֻּכוֹת	tahpukhôth	perversity
7460.151	v Qal act ptc ms	קֹרֵץ	qōrēts	pursing
8004	n fd, ps 3ms	שְׂפָתָיו	sephāthâv	his lips
3735.311	v Piel pf 3ms	כִּלָּה	killāh	he brings to completion
7750	n fs	רָעָה	rā'āh	evil

31.

Strong's	Parsing	Hebrew	Translit.	Gloss
6065	n fs	עֲטֶרֶת	'ăṭereth	a crown of
8930	n fs	תִּפְאֶרֶת	tiph'ereth	splendor
7939	n fs	שֵׂיבָה	sêvāh	gray hair
904, 1932	prep, n ms	בְּדֶרֶךְ	bedherekh	in the way of
6930	n fs	צְדָקָה	tsedhāqāh	righteousness
4834.221	v Niphal impf 3ms	תִּמָּצֵא	timmātsē'	it is found

32.

Strong's	Parsing	Hebrew	Translit.	Gloss
3005	adj	טוֹב	ṭôv	better
774	adj	אֶרֶךְ	'erekh	long of
653	n md	אַפַּיִם	'appayim	nostrils
4623, 1399	prep, adj	מִגִּבּוֹר	miggibbôr	than a mighty man
5090.151	cj, v Qal act ptc ms	וּמֹשֵׁל	ûmōshēl	and one who rules
904, 7593	prep, n fs, ps 3ms	בְּרוּחוֹ	berûchô	in his spirit
4623, 4058.151	prep, v Qal act ptc ms	מִלֹּכֵד	millōkhēdh	than one who captures
6111	n fs	עִיר	'îr	a city

33.

Strong's	Parsing	Hebrew	Translit.	Gloss
904, 2536	prep, art, n ms	בַּחֵיק	bachêq	in the lap
3014.621	v Hophal impf 3ms	יוּטַל	yûṭal	it is cast
881, 1518	do, art, n ms	אֶת־הַגּוֹרָל	'eth-haggôrāl	the lot
4623, 3176	cj, prep, pn	וּמֵיְהוָה	ûmēyehwāh	but from Yahweh
3725, 5122	adj, n ms, ps 3ms	כָּל־מִשְׁפָּטוֹ	kol-mishpāṭô	all its judgments

17:1

Strong's	Parsing	Hebrew	Translit.	Gloss
3005	adj	טוֹב	ṭôv	better
6846	n fs	פַּת	path	a morsel
2818	adj	חֲרֵבָה	chărēvāh	dry
8358, 904	cj, n fs, prep, ps 3fs	וְשַׁלְוָה־בָהּ	weshalwāh-vāhh	and quietness with it

---

slanderer separates intimate friends, *NASB.*

29. A violent man enticeth his neighbour, and leadeth him into the way that is not good: ... A lawless man allures his neighbor, *Douay* ... Cruel people trick their neighbors and lead them to do wrong, *NCV* ... A violent man puts desire of evil into his neighbour's mind, and makes him go in a way which is not good, *BB* ... A criminal deceives his neighbor, *Beck.*

30. He shutteth his eyes to devise froward things: moving his lips he bringeth evil to pass: ... He whose eyes are shut is a man of twisted purposes, *BB* ... One who winks his eyes is plotting something crooked; one who bites his lips has finished his evil work, *Beck* ... Whoever narrows the eyes to think up tricks and purses the lips has already done wrong, *JB* ... He who winks his eye is plotting trickery; he who compresses his lips has mischief ready, *NAB.*

31. The hoary head is a crown of glory, if it be found in the way of righteousness: ... Gray hair is a crown of glory; it is gained by virtuous living, *NAB* ... Gray hair is like a crown of honor; it is earned by living a good life, *NCV* ... Gray hair is a crown of splendor; it is attained by a righteous life, *NIV* ... Gray hair is a beautiful crown, Won by a life of virtue, *Anchor.*

32. He that is slow to anger is better than the mighty; and he that ruleth his spirit than he that

taketh a city: ... A patient man is better than a mighty one, And to master oneself is better than to take a city, *Anchor* ... Being slow to get angry is better than being a fighter, and controlling your spirit is better than capturing a city, *Beck* ... It is better to be patient than powerful. It is better to win control over yourself than over whole cities, *Good News.*

33. The lot is cast into the lap; but the whole disposing thereof is of the LORD: ... In the fold of the garment the lot is thrown, but from Yahweh comes the decision, *JB* ... Into the lap's fold the lot falls haphazard, but the Lord rules the issue, *Knox* ... When the lot is cast into the lap, its decision depends entirely on the LORD, *NAB* ... But the decision rests wholly with the LORD, *Goodspeed.*

17:1. Better is a dry morsel, and quietness therewith, than an house full of sacrifices with strife: ... Better a dry crust with an easy mind, Than a houseful of feasting and quarreling, *Anchor* ... Better a bit of dry bread in peace, than a house full of feasting and violent behaviour, *BB* ... Better to eat a dry crust of bread with peace of mind than have a banquet in a house full of trouble, *Good News.*

protection is to refuse to be drawn into such behavior by refusing to listen to gossip and by refusing to pass on what may be heard.

16:28. Closely related to the preceding verse, this proverb warns by describing the potential consequences of entertaining "news." Slander is so insidious (cf. 18:8) that it can destroy the closest relationship, especially when someone intentionally gossips in order to spread strife. The point is to consider how to respond when offered a juicy tidbit via the grapevine, as well as how to evaluate reports that negatively affect someone else. The wise do not listen to or spread gossip, malicious or not. The results could be disastrous.

16:29. The way of wisdom is peaceable, so that the violent are not a source of good or wise guidance. They hide their purposes with lies, so that they can destroy those who trust them. The proverb may mean that the violent are self-deceived, and so deceive others because they themselves are already lost (i.e., the "blind leaders of the blind"; Matt. 15:14), or it may warn that their motives are only wicked. In either case, their counsel leads to destruction.

16:30. Although the cultural significance of the wink is obscure, it is consistently condemned (cf. 6:13; 10:10) as a sign of malice (Ps. 35:19). Here both those who close the eyes and lips (which uses the word translated "wink" in the references cited above) are condemned as wicked planners who work toward malicious ends. The wise notice the behavior of those around them and, by careful reflection, draw conclusions about their purposes and, therefore, the value of their words.

16:31. Since long life is a reward of wisdom (cf. 3:2; 4:9f), white hair deserves honor (cf. 20:29) as proof of a righteous life. This verse also encourages the general attitude of courtesy and respect which is to characterize the wise (cf. 17:6).

16:32. Cities captured can be lost to a stronger force—strength and power decay or decline.

Patience, however, cannot be taken away. It is an internal quality of the wise (14:29) that helps avoid trouble (21:23), calms the strife caused by the impatient (15:18) and accomplishes its purpose despite its apparent weakness (25:15). The fool, on the other hand, has no patience; he bursts with anger and indignation at every slight, real or imagined (cf. 12:16; 14:29; 19:11; 20:3; 29:11).

Proverbs consistently condemns impetuous words or actions. These are not the product of reflection and thought, but the outpourings of a heart empty of all wisdom or understanding (cf. 10:21; 13:16; 15:28).

16:33. Rounding off Prov. 16 with its subtheme of divine sovereignty (cf. on 16:1), this verse points out that an event which cannot be determined ahead of time is under the LORD's control. If it is cast honestly, there is no planning for the disposals of the lot. Even the science of statistics, developed in the seventeenth century, reveals only what has happened. It can neither predict nor guarantee the results of any single throw. If this, the ultimately random act, is actually controlled by the LORD, how much more everything else that happens (cf. 18:18).

The lot (HED #1518) was probably a flat stick or bone with a mark on one side. By asking a series of "Yes/No" questions, the lot could single one person out of a group (Jon. 1:7) or nation (Josh. 7:16ff; 1 Sam. 10:20f; 14:40ff). The lot assigned tribal territories (cf. Josh. 14:2; 15:1; 16:1; 18:6 [N.B.: The word *gôrāl* can be translated "lot" or "allotment"—i.e., that determined by the lot—depending on the context]) and Levitical tasks (e.g., 1 Chr. 24:31; 25:8; 26:13f). Saul's use of it (1 Sam. 14:40ff) may have been superstitious, since the LORD would not answer him in any other way (1 Sam. 14:37), but Jonathan was chosen.

17:1. A peaceful life is both a goal and reward of wisdom. Peace is thus always better than turmoil, even if its price is poverty rather than the wealth that can afford sacrifice. By contrasting "sacrifices" with

2.

Strong's	Parsing	Hebrew	Translit.	English
904, 1158	prep, n ms	בְּבֵן	beven	over a son
5090.121	v Qal impf 3ms	יִמְשֹׁל	yimshōl	he will rule
5860, 7959.551	n ms, v Hiphil ptc ms	עֶבֶד־מַשְׂכִּיל	'evedh-maskîl	a slave who acts wisely
2160, 7663	n mp, n ms	זִבְחֵי־רִיב	zivchê-rîv	sacrifices of contention
4529	adj	מָלֵא	mālē'	full
4623, 1041	prep, n ms	מִבַּיִת	mibbayith	than a house

Strong's	Parsing	Hebrew	Translit.	English
991.551	v Hiphil ptc ms	מֵבִישׁ	mēvîsh	causing shame
904, 8761	cj, prep, n ms	וּבְתוֹךְ	ûvethôkh	and in the midst of
250	n mp	אַחִים	'achîm	brothers
2606.121	v Qal impf 3ms	יַחֲלֹק	yachălōq	he will divide
5338	n fs	נַחֲלָה	nachălāh	an inheritance

3.

Strong's	Parsing	Hebrew	Translit.	English
4876	n ms	מַצְרֵף	matsrēph	a crucible
3937, 3826B	prep, art, n ms	לַכֶּסֶף	lakkeseph	for the silver
3685	cj, n ms	וְכוּר	wekhûr	and a furnace
3937, 2174	prep, art, n ms	לַזָּהָב	lazzāhāv	for the gold
1010.151	cj, v Qal act ptc ms	וּבֹחֵן	ûvōchēn	and examining
3949	n mp	לִבּוֹת	libbôth	intentions
3176	pn	יְהוָה	yehwāh	Yahweh

4.

Strong's	Parsing	Hebrew	Translit.	English
7778.551	v Hiphil ptc ms	מֵרַע	mēra'	an evildoer
7477.551	v Hiphil ptc ms	מַקְשִׁיב	maqōshîv	one who pays attention
6142, 8004, 201	prep, n fs, n ms	עַל־שְׂפַת־אָוֶן	'al-sephath-'āwen	concerning a lip of iniquity
8632	n ms	שֶׁקֶר	sheqer	a liar
237.551	v Hiphil ptc ms	מֵזִין	mēzîn	one who listens
6142, 4098	prep, n fs	עַל־לְשׁוֹן	'al-leshôn	concerning a tongue of

5.

Strong's	Parsing	Hebrew	Translit.	English
2010	n fp	הַוֺּת	hawwōth	wickedness
4074.151	v Qal act ptc ms	לֹעֵג	lō'ēgh	a scoffer
3937, 7851	prep, art, n ms	לָרָשׁ	lārāsh	of the poor
2884.311	v Piel pf 3ms	חֵרֵף	chērēph	he taunts
6449.151	v Qal act ptc ms, ps 3ms	עֹשֵׂהוּ	'ōsēhû	his Maker
7976	adj	שָׂמֵחַ	sāmēach	joyful

6.

Strong's	Parsing	Hebrew	Translit.	English
3937, 344	prep, n ms	לְאֵיד	le'êdh	about calamity
3940	neg part	לֹא	lō'	not
5536.221	v Niphal impf 3ms	יִנָּקֶה	yinnāqeh	he will be innocent
6065	n fs	עֲטֶרֶת	'ătereth	a crown of
2292	n mp	זְקֵנִים	zeqēnîm	elders
1158	n mp	בְּנֵי	benê	sons of
1158	n mp	בָּנִים	vānîm	sons

7.

Strong's	Parsing	Hebrew	Translit.	English
8930	cj, n fs	וְתִפְאֶרֶת	wethiph'ereth	and the beauty of
1158	n mp	בָּנִים	bānîm	sons
1	n mp, ps 3mp	אֲבוֹתָם	'ăvôthām	their fathers
3940, 5173	neg part, adj	לֹא־נָאוָה	lō'-nā'wāh	not lovely
3937, 5210	prep, n ms	לְנָבָל	lenāvāl	to a fool
8004, 3615	n fs, n ms	שְׂפַת־יֶתֶר	sephath-yether	a lip of excess
652	cj	אַף	'aph	also

2. A wise servant shall have rule over a son that causeth shame, and shall have part of the inheritance among the brethren: ... A wise servant will rule over the master's disgraceful child and will even inherit a share of what the master leaves his children, *NCV* ... A wise slave may give orders to a disappointing son and share the inheritance with the brothers, *NEB* ... An intelligent slave will rule over a shameless son; he'll have a share of the property as one of the brothers, *Beck* ... and will have his part in the heritage among brothers, *BB*.

3. The refining pot is for silver, and the furnace for gold: but the LORD trieth the hearts: ... Like the smelter for silver, and the furnace, *Goodspeed* ... The heating-pot is for silver and the oven-fire for gold, but the Lord is the tester of hearts, *BB* ... Silver and gold are purified by fire, but God purifies hearts, *LIVB* ... Gold and silver are tested by fire, and a person's heart is tested by the LORD, *Good News*.

4. A wicked doer giveth heed to false lips; and a liar giveth ear to a naughty tongue: ... Only a base man listens to malicious words; only the false attend to mischievous talk, *Moffatt* ... The evil man gives heed to wicked lips, and listens to falsehood from a mischievous tongue, *NAB* ... A liar pays attention to a destructive tongue, *NASB* ... a liar listens to slander, *NEB*.

5. Whoso mocketh the poor reproacheth his Maker: and he that is glad at calamities shall not be unpunished: ... Whoever mistreats the poor insults their Maker; whoever enjoys someone's trouble will be punished, *NCV* ... He who mocks the poor shows contempt for their Maker; whoever gloats over disaster will not go unpunished, *NIV* ... he that is glad at calamity shall not be held innocent, *Darby* ... Whoever makes sport of the poor puts shame on his Maker; and he who is glad because of trouble will not go free from punishment, *BB.*

6. Children's children are the crown of old men; and the glory of children are their fathers: ... Grandchildren are the crown of old age, and the glory of children is in their fathers, *Berkeley* ... Grandchildren are the crown of old people, and parents are the glory of their children, *Beck* ... The crown of the aged is their children's children; the children's glory is their father, *JB* ... And fathers are the pride of their children, *Goodspeed.*

7. Excellent speech becometh not a fool: much less do lying lips a prince: ... Fine words do not become the foolish, false words become a prince still less, *JB* ... An excellent lip is not fitting for a fool; much less are lying lips fitting for a prince, *KJVII* ... Fools should not be proud, and rulers should not be liars, *NCV* ... Arrogant lips are unsuited to a fool—how much worse lying lips to a ruler!, *NIV.*

"morsel," the verse asserts that bread is better than meat, since "peace" or "fellowship" offerings were a main source of meat, part of the sacrificed animal being returned to the worshiper (Lev. 7:15–18).

Parallel to the "better than" proverbs that relate to the superiority of honest or peaceful poverty versus wealth acquired by wickedness or accompanied by strife (cf. 15:16; 16:8), this verse is especially close to 15:17. Like some of those, this proverb implies that contentment is great gain, especially if the price of advancement (financial, social or professional) is turmoil.

17:2. Wisdom prevails over folly without regard for social standing or cultural expectations. The Covenant specifies the right of the firstborn (Deut. 21:15ff), but does not forbid the scenario of this verse. If the head of a household recognized a servant's insight, he could actually make him one of his heirs, apparently even his primary heir. A wise servant could effectually manage, and in that sense "rule," the estate, much as Joseph did (but by Potiphar's appointment; Gen. 39:4ff). Whatever the legal requirements and historical precedent, the threat of disinheritance was to stimulate sons to seek wisdom (cf. 11:29; 13:22).

17:3. The first line of this verse is identical to 27:21a. The right amount of heat, applied by a skilled metalworker, always reveals any impurities in the metal. In the same way, the LORD tests the true state of every human heart, using external circumstances (cf. Judg. 7:4; Ps. 105:19; Isa. 48:10; and, apparently, Zech. 13:9; Mal. 3:2f) or examining them directly (Pss. 17:3; 26:2; 66:10; Jer. 9:7). Solomon, who had good opportunity to see metals tested and refined during the building of the Temple and his palace (cf. 1 Ki. 6–8), thus encourages the wise to examine themselves regularly and to make clean breast of their flaws and sins, since they cannot be hid, and are, in fact, fully known to God.

17:4. Like other verses that seem tautologous (see "Overview"), this proverb has two sides. The wicked seek out and follow wicked counsel. A person's nature is also revealed by the kind of advice that he accepts. The "destructive tongue" may be a tongue that counsels destruction (cf. 1:10–14), or one that gives advice that destroys its owner and all who follow it, or it may refer to both.

17:5. The words of the wise bring healing and comfort, not distress (cf. 10:11; 12:18; 15:4). Someone who mocks others for their circumstances or rejoices in their trouble reveals his ignorance (24:17f; cf. 12:10). Respect and compassion, which are required by the Covenant (Lev. 19:14, 18; cf. Deut. 27:18; Luke 10:25–37), characterize the wise. They understand that because God is the Maker of all (22:2), humble and gracious comfort is the only proper response to others, regardless of their condition. This verse is thus closely related to the following.

17:6. One mark of a culture typified by obedience to the teachings of Proverbs is mutual respect between people of all classes and circumstances (cf. 17:5), as well as across generations. Their "adornment" describes their delight in each other (cf. the same use of "crown" in 12:4; 16:31). This saying may also parallel verses that promise long life to the wise (e.g., 3:2, 16; 4:9f; 9:11; 10:27), meaning that living long enough to see grandchildren (and vice versa) demonstrates that the person has been blessed for living according to wisdom.

17:7. One theme of Proverbs is that some things are "not appropriate" (19:10; 26:1) because they threaten to overturn the moral order (30:21ff). Fools should be silent, because they have nothing to say that is worth hearing. They refuse to learn (18:2), and so speak only out of their own folly (10:14, 19). The wise must therefore evaluate the counsel that they are offered before accepting or acting upon it. Leaders

8.

3706, 3937, 5259	8004, 8632	63, 2682	8245	904, 6084	1196
cj, prep, n ms	n fs, n ms	n fs, n ms	art, n ms	prep, n fd	n mp, ps 3ms
כִּי־לְנָדִיב	שְׂפַת־שָׁקֶר	אֶבֶן־חֵן	הַשֹּׁחַד	בְּעֵינֵי	בְּעָלָיו
kî-lenādhîv	sephath-shāqer	'even-chēn	hashshōchadh	be'ênê	ve'ālâv
indeed to a leader	a lip of lying	a stone of favor	the bribe	in the eyes of	its owners

9.

420, 3725, 866	6680.121	7959.521	3803.351, 6840	1272.351
prep, adj, rel part	v Qal impf 3ms	v Hiphil impf 3ms	v Piel ptc ms, n ms	v Piel ptc ms
אֶל־כָּל־אֲשֶׁר	יִפְנֶה	יַשְׂכִּיל	מְכַסֶּה־פֶּשַׁע	מְבַקֵּשׁ
'el-kol-'ăsher	yiphneh	yaskîl	mekhasseh-pesha'	mevaqqēsh
to everywhere	he will turn	he will act wisely	the one who covers an offense	seeking

157	8521.151	904, 1745	6754.551	443
n fs	cj, v Qal act ptc ms	prep, n ms	v Hiphil ptc ms	n ms
אַהֲבָה	וְשֹׁנֶה	בְדָבָר	מַפְרִיד	אַלּוּף
'ahvāh	weshōneh	vedhāvār	maphrîdh	'allûph
love	and the one who repeats	about a matter	one who separates	close friends

10.

5365.122	1648	904, 1032.551	4623, 5409.541	3809
v Qal impf 3fs	n fs	prep, v Hiphil ptc ms	prep, v Hiphil inf con	n ms
תֵּחַת	גְּעָרָה	בְמֵבִין	מֵהַכּוֹת	כְּסִיל
tēchath	ge'ārāh	vemēvîn	mēhakkôth	kesîl
it will penetrate more	a rebuke	in one who discerns	than the striking of	the foolish

11.

4109	395, 4967	1272.321, 7737	4534	400
num	adv, n ms	v Piel impf 3ms, n ms	cj, n ms	n ms
מֵאָה	אַךְ־מְרִי	יְבַקֶּשׁ־רָע	וּמַלְאָךְ	אַכְזָרִי
mē'āh	'akh-merî	yevaqqesh-rā'	ûmal'ākh	'akhzārî
one hundred	only rebellion	an evil man seeks	and a messenger	a cruel man

12.

8365.421, 904	6539.142	1726	8316	904, 382	414, 3809
v Pual impf 3ms, prep, ps 3ms	v Qal inf abs	n ms	adj	prep, n ms	cj, adv, n ms
יְשֻׁלַּח־בּוֹ	פָּגוֹשׁ	דֹּב	שַׁכּוּל	בְּאִישׁ	וְאַל־כְּסִיל
yeshullach-bô	pāghôsh	dōv	shakkûl	be'îsh	we'al-kesîl
he will be sent against him	encountering	a bear	bereft	against a man	but not a fool

13.

904, 198	8178.551	7750	8809	3009B	3940, 4318.522	7750
prep, n fs, ps 3ms	v Hiphil ptc ms	n fs	prep	adj	neg part, v Hiphil impf 3fs	n fs
בְּאִוַּלְתּוֹ	מֵשִׁיב	רָעָה	תַּחַת	טוֹבָה	לֹא־תָמִישׁ	רָעָה
be'iwwaltô	mēshîv	rā'āh	tachath	tôvāh	lō'-thāmîsh	rā'āh
in his folly	one who returns to	evil	instead of	good	it will not depart	evil

14.

4623, 1041	6604.151	4448	7519	4209	3937, 6686	1607.711
prep, n ms, ps 3ms	v Qal act ptc ms	n md	n fs	n ms	cj, prep, n mp	v Hithpael pf 3ms
מִבֵּיתוֹ	פּוֹטֵר	מַיִם	רֵאשִׁית	מָדוֹן	וְלִפְנֵי	הִתְגַּלַּע
mibbêthô	pôtēr	mayim	rē'shîth	mādhôn	weliphnê	hithgalla'
from his house	letting flow	water	the beginning of	strife	and before	it will break out

8. A gift is as a precious stone in the eyes of him that hath it: whithersoever it turneth, it prospereth: ... A present is a precious stone in the eyes of its possessor; Wherever he turns, he prospers, *NKJV* ... A gift looks like a jewel to one who gets it; no matter how you turn it, it looks good, *Beck* ... A bribe is a precious stone in the eyes of the one receiving it; whatever he turns to, he causes to succeed, *Berkeley* ... wherever he goes, he does well, *BB*.

9. He that covereth a transgression seeketh love; but he that repeateth a matter separateth very friends: ... If you cover a friend's wrong, you seek his goodwill, but if you repeat the thing, you will break up the friendship, *Beck* ... If you want people to like you, forgive them when they wrong you. Remembering wrongs can break up a friendship, *Good News* ... Whoever covers an offence promotes love, whoever again raises the matter divides friends, *JB* ... Love forgets mistakes; nagging about them parts the best of friends, *LIVB*.

10. A reproof entereth more into a wise man than an hundred stripes into a fool: ... A rebuke entereth deeper into a man of understanding Than a hundred stripes, *MAST* ... rebuke sinks deeper into a man of sense than a hundred lashes into a fool, *Moffatt* ... A single reprimand does more for a man of intelligence than a hundred lashes, *NAB* ... A wise person will learn more from a warning than a fool will learn from a hundred lashings, *NCV.*

11. An evil man seeketh only rebellion: therefore a cruel messenger shall be sent against him: ... An evil man is set only on disobedience, but a messenger without mercy will be sent, *NEB* ... An uncontrolled man is only looking for trouble, so a cruel servant will be sent, *BB* ... a stern messenger will be sent, *Berkeley* ... a merciless official, *NIV.*

12. Let a bear robbed of her whelps meet a man, rather than a fool in his folly: ... Better to meet a bear robbed of her young than a fool involved with his nonsense, *Beck* ... It is better to meet a mother bear robbed of her cubs than to meet some fool busy with a stupid project, *Good News* ... than to meet a fool doing foolish things, *NCV.*

13. Whoso rewardeth evil for good, evil shall not depart from his house: ... Whoever gives evil in return for good will always have trouble at home, *NCV* ... Who repays a good turn with wrong, Distress departs not

who depend upon counselors must also evaluate the advice they receive and be certain it is truthful, i.e., that it is motivated by a concern for the justice required by the Covenant (16:12f; 22:11), so that they may rule securely (cf. 29:12).

By their words, a talkative fool and a corrupt minister of state disrupt the established moral order. The wise know to refuse both of them a hearing.

17:8. Without commending bribery (cf. 17:23), Solomon explains why some people are addicted to giving bribes—it works. Bribes lead to success at everything they try, so much so that they think of a bribe as a magical talisman or charm (lit., "gracious stone"). The warning is to consider the motivation underlying a "gift." It may, in the giver's eyes, obligate the recipient, just as it has always worked before.

17:9. This proverb is aimed directly at motives for repeating or not repeating bad news, whether it is a personal injury or something done to someone else. As the proverbs state often, talebearing destroys the trust that is the necessary foundation of close relationships (e.g., 16:28; 20:19; 22:10; 25:23; 26:20ff). The wise therefore note and avoid such people (20:19), knowing that they stand under the condemnation of God himself (6:19).

17:10. Like the rest of Proverbs, this verse denies any hope to fools (cf. esp. 27:22). They will not even learn from extreme punishment (a sentence of 100 blows was illegal under the Covenant [Deut. 25:1ff]), whereas the discerning respond positively to a simple rebuke, since they value correction and recognize its value. The proverbs generally warn that the folly of fools often leads them into behavior or words that make them prone to "blows" (10:13; 18:6f).

17:11. Those who incite rebellion must not expect any mercy. Insurrection was punished by

death (cf. 1 Ki. 11:40, and verses below). Since Proverbs was first addressed to young men who were preparing to become leaders in Israel, its warnings against sedition are especially strong (24:21f). Two of Solomon's half-brothers had been executed for rebellion: Absalom was killed by Joab (2 Sam. 18:9–15), and Adonijah was executed at Solomon's order (1 Ki. 2:19–25).

17:12. Although this verse lacks the explicit "better than" formula, it clearly recommends one of two options as the better situation. The English translations tend to invert the statements, which literally say, "Let a robbed bear meet a man, but not a fool in his folly." Rebellion and contumacy (i.e., folly) are so dangerous that death is better than falling or being drawn into them. As the opening chapters specify, to follow folly is to choose death (8:35f). This proverb is not weighing the relative values of life and death as much as it is warning about the dangers of sin.

17:13. The proverbs unanimously warn the wicked that they will be judged. How much more when they harm those who wish them well! "House" (HED #1041) is better translated "household" (or even, if applied to kings, "dynasty"). A leader should expect his example to be followed, so that betrayal and selfishness become a way of life throughout his household (cf. 2 Sam. 12:10). Since the wise seek the well-being of others, they not only return good for good, but good for evil (20:22; 24:29; 25:21f), knowing that they too face judgment (11:31).

17:14. Every quarrel has a prehistory. Those words and events, which may even seem innocent at the time, rarely presage their full effect. Many quarrels also begin with apparently minor disagreements, but quickly escalate into strife and conflict. The

15.

6926	7855.551	7857	6927.551	5389.131	7663
n ms	cj, v Hiphil ptc ms	n ms	v Hiphil ptc ms	v Qal impv 2ms	art, n ms
צַדִּיק	וּמַרְשִׁיעַ	רָשָׁע	מַצְדִּיק	נְטוֹשׁ	הָרִיב
tsaddîq	ûmarshîa'	rāshā'	matsdîq	neṭôsh	hārîv
the righteous	also declaring evil	the wicked	one who vindicates	disregard	the contention

16.

904, 3135, 3809	4378	4066, 2172	1612, 8530	3176	8774
prep, n fs, n ms	n ms	intrg, dem pron	cj, num, ps 3mp	pn	n fs
בְּיַד־כְּסִיל	מְחִיר	לָמָּה־זֶּה	גַּם־שְׁנֵיהֶם	יְהוָה	תּוֹעֲבַת
beyadh-kesîl	mechîr	lāmmāh-zeh	gam-shenêhem	yehwāh	tô'ăvath
in the hand of a fool	a price	why this	also the two of them	Yahweh	an abomination to

17.

7739	154.151	904, 3725, 6496	3949, 375	2551	3937, 7353.141
art, n ms	v Qal act ptc ms	prep, adj, n fs	cj, n ms, sub	n fs	prep, v Qal inf con
הָרֵעַ	אֹהֵב	בְּכָל־עֵת	וְלֵב־אָיִן	חָכְמָה	לִקְנוֹת
hārēa'	'ōhēv	bekhol-'ēth	welev-'āyin	chokhmāh	liqnôth
the friend	one who loves	during all times	but there is not a heart	wisdom	to buy

18.

3834	8965.151	2742, 3949	119	3314.221	3937, 7150	250
n fs	v Qal act ptc ms	adj, n ms	n ms	v Niphal impf 3ms	prep, n fs	cj, n ms
כָּף	תּוֹקֵעַ	חֲסַר־לֵב	אָדָם	יִוָּלֵד	לְצָרָה	וְאָח
kāph	tôqēa'	chăsar-lēv	'ādhām	yiwwālēdh	letsārāh	we'āch
palms	striking	lacking in heart	a man	he has been born	for adversity	but a brother

19.

6840	154.151	7739	3937, 6686	6401	6386.151
n ms	v Qal act ptc ms	n ms, ps 3ms	prep, n mp	n fs	v Qal act ptc ms
פֶּשַׁע	אֹהֵב	רֵעֵהוּ	לִפְנֵי	עֲרֻבָּה	עֹרֵב
pesha'	'ōhēv	rē'ēhû	liphnê	'ărubbāh	'ōrēv
a transgression	one who loves	his fellow	before	a pledge	giving security for

1272.351, 8133	6860	1391.551	4844	154.151
v Piel ptc ms, n ms	n ms, ps 3ms	v Hiphil ptc ms	n fs	v Qal act ptc ms
מְבַקֵּשׁ־שָׁבֶר	פִּתְחוֹ	מַגְבִּיהַּ	מַצָּה	אֹהֵב
mevaqqesh-shāver	pithchô	maghbîahh	matstsāh	'ōhēv
one who seeks ruin	his entrance	one who makes high	strife	one who loves

20.

904, 4098	2089.255	4834.121, 3008	3940	6379, 3949
prep, n fs, ps 3ms	cj, v Niphal ptc ms	v Qal impf 3ms, n ms	neg part	adj, n ms
בִּלְשׁוֹנוֹ	וְנֶהְפָּךְ	יִמְצָא־טוֹב	לֹא	עִקֶּשׁ־לֵב
bilshônô	wenehpākh	yimtsā'-ṭôv	lō'	'iqqesh-lēv
with his tongue	and one who is turned	he will find good	not	the perverse of heart

---

from his house, *Fenton* … calamity will not leave his house, *Berkeley*.

14. The beginning of strife is as when one letteth out water: therefore leave off contention, before it be meddled with: … Starting a quarrel is like opening a flood gate; so quit before the quarrel starts, *Beck* … The start of strife is like the opening of a dam; therefore, check a quarrel before it begins!, *NAB* … The start of an argument is like the first break in a dam; stop it before it goes any further, *Good News* … So abandon the quarrel before it breaks out, *NASB*.

15. He that justifieth the wicked, and he that condemneth the just, even they both are abomination to the LORD: … The LORD hates both of these things: freeing the guilty and punishing the innocent, *NCV* … Acquitting the guilty and condemning the innocent—the LORD detests them both, *NIV* … He who gives a decision for the evil-doer and he who gives a decision against the upright, are equally disgusting to the Lord, *BB* … Acquitting the bad, and convicting the good, Both alike are disgusting, *Fenton*.

16. Wherefore is there a price in the hand of a fool to get wisdom, seeing he hath no heart to it?: … Why should a fool have money in his hand to buy wisdom when he doesn't have a mind to grasp it?, *Beck* … Of what use is money in the hand of a fool, since he has no desire to get wisdom?, *NIV* … It is senseless to pay tuition to educate a rebel who has no heart for truth, *LIVB* … when he has no mind to learn?, *Moffatt*.

17. A friend loveth at all times, and a brother is born for adversity: … A friend shows his friendship at all times, and a brother is born to share troubles, *REB* ... At all times a friend is devoted, *Anchor* ... A friend is perpetually friendly, *Berkeley* ... of a brother's love there is no test like adversity, *Knox*.

18. A man void of understanding striketh hands, and becometh surety in the presence of his friend: ... A man with no understanding strikes hands and becomes surety, *KJVII* ... Senseless is the man who

gives his hand in pledge, who becomes surety for his neighbor, *NAB* ... It is not wise to promise to pay what your neighbor owes, *NCV* ... A man is without sense who gives a guarantee and surrenders himself to another as surety, *NEB*.

19. He loveth transgression that loveth strife: and he that exalteth his gate seeketh destruction: ... He who loves a quarrel loves sin; he who builds a high gate invites destruction,

NIV ... The lover of fighting is a lover of sin: he who makes high his doorway is looking for destruction, *BB* ... To like sin is to like making trouble. If you brag all the time, you are asking for trouble, *Good News* ... and he who opens wide his mouth seeks destruction, *Berkeley*.

20. He that hath a froward heart findeth no good: and he that hath a perverse tongue falleth into mischief: ... The tortuous of heart finds

---

verse thus carries a double warning: to consider carefully the long-term implications of words and deeds, and to be quick to drop out of or deflect (15:1) a conflict. The fool, unable to see beyond his own ends, cannot do this; the wise must.

17:15. Justice (often translated "righteousness") is a central concern of the Covenant, as demonstrated by Moses' appointment of judges, and especially his charge to them (Exo. 18:13–26; Deut. 1:9–18). The proper administration of justice (far more than conquest, wealth or fame) also determined the stability of the realm (cf. 16:12; 25:5; 29:4, 12, 14), since the people would grow increasingly restive under oppression, as happened during Solomon's own reign (1 Ki. 12:4).

Judges, who applied the law of God to the people (cf. Exo. 18:15f, 19; Deut. 1:17), revealed or perverted the justice of God by their decisions. To deny justice was thus to deny the God they purportedly represented (cf. 17:26; 18:5, where this is "not good"). Deceitful words and deeds were condemned as abominations (6:16–19; 11:1; 12:22; 20:23).

17:16. Students are often urged to purchase wisdom (4:5, 7; 16:16; 23:23). They are already on the path of knowledge, and so able to use the insight that they "buy." Even if wisdom could literally be bought, and even if fools could meet the asking price, they would not benefit; it would be an unusable tool in their hands (26:7).

Wisdom's price is submission and obedience (1:7; 4:1–7), attitudes that fools have rejected in their rebellion (2:22). This proverb, like many others, shows the utterly hopeless state of the fool: he has determined not to accept wisdom (15:12), thus he can neither recognize it (17:24) nor benefit from it. Having shut themselves off from its benefits, they cannot simply avail themselves at their convenience or need.

17:17. Since it is unlikely that strangers will offer succor in disaster or trouble, neighbors and relatives are one's primary source of help. This reminder of the importance of maintaining good relationships (18:19) and choosing friends wisely (18:24) also reminds the wise that they, who are also neighbors and relatives, must stand ready to help others (27:10).

17:18. Of six passages that discuss co-signing loans (6:1–5; 11:15; 20:16; 22:26f; 27:13), this is the only one that explains why someone would do such a thing. Solomon's explanation is quite simple—whoever does this lacks sense. To pledge oneself for someone else's debt is foolish because it is short-sighted. It fails to contemplate the possible consequences of the promise, which include the loss of money or property (cf. 22:26f). The money is also lost in the short term. The securitor must keep enough money on hand to repay the loan, which means that those funds are not available for any other use. To spend them might mean the loss of actual property (22:27). The wise person considers what might happen and, having considered it, refuses to take part in the contract.

17:19. The first line shows that those who enjoy creating interpersonal conflict do so because they enjoy sin (and hate wisdom and righteousness). The idiom in the second line—"exalts [or 'makes high'] his door [lit., 'opening']"—is unclear. It could describe a literal gate, and thus condemn self-exaltation (e.g., by building a bigger or fancier house than the neighbor's). It might also be a figure for the mouth, and condemn arrogant talk. The related adjective (gāvōahh [HED #1393]) often refers to pride (e.g., 16:5, 18). The line seems to condemn the arrogance that leads into troubling others, "shattering" relationships.

17:20. Since words, which reveal the orientation of the heart (15:28), determine the course of

21.

5489.121	904, 7750		3314.151	3809	3937, 8755	3937	3940, 7975.121
v Qal impf 3ms	prep, n fs		v Qal act ptc ms	n ms	prep, n fs	prep, ps 3ms	cj, neg part, v Qal impf 3ms
יִפּוֹל	בְּרָעָה		יֹלֵד	כְּסִיל	לְתוּגָה	לוֹ	וְלֹא־יִשְׂמַח
yippôl	berā'āh		yōlēdh	kesîl	lethûghāh	lô	welō'-yismach
he will fall	into evil		one who fathers	a fool	for grief	to him	and he will not be joyful

22.

1	5210		3949	7976	3296.521	1486	7593	5405
n ms	n ms		n ms	adj	v Hiphil impf 3ms	n fs	cj, n fs	adj
אֲבִי	נָבָל		לֵב	שָׂמֵחַ	יֵיטִב	גֵּהָה	וְרוּחַ	נְכֵאָה
'avî	nāvāl		lēv	sāmēach	yēṭiv	gēhāh	werûach	nekhē'āh
the father of	a fool		a heart	joyful	it causes to be good	a cure	and a spirit	dejected

23.

3111.322, 1678		8245	4623, 2536	7857	4089.121	3937, 5371.541
v Piel impf 3fs, n ms		n ms	prep, n ms	n ms	v Qal impf 3ms	prep, v Hiphil inf con
תְּיַבֶּשׁ־גָּרֶם		שֹׁחַד	מֵחֵיק	רָשָׁע	יִקָּח	לְהַטּוֹת
teyabbesh-gārem		shōchadh	mēchêq	rāshā'	yiqqāch	lehaṭṭôth
it will dry out the bones		a bribe	from the bosom	the wicked	he will take	to cause to lean

24.

758	5122		881, 6686	1032.551	2551	6084	3809
n fp	n ms		do, n mp	v Hiphil ptc ms	n fs	cj, n fd	n ms
אָרְחוֹת	מִשְׁפָּט		אֶת־פְּנֵי	מֵבִין	חָכְמָה	וְעֵינֵי	כְסִיל
'ārechôth	mishpāṭ		'eth-penê	mēvîn	chokhmāh	we'ênê	khesîl
the paths of	justice		the face of	one who discerns	wisdom	but the eyes of	a fool

25.

904, 7381, 800		3833	3937, 1	1158	3809	4612
prep, n ms, n ms		n ms	prep, n ms, ps 3ms	n ms	adj	cj, n ms
בִּקְצֵה־אָרֶץ		כַּעַס	לְאָבִיו	בֵּן	כְּסִיל	וּמֶמֶר
biqôtsēh-'arets		ka'as	le'āvîw	bēn	kesîl	ûmemer
on the ends of the earth		vexation	to his father	a son	foolish	and bitterness

26.

3937, 3314.153		1612	6294.141	3937, 6926	3940, 3005	3937, 5409.541
prep, v Qal act ptc fs, ps 3ms		cj	v Qal inf con	prep, art, n ms	neg part, adj	prep, v Hiphil inf con
לְיוֹלַדְתּוֹ		גַּם	עֲנוֹשׁ	לַצַּדִּיק	לֹא־טוֹב	לְהַכּוֹת
leyôladhtô		gam	'ānôsh	latstsaddîq	lō'-ṭôv	lehakkôth
to she who bore him		also	to fine	the righteous	not good	to strike

27.

5259	6142, 3598		2910.151	571	3156.151	1907
n mp	prep, n ms		v Qal act ptc ms	n mp, ps 3ms	v Qal act ptc ms	n fs
נְדִיבִים	עַל־יֹשֶׁר		חוֹשֵׂךְ	אֲמָרָיו	יוֹדֵעַ	דָּעַת
nedhîvîm	'al-yōsher		chôsēkh	'āmārâv	yôdhēa'	dā'ath
noble men	against uprightness		one who spares	his sayings	one who knows	knowledge

no happiness, the perverse of speech falls into misery, *JB* ... He who has a crooked mind finds no good, And he who is perverted in his language falls into evil, *NASB* ... False heart never found happiness, nor lying tongue escaped mischief, *Knox* ... And he who is crooked in speech will fall into trouble, *Goodspeed*.

21. He that begetteth a fool doeth it to his sorrow: and the father of a fool hath no joy: ... It is sad to have a foolish child; there is no joy in being the parent of a fool, *NCV* ... There is nothing but sadness and sorrow for a father whose son does foolish things, *Good News* ... To have a fool for a son brings grief, *NIV* ... And the father of an ill-natured youth has no happiness, *Anchor*.

22. A merry heart doeth good like a medicine: but a broken spirit drieth the bones: ... A glad heart makes a healthy body, but a crushed spirit makes the bones dry, *BB* ... A cheerful heart makes a good cure, but a broken spirit makes the bones dry up, *Berkeley* ... A happy mind is good medicine, but a depressed spirit saps one's strength, *Beck* ... A joyful heart promoteth healing, *Darby*.

23. A wicked man taketh a gift out of the bosom to pervert the ways of judgment: ... A wicked man will accept a bribe from the bosom To divert the course of justice, *Goodspeed* ... Bad men accept a secret bribe, to twist the course of justice, *Moffatt* ... The wicked man accepts a concealed bribe to pervert the course of justice, *NAB* ... A wicked man accepts a bribe under his cloak to pervert the course of, *NEB*.

24. Wisdom is before him that hath understanding; but the eyes of a fool are in the ends of the earth: … A discerning man keeps wisdom in view, but a fool's eyes wander to the ends, *NIV* … The discerning man sees the wise choice right in front of him, While the fool is looking to, *Anchor* … Wisdom is before the face of him who has sense; but the eyes of the foolish are on the ends, *BB* … Wisdom is never out of sight of those who are discerning, *REB*.

25. A foolish son is a grief to his father, and bitterness to her that bare him: … foolish son irritates his father and is a bitter grief to his mother, *Beck* … foolish son makes his father sad and causes his mother great sorrow, *NCV* … And a bitter sorrow to her who bore him, *Goodspeed* … and bitter pain to her who gave him birth, *BB*.

26. Also to punish the just is not good, nor to strike princes for equity: … To fine the upright is indeed a crime, to strike the noble is an unjustice, *JB* … It is not fair to fine the innocent, and most unfair to scourge a noble soul, *Moffatt* … It is not good to punish the innocent or to beat leaders for being honest, *NCV* … How short-sighted to fine the godly for being good! And to punish nobles for being honest!, *LIVB*.

27. He that hath knowledge spareth his words: and a man of

---

a person's life, those whose speech is devious should expect nothing but to fall into trouble (18:6f). They should certainly not expect blessing. Whether the judgment is physical, perhaps punishment for perjury that is uncovered in court, or social, as people begin to realize their perversity, their words, which come from their twisted hearts, will bring them and their followers into disaster. The wise know that their hearts determine the quality of their words and lives (4:23) and so examine their thoughts and words that they may guard their hearts.

17:21. Children affect their parents far more deeply than they may realize, especially as they grow old enough to make independent choices (cf. 10:1; 15:20). Parents who have this long view, however, also understand the value of discipline and work to help their children develop the self-discipline and wisdom that will enable them to live wisely. This verse thus encourages parents to discipline their children, and children to respond positively to that correction, knowing that they act out of love (cf. 3:11f; 13:24).

17:22. Not only is true joy difficult to conceal (15:13), it refreshes the soul, whereas an injured or wounded spirit eventually desicates a person. As this verse and others show, the Israelites understood the relationship between emotional and physical health (e.g., 14:30; 15:30) and encouraged discernment in personal relationships, as well as the knowledge that despair must not be allowed to go unchecked.

This and other proverbs (e.g., 15:13; 18:14) call for carefully chosen words in relating to others. They also warn that those lingering in sorrow (or wallowing in self-pity) must not be allowed or encouraged to do so. Brooding over injuries is ultimately self-destructive.

17:23. Anyone who knowingly accepts a bribe does so for a purpose, in order to accomplish what cannot be done legitimately. To seek or expect justice from such a person is futile, since the size of the bribe has already determined the outcome of the case. Bribes pervert justice (cf. 1 Sam. 8:3), encouraging perjury (contra Exo. 20:16), and are condemned by the Covenant (cf. Exo. 23:8; Deut. 16:19). Since judges represent God to the people (cf. Deut. 19:17), their justice must reflect his, which cannot be bribed (Deut. 10:17). Failure to observe this injunction brought the LORD's condemnation through his prophets (Mic. 3:11), which reflects the specific covenantal curse against accepting bribes (Deut. 27:25).

17:24. Fools, who reject wisdom's instruction, lack the insight and understanding to recognize true wisdom, even in its presence. They would rather search the ends of the earth than admit the wisdom of those who espouse what they despise. The wise, who recognize wisdom and insight, seek it where it may be found (10:13) and avoid those whose wisdom is actually folly (13:20; 14:7).

17:25. Children's words and choices reveal whether or not they follow their parents' instruction (20:11) and deeply affect their parents (cf. 10:1; 17:21). Fools engender bitter anger. This bitterness could be self-reproach for their own failure to discipline their children (cf. 19:18; 23:13f; 29:15), or it could be anger that their children rejected their counsel and correction (cf. 13:1; 17:21). This verse encourages parents to strive to raise their children, so that they will not be sources of vexation as they mature, and may warn children to consider the effect of their choices on those who love them.

17:26. Judges who fine the innocent for crimes that they did not commit (cf. the fines of restitution in Exo. 21:28–22:17), or who have leaders whipped (cf. Deut. 25:1ff) because of their honesty, are condemned for breaking the Law. The second line

7408, 7593	382	8722		1612	188	2896.551	2550
cj, adj, n fs	n ms	n fs	**28.**	cj	n ms	v Hiphil ptc ms	adj
וְקַר־רוּחַ	אִישׁ	תְּבוּנָה		גַּם	אֱוִיל	מַחֲרִישׁ	חָכָם
weqar-rûach	'îsh	tevûnāh		gam	'ĕwîl	machărîsh	chākhām
and cool in spirit	a man of	understanding		also	a fool	one who remains silent	wise

2913.221	334.151	8004	1032.255		3937, 8707
v Niphal impf 3ms	v Qal act ptc ms	n fd, ps 3ms	v Niphal ptc ms	**18:1**	prep, n fs
יֵחָשֵׁב	אֹטֵם	שְׂפָתָיו	נָבוֹן		לְתַאֲוָה
yēchāshēv	'ōṭēm	sephāthāv	nāvôn		letha'ăwāh
he will be considered to be	one who closes	his lips	being discerning		desire

1272.321	6754.255	904, 725, 8786	1607.721
v Piel impf 3ms	v Niphal ptc ms	prep, adj, n fs	v Hithpael impf 3ms
יְבַקֵּשׁ	נִפְרָד	בְּכָל־תּוּשִׁיָּה	יִתְגַּלָּע
yevaqqēsh	niphrādh	bekhol-tûshîyāh	yithgallā'
he will seek	someone separated	against all sound wisdom	he will break out

3940, 2759.121	3809	904, 8722	3706	524, 904, 1580.741	3949
2. neg part, v Qal impf 3ms	n ms	prep, n fs	cj	cj, prep, v Hithpael inf con	n ms, ps 3ms
לֹא־יַחְפֹּץ	כְּסִיל	בִּתְבוּנָה	כִּי	אִם־בְּהִתְגַּלּוֹת	לִבּוֹ
lō'-yachpōts	kesîl	bithvûnāh	kî	'im-behithgallôth	libbô
he does not delight	a fool	in understanding	because	that by revealing itself	his heart

904, 971.141, 7857	971.111	1612, 973	6196, 7320	2887	4448
3. prep, v Qal inf con, n ms	v Qal pf 3ms	cj, n ms	cj, prep, n ms	n fs	**4.** n md
בְּבוֹא־רָשָׁע	בָּא	גַּם־בּוּז	וְעִם־קָלוֹן	חֶרְפָּה	מַיִם
bevô'-rāshā'	bā'	gham-bûz	we'im-qālôn	cherpāh	mayim
when a wicked man coming	it will come	also contempt	and with dishonor	disgrace	waters

6233	1745	6552, 382	5337	5218.151	4888	2551
adj	n mp	n ms, n ms	n ms	v Qal act ptc ms	n ms	n fs
עֲמֻקִּים	דִּבְרֵי	פִי־אִישׁ	נַחַל	נֹבֵעַ	מְקוֹר	חָכְמָה
'ămuqqîm	divrê	phî-'îsh	nachal	nōvēa'	meqôr	chokhmāh
deep	the words of	the mouth of a man	a wadi	gushing	a fountain of	wisdom

understanding is of an excellent spirit: ... Experience uses few words; discernment keeps a cool head, *NEB* ... A man of knowledge uses words with restraint, and a man of understanding is even-tempered, *NIV* ... He who has knowledge says little: and he who has a calm spirit is a man of good sense, *BB* ... Whoever can control the tongue knows what knowledge is, someone of understanding keeps a cool temper, *JB* ... He who restrains his words has knowledge, and he who is calm of spirit is a man of understanding, *Berkeley*.

28. Even a fool, when he holdeth his peace, is counted wise: and he that shutteth his lips is esteemed a man of understanding: ... Even a fool is thought wise if he remains silent, and considered intelligent if he keeps his lips closed, *Beck* ... If the fool holds his tongue, he may pass for wise; if he seals his lips, he may pass for intelligent, *JB* ... Even a fool may pass for wise, if he says nothing; with closed lips he may be deemed sensible, *Moffatt* ... even a fool may be thought wise and intelligent if he stays quiet and keeps his mouth shut, *Good News*.

18:1. Through desire a man, having separated himself, seeketh and intermeddleth with all wisdom: ... He who keeps himself separate for his private purpose goes against all good sense, *BB* ... He who wilfully separates himself, seeks his own desire and breaks out against all sound wisdom, *Berkeley* ... He that separateth himself seeketh [his]

pleasure, *Darby* ... The unsociable man is out to get what he wants for himself; he opposes every wise undertaking, *Beck*.

2. A fool hath no delight in understanding, but that his heart may discover itself: ... A fool doesn't delight in reasoning but only in expressing what he thinks, *Beck* ... A fool has no pleasure in what is reasonable, But only in self-display, *Goodspeed* ... A fool takes no pleasure in understanding but only in airing an opinion, *JB* ... Fools do not want to understand anything. They only want to tell others what they think, *NCV*.

3. When the wicked cometh, then cometh also contempt, and with ignominy reproach: ... Do something evil, and people won't like you. Do something shameful, and they will make fun of you, *NCV* ... When wickedness comes, so does contempt, and with shame comes disgrace, *NIV* ... With the entrance of sin comes disgrace, And with shame-ful acts, reproach, *Fenton* ... When a wicked person appears, he brings shame, and with contempt there's insult, *Beck.*

4. The words of a man's mouth are as deep waters, and the wellspring of wisdom as a flowing brook: ... Deep streams are the words of man's mouth, A deep brook, and well of wisdom, *Fenton* ... A person's words can be a source of wisdom, deep as the ocean, fresh as a flowing stream, *Good News.*

---

implies their perversion of the very standards of justice, so that this verse parallels the first line of 17:15 (where what is "not good" here is called an "abomination to the LORD").

17:27–28. These two verses clearly reinforce each other, although they may not have originated as a unit. One who listens rather than speaking recognizes his own ignorance and the knowledge of others, from whom he wants to learn (cf. 15:14). On the other hand, he may already know what they are discussing, so he has no need to speak or to show off his knowledge (cf. 14:33; 18:2).

The person who has a "cool" temper ("spirit") possesses discernment (v. 27b). The process is cyclical: Patience lets a person wait for the outcome or result, rather than respond immediately (and intemperately). The result of that patient waiting is increased insight.

On the other hand, a fool who manages to keep silence (which, these verses imply, is antithetical to his or her nature) will for that reason seem wise. Silence is not, therefore, an adequate clue to wisdom or folly. It is what comes out of a person's heart (words and deeds) that reveals his true nature. The strong implication of Proverbs is that fools cannot not speak ("babble" [10:8, 10], "speak rashly" [12:18] and make their vexation known "at once" [12:16]), so that whoever is wise enough to wait will learn what is inside even the silent. Proverbs 17:28 therefore counsels patience even in drawing conclusions about others.

In one sense, fools who could manage to keep silent would be demonstrating some degree of wisdom. Since, however, wisdom is not simply right behavior, but right behavior in the fear of the LORD, they would remain fools unless their pilgrimage toward wisdom had already begun.

18:1. The first line is unclear because it does not indicate whether the subject is found apart from others by personal choice (cf. Gen. 13:9, 11, 14) or because he was driven away (cf. 19:4). Since this person is criticized by the parallel line (quarreling is not a virtue), and since community is highly valued in Proverbs, the subject of this verse is anyone who deliberately isolates or separates himself from others. Such a person seeks only his or her own counsel, rather than benefiting from the insights of others. Isolation (withdrawal from a community) is not a virtue in Proverbs, since wisdom is found in many counselors, never in hearing just one point of view. Furthermore, the tendency to quarrel reveals that the underlying cause of this withdrawal is anger, which is condemned throughout the Book.

18:2. Closely related in topic to Prov. 17:27f, this verse warns that it is useless to try to teach a fool, since his bent is to spout the folly that he knows (cf. 26:12; 29:20) rather than to learn from anyone else. Fools are, in fact, so delighted with what they already know that they see no need to learn from anyone else. What they reveal, however, is the depth of their foolishness.

Astuteness is a reward of patience (cf. 17:27), a quality which fools lack. They are unwilling to spend time and energy learning how to exercise discernment, because they are happy in their "knowledge," being unable to recognize ignorance and folly for what they are. Fools therefore interrupt others, finishing sentences and answering questions not asked (18:13), because they assume that they already know all that is necessary. Fools thus scoff at the wisdom of others (cf. 1:7; 2:22), rejecting correction (9:7f), since they already "know" everything.

18:3. Decisions have consequences; one is that there is no true respect for the wicked. They may be feared, but they are, secretly or openly, despised. This brings another consequence—their disgrace invites vilification. This personification of these consequences shows them as entering a house or other place together. As surely as friends are found together, so these consequences (disgrace and dishonor) are accompanied by their own consequence (reproach). The proverb thus warns those who might participate in or encourage some evil to rethink their choice, since its effect on their lives will probably be felt far beyond its immediate outcome.

18:4. "Deep water" is water in a well or cistern (cf. 20:5), and so is generally available at need. Wadis (HED #5337) are "torrent valleys," prone to harbor

5.

904, 5122	6926	3937, 5371.541	3940, 3005	6686, 7857	5558.141
prep, art, n ms	n ms	prep, v Hiphil inf con	neg part, adj	n mp, adj	v Qal inf con
בַּמִּשְׁפָּט	צַדִּיק	לְהַטּוֹת	לֹא־טוֹב	פְּנֵי־רָשָׁע	שְׂאֵת
bammishpāṭ	tsaddîq	lehaṭṭôth	lō'-ṭôv	penê-rāshā'	se'ēth
with justice	the righteous	to cause to lean	not good	the face of the wicked	lifting up

6.

8004	3809	971.126	904, 7663	6552	3937, 4253	7410.121
n fd	n ms	v Qal impf 3mp	prep, n ms	cj, n ms, ps 3ms	prep, n fp	v Qal impf 3ms
שִׂפְתֵי	כְסִיל	יָבֹאוּ	בְרִיב	וּפִיו	לְמַהֲלֻמוֹת	יִקְרָא
siphthê	khesîl	yāvō'û	verîv	ûphîw	lemahălumôth	yiqŏrā'
the lips of	a fool	they will enter	with contention	and his mouth	beatings	it calls for

7.

6552, 3809	4425, 3937	8004	4305	5497	**8.**	1745
n ms, n ms	n fs, prep, ps 3ms	cj, n fd, ps 3ms	n ms	n fs, ps 3ms		n mp
פִּי־כְסִיל	מְחִתָּה־לוֹ	וּשְׂפָתָיו	מוֹקֵשׁ	נַפְשׁוֹ		דִּבְרֵי
pî-khesîl	mechittāh-lô	ûsephāthâv	môqēsh	naphshô		divrê
the mouth of a fool	destruction to him	and his lips	a snare for	his life		the words of

7566.255	3626, 3996.752	2062	3495.116	2410, 1027	**9.**	1612
v Niphal ptc ms	prep, v Hithpael ptc mp	cj, pers pron	v Qal pf 3cp	n mp, n fs		cj
נִרְגָּן	כְּמִתְלַהֲמִים	וְהֵם	יָרְדוּ	חַדְרֵי־בָטֶן		גַּם
nirgān	kemithlahmîm	wehēm	yāredhû	chadhrê-vāṭen		gam
a slanderer	like tidbits	but they	they go down	the inmost parts of the belly		also

7791.751	904, 4536	250	2000	3937, 1196	5072
v Hithpael ptc ms	prep, n fs, ps 3ms	n ms	pers pron	prep, n ms	n ms
מִתְרַפֶּה	בִמְלַאכְתּוֹ	אָח	הוּא	לְבַעַל	מַשְׁחִית
mithrappeh	vimla'khtô	'āch	hû'	leva'al	mashchîth
one who is slack	in his work	a brother	he	to the owner of	destruction

10.

6010, 4166	8428	3176	904, 7608.121	6926
n ms, n ms	n ms	pn	prep, ps 3ms, v Qal impf 3ms	n ms
מִגְדַּל־עֹז	שֵׁם	יְהוָה	בּוֹ־יָרוּץ	צַדִּיק
mighdal-'ōz	shēm	yehwāh	bô-yārûts	tsaddîq
a tower of strength	the name of	Yahweh	into it he will run	the righteous

11.

7891.211	2019	6474	7439	6010	3626, 2440
cj, v Niphal pf 3ms	n ms	n ms	n fs	n ms, ps 3ms	cj, prep, n fs
וְנִשְׂגָּב	הוֹן	עָשִׁיר	קִרְיַת	עֻזּוֹ	וּכְחוֹמָה
wenisgāv	hôn	'āshîr	qiryath	'uzzô	ûkhechômāh
and he will be inaccessible	the wealth of	the rich	the city of	his strength	and like a wall

---

5. It is not good to accept the person of the wicked, to overthrow the righteous in judgment: ... It is not right to favor the guilty, Or to deny justice in court to the innocent, *Anchor* ... To have respect for the person of the evil-doer is not good, or to give a wrong decision against the upright, *BB* ... It is not good to show partiality to the wicked, to deprive a righteous man of justice, *Berkeley* ... It is wrong for a judge to favor the wicked and condemn the innocent, *LIVB*.

6. A fool's lips enter into contention, and his mouth calleth for strokes: ... A fool's talk gets him into trouble, his tongue brings him a beating, *Moffatt* ... The words of fools start quarrels. They make people want to beat them, *NCV* ... The fool's lips lead him into strife, and his mouth provokes a beating, *NAB* ... his mouth calls for blows, *NASB*.

7. A fool's mouth is his destruction, and his lips are the snare of his soul: ... A fool's mouth ruins him, and his lips trap him, *Beck* ... From his own words his undoing comes, from his own lips the snare, *Knox* ... When a fools speaks, he is ruining himself; he gets caught in the trap of his own words, *Good News*.

8. The words of a talebearer are as wounds, and they go down into the innermost parts of the belly: ... words of a gossip are swallowed greedily and they go down deeply into a person's being, *Beck* ... words of a gossip are tempting morsels, *Berkeley* ... are as dainty morsels, *Darby* ... Go down to the stomach's depths, *Fenton*.

9. He also that is slothful in his work is brother to him that is a great waster: ... A lazy person is as bad as someone who is destructive, *Good News* ... He who is slack at his work, *Goodspeed* ... Whoever is idle at work, *JB* ... If you're lazy in your work, you're a brother to him who loves to destroy, *Beck*.

10. The name of the LORD is a strong tower: the righteous runneth

into it, and is safe: ... No stronghold like the Lord's name; there the just take refuge, high above reach, *Knox* ... The Eternal is a tower of strength: good men run in and are secure, *Moffatt* ... into it runs the righteous and cannot be touched, *Berkeley* ... the upright runs to it and is secure, *JB*.

11. The rich man's wealth is his strong city, and as an high wall in his own conceit: ... Rich people, however, imagine that their wealth protects them like high, strong walls around a city, *Good News* ... The wealth of the rich is his castle, *Fenton* ... It shields him like a high wall, *Anchor*.

---

flash floods when it rains (Canaan has few perennial streams). Due to the porous soil and the narrow v-shaped profile of valleys, the water runs off quickly, so that within a few days the ravine is without surface water again (although the seeds, which had been dormant, spring quickly to life, to grow, to blossom and to increase while the ground is relatively moist).

Most people are willing to talk, especially when they have been asked to give advice, whether or not they have anything to say. True wisdom, however, is not always available, and must be sought out carefully and be based on knowledge of whose counsel is wise and worth consideration. If the choice lies between mere words and wisdom, choose the source of wisdom.

18:5. Injustice merits undiluted condemnation throughout the proverbs, whether it involves justifying the guilty or denying the rights of the innocent (cf. 11:10; 17:15; 28:4f, 12, 15f, 28; 29:4, 12, 14, 16, 26). Both are equally heinous, or, as Solomon laconically says, "not good" (as he also says in 17:26; 24:23; 28:21).

18:6–7. Although these verses contain separate sayings, they are linked topically and structurally (lips ... mouth ... mouth ... lips). Because of its foolish (and thus wicked) content, a fool's speech invites rebuke, correction and punishment. His words are therefore a source of his own ruin, since what comes out of his own mouth traps and condemns him (cf. 14:3). "Bring" (NRSV, NASB) involves a change of a vowel and reflects the Septuagint, but this change is not necessary and ignores the preposition.

18:8. Following two verses that warn about how fools' talk reveals their folly and thus affect them, this verse points out that gossips are fools. It is identical to 26:22, where it also follows two verses dealing with the strife that is the result of gossip (26:20ff). Those verses seem to be a deliberate literary context—these do not.

18:9. A half-hearted effort may seem to be merely less productive, but Solomon points out its

true nature. Indifference is destructive. The person who does not really care about how well something is done, or whether it ever gets done, will not do a good job, regardless of the task. The finished product will be poorly crafted, sloppily assembled, perhaps even dangerous, and those results may lead to loss of employment.

Apathy toward work reveals wrong thinking about the nature of work. The ability and opportunity to work are gifts of God (Gen. 2:15). They are not to be taken lightly, and they must not be squandered. To pursue a task with every tool and gift that God has given is the way of wisdom and righteousness (1 Cor. 15:58). Excellence requires skill, which comes from diligent practice. Diligence can only be maintained over the period of time needed to attain excellence by those who truly love their work. (It may even redound to the worker's credit; cf. 22:29; although that is not the motive in this verse.)

18:10–11. Juxtaposed, these verses contrast true and false security (the word translated "is safe" [v. 10, KJV] and "high" [v. 11, KJV] is the same word in Hebrew, used only one other time in Proverbs [29:25]). Wealth insulates, just as walled cities protect their inhabitants (cf. 10:15; its first line is identical with 18:11a). The security afforded by wealth, however, is illusory. Since the resources of the wealthy are not infinite (regardless of appearances), there is always the possibility that they will be overwhelmed by famine, war, plague or some other disaster. Nor do riches guarantee safety from turmoil, strife or dissension within the home (cf. 15:16f; 17:1), as the lives of Abraham and David showed (cf. Gen. 13:2; 16:4f; 2 Sam. 13–18).

The LORD is the only sure Refuge (cf., among many references, Pss. 18:1ff; 46:1–11; 62:1f, 5–8), and it is the righteous who understand this, but not necessarily the wealthy. This is not to deny that the wealthy may trust the LORD (cf. Matt. 19:23–26), but merely to note that the source of security is more easily interpreted by

7891.257	904, 5031	**12.**	3937, 6686, 8133	1391.121	3949, 382
v Niphal ptc fs	prep, n fs, ps 3ms		prep, *n mp*, n ms	v Qal impf 3ms	*n ms*, n ms
נִשְׂגָּבָה	בְּמַשְׂכִּיתוֹ		לִפְנֵי־שֶׁבֶר	יִגְבַּהּ	לֵב־אִישׁ
nisgāvāh	bᵉmaskîthô		liphnê-shever	yighbahh	lēv-'îsh
being inaccessible	in his imagination		before ruin	it will be high	the heart of a man

3937, 6686	3638	6265	**13.**	8178.551	1745	904, 3071	8471.121	198
cj, prep, *n mp*	n ms	n fs		v Hiphil ptc ms	n ms	prep, adv	v Qal impf 3ms	n fs
וְלִפְנֵי	כָבוֹד	עֲנָוָה		מֵשִׁיב	דָּבָר	בְּטֶרֶם	יִשְׁמָע	אִוֶּלֶת
wᵉliphnê	khāvôdh	'ănāwāh		mēshîv	dāvār	bᵉterem	yishmā'	'iwweleth
but before	honor	humility		one who returns	a word	before	he hears	foolishness

2026, 3937	3759	**14.**	7593, 382	3677.321	4382	7593
pers pron, prep, ps 3ms	cj, n fs		*n fs*, n ms	v Pilpel impf 3ms	n ms, ps 3ms	cj, *n fs*
הִיא־לוֹ	וּכְלִמָּה		רוּחַ־אִישׁ	יְכַלְכֵּל	מַחֲלֵהוּ	וְרוּחַ
hî'-lô	ûkᵉlimmāh		rûach-'îsh	yᵉkhalkēl	machălēhû	wᵉrûach
it to him	and dishonor		the spirit of a man	it will sustain	his sickness	but a spirit

5405	4449	5558.321	**15.**	3949	1032.255	7353.121, 1907
adj	intrg	v Piel impf 3ms, ps 3fs		n ms	v Niphal ptc ms	v Qal impf 3ms, n fs
נְכֵאָה	מִי	יִשָּׂאֶנָּה		לֵב	נָבוֹן	יִקְנֶה־דָּעַת
nᵉkhē'āh	mî	yissā'ennāh		lēv	nāvôn	yiqŏneh-dā'ath
dejected	who	he can bear it		a heart	being discerning	it will acquire knowledge

238	2550	1272.322, 1907	**16.**	5150	119	7620.521	3937
cj, n fs	n mp	v Piel impf 3fs, n fs		*n ms*	n ms	v Hiphil impf 3ms	prep, ps 3ms
וְאֹזֶן	חֲכָמִים	תְּבַקֶּשׁ־דָּעַת		מַתָּן	אָדָם	יַרְחִיב	לוֹ
wᵉ'ōzen	chăkhāmîm	tᵉvaqqesh-dā'ath		mattān	'ādhām	yarchîv	lô
and the ear of	the wise	it will seek knowledge		a gift of	a man	it makes wide	for him

3937, 6686	1448	5328.521	**17.**	6926	7518	904, 7663
cj, prep, *n mp*	n mp	v Hiphil impf 3ms, ps 3ms		adj	art, adj	prep, n ms, ps 3ms
וְלִפְנֵי	גְדֹלִים	יַנְחֶנּוּ		צַדִּיק	הָרִאשׁוֹן	בְּרִיבוֹ
wᵉliphnê	ghᵉdhōlîm	yanchennû		tsaddîq	hāri'shôn	bᵉrîvô
and before	the great	it will lead him		righteous	the first	in his lawsuit

971.121, 7739	2811.111	**18.**	4219	8139.521	1518
v Qal impf 3ms, n ms, ps 3ms	cj, v Qal pf 3ms, ps 3ms		n mp	v Hiphil impf 3ms	art, n ms
יָבֹא־רֵעֵהוּ	וַחֲקָרוֹ		מִדְיָנִים	יַשְׁבִּית	הַגּוֹרָל
yāvō'-rē'ēhû	wachăqārô		midhyānîm	yashbîth	haggôrāl
his fellow will come	and he will examine him		contentions	it will bring to an end	the lot

12. Before destruction the heart of man is haughty, and before honour is humility: ... before there can be glory there must be humility, *JB* ... hearts are proudest when ruin is nearest, *Knox* ... Haughtiness ends in disaster: to be humble is the way to honour, *Moffatt* ... Pride ends in destruction; humility ends in honor, *LIVB*.

13. He that answereth a matter before he heareth it, it is folly and shame unto him: ... To answer a question before you have heard it, is silly and shameful, *Moffatt* ... Anyone who answers without listening is foolish and confused, *NCV* ... it is folly to him and reproach, *Berkeley* ... Is absurd,— and reproach to yourself, *Fenton*.

14. The spirit of a man will sustain his infirmity; but a wounded spirit who can bear?: ... A [brave] spirit sustains a man when he is ill, But when the spirit is sick, who can cure it?, *Anchor* ... spirit of a man will be his support when he is ill; but how may a broken spirit be lifted up?, *BB* ... Sickness the human spirit can endure, but when the spirit is broken, who can bear this?, *JB* ... but a broken spirit who can carry?, *Berkeley*.

15. The heart of the prudent getteth knowledge; and the ear of the wise seeketh knowledge: ... The heart of the intelligent acquires learning, the ears of the wise search for knowledge, *JB* ... The thoughtful mind is eager to know more; the wise man longs to learn, *Moffatt* ... The intelligent man is always open to new ideas. In fact, he looks for them, *LIVB* ... the wise person listens to learn more, *NCV* ...

Knowledge comes to the discerning mind, *NEB*.

16. A man's gift maketh room for him, and bringeth him before great men: ... A gift opens the door to the giver and gains access to the great,

NEB ... man's gift clears the way for him, And brings him into the presence of the great, *Anchor* ... A man's bribe makes room for him, *KJVII* ... The gift made, how it opens a man's path for him, *Knox*.

17. He that is first in his own cause seemeth just; but his neighbour cometh and searcheth him: ... The man who pleads his case first seems to be in the right; then his opponent comes and puts him to the test, *NAB* ... The first to plead his case seems

---

what is seen and can be used than what is unseen and not in our control.

18:12. Those who are willing to listen to others, to weigh their words, to hear their counsel and to heed their rebuke, are thus protected, so that they avoid foolish decisions that may lead them into danger or distress. The arrogant, on the other hand, see no value in listening to anyone else's opinion. Heedless of the possible consequences of their decisions, they rush to their own destruction (14:16; 22:3). Thinking themselves wise, they demonstrate their foolishness. The second half of this verse is the same as the second line of 15:33, which parallels humility with the fear of the LORD as the teaching that leads to wisdom.

This verse puts Jesus' teachings about priority in the Kingdom of God into a larger biblical perspective. Humility means having time and energy to spare for others, serving and encouraging them (cf. Matt. 20:20–28).

18:13. The fool, who is so delighted with his own knowledge that he would rather "teach" than learn (18:2), is prone to answer questions before they are asked (which often turn out to be the wrong questions), to offer unwanted advice and to make promises before thinking through the consequences (cf. 20:25). Although this may seem precocious when it is right, and occasionally even impress others, it quickly becomes distracting and annoying, and insults others by implying that the speaker cannot think his own thoughts.

Attentive listening grows out of respect for others (a quality lacking in fools). Giving another person the time (and silence) to make a point, ask a question or request counsel is not only the part of wisdom—it is one way of fulfilling the second greatest commandment (cf. Lev. 19:18; Matt. 22:39).

18:14. Although the human spirit is resilient to recover from many types of spiritual and emotional illness, some wounds, especially those that are inflicted by others, may be too heavy to bear. This proverb encourages the wise to guard the well-being of others by considering (before they speak or act) the potential effect of their words and actions (cf. 25:20; Lev. 19:18).

18:15. The wise and discerning can be recognized by noting what they value, which echoes the prologue's exhortation to acquire wisdom and knowledge at any price (cf. 5:5, 7). Understanding the true worth of knowledge (cf. 3:13–26) and recognizing it when they see or hear it, they bend their energies toward seeking it (2:1–5) where it may be found (10:13; 17:24), and then do whatever is necessary to acquire it. This verse also implies that "enough knowledge" is a chimera and that to think oneself knowledgeable enough reveals either ignorance or that the beginning of losing whatever knowledge may have been possessed (19:27; cf. 1:5).

18:16. The parallel of the word translated "gift" (HED # 5150) with "bribe" (HED #8345; cf. 21:14), along with the mention of "the great" in the second line, shows that this verse probably refers to the influence that well-placed gifts or favors can bring. Those who can afford to be generous have many "friends" (19:6) and often find what they need or want. This proverb also implies that those who cannot afford to give gifts cannot gain access to the powerful and may thus warn those who would enter the upper reaches of society and government against using their wealth, and especially the favors that others may owe them, against the poor.

This is implied, however, not explicit in the text. The verse itself neither condemns nor condones using gifts for this purpose—it merely notes that this is often how bureaucracies work (17:23 and 29:4, however, explicitly condemn bribes or "gifts" that overturn justice).

18:17. Since the Covenant stipulates multiple witnesses, as well as a legal system of judges, accused and accuser (Deut. 19:15–21), this proverb warns judges not to decide too hastily, but to wait for cross-examination. Anyone can present a good case, but only the truth can stand up under careful study (cf. 25:8ff). Every decision, legal or not, must be based on as much information as possible; the wise do not answer hastily (cf. 18:13), but deliberately.

18:18. Since casting lots was a common means of determining the will of God (cf. verses cited in 16:33), it could also resolve disputes when no solu-

6839.255	250		6754.521	6335	1033
v Niphil ptc ms	n ms	**19.**	v Hiphil impf 3ms	n mp	cj, prep
נִפְשָׁע	אָח		יַפְרִיד	עֲצוּמִים	וּבֵין
niphshā'	'āch		yaphrîdh	'ătsûmîm	ûvên
having been transgressed against	a brother		it makes a separation	mighty ones	and between

4623, 6780	783		3626, 1308	4209	4623, 7439, 6010
prep, *n ms*	n ms	**20.**	prep, *n ms*	cj, n mp	prep, *n fs*, n ms
מִפְּרִי	אַרְמוֹן		כִּבְרִיחַ	וּמְדוֹנִים	מִקְרְיַת־עֹז
mipperî	'armôn		kivrîach	ûmedhônîm	miqqiryath-'ōz
from the fruit of	a citadel		like bars of	and contentions	from a city of strength

8004	8721	1027	7881.122	6552, 382
n fd, ps 3ms	*n fs*	n ms, ps 3ms	v Qal impf 3fs	n ms, n ms
שְׂפָתָיו	תְּבוּאַת	בִּטְנוֹ	תִּשְׂבָּע	פִּי־אִישׁ
sephāthâv	tevû'ath	biṭnô	tisba'	phî-'îsh
his lips	the produce of	his belly	it will be satisfied	the mouth of a man

154.152	904, 3135, 4098	2552	4323		7881.121
cj, v Qal act ptc mp, ps 3fs	prep, *n fs*, n fs	cj, n mp	n ms	**21.**	v Qal impf 3ms
וְאֹהֲבֶיהָ	בְּיַד־לָשׁוֹן	וְחַיִּים	מָוֶת		יִשְׂבָּע
we'ōhevêāh	beyadh-lāshôn	wechayyîm	māweth		yisbā'
and those who love it	in the power of the tongue	and life	death		he will be satisfied with

3008	4834.111	828	4834.111		6780	404.121
n ms	v Qal pf 3ms	n fs	v Qal pf 3ms	**22.**	n ms, ps 3fs	v Qal impf 3ms
טוֹב	מָצָא	אִשָּׁה	מָצָא		פִּרְיָהּ	יֹאכַל
ṭôv	māṣā'	'ishshāh	māṣā'		piryāhh	yō'khal
something good	he has found	a wife	he has found		its fruit	they will devour

6474	1744.321, 7851	8800		4623, 3176	7814	6572.521
cj, n ms	v Piel impf 3ms, n ms	n mp	**23.**	prep, pn	n ms	cj, v Hiphil impf 3ms
וְעָשִׁיר	יְדַבֶּר־רָשׁ	תַּחֲנוּנִים		מֵיְהוָה	רָצוֹן	וַיָּפֶק
we'āshîr	yedhabber-rāsh	tachănûnîm		mêyhwāh	rātsôn	wayyāpheq
but the rich	a poor man will speak	supplications		from Yahweh	favor	and he will obtain

154.151	3552	3937, 7778.741	7739	382		6006	6257.121
v Qal act ptc ms	cj, sub	prep, v Hithpoel inf con	n mp	*n ms*	**24.**	adv	v Qal impf 3ms
אֹהֵב	וְיֵשׁ	לְהִתְרֹעֵעַ	רֵעִים	אִישׁ		עַזּוֹת	יַעֲנֶה
'ōhēv	weyēsh	lehithrō'ēa'	rē'îm	'îsh		'azzôth	ya'ăneh
one who loves	but there is	to be broken	friends	a man of		harshly	he will answer

just, Until another comes and examines him, *NASB* ... The person who tells one side of a story seems right, until someone else comes and asks questions, *NCV* ... until another comes forward to cross-examine him, *REB*.

18. The lot causeth contentions to cease, and parteth between the mighty: ... The decision of chance puts an end to argument, parting the strong, *BB* ... lot puts an end to disputes and separates powerful men, *Berkeley* ... Settle a quarrel by casting lots; keep strong opponents apart,

Beck ... And decides between powerful rivals, *Goodspeed*.

19. A brother offended is harder to be won than a strong city: and their contentions are like the bars of a castle: ... brother offended is worse than a fortified city, and quarrels are like the locks of a keep, *JB* ... brother who has been insulted is harder to win back than a walled city, and arguments separate people like the barred gates of a palace, *NCV* ... It is harder to win back the friendship of an offended brother than to capture a fortified city, *LIVB*

... their disagreements are like the bars of, *KJVII*.

20. A man's belly shall be satisfied with the fruit of his mouth; and with the increase of his lips shall he be filled: ... From the fruit of his mouth a man's stomach is filled; with the harvest from his lips he is satisfied, *NIV* ... What a man says can provide food to fill his belly; the fruit of his lips can provide him a living, *Beck* ... the produce of his lips will be his in full measure, *BB* ... With the outcome of his lips will he be satisfied, *Goodspeed*.

21. Death and life are in the power of the tongue: and they that love it shall eat the fruit thereof: ... Death and life are determined by the tongue: the talkative must take the consequences, *Moffatt* ... What you say can mean life or death. Those who speak with care will be rewarded, *NCV* ... Death and life are in the gift of the tongue, those who indulge it must eat the fruit it yields, *JB* ... those who make it a friend shall eat its fruit, *NAB*.

22. Whoso findeth a wife findeth a good thing, and obtaineth favour of the LORD: ... When a man finds a wife, he finds something good. It shows that the LORD is pleased with him, *NCV* ... He who has found a wife has gained a goodly portion, and obtains favor, *Berkeley* ... and has the approval of the Lord, *BB* ... and the LORD will be pleased with you, *Beck*.

23. The poor useth entreaties; but the rich answereth roughly: ... A poor person must beg, but a rich man gives harsh answers, *Beck* ... The poor speaks humble requests, but the rich, *KJVII* ... poor man implores, *NAB* ... poor man pleads and the rich man answers with insults, *LIVB* ... When the poor man speaks, he has to be polite, but when the rich man answers, he is rude, *Good News*.

24. A man that hath friends must show himself friendly: and there is a friend that sticketh closer than a

---

tion could be reached by any other means. If they understood that the casting of the lot was under the sovereignty of God, and were willing to abide by what it revealed, then mighty opponents could come to a resolution, even if they were unwilling to listen to anyone else, however strong, clever or wise. Those who are wise also understand by this verse that the lot can succeed where reason and logic fail (cf. 18:19).

18:19. The Hebrew text is very difficult, as the translations show. The form of the verb (Niphal participle) in the first line suggests a translation like "A brother is more able to be [easily] offended than a strong city," so that the entire verse warns against provoking strife (cf. 6:12–19; 18:6; 20:3; 30:32f). Once conflict begins, it often proves extremely difficult to resolve (17:14). The preceding verse suggests one way to settle even major conflicts.

18:20. A number of the surrounding verses address how words affect the speaker (cf. 17:28; 18:6f, 13, 21; 19:5) and others (18:3, 6, 8, 21). The words of the wise lead others to bless and honor them (10:6), since they reveal that the speaker possesses the wisdom that leads to life for himself and others (10:11; 12:18).

18:21. This proverb reflects the power of words to affect others (it is not a superstitious view of the power of blessings and curses) and sums up many verses on the effect of words (e.g., 18:3, 6ff, 13, 19f). To rest "in the hand" or "power" suggests that words can be used to achieve either end. The wise, who understand this, seek to use the right words—words that will correct, heal, restore and strengthen those around them (cf. 12:18; 15:1, 4, 28; 25:11f). Fools who do not understand this principle often injure others with their words (12:18), but there are also fools who, knowing the power of words, twist them to their own ends (cf. 10:11f, 18; 12:20; 26:20–28; 29:5), without regard for their effect on others.

There are thus three groups: the wise, the foolish who deliberately use their words for good or harmful purposes and the fools who simply talk without considering the effect of their words, by which they harm others and condemn themselves. The first group is on the path of life; the words of the latter groups reveal that they are headed for death. The force of the entire Book of Proverbs is to encourage choices that lead to life, including one's words.

18:22. Not everyone who marries, marries well. Those who recognize their need for discernment in choosing a life partner and who therefore submit this aspect of their lives to the LORD are encouraged that they will receive more than they seek, for a good spouse is a good gift from God and a sign of his favor (cf. 19:14). Because it is a subtheme of the need to choose companions wisely, choosing a mate is only mentioned a few times in Proverbs (cf. 11:22; 21:9, 19; 25:24).

18:23. Poor people who depend upon the goodwill of those better off than themselves are often forced to beg for the help which they need, whatever form they require. This verse does not say that the rich refuse their prayers (this word usually refers to the psalmist's pleas for help from the LORD; e.g., Pss. 28:2; 28:6; 31:23); it does say that any answer comes from a position of strength, and may well be graceless. The status of the poor, as beggars, makes them liable to mistreatment. By standing in contrast to the verses that call for impartial justice (e.g., 29:14) and generosity (11:24ff), this verse warns the rich to heed the covenantal call (cf. Lev. 19:18). It also introduces the theme of poverty and wealth found in the next chapter (19:4, 6f).

18:24. The second line of this verse encourages the wise to seek companions who will be true friends (cf. 19:4, 6f). The first line, however, is difficult, because the first word (HED #382) is often

1742 adj	4623, 250 prep, n ms	**19:1**	3005, 7851 adj, n ms	2050.151 v Qal act ptc ms	904, 8866 prep, n ms, ps 3ms
דָּבֵק	מֵאָח		טוֹב־רָשׁ	הוֹלֵךְ	בְּתֻמּוֹ
dāvēq	mē'āch		ṭôv-rāsh	hôlēkh	bethummô
cleaving more	than a brother		better a poor man	walking	in his integrity

4623, 6379 prep, adj	8004 n fd, ps 3ms	2000 cj, pers pron	3809 n ms	**2.**	1612 cj	904, 3940, 1907 prep, neg part, n fs	5497 n fs	3940, 3005 neg part, adj
מֵעִקֵּשׁ	שְׂפָתָיו	וְהוּא	כְּסִיל		גַּם	בְּלֹא־דַעַת	נֶפֶשׁ	לֹא־טוֹב
mē'iqqēsh	sephāthâv	wehû'	khesîl		gam	belō'-dha'ath	nephesh	lō'-ṭôv
than perversity of	his lips	and he	a fool		also	when not knowledge	the soul	not good

211.151 cj, v Qal act ptc ms	904, 7559 prep, n fd	2490.151 v Qal act ptc ms	**3.**	198 n fs	119 n ms	5751.322 v Piel impf 3fs
וְאָץ	בְּרַגְלַיִם	חוֹטֵא		אִוֶּלֶת	אָדָם	תְּסַלֵּף
we'āts	beraghlayim	chôṭē'		'iwweleth	'ādhām	tesallēph
and one who hurries	with feet	one who misses		the foolishness of	a man	it will pervert

1932 n ms, ps 3ms	6142, 3176 cj, prep, pn	2280.121 v Qal impf 3ms	3949 n ms, ps 3ms	**4.**	2019 n ms	3362.521 v Hiphil impf 3ms	7739 n mp
דַּרְכּוֹ	וְעַל־יְהוָה	יִזְעַף	לִבּוֹ		הוֹן	יֹסִיף	רֵעִים
darkô	we'al-yehwāh	yiz'aph	libbô		hôn	yôṣîph	rē'îm
his way	and against Yahweh	it is incensed	his heart		wealth	it will add	friends

7521 adj	1859 cj, n ms	4623, 7739 prep, n ms, ps 3ms	6754.221 v Niphal impf 3ms	**5.**	5915 n ms	8632 n mp	3940 neg part
רַבִּים	וְדָל	מֵרֵעֵהוּ	יִפָּרֵד		עֵד	שְׁקָרִים	לֹא
rabbîm	wedhāl	mērē'hû	yippārēdh		'ēdh	sheqārîm	lō'
many	but a poor man	from his friend	he will be separated		a witness of	lies	not

5536.221 v Niphal impf 3ms	6558.521 cj, v Hiphil impf 3ms	3695 n mp	3940 neg part	4561.221 v Niphal impf 3ms	**6.**	7521 adj	2571.326 v Piel impf 3mp
יִנָּקֶה	וְיָפִיחַ	כְּזָבִים	לֹא	יִמָּלֵט		רַבִּים	יְחַלּוּ
yinnāqeh	weyāphîach	kezāvîm	lō'	yimmālēṭ		rabbîm	yechallû
he will be innocent	and he will blow	lies	not	he will escape		many	they will flatter

brother: ... man who has friends must himself be friendly, *NKJV* ... A man has many friends for companionship, but there is, *Berkeley* ... but some friends are more loyal than brothers, *Good News.*

19:1. Better is the poor that walketh in his integrity, than he that is perverse in his lips, and is a fool: ... Better a poor man who lives virtuously, *Anchor* ... Better is the poor man whose ways are upright, than the man of wealth whose ways are twisted, *BB* ... Better be poor and live innocently than fat and perverse in speech, *Beck* ... It is better to be poor but honest than to be a lying fool, *Good News.*

2. Also, that the soul be without knowledge, it is not good; and he

that hasteth with his feet sinneth: ... To act without reflection is not good; And to be over-hasty is to miss the mark, *Goodspeed* ... Where knowledge is wanting, zeal is not good; whoever goes too quickly stumbles, *JB* ... It is no use to act before you think, *Moffatt* ... and he who hurries with his feet sins, *KJVII* ... and he who acts hastily, blunders, *NAB.*

3. The foolishness of man perverteth his way: and his heart fretteth against the LORD: ... People's own foolishness ruins their lives, but in their minds they blame the LORD, *NCV* ... foolishness of a man twists his way, *NKJV* ... his heart is resentful against the LORD, *NAB* ... his heart rages against, *NASB* ... and then he bears a grudge against the LORD, *NEB.*

4. Wealth maketh many friends; but the poor is separated from his neighbour: ... Wealth adds many friends, but as for the poor, his only friend leaves him, *Berkeley* ... Wealth secures us many friends, But companions depart from the poor, *Fenton* ... Rich people are always finding new friends, but the poor cannot keep the few they have, *Good News* ... But the needy is parted from the one friend he has, *Anchor.*

5. A false witness shall not be unpunished, and he that speaketh lies shall not escape: ... Perjury will bring its own punishment; never was liar yet that escaped his doom, *Knox* ... A witness who lies will not go free; liars will never escape, *NCV* ... A dishonest witness shall not go unpunished, *Moffatt* ...

changed to (yēsh; HED #3552), following some manuscripts of the Septuagint, other ancient versions and the parallelism with the second line. A second problem is that the verbal form (HED #7778) can be assigned to different verbal roots (which explains the variety of translations), although only two are attested in the Hithpolel—"shout in triumph" and "be shattered."

Unless the first is interpreted in the sense of victory through the counsel of many friends (an interpretation not suggested by any commentators, and which fails to provide a meaningful parallel) the lines seem to stand in contrast. If the word "friends" in 24a is ironic (cf. 19:4, 6f), then the proverb could be warning that "friends" are not all equally worthy of friendship and trust. One genuine friend is better than crowds of sycophants, who will disappear at the first sign of trouble. As often in Proverbs, this verse underlines the importance of knowing those with whom we form close relationships.

19:1. It is better to live a life of integrity, even if this means poverty, than to be a fool whose heart (and mouth) is perverse. Since what comes out of the mouth reveals the true state of the heart (4:23; cf. Matt. 15:18ff), it is no surprise to read that fools are untrustworthy. If honest poverty is implicitly better than wealth gained through injustice or other wickedness, then possessions are not the measure of life's worth and value. This implies that truth, justice and righteousness, for example, are far more important in life than what is touched, tasted, seen and heard. There are many things more important than money—integrity is one of them.

Like other proverbs that compare poverty and wealth (e.g., 15:16f), this verse does not imply that poverty is superior to wealth. The real issue is trustworthiness, regardless of the circumstances or consequences.

The first line of this proverb is identical to 28:6a. Proverbs 28:6b has "ways" instead of "lips" and "rich" instead of "fool," both of which make the comparison much more consistent.

19:2. It takes time to gather information, get advice and reflect on possible courses of action (cf. 21:5). The ignorant, especially those who do not know their ignorance, do not understand the value of careful preparation and thus hurry into action without proper preparation. One consequence of this literal carelessness is a haste that often leads to error (29:20), poverty (21:5) or sin (28:20).

19:3. Rather than accepting responsibility for his disastrous choices, the fool blames the LORD for the consequences of his sin. The arrogance that blinded him to the coming ruin also keeps him from recognizing his guilt. Instead of repenting of his sin, he blames the LORD for what is his own fault. This blame may even have the appearance of theological orthodoxy, since he appears to recognize the sovereignty of God over his situation. His wrathful response, however, indicates that he does not understand the biblical teaching that God is sovereign, and individuals are responsible for their own actions. This verse commends wise planning that commits its plans to the sovereign LORD (cf. 16:1ff).

19:4. Circumstances often reveal the true nature of relationships. "Friendships" often grow out of self-interest. Friends who remain when there is no external motivation are rare and precious; the crowds that attend good fortune are fickle. Although these lines are probably not intended to describe consecutive scenes (i.e., the multitudinous friends of the wealthy melt away when the money disappears), they also warn the prudent against counting on help from "fair-weather friends." The proverb is thus both a caution and a call to self-examination (cf. 19:6f).

19:5. Solomon repeatedly warns against perverting justice, whether by bribes (17:23; cf. Isa. 5:23), favoritism (24:23) or lying under oath (19:5, 9). Liars may be clever, but their story will eventually break down, either because they cannot keep track of all that they have said or because some inadvertent circumstance will reveal the lie. A witness may even lie successfully in court. After the verdict has been reached, however, he has to live with those who know the truth, since the laws forbade reaching a verdict based on one person's testimony (Num. 35:30; Deut. 19:6; 19:15).

The warning is that no one is as clever as he thinks himself. A witness who lies often enough will eventually be caught (cf. 10:9). This was no light matter. In the covenantal statutes, if someone's testimony or accusation was found to be false, the accuser was given the punishment that the crime deserved (Deut. 19:16–19). For example, Someone whose false accusation of adultery was uncovered would have been stoned.

The irony of this warning is that the prudent, those who consider the outcomes of their choices (cf. 16:17; 22:3; 27:12), would not lie, even without this warning. The arrogant, who think that they can,

6686, 5259	3725, 7739	3937, 382	5150	**7.**	3725	250, 7851
n mp, n ms	cj, adj, art, n ms	prep, n ms	n ms		adj	n mp, n ms
פְּנֵי־נָדִיב	וְכָל־הָרֵעַ	לְאִישׁ	מַתָּן		כָּל	אֲחֵי־רָשׁ
phenê-nādhîv	wekhol-hārēa'	le'îsh	mattān		kol	'ăchê-rāsh
the face of a leader	and every friend	to a man	gifts		all	the brothers of a poor man

7983.116	652	3706	4623, 7739	7651.116	4623	7579.351
v Qal pf 3cp, ps 3ms	cj	cj	prep, n ms, ps 3ms	v Qal pf 3cp	prep, ps 3ms	v Piel ptc ms
שְׂנֵאֻהוּ	אַף	כִּי	מֵרֵעֵהוּ	רָחֲקוּ	מִמֶּנּוּ	מְרַדֵּף
senē'uhû	'aph	kî	merē'ēhû	rāchăqû	mimmennû	meraddēph
they hate him	also	indeed	more his friends	they go far away	from him	causing to pursue

571	3940, 2065	**8.**	7353.151, 3949	154.151	5497
n mp	neg part, pers pron		v Qal act ptc ms, n ms	v Qal act ptc ms	n fs, ps 3ms
אֲמָרִים	לֹא־הֵמָּה		קֹנֶה־לֵּב	אֹהֵב	נַפְשׁוֹ
'ămārîm	lō'-hēmmāh		qōneh-lēv	'ōhēv	naphshô
sayings	not they		the one who acquires a heart	one who loves	his life

8490.151	8722	3937, 4834.141, 3008	**9.**	5915	8632	3940
v Qal act ptc ms	n fs	prep, v Qal inf con, n ms		n ms	n mp	neg part
שֹׁמֵר	תְּבוּנָה	לִמְצֹא־טוֹב		עֵד	שְׁקָרִים	לֹא
shōmēr	tevûnāh	limtsō'-ṭôv		'ēdh	sheqārîm	lō'
one who guards	understanding	to find something good		a witness of	lies	not

5536.221	6558.521	3695	6.121	**10.**	3940, 5173	3937, 3809	8921
v Niphal impf 3ms	cj, v Hiphil impf 3ms	n mp	v Qal impf 3ms		neg part, adj	prep, n ms	n ms
יִנָּקֶה	וְיָפִיחַ	כְּזָבִים	יֹאבֵד		לֹא־נָאוֶה	לִכְסִיל	תַּעֲנוּג
yinnāqeh	weyāphîach	kezāvîm	yō'vēdh		lō'-nā'weh	likhsîl	ta'ănûgh
he will be innocent	and he will blow	lies	he will perish		not lovely	for a fool	luxury

652	3706, 3937, 5860	5090.141	904, 8015	**11.**	7961	119	773.511
cj	cj, prep, n ms	v Qal inf con	prep, n mp		n ms	n ms	v Hiphil pf 3ms
אַף	כִּי־לְעֶבֶד	מְשֹׁל	בְּשָׂרִים		שֵׂכֶל	אָדָם	הֶאֱרִיךְ
'aph	kî-le'evedh	meshōl	besārîm		sēkhel	'ādhām	he'ěrîkh
also	when a slave	ruling	over officials		the insight of	a man	it will lengthen

653	8930	5882.141	6142, 6840	**12.**	5278	3626, 3841
n ms, ps 3ms	cj, n fs, ps 3ms	v Qal inf con	prep, n ms		n ms	prep, art, n ms
אַפּוֹ	וְתִפְאַרְתּוֹ	עֲבֹר	עַל־פֶּשַׁע		נַהַם	כַּכְּפִיר
'appô	wethiph'artô	'ăvōr	'al-pāsha'		naham	kakkephîr
his nose	and his splendor	to pass on from	beside an offense		growling	like the lion

false witness will not go uncondemned, *Anchor*.

6. Many will entreat the favour of the prince: and every man is a friend to him that giveth gifts: ... Great numbers will make attempts to get the approval of a ruler: and every man is the special friend of him who has something to give, *BB* ... Everyone tries to gain the favor of important people; everyone claims the friendship of those who give out favors, *Good News* ... Many try to win the kindness of a generous person, *Beck* ... Many will beg the favor of, *KJVII*.

7. All the brethren of the poor do hate him: how much more do his friends go far from him? he pursueth them with words, yet they are wanting to him: ... All the poor man's brothers hate him; how much more do his friends shun him!, *NAB* ... A poor man's brothers all dislike him, *NEB* ... Poor people's relatives avoid them; even their friends stay far away. They run after them, begging, but they are gone, *NCV* ... He pursues them with words, but they are gone, *NASB*.

8. He that getteth wisdom loveth his own soul: he that keepeth under-standing shall find good: ... To learn sense is true self-love; cherish discernment and make sure of success, *REB* ... he who cherishes understanding prospers, *NIV* ... He who gets wisdom has love for his soul: he who keeps good sense will get what is truly good, *BB* ... He who gains wisdom loves his own life; he who maintains insight finds success, *Berkeley*.

9. A false witness shall not be unpunished, and he that speaketh lies shall perish: ... A lying witness will be punished, *Beck* ... whoever utters lies will be destroyed, *JB* ...

and the breather out of deceit will be cut off, *BB* ... Perjury will bring its own punishment, *Knox.*

10. Delight is not seemly for a fool; much less for a servant to have rule over princes: ... Luxury is not becoming for a fool, *KJVII* ... how much worse a slave in command of men of rank!, *NEB* ... It is not fitting that a fool should enjoy comfort, Any more than that a slave should rule

over, *Anchor* ... It doesn't seem right for a fool to succeed or for a slave to rule over princes!, *LIVB.*

11. The discretion of a man deferreth his anger; and it is his glory to pass over a transgression: ... A man's good sense makes him slow to wrath, and the overlooking of wrong-doing is his glory, *BB* ... It is intelligent to control your anger and beautiful to forgive a wrong, *Beck*

... it is his glory to overlook an offense, *Berkeley* ... And it is to his honor when he overlooks a fault, *Anchor.*

12. The king's wrath is as the roaring of a lion; but his favour is as dew upon the grass: ... The king's anger is as dangerous as a lion's. But his approval is as refreshing as the dew, *LIVB* ... A king's rage is like a lion's roar, *NEB* ... but his being

---

literally, "get away" with lying, are those who reject wisdom's counsel.

19:6–7. Although these are independent verses, their common topic, the effect of financial or social status on relationships, binds them closely together; they could each be considered an expansion of a line of 19:4 (cf. 18:23f). Rulers, who are in a position to bestow fortune or favor, are always the object of sycophantry, as are any with both the resources and desire to be generous. Those who lack money and power are ignored ("hated" is perhaps better translated "despised").

For the powerful and generous to take protestations of affection, support or agreement at face value is foolish. They are often merely manipulative, saying whatever will get them their desire. They will not entrust themselves to others naively. When a wealthier, more powerful or more generous person comes along, they, now relatively "poor," will be abandoned (cf. 19:4).

19:8. The parallel lines progress from acquiring wisdom (lit., "heart") to following the discernment provided by its teachings (cf. 16:17). Although the word nephesh (HED #5497) often functions as a reflexive pronoun, referring to a person "himself" (see "Overview"), the parallelism in this verse seems to imply that he cares about his own well-being (19:16). Diligence in learning demonstrates that someone cares deeply about the quality of his or her life; the promise is that obeying what one learns is a source of blessing (the same idiom occurs in 16:20; 17:20; 18:22). (Note the euphony created by the prominence of the vowel "holem" [ō], which occurs in all but two words.)

19:9. The only difference between this verse and 19:5 is that the consequence of lying is to perish, which may point this proverb specifically to capital crimes (cf. Deut. 19:16–19). It could also be a means of strengthening the warning. Someone

tempted to accuse another for gain or revenge should first reckon the potential risk of losing not just the case (and his desired end), but his life. The penalty for perjury, in capital cases at least, was death (cf. 21:28a).

The position of these two virtually identical proverbs, only a few lines apart, shows that they were meant to be understood in light of each other. This makes "will perish" the climax of the progression of the consequences described in the two verses.

19:10. Although this may seem to endorse determinism (e.g., that slaves are somehow not fit to rule over others), other proverbs warn that fools do prosper (13:22; 20:21; 21:6), if only temporarily, and that a wise slave may rule over his erstwhile masters (17:2). It does warn, however, that some things are not right. Fools ought not enjoy the fruits of wisdom, and masters must not be foolish, lest they be ruled by those under them.

Because fools reject wisdom, they should not enjoy its rewards (the word translated "luxury" [HED #8921] implies pleasure, delight, beauty; cf. S.S. 7:7; Mic. 2:9; Ecc. 2:8). For fools to enjoy these things, as for slaves to replace their rulers, unravels the moral order, and is thus "not fitting" (cf. 17:7; 26:1; 30:21ff).

19:11. The prudent understand that a wise life is one of self-discipline and development in light of God's standards (cf. 1:7). Patience is not only good, but can always be developed and strengthened, especially by training oneself to ignore the often unintended slights of others. A steadfast example of such forbearance will bring respect and, eventually, honor from both others and God (cf. 3:3f; 14:29).

19:12. Since the young men for whom Proverbs was originally intended were going to enter the higher levels of society and government service (cf. on 22:6), they needed to know how to deal with the king. The king exercised the power of

13.

3937, 1	2010		7814	6142, 6448	3626, 3030	4567	2281
prep, n ms, ps 3ms	n fp		n ms, ps 3ms	prep, n ms	cj, prep, n ms	n ms	n ms
לְאָבִיו	הַוֹּת	**13.**	רְצוֹנוֹ	עַל־עֵשֶׂב	וּכְטַל	מֶלֶךְ	זַעַף
leʾāvîw	hawwōth		reṭsōnô	ʿal-ʿēsev	ûkheṭal	melekh	zaʿaph
to his father	wickedness		his favor	on the vegetation	and like dew	a king	the wrath of

14.

2019	1041		828	4219	3065.151	1873	3809	1158
cj, n ms	n ms		n fs	n mp	v Qal act ptc ms	cj, n ms	adj	n ms
וָהוֹן	בַּיִת	**14.**	אִשָּׁה	מִדְיְנֵי	טֹרֵד	וְדֶלֶף	כְּסִיל	בֵּן
wāhôn	bayith		ʾishshāh	midhyenê	ṭōrēdh	wedheleph	kesîl	bēn
and wealth	a house		a wife	contentions of	continuing	and dripping	foolish	a son

15.

6340	7959.553	828	4623, 3176	1	5338
n fs	v Hiphil ptc fs	n fs	cj, prep, pn	n mp	n fs
עַצְלָה	מַשְׂכָּלֶת	אִשָּׁה	וּמֵיְהוָה	אָבוֹת	נַחֲלַת
ʿaṭslāh	maskoleth	ʾishshāh	ûmēyehwāh	ʾāvôth	nachălath
laziness	acting wisely	a wife	but from Yahweh	fathers	an inheritance of

16.

8490.151	7742.122	7711	5497	8976	5489.522
v Qal act ptc ms	v Qal impf 3fs	n fs	cj, n fs	n fs	v Hiphil impf 3fs
שֹׁמֵר	תִּרְעָב	רְמִיָּה	וְנֶפֶשׁ	תַּרְדֵּמָה	תַּפִּיל
shōmēr	thirʿāv	remîyāh	wenephesh	tardēmāh	tappîl
one who observes	it will be hungry	deceit	and the soul of	a deep sleep	it will cause to fall

4322.121	1932	995.151	5497	8490.151	4851
v Qal impf 3ms	n mp, ps 3ms	v Qal act ptc ms	n fs, ps 3ms	v Qal act ptc ms	n fs
יוּמָת	דְּרָכָיו	בּוֹזֶה	נַפְשׁוֹ	שֹׁמֵר	מִצְוָה
yavmuth	dherākhâv	bôzēh	naphshô	shōmēr	mitswāh
he will die	his ways	one who despises	his life	one who guards	a commandment

17.

1618	1859	2706.151	3176	4004.551
cj, n ms, ps 3ms	n ms	v Qal act ptc ms	pn	v Hiphil ptc ms
וּגְמֻלוֹ	דָּל	חוֹנֵן	יְהוָה	מַלְוֵה
ûghemulô	dāl	chônēn	yehwāh	malewēh
and his deed	the poor	one who has compassion on	Yahweh	lending to

18.

8951	3706, 3552	1158	3364.331		8396.321, 3937
n fs	cj, sub	n ms, ps 2ms	v Piel impv 2ms		v Piel impf 3ms, prep, ps 3ms
תִּקְוָה	כִּי־יֵשׁ	בִּנְךָ	יַסֵּר	**18.**	יְשַׁלֶּם־לוֹ
tiqŏwāh	kî-yēsh	binkhā	yassēr		yeshallem-lô
hope	when there is	your son	discipline		He will repay to him

---

pleased is like dew, *Beck* ... but his kindness is like, *NCV.*

13. A foolish son is the calamity of his father: and the contentions of a wife are a continual dropping: ... A stupid son is the despair of his father, And a wife's grumbling is a constant dripping, *Anchor* ... A foolish son is the destruction of his father; and the bitter arguments of a wife are like drops of rain falling without end, *BB* ... a nagging wife is like water dripping endlessly, *NEB* ... and a quarrelsome wife is like a constant dripping, *NIV.*

14. House and riches are the inheritance of fathers: and a prudent wife is from the LORD: ... House and wealth are a heritage from fathers, but a wife with good sense is from, *BB* ... A house and wealth descend from parents, But a sensible wife from, *Fenton* ... Home and possessions are an inheritance from parents, *NAB* ... but a wise wife is a gift from the LORD, *NCV.*

15. Slothfulness casteth into a deep sleep; and an idle soul shall suffer hunger: ... Lazy people sleep a lot, and idle people will go hungry, *NCV*

... Sloth leads to sleep and negligence to starvation, *REB* ... Hate of work sends deep sleep on a man: and he who has no industry will go without food, *BB.*

16. He that keepeth the commandment keepeth his own soul; but he that despiseth his ways shall die: ... He who keeps the law keeps his soul; but death will be the fate of him who takes no note of the word, *BB* ... Those who obey the commands protect themselves, *NCV* ... he that is careless of his ways shall die, *Darby* ... he who despises the LORD's authority will die, *Beck*.

17. He that hath pity upon the poor lendeth unto the LORD; and that which he hath given will he pay him again: ... Being kind to the poor is like lending to the LORD; he will reward you for what you have done, *NCV* ... He who is generous to the

poor lends to the LORD; he will repay him in full measure, *NEB* ... He who is gracious to the poor is lending to the LORD; He will repay him for his benevolent action, *Berkeley* ... and the Lord will give him his reward, *BB*.

18. Chasten thy son while there is hope, and let not thy soul spare

for his crying: ... Discipline your son, for there is hope, and do not set your heart on his destruction, *Berkeley* ... Correct your son, *Fenton* ... Give your son training while there is hope, *BB* ... Discipline your children while they are young enough to learn. If you don't, you are helping them destroy themselves, *Good News*.

---

life and death (cf. 16:14f); they therefore needed to deal with him wisely (14:35; 16:13, 15b), letting their deeds speak for them (22:29; 25:6f), and not provoking him (20:2). At the same time, however, kings needed honest counselors (16:13; 22:11; 29:12)—the requirements were for the right combination of diligence, tact and forthrightness, i.e., for wisdom in every area of life. (The first line is nearly identical to 20:2a.)

19:13. By juxtaposing phrases and images found elsewhere ("foolish son," cf. 10:1, 17, 25; "constant dripping," cf. 27:15; "quarrelsome wife," cf. 21:9, 19; 25:24; 27:15), this verse reveals that close relationships have great potential to affect the stability and quality of life. Roofs (mud-plaster over reeds laid across wooden beams) had to be re-plastered regularly (probably annually). A steadily leaking roof (if this is the referent of "constant dripping") could endanger the structural integrity of the entire house, since even a minimal flow of water into the mud-brick walls would quickly weaken them.

The contrast between a child's behavior (cf. 10:1) and that of a spouse is curious, since parents are responsible to discipline and teach their children (whom they do not choose), whereas the character of a spouse, who is chosen (cf. Gen. 24; Judg. 14), must be discerned before making that choice (cf. 11:22). It may also be intended to suggest that a quarrelsome household breeds ill-behaved and foolish children.

19:14. Having grown up with them, children know their parents' possessions and often count on inheriting a certain portion of the estate. A spouse, however, is relatively unknown, and so the discovery that someone has married well is a cause for delight and thanksgiving. Since this is in the hands of the LORD, the wise will understand their need to commit this decision to Him (cf. 18:22).

19:15. A sluggard is as useless as someone asleep. His laziness is actually self-destruction, since everything that he has, his fields and house,

will fall into ruin (24:30–34) because of his refusal to work (26:13–16), so that he has nothing with which to support himself or his household (6:10f; 24:33f). Proverbs does not automatically attribute poverty to laziness, but the slothful will impoverish themselves and starve.

19:16. The first line is ambivalent—either half could be the result of the other action. Since the proverb contrasts "whoever guards his life" and "whoever despises his way" (the subject of the second line), the first line probably says that covenantal obedience is the result of attention to well-being (cf. 19:8). Other verses (e.g., 13:13; 16:20) examine the consequences of obedience; this verse considers its motivation.

Since fools do not value the ultimate consequences of their decisions, they rarely look beyond the immediate outcome of their choices. Since they are fully satisfied with their own self-adequacy, they do not consider covenantal standards in decision-making. The consequences are disastrous—ultimately, if not immediately.

19:17. Lending anything is a business transaction. Lending to someone in need, regardless of their ability to repay is not regarded as "good business." When it is done, however, in the fear of the LORD and out of obedience to the Covenant (Deut. 15:7–11), repayment is certain. Underlying this statement is the reversal of values that is the delight of the gospel (cf. Luke 6:32–38), because true values reflect the character of God. Lending is closely related to generosity in Proverbs (cf. 14:21, 31).

19:18. The first line could be read as either "while there is hope" or "because there is hope." The first warns that discipline is profitable only up to a certain point, whereas the second is an encouragement that as long as a parent can discipline, hope is not lost. The second line strengthens this encouragement by warning that failure to discipline one's children is tantamount to seeking their death, because, as many proverbs teach, self-discipline is a

19.

1518, 2635	5497	414, 5558.123	420, 4322.541
n ms, n fs	n fs, ps 2ms	adv, v Qal juss 2ms	cj, prep, v Hiphil inf con, ps 3ms
גֹּרָל־חֵמָה	נַפְשֶׁךָ	אַל־תִּשָּׂא	וְאֶל־הֲמִיתוֹ
gōral-chēmāh	naphshekhā	'al-tissā'	we'el-hemîthô
a portion of wrath	your soul	do not lay on	but to kill him

3362.523	5968	524, 5522.523	3706	6296	5558.151
v Hiphil impf 2ms	cj, adv	cj, v Hiphil impf 2ms	cj	n ms	v Qal act ptc ms
תּוֹסִף	וְעוֹד	אִם־תַּצִּיל	כִּי	עֹנֶשׁ	נֹשֵׂא
tôsiph	we'ôdh	'im-tatstsîl	kî	'ōnesh	nōsē'
you will do again	then still	if you rescue	because	a penalty	one who carries

20.

2549.123	3937, 4775	4284	7186.331	6332	8471.131
v Qal impf 2ms	prep, prep	n ms	cj, v Piel impv 2ms	n fs	v Qal impv 2ms
תֶּחְכַּם	לְמַעַן	מוּסָר	וְקַבֵּל	עֵצָה	שְׁמַע
techkam	lema'an	mûsār	weqabbēl	'ētsāh	shema'
you will become wise	so that	correction	and accept	counsel	listen to

21.

3176	6332	904, 3949, 382	4422	7521	904, 321
pn	cj, n fs	prep, n ms, n ms	n fp	adj	prep, n fs, ps 2ms
יְהוָה	וַעֲצַת	בְּלֶב־אִישׁ	מַחֲשָׁבוֹת	רַבּוֹת	בְּאַחֲרִיתֶךָ
yehwāh	wa'ătsath	belev-'îsh	machăshāvôth	rabbôth	be'achărîthekhā
Yahweh	but the counsel of	in the heart of humankind	thoughts	many	in your future

22.

3005, 7851	2721	119	8707	7251.122	2026
cj, adj, n ms	n ms, ps 3ms	n ms	n fs	v Qal impf 3fs	pers pron
וְטוֹב־רָשׁ	חַסְדּוֹ	אָדָם	תַּאֲוַת	תָּקוּם	הִיא
wetôv-rāsh	chasdô	'ādhām	ta'ăwath	thāqûm	hî'
and better a poor man	his loyalty	a man	the longing of	it will rise	it

23.

4053.121	7884	3937, 2522	3176	3488	3695	4623, 382
v Qal impf 3ms	cj, adj	prep, n mp	pn	n fs	n ms	prep, n ms
יָלִין	וְשָׂבֵעַ	לְחַיִּים	יְהוָה	יִרְאַת	כָּזָב	מֵאִישׁ
yālîn	wesāvēa'	lechayyîm	yehwāh	yir'ath	kāzāv	mē'îsh
he will abide	and satisfied	to life	Yahweh	the fear of	falsehood	than a man of

24.

904, 7017	3135	6339	3045.111	7737	1118, 6734.221
prep, art, n fs	n fs, ps 3ms	n ms	v Qal pf 3ms	n ms	neg part, v Niphal impf 3ms
בַּצַּלָּחַת	יָדוֹ	עָצֵל	טָמַן	רָע	בַּל־יִפָּקֵד
batstsallāchath	yādhô	'ātsēl	tāman	rā'	bal-yippāqedh
in the dish	his hand	a sluggard	he hides	evil	he will not be punished with

19. A man of great wrath shall suffer punishment: for if thou deliver him, yet thou must do it again: ... The furious-tempered will suffer hurt, For if forgiven he never amends, *Fenton* ... A person who gets really angry will pay a price for it; if you rescue him you will have to do it again, *Beck* ... man of great wrath must bear his penalty, *Berkeley* ... for if you get him out of trouble you will have to do it again, *BB*.

20. Hear counsel, and receive instruction, that thou mayest be wise in thy latter end: ... Listen to advice and take criticism if you want to be wise the rest of your life, *Beck* ... Listen to advice, accept correction, to be the wiser in the time to come, *JB* ... Listen to counsel and accept discipline, That you may be wise the rest of your days, *NASB* ... and you will die a wise man, *NEB*.

21. There are many devices in a man's heart; nevertheless the counsel of the LORD, that shall stand: ... Many are the plans in a man's mind, But the Lord's will determines how things will turn out, *Anchor* ... Many schemes are in a man's mind, but the counsel of, *Berkeley* ... A man has many plans in his mind, but the LORD's plan will stand firm, *Beck* ... but it is the decision of the LORD that endures, *NAB*.

22. The desire of a man is his kindness: and a poor man is better than a liar: ... People want others to be loyal, so it is better to be poor than to be a liar, *NCV* ... The charm of a man is his kindness, *KJVII* ... Faithful love is what people look for in a person; they prefer the poor to a liar, *JB*.

23. The fear of the LORD tendeth to life: and he that hath it shall abide satisfied; he shall not be visited with evil: ... Reverence for the Eternal is the way to life; content with that, one never comes to harm, *Moffatt* ... fear of the LORD is an aid to life; one eats and sleeps without

being visited by misfortune, *NAB* ... fear of the LORD leads to life, *NASB* ... Those who respect the LORD will live and be satisfied, unbothered by trouble, *NCV.*

24. A slothful man hideth his hand in his bosom, and will not

so much as bring it to his mouth **again:** ... A lazy one hides his hand in, *KJVII* ... With folded hands the sluggard sits by, and never puts hand to mouth, *Knox* ... The sluggard buries his hand, *Goodspeed.*

---

primary trait of the wise. To fail to teach children discipline before they leave home may well condemn them to lives of foolish, and therefore self-destructive, behavior (cf. 27:5).

19:19. The anger that characterizes fools (9:7f; 20:3; 29:9) often gets them into trouble. Solomon counsels that it is best not to rescue or excuse them from whatever punishment is leveled against them, whether it is a monetary fine, social ostracism or some other form, since they inevitably return to their folly (10:23; 15:21; 26:11). If they are not rescued, they may understand the consequences of their folly, whereas if they are excused, they will never learn. This is perhaps the only verse in Proverbs that even begins to hint that there is any hope for a fool (cf. 23:35; 27:22; and the commentary on 26:12).

19:20. Proverbs does not commend the "lone thinker," and implies that one cannot arrive at good and wise conclusions, or act wisely, without help or counsel (cf. 12:15; 15:22). Merely listening, however, is not enough. Instead, whoever accepts instruction and discipline grows in wisdom. The expression translated "the rest of your days" (NASB), "in your latter days" (NKJV), "in the end" (NIV) and "the future" (NRSV) could refer to the end of life; i.e., by the end of your life you will have become wise. In Proverbs it often refers to the consequences of a course of action. (The person who heeds the counsel of others thereby demonstrates at least the beginning of wisdom (humility and obedience); whoever continues to do so ensures that the rest of his life will be increasingly characterized by wisdom.

19:21. In its restlessness, the human heart constantly turns from one idea to another, making more plans than any person could ever realize. In the providence of God, however, the universe is designed so that events happen one at a time. Like the cluster of verses that begins Prov. 16, this verse encourages the wise to live in the fear of the LORD, submitting their plans to his purposes.

19:22. The first line is ambiguous in Hebrew, meaning either "A man's desire is his shame" (cf.

chesedh [HED #2721] as "shame" in 14:34; Lev. 20:17, and the related verb as "causing shame" in Prov. 25:8) or "A man's desire is his loyalty [or kindness]." The second meaning (i.e., what others desire for him) is a possible, though by no means obvious, rendering of the text. It is the usual translation, mainly since it provides a clear parallel with the second line. The first rendition could mean that a person is faithful to what he desires, so he needs to choose carefully whether to set his heart on honesty or riches, when confronted with that choice. The second interpretation means that since people value honesty, it is better to tell the truth, regardless of the cost.

The second line closely parallels 19:1, which also asserts the superiority of honesty, even when it leads to poverty. Wealth gained by perjury is ultimately worthless (in Proverbs, kāzāv [HED #3695] always refers to a lying witness; cf. 6:19; 14:5, 25; 19:9; 21:28). The parallel with "perjurer" suggests that the man's faithfulness is his willingness to tell the truth in a court of law, unswayed by bribes.

19:23. The fear of the LORD is the first requirement of gaining wisdom (1:7), and wisdom is the source of life (3:18; 8:35), so that obedience to wisdom, which is the essence of the fear of the LORD yields life (10:27; 14:27; 22:4; cf. 16:6). Although complicated by the first word, the second line explains that one aspect of "life" is to sleep unharmed (3:21–26, esp. v. 24).

The first word might imply that whoever is satiated with the fear of the LORD (i.e., fully fears the LORD) will sleep safely, but this would be a strange use of "satisfied." It may also be a verb, so that the second line lists three results: sufficient food, a place to lodge or sleep and safety. Most translations make it adverbial: "sleeps satisfied" or "securely" (NASB, NRSV, NIV), which implies the latter interpretation.

19:24. The first line is identical to the first line of 26:15; the comical, and impossible, picture of someone too lazy to bring the food back to his mouth, so that his hand sits in the common dish. So laziness keeps someone from doing what is literally vital.

25.

1612, 420, 6552	3940	8178.521	4086	5409.523	6864
cj, prep, n ms, ps 3ms	neg part	v Hiphil impf 3ms, ps 3fs	n ms	v Hiphil impf 2ms	cj, n ms
גַּם־אֶל־פִּיהוּ	לֹא	יְשִׁיבֶנָּה	לֵץ	תַּכֶּה	וּפֶתִי
gam-'el-pîhû	lō'	yeshîvennāh	lēts	takkeh	ûphethî
also to his mouth	not	he will cause it to return	a mocker	you will strike	and the simple

6429.521	3306.541	3937, 1032.255	1032.121	1907
cj, v Hiphil impf 3ms	cj, v Hiphil inf con	prep, v Niphal ptc ms	v Qal impf 3ms	n fs
יַעְרִם	וְהוֹכִיחַ	לְנָבוֹן	יָבִין	דָּעַת
ya'ărim	wehôkhîach	lenāvôn	yāvîn	dā'ath
he will be prudent	and to chastise	a discerning one	he will discern	knowledge

26.

8161.351, 1	1300.521	525	1158	991.551
v Piel ptc ms, n ms	v Hiphil impf 3ms	n fs	n ms	v Hiphil ptc ms
מְשַׁדֶּד־אָב	יַבְרִיחַ	אֵם	בֵּן	מֵבִישׁ
meshaddedh-'āv	yavrîach	'ēm	bēn	mēvîsh
one who acts violently toward a father	he will cause to flee	a mother	a son	causing shame

27.

2763.551	2403.131, 1158	3937, 8471.141	4284
cj, v Hiphil ptc ms	v Qal impv 2ms, n ms, ps 1cs	prep, v Qal inf con	n ms
וּמַחְפִּיר	חֲדַל־בְּנִי	לִשְׁמֹעַ	מוּסָר
ûmachpîr	chadhal-benî	lishmōa'	mûsār
and behaving shamefully	cease my son	to listen to	chastisement

28.

3937, 8146.141	4623, 571, 1907	5915	1139	4054.121
prep, v Qal inf con	prep, n mp, n fs	n ms	n ms	v Qal impf 3ms
לִשְׁגוֹת	מֵאִמְרֵי־דָעַת	עֵד	בְּלִיַּעַל	יָלִיץ
lishghôth	mē'imrê-dhā'ath	'ēdh	beliyya'al	yālîts
to go astray	from the sayings of knowledge	a witness of	corruption	he will scoff at

5122	6552	7857	1142.321, 201
n ms	cj, n ms	n mp	v Piel impf 3ms, n ms
מִשְׁפָּט	וּפִי	רְשָׁעִים	יְבַלַּע־אָוֶן
mishpāṭ	ûphî	reshā'îm	yevalla'-'āwen
justice	and the mouth of	the wicked	it will swallow iniquity

29.

3679.216	3937, 4086
v Niphal pf 3cp	prep, art, n mp
נָכוֹנוּ	לַלֵּצִים
nākhônû	lallētsîm
they will prepare	for mockers

8572	4253	3937, 1490	3809
n mp	cj, n fp	prep, n ms	n mp
שְׁפָטִים	וּמַהְלֻמוֹת	לְגֵו	כְּסִילִים
shephāṭîm	ûmahlumôth	leghēw	kesîlîm
judgments	and beatings	for the back of	fools

20:1

4086	3302	2064.151
n ms	art, n ms	v Qal act ptc ms
לֵץ	הַיַּין	הֹמֶה
lēts	hayyayn	hōmeh
a mocker	the wine	making an uproar

---

25. Smite a scorner, and the simple will beware: and reprove one that hath understanding, and he will understand knowledge: ... When you strike an insolent fellow a fool may learn a lesson, When you admonish an intelligent man, it will add to [his] knowledge, *Anchor* ... When blows overtake the man of pride, the simple will get sense; say sharp words to the wise, and knowledge will be made clear to him, *BB* ... and when a discerning man is reproved, he will gain knowledge, *Berkeley* ... correct an intelligent person and he will get more intelligent, *Beck.*

26. He that wasteth his father, and chaseth away his mother, is a son that causeth shame, and bringeth reproach: ... A son who brings insult and shame assaults his father and drives away his mother, *Beck* ... He who ill-treats his father and drives out his mother is a child both worthless and depraved, *JB* ... He who mistreats his father, or drives away his mother, is a worthless and disgraceful son, *NAB* ... He who is violent to his father, driving away his mother, is a son causing shame and a bad name, *BB.*

27. Cease, my son, to hear the instruction that causeth to err from the words of knowledge: ... A son who no longer gives attention to teaching is turned away from the words of knowledge, *BB* ... Stop, my son, and listen to criticism, before you turn your back on words of knowledge, *Beck* ... My son, cease to hear that teaching which causes you to err, *KJVII* ... Cease listening, my son, to disipline, And you will stray from the words of, *NASB.*

28. An ungodly witness scorneth judgment: and the mouth of the

wicked devoureth iniquity: ... An evil witness makes fun of fairness, and wicked people love what is evil, *NCV* ... A corrupt witness mocks at justice, and the mouth of the wicked gulps down evil, *NIV* ... A worthless witness mocks at justice, *NRSV* ... A good-for-nothing witness makes sport of the judge's decision: and the mouth of evil-doers sends out evil like a stream, *BB*.

29. Judgments are prepared for scorners, and stripes for the back of fools: ... Rods are being made ready for the man of pride, and blows for the back of the foolish, *BB* ... Punishment is prepared for scoffers, and the lash for the back of, *Moffatt* ... Punishments were made for mockers, and beating for, *JB* ... and flogging for the back of fools, *Berkeley*.

20:1. Wine is a mocker, strong drink is raging: and whosoever is deceived thereby is not wise: ... Wine makes people scoff, and liquor makes them noisy, *Beck* ... strong drink a brawler, And whoever is intoxicated by it is not wise, *NASB* ... whoever is led astray by them is not wise, *NIV* ... no one addicted to their company grows wise, *NEB*.

19:25. By moving from the "scoffer" to the "naive" to the "discerning," this saying emphasizes the incorrigibility of the first group (cf. 21:11). The naive, when they see the trouble into which scoffers fall, can learn to fear the consequences of folly (whether "strike" is here being used as a legal term, as in, e.g., Deut. 25:1ff, or as a reference to punishment in general). The discerning respond to rebuke, because they understand their need of correction. The scoffer, however, is unmoved by correction (9:7f), nor does the example of the response of the discerning or the naive affect him.

The naive and discerning may actually seem "simple," because they submit to correction, whereas the mocker, who rejects any attempt to modify his behavior, may seem clever, independent or even wise. His refusal to learn, however, is the fundamental attitude of the fool (1:7). This verse commends self-examination, lest one be trapped by this form of conceit.

19:26. One of the basic requirements of the Covenant is respect for and obedience to parents (Exo. 20:12; Deut. 5:16), as the prologue reflects (e.g., 1:8; 2:1; 3:1; 4:1–4). Under the Covenant, a disrespectful son could be put to death (Deut. 21:18–21; although there is no record of this ever happening in Israel). As even Agur warns, such a child was cursed (30:11–14, 17; cf. Deut. 27:16).

To assault one's own father so that his mother was driven away would certainly shame the parents, since they, by implication, had failed to fulfill their duty of raising him into the obedience that characterizes the fear of the LORD (1:7). This verse thus warns parents not to neglect their children's discipline (cf. 13:24; 19:18; 22:6, 15; 23:13f; 29:15), lest they (the parents) be put to shame. It also warns those tempted to mistreat their parents that such behavior is always foolish; they will become odious (10:7).

19:27. This proverb stands in counterpoint to the exhortations of chs. 1–9, which encourage the son to "listen to" and "treasure" the teaching that he receives. To stop striving after wisdom is to stray (cf. 5:23). Wisdom and discipline are not objects to be acquired, stored up and used when needed. They are skills that must be practiced constantly in order to be maintained, and there is always room for growth (cf. 1:5f). The verse also parallels 10:17.

19:28. Justice is a major concern of Proverbs (e.g., 8:15f; 13:23; 17:15; 18:5; 20:8, 28; 24:23–26; 25:2, 4f; 28:5, 21; 29:2, 4, 7, 12, 14, 26), because the young men for whom the Book was written would play a major role in the justice system in Israel (cf. on 22:6). Witnesses who scorn the ideal of justice are untrustworthy, because they know no law outside themselves. The verb "swallows" may mean that they enjoy evil and so consume it (so, apparently, NKJV, NRSV, NIV), or it may mean that they destroy it (cf. 21:20), perhaps because they refuse to recognize guilt. Both meanings are unusual, but, in either case, judges need to discern a witness's attitude toward justice before accepting his testimony. (This verse and the next two refer to "mockers" [HED #4086] or "scoffers" [HED 4054], a link that is hidden in the translations.)

19:29. Closely tied to 19:28 by the term "mockers" or "scoffers" (cf. "mocks" or "scoffs"), this proverb warns that those who persistently reject wisdom are headed for trouble (cf. 18:6; 26:3). Although it was originally a general warning, its position after 19:28 is probably meant to encourage judges to punish those who mock justice and to warn witnesses against perjury. That they "are prepared" suggests that punishment is inevitable.

20:1. The person who tries to anticipate the consequences of actions avoids over-indulgence, recognizing that trouble usually accompanies drunkenness (23:20f). The arrogance that mocks others is antithetical to biblical wisdom, lying in folly's heart (1:7). The tacit warning is against trying to reason with drunkards, since they will either

3626, 3841	5278		2549.121	3940	904	3725, 8146.151	8336
prep, art, n ms	n ms	**2.**	v Qal impf 3ms	neg part	prep, ps 3ms	cj, *adj*, v Qal act ptc ms	n ms
כַּכְּפִיר	נַהַם		יְחַכָּם	לֹא	בּוֹ	וְכָל־שֹׁגֶה	שֵׁכָר
kakkephîr	naham		yechäkkam	lō'	bô	wekhol-shögheh	shēkhār
like the lion	growling		they are wise	not	because of it	and all going astray	strong drink

3937, 382	3638		5497	2490.151	5882.751	4567	372
prep, art, n ms	n ms	**3.**	n fs, ps 3ms	v Qal act ptc ms	v Hithpael ptc ms, ps 3ms	n ms	n fs
לָאִישׁ	כָּבוֹד		נַפְשׁוֹ	חוֹטֵא	מִתְעַבְּרוֹ	מֶלֶךְ	אֵימַת
lā'îsh	kāvôdh		naphshô	chôtē'	mith'abberô	melekh	'êmath
to the man	honor		his life	trespassing against	infuriating him	a king	the terror of

6339	4623, 2886		1607.721	3725, 188	4623, 7663	8140
n ms	prep, n ms	**4.**	v Hithpael impf 3ms	cj, *adj*, n ms	prep, n ms	n fs
עָצֵל	מֵחֹרֶף		יִתְגַּלָּע	וְכָל־אֱוִיל	מֵרִיב	שֶׁבֶת
'ātsēl	mēchōreph		yithgallä'	wekhol-'ĕwîl	mērîv	sheveth
a sluggard	from winter		he will break out	but every fool	from contention	cessation

6332	6233	4448		375	904, 7392	8068.121	3940, 2896.121
n fs	adj	n md	**5.**	cj, sub	prep, art, n ms	v Qal impf 3ms	neg part, v Qal impf 3ms
עֵצָה	עֲמֻקִּים	מַיִם		וָאַיִן	בַּקָּצִיר	יִשְׁאָל	לֹא־יַחֲרֹשׁ
'ētsāh	'ămuqqîm	mayim		wā'ayin	baqqātsîr	yish'al	lō'-yachărōsh
a plan	deep	water		but there is not	during the harvest	he will ask	he will not plow

7524, 119		1861.121	8722	382	904, 3949, 382
n ms, n ms	**6.**	v Qal impf 3ms, ps 3fs	n fs	cj, *n ms*	prep, *n ms*, n ms
רָב־אָדָם		יִדְלֶנָּה	תְּבוּנָה	וְאִישׁ	בְּלֶב־אִישׁ
rāv-'ādhām		yidhlennāh	tevûnāh	we'îsh	velev-'îsh
an abundance of men		he will draw it out	understanding	but a man of	in the heart of a man

4834.121	4449	551	382	2721	382	7410.121
v Qal impf 3ms	intrg	n mp	cj, *n ms*	n ms, ps 3ms	n ms	v Qal impf 3ms
יִמְצָא	מִי	אֱמוּנִים	וְאִישׁ	חַסְדּוֹ	אִישׁ	יִקְרָא
yimtsā'	mî	'ĕmûnîm	we'îsh	chasdô	'îsh	yiqōrā'
he will find	who	faithfulness	but a man of	his loyalty	a man	they will proclaim

	2050.751	904, 8866	6926	869	1158	313		4567
7.	v Hithpael ptc ms	prep, n ms, ps 3ms	adj	*n mp*	n mp, ps 3ms	prep, ps 3ms	**8.**	n ms
	מִתְהַלֵּךְ	בְּתֻמּוֹ	צַדִּיק	אַשְׁרֵי	בָּנָיו	אַחֲרָיו		מֶלֶךְ
	mithhallēkh	bethummô	tsaddîq	'ashrê	vānâv	'achărâv		melekh
	one who walks about	in his integrity	righteous	blessed	his children	after him		a king

2. The fear of a king is as the roaring of a lion: whoso provoketh him to anger sinneth against his own soul: ... A king's terror is like the roar of a lion; anyone who makes him angry puts his life in danger, *Beck* ... A king's threat scares men, like a lion roaring; he who provokes him is in danger, *Moffatt* ... wrath of a king is like the loud cry of a lion, *BB* ... fury of a king is like the roaring, *Berkeley.*

3. It is an honour for a man to cease from strife: but every fool will be meddling: ... A man is honorable when he stays away from a quarrel; any fool can start a fight, *Beck* ... Foolish people are always fighting, but avoiding quarrels will bring you honor, *NCV* ... To draw back from a dispute is honourable, *NEB* ... Any fool can start arguments; the honorable thing is to stay out of them, *Good News.*

4. The sluggard will not plow by reason of the cold; therefore shall he beg in harvest, and have nothing: ... The sluggard who does not plough in autumn goes begging at harvest and gets nothing, *NEB* ... sluggard does not plow in season; so at harvest time he looks but finds nothing, *NIV* ... At the onset of winter the idler does not plow; So at harvest time he looks for [a crop] and finds none, *Anchor* ... The hater of work will not do his ploughing because of the winter; so at the time of grain-cutting he will be requesting food and will get nothing, *BB.*

5. Counsel in the heart of man is like deep water; but a man of understanding will draw it out: ... A person's thoughts are like water in a deep well, but someone with insight can draw them out, *Good News* ... Planning in a man's mind is deep water, *Berkeley* ... The motive in a man's mind is like deep water, *Beck* ... The resources of the human heart are like deep waters, *JB* ... But a man of intelligence will draw it out, *Goodspeed*.

6. Most men will proclaim every one his own goodness: but a faithful man who can find?: ... Many a man professes good will, But where will you find one you can trust?,

Anchor ... Most men make no secret of their kind acts: but where is a man of good faith to be seen?, *BB* ... Many a man will profess to be kind, *Beck* ... but a faithful friend is hard to come by, *Knox*.

7. The just man walketh in his integrity: his children are blessed after him: ... just man walks in his purity, *KJVII* ... A blameless, upright man—happy are the children who come after him!, *Moffatt* ... The good people who live honest

lives will be a blessing to their children, *NCV* ... When a man lives a virtuous and honest life His sons are fortunate in their inheritance, *Anchor*.

8. A king that sitteth in the throne of judgment scattereth away all evil with his eyes: ... puts to flight all evil, *BB* ... winnows all evil, *Berkeley* ... knows evil when he sees it, *NCV* ... sifts out every evil, *Beck*.

---

mock or rage against wisdom (cf. 26:4; 29:9). Better to wait until they are sober.

The "error" of the second line is not only that those who are drunk cannot recognize or choose wisely, but that their very drunkenness proves that they are foolish.

20:2. Since the king had the power of life and death (16:14f), it was always wise to avoid doing anything that would provoke him. The verb in the second line is difficult to interpret, because it occurs infrequently and because of its form (Hithpael). It may mean "to provoke," "to stir up" (so NASB, NIV, NKJV, NRSV) or to "meddle" (cf. 26:17). In either case, the young men for whom Proverbs 1–24 was originally written (cf. 22:6) needed to understand how circumspect they needed to be around the king. The first line is nearly identical to 19:12a.

20:3. The virtue of patience and forbearance is a constant theme of Proverbs (cf. 12:16; 14:29; 15:18, 28; 29:11), as it is throughout ancient Near Eastern instructional materials (cf. Rom. 12:18). The fool, arrogant and rebellious by nature, refusing to recognize the wisdom of such restraint, is thus "free" to quarrel when and where he feels slighted. The slightly comic picture is of a fool raging against the wise man, who refuses to be drawn into the fool's quarrel (cf. 26:4f; 29:9).

20:4. The sluggard, who can always justify his refusal to work (26:16), cannot discern the need of the moment because he is more interested in his own immediate comfort. The long-term effect of this neglect, however, is a life reduced to beggary (cf. 20:13). Like 10:5 and 24:27, this proverb implies that there is activity appropriate to every season, whether gathering in harvest time or breaking up the soil after the "early rains" of autumn.

20:5. Water deep in a well is often invisible from the well's mouth. Since the wise do not advertise their wisdom (10:19; 17:27), their good counsel must be drawn out. Discernment is required, because someone seeking advice must first recognize those who have it, and draw out of them the counsel that he needs in order to be helped by it.

20:6. Although the syntax of the first line is not completely clear, the translations capture its essence, and the second line clarifies its intent. The rhetorical question expects the answer "No one," a case of implicit hyperbole that drives home the point (cf. 31:10; Ecc. 7:27ff). The repeated counsel of Proverbs is to choose friends carefully, since companions shape each other's thoughts (27:17) and, eventually, the course of our lives (13:20; 22:24f; 28:7).

20:7. Wise and foolish decisions extend far beyond the individual who makes them (cf. 10:1; 13:22; 14:26). This verse shows that those consequences extend not merely to those around them, but to those who come after them (cf. Exo. 34:6f). Because they are their children's template (cf. 17:13), parents bless their children's lives when their example encourages them to submit to the wisdom of God.

20:8. The king's responsibility was to administer justice (cf. 16:12; 17:15; 29:4, 12, 14). Solomon uses the image of winnowing ("scatters" [NASB, NKJV]) to describe the process of separating the wicked from the righteous. Cereal crops were tossed into the air so that the wind would separate the worthless chaff from the good grain by blowing it away (cf. Ps. 1:4). The king-as-judge was supposed to do the same for his people, using the Covenant as his guide (Deut. 17:18ff).

					9.
3553.151	6142, 3802, 1835	2306.351	904, 6084	3725, 7737	4449, 569.121
v Qal act ptc ms	prep, n ms, n ms	v Piel ptc ms	prep, n fd, ps 3ms	adj, n ms	intrg, v Qal impf 3ms
יוֹשֵׁב	עַל־כִּסֵּא־דִין	מְזָרֶה	בְּעֵינָיו	כָּל־רָע	מִי־יֹאמַר
yôshēv	'al-kissē'-dhîn	mezāreh	ve'ênâv	kol-rā'	mî-yō'mar
sitting	on a throne of judgment	winnowing	with his eyes	all evil	who can say

				10.		
2218.315	3949	3000.115	4623, 2496		63	63	380
v Piel pf 1cs	n ms, ps 1cs	v Qal pf 1cs	prep, n fs, ps 1cs		n fs	cj, n fs	n fs
זִכִּיתִי	לִבִּי	טָהַרְתִּי	מֵחַטָּאתִי		אֶבֶן	וָאֶבֶן	אֵיפָה
zikkîthî	libbî	ṭāhartî	mēchattā'thî		'even	wā'even	'êphâh
I have cleansed	my heart	I am pure	from my sin		a stone	and a stone	an ephah

			11.		
380	8774	3176	1612, 8530	1612	904, 4770
cj, n fs	n fs	pn	cj, num, ps 3mp	cj	prep, n mp, ps 3ms
וְאֵיפָה	תּוֹעֲבַת	יְהוָה	גַּם־שְׁנֵיהֶם	גַּם	בְּמַעֲלָלָיו
we'êphâh	tô'ăvath	yehwāh	gam-shenêhem	gam	bema'ălālâv
and an ephah	an abomination to	Yahweh	also the two of them	also	by his deeds

				12.	
5421.721, 5470	524, 2217	524, 3596	6714		238
v Hithpael impf 3ms, n ms	cj, adj	cj, cj, adj	n ms, ps 3ms		n fs
יִתְנַכֶּר־נָעַר	אִם־זַךְ	וְאִם־יָשָׁר	פָּעֲלוֹ		אֹזֶן
yithnakker-nā'ar	'im-zakh	we'im-yāshār	pā'ălô		'ōzen
a youth makes himself known	whether pure	or whether upright	his deeds		the ear

8471.153	6084	7495.153	3176	6449.111	1612, 8530
v Qal act ptc fs	cj, n fs	v Qal act ptc fs	pn	v Qal pf 3ms	cj, num, ps 3mp
שֹׁמַעַת	וְעַיִן	רֹאָה	יְהוָה	עָשָׂה	גַּם־שְׁנֵיהֶם
shōma'ath	we'ayin	rō'āh	yehwāh	'āsāh	gham-shenêhem
hearing	and an eye	seeing	Yahweh	He has made	both the two of them

13.					
414, 154.123	8517	6678, 3542.223		6741.131	6084
adv, v Qal juss 2ms	n fs	cj, v Niphal impf 2ms		v Qal impv 2ms	n fd, ps 2ms
אַל־תֶּאֱהַב	שֵׁנָה	פֶּן־תִּוָּרֵשׁ		פְּקַח	עֵינֶיךָ
'al-te'ěhav	shēnāh	pen-tiwwārēsh		peqach	'ênêkhā
do not love	sleep	so that you will not be dispossessed		open	your eyes

	14.					
7881.131, 4035		7737	7737	569.121	7353.151	234.151	3937
v Qal impv 2ms, n ms		n ms	n ms	v Qal impf 3ms	art, v Qal act ptc ms	cj, v Qal act ptc ms	prep, ps 3ms
שְׂבַע־לָחֶם		רַע	רַע	יֹאמַר	הַקּוֹנֶה	וְאָזֵל	לוֹ
seva'-lāchem		ra'	ra'	yō'mar	haqqôneh	we'ōzēl	lô
have plenty of bread		evil	evil	he will say	the buyer	but going away	with it

226	2054.721	15.	3552	2174	7524, 6689	3747
adv	v Hithpael impf 3ms		sub	n ms	cj, n ms, n fp	cj, n ms
אָז	יִתְהַלָּל		יֵשׁ	זָהָב	וְרָב־פְּנִינִים	וּכְלִי
'āz	yithhallāl		yēsh	zāhāv	werāv-penînîm	ûkheli
then	he will boast		there is	gold	and an abundance of pearls of coral	and an item of

9. Who can say, I have made my heart clean, I am pure from my sin?: ... I have cleansed myself of every fault?, *Knox* ... I am pure and sinless?, *Moffatt* ... I am innocent; I have never done anything wrong, *NCV* ... 'I have a clear conscience; I am purged from my sin'?, *NEB*.

10. Divers weights, and divers measures, both of them are alike abomination to the LORD: ... A double standard in weights and measures is an abomination, *NEB* ... Differing weights and differing measures—the LORD detests them both, *NIV* ... Unequal weights and unequal measures, Are both of them hateful to the Lord, *Anchor* ... they are all disgusting to the Lord, *BB*.

11. Even a child is known by his doings, whether his work be pure, and whether it be right: ... a child reveals himself by his acts, *Berkeley* ... child shows what he is by what he does, *Beck* ... if his work is free from sin and if it is right, *BB* ... you can tell if he is honest and good, *Good News.*

12. The hearing ear, and the seeing eye, the LORD hath made even both of them: ... LORD has given us eyes to see with and ears to listen with, *Good News* ... ear that listens, the watchful eye, are both of the Lord's fashioning, *Knox* ... Lord is the maker of them both, *Anchor* ... are equally the Lord's work, *BB.*

13. Love not sleep, lest thou come to poverty; open thine eyes, and

thou shalt be satisfied with bread: ... Be not overfond of sleep lest you come to poverty; keep your eyes open and have plenty of food, *Berkeley* ... Stay awake, work hard, and there will be plenty to eat!, *LIVB* ... lest you become poor, *Fenton* ... you will have ample food, *Moffatt.*

14. It is naught, it is naught, saith the buyer: but when he is gone his way, then he boasteth: ... Buyers say, "This is bad. It's no good." Then they go away and brag about what they bought, *NCV* ... 'A bad

bargain!' says the buyer to the seller, but off he goes to brag about it, *NEB* ... A poor thing, a poor thing, says he who is giving money for goods: but when he has gone on his way, then he makes clear his pride in what he has got, *BB* ... But as he goes away he congratulates himself, *Anchor.*

15. There is gold, and a multitude of rubies: but the lips of knowledge are a precious jewel: ... and a store of corals: but the lips of knowledge are a jewel of great price, *BB* ... and a mass of costly

20:9. The claim to have repented, to have cleansed his ways and motives, is untrustworthy of itself; it is merely words. Although the rhetorical question is similar to that in 20:6, here the answer is the opposite: "Anyone can make such a claim." Furthermore, these words are often self-serving, since they are protest to innocence; the wise will ask why anyone would feel the need to make such a statement, and then weigh the person's words and deeds to see whether his way is clean in fact, or merely in his own eyes (16:2; 21:2).

If the statement in the second line is merely religious, meaning that the person has offered the appropriate sacrifice(s), then it is still less credible, since the external act may not reflect the internal reality (cf. 7:14; 15:8; 21:27).

20:10. Repeating much of the language of 11:1, 20:23 and Deut. 25:13–16, this verse warns that whether measuring weight (stones of various sizes were used as weights on scales) or capacity (an "ephah" was a dry measure of about five gallons), honesty is imperative. Honesty is based on the second great commandment, the love of one's neighbor (cf. Lev. 19:33–37), and reflects the character of God. Dishonesty (using different weights and measures depending on whether the merchant is buying or selling) reveals that a person has rejected the standards of the Covenant and thus the fear of the LORD as a principle of life.

20:11. The verb could be either reflexive "makes himself known" (NRSV; cf. NASB) or passive "is known [recognized]" (NKJV, NIV), and may be intentionally ambiguous. Both interpretations emphasize the priority of deeds over aspirations or words. Many youths (cf. 22:6 on this word) may show promise, but not all live up to that potential. Many may also appear to live wisely, but it is

the evidence of their lives over a period of time that reveals whether that "wisdom" lies on the surface or grows out of hearts that truly fear the LORD.

20:12. Related to the prologue's commands to listen and observe ("obey"), this verse implies that since the LORD made the eye and ear, the wise will use them for his purposes—to grow in wisdom and righteousness. By linking the primary organs of learning to the LORD's activity (and by not mentioning, e.g., the mouth, feet or hands, which are organs of self-expression, not learning), He encourages the student to listen and learn.

20:13. Poverty could force Israelites to sell their property (Lev. 25:25, 29) or themselves as bondservants (cf. Exo. 21:2; Lev. 25:35–43, 47; Deut. 15:12). This verse warns against the laziness by which a person robs himself of his own inheritance and encourages in its place the diligence that provides the needs of life (cf. 6:6–11; 20:4; 24:30–34).

20:14. This reflection of human nature may be an intentionally humorous mini-parable that reflects a culture in which there were few fixed prices, and everything was purchased or bartered after haggling over the price. Its inclusion in Proverbs is due to the insight needed in selling, since no one would boast of a terrible purchase. It warns would-be sellers that buyers will always try to lower the price, regardless of their actual opinion, and is thus related to the larger theme of the need to weigh the words (and deeds) of others before accepting them.

20:15. A precious vessel deserves to be filled with something of great value. In the same way, the mouth of the wise is filled with something (knowledge) that is more valuable than gold and corals ("jewels"). To pursue worldly wealth rather than wisdom, if forced to choose between them, is foolish (cf. 3:14; 8:11, 19; 16:16).

3480	8004, 1907	16. 4089.131, 933	3706, 6386.111	2299
n ms	n fd, n fs	v Qal impv 2ms, n ms, ps 3ms	cj, v Qal pf 3ms	n ms
יְקָר	שִׂפְתֵי־דָעַת	לְקַח־בִּגְדוֹ	כִּי־עָרַב	זָר
yeqār	siphthê-dhā'ath	leqach-bighdhô	kî-'ārav	zār
preciousness	lips of knowledge	take his garments	when he has pledged for	a stranger

1185	5425	2341.131	17. 6388	3937, 382	4035	8632
cj, prep	n mp	v Qal impv 2ms, ps 3ms	adj	prep, art, n ms	n ms	n ms
וּבְעַד	נָכְרִים	חַבְלֵהוּ	עָרֵב	לָאִישׁ	לֶחֶם	שָׁקֶר
ûve'adh	nākherîm	chavlēhû	'ārēv	lā'îsh	lechem	shāqer
and on behalf of	foreigners	hold it in pledge	pleasant	to the man	food	deception

313	4527.221, 6552	2789	18. 4422	904, 6332
cj, adv	v Niphal impf 3ms, n ms, ps 3ms	n ms	n fp	prep, n fs
וְאַחַר	יִמָּלֵא־פִיהוּ	חָצָץ	מַחֲשָׁבוֹת	בְּעֵצָה
we'achar	yimmālē-phîhû	chātsāts	machăshāvôth	be'ētsāh
and afterward	his mouth will be filled with	gravel	plans	by counsel

3679.222	904, 8790	6449.131	4560	19. 1580.151, 5660
v Niphal impf 3fs	cj, prep, n fp	v Qal impv 2ms	n fs	v Qal act ptc ms, n ms
תִּכּוֹן	וּבְתַחְבֻּלוֹת	עֲשֵׂה	מִלְחָמָה	גּוֹלֶה־סּוֹד
thikkôn	ûvethachbulôth	'ăsēh	milchāmāh	gôleh-sôdh
they will be established	and with guidance	make	a battle	revealing a secret

2050.151	7689	3937, 6853.151	8004	3940	6386.723
v Qal act ptc ms	n ms	cj, prep, v Qal act ptc ms	n fd, ps 3ms	neg part	v Hithpael impf 2ms
הוֹלֵךְ	רָכִיל	וּלְפֹתֶה	שְׂפָתָיו	לֹא	תִתְעָרַב
hôlēkh	rākhîl	ûlăphôtheh	sephāthâv	lō'	thith'ārāv
one who goes	a slanderer	and with one who opens	his lips	not	you should associate

20. 7327.351	1	525	1906.121	5552	904, 386
v Piel ptc ms	n ms, ps 3ms	cj, n fs, ps 3ms	v Qal impf 3ms	n ms, ps 3ms	prep, n ms
מְקַלֵּל	אָבִיו	וְאִמּוֹ	יִדְעַךְ	נֵרוֹ	בְּאִישׁוֹן
meqallēl	'āvîw	we'immô	yidh'akh	nērô	be'îshôn
one who curses	his father	and his mother	it will be extinguished	his lamp	in the black of

2932	21. 5338	1009.457	904, 7518	321	3940
n ms	n fs	v Pual ptc fs	prep, art, adj	cj, n fs, ps 3fs	neg part
חֹשֶׁךְ	נַחֲלָה	מְבֻחֶלֶת	בָּרִאשֹׁנָה	וְאַחֲרִיתָהּ	לֹא
chōshekh	nachălāh	mevucheleth	bāri'shônāh	we'achărîthāhh	lō'
darkness	an inheritance	having been despised	at the first	then at the end of it	not

stones, but the understanding lips are a precious jewel, *Berkeley* ... but what a precious thing the lips of the wise are!, *Beck* ... but a priceless ornament is speech informed by knowledge, *JB*.

16. Take his garment that is surety for a stranger: and take a pledge of him for a strange woman: ... Take the coat of someone who promises to pay a stranger's debts, and keep it until he pays what the stranger owes, *NCV* ... Take a man's clothing if he makes himself responsible for a strange man, and get an undertaking from him who gives his word for strange men, *BB* ... Take the garment of one who guarantees a foreigner's debt, and hold the man responsible who makes a pledge in behalf of a stranger, *Beck* ... Take a man's garment if he becomes surety for a stranger; Hold him to account for the other, *Goodspeed*.

17. Bread of deceit is sweet to a man; but afterwards his mouth shall be filled with gravel: ... Bread is sweet when it is got by fraud, but later the mouth is full of grit, *JB* ... Ill-gotten wealth is bread most appetizing, that will yet turn to grit, *Knox* ... Bread obtained by falsehood is sweet, *NASB* ... Some men enjoy cheating, but the cake they buy with such ill-gotten gain will turn to gravel, *LIVB*.

18. Every purpose is established by counsel: and with good advice make war: ... Through consultation you will make up your mind, *Anchor* ... Every purpose is put into effect by wise help: and by wise guiding make war, *BB* ... Every plan is confirmed by counsel, *Berkeley* ... Get good advice and you will succeed; don't go charging into battle without a plan, *Good News* ... And make your war with precaution, *Fenton*.

19. He that goeth about as a tale-bearer revealeth secrets: therefore meddle not with him that flattereth with his lips: ... A gossip can never keep a secret. Stay away from people who talk too much, *Good News* ... He who goes about as a slanderer reveals secrets, *NASB* ... A gossip is always betraying confidences,

Anchor ... so have nothing to do with him whose lips are open wide, *BB* ... So have nothing to do with a gossip, *Goodspeed* ... have nothing to do with a tattler, *NEB*.

20. Whoso curseth his father or his mother, his lamp shall be put out in obscure darkness: ... If a man reviles father and mother, *NEB* ... lamp will be snuffed out in pitch darkness, *NIV* ... deep darkness, *NKJV* ... utter darkness, *NRSV* ... light will be put out in the blackest night, *BB*.

21. An inheritance may be gotten hastily at the beginning; but the end thereof shall not be blessed: ... An estate may be obtained hastily, *Berkeley* ... Wealth may be gotten quickly at first, But the results of it do not last, *Fenton* ... If you begin by amassing property in a hurry, in the end it will not be blessed, *Beck* ... The more easily you get your wealth, the less good it will do you, *Good News*.

22. Say not thou, I will recompense evil; but wait on the LORD, and he

---

20:16. This verse is virtually identical to Prov. 27:13, where it exemplifies the preceding verse, which says that wisdom entails looking ahead to the possible consequences of actions.

20:17. Whether the object of desire was obtained by outright theft or some other form of deceit, the anticipation is often greater than the enjoyment (cf. 20:21; 21:6; Job 20:12–16). The second line is usually translated as though "gravel" were a so-called adverbial accusative, but it could also be rendered as a separate exclamation: "but after his mouth is filled ... gravel!" This accords well with the proverbs on attainment through discipline and work (e.g., 10:4; 12:24, 27; 13:4; 21:5; 22:29) and their warning against avarice (23:4f).

20:18. Successful planning depends upon good advice. The wise person knows to seek and heed wise counsel (cf. 11:14; 15:22; 24:5f). Solomon uses the example of war, a matter of life and death, in an argument from the greater to the lesser. A king needs to plan carefully for a war, since he and his people could be destroyed (cf. Luke 14:32). How much more should individuals seek counsel when faced with decisions that will affect the course of their lives, even though they may not be "wars." Prudence involves counting the cost (Luke 14:26–35). Good advisors can help one see that cost, especially since people bent on a course of action can often see only its benefits (9:16ff; 16:2, 25).

20:19. It is unwise to entrust knowledge of one's private affairs or intentions to someone too foolish to keep his mouth shut (lit., "simple with regard to his lips"). Despite whether he intends to, he cannot help revealing others' secrets and must not be trusted (malice is not a necessary part of

being a "talebearer"). Since plans often take time to come to fruition, and since no one knows the full state of anyone else's thoughts (cf. 14:10; 25:3), premature or unauthorized revelation of incomplete deliberations may grievously harm the one making the decision.

The first line of this proverb is nearly identical to 11:13a. Like 11:13, this verse lies next to a proverb that addresses the importance of seeking help when making a decision (20:18; cf. 11:13f). It is foolish, and possibly even dangerous, to seek counsel from a gossip, who is likely to reveal private situations or dilemmas without permission.

20:20. The fifth commandment is the first one to include a promise (Exo. 20:12; cf. Eph. 6:1ff). Disrespect for parents attacks the moral order of both society and creation (cf. 30:21ff), so that cursing parents is a capital crime (Exo. 21:17; Lev. 20:9; Deut. 27:16). Whether they are accused by their own parents (Deut. 21:18–21) or by someone else, the guilty are under the curse of the Covenant and thus not even buried (cf. 30:17). Because they are wicked, their lamp will go out (cf. 13:9; 24:20; 2 Sam. 21:17).

20:21. An inheritance usually comes suddenly and creates relative wealth. Those who are unprepared for it may squander it, allow it to affect their relationships with others (18:23; 19:4) or destroy them in some other way. That which should have been a blessing (19:14) becomes a bane; their anticipation turns sour (cf. 20:6). The wise, who practice self-discipline in every facet of their lives, would understand from this proverb that they need to prepare for the time when they, too, may suddenly gain a fortune. It probably also warns against greed (23:4f), a ubiquitous form of idolatry (Col. 3:5).

1313.422 v Pual impf 3fs	**22.**	414, 569.123 adv, v Qal juss 2ms	8396.325, 7737 v Piel juss 1cs, n ms	7245.331 v Piel impv 2ms	3937, 3176 prep, pn
תְּבֹרָךְ		אַל־תֹּאמַר	אֲשַׁלְּמָה־רָע	קַוֵּה	לַיהוָה
thevōrākh		'al-tō'mar	'ăshallemāh-rā'	qawwēh	layhwāh
it will be blessed		do not say	let me repay evil	hope	toward Yahweh

3588.521 cj, v Hiphil juss 3ms	3937 prep, ps 2ms	**23.**	8774 n fs	3176 pn	63 n fs	63 cj, n fs	4118 cj, n md
וְיֹשַׁע	לָךְ		תּוֹעֲבַת	יְהוָה	אֶבֶן	וָאֶבֶן	וּמֹאזְנֵי
weyōsha'	lākh		tô'ăvath	yehwāh	'even	wā'āven	ûmō'zenê
and He will save	you		an abomination to	Yahweh	a stone	and a stone	and balances of

4983 n fs	3940, 3005 neg part, adj	**24.**	4623, 3176 prep, pn	4866, 1429 n mp, n ms	119 cj, n ms	4242, 1032.121 intrg, v Qal impf 3ms
מִרְמָה	לֹא־טוֹב		מֵיְהוָה	מִצְעֲדֵי־גָבֶר	וְאָדָם	מַה־יָבִין
mirmāh	lō'-ṭôv		mēyehwāh	mits'ădhê-ghāver	we'ādhām	mah-yāvîn
deceit	not good		from Yahweh	the steps of a man	so humankind	how can he discern

1932 n ms, ps 3ms	**25.**	4305 n ms	119 n ms	3324.121 v Qal impf 3ms	7231 n ms	313 cj, adv	5266 n mp
דַּרְכּוֹ		מוֹקֵשׁ	אָדָם	יָלַע	קֹדֶשׁ	וְאַחַר	נְדָרִים
darkô		môqēsh	'ādhām	yāla'	qōdhesh	we'achar	nedhārîm
his way		a snare to	a man	he speaks rashly	a holy thing	but afterward	vows

3937, 1266.341 prep, v Piel inf con	**26.**	2306.351 v Piel ptc ms	7857 n mp	4567 n ms	2550 adj	8178.521 cj, v Hiphil impf 3ms
לְבַקֵּר		מְזָרֶה	רְשָׁעִים	מֶלֶךְ	חָכָם	וַיָּשֶׁב
levaqqēr		mezāreh	reshā'îm	melekh	chākhām	wayyāshev
to examine		winnowing	the wicked	a king	wise	and he will cause to return

6142 prep, ps 3mp	210 n ms	**27.**	5552 n ms	3176 pn	5580 n fs	119 n ms	2769.151 v Qal act ptc ms
עֲלֵיהֶם	אוֹפָן		נֵר	יְהוָה	נִשְׁמַת	אָדָם	חֹפֵשׂ
'ălêhem	'ôphān		nēr	yehwāh	nishmath	'ādhām	chōphēs
over them	a wheel		the lamp of	Yahweh	the breath of	humankind	searching

---

shall save thee: ... Do not say, "I will repay a wrong"; Hope in the Lord and he will make you triumph, *Anchor* ... Do not say, I will give punishment for evil: go on waiting for the Lord, and he will be your saviour, *BB* ... Wait for the LORD to help you, *Goodspeed* ... Never promise thyself vengeance, *Knox* ... Wait for the Lord to handle the matter, *LIVB*.

23. Divers weights are an abomination unto the LORD; and a false balance is not good: ... One weight for getting and one for giving, the Lord cannot endure; a false balance is great wrong, *Knox* ... Varying weights are an abomination to the LORD, and false scales are not good, *NAB* ... A double standard in weights is an abomination, *NEB* ... Unequal weights are disgusting to the Lord, *BB*.

24. Man's goings are of the LORD; how can a man then understand his own way?: ... The LORD is the One who directs a man's steps; how else can a man understand which way to go?, *Beck* ... The LORD has determined our path; how then can anyone understand the direction his own life is taking?, *Good News* ... Yahweh guides human steps: how could anyone discern the way to go?, *JB* ... Man's steps are ordained by the LORD, *NASB*.

25. It is a snare to the man who devoureth that which is holy, and after vows to make inquiry: ... It is dangerous to dedicate a gift rashly, to make a vow and then have second thoughts, *REB* ... It is a trap for a man to dedicate something rashly and only later to consider his vows, *NIV* ... It is a danger to a man to say without

thought, It is holy, and, after taking his oaths, to be questioning if it is necessary to keep them, *BB* ... It disgraces a man to deny his promise, And after his vow to back out, *Fenton*.

26. A wise king scattereth the wicked, and bringeth the wheel over them: ... wise king sorts out the evil people, and he punishes them as they deserve, *NCV* ... sifts the wicked, And requites them for their guilt, *Goodspeed* ... wise king will find out who is doing wrong, and will punish him without pity, *Good News* ... winnows the wicked, And drives the threshing wheel over them, *NASB* ... threshes them under the cartwheel, *NAB*.

27. The spirit of man is the candle of the LORD, searching all the

20:22. Revenge, even in an apparently mild form such as mocking an enemy's misfortune, is condemned in Proverbs (24:17f, 28f; 25:21f; cf. Deut. 32:35; Matt. 5:43–47; Rom. 12:17, 19). The wise treat even their enemies well, knowing that there is only one Judge, and that He will reward each person, including themselves, according to the standard of the Covenant (cf. Lev. 19:18, 33f). Unlike fools, who explode with rage at every insult, real or imagined (14:29; 15:2; 19:3; 20:3), the wise remain calm (17:27) and continue to do good, knowing that the LORD will do what is right, in his own time.

20:23. "Not good" clearly indicates a litotes, as its parallel with "abomination unto the LORD" shows. Nearly identical to 11:1 and 20:10, this verse reflects the general covenantal concern with honesty (Deut. 25:13–16), a concern that is reiterated by the prophets (cf. Ezek. 45:9–12; Amos 8:5f; Mic. 6:9ff). Although honesty appears in Proverbs mainly in the language of commerce (weights and measures), it applies no less to any other aspect of dealings with a neighbor (Lev. 19:32–37).

20:24. If even the smallest elements of our "walk" are determined by the LORD (cf. 16:1f), then it is ultimately useless to try to answer the question of why. Not even the best analysis can fully explain experience, success or failure (although hindsight is occasionally clearer than foresight). It is better to leave those things with God and press on with the business of living, in the confidence of knowing that our steps are kept by God (cf. Ps. 121:3f). This verse is closely related to 16:1, 9.

This is not a warning against planning. Proverbs repeatedly commends careful planning (prudence; 14:16; 22:3), based on wise counsel (11:14; 12:15; 15:22; 19:20; 20:5, 18; 27:9), and condemns impetuosity as a mark of the fool (cf. 21:5). Planning, however, cannot overcome the purposes of God (16:1, 4, 9; 21:30f). It must be intentionally subordinated to his revealed purposes and the outcome accepted as accomplishing his will. This verse therefore counsels confidence in planning and work, knowing that the purposes of the LORD will stand.

Nor does this proverb condemn evaluation, trying to figure out "what went wrong." Analysis must, however, understand that it can only draw conclusions based on tangible realities and must, therefore, be tentative and humble, knowing that the ultimate reasons are probably unknowable.

20:25. Fools, who are ignorant of the value of speech, talk carelessly (12:18; 18:13; 29:20) and without thought for the consequences. The wise, who know better than to speak without thinking, reflect carefully on the cost of their words and actions, and so preserve themselves from many troubles (14:16; 22:3; 27:12).

This proverb probably describes a person who dedicates something to the Temple or Tabernacle on impulse (Lev. 7:16f; 22:18–23; 27:11–25; cf. Ecc. 5:4f) and only later realizes that it will be lost to his use. Such a vow was voluntary (Deut. 23:22), but once made, it had to be paid (Deut. 23:21, 23; Num. 30:2, 15).

20:26. Like 20:8, this verse uses harvest imagery to describe the king's judgment; the reversed order of the operations (winnowing before threshing) would have struck an ancient Israelite as impossible. This "dis-order" was probably intended to compel the reader's attention.

The first stage of separating the edible grain from the worthless chaff was threshing, which was done in one of three ways, each of which was designed to break the hull (the chaff) from the grain. They would drive an animal repeatedly over it (cf. Deut. 25:4), roll a weight ("wheel") over it (perhaps this was Samson's fate; Judg. 16:21) or beat it with wooden flails (known from Egyptian tomb paintings). On the second stage, winnowing, cf. the commentary on 20:8.

The king's activity in judgment was to be no less careful and just as thorough. The king was to determine guilt and innocence, and his sentences were to demonstrate which was which.

20:27. This verse could have either of two complementary meanings, or be deliberately ambiguous in order to entail both of them. The lamp of the human spirit or "breath" (cf. the same word in Gen 2:7) could refer to the LORD's ability to discover what is inside a person (cf. 15:3, 11; 16:2; 21:2 for the same idea) or to the LORD's illumination of the person's conscience (unparalleled in Proverbs; but cf. Rom. 2:14f, which Paul does not, however, link to the immediate activity of God). The first interpretation warns the wise that no motive or desire can be concealed from the LORD, as the other verses cited above also show. The second view encourages them to examine themselves, to ask God for insight as they do so and to respond to whatever self-understanding they may gain.

3725, 2410, 1027	28.	2721	583	5526.126, 4567
adj, n mp, n fs		n ms	cj, n fs	v Qal impf 3mp, n ms
כָּל־חַדְרֵי־בָטֶן		חֶסֶד	וֶאֱמֶת	יִצְּרוּ־מֶלֶךְ
kol-chadhrê-vāṭen		cheṣedh	we'ĕmeth	yitsts°rû-melekh
all the inmost parts of the belly		loyalty	and faithfulness	they will preserve a king

5777.111	904, 2721	3802	29.	8930	1005	3699
cj, v Qal pf 3ms	prep, art, n ms	n ms, ps 3ms		n fs	n mp	n ms, ps 3mp
וְסָעַד	בַּחֶסֶד	כִּסְאוֹ		תִּפְאֶרֶת	בַּחוּרִים	כֹּחָם
w°ṣā'adh	bacheṣedh	kiṣ'ô		tiph'ereth	bachûrîm	kōchām
and he will support	with the loyalty	his throne		the splendor of	the young men	their strength

1994	2292	7939	30.	2365	6729	5001.522	904, 7737
cj, n ms	n mp	n fs		n fp	n ms	v Hiphil impf 3fs	prep, n ms
וַהֲדַר	זְקֵנִים	שֵׂיבָה		חַבֻּרוֹת	פֶּצַע	תַּמְרִיק	בְּרָע
wahădhar	z°qēnîm	śêvāh		chabburôth	petsa'	tamrîq	b°rā'
and the beauty of	old men	gray hair		injuries from	a wound	it will cleanse	by evil

4485	2410, 1027	21:1	6631, 4448	3949, 4567
cj, n fp	n mp, n fs		n mp, n md	n ms, n ms
וּמַכּוֹת	חַדְרֵי־בָטֶן		פַּלְגֵי־מַיִם	לֶב־מֶלֶךְ
ûmakkôth	chadhrê-vāṭen		palghê-mayim	lev-melekh
and blows	the inmost parts of the belly		streams of water	the heart of a king

904, 3135, 3176	6142, 3725, 866	2759.121	5371.521
prep, n fs, pn	prep, adj, rel pron	v Qal impf 3ms	v Hiphil impf 3ms, ps 3ms
בְּיַד־יְהוָה	עַל־כָּל־אֲשֶׁר	יַחְפֹּץ	יַטֶּנּוּ
b°yadh-y°hwāh	'al-kol-'ăsher	yachpōts	yaṭṭennû
in the hand of Yahweh	onto all where	He is pleased	He will bend it

2.	3725, 1932, 382	3596	904, 6084	8834.151	3949	3176
	adj, n ms, n ms	adj	prep, n fd, ps 3ms	cj, v Qal act ptc ms	n mp	pn
	כָּל־דֶּרֶךְ־אִישׁ	יָשָׁר	בְּעֵינָיו	וְתֹכֵן	לִבּוֹת	יְהוָה
	kol-derekh-'îsh	yāshār	b°'ênâv	w°thōkhēn	libbôth	y°hwāh
	all the ways of a man	upright	in his eyes	but One Who examines	intentions	Yahweh

inward parts of the belly: ... The conscience of a man is the lamp of the LORD, Searching the whole innermost being, *Goodspeed* ... The LORD looks deep inside people and searches through their thoughts, *NCV* ... The LORD shines into a man's very soul, searching out his inmost being, *NEB* ... Lord keeps watch over the spirit of man, searching, *BB*.

28. Mercy and truth preserve the king: and his throne is upholden by mercy: ... Graciousness and integrity are a king's defense, And righteousness supports his throne, *Anchor* ... Mercy and good faith keep the king safe, and the seat of his power is based on upright acts, *BB* ... Faithful love and loyalty mount guard over the king, his throne is founded on saving justice, *JB* ... If a king is kind, honest and fair, his kingdom stands secure, *LIVB*.

29. The glory of young men is their strength: and the beauty of old men is the gray head: ... A young man's strength is his charm; and grey hairs make an old man beautiful, *Moffatt* ... Young men are admired for their strength, *Anchor* ... and the dignity of old men is gray hair, *NAB* ... the honor of old men is their gray hair, *NASB* ... gray hair the splendor of the old, *NIV*.

30. The blueness of a wound cleanseth away evil: so do stripes the inward parts of the belly: ... Wounds and bruises will scour the wicked man, And beatings will penetrate deep within him, *Anchor* ... Wounding strokes are good medicine for evil, blows have an effect on the inmost self, *JB* ... and a beating reaches the soul, *Beck* ... Sometimes it takes a painful experience to make us change our ways, *Good News*.

21:1. The king's heart is in the hand of the LORD, as the rivers of water: he turneth it whithersoever he will: ... Like flowing water is a king's heart in Yahweh's hand; he directs it wherever he pleases, *JB* ... The king's heart is like channels of water in the hand of the LORD; He turns it wherever He wishes, *NASB* ... The LORD can control a king's mind as he controls a river; he can direct it as he pleases, *NCV* ... He diverts it wherever he chooses, *Anchor*.

2. Every way of a man is right in his own eyes: but the LORD pondereth the hearts: ... You may think

The "chambers" portray a person as a series of rooms, each of which must be scrutinized, until the entire building (person) has been explored (cf. the same image in 18:8; 20:30).

20:28. This proverb warns kings that the primary standard for success was universal justice and that they were ultimately responsible to establish justice in the land (20:8, 26). A strong sense of justice reflected a king's commitment to the Covenant (Deut. 17:18ff) and established him securely on the throne (16:12; 29:4, 14). A king who understood this principle would seek honest counselors, lest his reign be threatened (29:12), and so the proverb also warns those who would serve the king that they too must be honest and just (16:13; 25:4f). (Cf. "Justice" in the topical index.)

20:29. The young may be naive, but they have energy and strength. The elderly may not have the strength that was once theirs, but the wisdom and insight that they have gained by their experience make up for their lack of physical ability. Every circumstance affords strengths and weaknesses; in this case, they are complementary. In addition, age is a sign of the blessing that attends a life wisely lived (3:2, 16; 4:10; 9:11). Like many other proverbs, this verse encourages mutual respect and joy for each other's gifts and abilities (cf. 16:31; 17:6).

20:30. A difficult verse (cf. the translations) due to the otherwise unknown word translated "cleanseth" in the first line ("cleanseth" reflects a slight change in the spelling that follows the scribal interpretation) and to the lack of a verb in the second line and resulting incomplete parallelism. Like other verses that encourage parents to discipline their children, this refers to the goal more than to the means. The wise understand the need to correct those who are in their care (cf. 13:24; 19:18; 22:15; 23:13f; 29:15, 17) and to do so thoughtfully, applying the right form of rebuke at the appropriate time (25:11f). They also understand that correction, though often unpleasant and unappreciated, demonstrates their love (3:11f; 13:24; cf. Heb. 12:5–13). The further implication of this verse, within the context of the Book of Proverbs, is that the person being corrected is open to rebuke (e.g., 9:7f; 17:10).

21:1. Irrigation ditches ran between banks of earth. A farmer who needed to direct the water to a particular field simply dug a hole in the bank at the spot that led to that field. As easily as that the LORD guides the king so that he accomplishes God's purposes. This is a constant theme of the prophetic oracles about the nations. In Isaiah, for example, the LORD calls the Babylonians those whom He has set apart, his mighty warriors (Isa. 13:3) and instruments of wrath (Isa. 13:5). He raises them up to punish the sin of Judah and judges them in turn for their arrogance (Hab. 1:5–11), just as he judged Assyria, which is like an ax in the hand of the woodchopper (Isa. 10:12–15). In sum, every prophetic declaration of judgment against a nation demonstrates the truth of this verse, since the LORD uses one nation to punish another, just as a farmer directs the flow of water into this field and that, as he sees fit.

This proverb is both a warning and a comfort, reminding the king that he rules by the will of God, not by his own strength. It also reminds him that he is not the sovereign power, but rules under the requirements of the Covenant (Deut. 17:18ff). His true role is that of regent, exercising dominion on behalf of and in the name of the LORD. His responsibility, therefore, is not to amass wealth (or horses or wives), but to ensure justice and faithfulness to the LORD. Those who are not kings, but who live under and serve them, should remember that their first duty is not to fear them, but the God Who rules over those human kings, the God Whom they themselves serve, however unwittingly. This is also a great encouragement to pray for one's rulers, that God would turn their hearts to justice, ruling in the fear of God (cf. 2 Sam. 23:3f). Proverbs 21:1 is thus a more specific example of the general truth of such verses as 16:1, 9.

21:2. The difference between the singular and plural of this verse and 16:2 is the difference between the totality of decisions and each individual choice. The motives of both are under the scrutiny of God. The wise person searches his own heart, knowing that he will render an account to a greater Judge. This verse is nearly identical to 16:2, where it follows a verse with a message similar to that of 21:1.

21:3. The requirements of the Covenant include sacrifice (cf. Lev. 1–7), but the most important commandments are that we love the LORD and those around us with all that is within us (Lev. 19:18; Deut. 6:5; Matt. 22:34–40). Living according to the standards of the Covenant requires knowing the standards and understanding that they reflect the character of the God Who gave them (Deut. 10:12–19).

3.

4623, 2160	3937, 3176	1013.255	5122	6930	6449.141
prep, n ms	prep, pn	v Niphal ptc ms	cj, n ms	n fs	v Qal inf con
מִזָּבַח	לַיהוָה	נִבְחָר	וּמִשְׁפָּט	צְדָקָה	עֲשֹׂה
mizzāvach	layhwāh	nivchār	ûmishpāṭ	tsedhāqāh	'ăsōh
than a sacrifice	to Yahweh	being more chosen	and justice	righteousness	to do

4.

2496	7857	5552	7622, 3949	7599, 6084
n fs	n mp	n ms	cj, adj, n ms	n ms, n fd
חַטָּאת	רְשָׁעִים	נֵר	וּרְחַב־לֵב	רוּם־עֵינַיִם
chaṭṭā'th	reshā'îm	nēr	ûrechav-lēv	rûm-'ênayim
sin	the wicked	the lamp of	and broad of heart	haughtiness of eyes

5.

4422	2845	395, 3937, 4325	3725, 211.151	395, 3937, 4408
n fp	n ms	cj, prep, n ms	cj, adj, v Qal act ptc ms	adv, prep, n ms
מַחְשְׁבוֹת	חָרוּץ	אַךְ־לְמוֹתָר	וְכָל־אָץ	אַךְ־לְמַחְסוֹר
machshevôth	chārûts	'akh-lemôthār	wekhol-'āts	'akh-lemachsôr
the plans of	the diligent	surely for profit	but all who hurry	surely to poverty

6.

6714	212	904, 4098	8632	1961	5264.255	1272.352, 4323
n ms	n mp	prep, n fs	n ms	n ms	v Niphal ptc ms	v Piel ptc mp, n ms
פֹּעַל	אוֹצָרוֹת	בִּלְשׁוֹן	שָׁקֶר	הֶבֶל	נִדָּף	מְבַקְשֵׁי־מָוֶת
pō'al	'ôtsārôth	bilshôn	shāqer	hevel	niddāph	mevaqŏshê-māweth
the accomplishing of	storehouses	by a tongue of	deception	a breath	something exhaled	seekers of death

7.

8160, 7857	1688.121	3706	4126.316	3937, 6449.141	5122
n ms, adj	v Qal impf 3ms, ps 3mp	cj	v Piel pf 3cp	prep, v Qal inf con	n ms
שֹׁד־רְשָׁעִים	יְגוֹרֵם	כִּי	מֵאֲנוּ	לַעֲשׂוֹת	מִשְׁפָּט
shōdh-reshā'îm	yeghôrēm	kî	mē'ănû	la'ăsôth	mishpāṭ
the violence of the wicked	it will chew them up	because	they refused	to do	justice

8.

2092	1932	382	2139	2217	3596
adj	n ms	n ms	adj	cj, adj	n ms
הֲפַכְפַּךְ	דֶּרֶךְ	אִישׁ	וָזָר	וְזַךְ	יָשָׁר
hăphakhpakh	derekh	'îsh	wāzār	wezakh	yāshār
twisted	the way of	a man	guilty	but pure	the upright

9.

6714	3005	3937, 3553.141	6142, 6682, 1437	4623, 828	4219	1041	2360
n ms, ps 3ms	adj	prep, v Qal inf con	prep, n fs, n ms	prep, n fs	n mp	cj, n ms	n ms
פָּעֳלוֹ	טוֹב	לָשֶׁבֶת	עַל־פִּנַּת־גָּג	מֵאֵשֶׁת	מִדְיָנִים	וּבֵית	חָבֶר
pā'ŏlô	ṭôv	lāsheveth	'al-pinnath-gāgh	mē'ēsheth	midhyānîm	ûvêth	chāver
his deeds	better	to dwell	on the corner of a roof	than a woman of	contentions	and a house of	association

---

that everything you do is right, but remember that the LORD judges your motives, *Good News* ... seems right to himself, but the Lord is the tester of hearts, *BB* ... the LORD weighs hearts, *Berkeley* ... the LORD will weigh his intents, *Fenton.*

3. To do justice and judgment is more acceptable to the LORD than sacrifice: ... Mercy shewn and justice done win the Lord's favour beyond any sacrifice, *Knox* ... God is more pleased when we are just and fair than when we give him gifts, *LIVB* ... justice and judgment is more pleasing to the LORD, *KJVII* ... Is desired by the LORD rather than sacrifice, *NASB* ... is more important to the LORD than sacrifices, *NCV.*

4. An high look, and a proud heart, and the plowing of the wicked, is sin: ... Proud looks, proud thoughts, and evil actions are sin, *NCV* ... Haughty looks and a proud heart, *NEB* ... conceited look, a proud mind, *Beck* ... Because of their pride and arrogance, The vow of evil men is a sin, *Anchor* ... A haughty eye, and a greedy heart, Are the seeds of sin in the bad, *Fenton.*

5. The thoughts of the diligent tend only to plenteousness; but of every one that is hasty only to want: ... The planning of an industrious man surely leads to plenty, but if you try to get it quick, you only get poor, *Beck* ... The plans of hard-working people earn a profit, but those who act too quickly become poor, *NCV* ... plans of the keen man show a profit, But all who are too hasty show a lost, *Anchor* ... Plan carefully and you will have plenty; if you act too quickly, you will never have enough, *Good News.*

6. The getting of treasures by a lying tongue is a vanity tossed to and fro of them that seek death: ... He who gets stores of wealth by a false tongue, is going after what is only breath, and searching for death, *BB* ... To make a fortune with the help of a lying tongue: such is the idle fantasy of those who look for death, *JB* ... The riches you get by dishon-

esty soon disappear, but not before they lead you into the jaws of death, *Good News.*

7. The robbery of the wicked shall destroy them; because they refuse to do judgment: ... The oppression of the wicked will sweep them away, because they refuse to do what is right, *NAB* ... The wicked are caught

up in their own violence, because they refuse, *NEB* ... By their violent acts the evil-doers will be pulled away, because they have no desire to do what is right, *BB* ... The violence of the wicked snares them, for they refuse to act with fairness, *Berkeley.*

8. The way of man is froward and strange: but as for the pure, his

---

Those who can afford the best sacrifices are also those who have the wealth, influence or power to pervert the course of justice to take advantage of widows, orphans, sojourners or the poor (Exo. 18:19–22; Deut. 24:17f; cf. Ezek. 22:25–29). Their sacrifices will not be chosen by the LORD, for they are guilty of the weightier matters of the Covenant.

21:4. Conceit ("lofty eyes") reveals a prideful heart, but the terms may also be progressive. What the eyes see enters the heart, and each pollutes the other, so that a haughty spirit also distorts a person's perception. If the image of the lamp refers primarily to the eyes (i.e., as the place through which light enters the body; cf. Matt. 6:22f; Luke 11:34ff), then the proverb may warn that the arrogant are so ruined that even their light is darkness (cf. 4:19; 2:12–15). Such a person must be avoided, since his or her friendship and counsel are ruinous (cf. 10:32).

21:5. The occasional success of an impetuous decision does not obviate the need for careful planning if one is to succeed. The very best plans may fail, since God, not man, is in control (cf. 16:1, 9; 20:24; 20:1), but the haste that acts without planning (as the parallelism implies) leads inevitably, if only eventually, to disaster. Wise planning also entails discipline (21:4) and setting worthwhile goals (cf. 28:20), but it is not limited to projects. Solomon also warns against hasty speech (29:20).

21:6. Deception can help someone get a fortune, but that wealth is deceptive. The second line is difficult because the relationship between its parts is unclear. The first image, "a driven breath," shows that wealth can be lost as easily as a puff of breath (cf. 23:4f) and combines ideas found in other wisdom writings (hevel [HED #1961], a motif of Ecclesiastes, where it is traditionally rendered "vanity"; the image of the wicked being blown away is found in, e.g., Ps. 1:4 and Job 21:18, which uses different vocabulary).

The main difficulty, however, is the participle "those who seek" (HED #1272). It might be in apposition to "driven breath," meaning that getting

treasure in this way is to pursue death, describing the fate of liars (so NASB, NKJV). Many interpreters and modern versions, however, follow the Septuagint and Vulgate, reading "snares" (HED #4305), instead of ("seekers" HED #1272; so NIV, NRSV). These readings do not differ greatly in force. Either way, liars are in danger of death. They may appear to prosper, but wealth gained by deception is itself deceptive (cf. 13:22; 20:17).

21:7. Those who refuse to pursue justice (lit., "act justly") often prefer violence, which might be physical, financial (e.g., by not showing mercy to creditors), through manipulating the legal system (e.g., by bribing witnesses), or being their own law in some other way. They may succeed (cf. 21:6), but they will eventually fall, as Solomon repeatedly warns (cf. 1:18f; 12:13; 21:10; 26:27). By refusing to act justly, they have set themselves in opposition to the Covenant (e.g., Deut. 16:18ff) and to the LORD (cf. 22:22f; 23:10f). The readers of Proverbs, the future leaders of Israel (cf. the commentary on 22:6), might be in positions of power, but they must not abuse their privilege, lest they be destroyed. (Cf. "Justice" in the topical index.)

21:8. Although it seems tautologous (cf. comments on 14:5), this proverb warns that deeds reveal the heart. This is not always immediately apparent, of course, especially for the wicked, who are often clever at concealing their true intentions (10:18; 26:24ff), but the discerning will eventually discover their wisdom or folly from their behavior and speech.

If the word wāzār (HED #2139) which only occurs here, means "guilty," then it was probably used to pun with the next word, wᵉzākh (HED #2217), "but clean." The creator of this verse was doubly ingenious, because the syntax of the first line is itself fairly contorted, whereas the second line is straightforward, just like the man that each describes.

21:9. This verse is identical to 25:24, which follows an emblematic proverb about the problems caused by gossip or slander (cf. 21:19).

10.

5497	7857	181.312, 7737	3940, 2706.621	904, 6084
n fs	n ms	v Piel pf 3fs, n ms	neg part, v Hophal impf 3ms	prep, n fd, ps 3ms
נֶפֶשׁ	רָשָׁע	אִוְּתָה־רָע	לֹא־יֻחַן	בְּעֵינָיו
nephesh	rāshā'	'iwwethāh-rā'	lō'-yuchan	be'ênâv
the soul of	the wicked	it desires evil	he will not be treated with compassion	in his eyes

11.

7739		904, 6294.141, 4086	2549.121, 6864
n ms, ps 3ms		prep, v Qal inf con, n ms	v Qal impf 3ms, adj
רֵעֵהוּ		בַּעֲנָשׁ־לֵץ	יֶחְכַּם־פֶּתִי
rē'ēhû		ba'ănāsh-lēts	yechăkkam-pethî
his fellow		when the punishing of a mocker	the simple will become wise

12.

904, 7959.541	3937, 2550	4089.121, 1907	7959.551	6926
cj, prep, v Hiphil inf con	prep, n ms	v Qal impf 3ms, n fs	v Hiphil ptc ms	n ms
וּבְהַשְׂכִּיל	לְחָכָם	יִקַּח־דָּעַת	מַשְׂכִּיל	צַדִּיק
ûvehaskîl	lechākhām	yiqqach-dā'ath	maskîl	tsaddîq
and when being wise	a wise man	he will get knowledge	being wise	the righteous

13.

3937, 1041	7857	5751.351	7857	3937, 7737	334.151
prep, n ms	n ms	v Piel ptc ms	n mp	prep, art, n ms	v Qal act ptc ms
לְבֵית	רָשָׁע	מְסַלֵּף	רְשָׁעִים	לָרָע	אֹטֵם
levêth	rāshā'	mesallēph	reshā'îm	lārā'	'ōṭēm
about the household of	the wicked	ruining	the wicked	to the disaster	one who stops up

238	4623, 2285, 1859	1612, 2000	7410.121	3940	6257.221
n fs, ps 3ms	prep, n fs, n ms	cj, pers pron	v Qal impf 3ms	cj, neg part	v Niphal impf 3ms
אָזְנוֹ	מִזַּעֲקַת־דָּל	גַּם־הוּא	יִקְרָא	וְלֹא	יֵעָנֶה
'āzenô	mizza'ăqath-dāl	gam-hû'	yiqǒrā'	welō'	yē'āneh
his ear	from the outcry of the poor	also he	he will call	and not	he will be answered

14.

5150	904, 5848	3836.121, 653	8245	904, 2536	2635	6006
n ms	prep, art, n ms	v Qal impf 3ms, n ms	cj, n ms	prep, art, n ms	n fs	adj
מַתָּן	בַּסֵּתֶר	יִכְפֶּה־אָף	וְשֹׁחַד	בַּחֵק	חֵמָה	עַזָּה
mattān	bassēther	yikhpeh-'āph	weshōchadh	bachēq	chēmāh	'azzāh
a gift	in a secret place	it will avert anger	and a bribe	in the bosom	wrath	strong

15.

7977	3937, 6926	6449.141	5122	4425	3937, 6713.152	201
n fs	prep, art, n ms	v Qal inf con	n ms	cj, n fs	prep, v Qal act ptc mp	n ms
שִׂמְחָה	לַצַּדִּיק	עֲשׂוֹת	מִשְׁפָּט	וּמְחִתָּה	לְפֹעֲלֵי	אָוֶן
simchāh	latstsaddîq	'ăsôth	mishpāṭ	ûmechittāh	lephō'ălê	'āwen
joy	to the righteous	to act with	justice	but terror	to those practicing	iniquity

---

work is right: ... Guilty people walk a crooked path; the innocent do what is right, *Good News* ... The way of the felon is devious, the conduct of the innocent straight, *JB* ... way of man is perverted and strange; but as for the pure, *KJVII* ... Guilty people live dishonest lives, but honest people do right, *NCV*.

9. It is better to dwell in a corner of the housetop, than with a brawling woman in a wide house: ... better to live in a corner on the roof than inside the house with a quarreling wife, *NCV* ... than have a nagging wife and a brawling household, *NEB* ... than with a bitter-tongued woman in a wide house, *BB* ... than to share a house with a contentious woman, *Berkeley*.

10. The soul of the wicked desireth evil: his neighbour findeth no favour in his eyes: ... The mind of a vicious man yearns to make trouble, He has no mercy for his fellow man, *Anchor* ... mind of a wicked person wants to do wrong and has no compassion on his fellow man, *Beck* ... Evil people only want to harm others. Their neighbors get no mercy from them, *NCV* ... wicked man is set on evil; he has no pity to spare for his friend, *NEB*.

11. When the scorner is punished, the simple is made wise: and when the wise is instructed, he receiveth knowledge: ... The simple learns a lesson [only] when a scoffer comes to grief, But the intelligent man understands when a matter is explained, *Anchor* ... When the man of pride undergoes punishment, the simple man gets wisdom; and by watching the wise he gets knowledge, *BB* ... when one is considerate of the wise man, he acquires knowledge, *Berkeley* ... When someone who is conceited gets his punishment, even an unthinking person learns a lesson. One who is wise will learn from what he is taught, *Good News*.

12. The righteous man wisely considereth the house of the wicked: but God overthroweth the wicked for their wickedness: ... The Upright One watches the house of the wicked; he hurls the wicked to destruction, *JB* ... Righteous One takes note of the house of the wicked, *NIV* ... Upright One, looking on the house of the evildoer, lets sinners be overturned to their destruction, *BB* ... God, the Righteous One, knows what is going on in the homes of the wicked, and will bring the wicked to judgment, *LIVB*.

13. Whoso stoppeth his ears at the cry of the poor, he also shall cry himself, but shall not be heard: ... He who closes his ears to the cry of the poor will himself also cry and not be heard, *Berkeley* ... If you shut your ears to the crying of the poor, you too will call and get no answer, *Beck* ... Whoever refuses to listen to the cry of the weak, will in turn plead and not be heard, *JB* ... He will cry, and none will answer, *Fenton*.

14. A gift in secret pacifieth anger: and a reward in the bosom strong wrath: ... By a secret offering wrath is turned away, and the heat of angry feelings by money in the folds of the robe, *BB* ... A gift in secret quiets anger; and a bribe in the bosom quiets strong wrath, *KJVII* ... and a concealed present, violent wrath, *NAB* ... A secret gift will calm an angry person; a present given in secrecy will quiet great anger, *NCV*.

15. It is joy to the just to do judgment: but destruction shall be to the workers of iniquity: ... The doing of justice is a joy to the right-

---

21:10. The first line states a general principle, which the second applies to a specific situation. The wicked always desire what is evil because of their wickedness. Against the covenantal requirement (Lev. 19:18, 33f; Prov. 3:29), they despise those around them (11:12; 14:21), seeing them only as tools by which to accomplish their own ends (cf. 12:26). It is therefore useless to seek or hope for mercy, wise counsel or help from such a person. Furthermore, the wicked reveal the true state of their hearts by despising their neighbors (cf. 21:8).

21:11. The ambiguity of the second line makes the details of this verse somewhat murky (like its close parallel in 19:25), although its overall import is clear. The second line could mean that the wise or the naive gain knowledge either because they are instructed or because they consider things (probably the punishment of the scornful). The main contrast is probably between the scoffer, who refuses to benefit from correction the naive, who learns from the scoffer's punishment, and the wise, who learns from mere instruction. The point would thus be the teachability of the naive and wise and the incorrigible nature of mockers (cf. 19:25). This seems to be the most likely meaning of this verse, but it ignores the preposition l^e (HED #3937) on "wise," assuming that it was repeated from the end of the previous word (maskîl; HED #5030).

21:12. Since the LORD knows what is in every heart, He can judge correctly (12:2; 16:2; 17:3; 21:2) and reward behavior appropriately (13:9, 21; 14:11). The identity of the "righteous" is not clear, even though the translations generally capitalize it ("Righteous One," NASB, NIV, NRSV) or specify the "righteous God" (NKJV). Since every other occurrence of tsaddîq (HED #6926) in Proverbs refers to a human being, it is also possible that "the righteous" refers to a judge who may destroy the household of the wicked in rendering judgment (cf. Josh. 7:24f). This would fit the purpose of the Book and the many proverbs that address the need for justice.

21:13. Although this verse can certainly be explained on the level of a purely human response (those who refuse to help those in need will not be helped, and will even find trouble for their parsimony; cf. 11:26; 28:27), it also has theological underpinnings, since the Book of Proverbs (and Scripture in general) consistently presents the LORD as the helper of the poor and needy. The second great commandment (Lev. 19:18, 33f) is based on the nature of God and on his creation of every human being in his image. Generosity (of goods, time, talents) is therefore a duty, not an option.

21:14. Since gifts win friends (18:16; 19:6), they can resolve conflicts or even calm rage (but cf. 6:34f). Their secrecy suggests that these are bribes (the usual meaning of shāchadh [HED #8244]). Since conflict is condemned throughout Proverbs, however, this verse advocates using one's property or abilities to avoid conflict, not bribes that cause justice to miscarry (cf. 17:23; 29:4). It thus insinuates that it is better to stop a quarrel at any cost than to let opponents become entrenched in their positions (cf. 17:14).

21:15. The innocent have nothing to fear and everything to gain from justice, whereas the guilty can only fear the punishment (cf. 28:1) which will

16.

119	8912.151	4623, 1932	7959.542	904, 7235	7787
n ms	v Qal act ptc ms	prep, n ms	v Hiphil inf abs	prep, n ms	n mp
אָדָם	תּוֹעֶה	מִדֶּרֶךְ	הַשְׂכֵּל	בְּקְהַל	רְפָאִים
'ādhām	tô'eh	midderekh	haskēl	biqŏhal	rephā'îm
a man	wandering	from the way of	understanding	in the assembly of	dead spirits

17.

5299.121	382	4408	154.151	7977	154.151	3302, 8467
v Qal impf 3ms	n ms	n ms	v Qal act ptc ms	n fs	v Qal act ptc ms	n ms, cj, n ms
יָנוּחַ	אִישׁ	מַחְסוֹר	אֹהֵב	שִׂמְחָה	אֹהֵב	יַיִן־וָשֶׁמֶן
yānûach	'îsh	machsôr	'ōhēv	simchāh	'ōhēv	yayin-wāshemen
he will rest	a man of	lack	one who loves	rejoicing	one who loves	wine and oil

18.

3940	6483.521	3853	3937, 6926	7857	8809
neg part	v Hiphil impf 3ms	n ms	prep, art, n ms	n ms	cj, prep
לֹא	יַעֲשִׁיר	כֹּפֶר	לַצַּדִּיק	רָשָׁע	וְתַחַת
lō'	ya'ăshîr	kōpher	latstsaddîq	rāshā'	wethachath
not	he will become rich	a ransom	for the righteous	the wicked	and instead of

19.

3596	931.151	3005	3553.141	904, 800, 4198
n mp	v Qal act ptc ms	adj	v Qal inf con	prep, n fs, n ms
יְשָׁרִים	בּוֹגֵד	טוֹב	שֶׁבֶת	בְּאֶרֶץ־מִדְבָּר
yeshārîm	bôghēdh	tôv	sheveth	be'erets-midhbār
the upright	those who act deceitfully	better	to dwell	in the wilderness land

20.

4623, 828	4209	3833	212	2629.255	8467
prep, n fs	n mp	cj, n ms	n ms	v Niphal ptc ms	cj, n ms
מֵאֵשֶׁת	מִדְוָנִים	וָכָעַס	אוֹצָר	נֶחְמָד	וָשֶׁמֶן
mē'ēsheth	medhônîm	wākhā'as	'ôtsār	nechmādh	wāshemen
than a woman of	contentions	and vexation	a treasure	something desired	and oil

21.

904, 5295	2550	3809	119	1142.321	7579.151
prep, n ms	n ms	cj, n ms	n ms	v Piel impf 3ms, ps 3ms	v Qal act ptc ms
בִּנְוֵה	חָכָם	וּכְסִיל	אָדָם	יְבַלְּעֶנּוּ	רֹדֵף
binwēh	chākhām	ûkhesîl	'ādhām	yevalle'ennû	rōdhēph
in the habitation of	the wise	but a fool	a man	he will devour it	one who pursues

22.

6930	2721	4834.121	2522	6930	3638	6111	1399
n fs	cj, n ms	v Qal impf 3ms	n mp	n fs	cj, n ms	n fs	n mp
צְדָקָה	וָחֶסֶד	יִמְצָא	חַיִּים	צְדָקָה	וְכָבוֹד	עִיר	גִּבֹּרִים
tsedhāqāh	wāchesedh	yimtsā'	chayyîm	tsedhāqāh	wekhāvôdh	'îr	gibbōrîm
righteousness	and loyalty	he will find	life	righteousness	and honor	a city of	warriors

eous, but to the workers of iniquity it is a calamity, *Berkeley* ... The practice of justice delights the innocent but terrifies those who do wrong, *Beck* ... The execution of justice is a joy to the righteous, But ruin to those who do evil, *Goodspeed* ... When justice is done, good people are happy, but evil people are brought to despair, *Good News.*

16. The man that wandereth out of the way of understanding shall remain in the congregation of the dead: ... man who takes leave of common sense comes to rest in the company of, *NEB* ... man who wanders from the way of wisdom Will rest in the assembly of the Shades, *Goodspeed* ... Whoever strays far from the way of prudence will rest in the assembly of shadows, *JB* ... man who wanders out of the right road will find his rest among the dead below, *Moffatt.*

17. He that loveth pleasure shall be a poor man: he that loveth wine and oil shall not be rich: ... poor man who loves enjoyment,—And wine and oil, will never be rich, *Fenton* ... Pleasure-lovers stay poor, no one will grow rich who loves wine and good living, *JB* ... Indulging in luxuries, wine, and rich food will never make you wealthy, *Good News* ... One who loves pleasure will end in poverty, *Anchor* ... lover of wine and oil will not get wealth, *BB.*

18. The wicked shall be a ransom for the righteous, and the transgressor for the upright: ... wicked is a ransom for the upright; and the law-breaker for the honest, *JB* ... Wicked people will suffer instead of good people, and those who cannot be trusted will suffer instead of those who do right, *NCV* ... And the treacherous is in the place of the upright, *NASB* ... and the faithless man takes the place of the upright, *Goodspeed*.

19. It is better to dwell in the wilderness, than with a contentious and an angry woman: ... better to live alone in the desert than with a quarreling and complaining wife, *NCV* ... better to be living in a waste land, than with a bitter-tongued and angry woman,

BB ... than with a nagging and ill-tempered wife!, *REB* ... contentious and fretful wife, *NRSV* ... quarrelsome and discontented wife, *Anchor*.

20. There is treasure to be desired and oil in the dwelling of the wise; but a foolish man spendeth it up: ... There is a store of great value in the house of the wise, but it is wasted by the foolish man, *BB* ... wise has valuables and oil at home, but a fool soon runs through both, *JB* ... The

wise man saves for the future, but the foolish man spends whatever he gets, *LIVB* ... foolish man devours it, *Berkeley* ... fool consumes it, *NAB*.

21. He that followeth after righteousness and mercy findeth life, righteousness, and honour: ... Whoever tries to live right and be loyal finds life, success, and honor, *NCV* ... Persevere in right conduct and loyalty and you shall find life and honour, *NEB* ... He who seeks

---

surely overtake them, if justice is zealously pursued (cf. 10:24; 11:23). The message is clear: which state is preferable—joy or anxiety? There may also be a subtle word here to judges. If a judge is known as honest and just, the emotional state of those before him may point toward their innocence or guilt (cf. 21:29).

21:16. This verse encourages diligence by warning of the dreadful consequence of straying from "the path." This path may be either the path that is characterized by understanding or the path that leads to success (the verb is ambiguous). Since the verb translated "wanders" (HED #8912) often implies that a person is lost or moving about aimlessly, this is not warning against rebellion as much as against casual or careless choices that by insensible degrees lead away from the path of life (cf. 2:18f; 9:18; 16:17).

21:17. One characteristic of a disciplined life is the ability to avoid immediate gratification for the sake of long-term goals. Diligence, not self-indulgence, is the path to true satisfaction. The "joy" of feasting and revelry may be real, but squandering resources (whether they be financial, temporal or gifts and abilities) rather than conserving and using them appropriately (cf. 24:27) impoverishes the quality of every aspect of life. Life, in other words, is a marathon, not a sprint.

21:18. The Covenant demands that perjurers be punished with the sentence that the accused would have received had they been guilty (Deut. 19:15–21; cf. Prov. 11:8). If this idea underlies this verse, as "treacherous" may imply, then it reminds judges to fulfill their obligation (cf. esp. Deut. 19:21) and reminds witnesses of the possible consequences of perjury (cf. the warning of 24:28f). It also reiterates the general proverbial assertion that wickedness rebounds on those who practice it (26:27). Rashi, one of the greatest rabbinic commentators, related this to the reversal of Haman's intentions (Est. 7:10).

21:19. Like the verses that commend a peaceful but simple meal over a feast accompanied by strife and hatred (15:17; 17:1), this proverb commends choosing a wife based on her personality. A woman who lacks a compatible personality may drive her husband out of the house, town or even beyond the cultivated land into the territory used only for herds and flocks. A contentious spouse destroys the peace of one's household, so that the goal becomes escape from his or her presence (cf. 21:9; 25:24).

21:20. The wise, who know how to set priorities (24:27) and work diligently to accomplish their goals, find their work blessed (8:21). Fools, on the other hand, who refuse to think ahead or to accept counsel concerning the consequences of their actions (14:16; 22:3; 27:12), waste even that which they have (21:17; 23:19ff). As often, the choice set before the student concerns which type of person he aspires to become. "Treasure" and "oil" probably refer to property in general (a double synecdoche), rather than to specific possessions.

21:21. The goals a person pursues in his life determine how his life will turn out (cf. 11:19; 12:28). Many proverbs contrast outcomes in order to clarify the consequences of choices (cf. 21:20). This verse presents the positive side only and implies that the results often outweigh (for better or worse) the goal (cf. 22:4). If this is true, how carefully each person must choose the guiding principle or purpose for his life!

Some translations follow the Septuagint and some manuscripts of the Vulgate in leaving "righteousness" out of the second line (e.g., NRSV). Its presence, however, clarifies the point; there is no compelling reason to omit it.

21:22. Wisdom is strength, especially when it is augmented by wise counsel (11:14; 15:22; 24:5f; cf. Ecc. 9:13–16). The wise, therefore, are quick to

6148.111	2550	3495.521	6010	4148		8490.151
v Qal pf 3ms	n ms	cj, v Hiphil impf 3ms	*n ms*	n ms, ps 3fs	**23.**	v Qal act ptc ms
עָלָה	חָכָם	וַיֹּרֶד	עֹז	מִבְטֶחָה		שֹׁמֵר
'ālāh	chākhām	wayyōredh	'ōz	mivṭechāh		shōmēr
he will go up	a wise man	and he will bring down	the strength of	its security		one who guards

6552	4098	8490.151	4623, 7150	5497		2170	3195
n ms, ps 3ms	cj, n fs, ps 3ms	v Qal act ptc ms	prep, n fp	n fs, ps 3ms	**24.**	adj	adj
פִּיו	וּלְשׁוֹנוֹ	שֹׁמֵר	מִצָּרוֹת	נַפְשׁוֹ		זֵד	יָהִיר
pîw	ûlāshônô	shōmēr	mitstsārôth	naphshô		zēdh	yāhîr
his mouth	and his tongue	one who guards	from adversities	his life		presumptuous	proud

4086	8428	6449.151	904, 5887	2171		8707	6339
n ms	n ms, ps 3ms	v Qal act ptc ms	prep, *n fs*	n ms	**25.**	*n fs*	n ms
לֵץ	שְׁמוֹ	עוֹשֶׂה	בְּעֶבְרַת	זָדוֹן		תַּאֲוַת	עָצֵל
lēts	shᵉmô	'ôseh	bᵉ'evrath	zādhôn		ta'awath	'ātsēl
a mocker	his name	one who acts	with boiling up	presumptuousness		the longing of	a sluggard

4322.522	3706, 4126.316	3135	3937, 6449.141		3725, 3219
v Hiphil impf 3fs, ps 3ms	cj, v Piel pf 3cp	n fd, ps 3ms	prep, v Qal inf con	**26.**	*adj*, art, n ms
תְּמִיתֶנּוּ	כִּי־מֵאֲנוּ	יָדָיו	לַעֲשׂוֹת		כָּל־הַיּוֹם
tᵉmîthennû	kî-mē'ānû	yādhâv	la'asôth		kol-hayyôm
it will kill him	because they refuse	his hands	to do		all the day

181.721	8707	6926	5598.121	3940	2910.121		2160
v Hithpael impf 3ms	n fs	cj, n ms	v Qal impf 3ms	cj, neg part	v Qal impf 3ms	**27.**	*n ms*
הִתְאַוָּה	תַאֲוָה	וְצַדִּיק	יִתֵּן	וְלֹא	יַחְשֹׂךְ		זֶבַח
hith'awwāh	tha'awāh	wᵉtsaddîq	yittēn	wᵉlō'	yachôskh		zevach
he longs for	delight	but the righteous	he gives	and not	he withholds		the sacrifice of

7857	8774	652	3706, 904, 2239		971.521
n mp	n fs	cj	cj, prep, n fs		v Hiphil impf 3ms, ps 3ms
רְשָׁעִים	תּוֹעֵבָה	אַף	כִּי־בְזִמָּה		יְבִיאֶנּוּ
rᵉshā'îm	tô'ēvāh	'aph	kî-vᵉzimmāh		yᵉvî'ennû
the wicked	a detestable thing	also	indeed by a shameful deed		he brings it

	5915, 3695	6.121	382	8471.151	3937, 5516
28.	*n ms*, n mp	v Qal impf 3ms	cj, n ms	v Qal act ptc ms	prep, art, n ms
	עֵד־כְּזָבִים	יֹאבֵד	וְאִישׁ	שׁוֹמֵעַ	לָנֶצַח
	'ēdh-kᵉzāvîm	yō'vēdh	wᵉ'îsh	shômēa'	lānetsach
	a witness of lies	he will perish	but a man	one who listens	unto forever

earnestly what is right and kind, Will find life and respect, *Anchor* ... finds life, prosperity and honor, *NIV*.

22. A wise man scaleth the city of the mighty, and casteth down the strength of the confidence thereof: ... A wise man goes up into the town of the strong ones, and overcomes its strength in which they put their faith, *BB* ... wise man can attack a city of warriors and push down the strong defenses they trust in, *Beck* ... clever man can scale a mighty city, *Moffatt* ... and brings down the stronghold in which they trust, *Berkeley*.

23. Whoso keepeth his mouth and his tongue keepeth his soul from troubles: ... Those who are careful about what they say keep themselves out of trouble, *NCV* ... Watch kept over mouth and tongue keeps the watcher safe from disaster, *JB* ... keeps himself from calamity, *NIV* ... Saves himself from many trials, *Anchor*.

24. Proud and haughty scorner is his name, who dealeth in proud wrath: ... The man of pride, lifted up in soul, is named high-hearted; he is acting in an outburst of pride, *BB* ... who acts with arrogant pride,

Berkeley ... A proud and conceited person is called a scoffer; there is arrogance and conceit in what he does, *Beck* ... People who act with stubborn pride are called "proud," "bragger," and "mocker," *NCV*.

25. The desire of the slothful killeth him; for his hands refuse to labour: ... Lazy people's desire for sleep will kill them, because they refuse to work, *NCV* ... desire of the hater of work is death to him, for his hands will do no work, *BB* ... desire of the sluggard slays him, *Berkeley* ... desire of the idle kills him, *Fenton*.

26. He coveteth greedily all the day long: but the righteous giveth and spareth not: ... He longs all day for his wish, While the honest work and want not, *Fenton* ... He is always feeling greedy; but a righteous person gives and doesn't hold back, *Beck* ... All day long the godless is racked by desire, the upright gives without ever refusing, *JB* ... all he does is think about what he would like to have. A righteous man, however, can give, and give generously, *Good News*.

27. The sacrifice of the wicked is abomination: how much more, when he bringeth it with a wicked mind?: ... LORD hates sacrifices brought by evil people, particularly when they offer them for the wrong reasons, *NCV* ... sacrifice of the wicked is hateful to God, *KJVII* ... above all if it is offered for bad motives, *JB* ... the more so when they offer it with a bad intention, *NAB*.

28. A false witness shall perish: but the man that heareth speaketh constantly: ... A lying witness will be forgotten, but a truthful witness will speak on, *NCV* ... false witness will be cut off, *BB* ... but a man who listens to advice may speak, *Beck* ... testimony of a liar is not believed, but the word of someone who thinks matters through is accepted, *Good News* ... no one who knows how to listen will ever be silenced, *JB*.

---

think before acting, and to seek and weigh advice (12:15). They also know, however, that all human plans are uncertain—the LORD's will ultimately prevails (19:21; 21:30f).

21:23. Whoever understands the power of words (cf. 12:18; 18:21; Jam. 3:1–12) recognizes the need to use them carefully. To "guard" or "keep watch" over words requires prudence to understand what needs most to be said. This understanding requires reflection rather than a quick response—wisdom does not speak out of frustration or anger. Also, at times, the right "words" are no words at all—to see this probably takes the greatest wisdom; silence certainly requires the greatest self-control.

21:24. The syntax in this verse is unclear—is he called "Proud," "Insolent" and "Scoffer" (so NASB), or is the proud and insolent named "Scoffer" (so NIV, NKJV, NRSV)? However, its message is straightforward. Anyone who treats others with arrogant fury will be noted by those around him and avoided (22:24f). Heaping up synonyms in the first line, and beginning and ending the proverb with closely related words for "insolence" only strengthens the point.

21:25–26. Those who are lazy would rather dream and wish than work toward their dreams. They do not really understand (or if they understand it intellectually, they do not believe) that physical life itself depends on work. Since they are contrasted with sluggards (v. 26b should begin with "but"), the "righteous" are the diligent who do what needs to be done (cf. 15:19). This implies a certain amount of insight: they understand what is most important at any given moment and then pursue it.

The result of diligence is the ability to help those in need. Their work flourishes, so that they have more than enough for themselves. Because they have the insight that underlies diligence, they

also understand that it is better to give than to receive, and are open-handed and generous. The sluggard, however, will never have enough to be generous, not even when confronted with a need that he wants to meet. His laziness destroyed his ability to fulfill the second great commandment (cf. 18:9). Laziness and diligence thus affect not only the individuals themselves, but those around them.

21:27. Like Prov. 15:8f, this is an argument *a fortiori*. If the perfunctory sacrifices of the wicked are rejected before they reach the altar, how much worse is it to offer a sacrifice under false pretenses, whether the fraud be an unrepentant heart (as this verse implies) or an oath in court (cf. Exo. 22:10f). Although this verse does not mention the LORD, his role as judge is clearly implied (15:8a, which is nearly identical to 21:27a, specifies his role). Sacrifice in the ancient Near East was often an attempt to trick or manipulate gods into helping the offerer, or leaving him alone. The LORD, however, is not deceived by dissembling—religious or otherwise.

21:28. Under the Covenant, perjury was punishable according to the nature of the false accusation (Deut. 19:15–21), so that a perjurer in a capital case faced execution. If listening here refers to the judge's role, the proverb may mean that a judge who listens carefully and thus renders justice will endure (cf. 18:17; 25:8f).

The parallelism suggests, however, that the contrast is between true and false witnesses. Listening is a primary requirement of gaining wisdom and its attendant righteousness (cf. 1:8; 2:2; 4:1f, 20; 22:17; 23:22), which may explain the contrast between one who listens (i.e., to wisdom) and therefore tells the truth and a false witness. Unlike a perjurer, a truthful witness can speak freely and without fear.

1744.321	6022.511	382	7857	904, 6686	3596	2000
v Piel impf 3ms	v Hiphil pf 3ms	n ms	adj	prep, n mp, ps 3ms	cj, adj	pers pron
יְדַבֵּר **29.**	הֵעֵז	אִישׁ	רָשָׁע	בְּפָנָיו	וְיָשָׁר	הוּא
yedhabbēr	hē'ēz	'îsh	rāshā'	bephānâv	weyāshār	hû'
he will speak	he will prevail	a man	wicked	with his face	but the upright	He

3679.521	1932	375	2551	375	8722
v Hiphil impf 3ms	n mp, ps 3ms **30.**	sub	n fs	cj, sub	n fs
יָכִין	דְּרָכָיו	אֵין	חָכְמָה	וְאֵין	תְּבוּנָה
yākhîn	derākhâv	'ên	chokhmāh	we'ên	tevûnāh
He will establish	his ways	there is not	wisdom	and there is not	understanding

375	6332	3937, 5224	3176	5670	3679.655	3937, 3219
cj, sub	n fs	prep, prep	pn **31.**	n ms	v Hophal ptc ms	prep, n ms
וְאֵין	עֵצָה	לְנֶגֶד	יְהוָה	סוּס	מוּכָן	לְיוֹם
we'ên	'ētsāh	leneghedh	yehwāh	sûs	mûkhān	leyôm
and there is not	counsel	before	Yahweh	a horse	having been prepared	for the day of

4560	3937, 3176	9009	1013.255	8428	4623, 6484	7521
n fs	cj, prep, pn	art, n fs **22:1**	v Niphal ptc ms	n ms	prep, n ms	adj
מִלְחָמָה	וְלַיהוָה	הַתְּשׁוּעָה	נִבְחָר	שֵׁם	מֵעֹשֶׁר	רָב
milchāmāh	welayhwāh	hatteshû'āh	nivchār	shēm	mē'ōsher	rāv
a battle	but of Yahweh	the deliverance	what is chosen	a name	than riches	abundant

4623, 3826B	4623, 2174	2682	3005	6474	7851	6539.216	6449.151
prep, n ms	cj, prep, n ms	n ms	adj **2.**	n ms	cj, n ms	v Niphal pf 3cp	v Qal act ptc ms
מִכֶּסֶף	וּמִזָּהָב	חֵן	טוֹב	עָשִׁיר	וָרָשׁ	נִפְגָּשׁוּ	עֹשֵׂה
mikkeseph	ûmizzāhāv	chēn	tôv	'āshîr	wārāsh	niphgāshû	'ōsēh
than silver	and than gold	favor	better	the rich	and the poor	they will meet	the Maker of

3725	3176	6415	7495.111	7750	5846.121	6864
adj, ps 3mp	pn **3.**	n ms	v Qal pf 3ms	n fs	cj, v Qal impf 3ms	cj, n mp
כֻּלָּם	יְהוָה	עָרוּם	רָאָה	רָעָה	וְיִסָּתֵר	וּפְתָיִים
khullām	yehwāh	'ārûm	rā'āh	rā'āh	weyissāthēr	ûphethāyîm
all of them	Yahweh	a prudent man	he will see	evil	and he hides	but the simple

5882.116	6294.216	6358	6265	3488	3176	6484
v Qal pf 3cp	cj, v Niphal pf 3cp **4.**	n ms	n fs	n fs	pn	n ms
עָבְרוּ	וְנֶעֱנָשׁוּ	עֵקֶב	עֲנָוָה	יִרְאַת	יְהוָה	עֹשֶׁר
'āverû	wene'ēnāshû	'ēqev	'ănāwāh	yir'ath	yehwāh	'ōsher
they will pass on	and they will be punished	the result of	humility	the fear of	Yahweh	riches

---

29. A wicked man hardeneth his face: but as for the upright, he directeth his way: ... The wicked man's strength shows on his face, but the honest it is whose steps are firm, *JB* ... Wicked people are stubborn, but good people think carefully about what they do, *NCV* ... but the upright man pays heed to his ways, *NAB*.

30. There is no wisdom nor understanding nor counsel against the LORD: ... or advice that can succeed against the LORD, *NCV* ... Face to face with the LORD, wisdom, understanding, counsel go for nothing,

NEB ... no wisdom, no thought, no policy, Which can avail against the Lord, *Anchor* ... Wisdom and knowledge and wise suggestions are of no use against the Lord, *BB*.

31. The horse is prepared against the day of battle: but safety is of the LORD: ... Train the horse for the time of war; Yet the victory, *Fenton* ... but the victory belongs to the LORD, *Berkeley* ... but power to overcome is from the Lord, *BB* ... But deliverance is of the LORD, *NKJV*.

22:1. A good name is rather to be chosen than great riches, and loving favour rather than silver and gold: ... Reputation is a better choice than riches; esteem is more than money, *Moffatt* ... is more to be desired than great wealth, and to be respected is better than, *BB* ... A good reputation than silver and gold, *Goodspeed* ... to be gracious is better than silver or gold, *Beck*.

2. The rich and poor meet together: the LORD is the maker of them all: ... Rich and poor stand side by side, *Moffatt* ... Rich and

198

poor have a common bond, *NAB* ... rich and poor are alike, *NCV* ... rich and the poor mix together, *Fenton.*

3. A prudent man foreseeth the evil, and hideth himself: but the simple pass on, and are punished: ... prudent sees danger and hides, The foolish go on and suffer, *Fenton* ... shrewd person foresees trouble and avoids it, but thoughtless people

go ahead and suffer for it, *Beck* ... The discreet sees danger and takes shelter, *JB* ... cautious man sees danger and takes cover, *Moffatt* ... Sensible people will see trouble coming and avoid it, but an unthinking person will walk right into it and regret it later, *Good News.*

4. By humility and the fear of the LORD are riches, and honour, and

life: ... Respecting the LORD and not being proud will bring you wealth, honor and life, *NCV* ... The reward of a gentle spirit and the fear of the Lord is wealth and honour and life, *BB* ... The results of humility—reverence for the LORD—are riches, *Berkeley* ... Lord has provided reward for the meek, With riches, honour, life, *Fenton.*

21:29. Although this proverb might describe a general difference between the wicked and righteous (appearance vs. reality), it may also be designed to correct the mis-application of 21:15, lest a judge be tempted to interpret brazenness as innocence (cf. the same expression in 7:13). The textual variant in the second line does not materially affect the meaning of the proverb. Whether the upright "establishes" or "discerns" his way (cf. the same expression in 14:8; 20:24), he lives obedient to wisdom and thus has the confidence that comes from doing what is right (28:1).

21:30–31. The proverbial emphasis on preparation by counsel and advice (11:14; 12:15; 15:22; 19:20; 20:5, 18; 24:5f; 27:9) must not be misinterpreted to mean that proper planning guarantees the plan's success. Neither human counsel, however wise and insightful, nor the best preparation can frustrate the plan of God (cf. Isa. 14:27). Proper planning, therefore, requires more than simply gathering, analyzing and discussing information in order to come to a wise decision. Wise planning entails submitting plans to the LORD, knowing that in the end it is his cause that shall prevail (16:3f).

These proverbs may have been originally independent, but neither their juxtaposition nor their position at the end of this chapter is accidental. When the Hebrew Bible was divided into chapters in the sixteenth century A.D. (the first Hebrew Bible with verse numbers, which implies chapter divisions, was published in 1571), Prov. 21 may have been marked off as a chapter because its first and last verses address divine sovereignty (cf. 16:1 and 16:33).

22:1. A good reputation is better than wealth measured in silver and gold. As the parallelism shows, the fame of the first line is a good reputation, which may not be the same as a great one. It is the result of a life that gains the approval of others, rather than one that seeks its own fame (cf. 25:6f). The choice between pursuing wealth, which

provides a certain type of fame, and doing that which elicits a gracious response from others is an easy one for the wise, because he realizes the true worth of each. Although only the second line actually uses the words "better than," "more desireable" in 22:1a shows that each line contains this type of saying (cf. 15:16f; 16:32).

22:2. This proverb again looks at wealth and poverty. Although the wealthy and the poor appear far removed from each other, socially as well as economically (and perhaps in other ways as well), they have the same Maker. Neither the wealthy nor the poor are other than human, which should humble the wealthy (who are inclined to glory in their riches; cf. 18:11) and encourage the poor (who may well be treated as less than human).

On the other hand, the verse also addresses their interaction. The rich should not look down on or despise the poor, nor should the poor envy or despise the wealthy. They will each give an account to the same master for their own attitudes and deeds, and will not be called upon to judge the other (cf., in a different context, Rom. 14:4; Prov. 29:13 closely parallels this verse).

22:3. This verse is identical to 27:12, which precedes a specific example of someone who fails to consider the consequences of a foolish decision.

22:4. These four benefits of humility are listed so that the most important, life and the fear of the LORD, bracket the other two. The thrust of Solomon's exhortations throughout chs. 1–9 is that whoever finds wisdom finds the fear of the LORD (1:29; 2:5) and gains life (3:18, 22; 4:13; 8:35; 9:6). Humility, the willingness to be subject to another, is the beginning of this process.

The need for humility appears in the very beginning of the Book (cf. 1:7; 3:5f), since only the humble respond wisely to teaching and correction (9:7–12). The inevitable outcome of pride and arrogance is disaster (16:18; 29:1), whereas a humble, obedient atti-

5.

5497	8490.151	6379	904, 1932	6583	7060	2552	3638
n fs, ps 3ms	v Qal act ptc ms	n ms	prep, n ms	n mp	n mp	cj, n mp	cj, n ms
נַפְשׁוֹ	שׁוֹמֵר	עִקֵּשׁ	בְּדֶרֶךְ	פַּחִים	צִנִּים	וְחַיִּים	וְכָבוֹד
naphshô	shômēr	'iqqēsh	bedherekh	pachîm	tsinîm	wechayyîm	wekhāvôdh
his life	one who guards	the perverse	in the way of	snares	thorns	and life	and honor

6.

1612	1932	6142, 6552	5470	2699.131	4623	7651.121
cj	n ms, ps 3ms	prep, n ms	prep, art, n ms	v Qal impv 2ms	prep, ps 3mp	v Qal impf 3ms
גַּם	דַּרְכּוֹ	עַל־פִּי	לַנַּעַר	חֲנֹךְ	מֵהֶם	יִרְחָק
gam	dharkô	'al-pî	lanna'ar	chănōkh	mēhem	yirchaq
also	his way	about the edge of	the child	train	from them	he will be far

7.

5090.121	904, 7851	6474	4623	3940, 5681.121	3706, 2290.521
v Qal impf 3ms	prep, n mp	n ms	prep, ps 3fs	neg part, v Qal impf 3ms	cj, v Hiphil impf 3ms
יִמְשׁוֹל	בְּרָשִׁים	עָשִׁיר	מִמֶּנָּה	לֹא־יָסוּר	כִּי־יַזְקִין
yimshôl	berāshîm	'āshîr	mimmennāh	lō'-yāsûr	kî-yazqîn
he will rule	over the poor	the rich	from it	he will not turn aside	when he is old

8.

5983	2319.151	4004.551	3937, 382	4004.151	5860
n fs	v Qal act ptc ms	v Hiphil ptc ms	prep, n ms	v Qal act ptc ms	cj, n ms
עַוְלָה	זֹרֵעַ	מַלְוֶה	לְאִישׁ	לֹוֶה	וְעֶבֶד
'awlāh	zōrēa'	malweh	le'îsh	lôweh	we'evedh
wrongdoing	a sower	a lender	to a man	a borrower	and a slave

9.

2000	3005, 6084	3735.121	5887	8101	7403.121, 201
pers pron	adj, n fs	v Qal impf 3ms	n fs, ps 3ms	cj, n ms	v Qal impf 3ms, n ms
הוּא	טוֹב־עַיִן	יִכְלֶה	עֶבְרָתוֹ	וְשֵׁבֶט	יִקְצוֹר־אָוֶן
hû'	tôv-'ayin	yikhleh	'evrātô	weshēvet	yiqtsôr-'āwen
he	a good eye	it will come to an end	his fury	and the stick of	he will harvest calamity

10.

4086	1691.331	3937, 1859	4623, 4035	3706, 5598.111	1313.421
n ms	v Piel impv 2ms	prep, art, n ms	prep, n ms, ps 3ms	cj, v Qal pf 3ms	v Pual impf 3ms
לֵץ	גָּרֵשׁ	לַדָּל	מִלַּחְמוֹ	כִּי־נָתַן	יְבֹרָךְ
lēts	gārēsh	laddāl	millachmô	kî-nāthan	yevōrākh
a mocker	drive out	to the poor	from his food	because he gives	he will be blessed

5. Thorns and snares are in the way of the froward: he that doth keep his soul shall be far from them: ... whoever values life will stay at a distance, *JB* ... a careful man avoids them, *Moffatt* ... he who would safeguard his life will shun them, *NAB* ... Evil people's lives are like paths covered with thorns and traps. People who guard themselves don't have such problems, *NCV*.

6. Train up a child in the way he should go: and when he is old, he will not depart from it: ... Start a boy on the right road, and even in old age he will not leave it, *NEB* ... Give a lad the training he needs for life, Even when he is old it will stay with him, *Anchor* ... Educate a child according to his life requirements; even when he is old, he will not veer from it, *Berkeley* ... Teach a child how he should live, and he will remember it all his life, *Good News*.

7. The rich ruleth over the poor, and the borrower is servant to the lender: ... rich man dominates the poor, *Anchor* ... borrower is a slave to the lender, *Goodspeed* ... debtor must wait on creditor, *Knox*.

8. He that soweth iniquity shall reap vanity: and the rod of his anger shall fail: ... By planting the seed of evil a man will get in the grain of sorrow, and the rod of his wrath will be broken, *BB* ... He who sows injustice will reap nothing, and the rod of his fury will fail, *Berkeley* ... He that soweth unrighteousness shall reap iniquity, and the rod of his wrath shall have an end, *Darby* ... If you sow injustice, you reap disaster; the rod of your own anger will do you in, *Beck*.

9. He that hath a bountiful eye shall be blessed; for he giveth of his bread to the poor: ... A kindly eye will earn a blessing, such a person shares out food with the poor, *JB* ... For every loaf of bread given to the hungry, blessing shall be the reward of kindly hearts, *Knox* ... generous man will have God's blessing, because he shares his food with poor folk, *Moffatt* ... When he gives of his own food to the needy, *Anchor*.

10. Cast out the scorner, and contention shall go out; yea, strife and reproach shall cease: ... Send away the man of pride, and argument will go out; truly fighting and shame will come to an end, *BB* ... and strife will

tude reaps rewards (15:33 also links the fear of the LORD with honor and humility; cf. Isa. 66:2; Luke 14:11; 18:14; Jam. 4:10). Several proverbs contrast the two attitudes and their fruit (18:12; 29:23).

The paradox is only apparent. A biblical law is that self-exaltation fails (27:1f), because only God can truly exalt (1 Sam. 2:2–10; Ps. 113:7ff; Luke 1:51f). The fame of success is therefore illusory, an occasion to realize the goodness of God rather than an excuse to exult in one's accomplishments.

22:5. Trouble can be avoided by guarding one's heart (4:23). This proverb implies that those who practice deceit (the "crooked") are blinded by their own way of thinking and so cannot avoid either the troubles of life or the problems created by others. Other verses also contrast the well-being of the wise with the trouble that accompanies wickedness (cf. 14:16; 15:19; 16:17; 22:3; 27:12).

22:6. Although the meaning of the second line of this verse is clear, the first line contains three difficulties: (1) elsewhere in Scripture the verb translated "train [up]" (HED #2699) in most English versions refers only to dedicating a building (1 Ki. 8:63; cf. 2 Chr. 7:5), or using it for the first time (Deut. 20:5); (2) the word rendered "child[ren]" (HED #5470) in most English versions generally refers to social status rather than to age; and (3) the phrase "in the way he should go" (KJV, NASB, NKJV, NIV) or "in the right way" (NRSV) is literally, "according to his way."

Although some think that "his" refers to God (cf. the references to the LORD in 21:30f; 22:2, 4), its nearest, and most obvious, referent is the upper class "youth" whose training is addressed by Proverbs in general (see "Overview"). Nor does Proverbs encourage the interpretation of "way" as personal aptitude (i.e., the most personally appropriate way for that individual). The Book focuses on submission to the LORD and wisdom's way and warns against discovering one's own way (cf. 18:1).

The biblical and extra-biblical use of Hebrew na'ar (HED #5470) suggests that it refers primarily to social standing, that is, to members of the upper class who are beginning or about to enter into their majority or appointed role in life (cf. Gen. 37:2; 1 Ki. 3:7). This, together with the verb's overtones of initiation and "his way" as the aspect of life which one is about to enter, suggests that the verse originally exhorted parents or teachers to celebrate the occasion of a young man's initiation into his full station in life.

Spending time, effort and energy to celebrate such a step implies its importance and worth, and would encourage the young to maintain themselves in their new status. (See Ted Hildebrandt, "Proverbs 22:6a: Train Up a Child?" *Grace Theological Journal* 9/1 (1988): 3–19, and other literature cited in his article.)

22:7. Let the borrower beware—he puts himself in the power of the lender. This proverb reveals a simple truth: the borrower works for the lender, not for himself. Since there were no banks in ancient Israel, borrowing was a personal affair arranged between individuals or families. With relatively few covenantal constraints upon lenders (cf. Exo. 22:25ff; Lev. 25:36f; Deut. 23:19f), a borrower needed to consider carefully whether a particular lender might prove benevolent or tyrannical, even to the point of requiring him to sell his family or himself into slavery to repay the loan (Exo. 21:2–7). Those in a position to lend money must also understand their relationship to their borrowers in light of the covenantal stipulations (cf. 19:17).

22:8. Only what is sown can be reaped. The second line is difficult, but seems to refer to the rod that expresses the anger of the one who sows wickedness—the means by which he expresses his anger. If this is correct, then the verse warns the wicked that not only will their wickedness bring them to grief, but they will eventually lose the ability to injure others. It would then also comfort the righteous that the wicked shall not always be oppressive. A verse between 22:8 and 22:9 in the Septuagint, but not the Hebrew text (22:8a) is the apparent source of 2 Cor. 9:7.

22:9. The "good eye" is generous, as the parallel line shows. Generosity is rewarded by being blessed, both by God (19:17) and by the objects of its charity. This "giving" should not be contrasted with the one who sells grain (14:26), although this verse may describe the greater generosity ("some of his food"). Both are contrasted, implicitly or explicitly, with those who refuse to share with those in need. Generosity is encouraged throughout Scripture. It grows out of understanding the person and nature of God and depending upon Him. The source of confidence is not what one has accumulated, but the foundation of one's trust (cf. Matt. 6:19–34).

22:10. Mockery alienates friends and destroys relationships, especially since it is often malevolent.

11.

154.151	7320	1835	8139.121	4209	3428.121
v Qal act ptc ms	cj, n ms	n ms	cj, v Qal impf 3ms	n ms	cj, v Qal impf 3ms
אֹהֵב	וְקָלוֹן	דִין	וְיִשְׁבֹּת	מָדוֹן	וְיֵצֵא
'ōhēv	weqālôn	dîn	weyishbōt	mādhôn	weyētsē'
one who loves	and disgrace	condemnation	and it will cease	strife	that it may go out

12.

5526.116	3176	6084	4567	7739	8004	2682	2999, 3949
v Qal pf 3cp	pn	n fd	n ms	n ms, ps 3ms	n fd, ps 3ms	n ms	adj, n ms
נָצְרוּ	יְהוָה	עֵינֵי	מֶלֶךְ	רֵעֵהוּ	שְׂפָתָיו	חֵן	טְהָר־לֵב
nātserû	yehwāh	'ênê	melekh	rē'ēhû	sephāthāv	chēn	tehôr-lēv
they preserve	Yahweh	the eyes of	the king	his friend	his lips	grace	pure of heart

13.

6339	569.111	931.151	1745	5751.321	1907
n ms	v Qal pf 3ms	v Qal act ptc ms	n mp	cj, v Piel impf 3ms	n fs
עָצֵל	אָמַר	בֹגֵד	דִּבְרֵי	וַיְסַלֵּף	דָעַת
'ātsēl	'āmar	vōghēdh	divrê	waysallēph	dhā'ath
a sluggard	he will say	one who acts treacherously	the words of	but He ruins	knowledge

14.

6230	8192	7815.225	7624	904, 8761	904, 2445	761
adj	n fs	v Niphal impf 1cs	n fp	prep, n ms	prep, art, n ms	n ms
עֲמֻקָּה	שׁוּחָה	אֶרְצֵחַ	רְחֹבוֹת	בְּתוֹךְ	בַּחוּץ	אֲרִי
'āmuqqāh	shûchāh	'ērātsēach	rechōvôth	bethôkh	vachûts	'ărî
deep	a pitfall	I will be killed	the open squares	in the middle of	in the street	a lion

5489.121, 8427	3176	2278.155	2299	6552
v Qal impf 3ms, adv	pn	v Qal pass ptc ms	n fp	n ms
יִפּוֹל־שָׁם	יְהוָה	זְעוּם	זָרוֹת	פִּי
yippôl-shām	yehwāh	ze'ûm	zārôth	pî
he will fall there	Yahweh	one who has been cursed by	foreign women	the mouth of

15.

4284	8101	904, 3949, 5470	7489.157	198
n ms	n ms	prep, n ms, n ms	v Qal pass ptc fs	n fs
מוּסָר	שֵׁבֶט	בְּלֶב־נָעַר	קְשׁוּרָה	אִוֶּלֶת
mûsār	shēvet	velev-nā'ar	qōshûrāh	'iwweleth
discipline	the rod of	on the heart of a child	being bound	foolishness

16.

3937, 7528.541	1859	6479.151	4623	7651.521
prep, v Hiphil inf con	n ms	v Qal act ptc ms	prep, ps 3ms	v Hiphil impf 3ms, ps 3fs
לְהַרְבּוֹת	דָּל	עֹשֵׁק	מִמֶּנּוּ	יַרְחִיקֶנָּה
leharbôth	dāl	'ōshēq	mimmennû	yarchîqennāh
to make abundant	the poor	one who oppresses	from him	it will cause it to be far

go out, and contention and abuse will cease, *Berkeley* ... and quarreling will leave; disputing and abusing each other will cease, *Beck* ... discord will vanish; Strife and insult will cease, *Goodspeed*.

11. He that loveth pureness of heart, for the grace of his lips the king shall be his friend: ... the man of winning speech has the king for his friend, *NAB* ... Whoever loves pure thoughts and kind words will have even the king as a friend, *NCV* ... [The Lord] loves a man of pure mind; Gracious speech wins the friendship of a king, *Anchor* ... He who values grace and truth is the king's friend, *LIVB*.

12. The eyes of the LORD preserve knowledge, and he overthroweth the words of the transgressor: ... eyes of the Lord keep knowledge, but by him the acts of the false man will be overturned, *BB* ... eyes of the LORD protect knowledge, and He turns aside the words of the treacherous, *Berkeley* ... eyes of the Lord watch over knowledge, And he contradicts the words of a deceiver, *Anchor* ... LORD's eyes are watching over knowledge, but He overturns those who talk disloyally, *Beck*.

13. The slothful man saith, There is a lion without, I shall be slain in the streets: ... In the streets I shall be killed!, *Anchor* ... hater of work says, There is a lion outside: I will be put to death in the streets, *BB* ... sluggard says, "There is a lion outside, *Berkeley* ... lazy person says, *Beck* ... I am sure to be killed in the streets!, *Fenton*.

14. The mouth of strange women is a deep pit: he that is abhorred of

the LORD shall fall therein: ... mouth of adulterous women is a deep pit; anyone with whom the LORD is angry will fall into it, *Beck* ... Adultery is a trap—it catches those with whom the LORD is angry, *Good News* ... wiles of a loose woman are a deep, deep pit, *Moffatt* ... He who is cursed of the LORD will fall into it, *NASB* ... words of an unfaithful wife are like a deep trap. Those who make the LORD angry will get caught by them, *NCV*.

15. Foolishness is bound in the heart of a child; but the rod of correction shall drive it far from him: ... Every child is full of foolishness, but punishment can get rid of it, *NCV* ... Folly is deep-rooted in the heart of a boy; a good beating will drive it right out of him, *NEB* ... Willful ignorance is ingrained in the mind of a boy, [Only] the teacher's cane will rid him of it, *Anchor* ... the rod of discipline will drive it far from him, *NIV* ... a rod to chastise him will rid him of it, *Beck*.

16. He that oppresseth the poor to increase his riches, and he that giveth to the rich, shall surely come to want: ... He who is cruel to the poor for the purpose of increasing his profit, and he who gives to the man of wealth, will only come to be in need, *BB* ... He who crushes the poor to gain for himself, and he who gives to the rich, shall surely come to poverty, *KJVII* ... Whoever gets rich by mistreating the poor, and gives presents to the wealthy, will become poor, *NCV*.

The only cure is to root it out. Better to have peace without whatever the scornful person brings to the relationship, than to have those benefits but ruined fellowship (26:20ff). The three terms are pleonastic, not a list of different types of action (mādhôn and dîn share the same root).

The nature of relationships is a major proverbial concern. This is one of the few directive or imperatival proverbs (cf. 22:24f). The same thought probably underlies 26:18f.

22:11. A word-by-word translation reveals this verse's difficulty: "One who loves [the] pure of heart, [the] grace of his lips—the king is his friend." The Septuagint reads "The LORD loves holy hearts, acceptable to him are all the blameless; [the] king rules with [his] lips." The original text of this verse seems beyond recovery.

Although there is little agreement among commentators, the general sense may parallel Prov. 16:13 and commend honest and gracious speech as the best policy in court and, by implication, throughout life. This understanding of the verse is at least consonant with other verses that commend gracious and truthful words (cf. 15:1), but it is at best only a probable interpretation.

22:12. Reflecting the prologue's repeated promise that wisdom, knowledge, etc. will protect and rescue the wise (cf. 2:7f, 12), this saying also warns that God is omniscient (15:3) and not only preserves the righteous, but executes judgment upon the wicked—specifically, the treacherous—by overthrowing and ruining the plans by which they hope to overthrow the upright.

22:13. This verse parallels 26:13, but here the sluggard explains his excuse instead of repeating it. Any excuse, no matter how ridiculous, serves his purpose (to avoid doing what is necessary). The irony is that laziness impoverishes and ultimately

destroys itself (10:4; 20:4; 21:25f)—a lion is not necessary.

22:14. The opening chapters repeatedly warn against the seductively flattering words of the strange woman (2:16; 5:3; 6:24; 7:5, 13–21), which are here likened to a "deep pit" (23:27 calls the prostitute herself a deep pit). This verse warns that sexual licentiousness, which appears to be purely self-indulgent, is actually a judgment of God upon those who are under his curse (cf. Rom. 1:24). Those who are tempted to toy with such sins (or any sin) are hereby warned.

22:15. Whether "folly" refers primarily to a heart that is naive (inexperienced) or rebellious, it is endemic to human beings, including children. The only antidote or corrective is discipline wisely administered (cf. 25:12) out of love and concern for his or her ultimate well-being (cf. 19:18). Since not all children are equally rebellious or contentious, however, parents need discretion to discipline each as best fits the child and the situation. "Rod" does not refer only to corporal punishment, but is a metonymy for any form of discipline.

22:16. Taking advantage of the weakness of the poor in order to aggrandize or enrich oneself, and giving generously to the rich for the same purpose are both wrong and will fail (cf. 14:24, which ends with the same expression). This failure is not because this behavior is not good business sense, but because it violates the standards of the Covenant and sets a course against that required by God (Deut. 15:7–11; cf. Prov. 22:22f).

22:17–24:22. On the translation of "the words of the wise" (22:17; e.g., NRSV) as a title, and the relationship of this section of Proverbs to the Wisdom of Amenemope see the "Overview."

This section of the Book presents another type of saying, different from both the extended wisdom

| 238
n fs, ps 2ms
אָזְנֶךָ
'oznekha
your ear | 5371.531
v Hiphil impv 2ms
הַט
hat
incline | **17.** | 395, 3937, 4408
adv, prep, n ms
אַךְ־לְמַחְסוֹר
'akh-lemachsôr
only to poverty | 3937, 6474
prep, n ms
לְעָשִׁיר
le'āshîr
to the rich | 5598.151
v Qal act ptc ms
נֹתֵן
nōthēn
giving | 3937
prep, ps 3ms
לוֹ
lô
for himself |

| 3937, 1907
prep, n fs, ps 1cs
לְדַעְתִּי
ledha'attî
to my knowledge | 8308.123
v Qal impf 2ms
תָּשִׁית
tāshîth
you should set | 3949
cj, n ms, ps 2ms
וְלִבְּךָ
welibbekha
and your heart | 2550
n mp
חֲכָמִים
chākhāmîm
the wise | 1745
n mp
דִּבְרֵי
divrê
the words of | 8471.131
cj, v Qal impv 2ms
וּשְׁמַע
ûshema'
and listen to |

| **18.** | 3706, 5456
cj, adj
כִּי־נָעִים
kî-nā'îm
because pleasant | 3706, 8490.123
cj, v Qal impf 2ms, ps 3mp
כִּי־תִשְׁמְרֵם
kî-thishmerēm
when you are observing them | 904, 1027
prep, n fs, ps 2ms
בְּבִטְנֶךָ
bevitnekha
in your inmost part | 3679.226
v Niphal impf 3mp
יִכֹּנוּ
yikkōnû
they will be established |

| 3267
adv
יַחְדָּו
yachdāw
together | 6142, 8004
prep, n fd, ps 2ms
עַל־שְׂפָתֶיךָ
'al-sephāthêkha
on your lips | **19.** | 3937, 2030.141
prep, v Qal inf con
לִהְיוֹת
lihyôth
to be | 904, 3176
prep, pn
בַּיהוָה
bayhwāh
in Yahweh | 4148
n ms, ps 2ms
מִבְטַחֶךָ
mivtachekha
your trust | 3156.515
v Hiphil pf 1cs, ps 2ms
הוֹדַעְתִּיךָ
hôdha'attîkha
I have made known to you |

| 3219
art, n ms
הַיּוֹם
hayyôm
today | 652, 887
cj, pers pron
אַף־אָתָּה
'aph-'āttāh
indeed you | **20.** | 1950B, 3940
intrg part, neg part
הֲלֹא
hălō'
have not | 3918.115
v Qal pf 1cs
כָּתַבְתִּי
khāthavtî
I have written | 3937
prep, ps 2ms
לְךָ
lekha
for you | 8425
adv
שִׁלְשׁוֹם
shilshôm
three days ago | 904, 4292
prep, n fp
בְּמוֹעֵצוֹת
bemô'ētsôth
with counsel |

| 1907
cj, n fs
וְדַעַת
wādha'ath
and knowledge | **21.** | 3937, 3156.541
prep, v Hiphil inf con, ps 2ms
לְהוֹדִיעֲךָ
lehôdhî'ăkha
to cause you to know | 7485
n ms
קֹשְׁט
qōsht
truth | 571
n mp
אִמְרֵי
'imrê
sayings of | 583
n fs
אֱמֶת
'emeth
reliability | 3937, 8178.541
prep, v Hiphil inf con
לְהָשִׁיב
lehāshîv
to bring back |

| 571
n mp
אֲמָרִים
'ămārîm
sayings | 583
n fs
אֱמֶת
'emeth
reliability | 3937, 8365.152
prep, v Qal act ptc mp, ps 2ms
לְשֹׁלְחֶיךָ
leshōlechêkha
to those sending you | **22.** | 414, 1528.123, 1859
adv, v Qal juss 2ms, n ms
אַל־תִּגְזָל־דָּל
'al-tighzāl-dāl
do not rob the poor | 3706
cj
כִּי
kî
because | 1859, 2000
adj, pers pron
דַל־הוּא
dhal-hû'
poor he |

17. Bow down thine ear, and hear the words of the wise, and apply thine heart unto my knowledge: ... Incline your ear and hear my words, And apply your mind to my learning, *Anchor* ... Attend, and hear the words of the wise, And apply your heart to My teachings, *Fenton* ... Wouldst thou but give heed, and listen to wise counsels, take these my warnings to heart!, *Knox* ... and apply your heart to my doctrine, *NAB*.

18. For it is a pleasant thing if thou keep them within thee; they shall withal be fitted in thy lips: ... It will be good to keep these things in mind so that you are ready to repeat them, *NCV* ... to keep them in your heart will be a pleasure, and then you will always have them ready on your lips, *NEB* ... For it will be a delight to cherish within you, *Anchor* ... Let them all be fixed upon your lips, *NKJV*.

19. That thy trust may be in the LORD, I have made known to thee this day, even to thee: ... So that your faith may be in the Lord, I have made them clear to you this day, even to you, *BB* ... That thy confidence may be in, *Darby* ... it is you whom I wish to instruct today, *JB* ... I have informed you this day, even you, *Berkeley* ... Words of life I teach you this day, That your trust may be in the LORD, *Goodspeed*.

20. Have not I written to thee excellent things in counsels and knowledge: ... Didn't I write you formerly with advice and knowledge, *Beck* ... Not once nor twice have I warned thee and instructed thee, *Knox* ... I have written thirty sayings for you, which give knowledge and good advice, *NCV* ... thirty sayings, with wise suggestions and knowledge, *BB*.

21. That I might make thee know the certainty of the words of truth; that thou mightest answer the words of truth to them that send unto thee?: ... To make you see how certain are true words, so that you may give a true answer to those who put questions to you?, *BB* ... to teach you the very words of truth, so you can give a true report to him who

sent you?, *Beck* ... and will teach you what the truth really is. Then when you are sent to find it out, you will bring back the right answer, *Good News* ... To acquaint you with the reality of true words, That you may bring back a true report, *Goodspeed*.

22. Rob not the poor, because he is poor: neither oppress the afflicted

in the gate: ... Do not despoil the weak, for he is weak, and do not oppress the poor at the gate, *JB* ... Never rob a helpless man because he is helpless, *NEB* ... Do not take advantage of the helpless poor man, *Anchor* ... Do not abuse poor people because they are poor, *NCV* ... And crush not the needy in the gate, *Goodspeed*.

---

poems of Prov. 1–9 and the two-line proverbs of Prov. 10:1–22:16. The sayings in these chapters are generally two or three verses long; there are also two longer poems (23:29–35; 24:30–34). Another difference is their nature—most of these sayings are hortatory, beginning with a prohibition, followed by an argument, reason or motive (cf. 22:22f, 24f, 26f; 23:26ff; 24:1f, 11f). Positive commands reflect those of the prologue, commanding attention to the teacher's instruction (cf. 22:17; 23:17b, 19, 22f, 26). Relatively few are the sort of observations that typify Prov. 10:1–22:16 (e.g., 24:7, 8ff).

These verses warn against, for example, injustice (22:22f, 28; 23:10ff; 24:11f, 15f, 23–26, 28f), immoderate living (23:19ff, 29–35), sexual immorality (23:26ff), response to the wicked (23:1ff, 6ff, 17f; 24:1f, 10, 17–22) and laziness (22:29; 24:30–34)—all topics addressed in the rest of the Book.

***22:17–21.** Much like many of the hortatory introductions of the prologue (e.g., 1:8f; 3:1f; 4:1–4, 10f, 20f), this larger section (22:17–24:34) opens with a call to attention that equates the teacher's words with the teachings of "the wise" (22:17–21). The motive given in these verses is that the son or student will trust the LORD (22:19a) and know how to speak truthfully and wisely (22:18b, 21b). The main difference between this summons and those in the prologue is that this one is followed by individual sayings rather than an extended wisdom poem, and its motive statements are positive, rather than promises of protection.*

22:17–18. These verses call for attention ("incline," "listen") and internalization of the father's teaching, and commend it as "pleasant" (the plural nāʿîm [HED #5456] encompasses both his "words" [v. 17a] and his "knowledge" [v. 17b]). They are not pleasing until they have been internalized, that is, made part of his way of thinking. Once this has happened, however, they are ready to be used (v. 18b). These verses thus outline three stages of wise living:

listening (v. 17a), learning (vv. 17b–18a) and using (v. 18b). The third stage—speaking wisely and truthfully (v. 18b; cf. v. 21)—is the reason for both listening and learning, and grows out of the trust in the LORD that results from this knowledge.

22:19. Although a word-for-word rendering of the second line of this verse makes sense—"I teach you today, even you"—it is in fact problematic, since the pronoun that ends the verse is used only to indicate the subject of a verb, not its object. The Septuagint apparently read a different Hebrew text: "I will teach you your [or 'his'] way." Despite this difficulty, the verse offers another motivation for the exhortations of v. 17—that the son's trust may have its proper object in the LORD and his wisdom, rather than in his own understanding (3:5f).

22:20. The translation "thirty" reflects the thirty "houses" of the Wisdom of Amenemope, which are supposedly paralleled by thirty "words of the wise" in 22:17–24:34 (see the "Overview"). The external parallelism with "today" (22:19b), however, suggests that "formerly" (22:20a) is the correct reading of the text, and the point is that the teacher's instruction is and has been consistent. The almost incidental mention of written instruction reveals that reading and perhaps writing were part of the training.

22:21. The rare word for truth, qōsht (HED #7485; used only here in Biblical Hebrew), is apparently explained by "sayings of truth," just as the "words" of the second line are explained by "truth." The purpose of his teaching (v. 20) was that the youth might know what was true. The result of knowing and understanding the truth (v. 21a) is the ability to discern and apply it at the appropriate time (v. 21b). The process outlined in 22:17f is thus reiterated at the end of this introductory section, leaving the greater purpose, to encourage his trust in the LORD (v. 20), as the focus of the text.

22:22–23. The terms "gate" (v. 22) and "plead" (v. 23) reveal that this saying refers pri-

23.

7662.121	3706, 3176		904, 8554	6270	414, 1850.323
v Qal impf 3ms	cj, pn		prep, art, n ms	n ms	adv, v Piel juss 2ms
יָרִיב	כִּי־יְהוָה	**23.**	בַשַּׁעַר	עָנִי	וְאַל־תְּדַכֵּא
yārîv	kî-yehwāh		vashshā'ar	'ānî	we'al-tedhakkē'
He will plead the case	because Yahweh		in the gate	the afflicted	and do not crush

414, 7749.723	5497	881, 7190.152	7190.111	7663
adv, v Hithpael juss 2ms	n fs	do, v Qal act ptc mp, ps 3mp	cj, v Qal pf 3ms	n ms, ps 3mp
אַל־תִּתְרַע	נָפֶשׁ	אֶת־קֹבְעֵיהֶם	וְקָבַע	רִיבָם
'al-tithra'	nāphesh	'eth-qōve'êhem	weqāva'	rîvām
do not become friends	life	those who snatch from them	and He will snatch	their lawsuit

24.

971.123	3940	2635	882, 382	653	882, 1196
v Qal impf 2ms	neg part	n fp	cj, prep, n ms	n ms	prep, n ms
תָבוֹא	לֹא	חֵמוֹת	וְאֶת־אִישׁ	אַף	אֶת־בַּעַל
thāvô'	lō'	chēmôth	we'eth-'îsh	'āph	'eth-ba'al
you should go	not	wrath	or with a man of	anger	with an owner of

25.

4305	4089.113	758	6678, 509.123	
n ms	cj, v Qal pf 2ms	n ms, ps 3ms	adv, v Qal impf 2ms	
מוֹקֵשׁ	וְלָקַחְתָּ	אֹרְחֹתוֹ	פֶּן־תֶּאֱלַף	**25.**
môqēsh	welāqachtā	'ārechāthô	pen-te'ĕlaph	
a snare	for you will receive	his pathway	so that you do not become familiar with	

26.

904, 6386.152	904, 8965.152, 3834	414, 2030.123	3937, 5497
prep, art, v Qal act ptc mp	prep, v Qal act ptc mp, n fs	adv, v Qal juss 2ms	prep, n fs, ps 2ms
בַּעֹרְבִים	בְתֹקְעֵי־כָף	אַל־תְּהִי	לְנַפְשֶׁךָ
ba'ōrevîm	vethōqe'ê-khāph	'al-tehî	lenaphshekhā
with those who gives surety for	with those who strike palms	do not be	for your soul

27.

5085	4089.121	4066	3937, 8396.341	524, 375, 3937	5044
n ms, ps 2ms	v Qal impf 3ms	intrg	prep, v Piel inf con	cj, sub, prep, ps 2ms	n fp
מִשְׁכָּבְךָ	יִקַּח	לָמָּה	לְשַׁלֵּם	אִם־אֵין־לְךָ	מַשָּׁאוֹת
mishkāvekhā	yiqqach	lāmmāh	leshallēm	'im-'ên-lekhā	mashshā'ôth
your bed	should he take	why	to pay	if there is not to you	debts

28.

6449.116	866	5986	1397	414, 5657.523	4623, 8809
v Qal pf 3cp	rel part	n ms	n ms	adv, v Hiphil juss 2ms	prep, prep, ps 2ms
עָשׂוּ	אֲשֶׁר	עוֹלָם	גְּבוּל	אַל־תַּסֵּג	מִתַּחְתֶּיךָ
'āsû	'asher	'ôlām	gevûl	'al-tassēgh	mittachtêkhā
they put	which	ancient times	the boundary of	do not deviate	from beneath you

---

23. For the LORD will plead their cause, and spoil the soul of those that spoiled them: ... the Lord will take up their cause, And will rob those who rob them of life, *Anchor* ... Lord will give support to their cause, *BB* ... and strip the soul of those who plunder them, *KJVII* ... The LORD will argue their case for them and threaten the life of anyone who threatens theirs, *Good News* ... For the Lord is their defender. If you injure them he will punish you, *LIVB*.

24. Make no friendship with an angry man; and with a furious man thou shalt not go: ... Never join any man who gets angry, never deal with a hot-tempered man, *Moffatt* ... Be not friendly with a hotheaded man, nor the companion of a wrathful man, *NAB* ... Don't make friends with quick-tempered people or spend time with those who have bad tempers, *NCV* ... Nor accompany one given to violent outbursts, *Anchor*.

25. Lest thou learn his ways, and get a snare to thy soul: ... For fear of learning his ways and making a net ready for your soul, *BB* ... For fear you should copy his paths, And acquire a risk for your mind, *Fenton* ... for fear you learn such behaviour, *JB* ... and get yourself into a trap, *Beck* ... You might learn their habits and not be able to change, *Good News*.

26. Be not thou one of them that strike hands, or of them that are sureties for debts: ... Be not one of those who pledge themselves, Of those who become surety, *Goodspeed* ... Leave it to others to engage themselves, and go bail for their neighbour's debts, *Knox* ... Don't promise to pay what someone else owes, and don't guarantee anyone's loan, *NCV* ... Never be one to give guarantees, or to pledge yourself as surety for another, *REB*.

27. If thou hast nothing to pay, why should he take away thy bed from under thee?: ... if you do not have the means to pay, why should your bed be taken, *Berkeley* ... If you cannot pay the loan, your own bed may be taken right out from under you, *NCV* ...

Why risk everything you own? They'll even take your bed!, *LIVB*.

28. Remove not the ancient landmark, which thy fathers have set: ... Do not move the ancient boundary-stone which your forefathers set up, *NEB* ... Do not move back an ancient boundary line Which your ancestors established, *Anchor* ... Let not the old landmark be moved

which your fathers have put in place, *BB* ... Don't move an old stone that marks a border, because those stones were set up by your ancestors, *NCV*.

29. Seest thou a man diligent in his business? he shall stand before kings; he shall not stand before mean men: ... Do you see people skilled in their work? They will

---

marily to legal justice, when the poor were especially vulnerable (cf. the condemnation of bribes in, e.g., 28:21). The second clause of v. 22 could either warn against taking advantage of someone else's poverty ("Do not rob the poor because he is poor"), or mean that his very poverty is the reason for not taking advantage of him ("Do not rob the poor, since he *is* poor"). The explanation or motive for the command is the warning that the poor have a Defender Who will both protect them and execute judgment upon the offender (cf. 23:10f). Since the gate is one of the places in which wisdom stands ready to teach all who will listen (1:21; 8:3), justice is a primary concern of wisdom, not merely legal niceties.

22:24–25. Like other proverbs that address friendship, these verses warn that we become like our friends. Familiarity can breed complacency, so that what may have repelled us at first becomes increasingly acceptable and eventually characterizes us as well. In this case, the warning is that we will not only begin to share their behavior, but also the problems that result from it.

The proverbs repeatedly condemn anger as a sign of folly. This saying shows that it is also a source of trouble. Since behavior reveals the state of the heart, and because attitudes are often assimilated unconsciously, we need friends who will strengthen, not inhibit, our righteousness.

22:26–27. Other references to co-signing agreements explain that this is foolish (17:18), urging all who have done so to escape the trap that they are in (6:1–5), maintaining that one aspect of a secure life is to avoid co-signing (11:15). This couplet explains the danger, that is, loss of possessions.

The first verse does not warn against associating with those who co-sign loans as much as it cautions against actually doing it. The following verse explains the prohibition: if the person for whom you have co-signed defaults, then you are

liable. If you have no money with which to repay the loan, then the loan agent will take your property in satisfaction. In other words, the co-signer pledges his or her guarantee that the loan will be repaid. But life is uncertain, and who can know whether they will have the money at hand when the time comes. They thus endanger their property and perhaps their well-being and that of their family. Thus the urgency with which Solomon presses the co-signer to escape (6:1–5).

22:28. Because the land was the LORD's and the Israelites were merely his tenants (Lev. 25:23), it was his to apportion (cf. Josh. 14–21). To steal someone's property was thus to reject God's lordship, his right to use the land as He wished. In an agrarian society, the ability to feed one's family (to survive) might depend on the produce from an acre or so of cultivable land. Moving a boundary marker stole not only property, but crops. This loss could well ruin the life of the small farmer.

In a land without obvious property lines, such as windbreaks, hedges or fences, permanent objects (probably stones) were used to mark boundaries. The prohibition against changing boundaries is found in Mesopotamian law codes, along with strict punishments for breaking the law.

This prohibition is unusual in that it is not supported by a motive statement (cf. the preceding verses). Other proverbs warn that the helpless will be defended by God (cf. 15:25; 23:10f), a warning based on the commandment (Exo. 20:15), and echoed in the Psalms (Pss. 68:5; 146:9). The Covenant cursed anyone who moved a boundary marker (Deut. 19:14; 27:17), a curse reiterated by Hosea (Hos. 5:10).

The proverb also contains an implicit argument against changing boundary markers. Those who had inherited, not established, the "ancient" boundaries had no right to change what their ancestors had set up.

| 1
n mp, ps 2ms
אֲבוֹתֶיךָ
'ăvôthêkhā
your ancestors | 29. | 2463.113
v Qal pf 2ms
חָזִיתָ
chāzîthā
you have beheld | 382
n ms
אִישׁ
'îsh
a man | 4248
adj
מָהִיר
māhîr
skillful | 904, 4536
prep, n fs, ps 3ms
בִּמְלַאכְתּוֹ
bimla'khtô
in his work | 3937, 6686, 4567
prep, n mp, n mp
לִפְנֵי־מְלָכִים
liphnê-melākhîm
before kings |

| 3429.721
v Hithpael impf 3ms
יִתְיַצָּב
yithyatstsāv
he will take his position | 1118, 3429.723
neg part, v Hithpael impf 3ms
בַּל־יִתְיַצֵּב
bal-yithyatstsêv
he will not take his position | 3937, 6686
prep, n mp
לִפְנֵי
liphnê
before | 2933
n mp
חֲשֻׁכִּים
chăshukkîm
obscure men |

| 23:1 | 3706, 3553.123
cj, v Qal impf 2ms
כִּי־תֵשֵׁב
kî-thêshêv
when you are sitting | 3937, 4033.141
prep, v Qal inf con
לִלְחוֹם
lilchôm
to eat | 882, 5090.151
prep, v Qal act ptc ms
אֶת־מוֹשֵׁל
'eth-môshêl
with a ruler | 1032.142
v Qal inf abs
בִּין
bîn
discerning | 1032.123
v Qal impf 2ms
תָּבִין
tāvîn
you must carefully discern |

| 881, 866
do, rel pron
אֶת־אֲשֶׁר
'eth-'ăsher
who | 3937, 6686
prep, n mp, ps 2ms
לְפָנֶיךָ
lephānêkhā
before you | 2. | 7947.113
cj, v Qal pf 2ms
וְשַׂמְתָּ
wesamtā
and you must put | 7956
n ms
שַׂכִּין
sakkîn
a dagger | 904, 4072
prep, n ms, ps 2ms
בְּלֹעֶךָ
belō'ekhā
on your throat |

| 524, 1196
cj, n ms
אִם־בַּעַל
'im-ba'al
if a master of | 5497
n fs
נֶפֶשׁ
nephesh
an appetite | 887
pers pron
אָתָּה
'āttāh
you | 3. | 414, 181.723
adv, v Hithpael juss 2ms
אַל־תִּתְאָו
'al-tith'āw
do not desire | 3937, 4440
prep, n mp, ps 3ms
לְמַטְעַמּוֹתָיו
lematammôthâv
his delicacies | 2000
cj, pers pron
וְהוּא
wehû'
for it |

| 4035
n ms
לֶחֶם
lechem
food of | 3695
n mp
כְּזָבִים
kezāvîm
lies | 4. | 414, 3129.123
adv, v Qal juss 2ms
אַל־תִּיגַע
'al-tîga'
do not become weary | 3937, 6483.541
prep, v Hiphil inf con
לְהַעֲשִׁיר
leha'ăshîr
to get rich | 4623, 1035
prep, n fs, ps 2ms
מִבִּינָתְךָ
mibbînāthekhā
from your discernment | 2403.141
v Qal inf con
חֲדָל
chădhāl
to forego |

| 5. | 1950B, 5990.522
intrg part, v Hiphil impf 3fs
הֲתָעוּף
hăthā'ûph
will they fly | 6084
n fd, ps 2ms
עֵינֶיךָ
'ênêkhā
your eyes | 904, ps 3ms
בּוֹ
bô
over it | 375
cj, sub, ps 3ms
וְאֵינֶנּוּ
we'ênennû
then it is not | 3706
cj
כִּי
kî
because | 6449.142
v Qal inf abs
עָשֹׂה
'āsōh
making |

| 6449.121, 3937
v Qal impf 3ms, prep, ps 3ms
יַעֲשֶׂה־לּוֹ
ya'ăseh-lô
it will certainly make for itself | 3796
n fd
כְּנָפַיִם
khenāphayim
wings | 3626, 5585
prep, n ms
כְּנֶשֶׁר
kenesher
like an eagle | 5990.111
cj, v Qal pf 3ms
וְעָיֵף
we'āyêph
and it will fly away | 8452
art, n md
הַשָּׁמָיִם
hashshāmāyim
the heavens |

work for kings, not for ordinary people, *NCV* ... You see a man skilful at his craft: he will serve kings, he will not serve common men, *NEB* ... Have you seen a man who is expert in his business? he will take his place before kings; his place will not be among low persons, *BB* ... he shall not stand before the undistinguished, *Berkeley*.

23:1. When thou sittest to eat with a ruler, consider diligently what is before thee: ... give thought with care to what is before you, *BB* ... pay close attention to what is set before you, *Beck* ... be careful how you eat, *Moffatt*.

2. And put a knife to thy throat, if thou be a man given to appetite: ...

Control yourself if you have a big appetite, *NCV* ... if you are given to gluttony, *NIV* ... if you are a man of hearty appetite, *Anchor* ... if you have a strong desire for food, *BB* ... If you're a big eater, *Beck*.

3. Be not desirous of his dainties: for they are deceitful meat: ... Don't go on craving his delicacies.

This is a food that deceives you, *Beck* ... Don't be greedy for the fine food he serves, *Good News* ... they are bait to lure thee, *Knox* ... Have no desire for his delicate food, for it is the bread of deceit, *BB*.

4. Labour not to be rich: cease from thine own wisdom: ... Take no care to get wealth; let there be an end to your desire for money, *BB* ... Do not wear yourself out in pursuit of wealth, No longer let your thoughts dwell on it, *Anchor* ... Don't wear yourself out to get rich. Be smart enough to stop, *Beck* ... surrender that personal ambition, *Berkeley* ... stop applying your mind to this, *JB*.

5. Wilt thou set thine eyes upon that which is not? for riches certainly make themselves wings; they fly away as an eagle toward heaven: ... Fix your gaze on it, and it is there no longer, for it is able to sprout wings like an eagle that flies off to the sky, *JB* ... Wealth can vanish in the wink of an eye. It can seem to grow wings and fly away like an eagle, *NCV* ... Before you can look round, it will be gone; it will surely grow wings like an eagle, *NEB* ... For riches can disappear as though they had the wings of a bird!, *LIVB*.

22:29. The phrase "You see" is not a question in Hebrew. Rather, it sets off the subject (a skillful person) in order to focus attention on what is said about him (cf. 29:20) and to encourage the reader to think of someone who stands out for his or her ability. Excellence has rewards, one of which is to be recognized by the most important members of society (and who could also best reward quality).

Whether applied to working in metals (1 Ki. 7:13f), political expertise (2 Sam. 16:20–17:4) or anything else, skill is the result of practice under the oversight of someone who is already accomplished at that skill, trade or profession. Wisdom recognizes someone else's expertise, is humble to see its own need, and is then willing to submit to being taught so that it can gain that skill. Mastery, however, comes only through tutored diligence. Dabbling in many areas may be recreational, but it cannot lead to excellence, which comes only from focused effort over a period of time. Excellence, in turn, leads to enjoyment, which encourages further effort.

23:1–8. The three prohibitions that open this chapter are closely linked by the exact repetition of 23:3a in 23:6b. Together they address the futility of pursuing wealth by revealing that wealth and its potential sources (rulers, the wealthy but stingy) are all deceitful. A ruler's gifts (represented by food) are deceitful, because he expects a return for his "investment" (23:1ff). Wealth itself is deceitful, because its benefits are only temporary, and it tends to disappear (23:4f; cf. 20:21). Finally, it is useless to attempt to ingratiate oneself to a miser. He appears to be generous (again represented by food), but his words are deceitful, and those who look to him will choke on their own words (23:6ff).

Although these poems are often applied to controlling appetite (23:1ff, 6ff) and contentment (23:4f), they actually warn against seeking riches from the wealthy. Rulers and misers are well-to-do, but sycophants hope in vain for wealth from either, since rulers' gifts are rarely "free" (and the cost of the expectations that accompany them may far outweigh their temporary value), and misers only appear to be generous (and for deceitful reasons).

23:1–3. The second half of 23:1 could refer to either the food "that is before you" or the ruler who set it there. If it refers to the food, then the real reference is to the intent behind the gift (and thus to the giver). Proverbs usually applies discernment to persons or to situations, rather than to objects.

The second and third commands (vv. 2a, 3a) are consequences of the first ("discern carefully" [v. 1b]). Understanding the real nature of a situation enables the wise to resist the temptation to become obligated by eating what will prove to be "food of lies." It tastes good, but will turn to ashes when its real cost is revealed. In addition to cautioning against seeking wealth from the powerful, this poem may therefore be related to other warnings against flattery (e.g., 29:5; cf. 26:28). A dinner invitation from a ruler would certainly flatter the "favored guest," but it would just as certainly place him under obligation.

23:4–5. Proverbs is generally positive toward wealth gained through hard work, warning that wealth gained illicitly neither satisfies nor lasts (e.g., 10:2; 11:4, 18; 15:6; 20:17; 21:6), but that a fortune gained through diligence does (e.g., 12:27; 14:23; 28:20). The position of these verses between two poems warning against entrusting oneself to the wealthy sharpens the warning that wealth is a vain pursuit (emphasized by the pun on the word "fly" [HED #5990]: "will you make your eyes *fly* upon it and it is not? ... like an eagle *it flies* to the sky" [v. 5]).

The attitude of the Book of Proverbs toward wealth may be more complex than it seems at first sight—a reminder of the importance of applying each proverb to the appropriate situation. This saying may also reflect the Book's concern that integrity should

414, 4032.123	881, 4035	7737	6084	414, 181.723	3937, 4440	3706
adv, v Qal juss 2ms	do, n ms	adj	n fs	cj, v Hithpael juss 2ms	prep, n mp, ps 3ms	cj
6. אַל־תִּלְחַם	אֶת־לֶחֶם	רַע	עָיִן	וְאַל־תִּתְאָו	לְמַטְעַמֹּתָיו	7. כִּי
'al-tilcham	'eth-lechem	ra'	'āyin	we'al-tith'āw	lemaṭ'ammōthâv	kî
do not eat	the bread of	an evil	an eye	and do not desire	his delicacies	because

3765, 8553.111	904, 5497	3772, 2000	404.131	8685.131	569.121
cj, v Qal pf 3ms	prep, n fs, ps 3ms	adv, pers pron	v Qal impv 2ms	cj, v Qal impv 2ms	v Qal impf 3ms
כְּמוֹ־שָׁעַר	בְּנַפְשׁוֹ	כֶּן־הוּא	אֱכֹל	וּשְׁתֵה	יֹאמַר
kemô-shā'ar	benaphshô	ken-hû'	'ēkhōl	ûshethēh	yō'mar
as he has measured	in his soul	so he	eat	and drink	he will say

3937	3949	1118, 6196	8.	6846, 404.113	7287.123
prep, ps 2ms	cj, n ms, ps 3ms	neg part, prep, ps 2ms		n fs, ps 2ms, v Qal pf 2ms	v Qal impf 2ms, ps 3fs
לָךְ	וְלִבּוֹ	בַּל־עִמָּךְ		פִּתְּךָ־אָכַלְתָּ	תְקִיאֶנָּה
lākh	welibbô	bal-'immākh		pittekhā-'ākhaltā	theqî'ennāh
to you	but his heart	not with you		your morsels you have eaten	you will vomit it

8271.313	1745	5456	9.	904, 238	3809	414, 1744.323
cj, v Piel pf 2ms	n mp, ps 2ms	art, adj		prep, n fd	n ms	adv, v Piel juss 2ms
וְשִׁחַתָּ	דְּבָרֶיךָ	הַנְּעִימִים		בְּאָזְנֵי	כְסִיל	אַל־תְּדַבֵּר
weshichattā	devārêkha	hanne'îmîm		be'āzenê	khesîl	'al-tedhabbēr
and you will spoil	your words	the pleasant		in the ears of	a fool	do not speak

3706, 972.121	3937, 7961	4543	10.	414, 5657.523	1397
cj, v Qal impf 3ms	prep, n ms	n fp, ps 2ms		adv, v Hiphil juss 2ms	n ms
כִּי־יָבוּז	לְשֵׂכֶל	מִלֶּיךָ		אַל־תַּסֵּג	גְּבוּל
kî-yāvûz	lesēkhel	millêkha		'al-tassēgh	gevûl
because he will despise	the wisdom of	your words		do not deviate	the boundary of

5986	904, 7898	3605	414, 971.123	11.	3706, 1381.151	2481
n ms	cj, prep, n mp	n mp	adv, v Qal juss 2ms		cj, v Qal act ptc ms, ps 3mp	adj
עוֹלָם	וּבִשְׂדֵי	יְתוֹמִים	אַל־תָּבֹא		כִּי־גֹאֲלָם	חָזָק
'ôlām	ûvisdhê	yethômîm	'al-tāvō'		kî-ghō'ālām	chāzāq
ancient times	and on the fields of	orphans	do not enter		because their Redeemer	strong

2000, 7662.121	881, 7663	882	12.	971.531	3937, 4284
pers pron, v Qal impf 3ms	do, n ms, ps 3mp	prep, ps 2ms		v Hiphil impv 2ms	prep, art, n ms
הוּא־יָרִיב	אֶת־רִיבָם	אִתָּךְ		הָבִיאָה	לַמּוּסָר
hû'-yārîv	'eth-rîvām	'ittākh		hāvî'āh	lammûsār
He He will plead the case	their lawsuit	with you		bring	toward discipline

3949	238	3937, 571, 1907	13.	414, 4661.123	4623, 5470
n ms, ps 2ms	cj, n fs, ps 2ms	prep, n mp, n fs		adv, v Qal juss 2ms	prep, n ms
לִבֶּךָ	וְאָזְנֶךָ	לְאִמְרֵי־דָעַת		אַל־תִּמְנַע	מִנַּעַר
libbekhā	we'āzenekhā	le'imrê-dhā'ath		'al-timna'	minna'ar
your heart	and your ear	to the sayings of knowledge		do not withhold	from a child

6. Eat thou not the bread of him that hath an evil eye, neither desire thou his dainty meats: ... Do not eat the food of a stingy man, do not crave his delicacies, *NIV* ... Eat not the bread of him whose eye is selfish, neither desire his delicacies, *Berkeley* ... Eat not the bread of the grudger And desire none of his sweets, *Fenton* ... Do not eat the food of anyone whose eye is jealous, do not hanker for his delicacies, *JB*.

7. For as he thinketh in his heart, so is he: Eat and drink, saith he to thee; but his heart is not with thee: ... what he is really thinking about is himself: 'Eat and drink,' he tells you, but his heart is not with you, *JB* ... For as he estimates his own appetite, so he will yours, *Anchor* ... he is the kind of man who is always thinking about the cost, *NIV* ... for as one who inwardly figures the cost, so is he, *Berkeley*.

8. The morsel which thou hast eaten shalt thou vomit up, and lose thy sweet words: ... you will vomit up the bit you have eaten, and spoil your compliments, *Berkeley* ... You will throw up the little you have eaten, and you will have wasted your kind words, *NCV* … and spoil your pleasant talk, *Beck* … and all your flattery will be wasted, *Good News.*

9. Speak not in the ears of a fool: for he will despise the wisdom of thy words: … Don't speak to fools; they will only ignore your wise words, *NCV* … Say nothing in the hearing of a foolish man, for he will put no value on the wisdom of your words, *BB* … Do not waste words on a fool, who will not appreciate the shrewdness of your remarks, *JB* … he will despise the wise things you say, *Beck.*

10. Remove not the old landmark; and enter not into the fields of the fatherless: … Do not move back an ancient boundary line, Nor intrude on the lands of orphans, *Anchor* … Do not let the landmark of the widow be moved, and do not go into the fields of those who have no father, *BB* … or trespass into the fields of orphans, *Beck* … nor invade the fields of orphans, *NAB.*

11. For their redeemer is mighty; he shall plead their cause with thee: … redeemer is strong; he will defend their cause against you, *NAB* … God, their defender, is strong; he will take their side against you, *NCV* … they

have a powerful guardian who will take up their cause against you, *NEB* … plead their case against you, *NASB.*

12. Apply thine heart unto instruction, and thine ears to the words of knowledge: … Give your heart to teaching, and your ears to the words, *BB* … Allow your mind to be trained and listen to intelligent words, *Beck* … Apply your heart to discipline and your ears to instructive sayings, *JB* … your ears to the teachings of fact, *Fenton.*

13. Withhold not correction from the child: for if thou beatest him with the rod, he shall not die: … Don't fail to punish children. If you

---

be pursued without regard for the outcome (cf. 19:1), and—again, by virtue of its position—that currying the favor of the wealthy may lead to compromising one's values. The image of wealth as a bird is one of the closest contacts between this section and the Wisdom of Amenemope (see "Overview").

23:6–8. These verses contain an even stronger warning than the opening poem by forbidding the discerning (23:1b) to eat the miser's food (23:6b is identical to 23:3a). When the miser's real motivations become known, they will contradict his gracious words (23:7c), turn the joy of the banquet to bile (23:8a) and reveal that the gracious words of his guest were wasted.

The host's favor and generosity had nothing to do with his guest's person or words, but only with his own wicked reasons (cf. 26:23–28). Discernment is needed in order to avoid such a person, especially when the bait of gifts (his food), wealth (the topic of 23:1–8) or both, is dangled.

23:9. What fools cannot understand they despise. Their normal response to wise advice is therefore to mock it. The person of understanding, who knows the worth of his own counsel, thus also knows better than to evaluate his ideas by the response that they engender, especially when that response is mockery. Having learned from his listeners' replies to his suggestions, he then knows who is and is not likely to accept his advice, and does not waste words on fools.

Mockery may be clever, but it is never commended in Scripture, except when directed by God toward his enemies (cf. 2 Ki. 19:21; Pss. 2:4; 59:8), and is specifically condemned in Proverbs,

where it characterizes fools (cf. 1:7; 11:12; 13:13; 14:21; 30:17). Whoever, therefore, finds himself scoffing at the suggestions and counsel of others may well be a fool.

23:10–11. With no near relations to look out for their well-being, orphans were especially susceptible to legal and financial oppression (as were widows and foreign settlers or "sojourners"). The Covenant therefore includes warnings against oppressing or taking advantage of these groups (Exo. 22:21; Deut. 27:19), as well as statutes directing Israel to treat them well (cf. Deut. 10:12–19; 14:28f; 24:19–22; 26:12–15)—their attitude toward the helpless was to reflect God's attitude toward Israel in Egypt.

An important theme of the Covenant is justice without regard for social class or position. Solomon warns those who are able because of their standing in the community to oppress the weak that doing so will bring them God's condemnation and enmity (cf. 15:25; 22:28). In the absence of a human redeemer, the LORD himself will fight for them (Exo. 22:23f).

23:12. Like 22:17–21, this exhortation begins a new section that addresses some dangers that may especially tempt youthful naiveté: drunkenness and gluttony (23:19ff, 29–35), sexual immorality (23:26ff) and the temptation to reject parental teaching (22:15f, 22, 24ff). The sayings in the rest of this chapter thus deal with problems that can ensue from failure to discipline children, which is specifically addressed in the next saying (23:13f).

23:13–14. Like other verses that address parental discipline, this one assures parents that children need correction, so that their immediate response, which will rarely be positive, should not

14.

904, 8101	887		4322.121	3940	904, 8101	3706, 5409.523	4284
prep, art, n ms	pers pron	**14.**	v Qal impf 3ms	neg part	prep, art, n ms	cj, v Hiphil impf 2ms, ps 3ms	n ms
בַּשֵּׁבֶט	אַתָּה		יָמוּת	לֹא	בַּשֵּׁבֶט	כִּי־תַכֶּנּוּ	מוּסָר
bashshēveṭ	'attāh		yāmûth	lō'	vashshēveṭ	kî-thakkennû	mûsār
with the rod	you		he will die	not	with the rod	rather you will strike him	correction

15.

524, 2550	1158		5522.523	4623, 8061	5497	5409.523
cj, adj	n ms, ps 1cs	**15.**	v Hiphil impf 2ms	prep, pn	cj, n fs, ps 3ms	v Hiphil impf 2ms, ps 3ms
אִם־חָכָם	בְּנִי		תַּצִּיל	מִשְּׁאוֹל	וְנַפְשׁוֹ	תַּכֶּנּוּ
'im-chākham	benî		tatstsîl	mishshe'ôl	wenaphshô	takkennû
if wise	O my son		you will deliver	from Sheol	and his soul	you will strike him

16.

3949	7975.121	3949	1612, 603		6159.127	3749	904, 1744.341
n ms, ps 2ms	v Qal impf 3ms	n ms, ps 1cs	cj, pers pron	**16.**	cj, v Qal impf 3fp	n fp, ps 1cs	prep, v Piel inf con
לִבֶּךָ	יִשְׂמַח	לִבִּי	גַם־אָנִי		וְתַעְלֹזְנָה	כִּלְיוֹתָי	בְּדַבֵּר
libbekhā	yismach	libbî	gham-'ānî		wetha'lōzenāh	khilyôthāy	bedhabbēr
your heart	it will be glad	my heart	also I		they will exult	my kidneys	when speaking

17.

8004	4478		414, 7353.321	3949	904, 2492	3706
n fd, ps 2ms	n mp	**17.**	adv, v Piel juss 3ms	n ms, ps 2ms	prep, art, n mp	cj
שְׂפָתֶיךָ	מֵישָׁרִים		אַל־יְקַנֵּא	לִבֶּךָ	בַּחַטָּאִים	כִּי
sephāthêkhā	mêshārîm		'al-yeqannē'	libbekhā	bachaṭṭā'îm	kî
your lips	uprightness		may it not be jealous	your heart	because of the sinners	yet

18.

524, 904, 3488, 3176	3725, 3219		3706	524, 3552	321	8951
cj, prep, n fs, pn	adj, art, n ms	**18.**	cj	cj, sub	n fs	cj, n fs, ps 2ms
אִם־בְּיִרְאַת־יְהוָה	כָּל־הַיּוֹם		כִּי	אִם־יֵשׁ	אַחֲרִית	וְתִקְוָתְךָ
'im-beyir'ath-yehwāh	kol-hayyôm		kî	'im-yēsh	'achărîth	wethiqwāthekhā
rather in the fear of Yahweh	all the day		because	surely there is	an end	and your hope

19.

3940	3901.222		8471.131, 887	1158	2549.131	861.331
neg part	v Niphal impf 3fs	**19.**	v Qal impv 2ms, pers pron	n ms, ps 1cs	cj, v Qal impv 2ms	cj, v Piel impv 2ms
לֹא	תִּכָּרֵת		שְׁמַע־אַתָּה	בְּנִי	וַחֲכָם	וְאַשֵּׁר
lō'	thikkārēth		shema'-'attāh	venî	wachăkhām	we'ashshēr
not	it will be cut off		you hear	O my son	and be wise	and be happy

20.

904, 1932	3949		414, 2030.123	904, 5617.152, 3302	904, 2236.152
prep, art, n ms	n ms, ps 2ms	**20.**	adv, v Qal juss 2ms	prep, v Qal act ptc mp, n ms	prep, v Qal act ptc mp
בַּדֶּרֶךְ	לִבֶּךָ		אַל־תְּהִי	בְּסֹבְאֵי־יָיִן	בְּזֹלֲלֵי
badderekh	libbekhā		'al-tehî	vesōve'ê-yāyin	bezōlelê
on the way	your heart		do not be	among drunkards of wine	among gluttons of

21.

1340	3937		3706, 5617.151	2236.151	3542.221
n ms	prep, ps 3mp	**21.**	cj, v Qal act ptc ms	cj, v Qal act ptc ms	v Niphal impf 3ms
בָּשָׂר	לָמוֹ		כִּי־סֹבֵא	וְזוֹלֵל	יִוָּרֵשׁ
vāsār	lāmô		kî-sōvē'	wezōlēl	yiwwārēsh
flesh	for themselves		because a drunkard	and a glutton	he will become impoverished

---

spank them, they won't die, *NCV* ... Do not hesitate to discipline a youth; Though you beat him with a stick, he will not die, *Anchor* ... Nor ever from child of thine withhold chastisement; he will not die under the rod, *Knox* ... Don't fail to correct your children; discipline won't hurt them!, *LIVB*.

14. Thou shalt beat him with the rod, and shalt deliver his soul from hell: ... Give him blows with the rod, and keep his soul safe from the underworld, *BB* ... You must whip him with the rod, and so preserve his life, *Moffatt* ... If you spank them, you will save them from death, *NCV*.

15. My son, if thine heart be wise, my heart shall rejoice, even mine: ... how I will rejoice if you become a man of common sense, *LIVB* ... I, even I, will be glad in heart, *BB* ... My own mind will be content, *Anchor* ... then I will be happy, *NCV*.

16. Yea, my reins shall rejoice, when thy lips speak right things:

... You will make my inmost being rejoice When your lips speak what is right, *Anchor* ... my thoughts in me will be full of joy when your lips, *BB* ... My heart will be delighted when you say what is right, *Beck* ... my inmost self rejoices when from your lips come honest words, *JB* ... I will be proud when I hear you speaking words of wisdom, *Good News*.

17. Let not thine heart envy sinners: but be thou in the fear of the LORD all the day long: ... Do not envy sinners their good fortune, but abide in the fear of the Lord continually, *Knox* ... Let not your heart emulate sinners, but be zealous for the fear of the LORD always, *NAB* ... but always respect the LORD,

NCV ... always reverence the Eternal, *Moffatt*.

18. For surely there is an end; and thine expectation shall not be cut off: ... For without doubt there is a future, *BB* ... And your hope will not be disappointed, *Anchor* ... the future holds blessings for thee, *Knox* ... and your hope will not come to nothing, *JB* ... Then you will have hope for the future, and your wishes will come true, *NCV*.

19. Hear thou, my son, and be wise, and guide thine heart in the way: ... Listen, my child, and be wise. Keep your mind on what is right, *NCV* ... Hear now, my son, and gain wisdom, Give attention to following

the right path, *Anchor* ... set your mind on the right course, *NEB* ... and keep your mind going in the right direction, *Beck*.

20. Be not among winebibbers; among riotous eaters of flesh: ... Don't keep company with those who drink too much wine or eat too much meat for pleasure, *Beck* ... Do not be one of those forever tippling wine nor one of those who gorge themselves with meat, *JB* ... Do not keep company with drunkards, *NEB* ... never sit down with tipsy men or among gluttons, *Moffatt*.

21. For the drunkard and the glutton shall come to poverty: and drowsiness shall clothe a man

---

deter parents from correcting them. The central lines of this couplet reiterate by contrast ("when you strike him with the rod ... you shall strike him with the rod") the link between discipline and love (cf. 13:24; 22:15; 21:5), which is also revealed in the discipline of God (cf. 3:11f). (On the meaning of "rod" [HED #8101], cf. 13:24; 22:15.) Far from being a child's death, discipline (properly applied) guarantees his or her life (cf. 19:18).

23:15–16. This chiastic couplet describes parents' joy (vv. 15b–16a) when their children's words and actions reveal their wisdom (vv. 15a, 16b) in order to encourage children to respond positively to their parents' instruction (22:17–21; 23:22–28) and discipline (23:13f). Like all such statements found throughout the Book (especially in chs. 1–9, beginning in 1:8f), this verse implies a healthy relationship between parents and children. It assumes that parental well-being is a positive motivation for children.

23:17–18. Naiveté may be especially prone to value appearances without thinking beyond the surface to greater or eventual realities. This warning cautions against wanting what the wicked have, and thus being tempted to turn away from the fear of the LORD (cf. 24:1f). "End" parallels "your hope" (v. 18 is chiastic), so that, even though the substance of the hope is not described (possibly hope for the wealth or "freedom" that characterize the wicked), its arrival is certain.

This verse may point only to the tendency for justice to be served, or it may look beyond this life to the certain eventuality of divine justice. Such jus-

tice will reward both the wicked and those who continue in the fear of the LORD according to the many warnings and promises of this Book. It thus encourages patience and perseverance in believing and living according to what is right.

23:19–21. Overindulging appetites shows that a person does not understand his proper function—to sustain life and enjoy what God has created. The three parts of this brief saying correspond to the verses: summons to listen (v. 19), prohibition (v. 20) and reason for the prohibition (v. 21). In this case, the warning is that either gluttony or drunkenness, or both (the verse does not prioritize them), reveal a lack of self-control that can have disastrous consequences. The typical opening exhortation to listen signals a new section, however small it may be (cf. 22:17; 23:12, 22, 26).

Those who prefer self-indulgence to diligence may endanger their inheritance. Their failure to work may impoverish them to the extent that they need to sell themselves or their property in order to pay their debts (cf. 20:13). The torpor that is the natural result of over-eating and drinking only contributes to this fate.

A person's desires are not the ultimate arbiter of what he or she needs or should have. Instead, the wise understand that food and drink are to be enjoyed as gifts of God. They are also the product of labor, which implies that we must continue to work to earn or produce them. Sleep in time of harvest leads to shame (10:5); laziness—whether due to over-indulgence or not—brings starvation and penury (cf. 6:10f; 24:30–34).

Proverbs 23:22–28

22.

| 2172 / dem pron / זֶה / zeh / this one | 3937,1 / prep, n ms, ps 2ms / לְאָבִיךָ / leʾāvîkhā / to your father | 8471.131 / v Qal impv 2ms / **22.** שְׁמַע / shemaʿ / listen | 5306 / n fs / נוּמָה / nûmāh / drowsiness | 3980.522 / v Hiphil impf 3fs / תַּלְבִּישׁ / talbîsh / it will clothe with | 7459 / cj, n mp / וּקְרָעִים / ûqŏrāʿîm / and rags |

23.

| 583 / n fs / **23.** אֱמֶת / ʾĕmeth / truth | 525 / n fs, ps 2ms / אִמֶּךָ / ʾimmekhā / your mother | 3706,2290.112 / cj, v Qal pf 3fs / כִּי־זָקְנָה / kî-zāqŏnāh / when she has become old | 414,972.123 / cj, adv, v Qal juss 2ms / וְאַל־תָּבוּז / weʾal-tāvûz / and do not despise | 3314.111 / v Qal pf 3ms, ps 2ms / יְלָדֶךָ / yelādhekhā / he fathered you |

24.

| 1559.131 / v Qal inf abs / **24.** גּוֹל / gîwl / rejoicing | 1035 / cj, n fs / וּבִינָה / ûvînāh / and understanding | 4284 / cj, n ms / וּמוּסָר / ûmûṣār / and instruction | 2551 / n fs / חָכְמָה / chokhmāh / wisdom | 414,4513.123 / cj, adv, v Qal juss 2ms / וְאַל־תִּמְכֹּר / weʾal-timkōr / and do not sell | 7353.131 / v Qal impv 2ms / קְנֵה / qŏnēh / buy |

| 2550 / n ms / חָכָם / chākhām / someone wise | 3314.151 / v Qal act ptc ms / יוֹלֵד / yôlēdh / one who fathers | 6926 / n ms / צַדִּיק / tsaddîq / someone righteous | 1 / n ms / אֲבִי / ʾăvî / the father of | 1559.121 / v Qal impf 3ms / יָגִיל / yāghîwl / he will greatly rejoice |

25.

| 525 / cj, n fs, ps 2ms / וְאִמֶּךָ / weʾimmekhā / and your mother | 7975.121,1 / v Qal juss 3ms, n ms, ps 2ms / **25.** יִשְׂמַח־אָבִיךָ / yismach-ʾāvîkhā / may your father be glad | 7975.121,904 / cj, v Qal impf 3ms, prep, ps 3ms / וְיִשְׂמַח־בּוֹ / weyismach-bô / and he will be glad because of him |

26.

| 3937 / prep, ps 1cs / לִי / lî / to me | 3949 / n ms, ps 2ms / לִבְּךָ / libbekhā / your heart | 5598.131,1158 / v Qal impv 2ms, n ms, ps 1cs / **26.** תְּנָה־בְנִי / tenāh-venî / give my son | 3314.153 / v Qal act ptc fs, ps 2ms / יוֹלַדְתֶּךָ / yôladhtekhā / the one who bore you | 1559.122 / cj, v Qal juss 3fs / וְתָגֵל / wethāghēl / and may she rejoice |

27.

| 2193 / n fs / זוֹנָה / zônāh / a prostitute | 6233 / adj / עֲמֻקָּה / ʾămuqqāh / deep | 3706,8192 / cj, n fs / כִּי־שׁוּחָה / kî-shûchāh / because a pitfall | 7813.127 / v Qal juss 3fp / **27.** תִּרְצֶנָה / tirtsenāh / let them delight in | 1932 / n mp, ps 1cs / דְּרָכַי / derākhay / my ways | 6084 / cj, n fd, ps 2ms / וְעֵינֶיךָ / weʿênêkhā / and your eyes |

28.

| 717.122 / v Qal impf 3fs / תֶּאֱרֹב / teʾĕrōv / she lies in wait | 3626,2971 / prep, n ms / כְּחֶתֶף / kechetheph / like a robber | 652,2026 / cj, pers pron / אַף־הִיא / ʾaph-hîʾ / also she | 5425 / n fs / **28.** נָכְרִיָּה / nākheriyāh / a foreign woman | 7140 / adj / צָרָה / tsārāh / narrow | 908 / cj, n fs / וּבְאֵר / ûveʾēr / and a well |

with rags: ... heavy drinker and the glutton will be disinherited, And sleep will clothe a man in rags, *Anchor* ... those who take delight in drink and feasting will come to be in need; and through love of sleep a man will be poorly clothed, *BB* ... Those who drink and eat too much become poor. They sleep too much and end up wearing rags, *NCV* ...

being in a stupor will dress you in rags, *Beck*.

22. Hearken unto thy father that begat thee, and despise not thy mother when she is old: ... Listen to your father, who gave you life, and do not forget your mother when, *NCV* ... Give ear to your father whose child you are, and do not keep

honour from your mother when, *BB* ... Listen to your father—you are his son, and don't despise your mother, *Beck* ... Listen to your father; without him you would not exist. When your mother is old, show her your appreciation, *Good News*.

23. Buy the truth, and sell it not; also wisdom, and instruction, and

understanding: … Purchase truth—never sell it—wisdom, discipline, and discernment, *JB* … truth to covet, hold wisdom, and self-command, and discernment for treasured heirlooms, *Knox* … Learn the truth and never reject it. Get wisdom, self-control, and understanding, *NCV* … Get for yourself that which is true, and do not let it go for money; get wisdom and teaching and good sense, *BB*.

24. The father of the righteous shall greatly rejoice: and he that begetteth a wise child shall have joy of him: … father of a just man will exult with glee, *NAB* … one who has a wise son will take delight in him, *Beck* … A righteous man's father has good reason to be happy. You can take pride in a wise son, *Good News* … The father of a godly man has cause for joy—what pleasure a wise son is!, *LIVB*.

25. Thy father and thy mother shall be glad, and she that bare thee shall rejoice: … Make your father and mother happy; give your mother a reason to be glad, *NCV* … Give your father and your mother cause for delight, *NEB* … Make your father and mother content, *Fenton* … let her rejoice who gave birth to you, *NASB*.

26. My son, give me thine heart, and let thine eyes observe my ways: … Give me your attention, my son, And may your eyes admire my ways, *Anchor* … Pay close attention, son, and let my life be your example, *Good News* … let your eyes take delight in my ways, *BB* … let your eyes take pleasure in my way, *JB*.

27. For a whore is a deep ditch; and a strange woman is a narrow pit: … a prostitute is a deep pit, a narrow well, the woman who belongs to another, *JB* … a harlot is a deep pit, *Anchor* … a loose woman is a deep hollow, *BB* … and an immoral woman a narrow well, *Beck* … and an unfaithful wife is like a narrow, *NCV* … And an adulterous woman is a narrow well, *NASB*.

28. She also lieth in wait as for a prey, and increaseth the transgressors among men: … They ambush you like robbers and cause many men to be unfaithful to their wives, *NCV* … Like a bandit she lies in wait, and multiplies the unfaithful among men, *NIV* … she is waiting secretly like a beast for its food, and deceit by her is increased among men, *BB* … and betrays her husband with man after man, *NEB* … and increases the treacherous among men, *Berkeley*.

23:22–23. Like other sayings in 23:12–35, this warns the young against a temptation to which they especially are prone—despising their parents. The negative complement of the fifth commandment (Exo. 20:12; cf. Eph. 6:1f), this saying recognizes that those who reject their parents' counsel thereby reject wisdom, and are headed for destruction (cf. 30:17). The exhortation of v. 23, however, prevents this from being obeyed in a negative way (i.e., by *not* doing what is wrong), since it exhorts the youth to respond positively to his parents' teaching. "Buying" (getting) and "not selling" (not losing or letting go) show its value (this verse does not forbid, e.g., being paid for teaching). Wisdom (parents' instruction) is worth any cost; nothing can replace its loss.

23:24–25. Like 23:15f, this couplet describes how parents respond when their children make wise decisions. The English versions unanimously render v. 24 as an observation, which is the basis of the exhortation in v. 25 (i.e., "since [v. 24], [you should act in such a way that] your father and mother will rejoice"). This is probable, but not necessary. Both may be indicative, which would still implicitly exhort children to honor their parents by responding appropriately to their direction and discipline (cf. 29:17).

23:26–28. As in 22:17, the entire person (inner ["heart"] and outer ["eyes"]) is summoned to obey the father's instruction. Their parallelism is both meristic and sequential—the heart is crucial, since, if it is right, the eyes must follow (cf. 4:23).

In this case, the father is warning against sexual license (v. 27a parallels 22:14), which is as dangerous as a deadfall or pit (cf. Gen. 37:22ff; Jer. 38:6). These behaviors, which are so often seen as demonstrations of liberty, actually trap and enslave those who participate in them. The emphasis is not on two "types" of women—both stand outside one's marriage covenant—but on the consequences. The covenantal warnings against the snare of marital relationships with other peoples (e.g., Exo. 34:11–16) also show the power and consequent danger of sexual and emotional entanglement. As in the prologue, where the immoral woman's house leads to Sheol (2:18; 7:27; 9:18), the warning is not against sexual relations, but against those outside marriage (2:16–19; 5:1–20; 6:20–35; 7:1–27).

She lurks in ambush (cf. 7:12), so that the son must keep to his father's ways (23:26b) in order to avoid her. Although different interpretations have been suggested for 23:28b, it makes good sense as it stands. Because many do not heed the counsel of the wise (23:26), they fall prey to her (23:27–28a) and betray their marital oaths (23:28b).

In keeping with the masculine orientation of the Book of Proverbs, these verses portray the

Verse 29

| אֲבוֹי (15, n ms) 'ăvôy — sorrow | לְמִי (3937, 4449; prep, intrg) lᵉmî — to whom | אוֹי (186, intrj) 'ôy — woe | לְמִי (3937, 4449; prep, intrg) lᵉmî — to whom | **29.** | תוֹסִף (3362.522, v Hiphil impf 3fs) tôsiph — she will continue | בְּאָדָם (904, 119; prep, n ms) bᵉ'ādhām — with a man | וּבוֹגְדִים (931.152, cj, v Qal act ptc mp) ûvôghdhîm — and those who act with deceit |

| לְמִי (3937, 4449; prep, intrg) lᵉmî — to whom | מִדוֹנִים (4209, n mp) midhônîm — contentions | לְמִי (3937, 4449; prep, intrg) lᵉmî — to whom | שִׂיחַ (7945, n ms) sîach — a complaint | לְמִי (3937, 4449; prep, intrg) lᵉmî — to whom | פְּצָעִים (6729, n mp) pᵉtsā'îm — wounds | חִנָּם (2703, adv) chinnām — without cause | לְמִי (3937, 4449; prep, intrg) lᵉmî — to whom |

Verse 30

| חַכְלִלוּת (2548, n fs) chakhlilûth — redness of | עֵינָיִם (6084, n fd) 'ênāyim — eyes | **30.** | לַמְאַחֲרִים (3937, 310.352; prep, art, v Piel ptc mp) lam'achărîm — to those who delay | עַל־הַיָּיִן (6142, 3302; prep, art, n ms) 'al-hayyāyin — over the wine | לַבָּאִים (3937, 971.152; prep, art, v Qal act ptc mp) labbā'îm — to those who go | לַחְקֹר (3937, 2811.141; prep, v Qal inf con) lachqōr — to search for |

Verse 31

| מִמְסָךְ (4611, n ms) mimsākh — mixed alcohol | **31.** | אַל־תֵּרֶא (414, 7495.123; adv, v Qal juss 2ms) 'al-tēre' — do not look at | יַיִן (3302, n ms) yayin — wine | כִּי (3706, cj) kî — when | יִתְאַדָּם (118.721, v Hithpael impf 3ms) yith'addām — it becomes red | כִּי־יִתֵּן (3706, 5598.121; cj, v Qal impf 3ms) kî-yittēn — when it gives | בַּכִּיס (904, 3719; prep, art, n fs) bakkîs — in the cup |

Verse 32

| עֵינוֹ (6084, n fs, ps 3ms) 'ênô — its eye | יִתְהַלֵּךְ (2050.721, v Hithpael impf 3ms) yithhallēkh — it is going | בְּמֵישָׁרִים (904, 4478; prep, n mp) bᵉmêshārîm — with smoothness | **32.** | אַחֲרִיתוֹ (321, n fs, ps 3ms) 'achărîthô — it end | כְּנָחָשׁ (3626, 5357; prep, n ms) kᵉnāchāsh — like a poisonous snake | יִשָּׁךְ (5574.121, v Qal impf 3ms) yishshākh — it will bite |

Verse 33

| וּכְצִפְעֹנִי (3626, 7126; cj, prep, n ms) ûkhetsiph'ōnî — and like an adder | יַפְרִשׁ (6816.521, v Hiphil impf 3ms) yaphrish — it will sting | **33.** | עֵינֶיךָ (6084, n fd, ps 2ms) 'ênêkhā — your eyes | יִרְאוּ (7495.126, v Qal impf 3mp) yir'û — they will see | זָרוֹת (2299, n fp) zārôth — strange things | וְלִבְּךָ (3949, cj, n ms, ps 2ms) wᵉlibbᵉkhā — and your heart |

Verse 34

| יְדַבֵּר (1744.321, v Piel impf 3ms) yᵉdabbēr — it will speak | תַּהְפֻּכוֹת (8749, n fp) tahpukhôth — perversity | **34.** | וְהָיִיתָ (2030.113, cj, v Qal pf 2ms) wᵉhāyîthā — and you will be | כְּשֹׁכֵב (3626, 8311.151; prep, v Qal act ptc ms) kᵉshōkhēv — like one who lies down | בְּלֶב־יָם (904, 3949, 3328; prep, n ms, n ms) bᵉlev-yām — on the middle of the sea |

Verse 35

| וּכְשֹׁכֵב (3626, 8311.151; cj, prep, v Qal act ptc ms) ûkheshōkhēv — and like one who lies | בְּרֹאשׁ (904, 7513; prep, n ms) bᵉrō'sh — on the top of | חִבֵּל (2348, n ms) chibbēl — mast | **35.** | הִכּוּנִי (3679.516, v Hiphil pf 3cp) hikkûnî — they have struck me down | בַּל־חָלִיתִי (1118, 2571.115; neg part, v Qal pf 1cs) val-chālîthî — but I was not sick |

---

29. Who hath woe? who hath sorrow? who hath contentions? who hath babbling? who hath wounds without cause? who hath redness of eyes?: ... Who has sorrow? Who has woe? Who has strife? Who has complaints? Who feels hurt without cause? Who has bloodshot eyes?, *Berkeley* ... who have misery and brawls? Who have wounds? who have objectless strife? With whom are the red gleaming eyes?, *Fenton* ... Who has woe? Who has misery? Who has quarrels and who is groaning? Who gets wounded without a reason? Whose eyesight is blurred?, *Beck* ... I will show you someone miserable and sorry for himself, always causing trouble and always complaining. His eyes are bloodshot, and he has bruises that could have been avoided, *Good News*.

30. They that tarry long at the wine; they that go to seek mixed wine: ... For those who linger over wine too long, ever on the look-out for the blended liquors, *JB* ... It is people who drink too much wine, who try out all different kinds of strong drinks, *NCV* … Those who linger late over their wine, those who are always trying some new spiced liquor, *NEB* … they who go to sample mixed wine, *Berkeley*.

31. Look not thou upon the wine when it is red, when it giveth his colour in the cup, when it moveth itself aright: … Look not at the wine's tawny glow, sparkling there in the glass, *Knox* … Do not gaze at wine, how red it is, how it sparkles in the cup! How smoothly it slips down the throat!, *JB* … Don't let wine tempt you, even though it is rich red, and it sparkles in the cup, and it goes down smoothly, *Good News*.

32. At the last it biteth like a serpent, and stingeth like an adder: … Afterwards it will bite like a snake, It secretes the venom of a viper, *Anchor* … In the end, its bite is like that of a snake, its wound like the wound of a poison-snake, *BB* … And stings like a viper, *NASB*.

33. Thine eyes shall behold strange women, and thine heart shall utter perverse things: … Your eyes will see strange sights, and your mind will be confused, *NCV* … your wits and your speech are confused, *NEB* … you will say twisted things, *BB* … And will utter weird words, *Goodspeed*.

34. Yea, thou shalt be as he that lieth down in the midst of the sea, or as he that lieth upon the top of a mast: … You will feel dizzy as if you're in a storm on the ocean, as if you're on top of a ship's sails, *NCV* … You will be like a man asleep at sea, Asleep in the midst of a violent storm, *Goodspeed* … You will be like someone sleeping in mid-ocean, like one asleep at the mast-head, *JB* … You will stagger like a sailor tossed at sea, clinging to a swaying mast, *LIVB*.

35. They have stricken me, shalt thou say, and I was not sick; they have beaten me, and I felt it not: when shall I awake? I will seek it

---

woman as the aggressor, but neither sex has a monopoly on this sin, or any other.

23:29–35. Like the earlier poem on drunkenness (23:19ff), this one also has three main parts: introduction (vv. 29f), prohibition (v. 31) and reasons supporting the prohibition (vv. 32–35). It satirizes drunkenness, showing the drunk what he looks like to others (vv. 33f), as well as describing his own view of his experience (v. 35a). It thus resembles other "character" poems, such as the description of the sluggard (24:30–34; 26:13–16) and a wicked society (30:11–14).

23:29–30. The first part of the introduction entails a series of rhetorical questions in v. 29. These are actually a compound riddle, designed to draw the reader or listener into the topic by encouraging him or her to ask what kind of person might fit such a description. The description includes his inner state (v. 29a), his relationships with others (v. 29b) and his physical condition (v. 29c–d), some of which may even be the result of his relationships with others (if the wounds are not self-inflicted). The correct answer (v. 30) is not those who drink wine, but those who drink too much of it, lingering when those with more self-control and understanding have gone.

23:31. The actual heart of the poem, the prohibition (v. 31), warns that it is better to stay away from temptation (some read this as an alternate form of the verb meaning "to drink deeply," which is possible, but not necessary). Looking at wine is not dangerous in itself, but it must be sought so that it can be considered. The environment in which it is

found is not likely to be conducive to behaving wisely. Since the person most likely to be tempted, however, does not recognize the source of his problems (v. 35b), but seeks it out, the proverb warns that it is better not to put oneself in the way of temptation. The wise will read this and recognize a responsibility to help those who are tempted by keeping them out of harm's way—or, at least, by not encouraging their self-destructive behavior.

23:32–35. The reasons are both internal and external. Drunkenness is a poisonous snake. It may initially be attractive (v. 31), but it is ultimately deadly (v. 32). Rather than physical diseases or disorders, this probably refers to the chaos and destruction that it brings into the lives of those enraptured by it. It also hints at the real problem—drunkards are fools. They have rejected wisdom and chosen death (8:36).

The drunkard lacks the ability to understand what is around him (v. 33a) and cannot even control his own thoughts and tongue (v. 33b). Therefore whatever comes out is more likely than not to be perverse. The enigmatic v. 34 probably refers to the vertigo that afflicts many who are drunk, a state of disequilibrium actually caused by their untrustworthy sense perceptions. Whether the blows and injuries described in v. 35 are self-inflicted (by, e.g., falling down) or the result of the strife mentioned in v. 29, his lack of perception extends even to his own body. The pain will be felt, but not right in his condition.

The gravest problem, however, is not the injuries that often accompany drunkenness, but the inability of this person to understand and learn from his expe-

2056.116	1118, 3156.115	5146	7301.525	3362.525	1272.325
v Qal pf 3cp, ps 1cs	neg part, v Qal pf 1cs	intrg	v Hiphil impf 1cs	v Hiphil impf 1cs	v Piel impf 1cs, ps 3ms
הֲלָמוּנִי	בַּל־יָדָעְתִּי	מָתַי	אָקִיץ	אוֹסִיף	אֲבַקְשֶׁנּוּ
hălāmûnî	bal-yādhā'ttî	māthay	'āqîts	'ôsîph	'ăvaqŏshennû
they have struck me	I do not realize	when	will I wake up	I will do again	I will search for it

24:1

5968	414, 7349.323	904, 596	7750	414, 181.723	3937, 2030.141	882
adv	adv, v Piel juss 2ms	prep, n mp	n fs	cj, v Hithpael juss 2ms	prep, v Qal inf con	prep, ps 3mp
עוֹד	אַל־תְּקַנֵּא	בְּאַנְשֵׁי	רָעָה	וְאַל־תִּתְאָו	לִהְיוֹת	אִתָּם
'ôdh	'al-teqannē'	be'anshê	rā'āh	we'al-tith'āw	lihyôth	'ittām
again	do not be envious	about men of	evil	and do not desire	to be	with them

2.

3706, 8160	1965.121	3949	6219	8004	1744.327
cj, n ms	v Qal impf 3ms	n ms, ps 3mp	cj, n ms	n fd, ps 3mp	v Piel impf 3fp
כִּי־שֹׁד	יֶהְגֶּה	לִבָּם	וְעָמָל	שִׂפְתֵיהֶם	תְּדַבֵּרְנָה
kî-shōdh	yehgeh	libbām	we'āmāl	siphthêhem	tedhabbērenāh
because violence	it will mutter	their heart	and trouble	their lips	they will speak

3.

904, 2551	1161.221	1041	904, 8722	3679.721
prep, n fs	v Niphal impf 3ms	n ms	cj, prep, n fs	v Hithpolal impf 3ms
בְּחָכְמָה	יִבָּנֶה	בָּיִת	וּבִתְבוּנָה	יִתְכּוֹנָן
bechokhmāh	yibbāneh	bāyith	ûvithvûnāh	yithkônān
by wisdom	it will be built	a household	and with understanding	it will be established

4.

904, 1907	2410	4527.226	3725, 2019	3479	5456
cj, prep, n fs	n mp	v Niphal impf 3mp	adj, n ms	adj	cj, adj
וּבְדַעַת	חֲדָרִים	יִמָּלְאוּ	כָּל־הוֹן	יָקָר	וְנָעִים
ûvedha'ath	chădhārîm	yimmāle'û	kol-hôn	yāqār	wenā'îm
and by knowledge	rooms	they are filled with	all goods	precious	and pleasant

5.

1429, 2550	904, 6010	382, 1907	563.351, 3699	3706
n ms, adj	prep, art, n ms	cj, n ms, n fs	v Piel ptc ms, n ms	cj
גֶּבֶר־חָכָם	בַּעוֹז	וְאִישׁ־דַּעַת	מְאַמֶּץ־כֹּחַ	**6.** כִּי
gever-chākhām	ba'ôz	we'îsh-da'ath	me'ammets-kōach	kî
a wise man	with the strength	and a man of knowledge	making strong power	because

904, 8790	6449.123, 3937	4560	9009	904, 7524
prep, n fp	v Qal impf 2ms, prep, ps 2ms	n fs	cj, n fs	prep, n ms
בְּתַחְבֻּלוֹת	תַּעֲשֶׂה־לְּךָ	מִלְחָמָה	וּתְשׁוּעָה	בְּרֹב
vethachbulôth	ta'ăseh-lekhā	milchāmāh	ûtheshû'āh	berōv
with guidance	you will make for yourself	a battle	and victory	in the abundance of

yet again: … You will think, "They hit me, but I'm not hurt. They beat me up, but I don't remember it. I wish I could wake up. Then I would get another drink," *NCV* … They have overcome me, you will say, and I have no pain; they gave me blows without my feeling them: when will I be awake from my wine? I will go after it again, *BB* … "Let them strike me! I suffer no pain! Let them beat me;—I never shall care!—When I wake, I will seek it again!, *Fenton* … I'll ask for more of it!, *JB*.

24:1. Be not thou envious against evil men: … Do not be envious of the wicked, *JB* … Do not be jealous, *KJVII* … Not for thee to emulate wrong-doers, *Knox* … Don't envy evil people, *NCV*.

neither desire to be with them: … nor wish for their company, *Anchor* … and aspire to be of their company, *Knox* … or long to make friends with them, *NEB* … desire their friendship, *REB*.

2. For their heart studieth destruction: … they think of noth- ing but creating havoc, *Anchor* … they spend their days plotting violence and cheating, *LIVB* … their one thought is plunder, *Moffatt* … violence is all they think of, *NEB* … For violence their heart muttereth, *Rotherham*.

and their lips talk of mischief: … every time they open their mouth someone is going to be hurt, *Good News* … what talk, whose every word is treachery!, *Knox* … mischief is their theme, *Moffatt* … their lips speak of foul play, *NAB* … their whole talk is about causing trouble, *Anchor*.

3. Through wisdom is an house builded: ... No foundation for a house like wisdom, *Knox* ... Any enterprise is built by wise planning, *LIVB* ... It takes wisdom to have a good family, *NCV*.

and by understanding it is established: ... it is set firm on its foundation, *Anchor* ... and by reason it is made strong, *BB* ... good judgement makes it secure, *NEB* ... it is erected by intelligence, *Moffatt*.

4. And by knowledge shall the chambers be filled: ... Through knowledge its rooms are furnished, *Anchor* ... its storerooms are filled, *JB* ... no furnishing may be found for the rooms of it, *Knox* ... and profits

wonderfully by keeping abreast of the facts, *LIVB*.

with all precious and pleasant riches: ... all dear and pleasing things, *BB* ... with riches of every kind, rare and desirable, *JB* ... with rare and beautiful treasures, *NCV* ... With all acquisitions costly and fair, *Rotherham* ... with costly and pleasing furnishings, *REB*.

5. A wise man is strong: ... A wise man is superior to a strong one, *Anchor* ... Anyone wise is mighty in force, *JB* ... Wise men are better than warriors, *Moffatt*.

yea, a man of knowledge increaseth strength: ... a learned man is better

than one who is physically powerful, *Anchor* ... well taught is firm of sinew, *Knox* ... brain is better than brawn, *Moffatt* ... a man of knowledge becometh alert in vigour, *Rotherham*.

6. For by wise counsel thou shalt make thy war: ... planning is necessary to conduct a war, *Anchor* ... it is by strategy that you wage war, *JB* ... for you need policy in war, *Moffatt* ... Surely with concerted measures shalt thou make for thyself war, *Rotherham*.

and in multitude of counsellors there is safety: ... in a number of wise guides there is salvation, *BB* ... the more good advice you get, the more likely you are to win, *Good*

rience. His goal, upon recovering, is to seek more, apparently so that he can repeat the experience.

Those who are wise are self-controlled and cautious, carefully weighing every decision in the light of its outcomes. Because they are thoughtful, they learn from their experience, growing in insight and the ability to choose wisely. This is possible because they live in the fear of the LORD, submitting themselves and their lives to his standards and control. Drunkenness is absolutely opposed to this type of behavior, as its primary motivation is to repeat the experience.

This poem's humor is thus real, but macabre rather than hilarious. Solomon makes his point deftly, but surely, using the drunkard's own words against himself.

24:1–2. Envy is a powerful motivator. Like 23:17f, this saying warns against being drawn into folly's rebellion by jealous desires. Unlike those verses, however, which address the well-being that attends the pursuit of wisdom, 24:1f reveals the true nature of the envied. They are dangerous; their minds are preoccupied with how they may trouble their neighbors (cf. 1:10–18).

These verses also warn those who would be wise that violent thoughts are signs of folly and wickedness, not of wisdom. Those who find themselves preoccupied with such things—using or abusing others to their destruction or their own advantage—have set themselves on the path of death.

With this saying, the warnings of this larger section (22:17–24:34) again become more general

and less focused on the troubles of the naive and immature (cf. 23:12–35).

24:3–6. These two sayings testify that wisdom is crucial to success, whether building and furnishing a house (vv. 3f; cf. 14:1) or waging war (vv. 5f). The two actions could hardly be more distinct. Building houses and establishing households are peacetime activities. They also belong to both the private and public spheres. By their juxtaposition, therefore, these four verses encompass major aspects of human life and activity (domestic peace and international war) and assert that wisdom is equally necessary in each of these areas of life, thus encouraging those who seek success to seek it through wisdom.

To build a house, however, refers to more than architecture and construction techniques. The second line (v. 3b) describes establishing a household so that it is secure. This is the legacy of the wise (13:22; cf. 12:7, contrast 11:29).

If this is true for the commonalities of life, how much more so for those who rule. The humility that encourages a person to seek advice comes from knowing that no one is omniscient or omnicompetent and that wisdom must be sought (2:1–5). The wise person therefore looks for ways to strengthen his ability to meet daily needs by increasing the knowledge that he already possesses. Then the plans, which are based on the insights of a number of people, are much more likely to succeed, since their joint strengths will (or, at least, should) cancel out each other's weaknesses (cf. 11:14 [11:14b is identical to 24:6b]; 12:15; 15:22).

7.

3398.151	7509	3937, 188	2554	904, 8554	3940	6858.121, 6552
v Qal act ptc ms	n fp	prep, n ms	n fp	prep, art, n ms	neg part	v Qal impf 3ms, n ms, ps 3ms
יוֹעֵץ	רָאמוֹת	לֶאֱוִיל	חָכְמוֹת	בַּשַּׁעַר	לֹא	יִפְתַּח־פִּיהוּ
yô'ēts	rā'môth	le'ĕwîl	chokhmôth	bashsha'ar	lō'	yiphtach-pîhû
counselors	corals	for a fool	wisdom	in the gate	not	he will open his mouth

8.

2913.351	3937, 7778.541	3937	1196, 4343	7410.126	9. 2239
v Piel ptc ms	prep, v Hiphil inf con	prep, ps 3ms	n ms, n fp	v Qal impf 3mp	n fs
מְחַשֵּׁב	לְהָרֵעַ	לוֹ	בַּעַל־מְזִמּוֹת	יִקְרָאוּ	זִמַּת
mechashshēv	lehārēa'	lô	ba'al-mezimmôth	yiqrā'û	zimmath
one who plots	to cause evil	to him	a master of plans	they will call	plotting of

10.

198	2496	8774	3937, 119	4086	7791.713
n fs	n fs	cj, n fs	prep, n ms	n ms	v Hithpael pf 2ms
אִוֶּלֶת	חַטָּאת	וְתוֹעֲבַת	לְאָדָם	לֵץ	הִתְרַפִּיתָ
'iwweleth	chaṭṭā'th	wethô'ăvath	le'ādhām	lēts	hithrappîthā
foolishness	a sin	and an abomination to	a man	a mocker	you have become lax

11.

904, 3219	7150	7140	3699	5522.531	4089.156	3937, 4323
prep, n ms	n fs	adj	n ms, ps 2ms	v Hiphil impv 2ms	v Qal pass ptc mp	prep, art, n ms
בְּיוֹם	צָרָה	צַר	כֹּחֶכָה	הַצֵּל	לְקֻחִים	לַמָּוֶת
beyôm	tsārāh	tsar	kōchekhāh	hatstsēl	lequchîm	lammāweth
on the day of	adversity	narrow	your strength	rescue	those being taken	to the death

12.

4267.152	3937, 2104	524, 2910.123	3706, 569.123	2075
cj, v Qal act ptc mp	prep, art, n ms	cj, v Qal impf 2ms	cj, v Qal impf 2ms	intrj
וּמָטִים	לַהֶרֶג	אִם־תַּחְשׂוֹךְ	כִּי־תֹאמַר	הֵן
ûmāṭîm	laheregh	'im-tachsôkh	kî-thō'mar	hēn
and those stumbling	to the slaughter	surely you will keep back	when you say	behold

3940, 3156.119	2172	1950B, 3940, 8834.151	3949	2000, 1032.121
neg part, v Qal pf 1cp	dem pron	intrg part, neg part, v Qal act ptc ms	n mp	pers pron, v Qal impf 3ms
לֹא־יָדַעְנוּ	זֶה	הֲלֹא־תֹכֵן	לִבּוֹת	הוּא־יָבִין
lō'-yādha'ănû	zeh	hălō'-thōkhēn	libbôth	hû'-yāvîn
we did not know	this	does not He who examines	hearts	He He will discern

5526.151	5497	2000	3156.121	8178.511	3937, 119
cj, v Qal act ptc ms	n fs, ps 2ms	pers pron	v Qal impf 3ms	cj, v Hiphil pf 3ms	prep, n ms
וְנֹצֵר	נַפְשְׁךָ	הוּא	יֵדָע	וְהֵשִׁיב	לְאָדָם
wenōtsēr	naphshekhā	hû'	yēdhā'	wehēshîv	le'ādhām
and the One Who keeps	your life	He	He knows	and He will return	to a man

---

News ... success lieth in the greatness of the counsellor, Rotherham ... what saves the state is many a counsellor, Moffatt ... victory is the fruit of long planning, NEB.

7. Wisdom is too high for a fool: ... Wise sayings are beyond the understanding of the fool, Anchor ... For a fool, to be silent is wisdom, NAB ... For a fool wisdom is an inaccessible fortress, JB ... wisdom hangs high beyond the fool's reach, Knox ... Wisdom is as unattainable to a fool as corals, MAST.

he openeth not his mouth in the gate: ... he keeps his mouth shut in the public place, BB ... he remains tongue-tied in the public assembly, REB ... They have nothing to say in a discussion, NCV ... he dare not open his mouth in court, NEB.

8. He that deviseth to do evil: ... He who is [always] scheming to create trouble, Anchor ... He whose purposes are bad, BB ... Whoever is intent on evil-doing, JB ... Consecrate close thought to evil ends, Knox ... A man who is bent on mischief, NEB.

shall be called a mischievous person: ... Becomes known as a master of trickery, Anchor ... will be named a man of evil designs, BB ... shall be called a master of intrigues, Darby ... men shall call him an author of wicknesse, Geneva ... you will earn a reputation as a troublemaker, Good News.

9. The thought of foolishness is sin: ... Sin is the scheme of a fool, Anchor ... The purpose of the foolish is sin, BB ... Folly dreams of nothing but sin, JB ... Craft of his own the fool has, but all used amiss, Knox ... the intrigues of foolish men misfire, NEB.

and the scorner is an abomination to men: ... the hater of authority is disgusting to others, *BB* ... People hate a person who has nothing but scorn for others, *Good News* ... men detest a mocker, *NIV* ... the insidious rogue no man can stomach, *Knox* ... and the insolent man is odious to his fellows, *NEB*.

10. If thou faint in the day of adversity: ... If you show weakness in a crisis, *Anchor* ... If you have been slack when times are hard, *Goodspeed* ... If you give up when trouble comes, *NCV* ... If you lose heart when things go wrong, *JB* ... Thou hast been slothful in the day of straitness, *Rotherham*.

thy strength is small: ... it shows that you are weak, *NCV* ... Your

means will be scanty, *Goodspeed* ... You are a poor specimen, *LIVB* ... Straitened is thy power, *Young* ... how helpless will you be on a day of disaster!, *NEB*.

11. If thou forbear to deliver them that are drawn unto death: ... Be the saviour of those who are given up to death, *BB* ... Don't hesitate to rescue someone who is about to be executed unjustly, *Good News* ... Save those being dragged towards death, *JB* ... What, hang thy hands down in time of peril?, *Knox* ... Rescue those who are unjustly sentenced to death, *LIVB*.

and those that are ready to be slain: ... do not keep back help from those who are slipping to destruction, *BB* ... from those staggering toward slaughter will you withhold your-

self?, *Berkeley* ... save those being hauled off to execution, *REB* ... cheat the gallows of its prey, *Knox* ... deliver any who go trembling to their doom, *Moffatt*.

12. If thou sayest, Behold, we knew it not: ... See, this is none of my business, *Anchor* ... we had no knowledge of this, *BB* ... not plead thy lack of strength, *Knox* ... Don't try to disclaim responsibility, *LIVB* ... I know not this man!, *NAB*.

doth not he that pondereth the heart consider it?: ... God knows and judges your motives, *Good News* ... will the Weigher of the heart pay no attention?, *JB* ... does not he who tests hearts perceive it?, *NAB* ... God, who knows what's in your mind, will notice, *NCV* ... Shall not

---

All of the verses that deal with planning and counsel imply the need to act based on knowledge and insight gleaned from different sources (including some who disagree with one another, or with the plan, or goal). This in turn reflects the proverbial doctrine that nothing be done in haste or impulsively (cf. 21:5). The theme of planning is thus integrally related to that of diligence, since success crowns diligent planning, whether one is building a house, establishing a household or preparing for war.

These verses do not guarantee success in such enterprises. They do, however, reflect the overwhelming conviction of Proverbs concerning diligence and care. These characterize a life lived in the fear of the LORD and tend to success, a fact especially evident when contrasted with the haste, carelessness and arrogance that characterize the fool (cf. 24:7).

24:7. The gate was the center of commercial and legal activities (cf. Ruth 4:1–12), and thus a place of honor (cf. Prov. 31:23, 31; Job 29:7–25). It was also a place where Wisdom was found (1:21; 8:3). Because Hebrew verbs rarely indicate specific "modes," this verse might be translated using such modals as "should," "must" or "ought." It may, however, simply be indicative (i.e., "He does not open his mouth in the gate"), because he is unable to understand or participate in the discussion.

At the same time, however, the context of the Book suggests that, if it is rarely appropriate for fools to speak (since their words are rarely worth

hearing), how much more inappropriate for them to speak in a place characterized by wisdom. It thus warns those who might be tempted to display their ignorance (cf. 17:28).

24:8–9. Unlike most of the following sayings, these verses do not contain a command or prohibition, but describe how others respond to the wicked. A ba'al (HED #1196) was a master of, or someone characterized by, some quality or type of deed (cf. 22:24; Gen. 37:19; Exo. 24:14). Those who use their time and energy to further their own wicked plans will eventually be discovered and condemned. Instead, the scornful are condemned and hated (9b; cf. 14:17; 15:26). The warning is thus against either being or trusting such a person. All such plotting is sin and leads to further sin. The verses are connected by the repeated root *zmm* (vv. 8b, 9a).

24:10–12. The boldness of the statement in Hebrew makes 24:10 nearly an accusation and conclusion drawn from that conclusion (lit., "You are weak in the day of distress! Your strength is weak.") Hence most versions translate this as a condition: "If you are weak." This verse is best understood as introducing 24:11f, which urges action (v. 11) and warns that excuses (v. 12a) will not suffice against the One Who knows the real reasons of the heart (v. 12b–c; cf. the nearly identical statement in 16:2; 21:26) and judges accordingly (v. 12d).

The chiastic arrangement of v. 10 is unusual, since its extremes depend on contrasting meanings

13.

3626, 6714	404.131, 1158	1756	3706, 3005	5499
prep, n ms, ps 3ms	v Qal impv 2ms, n ms, ps 1cs	n ms	cj, adj	cj, n ms
כְּפָעֳלוֹ	אֱכָל־בְּנִי	דְּבַשׁ	כִּי־טוֹב	וְנֹפֶת
kephā'ålô	'ekhāl-benî	dhevash	kî-ṭôv	wenōpheth
according to his deed	eat O my son	honey	because good	and a honeycomb

14.

5142	6142, 2541	3772	3156.131	2551	3937, 5497	524, 4834.113
adj	prep, n ms, ps 2ms	adv	v Qal impv 2ms	n fs	prep, n fs, ps 2ms	cj, v Qal pf 2ms
מָתוֹק	עַל־חִכֶּךָ	כֵּן	דְּעֵה	חָכְמָה	לְנַפְשֶׁךָ	אִם־מָצָאתָ
māthôq	'al-chikkekhā	kēn	de'eh	chokhmāh	lenaphshekhā	'im-mātsā'thā
sweet	on your palate	so	know	wisdom	for your soul	if you will find

15.

3552	321	8951	3940	3918.222	414, 717.123
cj, sub	n fs	cj, n fs, ps 2ms	neg part	v Niphal impf 3fs	adv, v Qal juss 2ms
וְיֵשׁ	אַחֲרִית	וְתִקְוָתְךָ	לֹא	תִכָּרֵת	אַל־תֶּאֱרֹב
weyēsh	'achărîth	wethiqŏwāthekhā	lō'	thikkārēth	'al-te'ěrōv
and there is	an end	and your hope	not	it will be cut off	do not lie in wait

16.

7857	3937, 5295	6926	414, 8161.323	7548	3706
n ms	prep, n ms	n ms	adv, v Piel juss 2ms	n ms, ps 3ms	cj
רָשָׁע	לִנְוֵה	צַדִּיק	אַל־תְּשַׁדֵּד	רִבְצוֹ	כִּי
rāshā'	linwēh	tsaddîq	'al-teshaddēdh	rivtsô	kî
O wicked man	at the abode of	the righteous	do not ravage	his home	because

8124	5489.121	6926	7251.111	7857	3911.226
num	v Qal impf 3ms	n ms	cj, v Qal pf 3ms	cj, n mp	v Niphal impf 3mp
שֶׁבַע	יִפּוֹל	צַדִּיק	וָקָם	וּרְשָׁעִים	יִכָּשְׁלוּ
sheva'	yippôl	tsaddîq	wāqām	ûreshā'îm	yikkāshelû
seven times	he will fall	the righteous	but he will rise	but the wicked	they will stumble

17.

904, 7750	904, 5489.141	342.152	414, 7975.123
prep, n fs	prep, v Qal inf con	v Qal act ptc mp, ps 2ms	adv, v Qal juss 2ms
בְּרָעָה	בִּנְפֹל	אוֹיְבֶיךָ	אַל־תִּשְׂמָח
verā'āh	binphōl	'ôyvêkhā	'al-tismāch
into disaster	when the falling of	your enemies	do not be glad

---

he that proveth hearts himself discern, *Rotherham*.

and he that keepeth thy soul: ... who keeps watch on your life, *Anchor* ... that preserveth thy soul, *Darby* ... is not he who guards your life, *Goodspeed* ... the Saviour of thy life, *Knox* ... He is watching you, *NCV*.

doth not he know it?: ... aware of it, *Goodspeed*.

and shall not he render to every man: ... will requite a man, *Anchor* ... shall He not repay each man, *Berkeley* ... recompense every man, *Geneva* ... reward each person, *NCV*.

according to his works?: ... the reward of his work?, *BB* ... as your deeds deserve?, *JB* ... for what he has done, *NCV*.

13. My son, eat thou honey, because it is good; and the honeycomb, which is sweet to thy taste: ... flowing honey, *BB* ... its drippings are sweet to your taste, *Berkeley* ... Sweet to thy palate, my son, is honey from the comb, *Knox* ... so sweet upon the tongue, *NEB* ... if virgin honey is sweet to your taste, *NAB*.

14. So shall the knowledge of wisdom be unto thy soul: ... So, be assured, is wisdom to your mind, *Goodspeed* ... but wise teaching is no less thy soul's food, *Knox* ... In the same way, wisdom is pleasing to you, *NCV* ... Know also that wisdom is sweet to your soul, *NIV* ... Seek wisdom for yourself, *REB* ... Make wisdom too your own, *NEB*.

when thou hast found it: ... If you possess that, *Anchor* ... When you enjoy becoming wise, *LIVB*.

then there shall be a reward: ... you will have a future, *Anchor* ... there shall be a result, *Darby* ... tomorrow's resource, *Knox* ... there is hope for you!, *LIVB* ... there is a prospect, *NKJV*.

and thy expectation shall not be cut off: ... your hope will not be disappointed, *Anchor* ... and a resource unfailing, *Knox* ... A bright future lies ahead!, *LIVB* ... your wishes will come true, *NCV* ... your thread of life will not be cut short, *NEB*.

15. Lay not wait, O wicked man: … Do not plot evil, *Anchor* … Do not lie in wait like an outlaw, *NIV* … Do not lurk, *JB* … O evil man, leave the upright man alone, *LIVB* … Villain, hands off, *Moffatt*.

against the dwelling of the righteous: … home of a just man, *Anchor* … habitation of the righteous, *ASV* … the fields of the upright man, *BB* … and attack a good family's house, *NCV* … like a felon at the good man's house, *NEB*.

spoil not his resting place: … do no violence to his home, *Berkeley* … do no violence to the place where the righteous live, *NRSV* … don't rob the place where they live, *NCV* … ransack not his abode, *Moffatt*.

16. For a just man falleth seven times: … No matter how often an honest man falls, *Good News* … seven times the just may stumble, *Knox* … though you trip him up seven times, *LIVB* … Even though good people may be bothered by trouble seven times, *NCV*.

and riseth up again: … he will get up again, *Anchor* … and rise to their feet again, *Knox* … they are never defeated, *NCV* … he is soon up again, *NEB*.

(slack/strength), but its center is created by a play on words (distress [HED #7150]/limited [HED #7140]), but this reveals that attempts to add to it in order to create two full lines are misguided.

The exhortation (v. 11) to rescue those who are in mortal danger does not specify the source of that danger. The words used here are not used for covenantal or legal execution, nor does the Covenant provide for rescuing those sentenced to death. Even someone guilty of manslaughter could be killed by the blood-avenger if found outside the bounds of the city of refuge (Num. 35:1–28). The particle 'im (HED #524) could be read as either a wish—"*Would that* you hold [them] back!" or a negative—"*Do not* hold [yourself] back!"

Although the details of the verse are not entirely clear, its overall message is: rescue those threatened with death. They are apparently under wrongful attack, perhaps by the marauders described in the prologue (1:10–19; 3:31; 4:10–19; 6:12–19, esp. v. 17b). Some think that this might be a call for the wise to rescue the foolish, whose folly condemns them to death (8:36; 9:18), but the Book of Proverbs mildly discourages attempting to teach fools (9:17; 17:10; 26:11; 27:22).

A plea of ignorance does not excuse inaction, especially since 24:12b–d warns that the LORD himself knows (cf. virtually identical clauses in 16:2b; 21:2b) that this claim is no more true than the lame excuses of the sluggard (22:13; 26:13). The LORD's evaluation is based on true knowledge, not only of one's deeds, but of the motives underlying them.

These verses thus present a specific application of the second great commandment (Lev. 19:18) and remind us that the responsibility is ours and the results are the LORD's to dispense as He will. Wisdom responds to the needs that it sees.

24:13–14. These verses form a complex emblematic saying that compares honey to wisdom.

Since honey was the most potent sweetener known to the ancients, it was valuable and thus worth searching for. In the same way, wisdom should be sought out and, when found, devoured. Furthermore, as honey is sweet to the taste (lit., "palate"), the assurance and hope that wisdom gives will sweeten one's life. This hope is based on the well-being promised throughout Proverbs to the obedient. This saying does not contradict the verses that warn against eating too much honey (25:16, 27). They use the same image, but in a different way.

24:15–22. The next four sayings (24:15–22) address the relationship between the righteous and wicked. The first two warn the wicked (vv. 15f) and righteous (vv. 17f) not to plot against or rejoice over the downfall of the other, respectively. The last two warn the wise against envying (vv. 19f) or becoming partners with (vv. not a unified "poem," these sayings are juxtaposed in order to present a more complete message and are linked by their repeated words and themes.

The last two verses are the least connected of this set of four sayings. They begin with a positive command (all the others are negative), and address a specific circumstance, rather than the general situations found in the other sayings. This is not atypical, however, since the last verse or saying in a group may be set off slightly from the others as a way of marking the end of a section (cf. 24:23a).

24:15–16. Like other verses throughout the Book of Proverbs, this saying warns against violence (cf. 1:10–19). It is however, addressed to the wicked, warning them that they will not ultimately prevail. Even though they may defeat the righteous ("seven times" probably means completely), it is the evildoers themselves who will be destroyed (cf. 1:26–32; 2:21f; Ps. 1:6). The wicked are thus cautioned against trusting in their victories, which are only apparent. The general tenor of Proverbs is that

3176	6678, 7495.121		3949	414, 1559.121	904, 3911.241
pn	cj, v Qal impf 3ms	**18.**	n ms, ps 2ms	adv, v Qal juss 3ms	cj, prep, v Niphal inf con, ps 3ms
יְהוָה	פֶּן־יִרְאֶה		לִבֶּךָ	אַל־יָגֵל	וּבִכָּשְׁלוֹ
yehwāh	pen-yir'eh		libbekhā	'al-yāghēl	ûvikkāshelô
Yahweh	so that He will not see		your heart	may it not rejoice	and when his stumbling

653	4623, 6142	8178.511	904, 6084	7778.111
n ms, ps 3ms	prep, prep, ps 3ms	cj, v Hiphil pf 3ms	prep, n fd, ps 3ms	cj, v Qal pf 3ms
אַפּוֹ	מֵעָלָיו	וְהֵשִׁיב	בְּעֵינָיו	וְרַע
'appô	mē'ālâv	wehēshîv	be'ênâv	wera'
his anger	from on him	and He will turn back	in his eyes	then it will be evil

3706		904, 7857	414, 7349.323	904, 7778.552	414, 2835.723	
cj	**20.**	prep, art, n mp	adv, v Piel juss 2ms	prep, art, v Hiphil ptc mp	adv, v Hithpael juss 2ms	**19.**
כִּי		בָּרְשָׁעִים	אַל־תְּקַנֵּא	בַּמְּרֵעִים	אַל־תִּתְחַר	
kî		bāreshā'îm	'al-teqannē'	bammerē'îm	'al-tithchar	
because		about the wicked	do not be envious	with evildoers	do not be annoyed	

1906.121	7857	5552	3937, 7737	321	3940, 2030.123
v Qal impf 3ms	n mp	n ms	prep, art, n ms	n fs	neg part, v Qal impf 2ms
יִדְעָךְ	רְשָׁעִים	נֵר	לָרָע	אַחֲרִית	לֹא־תִהְיֶה
yidh'ākh	reshā'îm	nēr	lārā'	'achărîth	lō'-thihyeh
it will be extinguished	the wicked	the lamp of	for the evil man	a future	it will not be

414, 6386.723	6196, 8521.152	4567	1158	3486.131, 881, 3176	
adv, v Hithpael juss 2ms	prep, v Qal act ptc mp	cj, n ms	n ms, ps 1cs	v Qal impv 2ms, do, pn	**21.**
אַל־תִּתְעָרָב	עִם־שׁוֹנִים	וָמֶלֶךְ	בְּנִי	יְרָא־אֶת־יְהוָה	
'al-tith'ārāv	'im-shônîm	wāmelekh	benî	yerā'-'eth-yehwāh	
do not associate	with those who change	and the king	O my son	fear Yahweh	

4449	8530	6608	344	7251.121	3706, 6849	
intrg	num, ps 3mp	cj, n ms	n ms, ps 3mp	v Qal impf 3ms	cj, adv	**22.**
מִי	שְׁנֵיהֶם	וּפִיד	אֵידָם	יָקוּם	כִּי־פִתְאֹם	
mî	shenêhem	ûphîd	'êdhām	yāqûm	kî-phith'ōm	
who	the two of them	and ruin	their calamity	it will rise up	because suddenly	

but the wicked shall fall into mischief: ... wicked men will stumble on into ruin, *Anchor* ... but the rogue is brought headlong by misfortune, *REB* ... the wicked are overwhelmed by trouble, *NCV* ... an evil man is crushed by a calamity, *Moffatt* ... disaster destroys the wicked, *Good News* ... the rascal is brought down by misfortune, *NEB*.

17. Rejoice not when thine enemy falleth: ... Do not be glad at the fall of your hater, *BB* ... Don't be glad when your enemy meets disaster, *Good News* ... Not thine to triumph over a fallen foe, *Knox* ... Don't be happy when your enemy is defeated, *NCV* ... Do not gloat when your enemy falls, *NIV*.

and let not thine heart be glad when he stumbleth: ... let not your heart have joy at his downfall, *BB* ... that thrill of rejoicing in thy heart over his calamity, *Knox* ... never exult when he is overthrown, *Moffatt* ... don't be glad when he is overwhelmed, *NCV* ... do not gloat when he is brought down, *NEB*.

18. Lest the LORD see it, and it displease him: ... For fear that the Lord may see it, and it may be evil in his eyes, *BB* ... and it appear wrong in His eyes, *Berkeley* ... The LORD will know if you are gloating, and he will not like it, *Good News* ... the Lord will see, and little love, *Knox* ... and disapprove, *NIV*.

and he turn away his wrath from him: ... And suspend his anger

against him, *Anchor* ... and then maybe he won't punish him, *Good News* ... his vengeance may yet change its course, *Knox* ... divert his wrath from him to you, *Moffatt* ... He may not be angry with them anymore, *NCV*.

19. Fret not thyself because of evil men: ... Do not be troubled because of evil-doers, *BB* ... Don't let evil people worry you, *Good News* ... Do not be indignant about the wicked, *JB* ... Do not be impatient when the wicked thrive, *Knox* ... Burn not with vexation against evildoers, *Rotherham*.

neither be thou envious at the wicked: ... or have envy of sinners, *BB* ... do not be jealous, *KJVII* ... Don't covet his riches, *LIVB* ... or emulate the wicked, *NEB* ... Be not envious of lawless men, *Rotherham*.

20. For there shall be no reward to the evil man: ... For the bad man has nothing to look forward to, *Anchor* ... For there will be no future for the evil man, *BB* ... For there shall be none end of plagues, *Geneva* ... villainy has no hope in store, *Knox* ... For there will be no prospect for the evil man, *NKJV*.

the candle of the wicked shall be put out: ... their lamp will be extinguished, *REB* ... its light flickers and is gone, *Knox* ... the lamp of the wicked will be snuffed out, *NIV* ... their embers will be put out, *NEB* ... the wicked will die like a flame that is put out, *NCV*.

21. My son, fear thou the LORD and the king: ... Have reverence for the LORD, my son, and honor the King, *Good News* ... stand in awe of the Eternal, *Moffatt* ... respect the LORD, *NCV*.

and meddle not with them that are given to change: ... and do not join with the rebellious, *NIV* ... with the fickle have thou no fellowship, *Rotherham* ... do not disobey either of them, *NRSV* ... don't associate with radicals, *LIVB* ... have nothing to do with those who are in high positions, *BB* ... meddle not with them that are seditious, *Geneva* ... do not ally yourself with innovators, *JB*.

22. For their calamity shall rise suddenly: ... For overthrow may come from them at any moment, *Anchor* ... for those two will send sudden destruction upon them, *NIV* ... they will bring about disaster without warning, *NEB* ... How sudden their ruin, *Knox* ... they can crush you swiftly, *Moffatt*.

---

the wicked perish and the righteous prevail, but at least one other verse implies that the wicked can overcome the righteous (25:26).

Although He is not mentioned, these verses clearly imply that the LORD is the ultimate Guarantor of the righteous (23:10ff), which is a warning to the wicked and a great encouragement to the righteous. NASB properly interprets 24:16b as the "calamity" or "disaster," with which it is implied the LORD will judge them (cf. 24:18).

When the righteous are oppressed, their dwellings (which represent all that they have) may be destroyed or stolen, and they may be physically abused or worse. These events will be real, and truly wicked and disastrous. They are not, however, ultimate destruction, since the LORD guarantees the ultimate outcome.

24:17–18. Tightly bound to the preceding verse by the repetition of "falls" and "stumbles," this saying warns against exulting in divine judgment upon enemies (cf. 17:5; 25:21f), much like passages that warn against seeking vengeance (e.g., 20:22).

If these verses are also addressed to the wicked (as the repeated words suggest), then they warn the wicked that their triumph over the righteous is not due to their strength, but manifests the judgment of God, which is only temporary (24:16). It is, however, difficult to explain such an extended address to the wicked, who are hardly likely to read the Book of Proverbs in the first place. If this saying addresses the righteous, however, the motive clause warns the righteous that they are not to exult in the downfall of any (cf. Jon. 3:10f). They are not to be judges, nor do they understand the greater purposes of God.

Arrogating the divine role will bring judgment upon themselves, when the wicked are free to act.

24:19–20. The prohibition against envying the wicked parallels 23:17 and 24:1. This motive clause (v. 20) describes the fate of the wicked, whereas the others promised hope for the righteous (23:18) and explained that the wicked were absorbed with violence, not with enjoying the profits of their wickedness (24:1). The direct contrast between the fates of the wicked and righteous (24:20a; 23:18a) is also the topic of 13:9 (on the idiom of an extinguished lamp, cf. 20:20 and 2 Sam. 21:17).

Some commentators suggest that because these three sayings are so closely related (even to the point of overlapping) this section of the Book was composed of smaller collections that were simply collated without editing. It is, however, a highly effective teaching technique to examine the same prohibition (in this case, "do not envy the wicked") from several points of view. It may perhaps be even more effective because they are dispersed throughout the larger passage.

24:21–22. The human king is worthy of respect and obedience because he is the chosen regent of the LORD, the great King (cf. David's attitude toward Saul; 1 Sam. 24:6; 26:9ff). The positive and negative commandments in v. 21 present opposed options. To fear the LORD and king is to avoid the company of those who do not; to seek them out is to demonstrate lack of respect for the divinely ordained authority.

The participle translated "those who change" (HED #8521) could also mean "those who repeat [a matter]" (cf. 17:9), in which case the line would warn

3156.151	23.	1612, 431	3937, 2550	5421.542, 6686	904, 5122	1118, 3005
v Qal act ptc ms		cj, dem pron	prep, n mp	v Hiphil inf abs, n mp	prep, n ms	neg part, adj
יוֹדֵעַ		גַּם־אֵלֶּה	לַחֲכָמִים	הַכֵּר־פָּנִים	בְּמִשְׁפָּט	בַּל־טוֹב
yôdhēa'		gam-'ēlleh	lachăkhāmîm	hakkēr-pānîm	bemishpāṭ	bal-ṭôv
one who knows		also these	to the wise	recognizing faces	during judgment	not good

24.	569.151	3937, 7856	6926	887	7181.126	6194
	v Qal act ptc ms	prep, n ms	adj	pers pron	v Qal impf 3mp, ps 3ms	n mp
	אֹמֵר	לְרָשָׁע	צַדִּיק	אָתָּה	יִקְּבֻהוּ	עַמִּים
	'ōmēr	lerāshā'	tsaddîq	'āttāh	yiqqevuhû	'ammîm
	one who says	to the wicked	righteous	you	they will curse him	peoples

2278.126	3947	25.	3937, 3306.552	5459.121	6142
v Qal impf 3mp, ps 3ms	n mp		cj, prep, art, v Hiphil ptc mp	v Qal impf 3ms	cj, prep, ps 3mp
יִזְעָמֻהוּ	לְאֻמִּים		וְלַמּוֹכִיחִים	יִנְעָם	וַעֲלֵיהֶם
yiz'āmuhû	le'ummîm		welammôkhîchîm	yin'ām	wa'ălêhem
they will curse him	peoples		but to those who chastise	it will be pleasant	and on them

971.122	1318, 3008	26.	8004	5583.121	8178.551	1745
v Qal impf 3fs	n fs, n ms		n fd	v Qal impf 3ms	v Hiphil ptc ms	n mp
תָּבוֹא	בִּרְכַּת־טוֹב		שְׂפָתַיִם	יִשָּׁק	מֵשִׁיב	דְּבָרִים
tāvô'	virkath-ṭôv		sephāthayim	yishshāq	mēshîv	devārîm
it will come	a blessing of goodness		lips	he will kiss	one who turns back	words

5416	27.	3679.531	904, 2445	4536	6497.331	904, 7898
adj		v Hiphil impv 2ms	prep, art, n ms	n fs, ps 2ms	cj, v Piel impv 2ms, ps 3fs	prep, art, n ms
נְכֹחִים		הָכֵן	בַּחוּץ	מְלַאכְתֶּךָ	וְעַתְּדָהּ	בַּשָּׂדֶה
nekhōchîm		hākhēn	bachûts	mela'khtekhā	we'attedhāhh	bassādheh
straight		prepare	in the street	your work	and get it ready	in the field

3937	313	1161.113	1041	28.	414, 2030.123
prep, ps 2ms	adv	cj, v Qal pf 2ms	n ms, ps 2ms		adv, v Qal juss 2ms
לָךְ	אַחַר	וּבָנִיתָ	בֵּיתֶךָ		אַל־תְּהִי
lākh	'achar	ûvānîthā	vêthekhā		'al-tehî
for yourself	afterward	then you will build	your house		do not be

5915, 2703	904, 7739	6853.313	904, 8004
n ms, adv	prep, n ms, ps 2ms	cj, v Piel pf 2ms	prep, n fd, ps 2ms
עֵד־חִנָּם	בְּרֵעֶךָ	וַהֲפִתִּיתָ	בִּשְׂפָתֶיךָ
'ēdh-chinnām	berē'ekhā	wahăphittîthā	bisphāthêkhā
a witness without cause	against your fellow	then you will open wide	with your lips

---

and who knoweth the ruin of them both?: … what calamity either one may send?, *Anchor* … Those two can cause great disaster!, *NCV* … and the ruin from either one, who can measure?, *NAB* … how swift falls, from either hand, the blow!, *Knox* … and who knows where it all will end?, *LIVB*.

23. These things also belong to the wise: … These also are sayings of the sages, *Anchor* … More maxims of the wise, *Knox* … These things also concern the wise, *Rotherham*.

It is not good to have respect of persons in judgment: … To show partiality in a judicial decision is wrong, *Anchor* … To have respect for a person's position when judging is not good, *BB* … It is ill done, to let partiality sway thy judgement, *Knox* … It is not fair to favour one side in a suit, *Moffatt* … It is wrong to sentence the poor, and let the rich go free, *LIVB*.

24. He that saith unto the wicked, Thou art righteous: … if thou acquit the guilty, *Knox* … Don't tell the wicked that they are innocent,

NCV … He who says to a guilty man, "You are innocent", *Anchor*.

him shall the people curse: … what people will love thee?, *Knox* … Populations shall curse him, *Rotherham* … Peoples execrate him, *Young* … he will be cursed and hated by everyone, *Good News*.

nations shall abhor him: … nations revile him, *Anchor* … hated by nations, *BB* … people will execrate him, *Goodspeed* … what race will have a good word for thee, *Knox* … people will denounce him, *Moffatt*.

25. But to them that rebuke him shall be delight: ... those who rebuke [the guilty] will be well regarded, *Anchor* ... to reprovers one should be pleasant, *Rotherham* ... those who judge honestly will fare pleasantly, *Goodspeed* ... those who correct him, come out of it well, *JB* ... to them that decide justly, *MAST*.

and a good blessing shall come upon them: ... enjoy a good reputation, *Good News* ... On them will rest the blessing of prosperity, *Goodspeed* ... blessings shall fall on thy head, *Knox* ... good fortune shall be theirs, *Moffatt*.

26. Every man shall kiss his lips that giveth a right answer: ... It is an honor to receive a frank reply, *LIVB* ... He is a true friend who is honest with you, *Moffatt* ... An honest answer is a sign of true friendship, *Good News* ... A straightforward answer is as good as a kiss of friendship, *NEB* ... An honest answer is as pleasing as a kiss on the lips, *NCV*.

27. Prepare thy work without: ... Set your business in order, *Goodspeed* ... Plan what you want on the open ground, *JB* ... Be thy first care what lies without, *Knox* ... Complete your outdoor tasks, *NAB* ... First work your farm, *Moffatt*.

and make it fit for thyself in the field: ... put thy field in order, *Darby* ... until your fields are ready, and you are sure that you can earn a living, *Good News* ... make everything ready on the land, *NEB* ... till thy lands first with all diligence, *Knox*.

and afterwards build thine house: ... then you can marry and set up house, *Moffatt* ... Don't build your house and establish a home until, *Good News*.

28. Be not a witness against thy neighbour without cause: ... Do not for spite give evidence against your neighbor, *Anchor* ... Bear not unfounded witness, *Goodspeed* ...

---

against associating with gossips (cf. 20:19, which uses the same verb "associate [closely] with"). The warning could actually be two-sided: avoid those who plot together to change (i.e., rebel), as well as those who gossip, since gossip often seeds sedition.

The two-sided exhortation/caution is supported by the warning that although kings and the LORD are patient, they will act suddenly in judgment. "Their disaster" refers to the judgment that they bring upon the rebels, a disaster that is incalculable ("who knows?"), but could well entail capital punishment.

This principle is reflected in the general biblical conviction that all governments are established by the LORD for his own purposes, since He is the "King of [over all] kings" and "Lord of lords" (e.g., 1 Sam. 2:6–10; Isa. 10:5–19; 41:1–4; Hab. 1:5–11; Rom. 13:1–7). Those who are wise trust their greater King for peace, justice and well-being (29:26).

24:23a. On the subtitle, see "Overview."

24:23b–26. The first and last verses of this group are general truths applied specifically by vv. 24f. Justice is a major topic in Proverbs, especially its proper administration (cf. 8:15f; 17:15, 26; 18:5; 25:2, 4f; 28:5, 21; 29:2, 4, 14, 26; 31:4–9, and the verses cited below).

To favor one claimant over another for any reason, whether a bribe or favor, social position or personal relationship, is consistently and insistently condemned throughout the proverbs. As in several other verses, it is here simply called "not good" (cf. 17:26; 18:5; 28:21 [28:21a is nearly identical to 24:23b]), though it is also called an "abomination to the LORD" (17:15).

Acquitting or justifying the guilty earns outraged contempt (v. 24) from the innocent, who conclude that they have no hope of receiving justice, since truth is not the standard by which cases are decided. On the other hand, those who condemn the guilty are blessed for upholding the Law and for vindicating the innocent (v. 25). However, this blessing does not only come from people: God himself promises that He blesses the pursuit of justice in obedience to his law (cf. Deut. 4:1–8; 16:20).

Although v. 26 may have been originally independent, its position with these three "judicial" verses suggests that it should be interpreted as an encouragement to anyone in a position to determine guilt or innocence or to decide between opposing claims. The right answer is always encouraging: true justice is heartening indeed.

24:27. Although a house is more visible and tangible than crops (especially before they are fully grown), food is necessary to life, while a house is not. This proverb encourages the prudent to plan so that they do each job in its time (e.g., 10:5). The seed must be sown at the right time, or there will be no harvest, but after the grain is sown, while it is growing in the field, the house can be built (cf. 24:30–34; 28:19).

24:28–29. These verses were apparently originally separate, but were joined in order to make a slightly different point. That they were originally independent can be seen from the contrast between "without cause" (v. 28a) and the vengeance motif of v. 29, which says that the neighbor has, in fact, done something for which vengeance (or justice) could be

29.

414, 569.123	3626, 866	6449.111, 3937	3772	6449.125, 3937
adv, v Qal juss 2ms	prep, rel part	v Qal pf 3ms, prep, ps 1cs	adv	v Qal impf 1cs, prep, ps 3ms
אַל־תֹּאמַר	כַּאֲשֶׁר	עָשָׂה־לִי	כֵּן	אֶעֱשֶׂה־לּוֹ
'al-tō'mar	ka'ăsher	'āsāh-lî	kēn	'e'ĕseh-lô
do not say	according to what	he has done to me	so	I will do to him

8178.525	3937, 382	3626, 6714	**30.**	6142, 7898	382, 6339	5882.115
v Hiphil impf 1cs	prep, art, n ms	prep, n ms, ps 3ms		prep, n ms	n ms, adj	v Qal pf 1cs
אָשִׁיב	לָאִישׁ	כְּפָעֳלוֹ		עַל־שְׂדֵה	אִישׁ־עָצֵל	עָבַרְתִּי
'āshîv	lā'îsh	kephā'ălô		'al-sedhēh	'îsh-'ātsēl	'āvartî
I will return	to the man	according to his deed		beside the field of	a lazy man	I passed by

6142, 3884	119	2742, 3949	**31.**	2079	6148.111	3725
cj, prep, n ms	n ms	adj, n ms		cj, intrj	v Qal pf 3ms	adj, ps 3ms
וְעַל־כֶּרֶם	אָדָם	חֲסַר־לֵב		וְהִנֵּה	עָלָה	כֻּלּוֹ
we'al-kerem	'ādhām	chăsar-lēv		wehinnēh	'ālāh	khullô
and beside the vineyard of	a man	lacking in heart		and behold	it had gone up	all of it

7347B	3803.416	6686	2839	1474	63
n mp	v Pual pf 3cp	n mp, ps 3ms	n mp	cj, n ms	n fp, ps 3ms
קִמְּשֹׂנִים	כָּסּוּ	פָּנָיו	חֲרֻלִּים	וְגֶדֶר	אֲבָנָיו
qimmesōnîm	kāssû	phānâv	chărullîm	weghedher	'ăvānâv
thorny plants	they covered	its surface	nettles	and the stone wall of	his stones

2117.212	**32.**	2463.125	609	8308.125	3949	7495.115
v Niphal pf 3fs		cj, v Qal impf 1cs	pers pron	v Qal impf 1cs	n ms, ps 1cs	v Qal pf 1cs
נֶהֱרָסָה		וָאֶחֱזֶה	אָנֹכִי	אָשִׁית	לִבִּי	רָאִיתִי
nehĕrāsāh		wā'echĕzeh	'ānōkhî	'āshîth	libbî	rā'îtî
it had been broken down		and I looked	I	I will set	my heart	I saw

4089.115	4284	**33.**	4746	8535	4746	8900	4746	2355	3135
v Qal pf 1cs	n ms		sub	n fp	sub	n fp	sub	n ms	n fd
לָקַחְתִּי	מוּסָר		מְעַט	שֵׁנוֹת	מְעַט	תְּנוּמוֹת	מְעַט	חִבֻּק	יָדַיִם
lāqachtî	mûsār		me'at	shēnôth	me'at	tenûmôth	me'at	chibbuq	yādhayim
I took	instruction		a little	sleep	a little	slumber	a little	folding of	hands

Don't testify spitefully against an innocent neighbor, *LIVB* ... Never give baseless evidence against your neighbour, *Moffatt* ... Don't testify against your neighbor for no good reason, *NCV*.

and deceive not with thy lips: ... or say misleading things about him, *Good News* ... wouldst thou spread lying tales?, *Knox* ... So mightest thou open too wide thy lips, *Rotherham* ... nor misrepresent him in your evidence, *NEB* ... never mislead men by what you say, *Moffatt*.

29. Say not, I will do so to him as he hath done to me: ... Do not say, "I will treat my neighbour as my neighbour treated me, *JB* ... Nor be content to say, I am but serving him as he served me, *Knox* ... Don't say, "Now I can pay him back for all his meanness to me!", *LIVB*.

I will render to the man according to his work: ... I will repay the man for his act!, *Anchor* ... I'll get even with him!, *Good News* ... I pay off old scores, *Knox* ... I will pay them back for what they have done, *NRSV*.

30. I went by the field of the slothful: ... I walked through the field of the indolent, *Anchor* ... sluggard, *ASV* ... hater of work, *BB* ... I passed by the field of a lazy man, *Berkeley* ... By the idler's field I was passing, *JB*.

and by the vineyard of the man void of understanding: ... by the vine-garden of the man without sense, *BB* ... where idleness reigned and improvidence, *Knox* ... the thriftless, *Moffatt* ... the dull-witted, *Anchor* ... of a stupid person, *NRSV* ... a man lacking sense, *Rotherham*.

31. And, lo, it was all grown over with thorns: ... full of thorns, *BB* ... thistles, *Darby* ... full of thorn bushes, *Good News* ... there it all lay, deep in thorns, *JB* ... Nettles were everywhere, *Knox*.

and nettles had covered the face thereof: ... The surface covered with weeds, *Anchor* ... covered with waste plants, *BB* ... briers had covered the ground, *Knox*.

and the stone wall thereof was broken down: ... was in ruins, *NIV* ...

had fallen down, *NCV* … stones of its walls had been torn down, *NEB* … stone fence thereof had been thrown down, *Rotherham.*

32. Then I saw, and considered it well: … I looked, and took it to heart, *Anchor* … reflected upon it, *Goodspeed* … I saw and I took good note, *NEB* … I applied my heart to what I observed, *NIV.*

I looked upon it, and received instruction: … I saw, and I got

teaching from it, *BB* … I drew this lesson from the sight, *JB* … found a warning in that ill example, *Knox* … I looked—I accepted correction, *Rotherham* … I observed and received instruction, *Berkeley.*

33. Yet a little sleep, a little slumber: … Go ahead and take your nap, *Good News* … Sleep on (thought I) a little longer, yawn a little longer, *Knox* … A little extra sleep, A little more slumber, *LIVB* … You sleep a little; you take a nap, *NCV.*

a little folding of the hands to sleep: … A little longer with hands folded in repose, *Anchor* … Fold your hands and rest awhile, *Good News* … a little folding of the arms to lie back, *JB* … a little longer pillow head on hand, *Knox.*

34. So shall thy poverty come as one that travelleth: … soon you will be as poor as if you had been robbed, *NCV* … So loss will come on you like an outlaw, *BB* … yes, and poverty will pounce on you, *Moffatt* … and your

---

sought. Of itself, v. 28 is similar to other proverbs that condemn false testimony (cf. Exo. 20:16; 21:1ff; Lev. 19:16; Deut. 19:16–21), and v. 29, like 20:22, warns against seeking vengeance (cf. Deut. 32:35).

Together they condemn a spirit of belligerence that seeks confrontation, despite whether the other party deserves it. Fools lack self-control, and so vent their fury immediately upon being frustrated or injured. The wise, who understand the danger of angry words and the value of silence, are able to exercise self-control (cf. 10:19; 14:29; 17:27f).

24:30–34. Solomon addresses indolence in two brief poems (6:6–11; 24:30–34), as well as in many individual proverbs, and Hezekiah's men compiled four further sayings about laziness (26:13–16). All of this suggests that sloth was not a significant problem in ancient Israel, perhaps especially among relatively well-to-do youths (see "Overview").

This poem describes a process of observation, reflection and conclusion, ending with a proverb (24:33f) that is identical to an earlier saying (6:10f). This description has led scholars to see these steps as the process by which proverbs were created. Proverbs, after all, draw principles from an apparent variety of experiences by identifying their common elements. Though some scholars draw the conclusion that the underlying message of this poem is that the wise did not claim divine authority for their insights, this is untenable in light of such passages as Prov. 2:5f.

24:30. The wise man, passing a ruinous property, realized that it belonged to someone who did not understand prudence. His laziness had destroyed all that he had and left it a worthless wreck (cf. Ecc. 10:18).

Although nearly any type of work can illustrate slothfulness, agricultural imagery was especially appropriate in an agrarian economy in which no one was far removed from the land and its care. Successful farming requires doing each season's work in its time (cf. 10:5; 20:4). The cycle of loosening the soil, sowing, guarding (from birds), reaping, threshing, winnowing and storing is necessarily sequential and cannot be changed. This analogy, that success requires the proper pursuit at the right time, thus fits life, which is likewise seasonal.

24:31. None of these conditions is an immediate result of laziness. They are all products of long-term neglect that fail to address the most pressing need. It usually takes one or two seasons of failing to plow or sow for weeds to "cover the face" of a field. Stone walls do not collapse at once, but gradually, one or two stones at a time, due to frost heaves and other effects of weather during the year. Similarly, laziness is not the result of a conscious decision, but is revealed in the cumulative effect of many minor choices—not to plow, not to sow, not to fix the wall.

24:32. The wise man realizes that every situation is an opportunity to learn. One difference between the wise and fools is that the wise constantly seek to increase their wisdom, looking for opportunities from which they can learn. Fools, on the other hand, thinking themselves wise (26:12), despise any opportunity to learn, whether by their own observation and reflection, as here, or from the lips of others (12:15).

24:33–34. These verses are virtually identical to 6:10f. Because the preceding verses are quite different, however, they have a slightly different function. The earlier poem is addressed to the sluggard in its entirety. These verses are preceded by a soliloquy, in which the wise man relates his observations and thoughts. Proverbs 6:6–11 involves the sluggard from the first, encouraging him to observe

24:34

3937, 8311.141	34.	971.111, 2050.751	7677	4408
prep, v Qal inf con		cj, v Qal pf 3ms, v Hithpael ptc ms	n ms, ps 2ms	cj, n mp, ps 2ms
לִשְׁכָּב		וּבָא־מִתְהַלֵּךְ	רֵישֶׁךָ	וּמַחְסֹרֶיךָ
lishkāv		ûvā'-mithhallēkh	rēyōshekhā	ûmachşōrêkhā
to rest		and what goes back and forth will come	your poverty	and your lack

25:1

3626, 382	4182	25:1	1612, 431	5091	8406	866	6514.516
prep, n ms	n ms		cj, dem pron	n mp	pn	rel part	v Hiphil pf 3cp
כְּאִישׁ	מָגֵן		גַּם־אֵלֶּה	מִשְׁלֵי	שְׁלֹמֹה	אֲשֶׁר	הֶעְתִּיקוּ
keʾîsh	māghēn		gam-'ēlleh	mishlê	sheʹlōmōh	'āsher	heʹättîqû
like a man with	a shield		also these	the proverbs of	Solomon	which	they transcribed

596	2488	4567, 3171	2.	3638	435	5846.541	1745
n mp	pn	n ms, pn		n ms	n mp	v Hiphil inf con	n ms
אַנְשֵׁי	חִזְקִיָּה	מֶלֶךְ־יְהוּדָה		כְּבֹד	אֱלֹהִים	הַסְתֵּר	דָּבָר
'anshê	chizqîyāh	melekh-yeʹhûdhāh		keʹvōdh	'ĕlōhîm	hastēr	dāvār
the men of	Hezekiah	the king of Judah		the glory of	God	to hide	a matter

3638	4567	2811.141	1745	3.	8452	3937, 7599	800
cj, n ms	n mp	v Qal inf con	n ms		n md	prep, art, n ms	cj, n fs
וּכְבֹד	מְלָכִים	חֲקֹר	דָּבָר		שָׁמַיִם	לָרוּם	וָאָרֶץ
ûkheʹvōdh	meʹlākhîm	chăqōr	dāvār		shāmayim	lārûm	wā'ārets
and the glory of	kings	to explore	a matter		the heavens	for the height	and the earth

3937, 6232	3949	4567	375	2812	4.	1965.142	5698
prep, art, n ms	cj, n ms	n mp	sub	n ms		v Qal inf abs	n mp
לָעֹמֶק	וְלֵב	מְלָכִים	אֵין	חֵקֶר		הָגוֹ	סִיגִים
lā'ōmeq	weʹlēv	meʹlākhîm	'ên	chēqer		hāghô	sîghîm
for the depth	and the heart of	kings	there is not	examination		considering	dross

4623, 3826B	3428.121	3937, 7170.151	3747	5.	1965.142	7857
prep, n ms	cj, v Qal impf 3ms	prep, art, v Qal act ptc ms	n ms		v Qal inf abs	n ms
מִכָּסֶף	וַיֵּצֵא	לַצֹּרֵף	כְּלִי		הָגוֹ	רֶשַׁע
mikkāseph	wayyētsē'	latstsōrēph	keʹlî		hāghô	rāshā'
from the silver	and it will go out	for the smith	a vessel		considering	the wicked

poverty will come upon you as a bandit, *Berkeley* … ay, but poverty will not wait, *Knox* … like a footpad, *REB* … [as] a roving plunderer, *Darby*.

and thy want as an armed man: … your destitution like a beggar, *Anchor* … your want like an unyielding warrior, *Berkeley* … you will have as little as if you had been held up, *NCV* … the day of distress will not wait, *Knox* … violently like a bandit, *LIVB*.

25:1. These are also proverbs of Solomon: … parables, *Geneva* … The following also are maxims, *Moffatt*.

which the men of Hezekiah king of Judah copied out: … transmitted by the men of, *Anchor* … edited, *Goodspeed* … transcribed at the court of Hezekiah, *JB* … copied out by scholars under Hezekiah, *Moffatt* … that the officials of King Hezekiah of Judah copied, *NRSV*.

2. It is the glory of God to conceal a thing: … to keep a thing secret, *BB* … to hide a thing, *KJVII* … We honor God for what he conceals, *Good News* … For mysteries unfathomable, praise God, *Knox* … The glory of God lies in what he conceals, *Anchor*.

but the honour of kings is to search out a matter: … The glory of kings in what they bring to light, *Anchor* … the glory of kings to fathom a matter, *Goodspeed* … to sift it thoroughly, the glory of kings, *JB* … for mysteries revealed, the king, *Knox* … Kings are honored for what they can discover, *NCV*.

3. The heaven for height, and the earth for depth: … As the heavens above are high and the world below is deep, *Anchor* … High as heaven thou must look, deep as earth, *Knox* … You cannot understand the height of heaven, the size of the earth, *LIVB* … No one can measure the height of the skies or the depth of the earth, *NCV*.

and the heart of kings is unsearchable: … The mind of kings is unfathomable, *Anchor* … there is no searching out the mind of a king, *Berkeley* … You never know what a king is thinking, *Good News* … ere the mind of kings shall be made known to thee, *Knox* … or all that goes on in the king's mind!, *LIVB*.

4. Take away the dross from the silver: … By the removal of impurities

the ant and draw his own conclusion (which is dictated in vv. 10f). This poem, on the other hand, draws the reader along by narrating a story—the "punch line" is delayed until the end.

The ant's diligent busyness (6:7ff) contrasts with the ruinous result of the sluggard's laziness (24:31f). The point, however, is identical: whoever is not diligent has chosen ruination (cf. 10:4; 14:23; 15:19; 20:4; 21:25f; 23:20f).

25:1–29:27. *There are some differences between these materials and the earlier Solomonic collection (see the "Overview"). Proverbs 25–29 contain nearly all of the emblematic proverbs in the Book (35 proverbs, encompassing 36 of 138 verses, more than one-quarter of these 5 chapters).*

There are also some thematic groups, although these are not poems per se (with the exception of 27:23–27), such as the proverbs about the king (25:2–7), the sluggard (26:13–16) and destructive speech (26:23–28). Although these proverbs vary, chs. 25–27 contain quite a few emblematic proverbs, and chs. 28–29 are characterized by antithetical sayings. Chapters 28–29 have also been called "the book of kingship," because of the many verses related to the king.

25:1. Hezekiah, the fourteenth king of Judah, reigned more than 200 years after Solomon's death. He ruled alongside his father Ahaz as co-regent (ca. 729–716), before he became king in his own right. According to Kings and Chronicles (2 Ki. 18:1–6; 2 Ch. 29:1f), Hezekiah was a good king, who rejected his father's paganism, "opened the doors of the Temple" (2 Chr. 29:3) and ordered the priests to restore the true worship of the LORD (2 Ch. 29:4–11).

At some point during his long reign (716–687/86 B.C.), he (or someone working for him) discovered one or more documents—probably scrolls—containing some of Solomon's proverbs. Since the major religious activity of Hezekiah was the cleansing of the Temple, they may well have been in one of the temple storerooms. It is also possible, however, that these materials had always been available and that someone decided during Hezekiah's reign to add them to Solomon's other proverbs.

Hezekiah's response, however, demonstrates his great respect for the traditions of his fathers. His great-grandson, Josiah, responded in a similar way a century later when the scroll of the Law was discovered while the Temple was being cleansed (cf. 2 Ki. 22:8–23:25; 2 Ch. 34:14–35:19). Hezekiah some-

how recognized that these proverbs were Solomonic and ordered them added to the Book of Proverbs, which probably only consisted of Prov. 1–24 and Prov. 30–31 (see the "Overview"). They put these materials before the non-Israelite materials, probably in order to keep the Solomonic corpus intact.

25:2–7. *Five of these six verses mention the king, forming a topical group (vv. 4f and 6f are compound proverbs), which is probably the result of editorial work by Hezekiah's men (see comments on 25:1–29:27, above).*

25:2–3. These verses are carefully interwoven. Their first and last lines describe what cannot be known (the mind of God and of the king), while the inner lines (vv. 2b–3a) describe the searching king and the searched universe. The lines may have been originally independent; if they were, Hezekiah's men combined them brilliantly.

God could give rulers the knowledge that they need in order to rule justly—either directly or through his prophets. However, if He does not do this, the king's responsibility is to study the affairs of justice so that he judges righteously. To determine how the standards of God apply to a given situation and then to obey them is to be established in righteousness (cf. 29:14).

Kings' thoughts and intents are ultimately as unknowable as heaven and earth (a biblical merism for "everything" or "the universe"). Some Israelites of Solomon's day would probably have known of the astronomical observations and data of the Babylonians, and mining was an important part of the ancient Near Eastern economy (cf. Job 28:1–11), so whereas heaven and earth could be studied and known, if only in a very limited sense, the hearts of kings are inscrutable. The wise, therefore, never presume to understand what the king is thinking (cf. 14:10, 13). Instead, they listen and offer counsel when it is sought.

The theme of the unseen heart, unknown by anyone except God, lies behind this proverb (cf. 16:2; 17:3; Pss. 7:9; 26:2; 139:23f; Jer. 17:9f). It also demonstrated Jesus' divinity when He discerned the motives of those around Him (cf. Matt. 22:18; John 2:24f), as well as the divine origin of the Scripture (Heb. 3:12).

25:4–5. In order to be cast effectively, silver must be as pure as possible, since impurities can discolor and weaken the casting (alloys are not in view here). The first step in creating utensils, then, is to purify the silver. Similarly, a king's throne is made

3937, 6686, 4567	3679.221	904, 6928	3802
prep, n mp, n ms	cj, v Niphal impf 3ms	prep, art, n ms	n ms, ps 3ms
לִפְנֵי־מֶלֶךְ	וְיִכּוֹן	בַּצֶּדֶק	כִּסְאוֹ
liphnê-melekh	weyikkôn	batstsedheq	kis'ô
the presence of the king	and it will be established	in righteousness	his throne

6.

414, 1991.723	3937, 6686, 4567	904, 4887	1448	414, 6198.123
adv, v Hithpael juss 2ms	prep, n mp, n ms	cj, prep, n ms	n mp	adv, v Qal juss 2ms
אַל־תִּתְהַדַּר	לִפְנֵי־מֶלֶךְ	וּבִמְקוֹם	גְּדֹלִים	אַל־תַּעֲמֹד
'al-tithhaddar	liphnê-melekh	ûvimqôm	gedhōlîm	'al-ta'āmōdh
do not honor yourself	the presence of a king	and in a place of	great ones	do not stand

7.

3706	3005	569.141, 3937	6148.131	2077	4623, 8584.541
cj	adj	v Qal inf con, prep, ps 2ms	v Qal impv 2ms	adv	prep, v Hiphil inf con, ps 2ms
כִּי	טוֹב	אֲמָר־לְךָ	עֲלֵה	הֵנָּה	מֵהַשְׁפִּילְךָ
kî	tôv	'āmār-lekhā	'ălēh	hēnnāh	mēhashpîlekhā
because	better	to be said to you	come up	here	than your being made low

3937, 6686	5233	866	7495.116	6084	414, 3428.123	3937, 7662.141
prep, n mp	n ms	rel part	v Qal pf 3cp	n fd, ps 2ms	adv, v Qal juss 2ms	prep, v Qal inf con
לִפְנֵי	נָדִיב	אֲשֶׁר	רָאוּ	עֵינֶיךָ	אַל־תֵּצֵא	לָרִב
liphnê	nādhîv	'ăsher	rā'û	'ênêkhā	'al-tētsē'	lāriv
before	a leader	what	they have seen	your eyes	do not go out	to plead a case

(**8.** preceding אַל־תֵּצֵא)

4257.341	6678	4242, 6449.123	904, 321	904, 3757.541	881
v Piel inf con	cj	intrg, v Qal impf 2ms	prep, n fs, ps 3fs	prep, v Hiphil inf con	do, ps 2ms
מַהֵר	פֶּן	מַה־תַּעֲשֶׂה	בְּאַחֲרִיתָהּ	בְּהַכְלִים	אֹתְךָ
mahēr	pen	mah-ta'āseh	be'achārîthāhh	behakhlîm	'ōthekhā
acting quickly	otherwise	what will you do	at its end	when humiliating	you

9.

7739	7662.141	7663	882, 7739	5660	311
n ms, ps 2ms	v Qal inf con, ps 2ms	n ms	prep, n ms, ps 2ms	cj, n ms	adj
רֵעֶךָ	רִיבְךָ	רִיב	אֶת־רֵעֶךָ	וְסוֹד	אַחֵר
rē'ekhā	rîvekhā	rîv	'eth-rē'ekhā	wesôdh	'achēr
your fellow	your pleading of a case	a lawsuit	with your fellow	but a secret of	another

10.

414, 1581.123	6678, 2720.321	8471.151	1730	3940
adv, v Qal juss 2ms	cj, v Piel impf 3ms, ps 2ms	v Qal act ptc ms	cj, n fs, ps 2ms	neg part
אַל־תְּגַל	פֶּן־יְחַסֶּדְךָ	שֹׁמֵעַ	וְדִבָּתְךָ	לֹא
'al-teghal	pen-yechassedhkhā	shōmēa'	wedhibbāthekhā	lō'
do not reveal	so he will not shame you	one who hears	and your slander	not

from silver, *Anchor* ... Take away the waste from silver, *BB* ... Rid silver of dross, *Knox* ... Remove the scum from the silver, *NCV*.

and there shall come forth a vessel for the refiner: ... the artist can produce a thing of beauty, *Good News* ... it emerges wholly purified, *JB* ... it will go to the silversmith for jewelry, *NKJV* ... the cup shines bright, *Knox* ... the silver shines out pure, *Moffatt*.

5. Take away the wicked from before the king: ... [So] by the expulsion of a wicked man from the king's presence, *Anchor* ... Keep evil advisers away from the king, *Good News* ... rid the court of knaves, *Knox* ... When you remove corrupt men from the king's court, *LIVB* ... remove scoundrels from a king, *Moffatt*.

and his throne shall be established in righteousness: ... His throne is firmly founded in right, *Anchor* ... his government will be known for its justice, *Good News* ... and on uprightness his throne is founded, *JB* ... and the throne stands firm, *Knox* ... then his government will be honest and last a long time, *NCV*.

6. Put not forth thyself in the presence of the king: ... Do not give yourself airs at a royal court, *Anchor* ... Do not take glory for yourself before the king, *BB* ... When you stand before the king, don't try to impress him, *Good News* ... Claim not honor, *Goodspeed* ... Never play the great lord at court, *Knox*.

and stand not in the place of great men: ... Or take up your position where the great belong, *Anchor* ... as though you were some powerful prince, *LIVB* ... do not claim a place among great men, *NIV* ... don't ...

pretend to be important, *Good News* ... mingle with men of rank, *Knox*.

7. For better it is that it be said unto thee, Come up hither: ... It is better to be asked to take a higher position, *Good News* ... who would not rather be beckoned to a higher place, *Knox*.

than that thou shouldest be put lower: ... Than to be humiliated, *Anchor* ... than to be told to give your place to someone more important, *Good News* ... than to be humbled, *Goodspeed* ... than be put to the blush, *Knox* ... than to be sent back to the end of the line, *LIVB*.

in the presence of the prince: ... before the ruler, *BB* ... before the noble, *Goodspeed* ... in the king's presence?, *Knox*.

whom thine eyes have seen: ... Because of something you have seen, *NCV* ... What you have witnessed, *REB*.

8. Go not forth hastily to strive: ... Don't be hot-headed and rush to court!, *LIVB* ... Do not be quick to go to law about what you have seen, *BB* ... be in no hurry to tell everyone, *REB* ... Report not hastily to the multitude, *Goodspeed* ... do not disclose hastily what thy eyes have witnessed, *Knox*.

lest thou know not what to do in the end thereof: ... else what will you do in its outcome, *Berkeley* ... and there is no undoing the mischief, *Knox* ... You may start something you can't finish, *LIVB* ... for what will you do later on, *Douay*.

when thy neighbour hath put thee to shame: ... if the other man later confounds you?, *Anchor* ... If another witness later proves you wrong, *Good News* ... and go down before your neighbor in shameful defeat, *LIVB* ... when you are taxed with it?, *Moffatt* ... or it will end in bitter reproaches from your friend, *NEB*.

9. Debate thy cause with thy neighbour himself: ... Argue your cause with your neighbor, *Berkeley* ... settle it between yourselves, *Good News* ... Have the quarrel out with your neighbour, *JB* ... To thy friend's private ear open thy wrongs, *Knox* ... Talk the thing over with the other man, *Moffatt*.

and discover not a secret to another: ... do not betray another man's confidence, *NIV* ... disclose not the secret of another, *ASV* ... do not uncover a secret to another, *KJVII*.

10. Lest he that heareth it put thee to shame: ... Lest someone who hears it denounce you, *Anchor* ... Or your hearer may say evil of you, *BB* ... lest he that heareth [it] disgrace thee, *Darby* ... expose your shame, *NIV* ... lest he accuse you of slander, *LIVB* ... hearing it, will turn on thee with reproaches, *Knox*.

and thine infamy turn not away: ... and your reputation be ruined, *NKJV*

---

secure by justice and righteousness (16:12; 29:14), because he is responsible to establish justice in the land; thus, the first step in doing this is to eliminate graft and corruption in the government. A king cannot rule justly if his officials are corrupt. The king must not, therefore, be naive about the qualities of those serving under him. Their performance creates satisfaction or unrest in the nation, which, in turn, establishes or threatens his reign. If the metal were too impure, it would be rejected as useless for the smith's purposes; if the nation had too much dross, it would be rejected (cf. Jer. 6:27–30).

25:6–7. Modesty in the presence of a superior is not merely good etiquette, it is good sense. Self-aggrandizement may well lead to embarassment (cf. Luke 14:7–11) or disaster (cf. 29:23). Even knowing the rest of the guest list may not be enough to enable a person to determine who is most distinguished or important. Arrogance, in fact, renders people incapable of discernment, since it always exalts its own importance and denigrates the accomplishments of others. These verses are also closely related to 27:1f, which warn against boasting about what someone will do (v. 1) or has done (v. 2).

25:8. Proverbs never commends haste, preferring in its stead action after reflection on the possible consequences of each choice. One side in a conflict may seem clearly right (or wrong), but even such a case must still be studied with care. There is nearly always someone else who knows more about the situation and who can humiliate those who rushed to pursue or decide a case without sufficient knowledge.

25:9–10. Tied to the preceding verse by the idea of strife or legal contention, this proverb warns that betraying confidentiality can have dire consequences. The first line could be translated, "Pursue your lawsuit with your neighbor." Verse 9b, however, warns that whatever is learned in the course of the case should remain confidential. Overcoming the bad reputation that comes from betrayal is not easy, if even possible. And such a reputation is unavoidable, since bad news travels quickly and is not easily forgotten (cf. 26:22), which means that word will eventually get back to the one whose confidence was betrayed. This proverb is another warning to consider carefully both the content and effect of words, in this case, because they will rebound on the speaker, to his or her detriment.

11.

Strong's	Parsing	Hebrew	Translit	English
8178.122	v Qal impf 3fs	תָּשׁוּב	thāshûv	it will turn back
8931	n mp	תַּפּוּחֵי	tappûchê	apples of
2174	n ms	זָהָב	zāhāv	gold
904, 5031	prep, n fp	בְּמַשְׂכִּיּוֹת	bemaskîyôth	in images of
3826B	n ms	כָּסֶף	kāseph	silver
1745	n ms	דָּבָר	dāvār	a word
1744.155	v Qal pass ptc ms	דָּבֻר	dāvur	being spoken

12.

Strong's	Parsing	Hebrew	Translit	English
6142, 673	prep, n mp, ps 3ms	עַל־אָפְנָיו	'al-'āphenâv	at its proper time
5321	n ms	נֶזֶם	nezem	the ring of
2174	n ms	זָהָב	zāhāv	gold
2583, 3929	cj, n ms, n ms	וַחֲלִי־כָתֶם	wachălî-khāthem	and an ornament of gold
3306.551	v Hiphil ptc ms	מוֹכִיחַ	môkhîach	chastising
2550	n ms	חָכָם	chākhām	a wise man

13.

Strong's	Parsing	Hebrew	Translit	English
6142, 238	prep, n fs	עַל־אֹזֶן	'al-'ōzen	on an ear
8471.153	v Qal act ptc fs	שֹׁמָעַת	shōmā'ath	listening
3626, 7064, 8345	prep, n fs, n ms	כְּצִנַּת־שֶׁלֶג	ketsinnath-shelegh	like the coldness of snow
904, 3219	prep, n ms	בְּיוֹם	beyôm	on the day of
7392	n ms	קָצִיר	qātsir	the harvest
7005	n ms	צִיר	tsîr	an envoy

Strong's	Parsing	Hebrew	Translit	English
548.255	v Niphal ptc ms	נֶאֱמָן	ne'ĕmān	being reliable
3937, 8365.152	prep, v Qal act ptc mp, ps 3ms	לְשֹׁלְחָיו	leshōlechâv	to the ones who send him
5497	cj, n fs	וְנֶפֶשׁ	wenephesh	and the soul of
112	n mp, ps 3ms	אֲדֹנָיו	'ădhōnâv	his master
8178.521	v Hiphil impf 3ms	יָשִׁיב	yāshîv	he will cause to return

14.

Strong's	Parsing	Hebrew	Translit	English
5563	n mp	נְשִׂיאִים	nesî'îm	clouds
7593	cj, n fs	וְרוּחַ	werûach	and wind
1700	cj, n ms	וְגֶשֶׁם	wegheshem	but rain
375	sub	אַיִן	'ayin	there is not
382	n ms	אִישׁ	'îsh	a man
2054.751	v Hithpael ptc ms	מִתְהַלֵּל	mithhallēl	one who boasts
904, 5164, 8632	prep, n fs, n ms	בְּמַתַּת־שָׁקֶר	bemattath-shāqer	with a gift of deception

15.

Strong's	Parsing	Hebrew	Translit	English
904, 775	prep, n ms	בְּאֹרֶךְ	be'ōrekh	with length of
653	n md	אַפַּיִם	'appayim	nostrils
6853.421	v Pual impf 3ms	יְפֻתֶּה	yephutteh	he will be persuaded
7389	n ms	קָצִין	qātsîn	a leader
4098	cj, n fs	וְלָשׁוֹן	welāshôn	and a tongue
7679	adj	רַכָּה	rakkāh	tender

16.

Strong's	Parsing	Hebrew	Translit	English
8132.122, 1678	v Qal impf 3fs, n ms	תִּשְׁבָּר־גָּרֶם	tishbār-gārem	it will shatter a bone
1756	n ms	דְּבַשׁ	devash	honey
4834.113	v Qal pf 2ms	מָצָאתָ	mātsā'thā	you have found
404.131	v Qal impv 2ms	אֱכֹל	'ĕkhōl	eat
1823	sub, ps ms	דַּיֶּךָ	dayyekkā	your ample amount

... and your indiscretion will then be beyond recall, *NEB* ... and you might not ever be respected again, *NCV* ... and you can't withdraw what you said, *LIVB* ... to your lasting shame, *Moffatt* ... nor wilt thou lightly recover thy good name, *Knox*.

11. A word fitly spoken: ... A word at the right time, *BB* ... a word spoken in season, *Darby* ... a word spoken in right circumstances, *NASB* ... Timely advice, *LIVB* ... Is a secret which has been whispered in the ear, *Anchor*.

is like apples of gold in pictures of silver: ... Like gold inlay in objects of wrought silver, *Anchor* ... like a design of gold, set in silver, *Good News* ... Like a boss of gold amid silver tracery, *Knox* ... is as lovely as gold apples in a silver basket, *LIVB* ... is like a golden apple laid on silver network, *Moffatt*.

12. As an earring of gold, and an ornament of fine gold: ... Like a nose-ring of gold and an ornament of the best gold, *BB* ... is more valuable than gold rings or jewelry made of the finest gold, *Good News* ... Golden

ear-ring nor pearl drop fits so well, as, *Knox* ... A ring of gold and a vessel of precious metal, *Rotherham*.

so is a wise reprover upon an obedient ear: ... Is a sage's reprimand to an ear that listens, *Anchor* ... is a wise man who says sharp words to an ear ready to give attention, *BB* ... is a wise rebuke to an attentive ear, *JB* ... as wise reproof given to a wise listener, *Knox* ... to accept valid criticism, *LIVB*.

13. As the cold of snow in the time of harvest: ... Like the coolness of snow in the heat of harvest time, *Anchor* … like cold water in the heat of harvest time, *Good News* … Like a draught of snow-cooled water in the time of harvest, *Goodspeed* … as a cool day in the hot summertime, *LIVB* … Like snow that cools a harvest drink, *Moffatt*.

so is a faithful messenger to them that send him: … a reliable messenger, *Anchor* … a trusty messenger, *Knox* … A faithful employee, *LIVB*.

for he refresheth the soul of his masters: … for he gives new life to the soul of his master, *BB* … he

revives the soul of his master, *JB* … will bring thee more relief, *Knox* … he is a treat to those who send him, *Moffatt* … When the life of his masters he restoreth, *Rotherham*.

14. Whoso boasteth himself of a false gift: … so is one who takes credit for an offering he has not given, *BB* … People who promise things that they never give, *Good News* … such is anyone whose promises are princely but never kept, *JB* … such thanks he wins that boasts much, and nothing accomplishes, *Knox* … Whoever falsely boasts of giving, *NKJV*.

is like clouds and wind without rain: … Storm-wrack and cloud and no rain to follow, *Knox* … is like a cloud blowing over a desert without dropping any rain, *LIVB*.

15. By long forbearing is a prince persuaded: … With patience you can convince a ruler, *NCV* … A judge is moved by one who for a long time undergoes wrongs without protest, *BB* … Be patient and you will finally win, *LIVB* … A prince, in his forbearance, may yet be won over to thy cause, *Knox* … With patience a judge may be cajoled, *JB* … By forbearance a ruler is pacified, *Goodspeed*.

25:11. The right word at the right time is like well-crafted jewelry, which is admired and appreciated. Though remarks may appear clever or witty in casual conversation or impromptu remarks, words that are remembered, and thus become effectual, are the product of one who has a disciplined inner life, constantly pondering what he will say under various circumstances (cf. Col. 4:6). This extends even to the proverbs themselves, for one aspect of wisdom is knowing when to apply a particular proverb to a situation.

25:12. This verse could be interpreted as a specific example of the general principle of 25:11. Just as the right jewelry enhances the appearance of the one who wears it, the right word of rebuke makes life more attractive by encouraging somebody to act wisely. A wise person knows how to correct others to their true benefit. The word "listening" (HED #8471), however, implies that wisdom entails knowing who is ready to hear that correcting word. It involves more than being able to point out faults or errors (even in a winsome way); it requires discretion and the ability to understand character.

25:13. Snow during harvest (roughly April through September) would have been a prodigy, remembered and discussed for generations. Any precipitation was unusual during harvest (cf. 1 Sam. 12:17f, where the people feared the event because of the season, not merely because it was in response to Samuel's prayer). But in the heat and dust of harvest, a shower of snow would have revitalized tired workers. Faithfulness is equally rare, just as refreshing, and therefore to be pursued (cf. 10:26). Unlike most, this emblematic proverb explains the emblem.

25:14. We are now given another proverb that relates human behavior to the weather (cf. 25:13, 23; 26:1), from a time when wind and clouds meant life or death, rain or drought. The word used for the type of clouds mentioned here is always associated with lightning and rainstorms in its other biblical occurrences (cf. Ps. 135:7; Jer. 10:13; 51:16). The appearance of these clouds would have been an encouragement, and their dissolution a great disappointment, just like a lying braggart's empty words. The faithfulness of those who make promises must be weighed before putting hope in their words. Although the implication of "falsehood" is that there is no intention of fulfilling the promise, this verse also cautions those who would commit themselves to a course of action. Promises must not be made without forethought, lest those who are depending on their fulfillment be disheartened. It is better not to speak than to promise too much.

25:15. That patience is a virtue is patent throughout Proverbs (e.g., 12:16; 14:17, 29; 15:18). That it is also powerful is not as obvious. This verse is not describing a patiently presented petition that finally wins the day (cf. Luke 18:1–8), as much as the ability to remain unprovoked (cf. the same word "soft" in 15:1), a patience that will be noted and rewarded by those in authority. The resulting victories will confirm the insights of the wise, but astound those who do not understand the nature of true power.

25:16–17. This is a rare two-verse emblematic proverb, in which the first verse is the image which the second applies. In itself, v. 16 clearly cautions against over-indulgence. The combination, however, extends the virtue of moderation beyond physical appetites to human relationships (and, by implication,

17.

3478.531 v Hiphil impv 2ms	7559 n fs, ps 2ms
הֹקַר hōqar — cause it to be rare	רַגְלְךָ raghlekhā — your foot

6678, 7881.123 cj, v Qal impf 2ms, ps 3ms	7287.513 cj, v Hiphil pf 2ms, ps 3ms
פֶּן־תִּשְׂבָּעֶנּוּ pen-tisbā'ennû — so that you will not be satiated	וַהֲקֵאתוֹ wahqē'thô — then you will vomit it

7983.111 cj, v Qal pf 3ms, ps 2ms	6678, 7881.121 cj, v Qal impf 3ms, ps 2ms	7739 n ms, ps 2ms	4623, 1041 prep, n ms
וּשְׂנֵאֶךָ ûsenē'ekhā — then he will hate you	פֶּן־יִשְׂבָּעֲךָ pen-yisbā'äkhā — so that he will not become full of you	רֵעֶךָ rē'ekhā — your fellow	מִבֵּית mibbêth — from the house of

18.

904, 7739 prep, n ms, ps 3ms	6257.151 v Qal act ptc ms	382 n ms	8532.155 v Qal pass ptc ms	2777 cj, n ms	2820 cj, n fs	4812 n ms
בְּרֵעֵהוּ verē'ēhû — against his fellow	עֹנֶה 'ōneh — answering	אִישׁ 'îsh — a man	שָׁנוּן shānûn — being sharpened	וְחֵץ wechēts — and an arrow	וְחֶרֶב wecherev — and a sword	מֵפִיץ mēphîts — a club

19.

4148 n ms	4726.457 v Pual ptc fs	7559 cj, n fs	7753.153 v Qal act ptc fs	8514 n fs	8632 n ms	5915 n ms
מִבְטָח mivṭāch — trust	מוּעָדֶת mû'ādheth — having faltered	וְרֶגֶל wereghel — and a foot	רֹעָה rō'āh — being bad	שֵׁן shēn — a tooth	שָׁקֶר shāqer — deception	עֵד 'ēdh — a witness of

20.

933 n ms	5917.551 v Hiphil ptc ms	7150 n fs	904, 3219 prep, n ms	931.151 v Qal act ptc ms
בֶּגֶד beghedh — a garment	מַעֲדֶה ma'ādheh — one who causes to put on	צָרָה tsārāh — adversity	בְּיוֹם beyôm — on the day of	בּוֹגֵד bôghēdh — one who acts deceitfully

3949, 7737 n ms, adj	6142 prep	904, 8302 prep, art, n mp	8301.151 cj, v Qal act ptc ms	6142, 5611 prep, n ms	2663 n ms	7426 n fs	904, 3219 prep, n ms
לֶב־רָע lev-rā' — a bad heart	עַל 'al — on	בַּשִּׁירִים bashshirîm — with the songs	וְשָׁר weshār — even a singer	עַל־נָתֶר 'al-nāther — on baking soda	חֹמֶץ chōmets — vinegar	קָרָה qārāh — cold	בְּיוֹם beyôm — on a day of

21.

524, 7041 cj, cj, adj	4035 n ms	404.531 v Hiphil impv 2ms, ps 3ms	7983.151 v Qal act ptc ms, ps 2ms	524, 7744 cj, adj
וְאִם־צָמֵא we'im-tsāmē' — and if thirsty	לָחֶם lāchem — food	הַאֲכִלֵהוּ ha'äkhilēhû — feed him	שֹׂנַאֲךָ sōna'äkhā — one who hates you	אִם־רָעֵב 'im-rā'ēv — if hungry

and a soft tongue breaketh the bone: ... can even convince rulers, *Good News* ... hard heart gives place to soft tongue, *Knox* ... gentle words abate his ire, *Moffatt* ... a gentle word can get through to the hard-hearted, *NCV* ... a soft tongue may break down authority, *REB*.

16. Hast thou found honey?: ... When you find honey, *Anchor* ... Do you like honey?, *LIVB*.

eat so much as is sufficient for thee: ... eat just enough for you, *Anchor* ... Eat only what you need, *Berkeley* ... Eat to your satisfaction ... but not to excess, *JB* ... eat thy fill and no more, *Knox* ... Don't eat too much of it, *LIVB*.

lest thou be filled therewith, and vomit it: ... for fear that, being full of it, you may not be able to keep it down, *BB* ... or you will bring it up again, *JB* ... nothing comes of surfeit but vomiting, *Knox* ... too much of it will make you sick, *NEB* ... it will make you throw up, *NCV*.

17. Withdraw thy foot from thy neighbour's house: ... [So] be infre-quent in visiting your neighbor's home, *Anchor* ... Don't visit your neighbor too often, *Good News* ... Set your foot but sparingly in your neighbor's house, *Goodspeed*.

lest he be weary of thee, and so hate thee: ... Lest he see too much of you and begin to dislike you, *Anchor* ... Lest he be sated with you, and give you a cool reception, *Goodspeed* ... you will outwear your welcome!, *LIVB* ... he may grow tired of you, and turn against you, *Moffatt* ... lest he have more than enough of you, and hate you, *NAB*.

18. A man that beareth false witness against his neighbour: … A false accusation, *Good News* … Telling lies about someone, *LIVB* … When you lie about your neighbors, *NCV* … a false witness who denounces his friend, *NEB*.

is a maul, and a sword, and a sharp arrow: … a mace, *Anchor* … a hammer, *BB* … a scattering club, *Berkeley* … What is worse than javelin, sword, and arrow all at once?, *Knox* … Like a war club, *NRSV*.

19. Confidence in an unfaithful man in time of trouble: … so is trust in a faithless man in a time of adversity, *Berkeley* … Depending on an unreliable person in a crisis, *Good News* … such is the fickle when trusted in time of trouble, *JB* … Is confidence in the treacherous in the day of danger, *Rotherham* … is a traitor relied on, *NEB*.

is like a broken tooth, and a foot out of joint: … like having a loose tooth or a palsied foot, *Anchor* … Like a decaying tooth or a sprained ankle, *REB* … a tooth decayed or a foot limping, *NEB* … What is more frail than rotting tooth, or sprained foot?, *Knox* … like trying to chew with a loose tooth or walk with a crippled foot, *Good News*.

20. As he that taketh away a garment in cold weather: … like Disrobing a man on a cold day, *Anchor* … take off your coat in bitter weather, *JB* … lose thy cloak in mid winter, *Knox* … As splendour of dress on a cold day, *Rotherham* … Like a moth in clothing, *NAB*.

and as vinegar upon nitre: … adding sour wine to soda, *Anchor* … like rubbing salt in a wound, *Good News* … Vinegar goes ill with natron, *Knox* … a maggot in wood, *NAB* … Like one who dresses a wound with vinegar, *NEB*.

so is he that singeth songs to an heavy heart: … is he who makes melody to a sad heart, *BB* … Singing to a person who is depressed, *Good News* … Being happy-go-lucky around a person whose heart is heavy, *LIVB* … Singing music to a saddened soul, *Moffatt* … sorrow gnaws at the human heart, *NAB*.

21. If thine enemy be hungry, give him bread to eat: … If your hater is in need of food, give him bread, *BB* … Here is thy chance; feed him, *Knox*.

and if he be thirsty, give him water to drink: … Thirsts he? Of thy well let him drink, *Knox*.

22. For thou shalt heap coals of fire upon his head: … You will make him burn with shame, *Good News* … This will make him feel ashamed of himself, *LIVB* … for so you shall quench blazing passions, *Moffatt*.

---

to every area of life). "Hatred" (HED #7983) in v. 17b could merely refer to being tired of someone's constant presence, although the parallel "vomit" (HED #7287) suggests a stronger emotion. Proverbs encourages balance in relationships (e.g., 27:10).

25:18. Deliberate lies are as deadly as any weapon (cf. 18:21), threatening the life of the falsely accused. Deceitful testimony not only violates the commandment, which the second line virtually duplicates (cf. Exo. 20:16), it is also double-edged. Just as weapons can be used against the ones wielding them, so false testimony can lead to the destruction of the perjuror (cf. Deut. 19:16–20). The nearly universal correction of the first word from "one who scatters" (Masoretic text) to "club" or "war club" reflects the Septuagint and fits the sense (cf. Jer. 51:20), although the only other occurrence of mēphîts (participle of pûts; HED #4812; Nah. 2:1) is also in a military context.

25:19. Knowing the character of friends is a major theme in Proverbs. This verse warns that putting trust in, or confiding in, a treacherous person is as useless (and possibly as dangerous) as a bad tooth or a fall. The insight to recognize the trustworthiness of others so that they can be avoided is a fruit of wisdom. The anomalous forms of both participles

in the first line have been repointed by many to rā'āh, "bad," and mô'adheth, "slipping," respectively.

25:20. By not caring enough to consider the other person's emotional state, fools' careless words (cf. 15:2, etc.) are often irritating. A song that is due to high spirits can be even more irritating than one intended to encourage or cheer. Since external appearances usually disguise inner conditions (14:10; cf. 14:13), the discretion required to know just how to encourage or cheer someone else takes observation and thought. The wise are gracious to recognize and respond to the feelings of others (cf. Rom. 12:15; 1 Cor. 12:26). Proverbs 25:11 shows the difference that discretion makes (cf. 15:23).

25:21–22. These verses seem to address a situation in which an injured party has the upper hand over a former adversary or oppressor who needs the basic necessities of bread and water. In other proverbs, the same idea is much milder: one is to refrain from taking revenge (e.g., 20:22) or from rejoicing when one's enemy falls into disaster (e.g., 24:17f).

The difficult aspect of these verses is the meaning of the "burning coals." There are several possibilities: (1) This may be an image. Treating an enemy kindly is like putting coals in a clay pot so that someone whose cooking fire had gone out could carry

22.

8615.531	4448		3706	1544	887	2954.151	6142, 7513
v Hiphil impv 2ms, ps 3ms	n mp	**22.**	cj	n fp	pers pron	v Qal act ptc ms	prep, n ms, ps 3ms
הַשְׁקֵהוּ	מָיִם		כִּי	גֶּחָלִים	אַתָּה	חֹתֶה	עַל־רֹאשׁוֹ
hashqēhû	māyim		kî	ghechālîm	'attāh	chōtheh	'al-rō'shô
give him a drink	water		because	coals	you	snatching	on his head

23.

3176	8396.321, 3937		7593	7103	2523.322	1700
cj, pn	v Piel impf 3ms, prep, ps 2ms	**23.**	n fs	n ms	v Polel impf 3fs	n ms
וַיהוָה	יְשַׁלֶּם־לָךְ		רוּחַ	צָפוֹן	תְּחוֹלֵל	גָּשֶׁם
wayhwāh	yeshallem-lākh		rûach	tsāphôn	techôlēl	gāshem
and Yahweh	He will repay you		the wind from	the north	it will bring forth	rain

24.

6686	2278.256	4098	5848	3005	3553.141	6142, 6682, 1437
cj, n mp	v Niphal ptc mp	n fs	n ms	adj	v Qal inf con	prep, n fs, n ms
וּפָנִים	נִזְעָמִים	לְשׁוֹן	סָתֶר	טוֹב	שֶׁבֶת	עַל־פִּנַּת־גָּג
ûphānîm	niz'āmîm	leshôn	sāther	ṭôv	sheveth	'al-pinnath-gāgh
and faces	being cursed	the tongue of	secrecy	better	to dwell	on the corner of a roof

25.

4623, 828	4209	1041	2360		4448	7426
prep, n fs	n mp	cj, n ms	n ms	**25.**	n md	adj
מֵאֵשֶׁת	מִדְוֹנִים	וּבֵית	חָבֶר		מַיִם	קָרִים
mē'ēsheth	midhônîm	ûvêth	chāver		mayim	qārîm
than a woman of	contentions	and the household of	association		water	cold

26.

6142, 5497	6106	8444	3009B	4623, 800	4963		4754
prep, n fs	adj	cj, n fs	adj	prep, n fs	n ms	**26.**	n ms
עַל־נֶפֶשׁ	עֲיֵפָה	וּשְׁמוּעָה	טוֹבָה	מֵאֶרֶץ	מֶרְחָק		מַעְיָן
'al-nephesh	'ăyēphāh	ûshemû'āh	ṭôvāh	mē'erets	merchāq		ma'ăyān
concerning a soul	weary	and news	good	from a land of	distance		a place of springs

7806.255	4888	8271.655	6926	4267.151
v Niphal ptc ms	cj, n ms	v Hophal ptc ms	n ms	v Qal act ptc ms
נִרְפָּשׂ	וּמָקוֹר	מָשְׁחָת	צַדִּיק	מָט
nirpās	ûmāqôr	māshechāth	tsaddîq	māṭ
being muddied	and a spring	having been spoiled	a righteous man	faltering

27.

3937, 6686, 7857		404.142	1756	7528.541	3940, 3005	2812
prep, n mp, n ms	**27.**	v Qal inf abs	n ms	v Hiphil inf con	neg part, adj	cj, n ms
לִפְנֵי־רָשָׁע		אָכֹל	דְּבַשׁ	הַרְבּוֹת	לֹא־טוֹב	וְחֵקֶר
liphnê-rāshā'		'ākhōl	devash	harbôth	lō'-ṭôv	wecheqer
before a wicked man		eating	honey	being much	not good	and the exploration of

---

and the Lord shall reward thee: ... will recompense you, *Anchor* ... will vindicate you, *NAB.*

23. The north wind driveth away rain: ... As surely as the north wind brings rain, *Anchor* ... As the north wind gives birth to rain, *BB* ... The north wind stops rain, *Knox* ... As surely as a wind from the north brings cold, *LIVB* ... produces rain, *NRSV.*

so doth an angry countenance a backbiting tongue: ... A whispering tongue brings angry looks, *Anchor* ... and a concealed tongue an angry face, *Berkeley* ... Gossip brings anger, *Good News* ... so an angry glance holds back slander, *NEB* ... a face stirred with indignation, a secretive tongue, *Rotherham.*

24. It is better to dwell in the corner of the housetop: ... corner of a roof, *Anchor* ... better to be living in an angle of the house-top, *BB* ... Better to live on the roof, *Good News* ... Better lodge in a garret, *Knox* ... better to live in a corner of an attic, *LIVB.*

than with a brawling woman and in a wide house: ... than with a bitter-tongued woman, *BB* ... Than to share a spacious house with a quarrelsome wife, *Goodspeed* ... than have a nagging wife and a brawling household, *NEB* ... than in a beautiful home with a cranky, quarrelsome woman, *LIVB* ... Than in a house in common with a contentious woman, *MAST.*

25. As cold waters to a thirsty soul: ... Like a drink of cold water to a weary man, *Anchor* ... Cold water to a thirsty throat, *JB* ... refreshing as cold water to parched lips, *Knox* ... cold waters to a faint soul, *MAST* ... like a cool drink when you are tired, *NCV.*

so is good news from a far country: ... Good news from a distant land, *Anchor* ... from far away, *LIVB* ... good news from a far land is refreshing, *Moffatt.*

26. A righteous man falling down before the wicked: ... a just man who quails before a wicked one, *Anchor* ... such is the upright person trembling before the wicked, *JB* ... when honest men bow down before knaves, *Knox* ... If a godly man compromises with the wicked, *LIVB* ... a righteous man tottering before one who is lawless, *Rotherham.*

is as a troubled fountain, and a corrupt spring: ... Like a trampled fountain, or a polluted spring, *Berkeley* ... A churned-up spring, a fountain fouled, *JB* ... Fouled the spring, poisoned the well, *Knox* ... is like a muddy spring or a dirty well, *NCV* ... like a murky spring and a polluted well, *NKJV* ... Like a spring fouled by animals, *Anchor.*

27. It is not good to eat much honey: ... A surfeit harms, though it be of honey, *Knox* ... It is bad to indulge overmuch in honey, *Moffatt* ... A surfeit of honey is bad for a man, *NEB* ... To eat honey in abundance is not good, *Rotherham.*

---

them home and restart it. This would then be a two-verse emblematic proverb, interpreting the conjunction at the beginning of v. 22 as "for [doing so is like] heaping coals." (2) It may be related to a putative Egyptian ceremony in which a penitent sinner would possibly "wear" coals on his head as a sign of contrition. The coals may signify shame and repentance (and, some suggest, lead to the former enemies' reconciliation). (3) The coals may represent judgment (cf. Pss. 11:6; 140:9f), so that the proverb means that we should act rightly and leave any vengeance to God. This may have been Paul's interpretation. He combined this verse with Deut. 32:35 and used these verses to deny the right of personal vengeance (cf. Rom. 12:20). (4) The verb for "heaping" is literally "snatching" (HED #2954), which may mean "to remove," and thus would be related to Prov. 15:1.

The command is clear (v. 21), even though the explanation or motivation is not. Scripture generally enjoins doing good to everyone, even enemies (e.g., Exo. 23:4f; Matt. 5:43–48). As in other proverbs, the consequence of kindness to those in need is the LORD's blessing (19:17; cf. 14:31; 21:13; 28:27). The basic command is to overcome evil with good.

25:23. Since rain in Canaan is produced by moist air from the Mediterranean colliding with hot, dry air off the eastern desert, rain comes from the west, not the north. This inconsistency with Israelite experience may mean that this proverb originated in a place where rain comes from the north (e.g., Egypt). It is curious that Solomon would not have adapted the proverb to accord with his own knowledge, but this may reflect its great antiquity. The more familiar a saying, the less likely it is to change.

Just as people who spend time outdoors know which weather patterns forecast rain, so those who are attentive to those around them know that certain behaviors yield problems. It is axiomatic that good news is not spread by tale-bearers, but that negative reports are the principal subjects of gossip. In this case, knowing that they bring trouble, the wise avoid people who bear tales in secret (cf. 26:20ff).

25:24. Since roofs were flat, they were often used for living. The Covenant implies this by ordering people to build parapets around their roofs so that they would not be guilty if someone were to fall off (cf. Deut. 22:8). Life on the roof would not have been pleasant; it would have been blistering in summer, wet and chilly during the rainy season. But it would be better to live there than to live in a house with a contentious spouse. This verse is identical to 21:9, and parallel to 21:19, but here it follows another verse about strife (25:23).

25:25. At a time when messages were carried by foot, news from afar would have been somewhat rare. Because Abraham was in Canaan, he did not hear that his brother Nahor had an heir until two more generations had past (Gen. 22:20ff). The effect of hearing good news is, like that of the faithful messenger described in 25:13, cool water, not merely to anyone, but to those who need it desperately. The wise person knows the importance and value to others of maintaining relationships, even from a territory several days' journey away ("a distant land").

25:26. Since the verb môṯ (HED #4267) means "to fall" or "to stumble" (often as a synecdoche for death; cf. Ps. 121:3), this is one of the few verses in Proverbs that warns that the wicked may overcome the righteous (e.g., 24:15f; cp. 12:3, where the same word occurs). The consequences of this "victory" are deadly even for the wicked. The righteous will no longer be a source of life (cf. 10:11; 13:14). The wise therefore need to guard themselves, but also to recognize that this is no guarantee of success or victory.

25:27. Like Prov. 25:16, the first line encourages moderation. It is difficult, however, to determine the function of the second line, which reads, "and the investigation of their glory is glory." The

866 rel pron	382 n ms	2440 n fs	375 sub	6805.157 v Qal pass ptc fs	6111 n fs	28.	3638 n ms	3638 n ms, ps 3mp
אֲשֶׁר	אִישׁ	חוֹמָה	אֵין	פְּרוּצָה	עִיר		כָּבוֹד	כְּבֹדָם
'ăsher	'îsh	chômāh	'ên	pᵉrûtsāh	'îr		kāvôdh	kᵉvōdhām
who	a man	a wall	there is not	having been broken into	a city		glory	their glory

3626, 4443 cj, prep, art, n ms	904, 7302 prep, art, n ms	3626, 8345 prep, art, n ms	26:1	3937, 7593 prep, n fs, ps 3ms	4785 n ms	375 sub
וְכַמָּטָר	בַּקַּיִץ	כַּשֶּׁלֶג		לְרוּחוֹ	מַעְצָר	אֵין
wᵉkhammāṭār	baqqayits	kashshelegh		lᵉrûchô	ma'ătsār	'ên
and like the rain	in the summer	like the snow		to his spirit	self-control	there is not

3937, 5290.141 prep, v Qal inf con	3626, 7109 prep, art, n fs	2.	3638 n ms	3937, 3809 prep, n ms	3940, 5173 neg part, adj	3772 adv	904, 7392 prep, art, n ms
לָנוּד	כַּצִּפּוֹר		כָּבוֹד	לִכְסִיל	לֹא־נָאוֶה	כֵּן	בַּקָּצִיר
lānûdh	katstsippôr		kāvôdh	likhsîl	lō'-nā'weh	kēn	baqqātsîr
for flitting about	like the bird		honor	for a fool	not lovely	so	during the harvest

8199 n ms	3.	971.122 v Qal impf 3fs	3940 neg part	2703 adv	7329 n fs	3772 adv	3937, 5990.141 prep, v Qal inf con	3626, 1925 prep, art, n fs
שׁוֹט		תָבֹא	לֹא	חִנָּם	קִלְלַת	כֵּן	לָעוּף	כַּדְּרוֹר
shôṭ		thāvō'	lō'	chinnām	qilᵉlath	kēn	lā'ûph	kaddᵉrôr
a whip		it will come	not	without cause	a curse	so	for flying	like the swallow

414, 6257.123 adv, v Qal juss 2ms	4.	3809 n mp	3937, 1490 prep, n ms	8101 cj, n ms	3937, 2645 prep, art, n ms	5141 n ms	3937, 5670 prep, art, n ms
אַל־תַּעַן		כְּסִילִים	לְגֵו	וְשֵׁבֶט	לַחֲמוֹר	מֶתֶג	לַסּוּס
'al-ta'an		kᵉsîlîm	lᵉghēw	wᵉshēveṭ	lachămôr	metheg	lassûs
do not answer		fools	for the back of	and a rod	for the donkey	a bridle	for the horse

so for men to search their own glory is not glory: ... or to seek honor on top of honor, *NRSV* ... the quest for honour is burdensome, *NEB* ... nor does it bring you honor to brag about yourself, *NCV* ... Therefore be sparing of your compliments, *Goodspeed* ... to search into weighty matters is [itself] a weight, *Darby* ... search too high, and the brightness shall dazzle thee, *Knox*.

28. He that hath no rule over his own spirit: ... He whose spirit is without restraint, *ASV* ... A man that refraineth not his appetite, *Geneva* ... such is anyone who lacks self-control, *JB* ... he lies defenceless, that cannot master himself, but ever speaks his mind, *Knox* ... is the man with no check on his feelings, *NAB*.

is like a city that is broken down, and without walls: ... Like a city overthrown because it has no wall, *Anchor* ... Like a city breached and defenseless, *Goodspeed* ... Like an open city with no defenses, *NAB* ...

Like a city that has burst out of its confining walls, *NEB* ... Like a city that is broken into, *NASB*.

26:1. As snow in summer, and as rain in harvest: ... rain when the grain is being cut, *BB*.

so honour is not seemly for a fool: ... so honour is not natural for the foolish, *BB* ... Praise for a fool is out of place, *Good News* ... Honor is unseasonable for a fool, *Goodspeed* ... So unbecoming to a dullard is honour, *Rotherham* ... honour is unseasonable in a stupid man, *NEB*.

2. As the bird by wandering, as the swallow by flying: ... Like a fluttering bird or a swooping swallow, *Anchor* ... They are like birds that fly by and never light, *Good News* ... As the sparrow escapes, and the swallow flies away, *JB* ... Light as a bird of passage, light as sparrow on the wing, *Knox* ... they are like sparrows or swallows that fly around and never land, *NCV*.

so the curse causeless shall not come: ... so an unjustified curse does not alight, *Berkeley* ... groundless abuse gets nowhere, *NEB* ... Curses cannot hurt you unless you deserve them, *Good News* ... so the undeserved curse will never hit its mark, *JB* ... the baseless curse never goes home, *Moffatt*.

3. A whip for the horse, a bridle for the ass: ... Guide a horse with a whip, a donkey with a bridle, *LIVB* ... harnesses are for donkeys, *NCV* ... halter for the donkey, *NIV*.

and a rod for the fool's back: ... you have to beat a fool, *Good News* ... and for the backs of fools, a stick, *JB* ... and a rebel with a rod to his back!, *LIVB* ... so paddles are good for fools, *NCV*.

4. Answer not a fool according to his folly: ... Do not answer a fool in his own foolish terms, *Anchor* ... Do not give to the foolish man a foolish answer, *BB* ... If you answer a silly

two lines seem unrelated, nor does "their" have an antecedent. It is somewhat possible that the second line means that true honor consists of seeking to honor others rather than oneseslf (cf. 25:6f; 27:1f). Eating too much honey is thus implicitly compared to self-puffery, perhaps because both can easily be done to excess.

It is not at all obvious that this is the sense of the text. There are almost as many interpretations as interpreters. This may be one of the "riddles and dark sayings" (1:6), it may be a conflation of halves of two originally unrelated proverbs, as some suggest, or it may be an example of an unresolvable text.

25:28. Conquerors of ancient cities usually broke large gaps in the walls in order to make them defenseless. This included destroying the gates (cf. Neh. 1:3; 3:1–32). Anyone who lacks self-control is just as defenseless, because this behavior demonstrates his lack of knowledge and understanding, which in turn allows him to be dominated and controlled by others, especially by those who recognize and know how to take advantage of his weakness. Self-control is a singular mark of the patience that typifies the wise; its lack demonstrates folly (cf. 14:17, 29).

26:1–11. These verses are bound together by their common topic of the fool (vv. 1, 3–11). The "better than" proverb that pinpoints the break between this section and the one dealing with the sluggard (vv. 12–16) also reflects the central concern of these verses—dealing with fools. It is inappropriate to honor them (vv. 1, 8), because what they deserve is discipline (v. 3). The center of this section, vv. 4f, poses the dilemma that faces everyone dealing with fools. They need to be answered (v. 5), but it is difficult to do this well (v. 4). Fools are not only frustrating (v. 6), but even wisdom cannot help them (vv. 7ff), since, failing to learn from their experience, they return to it again and again (v. 11). Several verses in this section share the form of "double emblems" (26:1ff, 6; e.g., 25:12, 19, 20; see "Overview"), which further links them.

26:1. This proverb not only asserts that honor is not fitting for a fool, but it implies that those who honor fools are even more foolish than the objects of their respect. The references to the climate also imply that fools simply cannot do anything to deserve honor, since snow in summer and rain during harvest are so rare in Palestine as to be the subject of an implied covenantal curse (cf. 25:13; 1 Sam. 12:16ff). These weather conditions

are as probable as a fool who deserves honor. A further implication is that honoring a fool overturns the moral order of creation, and thus upsets the seasons themselves (cf. 30:21f). This statement is bound closely to the biblical idea of "fool" (see "Overview").

26:2. Birds do not stop flying until they have a reason to do so. So it is with curses: those who live wisely, seeking the peace and welfare of their neighbors, giving no one cause to wish them harm, live free from the fear of a curse. This curse may refer to the penalties for breaking the Covenant (cf. Lev. 26:14–39; Deut. 28:15–68): covenantal obedience brings blessing and life, while disobedience brings the curse (cf. Deut. 30:15–20). The curses of the imprecatory Psalms (e.g., Pss. 35; 69; 109) are also covenantal, called forth in response to covenantal sins of the psalmist's enemies.

Here, however, the curse is more probably a personal curse uttered by a neighbor in response to something that was said or done. The verse thus encourages the wise to live, so far as is possible, without offending or harming others.

26:3. Just as different kinds of equipment are appropriate for different draft animals, so there is a proper means of controlling a fool. Whips and bridles are not primarily instruments of punishment, but of control. Proverbs 26:1, 8 assert that honor is inappropriate for fools. This verse says that the rod, which represents any type of discipline or control, is fitting for them. It further implies that, just as those who handle horses and donkeys use whips and bridles to control them, so a fool needs someone willing to exert a strong degree of control over his or her life.

26:4–5. These verses could have been originally independent sayings, juxtaposed by the men of Hezekiah (25:1) or an extended proverb that warns against one type of response while commending another. If they were an original unit, they encourage discernment of a different type, warning that fools should not be answered by using their own fallacious reasoning, but by reasoning with them "as [their] folly deserves" in a way which strips their folly bare. This interpretation requires two different uses of the same prepositional construction in Hebrew, which, given the strict parallelism of these verses, seems unlikely.

On the other hand, even if these verses were originally independent, they now lie within a carefully constructed passage dealing with fools

| 3809
n ms
כְּסִיל
keṣîl
a fool | 3626, 198
prep, n fs, ps 3ms
כְּאִוַּלְתּוֹ
keʾiwwaltô
according to his foolishness | 6678, 8187.123, 3937
cj, v Qal impf 2ms, prep, ps 3ms
פֶּן־תִּשְׁוֶה־לּוֹ
pen-tishweh-lô
so that you will not be like him | 1612, 887
cj, pers pron
גַּם־אָתָּה
gham-ʾāttāh
also you | 6257.131
v Qal impv 2ms
עֲנֵה
ʿᵃnēh
answer | **5.** |

| 3809
n ms
כְּסִיל
kheṣîl
a fool | 3626, 198
prep, n fs, ps 3ms
כְּאִוַּלְתּוֹ
keʾiwwaltô
according to his foolishness | 6678, 2030.121
cj, v Qal impf 3ms
פֶּן־יִהְיֶה
pen-yihyeh
so that he will not be | 2550
adj
חָכָם
chākhām
wise | 904, 6084
prep, n fd, ps 3ms
בְּעֵינָיו
beʿênāv
in his eyes |

| **6.** | 7380.351
v Piel ptc ms
מְקַצֶּה
meqatstseh
one who cuts off | 7559
n fd
רַגְלַיִם
raghlayim
feet | 2660
n ms
חָמָס
chāmās
violence | 8685.151
v Qal act ptc ms
שֹׁתֶה
shōtheh
drinking | 8365.151
v Qal act ptc ms
שֹׁלֵחַ
shōlēach
one who sends | 1745
n mp
דְּבָרִים
devārîm
words |

| 904, 3135, 3809
prep, n fs, n ms
בְּיַד־כְּסִיל
beyadh-keṣîl
in the hand of a fool | **7.** | 1861.116
v Qal pf 3cp
דַּלְיוּ
dalyû
they dangle more | 8225
n fd
שֹׁקַיִם
shōqayim
legs | 4623, 6701
prep, adj
מִפִּסֵּחַ
mippisseach
than a lame man | 5091
cj, n ms
וּמָשָׁל
ûmāshāl
even a proverb |

| 904, 6552
prep, n ms
בְּפִי
bephî
in the mouth of | 3809
n mp
כְּסִילִים
kheṣîlîm
fools | **8.** | 3626, 7173.141
prep, v Qal inf con
כִּצְרוֹר
kitsrôr
like one who binds | 63
n fs
אֶבֶן
ʾeven
a stone | 904, 4935
prep, n fs
בְּמַרְגֵּמָה
bemargēmāh
in the sling | 3772, 5598.151
cj, v Qal act ptc ms
כֵּן־נוֹתֵן
kēn-nôthēn
so one who gives | 3937, 3809
prep, n ms
לִכְסִיל
likhṣîl
to a fool |

| 3638
n ms
כָּבוֹד
kāvôdh
honor | 2430
n ms
חוֹחַ
chôach
a thorn | **9.** | 6148.111
v Qal pf 3ms
עָלָה
ʿālāh
it will go up | 904, 3135, 8318
prep, n fs, n ms
בְּיַד־שִׁכּוֹר
veyadh-shikkôr
into the hand of a drunkard | 5091
cj, n ms
וּמָשָׁל
ûmāshāl
even a proverb | 904, 6552
prep, n ms
בְּפִי
bephî
in the mouth of |

| 3809
n mp
כְּסִילִים
kheṣîlîm
fools | **10.** | 7521
adj
רַב
rav
much | 2523.351, 3725
v Polel ptc ms, n ms
מְחוֹלֵל־כֹּל
mechôlēl-kōl
one who causes anguish to everyone | 7963.151
cj, v Qal act ptc ms
וְשֹׂכֵר
wesōkhēr
one who hires | 3809
n ms
כְּסִיל
keṣîl
a fool |

question, you are just as silly as the person who asked it, *Good News* ... Leave the fool's challenge unanswered, *Knox* ... don't use foolish arguments as he does, *LIVB*.

lest thou also be like unto him: ... Lest you put yourself on his level, *Anchor* ... for fear you grow like him yourself, *JB* ... and prove thyself wise, *Knox* ... or you will be a fool yourself, *NRSV*.

5. Answer a fool according to his folly: ... Give a foolish man a foolish answer, *BB* ... or answer it, if thou

wilt, and prove him fool, *Knox* ... Prick his conceit with silly replies!, *LIVB* ... Answer a fool as his folly deserves, *NASB* ... answer fools as they should be answered, *NCV*.

lest he be wise in his own conceit: ... So he will not think himself wise, *Anchor* ... the one who asked it will realize that he's not as smart as he thinks, *Good News* ... lest he imagines he is wise, *Moffatt*.

6. He that sendeth a message by the hand of a fool: ... If you let a fool deliver a message, *Good News* ... Send

a fool on thy errand, *Knox* ... To trust a rebel to convey a message, *LIVB*.

cutteth off the feet, and drinketh damage: ... One chops off his own feet and invites violence, *Anchor* ... you might as well cut off your own feet; you are asking for trouble, *Good News* ... He wounds himself, he takes violence for his drink, *JB* ... cuts his own leg off and displays the stump, *NEB* ... thou hast a lame journey, and mischief brewing for thee, *Knox*.

7. The legs of the lame are not equal: ... dangles helpless as the legs of the lame, *REB* … Unreliable as the legs of the lame, *JB* … it is all fair legs and no walking, *Knox* … becomes as useless as a paralyzed leg, *LIVB* … As they that lift up the legs of the lame, *Geneva*.

so is a parable in the mouth of fools: … A maxim quoted by fools, *Anchor* … so is a wise saying in the mouth of the foolish, *BB* … so maxims limp on the lips of a fool, *Moffatt* … A proverb in the mouth of stupid men, *NEB*.

8. As he that bindeth a stone in a sling: … is like tying a stone firmly in a catapult, *Anchor* … attempting

to keep a stone fixed in a cord, *BB* … As a bag of gems in a stone-heap, *Darby* … Like one who gets the stone caught in his sling, *NEB* … thou hast wasted one more stone on Mercury's cairn, *Knox*.

so is he that giveth honour to a fool: … giveth glory to a foole, *Geneva* … Praising someone who is stupid makes as much sense, *Good News* … Pay a fool reverence, *Knox* … Honoring a rebel will backfire, *LIVB*.

9. As a thorn goeth up into the hand of a drunkard: … like a thornstick in a drunkard's hand,

Anchor … a drunk man trying to pick a thorn out of his hand, *Good News* … as branch of bramble in the hand of a drunkard, *Knox* … Like thorny branches brandished by a drunkard, *Moffatt* … A brier cometh into the hand of a drunken-man, *Rotherham*.

so is a parable in the mouth of fools: … so is a wise saying, *BB* … A fool quoting a wise saying, *Good News* … A rebel will misapply an illustration, *LIVB*.

10. The great God that formed all things: … As an archer that woundeth all, *MRB* … A master

(26:1–12). In that context, they call for discernment that recognizes both the danger of answering a fool (cf. 29:9) and the importance of doing so (a fool who is "wise in his own eyes" is in even a worse state than the average fool; cf. 26:12). Their juxtaposition demonstrates the need and the danger, and, by thus encouraging reflection on what to say and how to say it, they fit within the larger teaching of Proverbs that the wise speak seldom and carefully.

26:6. A messenger is an extra pair of legs, but to send a message by a fool is to cut off those legs. Like other verses in this chapter (e.g., vv. 1, 8), this proverb also says that certain things are inappropriate for fools. The use of "words" may imply an oral message rather than a written one, but it may simply specify a message rather than, e.g., money or animals. Equating this with "drinking violence" is probably hyperbolic, strengthening the warning. This verse warns the wise to consider carefully the character of the person that they are going to entrust with a charge by warning them of the probable outcome of trusting the wrong person. There may be circumstances where a decision is made to entrust an errand or project to someone who may not be quite adequate for the task. The decision is a calculated risk that Proverbs says is not worth it.

26:7. It is senseless for fools to learn, or even to memorize, proverbs, since they cannot use them properly (cf. 17:16; 26:9). They may as well be lame men trying to walk on useless legs. (This interpretation depends upon an emendation of the first line, which is very difficult in Hebrew.) This verse, as well as the others cited above, shows that knowledge is not wisdom. Even when a fool has the trappings of wisdom (even when he can quote a

proverb), he is not wise. Wisdom is the ability to understand and properly use what one knows.

26:8. The first verse of this chapter illustrates the incongruity of honoring a fool. This proverb uses another image for nearly the same purpose. The biblical sling was the early equivalent of the Welsh longbow, which was a long-distance weapon that could be used en masse in battle or singly for hunting (cf. Judg. 20:16; 1 Sam. 17:40; 1 Chr. 12:2). It consisted of a strap of leather with a widened middle section into which the stone was set. The two ends were held, the sling whirled around and one end released. The centrifugal force could carry the stone more than 100 yards. Tied into the sling it would be useless. Whoever honors a fool misunderstands the significance of, and so misuses, honor as badly as someone who uses slings as carrying-cases for sling-stones.

26:9. The ambiguity of "goes up" (HED #6148) makes the entire verse enigmatic. A drunkard may fall on or grab a thornbush for support or wield a switch of thorns (the latter would imply a unique use of "go up"). Both senses reflect wisdom's uselessness to a fool (cf. v. 7), because he will injure himself or others. The verse also warns that to teach fools endangers them, since they do understand what they have "learned." It may also endanger others, as fools pass on their "wisdom." They may quote proverbs that are true, but they will do so without the discernment necessary to ensure that they are addressing them to proper circumstances. Their counselees may well be injured by such advice.

26:10. This is "probably the most obscure verse in Proverbs" (as ancient and modern translations show), and still awaits a convincing explanation. The "archer" (NASB, NRSV, NIV) could also

11.

7963.151	5882.152	3626, 3732	8178.151	6142, 7178	3809
cj, v Qal act ptc ms	v Qal act ptc mp	prep, n ms	v Qal act ptc ms	prep, n ms, ps 3ms	n ms
וְשֹׂכֵר	עֹבְרִים	כְּכֶלֶב	שָׁב	עַל־קֵאוֹ	כְּסִיל
wesōkhēr	'ōverîm	kekhelev	shāv	'al-qē'ô	kesîl
and one who hires	those passing by	like a dog	returning	unto his vomit	a fool

12.

8521.151	904, 198	7495.113	382	2550	904, 6084	8951
v Qal act ptc ms	prep, n fs, ps 3ms	v Qal pf 2ms	n ms	adj	prep, n fd, ps 3ms	n fs
שׁוֹנֶה	בְּאִוַּלְתּוֹ	רָאִיתָ	אִישׁ	חָכָם	בְּעֵינָיו	תִּקְוָה
shôneh	ve'iwwaltô	rā'îthā	'îsh	chākhām	be'ênâv	tiqŏwāh
repeating	in his foolishness	you have seen	a man	wise	in his eyes	hope

13.

3937, 3809	4623	569.111	6339	8256	904, 1932	761	1033
prep, n ms	prep, ps 3ms	v Qal pf 3ms	n ms	n ms	prep, art, n ms	n ms	prep
לִכְסִיל	מִמֶּנּוּ	אָמַר	עָצֵל	שַׁחַל	בַּדָּרֶךְ	אֲרִי	בֵּין
likhsîl	mimmennû	'āmar	'ātsēl	shachal	baddārekh	'ărî	bên
for a fool	more than him	he will say	a sluggard	a young lion	on the road	a lion	between

14.

7624	1878	5621.122	6142, 7008	6339	6142, 4433
art, n fp	art, n fs	v Qal impf 3fs	prep, n ms, ps 3fs	cj, adj	prep, n fs, ps 3ms
הָרְחֹבוֹת	הַדֶּלֶת	תִּסּוֹב	עַל־צִירָהּ	וְעָצֵל	עַל־מִטָּתוֹ
hārechōvôth	haddeleth	tissôv	'al-tsîrāhh	we'ātsēl	'al-mittāthô
the open places	the door	it rotates	on its hinge	and a sluggard	on his bed

15.

3045.111	6339	3135	904, 7017	3942.211
v Qal pf 3ms	n ms	n fs, ps 3ms	prep, art, n fs	v Niphal pf 3ms
טָמַן	עָצֵל	יָדוֹ	בַּצַּלָּחַת	נִלְאָה
tāman	'ātsēl	yādhô	batstsallāchath	nil'āh
he will hide	a sluggard	his hand	in the bowl	he will become weary

16.

3937, 8178.541	420, 6552	2550	6339	904, 6084	4623, 8124
prep, v Hiphil inf con, ps 3fs	prep, n ms, ps 3ms	adj	n ms	prep, n fd, ps 3ms	prep, num
לְהָשִׁיבָהּ	אֶל־פִּיו	חָכָם	עָצֵל	בְּעֵינָיו	מִשִּׁבְעָה
lahshîvāhh	'el-pîw	chākhām	'ātsēl	be'ênâv	mishshiv'āh
to bring it back	to his mouth	wiser	a sluggard	in his eyes	than seven

roughly worketh every one, *Darby* ... The master workman does everything himself, *Goodspeed* ... The law settles quarrels at last, *Knox* ... An able man does everything himself, *Moffatt*.

both rewardeth the fool, and rewardeth transgressors: ... but he who hires a fool, hires a passer-by, *Berkeley* ... Gives the fool his hire and the transgressor his wages, *NKJV* ... An employer who hires any fool that comes along, *Good News* ... yet silence the fool, and feud there shall be none, *Knox* ... may get better work from an untrained apprentice than from a skilled rebel!, *LIVB*.

11. As a dog returneth to his vomit: ... Like a dog going back to the food which he has not been able to keep down, *BB* ... like a dog that goes back to what it has thrown up, *NCV*.

so a fool returneth to his folly: ... the foolish man doing his foolish acts over again, *BB* ... a fool repeateth his folly, *Darby* ... reverts to his folly, *JB* ... repeats his foolishness, *NCV*.

12. Seest thou a man wise in his own conceit?: ... Have you observed the man who thinks he is wise?, *Anchor* ... someone who thinks he is wise when he is not, *Good News* ... The man who lays claim to wisdom, *Knox* ... You see a man of self-conceit?, *Moffatt*.

there is more hope of a fool than of him: ... The most stupid fool is better off, *Good News* ... Who is in more perilous case than the fool him-

self?, *Knox* ... There is one thing worse than a fool, *LIVB*.

13. The slothful man saith, There is a lion in the way: ... Why doesn't the lazy man ever get out of the house? What is he afraid of? Lions?, *Good News* ... The sluggard says, "There is a roaring beast on the road," *Goodspeed* ... What, go abroad? says Sloth; there is a lion there, *Knox* ... says the idler, *JB*.

a lion is in the streets: ... trust me, a lion's dam loose in the street, *Knox* ... a lion in the middle of the square!, *NAB* ... a lion at large in the streets, *NEB* ... there's a lion outside!, *Moffatt*.

14. As the door turneth upon his hinges: ... A door is turned on its pillar, *BB* ... He gets no farther than a door swinging on its hinges, *Good News* … Like a door turning back and forth, *NCV* … on its sockets, *Goodspeed*.

so doth the slothful upon his bed: … The lazy man turns over in bed, *Good News* … Sloth turns about, but keeps his bed, *Knox* … the sluggard is still upon his bed, *MAST* … the hater of work on his bed, *BB*.

15. The slothful hideth his hand in his bosom: … The lazy man puts his hand into the dish, *Anchor* … The sluggard burieth his hand in the dish, *ASV* … The hater of work puts his hand deep into the basin, *BB* …

With folded hands the sluggard sits by, *Knox*.

it grieveth him to bring it again to his mouth: … But he is too weary to raise it to his mouth, *Anchor* … it tires him to return it to his mouth, *Berkeley* … Some people are too lazy to put food in their own mouths,

---

be a "captain" (cf. 2 Ki. 18:17; Jon. 1:6) or "great one" (hence "great [God]" in KJV, NKJV). The translation "archer" reflects a rare noun (Job 16:13; Jer. 50:29; cf. the related verb in Gen. 49:23; Ps. 18:14; and, possibly, Gen. 21:20). The second word may come from one of two verbal roots, one of which would mean "brings forth" in the sense of "gives birth to" (cf. Ps. 29:9), and the other, "pierces" (i.e., "wounds"; cf. Isa. 51:9).

The second fits "archer" as a translation of the first word, yielding, "An archer wounds everyone." Nor is the meaning of the second line (lit. "whoever hires a fool and whoever hires passers-by") much more clear. If the second "whoever hires" is repointed as "drunkard" (RSV, NRSV), then the verse may compare someone who injures others to one who hires fools and those who pass by. If "passers-by" means "unqualified" (so NASB, NIV and, with some rearrangement of the text, NRSV), the point would be that hiring a fool is itself foolhardy and even dangerous to both the employer and others, just as an archer wounds everyone.

26:11. Every other occurrence of the noun "vomit" (HED #7178) describes the result of drunkenness (Isa. 19:14; 28:8; Jer. 48:29), as does one occurrence of the verb "vomit" (Jer. 25:27), which further strengthens the comparison between the fool and the drunk in these verses (26:9f). Since fools will not learn, as these verses show (vv. 7ff; cf. v. 12), they can only continue in their foolish behavior. That is all that they know. To try to teach a fool (v. 5) is thus an exercise in frustration. Even exceptions to the rule are only apparent, because folly is a state of the heart. As such, it can be concealed for a time, but will ultimately become visible again when they return to their foolish behavior.

26:12. Together with 26:16 (cf. the repeated "wise in his [own] eyes"), this verse envelopes the descriptions of laziness in 26:13–16 within the theme of arrogance (as it also reflects the central point of the preceding section; 26:4f). The second line is identical to 29:20b. Together these verses suggest that the

foolish and slothful have answers for any counsel before they even hear it. Their "understanding," because it refuses to consider the wisdom and insight of others, inevitably leads them astray, ultimately to destruction. Arrogance is a type of folly. Solomon holds out no hope for the fool (cf. 6:15f; 21:4; 30:13). These verses disabuse the smug. There is less hope for them than for the most helpless.

26:13–16. These four proverbs dealing with the sluggard are not a poem, despite their thematic unity. They show no development or climax, but comprise a topical group, like many verses in this section of the Book (see commentary on 25:1–29:27 and "Overview").

26:13. Closely linked to 22:13, the first proverb repeats the sluggard's silly excuse, which is even more foolish because no one believes it. The difference between the lazy and the diligent, with whom they are usually contrasted (cf. 10:4f; 12:24, 27; 13:4; 14:23), is the diligence that determines what is most important and then pursues that goal. Sluggards are content with any excuse, because their first value is to avoid their duty, whatever it may be. Nor will they accept reasoned argument, because they are fully satisfied with their own understanding of their situation (cf. 26:12, 16). The preceding verse may also imply that these excuses are the sluggard's response to inquiries about his failure to accept responsibility.

26:14. As a door swings back and forth, the indolent tosses to and fro in bed, perhaps a reflection of the repeated proverb, "A little sleep, a little slumber, a little folding of the hands to rest" (6:10; 24:33). Even when he gets up and appears to be working, his "work" accomplishes nothing. He may as well have stayed in bed. Even a door looks busy as it is opened and closed, but it goes nowhere. Unlike the sloth, however, the door accomplishes its purpose simply by swinging to and fro; all the sluggard's tossing and turning achieves nothing.

26:15. The first line is identical to 19:24. The slothful person buries his hand out of sight in the dish

Proverbs 26:17–22

17.

8178.552	3051	2480.551	904, 238, 3732	5882.151
v Hiphil ptc mp	n ms	v Hiphil ptc ms	prep, n fd, n ms	v Qal act ptc ms
מְשִׁיבֵי	טָעַם	מַחֲזִיק	בְּאָזְנֵי־כָלֶב	עֹבֵר
mᵉshîvê	ṭā'am	machăzîq	be'āzᵉnê-khālev	'ōvēr
returning	a taste	one who seizes	by the ears of a dog	one who passes by

18.

5882.751	6142, 7663	3940, 3937	3626, 3992.751
v Hithpael ptc ms	prep, n ms	neg part, prep, ps 3ms	prep, v Hithpalpel ptc ms
מִתְעַבֵּר	עַל־רִיב	לֹא־לוֹ	כְּמִתְלַהְלֵהַּ
mith'abbēr	'al-rîv	lō'-lô	kᵉmithlahlēahh
passes himself	into a contention	not to him	like a madman

19.

3498.151	2289	2777	4323	3772, 382	7700.311
art, v Qal act ptc ms	n mp	n mp	cj, n ms	cj, n ms	v Piel pf 3ms
הַיֹּרֶה	זִקִּים	חִצִּים	וָמָוֶת	כֵּן־אִישׁ	רִמָּה
hayyōreh	ziqqîm	chitstsîm	wāmāweth	kēn-'îsh	rimmāh
the one who shoots	flaming arrows	arrows	and death	so a man	he will deceive

20.

881, 7739	569.111	1950B, 3940, 7925.351	603	904, 675	6320
do, n ms, ps 3ms	cj, v Qal pf 3ms	intrg part, neg part, v Piel ptc ms	pers pron	prep, n ms	n mp
אֶת־רֵעֵהוּ	וְאָמַר	הֲלֹא־מְשַׂחֵק	אָנִי	בְּאֶפֶס	עֵצִים
'eth-rē'ēhû	we'āmar	hălō'-mᵉsacheq	'ānî	be'ephes	'ētsîm
his fellow	and he will say	am I not joking	I	when an end	wood

21.

3637.122, 813	904, 375	7566.255	8698.121	4209	6595
v Qal impf 3fs, n fs	cj, prep, neg part	v Niphal ptc ms	v Qal impf 3ms	n ms	n ms
תִּכְבֶּה־אֵשׁ	וּבְאֵין	נִרְגָּן	יִשְׁתֹּק	מָדוֹן	פֶּחָם
tikhbeh-'ēsh	ûve'ên	nirgān	yishtōq	mādhôn	pechām
a fire will go out	and when there is not	a slanderer	it will be silent	strife	charcoal

3937, 1544	6320	3937, 813	382	4209	3937, 2893.341, 7663
prep, n fp	cj, n mp	prep, n fs	cj, n ms	n mp	prep, v Pilpel inf con, n ms
לְגֶחָלִים	וְעֵצִים	לְאֵשׁ	וְאִישׁ	מִדְוֹנִים	לְחַרְחַר־רִיב
lᵉghechālîm	wᵉ'ētsîm	lᵉ'ēsh	wᵉ'îsh	midhônîm	lᵉcharchar-rîv
for coals	and wood	for fire	and a man of	contentions	for causing contention to burn

22.

1745	7566.255	3626, 3996.752	2062	3495.116
n mp	v Niphal ptc ms	prep, v Hithpael ptc mp	cj, pers pron	v Qal pf 3cp
דִּבְרֵי	נִרְגָּן	כְּמִתְלַהֲמִים	וְהֵם	יָרְדוּ
divrê	nirgān	kᵉmithlahmîm	wᵉhēm	yārᵉdhû
the words of	a slanderer	like tidbits	but they	they will go down

---

Good News … it wears him out to bring it back to his mouth, *RSV*.

16. The sluggard is wiser in his own conceit: … The hater of work seems to himself wiser, *BB* … A lazy man will think he is smarter, *Good News* … Yet in his own opinion he is smarter, *LIVB* … The lazy man imagines he is wiser, *Moffatt* … The lazy person is wiser in self-esteem, *NRSV*.

than seven men that can render a reason: … Than seven men who can give an apt answer, *Anchor* … who are able to give an answer with good

sense, *BB* … who can give good reasons for their opinions, *Good News* … who can answer with judgment, *Rotherham* … than a dozen men who argue ably, *Moffatt*.

17. He that passeth by, and meddleth with strife belonging not to him: … One who mixes in a quarrel which is none of his business, *Anchor* … He who gets mixed up in a fight which is not his business, *BB* … Getting involved in an argument, *Good News* … who meddles in someone else's quarrel, *JB* … interfering in an argument, *LIVB*.

is like one that taketh a dog by the ears: … Is taking a mad dog by the tail, *Anchor* … is like going down the street and grabbing a dog by the ears, *Good News* … Yanking a dog's ears is no more foolish than, *LIVB* … Like a man who seizes a passing cur, *NEB*.

18. As a mad man who casteth firebrands, arrows, and death: … is like a crazy man playing with a deadly weapon, *Good News* … like a madman throwing around firebrands, *LIVB* … Like a lunatic who lets fly deadly brands and arrows, *Moffatt* …

a madman shooting at random his deadly darts, *NEB*.

19. So is the man that deceiveth his neighbour, and saith: ... So is the man who gets the better of his neighbour by deceit, *BB* ... A man who tricks someone, *Good News* ... so is anyone who lies to a companion, *JB* ... nor he either, that hurts a friend by treachery, *Knox*.

Am not I in sport?: ... I was only joking, *Anchor* ... Aren't I amusing?, *JB* ... and pleads that it was done in jest, *Knox* ... I was just fooling, *LIVB* ... then says it was in fun, *Moffatt*.

20. Where no wood is, there the fire goeth out: ... If no wood is added a fire goes out, *Anchor* ... No fuel, no fire, *Knox* ... The fire goes out when the wood fails, *Moffatt* ... For lack of wood a fire dies down, *REB*.

so where there is no talebearer, the strife ceaseth: ... so, "No calumny, no quarrel", *Anchor* ... where there is no secret talk, argument is ended, *BB* ... where there is no tattler strife is hushed, *Rotherham* ... quarrels cease when slanderers are away, *Moffatt* ... tensions disappear when gossip stops, *LIVB*.

21. As coals are to burning coals, and wood to fire: ... Charcoal keeps the embers glowing, *Good News* ... Coal needs ember, and fire tinder, *Knox* ... as easily as a match sets fire to paper, *LIVB* ... What a bellows is

to live coals, *NAB* ... Black coal to burning blocks, *Rotherham*.

so is a contentious man to kindle strife: ... A quarrelsome man rekindles a dispute, *Anchor* ... so a man given to argument gets a fight started, *BB* ... troublemakers keep arguments alive, *Good News* ... and strife a quarreller, for their kindling, *Knox* ... a quarrelsome person keeps an argument going, *NCV*.

22. The words of a talebearer are as wounds: ... The words of a slanderer are swallowed greedily, *Anchor* ... The words of a whisperer are as dainty morsels, *ASV* ... The words of a tattler are dainties, *Rotherham* ... Gossip is so tasty!, *Good News* ... Innocent enough

---

of food (the word translated "buries" [HED #3045] is often used of concealing something by covering it; cf. Exo. 2:12; Josh. 2:6; 7:21, 22). Even the effort required to do that tires him to the point that he cannot force his hand back to his mouth with the food that he needs. Not only does he need this food (apparently he wanted it badly enough to reach for it), but he cannot sustain his initial effort. Unless he gets the food to his mouth, he will die (cf. 21:25f). People rarely set out to become sluggards, but their choices, insignificant as they seem at the time, dull their spirits (cf. 6:10; 24:33) into a state that leads to destruction.

26:16. With 26:12, this verse frames the description of the sluggard within the larger theme of self-satisfied arrogance. Facts and reasoning do not shake their faulty reasoning, nor do they move them away from their typically silly excuses (v. 13), since they are fully satisfied with their own understanding (16:2; 19:3; 21:2), even though it may lead to their destruction (cf. 16:25).

Complacency (self-satisfaction) grows out of arrogance, since pride lends its object far more importance than it might otherwise deserve. When the object is oneself, the tendency is self-justification, (v. 13) regardless of one's behavior.

26:17. To grab a dog by the ears was to invite it to bite (or worse). Dogs were rarely domesticated: they typified disgusting behavior (26:11), and they were considered unclean. Their low reputation in Israel is clear from the use of "dog" as a term of derision or self-abegnation shows (cf. 1 Sam. 17:43;

24:14; 2 Sam. 3:8; 9:8). To grab the ears of a wild scavenger would be an act of insanity or stupidity. To interfere in someone else's problem invites trouble. This warns those who are inclined by their own personality, by relationship with one of the parties involved, or for some other reason, to involve themselves in a problem not their own. It also cautions those who are asked to intervene. The proverb does not forbid involvement, but the warning is clear.

26:18–19. Like the preceding verse, this proverb warns that stupid behavior can bring disaster in its wake. Lying is as destructive as throwing coals into a field or house and as deadly as arrows, even if done by a "madman" who knows no better. Deception, even as a practical joke, can easily backfire, destroying friendships and trust (cf. 6:12–19). The wise person considers the possible consequences before doing something "for the fun of it," especially when that "fun" comes at someone else's expense.

26:20–22. These three emblematic proverbs describe the havoc that words can wreak on interpersonal relationships. The chiasm of "slanderer" (v. 20), "contentious" person (v. 21) and "slanderer (v. 22) closely links these verses, and v. 22 explains why the behavior described negatively (v. 20) and positively (v. 21) so effectively destroys relationships. Proverbs 26:22 is identical to 18:8, which also follows two proverbs that describe the trouble caused by words.

As a fire without fuel dies (cf. 30:16c), interpersonal conflict tends to die down when gossips and people who stir up trouble are removed. The quarrel-

23.

2410, 1027		3826B	5698	7099.455	6142, 2895	8004
n mp, n fs	**23.**	n ms	n mp	v Pual ptc ms	prep, n ms	n fd
חַדְרֵי־בָטֶן		כֶּסֶף	סִיגִים	מְצֻפֶּה	עַל־חָרֶשׂ	שְׂפָתַיִם
chadhrê-vāten		keseph	sîghîm	metsuppeh	'al-chāres	sephathayim
the inmost parts of the belly		silver with	dross	having been overlaid	on pottery	lips

24.

1875.152	3949, 7737		904, 8004	5421.221	7983.151
v Qal act ptc mp	cj, n ms, adj	**24.**	prep, n fs, ps 3ms	v Niphal impf 3ms	v Qal act ptc ms
דֹּלְקִים	וְלֶב־רָע		בִּשְׂפָתָו	יִנָּכֵר	שׂוֹנֵא
dōleqîm	welev-rā'		bisphāthāô	yinnākhēr	sônē'
burning	and an evil heart		with his lip	he disguises himself	one who hates

25.

904, 7419	8308.121	4983		3706, 2706.321	7249
cj, prep, n ms, ps 3ms	v Qal impf 3ms	n fs	**25.**	cj, v Piel impf 3ms	n ms, ps 3ms
וּבְקִרְבּוֹ	יָשִׁית	מִרְמָה		כִּי־יְחַנֵּן	קוֹלוֹ
ûveqirbô	yāshîth	mirmāh		kî-yechannēn	qôlô
and in his inward parts	he puts	deceit		when he causes to be gracious	his voice

414, 548.523, 904	3706	8124	8774	904, 3949
adv, v Hiphil juss 2ms, prep, ps 3ms	cj	num	n fp	prep, n ms, ps 3ms
אַל־תַּאֲמֶן־בּוֹ	כִּי	שֶׁבַע	תּוֹעֵבוֹת	בְּלִבּוֹ
'al-ta'āmen-bô	kî	sheva'	tô'ēvôth	belibbô
do not believe in it	because	seven	abominable things	in his heart

26.

3803.722	7985	904, 5046	1580.222	7750	904, 7235
v Hithpael impf 3fs	n fs	prep, n ms	v Niphal impf 3fs	n fs, ps 3ms	prep, n ms
תִּכַּסֶּה	שִׂנְאָה	בְּמַשָּׁאוֹן	תִּגָּלֶה	רָעָתוֹ	בְקָהָל
tikkasseh	sin'āh	bemashshā'ôn	tiggāleh	rā'āthô	veqāhāl
it is covered	hatred	with deception	it will be uncovered	his evil	in the assembly

27.

3868.151, 8273	904	5489.121	1597.151	63	420
v Qal act ptc ms, n fs	prep, ps 3fs	v Qal impf 3ms	cj, v Qal act ptc ms	n fs	prep, ps 3ms
כֹּרֶה־שַׁחַת	בָּהּ	יִפֹּל	וְגֹלֵל	אֶבֶן	אֵלָיו
kōreh-shachath	bāhh	yippōl	weghōlēl	'even	'ēlâv
one who digs a pit	in it	he will fall	and one who rolls	a stone	to him

seem the words of the backbiter, *Knox* … The words of one who says evil of his neighbour secretly are like sweet food, *BB*.

and they go down into the innermost parts of the belly: … How we love to swallow it!, *Good News* … swallowed right down, *REB* … swallowed and relished to the full, *Moffatt* … yet their poison sinks deep into a man's belly, *Knox* … people like to gobble them up, *NCV*.

23. Burning lips and a wicked heart: … smooth talk concealing an evil intention, *Anchor* … Glib speech that covers a spiteful heart, *NEB* … Insincere talk that hides what you are really thinking, *Good News* … Kind words from a wicked mind, *NCV* … Ardent lips, *Darby*.

are like a potsherd covered with silver dross: … Like glaze on the surface of earthenware, *Anchor* … like a vessel of earth plated with silver waste, *BB* … fine glaze on a cheap clay pot, *Good News* … a pot overlaid with silver slag, *Goodspeed* … is but lustre ware, *Knox*.

24. He that hateth dissembleth with his lips: … A man filled with hate disguises it in his words, *Anchor* … With his lips the hater makes things seem what they are not, *BB* … He who hates, pretends with his lips, *Berkeley* … Those who hate you may try to fool you with their words, *NCV* … Whoever hates may hide it in his speech, *JB*.

and layeth up deceit within him: … While inwardly he plots to

betray you, *Anchor* … but deceit is stored up inside him, *BB* … deep within him lies treachery, *JB* … inwardly he harbours guile, *Moffatt* … in their minds they are planning evil, *NCV*.

25. When he speaketh fair, believe him not: … When his speech is ingratiating, do not trust him, *Anchor* … Though his speech is charming, *NIV* … When he says fair words, *BB* … when he speaks pleasantly, *Berkeley* … People's words may be kind, but don't believe them, *NCV*.

for there are seven abominations in his heart: … because his heart is filled to the brim with hate, *Good News* … here are seven depths of wickedness in a single heart, *Knox* … for he has many a foul thought in mind, *Moffatt* … for seven hateful things are in his heart, *KJVII.*

26. Whose hatred is covered by deceit: … Though his hatred be craftily hidden, *Anchor* … Lies can hide hate, *NCV* … Vain the pretences that cloak his malice, *Knox* … Though he pretends to be so kind, *LIVB* … A man may conceal hatred under dissimulation, *NAB.*

his wickedness shall be shown before the whole congregation: … but everyone will see the evil things he does, *Good News* … shall be disclosed in the convocation, *Rotherham* … to reveal its wickedness later in the assembly, *JB* … but the evil will be plain to everyone, *NCV* … his malice shall be publicly exposed, *Moffatt.*

27. Whoso diggeth a pit shall fall therein: … He who digs a pit [for another] will fall into it [himself], *Anchor* … People who set traps for others get caught themselves, *Good News.*

and he that rolleth a stone, it will return upon him: … People who start landslides get crushed, *Good News* … shift rock, and it shall roll back on thee, *Knox* … the stone a man sets rolling recoils upon himself, *Moffatt.*

---

some person (v. 21) may be deliberately troublesome, creating conflict for personal gain or for the mere pleasure of controlling others, or may merely be guilty of careless talk (cf. 12:18). Proverbs consistently portrays gossip, however, as maliciously manipulating other people for spiteful ends.

Gossip and slander breed quarrels, envy and factions, which can be exhibited by many kinds of strife, because the heart responds to this kind of information like the body craves good food (v. 22). If words could be heard and forgotten, they would not be as damaging. Disclaimers notwithstanding, these words enter the core of the hearer's being ("the chambers of the belly"), so that the conflict grows as it is fueled by gossip and strife feeding on each other.

The wise person understands that the only way to eliminate dissension may be to get rid of the troublemaker, as Korah, Dathan, Abiram and On, who stirred up 250 well-known leaders against Moses and Aaron, were destroyed (Num. 16:1–35). Their rebellion, stifled though it was, nevertheless led to the people's complaint against Moses and Aaron (Num. 16:41).

26:23–28. The first four proverbs (vv. 23–26) describe the hypocrisy that disguises hatred, ending with a warning that it cannot remain hidden indefinitely (v. 26b). The last verse then returns to the opening theme of hypocrisy (v. 28), after a warning that sin often destroys those who practice it (v. 27). They are probably a collection of independent proverbs, rather than an original poem, but are closely linked by their common theme and terms (which include "lips," "heart," "wicked," "hatred," etc.), which come to a climax in v. 28. A "lying tongue hates" and a "flattering mouth" wreaks ruin.

All of these verses, in other words, show that the intended consequence of words reveals their true motivation. Flattery is hypocritical, since it

views the other person as an object to be manipulated, but flattery that encourages others to take paths to their ruin reveals deep animosity.

26:23–25. The image in v. 23 sets the stage for the others by underlining the difference between appearance and reality. English lustreware used special glazes so that the less-than-wealthy could have "silver" tableware. Unlike silverware, however, it broke, revealing its clay core. Fervid protestations of respect, affection and friendship can disguise hatred, envy and a multitude of other sins.

Enmity disguises itself by dissembling, which comes naturally to those who depend upon deceit to preserve their personal relationships (v. 24f), even as they plan the destruction of the object(s) of their hatred. In this context, v. 25 cautions against accepting words at their face value, especially when there has been a history of strife, since the underlying cause of the problem (envy or some other sin) may not have changed. If someone's encouragement has led to disaster, only a fool would implicitly trust that person's counsel a second time (especially if the counselor escaped harm). If the advice was honest (heartfelt but unwise) then no harm is done by weighing it carefully. If it rose out of malice, the wise will turn a deaf ear.

26:26. The first half of this verse sounds like the preceding (hatred hidden by hypocrisy), but the second line warns that deceit cannot be maintained indefinitely. As the circle of those who hear grows, it becomes increasingly difficult to hide true feelings, and the likelihood that the hated object will discover the truth only grows. The mention of the assembly (HED #7235) may suggest a legal setting in which the true motives eventually come out, uncovering the wickedness of the hypocrisy.

26:27. At first glance, this verse may appear to be out of place, warning that wickedness often rebounds upon those who practice it. It is, however,

8178.122		4098, 8632	7983.121	1847	6552	2607
v Qal impf 3fs	**28.**	n fs, n ms	v Qal impf 3ms	n mp, ps 3ms	cj, n ms	adj
תָּשׁוּב		לְשׁוֹן־שֶׁקֶר	יִשְׂנָא	דַּכָּיו	וּפֶה	חָלָק
tāshûv		leshôn-sheqer	yisnā'	dhakkâv	ûpheh	chālāq
it will return		a tongue of lies	it will hate	its oppressed	and a mouth	flattering

6449.121	4214		414, 2054.723	904, 3219	4417	3706
v Qal impf 3ms	n ms	**27:1**	adv, v Hithpael juss 2ms	prep, n ms	adv	cj
יַעֲשֶׂה	מִדְחֶה		אַל־תִּתְהַלֵּל	בְּיוֹם	מָחָר	כִּי
ya'ăseh	midhcheh		'al-tithhallēl	beyôm	māchār	kî
it will execute	stumbling		do not boast	about a day	later	because

3940, 3156.123		4242, 3314.121	3219		2054.321	2299
neg part, v Qal impf 2ms		intrg, v Qal impf 3ms	n ms	**2.**	v Piel juss 3ms, ps 2ms	n ms
לֹא־תֵדַע		מַה־יֵּלֶד	יוֹם		יְהַלֶּלְךָ	זָר
lō'-thēdha'		mah-yēledh	yôm		yehallelkhā	zār
you do not know		what it will bring forth	a day		let him praise you	a stranger

3940, 6552	5425	414, 8004		3635, 63	5377	2437
cj, neg part, n ms, ps 2ms	n ms	cj, adv, n fd, ps 2ms	**3.**	n ms, n fs	cj, n ms	art, n ms
וְלֹא־פִיךָ	נָכְרִי	וְאַל־שְׂפָתֶיךָ		כֹּבֶד־אֶבֶן	וְנֵטֶל	הַחוֹל
welō'-phîkhā	nākherî	we'al-sephāthêkhā		kōvedh-'even	wenēṭel	hachôl
and not your mouth	a foreigner	and not your lips		heaviness of a stone	and a burden of	the sand

3833	188	3633	4623, 8530		401	2635	8279	653
cj, n ms	n ms	adj	prep, num, ps 3mp	**4.**	n fs	n fs	cj, n ms	n ms
וְכַעַס	אֱוִיל	כָּבֵד	מִשְּׁנֵיהֶם		אַכְזְרִיּוּת	חֵמָה	וְשֶׁטֶף	אַף
wekha'as	'ĕwîl	kāvēdh	mishshenêhem		'akhzerîyûth	chēmāh	wesheṭeph	'āph
but vexation by	a fool	heavier	than both of them		cruelty with	wrath	even a flood of	anger

4449	6198.121	3937, 6686	7352	3009B		8763	1580.455	4623, 157
cj, intrg	v Qal impf 3ms	prep, n mp	n fs	adj	**5.**	n fs	v Pual ptc ms	prep, n fs
וּמִי	יַעֲמֹד	לִפְנֵי	קִנְאָה	טוֹבָה		תּוֹכַחַת	מְגֻלָּה	מֵאַהֲבָה
ûmî	ya'ămōdh	liphnê	qin'āh	ṭôvāh		tôkhachath	meghullāh	mē'ahăvāh
but who	he can stand	before	anger	better		correction	having been revealed	than love

---

28. A lying tongue hateth those that are afflicted by it: ... A lying tongue is the enemy of the innocent, *REB* ... Liars hate the people they hurt, *NCV* ... Fie on the glib tongues that hate all honesty, *Knox* ... A lying tongue brings destruction to itself, *Goodspeed* ... A lying tongue makes innocence seem guilty, *NEB*.

and a flattering mouth worketh ruin: ... smooth talk leads to downfall, *Anchor* ... smooth words conceal their sting, *NEB* ... the treacherous lips that plot men's downfall!, *Knox* ... the wheedling mouth causes ruin, *JB* ... false praise can ruin others, *NCV*.

27:1. Boast not thyself of tomorrow: ... Do not make a noise about tomorrow, *BB* ... Do not congratulate your-self about tomorrow, *JB* ... Do not flatter thyself with hopes of to-morrow, *Knox* ... Don't brag about tomorrow, *NCV* ... Do not praise yourself for tomorrow's success, *REB*.

for thou knowest not what a day may bring forth: ... For you do not know what may happen in a day, *Anchor* ... for you are not certain what a day's outcome may be, *BB* ... You don't know what will happen between now and then, *Good News* ... what lies in the womb of the future thou canst not tell, *Knox* ... wait and see what happens, *LIVB*.

2. Let another man praise thee, and not thine own mouth: ... Let other people praise you—even strangers; never do it yourself, *Good News* ... Let someone else sing your praises, *JB* ... Seek praise, but not of thy own bestowing, *Knox* ... Let flattery come from a stranger, not from yourself, *NEB*.

a stranger, and not thine own lips: ... A foreigner, rather than your own lips, *Anchor* ... another's lips, not thine, must sound it, *Knox* ... from the lips of an outsider and not from your own, *REB*.

3. A stone is heavy, and the sand weighty: ... A stone has great weight, and sand is crushing, *BB* ... What is more crushing than stone, more burdensome than sand?, *Knox* ... Stone is a burden and sand a dead weight, *NEB*.

but a fool's wrath is heavier than them both: ... But a provoking fool is harder to bear than both together, *Anchor* … compared to the trouble that stupidity can cause, *Good News* … but the annoyance caused by a fool is heavier than both, *Goodspeed* … heavier than both—a grudge borne by a fool, *JB* … but a vexatious fool is worse to bear than both, *Moffatt*.

4. Wrath is cruel, and anger is outrageous: … O, the cruelty of anger and the overflowing of wrath!, *Anchor* … and angry feeling an overflowing stream, *BB* … Fierce, fierce is rage, and indignation mounts like a flood, *Knox* … The cruelty of rage and the overflow of anger!, *Rotherham* … Anger is relentless, and wrath overwhelming, *NAB*.

but who is able to stand before envy?: … but who does not give way before envy?, *BB* … but it is nothing compared to jealousy, *Good News* … but the pangs of jealousy, these there is no resisting, *Knox* … Jealousy is more dangerous and cruel than anger, *LIVB* … but no one can put up with jealousy!, *NCV*.

5. Open rebuke is better than secret love: … Better is open protest than love kept secret, *BB* … It is bet-

---

a warning to those who would try to trap or destroy others by lies. All actions have unforeseen consequences, whether good (cf. 21:21; 22:4) or bad (cf. 21:16; 22:8). This includes hypocrisy, flattery and other lies. The lie will trap the liar. Neither cleverness, a good memory, nor any other skill will enable the hypocrite to escape.

26:28. Unlike the preceding verses, this proverb does not contrast outward words with true inner feelings. It instead shows that encouraging words may be lies, designed to crush the objects of secret hatred. Flattery ("a smooth mouth") is intended to manipulate someone else, whether for the flatterer's personal gain or for the ruin of the one being flattered (cf. 29:5).

27:1. As in the proverbs that describe the chasm that can exist between the plans and actual direction of life (e.g., 16:1, 9; 19:21), Solomon cautions against the presumptive arrogance that acts as though any human being can control or determine the future. He does this by contrasting boasting and knowledge. To boast about what cannot be known or controlled is foolish. James quotes this verse and comments that such boasting is sin because it fails to remember that human life is as fleeting as a cloud (Jam. 4:13–16), and so all plans must be made in conscious dependence upon God (cf. 16:3; Luke 12:20).

Human transience is a common scriptural theme (cf. Pss. 39:5f; 90:3–6; Isa. 40:6ff) that is consistently set over against the permanence of God (Ps. 90:1f) and his Word (Isa. 40:8c). Knowledge and control of the future is limited to Him alone (Isa. 41:21–26; 44:6ff).

There is another implicit rebuke here. The sluggard dies because he would rather dream and boast about what he will accomplish than to actively pursue his dreams (14:23; 21:25f). Planning is vital (11:14; 15:22; 16:1ff; 24:6), but action is necessary. The only time available is the present, but the lazy fool would rather misuse it.

27:2. This proverb is related to the preceding verse (the Hebrew words translated "boast" and "praise" are different forms of the same verb; HED #2054). If boasting about what will be accomplished tomorrow represents the sin of presumption, parading one's knowledge or accomplishments is no less arrogance, which leads to destruction (15:33; 16:18; 18:12). Pressing a claim for self-adulation or honor also runs the risk of rejection, since others, including God, may not see those "accomplishments" in the same light. Better to spend one's energy and time on the task at hand, which never involves praising oneself, but growing in skill and ability (cf. 22:29).

27:3. Most construction in ancient Israel was stone and mud (beaten earth). The comparison between a stone and grains of sand seems ludicrous at first, but a load is just as burdensome as one of stone in the long run, since sand is stone. Both images are easily understood by anyone who has carried either stone or sand even a relatively short distance. A fool's anger may seem relatively insignificant at first, but it becomes unbearable when faced with it repeatedly. If possible, it is wise to avoid an angry person, since anger does not correct itself (cf. 19:19), and what begins as a minor irritation will become intolerable.

27:4. Like the preceding verse, this is a double emblematic proverb (see "Overview"). Jealousy is much more fierce and destructive than anger (cf. 6:34). Nor can it be easily defused, since it feeds on suspicion. Only a sustained demonstration that the suspicions are false lulls jealousy to sleep (or the ordeal of jealousy; Num. 5:11–31). It is best to avoid any behavior that might give rise to jealousy, since one never knows how fierce a flood might be loosed.

27:5. A rebuke given in order to correct, or protect someone from, a foolish or sinful choice does far more good, however uncomfortable it may be at the moment, than unexpressed affection or encouragement. A rebuke can therefore express

5846.457		548.256	6729	154.151	6518.258	5573
v Pual ptc fs	**6.**	v Niphal ptc mp	n mp	v Qal act ptc ms	cj, v Niphal ptc fp	n fp
מְסֻתָּרֶת		נֶאֱמָנִים	פִּצְעֵי	אוֹהֵב	וְנַעְתָּרוֹת	נְשִׁיקוֹת
mᵉsuttāreth		ne'ĕmānîm	pits'ê	'ôhēv	wᵉna'ăttārôth	nᵉshîqôth
having been hidden		what is reliable	the wounds of	one who loves	but begging	the kisses of

7983.151		5497	7884	983.122	5499	5497	7744	3725, 4914
v Qal act ptc ms	**7.**	n fs	adj	v Qal impf 3fs	n ms	cj, n fs	adj	*adj*, adj
שׂוֹנֵא		נֶפֶשׁ	שְׂבֵעָה	תָּבוּס	נֹפֶת	וְנֶפֶשׁ	רְעֵבָה	כָּל־מַר
sônē'		nephesh	sᵉvē'āh	tāvûs	nōpheth	wᵉnephesh	rᵉ'ēvāh	kol-mar
one who hates		the soul	satisfied	it will despise	honey	but a person	hungry	all bitter

5142		3626, 7109	5252.153	4623, 7348	3772, 382	5252.151	4623, 4887
adj	**8.**	prep, n fs	v Qal act ptc fs	prep, n ms, ps 3fs	adv, n ms	v Qal act ptc ms	prep, n ms, ps 3ms
מָתוֹק		כְּצִפּוֹר	נוֹדֶדֶת	מִן־קִנָּהּ	כֵּן־אִישׁ	נוֹדֵד	מִמְּקוֹמוֹ
māthôq		kᵉtsippôr	nôdhedheth	min-qinnāhh	kēn-'îsh	nôdhēdh	mimmᵉqômô
sweet		like a bird	wandering	from its nest	so a man	wandering about	from his place

	8467	7285	7975.321, 3949	5161	7739
9.	n ms	cj, n fs	v Piel impf 3ms, n ms	cj, *n ms*	n ms, ps 3ms
	שֶׁמֶן	וּקְטֹרֶת	יְשַׂמַּח־לֵב	וּמֶתֶק	רֵעֵהוּ
	shemen	ûqᵉtōreth	yᵉsammach-lēv	ûmetheq	rē'ēhû
	oil	and incense	the heart will rejoice about	and the sweetness of	his friend

4623, 6332, 5497		7751	7739	1	414, 6013.123
prep, *n fs*, n fs	**10.**	n ms, ps 2ms	cj, *n ms*	n ms, ps 2ms	adv, v Qal juss 2ms
מֵעֲצַת־נָפֶשׁ		רֵעֲךָ	וְרֵעֶה	אָבִיךָ	אַל־תַּעֲזֹב
mē'ătsath-nāphesh		rē'ăkhā	wᵉrē'eh	'āvîkhā	'al-ta'ăzōv
from the counsel of the soul		your friend	and the friend of	your father	do not abandon

1041	250	414, 971.123	904, 3219	344	3005	8333
cj, *n ms*	n ms, ps 2ms	adv, v Qal juss 2ms	prep, *n ms*	n ms, ps 2ms	adj	n ms
וּבֵית	אָחִיךָ	אַל־תָּבוֹא	בְּיוֹם	אֵידֶךָ	טוֹב	שָׁכֵן
ûvêth	'āchîkhā	'al-tāvô'	bᵉyôm	'ēdhekhā	ṭôv	shākhēn
and the household of	your brother	do not enter	on the day of	your calamity	better	a neighbor

---

ter to correct someone openly than to have love and not show it, *NCV* ... Better a rebuke revealed than love concealed, *Berkeley* ... Better open reproof than feigned love, *JB* ... Better a frank word of reproof than the love that will not speak, *Moffatt*.

6. Faithful are the wounds of a friend: ... The blows of a friend are well meant, *Anchor* ... A friend means well, even when he hurts you, *Good News* ... The slap of a friend can be trusted to help you, *NCV* ... The wounds of a lover are faithfull, *Geneva* ... Wounds from a friend are better than kisses from an enemy!, *LIVB*.

but the kisses of an enemy are deceitful: ... like knives are the kisses of an enemy, *Anchor* ... profuse are

the kisses of an enemy, *Berkeley* ... but an enemy multiplies kisses, *NIV* ... but the greetings of an enemy one prays against, *NAB* ... the kisses of an enemy are importunate, *MAST*.

7. The full soul loatheth an honeycomb: ... The surfeited soul trampleth upon droppings from the comb, *Rotherham* ... The sated appetite spurns honey, *NRSV* ... When you are full, not even honey tastes good, *NCV* ... The gorged throat revolts at honey, *JB* ... The full soul is not interested in a honeycomb, *KJVII*.

but to the hungry soul every bitter thing is sweet: ... to Hunger's lips, bitter is sweet, *Knox* ... to a famished man, *NASB* ... to a ravenous appetite, *NRSV*.

8. As a bird that wandereth from her nest: ... Like a bird wandering from the place of her eggs, *BB* ... that strays from its nest, *JB*.

so is a man that wandereth from his place: ... A man away from home, *Good News* ... so is anyone who strays from his native land, *JB* ... a man who is far from his home, *NAB*.

9. Ointment and perfume rejoice the heart: ... As perfume and incense gratify the senses, *Anchor* ... Friendly suggestions are as pleasant as perfume, *LIVB* ... Perfume and scent are a delight, *Moffatt* ... Sweeter than ointment, sweeter than any perfume, *Knox*.

so doth the sweetness of a man's friend by hearty counsel: ... So a friend's cordiality strengthens one's spirit, *Anchor* ... The sweetness of one's friend more than fragrant wood, *Rotherham* ... the sweetness of a friend is an aromatic forest, *Beck* ... the sweetness of friendship rather than self-reliance, *JB* ... sweet counsel is a strength, *Moffatt*.

10. Thine own friend, and thy father's friend, forsake not: ...

Never abandon a friend—either yours or your father's, *LIVB* ... Drop not a friend who was your father's friend, *Moffatt* ... Don't forget your friend, *NCV*.

neither go into thy brother's house in the day of thy calamity: ... Don't go to your brother's home only when you're in trouble, *Beck* ... so, in thy sore need, no kinsman's door thou

shalt need to enter, *Knox* ... but if ruin befalls you, enter not a kinsman's house, *NAB* ... Don't always go to your family for help when trouble comes, *NCV*.

for better is a neighbour that is near than a brother far off: ... Neighbour over the way is better than kinsman at a distance, *Knox*.

---

love, so that affection, which may have been concealed, is revealed in the reproof. This implies that depth of love is demonstrated by willingness to confront someone else. Love that allows someone to drift from the path of righteousness is not true love.

27:6. True friends neither expect nor offer effusive praise, knowing that their relationship gives their words a great deal of weight. At the same time, their commitment to one another's well-being may lead them to confront or correct some fault or blind spot (27:5, 17). On the other hand, effusive praise (flattery) does not grow out of a desire for the other's good (29:5), and may even mask bitterness or hatred (26:23–28). The wise person, therefore, understands that words may not immediately reveal their underlying motive, and so weighs both their effect and their purpose.

27:7. On its surface, this observation means that a person's situation determines how he or she evaluates something else (an Israelite version of "One man's junk is another's treasure"). It also, however, points to the broader principle that someone's surface response often reveals his or her inner state. When, for example, the stimulus is morally charged, such as Wisdom's teaching, a negative or positive response indicates whether or not the person is wise or rebellious. The principle is thus a diagnostic tool that can be used externally (to understand someone else), or internally (to analyze the proper response is to gain self-understanding).

27:8. This contrary-to-nature saying shows how unseemly it is to desert our proper place in life. Most birds do not abandon their nests until their young are grown and gone. It may describe marital infidelity, if the image of the nest equates his "place" with his home and domestic responsibilities. Or it could be comparing the misery of a person force to leave home with that of a bird who has abandoned a destroyed nest.

On the other hand, this verse could have wider social implications. It could support the need to stay in a station in order to maintain the social sphere (cf. 30:21ff), or it could warn Israelites against leaving the land of promise in order to sojourn in other countries (cf. Ruth 1:1ff). (Proverbs 26:2 also uses the image of a wandering bird, but with quite different import.)

27:9. Since "oil" and "incense" occur together only twice (Ezek. 16:18; 23:41), in descriptions of illicit sexual relations as a metaphor for apostasy, this may be the pleasure described in the first line. They are also associated in cultic contexts (e.g., Exo. 35:8, 15; Isa. 1:13), but the non-cultic nature of Wisdom literature, and especially of the proverbs, argues against worship as the appropriate context for this verse.

The first line, which was probably the image half of an emblematic proverb, is clear, but the second line (which should explain the image) is not, as the translations show. The Hebrew could mean either "and/but the sweetness of his friend is a soul's [another's?] counsel" or "and/but his friend is sweeter than a soul's [another's?] counsel." If this is an emblematic proverb, then NASB, NIV, NKJV are probably close to the original (although they interpret, rather than translate, the Hebrew text).

If this is the proper interpretation of the text as it stands, it parallels other proverbs that encourage the wise to both give and accept counsel (15:23; 25:11f).

27:10. This "better than" proverb is a reminder that any help is better than none. The first line warns against abandoning a friend or acquaintance, since one never knows whose help may be needed. The contrasting warning is that it is dangerous to overburden relatives with troubles, since that may drive them away, so that they are unavailable in a time of real need (although the word "brother" [HED #250] in the Bible often means simply another Israelite, the contrast with "friend" probably implies a familial relationship).

11.

7427 adj	4623, 250 prep, n ms	7632 adj	2549.131 v Qal impv 2ms	1158 n ms, ps 1cs	7975.331 cj, v Piel impv 2ms	3949 n ms, ps 1cs
קָרוֹב	מֵאָח	רָחוֹק	חֲכַם	בְּנִי	וְשַׂמַּח	לִבִּי
qārôv	mē'āch	rāchôq	chăkham	benî	wesammach	libbî
near	than a brother	far away	be wise	O my son	and make glad	my heart

12.

8178.525 cj, v Hiphil juss 1cs	2884.151 v Qal act ptc ms, ps 1cs	1745 n ms	6415 n ms	7495.111 v Qal pf 3ms	7750 n fs	5846.255 v Niphal ptc ms
וְאָשִׁיבָה	חֹרְפִי	דָּבָר	עָרוּם	רָאָה	רָעָה	נִסְתָּר
we'āshîvāh	chôrephî	dhāvār	'ārûm	rā'āh	rā'āh	nistār
that I may return	one who taunts me	a word	a prudent man	he will see	evil	being hidden

13.

6848 adj	5882.116 v Qal pf 3cp	6294.216 v Niphal pf 3cp	4089.131, 933 v Qal impv 2ms, n ms, ps 3ms
פְּתָאיִם	עָבְרוּ	נֶעֱנָשׁוּ	קַח־בִּגְדוֹ
pethā'yim	'āverû	ne'ĕnāshû	qach-bighdhô
the simple	they will pass on	they will be punished	take his garment

3706, 6386.111 cj, v Qal pf 3ms	2299 n ms	1185 cj, prep	5425 n fs	2341.131 v Qal impv 2ms, ps 3ms
כִּי־עָרַב	זָר	וּבְעַד	נָכְרִיָּה	חַבְלֵהוּ
kî-'ārav	zār	ûve'adh	nākheriyāh	chavlēhû
when he has pledged for	a foreigner	and on behalf of	a foreign woman	take him as pledge

14.

1313.351 v Piel ptc ms	7739 n ms, ps 3ms	904, 7249 prep, n ms	1448 adj	904, 1269 prep, art, n ms	8326.542 v Hiphil inf abs	7329 n fs
מְבָרֵךְ	רֵעֵהוּ	בְּקוֹל	גָּדוֹל	בַּבֹּקֶר	הַשְׁכֵּים	קְלָלָה
mevārēkh	rē'ēhû	beqôl	gādhôl	babbōqer	hashkēm	qelālāh
one who blesses	his friend	with a voice	great	in the morning	causing to rise early	a curse

15.

2913.222 v Niphal impf 3fs	3937 prep, ps 3ms	1873 n ms	3065.151 v Qal act ptc ms	904, 3219 prep, n ms	5648 n ms
תֵּחָשֵׁב	לוֹ	דֶּלֶף	טוֹרֵד	בְּיוֹם	סַגְרִיר
tēchāshev	lô	deleph	tôrēdh	beyôm	saghrîr
it will be considered	to him	a leaking roof	continually dripping	on the day of	steady rain

---

11. My son, be wise, and make my heart glad: ... If you gain wisdom, my son, you will make me happy, *Anchor* ... be wise, and rejoyce mine heart, *Geneva* ... My son, wouldst thou be thy father's pride? Court wisdom, *Knox* ... Delight my heart by being wise, *Moffatt.*

that I may answer him that reproacheth me: ... so that I may give back an answer to him who puts me to shame, *BB* ... so I can answer anyone who insults me, *Beck* ... I shall be able to forestall my critics, *NEB* ... And I return my reproacher a word, *Young* ... then I can answer anyone who treats me with contempt, *NIV.*

12. A prudent man foreseeth the evil, and hideth himself: ... The sharp man sees the evil and takes cover, *BB* ... Sensible people will see trouble coming and avoid it, *Good News* ... The discreet sees danger and takes shelter, *JB* ... When ill times come, prudence is on its guard, and takes refuge, *Knox* ... The clever see danger and hide, *NRSV* ... The prudent path seen the evil, he is hidden, *Young.*

but the simple pass on, and are punished: ... simpletons go right ahead and must pay the penalty, *Anchor* ... the simple pass on, and suffer for it, *ASV* ... an unthinking person will walk right into it and regret it later, *Good News* ... fools keep going and get into trouble, *NCV* ... the thoughtless pass on, and are punished, *MAST* ... but the simple go on, and suffer for it, *NRSV.*

13. Take his garment that is surety for a stranger: ... Take the garment of one who guarantees a foreigner's debt, *Beck* ... Does a man go bail for a stranger? Without more ado, take his garment from him, *Knox* ... Take the coat of someone who promises to pay a stranger's loan, *NCV* ... He has gone bail for a man?—seize him!, *Moffatt* ... Take his garment, when a stranger hath been surety, *Young.*

and take a pledge of him for a strange woman: ... And hold him to his promise who has done so for foreigners, *Anchor* ... and hold it in pledge when he is surety for a seductress, *NKJV* ... Take a pledge from him, for persons unknown, *JB* ... who trusts without knowledge, forfeits the pledge, *Knox* ... for an adulterous woman hold him in pledge, *NASB* ... seize the pledge given as surety for foreigners, *NRSV*.

14. He that blesseth his friend with a loud voice: ... Whoever at dawn loudly blesses his neighbour with a, *JB* ... so loudly wishing thy neighbour well?, *Knox* ... If you shout a pleasant greeting to a friend, *LIVB* ...

Loud blessing lavished by one man on another, *Moffatt* ... If one man greets another too heartily, *NEB*.

rising early in the morning: ... [Rousing] him in the morning, *Anchor* ... So early abroad, *Knox* ... too early, *LIVB* ... wake him up early, *Good News* ... Will be counted as cursing, *NRSV*.

it shall be counted a curse to him: ... This is curse, not blessing, *Knox* ... he might as well curse him!, *REB* ... he may give great offence, *NEB* ... A reproach shall it be reckoned to him, *Rotherham* ... it shall be counted as foolishness to him, *KJVII*.

15. A continual dropping in a very rainy day: ... A constant dripping

---

As often in the proverbs, this does not mean that someone should never approach a relative with a need. It does caution against constantly seeking help without discerning whether or not that help is truly needed. It also commends long-term relationships, since long acquaintance and friendship can be the foundation of much help in need. This may also reflect the proverbial value that fathers affect their children's lives (cf. 13:22), since a father's friends may well be faithful to the memory of their friendship, and, for his sake, help his children.

27:11. Wisdom in children is a twofold blessing: it cheers and encourages the parents themselves, and increases their stature in the community. It also takes away at least one avenue of attack by their enemies or opponents. The command to be[come] wise appeals to the well-being of the parents, as in Prov. 10–29 (e.g., 10:1; 23:15f, 24f), whereas in Prov. 1–9 it is to the child's (e.g., 2:1–22; 3:1–10; 4:20–27), implying the close relationship between the two results.

27:12–13. Although these verses were probably originally independent sayings (27:12 is virtually identical to 22:3; 27:13 is nearly identical to 20:16), their combination here is an example of a general principle followed by a specific application of that principle. Insight understands that certain actions have disastrous consequences, and so "hides" from those outcomes by choosing a wiser or more righteous course (cf. 14:16). The naive, lacking the experience that lends insight, press on and suffer for it.

Verse 12 implicitly encourages the reader to seek insight (i.e., to strive toward wisdom) in order to be able to avoid the disaster that flows from foolish decisions. But it also warns against associating with the naive in their plans, because they do not have knowledge or experience to plan wisely. Their plans bring only trouble.

Specifically, since they do not understand the nature of the obligation under which they have placed themselves, the naive may find themselves trapped by their words (cf. 6:1–5), whether they have foolishly co-signed a loan for someone that they do not know well, or have been drawn into an illicit relationship (i.e., with a "foreign woman"; cf. 2:16–19; 5:3–14, 20; 6:24–35; 7:1–27). If it is dangerous to pledge property for a friend or neighbor, how much more foolish for someone unknown or immoral.

The specific application of the general principle is that the wise need to protect the naive by keeping them from pledging, whether by holding their property (exemplified by their "garment") for them so that it cannot be lost if the original borrower defaults, or by doing whatever is necessary to protect him from the type of relationship that brings only trouble ("binding" is surely hyperbolic).

27:14. A greeting shouted too early in the morning is a negative illustration of Prov. 25:11. There is nothing wrong with any of the pieces of this statement: it is good to bless friends, loud voices are acceptable (unless they are raised in strife) and rising early in the morning fits the general theme of diligence. It is the combination that turns a blessing into a curse. Even knowing what is good does not mean that it can simply be done at whim or in our own timing, without considering the circumstances or feelings of others (cf. 25:20). To exercise discretion is to consider as much as possible the entire situation before speaking or acting, so that the word truly fits, in content and volume, its setting.

27:15–16. These verses are connected by the pronoun "her" in v. 16a, since it has no antecedent apart from v. 15. The first is an emblematic proverb, offering counsel like that of other verses that warn about the importance of personality in a spouse (e.g., 19:13; 21:9, 19; 25:24; 26:21) and, by implication, any close associate, such as a business partner or friend.

The second verse seems to address a slightly different topic, the difficulty of controlling the fac-

828	4209	8187.712		7121.152	7121.111, 7593
cj, n fs	n mp	v Nithpael pf 3fs	**16.**	v Qal act ptc mp, ps 3fs	v Qal pf 3ms, n fs
וְאֵשֶׁת	מִדוֹנִים	נִשְׁתָּוָה		צֹפְנֶיהָ	צָפַן־רוּחַ
weʾēsheth	midhônîm	nishtāwāh		tsōphᵉnêāh	tsāphan-rûach
even a wife of	contentions	she will become like		one who stores her	he will store the wind

8467	3332	7410.121		1298	904, 1298	3266	382	3266
cj, n ms	n fs, ps 3ms	v Qal impf 3ms	**17.**	n ms	prep, n ms	adv	cj, n ms	adv
וְשֶׁמֶן	יְמִינוֹ	יִקְרָא		בַּרְזֶל	בְּבַרְזֶל	יָחַד	וְאִישׁ	יַחַד
weshemen	yemînô	yiqŏrāʾ		barzel	bevarzel	yāchadh	weʾîsh	yachadh
and oil	his right hand	he will call		iron	with iron	together	and a man	together

6686, 7739		5526.151	8711	404.121	6780
n mp, n ms, ps 3ms	**18.**	v Qal act ptc ms	n fs	v Qal impf 3ms	n ms, ps 3fs
פְּנֵי־רֵעֵהוּ		נֹצֵר	תְּאֵנָה	יֹאכַל	פִּרְיָהּ
penê-rēʾēhû		nōtsēr	teʾēnāh	yōʾkhal	piryāhh
the presence of his fellow		one who keeps	a fig tree	he will eat	its fruit

8490.151	112	3632.421		3626, 4448	6686	3937, 6686
cj, v Qal act ptc ms	n mp, ps 3ms	v Pual impf 3ms	**19.**	prep, art, n md	art, n mp	prep, art, n mp
וְשֹׁמֵר	אֲדֹנָיו	יְכֻבָּד		כַּמַּיִם	הַפָּנִים	לַפָּנִים
weshshōmēr	ʾădhōnâv	yekhubbādh		kammayim	happānîm	lappānîm
and the one who guards	his master	he will be honored		like the water	the faces	to the faces

3772	3949, 119	3937, 119		8061	10	3940	7881.127
adv	n ms, art, n ms	prep, art, n ms	**20.**	pn	cj, pn	neg part	v Qal impf 3fp
כֵּן	לֵב־הָאָדָם	לָאָדָם		שְׁאוֹל	וַאֲבַדֹּה	לֹא	תִשְׂבַּעְנָה
kēn	lēv-hāʾādhām	lāʾādhām		sheʾôl	waʾăvaddōh	lōʾ	thisbaʿănāh
so	the heart of the man	to the man		Sheol	and Abaddon	not	they can be satisfied

6084	119	3940	7881.127		4876	3937, 3826B
cj, n fd	art, n ms	neg part	v Qal impf 3fp	**21.**	n ms	prep, art, n ms
וְעֵינֵי	הָאָדָם	לֹא	תִשְׂבַּעְנָה		מַצְרֵף	לַכֶּסֶף
weʿênê	hāʾādhām	lōʾ	thisbaʿănāh		matsrēph	lakkeseph
and the eyes of	humankind	not	they can be satisfied		a crucible	for the silver

on a day of winter rain, *Anchor* ... The dripping of a gutter on a rainy day, *JB* ... Between a scold and a roof that drips in winter there is nothing to choose, *Knox* ... a persistent leak, *NAB* ... A continuous dripping on a day of downpour, *Rotherham*.

and a contentious woman are alike: ... is a bitter-tongued woman, *BB* ... and a quarrelsome woman are alike, *JB* ... and a cranky woman are much alike!, *LIVB* ... the match is a quarrelsome woman, *NAB* ... A quarreling wife is as bothersome, *NCV* ... that is what a nagging wife is like, *NEB* ... And a woman of contentions are alike, *Young*.

16. Whosoever hideth her hideth the wind: ... To try to restrain her is like trying to restrain the wind, *Anchor* ... whoever can restrain her, can restrain the wind, *JB* ... As well try to store up the wind in thy house, *Knox* ... He who keeps her stores up a stormwind, *NAB* ... The north wind is a harsh wind, *Moffatt* ... He who keeps secret the secret of his friend, *BB* ... As well try to control the wind as to control her!, *REB*.

and the ointment of his right hand, which betrayeth itself: ... One cries out that "his hand is slippery," *Anchor* ... and take a firm hold on grease, *JB* ... he cannot tell north from south, *NAB* ... grasps oil with his right hand, *NASB* ... but it has an auspicious name, *Moffatt* ... or hold on to anything with oil-slick hands, *LIVB* ... though thou call her the marrow of thy right hand, *Knox* ... As well try to pick up oil in one's fingers!, *REB* ... ointment of his right hand calleth out, *Young*.

17. Iron sharpeneth iron: ... As one iron implement is sharpened by another, *Anchor* ... iron is sharpened by iron, *JB* ... the sparks that fly when iron strikes iron, *LIVB* ... As iron whets iron, *Moffatt* ... Let iron by iron become sharp, *Rotherham*.

so a man sharpeneth the countenance of his friend: ... so one man sharpens the wits of another, *Beck* ... one person is sharpened by contact with another, *JB* ... and a man sharpens the face of his friend, *KJVII* ... so one man sharpens another, *NIV* ... People learn from one another, *Good*

News ... one person is sharpened by contact with another, *JB* ... friend shapes friend, *Knox* ... so people can improve each other, *NCV*.

18. Whoso keepeth the fig tree shall eat the fruit thereof: ... He who watches over the fig tree will eat its fruit, *Berkeley* ... If figs thou wouldst eat, tend thy fig-tree well, *Knox* ... A workman may eat from the orchard he tends, *LIVB*.

so he that waiteth on his master shall be honoured: ... if honour thou wouldst have, wait well on thy master, *Knox* ... anyone should be rewarded who protects another's interests, *LIVB* ... and he who is attentive to his mas-

ter will be enriched, *NAB* ... and he who watches his master's interests will come to honour, *NEB*.

19. As in water face answereth to face: ... As a face is reflected in water, *Anchor* ... Clear as a face mirrored in water, *Knox* ... As one face is like another, *Moffatt* ... As one face differs from another, *NAB*.

so the heart of man to man: ... So a man's thoughts are reflected in the man, *Anchor* ... so your mind shows what kind of person you are, *NCV* ... the wise see men's hearts, *Knox* ... but what he is really like is shown by the kind of friends he chooses, *LIVB*.

20. Hell and destruction are never full: ... People will never stop dying and being destroyed, *NCV* ... like the world of the dead—there is always room for more, *Good News* ... Sheol and Perdition are never satisfied, *JB* ... Death and the grave were never yet content, *Knox*.

so the eyes of man are never satisfied: ... Man's desire is insatiable, *Anchor* ... Human desires, *Good News* ... nor man's eyes with gazing, *Knox* ... and they will never stop wanting more than they have, *NCV*.

21. As the refining pot for silver, and the furnace for gold: ... As a crucible for silver and a smelter for

tious spouse of v. 15. It apparently compares controlling such a person to controlling the wind (v. 16a), and holding oil in one's hand (v. 16b). Both lines present translation difficulties, although the meaning of "restrain" for tsāphan (HED #7121) may be attested in Hos. 13:12, and the root qrh (HED #7424) must be read for qr' (HED #7410), "meets," rendering the phrase, "and oil meets his right [hand]."

27:17. An iron file or hammer can be used to sharpen iron tools (cf. Ezek. 21:14ff). Since the word "face" (HED #6686) can refer to the edge of a sword (Ezek. 21:16) or ax (Ecc. 10:10), "his friend's face" may both continue the imagery of the first line and describe his friend's words by metonymy. The interaction within a friendship is mutual, so that friends shape one another's ways of thinking and living. The verse thus commends the benefits of friendship and warns the wise to choose their friends carefully.

27:18. Good service is usually recognized and, if the master is both gracious and wise, rewarded. The image of the gardener of figs may encourage service over a period of time, since fig trees are extremely long-lived, and mature slowly.

27:19. The inner and outer person correspond as clearly as a face corresponds to its own image in the water. Thus, to observe and analyze someone's words and deeds is to come to understand his heart, since the heart is the essence of the person and inevitably makes its true state known in and through the life of the person. The "someone" may, be understood as "anyone." The wise person can use his own thoughts, words and deeds in order to understand the state of his heart, as well as the

heart of others. This is probably the implication of the article, which is used throughout this verse: "so the man's heart [is] the man."

27:20. This verse "applies" the number-saying in Prov. 30:15f, where Agur lists four things that are never satisfied, but does not draw a conclusion from his observation. Since everyone and everything either has died or will die, death has not yet had enough. Human appetites are equally insatiable (cf. Ecc. 1:8; 4:8; 5:10ff).

It is fruitless to try to satisfy desires by obtaining their objects. Nothing in this life can satisfy human hearts. The proof of this is that as soon as the object of desire is obtained, the eyes fix on something else. This is true on any scale, from emperor (Alexander the Great supposedly wept when his army refused to cross the Indus River, since there were "no more worlds to conquer"; cf. Hab. 2:5) to the worker who thinks that an increased wage would solve all his problems.

The proverb thus points beyond the desires of this life to God himself, the only Source of life and wisdom. And wisdom, in turn, yields satisfaction (cf. 3:1–19; 5:15–19; 9:1–6), since it recognizes the adequacy of God alone. As Augustine said, "You have made us for yourself, O God, and our hearts are restless until they find their rest in you" (*Confessions* I.1).

27:21. The first line of this verse is identical to 17:3a. That verse presents the LORD as the unseen Examiner of hearts, whereas this proverb considers how praise affects a person. The Israelites knew how to refine precious metals by heating them so that the impurities either burned off or floated to the

22.

3685 cj, n ms	3937, 2174 prep, art, n ms	382 cj, n ms	3937, 6552 prep, n ms	4251 n ms, ps 3ms	524 cj
וְכוּר	לַזָּהָב	וְאִישׁ	לְפִי	מַהֲלָלוֹ	אִם
wekhûr	lazzāhāv	we'îsh	lephî	mahlālô	'im
and a furnace	for the gold	and a man	for the mouth of	his praise	if

3935.123, 881, 188 v Qal impf 2ms, do, art, n ms	904, 4525 prep, art, n ms	904, 8761 prep, n ms	7669 art, n fp	904, 6166 prep, art, n ms
תִּכְתּוֹשׁ־אֶת־הָאֱוִיל	בַּמַּכְתֵּשׁ	בְּתוֹךְ	הָרִיפוֹת	בַּעֱלִי
tikhtôsh-'eth-hā'ĕwîl	bammakhtēsh	bethôkh	hārîphôth	ba'ĕlî
you could pound the fool	in the mortar	in the middle of	the loose grain	with the pestle

23.

3940, 5681.122 neg part, v Qal impf 3fs	4623, 6142 prep, prep, ps 3ms	198 n fs, ps 3ms	3156.142 v Qal inf abs	3156.123 v Qal impf 2ms
לֹא־תָסוּר	מֵעָלָיו	אִוַּלְתּוֹ	יָדֹעַ	תֵּדַע
lō'-thāsûr	mē'ālâv	'iwwaltô	yādhōa'	tēdha'
it would not depart	from beside him	his foolishness	knowing	you will surely know

24.

6686 n mp	6887 n fs, ps 2ms	8308.131 v Qal impv 2ms	3949 n ms, ps 2ms	3937, 5953 prep, n mp	3706 cj	3940 neg part	3937, 5986 prep, n ms
פְּנֵי	צֹאנֶךָ	שִׁית	לִבְּךָ	לַעֲדָרִים	כִּי	לֹא	לְעוֹלָם
penê	tsō'nekhā	shîth	libbekhā	la'ădhārîm	kî	lō'	le'ôlām
the faces of	your sheep	put	your heart	to herds	because	not	unto eternity

25.

2738 n ms	524, 5325 cj, cj, n ms	3937, 1810 prep, n ms	1810 n ms	1580.111 v Qal pf 3ms	2785 n ms
חֹסֶן	וְאִם־נֵזֶר	לְדוֹר	דּוֹר	גָּלָה	חָצִיר
chōsen	we'im-nēzer	ledhôr	dhôr	gālāh	chātsîr
storage	and with a headband	to a generation	a generation	it will uncover	grass

26.

7495.211, 1940 cj, v Niphal pf 3ms, n ms	636.216 cj, v Niphal pf 3cp	6448 n mp	2098 n mp	3904 n mp
וְנִרְאָה־דֶשֶׁא	וְנֶאֶסְפוּ	עֶשְׂבוֹת	הָרִים	כְּבָשִׂים
wenir'āh-dheshe'	wene'esphû	'issevôth	hārîm	kevāsîm
and fresh growth will be seen	and they will be gathered	the herbs of	the mountains	lambs

gold, Anchor ... Silver is refined in a melting-pot and gold in a furnace, Beck ... Fire tests gold and silver, Good News ... Silver and gold are judged by furnace and crucible, Knox ... A furnace for silver, a foundry for gold, JB.

so is a man to his praise: ... Flattery will show what a man is, Anchor ... a man is tested by his reaction to men's praise, LIVB ... praise is the test of character, NEB ... a man is valued by what others say of him, NKJV ... a person is worth what his reputation is worth, JB.

22. Though thou shouldest bray a fool in a mortar among wheat with a pestle: ... Even if you ground up a foolish person like grain in a bowl, NCV ... Though

you pound a fool with a pestle, Among grit in a mortar, Goodspeed ... Though you should pound the fool to bits, NAB ... though you crush him to powder, LIVB.

yet will not his foolishness depart from him: ... even then his nonsense won't leave him, Beck ... he will be a fool still, Knox ... his folly will never be knocked out of him, NEB ... You can't separate a rebel from his foolishness, LIVB.

23. Be thou diligent to know the state of thy flocks: ... Be careful to know your own sheep, NEB ... Be well acquainted with the appearance of thy flocks, Darby ... Spent be thy care, thy eyes watchful over flock and herd of thine, Knox ... Be sure you know how your sheep are doing, NCV.

and look well to thy herds: ... take good care of your herds, JB ... Apply thy mind to thy herds, Rotherham ... Set thy heart to the droves, Young ... pay attention to the condition of your cattle, NCV.

24. For riches are not for ever: ... possessions are impermanent, Anchor ... wealth is not for ever, Darby ... riches remain not alway, Geneva ... riches will slip from thy grasp, Knox ... Riches can disappear fast, LIVB.

and doth the crown endure to every generation?: ... no treasure lasts for generations, Anchor ... Not even nations last forever, Good News ... crowns do not hand themselves on from age to age, JB ... nor do governments go on forever, NCV ... Nor is the diadem from generation to generation, *Rotherham*.

25. The hay appeareth, and the tender grass showeth itself: … when hay is stored away, tender grass can be seen, *Beck* … See, where the meadows are laid bare, and the aftermath is

springing, *Knox* … When haytime is over and the aftermath mowed, *Moffatt* … when the hay has been cut and the second growth appears, *Anchor*.

and herbs of the mountains are gathered: … When the crop has been gathered in from the hillsides, *Anchor*

… the mountain plants are got in, *BB* … vegetables are gathered from the hills, *Beck* … the hay all carried, now, from the hill-slopes!, *Knox* … the mountain greens are gathered in, *NAB*.

26. The lambs are for thy clothing: … Pasture for the lambs that shall

---

top where they could be skimmed off. Having been purified, the metal could then be cast in a mold (cf. 25:4). The heat thus refines and tests the metal, since it reveals and burns off impurities. Whether a person becomes prideful in response to praise reveals the state of his heart.

27:22. The Book of Proverbs holds out no hope for the fool (17:10, 16; 26:7, 9). Not even the most severe punishment will drive his folly from him or turn him from his self-destructive course, since it is his natural way of life (cf. 26:11). Verses that seem to suggest the possibility that fools can change (e.g., 26:12; 29:20) actually prove their point by the impossibility of any change. This verse may warn against futile efforts at reform or against dallying with folly oneself.

27:23–27. This brief poem on the importance and benefits of diligent stewardship of flocks may seem a strange topic for kings. Solomon, however, was only one generation away from the sheepfold. David's humble heritage (cf. 1 Sam. 16:11ff, 19; 17:15, 20, 28, 34) was not forgotten by the people (2 Sam. 5:2). The LORD reminded David of his background (2 Sam. 7:8), and Nathan undoubtedly used a lamb in his parable because of David's background, both to arouse his sympathy and to remind him of how much the LORD had done for him (2 Sam 12:1–4).

The poem consists of a command (v. 23), followed by a complex motive clause (vv. 24–27). The thrust of the poem is that one must care for one's flocks and herds (v. 23), because life's trophies are not permanent (v. 24). The animals are the true basis of one's life, since to have them is to have what is most important—food, clothing and property (vv. 25ff). Successful life, therefore, requires focusing on what is most important and not allowing other things to distract one from maintaining the foundation.

In addition to his personal background, Solomon would have known the ancient Near Eastern tradition that viewed kings as shepherds, common to Sumer, Babylon (Code of Hammurabi), Assyria and Neo-Babylonia, and also found in Egypt, so that their manifold titles often included "shep-

herd." Centuries after Solomon, the LORD would use this same image in the mouths of his prophets to condemn evil rulers and false prophets as wicked shepherds (cf. Jer. 49:19; 50:6; 51:23; Zech. 13:7).

Scripture speaks, in fact, of five good shepherds: Moses (cf. Isa. 63:11); David (by implication); Cyrus king of Persia (cf. Isa. 44:28); the LORD himself (cf. Pss. 23:1; 80:1; Isa. 40:11); and Jesus Christ (cf. John 10:1–30). As God is a shepherd to his people (e.g., Pss. 95:7; 100:3), the king is to shepherd them as well. The entire poem is thus a conceit (an extended metaphor) on the nature of covenantal kingship, extending far beyond the farm or sheepfold. The imagery is thus both royal and divine.

Since themes related to kingship and governance dominate Prov. 28–29, this poem was probably set here in order to introduce them. (The chapter break is both misplaced and misleading.)

27:23–24. Flocks and herds were signs of wealth in the ancient world. When Pharaoh wanted to honor Abram for Sarai's sake, he gave him "sheep, oxen, donkeys, male and female servants, female donkeys, and camels" (Gen. 12:16). A few verses later, Abram is described as wealthy in "flocks, silver, and gold" (Gen. 13:2), probably listed from the least to most intrinsically valuable (gold is worth more than goat meat or hair), but in decreasing order of quantity. The well-being of flocks must not be taken for granted (cf. Gen. 30:32–31:1).

This emblematic proverb likens the care needed to preserve flocks with that required for successful rulers. Power can dissipate, corrode or be lost just as surely as flocks and herds. The wise king watches over his dominion with as much care as a good shepherd.

27:25. Each season, spring and harvest, brings its own needs. They also follow upon each other inexorably, so that all that the farmer king can do is whatever task is at hand, whether rotating the flocks to the new grass or reaping a harvest (or going to war; cf. 2 Sam. 11:1; 1 Ki. 20:22, 26).

27:26–27. The result of this attention to the daily matters of the vocation (the well-being of the

3937, 3961	4378	7898	6500		1823	2560	6008
prep, n ms, ps 2ms	cj, n ms	n ms	n mp	27.	cj, sub	n ms	n fp
לִלְבֻשֶׁךָ	וּמְחִיר	שָׂדֶה	עַתּוּדִים		וְדֵי	חֲלֵב	עִזִּים
lilvushekhā	ûmechîr	sādheh	'attûdhîm		wedhê	chălēv	'izzîm
for your clothing	and the price of	a field	he-goats		and enough of	the milk of	goats

3937, 4035	3937, 4035	1041	2552	3937, 5472
prep, n ms, ps 2ms	prep, n ms	n ms, ps 2ms	cj, n mp	prep, n fp, ps 2ms
לְלַחְמְךָ	לְלֶחֶם	בֵּיתֶךָ	וְחַיִּים	לְנַעֲרוֹתֶיךָ
lelachmekhā	lelechem	bêthekhā	wechayyîm	lena'ărôthêkhā
for your food	for the food of	your household	and life	for your maidservants

28:1	5308.116	375, 7579.151	7857	6926	3626, 3841
	v Qal pf 3cp	cj, sub, v Qal act ptc ms	n ms	cj, n mp	prep, n ms
	נָסוּ	וְאֵין־רֹדֵף	רָשָׁע	וְצַדִּיקִים	כִּכְפִיר
	nāsû	we'ên-rōdhēph	rāshā'	wetsaddîqîm	kikhphîr
	they will flee	when there is not a pursuer	the wicked	but the righteous	like a lion

1019.121		904, 6840	800	7521	8015	904, 119
v Qal impf 3ms	2.	prep, n ms	n fs	adj	n mp, ps 3fs	cj, prep, n ms
יִבְטָח		בְּפֶשַׁע	אֶרֶץ	רַבִּים	שָׂרֶיהָ	וּבְאָדָם
yivṭāch		bephesha'	'erets	rabbîm	sārêāh	ûve'ādhām
he will be confident		by the transgression of	a land	many	its officials	but with a man

1032.551	3156.151	3772	773.521		1429	7851
v Hiphil ptc ms	v Qal act ptc ms	adv	v Hiphil impf 3ms	3.	n ms	n ms
מֵבִין	יֹדֵעַ	כֵּן	יַאֲרִיךְ		גֶּבֶר	רָשׁ
mēvîn	yōdhēa'	kēn	ya'ărîkh		gever	rāsh
giving discernment to	one who knows	so	it will be long		a man	a poor man

6479.151	1859	4443	5691.151	375	4035
cj, v Qal act ptc ms	n mp	n ms	v Qal act ptc ms	cj, sub	n ms
וְעֹשֵׁק	דַּלִּים	מָטָר	סֹחֵף	וְאֵין	לָחֶם
we'ōshēq	dallîm	māṭār	sōchēph	we'ên	lāchem
and one who oppresses	the poor	rain	sweeping away	and there is not	bread

clothe thee, *Knox* ... your sheep will furnish you with clothing then, *Moffatt* ... Make clothes from the lambs' wool, *NCV*.

and the goats are the price of the field: ... goats will provide profit from the land, *Anchor* ... the he-goats make the value of a field, *BB* ... the goats furnish money for a field, *Berkeley* ... the goats that shall be the price of more fields yet, *Knox*.

27. And thou shalt have goats' milk enough for thy food: ... to feed you and your family, *Beck* ... goat's milk, too, shall suffice to feed thee, *Knox*.

for the food of thy household: ... give life and strength to thy men, *Knox*.

and for the maintenance for thy maidens: ... and sustenance for your maidservants, *Anchor* ... and it will keep your maids alive, *Beck* ... to make your servant girls healthy, *NCV* ... nourishment for your maidens, *NEB* ... life to thy damsels!, *Young*.

28:1. The wicked flee: ... A rogue runs away, *Anchor* ... The evil man goes running away, *BB* ... Bad conscience takes to its heels, *Knox* ... Rascals will run away, *Moffatt*.

when no man pursueth: ... when no one is chasing him, *Anchor* ... is after him, *BB*.

but the righteous are bold as a lion: ... like a lion are confident, *Rotherham* ... like a lion, feels sure of himself, *NAB* ... is like a young

lion in repose, *NEB* ... are braver than lions, *Anchor* ... feel safe as a young lion, *Beck*.

2. For the transgression of a land: ... When a land is in revolt, *Anchor* ... When there is moral rot within a nation, *LIVB* ... When a country is rebellious, *NIV* ... where a land is plagued for its guilt, *Knox* ... By the transgression of a land, *NASB*.

many are the princes thereof: ... it has many [would-be] rulers, *Anchor* ... it will have one ruler after another, *Good News* ... its government topples easily, *LIVB*.

but by a man of understanding and knowledge: ... only with a man of intelligence, *Beck* ... when it has intelligent, sensible leaders, *Good*

News ... with one person wise and experienced, *JB* ... by wise counsel, and men's talk overheard, *Knox* ... with a prudent man, *NAB*.

the state thereof shall be prolonged: ... a nation will be strong and endure, *Good News* ... you have stability, *JB* ... will it last long, *Beck* ... long lives the king, *Knox* ... it knows security, *NAB*.

3. A poor man that oppresseth the poor: ... A man of wealth who is cruel to the poor, *BB* ... A man in authority who oppresses poor people, *Good News* ... A needy man, *MRB* ... Rulers who mistreat the poor, *NCV* ... who crushes the poor, *KJVII*.

is like a sweeping rain: ... here is a devastating rain, *JB* ... beating rain,

NRSV ... violent rain, *BB* ... driving rain, *Good News* ... Tempest threatens, *Knox*.

which leaveth no food: ... which ruins the harvest, *Anchor* ... causing destruction of food, *BB* ... that destroys the crops, *Good News* ... sweeping away their last hope, *LIVB* ... farewell, bread!, *JB*.

---

flocks and herds) is that there will be resources to feed and clothe all the members of the household, and even enough to purchase land. How important is this? The last line says, literally, "and life for your maidens." This is not a description of superfluous luxuries, but of what is truly vital.

Understanding and maintaining what is most important is the part of wisdom. Solomon uses flocks and herds to illustrate and encourage reflection upon the primary issues of the monarch's responsibilities. Like flocks and herds, wisdom, knowledge and dominion must be constantly guarded and kept.

28:1–29:27. In these chapters, the proverbs return to the antithetical style of chs. 10–15. As in those chapters, any apparent "organization" (i.e., repeated verses and ideas) results from the use of themes common to the entire Book (e.g., the righteous and the wicked).

Two aspects of these chapters, however, point to their overall focus on a specific aspect of wisdom, namely leadership. First, in sharp contrast to the earlier chapters, there are only four references to "fools" (28:26; 29:9, 11, 20). Second, many verses throughout these chapters refer to or describe various aspects of leadership (e.g., 28:7, 12, 15f, 28; 29:2, 12, 16, 18), especially justice (e.g., 28:2, 4f, 9, 17, 21; 29:4, 14, 25f), and nearly all of them can be applied directly to royal concerns (cf. 28:23 and 29:5 on the danger of flattering counselors). In this light, the preceding poem (27:23–27, which is unfortunately disconnected by a poor chapter break), uses the common ancient Near Eastern and biblical metaphor of the king as shepherd to introduce the general topic of these chapters.

Although rulership seems to dominate these chapters, and although many of the proverbs in them may be especially applicable to kings and their counselors, they also apply to all readers, even allowing for different stations in life. This needs to *be kept in mind, since the comments emphasize either the specific (royal) or general application of each verse, but rarely both.*

28:1. A guilty conscience can make even the wicked timorous, although they are usually portrayed as being boldly on the offensive (e.g., 26:23–28). The real point of the verse is the contrast with the confidence of those who do what is right, although their confidence rests not in their own righteousness, but, based on the context of the entire Book, in the LORD's faithfulness toward them (16:20; 28:25). The lion's boldness is itself proverbial (30:30, even though a different word for lion is used).

The lack of grammatical concord (a plural verb with a singular subject in the first line and the opposite in the second) is not atypical of Hebrew poetic style, in which grammatical concerns were not always as important as structure, contrasts and other considerations. The entire grammatical and semantic structure is chiastic:

They flee (plural, perfect) without a pursuer, the wicked (singular);

The righteous (plural) like a lion are confident (singular, imperfect).

28:2. The first line connects moral decline with political turmoil, and, possibly, military defeat, but the second line is extremely difficult. Since the majority of verses in these chapters are antithetical, we may conjecture a contrast between a land's stability and welfare under wise and wicked rulers (cf. the relative stability of the Davidic line in Judah versus the multiple "dynasties" of the north). The Septuagint's reading of the verse is so different that it cannot be related to the Hebrew text: "Because of the sins of the ungodly quarrels arise, but a wise man will quiet them."

28:3. Although the text is clear, several suggestions have been made for different readings of the word "poor," apparently because it is difficult to imagine a situation in which the poor could oppress

4.

6013.152	8784	2054.326	7857	8490.152	8784
v Qal act ptc mp	n fs	v Piel impf 3mp	n ms	cj, v Qal act ptc mp	n fs
עֹזְבֵי	תּוֹרָה	יְהַלְלוּ	רֶשַׁע	וְשֹׁמְרֵי	תּוֹרָה
'ōzevê	thôrāh	yehalelû	rāshā'	weshōmerê	thôrāh
those who abandon	the Law	they will praise	the wicked	but those who observe	the Law

5.

1667.726	904	596, 7737	3940, 1032.126	5122	1272.352
v Hithpael impf 3mp	prep, ps 3mp	n mp, n ms	neg part, v Qal impf 3mp	n ms	cj, v Piel ptc mp
יִתְגָּרוּ	בָם	אַנְשֵׁי־רָע	לֹא־יָבִינוּ	מִשְׁפָּט	וּמְבַקְשֵׁי
yithgārû	vām	'anshê-rā'	lō'-yāvînû	mishpāt	ûmevaqōshê
they will contend	with them	men of evil	they do not understand	justice	but those who seek

6.

3176	1032.126	3725	3005, 7851	2050.151	904, 8866
pn	v Qal impf 3mp	n ms	adj, n ms	v Qal act ptc ms	prep, n ms, ps 3ms
יְהוָה	יָבִינוּ	כֹּל	טוֹב־רָשׁ	הוֹלֵךְ	בְּתֻמּוֹ
yehwāh	yāvînû	khōl	tōv-rāsh	hōlēkh	bethummô
Yahweh	they will understand	everything	better a poor man	walking	in his integrity

7.

4623, 6379	1932	2000	6474	5526.151	8784	1158
prep, adj	n md	cj, pers pron	adj	v Qal act ptc ms	n fs	n ms
מֵעִקֵּשׁ	דְּרָכַיִם	וְהוּא	עָשִׁיר	נוֹצֵר	תּוֹרָה	בֵּן
mē'iqqēsh	derākhayim	wehû'	'āshîr	nôtsēr	tôrāh	bēn
than perversity of	ways	but he	rich	one who keeps	the Law	a son

1032.551	7749.151	2236.152	3757.521	1
v Hiphil ptc ms	cj, v Qal act ptc ms	v Qal act ptc mp	v Hiphil impf 3ms	n ms, ps 3ms
מֵבִין	וְרֹעֶה	זוֹלְלִים	יַכְלִים	אָבִיו
mēvîn	werō'eh	zôlelîm	yakhlîm	'āvîw
giving discernment	but a companion of	vile men	he will humiliate	his father

8.

7528.551	2019	904, 5575	904, 8974
v Hiphil ptc ms	n ms, ps 3ms	prep, n ms	cj, prep, n fs
מַרְבֶּה	הוֹנוֹ	בְּנֶשֶׁךְ	וּבְתַרְבִּית
marbeh	hônô	beneshekh	ûvetharbîth
one who makes much	his wealth	with interest	and with usury

---

4. They that forsake the law: … Those who disobey what they have been taught, *NCV* … Those who have forsaken morality, *Anchor* … Those who abandon the law, *NAB* … Sound teaching is forgotten, *Knox* … Apostates, *Moffatt*.

praise the wicked: … give praise to the evil-doer, *BB* … praise pagans, *Moffatt* … you are on the side of the wicked, *Good News* … where the wrong-doer is well spoken of, *Knox*.

but such as keep the law: … the law-abiding, *Anchor* … honest folk, *Knox* … they who keep instruction, *Rotherham* … but if you obey it, *Good News*.

contend with them: … resist them, *NIV* … are angered by them, *JB* … will still be up in arms, *Knox* … struggle against them, *NRSV* … plead against them, *KJVII*.

5. Evil men understand not judgment: … have no knowledge of what is right, *BB* … Wicked men don't know right from wrong, *Beck* … Evil people do not know what justice is, *Good News* … No skill the knave has to discern the right, *Knox*.

but they that seek the LORD: … the Lord's servants, *Anchor* … those who go after the Lord, *BB* … those who worship the LORD, *Good News* … those who seek Yahweh, *JB* … quest of the Lord's will, *Knox*.

understand all things: … understand everything, *JB* … have discretion, *Beck* … know all about it, *Anchor* … makes that craft perfect, *Knox* … understand it completely, *NRSV*.

6. Better is the poor that walketh in his uprightness: … A poor man who maintains his integrity, *Anchor* … Better to be poor and honest, *Good News* … to be poor and innocent, *NCV* … poor and above reproach, *REB*.

than he that is perverse in his ways, though he be rich: … than the man of wealth whose ways are not straight, *BB* … than rich and dishonest, *Good News* … than crooked ways that bring riches, *Knox* … than rich and a cheater, *LIVB*.

7. Whoso keepeth the law is a wise son: … An intelligent son does as he is instructed, *Beck* … A young man who obeys the law is intelligent,

Good News ... A son's wisdom is to obey his father's teaching, *Knox* ... Children who obey what they have been taught are smart, *NCV* ... A discerning son observes the law, *NEB*.

but he that is a companion of riotous men: ... a companion of squanderers, *Rotherham* ... companion of gluttons, *Anchor* ... a friend of dissolute men, *Moffatt* ... One who makes friends with good-for-nothings, *Good News* ... he who keeps company with feasters, *BB*.

shameth his father: ... humiliates, *Anchor* ... disgraces, *Beck* ... wounds, *NEB* ... Doth cause his father to blush, *Young*.

8. He that by usury and unjust gain: ... through usury and rents, *Anchor* ... by taking interest and making loans, *Beck* ... by interest and overcharge, *NAB* ... by lending at discount or at interest, *NEB*.

increaseth his substance: ... grows wealthy, *Anchor* ... makes his wealth

greater, *BB* ... augmenteth his substance, *MAST* ... augments wealth, *NRSV*.

he shall gather it for him: ... gets it together, *BB* ... amasses it for someone else, *JB* ... Accumulates to benefit a patron, *Anchor*.

that will pity the poor: ... who is kind to, *Beck* ... who will bestow it on, *JB* ... who is gracious to, *NASB*.

---

anyone. On the basis of the Septuagint, it may be read "wicked"; another suggestion is either "rich" or "chief" (i.e., ruler). Poverty, however, can be relative, as Jesus' parable shows (Matt. 18:23–35).

Though rain should nourish crops, a hard driving rain can destroy standing grain and ruin the harvest (the verb may suggest rain that is blown horizontal by the wind). Similarly, a poor man can destroy the lives of the less fortunate. This is doubly wicked, since his own experience probably includes the straits of oppression at the hands of the wealthy.

28:4. In Proverbs, the word tôrāh (HED #8784) often refers to the teacher's words (e.g., 1:8; 3:1; 4:2; 6:20, 23; 7:2; 13:14), but in chs. 28–29 it primarily refers to the teachings and laws of the Covenant (e.g., 28:7, 9; 29:18). A person's attitude toward the Covenant can be discerned by his actions with regard to evil, whether he praises it or fights against it. This verse also provides an internal check, since our own attitude toward wickedness and sin reveals whether we are in the process of abandoning or observing the Covenant and its standards.

28:5. Reflecting the theme of justice that is especially prevalent in chs. 28–29, this saying warns that some people ought not to be placed in situations that require moral insight. They will be unable to fulfill their basic duty (upholding justice), since their hearts are inclined away from justice (cf. the problems of attitude toward the Covenant and favoritism in the adjacent verses). This reflects the basic ancient Near Eastern concept of the king as the highest court (cf. 1 Ki. 3:9), as well as his responsibility to appoint judges who will uphold the standards of covenantal justice (Exo. 18:13–26; Deut. 1:9–18; 1 Sa. 8:1–5). It also shows that character may or may not make people fit for particular

responsibilities, so that they must be well-known before being given those duties.

28:6. Honesty and integrity are always the better choice, regardless of the outcome. Like other "better than" proverbs, this verse asserts their superiority over lies that lead to wealth (e.g., 15:16; 16:17; 19:1, 22). Its first line is identical to 19:1a, which highlights the source of his perversity, whereas this proverb reveals that his "reward" does not outweigh or neutralize the wickedness that gained it. The wicked is described here and in 28:18 as "twisted [perverse] of two ways" (the only occurrences of this idea), which may mean someone who plays both ends against the middle, betraying everyone for his own advantage. The proverb warns that the wicked may seem to end up ahead of the righteous in this life, but an unseen scale weighs all things.

28:7. Living by the Covenant reveals the ability to discern what is true and valuable. One proof that discernment is lacking is poor choice in companions (cf. 1:10–19; 22:24f; 23:19ff; 29:3). Those who lack the understanding that comes from experience, and who continually choose companions for the wrong reasons (including friends who encourage them to indulge their own appetites) will end up living in ways that both insult and humiliate their parents. Like other verses that address the effect of children's choices on their parents, this proverb encourages parents to discipline their children (e.g., 19:18; 29:15, 17) and exhorts children to consider how their decisions affect others.

28:8. Both normal and excessive interest (usury) were forbidden under the Covenant (Exo. 22:25; Lev. 25:35ff; Deut. 23:19f), a statute that remained in force through and after the exile (Ezek. 18:8, 13, 17; 22:12). The verse warns that though the wicked may enjoy the fruits of their wickedness for

Proverbs 28:9–13

			9.
3937, 2706.151	1859	7192.121	5681.551
prep, v Qal act ptc ms	n mp	v Qal impf 3ms, ps 3ms	v Hiphil ptc ms
לְחוֹנֵן	דַּלִּים	יִקְבְּצֶנּוּ	מֵסִיר
lechônēn	dallîm	yiqŏbbetsennû	mēsîr
for one who acts compassionately with	the poor	he will gather it	one who turns away

238	4623, 8471.141	8784	1612, 8940	8774
n fs, ps 3ms	prep, v Qal inf con	n fs	cj, n fs, ps 3ms	n fs
אָזְנוֹ	מִשְּׁמֹעַ	תּוֹרָה	גַּם־תְּפִלָּתוֹ	תּוֹעֵבָה
'āzenô	mishshemōa'	tôrāh	gam-tephillāthô	tô'ēvāh
his ear	from listening to	the Law	also his prayer	a detestable thing

10.

8146.551	3596	904, 1932	7737	904, 8248	2000, 5489.126
v Hiphil ptc ms	n mp	prep, n ms	n ms	prep, n fs, ps 3ms	pers pron, v Qal impf 3mp
מַשְׁגֶּה	יְשָׁרִים	בְּדֶרֶךְ	רָע	בִּשְׁחוּתוֹ	הוּא־יִפּוֹל
mashgeh	yeshārîm	bedherekh	rā'	bishchûthô	hû'-yippôl
one who causes to stray	the upright	in the way of	evil	in his pit	he he will fall

11.

8879	5336.126, 3008	2550	904, 6084	382	6474
cj, n mp	v Qal impf 3mp, n ms	adj	prep, n fd, ps 3ms	n ms	adj
וּתְמִימִים	יִנְחֲלוּ־טוֹב	חָכָם	בְּעֵינָיו	אִישׁ	עָשִׁיר
ûthemîmîm	yinchălû-ṭôv	chākhām	be'ênâv	'îsh	'āshîr
but the blameless	they will inherit good	wise	in his eyes	a man	rich

12.

1859	1032.551	2811.121	904, 6192.141
cj, n ms	v Hiphil ptc ms	v Qal impf 3ms, ps 3ms	prep, v Qal inf con
וְדַל	מֵבִין	יַחְקְרֶנּוּ	בַּעֲלֹץ
wedhal	mēvîn	yachqŏrennû	ba'ălōts
but a poor man	giving discernment	he will search him out	when the rejoicing of

6926	7521	8930	904, 7251.141	7857	2769.421	119
n mp	adj	n fs	cj, prep, v Qal inf con	n mp	v Pual impf 3ms	n ms
צַדִּיקִים	רַבָּה	תִּפְאָרֶת	וּבְקוּם	רְשָׁעִים	יְחֻפַּשׂ	אָדָם
tsaddîqîm	rabbāh	thiph'āreth	ûveqûm	reshā'îm	yechuppas	'ādhām
the righteous	much	splendor	but when the rising up of	the wicked	they will hide	men

13.

3803.351	6840	3940	7014.521	3142.551
v Piel ptc ms	n mp, ps 3ms	neg part	v Hiphil impf 3ms	cj, v Hiphil ptc ms
מְכַסֶּה	פְּשָׁעָיו	לֹא	יַצְלִיחַ	וּמוֹדֶה
mekhasseh	peshā'âv	lō'	yatslîach	ûmôdheh
one who conceals	his transgressions	not	he will succeed	but one who confesses

9. He that turneth away his ear from hearing the law: ... If anyone refuses to listen to divine instruction, *Beck* ... Turn a deaf ear to thy teachers, *Knox* ... If a man is deaf to all admonition, *Moffatt* ... If one shuts his ears against moral instruction, *Anchor*.

even his prayer shall be abomination: ... even his prayer is disgusting, *BB* ... God will find your prayers too hateful to hear, *Good News* ... thy prayer shall be all sacrilege, *Knox* ... his very prayer is loathsome, *Moffatt* ... even his prayers are detestable, *NIV*.

10. Whoso causeth the righteous to go astray in an evil way: ... Anyone causing the upright to go wandering, *BB* ... If anyone leads good people astray, *Beck* ... If you trick an honest person into doing evil, *Good News* ... Whoever seduces the honest to evil ways, *JB* ... The man who leads upright men into a wrong path, *Anchor* ... He who tempts the upright into evil courses, *NEB*.

he shall fall himself into his own pit: ... will himself go down into the hole he has made, *BB* ... you will fall into your own trap, *Good*

News ... will be ruined by their own evil, *NCV*.

but the upright shall have good things in possession: ... But the perfect shall inherit good, *ASV* ... [While the innocent will become prosperous], *Anchor* ... The blameless are the heirs to happiness, *JB* ... The honest shall inherit a fortune, *NEB* ... The innocent will be well rewarded, *Good News*.

11. The rich man is wise in his own conceit: ... A rich man may pride himself on his wisdom, *Anchor* ...

264

The man of wealth seems to himself to be wise, *BB* ... Rich people always think they are wise, *Good News* ... Rich men are conceited, *LIVB* ... The rich is wise in self-esteem, *NRSV*.

but the poor that hath understanding: ... an intelligent poor person, *NRSV* ... a discerning poor man, *Anchor* ... but the poor man who has sense, *BB* ... possessed of intelligence, *Goodspeed*.

searcheth him out: ... will test him, *Goodspeed* ... can expose him, *Anchor* ... has a low opinion of

him, *BB* ... can see through him, *Beck.*

12. When righteous men do rejoice: ... When good men are in the ascendant, *Anchor* ... When the upright do well, *BB* ... When good men come to power, *Good News* ... When the upright triumph, *JB*.

there is great glory: ... everything is splendid, *Anchor* ... everybody celebrates, *Good News* ... there is great exultation, *JB* ... jubilation, *NAB* ... morale is high, *REB*.

but when the wicked rise: ... rise to power, *Anchor* ... when evil-doers are lifted up, *BB* ... are in the ascendant, *JB* ... gain preeminence, *NAB* ... come to the top, *NEB*.

a man is hidden: ... one keeps out of their way, *Anchor* ... men hide themselves, *ASV* ... people take cover, *JB* ... men do not let themselves be seen, *BB* ... men must be sought for, *MAST*.

13. He that covereth his sins: ... conceals his transgressions, *Anchor* ... keeps his sins secret, *BB*.

---

a season, they will eventually pass on to the righteous (cf. 13:22). Proverbs dealing with greed are scattered throughout this chapter.

28:9. Closely related to the first line of 28:4, this saying warns that those who deliberately reject the teachings of the Covenant will not be accepted (on the word tôrāh in Proverbs, see comments on 28:4). It is scarcely possible to do justice to the strength of "abomination" in English. Abominations are those who are under God's judgmental wrath (6:16–19); their attempts at worship, prayer and sacrifice, are rejected, since they do not offer them out of pure or repentant hearts (15:8, 9; 21:27).

This verse may demonstrate the underlying cause of such a divine response to the actions described as abominable (cheating, violence). Although God holds the wicked guilty (11:1; 20:23, and the verses cited above), their primary sin is that they despise and turn away from the Covenant (contrast 13:19). Although the word tôrāh refers primarily to the Covenant, this verse contrasts sharply with the prologue's ubiquitous call to attend closely to the teacher's tôrāh (e.g., 1:8; 3:1; 4:2; 6:20, 23; 7:2; 13:14). This verse describes the "or else proverb."

28:10. Although the verse contrasts trying to guide someone into a trap (cf. Deut. 27:18) with honesty, it focuses on the results of both ways of life. The former actually endangers the wicked himself (cf. 1:18f; 26:27), whereas the latter promises peace and security as the consequences of honesty (12:20ff). The principle of exact retribution (righteousness rewarded and sin punished) is the theme of the Job's "counselors," who urged him to confess the sin that, in their minds, underlay the recent dreadful events of his life.

28:11. The wealthy may be especially prone to think that their prosperity reflects their own abili-

ties. The parallelism implies that they lack insight. Insight, however, is not limited by social standing. It enables those who possess it to see through those around them. The primary contrast, however, is between false self-confidence and true discernment, not social or economic class.

This verse neither condemns wealth nor exalts poverty. None of the proverbs present poverty as a virtue. Poverty is preferable to illicit wealth (19:1) and, in this verse, to wealth, if possessing it would blunt insight and understanding.

28:12. Seen in light of its parallels (11:10; 28:28; 29:2), this verse also asserts the consequences of true justice. When the innocent, having been exonerated, rejoice, fame and splendor increase, because justice is a sign of wisdom and understanding (cf. Deut. 4:6). The opposite is true, however, when justice is perverted and the guilty are set free. Then, knowing their own peril (even if they are innocent), men and women stay out of sight, since to call attention to oneself is to invite trouble.

All of the verses on this topic must be seen within the general theme of justice (e.g., 25:4f; 29:12, 14), and the covenantal promises that a land is established by its righteousness (e.g., Deut. 16:19f; Isa. 2:3; 32:16ff), which are a reminder that the standards are eternal.

28:13. Honest confession often encourages a positive response, especially in contrast to the condemnation that results when self-protective lies and deceit are stripped away and the truth laid bare under protest of innocence despite the facts. Open confession is also better because deceit cannot be sustained indefinitely (10:9).

This verse addresses the person who "covers" his own sin in order to escape the consequences of

14.

869 n ms	119 n ms	6585.351 v Piel ptc ms	8878 adv
אַשְׁרֵי	אָדָם	מְפַחֵד	תָּמִיד
'ashrê	'ādhām	mephachēdh	tāmîdh
blessed	a man	one who fears	continually

6013.151 cj, v Qal act ptc ms	7638.421 v Pual impf 3ms
וְעֹזֵב	יְרֻחָם
we'ōzēv	yeruchām
and one who abandons	he will be shown mercy

15.

761, 5277.151 n ms, v Qal act ptc ms	1726 cj, n ms
אֲרִי־נֹהֵם	וְדֹב
'ărî-nōhēm	wedhōv
a roaring lion	and a bear

7481.551 cj, v Hiphil ptc ms	3949 n ms, ps 3ms	5489.121 v Qal impf 3ms	904, 7750 prep, n fs
וּמַקְשֶׁה	לִבּוֹ	יִפּוֹל	בְּרָעָה
ûmaqōsheh	libbô	yippôl	berā'āh
but one who makes hard	his heart	he will fall	into evil

16.

5233 n ms	2742 adj	8722 n fp
נָגִיד	חֲסַר	תְּבוּנוֹת
nāghîdh	chăsar	tevûnôth
a leader	lacking in	understanding

8630.151 v Qal act ptc ms	5090.151 v Qal act ptc ms	7857 adj	6142 prep	6194, 1859 n ms, adj
שֹׁקֵק	מֹשֵׁל	רָשָׁע	עַל	עַם־דָּל
shôqēq	mōshēl	rāshā'	'al	'am-dāl
onrushing	a ruler	wicked	over	a poor people

17.

119 n ms	3219 n mp	773.521 v Hiphil impf 3ms	1240 n ms	7983.152 v Qal act ptc mp	4805 n fp	7521 cj, adj
אָדָם	יָמִים	יַאֲרִיךְ	בֶּצַע	שֹׂנְאֵי	מַעֲשַׁקּוֹת	וְרַב
'ādhām	yāmîm	ya'ărîkh	vetsa'	sōne'ê	ma'ăshaqqôth	werav
a man	days	he will lengthen	unjust gain	those who hate	extortions	and great in

414, 8881.126, 904 adv, v Qal juss 3mp, prep, ps 3ms	5308.121 v Qal impf 3ms	5912, 908 prep, n ms	904, 1879, 5497 prep, n ms, n fs	6479.155 v Qal pass ptc ms
אַל־יִתְמְכוּ־בוֹ	יָנוּס	עַד־בּוֹר	בְּדַם־נָפֶשׁ	עָשֻׁק
'al-yithmekhû-vô	yānûs	'adh-bôr	bedham-nāphesh	'āshuq
may they not take hold on him	he will flee	unto a pit	with the blood of a life	being oppressed

18.

2050.151 v Qal act ptc ms	8879 adv	3588.221 v Niphal impf 3ms	6378.255 cj, v Niphal ptc ms	1932 n md	5489.121 v Qal impf 3ms
הוֹלֵךְ	תָּמִים	יִוָּשֵׁעַ	וְנֶעְקַשׁ	דְּרָכַיִם	יִפּוֹל
hôlēkh	tāmîm	yiwwāshēa'	wene'āqash	derākhayim	yippôl
one who walks	blamelessly	he will be saved	but one who perverts	ways	he will fall

19.

904, 259 prep, num	5856.151 v Qal act ptc ms	124 n fs, ps 3ms	7881.121, 4035 v Qal impf 3ms, n ms	7579.351 cj, v Piel ptc ms
בְּאַחַת	עֹבֵד	אַדְמָתוֹ	יִשְׂבַּע־לָחֶם	וּמְרַדֵּף
be'echāth	'ōvēdh	'adhmāthô	yisba'-lāchem	ûmeraddēph
on one	one who cultivates	his ground	he will have plenty of bread	but one who pursues

---

shall not prosper: ... will not do well, *BB* ... You will never succeed in life, *Good News*.

but whoso confesseth and forsaketh them: ... but one who is open about them, and gives them up, *BB* ... whoever confesses and renounces them, *JB*.

shall have mercy: ... if thou wouldst find pardon, *Knox* ... will find compassion, *NASB*.

14. Happy is the man that feareth always: ... who is scrupulous in conduct, *NEB* ... who is always on his guard, *NAB* ... who is always reverent, *Berkeley* ... You will be blessed if you always stand in awe, *Beck*.

but he that hardeneth his heart: ... but if you get stubborn, *Beck* ... reckless men, *Moffatt*.

shall fall into mischief: ... calamity, *Anchor* ... come into trouble, *BB* ... distress, *JB* ... come to grief, *Moffatt*.

15. As a roaring lion, and a ranging bear: ... growling lion or a prowling bear, *Anchor* ... loud-voiced lion and a wandering bear, *BB* ... ravening lion and hungry bear all at once, *Knox* ... a starving lion or a thirsty bear, *NEB*.

so is a wicked ruler over the poor people: ... wicked ruler of a powerless people, *JB* ... Nation without bread and prince without scruple, *Knox*.

16. The prince that wanteth understanding: ... who has no sense, *BB* ... void of intelligence, *Darby* ... destitute of understanding, *Geneva* ... The man who is stupid and grasping, *NEB* ... A tyrannical ruler, *NIV* ... A ruler without wisdom, *NCV*.

is also a great oppressor: ... a cruel ruler, *BB* ... is rich in rapacity, *JB* ... lacks judgment, *NIV*.

but he that hateth covetousness: ... he who hates unjust gain, *KJVII* ... ill-gotten gain, *NAB* ... one who hates greed, *JB* ... those who hate plunder, *Beck* ... he who has no desire to get profit for himself, *BB*.

shall prolong his days: ... will have long life, *BB*.

17. A man that doeth violence to the blood of any person: ... A man oppressed with the blood of a soul, *Young* ... A man that is laden with the blood of any person, *ASV* ... A man guilty of murder, *Beck* ... A homicide must hide, *Moffatt* ... Compass thou a man's death, *Knox*.

shall flee to the pit: ... will jump into a well to escape arrest, *NEB* ... Will come quickly to the grave, *Anchor* ... will go in flight to the underworld, *BB* ... Will be a fugitive until death, *NASB*.

let no man stay him: ... let no one support him, *NASB* ... let no man give him help, *BB* ... let them run until they die, *NCV* ... let no one shelter him, *Moffatt*.

18. Whoso walketh uprightly shall be saved: ... He who lives blamelessly will be delivered, *Anchor* ... Whoever walks wholeheartedly, *Berkeley* ... will be rescued from harm, *LIVB*.

but he that is perverse in his ways: ... the corrupt man, *Anchor* ... him whose ways are twisted, *BB* ... the perverse in his double-dealing, *Berkeley* ... whoever wavers between two ways, *JB* ... the man of crooked courses, *Moffatt*.

shall fall at once: ... will fall to destruction, *Anchor* ... will fall in a moment, *Berkeley* ... falls down in one of them, *JB*.

19. He that tilleth his land: ... By ploughing his land, *BB* ... If you work your ground, *Beck* ... A hard-working farmer, *Good News* ... The man who works his farm, *Moffatt*.

his act, rather than the person who refuses to discuss others' transgressions out of a desire for peace and harmony (cf. 10:12; 17:9).

28:14. The wise are cautious, knowing the deadfalls that await the unwary (cf. 2:18f; 9:18). Because they understand the importance of foresight, they seek counsel and weigh the outcomes of their choices, which enables them to choose wisely (cf. 14:16; 22:3; 27:12), whereas the arrogant, who refuse to listen to counsel or rebuke, come to disaster (cf. 16:18; 29:1).

28:15. Just as these predators (the largest known to ancient Israel) constantly seek prey, so a rapacious ruler terrorizes his subjects by hunting out everything of value (including them). When leaving his homeland due to famine or plague or fleeing the destruction of war, a wise sojourner considers the nature of a land's ruler and the state of its people before settling in it. The bear, the lion and the wicked ruler hunt because it is their nature.

28:16. The Hebrew text of the first line of this verse is difficult, as the English versions show: "A leader who is a great oppressor lacks understanding" (NASB); "A ruler who lacks understanding is a great oppressor" (NKJV); "A tyrannical ruler lacks judgment" (NIV). The contrast with the second line (which is clear) shows that a leader may be tempted to oppress his people for quick wealth. The wise ruler, however, understands that peace and security are more important and valuable in the long run, and avoids the temptation.

28:17. The first line, literally translated, describes one "oppressed by [the] blood of a life," pronouncing him a fugitive until death (if "pit" is a metaphor for death). The second line is also ambiguous, since the verb could mean either "to seize" or "to support." This proverb warns that the guilty must bear their guilt until judgment has been meted out and that no one is to help them escape punishment. Murder attacks the fabric of the covenant community, so that murder must be punished. This reiterates the Covenant's view of the severity of murder (Gen. 9:6; Exo. 21:12, 14; Lev. 24:17). Guilt ostracizes the guilty, leaving them without refuge or aid.

28:18. Like other proverbs that contrast integrity with an unscrupulous life (e.g., 10:9; 19:1; 28:6), this verse reveals the result of the choices that lead down these paths. The unethical (lit., "twisted [perverse] of two ways") is willing to do whatever is necessary to gain his own ends, even betraying those who trust him (cf. 28:6). When different parties realize that their trust has been abused, the traitor has no refuge. This is true in both this life and the judgment to come.

28:19. Work bears fruit, regardless of the goal. The wise person works his land and does not waste time or energy chasing empty or worthless goals. Working at what is most important (providing for himself and his family), the worker gained his bread by his labor. In Israel's economy, this was literally true. Most people ate what they themselves grew or gleaned (cf. Ruth 2–3). Foolish goals, however dili-

7673	7881.121, 7677		382	536	7521, 1318
n mp	v Qal impf 3ms, n ms	**20.**	n ms	n fp	adj, n fp
רֵקִים	יִשְׂבַּע־רִישׁ		אִישׁ	אֱמוּנוֹת	רַב־בְּרָכוֹת
rēqîm	yisba'-rîsh		'îsh	'emûnôth	rav-berākhôth
the vain	he will have plenty of poverty		a man of	reliability	great with blessings

211.151	3937, 6483.541	3940	5536.221	5421.542, 6686
cj, v Qal act ptc ms	prep, v Hiphil inf con	neg part	v Niphal impf 3ms	**21.** v Hiphil inf abs, n mp
וְאָץ	לְהַעֲשִׁיר	לֹא	יִנָּקֶה	הַכֵּר־פָּנִים
we'āts	leha'ashîr	lō'	yinnāqeh	hakkēr-pānîm
but one who hurries	to become rich	not	he will be innocent	recognizing faces

3940, 3005	6142, 6846, 4035	6839.121, 1429	963.255
neg part, adj	cj, prep, n fs, n ms	v Qal impf 3ms, n ms	**22.** v Niphal ptc ms
לֹא־טוֹב	וְעַל־פַּת־לֶחֶם	יִפְשַׁע־גָּבֶר	נִבְהָל
lō'-ṭôv	we'al-path-lechem	yiphsha'-gāver	nivhāl
not good	then because of a morsel of bread	a man will commit an offense	being dismayed

3937, 2019	382	7737	6084	3940, 3156.121	3706, 2743	971.121
prep, art, n ms	n ms	adj	n fs	cj, neg part, v Qal impf 3ms	cj, n ms	v Qal impf 3ms, ps 3ms
לַהוֹן	אִישׁ	רַע	עָיִן	וְלֹא־יֵדַע	כִּי־חֶסֶר	יְבֹאֶנּוּ
lahôn	'îsh	ra'	'āyin	welō'-yēdha'	kî-cheser	yevō'ennû
for the wealth	a man	evil of	eye	and he does not know	that lack	it will come to him

3306.551	119	313	2682	4834.121	4623, 2606.551
23. v Hiphil ptc ms	n ms	prep, ps 1cs	n ms	v Qal impf 3ms	prep, v Hiphil ptc ms
מוֹכִיחַ	אָדָם	אַחֲרַי	חֵן	יִמְצָא	מִמַּחֲלִיק
môkhîach	'ādhām	'acharay	chēn	yimtsā'	mimmachălîq
he who chastises	a man	after me	favor	he will find more	than one who flatters with

4098	1528.151	1	525	569.151
n ms	**24.** v Qal act ptc ms	n ms, ps 3ms	cj, n fs, ps 3ms	cj, v Qal act ptc ms
לָשׁוֹן	גּוֹזֵל	אָבִיו	וְאִמּוֹ	וְאֹמֵר
lāshôn	gôzēl	'āvîw	we'immô	we'ōmēr
the tongue	a robber	his father	or his mother	but saying

shall have plenty of bread: ... shall have bread and to spare, *JB* ... will have plenty to eat, *Anchor* ... will have bread in full measure, *BB* ... abundant food, *NIV*.

but he that followeth after vain persons: ... he that pursueth empty-heads, *Rotherham* ... goes after good-for-nothing persons, *BB* ... he who follows worthless pursuits, *Berkeley* ... he that followeth the idle, *Geneva* ... whoever chases fantasies, *JB*.

shall have poverty enough: ... you'll get plenty of nothing, *Beck* ... has no sense, *JB* ... a bellyful of nothing, *Knox* ... will have poverty in plenty, *NASB*.

20. A faithful man shall abound with blessings: ... A trustworthy man will be amply blessed, *Anchor* ... A trustworthy person will be overwhelmed with blessings, *JB* ... A man of steady character will enjoy many blessings, *NEB* ... man of fidelity aboundeth in blessings, *Rotherham*.

but he that maketh haste to be rich: ... one attempting to get wealth quickly, *BB* ... he who chases wealth, *Berkeley* ... if you are in a hurry to get rich, *Good News* ... how shall wealth reach thee suddenly, *Knox*.

shall not be innocent: ... shall not escape the penalty, *Berkeley* ... will not go free from punishment, *BB* ... will be held accountable, *Anchor* ... you are going to be punished, *Good News* ... is not acquitted, *Young*.

21. To have respect of persons is not good: ... To show partiality [in a judicial decision] is wrong, *Anchor* ... It's bad to show special favors to anyone, *Beck* ... Prejudice is wrong, *Good News* ... Great wrong it is to sell judgement, *Knox* ... It is not good for a judge to take sides, *NCV*.

for for a piece of bread: ... over a morsel of food, *Anchor* ... for a bite of food, *Beck* ... for a mouthful of bread, *JB* ... a mere crust of bread, *NEB*.

that man will transgress: ... A man may be at fault, *Anchor* ... a man will do wrong, *Beck* ... some will sin, *NCV*.

22. He that hasteth to be rich hath an evil eye: ... The avaricious man is perturbed about his wealth, *NAB* ...

A greedy person is in a hurry to get rich, *Beck* … The person of greedy eye chases after wealth, *JB* … The selfish man is eager to get rich, *Moffatt* … Eye on his rivals in the race for wealth, *Knox*.

and considereth not that poverty shall come upon him: … not realizing that want is about to overtake him, *Beck* … does not know that want will come upon him, *Berkeley* … not knowing that want will be the

result, *JB* … sees nothing, when want is hard at his heels, *Knox* … never dreams he may be in distress, *Moffatt*.

23. He that rebuketh a man afterwards: … He who says words of protest to a man will later, *BB* … In the end, people appreciate frankness, *LIVB* … In the long run, a man who will reprove, *Moffatt* … Those who correct others, *NCV*.

shall find more favour: … have more approval, *BB* … he'll be kindlier, *Beck* … will get more thanks, *Goodspeed* … will later be liked, *NCV*.

than he that flattereth with the tongue: … than one who says smooth words with his tongue, *BB* … more than those who give false praise, *NCV*.

24. Whoso robbeth his father or his mother: … He who defrauds, *Douay*.

---

gently worked at, lead only to poverty. The end is the same in both cases: both are satisfied or satiated with something. The wise worker's satisfaction is real, because he is fed with what he needs for life. The fool who pursues worthless things also gets his fill, but it is an empty filling. There is no satisfaction, since he does not work on what is vital. The wise person is prudent to distinguish what is most important, and works diligently toward that goal. The fool chases whatever is most attractive (laboring in the field is rarely attractive) and starves.

The first three-quarters of this proverb are identical to 12:11 (cf. 10:5; 20:4). This verse addresses the nature and value of one's goals. Those verses deal with the effects of laziness. Together they demonstrate the close connection between motivation, attitude and action.

28:20. Haste is rarely a virtue in Proverbs (the only positive reference to doing something quickly is Prov. 6:1–5), especially when it leads to sin, as this verse implies. Wealth is not sinful, nor is it wrong to work toward that goal. Someone in a hurry to get rich is likely to be willing to lie or prove unfaithful in some other way. Having misled others, he will not find it easy, and may find it impossible, to be forgiven for his sin. The faithful, however, are free from guilt and blessed for their faithfulness, whether or not that blessing includes wealth.

28:21. Injustice and bribery must have been perennial in ancient Israel, if the number of proverbs devoted to injustice is any indication (e.g., 17:23; 24:23). The size of the bribe is clearly a meiosis, underscoring the human tendency to sin. If such a small bribe "leads" a person astray, how desperate is the heart to do right? The warning is also for those who appoint judges. The person who is unfaithful in small things is not likely to resist when the gifts and stakes are higher.

28:22. The constant desire for "a little more" reveals a greedy heart. Wealth is a dangerous goal, however, since the desire may encourage compromising of principles of integrity, which could lead in turn to the loss of everything that was gained (cf. 20:21). The second line may also refer to the increasing poverty that comes by feeding avarice. At any rate, greed entails sin (Eph. 5:5), because it seeks to supply what can only be supplied by God, that is, security and meaning in life. In 22:9, the phrase "a good eye" describes the generous (cf. 23:6).

28:23. The rebuke that saves someone from the consequences of a foolish course of action (cf. 6:23; 15:10), although less pleasant to hear, is far more appreciated in the long run than the flattery that hastens him toward disaster (cf. 29:5). Solomon portrays flattery as lying with evil intent (cf. 26:28), but it can also be simply telling someone what they want to hear, without considering the consequences to them (or oneself).

This reproof is clearly a warning "in its season" (cf. 25:11), since a rebuke after the fact (i.e., "I told you so") is hardly appreciated. Underlying such a rebuke is a care that watches out for the other person's welfare (cf. Phil. 2:3f), thus fulfilling the commandment (Lev. 19:18, 34; Matt. 22:39f). The love that this reveals may only be recognized in the long run. Solomon's assurance is that it is always the better choice.

28:24. Some rebel against the Covenant by substituting their own interests as the standard. Their defiance in breaking two of the basic commandments, by stealing (Exo. 20:15) and not honoring their parents (Exo. 20:12), shows the depth of their rebellion. They blind themselves against recognizing their guilt, saying that there has been "no transgression." This attitude leads to increasingly anti-social behavior (cf.

25.

7622, 5497	8271.551	3937, 382	2000	2358	375, 6840
adj, n fs	v Hiphil ptc ms	prep, n ms	pers pron	n ms	sub, n ms
רְחַב־נֶפֶשׁ	מַשְׁחִית	לְאִישׁ	הוּא	חָבֵר	אֵין־פֶּשַׁע
rechav-nephesh	mashchîth	le'îsh	hû'	chāvēr	'ên-pāsha'
wide of soul	one who destroys	to a man	he	a companion	there is not a transgression

26.

1019.151	1941.421	6142, 3176	1019.151	4209	1667.321
v Qal act ptc ms	v Pual impf 3ms	prep, pn	cj, v Qal act ptc ms	n ms	v Piel impf 3ms
בּוֹטֵחַ	יְדֻשָּׁן	עַל־יְהוָה	וּבוֹטֵחַ	מָדוֹן	יְגָרֶה
bôtēach	yedhushshān	'al-yehwāh	ûvôtēach	mādhôn	yeghāreh
one who trusts	he will be fattened	on Yahweh	but one who trusts	strife	he will contend

4561.221	2000	904, 2551	2050.151	3809	2000	904, 3949
v Niphal impf 3ms	pers pron	prep, n fs	cj, v Qal act ptc ms	n ms	pers pron	prep, n ms, ps 3ms
יִמָּלֵט	הוּא	בְּחָכְמָה	וְהוֹלֵךְ	כְּסִיל	הוּא	בְּלִבּוֹ
yimmālēt	hû'	bechokhmāh	wehôlēkh	khesîl	hû'	belibbô
he will escape	he	in wisdom	but one who walks	a fool	he	in his heart

27.

5598.151	3937, 7851	375	4408	6180.551	6084	7521, 4134
v Qal act ptc ms	prep, art, n ms	sub	n ms	cj, v Hiphil ptc ms	n fd, ps 3ms	adj, n fp
נוֹתֵן	לָרָשׁ	אֵין	מַחְסוֹר	וּמַעְלִים	עֵינָיו	רַב־מְאֵרוֹת
nôthēn	lārāsh	'ên	machsôr	ûma'ālîm	'ênâv	rav-me'ērôth
one who gives	to the poor	there is not	lack	but he who hides	his eyes	many curses

28.

904, 7251.141	7857	5846.221	119	904, 6.141
prep, v Qal inf con	n mp	v Niphal impf 3ms	n ms	cj, prep, v Qal inf con, ps 3mp
בְּקוּם	רְשָׁעִים	יִסָּתֵר	אָדָם	וּבְאָבְדָם
bequm	reshā'îm	yissāthēr	'ādhām	ûve'āvedhām
when rising up	the wicked	they will hide	men	but when their perishing

29:1

7528.126	6926	382	8763	7481.551, 6439	6875
v Qal impf 3mp	n mp	n ms	n fp	v Hiphil ptc ms, n ms	adv
יִרְבּוּ	צַדִּיקִים	אִישׁ	תּוֹכָחוֹת	מַקְשֶׁה־עֹרֶף	פֶּתַע
yirbû	tsaddîqîm	'îsh	tôkhāchôth	maqōsheh-'ōreph	petha'
they will multiply	the righteous	a man with	reprimands	he will stiffen the neck	suddenly

2.

8132.221	375	4995	904, 7528.141	6926
v Niphal impf 3ms	cj, sub	n ms	prep, v Qal inf con	adj
יִשָּׁבֵר	וְאֵין	מַרְפֵּא	בִּרְבוֹת	צַדִּיקִים
yishshāvēr	we'ên	marpē'	birvôth	tsaddîqîm
it will be broken	and there is not	healing	when being abundant	the righteous

and saith, It is no transgression: ... And says he has done nothing wrong, *Anchor* ... and says, It is no sin, *BB*.

the same is the companion of a destroyer: ... is no better than wanton destruction, *NEB* ... is the same as a taker of life, *BB* ... might as well be an anarchist, *Beck* ... is partner to a thug, *NRSV* ... He is next door to a murderer, *Knox*.

25. He that is of a proud heart: ... An arrogant man, *NASB* ... A greedy man, *Anchor* ... The covetous, *JB* ... He who is ever desiring profit, *BB* ... He that is puffed up in soul, *Darby*.

stirreth up strife: ... stirs up contention, *Anchor* ... stirs up trouble, *Beck* ... exciteth contention, *Darby* ... stirs up enmity, *Knox* ... provokes disputes, *JB*.

but he that putteth his trust in the LORD: ... that relieth upon, *Darby* ... whoever trusts in Yahweh, *JB* ... who trusts in the Eternal, *Moffatt*.

shall be made fat: ... will prosper, *Anchor* ... will be enriched, *Berkeley* ... will flourish, *Goodspeed* ... thrives, *Moffatt* ... grows fat and prosperous, *NEB*.

26. He that trusteth in his own heart is a fool: ... He whose faith is in himself is foolish, *BB* ... If you trust your own mind, you're a fool, *Beck* ... Whoever trusts his own wit is a fool, *JB* ... the same is a dullard, *Rotherham*.

but whoso walketh wisely: ... if you live wisely, *Beck* ... anyone whose ways are wise, *JB* ... but he whose guide is wisdom, *REB*.

he shall be delivered: ... will be kept safe, *BB* ... you will survive, *Beck* ... is secure, *Moffatt* ... will come safely through, *REB*.

27. He that giveth unto the poor shall not lack: ... will never be in need, *BB* ... will ever go short, *JB*.

but he that hideth his eyes: ... But one who shuts his eyes [to their need], *Anchor* ... who gives no attention to them, *BB* ... turn away from their plea, *Knox* ... but he who turns a blind eye, *NEB*.

shall have many a curse: ... will be roundly cursed, *Anchor* ... blessing thou shalt have none, *Knox*.

28. When the wicked rise: ... When evil-doers are lifted up, *BB* ... When the wicked are in the ascendant, *JB* ... When knaves flourish, *Knox* ... When the wicked get control, *NCV* ... When the wicked gain pre-eminence, *Douay* ... When the wicked come to the top, *NEB*.

men hide themselves: ... one takes cover, *Anchor* ... all the world takes to hiding, *Knox* ... everybody hides, *NCV* ... others are pulled down, *NEB*.

but when they perish: ... when destruction overtakes them, *BB* ... come they by their end, *Knox* ... when they die, *NCV* ... at their fall, *Douay*.

the righteous increase: ... the upright are increased, *BB* ... the righteous flourish, *Beck* ... the upright multiply, *JB* ... thou shalt see honest folk abroad, *Knox* ... good people do well, *NCV*.

29:1. He that being often reproved: ... one who resents rebukes, *Anchor* ... One who is corrected, *Beck* ... Who spurns the yoke of correction, *Knox* ... after being often warned, *KJVII* ... in spite of many a warning, *Moffatt*.

hardeneth his neck: ... becomes stubborn, *Anchor* ... stiffens his neck, *Berkeley* ... refuses to accept criticism, *LIVB* ... is obstinate, *Moffatt*.

30:11–14) that will, however, be judged (cf. 30:17). This verse does not merely describe, but it warns against associating with or being such a person.

This proverb may even implicate the lazy, who are also related to the "destroyer" (18:9). Unwilling to provide for themselves, they need to steal to support themselves.

28:25. Greed reveals a lack of trust in the LORD, as the parallelism shows. Greedy people also cause strife (cf. 15:18; 29:22); they not only trouble the lives of those around them, but they themselves are doomed to frustration, since greed is never satisfied (cf. 27:20; 30:15f; Ecc. 1:8; 4:8; 5:10f). The concentration of proverbs dealing with acquisitiveness (28:6, 8, 16, 20, 22, 24, 27) is intentional and addresses one of the temptations of kings.

This contrasts with the blessing of trusting in the LORD, a constant refrain of Proverbs (e.g., 16:20). This proverb and the next were probably juxtaposed because of the contrasting objects of trust (vv. 25b, 26a; "he who trusts in" is identical), even though they make different points (cf. 28:1).

28:26. One mark of folly is that because fools assume that they are wise (12:15), they are not willing to seek or accept help (cf. the contrasting object of trust in v. 25). Their refusal to consider the consequences of their decisions often leads them into trouble (14:16; 22:3). Those who understand how little they actually know often escape potential problems by seeking counsel from others who are wise (cf. 20:5).

28:27. Refusing to recognize and address the needs of others disrupts the community. Although

this verse can be explained as describing a purely human response, it reveals that selfishness breaks the Covenant (cf. Deut. 15:7–11), bringing the covenantal curse of poverty (cf. Deut. 28:44) upon the arrogant, whereas God himself repays those willing to help (19:17).

28:28. Several verses in Proverbs address the relationship between the well-being of a land or city and its rulers, especially under the general topic of "justice." When the leaders are wicked, most people stay out of the way. Anonymity may be the best protection in an unjust society. When, however, those leaders fall out of power or die, those who promote justice are again able to rise to prominence (cf. 11:10; 28:12; 29:2).

29:1. A variation of "pride before a fall" (e.g., 12:1; 15:10, 32f; 16:18), this verse uses the image of a "hard neck" to describe Israel's rebellion at Sinai (cf. Exo. 32:9; 33:3, 5; 34:9; Deut. 9:6, 13; Neh. 9:16ff). In most of its post-Solomonic uses, however, this phrase refers to the behavior described here, turning the back, thus demonstrating stubborn refusal to listen (2 Ki. 17:14; 2 Ch. 36:13; Neh. 9:29; Jer. 7:26; 17:23; 19:15). The consequence of conceit is disaster, and the greater the arrogance the more devastating the defeat of its pretensions.

The proper response—to listen and respond obediently—is encouraged by Solomon when he points out that the LORD rebukes out of love (3:11f) and that reproof gives life (6:23).

29:2. Like other verses in Prov. 28–29, this addresses the question of justice (e.g., 28:4f, 12, 15f, 28; 29:4, 12, 14, 16, 26). When a ruler consis-

6194	598.221	7857	904, 5090.141	6194	7975.121
n ms	v Niphal impf 3ms	n ms	cj, prep, v Qal inf con	art, n ms	v Qal impf 3ms
עָם	יֵאָנַח	רָשָׁע	וּבִמְשֹׁל	הָעָם	יִשְׂמָח
'ām	yē'ānach	rāshā'	ûvimshōl	hā'ām	yismach
the people	they will sigh	the wicked	but when ruling	the people	they will be glad

3.

2193	7749.151	1	7975.321	2551	382, 154.151
n fp	cj, v Qal act ptc ms	n ms, ps 3ms	v Piel impf 3ms	n fs	n ms, v Qal act ptc ms
זוֹנוֹת	וְרֹעֶה	אָבִיו	יְשַׂמַּח	חָכְמָה	אִישׁ־אֹהֵב
zônôth	werō'eh	'āvîw	yesammach	chokhmāh	'ish-'ōhēv
prostitutes	but the companion of	his father	he will make glad	wisdom	a man loving

4.

8978	382	800	6198.521	904, 5122	4567	6.321, 2019
n fp	cj, n ms	n fs	v Hiphil impf 3ms	prep, n ms	n ms	v Piel impf 3ms, n ms
תְּרוּמוֹת	וְאִישׁ	אָרֶץ	יַעֲמִיד	בְּמִשְׁפָּט	מֶלֶךְ	יְאַבֶּד־הוֹן
terûmôth	we'îsh	'ārets	ya'ămîdh	bemishpāṭ	melekh	ye'abbedh-hôn
tributes	but a man of	a land	he will cause to stand	with justice	a king	he will destroy wealth

5.

6816.151	7862	6142, 7739	2606.551	1429	2117.121
v Qal act ptc ms	n fs	prep, n ms, ps 3ms	v Hiphil ptc ms	n ms	v Qal impf 3ms, ps 3fs
פֹּרֵשׂ	רֶשֶׁת	עַל־רֵעֵהוּ	מַחֲלִיק	גֶּבֶר	יַהְרְסֶנָּה
pôrēs	resheth	'al-rē'ēhû	machălîq	gever	yehersennāh
spreading	a net	concerning his fellow	flattering	a man	he will break it down

6.

6926	4305	7737	382	904, 6840	6142, 6718
cj, n ms	n ms	adj	n ms	prep, n ms	prep, n fp, ps 3ms
וְצַדִּיק	מוֹקֵשׁ	רָע	אִישׁ	בְּפֶשַׁע	עַל־פְּעָמָיו
wetsaddîq	môqēsh	rā'	'îsh	bephesha'	'al-pe'āmâv
but a righteous man	a snare	evil	a man	by a transgression	beside his steps

7.

1835	6926	3156.151	7975.111	7728.121
n ms	n ms	v Qal act ptc ms	cj, v Qal pf 3ms	v Qal impf 3ms
דִּין	צַדִּיק	יֹדֵעַ	וְשָׂמֵחַ	יָרוּן
dîn	tsaddîq	yōdhēa'	wesāmēach	yārûn
the vindication of	a righteous man	one who knows	and he will be glad	he will shout for joy

8.

6558.521	4087	596	1907	3940, 1032.121	7857	1859
v Hiphil impf 3ms	n ms	n mp	n fs	neg part, v Qal impf 3ms	n ms	n mp
יָפִיחוּ	לָצוֹן	אַנְשֵׁי	דָּעַת	לֹא־יָבִין	רָשָׁע	דַּלִּים
yāphîchû	lātsôn	'anshê	dā'ath	lō'-yāvîn	rāshā'	dallîm
they will fan	mocking	men of	knowledge	he does not understand	a wicked man	the poor

---

shall suddenly be destroyed: … will be crushed, *NAB* … will be ruined, *Beck* … will suddenly be done for, *Moffatt*.

and that without remedy: … will not be made well again, *BB* … there will be no cure, *Beck* … never have another chance, *LIVB* … beyond healing, *NRSV* … past mending, *NEB*.

2. When the righteous are in authority: … When just men are numerous, *Anchor* … When the upright have power, *BB*.

the people rejoice: … a people is happy, *Anchor* … people are glad, *BB* … the city is all rejoicing, *Knox*.

but when the wicked beareth rule: … when the wicked hold office, *NEB*.

the people mourn: … a people groans, *Anchor* … grief comes on the people, *BB* … all lament, *Knox*.

3. Whoso loveth wisdom: … when the son takes wisdom for his mistress, *Knox* … A child who loves wisdom, *NRSV*.

rejoiceth his father: … is a joy to his father, *BB* … Glad the father's heart, *Knox* … makes a parent glad, *NRSV*.

but he that keepeth company with harlots: … he who goes in the company of loose women, *BB* … one who keeps company with prostitutes, *Beck*.

spendeth his substance: … consumes his patrimony, *Anchor* … is a waster of wealth, *BB*.

4. The king by judgment establisheth the land: … by right rule, makes the land safe, *BB* ... by justice or exaction make the fortunes of a state, *Knox* ... make the country flourish by his justice, *Moffatt* ... makes his land secure, *Anchor* ... gives stability to the land, *NAB*.

but he that receiveth gifts: ... he who imposes heavy taxes, *NAB* ... a negligent one, *Anchor* ... one full of desires, *BB* ... by forced contributions, *NEB* ... an extortioner, *JB*.

overthroweth it: ... ruins it, *Anchor* ... makes it a waste, *BB* ... mar them, *Knox* ... tears his country down, *NCV*.

5. A man that flattereth his neighbour: ... The man who cajoles his companion, *Anchor* ... who says smooth things to his neighbour, *BB*

... By empty flattery, *Knox* ... Those who give false praise, *NCV* ... taking a portion above his neighbour, *Young*.

spreadeth a net for his feet: ... is stretching out a net for his steps, *BB* ... to trip him, *Moffatt* ... setting a trap for them, *NCV* ... you set a trap for yourself, *Good News* ... thou mayst lay a snare for thy friend's feet, *Knox*.

6. In the transgression of an evil man there is a snare: ... By his own false steps the sinner is entangled, *Knox* ... In an evil man's sin, *Goodspeed* ... trapped in their own sins, *Good News*.

but the righteous doth sing and rejoice: ... a righteous man sings

with joy, *Goodspeed* ... the just man runs on joyfully, *NAB* ... the good man runs away, happy to escape, *Anchor* ... good men can go forward happily, *Moffatt*.

7. The righteous considereth the cause of the poor: ... One who knows what is right pleads the case of the poor, *Anchor* ... The upright man gives attention to the cause of the poor, *BB* ... A person who knows what is right champions the cause of the weak, *Beck* ... The righteous listens to the plea of the poor, *KJVII*.

but the wicked regardeth not to know it: ... an evil man has no such knowledge, *Anchor* ... the evil-doer gives no thought to it, *BB* ... A wicked man knows no respect, *Goodspeed* ...

---

tently exonerates the innocent and condemns the guilty, the people, assured of justice, rejoice in their king's wisdom and rule. A ruler who oppresses his people causes them to groan for deliverance (cf. 11:10; 28:12, 28).

29:3. Harking back to the prologue's warnings against sexual immorality (2:16–19; 5:3–23; 6:20–35; 7:6–27), and using the language of the first "proper" proverb (10:1), this verse implies that it is no waste to lavish affection on a person's spouse. Such care, in fact, is a sign of wisdom, demonstrating that priorities are covenantal.

Self-indulgence, on the other hand, is never wise, since it consumes without replenishing. The lack of prudence that this displays, and the future trouble that such folly portends, would grieve any parent.

29:4. The just administration of the Law assures the populace that they will receive justice, so that the land is at peace (cf. 29:2). A corrupt judgeship, however, incites the people to reject or rebel against the government (cf. 1 Sam. 8:4f). Since Israel's king was ultimately responsible for the administration of justice throughout the land (Deut. 17:18ff; cf. Ps. 72:1–4; Isa. 11:3f; Jer. 22:3, 16), he had to protect his people from the perversion of justice caused by bribes (this is apparently a unique use of the word usually translated "wave offering").

29:5. Flattery, which is ascribed to malicious motives by Solomon (cf. 26:23–28), is a trap for anyone foolish enough to believe it. To praise others in order to manipulate them for any purpose is

to run the danger of destroying them. It also reveals the true problem with flattery: it sees people as objects to be manipulated for a goal. This could be the flatterer's intent (cf. 26:28), or it could come from persuading someone to try something which he cannot do.

The proverb is somewhat enigmatic, however, since the "steps" could belong to either person. Flatterers may find themselves trapped by their own words when their attempts to manipulate others are uncovered (cf. 10:9). Another deliberate ambiguity of this verse is the relationship between the lines. Either line could be the emblem.

29:6. The first line reads, literally, "In a wicked man's transgression is a snare," implying that the wicked are trapped by their own actions (cf. 1:18f; 26:27). Those who obey the Covenant live without fear (cf. 29:1), since obedience frees those who submit so that they can rejoice.

29:7. Honesty in court depends on impartiality, without regard for the standing (financial, social, etc.) of either party. Since human nature tends to favor those who are already favored (cf. Jam. 2:1ff), or who dress well and behave "properly," specific effort is normally required to overcome these natural prejudices. This, however, requires a prior decision to uphold justice, which comes from a heart that has determined to seek and fear the LORD (cf. 4:23).

29:8. The other six proverbial occurrences of the verb in the first line (HED #6558) mean "to breathe out" truth (12:17) or falsehood (6:19; 14:5,

188 adj	882, 382 prep, n ms	8570.255 v Niphal ptc ms	382, 2550 n ms, adj	**9.**	653 n ms	8178.526 v Hiphil impf 3mp	2550 cj, n mp	7439 n fs
אֱוִיל	אֶת־אִישׁ	נִשְׁפָּט	אִישׁ־חָכָם		אַף	יָשִׁיבוּ	וַחֲכָמִים	קִרְיָה
'ĕwîl	'eth-'îsh	nishpāt	'îsh-chākhām		'āph	yāshîvû	wachăkhāmîm	qiryāh
foolish	with a man	being judged	a wise man		anger	they will turn back	but the wise	a city

1879 n mp	596 n mp	**10.**	5369 n fs	375 cj, sub	7925.111 cj, v Qal pf 3ms	7553.111 cj, v Qal pf 3ms
דָּמִים	אַנְשֵׁי		נָחַת	וְאֵין	וְשָׂחַק	וְרָגַז
dhāmîm	'anshê		nāchath	we'ên	wesāchaq	werāghaz
bloodshed	men of		calmness	and there is not	and he will laugh	then he will tremble

3725, 7593 adj, n fs, ps 3ms	**11.**	5497 n fs, ps 3ms	1272.326 v Piel impf 3mp	3596 cj, n mp	7983.126, 8865 v Qal impf 3mp, n ms
כָּל־רוּחוֹ		נַפְשׁוֹ	יְבַקֵּשׁוּ	וִישָׁרִים	יִשְׂנְאוּ־תָם
kol-rûchô		naphshô	yevaqōshû	wîshārîm	yisne'û-thām
all his spirit		his life	they will seek	but the upright	they will hate the blameless

8099.321 v Piel impf 3ms, ps 3fs	904, 268 prep, adv	2550 cj, n ms	3809 n ms	3428.521 v Hiphil impf 3ms
יְשַׁבְּחֶנָּה	בְּאָחוֹר	וְחָכָם	כְּסִיל	יוֹצִיא
yeshabbechennāh	be'āchôr	wechākhām	khesîl	yôtsî'
he will consider it fortunate	when afterward	but a wise man	a fool	he will cause to go out

12.	5090.151 v Qal act ptc ms	7477.551 v Hiphil ptc ms	6142, 1745, 8632 prep, n ms, n ms
	מֹשֵׁל	מַקְשִׁיב	עַל־דְּבַר־שָׁקֶר
	mōshēl	maqōshîv	'al-devar-shāqer
	a ruler	one who pays attention	on account of a word of a lie

3725, 8664.352 adj, v Piel ptc mp, ps 3ms	7857 adj	**13.**	7851 n ms	382 cj, n ms	8830 n mp	6539.216 v Niphal pf 3cp
כָּל־מְשָׁרְתָיו	רְשָׁעִים		רָשׁ	וְאִישׁ	תְּכָכִים	נִפְגָּשׁוּ
kol-meshārethâv	reshā'îm		rāsh	we'îsh	tekhākhîm	niphgāshû
all those ministering to him	wicked		a poor man	and a man of	afflictions	they will meet

the wicked does not care to know it, *KJVII* ... the godless don't care, *LIVB*.

8. Scornful men bring a city into a snare: ... Insolent men put the city in an uproar, *Anchor* ... Men of pride are the cause of violent acts in a town, *BB* ... Scoffers put a city in an uproar, *Beck* ... Unprincipled men set the city in a blaze, *Goodspeed* ... Unscrupulous men kindle strife in a city, *Moffatt*.

but wise men turn away wrath: ... wise men assuage popular anger, *Anchor* ... the wise moderate anger, *JB* ... that madness, wisdom must turn aside, *Knox* ... the sensible discourage party-spirit, *Moffatt*.

9. If a wise man contendeth with a foolish man: ... When a wise man has a controversy with a foolish man, *NASB* ... When a wise man goes to law, *Anchor* ... takes a fool to court, *Moffatt* ... Let someone wise argue with a fool, *JB*.

whether he rage or laugh: ... anger and good humour alike will be wasted, *JB* ... Between bluster and mockery, *Knox* ... he will meet abuse or derision, *NEB* ... there is ranting and ridicule, *NRSV*.

there is no rest: ... there will be no peace, *Goodspeed* ... there is no end to it, *Knox* ... he gets no peace, *Moffatt* ... there is no settlement, *Rotherham*.

10. The bloodthirsty hate the upright: ... detest a blameless man, *Anchor* ... hate him that is perfect, *ASV* ... hate the man of integrity, *Berkeley* ... Men of blood are haters of the good man, *BB*.

but the just seek his soul: ... the upright are concerned for his welfare, *Anchor* ... good people seek to live like him, *Beck* ... seek the life of the upright, *Goodspeed* ... the just seek his well-being, *NKJV*.

11. A fool uttereth all his mind: ... All his anger doth a dullard let go, *Rotherham* ... A foolish man lets out all his wrath, *BB* ... A fool gives full vent to his anger, *Berkeley* ... A stupid man gives free rein to his anger, *NEB* ... Folly blurts out its whole mind, *Knox*.

but a wise man keepeth it in till afterwards: ... keeps his anger to himself, *Moffatt* ... restrains his anger, *Goodspeed* ... keeps himself under control, *NIV* ... wise men reserve utterance till by and by, *Knox* ... but by biding his time, the wise man calms it, *NAB*.

12. If a ruler hearken to lies: ... When a ruler pays attention to false reports, *Anchor* ... listens to false accusations, *Moffatt* ... King that listens to false rumour, *Knox* ... If a prince listens to falsehood, *NEB*.

all his servants are wicked: ... All his attendants become lawless, *Rotherham* ... all his officials will be wicked, *Berkeley* ... all his ministers will be scoundrels, *JB* ... will have wicked aides on his staff, *LIVB*.

13. The poor and the deceitful man meet together: ... The poor man and his oppressor have this in common, *Anchor* ... The poor man and his creditor come face to face, *BB* ... The indigent and the oppressor meet

together, *Darby* ... Poor men and ·their masters dwell side by side, *Knox* ... Rich and poor are alike in this, *LIVB*.

the LORD lighteneth both their eyes: ... The Lord permitted both to see the light of day, *Anchor* ... Yahweh gives light to the eyes of both, *JB* ... each depends on God for light, *LIVB* ... what happiness each has comes from the LORD, *NEB*.

25; 19:5, 9), which does not fit this context. The contrast with the peacemaking efforts of the wise, who know how to turn aside wrath (15:1), suggests that the first line describes those whose arrogance causes trouble for themselves and everyone around them (cf. 11:11).

29:9. Because fools are not interested in learning (18:2), they will not listen to reason. Contending with fools thus brings frustration. There will be "no rest," because they are incapable of resolving conflict. A wise person will recognize this and avoid conflict with fools if possible. On the other hand, if an opponent's folly becomes apparent after the case is in process, the wise, knowing that a peaceful resolution is impossible, will drop it (cf. 26:4f), even if this means suffering loss. Other verses also warn that it is usually best to avoid fools (e.g., 13:20; 14:7).

29:10. The differences between the translations reveals some of the difficulty of this verse. The first line echoes other proverbs (e.g., 29:27), but the second line seems contradictory, saying literally, "But the upright [plural] seek his life." Since the antecedent of "his" seems to be the "upright" (v. 10a), and since the idiom "seek the life of X" means to "seek X [in order to kill him]" (e.g., Exo. 4:19; 1 Sam. 23:15; 25:29; 2 Sam. 4:8), the verse thus seems to say that both the wicked and the upright seek to kill those who have integrity.

In order to make sense of this verse, various suggestions have been made, such as emending "upright" to "wicked" by shifting the letters and adding one (reading ûrshā'îm for wîshārîm, which are actually closer in Hebrew than they appear in transliteration), or by changing the verb from "to seek" to "to be concerned for," based loosely on Ezek. 34:11 (a change of one letter). Neither suggestion is supported by any ancient version or

Hebrew manuscript. Another possibility is that "his" refers not to the upright, but to the "men of blood" (words with different grammatical number are often parallel in Proverbs), so that the verse parallels 29:27. Proverbs 29:27 would then reveal their opinion of each other, whereas this verse shows that their animosity goes beyond merely thinking each other "abominable."

29:11. The fool, lacking self-restraint, holds nothing back (apparently in a quarrel; cf. 29:9), unlike the wise, who know the value of patience. The wise also, unlike the fool, understand the importance of words, so that when they speak, their words are careful and peaceful, having been well thought out, rather than poured out (cf. 15:28; 17:27f; 20:3).

29:12. A ruler may prefer lies to the truth, so they tell him what he wants to hear, or he may be a fool, and so lack the insight to distinguish truth from lies. (N.B.: A ruler who prefers lies is also a fool, but of a different sort.) Whatever the cause, the result will be an increasingly crooked government, as its members emulate their head. Corruption rarely works its way up from the bottom, but it often streams down from the top. A ruler who wants a stable administration must first realize that it comes about only through justice (29:14), and then rid his land of wickedness (20:8, 26; 25:4f). (Note the close connection of this verse and the next two, which address poverty and justice.)

29:13. When the poor and those who oppress them meet, as is inevitable in the normal course of life, both groups need to remember that they live by the grace of the same God (cf. Ps. 13:3). Those in positions to exercise their will over others must realize that their own lives are in the hands of God and therefore treat the poor with respect (cf. 14:31; 17:5). The poor must recognize that they, too, gain their lives from God.

14.

904, 583	8570.151	4567	3176	8530	213.551, 6084
prep, n fs	v Qal act ptc ms	n ms	pn	num, ps 3mp	v Hiphil ptc ms, n fd
בֶּאֱמֶת	שׁוֹפֵט	מֶלֶךְ	יְהוָה	שְׁנֵיהֶם	מֵאִיר־עֵינֵי
be'emeth	shôphēt	melekh	yehwāh	shenêhem	mē'îr-'ênê
in truth	administering justice	a king	Yahweh	the two of them	illuminating the eyes of

15.

5598.121	8673	8101	3679.221	3937, 5911	3802	1859
v Qal impf 3ms	cj, n fs	n ms	v Niphal impf 3ms	prep, n ms	n ms, ps 3ms	n mp
יִתֵּן	וְתוֹכַחַת	שֵׁבֶט	יִכּוֹן	לָעַד	כִּסְאוֹ	דַּלִּים
yittēn	wethôkhachath	shēveṭ	yikkôn	lā'adh	kis'ô	dallîm
it will give	and correction	a rod	it will be established	unto eternity	his throne	the poor

16.

904, 7528.141	525	991.551	8365.455	5470	2551
prep, v Qal inf con	n fs, ps 3ms	v Hiphil ptc ms	v Pual ptc ms	cj, n ms	n fs
בִּרְבוֹת	אִמּוֹ	מֵבִישׁ	מְשֻׁלָּח	וְנַעַר	חָכְמָה
birvôth	'immô	mēvîsh	meshullāch	wena'ar	chokhmāh
when being abundant	his mother	causing shame	having been sent out	but a child	wisdom

7495.126	904, 4816	6926	7528.121, 6840	7857
v Qal impf 3mp	prep, n fs, ps 3mp	cj, n mp	v Qal impf 3ms, n ms	n mp
יִרְאוּ	בְּמַפַּלְתָּם	וְצַדִּיקִים	יִרְבֶּה־פָּשַׁע	רְשָׁעִים
yir'û	bemappaltām	wetsaddîqîm	yirbeh-pāsha'	reshā'îm
they will see	when their falling	but the righteous	transgression will be abundant	the wicked

17.

4729	5598.121	5299.521	1158	3364.331
n mp	cj, v Qal impf 3ms	cj, v Hiphil impf 3ms, ps 2ms	n ms, ps 2ms	v Piel impv 2ms
מַעֲדַנִּים	וְיִתֵּן	וִינִיחֶךָ	בִּנְךָ	יַסֵּר
ma'ădhannîm	weyittēn	wînîchekhā	binkhā	yassēr
delicacies	and he will give	and he will cause you to rest	your son	discipline

18.

8490.151	6194	6797.221	2469	904, 375	3937, 5497
cj, v Qal act ptc ms	n ms	v Niphal impf 3ms	n ms	prep, sub	prep, n fs, ps 2ms
וְשֹׁמֵר	עָם	יִפָּרַע	חָזוֹן	בְּאֵין	לְנַפְשֶׁךָ
weshōmēr	'ām	yippāra'	chāzôn	be'ên	lenaphshekhā
but one who observes	a people	they will get out of control	a vision	without	to your soul

14. The king that faithfully judgeth the poor: ... The king who is a true judge in the cause of the poor, *BB* ... When a king honestly provides justice for the poor, *Beck* ... who judges the poor with equity, *Goodspeed* ... A king who steadfastly deals out justice to the weak, *NEB*.

his throne shall be established for ever: ... A king's throne will be established in perpetuity, *Anchor* ... will be safe for ever on the seat of his power, *BB* ... his government will continue forever, *NCV* ... His throne to futurity shall be established, *Rotherham*.

15. The rod and reproof give wisdom: ... Scolding and spanking a child, *LIVB* ... Punishment and rebuke, *Anchor* ... rod and sharp words, *BB* ... The stick and the reprimand, *JB*.

but a child left to himself: ... a boy who runs wild, *NEB* ... boy who gets his own way, *Anchor* ... a childe set at libertie, *Geneva* ... a neglected child, *NRSV* ... a youth unrestrained, *Rotherham*.

bringeth his mother to shame: ... a mother's care is wasted, *Knox*.

16. When the wicked are multiplied: ... are numerous, *Anchor* ... are in power, *BB* ... are on the increase, *JB* ... thrive, *NIV*.

transgression increaseth: ... crime is rampant, *Anchor* ... sin multiplies, *JB* ... sin is in power, *NEB*.

but the righteous shall see their fall: ... good men will see their collapse, *Anchor* ... upright will have pleasure when they see their downfall, *BB* ... good men will yet gloat over their downfall, *Moffatt*.

17. Correct thy son, and he shall give thee rest: ... Instruct your son, *Anchor* ... Chasten thy son, *Darby* ... Discipline your son and you can always be proud of him, *Good News* ... Correct your child, and he will give you peace of mind, *JB* ... A son well schooled is rest well earned, *Knox*.

yea, he shall give delight unto thy soul: ... pleasures to thy soule, *Geneva* ... great joy thou shalt have of him, *Knox* ... he will be a comfort to you, *NEB*.

18. Where there is no vision: ... Where there is no wisdom, *KJVII* ... no divine revelation, *Beck* ... Without prophecy, *NAB* ... Without inspired guidance, *Anchor* ... What revel among the host, the power of prophecy once withdrawn!, *Knox.*

the people perish: ... cast off restraint, *ASV* ... are uncontrolled, *BB* ... run wild, *Beck* ... decay, *Geneva* ... is a people made naked, *Young.*

but he that keepeth the law, happy is he: ... Hence a law-abiding peo-

ple is fortunate, *Anchor* ... but what a wonderful thing ... to know and keep his laws, *LIVB* ... a guardian of the law keeps them on the straight path, *NEB* ... But he that keepeth instruction, *Rotherham.*

Although this verse parallels Prov. 22:2, it is illegitimate to infer from these two verses that the wealthy are guilty oppressors and that the poor are always righteous. Poverty is not exalted in Proverbs (cf. the conditions in 17:1). God is the Giver of life and all things, including our station in life, which should condition attitude toward the circumstance, as well as toward the less (or more) fortunate. This should not encourage a passive acceptance of "fate," as though to work toward changing circumstance were a sinful rejection of what God has ordained. Gifts, talents, abilities and opportunities are likewise part of circumstance, and should be viewed and used as such. It is instead a warning to both groups to beware of arrogance and to realize that before God such differences which are significant to human beings are of little or no import.

29:14. Since the poor are powerless and cannot benefit their benefactors, a king who deals justly with them is truly concerned to establish justice in his land, dealing with the powerful and weak alike (cf. Deut. 1:17). Diametrically opposed to the behavior described in 29:12, this verse reflects the covenantal concern for justice for the weak and helpless, who are typified as the orphan, the widow and the sojourner (cf. Exo. 22:21f; Deut. 24:17f).

This king's throne will be established because he will be fulfilling his responsibility to reveal the justice of God by his apportionment of covenantal justice to the people (cf. Deut. 10:17; 16:19f; 17:18ff). The warning of the Covenant is also that failure to deal justly with these people will lead to the destruction throughout the land (Exo. 22:23f).

29:15. Wisdom comes through experience, but not through experience alone. It must be guided, which is the function of discipline. To allow a child to go his own way (lit., "sent away") may be easier than struggling with the trauma of discipline (23:13f), but the end of such negligence will be the parents' shame and sorrow. Parents who understand this, and who love their children, will discipline them, so that they grow up in wisdom, not as fools. (On the meaning of "rod," see 13:24; 22:15.)

29:16. As the wicked multiply, wickedness increases and even prevails. Since there are more who act wickedly, their prevalence in society encourages others, who might otherwise resist temptation, to imitate and join their sin. The verse, however, contrasts the temporary and apparent strength of the transgressors with the abiding and real endurance of truth by noting that when judgment comes, the wicked fall but the righteous remain (cf. Ps. 1:5f).

The word translated "fall" (NASB, NKJV) or "downfall" (NIV, NRSV) occurs most frequently in Ezekiel (six of eight occurrences), where it describes the act or result of God's judgment against a king or kingdom (HED #4567; 4577; Ezek. 26:15, 18; 27:27; 31:13, 16; 32:10), which may imply a similar force here. The theme of the rise and fall of the wicked (or righteous) occurs several times in the surrounding verses (e.g., 28:28; 29:2; cf. 10:25).

29:17. Well-raised children free their parents from turmoil, such as that described in 29:15 (lit., "give rest to"). Their behavior delights their parents as much as the most desirable delicacies. Unlike most other verses on parental discipline, which focus on how discipline benefits the child (but cf. 29:15), this verse focuses on its effects on the parents (it begins just like 19:18). Discipline thus has a twofold prospect—parental peace and delight in its fruits (cf. 10:1; 23:15f, 24f) and the well-being of the child. Although the verse does not specify this, it is clear that this benefit is both short-term and long-term, referring to a well-behaved and obedient child, as well as to a self-disciplined adult able to live wisely.

29:18. Divine revelation constrains its recipients. When it is, or seems to be, lacking, only those who understand the divine origin and authority of the Covenant will order their lives according to its standards. The proverb contrasts those who depend upon special acts of divine communication with the one who heeds the Covenant as already given, describing the response of the former and the consequences for the latter.

The usual pattern is that the apparent lack of revelation leads to license. For example, in Exo.

19.

8784	869		904, 1745	3940, 3364.221	5860	3706, 1032.121
n fs	n ms, ps 3ms	**19.**	prep, n mp	neg part, v Niphal impf 3ms	n ms	cj, v Qal impf 3ms
תּוֹרָה	אַשְׁרֵהוּ		בִּדְבָרִים	לֹא־יִוָּסֵר	עֶבֶד	כִּי־יָבִין
tôrāh	'ashrēhû		bidhvārîm	lō'-yiwwāṣēr	'āvedh	kî-yāvîn
the Law	his happiness		by words	he will not be disciplined	a slave	although he understands

20.

375	4776		2463.113	382	211.151	904, 1745
cj, sub	n ms	**20.**	v Qal pf 2ms	n ms	v Qal act ptc ms	prep, n mp, ps 3ms
וְאֵין	מַעֲנֶה		חָזִיתָ	אִישׁ	אָץ	בִּדְבָרָיו
we'ên	ma'āneh		chāzîthā	'îsh	'āts	bidhvārâv
yet there is not	an answer		you will behold	a man	one who hurries	with his words

21.

8951	3937, 3809	4623		6691.351	4623, 5471	5860	321
n fs	prep, n ms	prep, ps 3ms	**21.**	v Piel ptc ms	prep, n ms	n ms, ps 3ms	cj, n fs, ps 3ms
תִּקְוָה	לִכְסִיל	מִמֶּנּוּ		מְפַנֵּק	מִנֹּעַר	עַבְדּוֹ	וְאַחֲרִיתוֹ
tiqŏwāh	likhşîl	mimmennû		mephannēq	minnō'ar	'avdô	we'achărîthô
more hope	for a fool	than he		one who pampers	from youth	his servant	then its result

22.

2030.121	4641		382, 653	1667.321	4209	1196
v Qal impf 3ms	n ms	**22.**	n ms, n ms	v Piel impf 3ms	n ms	cj, n ms
יִהְיֶה	מָנוֹן		אִישׁ־אַף	יְגָרֶה	מָדוֹן	וּבַעַל
yihyeh	mānôn		'îsh-'aph	yeghāreh	mādhôn	ûva'al
he will be	an insolent person		a man of anger	he will contend	strife	and an owner of

23.

2635	7521, 6840		1375	119	8584.522
n fs	adj, n ms	**23.**	n fs	n ms	v Hiphil impf 3fs, ps 3ms
חֵמָה	רַב־פֶּשַׁע		גַּאֲוַת	אָדָם	תַּשְׁפִּילֶנּוּ
chēmāh	rav-pāsha'		ga'ăwath	'ādhām	tashpîlennû
wrath	much in transgression		the pride of	a man	it will bring him low

24.

8587, 7593		8881.121	3638		2606.151	6196, 1631
cj, adj, n fs		v Qal impf 3ms	n ms	**24.**	v Qal act ptc ms	prep, n ms
וּשְׁפַל־רוּחַ		יִתְמֹךְ	כָּבוֹד		חוֹלֵק	עִם־גַּנָּב
ûshephal-rûach		yithmōkh	kāvôdh		chôlēq	'im-gannāv
but the lowly in spirit		he will take hold of	honor		one who divides	with a thief

---

19. A servant will not be corrected by words: … You can't correct a slave with words, *Beck* … A servant will not be chastised with words, *Geneva* … Word was never yet that would check a slave, *Knox* … By words no servant can be trained, *Douay*.

for though he understand: … though the sense of the words is clear, *BB* … he listens only to defy it, *Knox* … For the words may not be heeded, *LIVB*.

he will not answer: … will not respond, *Anchor* … will not give attention, *BB* … will take no notice, *JB*.

20. Seest thou a man that is hasty in his words?: … Do you notice the man who speaks too soon?, *Anchor* … Have you seen a man who is quick with his tongue?, *BB* … Do you see someone who is quick to talk?, *Beck* … When you see someone over-eager to speak, *NEB*.

there is more hope of a fool than of him: … more hope for the stupid, *Anchor* … a dullard, *Rotherham*.

21. He that delicately bringeth up his servant from a child: … If a servant is gently cared for from his early years, *BB* … Pamper thy slave young, *Knox* … A spoiled boy sinks to be a slave, *Moffatt* … He who pampers his slave from childhood, *NASB* … At his latter end also he is his continuator, *Young*.

shall have him become his son at the length: … he will become a cause of sorrow in the end, *BB* …

Will in the end find him to be a son, *NASB* … Will in the end gain nothing but ingratitude, *Goodspeed* … he will expect you to treat him as a son!, *LIVB* … Shall have him become a master at the last, *MAST*.

22. An angry man stirreth up strife: … is the cause of fighting, *BB* … exciteth contention, *Darby* … A man of passion stirs up discord, *Goodspeed* … The hot-head provokes disputes, *JB* … Ever the quarreller breeds strife, *Knox*.

and a furious man: … bad-tempered, *Anchor* … given to wrath, *BB* … a hot-head, *Beck* … someone in a rage, *JB* … quick temper, *Knox*.

aboundeth in transgression: … causes much mischief, *Anchor* …

does much wrong, *BB* ... commits all sorts of sins, *JB* ... sins a lot, *NCV*.

23. A man's pride shall bring him low: ... will be the cause of his fall, *BB* ... Arrogance will bring your downfall, *Good News* ... Pride brings humiliation, *JB* ... The loftiness of a man layeth him low, *Rotherham*.

but honour shall uphold the humble in spirit: ... the modest will attain to honor, *Anchor* ... he who has a gentle spirit, *BB*.

24. Whoso is partner with a thief hateth his own soul: ... A thief's accomplice is his own enemy, *Anchor* ... As thou lovest thy life, aid thieves never, *Knox* ... a man who goes shares with a thief, *NEB*.

he heareth cursing: ... Execration he heareth, *Young* ... He heareth the adjuration, *ASV* ... he is put under oath, *BB* ... he knows the consequence, *LIVB* ... If they have to testify in court, *NCV*.

and betrayeth it not: ... says nothing, *BB* ... but won't give evidence, *Beck* ... but does it anyway, *LIVB* ... they are afraid to say anything, *NCV*.

32:25, the same verb describes the people's sinful activity around the golden calf. Eli and his sons, who were as priests supposed to teach the Covenant, responded to the relative lack of divine revelation in their time (1 Sam. 3:1f) by failing to live up to the light that they already had (the laws of sacrifices; Lev. 1–7), even when corrected by the people (1 Sam 2:16). In contrast, stand Samuel's continued faithfulness (1 Sam. 2:11, 18, 21, 26) and Josiah's immediate response to the scroll found in the Temple (2 Ki. 22:11ff).

Although references to revelation are rare in Proverbs (cf. 2:6), the theme of one's response to the "law" is also found in 28:4, 7.

29:19. Discipline was as necessary for servants as for children (13:24; 29:15, 17). Even when they understand what is meant, they rebel by refusing to respond by obedience, unless compelled by force. No one, in any situation, is free of the need for instruction and training in discipline.

29:20. Proverbs consistently portrays fools as those who cannot control their words. They answer questions before they hear them (18:13), and are far more interested in hearing their own opinion than learning from the counsel and wisdom of others (18:2). This proverb appears to hold out some hope for fools (cf. 26:12, which is nearly identical; cp. 27:22), but his inability even to appear wise by holding his tongue (17:27f) shows the depth of his folly. He is so satisfied with his own wisdom that he cannot hear the wisdom of others. Someone wise in his own eyes is a fool indeed (cf. 26:12).

29:21. The translations reflect the uncertain meaning of the last word in the verse, mānôn (HED #4641), which occurs only here in the Bible. NASB and NKJV, for example, relate it to a rare verb (only in Ps. 72:17) and noun ("offspring"; only in Gen. 21:23; Job 18:19; Isa. 14:22) and so interpret it as "son" (i.e., "heir"). NIV and NRSV, on the other hand, change one letter so that it reads "grief" or "sorrow" and then apply this to the slave's effect on his owner (NIV) or himself (NRSV, which follows the Vulgate).

Although the word translated "pampers" (HED #6691) also occurs only here, it has this meaning in post-biblical Hebrew. Whatever the precise meaning of the verse, it seems to warn against pampering a servant, for the sake of the master, as well as the slave.

29:22. A self-evident proverb (see the "Overview"), this verse warns that it is important to know others before becoming involved with them as friends, business associates or in some other relationship. People who are angered easily because they lack self-control are inevitably sources of trouble, for themselves (19:19) as well as for those who associate with them (22:24f). In common with many verses that describe the fool, this proverb warns that the rebellious rarely, if ever, change (e.g., 26:9; 27:22; 29:20). To expect that the impatient and easily provoked will suddenly become models of self-control is futile. (The first line is similar to 15:18a; that verse is antithetical, rather than synonymous.)

29:23. Unwillingness to consider the opinions, corrections or advice of others often leads to disaster (16:18). Humility, however, enables its possessor to seize and hold onto that which brings true honor (cf. 18:12). The main difference between this verse and the others on this theme is that here the humble actively grasp the honor that in other proverbs they receive (13:18; 15:33).

29:24. Whoever refuses to testify upon hearing a public summons is condemned as a covenant-breaker (Lev. 5:1). On the other hand, a witness who was party to a crime (this verse implies that the crime was receiving stolen goods) cannot testify without incriminating himself. The verse warns of the dilemma that criminal activity can bring and hints at the consequences, neither of which are good (cf. 1:10–19).

Verse 25

| 2832
n fs
חֶרְדַּת
cherdath
the terror of | **25.** | 5222.521
v Hiphil impf 3ms
יַגִּיד
yaggîdh
he will disclose | 3940
cj, neg part
וְלֹא
welō'
yet not | 8471.121
v Qal impf 3ms
יִשְׁמַע
yishma'
he will hear | 427
n fs
אָלָה
'ālāh
cursing | 5497
n fs, ps 3ms
נַפְשׁוֹ
naphshô
his life | 7983.151
v Qal act ptc ms
שׂוֹנֵא
sônê'
one who hates |

Verse 26

| 7521
adj
רַבִּים
rabbîm
many | **26.** | 7891.421
v Pual impf 3ms
יְשֻׂגָּב
yesuggāv
he will be inaccessible | 904, 3176
prep, pn
בַּיהוָה
bayhwāh
in Yahweh | 1019.151
cj, v Qal act ptc ms
וּבוֹטֵחַ
ûvôtēăch
but one who trusts | 4305
n ms
מוֹקֵשׁ
môqēsh
a snare | 5598.121
v Qal impf 3ms
יִתֵּן
yittēn
it will put | 119
n ms
אָדָם
'ādhām
a man |

| 5122, 382
n ms, n ms
מִשְׁפַּט־אִישׁ
mishpaṭ-'îsh
the judgment for a man | 4623, 3176
cj, prep, pn
וּמֵיהוָה
ûmēyehwāh
but from Yahweh | 6686, 5090.151
n mp, v Qal act ptc ms
פְּנֵי־מוֹשֵׁל
penê-môshēl
the presence of a ruler | 1272.352
v Piel ptc mp
מְבַקְשִׁים
mevaqŏshîm
seeking |

Verse 27

| **27.** | 8774
n fs
תּוֹעֵבַת
tô'ăvath
an abomination to | 6926
n mp
צַדִּיקִים
tsaddîqîm
the righteous | 382
n ms
אִישׁ
'îsh
a man of | 5982
n ms
עָוֶל
'āwel
perverseness | 8774
cj, *n fs*
וְתוֹעֵבַת
wethô'ăvath
but an abomination to | 7857
n ms
רָשָׁע
rāshā'
the wicked |

30:1

| 5177
n ms
נְאֻם
ne'um
a declaration of | 5016
art, pn
הַמַּשָּׂא
hammassā'
Massa | 1158, 3458
n ms, pn
בִּן־יָקֶה
bin-yāqeh
the son of Jakeh | 91
pn
אָגוּר
'āghûr
Agur | 1745
n mp
דִּבְרֵי
divrê
the words of | **30:1** | 3596, 1932
adj, n ms
יֶשַׁר־דָּרֶךְ
yeshar-dārekh
uprightness in way |

| 4623, 382
prep, *n ms*
מֵאִישׁ
mē'îsh
than a man | 609
pers pron
אָנֹכִי
'ānōkhî
I | 1221
adj
בַעַר
va'ar
more stupid | 3706
cj
כִּי
kî
because | **2.** | 407
cj, pn
וְאֻכָל
we'ukhāl
and Ucal | 3937, 391
prep, pn
לְאִיתִיאֵל
le'îthî'ēl
to Ithiel | 3937, 391
prep, pn
לְאִיתִיאֵל
le'îthî'ēl
to Ithiel | 1429
art, n ms
הַגֶּבֶר
haggever
the man |

| 2551
n fs
חָכְמָה
chokhmāh
wisdom | 3940, 4064.115
cj, neg part, v Qal pf 1cs
וְלֹא־לָמַדְתִּי
welō'-lāmadhtî
and I have not learned | **3.** | 3937
prep, ps 1cs
לִי
lî
to me | 119
n ms
אָדָם
'ādhām
a man | 3940, 1035
cj, neg part, *n fs*
וְלֹא־בִינַת
welō'-vînath
and not the understanding of |

---

25. The fear of man bringeth a snare: ... sets a trap [for him], *Anchor* ... To be afraid of human beings, *JB* ... Being afraid of people can get you into trouble, *NCV* ... A man's fears will prove a snare to him, *NEB*.

but whoso putteth his trust in the LORD shall be safe: ... From which the believer in the Lord is protected, *Anchor* ... whoever trusts in Yahweh is secure, *JB* ... he who trusts in the LORD will be exalted, *NASB* ... trust in the LORD is a tower of refuge, *REB*.

26. Many seek the ruler's favour: ... court the ruler's favor, *Goodspeed* ... curry favor, *NAB* ... seek audience of a prince, *NEB* ... approval of a ruler, *BB*.

but every man's judgment cometh from the LORD: ... [only] from the Lord may one expect justice, *Anchor* ... the decision in a man's cause comes from the Lord, *BB* ... in every case the LORD decides, *NEB* ... a man's fate is fixed by the Eternal, *Moffatt*.

27. An unjust man is an abomination to the just: ... A depraved man is abominable to the just, *Anchor* ... An evil man is disgusting to the upright, *BB* ... Abhorrent to the upright is the sinful, *JB* ... hate those who are dishonest, *NCV* ... The righteous cannot abide an unjust man, *NEB*.

and he that is upright in the way is abomination to the wicked: ... is disgusting to evil-doers, *BB* ... the villain loathes the upright, *Moffatt* ... nor the wicked a man whose conduct is upright, *NEB*.

30:1. The words of Agur the son of Jakeh, even the prophecy: the man

spake unto Ithiel, even unto Ithiel and Ucal: ... the oracle, *ASV.*

2. Surely I am more brutish than any man: ... I'm only an animal, *Beck* ... I am a dumb brute, *NEB* ... I am more foolish, *Geneva* ... I am too stupid to be a man, *Berkeley.*

and have not the understanding of a man: ... scarcely a man, *Beck* ... and have not even human intelligence, *NAB.*

3. I neither learned wisdom: ... I lack the knowledge of the holy ones, *JB* ... no power of reasoning like a

man, *BB* ... dull as a clod, with no quick brain, *Moffatt.*

nor have the knowledge of the holy: ... wisdom's dull pupil, without skill in holy lore?, *Knox* ... no master of thought, of the Deity I know nought, *Moffatt.*

29:25. Being overly concerned with (lit., "dread" of) what others may think or do can lead to foolish decisions, since expectations and demands may be inappropriate, unrealistic or even wicked. Trust in the LORD, however, lifts us above the influence of his opinions, since God's standards and approval are now the basis of decisions and actions (3:21–26; 14:26, 27; 18:10).

29:26. Although many verses in this chapter address the issue of governmental justice (e.g., vv. 4, 12, 14), this proverb warns that justice is ultimately not a human product. It exists only insofar as it is revealed by the LORD and enacted by those human beings who justly apply his decrees to the cases before them (cf. 29:12, 14). The further implication, however, is that only the LORD ensures justice and that to trust any human judge or system apart from his control is to be disappointed in the long run.

29:27. The wicked and honest build their lives upon mutually exclusive foundations, so that even if they are not personal enemies, their ways of life call attention to the differences between them at every turn and also implicitly condemn one another's choices. As long as both follow their convictions, the inherent contradiction between the motives underlying their decisions warns that they cannot work together for long (cf. 11:20).

30:1. This is the only biblical reference to Agur. The son of Jakeh the Massa'ite, Agur was probably a wise man from the Arabian region known as Massa'. This territory was on the border of the region controlled by Solomon when his empire was at its height. Solomon's wisdom attracted attention from across the ancient world (1 Ki. 4:29–34), and wise men (and the queen of Sheba) traveled to Jerusalem to test his reputed wisdom against their own (1 Ki. 10:1–10). Agur may have visited Solomon in person, or his sayings may have come into Solomon's hands by some other means. At any rate, Solomon approved them as fit for his Book (see "Overview").

This interpretation reflects a slightly different form of the word translated "oracle" (HED #5177; e.g., NASB, NIV) or "utterance" (NKJV) here and

in Prov. 31:1. This term is used most frequently by the prophets, especially Isaiah, to introduce a message: "The oracle concerning [or "against"] Babylon" (Isa. 13:1), or "Moab" (Isa. 15:1; cf. 17:1; 19:1; 21:1, 11, 13; Nah. 1:1; Hab. 1:1; Zech. 9:1; 12:1; Mal. 1:1). It is identical to another word meaning "burden" (cf. Num. 4:15, 19, 24, 27), which creates some debate about its precise significance in the prophetic texts. Since the term does not seem to have been used with this meaning until at least two centuries after Solomon's death, it is unlikely that these two chapters of Proverbs were considered "prophetic oracles." The ethnic or political interpretation is preferable, since it also reflects the political realities of Solomon's reign and explains how the wisdom of foreigners could be included in Solomon's work. This is only an argument for probability, however, as both interpretations are possible.

The first phrase of v. 1b occurs in only three other passages (Num. 24:4, 15; 2 Sam. 23:1). If this is an intentional allusion to Balaam, then the use of the word "stupid" (v. 2) is especially striking, because it has the same consonants as "Beor," the name of Balaam's father (cf. Num. 22–24). In 2 Sam. 23:1, the phrase introduces the last words of David, who is "the man."

The rest of the line is extremely difficult. It may be addressed to two of Agur's disciples, "to Ithiel, to Ithiel and Ucal" (so KJV, NASB, NIV). The name "Ithiel," which probably means "God [is] with me," occurs elsewhere only in a Benjamite genealogy (Neh. 11:7). Other proposals divide the consonants differently and change some of the vowels, resulting in such translations as, "I am weary, O God, I am weary, O God, but I will prevail" (so NRSV) or, if the verse is actually Aramaic (cf. Dan. 3:29), "There is no God, there is no God, nor can I [know anything]" (based on what follows in v. 2).

30:2–3. Agur confesses the depth of his ignorance. He is not claiming to be an animal, nor is he confessing stupidity. Instead, his statement resembles Job's response to the LORD's questions (Job 40:2f; 42:2–6). His wisdom, compared to the

4.

Strong's	Parsing	Hebrew	Translit.	English
6148.111, 8452	v Qal pf 3ms, n md	עָלָה־שָׁמַיִם	'ālāh-shāmayim	He has gone up to the heavens
4449	intrg	מִי	mî	Who
3156.125	v Qal impf 1cs	אֵדָע	'ēdhā'	I will know
7202	adj	קֹדֹשִׁים	qŏdhōshîm	the Holy One
1907	cj, n fs	וְדַעַת	wᵉdha'ath	nor knowledge of
4449	intrg	מִי	mî	Who
904, 2756	prep, n md, ps 3ms	בְּחָפְנָיו	bᵉchāphᵉnâv	in the hollow of his hands
636.111, 7593	v Qal pf 3ms, n fs	אָסַף־רוּחַ	'āsaph-rûach	He has gathered the wind
4449	intrg	מִי	mî	Who
3495.121	cj, v Qal impf 3ms	וַיֵּרַד	wayyēradh	and He has come down
3725, 675, 800	adj, n mp, n fs	כָּל־אַפְסֵי־אָרֶץ	kol-'aphsê-'ārets	all the ends of the earth
7251.511	v Hiphil pf 3ms	הֵקִים	hēqîm	He has raised up
4449	intrg	מִי	mî	Who
904, 7980	prep, art, n fs	בַּשִּׂמְלָה	bassimlāh	in the cloak
7173.111, 4448	v Qal pf 3ms, n md	צָרַר־מַיִם	tsārar-mayim	He has enclosed the waters

5.

Strong's	Parsing	Hebrew	Translit.	English
438	n ms	אֱלוֹהַּ	'ĕlôahh	God
3725, 577	adj, n fs	כָּל־אִמְרַת	kol-'imrath	every saying of
3156.123	v Qal impf 2ms	תֵּדַע	thēdhā'	you know
3706	cj	כִּי	kî	surely
4242, 8428, 1158	cj, intrg, n ms, n ms, ps 3ms	וּמַה־שֶּׁם־בְּנוֹ	ûmah-shem-bᵉnô	and what the name of his Son
4242, 8428	intrg, n ms, ps 3ms	מַה־שְּׁמוֹ	mah-shᵉmô	what his name

6.

Strong's	Parsing	Hebrew	Translit.	English
414, 3362.523	adv, v Hiphil juss 2ms	אַל־תּוֹסְףְ	'al-tôsp	do not add
904	prep, ps 3ms	בּוֹ	bô	in Him
3937, 2725.152	prep, art, v Qal act ptc mp	לַחֹסִים	lachōsîm	to those who seek refuge
2000	pers pron	הוּא	hû'	He
4182	n ms	מָגֵן	māghēn	a shield
7170.157	v Qal pass ptc fs	צְרוּפָה	tsᵉrûphāh	having been refined

7.

Strong's	Parsing	Hebrew	Translit.	English
8692	num	שְׁתַּיִם	shᵉttayim	two
3694.213	cj, v Niphal pf 2ms	וְנִכְזָבְתָּ	wᵉnikhzāvettā	then you will be declared a liar
904	prep, ps 2ms	בָּךְ	bᵉkhā	with you
6678, 3306.521	cj, v Hiphil impf 3ms	פֶּן־יוֹכִיחַ	pen-yôkhîach	so that He will not chastise
6142, 1745	prep, n mp, ps 3ms	עַל־דְּבָרָיו	'al-dᵉvārâv	onto his words

8.

Strong's	Parsing	Hebrew	Translit.	English
8175	n ms	שָׁוְא	shāwᵉ'	vanity
4322.125	v Qal impf 1cs	אָמוּת	'āmûth	I will die
904, 3071	prep, adv	בְּטֶרֶם	bᵉterem	before
4623	prep, ps 1cs	מִמֶּנִּי	mimmenî	from me
414, 4661.123	adv, v Qal juss 2ms	אַל־תִּמְנַע	'al-timna'	do not withhold
4623, 882	prep, prep, ps 2ms	מֵאִתָּךְ	mē'ittākh	from You
8068.115	v Qal pf 1cs	שָׁאַלְתִּי	shā'altî	I asked

---

4. Who hath ascended up into heaven, or descended?: ... Who has scaled the heavens and come down?, *Goodspeed* ... Who has mounted to the heavens, *JB* ... Who may he be that has scaled heaven, and come back to tell its secrets, *Knox*.

who hath gathered the wind in his fists?: ... Who has grabbed the wind in His hand, *Beck* ... Who has gathered the wind in the clasp of his hand?, *JB* ... who has cupped the wind in his hands?, *NAB*.

who hath bound the waters in a garment?: ... Who has wrapped up the waters in his garment?, *Berkeley* ... wrapped up water in a piece of cloth?, *Good News* ... wrapped away the storm-clouds under his mantle, *Knox* ... wraps up the oceans in his cloak?, *LIVB* ... prisoning the waters in his robe?, *BB*.

who hath established all the ends of the earth?: ... Who has set up the boundaries, *Beck* ... Who but God has created the world?, *LIVB* ... by whom have all the ends of the earth been fixed?, *BB* ... who has marked out all the ends of the earth?, *NAB*.

what is his name, and what is his son's name: ... What is his child's name?, *JB* ... where son of his may be found?, *Knox*.

if thou canst tell?: ... since you must know?, *Beck* ... Surely you know!, *Berkeley* ... if you are able to say?, *BB*.

5. Every word of God is pure: ... is tried, *ASV* ... is tested, *Goodspeed* ... is unalloyed, *JB* ... are like metal tested in the fire, *Knox* … is flawless, *NIV* … has proved to be true, *Beck*.

he is a shield unto them that put their trust in him: … that take refuge in him, *ASV* … he is the sure defence, *Knox* … He defends all who come to him for protection, *LIVB* … he is a breast-plate, *BB*.

6. Add thou not unto his words: … To his words make no addition, *JB*.

lest he reprove thee, and thou be found a liar: … he will reprimand, *Good News* … Lest he call you to account, *Goodspeed* … speedily thy practices shall come to light, *Knox* … he will make clear your error, *BB*.

7. Two things have I required of thee: … Two requests, *Knox* … two favors, *LIVB* … two boons, *Moffatt*.

deny me them not before I die: … do not grudge me them, *JB* … be they mine while life lasts, *Knox*.

8. Remove far from me vanity and lies: … falsehood and lying, *Berkeley* … treachery, *Knox* … deception, *NASB*.

give me neither poverty nor riches; feed me with food convenient for me: … food You prescribe for me, *NKJV* … my portion of nourishment, *Berkeley* … food that is needful, *ASV* … grant me only my share of food, *JB* … the livelihood I need, *Knox* … just enough to satisfy my needs!, *LIVB*.

---

knowledge which God possesses, is less than that of an animal compared with a human's. These statements anticipate his next point, God's sovereign control of creation (v. 4), which strengthens the parallel with Job's confession.

There are two possible interpretations of the second line of v. 3. It could parallel v. 3a, "I have not learned wisdom, nor do I have knowledge of holy things [or the Holy One]" (cf. NKJV), or contrast with it, "but I have knowledge of the Holy One [or holy things]" (cf. NASB). The next three verses support the second interpretation (cf. Pss. 73:22–23a; 92:5f).

This claim needs to be understood in light of the preceding line. He is going to address the issue of God's absolute dependability under the rubrics of sovereignty (v. 4) and revelation (vv. 5f). Agur confesses that even the understanding that he possesses is insignificant compared with all that there is to know about God and his creation, lest his questions or warnings be thought arrogant.

30:4. Rhetorical questions are asked to make a point by provoking a response in the reader. They are not meant to be answered. By these questions Agur argues that God's superiority is matchless (they allow no other answer) in order to lead into his warning about tampering with the words of God (vv. 5f). The first question reflects Moses' statement that the Covenant was not secreted in heaven, so that they did not need to ask, "Who will go up to heaven for us and get it for us and make it known to us, so that we may do it?" (Deut. 30:12). They were without excuse since they already had the Covenant "in their mouth and heart" (Deut. 30:14).

The questions in this verse reflect the creation poem of Prov. 8:22–31, which mentions the heaven, sea and earth. The picture of God "wrapping" the

sea also occurs in Job 26:8; 38:8–11, and parallels the creation story (Gen. 1:9; cf. Ps. 104:1–9). By reflecting the themes of creation and revelation found in Prov. 8:22–31, these questions create a "bookend" around the central proverbial collection.

30:5–6. Because God's words are all pure (the reference is to gold and silver refined of dross), He protects everyone who takes refuge by learning and understanding those words. They reveal Him, and thus the nature of the protection that He offers. On the other hand, whoever mixes his or her own words with God's demonstrates a lack of trust; that person has not truly taken refuge in the Word of God, but in his own (cf. 3:5f). (Verse 5 is nearly identical to Ps. 18:30a–b.)

A standard part of ancient Near Eastern covenants was a prohibition against changing the text of the treaty. Verse 6 echoes Deut. 4:2 and 12:31, as does Rev. 22:18. Agur addresses the problem by forbidding anyone to claim to speak for God, choosing to infer the opposite prohibition (against removing any of the text) by mentioning only half of the formula. He may also view the temptation to claim to speak for God as stronger, and as having more serious consequences, than the temptation to be silent (throughout Proverbs fools are described as those who would rather speak than be silent).

30:7–9. *Agur announces both the substance of his prayer (v. 8) and the reason for his request (v. 9). These verses display the same humility that he has displayed in vv. 2–6—an attitude of deep dependence upon God and a desire to honor Him.*

30:7–8. Among his requests, Agur asked the Lord to protect him from those who would mislead him (cf. 20:26), by removing them from his presence. In order to take refuge in God and his Word

1745, 3695	7651.531	4623	7677	6484	414, 5598.123, 3937
cj, n ms, n ms	v Hiphil impv 2ms	prep, ps 1cs	n ms	cj, n ms	adv, v Qal juss 2ms, prep, ps 1cs
וּדְבַר־כָּזָב	הַרְחֵק	מִמֶּנִּי	רֵאשׁ	וָעֹשֶׁר	אַל־תִּתֶּן־לִי
ûdhevar-kāzāv	harchēq	mimmenî	rē'sh	wā'ōsher	'al-titten-lî
and a word of a lie	cause to be far	from me	poverty	and riches	do not give to me

3072.531	4035	2805		6678	7881.125
v Hiphil impv 2ms, ps 1cs	n ms	n ms, ps 1cs	**9.**	cj	v Qal impf 1cs
הַטְרִיפֵנִי	לֶחֶם	חֻקִּי		פֶּן	אֶשְׂבַּע
haṭrîphēnî	lechem	chuqqî		pen	'esba'
feed me	food of	what is prescribed for me		otherwise	I will be satisfied

3703.315	569.115	4449	3176	6678, 3542.225
cj, v Piel pf 1cs	cj, v Qal pf 1cs	intrg	pn	cj, cj, v Niphal impf 1cs
וְכִחַשְׁתִּי	וְאָמַרְתִּי	מִי	יְהוָה	וּפֶן־אִוָּרֵשׁ
wekhichashtî	we'āmartî	mî	yehwāh	ûphen-'iwwārēsh
and I will disavow	and I will say	who	Yahweh	and so that I will not be dispossessed

1630.115	8945.115	8428	435		414, 4102.523	5860
cj, v Qal pf 1cs	cj, v Qal pf 1cs	n ms	n mp, ps 1cs	**10.**	adv, v Hiphil juss 2ms	n ms
וְגָנַבְתִּי	וְתָפַשְׂתִּי	שֵׁם	אֱלֹהַי		אַל־תַּלְשֵׁן	עֶבֶד
weghānavtî	wethāphastî	shēm	'ĕlōhay		'al-talshēn	'evedh
then I will steal	and I will take hold of	the name of	my God		do not slander	a servant

420, 112	6678, 7327.321	843.113		1810	1
prep, n ms, ps 3ms	cj, v Piel impf 3ms, ps 2ms	cj, v Qal pf 2ms	**11.**	n ms	n ms, ps 3ms
אֶל־אֲדֹנוֹ	פֶּן־יְקַלְלֶךָ	וְאָשָׁמְתָּ		דּוֹר	אָבִיו
'el-'ădhōnô	pen-yeqallelkhā	we'āshāmettā		dôr	'āwîw
to his master	so that he will not curse you	then you will be guilty		a generation	their father

7327.321	881, 525	3940	1313.321		1810	2999	904, 6084
v Piel impf 3ms	cj, do, n fs, ps 3ms	neg part	v Piel impf 3ms	**12.**	n ms	adj	prep, n fd, ps 3ms
יְקַלֵּל	וְאֶת־אִמּוֹ	לֹא	יְבָרֵךְ		דּוֹר	טָהוֹר	בְּעֵינָיו
yeqallēl	we'eth-'immô	lō'	yevārēkh		dôr	ṭāhôr	be'ênâw
they will curse	and their mother	not	they will bless		a generation	pure	in their eyes

4623, 6884	3940	7647.411		1810	4242, 7597.116
cj, prep, n fs, ps 3ms	neg part	v Pual pf 3ms	**13.**	n ms	intrg, v Qal pf 3cp
וּמִצֹּאָתוֹ	לֹא	רֻחָץ		דּוֹר	מָה־רָמוּ
ûmitstsō'āthô	lō'	ruchāts		dôr	māh-rāmû
and from their excrement	not	they have been washed		a generation	to what will they rise

9. Lest I be full: ... Or I may feel satisfied, *Beck* ... so shall not abundance tempt me, *Knox* ... if I grow rich, I may become content without God, *LIVB*.

and deny thee, and say: ... and disown thee, *Goodspeed* ... discrediting my God, *Moffatt* ... blacken the name of my God, *NEB* ... do violence to the Name of my God, *Rotherham*.

Who is the LORD?: ... who is Yahweh?, *JB* ... and doubt if Lord there be, *Knox*.

or lest I be poor, and steal: ... lest I be in want, *Goodspeed* ... or else, in destitution, *JB* ... if I am reduced to poverty I shall steal, *REB*.

and take the name of my God in vain: ... use profanely, *ASV* ... violate God's name, *Berkeley* ... dishonour my God's name with perjury, *Knox* ... insult God's holy name, *LIVB* ... besmirch the name of my God, *REB*.

10. Accuse not a servant unto his master: ... Slander not a servant, *ASV* ... Do not malign, *NKJV* ... Do not inform on a servant, *Anchor* ...

Do not blacken a slave's name, *JB* ... Never disparage a slave, *NEB*.

lest he curse thee: ... or he will speak ill of you, *NEB* ... Lest he revile thee, *Rotherham*.

and thou be found guilty: ... you incur guilt, *Anchor* ... you will have to pay for it, *Beck* ... since you are guilty, *Berkeley* ... and suffer for it, *Good News* ... you have to pay the penalty, *NAB*.

11. There is a generation that curseth their father: ... There is one kind of man, *Anchor* ... There is a class of people, *Goodspeed* ... A bad breed it is, *Knox*.

and doth not bless their mother: ... do not show their appreciation, *Good News* ... have no good word, *Knox* ... speak ill of their own mothers, *REB*.

12. There is a generation that are pure in their own eyes: ... who seem to themselves to be free from sin, *BB*.

and yet is not washed from their filthiness: ... all unpurged from its defilement, *Knox* ... with stains still on them!, *Moffatt* ... from its filth hath it not been bathed, *Rotherham*.

13. There is a generation, O how lofty are their eyes!: ... whose eyes are ever so proud, *Anchor*.

and their eyelids are lifted up: ... his glances haughty!, *Anchor* ... scornful brow, *Knox* ... supercilious

looks, *Moffatt* ... are raised in arrogance, *NASB*.

14. There is a generation, whose teeth are as swords: ... whose incisors are swords, *NAB*.

and their jaw teeth as knives: ... whose jaws are [like] butcher knives, *Anchor* ... whose fangs are knives, *Goodspeed* ... jaws that grind slowly on, *Knox* ... knives within their mouths, *Moffatt*.

(30:5), he must avoid liars. He is probably talking here specifically about those who claim to speak for God, whether as prophets or as interpreters of his word, since they are the ones most likely to attempt to "add to God's words" (30:6). His request reflects his status (for only a ruler would be in a position to hear their counsel and "prophecy") and his desire to rule with justice. This was Solomon's prayer (1 Ki. 3:9). Perversion of justice became one of the great failures of the post-Solomonic leaders of both Israel and Judah, according to the repeated testimony of the prophets.

He also asks God to provide neither more nor less than what he truly needs, but refers merely to his allotted food, rather than to a "dollar value" or list of possessions. If he has the food that he needs, then he will have enough of what he needs.

30:9. He concludes his prayer by explaining his second request (the first request refers to 30:5f). He fears both his tendency to self-sufficiency and the temptation to meet his own needs sinfully, which he could justify by establishing himself as the standard of right and wrong, a temptation that would only be exacerbated by wicked advisors (30:8a). Moses warned Israel that when they were settled in the land they would be tempted to forget that the LORD had provided their homes, vineyards and wells, etc., and imagine that they had gotten them for themselves (Deut 6:10–19; 8:1–20).

30:10. To injure people by accusing them falsely may cause them trouble (cf. 26:20ff), but anyone, including a slave, can slander someone else. In fact, slaves, because of their opportunities to be around their masters, may know things that would cause great trouble for them. This proverb is another application of the general principle that people sow what they reap, whether for good (cf. 21:21; 22:4) or ill (21:16; 22:8). Even if an accusa-

tion is not technically slanderous, everyone is responsible for his own actions, and should not be accusing others, especially those over whom they have no authority (cf. Rom. 14:4).

30:11–14. This poem describes the violent and arrogant who reject parental authority (v. 11), justify their wickedness (v. 12) and afflict those weaker than themselves for their own gain (v. 13f). It is yet another warning about companions, as it moves from "lesser" to "greater" evils. Someone's attitude toward his parents may seem relatively minor. These verses warn that those who begin by despising their parents end by becoming a wicked and violent law unto themselves. As Solomon says at the beginning of the Book, they not only stand condemned, but will be destroyed (Prov. 1:8–19), as will those who associate with them. This warning is made explicit three verses later (Prov. 30:17).

30:11. As with many proverbs, this verse can be tied directly to one of the Ten Commandments (Exo. 20:12). A person's relationship with his parents is not usually thought of as especially significant for the quality of his life. This verse, however, shows that our attitude toward our parents reveals a deeper attitude toward all authority, including the authority that judges our actions (cf. 2 Tim. 3:2–5).

30:12–13. Those who despise their parents have already justified their sinful actions. They have chosen or established a standard that does not condemn their actions, nor does it require them to seek forgiveness and grace. Any such standard always denies the law of God, since it springs from the human heart, which is "more deceitful than anything" (Jer 17:9). Such wicked self-righteousness (v. 12) displays the true arrogance of the person's heart. Both exalted eyes and raised eyelids are signs of arrogance (v. 13).

14.

6084	6310	5558.226	1810	2820	8514
n fd, ps 3ms	cj, n md, ps 3ms	v Niphal impf 3mp	n ms	n fp	n fp, ps 3ms
עֵינָיו	וְעַפְעַפָּיו	יִנָּשֵׂאוּ	דּוֹר	חֲרָבוֹת	שִׁנָּיו
'ênâv	we'aph'appâv	yinnāsē'û	dôr	chărāvôth	shinnâv
their eyes	and their eyelids	will they be lifted to	a generation	swords	their teeth

4121	5148	3937, 404.141	6270	4623, 800	33
cj, n fp	n fp, ps 3mp	prep, v Qal inf con	n mp	prep, n fs	cj, adj
וּמַאֲכָלוֹת	מְתַלְּעֹתָיו	לֶאֱכֹל	עֲנִיִּים	מֵאֶרֶץ	וְאֶבְיוֹנִים
ûma'ăkhālôth	methalle'ōthâv	le'ĕkhōl	'ănîyîm	mē'erets	we'evyônîm
and knives	their jaws	to devour	the afflicted	from the earth	and the needy

15.

4623, 119	3937, 6158	8692	1351	1957.131	1957.131	8421	2079
prep, n ms	prep, n fs	num	n fp	v Qal impv 2ms	v Qal impv 2ms	num	intrj
מֵאָדָם	לַעֲלוּקָה	שְׁתֵּי	בָנוֹת	הַב	הַב	שָׁלוֹשׁ	הֵנָּה
mē'ādhām	la'ălûqāh	shettê	vānôth	hav	hav	shālôsh	hēnnāh
from humankind	to a leech	two	daughters	give	give	three	behold

16.

3940	7881.127	727	3940, 569.116	2019	8061	6354
neg part	v Qal impf 3fp	num	neg part, v Qal pf 3cp	n ms	pn	cj, n ms
לֹא	תִשְׂבַּעְנָה	אַרְבַּע	לֹא־אָמְרוּ	הוֹן	שְׁאוֹל	וְעֹצֶר
lō'	thisba'ănāh	'arba'	lō'-'āmerû	hôn	she'ôl	we'ōtser
not	they can be satisfied	four	they do not say	wealth	Sheol	and barrenness of

17.

7641	800	3940, 7881.112	4448	813	3940, 569.112	2019	6084
n ms	n fs	neg part, v Qal pf 3fs	n md	cj, n fs	neg part, v Qal pf 3fs	n ms	n fs
רָחַם	אֶרֶץ	לֹא־שָׂבְעָה	מַיִם	וְאֵשׁ	לֹא־אָמְרָה	הוֹן	עַיִן
rācham	'erets	lō'-sāve'āh	mayim	we'ēsh	lō'-'āmerāh	hôn	'ayin
the womb	the earth	it is not satisfied with	water	and fire	it does not say	wealth	the eye

4074.122	3937, 1	972.122	3937, 3459, 525	5548.126
v Qal impf 3fs	prep, n ms	cj, v Qal impf 3fs	prep, n fs, n fs	v Qal impf 3mp, ps 3fs
תִּלְעַג	לְאָב	וְתָבוּז	לִיקֲּהַת־אֵם	יִקְּרוּהָ
til'agh	le'āv	wethāvûz	lîqqehath-'ēm	yiqqerûhā
it will deride	a father	and it will despise	about the obedience to a mother	they will gouge it out

to devour the poor from off the earth: ... till poor folk none are left, *Knox* ... to cut off weak folk, *Moffatt* ... they eat the wretched out of the country, *NEB*.

and the needy from among men: ... their friendless neighbours, *Knox* ... the helpless from the land, *Moffatt* ... the needy out of house and home, *NEB*.

15. The horseleach hath two daughters: ... A leech, *Anchor* ... The blood-sucker, *Beck* ... Two sisters there are, men say, brood of the leech, *Knox* ... The night-spirit, *BB* ... The vampire, *Rotherham*.

crying, Give, give: ... Give us morè, give us more!, *Knox*.

There are three things that are never satisfied, yea, four things say not, It is enough: ... But stay, there is a third Insatiable; nay, a fourth I can name that never says, Enough!, *Knox*.

16. The grave: ... Sheol, *Anchor* ... underworld, *BB* ... world of the dead, *Good News* ... nether world, *NAB* ... cemetery, *NCV* ... Hades, *Rotherham*.

and the barren womb: ... woman without a child, *BB* ... childless mother, *NCV* ... restrained womb, *Young*.

the earth that is not filled with water: ... the earth over-thirsty for water, *Berkeley* ... unsated with water, *Goodspeed* ... that is never saturated with water, *NAB* ... dry ground that needs rain, *Good News* ... a land short of water, *Anchor*.

and the fire that saith not, It is enough: ... a fire burning out of control, *Good News* ... And fire—it hath not said, 'Sufficiency', *Young*.

17. The eye that mocketh at his father: ... The eye which makes sport of a father, *BB* ... which looks jeeringly on a father, *JB* ... If you make fun of your father, *NCV*.

and despiseth to obey his mother: ... scorns his aged mother, *Anchor* ... sees no value in a mother when she is old, *BB* ... despiseth the instruction of his mother, *Geneva* ... a mother's pangs despised!, *Knox*.

the ravens of the valley shall pick it out: … His eye will be plucked out by the ravens of the canyon, *Anchor* … will be picked out by crows, *Beck* … plucked out by magpies, *NEB* … ravens shall pick the eyes out of his corpse, *Moffatt* …	the birds of the valley will peck out your eyes, *NCV*. **and the young eagles shall eat it:** … and eaten by vultures, *Beck* … or eaten by the vulture's young, *NEB*.	**18. There be three things which are too wonderful for me:** … Three things astonish me, *Anchor* … the wonder of which overcomes me, *BB* … beyond my comprehension, *JB* … make me marvel, *Moffatt*.

30:14. Kindness toward the helpless (the widow, orphan and stranger) is a constant theme of the Covenant (cf. Exo. 22:21–24; Lev. 19:33f; Deut. 1:16f; 27:19). Throughout Proverbs, Solomon repeatedly commends generosity and condemns the selfishness epitomized in the violence described in this verse (cf. 14:31; 19:17; 21:13; 22:9; 22:22f; 23:10ff; 28:27). In the same way, Agur warns that the arrogance which is displayed by disrespect for one's parents reveals an attitude of the heart that, unless checked, can lead to violence, even murder, in order to satisfy desires. This contrasts with the spirit of humility and contentment which he exemplifies in his prayer (30:8f).

30:15–16. This is the first of five numeric sayings that list "three, even four" things grouped around a common theme (30:15–31; cf. 6:16–19). The first three numeric sayings include women among other subjects ("barren womb" [v. 16], "a man with a maid" [v. 19d], "an unloved woman" and "a maidservant" [v. 23]). The last two end with ironic comments on the the nature of royalty (vv. 28, 31b).

This complex emblematic proverb consists of two parts, the emblem (v. 15a) and its explanation, which, in this case, is a list rather than a statement (vv. 15b–16; cf. 25:11–14). The leech's offspring are also leeches, and, like the leech herself, know only one task in life, that is, to gorge on blood. Like their mother, none of her children are ever satisfied. Everything has died, and everything continues to die. Thus death is not yet satiated. Do not think that you, or anyone else, will escape, and live accordingly. Sarai (Gen. 16:1–5), Rachel (Gen. 30:1f, 14ff), Hannah (1 Sam. 1:5–16) and others reveal the desperation that barrenness can cause, and how, in each case, it was satisfied only when a child was born. Even when floods fill the wadis and the Jordan overflows, the water subsides, and the more fire is fed, the larger it grows. To stop feeding it is to kill it, just as to stop watering the earth is to make it fruitless and unproductive.

The insight that enables Agur to see similarities between seemingly disparate animals and types of people is a striking sign of his wisdom. Agur's list of things that share this attribute is not as long as it could be (cf. 27:20; Ecc. 1:8; 4:8; 5:10ff), which may be one purpose of these types of sayings. By making a brief list, he encourages others to look for similarities in the human and non-human created orders, either to add to this list or to create their own. In this case, it is as futile to try to comfort a barren woman by gifts or personal reassurances (cf. 1 Sam. 1:8), as it would be to try to satisfy the grave's appetite for life or earth's for water or fire's for fuel. The wise person notes the similarities, and does not try.

30:17. This is the fate of those characterized in vv. 11–14. According to Deut. 21:18–21, the Covenant allowed parents to have a disobedient and truculent son executed by stoning, though there is no biblical evidence that this particular law was ever acted upon (its mere existence may have been sufficient deterrent). The next statute in Deuteronomy, however, specifies that the corpse of someone who has been executed must not be left out as carrion for wild beasts and birds, but buried (Deut. 21:22f), while the Covenant warned that the corpses of those killed by the judgments of natural disaster and military defeat would be left as "food for all the birds of the sky and the beasts of the earth, without anyone to frighten them away" (Deut. 28:26). The horror which this curse elicited in the ancient world is seen in Rizpah, Saul's concubine, who risked King David's wrath by protecting the corpses of her sons and Saul's other five grandsons from scavengers (2 Sam. 21:10). Goliath and David taunted each other with the same promise, since the enemy dead were normally stripped of plunder and left as they lay (1 Sam. 17:45ff).

Jezebel was a king's daughter (her father was Eth-Baal, priest-king of Tyre and Sidon; cf. 1 Ki. 16:31ff). Despite her wickedness and promotion of Baal, Jehu respected her rank enough to order his men to bury her, although they found only pieces (2 Ki. 9:34f). This passage explains that to be left unburied as food for wild beasts was to be treated as dung (2 Ki. 9:37). The prophets would also apply

6397, 5337	404.126	1158, 5585		8421	2065
n mp, n ms	cj, v Qal impf 3mp, ps 3fs	*n mp*, n ms		num	pers pron
עֹרְבֵי־נַחַל	וְיֹאכְלוּהָ	בְנֵי־נָשֶׁר	**18.**	שְׁלֹשָׁה	הֵמָּה
'ōrevê-nachal	weyō'khelûāh	venê-nāsher		shelōshāh	hēmmāh
the ravens of the wadi	and they will eat it	the young of the vulture		three	they

6623.216	4623	727	3940	3156.115		1932
v Niphal pf 3cp	prep, ps 1cp	cj, num	neg part	v Qal pf 1cs, ps 3mp		*n ms*
נִפְלְאוּ	מִמֶּנִּוּ	וְאַרְבָּע	לֹא	יְדַעְתִּים	**19.**	דֶּרֶךְ
niphle'û	mimmeniû	we'arbā'	lō'	yedha'ăttîm		derekh
they are more extraordinary	than we	even four	not	I know them		the way of

5585	904, 8452	1932	5357	6142	6962	1932, 605
art, n ms	prep, art, n md	*n ms*	n ms	prep	n ms	*n ms*, n fs
הַנֶּשֶׁר	בַּשָּׁמַיִם	דֶּרֶךְ	נָחָשׁ	עֲלֵי	צוּר	דֶּרֶךְ־אֳנִיָּה
hannesher	bashshāmayim	derekh	nāchāsh	'ălê	tsûr	derekh-'ănîyāh
the eagle	in the heavens	the way of	a serpent	on	a rock	the way of a ship

904, 3949, 3328	1932	1429	904, 6183		3772	1932	828
prep, *n ms*, n ms	cj, *n ms*	n ms	prep, n fs		adv	*n ms*	n fs
בְלֶב־יָם	וְדֶרֶךְ	גֶּבֶר	בְּעַלְמָה	**20.**	כֵּן	דֶּרֶךְ	אִשָּׁה
velev-yām	wedherekh	gever	be'almāh		kēn	derekh	'ishshāh
in the heart of the sea	and the way of	a man	with a young woman		so	the way of	a woman

5178.353	404.112	4364.112	6552	569.112	3940, 6713.115
v Piel ptc fs	v Qal pf 3fs	cj, v Qal pf 3fs	n ms, ps 3fs	cj, v Qal pf 3fs	neg part, v Qal pf 1cs
מְנָאָפֶת	אָכְלָה	וּמָחֲתָה	פִּיהָ	וְאָמְרָה	לֹא־פָעַלְתִּי
menā'āpheth	'ākhelāh	ûmāchăthāh	phîāh	we'āmerāh	lō'-phā'altî
an adultress	she will eat	then she will wipe off	her mouth	then she will say	I have not committed

201		8809	8421	7553.112	800	8809	727	3940, 3310.122
n ms		prep	num	v Qal pf 3fs	n fs	cj, prep	num	neg part, v Qal impf 3fs
אָוֶן	**21.**	תַּחַת	שָׁלוֹשׁ	רָגְזָה	אֶרֶץ	וְתַחַת	אַרְבַּע	לֹא־תוּכַל
'āwen		tachath	shālôsh	rāghezāh	'erets	wethachath	'arba'	lō'-thûkhal
iniquity		under	three	it will tremble	the earth	yes under	four	it will not be able

5558.141		8809, 5860	3706	4566.121	5210	3706
v Qal inf con		prep, n ms	cj	v Qal impf 3ms	cj, n ms	cj
שְׂאֵת	**22.**	תַּחַת־עֶבֶד	כִּי	יִמְלוֹךְ	וְנָבָל	כִּי
se'ēth		tachath-'evedh	kî	yimlôkh	wenāvāl	kî
to bear		under a slave	when	he becomes a king	and a fool	when

yea, four which I know not: … There are four I cannot fathom, *Anchor* … four things outside my knowledge, *BB* … four which I do not comprehend, *Berkeley* … I do not understand, *JB*.

19. The way of an eagle in the air: … How an eagle makes his way through the sky, *Beck* … a vulture in the air, *Goodspeed*.

the way of a serpent upon a rock: … viper that crawls on rock, *Knox* … on a crag, *Goodspeed*.

the way of a ship in the midst of the sea; and the way of a man with a maid: … how a man wins his way with a girl, *Anchor* … how a man makes his way with a virgin, *Beck* … a man and a woman falling in love, *Good News* … a man that goes courting maid, *Knox* … The growth of love between a man and a girl, *LIVB* … the way of a man in youth, *Young*.

20. Such is the way of an adulterous woman: … a false wife, *BB* … an unfaithful wife, *Good News* … wanton wife, *Knox* … a prostitute, *LIVB* … a woman committing adultery, *Rotherham*.

she eateth, and wipeth her mouth: … she commits adultery, takes a bath, *Good News* … licks her greedy lips, *Knox* … she gratifies her appetite, *Moffatt*.

and saith, I have done no wickedness: … I have not committed iniquity, *Geneva* … I haven't done anything wrong!, *Good News* … will have it that she did no harm, *Knox* … What's wrong with that?, *LIVB* … calmly says, "No harm!", *Moffatt*.

21. For three things the earth is disquieted: … the earth shudders, *Anchor* … trembles, *Beck* … is mooved, *Geneva* … quakes, *Goodspeed* … is perturbed, *NKJV* … a land is stirred, *Rotherham*.

and for four which it cannot bear: … it cannot tolerate, *Anchor* …

which it will not put up with, *BB* … and can't bear up under, *Beck* … cannot susteine it selfe, *Geneva* … it cannot endure, *JB*.

22. For a servant when he reigneth: … A slave who has become a king, *Anchor*.

and a fool when he is filled with meat: … An obstinate fool when he is filled with food, *Anchor* … a man without sense when his wealth is increased, *BB* … a brute gorged with food, *JB* … A rebel who prospers, *LIVB* … a fool when he is glutted with food, *NAB* … a churl gorging himself, *NEB*.

---

this curse to the nations (cf. Isa. 18:6; 56:9; Ezek. 39:1–4, 17–20), as does John (Rev. 19:17–21).

If "the first commandment with promise" (Eph. 6:1ff) is violated, the judgment is a despicable death, unmitigated by burial or posthumous respect.

30:18–19. Although numerical sayings draw disparate objects or circumstances together by revealing their underlying unity, that common thread may well be the wise man's own response, as here. Agur professes himself baffled by four things. The first three encompass the realms of air, land and sea, and of the created order and human achievement. The first two, the eagle's flight and the serpent's movement, are virtually inexplicable without a fairly sophisticated understanding of Bernoulli's principle or the musculoskeletal system. Understanding displacement would also help him understand how something as heavy as a ship could float. But the common thread between these three is that their elements (air, rock, sea) are trackless. How can they find their way?

By the same token, how can a man find his way with a woman? Although the exact reference may be to seduction or to falling in love, the point is the mystery of the process. It is also, as are so many of these numerical sayings, a mildly ironic warning against trying to figure it out. The inquisitor may as well try to track the roads of the sky or sea or rock.

30:20. Closely tied to the preceding saying (by the repetition of "way") and the following (by the implication of the last line of v. 23), this verse warns that illicit sexual activity leads people to redefine morality in order to justify, or to excuse in this case, their actions. The word "this," with which the verse begins, may refer to the entire range of her activity (cf. 6:26 for another image relating food to illicit sexual activity). She may commit adultery as freely as she eats, or she may consider adultery no more blameworthy than feeding herself. In either case, the focus of the verse is on her denial with which the verse ends. Those blinded by sin cannot admit their guilt; they literally cannot see anything of

which they need to repent. To entertain romantic hope of change is to deny such a person's very nature, because, until sin's blinders are removed, they will continue to sin without guilt or compunction. This verse is thus related to all those that warn against choosing friends or companions (or a spouse) without first considering their character (cf. 11:22; 13:20; 22:24f).

30:21–23. The frequent use of the verb translated "trembles" (NASB, NIV) or "is perturbed" (NKJV) in contexts of judgment or war (e.g., Exo. 15:14; Deut. 2:25; 1 Sam. 14:15) frequently in the prophets (e.g., Isa. 5:25; 14:9; 28:21; 32:10, 11; Joel 2:1, 10) or in response to troubling news (Gen. 45:24; 2 Sam. 19:1) shows that this trembling arises out of deep distress, usually terror that results from upsetting the moral order. These verses should not be used to support slavery (v. 22a), starvation (v. 22b) or spinsterhood (v. 23a). They are concerned to uphold the established moral order, whether political or familial (cf. 19:10, which closely parallels v. 22).

Since kingship was hereditary, servants (or "slaves") usually became king by coup or assassination. After the kingdom's division, this would be true in Israel's own history (cf. Omri [1 Ki. 16:9ff, 18] and Jehu [2 Ki. 9:24, 33]), in contrast with David's patience (e.g., 1 Sam. 24:6; 26:9ff), although he, too, had been anointed by a prophet of the LORD.

If, as seems likely, the word nāvāl (HED #5210) means "outlaw" (cf. Job 30:1–8), then in this context, the point is that honor and its accompanying luxury are inappropriate for lawbreakers (cf. 19:10a). To "be satisfied with bread" is the reward of diligence in Proverbs (20:13; 28:19; cf. 12:11; 31:27). Diligence is rarely ascribed to such persons, who are foragers and scavengers (cf. Job 30:3–7). Their appropriate reward is that the bread they think will satisfy them turns to gravel (cf. 20:17).

An "unloved" (lit., "hated") wife was not married for her own sake, but for whatever she could bring to the marriage, either her dowry, the ability to

23.

7881.121, 4035	8809	7983.157	3706	1195.222
v Qal impf 3ms, n ms	prep	v Qal pass ptc fs	cj	v Niphal impf 3fs
יִשְׂבַּע־לָחֶם	תַּחַת	שְׂנוּאָה	כִּי	תִּבָּעֵל
yisba'-lāchem	tachath	senû'āh	kî	thibbā'ēl
he will have plenty of bread	under	a hated woman	when	she will get married

24.

8569	3706, 3542.122	1435	727	2062	7278, 800
cj, n fs	cj, v Qal impf 3fs	n fs, ps 3fs	num	pers pron	adj, n fs
וְשִׁפְחָה	כִּי־תִירַשׁ	גְּבִרְתָּהּ	אַרְבָּעָה	הֵם	קְטַנֵּי־אָרֶץ
weshiphchāh	kî-thîrash	gevirtāhh	'arbā'āh	hēm	qŏtannê-'ārets
and a female slave	when she dispossesses	her mistress	four	they	small on the earth

25.

2065	2550	2549.456	5431	6194	3940, 6006
cj, pers pron	adj	v Pual ptc mp	art, n fp	n ms	neg part, adj
וְהֵמָּה	חֲכָמִים	מְחֻכָּמִים	הַנְּמָלִים	עַם	לֹא־עָז
wehēmmāh	chăkhāmîm	mechukkāmîm	hannemālîm	'am	lō'-'āz
but they	wise	being made very wise	the ants	a people	not strong

26.

3679.526	904, 7302	4035	8596	6194	3940, 6335	7947.126
cj, v Hiphil impf 3mp	prep, art, n ms	n ms, ps 3mp	n mp	n ms	neg part, adj	cj, v Qal impf 3mp
וַיָּכִינוּ	בַקַּיִץ	לַחְמָם	שְׁפַנִים	עַם	לֹא־עָצוּם	וַיָּשִׂימוּ
wayyākhînû	vaqqayits	lachmām	shephanîm	'am	lō'-'ātsûm	wayyāsîmû
but they prepare	in the summer	their food	coneys	a people	not mighty	but they put

27.

904, 5748	1041	4567	375	3937, 722	3428.121	2788.151
prep, art, n ms	n ms, ps 3mp	n ms	sub	prep, art, n ms	cj, v Qal impf 3ms	v Qal act ptc ms
בַסֶּלַע	בֵּיתָם	מֶלֶךְ	אֵין	לָאַרְבֶּה	וַיֵּצֵא	חֹצֵץ
vassela'	bêthām	melekh	'ên	lā'arbeh	wayyētsē'	chōtsēts
in the rocks	their house	a king	there is not	to the locust	but they go out	dividing

28.

3725	7982	904, 3135	8945.323	2026	904, 2033	4567
adj, ps 3ms	n fs	prep, n fd	v Piel impf 2ms	cj, pers pron	prep, n mp	n ms
כֻּלּוֹ	שְׂמָמִית	בְּיָדַיִם	תְּתַפֵּשׂ	וְהִיא	בְּהֵיכְלֵי	מֶלֶךְ
kullô	semāmîth	beyādhayim	tethappēs	wehî'	behêkhelê	melekh
all of them	a gecko	in the hands	you can grasp	yet it	in the palaces of	kings

29.

8421	2065	3296.552	7082	727	3296.552	2050.141
num	pers pron	v Hiphil ptc mp	n ms	cj, num	v Hiphil ptc mp	v Qal inf con
שְׁלֹשָׁה	הֵמָּה	מֵטִיבֵי	צָעַד	וְאַרְבָּעָה	מֵטִיבֵי	לָכֶת
shelōshāh	hēmmāh	mêtîvê	tsā'adh	we'arbā'āh	mêtîvê	lākheth
three	they	causing to go well	a march	yes four	causing to go well	proceeding

23. For an odious woman when she is married: ... a plain girl who at last gets married, *Moffatt* ... an unloved woman who is married, *NIV* ... a shunned woman getting married, *Beck* ... a hateful woman wed at last, *JB* ... under a bypast woman when she gets a husband, *Berkeley*.

and an handmaid that is heir to her mistress: ... a servant-girl who takes the place of her master's wife, *BB* ... who succeeds her mistress, *Berkeley* ... when she supplants her mistress, *Goodspeed* ... who marries her mistress' husband, *LIVB*.

24. There be four things which are little upon the earth: ... Four are little ones, *Young*.

but they are exceeding wise: ... but extremely shrewd, *Moffatt*.

25. The ants are a people not strong: ... ants are a frail species, *Anchor* ... pismires a people not strong, *Geneva* ... How puny a race the ants, *Knox*.

yet they prepare their meat in the summer: ... put by a store of food, *BB* ... that hoard their food in harvest time, *Knox*.

26. The conies are but a feeble folk: ... Marmots are a feeble species, *Anchor* ... rock-badgers aren't a mighty species, *Douay* ... rabbits are but a feeble folk, *Berkeley* ... how defenceless the rock-rabbits, *Knox* ... Cliff badgers: delicate little animals, *LIVB*.

yet make they their houses in the rocks: ... hide their burrows in the clefts!, *Knox* ... they can burrow in the rocks, *Moffatt* ... they can live among the rocks, *NCV* ... they place in a rock their house, *Young*.

27. The locusts have no king: … grashopper, *Geneva*.

yet go they forth all of them by bands: … they take the field in battalions, *Anchor* … they move in formation, *Good News* … they migrate all in array. *NAB* … they all sally forth in detachments, *NEB* … they all advance in ranks, *NKJV*.

28. The spider taketh hold with her hands: … The spider skillfully grasps with its hands, *NKJV* … The lizard—she holds on by her forefeet, *Goodspeed* … the lizard—you may lift it in your hand, *Moffatt* … you can catch them with your hands, *NAB*.

and is in kings' palaces: … [makes its way] into royal palaces, *Anchor* … yet they frequent the palaces of kings, *JB* … it will push into a palace, *Moffatt*.

29. There be three things which go well: … which stride proudly, *Anchor* … whose steps are good to see, *BB* … that are stately in their tread, *Berkeley* … that are impressive to watch, *Good News* … that walk majestically, *Knox*.

yea, four are comely in going: … carry themselves with dignity, *Anchor* … stately in gait, *Goodspeed* … stately tread, *Moffatt* … stately in their march, *MRB* … stately in their carriage, *NAB*.

---

bear children or the necessity to clear the way for a more desirable sister (if Laban's excuse is genuine; Gen. 29:26). She might also be a barren first wife, whose status would be reduced by a fertile rival. "Hated" is probably a relative term that describes the less-favored wife (cf. Gen. 29:31, 33, where the same term occurs). Deuteronomy 21:15ff, a law of inheritance that contrasts "hated" and "beloved" wives and their sons, illustrates the potential for abuse in such a relationship. This line does not specify who hates her. It may be her husband because she was barren, or because he wanted her for some further reason only. It might also be a rival, especially in the case of infertility (cf. Gen. 16:1–4; 1 Sam. 1:6f). Marriage is so significant that love, respect and affection must lie at its heart (even in a culture where marriages may have been arranged). When they do not, the moral order is undermined.

Like the slave (v. 22), a female servant or slave could become a wife only by supplanting her mistress, whether by innocently alienating her master's affections because of his inability to control his own desires or by deliberately inciting his lusts (cf. v. 20). Whether the fault is his or hers the verse does not specify, but the result disrupts the marriage, which is meant to be unbroken from within or without.

This verse thus underlines the essential biblical teaching that loving monogamy is God's standard for marriage (cf. Gen. 2:23ff; Eph. 5:25–31), despite the lapses of the patriarchs and leaders of Israel. Marriage is to be protected as integral to the moral order.

30:24–28. According to the "introduction" (v. 24), the four things that he is about to name are not prepossessing, but they have impressed him by their great wisdom. Ants are so small that they can carry only tiny crumbs. They are, however, ceaselessly active, diligent and self-disciplined to pursue the right activity in its time. Because they gather food when it is available, they are prepared for those times when it is not (cf. 6:6–11).

Cliffs (stone outcroppings) formed the ultimate refuge (cf. Jer. 49:16; Obad. 3). Rock badgers, about the size of a wild rabbit, are not powerful enough to build fortresses or city walls, but they live securely. These two examples are rather innocuous, preparing the reader to accept the third and fourth members of the group, and their application.

Verses 27f focus on the king. Unfortunately, this is obscured in translation. In the Hebrew text, v. 27a uses an unusual syntactical construction so that the word "king" begins the verse; v. 28 ends with the same word. The inverted structure of v. 27a thus deliberately focuses both verses on the king, who is the point of the entire saying. Naming the king first also leads the reader to expect that the king is the grammatical subject of the verse (which he is not), as were the animals named in the previous verses. This expectation contradicts the theme announced in v. 24—how could a king be considered insignificant? The verse is cleverly written to compel attention (and admiration).

Locusts have no king (cf. 6:7), but are self-disciplined without one (cf. v. 25). They are able to form into companies and ranks as they go out to "war" (cf. Joel 2:5–9). By contrast, a king constantly struggles to maintain order and control over those under him, and, especially in time of war, order in the ranks may be his greatest challenge. What the king cannot do, locusts do by nature. In the same way, lizards ("spider," KJV), which can be caught by hand, live in the most desirable dwelling in the land—the king's palace. They have no power or wealth to commend them, but they live where even the powerful and wealthy may not.

30.

| 4055
n ms
לַיִשׁ
layish
a lion | 1399
n ms
גִּבּוֹר
gibbôr
a warrior | 904, 966
prep, art, n fs
בַּבְּהֵמָה
babbehēmāh
among the beasts | 3940, 8178.121
cj, neg part, v Qal impf 3ms
וְלֹא־יָשׁוּב
welō'-yāshûv
and it does not go back | 4623, 6686, 3725
prep, n mp, n ms
מִפְּנֵי־כֹל
mippenê-khōl
from before anything |

31.

| 2310
n ms
זַרְזִיר
zarzîr
a strutting bird | 5158
n md
מָתְנַיִם
māthenayim
the hips | 173, 8825
cj, n ms
אוֹ־תָיִשׁ
'ô-thāyish
or a he-goat | 4567
cj, n ms
וּמֶלֶךְ
ûmelekh
and a king | 518
n ms
אַלְקוּם
'alqûm
an uprising | 6196
prep, ps 3ms
עִמּוֹ
'immô
with him |

32.

| 524, 5209.113
cj, v Qal pf 2ms
אִם־נָבַלְתָּ
'im-nāvaltā
if you have acted foolishly | 904, 5558.741
prep, v Hithpael inf con
בְהִתְנַשֵּׂא
vehithnassē'
by lifting yourself up | 524, 2246.113
cj, cj, v Qal pf 2ms
וְאִם־זַמּוֹתָ
we'im-zammôthā
or if you have plotted | 3135
n fs
יָד
yādh
a hand | 3937, 6552
prep, n ms
לְפֶה
lepheh
to the mouth |

33.

| 3706
cj
כִּי
kî
because | 4468
n ms
מִיץ
mîts
pressing of | 2560
n ms
חָלָב
chālāv
milk | 3428.521
v Hiphil impf 3ms
יוֹצִיא
yôtsî'
it will cause to come out | 2628
n fs
חֶמְאָה
chem'āh
curds | 4468, 652
cj, n ms, n ms
וּמִיץ־אַף
ûmîts-'aph
and pressing of a nose |

| 3428.521
v Hiphil impf 3ms
יוֹצִיא
yôtsî'
it will cause to come out | 1879
n ms
דָם
dhām
blood | 4468
cj, n ms
וּמִיץ
ûmîts
and pressing of | 653
n md
אַפַּיִם
'appayim
nostrils | 3428.521
v Hiphil impf 3ms
יוֹצִיא
yôtsî'
it will cause to come out | 7663
n ms
רִיב
rîv
contention |

31:1

| 1745
n mp
דִּבְרֵי
divrê
the words of | 4068
pn
לְמוּאֵל
lemû'ēl
Lemuel | 4567
n ms
מֶלֶךְ
melekh
the king of | 5016
pn
מַשָּׂא
massā'
Massa | 866, 3364.312
rel part, v Piel pf 3fs, ps 3ms
אֲשֶׁר־יִסְּרַתּוּ
'āsher-yisserattû
which she instructed him in | 525
n fs, ps 3ms
אִמּוֹ
'immô
his mother |

30. A lion which is strongest among beasts: ... the mightiest among animals, *Beck*.

and turneth not away for any: ... yielding to none, *Anchor* ... turning back from no one, *Beck* ... turneth not at the sight of any, *Geneva* ... that fears no encounter, *Knox* ... runs from nothing, *NCV* ... which will not turn tail for anyone, *NEB*.

31. A greyhound; an he goat also: ... strutting cock; the old ram, *Anchor* ... The war-horse, *BB* ... a vigorous cock, *JB* ... the cock (Loins-girt they call him), and the ram, *Knox* ... A girt one of the loins, *Young*.

and a king, against whom there is no rising up: ... the king whom no man dare resist, *Anchor* ... at the head of his army, *Beck* ... against whom none can rise up, *Darby* ... when he harangues his people, *JB* ... a king whose troops are with him, *NKJV*.

32. If thou hast done foolishly in lifting up thyself: ... If you have been such a fool as to give yourself airs, *Anchor* ... If you have played the fool in exalting yourself, *Berkeley* ... If you are churlish and arrogant, *NEB*.

or if thou hast thought evil: ... If you have schemed, *Anchor* ... devised evil, *Berkeley* ... hatched a scheme, *Goodspeed* ... plotting evil, *LIVB* ... You urge in your conceit some silly plan?, *Moffatt* ... If you have foolishly been proud or presumptuous, *NAB* ... and fond of filthy talk, *NEB*.

lay thine hand upon thy mouth: ... lay your hand on your lips, *JB* ... he had been better advised to hold his tongue, *Knox* ... shut your mouth, *NCV* ... clap your hand over your mouth!, *NIV*.

33. Surely the churning of milk bringeth forth butter: ... As the pressing of milk yields curds, *Anchor* ... Just as stirring milk makes butter, *NCV*.

and the wringing of the nose bringeth forth blood: ... the pressing of the nostrils leads to strife], *Anchor* ... and squeezing a nose produces blood, *Beck* ... twisting the nose produces blood, *NIV* ... a blow to the nose, *LIVB* ... blow thy nose lustily, and blood shall flow at last, *Knox*.

Kings may not be as powerful or, perhaps, as wise as they often claim. Even if they are, the animal kingdom reveals that some of their claims (to provide food and protection, to maintain order and to occupy a higher plane) are rather empty boasts. This may seem surprising in light of the generally high view of kingship throughout the Book of Proverbs, but it is probably an ironic warning to kings (and others in authority) not to take themselves too seriously.

30:29–31. This saying is difficult because the second animal listed is unknown (the term occurs only here), and the word that describes the king is also unique. Nonetheless, the general principle seems clear, thanks to the "introduction" (v. 29) and the fullness of the description in v. 30.

Again, the king is mentioned last, following three animals that walk or move well (the Hebrew is not more precise than this). The majesty of the lion, symbolic throughout the ancient Near East of kingship, is that it fears nothing; indeed, every animal maintains a respectful distance.

The word translated "lion" (HED #4055) is relatively rare in the Bible (only here, Job 4:11 and Isa. 30:6), but its meaning is not in doubt. The next animal is unknown. Suggestions range from birds (rooster, raven) to the war-horse and greyhound. The term of difficulty means, literally, "pinched [pressed?] in the loins," which may have been either an animal's name or a descriptive term that was understood by Agur's contemporaries. The third animal, the male goat (cf. Gen. 30:35; 32:14; 2 Chr. 17:11), like the lion, is well-known. Wild goats' habitat protects them from predators, but, if attacked, they tend to turn to face them, rather than retreat. These three animals have in common grace or majesty of movement.

If the key word ('alqûm; HED #518) in the last phrase refers to the king's army, then this entire saying is probably ironic—kings are majestic only when surrounded by the panoply of state. Unlike the beasts listed before him, he needs more than his own person to inspire the respect, awe, and fear that they think is their due by right (those who can have others executed on a whim are usually treated respectfully). Even if it does not mean "army" (NASB, NIV) or "troops" (NKJV), this seems to be the general sense of the saying. It is another warning to kings to realize that respectful treatment is not necessarily heartfelt and that some animals receive as much respect as any king.

30:32–33. This saying concludes Agur's writings with a final warning to kings and rulers that flows directly from the preceding numerical sayings (vv. 24–31). Both of them, with gentle humor, warn kings not to think too highly of themselves. The verses here repeat that warning, albeit more pointedly. The opening line explicitly condemns arrogance ("lifting up yourself") as stupid. Its parallel with "planned" implies that those plans were wicked. Since v. 32b contains neither verb nor pronouns (lit., "hand to mouth"), it may be directive: "Put your hand on your mouth" (NASB, NKJV; "clap" [NIV]) so that you stop making such plans. Or this phrase may be adverbial, "If you have planned, hand on mouth" (i.e., in secret), with a rebuke implied from the first line.

A more literal translation reveals the symmetry of v. 33:

> For pressing milk yields curds,
> and pressing a nose yields blood,
> and pressing anger yields strife.

The same term is used for "nose" and "anger" (HED #652), and the extended meaning of the term translated "blood" is "bloodshed." Thus the interconnections of these lines are strengthened by the language.

Arrogance leads to contention, and arrogance in kings leads to bloodshed. These verses conclude the preceding sayings by reminding kings of the terrible consequences of pride, especially when pride characterizes those in their position. Technically, this is not a numerical saying; the change in pattern makes it an effective close to Agur's words.

31:1–9. Lemuel's mother's opening words are designed to focus her son's attention on what she is about to say. The threefold exclamation reinforces his relationship to her. He may be the king, but he remains her son, and thus beholden to listen to her. She may have offered her "vows" in hopes of conception (cf. 1 Sam. 1:11), or in thanksgiving for his birth; that she mentions it reveals the weight which she reckons to her counsel. This counsel addresses two topics. She warns him against diluting his energies with women (v. 3; cf. 29:3) and against abusing alcohol (vv. 4–9; cf. 20:1; 23:19ff, 29–35).

31:1–2. This is the only biblical reference to King Lemuel of Massa', a region of Arabia (see 30:1 and "Overview"). The words are not his, however, but his mother's. The counsel of Lemuel's

2.

4242, 1275	4242, 1118, 1027	4242	1118, 5266	**3.** 414, 5598.123
intrg, n ms, ps 1cs	cj, intrg, n ms, n fs, ps 1cs	cj, intrg	n ms, n mp, ps 1cs	adv, v Qal juss 2ms
מַה־בְּרִי	וּמַה־בַּר־בִּטְנִי	וּמֶה	בַּר־נְדָרָי	אַל־תִּתֵּן
mah-berî	ûmah-bar-biṭnî	ûmeh	bar-nedhārāy	'al-tittēn
what O my son	even what O son of my womb	and what	O son of my vows	do not give

3937, 5571	2524	1932	3937, 4364.154	4567	**4.** 414	3937, 4567
prep, art, n fp	n ms, ps 2ms	cj, n mp, ps 2ms	prep, v Qal act ptc fp	n mp	adv	prep, art, n mp
לַנָּשִׁים	חֵילֶךָ	וּדְרָכֶיךָ	לַמְחוֹת	מְלָכִין	אַל	לַמְלָכִים
lannāshîm	chêlekhā	ûderākhêkhā	lamchôth	melākhîn	'al	lamlākhîm
to the women	your army	and your ways	the destroyers of	kings	not	for the kings

4068	414	3937, 4567	8685.141, 3302	3937, 7619.152	173	8336
pn	adv	prep, art, n mp	v Qal inf con, n ms	cj, prep, v Qal act ptc mp	cj	n ms
לְמוֹאֵל	אַל	לַמְלָכִים	שְׁתוֹ־יָיִן	וּלְרוֹזְנִים	אוֹ	שֵׁכָר
lemô'ēl	'al	lamlākhîm	shethô-yāyin	ûlerôznîm	'ô	shēkhār
O Lemuel	not	for the kings	to drink wine	or for dignitaries	or	strong drink

5.

6678, 8685.121	8319.121	2809.455	8521.321	1833
cj, v Qal impf 3ms	cj, v Qal impf 3ms	v Pual ptc ms	cj, v Piel impf 3ms	n ms
פֶּן־יִשְׁתֶּה	וְיִשְׁכַּח	מְחֻקָּק	וִישַׁנֶּה	דִּין
pen-yishteh	weyishkach	mechuqqāq	wîshanneh	dîn
otherwise he will drink	and he will forget	what is decreed	and he will alter	the judgment of

3725, 1158, 6271	**6.** 5598.133, 8336	3937, 6.151	3302
adj, n mp, n ms	v Qal impv 2mp, n ms	prep, v Qal act ptc ms	cj, n ms
כָּל־בְּנֵי־עֹנִי	תְּנוּ־שֵׁכָר	לְאוֹבֵד	וְיַיִן
kol-benê-'ōnî	tenû-shēkhār	le'ôvēdh	weyayin
all the children of the afflicted	give strong drink	to the one who is perishing	and wine

3937, 4914	5497	**7.** 8685.121	8319.121	7677	6219	3940
prep, adj	n fs	v Qal impf 3ms	cj, v Qal impf 3ms	n ms, ps 3ms	cj, n ms, ps 3ms	neg part
לְמָרֵי	נָפֶשׁ	יִשְׁתֶּה	וְיִשְׁכַּח	רִישׁוֹ	וַעֲמָלוֹ	לֹא
lemārê	nāphesh	yishteh	weyishkach	rîshô	wa'amālô	lō'
to the bitter of	soul	he will drink	and he will forget	his poverty	and his misfortune	not

2226.121, 5968	**8.** 6858.131, 6552	3937, 489	420, 1835
v Qal impf 3ms, adv	v Qal impv 2ms, n ms, ps 2ms	prep, adj	prep, n ms
יִזְכָּר־עוֹד	פְּתַח־פִּיךָ	לְאִלֵּם	אֶל־דִּין
yizkār-'ôdh	pethach-pîkhā	le'illēm	'el-dîn
he will remember anymore	open your mouth	for the mute	for the justice of

so the forcing of wrath bringeth forth strife: ... churning of anger brings forth strife, *Berkeley* ... pressure of anger leads to bloodshed, *Anchor* ... so provocation leads to strife, *NEB*.

31:1. The words of king Lemuel, the prophecy that his mother taught him: ... A solemn injunction which his mother lays on him, *Anchor* ... learned from his mother, *Moffatt* ... a revelation, *Beck*.

2. What, my son? and what, the son of my womb? and what, the son of my vows?: ... sonne of my desires!, *Geneva* ... answer to my prayers, *Good News* ... whom I have dedicated to the Lord, *LIVB* ... my first-born!, *Douay*.

3. Give not thy strength unto women: ... Don't spend all your energy on sex and all your money on women, *Good News* ... Wouldst thou give thyself up to the love of women, *Knox* ... Yield not your virility, *Anchor* ... Give not your vigor, *Douay* ... the vigour of your manhood, *NEB*.

nor thy ways to that which destroyeth kings: ... or your power to those who ruin kings, *Beck* ... nor consort with those who make eyes at kings, *NEB* ... And thy ways to wiping away of kings, *Young*.

4. It is not for kings, O Lemuel, it is not for kings to drink wine: ... Wine was never made for kings, *Knox* ... It is not for kings to be quaffing wine, *Moffatt*.

nor for princes strong drink: ... nor princes to be fond of beer, *Anchor* ... or have a craving for alcohol, *Good News* … For princes to quaff strong drink, *Goodspeed* … carouse befits ill thy council-chamber, *Knox* … for princes to be swilling liquor, *Moffatt*.

5. Lest they drink, and forget the law: … he forget his duty, *Anchor* … they may forget what is right, *Beck* … forget what is decreed, *Berkeley* … lest in their cups they forget, *Moffatt*.

and pervert the judgment of any of the afflicted: … change the judgement of all the children of affliction, *Geneva* … violate the rights of any in trouble, *Goodspeed* … misjudge the plea of the friendless, *Knox* … twist the law against their wretched vic-tims, *NEB* … deprive all the oppressed of their rights, *NIV* … alter the plea of any who are sorely oppressed, *Rotherham*.

6. Give strong drink unto him that is ready to perish: … Give beer [rather] to one who is in extremity, *Anchor* … Alcohol is for people who are dying, *Good News* … Strong drink for the mourner, *Knox* … Hard liquor is for sick men at the brink of death, *LIVB*.

and wine unto those that be of heavy hearts: … whose life is bitter, *Anchor* … for the afflicted heart, *Knox* … for those in deep depression, *LIVB* … to those who are in anguish, *NIV*.

7. Let him drink, and forget his poverty: … misfortune, *JB*.

and remember his misery no more: … no longer remember his troubles, *Anchor* … think no more of their burdens, *NAB* … his wearying toil let him remember no more, *Rotherham*.

8. Open thy mouth for the dumb: … Speak out for the one who cannot speak for himself, *Anchor* … Make your views heard, *JB* … give thy voice for dumb pleader, *Knox* … Do justice to a widow, *Moffatt*.

in the cause of all such as are appointed to destruction: … let

---

mother (31:1–9) may seem to reveal concerns especially important to women, but it is simply good advice for any leader. If Lemuel cannot rule his own appetites, how will he be able to rule Massa'? Solomon approved the counsel of Lemuel's mother as fitting the purposes of his Book.

Despite the masculine tone of Proverbs, these verses show that both fathers and mothers taught their children (1:8; 4:3f; 6:20) and that mothers were worthy of equal respect, as many warnings also reveal (15:20; 19:26; 20:20; 23:22; 28:24; 30:11, 17; cf. Exo. 20:12). The queen mother was in a privileged position in Israel (cf. 1 Ki. 2:17–20), no less than in other nations, although not to the extent that Athaliah's usurpation was tolerated (2 Ki. 11:1–16).

31:3. She first warns him against multiplying his harem, since to do so is to endanger his throne. It is not clear how women "destroy kings," but this may reflect the turmoil that accompanies the many sons, all potential heirs, of a large harem (cf. the dynastic struggles between David's sons, Amnon, Absalom, Adonijah and Solomon described in 2 Sam. 13 and 1 Ki. 2). The further danger is that by giving his "ways" to women, he may find that the harem in fact comes to rule the kingdom behind his back, undermining his authority and undoing his work. The Aramaic form of the word "kings" further suggests the Massa'ite origin of Prov. 30–31.

31:4–7. The establishment of justice in a land was primarily the responsibility of the king, hence Solomon's prayer for wisdom to judge wisely (1 Ki. 3:9), and the theme of royal justice throughout Proverbs (cf. 16:10; 20:8, 26; 29:4, 14). The boast of a number of ancient Near Eastern kings was that their gods had enabled them to establish justice in the land (cf. the Code of Hammurabi and the inscriptions of Darius). Injustice is condemned throughout writings of the ancient Near East, including the Bible.

Drunkenness befuddles the mind, making it difficult to remember what has been decreed and impossible to discern truth from falsehood (cf. 23:33). Using the same words that described the deleterious effects of drunkenness on judgment ("let him drink and forget"), Lemuel's mother shows alcohol's effect as a sedative or soporific for those in deep trouble. This description of drunkenness as a "medical" treatment for depression (vv. 6f) actually proves her point about the effect of alcohol on the memory and judgment. It reduces a person to a stupor, so that even those who are upset for good cause forget their troubles. Much more seriously will be its affect on the ability to judge wisely.

31:8–9. She now turns from the problem of perverting justice due to drunkenness to encouraging him to pursue justice for those who cannot expect it. The "dumb" (v. 8a) may be literally unable to speak or those who, because of their social standing, would normally be unheard. The king's responsibility is to be sure that their voices are heard (not necessarily to speak for them). He is also to judge the poor of the land with justice (v. 9), rather than to prefer the wealthy. This is an implicit warning against accepting bribes (cf. 17:23), since verdicts determined by bribery never favor the poor. At the same time, these verses are not exalting the poor at the expense of the rich, so that poverty equals

9.

8570.131, 6928	6858.131, 6552	2576	3725, 1158
v Qal impv 2ms, n ms	v Qal impv 2ms, n ms, ps 2ms	n ms	adj, n mp
שְׁפָט־צֶדֶק	פְּתַח־פִּיךָ	חֲלוֹף	כָּל־בְּנֵי
shephāṭ-tsedheq	pethach-pîkhā	chălôph	kol-benê
judge with righteousness	open your mouth	passing away	all the children of

10.

4834.121	4449	828, 2524	33	6270	1833.131
v Qal impf 3ms	intrg	n fs, n ms	cj, adj	n ms	cj, v Qal impv 2ms
יִמְצָא	מִי	אֵשֶׁת־חַיִל	וְאֶבְיוֹן	עָנִי	וְדִין
yimtsā'	mî	'ēsheth-chayil	we'evyôn	'ānî	wedhîn
he will find	who	a wife of strength	and needy	the afflicted	and vindicate

11.

3949	904	1019.111	4509	4623, 6689	7632
n ms	prep, ps 3fs	v Qal pf 3ms	n ms, ps 3fs	prep, n fp	cj, adj
לֵב	בָּהּ	בָּטַח	מִכְרָהּ	מִפְּנִינִים	וְרָחֹק
lēv	bāhh	bāṭach	mikhrāhh	mippenînîm	werāchōq
the heart of	in her	it has trusted	her value	than pearls of coral	and more remote

12.

3725	3940, 7737	3008	1621.112	2742.121	3940	8395	1197
n ms	cj, neg part, n ms	n ms	v Qal pf 3fs, ps 3ms	v Qal impf 3ms	neg part	cj, n ms	n ms, ps 3fs
כֹּל	וְלֹא־רָע	טוֹב	גְּמָלַתְהוּ	יֶחְסָר	לֹא	וְשָׁלָל	בַּעְלָהּ
kōl	welō'-rā'	ṭôv	gemālathhû	yechăsār	lō'	weshālāl	ba'ălāhh
all	and not evil	good	she rewards him	he will lack	not	and gain	her husband

orphans have their rights, *Moffatt* ... for the rights of all the unfortunate, *Anchor* ... for the rights of the destitute, *NAB* ... such as are left desolate, *ASV* ... For the right of all sons of change, *Young*.

9. Open thy mouth, judge righteously: ... See justice done, *Anchor* ... pronounce an upright verdict, *JB* ... decide your cases fairly, *Moffatt*.

and plead the cause of the poor and needy: ... defend the afflicted poor!, *Anchor* ... render fair decisions, *Beck* ... giving redress to the friendless and the poor, *Knox* ...

champion the weak and wretched, *Moffatt* ... decree what is just, *Douay*.

10. Who can find a virtuous woman?: ... A capable wife is a rare find, *Anchor* ... A worthy woman, *ASV* ... a good wife?, *Beck* ... A wife with strength of character, *Berkeley* ... a vigorous wife, *Knox*.

for her price is far above rubies: ... far greater than jewels, *Anchor* ... farre above the pearles, *Geneva* ... worth far more than corals, *Goodspeed* ... a rare treasure, *Knox* ... far beyond red coral, *REB*.

11. The heart of her husband doth safely trust in her: ... Her husband gives her his confidence, *Anchor* ... trusts her, *Beck* ... may depend on her, *Moffatt* ... entrusting his heart to her, *NAB*.

so that he shall have no need of spoil: ... he will never lack profit, *Berkeley* ... he has everything he needs, *NCV* ... children are not lacking, *NEB* ... lacks nothing of value, *NIV*.

12. She will do him good and not evil: ... She rewards him with good and not harm, *Anchor* ... She helps him and doesn't harm him, *Beck* ...

innocence or wealth guilt. That would not be justice, which must be based on the facts in the case. The judge must apply the Law impartially, deciding the case on its own merits. The covenantal warnings are explicit (cf. Deut. 1:16f), as are the exhortations (cf. Deut. 16:18ff). The thrust of her exhortation is that he must be sure the people from all strata of society have equal standing and opportunity before the Law. If the king does not pursue this, neither will his ministers, and the land will become corrupt (cf. 29:4, 12, 14).

31:10–31. The verses of this poem begin with the consecutive letters of the Hebrew alphabet. Poets

probably wrote acrostics (cf. Pss. 111; 112; 119; Lam. 1–4) much as they now use sonnets, or any other carefully defined form, that is, to exercise and reveal the poet's skill and delight in poetic composition. Poetry is highly manipulated language. The most obvious artifice of an acrostic is its alphabetic structure. At the same time, closing the Book with this acrostic brings a sense of finality and completion.

This poem comprises three sections. The introduction (vv. 10ff) announces the theme of the excellent wife (v. 10) and her effect on her husband (v. 11f). The central portion (vv. 13–24) focuses on her life, interrupted by a brief description of her person (vv. 17f) and a further note on her effect on her husband's reputation (v. 23), before ending as it began with her industry (v. 24). The poem then ends by focusing on her person (vv. 25ff) and reward (vv. 28–31). The "interruptions" in the main section (vv. 17f, 23) are not incidental, but follow the general pattern of the poem:

A her value (v. 10)
  B her effect on her husband (vv. 11–12)
    C her industry (vv. 13–16)
      D her person (vv. 17–18)
    C her industry (vv. 19–22)
  B her effect on her husband (v. 23)
    C her industry (v. 24)
      D her person (vv. 25–27)
A her value and praise (vv. 28–31)

These verses certainly present an ideal picture, probably in order to show what it means to live in the fear of the LORD. Her life thus concretizes the theory of the rest of the Book. Although the portrait is ideal, there is no point at which its principles cannot be emulated. The particulars of her life and work may not fit everyone's circumstance (few people have servants or buy and sell property as part of everyday life), but her industry, piety and the quality of her relationships do not depend on her financial or social standing.

A natural question upon reading this poem is how anyone could possibly do all this. The poet cleverly delays answering this question, not revealing that her life demonstrates her fear of the LORD until the end of the poem (v. 30). This reflection of Prov. 1:7 is thus a "bookend" of the entire Book, showing what a life lived in the fear of the LORD, a life lived wisely, looks like. The point lies not in the particulars, but in the principles. It is thus an encouragement to fear the LORD, and to let that attitude permeate every aspect of life.

These verses also affirm that the fear of the LORD applies to all of life. Nothing in daily life, whether business transactions or providing the necessities of life, such as food and clothing, is free from the need to depend upon God's wisdom and counsel. This transforms every aspect of the woman's life from merely mundane to truly spiritual, since it is all done in the fear of God, or in the presence of God. There is no separation of secular and sacred, for everything is sacred by

virtue of her conscious dependence upon the wisdom of God.

The poem describes a prosperous and extensive household of the upper class. She is not, however, a woman "of leisure." She oversees the production of food and clothing for the household (vv. 13ff, 19, 21f), as well as for trade or barter (v. 24), and has financial resources to buy and develop property (v. 16), although whether these resources are her own or her husband's is not specified. Part of this freedom is the result of her husband's trust (v. 11), which she has earned by the pattern of her life (v. 12).

Another caution against the despair that often attends reading this poem is that, although the poem certainly emphasizes her industry, it does not necessarily teach that she does all these deeds personally, any more than the statements that Solomon built the Temple mean that he carved and set the stones or poured the bronze himself (1 Ki. 5:17–7:51). She had servants who doubtless did some of it (v. 15), although she also participated and was ultimately responsible. The clear implication is that she understood her responsibilities and submitted to the LORD her plans for meeting them.

31:10–12. An excellent wife is rare and therefore precious (cf. Ecc. 7:27ff). Since she is rare, she must be "found," like rare jewels and wisdom itself (cf. Prov. 2:1–4). This implies a careful search, a search that is rewarded by the favor of God (cf. 18:22; 19:14). Her way of life gains her husband's trust (v. 11), since everything that she does is good for him also (v. 12; cf. 12:4). The rest of the poem expands this theme of the blessing that her diligence brings to her household, and thus to her husband.

Her husband's "good" (v. 12) is literally "spoil" or "booty," a military image that seems out of place in this portrait of domestic life, but that probably reflects the variety of good that she brings him. Just as the spoils of war might include cattle, slaves, precious metals and valuable clothing, her bounty provides many kinds of benefits.

31:13–14. When it is time to find materials, she does so intentionally and carefully, searching out the best wool and flax, whether from her own property or in the marketplace. These are the raw materials from which she will make clothing for herself (v. 22), her household (v. 21), and to sell (v. 24). Her delight in her work grows out of her relationship to

13.

3219	2522	1938.112	7055	6844	6449.122	904, 2761
n mp	n mp, ps 3fs	v Qal pf 3fs	n ms	cj, n mp	cj, v Qal impf 3fs	prep, n ms
יְמֵי	חַיֶּיהָ	דָּרְשָׁה	צֶמֶר	וּפִשְׁתִּים	וַתַּעַשׂ	בְּחֵפֶץ
yᵉmê	chayyêh	dārᵉshāh	tsemer	ûphishtîm	watta'as	bᵉchêphets
the days of	her life	she searches for	wool	and flax	and she makes	with the delight of

14.

3834	2030.112	3626, 605	5692.151	4623, 4963	971.522
n fd, ps 3fs	v Qal pf 3fs	prep, n fp	v Qal act ptc ms	prep, n ms	v Hiphil impf 3fs
כַּפֶּיהָ	הָיְתָה	כָּאֳנִיּוֹת	סוֹחֵר	מִמֶּרְחָק	תָּבִיא
kappêāh	hāyᵉthāh	kā'ānîyôth	sôchēr	mimmerchāq	tāvî'
her palms	she is	like the ships of	a merchant	from a far distance	she brings

15.

4035	7251.122	904, 5968	4050	5598.122	3073	3937, 1041
n ms, ps 3fs	cj, v Qal impf 3fs	prep, adv	n ms	cj, v Qal impf 3fs	n ms	prep, n ms, ps 3fs
לָחְמָהּ	וַתָּקָם	בְּעוֹד	לַיְלָה	וַתִּתֵּן	טֶרֶף	לְבֵיתָהּ
lachmāhh	wattāqām	bᵉ'ôdh	laylāh	wattittēn	tereph	lᵉvêthāhh
her food	and she rises up	when yet	at night	and she gives	food	to her household

16.

2805	3937, 5472	2246.112	7898	4089.122
cj, n ms	prep, n fp, ps 3fs	v Qal pf 3fs	n ms	cj, v Qal impf 3fs, ps 3ms
וְחֹק	לְנַעֲרֹתֶיהָ	זָמְמָה	שָׂדֶה	וַתִּקָּחֵהוּ
wᵉchōq	lᵉna'ărōthêāh	zāmᵉmāh	sādheh	wattiqqāchēhû
and prescribed actions	to her young women	she considers	a field	then she acquires it

17.

4623, 6780	3834	5378.112	3884	2391.112	904, 6010	5158
prep, n ms	n fd, ps 3fs	v Qal pf 3fs	n ms	v Qal pf 3fs	prep, n ms	n md, ps 3fs
מִפְּרִי	כַּפֶּיהָ	נָטְעָה	כָּרֶם	חָגְרָה	בְעוֹז	מָתְנֶיהָ
mippᵉrî	khappêāh	nātᵉ'ā	kārem	chāghᵉrāh	vᵉ'ôz	māthᵉnêāh
from the fruit of	her palms	she plants	a vineyard	she girds	with strength	her hips

18.

563.322	2307	3049.112	3706, 3005	5693	3940, 3637.121
cj, v Piel impf 3fs	n fp, ps 3fs	v Qal pf 3fs	cj, adj	n ms, ps 3fs	neg part, v Qal impf 3ms
וַתְּאַמֵּץ	זְרֹעוֹתֶיהָ	טָעֲמָה	כִּי־טוֹב	סַחְרָהּ	לֹא־יִכְבֶּה
wattᵉ'ammēts	zᵉrō'ôthêāh	ṭā'ămāh	kî-ṭôv	sachrāhh	lō'-yikhbeh
and she makes firm	her arms	she perceives	that good	her profit	she does not extinguish

19.

904, 4050	5552	3135	8365.312	904, 3721	3834
prep, art, n ms	n ms, ps 3fs	n fd, ps 3fs	v Piel pf 3fs	prep, art, n ms	cj, n fd, ps 3fs
בַּלַּיִל	נֵרָהּ	יָדֶיהָ	שִׁלְּחָה	בַכִּישׁוֹר	וְכַפֶּיהָ
vallayil	nērāhh	yādhêāh	shillᵉchāh	vakkîshôr	wᵉkhappêāh
in the night	her lamp	her hands	she put forth	on the spindle whorl	and her palms

---

Content, not sorrow, she will bring him, *Knox.*

all the days of her life: ... as long as she lives, *Beck* ... from first to last, *Moffatt.*

13. She seeketh wool, and flax: ... Does she not busy herself with wool and thread, *Knox.*

and worketh willingly with her hands: ... delights to work with her hands, *Anchor* ... works it up as she wills, *Goodspeed* ... does her work with eager hands, *JB.*

14. She is like the merchants' ships; she bringeth her food from afar: ... She buys imported foods, *LIVB* ... She brings home food from out-of-the-way places, *Good News* ... fetching foodstuffs from afar, *Moffatt* ... secures her provisions from afar, *Douay* ... bringeth in her bread, *Young.*

15. She riseth also while it is yet night: ... when it is still dark, *Beck* ... before dawn, *LIVB.*

and giveth meat to her household: ... To provide food, *Anchor* ...

assigns jobs to her maids, *Beck* ... to prepare breakfast for her household, *LIVB* ... giving orders to her serving girls, *JB* ... sets meat before her household, *NEB.*

and a portion to her maidens: ... feeds her servant girls, *NCV* ... give instructions to her maids, *Anchor* ... handing her maids their rations, *Moffatt* ... a portion to her damsels, *Young* ... each waiting-woman has her share, *Knox.*

16. She considereth a field, and buyeth it: ... examines, *Anchor* ...

inspect, *LIVB* ... picks out, *Douay* ... buys land prudently, *Moffatt* ... Ground must be examined, and bought, *Knox*.

with the fruit of her hands she planteth a vineyard: ... From her earnings, *Anchor* ... with what her hands have produced, *Beck*.

17. She girdeth her loins with strength: ... She puts on strength like a garment, *Beck* ... puts her back into her work, *JB* ... How briskly she girds herself to the task, *Knox* ... She sets about her duties resolutely, *REB*.

and strengtheneth her arms: ... goes to work with a will, *Anchor* ... goes to work with her arms, *Beck* ... shows how strong her arms can be, *JB* ... braces herself for the work, *NEB* ... strong and industrious, *Good News*.

18. She perceiveth that her merchandise is good: ... Industry, she knows, is well rewarded, *Knox* ... samples merchandise to be sure it is good, *Anchor* ... perceiveth that her merchandise is profitable, *ASV* ... watches for bargains, *LIVB* ... enjoys the success of her dealings, *NAB*.

her candle goeth not out by night: ... Her lamp burns late at night, *Anchor* ... the lamp burns all night in her house, *Moffatt* ... at night her lamp is undimmed, *NAB*.

19. She layeth her hands to the spindle: ... puts her hand to the spindle whorl, *Anchor* ... She spins her own thread, *Good News* ... makes thread with her hands, *NCV*.

and her hands hold the distaff: ... her fingers ply the spindle, *Anchor* ... she manipulates the spindle, *Berkeley* ... weaves her own cloth, *Good News*.

---

the Lord (v. 30), since every part of her life, even this chore, lies within that relationship.

Verse 14 also shows her willingness to search out that which is best for her household. The point is not the distance that she travels, but that she does whatever is necessary to provide their needs.

31:15. Not only is she careful to seek what is best, she disciplines herself to meet their needs at the right time. Since they worked mainly with hand tools, and since they could not work after dark, every moment of daylight would have been precious. Rising before sunrise to feed them would enable them to work in the fields throughout the entire day.

The third line could mean either that she provided specifically for her maidservants (cf. 27:27) or that she prescribed tasks for them, since the word can mean "prescribed portion" (cf. Prov. 30:8) or "prescribed duty" (the word is most frequently translated "statute"). The parallel with "food" (v. 5b; lit., "prey") suggests that this is their portion of food, but, since they would have been part of her household (v. 15b), this is probably intended to suggest that she is as careful about seeing that the servants fulfill their duties as she is to see that they (and everyone else) are fed.

31:16. Just as she seeks out the best materials (vv. 13ff), she also acts carefully when dealing in real estate. The yield of this field and vineyard will be two further means of supporting her household, either directly, by providing food for them, or by providing income from the sale of the produce. Her care in choosing demonstrates that she is weighing the consequences of this choice. Nothing is done out of impulse. The process described here also needs to be understood in light of the emphasis in

Proverbs on the wisdom of seeking counsel. She knows where and how to get good advice when making decisions (cf. 11:14; 12:15; 15:22; 19:20; 20:18; 21:30f; 24:5f; 27:9).

31:17. Like v. 13b, which says that she delights in the work she has to do, this verse also shows that she works industriously and diligently, not reluctantly or with a slack hand (cf. the warnings against laziness throughout the Book). Both images can refer to preparation for a task (on "gird," cf. Exo. 12:11; 2 Ki. 4:29; 9:1; "strengthen," cf. Amos 2:14; Nah. 2:1). She understands that whatever must be done should be done well (cf. Ecc. 9:10).

31:18. She knows by experience ("tastes," cf. Ps. 34:9) that her return for her labor is worthwhile. This verse strengthens the parallel of a life lived wisely with wisdom itself, since the word for "gain" (HED #5693; so NASB; "merchandise," NRSV) occurs in only one other verse in Proverbs, where it describes the value of wisdom itself (3:14). Together with v. 15a, the second line of this verse implies that she is the first to rise and the last to go to bed. This may reflect the self-sacrifice inherent in such a life.

31:19–20. Although these verses appear to address two different topics, industry and generosity, they are bound by their objects, which are named chiastically ("Her hands she reaches ... and her palms," "Her palm ... and her hands she reaches"). This structure underlines the close connection between industry and generosity, which is addressed in 21:25f. Only the diligent have enough to be generous; the lazy lack even what they need for themselves (cf. 19:15; 20:13). Generosity in its turn is frequently commended as evidence of wise living, in the fear of the Lord

20.

3135 cj, n fd, ps 3fs	3937, 6270 prep, art, n ms	6816.112 v Qal pf 3fs	3834 n fs, ps 3fs	6661 n ms	8881.116 v Qal pf 3cp
וְיָדֶיהָ	לֶעָנִי	פָּרְשָׂה	כַּפָּהּ	פָּלֶךְ	תָּמְכוּ
weyādhêāh	le'ānî	pāresāh	kappāhh	phālekh	tāmekhû
and her hands	to the afflicted	she stretches out	her palm	the spindle whirl	they take hold of

21.

3706 cj	4623, 8345 prep, n ms	3937, 1041 prep, n ms, ps 3fs	3940, 3486.123 neg part, v Qal impf 2ms	3937, 33 prep, art, adj	8365.312 v Piel pf 3fs
כִּי	מִשָּׁלֶג	לְבֵיתָהּ	לֹא־תִירָא	לָאֶבְיוֹן	שִׁלְּחָה
kî	mishshālegh	levêthāhh	lō'-thîrā'	lā'evyôn	shillechāh
because	from snow	for her household	you will not be afraid	to the needy	she puts forth

22.

8668 n ms	6449.112, 3937 v Qal pf 3fs, prep, ps 3fs	4926 n mp	8528 n mp	3980.155 v Qal pass ptc ms	3725, 1041 adj, n ms, ps 3fs
שֵׁשׁ	עָשְׂתָה־לָּהּ	מַרְבַדִּים	שָׁנִים	לָבֻשׁ	כָּל־בֵּיתָהּ
shēsh	'āsethāh-lāhh	marvaddîm	shānîm	lāvush	khol-bêthāhh
linen	she makes for herself	coverings	crimson	having been clothed with	all her household

23.

904, 3553.141 prep, v Qal inf con, ps 3ms	1197 n ms, ps 3fs	904, 8554 prep, art, n mp	3156.255 v Niphal ptc ms	3961 n ms, ps 3fs	736 cj, n ms
בְּשִׁבְתּוֹ	בַּעְלָהּ	בַּשְּׁעָרִים	נוֹדָע	לְבוּשָׁהּ	וְאַרְגָּמָן
beshivtô	ba'ălāhh	bashshe'ārîm	nôdhā'	levushāhh	we'argāmān
when his sitting	her husband	in the gates	being known	her clothes	and purple cloth

24.

2382 cj, n ms	4513.122 cj, v Qal impf 3fs	6449.112 v Qal pf 3fs	5650 n ms	6196, 2292, 800 prep, n mp, n fs
וַחֲגוֹר	וַתִּמְכֹּר	עָשְׂתָה	סָדִין	עִם־זִקְנֵי־אָרֶץ
wachăghôr	wattimkōr	'āsethāh	sādhîn	'im-ziqōnê-'ārets
and girdles	and she sells	she makes	undergarments	with the elders of the land

25.

7925.122 cj, v Qal impf 3fs	3961 n ms, ps 3fs	6010, 1994 n ms, cj, n ms	3937, 3793 prep, art, pn	5598.112 v Qal pf 3fs
וַתִּשְׂחַק	לְבוּשָׁהּ	עֹז־וְהָדָר	לַכְּנַעֲנִי	נָתְנָה
wattischaq	levushāhh	'ōz-wehādhār	lakkena'ănî	nāthenāh
and she laughs	her clothes	strength and honor	to the merchant	she appropriates

26.

8784, 2721 cj, n fs, n ms	904, 2551 prep, n fs	6858.112 v Qal pf 3fs	6552 n ms, ps 3fs	315 adv	3937, 3219 prep, n ms
וְתוֹרַת־חֶסֶד	בְחָכְמָה	פָּתְחָה	פִּיהָ	אַחֲרוֹן	לְיוֹם
wethôrath-chesedh	vechokhmāh	pāthechāh	pîāh	'achărôn	leyôm
and instruction about kindness	in wisdom	she opens	her mouth	afterward	about the day of

---

20. She stretcheth out her hand to the poor: ... opens her hands to the unfortunate, *Anchor* ... Kindly is her welcome, *Knox* ... To poor folk she is generous, *Moffatt* ... welcomes the poor, *NCV*.

yea, she reacheth forth her hands to the needy: ... stretches out her arms to the poor, *Anchor* ... lends a hand to the forlorn, *Moffatt* ... her purse ever open to those in need, *Knox*.

21. She is not afraid of the snow for her household: ... Let the snow lie cold if it will, *Knox*.

for all her household are clothed with scarlet: ... no servant of hers but is warmly clad, *Knox* ... they all have fine clothes to keep them warm, *NCV* ... all her charges are doubly clothed, *NAB* ... clothed in crimson, *NRSV* ... wrapped in double cloaks, *REB*.

22. She maketh herself coverings of tapestry: ... She makes her own bedcovers, *Anchor* ... carpets of tapestry, *ASV* ... She makes quilts for herself, *Beck* ... Ornamental coverings, *Young*.

her clothing is silk and purple: ... She clothes herself in fine linen and dyed wool, *Anchor* ... her clothing is fair linen and purple, *BB* ... linen and other expensive material, *NCV* ... white linen, *Rotherham*.

23. Her husband is known in the gates: ... is respected, *JB* ... is a man of note, *Moffatt* ... is prominent, *NAB* ... well known, *REB*.

when he sitteth among the elders of the land: ... elders of the country, *Beck* ... one of the leading citizens, *Good News* ... he sits with the sheikhs in council, *Moffatt* ... where he makes decisions, *NCV*.

24. She maketh fine linen, and selleth it: ... She makes a wrapper and sells it, *Anchor*.

and delivereth girdles unto the merchant: ... make a girdle for the travelling merchant, *Knox* ... supplies a sash to the merchant, *Anchor* ... stocks the merchants with belts, *NAB* ... supplies belts to the tradesmen, *NASB*.

25. Strength and honour are her clothing: ... Her clothing is of good quality and elegant, *Anchor* ... Protected by her own industry and good repute, *Knox* ... Strong and secure is her position, *Moffatt*.

and she shall rejoice in time to come: ... can afford to laugh at tomorrow, *NEB* ... She happily looks forward to the morrow, *Anchor* ... she smiles at the future, *Beck* ... she rejoiceth at a latter day, *Young* ... has no fear of old age,

LIVB ... she greets the morrow with a smile, *Knox*.

26. She openeth her mouth with wisdom: ... When she opens her mouth she speaks wisely, *Anchor* ... She talks shrewd sense, *Moffatt*.

and in her tongue is the law of kindness: ... kindly instruction is on her tongue, *Anchor* ... gentle teaching is on her tongue, *Berkeley* ... Ripe wisdom governs her speech, *Knox* ... loyalty is the theme of her teaching, *NEB*.

(cf. 11:24ff; 14:31; 17:5; 19:17; 21:13; 22:9, 16; 28:27).

31:21–22. Red dye was expensive; scarlet clothing was a sign that they were well-prepared for harsh weather with the best clothing that could be made. Her own clothing is also of the highest quality. Perhaps the linen had been spun and woven from the flax that she had purchased (v. 13), although some scholars think that "linen" and "purple" specify imported goods. Although there is a difference between "red" and "purple" (both most frequently describe the materials of the Tabernacle; cf. Exo. 25–28, 35–39), the exact shade of these colors is unknown, although both here refer to clothing made from dyed fabric, and both, whether purchased as fabric, dye or dyed fabric, would have been quite expensive. It is easy (and misleading) to over-interpret differences between parallel lines (see "Overview"), but the poet does mention the wife's concern and provision for her household before describing her own clothing.

31:23. The master of a household that is run with the efficiency, generosity and wisdom described in this poem will be widely respected, and seated as a leader. If he had the discretion to choose such a wife, he may also have the insight necessary to rule as a judge (cf. Ruth 4:2–11). He will, at least, be given that opportunity. His wife is his crown (cf. 12:4).

31:24. Under her supervision, the household is so efficient that they produce more clothing than they themselves need, so that they can sell some. "Canaanite" (Hebrew text) refers to merchants (NKJV, NRSV) or tradesmen (NASB), probably because the Phoenicians, the traders par excellence of that part of the world, spoke a dialect of Canaanite, and so were reckoned Canaanites. Their

interest in trading with her hints that her work was of high quality.

31:25–27. This summary describes her metaphorical clothing (v. 25a; cf. v. 22b) and confidence (v. 25b), and shows that her concern for her household (v. 27a) is driven by more than business. It grows out of her fear of the LORD, which she attempts to pass on to those for whom she cares, certainly her own children (v. 26; cf. 1:8; 4:3f; 6:20; 31:1) and perhaps everyone around her. These lessons need not be formal. Just as her life instructs the reader of Proverbs, so it teaches those who live and work with her daily, and who thus see the fruit of the fear of the LORD in her life.

Metaphorical clothing (v. 25a) is often used in poetic passages to describe the person "wearing" those qualities (cf. Ps. 93:1). In this case, the fruit of her diligent use of her strength and ability not only bring her honor (anticipating vv. 28–31), they also give her confidence to face the future. She has sufficient food, clothing and property to ensure her ability to continue to provide for her household.

The "teaching of kindness" could refer either to teaching that is kind (i.e., she teaches in a kind manner) or to teaching that has as its object kindness (i.e., teaching with the content of kindness). The parallel with "wisdom" (v. 26a) probably means that this is kind teaching. She may be a demanding mistress, but she is not difficult or harsh. Her words are words of healing and life, thoughtful and wise.

Although the grammar, vocabulary and syntax of the first line of v. 27 are unusual ("[She is] one who watches over the goings of"), this line also reflects her interest in and concern for those under her care. The last line of this section is a classic understatement, especially coming after the verses

27.

6341	4035	1041	2049	7099.153	6142, 4098
n fs	cj, n ms	n ms, ps 3fs	n fp	v Qal act ptc fs	prep, n fs, ps 3fs
עַצְלוּת	וְלֶחֶם	בֵּיתָהּ	הֲלִיכוֹת	צוֹפִיָּה	עַל־לְשׁוֹנָהּ
'atslûth	welechem	bêthāhh	hǎlîkhôth	tsôphîyāh	'al-leshônāhh
laziness	and the bread of	her household	the proceedings of	a watchful woman	on her tongue

28.

3940	404.122	7251.116	1158	861.326	1197
neg part	v Qal impf 3fs	v Qal pf 3cp	n mp, ps 3fs	cj, v Piel impf 3mp, ps 3fs	n ms, ps 3fs
לֹא	תֹאכֵל	קָמוּ	בָנֶיהָ	וַיְאַשְּׁרוּהָ	בַּעֲלָהּ
lō'	thō'khēl	qāmû	vānêhā	way'ashsherûāh	ba'ǎlāhh
not	she will eat	they will rise	her children	and they will declare her blessed	her husband

29.

2054.321	7521	1351	6449.116	2524	879
cj, v Piel impf 3ms, ps 3fs	adj	n fp	v Qal pf 3cp	n ms	cj, pers pron
וַיְהַלְלָהּ	רַבּוֹת	בָּנוֹת	עָשׂוּ	חָיִל	וְאַתְּ
wayhalelāhh	rabbôth	bānôth	'āsû	chāyil	we'atte
he will praise her	many	daughters	they have acted with	valiance	but you

30.

6148.114	6142, 3725	8632	2682	1961	3418
v Qal pf 2fs	prep, n ms, ps 3fp	n ms	art, n ms	cj, n ms	art, n ms
עָלִית	עַל־כֻּלָּנָה	שֶׁקֶר	הַחֵן	וְהֶבֶל	הַיֹּפִי
'ālîth	'al-kullānāh	sheqer	hachēn	wehevel	hayyōphî
you went up	above all of them	a lie	the grace	and a breath	the beauty

31.

828	3488, 3176	2026	2054.722	5598.131, 3937
n fs	n fs, pn	pers pron	v Hithpael impf 3fs	v Qal impv 2ms, prep, ps 3fs
אִשָּׁה	יִרְאַת־יְהוָה	הִיא	תִּתְהַלָּל	תְּנוּ־לָהּ
'ishshāh	yir'ath-yehwāh	hî'	thithhallāl	tenû-lāhh
a wife	the fear of Yahweh	she	she will be praised	give to her

4623, 6780	3135	2054.326	904, 8554	4801
prep, n ms	n fd, ps 3fs	cj, v Piel juss 3mp, ps 3fs	prep, art, n mp	n mp, ps 3fs
מִפְּרִי	יָדֶיהָ	וִיהַלְלוּהָ	בַשְּׁעָרִים	מַעֲשֶׂיהָ
mipperî	yādhêhā	wîhalelûāh	vashshe'ārîm	ma'ǎsêāh
from the fruit of	her hands	and may they praise her	in the gates	her deeds

---

27. She looketh well to the ways of her household: ... watches closely what goes on, *Anchor* ... the conduct of her family, *Beck* ... surveyeth the ways, *Darby*.

and eateth not the bread of idleness: ... permits no one to eat food in idleness, *Anchor* ... not content to go through life eating and sleeping, *Knox* ... never wastes her time, *NCV*.

28. Her children arise up, and call her blessed: ... pronounce blessings on her, *Anchor* ... congratulate her, *Moffatt* ... with one accord call her happy, *NEB* ... extol her virtues, *REB*.

her husband also, and he praiseth her: ... sings her praises, *Anchor* ... is loud in her praise, *Knox* ... extols her, *NAB*.

29. Many daughters have done virtuously: ... have done nobly, *Berkeley* ... women have done fine work, *Beck* ... have done admirable things, *JB* ... are the women of proven worth, *NAB*.

but thou excellest them all: ... you have surpassed them all, *Anchor* ... transcend them all, *Berkeley* ... surmountest, *Geneva* ... Unrivalled art thou among all the women, *Knox*.

30. Favour is deceitful: ... Vain are the winning ways, *Knox* ... Grace is deceitful, *ASV* ... Charm is deceitful, *Berkeley* ... Charm is a delusion, *NEB*.

and beauty is vain: ... beauty is a snare, *Knox* ... a breath, *Goodspeed* ... beauty can trick you, *NCV*.

but a woman that feareth the LORD, she shall be praised: ... The intelligent woman [who reverences the Lord] is the one deserving praise, *Anchor* ... keep your praise for a wife with brains, *Moffatt*.

31. Give her of the fruit of her hands: ... Give her the reward she has earned, *Anchor* ... Give her credit for what she has done, *Beck* ... Work such as hers claims its reward, *Knox* ... Give her the product of her hands, *NASB*.

and let her own works praise her in the gates: ... let the gates ring with praise of her deeds, *Anchor* ... let her deeds praise her, *Beck* ... she should be praised in public, *NCV*.

that describe the activities of her life. To "eat the bread of idleness" means to be (or become) idle. Her activity is not, however, the frenetic rushing of the fool, unable to discern what is most important, and so shifting his or her energy from object to object. She is busy because she knows what is most important and, understanding this, bends her energies to accomplishing it, both for her own sake and for the sakes of those around her.

31:28–31. The last four verses show the response of all who know her, from her immediate family (vv. 28f) to all the people of her town (v. 31). Her worth is evaluated or described by the poet (v. 10), herself (v. 18a), her children and husband (vv. 11, 28–31a), and others (v. 31b). The latter (v. 31b) also reflects her beneficial effect on her husband's reputation (v. 23). Her household unites in honoring her, and their song of praise, quoted here (v. 29), shows how difficult it is to find someone who lives and acts as wisely as she has (cf. v. 10).

31:28–29. The repeated verb hālal, "praise" (HED #2054; vv. 28b, 30b, 31b), shows that this entire poem is organized as a hymn of praise, not to God, but to the person who fears God. It thus resembles another biblical acrostic, Ps. 112, which praises "the man that feareth the LORD" (Ps. 112:1). Although the two portraits are quite different (Ps. 112 does not describe the person's life as specifically as does Prov. 31:10–31), they contain striking parallels, including their blessedness, generosity and honor. Both also follow the general format of

the hymn: call to praise (here a question, v. 10a), then a list of the person's praiseworthy deeds (vv. 11–27), concluding with a final call to praise (cf. the imperative in v. 31).

31:30. Nor is her value based on such superficialities as her appearance, since beauty does not provide food (vv. 13–16, 19, 21), nor does it last. Beauty is perhaps more frequently associated with selfishness and a lack of care for others, qualities opposite those which characterize this woman's life. She is honored because in her life people have seen the fear of the LORD.

31:31. Boaz says that everyone in his town (lit., "gates") knows that Ruth is an "excellent woman" (the term used in 31:10 and repeated in 31:29a). She was highly esteemed because they had seen her faithfulness toward Naomi, both in coming with her from Moab and in gleaning grain for the two of them (Ruth 3:11; in Ruth 2:1, Boaz is called the male equivalent).

Although the woman is not praised for her beauty (v. 30), she is honored and respected for her chosen way of life. This choice is implied in the placement of this poem at the end of the Book. Proverbs says repeatedly that wisdom must be sought and, when found, obeyed. This life is not one of privilege and rank, but the result of deliberate and repeated decisions to act, speak and live wisely. Just as the craftsman is honored for his skill (22:29), the person who lives in a wise way will be recognized.

THE BOOK OF

ECCLESIASTES

Expanded Interlinear
Various Versions
Verse-by-Verse Commentary

THE BOOK OF
ECCLESIASTES קֹהֶלֶת

	1745 *n mp* דִּבְרֵי divrê the words of	7237 n ms קֹהֶלֶת qōheleth the preacher	1158, 1784 *n ms, pn* בֶּן־דָּוִד ben-dāwidh the son of David	4567 n ms מֶלֶךְ melekh a king	904, 3503 prep, pn בִּירוּשָׁלָם bîrûshālām in Jerusalem	**2.**	1961 *n ms* הֲבֵל hevēl a vanity of	1961 n mp הֲבָלִים hevālîm the vanities

1:1

569.111 v Qal pf 3ms אָמַר 'āmar he has said	7237 n ms קֹהֶלֶת qōheleth the preacher	1961 *n ms* הֲבֵל hevēl a vanity of	1961 n mp הֲבָלִים hevālîm the vanities	3725 art, n ms הַכֹּל hakkōl everything	1961 n ms הֲבֵל hāvel a vanity	**3.**	4242, 3620 intrg, n ms מַה־יִּתְרוֹן mah-yithrôn what is the profit

3937, 119 prep, art, n ms לָאָדָם lā'ādhām to humankind	904, 3725, 6219 prep, *adj*, n ms, ps 3ms בְּכָל־עֲמָלוֹ bekhol-'āmālô because of all his toil	8054, 6218.121 rel part, v Qal impf 3ms שֶׁיַּעֲמֹל sheya'amōl which he toils	8809 prep תַּחַת tachath under	8507 art, n ms הַשָּׁמֶשׁ hashshāmesh the sun	**4.**	1810 n ms דּוֹר dôr a generation

2050.151 v Qal act ptc ms הֹלֵךְ hōlēkh going	1810 cj, n ms וְדוֹר wedhôr and a generation	971.151 v Qal act ptc ms בָּא bā' coming	800 cj, art, n fs וְהָאָרֶץ wehā'ārets yet the earth	3937, 5986 prep, n ms לְעוֹלָם le'ôlām unto eternity	6198.153 v Qal act ptc fs עֹמָדֶת 'ōmādheth standing

5.	2311.111 cj, v Qal pf 3ms וְזָרַח wezārach and it rises	8507 art, n ms הַשָּׁמֶשׁ hashshemesh the sun	971.111 cj, v Qal pf 3ms וּבָא ûvā' and it goes	8507 art, n ms הַשָּׁמֶשׁ hashshāmesh the sun	420, 4887 cj, prep, n ms, ps 3ms וְאֶל־מְקוֹמוֹ we'el-meqômô and to its place	8079.151 v Qal act ptc ms שׁוֹאֵף shô'ēph panting

2311.151 v Qal act ptc ms זוֹרֵחַ zôrēach rising	2000 pers pron הוּא hû' it	8427 adv שָׁם shām there	**6.**	2050.151 v Qal act ptc ms הֹלֵךְ hōlēkh proceeding	420, 1924 prep, n ms אֶל־דָּרוֹם 'el-dārôm toward the south	5621.151 cj, v Qal act ptc ms וְסוֹבֵב wesôvēv and going around	420, 7103 prep, n fs אֶל־צָפוֹן 'el-tsāphôn to the north

1:1. The words of the Preacher, the son of David: ... Composition of Qoheleth son of David, *JB* ... Words of the Spokesman, king David's son, *Knox* ... Sayings of the Speaker, David's son, *Moffatt* ... words of the Teacher, a son of David, *NCV, NIV.*

king in Jerusalem: ... that reigned once at Jerusalem, *Knox.*

2. Vanity of vanities, saith the Preacher: ... Futility of futilities, *Berkeley* ... All is to no purpose, *BB* ... Sheer futility, *JB* ... "Meaningless! Meaningless!", *NIV.*

vanity of vanities: ... futility of futilities, *Berkeley* ... Sheer futility, *JB* ... a shadow's shadow, *Knox* ... Utterly meaningless!, *NIV.*

all is vanity: ... all is futile, *Berkeley* ... all the ways of man are to no purpose, *BB* ... everything is futile!, *JB* ... Everything is meaningless, *NIV.*

3. What profit hath a man of all his labour: ... What advantage does man have in all his work, *NASB* ... What do people really gain, *NCV* ... What has a man to show for all his trouble and effort, *Anchor.*

which he taketh under the sun?: ... which he toils at, *NAB, Douay* ... Which he does, *NASB* ... they do here on earth?, *NCV* ... that he laboureth at, *Young.*

4. One generation passeth away, and another generation cometh: ... One generation goes and another comes, *Beck* ... Age succeeds age, *Knox* ... People live, and people die, *NCV.*

but the earth abideth for ever: ... earth remains forever, *Berkeley* ... earth standeth for ever, *Darby* ...

earth endures for ever!, *Fenton* … the world goes on unaltered, *Knox*.

5. The sun also ariseth, and the sun goeth down: … The rising sun goes down, *Moffatt* … the sun rises and the sun sets, *NASB* … the sun breaketh forth and the sun goeth in, *Rotherham* … the sun hath risen, and the sun hath gone in, *Young*.

and hasteth to his place where he arose: … hurries to its place, *KJVII* … hurries round only to rise again, *Moffatt* … presses on to the place where it rises, *NAB* … speeds to its place and rises there again, *REB*.

6. The wind goeth toward the south, and turneth about unto the north: … Blowing toward the south and veering toward the north, *Anchor* … blows south and turns north, *Beck* … travels to the South, and revolves towards the North, *Fenton* … Southward goes the wind, then turns to the north, *JB*.

it whirleth about continually: … ever circling goes the wind, *Anchor* … going around and around, *Beck* …

No common words begin this Book. We may take them not only as the words of Solomon, the wisest of men, but as the words of "the only wise God." And we must humble ourselves (Matt. 18:3f), if we would profit by their precious instruction.

1:1. In Ecclesiastes, Solomon is given a unique name—the Preacher (HED #7237). The Preacher's ordinary course combined oral and written instruction: "He still taught the people knowledge … and that which was written was upright, even words of truth" (12:9f). Because his oral teaching was wondrously diversified in every track of science, people from all nations and all ranks flocked to hear his wisdom (v. 34). Indeed, he was the "encyclopedia" of his age (cf. 1 Ki. 4:30–33). Jesus himself taught a lesson of conviction using one of these illustrious foreigners: "The queen of the south shall rise up in the judgment with this generation, and shall condemn it: for she came from the uttermost parts of the earth to hear the wisdom of Solomon; and, behold, a greater than Solomon is here" (Matt. 12:42).

The Preacher's parentage also added weight to his instructions—he was the son of David, and he undoubtedly owed much to his father's godly and affectionate counsel. Further, he had dignity of station—he was king of Jerusalem. His royal influence must indeed have been shaken by the gross display of idolatrous lust. On the other hand, the special credentials of his birth (2 Sam. 7:12ff), the seal of divine love upon him (Neh. 13:26) and his rich endowments (1 Ki. 3:5–12) could not be forgotten.

1:2. This verse appears to have been intended as the compendium of the whole treatise. The subject of vanity opens upon us abruptly; this is not surprising considering the Preacher's heart was filled with it. He brings out his subject with a vast variety of illustrations, and then closes by emphatically repeating his judgment. It is not only vain, but vanity itself.

Yet the Preacher's verdict casts no reflection on the works of God, which were pronounced "very good" at their formation. Instead, he speaks of the works not as God made them, but as sin marred them. Things intrinsically excellent are perverted by their abuse: the "creature" is now "made subject to vanity" (Rom. 8:20).

Repeatedly Solomon reminds us that the blessings of the creature, when used for the glory of God, are lawful in themselves, and become the source of rich and legitimate enjoyment. Man, however, buries his heart in their vanity. To give a deeper impression of this error, the wise man makes a vehement exclamation, as if overwhelmed with his own perception of it, and wondering at the delusion of seeking happiness from a mere vapor. So deeply has the love of vanity struck its roots into the heart, that the delusion cannot be too strongly exposed.

1:3. The mass of mankind revolt from the Preacher's judgment. He therefore throws down the challenge, "What profit hath a man of all his labour?" Apart from God, the world is poor indeed. Disappointment brings weariness, and success leaves no permanent satisfaction.

In fact, men are so willing to be deceived that they take up with the very shadow of profit—what appears to be substance has no real being at all. The appetite for wisdom, riches, honor and sensual indulgence may be indefinitely enlarged, but, as Jesus asked, "What is a man profited, if he shall gain the whole world, and lose his own soul?" (Matt. 16:26). The man of the world may be orthodox in his creed and moral in his practice, but he has stumbled at the very threshold. He has placed the world before God, the body before the soul, time before eternity.

What will it be at the last, when the account of all our labor must be rendered up? The question is, "What fruit have you produced?" For the person of sin, the answer will consist of darkness and despair. Such is the fruitless labor under the sun.

1:4–7. The changeableness of man, as contrasted with the relative permanence of the universe, seems another proof of utter vanity. Man and his labor are swept away, as if they had never been.

307

7593	8178.151	6142, 5623	7593	2050.151	5621.151	5621.151
art, n ms	v Qal act ptc ms	cj, prep, sub, ps 3ms	art, n ms	v Qal act ptc ms	v Qal act ptc ms	v Qal act ptc ms
הָרוּחַ	שָׁב	וְעַל־סְבִיבֹתָיו	הָרוּחַ	הוֹלֵךְ	סֹבֵב	סוֹבֵב
hārûach	shāv	we'al-sevîvōthâv	hārûach	hôlēkh	sōvēv	sôvēv
the wind	turning back	and on its circuits	the wind	proceeding	going around	going around

7.

420, 4887	4529	375	3328	420, 3328	2050.152	3725, 5337
prep, n ms	adj	sub, ps 3ms	cj, art, n ms	prep, art, n ms	v Qal act ptc mp	adj, art, n mp
אֶל־מְקוֹם	מָלֵא	אֵינֶנּוּ	וְהַיָּם	אֶל־הַיָּם	הֹלְכִים	כָּל־הַנְּחָלִים
'el-meqôm	mālē'	'ênennû	wehayyām	'el-hayyām	hōlekhîm	kol-hannechālîm
to the place	full	there is not	yet the sea	to the sea	proceeding	all the streams

8.

3725, 1745	3937, 2050.141	8178.152	2062	8427	2050.152	8054, 5337
adj, art, n mp	prep, v Qal inf con	v Qal act ptc mp	pers pron	adv	v Qal act ptc mp	rel part, art, n mp
כָּל־הַדְּבָרִים	לָלָכֶת	שָׁבִים	הֵם	שָׁם	הֹלְכִים	שֶׁהַנְּחָלִים
kol-haddevārîm	lālākheth	shāvîm	hēm	shām	hōlekhîm	shehannechālîm
all the matters	to proceed	returning	they	there	proceeding	which the streams

6084	3940, 7881.122	3937, 1744.341	382	3940, 3310.121	3131
n fs	neg part, v Qal impf 3fs	prep, v Piel inf con	n ms	neg part, v Qal impf 3ms	adj
עַיִן	לֹא־תִשְׂבַּע	לְדַבֵּר	אִישׁ	לֹא־יוּכַל	יְגֵעִים
'ayin	lō'-thisba'	ledhabbēr	'îsh	lō'-yûkhal	yeghē'îm
the eye	it is not satisfied	to speak	a man	he is not able	wearisome

9.

4242, 8054, 2030.111	4623, 8471.141	238	3940, 4527.222	3937, 7495.141
intrg, rel part, v Qal pf 3ms	prep, v Qal inf con	n fs	cj, neg part, v Niphal impf 3fs	prep, v Qal inf con
מַה־שֶׁהָיָה	מִשְּׁמֹעַ	אֹזֶן	וְלֹא־תִמָּלֵא	לִרְאוֹת
mah-shehāyāh	mishshemōa'	'ōzen	welō'-thimmālē'	lir'ôth
what that it has been	of hearing	the ear	and it is not filled	to see

8054, 6449.221	2000	4242, 8054, 6449.211	8054, 2030.121	2000
rel part, v Niphal impf 3ms	pers pron	cj, intrg, rel part, v Niphal pf 3ms	rel part, v Qal impf 3ms	pers pron
שֶׁיֵּעָשֶׂה	הוּא	וּמַה־שֶׁנַּעֲשָׂה	שֶׁיִּהְיֶה	הוּא
sheyē'āseh	hû'	ûmah-shenna'ăsāh	sheyihyeh	hû'
what it will be done	it	and what that it has been done	what it will be	it

10.

375	3725, 2413	8809	8507	3552	1745	8054, 569.121
cj, sub	adj, adj	prep	art, n ms	sub	n ms	rel part, v Qal impf 3ms
וְאֵין	כָּל־חָדָשׁ	תַּחַת	הַשָּׁמֶשׁ	יֵשׁ	דָּבָר	שֶׁיֹּאמַר
we'ên	kol-chādhāsh	tachath	hashshāmesh	yēsh	dāvār	sheyō'mar
and there is not	anything new	under	the sun	there is	a thing	which someone will say

7495.131, 2172	2413	2000	3647	2030.111	3937, 5986	866	2030.111
v Qal impv 2ms, dem pron	adj	pers pron	adv	v Qal pf 3ms	prep, n mp	rel part	v Qal pf 3ms
רְאֵה־זֶה	חָדָשׁ	הוּא	כְּבָר	הָיָה	לְעֹלָמִים	אֲשֶׁר	הָיָה
re'ēh-zeh	chādhāsh	hû'	kevār	hāyāh	le'ōlāmîm	'ăsher	hāyāh
see this	new	it	already	it has been	of a long time	which	it has been

travelling in circles, *Fenton* ... Turning, turning, the wind blows, *Goodspeed*.

and the wind returneth again according to his circuits: ... returning upon its tracks, *Anchor* ... makes its rounds, *Beck* ... in its revolutions returns to its place of origin!, *Fenton* ... back to its circling goes the wind, *JB*.

7. All the rivers run into the sea: ... flow into, *Knox* ... streams all flow into the sea, *Moffatt* ... go to the sea, *NAB* ... All the streams are going unto the sea, *Young*.

yet the sea is not full: ... yet never the sea grows full, *Knox* ... the sea they never fill, *Moffatt* ... yet the sea never overflows, *NEB, REB*.

unto the place from whence the rivers come, thither they return again: ... back to their springs they find their way, *Knox* ... To the place where they go, the rivers keep on going, *NAB, Douay* ... back to the place from which the streams ran they return to run again, *NEB*.

8. All things are full of labour: … All words fail through weariness, *Anchor* … Everything is a bore, *Beck* … All things are unspeakably tiresome, *Berkeley* … All things are full of toil, *Darby*.

man cannot utter it: … a man becomes speechless, *Anchor* … more than anyone can tell, *Beck* … none can express it, *Darby* … man may not give their story, *BB*.

the eye is not satisfied with seeing: … the eye cannot see it all, *Anchor* … more than any eye can see, *Beck* …

the eye has never enough of its seeing, *BB* … Eye looks on unsatisfied, *Knox*.

nor the ear filled with hearing: … nor the ear hear the end of it, *Anchor* … more than any ear can hear, *Beck* … nor does the ear get enough hearing, *Berkeley* … ear listens, ill content, *Knox*.

9. The thing that hath been, it is that which shall be: … What has been is what shall be, *Moffatt* … All things continue the way they have been since the beginning, *NCV* … What has happened will happen again, *NEB*.

and that which is done is that which shall be done: … that which has happened once shall happen again, *Knox* … what has gone on is what shall go on, *Moffatt*.

and there is no new thing under the sun: … nothing new here on earth, *NCV* … there is not an entirely new thing under the sun, *Young*.

10. Is there any thing whereof it may be said, See, this is new?: … Take anything which people acclaim as being new, *JB*.

"The earth is a stage—persons passing and vanishing before our eyes." Continually shifting the inhabitants, one generation passes away to make room for another: the house stands, but the tenants are continually changing. Could they remain to enjoy it, there might be some permanent profit. Still eternity and unchangeableness are the necessary grounds of happiness. Indeed, the ultimate destiny of the earth is that it will be "burned up" (2 Pet. 3:10). Yet a substratum for the "new earth," which "we, according to his promise, look for" (2 Pet. 3:13), may be reserved. At all events, as compared with man's passing away, the earth abides forever until its end in connection with the purpose of God is eternally accomplished. So long as there will remain a seed to serve Him (Ps. 22:30) and one generation to praise his works to another (Ps. 145:4), it stands.

See how everything presents the same picture. The sun, after so many thousand courses, rises and sets, hasting to its place (Pss. 19:4ff; 104:19–22). The wind is always shifting, returning again according to its circuits (Ps. 135:7; Jer. 10:13). The currents of the rivers run into the sea, which yet is not full, but returns in clouds and vapors to water the earth (Ps. 104:8f). All this seems a weary go-round, constant movement while everything stays the same. So many emblems of man's restless state! Should they not rouse us to work while it is day (John 9:4)—filling up our own little sphere of service according to the will of God in our generation (Acts 13:36)—looking to fall asleep in Jesus, resting from our labors, and our works following us? (Rev. 14:13).

1:8. Every step of advance shows more clearly the "weary land." Labor, rather than rest, is our lot (2:11f). Man riseth up early, and late taketh rest, and

eateth the bread of carefulness (cf. Ezek. 12:19). All things, even the most cheerful exercises, are full of labor. What therefore brings toil also brings additional proof that all is vanity. Indeed, this weariness is felt in so many ways that man cannot utter it. Men seek and they find; and yet they toil again, no nearer the prize than at the beginning. Even the delights enjoyed through the senses grow tiresome. Seeing and hearing bring no permanent satisfaction (4:8; 5:10f; cp. Prov. 27:20; 30:15f). People cry for more and more of the world, but when it comes, it does not satisfy.

We can never find satisfaction in this life until we focus our affections on God. Is it not the real knowledge of the Savior that gives life, energy and joy to our religion? The appetite is fully satisfied early with the gratification we find in the LORD during this life. Later, eternity opens with the bright anticipation of perfect enjoyment. Jesus said, "He who comes to me will never hunger; and he who believes on me will never thirst" (John 6:35; cp. 4:13f).

1:9–10. The Preacher extends his view on all sides. He includes all ages to the very end of time. He asserts that everything which will be done has already been done. This, indeed, must be a qualified statement. Amid endlessly diversified changes and modifications, there are some things, doubtless, which have not been already of old time. Yet the main features of the universe are the same. Animate and inanimate objects remain as they were from the beginning (2 Pet. 3:4). The same causes produce the same effects; the laws of the heavenly bodies, the courses of the seasons (Gen. 8:22; Ps. 74:16f; Jer. 5:24), the arrangements relative to the animal world and the chemical properties of nat-

11.

3937, 315	1612	3937, 7518	2230	375	4623, 3937, 6686
prep, art, adj	cj, cj	prep, art, adj	n ms	sub	prep, prep, n mp, ps 1cp
לָאַחֲרֹנִים	וְגַם	לָרִאשֹׁנִים	זִכְרוֹן	אֵין	מִלְּפָנֵנוּ
lā'achărōnîm	wegham	lāri'shōnîm	zikhrōn	'ên	millephānēnû
of what is latter	and also	of what is former	a remembrance	there is not	from before us

8054, 2030.126	6196	2230	3937	3940, 2030.121	8054, 2030.126
rel part, v Qal impf 3mp	prep	n ms	prep, ps 3mp	neg part, v Qal impf 3ms	rel part, v Qal impf 3mp
שֶׁיִּהְיוּ	עִם	זִכָּרוֹן	לָהֶם	לֹא־יִהְיֶה	שֶׁיִּהְיוּ
shêyihyû	'im	zikkārôn	lāhem	lō'-yihyeh	shêyihyû
which they will be	with	a remembrance	to them	it will not be	which they will be

12.

904, 3503	6142, 3547	4567	2030.115	7237	603	3937, 7518
prep, pn	prep, pn	n ms	v Qal pf 1cs	n ms	pers pron	prep, art, adj
בִּירוּשָׁלָם	עַל־יִשְׂרָאֵל	מֶלֶךְ	הָיִיתִי	קֹהֶלֶת	אֲנִי	לָאַחֲרֹנָה
bîrûshālām	'al-yisrā'ēl	melekh	hāyîthî	qōheleth	'ănî	lā'achărōnāh
in Jerusalem	over Israel	a king	I have been	the preacher	I	of what is latter

13.

6142	904, 2551	3937, 8780.141	3937, 1938.141	881, 3949	5598.115
prep	prep, art, n fs	cj, prep, v Qal inf con	prep, v Qal inf con	do, n ms, ps 1cs	cj, v Qal pf 1cs
עַל	בַּחָכְמָה	וְלָתוּר	לִדְרוֹשׁ	אֶת־לִבִּי	וְנָתַתִּי
'al	bachokhmāh	welāthûr	lidhrôsh	'eth-libbî	wenāthattî
about	with the wisdom	and to investigate	to seek	my heart	and I set

435	5598.111	7737	6275	2000	8452	8809	6449.211	3725, 866
n mp	v Qal pf 3ms	adj	n ms	pers pron	art, n md	prep	v Niphil pf 3ms	adj, rel part
אֱלֹהִים	נָתַן	רָע	עִנְיַן	הוּא	הַשָּׁמַיִם	תַּחַת	נַעֲשָׂה	כָּל־אֲשֶׁר
'ĕlōhîm	nāthan	rā'	'inyan	hû'	hashshāmayim	tachath	na'ăsāh	kol-'ăsher
God	He has given	evil	occupation	it	the heavens	under	it is done	all that

14.

881, 3725, 4801	7495.115	904	3937, 6257.141	119	3937, 1158
do, adj, art, n mp	v Qal pf 1cs	prep, ps 3ms	prep, v Qal inf con	art, n ms	prep, n mp
אֶת־כָּל־הַמַּעֲשִׂים	רָאִיתִי	בּוֹ	לַעֲנוֹת	הָאָדָם	לִבְנֵי
'eth-kol-hamma'ăsîm	rā'îthî	bô	la'ănôth	hā'ādhām	livnê
all the deeds	I have seen	with it	to be afflicted	humankind	to the sons of

7758	1961	3725	2079	8507	8809	8054, 6449.116
cj, n fs	n ms	art, n ms	cj, intrj	art, n ms	prep	rel part, v Niphal pf 3cp
וּרְעוּת	הֶבֶל	הַכֹּל	וְהִנֵּה	הַשָּׁמֶשׁ	תַּחַת	שֶׁנַּעֲשׂוּ
ûre'ûth	hevel	hakkōl	wehinnēh	hashshāmesh	tachath	shenna'ăsû
and a striving for	a vanity	everything	and behold	the sun	under	which they have been done

it hath been already of old time, which was before us: ... in the ages which were before us, *ASV* ... has been there already long before us, *Beck* ... existed long ago in times past, *Berkeley* ... was already in existence in the ages Which were before us, *Goodspeed.*

11. There is no remembrance of former things: ... no remembrance of the former generations, *ASV* ... Nothing in the past is remembered, *Beck* ... no memory of those who have gone before, *BB* ... there is no record of past events, *Fenton.*

neither shall there be any remembrance of things that are to come with those that shall come after: ... of later things which have yet to be there will be no recollection among men of a still later time, *Anchor* ... in the future nothing will be remembered by those who come later, *Beck* ... of those who come after there will be no memory for those who are still to come after them, *BB* ... the fame of to-morrow's doings will be forgotten by the men of a later time, *Knox.*

12. I the Preacher was king over Israel in Jerusalem: ... I, the Spokesman, *Knox* ... I the Speaker, *Moffatt* ... I, the Teacher, *NCV.*

13. And I gave my heart: ... applied my mind, *Anchor* ... applied my heart, *ASV* ... I used my wisdom, *Beck* ... I devoted my mind, *Fenton.*

to seek and search out by wisdom: ... to search and investigate, *Anchor* ... to study, search and explore, *Beck* ... to investigation, and to scientific Research, *Fenton* ... to investigation and exploration, *JB.*

concerning all things that are done under heaven: ... all that is done beneath the sky, *Anchor* ... everything done under the sun, *Beck* ... over everything that occurs under the skies, *Fenton* ... all that men do, here under the sun, *Knox*.

this sore travail hath God given to the sons of man to be exercised therewith: ... a grievous affliction God has put on human beings to afflict them, *Anchor* ... a sorry task God has given human beings to weary themselves with, *Beck* ... it is a hard thing which God has put on the sons of men to do, *BB*.

14. I have seen all the works that are done under the sun: ... all that goes on in this world, *Moffatt* ... everything done on earth, *NCV* ... all the deeds that are done here under the sun, *NEB*.

and, behold, all is vanity and vexation of spirit: ... it is a vain, futile

ural bodies and objects have never changed. There is no new thing under the sun.

Solomon had just before beautifully described the process of evaporation—the waters of the sea forming clouds, which empty themselves upon the earth, and fill the rivers, which again carry them into the sea (vv. 6f). But here is no new creation of waters; only the successive reproduction of the clouds, vapors and rivers. In the wondrous economy of nature, there is, therefore, no new thing under the sun.

Look again at man in all his pleasures, pursuits and changes of life. His intellect may be gratified, and his appetite for novelty supplied in the multiplied new openings of science, but no new springs of vital happiness are opened to him. He is as far as ever from true rest. Our disappointed forefathers in bygone days never found it. We will find the world as they did, and so we will leave it to our children—a world of vexation, a shadow and a bubble.

1:11. Like the last, this is a general, rather than universal, truth. Not only the former things themselves, but even their remembrance passes. Time blots out a multitude of events, as if they had never been. Men, as well as events, have passed away. How little is the remembrance of the great empire of Nimrod, of the early beginnings of Rome or the first dynasty of France! The idols and heroes of the world—the mighty and illustrious, with all their titles and grandeur, pass away and are forgotten.

Now contrast with this oblivion of former things the great miracle of Providence, the preservation of the Bible, God's Word. Here is indeed the remembrance of former things, free from the injury of time, still full and clear, as from the beginning. What do we owe to the divine Keeper for this precious transcript of himself and his love!

1:12. The Preacher up to this point has only given a general view of this world's vanity. He now confirms it from his own history. His royal dignity gave him every advantage of observation. He was king, not of a barbarous and ignorant people, but of Israel, the only people on the face of the earth who

professed the true knowledge of God and the right standard of principle (Deut. 4:7f). He was in Jerusalem, the city which God had fixed as the habitation of his glory.

Who does not know his sadly instructive history? He was the son of a godly king and beloved of God. But how could Solomon thus fall? Could he, who so highly exalted wisdom, degrade himself into the lowest folly? Could he, who was so conscious of the snares of sin, and warned so wisely, fall, so as to become a proverb of apostasy?

Only those who have been taught by experience, no less than by Scripture, the total corruption of the heart, can solve the mystery. But to such the lesson is most valuable. The most experienced is exposed, no less than the weakest babe in the family. Oh! what need is there to "watch unto prayer" (1 Pet. 4:7), and to walk closely with God!

1:13. The wise man throws himself with intense energy into his hazardous inquiry. All his extraordinary treasures of wisdom are employed to know why man, the noblest of God's creatures, is placed in the world to be exercised with travail, during his short life. The Preacher himself subsequently explains the problem, "God hath made man upright; but they have sought out many inventions" (7:29). Man by his fall alienated himself from the only Source of life and rest. Fallen man of himself cannot recover one atom of his former perfection. God has given him this travail as the chastening for his apostasy.

All is dark with him, till he will see that all is vanity, and himself the chiefest of all vanities. Thus the LORD will bring him to his home, wearied with the unsuccessful efforts. Once brought home, he finds the LORD an unfailing confidence for time and eternity. He has engaged to take charge of all, and we should bid our souls return unto their rest (Ps. 116:7), upon the engagements of an unchangeable, covenant-keeping God.

1:14. Solomon's research extended to all the works done under the sun: all this he had seen with his own eye. He had earnestly heeded, and clearly

7593		6003.455	3940, 3310.121	3937, 8963.141	2747
n ms	**15.**	v Pual ptc ms	neg part, v Qal impf 3ms	prep, v Qal inf con	cj, n ms
רוּחַ		מְעֻוָּת	לֹא־יוּכַל	לִתְקֹן	וְחֶסְרוֹן
rûach		me'uwwāth	lō'-yûkhal	lithqōn	wechesrôn
wind		something made completely crooked	it is not able	to become straight	and want

3940, 3310.121	3937, 4630.241		1744.315	603	6196, 3949	3937, 569.141
neg part, v Qal impf 3ms	prep, v Niphal inf con	**16.**	v Piel pf 1cs	pers pron	prep, n ms, ps 1cs	prep, v Qal inf con
לֹא־יוּכַל	לְהִמָּנוֹת		דִּבַּרְתִּי	אֲנִי	עִם־לִבִּי	לֵאמֹר
lō'-yûkhal	lehimmānôth		dibbartî	'ănî	'im-libbî	lē'mōr
it is not able	to be counted		I spoke	I	with my heart	saying

603	2079	1461.515	3362.515	2551	6142
pers pron	intrj	v Hiphil pf 1cs	cj, v Hiphil pf 1cs	n fs	prep
אֲנִי	הִנֵּה	הִגְדַּלְתִּי	וְהוֹסַפְתִּי	חָכְמָה	עַל
'ănî	hinnēh	highdaltî	wehôsaphtî	chokhmāh	'al
I	behold	I have caused to be great	and I have added	wisdom	above

3725, 866, 2030.111	3937, 6686	6142, 3503	3949	7495.111	7528.542
adj, rel pron, v Qal pf 3ms	prep, n mp, ps 1cs	prep, pn	cj, n ms, ps 1cs	v Qal pf 3ms	v Hiphil inf abs
כָּל־אֲשֶׁר־הָיָה	לְפָנַי	עַל־יְרוּשָׁלָם	וְלִבִּי	רָאָה	הַרְבֵּה
kol-'ăsher-hāyāh	lephānay	'al-yerûshālām	welibbî	rā'āh	harbēh
any who he was	before me	over Jerusalem	and my heart	it saw	making abundant

2551	1907		5598.125	3949	3937, 3156.141	2551	3156.141
n fs	cj, n fs	**17.**	cj, v Qal impf 1cs	n ms, ps 1cs	prep, v Qal inf con	n fs	cj, v Qal inf con
חָכְמָה	וָדַעַת		וָאֶתְּנָה	לִבִּי	לָדַעַת	חָכְמָה	וְדַעַת
chokhmāh	wādhā'ath		wā'ettenāh	libbî	lādha'ath	chokhmāh	wedha'ath
wisdom	and knowledge		and I set	my heart	to know	wisdom	and to know

2014	5724	3156.115	8054, 1612, 2172	2000	7763	7593
n fp	cj, n fs	v Qal pf 1cs	rel part, cj, dem pron	pers pron	n ms	n ms
הוֹלֵלוֹת	וְשִׂכְלוּת	יָדַעְתִּי	שֶׁגַּם־זֶה	הוּא	רַעְיוֹן	רוּחַ
hôlēlôth	wesikhlûth	yādha'ttî	sheggam-zeh	hû'	ra'ăyôn	rûach
folly	and foolishness	I understood	that also this	it	a striving for	wind

	3706	904, 7524	2551	7524, 3833	3362.521
18.	cj	prep, n ms	n fs	n ms, n ms	cj, v Hiphil impf 3ms
	כִּי	בְּרֹב	חָכְמָה	רָב־כָּעַס	וְיוֹסִיף
	kî	berōv	chokhmāh	rāv-kā'as	weyôsîph
	because	in the abundance of	wisdom	an abundance of vexation	when someone will add

1907	3362.521	4480		569.115	603	904, 3949	2050.131, 5167
n fs	v Hiphil impf 3ms	n ms	**2:1**	v Qal pf 1cs	pers pron	prep, n ms, ps 1cs	v Qal impv 2ms, part
דַּעַת	יוֹסִיף	מַכְאוֹב		אָמַרְתִּי	אֲנִי	בְּלִבִּי	לְכָה־נָּא
da'ath	yôsîph	makh'ôv		'āmartî	'ănî	belibbî	lekhāh-nā'
knowledge	he will add	pain		I said	I	in my heart	come please

affair, *Moffatt* ... it is all useless, like chasing the wind, *NCV* ... they are all emptiness and chasing the wind, *NEB*.

15. That which is crooked cannot be made straight: ... What is bent cannot be straightened, *Anchor* ... You can't straighten out what is twisted, *Beck* ... The crooked could

not be straightened, *Fenton* ... there was no curing men's cross-grained nature, *Knox*.

and that which is wanting cannot be numbered: ... what is missing cannot be made up, *Anchor* ... you can't count what is not there, *Beck* ... what is lacking cannot be counted, *Berkeley* ... the wrong could not be

righted, *Fenton* ... nor can you count up the defects in life, *Moffatt*.

16. I communed with mine own heart: ... Said I to myself, *Moffatt* ... I thought to myself, *NIV*.

saying, Lo, I am come to great estate: ... Behold, I have become great, *NAB* ... I have amassed great wisdom, *NEB* ... I have attained greatness, *NKJV*.

and have gotten more wisdom than all they that have been before me in Jerusalem: ... gained far more wisdom than any, *Moffatt* ... stored up wisdom beyond all who were before me in Jerusalem, *NAB* ... I have magnified and increased wisdom more, *NASB* ... have gathered wisdom, beyond any one who hath been before me, *Rotherham*.

yea, my heart had great experience of wisdom and knowledge: ... my mind has such experience of wisdom and knowledge, *Moffatt* ... my mind

has broad experience of wisdom and knowledge, *NAB* ... my mind has observed a wealth of wisdom and knowledge, *NASB* ... I have become familiar with wisdom and knowledge, *NEB*.

17. And I gave my heart to know wisdom: ... I turned my attention to the nature of, *Anchor* ... I applied my heart to know, *ASV* ... I've studied to master wisdom, *Beck* ... to getting knowledge of wisdom, *BB* ... gave my mind to the investigation of Science, *Fenton*.

and to know madness and folly: ... and of foolish behavior and vulgarity, *Anchor* ... madness and foolishness,

Beck ... the ways of the foolish, *BB* ... stupidity and folly, *JB*.

I perceived that this also is vexation of spirit: ... I learned that this too was a grasping at the wind, *Anchor* ... I'm convinced this also is like trying to catch the wind, *Beck* ... I found that this too was labour lost, *Knox* ... I find it futile, *Moffatt*.

18. For in much wisdom is much grief: ... with more wisdom comes more worry, *Anchor* ... If you have a lot of wisdom, you have a lot of irritation, *Beck* ... in more wisdom is more vexation, *Berkeley* ... much wisdom, much woe, *Knox*.

---

understood it. He had given his judgment before in part—all is vanity. A fuller investigation brings in a more complete verdict—all is vexation of spirit. Disappointment possesses us in trifles, as well as in matters of moment. The golden opportunity of feeding our faith upon the promises of God—of nourishing our graces in the pastures of the Good Shepherd—is stolen from us by the over-eager pursuit of comparatively unworthy objects. Is not this vexation of spirit?

1:15. The wise man directs our attention to two points, the things that are and the countless multitude of things that are lacking. The world in its present constitution from the Fall is full of crookedness and defect. Yet a reverential inquiry will show many apparent irregularities to be component parts of a system, which God has made beautiful (3:11).

But let us look at this aphorism more minutely. Physically, it lies upon the surface. We have no power to change one hair of our heads, or alter our stature (Matt. 5:36; 6:27). Intellectually, man's wisdom can never discover—much less remove—the causes of his restless misery. Spiritually, every faculty of man is under the perversity of the fall, and we have no more power to make straight its crookedness, than to restore the whole work of God to its original "uprightness." Man in "the fulness of his sufficiency he shall be in straits" (Job 20:22). He is a creature of so many wants.

1:16–18. Wisdom was Solomon's first experiment in the pursuit of rest. He investigated all the advantage of great estate, large wisdom and experience, but here he lost his path. He sought to know

wisdom under the sun. So far from increasing his happiness, it only added a deeper stamp to his decision.

Yet we are no patrons of ignorance. Far be it from us to deny the highly valuable pleasures of wisdom and knowledge. Still, if we attempt their pursuit, as Solomon seems to have done, by making an idol of our gifts—putting God out of his supremacy—we can only expect to add our testimony, attesting to their disappointment.

What a contrast is the substance and reality of the Gospel! "The way of life is above to the wise" (Prov. 15:24), higher than the highest pinnacle of this world's glory. On the other hand, who can read the gloomy pathway into eternity of one of the most amiable of philosophers without sorrowful conviction?

Hard indeed is it for the philosopher to "receive the kingdom of God," for there is only one way in which it can be received—"as a little child" (Mark 10:15). Here he will find the only remedy for his grief and sorrow. Intelligence in all the branches of natural science gives no help to a right understanding of the Gospel. If Solomon with his mighty grasp of intellect could find no rest in earthly wisdom, who else can expect it? Let the glowing stimulus be given to the pursuit of heavenly wisdom. This wisdom stands out in striking contrast to every "vain show": it is life eternal (John 17:3).

2:1–2. Solomon was disappointed in the thorny path of wisdom and knowledge. Grief and sorrow, rather than happiness and rest, were the culmination of that course. Yet not disheartened by the failure, he would try a new path. The man of wisdom turned himself into a man of pleasure. In a fever of excite-

1961	1612, 2000	2079	904, 3005	7495.131	904, 7977	5441.325
n ms	cj, pers pron	cj, intrj	prep, adj	cj, v Qai impv 2ms	prep, n fs	v Piel juss 1cs, ps 2ms
הָבֶל	גַם־הוּא	וְהִנֵּה	בְטוֹב	וּרְאֵה	בְּשִׂמְחָה	אֲנַסְּכָה
hāvel	gham-hû'	wehinnēh	vetôv	ûre'ēh	vesimchāh	'ănassekhāh
a vanity	also it	and behold	with good	and see	with gladness	let me test you

2.

6449.153	4242, 2173	3937, 7977	2054.451	569.115	3937, 7926
v Qal act ptc fs	intrg, dem pron	cj, prep, n fs	v Pual ptc ms	v Qal pf 1cs	prep, n ms
עֹשָׂה	מַה־זֹּה	וּלְשִׂמְחָה	מְהוֹלָל	אָמַרְתִּי	לִשְׂחוֹק
'ōsāh	mah-zōh	ûlăsimchāh	mehôlāl	'āmartî	lischôq
accomplishing	what this	and about rejoicing	mocking	I said	about laughter

3.

3949	881, 1340	904, 3302	3937, 5082.141	904, 3949	8780.115
cj, n ms, ps 1cs	do, n ms, ps 1cs	prep, art, n ms	prep, v Qal inf con	prep, n ms, ps 1cs	v Qal pf 1cs
וְלִבִּי	אֶת־בְּשָׂרִי	בַּיַּיִן	לִמְשׁוֹךְ	בְלִבִּי	תַּרְתִּי
welibbî	'eth-besārî	bayyayin	limshôkh	velibbî	tartî
and my heart	my body	with the wine	to draw	in my heart	I investigated

866, 7495.125	5912	904, 5724	3937, 270.141	904, 2551	5268.151
rel part, v Qal impf 1cs	adv	prep, n fs	cj, prep, v Qal inf con	prep, art, n fs	v Qal act ptc ms
אֲשֶׁר־אֶרְאֶה	עַד	בְּסִכְלוּת	וְלֶאֱחֹז	בַּחָכְמָה	נֹהֵג
'ăsher-'er'eh	'adh	besikhlûth	wele'ěchōz	bachokhmāh	nōhēgh
that I would see	until	on foolishness	and to seize	with the wisdom	leading

8452	8809	6449.126	866	119	3937, 1158	3005	338, 2172
art, n md	prep	v Qal impf 3mp	rel part	art, n ms	prep, n mp	adj	intrg, dem pron
הַשָּׁמַיִם	תַּחַת	יַעֲשׂוּ	אֲשֶׁר	הָאָדָם	לִבְנֵי	טוֹב	אֵי־זֶה
hashshāmayim	tachath	ya'ăsû	'ăsher	hā'ādhām	livnê	tôv	'ê-zeh
the heavens	under	they will do	which	humankind	for the sons of	good	where this

4.

1161.115	4801	1461.515	2522	3219	4709
v Qal pf 1cs	n mp, ps 1cs	v Hiphil pf 1cs	n mp, ps 3mp	n mp	n ms
בָּנִיתִי	מַעֲשָׂי	הִגְדַּלְתִּי	חַיֵּיהֶם	יְמֵי	מִסְפַּר
bānîthî	ma'ăsāy	highdaltî	chayyêhem	yemê	mispar
I built	my deeds	I have caused to be great	their life	the days of	the number of

5.

1634	3937	6449.115	3884	3937	5378.115	1041	3937
n fp	prep, ps 1cs	v Qal pf 1cs	n mp	prep, ps 1cs	v Qal pf 1cs	n mp	prep, ps 1cs
גַּנּוֹת	לִי	עָשִׂיתִי	כְּרָמִים	לִי	נָטַעְתִּי	בָּתִּים	לִי
gannôth	lî	'āsîthî	kerāmîm	lî	nāta'ăttî	bāttîm	lî
gardens	for myself	I made	vineyards	for myself	I planted	houses	for myself

6.

4448	1320	3937	6449.115	3725, 6780	6320	904	5378.115	6758
n mp	n fp	prep, ps 1cs	v Qal pf 1cs	adj, n ms	n ms	prep, ps 3mp	cj, v Qal pf 1cs	cj, n mp
מָיִם	בְּרֵכוֹת	לִי	עָשִׂיתִי	כָּל־פְּרִי	עֵץ	בָּהֶם	וְנָטַעְתִּי	וּפַרְדֵּסִים
māyim	berēkhôth	lî	'āsîthî	kol-perî	'ēts	vāhem	wenāta'ăttî	ûphardēsîm
water	pools of	for myself	I made	all fruits	trees	in them	and I planted	and orchards

and he that increaseth knowledge increaseth sorrow: ... he who adds to his knowledge adds to his pain, *Anchor* ... the more knowledge, the more grief you have, *Beck* ... increasing one's knowledge increases one's distress, *Berkeley* ... who adds to learning, adds to the load we bear, *Knox*.

2:1. I said in mine heart, Go to now: ... I said to myself, Come now, *Berkeley* ... I thought to myself, *JB*.

I will prove thee with mirth: ... test you in gladness, *Berkeley* ... give you joy for a test, *BB* ... I will try pleasure, *JB* ... I will try having fun, *NCV*.

therefore enjoy pleasure: ... have a good time, *Berkeley* ... so take your pleasure, *BB* ... see what enjoyment has to offer, *JB* ... I will enjoy myself, *NCV*.

and, behold, this also is vanity: ... is worthless, *Berkeley* ... was to no purpose, *BB* ... was futile too, *JB* ... is also useless, *NCV*.

2. I said of laughter, It is mad: ... is foolish, *NIV, BB* ... doesn't make any sense, *Beck* ... an empty thing, *Knox* ... Mirth is madness, *Moffatt*.

and of mirth, What doeth it?: ... of pleasure, 'What is the good of that?', *NEB* ... what does pleasure accomplish?, *NIV* ... of pleasure, "What use is it?", *NRSV* ... What availeth it?, *Darby*.

3. I sought in mine heart to give myself unto wine: ... I tried to find out what happened when I stimulate my body with wine, *Beck* ... searched in my heart how to cherish my flesh with wine, *Darby* ... to give pleasure to my flesh with wine, *BB* ... intentionally tried to embolden my body by wine, *Fenton*.

yet acquainting mine heart with wisdom: ... (my mind being wisely in control), *Beck* ... while my heart was acting with wisdom, *Berkeley* ... still guiding my heart with wisdom, *BB* ... with my intellect scientifically guiding me, *Fenton*.

and to lay hold on folly: ... I also took hold of foolishness, *Beck* ... to lay hold of frivolity, *Berkeley* ... I resolved to embrace folly, *JB*.

till I might see what was that good for the sons of men, which they should do under the heaven all the days of their life: ... till I could see what is best for human beings to do, *Beck* ... so that I might see what was good for man to do, *Berkeley* ... to discover the best way for people to spend their days, *JB*.

4. I made me great works: ... I accomplished some great things, *Beck* ... undertook great works, *BB* ... I extended my operations, *Fenton* ... I worked on a grand scale, *JB*.

I builded me houses: ... building myself houses, *BB* ... built myself palaces, *JB* ... built mansions, *Moffatt*.

I planted me vineyards: ... planting vine-gardens, *BB*.

5. I made me gardens and orchards: ... made for myself gardens and parks, *Anchor* ... and fruit-gardens, *BB* ... and paradises, *Young*.

and I planted trees in them of all kind of fruits: ... bearing all kinds of fruit, *Anchor* ... every kind of fruit tree, *Beck* ... fruit-trees of all sorts, *BB*.

---

ment he urged on his heart, as if it were too sluggish for the plunge. "Go to now, I will prove thee with mirth, therefore enjoy pleasure."

Contrast this attitude with Solomon's godly father. A great downward step indeed was it from the ways of God, or even from the pleasures of enlarged intellect, to the froth of an empty mind and the brutal pleasures of sense. A fearful experiment! One pleasure might bring a thousand woes.

Surely at this time he must have been a wanderer. Had he not commended to others the "pleasantness" and "peace" of wisdom's ways? (Prov. 3:13–18). And now was he looking to sensual mirth as the only substantial good? The wisest among men was in a very strange atmosphere. This, however, is man's common delusion—to suppose that happiness is the creature of circumstances. Therefore, if he is disappointed in one course, he will seek it in another. Little does the self-deluded victim know that he carries the principle of his misery in his own bosom.

We need not go to the world for happiness, for its resources have their end. Here is a principle, that has all the elements of true joy in itself—"a well of water springing up into everlasting life" (John 4:14). True joy has its own character. It centers in truth. It is the natural ebullition of redeemed souls, singing (Ps. 126:1f) on their way Zionward, and tuning their hearts for the everlasting song (Isa. 35:10).

2:3. Solomon here records a third extraordinary experiment to discover the object of his search.

Wisdom says, "It is not in me." Pleasure, with the same impressive emphasis, says, "It is not in me." If neither possesses rest by itself, let them both be tried together—the intellectual with the sensual pleasure. His purpose was to give himself to wine, while acquainting his heart with wisdom.

We cannot suppose that Solomon sympathized in taste with the carousels of wine. Indeed, he declares that he did it to make an experiment, one filled with danger. True godliness might flow out and waste away in the experiment. Every indulgence would tend to fix the heart to a most ruinous choice. The wisdom, with which his heart was acquainted, could not give a right balance in such a mass of defilement. Much less could he expect to find here that good thing for the sons of men, while he was making "provision for the flesh, to fulfil the lusts thereof" (Rom. 13:14).

Elsewhere he directs a moderate use of wine (9:7; Prov. 31:6f; cp. Ps. 104:15). Although his wisdom might have, to some degree, kept him master of his pleasures and restrained him from foul excess (which is not numbered among his sins), yet to give himself to wine was transgressing the bounds of godly liberty.

2:4–11. Perhaps the whole course of this world's experience does not furnish a more vivid picture of the unsatisfactory nature of earthly greatness. No element of rest or pleasure seems to be wanting, yet the result is barren indeed. It is the

5860 n mp עֲבָדִים 'ăvādhîm male slaves	7353.115 v Qal pf 1cs קָנִיתִי qānîthî I bought	**7.**	6320 n mp עֵצִים 'ētsîm trees	7049.151 v Qal act ptc ms צוֹמֵחַ tsômēach sprouting	3402 n ms יַעַר ya'ar the forest	4623 prep, ps 3mp מֵהֶם mēhem from them	3937, 8615.541 prep, v Hiphil inf con לְהַשְׁקוֹת lehashqôth to irrigate

1267 n ms בָּקָר vāqār cows	4898 n ms מִקְנֶה miqŏneh livestock	1612 cj גַּם gam also	3937 prep, ps 1cs לִי lî to me	2030.111 v Qal pf 3ms הָיָה hāyāh they were	1158, 1041 cj, n mp, n ms וּבְנֵי־בַיִת ûvenê-vayith and sons of the household	8569 cj, n fp וּשְׁפָחוֹת ûshephāchôth and female slaves

8054, 2030.116 rel pron, v Qal pf 3cp שֶׁהָיוּ shehāyû who they were	4623, 3725 prep, n ms מִכֹּל mikkōl than all	3937 prep, ps 1cs לִי lî to me	2030.111 v Qal pf 3ms הָיָה hāyāh they were	7528.542 v Hiphil inf abs הַרְבֵּה harbēh making more abundant	6887 cj, n fs וְצֹאן wātsō'n and sheep

5643 cj, n fs וּסְגֻלַּת ûseghullath and the possession of	2174 cj, n ms וְזָהָב wezāhāv and gold	1612, 3826B cj, n ms גַּם־כֶּסֶף gam-keseph also silver	3937 prep, ps 1cs לִי lî for myself	3788.115 v Qal pf 1cs כָּנַסְתִּי kānastî I gathered	**8.**	904, 3503 prep, pn בִּירוּשָׁלָם bîrûshālām in Jerusalem	3937, 6686 prep, n mp, ps 1cs לְפָנַי lephānay before me

8301.154 cj, v Qal act ptc fp וְשָׁרוֹת weshārôth and female singers	8301.152 v Qal act ptc mp שָׁרִים shārîm male singers	3937 prep, ps 1cs לִי lî for myself	6449.115 v Qal pf 1cs עָשִׂיתִי 'āsîthî I appointed	4224 cj, art, n fp וְהַמְּדִינוֹת wehammedhînôth and the districts	4567 n mp מְלָכִים melākhîm kings

1461.115 cj, v Qal pf 1cs וְגָדַלְתִּי weghādhaltî and I became greater	**9.**	8162 cj, n fp וְשִׁדּוֹת weshiddôth and ladies	8162 n fs שִׁדָּה shiddāh a lady	119 art, n ms הָאָדָם hā'ādhām humankind	1158 n mp בְּנֵי benê the sons of	8921 cj, n mp וְתַעֲנוּגֹת wetha'ănûghōth and the pleasures of

2551 n fs, ps 1cs חָכְמָתִי chokhmāthî my wisdom	652 cj אַף 'aph also	904, 3503 prep, pn בִּירוּשָׁלָם bîrûshālām in Jerusalem	3937, 6686 prep, n mp, ps 1cs לְפָנַי lephānay before me	8054, 2030.111 rel pron, v Qal pf 3ms שֶׁהָיָה shehāyāh who he was	4623, 3725 prep, n ms מִכֹּל mikkōl than all	3362.515 cj, v Hiphil pf 1cs וְהוֹסַפְתִּי wehôsaphtî and I added more

702.115 v Qal pf 1cs אָצַלְתִּי 'ātsaltî I held back	3940 neg part לֹא lō not	6084 n fd, ps 1cs עֵינַי 'ênay my eyes	8068.116 v Qal pf 3cp שָׁאֲלוּ shā'ălû they requested	866 rel part אֲשֶׁר 'ăsher that	3725 cj, n ms וְכֹל wekhōl and all	**10.**	3937 prep, ps 1cs לִי lî to me	6198.112 v Qal pf 3fs עָמְדָה 'āmedhāh it remained

6. I made me pools of water: ... constructed reservoirs, *Anchor* ... made me ponds of water, *Darby* ... made myself pools and brooks, *Fenton* ... made myself waterpools, *NKJV*.

to water therewith the wood that bringeth forth trees: ... to irrigate the plantation of young trees, *Anchor* ... to water therefrom the forest where trees were reared, *ASV* ... with which to irrigate a young forest, *Goodspeed* ... to water a flourishing woodland, *Douay*.

7. I got me servants and maidens: ... bought slaves and slave girls, *Anchor* ... bought men-servants and maid-servants, *ASV* ... bought men and women slaves, *Beck*.

and had servants born in my house: ... children were born to me in, *Berkeley* ... they gave birth to sons and daughters in, *BB* ... they had children in, *Fenton* ... had a household of dependents, *Goodspeed*.

also I had great possessions of great and small cattle above all

that were in Jerusalem before me: … my possessions of cattle and sheep also were greater than those of all who had preceded me in, *Anchor* … owned many cows and sheep, more than any who had been before me in, *Beck* … had great wealth of herds and flocks, *BB* … having possessions in cattle and sheep in far greater numbers than any who had been in, *Goodspeed*.

8. I gathered me also silver and gold, and the peculiar treasure of kings and of the provinces: … wealth of kings and of countries, *BB* … royal treasures from my provinces, *Fenton* … revenues of subject king and subject province, *Knox* … treasures from kings and other areas, *NCV*.

I gat me men singers and women singers: … trained men and women singers, *Beck* … got makers of song, male and female, *BB* … minstrels, male and female, *REB*.

and the delights of the sons of men, as musical instruments, and

that of all sorts: … enjoyed the pleasures men have with concubines, *Beck* … the delights of men—mistresses galore, *Berkeley* … girls of all sorts to be my brides, *BB* … luxuries of the sons of men, women of all sorts, *Goodspeed*.

9. So I was great, and increased more than all that were before me in Jerusalem: … I became greater than any, *Anchor* … I became greater and wealthier than all, *Berkeley* … I enlarged and increased myself more, *Fenton* … Never had Jerusalem known such wealth, *Knox*.

also my wisdom remained with me: … my wisdom stayed with me, *Anchor* … I also kept my wisdom, *Beck* … while my wisdom continued with me, *Berkeley* … My scientific idea, however, remained with me, *Fenton* … yet my wisdom stood by me, *Goodspeed*.

10. And whatsoever mine eyes desired I kept not from them: … Eyes denied nothing that eyes could

covet, *Knox* … Nothing I coveted did I deny myself, *Moffatt* … Nothing that my eyes desired did I deny them, *NAB*.

I withheld not my heart from any joy: … a heart stinted of no enjoyment, *Knox* … I refused my heart no joy, *Moffatt* … nor did I deprive myself of any joy, *NAB* … Anything I saw and wanted, I got for myself, *NCV*.

for my heart rejoiced in all my labour: … all the pleasures I had devised for myself, *Knox* … my heart did feel joy in all this toil, *Moffatt* … was pleased because of all my labor, *NASB*.

and this was my portion of all my labour: … this was to be my reward, this the fruit of all my labours, *Knox* … so much did I get from all my efforts, *Moffatt* … this was my reward for all my labor, *NASB* … this pleasure was the reward for all my hard work, *NCV*.

converse of the Christian. He seems to be "possessing all things"; yet in reality it is "having nothing" (cp. 2 Cor. 6:10). God employed Solomon not only to show the picture, but to show it, as before hinted, from his own experience. The LORD therefore poured in upon him the full confluence of earthly happiness, that he might see, and prove, and tell its utter insufficiency for rest.

Solomon's metropolis must have been the wonder of the world. He made great works. His houses, from their description, must have been wonderful buildings, both as to art and magnificence—framed, probably, like the buildings of Babylon, for state or for pleasure (Dan. 4:28ff). His vineyards, orchards and gardens were filled with trees (S.S. 8:11; 6:2; 4:13), pools of water, with some mechanical contrivance for conveying it (cf. 2 Ki. 18:17). His retinue of servants, no less than his house, commanded the queen of Sheba's highest admiration (1 Ki. 10:5–8.) His extensive herds and flocks (1 Ki. 4:23, 26, 28) were beyond what had previously been known. Immense treasures of silver and gold flowed in from all quarters (1 Ki. 9:26ff; 10:10, 14f, 25, 27f). Vocal and instrumental music ministered

to his indulgence (cf. 2 Sam. 19:35; 2 Chr. 35:25). His intellectual wisdom remained with him to give the full scope to his comprehensive mind. Added to this, he had the most free and unabated enjoyment of his resources. There was little of outward tumult to disturb (1 Ki. 4:25). All therefore that royal treasures could procure, largeness of heart desire, vast wisdom contrive, was the portion of his labor.

Nevertheless, when he looked back on all the works which he had wrought and the labor which he had labored, it seemed only as the chasing of shadows. The pleasure faded with the novelty. Here, then, is the man who drank the fullest cup of earth's best joy. What the result is, hear from his own mouth—vanity and vexation. Thus, the lowest condition in godliness is far happier and far safer than the highest ground of earthly prosperity. Even so, the spell of delusion is so strong that Solomon continues to try the experiment with the same unvarying result. In so dark a cloud set one of the finest suns of human intellect!

Unrestrained desire was the source of this vanity and vexation. He kept back from his eyes nothing that they desired. Wisdom's voice warns not to

11.

7975.111	3706, 3949	4623, 3725, 7977	881, 3949	3940, 4661.115	4623
v Qal pf 3ms	cj, n ms, ps 1cs	prep, adj, n fs	do, n ms, ps 1cs	neg part, v Qal pf 1cs	prep, ps 3mp
שָׂמֵחַ	כִּי־לִבִּי	מִכָּל־שִׂמְחָה	אֶת־לִבִּי	לֹא־מָנַעְתִּי	מֵהֶם
sāmēcha	kî-libbî	mikkol-simchāh	'eth-libbî	lō'-māna'ttî	mēhem
it was glad	because my heart	from any gladness	my heart	I did not withhold	from them

6680.115	4623, 3725, 6219	2610	2172, 2030.111	4623, 3725, 6219
cj, v Qal pf 1cs	prep, adj, n ms, ps 1cs	n ms, ps 1cs	cj, dem pron, v Qal pf 3ms	prep, adj, n ms, ps 1cs
וּפָנִיתִי	מִכָּל־עֲמָלִי	חֶלְקִי	וְזֶה־הָיָה	מִכָּל־עֲמָלִי
ûphānîthî	mikkol-'āmālî	chelqî	wezeh-hāyāh	mikkol-'āmālî
then I turned	from all my toil	my portion	and this was	from all my toil

8054, 6218.115	904, 6219	3135	8054, 6449.116	904, 3725, 4801	603
rel part, v Qal pf 1cs	cj, prep, art, n ms	n fd, ps 1cs	rel part, v Qal pf 3cp	prep, adj, n mp, ps 1cs	pers pron
שֶׁעָמַלְתִּי	וּבֶעָמָל	יָדַי	שֶׁעָשׂוּ	בְּכָל־מַעֲשַׂי	אֲנִי
she'āmaltî	ûve'āmāl	yādhay	she'āsû	bekhol-ma'ăsay	'ănî
which I had toiled	and with the toil	my hands	which they had done	with all my deeds	I

375	7593	7758	1961	3725	2079	3937, 6449.141
cj, sub	n ms	cj, n fs	n ms	art, n ms	cj, intrj	prep, v Qal inf con
וְאֵין	רוּחַ	וּרְעוּת	הֶבֶל	הַכֹּל	וְהִנֵּה	לַעֲשׂוֹת
we'ên	rûach	ûre'ûth	hevel	hakkōl	wehinnēh	la'ăsôth
and there was not	wind	and a striving for	a vanity	everything	and behold	to do

12.

2014	2551	3937, 7495.141	603	6680.115	8507	8809	3620
cj, n fp	n fs	prep, v Qal inf con	pers pron	cj, v Qal pf 1cs	art, n ms	prep	n ms
וְהוֹלֵלוֹת	חָכְמָה	לִרְאוֹת	אֲנִי	וּפָנִיתִי	הַשֶּׁמֶשׁ	תַּחַת	יִתְרוֹן
wehôlēlôth	chokhmāh	lir'ôth	'ănî	ûphānîthî	hashshāmesh	tachath	yithrôn
and folly	wisdom	to see	I	then I turned	the sun	under	a profit

5724	3706	4242	119	8054, 971.121	313	4567	881
cj, n fs	cj	intrg	art, n ms	rel pron, v Qal impf 3ms	adv	art, n ms	do
וְסִכְלוּת	כִּי	מֶה	הָאָדָם	שֶׁיָּבוֹא	אַחֲרֵי	הַמֶּלֶךְ	אֵת
wesikhlûth	kî	meh	hā'ādhām	shêyāvô'	'achărê	hammelekh	'ēth
and foolishness	because	what	the man	who he will come	after	the king	

13.

866, 3647	6449.116	7495.115	603	8054, 3552	3620	3937, 2551
rel part, adv	v Qal pf 3cp, ps 3ms	v Qal pf 1cs	pers pron	rel part, sub	n ms	prep, art, n fs
אֲשֶׁר־כְּבָר	עֲשׂוּהוּ	וְרָאִיתִי	אֲנִי	שֶׁיֵּשׁ	יִתְרוֹן	לַחָכְמָה
'ăsher-kevār	'āsûhû	werā'îthî	'ănî	shêyēsh	yithrôn	lachokhmāh
what already	they have done it	and I saw	I	that there is	a profit	to the wisdom

14.

4623, 5724	3626, 3620	214	4623, 2932	2550	6084
prep, art, n fs	prep, n ms	art, n ms	prep, art, n ms	art, n ms	n fd, ps 3ms
מִן־הַסִּכְלוּת	כִּיתְרוֹן	הָאוֹר	מִן־הַחֹשֶׁךְ	הֶחָכָם	עֵינָיו
min-hassikhlûth	kîthrôn	hā'ôr	min-hachōshekh	hechākhām	'ênâv
from the foolishness	like the profit of	the light	from the darkness	the wise	his eyes

---

11. Then I looked on all the works that my hands had wrought: ... to observe all the work which my hands had done, *Berkeley* ... I saw all the works which my hands had made, *BB* ... I reflected on all the work that my hands had done, *Fenton* ... I reviewed all my works which my hands had made, *Goodspeed*.

and on the labour that I had laboured to do: ... the effort I exerted in doing it, *Berkeley* ... everything I had been working to do, *BB* ... the things I had striven to accomplish, *Fenton* ... the toil which I had expended in making them, *Goodspeed*.

and, behold, all was vanity and vexation of spirit: ... all was worthless, *Berkeley* ... all was to no purpose and desire for wind, *BB* ... What futility it all was, what chasing after the wind!, *JB* ... I found there but frustration and labour lost, *Knox*.

and there was no profit under the sun: ... was no gain, *Berkeley* ... they had no result, *Fenton* ... is nothing to be gained, *JB* ... so fugitive is all we cherish, *Knox.*

12. And I turned myself to behold wisdom, and madness, and folly: ... went again in search of wisdom and of foolish ways, *BB* ... I reflected, and examined my Science, and Madness, and Folly!, *Fenton* ... reflections then turned to wisdom, stupidity and folly, *JB* ... my mind went back to the thought of wisdom, of ignorance, too, and folly, *Knox.*

for what can the man do that cometh after the king?: ... what kind of man would succeed the King?, *Fenton* ... what can the successor of a king do?, *JB* ... should mortal king strive to imitate the sovereign power that made him?, *Knox.*

even that which hath been already done: ... thing which he has done before, *BB* ... Nothing but what the king has done already, *Moffatt* ...

can't do more than what the other king has already done, *NCV.*

13. Then I saw that wisdom excelleth folly: ... is better than foolishness, *Beck* ... there is a result to Science, more than to Ignorance, *Fenton* ... there is profit in wisdom more then in folly, *Geneva* ... More is to be gained from wisdom, *JB.*

as far as light excelleth darkness: ... surpasses, *Anchor* ... is better than, *Beck* ... there is a result to Light, more than to Darkness, *Fenton* ... light is more excellent than darkenesse, *Geneva.*

14. The wise man's eyes are in his head: ... wise have their eyes open, *JB* ... Wise people see where they are going, *NCV.*

but the fool walketh in darkness: ... the fool goes forward blindly, *Anchor* ... fools walk around in the

dark, *NCV* ... the fool in darkness is walking, *Young.*

and I myself perceived also that one event happeneth to them all: ... the same chance happens to them both, *Anchor* ... the same fate overtakes them all, *Goodspeed* ... one fate awaits them both, *JB* ... In their ending both were alike, *Knox* ... one lot befalls both of them, *NAB.*

15. Then said I in my heart: ... said to myself, *Anchor, Goodspeed* ... I was thinking, *Beck* ... I said to my heart, *Fenton* ... I thought to myself, *NCV.*

As it happeneth to the fool, so it happeneth even to me: ... The same thing that happens to a fool happens to me, *Beck* ... As it happens to the Ignorant, so it will also happen to me!, *Fenton* ... As it befalls the fool, so will it befall me, *Goodspeed* ... one and the same fate overtakes them both, *NEB.*

cast one hankering look toward the wilderness. Its unholy breath fades the freshness and purity of our enjoyment. It is in the spiritual world that we realize things in their true color.

Never mistake the glare of this world's glory for solid happiness. God would have us rejoice in our labor—enjoy our earthly blessings, but not rest in them. A momentary pleasure is all that can be looked for. Let earth be the cistern only, not the fountain. Let its best blessings be loved after Him as the sunbeam of his love. Let nothing of earth be our rest. God never intended so poor a portion for his redeemed ones. Our rest is built upon unchangeable promises. Meanwhile the real joy is found when God is the center, and the Savior. What were the pleasures of Solomon's earthly paradise, compared with the unspeakable delight of "eating of the tree of life, which is in the midst of the Paradise of God!" (Rev. 2:7).

2:12–15. Solomon had tried wisdom and folly, both separately and together, as independent sources of happiness. He had pronounced judgment upon them as vanity and vexation. But might he not have passed over some matters of weight in the decision? A second review might discover some error. He turns himself, therefore, as he had done before (1:17), to behold the two things and compare

together his contrary experiments of wisdom and folly. Still there is no retraction, no modifying of his judgment. The search for happiness in anything besides God must end in disappointment.

Though wisdom, as a source of rest, bears the stamp of vanity, we must not underrate its relative value. It is the gift of God, opening to us channels of rich pleasure and important usefulness to our fellow creatures. It excels folly as far as light excels darkness.

Now turn our eyes to the fool walking in darkness. It is as if his eyes, instead of being in his head, were at his back. He blunders on as if blind, or in the dark; his steps go backward, running in his own folly. Whatever be his earthly wisdom, an angel would say of such a man, "There goes a poor blind creature, groping his way to hell."

As wide as is the difference between the wise man and the fool, on some points they are one. Solomon himself was on the same level with the most common pauper. Both were subject to the same vicissitudes of providence. The same last event laid them low together. Surely the wise man becomes the fool, disputing the ways of God, looking for some elevation above his fellow creatures. Such is the depth of selfishness and depravity yet to be purged out! This is also vanity.

8054, 4907	1612, 603	3156.115	2050.151	904, 2932	3809	904, 7513
rel part, n ms	cj, pers pron	cj, v Qal pf 1cs	v Qal act ptc ms	prep, art, n ms	cj, art, n ms	prep, n ms, ps 3ms
שֶׁמִּקְרֶה	גַּם־אָנִי	וְיָדַעְתִּי	הֹלֵךְ	בַּחֹשֶׁךְ	וְהַכְּסִיל	בְּרֹאשׁוֹ
shemmiqŏreh	gham-'ānî	weyādha'ăttî	hôlēk	bachōshek	wehakkesîl	berō'shô
that an event	also I	and I knew	walking	in the darkness	but the fool	in his head

904, 3949	603	569.115	**15.**	882, 3725	7424.121	259
prep, n ms, ps 1cs	pers pron	cj, v Qal pf 1cs		prep, n ms, ps 3mp	v Qal impf 3ms	num
בְּלִבִּי	אָנִי	וְאָמַרְתִּי		אֶת־כֻּלָּם	יִקְרֶה	אֶחָד
belibbî	'ānî	we'āmartî		'eth-kullām	yiqŏreh	'echādh
in my heart	I	and I said		with all of them	it will happen to	one

603	2549.115	4066	7424.121	1612, 603	3809	3626, 4907
pers pron	v Qal pf 1cs	cj, intrg	v Qal impf 3ms, ps 1cs	cj, pers pron	art, n ms	prep, n ms
אָנִי	חָכַמְתִּי	וְלָמָּה	יִקְרֵנִי	גַּם־אָנִי	הַכְּסִיל	כְּמִקְרֵה
'ānî	chākhamtî	welāmmāh	yiqŏrēnî	gam-'ānî	hakkesîl	kemiqŏrēh
I	have I been wise	so why	it will happen to me	also I	the fool	like the event of

3706	**16.**	1961	8054, 1612, 2172	904, 3949	1744.315	3252	226
cj		n ms	rel part, cj, dem pron	prep, n ms, ps 1cs	cj, v Piel pf 1cs	n ms	adv
כִּי		הֶבֶל	שֶׁגַּם־זֶה	בְּלִבִּי	וְדִבַּרְתִּי	יוֹתֵר	אָז
kî		hāvel	sheggam-zeh	velibbî	wedhibbartî	yôthēr	'āz
because		a vanity	that also this	in my heart	and I spoke	a remainder	then

3219	904, 8054, 3647	3937, 5986	6196, 3809	3937, 2550	2230	375
art, n mp	prep, rel part, adv	prep, n ms	prep, art, n ms	prep, art, n ms	n ms	sub
הַיָּמִים	בְּשֶׁכְּבָר	לְעוֹלָם	עִם־הַכְּסִיל	לֶחָכָם	זִכְרוֹן	אֵין
hayyāmîm	beshekkevār	le'ôlām	'im-hakkesîl	lechākhām	zikhrōn	'ên
the days	in that already	unto eternity	with the fool	of the wise	a remembrance	there is not

6196, 3809	2550	4322.121	351	8319.255	3725	971.152
prep, art, n ms	art, n ms	v Qal impf 3ms	cj, adv	v Niphal ptc ms	art, n ms	art, v Qal act ptc mp
עִם־הַכְּסִיל	הֶחָכָם	יָמוּת	וְאֵיךְ	נִשְׁכָּח	הַכֹּל	הַבָּאִים
'im-hakkesîl	hechākhām	yāmûth	we'ēkh	nishkāch	hakkōl	habbā'îm
with the fool	the wise	will he die	and how	being forgotten	everything	those coming

17.	7983.115	881, 2522	3706	7737	6142	4801	8054, 6449.211
	cj, v Qal pf 1cs	do, art, n mp	cj	adj	prep, ps 1cs	art, n ms	rel part, v Niphal pf 3ms
	וְשָׂנֵאתִי	אֶת־הַחַיִּים	כִּי	רַע	עָלַי	הַמַּעֲשֶׂה	שֶׁנַּעֲשָׂה
	wesānē'thî	'eth-hachayyîm	kî	ra'	'ālay	hamma'ăseh	shenna'ăsāh
	and I hated	the life	because	evil	on me	the deed	which it had been done

8809	8507	3706, 3725	1961	7758	7593	**18.**	7983.115
prep	art, n ms	cj, art, n ms	n ms	cj, n fs	n ms		cj, v Qal pf 1cs
תַּחַת	הַשָּׁמֶשׁ	כִּי־הַכֹּל	הֶבֶל	וּרְעוּת	רוּחַ		וְשָׂנֵאתִי
tachath	hashshāmesh	kî-hakkōl	hevel	ûre'ûth	rûach		wesānē'thî
under	the sun	because everything	a vanity	and a striving for	wind		and I hated

603	881, 3725, 6219	8054, 603	6221	8809	8507
pers pron	do, adj, n ms, ps 1cs	rel part, pers pron	n ms	prep	art, n ms
אָנִי	אֶת־כָּל־עֲמָלִי	שֶׁאֲנִי	עָמֵל	תַּחַת	הַשָּׁמֶשׁ
'ānî	'eth-kol-'ămālî	she'ănî	'āmēl	tachath	hashshāmesh
I	all my toil	which I	a laborer	under	the sun

8054, 5299.525	3937, 119	8054, 2030.121	313	**19.**	4449
rel part, v Hiphil impf 1cs, ps 3ms	prep, art, n ms	rel pron, v Qal impf 3ms	adv, ps 1cs		cj, intrg
שֶׁאֲנִיחֶנּוּ	לָאָדָם	שֶׁיִּהְיֶה	אַחֲרַי		וּמִי
she'anîchennû	lā'ādhām	shêyihyeh	'achăray		ûmî
which I will leave it	to the man	who he will be	after me		and who

and why was I then more wise?: ... how then is wisdom an advantage?, *Anchor* ... what then is the good of my being wiser?, *Beck* ... why am I more instructed than the rest?, *Fenton* ... was not I the fool, that toiled to achieve wisdom more than he?, *Knox*.

Then I said in my heart, that this also is vanity: ... I concluded that this too was futility, *Anchor* ... is to no purpose, *BB* ... that also is useless!, *Fenton* ... I found labour lost, here too, *Knox*.

16. For there is no remembrance of the wise more than of the fool for ever: ... wise man, like the fool, will not be long remembered, *NIV* ... there is no enduring remembrance of the wise or of fools, *NRSV* ... The wise person is remembered no longer than the fool, *REB*.

seeing that which now is in the days to come shall all be forgotten: ... in days to come both will be forgotten, *NIV* ... in the days to come all will have been long forgotten, *NRSV* ... in the days to come both will have been forgotten, *REB*.

And how dieth the wise man? as the fool: ... Like the fool, the wise man too must die!, *NIV* ... How can the wise die just like fools?, *NRSV*

... both wise and foolish are doomed to die!, *REB*.

17. Therefore I hated life: ... I came to hate life, *Anchor* ... Life I have come to hate, *JB* ... I became weary of life itself, *Knox* ... I loathed life, *NAB*.

because the work that is wrought under the sun is grievous unto me: ... felt bad about everything accomplished under the sun, *Beck* ... the work which was done under the sun seemed bad to me, *Berkeley* ... everything under the sun was evil to me, *BB* ... for everything that is done under the sun seemed to me wrong, *Goodspeed*.

for all is vanity and vexation of spirit: ... only a vapor and a clutching at the wind, *Anchor* ... all is fruitless and chasing after wind, *Berkeley* ... all is to no purpose and desire for wind, *BB* ... all is futility and chasing after the wind, *JB*.

18. Yea, I hated all my labour which I had taken under the sun: ... Hate had I for all my work which I had done, *BB* ... all my works,— that I had striven for, *Fenton* ... hated all that I had toiled at, *Moffatt* ... I detested all the fruits of my labor, *NAB*.

because I should leave it unto the man that shall be after me: ... the man who comes after me will have its fruits, *BB* ... bequeath to my successor, *JB* ... knowing I must leave it to the man who follows me, *Moffatt* ... since I should have to leave its fruits to my successor, *NEB*.

19. And who knoweth whether he shall be a wise man or a fool?: ... I don't know if he will be wise or foolish, *NCV* ... What sort of a man will he be who succeeds me, *NEB*.

yet shall he have rule over all my labour wherein I have laboured: ... will have it all in his own hands, all I have won by my toil and trouble and skill, *Moffatt* ... will have control over all the fruits of my wise labor, *NAB* ... will control everything for which I worked so hard, *NCV* ... will be master of all for which I toiled, *RSV*.

and wherein I have shown myself wise under the sun: ... used my wisdom, *NRSV, RSV* ... wherein I had acted wisely, *Rotherham* ... I have done wisely, *Young*.

This is also vanity: ... is also useless, *NCV* ... is emptiness, *NEB* ... is meaningless, *NIV* ... is futility, *REB*.

2:16–17. We have been reminded before how fleeting is the remembrance of names mighty in their generation. To the mass there is often no remembrance of the wise more than the fool. Every new generation raises up a new race of rivals for renown. But after a short-lived day, that which now is, in the days to come will be forgotten. Few, comparatively, survive the wreck of time.

But take another contrast of the two classes. The one is secured everlasting remembrance; the other is doomed to degraded oblivion (Ps. 112:6; Prov. 10:7). Does the one die as the other? Darkness and light are not more different. Hear the wise man's history of them both. "The wicked is driven away in his wickedness: but the righteous hath hope in his death" (Prov. 14:32).

Yet this equalizing level was a source of deep exercise to the Preacher. Estranged as he now was from God, fretfulness stirred up a disgust and weariness of life. All became a grievous vanity. To die and to be forgotten as the fool seems living to no purpose to the man of wisdom. He would almost as soon be blotted out of life, as be disappointed of his airy vision—an enduring name. When self is thus the center of happiness—the great end of life—what a treasure of vanity do we lay in store for ourselves!

2:18–23. This passage presents another aspect of vanity, and to the wise man a great grief. All his great works of wisdom and labor, which had ministered to him a temporary satisfaction, after a while became to him objects of disgust. They must be left, and to whom he could not tell. David had no such

3156.151	2550	2030.121	173	5722	8375.121	904, 3725, 6219
v Qal act ptc ms	art, n ms	v Qal impf 3ms	cj	adj	cj, v Qal impf 3ms	prep, adj, n ms, ps 1cs
יוֹדֵעַ	הֶחָכָם	יִהְיֶה	אוֹ	סָכָל	וְיִשְׁלַט	בְּכָל־עֲמָלִי
yôdhēa'	hechākhām	yihyeh	'ô	sākhol	weyishlaṭ	bekhol-'ămālî
knowing	the wise	he will be	or	foolish	then he will gain power	by all my toil

8054, 6218.115	8054, 2549.115	8809	8507	1612, 2172	1961
rel part, v Qal pf 1cs	cj, rel part, v Qal pf 1cs	prep	art, n ms	cj, dem pron	n ms
שֶׁעָמַלְתִּי	וְשֶׁחָכַמְתִּי	תַּחַת	הַשָּׁמֶשׁ	גַּם־זֶה	הֶבֶל
she'āmaltî	weshechākhamtî	tachath	hashshāmesh	gam-zeh	hāvel
which I had toiled	and which I had become wise	under	the sun	also this	a vanity

20.

5621.115	603	3937, 3085.341	881, 3949	6142	3725, 6219
cj, v Qal pf 1cs	pers pron	prep, v Piel inf con	do, n ms, ps 1cs	prep	adj, art, n ms
וְסַבּוֹתִי	אֲנִי	לְיָאֵשׁ	אֶת־לִבִּי	עַל	כָּל־הֶעָמָל
wesabbôthî	'ănî	leya'ēsh	'eth-libbî	'al	kol-he'āmāl
so I turned around	I	to cause despair to	my heart	about	all the toil

8054, 6218.115	8809	8507	21.	3706, 3552	119	8054, 6219
rel part, v Qal pf 1cs	prep	art, n ms		cj, sub	n ms	rel part, n ms, ps 3ms
שֶׁעָמַלְתִּי	תַּחַת	הַשָּׁמֶשׁ		כִּי־יֵשׁ	אָדָם	שֶׁעֲמָלוֹ
she'āmaltî	tachath	hashshāmesh		kî-yēsh	'ādhām	she'āmālô
which I had toiled	under	the sun		because there is	a man	which his toil

904, 2551	904, 1907	904, 3917	3937, 119	8054, 3940
prep, n fs	cj, prep, n fs	cj, prep, n ms	cj, prep, n ms	rel pron, neg part
בְּחָכְמָה	וּבְדַעַת	וּבְכִשְׁרוֹן	וּלְאָדָם	שֶׁלֹּא
bechokhmāh	ûvedha'ath	ûvekhishrôn	ûlĕ'ādhām	shellō'
with wisdom	and with knowledge	and with skill	but to a man	who not

6218.111, 904	5598.121	2610	1612, 2172	1961	7750	7521
v Qal pf 3ms, prep, ps 3ms	v Qal impf 3ms, ps 3ms	n ms, ps 3ms	cj, dem pron	n ms	cj, n fs	adj
עָמַל־בּוֹ	יִתְּנֶנּוּ	חֶלְקוֹ	גַּם־זֶה	הֶבֶל	וְרָעָה	רַבָּה
'āmal-bô	yittenennû	chelqô	gam-zeh	hevel	werā'āh	rabbāh
he toiled with it	he will give him	his portion	also this	a vanity	and an evil	abundant

22.

3706	4242, 2030.151	3937, 119	904, 3725, 6219	904, 7763
cj	intrg, v Qal act ptc ms	prep, art, n ms	prep, adj, n ms, ps 3ms	cj, prep, n ms
כִּי	מֶה־הֹוֶה	לָאָדָם	בְּכָל־עֲמָלוֹ	וּבְרַעְיוֹן
kî	meh-hôweh	lā'ādhām	bekhol-'ămālô	ûvera'ăyôn
because	what being	to humankind	because of all his toil	and by the striving of

3949	8054, 2000	6221	8809	8507	23.	3706	3725, 3219	4480
n ms, ps 3ms	rel part, pers pron	n ms	prep	art, n ms		cj	adj, n mp, ps 3ms	n mp
לִבּוֹ	שֶׁהוּא	עָמָל	תַּחַת	הַשָּׁמֶשׁ		כִּי	כָּל־יָמָיו	מַכְאֹבִים
libbô	shehû'	'āmēl	tachath	hashshāmesh		kî	khol-yāmāv	makh'ōvîm
his heart	which it	a labor	under	the sun		because	all his days	pains

3833	6275	1612, 904, 4050	3940, 8311.111	3949	1612, 2172
cj, n ms	n ms, ps 3ms	cj, prep, art, n ms	neg part, v Qal pf 3ms	n ms, ps 3ms	cj, dem pron
וְכַעַס	עִנְיָנוֹ	גַּם־בַּלַּיְלָה	לֹא־שָׁכַב	לִבּוֹ	גַּם־זֶה
wākha'as	'inyānô	gam-ballaylāh	lō'-shākhav	libbô	gam-zeh
and a vexation	his occupation	also in the night	it has not lain	his heart	also this

1961	2000	24.	375, 3005	904, 119	8054, 404.121	8685.111
n ms	pers pron		sub, adj	prep, art, n ms	rel part, v Qal impf 3ms	cj, v Qal pf 3ms
הֶבֶל	הוּא		אֵין־טוֹב	בָּאָדָם	שֶׁיֹּאכַל	וְשָׁתָה
hevel	hû'		'ên-ṭôv	bā'ādhām	sheyō'khal	weshāthāh
a vanity	it		there is not good	with humankind	that he will eat	and he will drink

20. Therefore I went about to cause my heart to despair: … So once more I fell into despair, *Anchor* … So my mind was turned to grief, *BB* … So I abandoned my mind to despair, *Fenton* … So I became sad, *NCV.*

of all the labour which I took under the sun: … about all that I had achieved, *Anchor* … for all the trouble I had taken and all my wisdom, *BB* … over all the objects I had attempted, *Fenton* … about all the hard work I had done, *NCV.*

21. For there is a man whose labour is in wisdom, and in knowledge, and in equity: … here is one who has laboured wisely, skilfully and successfully, *JB* … a man who has toiled skilfully and thoughtfully and ably, *Moffatt* … People can work hard using all their wisdom, knowledge, and skill, *NCV* … a man who has worked hard with intelligence, knowledge, and skill, *Beck.*

yet to a man that hath not laboured therein shall he leave it for his portion: … must leave what is his own to someone who has not toiled for it at all, *JB* … has to leave all his gains to one who has never worked for them, *Moffatt* … they will die, and other people will get the things for which they worked, *NCV* … must leave his heritage to a man who has not labored for it, *NKJV.*

This also is vanity and a great evil: … is futile too, and grossly unjust, *JB* … is also unfair and useless, *NCV* … is emptiness and utterly wrong, *NEB* … is meaningless and a great misfortune, *NIV.*

22. For what hath man of all his labour, and of the vexation of his heart: … how does a man benefit from all the toil and stress, *Anchor* … What does a man get for all his work and striving, *Beck* … what does a man get for all his toil and for all his heart's striving, *Berkeley* … What

does a man get for all his work, and for the weight of care, *BB.*

wherein he hath laboured under the sun?: … of his lifelong struggle?, *Anchor* … with which he wearies himself, *Beck, Berkeley* … with which he has done his work, *BB* … that he has striven for, *Fenton.*

23. For all his days are sorrows, and his travail grief: … all his days are griefs, and his efforts sorrows, *Fenton* … all his days are sorrowful and his task is melancholy, *Goodspeed* … his days are full of sorrow, his work is full of stress, *JB* … His days all painfulness and care, *Knox.*

yea, his heart taketh not rest in the night: … and his mind does not rest at night!, *Fenton* … at night his mind finds no rest, *Goodspeed* … even at night he has no peace of mind?, *JB* … his very nights restless, *Knox.*

---

anxieties. His heart had not been set upon his treasures, and therefore it was no sacrifice to him to part with them. Besides, he well knew the consecrated use to which his wise son would apply them (1 Chr. 28:11–21; 29:1–22). But Solomon probably had his forebodings of the man who should come after him. And the history of the son fully justified the anxious question, Who knows whether he will be a wise man or a fool? (Ps. 49:10; cp. 39:6). Must he, after a life of labor in wisdom, knowledge, and equity, become a drudge to his successor, of whom he knows nothing with any certainty? What advantage has he of all his labor? He heaps up his words one upon another (labor, sorrow, grief, travail), to describe more emphatically the painfulness of his exercise.

And yet this great evil may have been overruled for Solomon's good. His heart had clung to the world, and it required sharp discipline to break it away. But repeated failures caused his heart to despair. And might not this restlessness of earthly rest have been his Father's restoring discipline? This is the canker on the supreme pursuit of this world's portion. We may possess the creature, but, we will never enjoy it until God is on the throne above it (Ps. 73:25). There will be no cleaving to God until the vanity of all, in comparison with Him,

has been experimentally acknowledged. O my God may I feel the vanity of everything that turns my heart away from You!

The special trial, however, to which Solomon here alludes, presses heavily upon many a Christian heart. Will the fruits of our labor descend from us into worthy or unworthy hands? to a wise man or a fool? Will they be devoted to the Church or be desecrated to the world? Will we be able to perpetuate a good name in godly, well-doing children and to commit our trust into their hands with peaceful confidence? How this anxious exercise urges upon us the obligation of training our children for God!

If this is a severe trial of faith to the Christian, what is the threatened chastisement to the ungodly without a refuge, covenant promises or sustaining support? (v. 26; Deut. 28:30–33). All his labor barren! All his days a mind racked with care. Even night brings no rest. All is vanity. Who will not listen to the pleading voice of the Savior, contrasting this field of fruitless disappointment with his own offer of solid peace and satisfaction? Welcome every sinner that feels his need of this precious remedy!

2:24–26. The surface view of this passage might seem to savor the rule, "Let us eat and drink: for tomorrow we die" (1 Cor. 15:32; cp. Luke

3706 cj	603 pers pron	7495.115 v Qal pf 1cs	1612, 2173 cj, dem pron	904, 6219 prep, n ms, ps 3ms	3005 adj	881, 5497 do, n fs, ps 3ms	7495.511 cj, v Hiphil pf 3ms
כִּי	אָנִי	רָאִיתִי	גַם־זֹה	בַּעֲמָלוֹ	טוֹב	אֶת־נַפְשׁוֹ	וְהֶרְאָה
kî	'ānî	rā'îthî	gam-zōh	ba'ămālô	tôv	'eth-naphshô	weher'āh
that	I	I have seen	also this	in his toil	good	his soul	and he will cause to see

4449 cj, intrg	404.121 v Qal impf 3ms	4449 intrg	3706 cj	25.	2026 pers pron	435 art, n mp	4623, 3135 prep, n fs
וּמִי	יֹאכַל	מִי	כִּי		הִיא	הָאֱלֹהִים	מִיָּד
ûmî	yō'khal	mî	kî		hî'	hā'ĕlōhîm	mîyadh
and who	he will eat more	who	because		it	God	from the hand of

3937, 6686 prep, n mp, ps 3ms	8054, 3005 rel pron, adj	3937, 119 prep, n ms	3706 cj	26.	4623 prep, ps 1cs	2445 n ms	2456.121 v Qal impf 3ms
לְפָנָיו	שֶׁטּוֹב	לְאָדָם	כִּי		מִמֶּנִּי	חוּץ	יָחוּשׁ
lephānâv	shettōv	le'ādhām	kî		mimmenî	chûts	yāchûsh
before Him	who good	to a man	because		than I	outside	he will hurry more

5598.111 v Qal pf 3ms	2551 n fs	1907 cj, n fs	7977 cj, n fs	3937, 2490.151 cj, prep, art, v Qal act ptc ms	5598.111 v Qal pf 3ms
נָתַן	חָכְמָה	וְדַעַת	וְשִׂמְחָה	וְלַחוֹטֵא	נָתַן
nāthan	chokhmāh	wedha'ath	wesimchāh	welachôte'	nāthan
He gives	wisdom	and knowledge	and gladness	but to the sinner	He gives

6275 n ms	3937, 636.141 prep, v Qal inf con	3937, 3788.141 cj, prep, v Qal inf con	3937, 5598.141 prep, v Qal inf con	3937, 3005 prep, adj	3937, 6686 prep, n mp
עִנְיָן	לֶאֱסוֹף	וְלִכְנוֹס	לָתֵת	לְטוֹב	לִפְנֵי
'inyān	le'ĕsôph	welikhnôs	lāthēth	letôv	liphnê
an occupation	to gather	and to gather in	to give	to the good	before

435 art, n mp	1612, 2172 cj, dem pron	1961 n ms	7758 cj, n fs	7593 n ms	3:1	3937, 3725 prep, art, n ms	2249 n ms
הָאֱלֹהִים	גַּם־זֶה	הֶבֶל	וּרְעוּת	רוּחַ		לַכֹּל	זְמָן
hā'ĕlōhîm	gam-zeh	hevel	ûre'ûth	rûach		lakkōl	zemān
God	also this	a vanity	and a striving for	wind		for everything	an appointed time

6496 cj, n fs	3937, 3725, 2761 prep, adj, n ms	8809 prep	8452 art, n md	2.	6496 n fs	3937, 3314.141 prep, v Qal inf con	6496 cj, n fs
וְעֵת	לְכָל־חֵפֶץ	תַּחַת	הַשָּׁמַיִם		עֵת	לָלֶדֶת	וְעֵת
we'ēth	lekhol-chēphets	tachath	hashshāmayim		'ēth	lāledheth	we'ēth
and a time	for every desire	under	the heavens		a time	to bear a child	and a time

This is also vanity: ... is futile too, *JB* ... what is here but frustration?, *Knox* ... is also useless, *NCV* ... is emptiness, *NEB* ... is meaningless, *NIV.*

24. There is nothing better for a man, than that he should eat and drink: ... is nothing good for man but that he eat and drink, *Goodspeed* ... can do nothing better than to eat and drink, *NIV.*

and that he should make his soul enjoy good in his labour: ... and find satisfaction in his work, *Goodspeed* ... and enjoy himself as he does his work, *Moffatt* ... and provide himself with good things by his labors, *NAB* ... and tell himself that his labor is good, *NASB.*

This also I saw, that it was from the hand of God: ... even this, I came to see, is in God's hands, *Anchor* ... I see that this too comes from God's hand, *JB* ... is what God grants, *Moffatt* ... does not come from any good in a person: it comes from God, *REB.*

25. For who can eat, or who else can hasten hereunto, more than I?: ... who can eat and rejoice apart from him?, *Anchor* ... Without God, who can eat and enjoy himself?, *Beck* ... who can eat with enjoyment apart from Him?, *Berkeley* ... Who may take food or have pleasure without him?, *BB.*

26. For God giveth to a man that is good in his sight wisdom, and knowledge, and joy: ... to a man whom he favors God assigns wisdom, knowledge, and happiness, *Anchor* ... To the man with whom he is pleased, God gives wisdom and knowledge and joy, *BB* ... to the man who pleases HIM, He gives science,

324

and knowledge and pleasure, *Fenton* ... Who wins God's favour, has wisdom and skill for his reward, and pleasure too, *Knox.*

but to the sinner he giveth travail, to gather and to heap up, that he may give to him that is good before God: ... he gives the work of getting goods together and storing up wealth, to give to him in whom God has pleasure, *BB* ... to the offender He gives the trouble to gather and accumulate, to give the product to the pleasing before GOD, *Fenton* ... he gives the task of gathering and collecting that he may give it to the one who is good in God's sight, *Goodspeed* ... on the sinner he lays the task of gathering and storing up for someone else who is pleasing to him, *JB.*

This also is vanity and vexation of spirit: ... is to no purpose and desire for wind, *BB* ... is futility and chasing after the wind, *JB* ... for him the labour lost, *Knox* ... is emptiness and chasing the wind, *NEB.*

3:1. To every thing there is a season: ... Everything has its season, *Anchor* ... is an appointed time for everything, *Beck* ... there is a fixed time, *BB* ... Everything must be done by turns, *Knox.*

and a time to every purpose under the heaven: ... there is a proper time for every happening, *Anchor* ... a right time for everything we want to do, *Beck* ... a time for every business, *BB* ... a time for every occupation, *JB.*

2. A time to be born, and a time to die: ... Men are born only to die, *Knox* ... a time for birth, a time for death, *Moffatt* ... time to bring forth, And a time to die, *Young.*

a time to plant, and a time to pluck up that which is planted: ... plant trees only to displant them, *Knox* ... a time to plant and a time to uproot,

---

12:19). But did Solomon really mean that there was nothing better for a man than sensual indulgence? Far from it! The case before us determines and limits his true meaning. A man is brooding over his disappointments. Let him rejoice in his temporal blessings in thanksgiving to God. This pleasure of eating and drinking is totally distinct from the mere animal appetite. It recognizes the Christian principle, Whether ye eat or drink, do all to the glory of God. The world, with all its legitimate enjoyments, is the Christian's portion (1 Cor. 3:22).

We might also ask where this enjoyment comes from. Is it not reached out to us from the hand of God? Can we think ill of anything that comes from this Source? Here we receive not only the good things themselves but the power to make a right use of them. The Preacher himself could speak with a deep-toned experience, for who can eat, or who haste hereunto, more than he?

No brightness beams upon the sinner's lot. He may be prudent and prosperous, but God gives him travail as his portion. The unfaithful steward is cast out. His privileges are transferred, for better improvement, to him who is good before God. "But to him that soweth righteousness shall be a sure reward" (Prov. 11:18).

3:1. Solomon is still pursuing his argument. Everything around us is in a perpetual change. What vanity, therefore, is it to seek solid happiness in so shifting a scene! As well might we find rest on the tossing ocean as in a fluctuating world. There is no stable center. To everything there is a season, a fixed time, a predetermined purpose on which everything depends. Of this purpose we know nothing, but

"known unto God are all his works from the beginning of the world" (Acts 15:18). His eye has been upon everything, great and small, from all eternity.

There is a season for every work of God. There was a season for Israel's deliverance from Egypt and for the return from Babylon. Nothing could either force on or keep back the time. "On the self-same day," the deliverance was at once developed and consummated (Exo. 12:41; Ezra 1:1). To have looked for it at any other time, whether sooner or later, would only have brought disappointment. There was "the fulness of time," the appointed season, the fittest time, for the Savior's advent (Gal. 4:4). An earlier period would have hindered many important purposes, or at least clouded their full development. The delay demonstrated the utter weakness of all other remedies.

To time things rightly is the property of wisdom. And here indeed "the LORD is a God of judgment: blessed are all they that wait for him" (Isa. 30:18). Remember, the Father's will appointed the season and determined the purpose.

3:2. Solomon begins with the life of man—his time of coming into the world and his time of going out. Neither is in his own purpose or will. Could we see with the eyes of God, we should find these points to be the fittest times that infinite wisdom could ordain, connected with our present responsibilities and our hopes for eternity.

A time to be born! What a moment! A wondrous miracle is wrought! An heir of immortality brought into being, "fearfully and wonderfully made!" "The spirit of God hath made me, and the breath of the Almighty hath given me life" (Job 33:4).

3937, 4322.141	6496	3937, 5378.141	6496	3937, 6369.141	5378.155	6496
prep, v Qal inf con	n fs	prep, v Qal inf con	cj, n fs	prep, v Qal inf con	v Qal pass ptc ms	3. n fs
לָמוּת	עֵת	לָטַעַת	וְעֵת	לַעֲקוֹר	נָטוּעַ	עֵת
lāmûth	'ēth	lāṭa'ath	we'ēth	la'ăqôr	nāṭûa'	'ēth
to die	a time	to plant	and a time	to uproot	what is planted	a time

3937, 2103.141	6496	3937, 7784.141	6496	3937, 6805.141	6496	3937, 1161.141
prep, v Qal inf con	cj, n fs	prep, v Qal inf con	n fs	prep, v Qal inf con	cj, n fs	prep, v Qal inf con
לַהֲרוֹג	וְעֵת	לִרְפּוֹא	עֵת	לִפְרוֹץ	וְעֵת	לִבְנוֹת
lahrōgh	we'ēth	lirpô'	'ēth	liphrôts	we'ēth	livnôth
to kill	and a time	to heal	a time	to break through	and a time	to build

6496	3937, 1098.141	6496	3937, 7925.141	6496	5792.141	6496	7833.141
4. n fs	prep, v Qal inf con	cj, n fs	prep, v Qal inf con	n fs	v Qal inf con	cj, n fs	v Qal inf con
עֵת	לִבְכּוֹת	וְעֵת	לִשְׂחוֹק	עֵת	סְפוֹד	וְעֵת	רְקוֹד
'ēth	livkôth	we'ēth	lischôq	'ēth	sephôdh	we'ēth	reqôdh
a time	to weep	and a time	to laugh	a time	to lament	and a time	to dance

6496	3937, 8390.541	63	6496	3788.141	63	6496	3937, 2354.141
5. n fs	prep, v Hiphil inf con	n fp	cj, n fs	v Qal inf con	n fp	n fs	prep, v Qal inf con
עֵת	לְהַשְׁלִיךְ	אֲבָנִים	וְעֵת	כְּנוֹס	אֲבָנִים	עֵת	לַחֲבוֹק
'ēth	lehashlîkh	'ăvānîm	we'ēth	kenôs	'ăvānîm	'ēth	lachăvôq
a time	to cast away	stones	and a time	to gather	stones	a time	to embrace

6496	3937, 7651.141	4623, 2354.341	6496	3937, 1272.341	6496	3937, 6.341
cj, n fs	prep, v Qal inf con	prep, v Piel inf con	6. n fs	prep, v Piel inf con	cj, n fs	prep, v Piel inf con
וְעֵת	לִרְחֹק	מֵחַבֵּק	עֵת	לְבַקֵּשׁ	וְעֵת	לְאַבֵּד
we'ēth	lirchōq	mēchabbēq	'ēth	levaqqēsh	we'ēth	le'abbēdh
and a time	to be far	from embracing	a time	to seek	and a time	to lose

6496	3937, 8490.141	6496	3937, 8390.541	6496	3937, 7458.141	6496
n fs	prep, v Qal inf con	cj, n fs	prep, v Hiphil inf con	7. n fs	prep, v Qal inf con	cj, n fs
עֵת	לִשְׁמוֹר	וְעֵת	לְהַשְׁלִיךְ	עֵת	לִקְרוֹעַ	וְעֵת
'ēth	lishmōr	we'ēth	lehashlîkh	'ēth	liqôrōa'	we'ēth
a time	to keep	and a time	to cast away	a time	to tear away	and a time

Moffatt, NIV … A time to plant, And a time to eradicate the planted, *Young.*

3. A time to kill, and a time to heal: … A time to put to death and a time to make well, *BB* … A time to wound, and a time to cure, *Fenton* … Now we take life, now we save it, *Knox* … A time to slay, And a time to heal, *Young.*

a time to break down, and a time to build up: … A time to wreck and a time to build, *Anchor* … a time for pulling down and a time for building up, *BB* … A time to tear down, and a time to rebuild, *Goodspeed* … now we are destroying, now building, *Knox.*

4. A time to weep, and a time to laugh: … A time for weeping and a time for laughing, *BB* … A time for tears, a time for laughter, *JB* … Weep first, then laugh, *Knox.*

a time to mourn, and a time to dance: … A time to lament and a time to dance for joy, *Anchor* … a time for sorrow and a time for dancing, *BB* … mourn we and dance, *Knox* … A time to wail, and a time to dance for joy, *Rotherham.*

5. A time to cast away stones, and a time to gather stones together: … A time to take stones away and a time to get stones together, *BB* … A time to pick stones, and a time to cast out, *Fenton* … A time for throwing stones away, a time for gathering them, *JB.*

a time to embrace, and a time to refrain from embracing: … a time to hug and a time to keep from hugging, *Beck* … a time for kissing and a time to keep from kissing, *BB* … A time to fold hands, and a time to unfold, *Fenton.*

6. A time to get, and a time to lose: … A time to seek and a time to give up, *Anchor* … a time to search and a time to lose, *Beck* … To-day's gain, to-morrow's loss, *Knox* … A time to search, and a time to give up as lost, *NASB.*

a time to keep, and a time to cast away: … a time to keep and a time to throw away, *Beck* … a time to retain, and a time to throw away, *Berkeley* … a time to keep and a time to give away, *BB* … A time to hoard, and a time to spend, *Fenton.*

There is also appointed to us a time to die. How came this time? Immortality was our original being (Gen. 1:26). "By one man sin entered into the world, and death by sin" (Rom. 5:12). Ever since, "it is appointed unto men once to die" (Gen. 3:19; Heb. 9:27). Our "days are determined, the number of his months are with thee; thou hast appointed his bounds that he cannot pass" (Job 14:5).

If our steps are ordered by the LORD (Ps. 37:23), much more is the last step of all—the step out of one world into another, out of time into eternity.

Within the boundary of life there is a time to plant and a time to pluck up that which is planted. Planting had been to Solomon a matter of primary interest (2:4f). But how soon might the season come to undo his own work and to pluck up that which was planted! A garden or estate is often laid out with plantation, whether for present pleasure or future advantage. Yet change of mind or of taste may induce the owner to pluck up.

3:3. "A time to kill, and a time to heal; a time to break down, and a time to build up." The time to die is the immediate appointment of God. The time to kill is the act of man under permissive providence. The same providence gives the healing blessing. In both cases God claims his own prerogative. Hezekiah's case displayed the exercise of both these branches of prerogative. For while the Sustainer of life declared his purpose to kill, He then showed his relenting mercy and healing (Isa. 38; also 2 Ki. 5:7).

The same changeableness belongs to our estates as to our persons. Solomon had been much occupied in building up (1 Ki. 9:15–19). But many of his buildings, even the walls of Jerusalem, were destined to be broken down (2 Ki. 25:4–10). Our confidence is secure in only one building—the "house not made with hands, eternal in the heavens" (2 Cor. 5:1).

3:4. These two instances are evidently a repetition with increasing emphasis. The mourning is the most poignant weeping. The dancing expresses not only the laughter of the lips but the exuberant excitement of the whole man. These are God's times. Beware of changing them. It is a fearful provocation to respond "joy and gladness" when "the Lord GOD of Hosts call to weeping, and to mourning" (Isa. 22:12ff).

Who has not found the time to weep and mourn? "Man is born unto trouble, as the sparks fly upward" (Job 5:7; 14:1). And yet lesson after lesson is needed to make us know the world to be a vale of tears. We look around to the right or the left to avoid this or that trouble. Is not this looking out for some side road where we will meet neither with promises, comfort, nor guidance? Be content with your appointed lot. The tears of the child of God have more of the element of happiness than the laughter of the ungodly. Yet we may look for a change of seasons in God's best and fittest time. A portion "double for all his sorrows" was poured into Job's bosom. The mouths "of the returning captives" were filled with laughter, and their tongue with singing (Ps. 106:1f).

3:5. The natural reference would be to casting away of stones when they were useless, or perhaps a hindrance to the soil, and gathering them when they were used for some profitable purpose. Such use was often made of them in olden times. They were the memorials of the covenant between Jacob and Laban (Gen. 31:44–51). They were the remembrance of God's miracle in the passage of Jordan (Josh. 4:1–9). Shortly after, they were the broad beacon of rebuke in Achan's sin (Josh. 7:26.) In later days, they were the trophy of the victory over Absalom (2 Sam. 18:17). In every such case there was a divine purpose and a suitable season.

Passing into the social sphere, the exercise of the affections affords instances of change—sometimes indulgence and sometimes restraint (1 Cor. 7:3ff). The embrace of parental love would naturally be warm (Prov. 23:24). Yet it might be wisely refrained toward a refractory child (Prov. 17:25).

3:6. We see men with their whole heart in their business. Industry is successful. Money flows in. Here is the time to get (Prov. 10:4f) and, for a while at least, a time to keep. But the providence of God has fixed a time to lose. Speculation or untoward circumstances have given wings to riches, and they have flown away (Prov. 23:5). Many a fortune, obtained by the toil of years and kept with care, has been lost in a day. Many an estate, received through inheritance, has been cast away by reckless extravagance. Such is the uncertainty of a worldly portion.

3:7. The reference to the garment is obvious. The rending was the sign of intense grief. The sewing, therefore, was probably the preparing of the garment for some joyful occasion. Here then we have again the time to weep and the time to laugh.

A time of sorrow also must be mentioned as a time of restraint. Precious words are often wasted at this season. The time of silence is more soothing. We had better restrain our words till the waters have somewhat assuaged. A talkative comforter adds to

3937, 8944	6496	3937, 2924.141	6496	3937, 1744.341		6496	3937, 154.141
prep, v Qal inf con	n fs	prep, v Qal inf con	cj, n fs	prep, v Piel inf con		n fs	prep, v Qal inf con
לִתְפּוֹר	עֵת	לַחֲשׁוֹת	וְעֵת	לְדַבֵּר	8.	עֵת	לֶאֱהֹב
lithpôr	'ēth	lachăshôth	w^{e}'ēth	l^{e}dhabbēr		'ēth	le'ěhōv
to sew	a time	to be silent	and a time	to speak		a time	to love

6496	3937, 7983.141	6496	4560	6496	8361		4242, 3620
cj, n fs	prep, v Qal inf con	*n fs*	n fs	cj, *n fs*	n ms		intrg, n ms
וְעֵת	לִשְׂנֹא	עֵת	מִלְחָמָה	וְעֵת	שָׁלוֹם	9.	מַה־יִּתְרוֹן
w^{e}'ēth	lisnō'	'ēth	milchāmāh	w^{e}'ēth	shālôm		mah-yithrôn
and a time	to hate	a time of	war	and a time of	peace		what is the profit

6449.151	904, 866	2000	6221		7495.115	881, 6275	866
art, v Qal act ptc ms	prep, rel part	pers pron	n ms		v Qal pf 1cs	do, art, n ms	rel part
הָעוֹשֶׂה	בַּאֲשֶׁר	הוּא	עָמֵל	10.	רָאִיתִי	אֶת־הָעִנְיָן	אֲשֶׁר
hā'ôseh	ba'ăsher	hû'	'āmēl		rā'îthî	'eth-hā'inyān	'ăsher
the worker	where	he	a laborer		I have seen	the occupation	that

5598.111	435	3937, 1158	119	3937, 6257.141	904		881, 3725
v Qal pf 3ms	n mp	prep, *n mp*	art, n ms	prep, v Qal inf con	prep, ps 3ms		do, art, n ms
נָתַן	אֱלֹהִים	לִבְנֵי	הָאָדָם	לַעֲנוֹת	בּוֹ	11.	אֶת־הַכֹּל
nāthan	'ělōhîm	livnê	hā'ādhām	la'ănôth	bô		'eth-hakkōl
He has given	God	to the sons of	humankind	to be afflicted	with it		everything

6449.111	3413	904, 6496	1612	881, 5986	5598.111	904, 3949	4623, 1136
v Qal pf 3ms	adj	prep, n fs, ps 3ms	cj	do, art, n ms	v Qal pf 3ms	prep, n ms, ps 3mp	prep, part
עָשָׂה	יָפֶה	בְעִתּוֹ	גַּם	אֶת־הָעֹלָם	נָתַן	בְּלִבָּם	מִבְּלִי
'āsāh	yāpheh	v^{e}'ittô	gam	'eth-hā'ōlām	nāthan	b^{e}libbām	mibb^{e}lî
He has made	beautiful	in its season	also	the eternity	He has given	in their heart	without

866	3940, 4834.121	119	881, 4801	866, 6449.111	435
rel part	neg part, v Qal impf 3ms	art, n ms	do, art, n ms	rel part, v Qal pf 3ms	art, n mp
אֲשֶׁר	לֹא־יִמְצָא	הָאָדָם	אֶת־הַמַּעֲשֶׂה	אֲשֶׁר־עָשָׂה	הָאֱלֹהִים
'ăsher	lō'-yimtsā'	hā'ādhām	'eth-hamma'ăseh	'ăsher-'āsāh	hā'ělōhîm
which	he will not find	humankind	the deeds	which He has done	God

4623, 7513	5912, 5677		3156.115	3706	375	3005	904	3706
prep, n ms	cj, adv, n ms		v Qal pf 1cs	cj	*sub*	adj	prep, ps 3mp	cj
מֵרֹאשׁ	וְעַד־סוֹף	12.	יָדַעְתִּי	כִּי	אֵין	טוֹב	בָּם	כִּי
mērō'sh	w^{e}'adh-s̱ôph		yādha'ttî	kî	'ên	ṯôv	bām	kî
from the first	even until the end		I know	that	there is not	good	in them	except

7. A time to rend, and a time to sew: ... A time to tear apart, and a time to sew together, *NASB* ... a time to tear and a time to mend, *NEB, NIV.*

a time to keep silence, and a time to speak: ... A time to keep quiet, and a time to talk, *Goodspeed* ... a time for silence and a time for speech, *Moffatt, REB.*

8. A time to love, and a time to hate: ... love alternating with hatred, *Knox* ... A time for love and a time for hate, *BB.*

a time of war, and a time of peace: ... A time for war and a time for peace, *Anchor.*

9. What profit hath he that worketh in that wherein he laboureth?: ... What does a worker get for wearing himself out?, *Beck* ... What benefit does the workman get from that for which he wears himself out?, *Berkeley* ... What do people gain from the efforts they make?, *JB* ... What does a busy man gain from his toil?, *Moffatt.*

10. I have seen the travail: ... the sore task, *Anchor* ... the employment, *Berkeley* ... saw the work, *BB* ... examined the endeavours, *Fenton.*

which God hath given to the sons of men to be exercised in it: ... assigns to men to afflict them, *Anchor* ... has granted men to be engaged, *Berkeley* ... has put on the sons of men, *BB* ... appointed for the children of Adam, *Fenton.*

11. He hath made every thing beautiful in his time: ... right in its time, *BB* ... beautiful in its season,

Goodspeed ... is apt for its time, *JB* ... assigned each to its proper time, *Moffatt.*

also he hath set the world in their heart: ... made their hearts without knowledge, *BB* ... has also implanted ignorance in their mind, *Goodspeed* ... has given us an awareness of the passage of time, *JB* ... for the mind of man he has appointed mystery, *Moffatt.*

so that no man can find out the work that God maketh from the beginning to the end: ... is unable to see the works of God, from the first to the last, *BB* ... cannot discover the work which God has done from beginning to end, *Goodspeed* ... we can grasp neither the beginning nor the end of what God does, *JB* ... that man may never fathom God's own purpose from beginning to end, *Moffatt.*

12. I know that there is no good in them: ... there is no happiness for a human being, *JB* ... there is nothing better for them, *MAST, MRB* ... the best thing for them, *NCV* ... there is nothing good for man, *NEB.*

but for a man to rejoice, and to do good in his life: ... except in pleasure and enjoyment through life, *JB* ... than to rejoice, and to get pleasure so long as they live, *MAST* ... than to

---

the trouble he professes to heal. He is rather a sore than a balm. Great wisdom is required to know when, as well as what, to speak.

The wise improvement of the time to speak brings a diversified and fruitful blessing. The fool is restrained (Prov. 26:5). The afflicted is comforted (2 Thess. 4:18; 5:14). Christian rebuke is rightly and lovingly administered. The ignorant is instructed (Prov. 10:21; Isa. 50:4). Succor is given in the time of extremity (Est. 7:4; Prov. 31:8f). Sound knowledge is dispersed in our respective spheres (Prov. 15:7).

3:8. The first clause probably refers to the individual feelings; the latter to public movements. Love is emphatically called "the bond of perfectness"—the very bond of peace and of all virtues. A time to love is, therefore, the appointed time and sphere for the exercise of love in the natural flow of sympathy, or gratitude, or the impulse of a natural affection. Hatred, under the most aggravated personal provocations, is forbidden (Matt. 5:43f). It can only therefore be admissible in our relation to God, which constrains us to count his enemies to be ours.

The same principles find the full sphere for their exercise in the wider field. There is a time of war, whether arising from men's ungoverned passions (Jam. 4:1), the just reparation of injury (Gen. 14:14–17) or some legitimate occasion of self-defense (2 Sam. 10:3–6). All this is not chance. It is the providence or permissive control of the Great Ruler of the universe. War is his chastisement; peace his returning blessing. It is his prerogative to "make wars to cease unto the ends of the earth" (Ps. 46:9); to "scatter the people that delight in war" (Ps. 68:30); and, when the sword has done its appointed work, to "make peace in the borders of his people" (Ps. 147:14). "When he gives quietness, who then can cause trouble? and when he hideth his face, who then can behold him? whether it be done against a nation, or against a man only" (Job 34:29).

3:9. The question is again repealed—What profit can man's labor bring out for his true happiness? We may thank God for a thousand disappointments, if only we have learned the valuable lesson, not to look for indulgence, where he intends discipline. He may permit some apparently casual event to sweep away the result of years. If the world has left you dissatisfied, restless and unhappy, let God's remedy be fairly tried. If this does not fill up the void, ease the disquietude, and sustain the heart in the conflict, let it be cast away.

3:10. Solomon had seen all the changes of life and marked the divine reason for them. They were not the fruit of blind confusion but the chastening travail, which God gives to the sons of men to be exercised in it. Never was it his purpose that earth should be his children's home. The consecrated pathway, therefore, to the "rest that remaineth to" them is appointed "through much tribulation." Christian confidence is the present fruit of this travail in the school of discipline. And all will end at last in the unclouded brightness of the eternal consummation.

3:11. This was the judgment of God of his created works: "very good" (Gen. 1:31). Each was marked by its own peculiar beauty. The minutest insect to the eye of Christian intelligence displays a beauty, as if the whole divine mind had been centered in its formation. Everything is suited to its appointed use and service, the combination of circumstances fitting in their proper places—all in due connection and dependence.

He has set the world in the heart of man as the object of his intense interest and delight. He has put into his heart a vast desire to study and great power to comprehend it in all its order and beauty. But no man can find out the work that God makes from beginning to the end.

3:12–13. This statement is often repeated in substance. The repetition shows its importance.

3725, 119	1612	**13.**	904, 2522	3005	3937, 6449.141	524, 3937, 7975.141
adj, art, n ms	cj, cj		prep, n mp, ps 3ms	adj	cj, prep, v Qal inf con	cj, pre, v Qal inf con
כָּל־הָאָדָם	וְגַם		בְּחַיָּיו	טוֹב	וְלַעֲשׂוֹת	אִם־לִשְׂמוֹחַ
kol-hā'ādhām	wegham		bechayyâv	tôv	wela'asôth	'im-lismôach
every man	and also		during their lifetime	good	and to do	to rejoice

435	5164	904, 3725, 6219	3005	7495.111	8685.111	8054, 404.121
n mp	*n fs*	prep, *adj*, n ms, ps 3ms	adj	cj, v Qal pf 3ms	cj, v Qal pf 3ms	rel part, v Qal impf 3ms
אֱלֹהִים	מַתַּת	בְּכָל־עֲמָלוֹ	טוֹב	וְרָאָה	וְשָׁתָה	שֶׁיֹּאכַל
'ĕlōhîm	mattath	bekhol-'āmālô	tôv	werā'āh	weshāthāh	shêyō'khal
God	a gift of	in all his toil	good	and he will see	and he will drink	that he will eat

2026	**14.**	3156.115	3706	3725, 866	6449.121	435	2000	2030.121
pers pron		v Qal pf 1cs	cj	*adj*, rel part	v Qal impf 3ms	art, n mp	pers pron	v Qal impf 3ms
הִיא		יָדַעְתִּי	כִּי	כָּל־אֲשֶׁר	יַעֲשֶׂה	הָאֱלֹהִים	הוּא	יִהְיֶה
hî'		yādha'ttî	kî	kol-'āsher	ya'aseh	hā'ĕlōhîm	hû'	yihyeh
it		I know	that	all that	He does	God	it	it will be

3937, 5986	6142	375	3937, 3362.541	4623	375	3937, 1686.141
prep, n ms	prep, ps 3ms	*sub*	prep, v Hiphil inf con	cj, prep, ps 3ms	*sub*	prep, v Qal inf con
לְעוֹלָם	עָלָיו	אֵין	לְהוֹסִיף	וּמִמֶּנּוּ	אֵין	לִגְרֹעַ
le'ôlām	'ālâv	'ên	lehôsîph	ûmimmennû	'ên	lighrōa'
unto eternity	onto it	there is not	of adding	and from it	there is not	of reducing

435	6449.111	8054, 3486.126	4623, 3937, 6686	**15.**	4242, 8054, 2030.111
cj, art, n mp	v Qal pf 3ms	rel part, v Qal impf 3mp	prep, prep, n mp, ps 3ms		intrg, rel part, v Qal pf 3ms
וְהָאֱלֹהִים	עָשָׂה	שֶׁיִּרְאוּ	מִלְּפָנָיו		מַה־שֶּׁהָיָה
wehā'ĕlōhîm	'āsāh	shêyir'û	millephānâv		mah-shehāyāh
and God	He has done	so that they will fear	from before Him		what that it has been

3647	2000	866	3937, 2030.141	3647	2030.111	435	1272.321
adv	pers pron	cj, rel part	prep, v Qal inf con	adv	v Qal pf 3ms	cj, art, n mp	v Piel impf 3ms
כְּבָר	הוּא	וַאֲשֶׁר	לִהְיוֹת	כְּבָר	הָיָה	וְהָאֱלֹהִים	יְבַקֵּשׁ
kevār	hû'	wa'asher	lihyôth	kevār	hāyāh	wehā'ĕlōhîm	yevaqqēsh
already	it	and what	to be	already	it has been	and God	He seeks

881, 7579.255	**16.**	5968	7495.115	8809	8507	4887	5122	8427
do, v Niphal ptc ms		cj, adv	v Qal pf 1cs	prep	art, n ms	*n ms*	art, n ms	adv
אֶת־נִרְדָּף		וְעוֹד	רָאִיתִי	תַּחַת	הַשֶּׁמֶשׁ	מְקוֹם	הַמִּשְׁפָּט	שָׁמָּה
'eth-nirdāph		we'ôdh	rā'îthî	tachath	hashshāmesh	meqôm	hammishpāṭ	shammâh
what is pursued		and still	I have seen	under	the sun	the place of	the justice	to there

7857	4887	6928	8427	7857	**17.**	569.115
art, n ms	cj, *n ms*	art, n ms	adv	art, n ms		v Qal pf 1cs
הָרֶשַׁע	וּמְקוֹם	הַצֶּדֶק	שָׁמָּה	הָרֶשַׁע		אָמַרְתִּי
hāresha'	ûmeqôm	hatstsedheq	shammâh	hāresha'		'āmartî
the wickedness	and the place of	the righteousness	to there	the wickedness		I said

be happy and enjoy themselves as long as they are alive, *Moffatt* ... to be glad and to do well during life, *NAB, Douay*.

13. And also that every man should eat and drink, and enjoy the good of all his labour: ... when a man can eat and drink and find satisfaction in his occupation, *Anchor* ... should eat and drink and be happy, *Moffatt* ... God wants all people to eat and drink and be happy in their work, *NCV* ... should eat and drink and take pleasure in all their toil, *NRSV*.

it is the gift of God: ... he has a gift from God, *Anchor* ... is indeed God's very gift to man, *Moffatt* ... which are gifts from God, *NCV*.

14. I know that, whatsoever God doeth, it shall be for ever: ... will endure, *Anchor* ... will remain for ever as he made it, *Knox* ... whatever God may do shall stand unchanged, *Moffatt* ... will continue forever, *NCV*.

nothing can be put to it, nor anything taken from it: ... can be added, and from it nothing can be subtracted, *Anchor* … nothing may be added to it and nothing may be withdrawn from it, *Goodspeed* … there is no adding to it, no taking away from it, *Knox* … People cannot add anything to what God has done, and they cannot take anything away from it, *NCV.*

and God doeth it, that men should fear before him: … men must stand in awe of him, *Anchor* … so that they should be reverent in His presence, *Berkeley* … that he may be revered, *NAB, Douay* … to make people respect him, *NCV.*

15. That which hath been is now: … Whatever is, it has already been, *Moffatt* … What now is has already been, *NAB* … What happens now has happened in the past, *NCV.*

and that which is to be hath already been: … whatever is to be, already is, *Moffatt* … what will happen in the future has happened before, *NCV.*

and God requireth that which is past: … he is ever repeating the history of the past, *Knox* … is ever bringing back what disappears, *Moffatt* … seeketh again that which is passed away, *MRB* … restores what would otherwise be displaced, *NAB, Douay.*

16. And moreover I saw under the sun the place of judgment, that wickedness was there: … where justice should be found, there wickedness is, *Anchor* … in the place of justice there is wrong, *Beck* … on the Seat of JUSTICE there was VILLAINY, *Fenton* … wickedness took the place of righteousness, *Goodspeed.*

and the place of righteousness, that iniquity was there: … where the just man should be, there is an evil-doer, *Anchor* … in the place of right-eousness there is wickedness, *Beck* … on the seat of RIGHTEOUSNESS,— WICKEDNESS!, *Fenton* … wickedness took the place of righteousness, *Goodspeed.*

17. I said in mine heart, God shall judge the righteous and the wicked: … the upright and the criminal will both be judged by God, *JB* … told myself that God would give judgement one day between the just and the sinners, *Knox* … God will deal one day with the just and the unjust, *Moffatt* … he will judge both good people and bad, *NCV.*

for there is a time there for every purpose and for every work: … since there is a time for every thing and every action here, *JB* … all things would reach their appointed end, *Knox* … 'tis he who appoints a time for everything, for all that men devise and practise, *Moffatt* … there is a time for every affair and on every work a judgment, *NAB.*

God would have us observe it. He encourages us to trust Him. And how does He return our trust by the overflowing fulfillment of promised grace beyond prayer and expectation! Surely joy should be our element. Endeavor to enjoy Him in everything and everything in Him. The man not only rejoices, but he does good all his days. And what an increase is it to our own happiness that our God and Savior should have indulged us with the privilege of thus promoting his glory!

3:14–15. Observe the striking view of God's unchangeableness. His works pass away when their use is finished, but his eternal counsel will be forever, not to be altered or set aside by man's will or power. "The counsel of the LORD standeth for ever, the thoughts of his heart to all generations" (Ps. 33:11; cp. Prov. 19:21; 21:30). Amid outward changes and seeming confusion all things are carried out unchangeably.

And yet, in the midst of all external changes there is substantial uniformity. That which has been is now, and that which is to be has already been. The work of God is the same in every age. The scene seems to be acting over again. God requires that which is past. He calls it back before Him as the precedent for the future. In providence the same laws of government are in force, as from the beginning. There are few events but what may find their counterpart from the annals of the past. The children of God are exercised in the same trials; and the same proofs of sustaining and delivering grace are vouchsafed to them, as to Noah, Abraham and the saints of old.

3:16–17. A thoughtful mind is often exercised on the apparent inequalities of the divine government. Solomon's observant eye could not overlook that which has been a stumblingblock to men of reason who only dispute about what they see and, therefore, are ready to find fault with the appointments far beyond their wisdom. May we not hope that Solomon found rest in his difficulties where his father had found it (Ps. 73:16f), in the sanctuary of God? This injustice is seen in the best governments. This evil has also sometimes been found where we should have little expected it. Samuel was directed to rebuke it in Eli, yet it afterward appeared in his own house (1 Sam. 3:13; 8:3ff). Power, if it be not the instrument of promoting godliness, only makes its possessor a wolf or a tiger to his fellow creatures. So dangerous is worldly elevation! The pinnacle is a hazardous position. Our corrupt nature can bear but

Ecclesiastes 3:18–21

603	904, 3949	881, 6926	881, 7857	8570.121	435	3706, 6496
pers pron	prep, n ms, ps 1cs	do, art, n ms	cj, do, art, n ms	v Qal impf 3ms	art, n mp	cj, n fs
אֲנִי	בְּלִבִּי	אֶת־הַצַּדִּיק	וְאֶת־הָרָשָׁע	יִשְׁפֹּט	הָאֱלֹהִים	כִּי־עֵת
'ănî	belibbî	'eth-hatstsaddîq	we'eth-hārāshā'	yishpōṭ	hā'ĕlōhîm	kî-'ēth
I	in my heart	the righteous	and the wicked	He will judge	God	because a time

3937, 3725, 2761	6142	3725, 4801	8427	**18.** 569.115	603	904, 3949
prep, adj, n ms	cj, prep	adj, art, n ms	adv	v Qal pf 1cs	pers pron	prep, n ms, ps 1cs
לְכָל־חֵפֶץ	וְעַל	כָּל־הַמַּעֲשֶׂה	שָׁם	אָמַרְתִּי	אֲנִי	בְּלִבִּי
lekhol-chēphets	we'al	kol-hamma'ăseh	shām	'āmartî	'ănî	belibbî
for every desire	and concerning	every work	there	I said	I	in my heart

6142, 1750	1158	119	3937, 1331.141	435	3937, 7495.141
prep, n fs	n mp	art, n ms	prep, v Qal inf con, ps 3mp	art, n mp	cj, prep, v Qal inf con
עַל־דִּבְרַת	בְּנֵי	הָאָדָם	לְבָרָם	הָאֱלֹהִים	וְלִרְאוֹת
'al-divrath	benê	hā'ādhām	levārām	hā'ĕlōhîm	welir'ôth
about the manner of	the sons of	humankind	to purge them	God	and to see

8054, 2062, 966	2065	3937	**19.** 3706	4907	1158, 119
rel part, pers pron, n fs	pers pron	prep, ps 3mp	cj	n ms	n mp, art, n ms
שֶׁהֵם־בְּהֵמָה	הֵמָּה	לָהֶם	כִּי	מִקְרֶה	בְּנֵי־הָאָדָם
shehem-behēmāh	hēmmāh	lāhem	kî	miqŏreh	venê-hā'ādhām
that they animals	they	to them	because	what happens to	the children of humankind

4907	966	4907	259	3937	3626, 4323	2172
cj, n ms	art, n fs	cj, n ms	num	prep, ps 3mp	prep, n ms	dem pron
וּמִקְרֶה	הַבְּהֵמָה	וּמִקְרֶה	אֶחָד	לָהֶם	כְּמוֹת	זֶה
ûmiqŏreh	habbehēmāh	ûmiqŏreh	'echādh	lāhem	kemôth	zeh
and what happens to	the animal	indeed an event	one	to them	like the death of	this one

3772	4323	2172	7593	259	3937, 3725	4325	119
adv	n ms	dem pron	cj, n ms	num	prep, art, n ms	cj, n ms	art, n ms
כֵּן	מוֹת	זֶה	וְרוּחַ	אֶחָד	לַכֹּל	וּמוֹתַר	הָאָדָם
kēn	môth	zeh	werûach	'echādh	lakkōl	ûmôthar	hā'ādhām
so	the death of	that one	and a breath	one	to everything	and an advantage to	humankind

4623, 966	375	3706	3725	1961	**20.** 3725	2050.151
prep, art, n fs	sub	cj	art, n ms	n ms	art, n ms	v Qal act ptc ms
מִן־הַבְּהֵמָה	אַיִן	כִּי	הַכֹּל	הָבֶל	הַכֹּל	הוֹלֵךְ
min-habbehēmāh	'ayin	kî	hakkōl	hāvel	hakkōl	hôlēkh
more than the animals	there is not	because	everything	a vanity	everything	proceeding

420, 4887	259	3725	2030.111	4623, 6312	3725	8178.111
prep, n ms	num	art, n ms	v Qal pf 3ms	prep, art, n ms	cj, art, n ms	v Qal pf 3ms
אֶל־מָקוֹם	אֶחָד	הַכֹּל	הָיָה	מִן־הֶעָפָר	וְהַכֹּל	שָׁב
'el-māqôm	'echādh	hakkōl	hāyāh	min-he'āphār	wehakkōl	shāv
to a place	one	everything	it was	from the dust	and everything	it will return

420, 6312	**21.** 4449	3156.151	7593	1158	119	6148.153
prep, art, n ms	intrg	v Qal act ptc ms	n fs	n mp	art, n ms	art, v Qal act ptc fs
אֶל־הֶעָפָר	מִי	יוֹדֵעַ	רוּחַ	בְּנֵי	הָאָדָם	הָעֹלָה
'el-he'āphār	mî	yôdhēa'	rûach	benê	hā'ādhām	hā'ōlāh
to the dust	who	one who knows	the spirit of	the children of	humankind	the one going up

2026	3937, 4762	7593	966	3495.153	2026	3937, 4432
pers pron	prep, adv	cj, n fs	art, n fs	art, v Qal act ptc fs	pers pron	prep, adv
הִיא	לְמַעְלָה	וְרוּחַ	הַבְּהֵמָה	הַיֹּרֶדֶת	הִיא	לְמַטָּה
hî'	lema'ălāh	werûach	habbehēmāh	hayyōredheth	hî'	lemaṭṭāh
it	upward	and the breath of	the animal	the one going down	it	downward

18. I said in mine heart concerning the estate of the sons of men: ... where human beings are concerned, *JB* ... As for the children of men, *NAB* ... God leaves it the way it is, *NCV* ... In dealing with men, *NEB*.

that God might manifest them, and that they might see that they themselves are beasts: ... this is so that God can test them and show them that they are animals, *JB* ... to let them see they are no better than the beasts, *Moffatt* ... to test people and to show them they are just like animals, *NCV* ... it is God's purpose to test them and to see what they truly are, *NEB, REB*.

19. For that which befalleth the sons of men befalleth beasts: ... the fate of men and the fate of animals is the same, *Anchor* ... What happens to people happens to animals, *Beck* ... man comes to the same ending as the beasts, *Knox* ... the lot of man and of beast is one lot, *NAB*.

even one thing befalleth them: ... the same happens to both, *Beck* ... there is nothing to choose between his lot and theirs, *Knox* ... one mischance awaits them all, *NEB* ... even one event is to them, *Young*.

as the one dieth, so dieth the other: ... One dies like the other, *Beck* ... both alike are doomed to die, *Knox* ... the one dies as well as the other, *NAB* ... death comes to both alike, *NEB*.

yea, they have all one breath: ... all have the same breath of life, *Anchor* ... all have one spirit, *BB* ... the same breath is in all of them, *Goodspeed* ... both have the selfsame breath, *JB* ... They have but one principle of life, *Knox*.

so that a man hath no preeminence above a beast: ... has no superiority over, *Anchor* ... is no better than, *Beck* ... the advantage of men over animals amounts to nothing, *Berkeley* ... Man is not higher than, *BB*.

for all is vanity: ... all are a breath that vanishes, *Anchor* ... for all is uselessness, *Berkeley* ... all is to no purpose, *BB* ... all is futile, *JB*.

20. All go unto one place: ... are bound for the same place, *Anchor* ... Everything goes to the same place, *JB* ... we are all making for the same goal, *Knox* ... Both end up the same way, *NCV*.

all are of the dust, and all turn to dust again: ... come from the ground, and all are returning to the ground, *Anchor* ... everything comes from the dust, everything returns to the dust, *JB* ... of earth we were made, and to earth we must return, *Knox*.

21. Who knoweth the spirit of man that goeth upward, and the spirit of the beast that goeth downward to the earth?: ... Who can be sure that, *Anchor* ... Does anyone know if, *Beck* ... Who has a right to tell us that, *Knox*.

22. Wherefore I perceive that there is nothing better, than that a man should rejoice in his own works: ... I became aware that it is best for man to busy himself here to his own content, *Knox* ... I saw the best thing for man was to be happy in his work, *Moffatt* ... I saw that the best thing people can do is to enjoy their work, *NCV*.

for that is his portion: ... this and nothing else is his allotted portion, *Knox* ... that is what he gets out of life, *Moffatt* ... this is his lot, *Douay* ... that is all they have, *NCV*.

---

little raising. There is one ever ready to help us to climb. But let it be our desire to be kept upon lowly ground. We cannot know what is in our heart till the stirring power of temptation has brought it before our eyes.

3:18–20. This confusion before the wise man's eyes pressed heavily upon his heart. He could not forget the sad retrospect when he had degraded himself from the dignity of a son of God to walk before men like a beast. He now had before him not only the mighty oppression just alluded to but the mass of mankind, the sons of men in the same bestial state. How could he restrain the saying of his heart concerning their estate that they might see that they themselves were beasts? For indeed they will never know their honor until they have known their shame. Yet this they will never see until God will manifest unto them their real state. So degraded is man that he cannot understand his own degradation.

Yet when we see men of vast capacity seeking happiness in sensual pleasures and never looking beyond the grave, does not man here sink his immortal nature to the very lowest "brutishness?" The testimony of God is true to the very letter: "Man that is in honour, and understandeth not, is like the beasts that perish" (Ps. 49:20; also 14). This is his spiritual level. As to animal life, all go unto one place, as are of the dust, and all turn to dust again (Gen. 2:7; 3:19). In the mere outward respect, both breathe, and live, and die alike. "Man hath no preeminence above a beast: for all is vanity."

3:21. Though there be no animal preeminence of man above the beast, yet vast indeed is the difference as to their spirits. The one goeth upward to "the Father of spirits," and shall "return unto God who gave it" (ch. 12:7 with Heb. 12:9). The other goeth downward to the earth. It dies with the body and perishes forever.

Ecclesiastes 3:22–4:4

119	7975.121	4623, 866	3005	375	3706	7495.115	**22.**	3937, 800
art, n ms	v Qal impf 3ms	prep, rel part	adj	sub	cj	v Qal pf 1cs		prep, art, n fs
הָאָדָם	יִשְׂמַח	מֵאֲשֶׁר	טוֹב	אֵין	כִּי	וְרָאִיתִי		לָאָרֶץ
hā'ādhām	yismach	mē'ăsher	ṭôv	'ên	kî	wᵉrā'îthî		lā'ārets
humankind	he will be glad	than that	better	there is not	that	and I saw		to the earth

3937, 7495.141	971.521	4449	3706	2610	3706, 2000	904, 4801
prep, v Qal inf con	v Hiphil impf 3ms, ps 3ms	intrg	cj	n ms, ps 3ms	cj, pers pron	prep, n mp, ps 3ms
לִרְאוֹת	יְבִיאֶנּוּ	מִי	כִּי	חֶלְקוֹ	כִּי־הוּא	בְּמַעֲשָׂיו
lir'ôth	yᵉvî'ennû	mî	kî	chelqô	kî-hû'	bᵉma'ăsâv
to see	he will bring him	who	because	his portion	because it	in his acts

7495.125	603	8178.115	**4:1**	313	8054, 2030.121	904, 4242
cj, v Qal impf 1cs	pers pron	cj, v Qal pf 1cs		prep, ps 3ms	rel part, v Qal impf 3ms	prep, intrg
וָאֶרְאֶה	אָנִי	וְשַׁבְתִּי		אַחֲרָיו	שֶׁיִּהְיֶה	בְּמֶה
wā'er'eh	'ānî	wᵉshavtî		'achărâv	shêyihyeh	bᵉmeh
and I saw	I	and I turned again		after him	what will it be	into what

1893	2079	8507	8809	6449.256	866	881, 3725, 6471
n fs	cj, intrj	art, n ms	prep	v Niphal ptc mp	rel part	do, n ms, art, n mp
דִּמְעַת	וְהִנֵּה	הַשָּׁמֶשׁ	תַּחַת	נַעֲשִׂים	אֲשֶׁר	אֶת־כָּל־הָעֲשֻׁקִים
dim'ath	wᵉhinnēh	hashshāmesh	tachath	na'ăsîm	'ăsher	'eth-kol-hā'ăshuqîm
the tears of	and behold	the sun	under	being practiced	that	all the oppression

4623, 3135	5341.351	3937	375	6479.156
cj, prep, n fs	v Piel ptc ms	prep, ps 3mp	cj, sub	art, v Qal pass ptc mp
וּמִיַּד	מְנַחֵם	לָהֶם	וְאֵין	הָעֲשֻׁקִים
ûmîyadh	mᵉnachēm	lāhem	wᵉ'ên	hā'ăshuqîm
and from the hand of	a comforter	to them	and there was not	those oppressed

5341.351	3937	375	3699	6479.152
v Piel ptc ms	prep, ps 3mp	cj, sub	n ms	v Qal act ptc mp, ps 3mp
מְנַחֵם	לָהֶם	וְאֵין	כֹּחַ	עֹשְׁקֵיהֶם
mᵉnachēm	lāhem	wᵉ'ên	kōach	'ōshᵉqêhem
a comforter	to them	but there was not	a power	their oppressors

4322.116	8054, 3647	881, 4322.152	603	8099.342	**2.**
v Qal pf 3cp	rel pron, adv	do, art, v Qal act ptc mp	pers pron	cj, v Piel inf abs	
מֵתוּ	שֶׁכְּבָר	אֶת־הַמֵּתִים	אָנִי	וְשַׁבֵּחַ	
mēthû	shekkᵉvār	'eth-hammēthîm	'ānî	wᵉshabbēach	
they had died	who already	the dead	I	so considering more fortunate	

881	4623, 8530	3005	**3.**	5946	2522	2065	866	4623, 2522
do	prep, num, ps 3mp	cj, adj		adv	adj	pers pron	rel pron	prep, art, n mp
אֵת	מִשְּׁנֵיהֶם	וְטוֹב		עֲדֶנָה	חַיִּים	הֵמָּה	אֲשֶׁר	מִן־הַחַיִּים
'ēth	mishshᵉnêhem	wᵉṭôv		'ădhenāh	chayyîm	hēmmāh	'ăsher	min-hachayyîm
	than the two of them	and better		still	living	they	who	than the living

866	7737	881, 4801	3940, 7495.111	866	2030.111	3940	866, 5940
rel part	art, adj	do, art, n ms	neg part, v Qal pf 3ms	rel pron	v Qal pf 3ms	neg part	rel part, adv
אֲשֶׁר	הָרָע	אֶת־הַמַּעֲשֶׂה	לֹא־רָאָה	אֲשֶׁר	הָיָה	לֹא	אֲשֶׁר־עֶדֶן
'ăsher	hārā'	'eth-hamma'ăseh	lō'-rā'āh	'ăsher	hāyāh	lō'	'ăsher-'edhen
which	the evil	the deeds	he has not seen	who	he has been	not	who yet

881	881, 3725, 6219	603	7495.115	**4.**	8507	8809	6449.211
cj, do	do, adj, n ms	pers pron	v Qal pf 1cs		art, n ms	prep	v Niphil pf 3ms
וְאֵת	אֶת־כָּל־עָמָל	אָנִי	וְרָאִיתִי		הַשָּׁמֶשׁ	תַּחַת	נַעֲשָׂה
wᵉ'ēth	'eth-kol-'āmāl	'ānî	wᵉrā'îthî		hashshāmesh	tachath	na'ăsāh
and	all toil	I	and I saw		the sun	under	they have been done

for who shall bring him to see what shall be after him?: … who can show him what the future will bring?, *Knox* … who can show him what is to happen afterwards?, *Moffatt* … Who will let him see what is to come after him?, *Douay* … No one can help another person see what will happen in the future, *NCV.*

4:1. So I returned, and considered all the oppressions that are done under the sun: … I turned to consider all the acts of oppression, *Anchor* … I saw all the cruel things which are done, *BB* … examined into all the wrongs, *Fenton* … I saw all the people who were mistreated, *NCV.*

and behold the tears of such as were oppressed: … I witnessed the tears of the oppressed, *Anchor* … weeping of those who have evil done to them, *BB*

… Innocent folk in tears, *Knox* … the tears of the victims, *NAB.*

and they had no comforter: … no one to comfort them, *Anchor* … they had no consolation, *Fenton* … no one to redress their wrongs, *Moffatt.*

and on the side of their oppressors there was power: … oppressors have power in their hands, *Anchor* … from the hands of the evil-doers there went out power, *BB* … tyrants in power, *Moffatt* … Cruel people had all the power, *NCV.*

but they had no comforter: … have no avenger, *Anchor* … for them not one sustainer, *Berkeley* … they had no consolation, *Fenton* … no one to redress their wrongs!, *Moffatt.*

2. Wherefore I praised the dead which are already dead more than

the living which are yet alive: … thought the dead who are already dead more fortunate than the living, *Anchor* … congratulated the dead who were already dead, rather than the living, *Beck, Goodspeed* … The dead, it seemed, were more to be envied than the living, *Knox* … judged the dead already in their graves to be more happy than the living, *Moffatt.*

3. Yea, better is he than both they, which hath not yet been: … happier than both of these are those who are yet unborn, *JB* … better than them both did I esteem him which hath not yet been, *MRB* … those who have never been born are better off still, *NCV* … More fortunate then either I reckoned the man yet unborn, *NEB.*

who hath not seen the evil work that is done under the sun: … has

3:22. Solomon is returning to his former statement. There is a godly as well as an infidel (1 Cor. 15:32) enjoyment of "things present." Let the Christian look for it in following the will of God. Here are his own works, not done in his own strength or for his own glory and reward. And here also is his portion. Here he remembers his God, and his God meets him with his acceptance (Isa. 64:5). Here we have our rejoicing with trembling indeed; yet with "the testimony of our conscience" (2 Cor. 1:12; Gal. 6:4f). Godliness is a bright atmosphere of Christian joy to the whole-hearted Christian.

And if our present portion be so precious, what will it be when we will grasp "the prize of our high calling of God in Christ Jesus?"

Meanwhile the future is uncertain. None can bring us to see what will be afterward. But the simple reliance for the day sweeps away the tossing cares for tomorrow (Matt. 6:34). Eternal rest soon will swallow up present anxieties.

4:1–3. A sinful world is a world of selfishness. Men, instead of feeling themselves to be members of one great body, live only to "seek their own" (Eph. 4:16; Phil. 2:21) at whatever cost to their fellow creatures. Solomon had already taken one view of this sad spectacle. He had seen with his father "the vilest men exalted—the throne of iniquity framing mischief by a law" (3:16f; Pss. 12:8;

94:20f). He now returns and considers. He takes a wider survey. He sees oppression in every corner. Twice he alludes to the deep and poignant aggravation: there is no comforter, no one to afford relief to soul or body. The tyranny of the oppressor here reaches his summit of cruelty.

Sympathy with sorrow is indeed a precious privilege. "Remember them that are in bonds, as bound with them" (Heb. 13:3). Might not prayer and effort be made to bring the sufferers to an interest in the endearing sympathy of "the Man of sorrows" Who was touched with the feeling of his people's sorrow? And yet how very little do we realize the sorrow of others, either because they are at a distance from us or because we have ourselves no intelligent and experimental acquaintance with the particular pages of the history of sorrow!

So keen were Solomon's sensibilities that, looking at the comparison merely in the light of temporal evil, he considered death or even nonexistence preferable as a refuge from this suffering lot. The patriarch, in his crushing sorrow, looked to the grave as his hope of rest. "There the wicked cease from troubling; and there the weary be at rest. There prisoners rest together; they hear not the voice of the oppressor" (Job 3:17f).

4:4. How vividly Solomon draws the picture of selfishness in all its features! A man pursues a right

3725, 3917	4801	3706	2026	7352, 382	4623, 7739	1612, 2172
adj, n ms	art, n ms	cj	pers pron	n fs, n ms	prep, n ms, ps 3ms	cj, dem pron
כָּל־כִּשְׁרוֹן	הַמַּעֲשֶׂה	כִּי	הִיא	קִנְאַת־אִישׁ	מֵרֵעֵהוּ	גַּם־זֶה
kol-kishrôn	hamma'ăseh	kî	hî'	qin'ath-'îsh	mērē'ēhû	gam-zeh
all the skill of	the work	because	it	the envy of a man	of his fellow	also this

1961	7758	7593	5. 3809	2354.151	881, 3135	404.151
n ms	cj, n fs	n fs	art, n ms	v Qal act ptc ms	do, n fp, ps 3ms	cj, v Qal act ptc ms
הֶבֶל	וּרְעוּת	רוּחַ	הַכְּסִיל	חֹבֵק	אֶת־יָדָיו	וְאֹכֵל
hevel	ûre'ûth	rûach	hakkesîl	chōvēq	'eth-yādhâv	we'ōkhēl
a vanity	and a striving for	wind	the fool	one who folds	his hands	and one who eats

6. 3005	4530	3834	5369	4623, 4530	2756	6219
adj	n ms	n fs	n fs	prep, n ms	n md	n ms
טוֹב	מְלֹא	כַף	נַחַת	מִמְּלֹא	חָפְנַיִם	עָמָל
tôv	melō'	khaph	nāchath	mimmelō'	chāphenayim	'āmāl
better	fullness of	a palm of	restfulness	than fullness of	the hollow of the hands	toil

7758	7593	7. 8178.115	603	7495.125	1961	8809
cj, n fs	n fs	cj, v Qal pf 1cs	pers pron	cj, v Qal impf 1cs	n ms	prep
וּרְעוּת	רוּחַ	וְשַׁבְתִּי	אָנִי	וָאֶרְאֶה	הֶבֶל	תַּחַת
ûre'ûth	rûach	weshavtî	'ănî	wā'er'eh	hevel	tachath
and a striving for	wind	and I turned again	I	and I saw	a vanity	under

8507	8. 3552	259	375	8530	1612	1158	250
art, n ms	sub	num	cj, sub	num	cj	n ms	cj, n ms
הַשָּׁמֶשׁ	יֵשׁ	אֶחָד	וְאֵין	שֵׁנִי	גַּם	בֵּן	וָאָח
hashshāmesh	yēsh	'echādh	we'ên	shēnî	gam	bēn	wā'āch
the sun	there was	one	and there was not	a second one	also	a son	and a brother

375, 3937	375	7377	3937, 3725, 6219	1612, 6084
sub, prep, ps 3ms	cj, sub	n ms	prep, adj, n ms, ps 3ms	cj, n fd, ps 3ms
אֵין־לוֹ	וְאֵין	קֵץ	לְכָל־עֲמָלוֹ	גַּם־עֵינָיו
'ên-lô	we'ên	qēts	lekhol-'āmālô	gam-'ênâv
there was not to him	and there was not	an end	to all his toil	also his eyes

3940, 7881.122	6484	3937, 4449	603	6221	2741.351
neg part, v Qal impf 3fs	n ms	cj, prep, intrg	pers pron	n ms	cj, v Piel ptc ms
לֹא־תִשְׂבַּע	עֹשֶׁר	וּלְמִי	אָנִי	עָמֵל	וּמְחַסֵּר
lō'-thisba'	'ōsher	ûlemî	'ănî	'āmēl	ûmechassēr
they were not satisfied with	riches	and for whom	I	a laborer	and causing to lack

881, 5497	4623, 3009B	1612, 2172	1961	6275	7737	2000	9. 3005
do, n fs, ps 1cs	prep, n fs	cj, dem pron	n ms	cj, n ms	adj	pers pron	adj
אֶת־נַפְשִׁי	מִטּוֹבָה	גַּם־זֶה	הֶבֶל	וְעִנְיַן	רָע	הוּא	טוֹבִים
'eth-naphshî	mittôvāh	gam-zeh	hevel	we'inyan	rā'	hû'	tôvîm
my soul	from goodness	also this	a vanity	and an occupation	evil	it	better

never known the misery that goes on, *Moffatt* ... has not seen the wicked work that is done, *NAB* ... who had not witnessed the wicked deeds done here, *NEB* ... who had not seen the vexatious work, which was done, *Rotherham*.

4. Again, I considered all travail, and every right work, that for this

a man is envied of his neighbour: ... saw that all a man's toil and skill is expended through the desire to surpass his neighbor, *Anchor* ... saw that all the hard work and all the skillful effort comes from jealous competition, *Beck* ... saw that all the toil and skill in activities bring envy between a man and his neighbor, *Berkeley* ... saw that all the labor and

all the hard work is due to men's jealousy of one another, *Goodspeed*.

This is also vanity and vexation of spirit: ... is an empty thing and a clutching at the wind, *Anchor* ... This, too, is futility and chasing after wind, *Berkeley* ... is to no purpose and a desire for wind, *BB* ... was frustration and lost labour here, *Knox*.

5. The fool foldeth his hands together: … sits idle, *Knox* … it is foolish to fold your hands and do nothing, *NCV.*

and eateth his own flesh: … starves to death?, *Knox* … lets life go to ruin, *Moffatt* … because you will starve to death, *NCV* … wastes away, *NEB.*

6. Better is an handful with quietness: … in peace, *Anchor* … a handful of rest is better, *Beck* … Better one hand full of repose, *JB.*

than both the hands full with travail and vexation of spirit: … won by toil and reaching for the wind, *Anchor* … than both fists full of hard work and trying to catch the wind, *Beck* … than two hands full of trouble and desire for wind, *BB* … than two hands full of achievements to chase after the wind, *JB.*

7. Then I returned, and I saw vanity under the sun: … something else futile I observe, *JB* … another kind of frustration I marked, *Knox* … saw something here on earth that was useless, *NCV* … I saw emptiness, *NEB.*

8. There is one alone, and there is not a second: … a solitary man with no companion, *Douay* … a man who had no family, *NCV* … a lonely man without a friend, *NEB* … a man all alone, *NIV.*

yea, he hath neither child nor brother: … neither son nor brother, *Douay* … even son or brother he hath not, *Young.*

yet is there no end of all his labour: … to all his toil, *Douay* … He always worked hard, *NCV* … toiling endlessly, *NEB.*

neither is his eye satisfied with riches: … riches do not satisfy his greed, *NAB, Douay* … was never satisfied with what he had, *NCV* … yet never satisfied with his wealth, *NEB.*

neither saith he, For whom do I labour, and bereave my soul of good?: … toil and deprive myself of good things?, *NAB* … never asked himself, "For whom am I working so hard? Why don't I let myself enjoy life?", *NCV.*

This is also vanity, yea, it is a sore travail: … is vanity and a worthless task, *NAB* … is very sad and useless, *NCV* … is emptiness, a sorry business, *NEB* … is meaningless—a miserable business!, *NIV.*

9. Two are better than one; because they have a good reward for their labour: … get a better return,

---

work. Yet his neighbor envies his rectitude. Whichever side of the world we look, it presents the same face of vanity.

The better the work the more is the man hated by those who have no heart to imitate him. Thus even godliness becomes a source of evil. If our godliness "condemn the world," we must expect to be hated by the world.

The true power of the gospel can alone root out this hateful principle. If there be a living union with Christ, will not his honor be our joy by whomever it be advanced? If there be a true communion with the body, the prosperity of one member will be the joy of the whole (1 Cor. 12:26; Eph. 4:16).

4:5–6. Another picture of vanity! The sluggard, wasting his precious time and opportunity and mistaking idleness for quietness, bears the stamp of a fool. And well does he deserve his name. He folds his hands together (Prov. 6:9f; 24:30–33) with heartless indifference, as if he would rather eat his very flesh from his bones than put forth any troublesome exertion. And yet an excuse was ready at hand. Above him he saw the tyranny of the oppressor. Many on his own level grudged their neighbor his happiness. And therefore for himself he deems a little with ease to be far better than much with toil and trouble. Nothing is to be gained without travail. And yet the fruit of successful travail becomes the object of envy. He thinks, therefore, that a handful of quietness is far better than both hands filled with the heavy burden of vexation of spirit.

4:7–8. Solomon's mind was in constant exercise. We find him returning from one side to another, only to fasten upon some new illustration of this world's vanity. The slothful fool sits with his folded hands preferring quietness at any cost. Contrasted with him, we have the covetous fool full of active energy. He has chosen money for his God. He cannot plead in excuse the necessary claims of a large family. He is alone, and there is not a second. He has neither child nor brother. Yet so long as he can add one farthing to his hoard, he cannot bear the thought of giving up. There is no end of his labor. Labor indeed it is, without rest or satisfaction, however he may heap up his treasure.

But it is not only the miser. Here also is the man that spends his money upon himself and upon his own selfish gratifications, forgetting its true use and responsibility. We are not our own (1 Cor. 6:19). Neither is our silver or our gold our own, but God's.

The man of covetousness would keep his money within his last grasp. He can realize no other satisfaction. But all this is vanity and severe travail. Never has he soberly calculated profit and loss.

4:9–12. We have seen the misery of solitary selfishness. Contrast with this dark picture the pleasures

10.

3706 cj	904, 6219 prep, n ms, ps 3mp	3005 adj	7964 n ms	3552, 3937 sub, prep, ps 3mp	866 cj	4623, 259 prep, art, num	8530 art, num
כִּי	בַּעֲמָלָם	טוֹב	שָׂכָר	יֵשׁ־לָהֶם	אֲשֶׁר	מִן־הָאֶחָד	הַשְּׁנַיִם
kî	ba'ămālām	ṭôv	sākhar	yēsh-lāhem	'ăsher	min-hā'echādh	hashshenayim
because	in their toil	good	a reward	there is to them	because	than the one	the two

259 art, num	341, 3937 cj, intrj, prep, ps 3ms	881, 2358 do, n ms, ps 3ms	7251.521 v Hiphil impf 3ms	259 art, num	524, 5489.126 cj, v Qal impf 3mp
הָאֶחָד	וְאִילוֹ	אֶת־חֲבֵרוֹ	יָקִים	הָאֶחָד	אִם־יִפֹּלוּ
hā'echādh	we'îlô	'eth-chăvērô	yāqîm	hā'echādh	'im-yippōlû
the one	but woe to him	his companion	he will raise up	the one	if they fall

11.

1612 cj	3937, 7251.541 prep, v Hiphil inf con, ps 3ms	8530 num	375 cj, sub	8054, 5489.121 rel pron, v Qal impf 3ms
גַּם	לַהֲקִימוֹ	שֵׁנִי	וְאֵין	שֶׁיִּפּוֹל
gam	lahqîmô	shēnî	we'ên	shêyippôl
also	to raise him up	a second one	and there is not	who he falls

2657.121 v Qal impf 3ms	351 intrg	3937, 259 cj, prep, num	3937 prep, ps 3mp	2657.111 cj, v Qal pf 3ms	8530 num	524, 8311.126 cj, v Qal impf 3mp
יֵחָם	אֵיךְ	וּלְאֶחָד	לָהֶם	וְחַם	שְׁנַיִם	אִם־יִשְׁכְּבוּ
yēchām	'êkh	ûlă'echādh	lāhem	wecham	shenayim	'im-yishkevû
will it be warm	how	but for one	for them	then it will be warm	two	if they will lie

12.

5224 sub, ps 3ms	6198.126 v Qal impf 3mp	8530 art, num	259 art, num	524, 8967.121 cj, cj, v Qal impf 3ms, ps 3ms
נֶגְדּוֹ	יַעַמְדוּ	הַשְּׁנַיִם	הָאֶחָד	וְאִם־יִתְקְפוֹ
neghdô	ya'amdhû	hashshenayim	hā'echādh	we'im-yithqŏphô
against him	they will stand	the two	the one	and if someone overpowers him

13.

3005 adj	5607.221 v Niphal impf 3ms	904, 4259 prep, n fs	3940 neg part	8420.455 art, v Pual ptc ms	2432 cj, art, n ms
טוֹב	יִנָּתֵק	בִּמְהֵרָה	לֹא	הַמְשֻׁלָּשׁ	וְהַחוּט
ṭôv	yinnāthēq	vimhērāh	lō'	hamshullāsh	wehachûṭ
better	it will be snapped in two	with haste	not	which is made from three	and a thread

3940, 3156.111 neg part, v Qal pf 3ms	866 rel pron	3809 cj, adj	2292 adj	4623, 4567 prep, n ms	2550 cj, adj	4693 adj	3315 n ms
לֹא־יָדַע	אֲשֶׁר	וּכְסִיל	זָקֵן	מִמֶּלֶךְ	וְחָכָם	מִסְכֵּן	יֶלֶד
lō'-yādha'	'ăsher	ûkhesîl	zāqēn	mimmelekh	wechākhām	miskēn	yeledh
he does not know	who	and foolish	old	than a king	and wise	needy	a child

14.

3937, 2178.241 prep, v Niphil inf con	5968 adv	3706, 4623, 1041 cj, prep, *n ms*	646.156 art, v Qal pass ptc mp	3428.111 v Qal pf 3ms
לְהִזָּהֵר	עוֹד	כִּי־מִבֵּית	הָסוּרִים	יָצָא
lehizzāhēr	'ôdh	kî-mibbêth	hāṣûrîm	yātsā'
to be warned	anymore	because from the house of	those bound	he came out

15.

3937, 4566.141 prep, v Qal inf con	3706 cj	1612 cj	904, 4577 prep, n fs, ps 3ms	3314.211 v Niphal pf 3ms	7609.151 v Qal act ptc ms	7495.115 v Qal pf 1cs
לִמְלֹךְ	כִּי	גַּם	בְּמַלְכוּתוֹ	נוֹלַד	רָשׁ	רָאִיתִי
limlōkh	kî	gam	bemalkhûthô	nôladh	rāsh	rā'îthî
to reign	yet	also	in his kingdom	he was born	being poor	I have seen

881, 3725, 2522 do, adj, art, adj	2050.352 art, v Piel ptc mp	8809 prep	8507 art, n ms	6196 prep	3315 art, n ms	8529 art, num
אֶת־כָּל־הַחַיִּים	הַמְהַלְּכִים	תַּחַת	הַשָּׁמֶשׁ	עִם	הַיֶּלֶד	הַשֵּׁנִי
'eth-kol-hachayyîm	hamhallekhîm	tachath	hashshāmesh	'im	hayyeledh	hashshēnî
all the living	those moving about vigorously	under	the sun	with	the boy	the second

Anchor … get a fine reward, *Beck* … get a good wage, *Goodspeed* … partnership brings advantage to both, *Knox.*

10. For if they fall, the one will lift up his fellow: … if one has a fall, the other will give him a hand, *BB* … if the one falls his companion can lift him up, *Fenton* … If one falls, the other will give support, *Knox* … if one falls the other man can raise his fellow, *Moffatt.*

but woe to him that is alone when he falleth; for he hath not another to help him up: … he has no helper, *BB* … there is not another to help him to rise!, *Fenton* … there is no partner to lift him up, *Goodspeed* … there is none to raise him, *Knox.*

11. Again, if two lie together, then they have heat: … each shall warm the other, *Knox* … they keep each other warm, *NAB, Douay* … they will be warm, *NCV* … then have they warmth, *Rotherham.*

but how can one be warm alone?: … for the lonely, there is no warmth, *Knox* … a person alone will not be warm, *NCV* … how hath one heat?, *Young.*

12. And if one prevail against him, two shall withstand him: … suppose somebody overpowers one who is alone, two can oppose him, *Beck* … two attacked by one would be safe, *BB* … one may be defeated, where two associated could stand, *Fenton* … Where one alone would be overcome, two will put up resistance, *JB.*

and a threefold cord is not quickly broken: … A triple cord, *Beck* … three cords twisted together, *BB* … A three-ply cord, *NAB* … cord of three strands, *NASB.*

13. Better is a poor and a wise child than an old and foolish king: … young man, lowly born and wise, is better than an old and silly king, *Moffatt* … a young man poor and wise than a king old and foolish, *NEB* … a boy poor and wise,—than a king old and stupid, *Rotherham.*

who will no more be admonished: … who will no longer take advice, *Moffatt* … who knoweth not how to receive admonition any more, *MRB* … who no longer knows caution, *NAB, Douay* … who no longer knows how to take warning, *NIV.*

14. For out of prison he cometh to reign: … had risen from a prison to the throne, *Anchor* … out of a prison the young man comes to be king, *BB*

and advantages of social bonds. In a variety of instances, we will readily admit Solomon's judgment: two are better than one. They have a good reward for their labor. For have they not richer enjoyment of the common good in the mutual effort to promote it?

The most sober principle of interpretation will admit a reference to all that glowing contact of united hearts, where each has a part and responsibility in helping and comforting the other. To begin at the beginning, "It is not good that the man should be alone" (Gen. 2:18; cp. Ps. 68:6). If it was "not good" in Paradise, much less is it in a wilderness world. When two are brought together by the LORD's providence (Gen. 2:22), and especially when each is fitted to each other by his grace, "being heirs together of the grace of life" (1 Pet. 3:7), who can doubt that two are better than one? Love sweetens toil, soothes the sting of trouble and gives a Christian zest of enjoyment to every course of daily life. The mutual exercises of sympathy give energy to prayer and furnish large materials for confidence and praise.

All the kindly offices of friendship, especially when cemented in the Christian bond, apply to this point. The united prayer of "any two, who will agree touching anything they will ask," is sealed with acceptance (Matt. 18:19). Mutual faithfulness (Gal. 2:11–14; 6:1), consideration, inspection and godly provocation (Heb. 10:24) all enter into the sphere of Christian responsibility and minister to the glory of our common Lord. Each of us has something to impart, to prevent discouragement, to receive, to teach us humility.

4:13–14. Riches were the last instance of vanity. Here Solomon affixes the stamp upon honor, man's highest condition. This is not indeed the ordinary course. God's people are often left in a low condition while the ungodly maintain a royal elevation. But such cases do occur. He probably had some example before his eyes of an old and foolish king beyond the border, raised to the throne without any fitness to reign and strewing his folly preeminently by unwillingness to be admonished.

The comparison between a poor, wise child and a rich, foolish king is confirmed by the different event happening to each. The child may for a while be in inglorious poverty. But may it not be the divine purpose to bring, as it were, another Joseph out of prison, or a Daniel out of captivity (Dan. 1:6; 6:1) to raise him to an honorable elevation? Wisdom may be the fruit of the prison's discipline and supply to the child what he wants in years (1 Ki. 3:6–12); while the old and foolish king—born to an empire and born in his kingdom as his rightful inheritance—dies a beggar in obscurity (2 Ki. 23:31–34; 24:12; 25:7; Lam. 4:20).

4:15–16. The Preacher now turns to the people. He finds the same vanity and vexation as else-

16. לְכֹל (3937, 3725 — prep, n ms) *lᵉkhōl* — to everyone | לְכָל־הָעָם (3937, 3725, 6194 — prep, adj, art, n ms) *lᵉkhol-hā'ām* — to all the people | אֵין־קֵץ (375, 7377 — sub, n ms) *'ên-qēts* — there is not an end | תַּחְתָּיו (8809 — prep, ps 3ms) *tachtâv* — instead of him | יַעֲמֹד (6198.121 — v Qal impf 3ms) *ya'ămōdh* — he will stand | אֲשֶׁר (866 — rel pron) *'ăsher* — who

אֲשֶׁר־הָיָה (866, 2030.111 — rel pron, v Qal pf 3ms) *'ăsher-hāyāh* — who they were | לִפְנֵיהֶם (3937, 6686 — prep, n mp, ps 3mp) *liphnêhem* — before them | גַּם (1612 — cj) *gam* — also | הָאַחֲרוֹנִים (315 — art, adv) *hā'achărônîm* — those afterward | לֹא (3940 — neg part) *lō'* — not | יִשְׂמְחוּ־בוֹ (7975.126, 904 — v Qal impf 3mp, prep, ps 3ms) *yismᵉchû-vô* — they will rejoice in him

כִּי־גַם־זֶה (3706, 1612, 2172 — cj, cj, dem pron) *kî-gham-zeh* — indeed also this | הֶבֶל (1961 — n ms) *hevel* — a vanity | וְרַעְיוֹן (7763 — cj, n ms) *wᵉra'ăyôn* — and a striving for | רוּחַ (7593 — n ms) *rûach* — wind

5:1 שְׁמֹר (8490.131 — v Qal impv 2ms) *shᵉmōr* — guard | רַגְלֶיךָ (7559 — n fd, ps 2ms) *raghlêkhā* — your feet | כַּאֲשֶׁר (3626, 866 — prep, rel part) *ka'ăsher* — when

מִתֵּת (4623, 5598.141 — prep, v Qal inf con) *mittēth* — from the giving of | לִשְׁמֹעַ (3937, 8471.141 — prep, v Qal inf con) *lishmōa'* — to listen | וְקָרוֹב (7414.142 — cj, v Qal inf abs) *wᵉqārôv* — and drawing near | הָאֱלֹהִים (435 — art, n mp) *hā'ĕlōhîm* — God | אֶל־בֵּית (420, 1041 — prep, n ms) *'el-bêth* — to the temple of | תֵּלֵךְ (2050.123 — v Qal impf 2ms) *tēlēkh* — you go

רָע (7737 — n ms) *rā'* — evil | לַעֲשׂוֹת (3937, 6449.141 — prep, v Qal inf con) *la'ăsôth* — to do | יוֹדְעִים (3156.152 — v Qal act ptc mp) *yôdh'îm* — one who knows | כִּי־אֵינָם (3706, 375 — cj, sub, ps 3mp) *kî-'ênām* — because there is not to them | זֶבַח (2160 — n ms) *zāvach* — a sacrifice | הַכְּסִילִים (3809 — art, n mp) *hakkᵉsîlîm* — the foolish

2. אַל־תְּבַהֵל (414, 963.323 — adv, v Piel juss 2ms) *'al-tᵉvahēl* — do not hasten | עַל־פִּיךָ (6142, 6552 — prep, n ms, ps 2ms) *'al-pîkhā* — concerning your mouth | וְלִבְּךָ (3949 — cj, n ms, ps 2ms) *wᵉlibbᵉkhā* — and your heart | אַל־יְמַהֵר (414, 4257.321 — adv, v Piel juss 3ms) *'al-yᵉmahēr* — do not hurry | לְהוֹצִיא (3937, 3428.541 — prep, v Hiphil inf con) *lᵉhôtsî'* — to cause to go out

דָּבָר (1745 — n ms) *dhāvār* — a word | לִפְנֵי (3937, 6686 — prep, n mp) *liphnê* — before | הָאֱלֹהִים (435 — art, n mp) *hā'ĕlōhîm* — God | כִּי (3706 — cj) *kî* — because | הָאֱלֹהִים (435 — art, n mp) *hā'ĕlōhîm* — God | בַּשָּׁמַיִם (904, 8452 — prep, art, n md) *bashshāmayim* — in the heavens | וְאַתָּה (887 — cj, pers pron) *wᵉ'attāh* — but you | עַל־הָאָרֶץ (6142, 800 — prep, art, n fs) *'al-hā'ārets* — upon the earth

עַל־כֵּן (6142, 3772 — prep, adv) *'al-kēn* — therefore | יִהְיוּ (2030.126 — v Qal juss 3mp) *yihyû* — may they be | דְּבָרֶיךָ (1745 — n mp, ps 2ms) *dhᵉvārêkhā* — your words | מְעַטִּים (4746 — sub) *mᵉ'attîm* — few | **3.** כִּי (3706 — cj) *kî* — because | בָּא (971.111 — v Qal pf 3ms) *bā'* — it will come | הַחֲלוֹם (2573 — art, n ms) *hachălôm* — the dream

---

... from a household of rebels he came forth to be king, *Goodspeed* ... though stepping from prison to the throne, *JB*.

whereas also he that is born in his kingdom becometh poor: ... in the very kingdom where he was born in poverty, *Anchor* ... though by birth he was only a poor man, *BB* ...

though in his own kingdom he was born poor, *Goodspeed* ... though born a beggar in that kingdom, *JB*.

15. I considered all the living which walk under the sun: ... all who live and move, *JB* ... the whole world, from east to west, *Knox* ... studied all life here, *REB*.

with the second child that shall stand up in his stead: ... round the young man who was to be ruler in place of the king, *BB* ... running with the youth who was to stand in his place, *Goodspeed* ... support the young newcomer who takes over, *JB* ... take part with the young man, the usurper that rises in the old king's stead, *Knox*.

16. There is no end of all the people, even of all that have been before them: ... endless numbers of the people in the past, *Anchor* ... was an endless crowd that he was leading, *Beck* ... no end of all the people, of all those whose head he was, *BB* ... He takes his place at the head of innumerable subjects, *JB.*

they also that come after shall not rejoice in him: ... would care nothing about him, *Anchor* ... those who came later weren't happy with him, *Beck* ... will have no delight in him, *BB* ... his successors will not think the more kindly of him for that, *JB.*

Surely this also is vanity and vexation of spirit: ... is an example of futility and grasping at the wind, *Anchor* ... is to no purpose and desire for wind, *BB* ... is frustration, and labour lost, *Knox* ... is vain and futile, *Moffatt.*

5:1. Keep thy foot when thou goest to the house of God: ... Watch your step, *Beck* ... Put your feet down with care, *BB* ... Never enter God's house carelessly, *Moffatt.*

and be more ready to hear, than to give the sacrifice of fools: ... It is better to listen, *Beck* ... it is better to give ear, *BB* ... to draw near to obey is better than that fools should offer sacrifice, *Goodspeed* ... draw near him to listen, *Moffatt.*

for they consider not that they do evil: ... in their ignorance do wrong, *Beck* ... whose knowledge is only of doing evil, *BB* ... do not understand that they do wrong, *Fenton* ... all a fool knows is how to do wrong, *Moffatt.*

2. Be not rash with thy mouth: ... Be in no hurry to speak, *JB* ... Be not hasty in your utterance, *NAB* ... Do not be hasty in word, *NASB* ... Think before you speak, *NCV.*

and let not thine heart be hasty to utter any thing before God: ... do not hastily declare yourself, *JB* ... never let your heart hurry you into words, *Moffatt* ... let not your heart be quick to make a promise, *NAB* ... be careful about what you say, *NCV.*

for God is in heaven, and thou upon earth: therefore let thy words be few: ... Be sparing, then, of speech, *JB* ... few words are best, *Knox* ... say only a few words to God, *NCV.*

3. For a dream cometh through the multitude of business: ... through much effort, *NASB* ... nightmares come with many cares, *Douay* ... Bad dreams come from too much worrying, *NCV* ... dream comes when there are many cares, *NIV.*

and a fool's voice is known by multitude of words: ... through many words, *NASB* ... too many words come from foolish people, *NCV* ...

---

where. He takes an extensive survey, considering all the living which walk under the sun. Generation after generation pass before his mind's eye. All have the same character.

This appeared to the Preacher to be the universal rude, human nature in every age alike. There was no end of all the people. The giddy and inconstant multitude go on from generation to generation. Solomon had seen it himself. So had others before him. So it would go on to the end. They would abandon the present idol as those had done who had been before them. The heir that is now worshiped with servility will have his turn of mortification. They that come after will not rejoice in him. "Cease ye from man, whose breath is in his nostrils"—is the much needed exhortation—"for wherein is he to be accounted of?" (Isa. 2:22). The smile of today may be changed for the frown of tomorrow (Mark 11:8; 15:8, 14). The love of change is a dominant principle of selfishness—insensible to our present blessings and craving for some imaginary good.

5:1. The Preacher has multiplied his illustrations of his subject. All is vanity. There is, however, one exception—the service of God. Let us then go into the sanctuary. Yet even here, what a mass is there of vacant service, the copy and dead imitation. How important, therefore, is the divine rule to maintain the vital sacredness of the service. Solomon's rule, "Be ready to hear," is that of our divine Master, Who said, "Take heed therefore how ye hear" (Luke 8:18).

Truly, the hindrances press heavily. Perhaps all (except those connected with our physical temperament) are summed up in one: "The word preached did not profit them, not being mixed with faith in them that heard it" (Heb. 4:2).

And yet, the heartless worshipers consider not that they do evil (cf. Hos. 7:2). But however well conceived be the outward form, the substance is "the sacrifice of the wicked, which is an abomination to the LORD" (Prov. 15:8). Account will be taken at the great day not only for the commission of sin but for the service of duty.

5:2–3. This is a divine rule for prayer. We need not restrict it to public worship. The vanity of the heart in prayer gives full scope for this rule of discipline. How much of our own spirit mingles with our communion with God! Our business with God is infinitely greater than with all the world beside.

The want of preparation of heart to speak in the Lord's ear makes the heart careless and irreverent and brings guilt upon the holy exercise. The thought

Row 1

1745	904, 7524	3809	7249	6275	904, 7524
n mp	prep, n ms	n ms	cj, n ms	n ms	prep, n ms
דְּבָרִים	בְּרֹב	כְּסִיל	וְקוֹל	עִנְיָן	בְּרֹב
devārîm	berōv	kesîl	weqôl	'inyān	berōv
words	by the abundance of	the foolish	and the voice of	an occupation	by the abundance of

4.

3706	3937, 8396.341	414, 310.323	3937, 435	5266	5265.123	3626, 866
cj	prep, v Piel inf con, ps 3ms	adv, v Piel juss 2ms	prep, n mp	n ms	v Qal impf 2ms	prep, rel part
כִּי	לְשַׁלְּמוֹ	אַל־תְּאַחֵר	לֵאלֹהִים	נֶדֶר	תִּדֹּר	כַּאֲשֶׁר
kî	leshallemô	'al-te'achēr	lē'lōhîm	nedher	tiddōr	ka'ăsher
because	to make it complete	do not delay	to God	a vow	you vow	when

5.

866	3005	8396.331	866, 5265.123	881	904, 3809	2761	375
rel part	adj	v Piel impv 2ms	rel part, v Qal impf 2ms	do	prep, art, n mp	n ms	sub
אֲשֶׁר	טוֹב	שַׁלֵּם	אֲשֶׁר־תִּדֹּר	אֶת	בַּכְּסִילִים	חֵפֶץ	אֵין
'ăsher	ṭôv	shallēm	'ăsher-tiddōr	'ēth	bakkesîlîm	chēphets	'ên
that	better	make complete	what you will vow	do	in the foolish	delight	there is not

Row 4

8396.323	3940	4623, 8054, 5265.123	3940, 5265.123
v Piel impf 2ms	cj, neg part	prep, rel part, v Qal impf 2ms	neg part, v Qal impf 2ms
תְשַׁלֵּם	וְלֹא	מִשֶּׁתִּדּוֹר	לֹא־תִדֹּר
theshallēm	welō'	mishshettiddôr	lō'-thiddōr
you will make it complete	and not	than that you make a vow	you do not vow

6.

3937, 6686	414, 569.123	881, 1340	3937, 2490.541	881, 6552	414, 5598.123
prep, n mp	cj, adv, v Qal juss 2ms	do, n ms, ps 2ms	prep, v Hiphil inf con	do, n ms, ps 2ms	adv, v Qal juss 2ms
לִפְנֵי	וְאַל־תֹּאמַר	אֶת־בְּשָׂרֶךָ	לַחֲטִיא	אֶת־פִּיךָ	אַל־תִּתֵּן
liphnê	we'al-tō'mar	'eth-besārekhā	lachăṭî'	'eth-pîkhā	'al-tittēn
before	and do not say	your body	to cause to sin	your mouth	do not allow

Row 6

435	7395.121	4066	2026	8145	3706	4534
art, n mp	v Qal impf 3ms	intrg	pers pron	n fs	cj	art, n ms
הָאֱלֹהִים	יִקְצֹף	לָמָּה	הִיא	שְׁגָגָה	כִּי	הַמַּלְאָךְ
hā'ĕlōhîm	yiqtsōph	lāmmāh	hi'	sheghāghāh	kî	hammal'ākh
God	will He be angry	why	it	an inadvertent sin	that	the messenger

7.

3706	3135	881, 4801	2341.311	6142, 7249
cj	n fd, ps 2ms	do, n ms	cj, v Piel pf 3ms	prep, n ms, ps 2ms
כִּי	יָדֶיךָ	אֶת־מַעֲשֵׂה	וְחִבֵּל	עַל־קוֹלֶךָ
kî	yādhêkhā	'eth-ma'ăsēh	wechibbēl	'al-qôlekhā
because	your hands	the work of	that He will take in pledge	about your voice

Row 8

881, 435	3706	7528.542	1745	1961	2573	904, 7524
do, art, n mp	cj	v Hiphil inf abs	cj, n mp	cj, n mp	n mp	prep, n ms
אֶת־הָאֱלֹהִים	כִּי	הַרְבֵּה	וּדְבָרִים	וַהֲבָלִים	חֲלֹמוֹת	בְּרֹב
'eth-hā'ĕlōhîm	kî	harbēh	ûdhevārîm	wahvālîm	chălōmôth	verōv
God	yet	making abundant	and words	and vanities	dreams	in the abundance of

8.

6928	5122	1530	7851	524, 6480	3486.131
cj, n ms	n ms	cj, n ms	n ms	cj, n ms	v Qal impv 2ms
וָצֶדֶק	מִשְׁפָּט	וְגֵזֶל	רָשׁ	אִם־עֹשֶׁק	יְרָא
wātsedheq	mishpāṭ	weghēzel	rāsh	'im-'ōsheq	yerā'
and righteousness	justice	and robbery of	a poor man	if the extortion of	fear

Row 10

4623, 6142	1393	3706	6142, 2761	414, 8867.123	904, 4224	7495.123
prep, prep	adj	cj	prep, art, n ms	adv, v Qal juss 2ms	prep, art, n fs	v Qal impf 2ms
מֵעַל	גָּבֹהַּ	כִּי	עַל־הַחֵפֶץ	אַל־תִּתְמַהּ	בַּמְּדִינָה	תִּרְאֶה
mē'al	ghāvōahh	kî	'al-hachēphets	'al-tithmahh	vammedhînāh	tir'eh
from over	higher	because	about the delight	do not be astonished	in the districts	you see

the fool talks and it is so much chatter, *NEB* … the voice of a fool by abundance of words, *Young*.

4. When thou vowest a vow unto God, defer not to pay it: … do not be slow in paying it, *Anchor* … don't delay to pay it, *Beck* … When you take an oath before God, put it quickly into effect, *BB* … discharge it without delay, *JB*.

for he hath no pleasure in fools: … he has no liking for fools, *Anchor* … for He is not pleased with evasions, *Fenton* … has no love for fools, *JB* … the vows of fools displease him), *Moffatt*.

pay that which thou hast vowed: … Pay what you vow to pay, *Anchor* … keep the oath you have taken, *BB* … Do what you have promised, *Fenton* … Discharge your vow, *JB*.

5. Better is it that thou shouldest not vow, than that thou shouldest

vow and not pay: … better that you make no vow, than that you make a vow and fail to keep it, *Anchor* … It is better not to promise anything than to promise something and not do it, *NCV* … Better that thou do not vow, than that thou dost vow and dost not complete, *Young*.

6. Suffer not thy mouth to cause thy flesh to sin: … Do not allow your tongue to put you in the wrong, *Anchor* … Don't let your mouth get you into sin, *Beck* … Let not your mouth make your flesh do evil, *BB* … Do not allow your mouth to make a sinner of you, *JB*.

neither say thou before the angel, that it was an error: … "It was just a mistake", *Anchor* … No thought I gave to it?, *Knox* … "I didn't mean what I promised", *NCV* … that it was unintentional, *REB*.

wherefore should God be angry at thy voice, and destroy the work of

thine hands?: … angered by your speech, and destroy what you have accomplished?, *Anchor* … get angry with what you say and destroy what you've done?, *Beck* … lest God be angry at your excuse and undo you, *Moffatt* … God will become angry with your words and will destroy everything you have worked for, *NCV*.

7. For in the multitude of dreams and many words there are also divers vanities: … "Like so many empty dreams are so many empty words", *Anchor* … Where there are many dreams, there is also much empty talk, *Beck* … much talk comes from dreams and things of no purpose, *BB* … through many empty dreams come many vows, *Goodspeed*.

but fear thou God: … Simply show respect to God!, *Anchor* … You shall revere God, *Berkeley* … content thyself rather with the fear of God, *Knox* … You should respect God, *NCV* … stand in awe of God, *NIV*.

of the Lord in heaven sitting on his throne and the defiled sinner on earth standing before Him (Isa. 6:5–8), the infinite distance between his greatness and our vileness should make us sober.

The few words here directed are words well chosen and ordered. They contrast strongly with the "vain repetitions," such as the frantic orgies of Baal. The fewness of the words is not the main concern, but whether they be the words of the heart.

But the few words imply the heart set in order before utterance—a thoughtful mind in a spiritual habit. There is more substance in a few minutes of real communion than in an hour of formal exercise. There is no artificial method. All is full of feeling and confidence, sealed with gracious acceptance.

Loose and incoherent impulses also contrast with the few sober, recollected words. They are like the confused images of a dream, flowing out of the hurry of distracting business.

5:4–7. The rules in the former verses apply to the ordinary service of God. This relates to a special exercise. The warning, however, against rashness and haste applies here also. A solemn engagement made with God is a transaction needing much prayer and consideration. It should rest upon the clear warrant of God's Word. It should concern a matter really

important, suitable and attainable. It should be so limited as to open a way for disentanglement under unforeseen contingencies or altered circumstances. It will be a hindrance or a help, according as it is the result of impulse or of intelligence.

Vows, however, are not like prayers at which we should be "without ceasing" (1 Thess. 5:17). We have burdens and infirmities enough pressing upon us. Let us be careful that we do not rashly or needlessly multiply them.

Here is not the direction to make a vow but the obligation, having made it, to cheerfully and instantly pay it. It is an engagement we should be careful to discharge to man and much more to God (Deut. 23:21; Ps. 76:11). The rule is therefore emphatically repeated: Defer not to pay it.

Every member, so active is the principle of sin, stirs the whole body. The rashness of the mouth causes the flesh to sin. To how many inconsiderate and unwarranted vows does this warning apply! (Judg. 11:30; 1 Sam. 14:24). Never suffer your mouth to promise what you cannot and ought not to perform.

5:8. We need not always expect continuous connection in this Book. It is not the regular dissertation upon a given subject but a rapid survey of the

9. (read right to left)

Strong's	Parsing	Hebrew	Translit	Gloss
800	n fs	אֶרֶץ	'erets	the land
3620	cj, n ms	וְיִתְרוֹן	weyithrôn	and the profit of
6142	prep, ps 3mp	עֲלֵיהֶם	'ălêhem	over them
1393	cj, adj	וּגְבֹהִים	ûghevōhîm	and those higher
8490.151	v Qal act ptc ms	שֹׁמֵר	shōmēr	One Who watches
1393	adj	גָּבֹהַּ	gāvōahh	high

10.

Strong's	Parsing	Hebrew	Translit	Gloss
3826B	n ms	כֶּסֶף	keseph	silver
154.151	v Qal act ptc ms	אֹהֵב	'ōhēv	someone who loves
5856.255	v Niphal ptc ms	נֶעֱבָד	ne'ĕvādh	being cultivated
3937, 7898	prep, n ms	לְשָׂדֶה	lesādheh	to the field
4567	n ms	מֶלֶךְ	melekh	a king
2026	pers pron	הִיא	hî'	it
904, 3725	prep, art, n ms	בַּכֹּל	bakkōl	among everyone

Strong's	Parsing	Hebrew	Translit	Gloss
3940	neg part	לֹא	lō'	not
904, 2066	prep, art, n ms	בֶּהָמוֹן	behāmôn	with the wealth
4449, 154.151	cj, intrg, v Qal act ptc ms	וּמִי־אֹהֵב	ûmî-'ōhēv	and who is someone who loves
3826B	n ms	כֶּסֶף	keseph	silver
3940, 7881.121	neg part, v Qal impf 3ms	לֹא־יִשְׂבַּע	lō'-yisba'	he will not be satisfied with

11.

Strong's	Parsing	Hebrew	Translit	Gloss
7525.116	v Qal pf 3cp	רַבּוּ	rabbû	they are more numerous
3009B	art, adj	הַטּוֹבָה	hattôvāh	the good
904, 7528.141	prep, v Qal inf con	בִּרְבוֹת	birvôth	when being abundant
1961	n ms	הֶבֶל	hāvel	a vanity
1612, 2172	cj, dem pron	גַּם־זֶה	gam-zeh	also this
8721	n fs	תְּבוּאָה	thevû'āh	gain

Strong's	Parsing	Hebrew	Translit	Gloss
524, 7506	cj, n fs	אִם־רְאִיַּת	'im-re'îyath	except the seeing of
3706	cj	כִּי	kî	because
3937, 1196	prep, n mp, ps 3fs	לִבְעָלֶיהָ	liv'ālêāh	to its owners
4242, 3917	cj, intrg, n ms	וּמַה־כִּשְׁרוֹן	ûmah-kishrôn	and what is the advantage
404.152	v Qal act ptc mp, ps 3fs	אֹכְלֶיהָ	'ōkhlêāh	the eaters of it

12.

Strong's	Parsing	Hebrew	Translit	Gloss
524, 4746	cj, sub	אִם־מְעַט	'im-me'at	whether a little
5856.151	art, v Qal act ptc ms	הָעֹבֵד	hā'ōvēdh	the worker
8517	n fs	שְׁנַת	shenath	the sleep of
5142	adj	מְתוּקָה	methûqāh	sweet
6084	n fd, ps 3ms	עֵינָיו	'ênāv	his eyes

Strong's	Parsing	Hebrew	Translit	Gloss
375	sub, ps 3ms	אֵינֶנּוּ	'ênennû	there is not of it
3937, 6474	prep, art, n ms	לֶעָשִׁיר	le'āshîr	of the rich
7882	cj, art, n ms	וְהַשָּׂבָע	wehassāvā'	but the surplus
404.121	v Qal impf 3ms	יֹאכֵל	yō'khēl	he will eat
524, 7528.542	cj, cj, v Hiphil inf abs	וְאִם־הַרְבֵּה	we'im-harbēh	or whether making abundant

13.

Strong's	Parsing	Hebrew	Translit	Gloss
8809	prep	תַּחַת	tachath	under
7495.115	v Qal pf 1cs	רָאִיתִי	rā'îthî	I have seen
2571.153	v Qal act ptc fs	חוֹלָה	chôlāh	being weak
7750	n fs	רָעָה	rā'āh	evil
3552	sub	יֵשׁ	yēsh	there is
3937, 3583.141	prep, v Qal inf con	לִישׁוֹן	lîshôn	to sleep
3937	prep, ps 3ms	לוֹ	lô	to him
5299.551	v Hiphil ptc ms	מֵנִיחַ	manîach	allowing rest

---

8. If thou seest the oppression of the poor: ... see the poor under a cruel yoke, *BB* ... In some places you will see poor people mistreated, *NCV*.

and violent perverting of judgment and justice in a province: ... denial of justice and right, *Anchor* ... robbed of what is just and right, *Beck* ... right being violently overturned in a country, *BB* ... distortion of justice and right, *Fenton*.

marvel not at the matter: ... do not be shocked, *Anchor* ... don't be surprised, *Beck* ... be not amazed at the situation, *Goodspeed* ... Let not such things bewilder thee, *Knox*.

for he that is higher than the highest regardeth: ... each official is being watched by his superior, *Anchor* ... a high official has one higher watching him, *Beck* ... one high official watches over another, *Goodspeed* ... it is one official preying on another, *Moffatt*.

and there be higher than they: ... over them all is the king, *Anchor* ...

and both have higher ones over them, *Beck* … there are those higher than both, *Goodspeed* … over both there is a supreme authority, *Moffatt.*

9. Moreover the profit of the earth is for all: … what the land yields is for the benefit of all, *JB* … the abundance of the earth is for all, *KJVII* … wealth of the country is divided up among them all, *NCV* … increase from the land is taken by all, *NIV.*

the king himself is served by the field: … the king [himself] is dependent upon the field, *Darby* … the king makes sure he gets his share of the profits, *NCV* … the king himself profits from the fields, *NIV.*

10. He that loveth silver shall not be satisfied with silver: … He who

loves money never has enough money, *Anchor* … love of money will never be satisfied with money, *Fenton* … The covetous man is never satisfied with money, *NAB, Douay.*

nor he that loveth abundance with increase: … whoever cares most about making money thinks his profits are too small, *Anchor* … if you love property, you will gain nothing, *Beck* … Nor he who loves riches with gain, *Goodspeed* … the lover of wealth reaps no fruit from it, *NAB.*

this is also vanity: … This is futility, *Anchor* … is to no purpose, *BB* … is also useless, *NCV* … is meaningless, *NIV.*

11. When goods increase, they are increased that eat them: … Where

goods abound, parasites abound, *JB* … riches will give thee more mouths to feed, *Knox* … The more a man gains, the more there are to spend it, *Moffatt* … The more wealth people have, the more friends they have to help spend it, *NCV.*

and what good is there to the owners thereof, saving the beholding of them with their eyes?: … where is the owner's profit, apart from feasting his eyes?, *JB* … profit he has none that owns them, save the feasting of his eyes on them if he will, *Knox* … while the owner can only look on, *Moffatt* … what is the advantage to their owners except to look on?, *NASB.*

12. The sleep of a labouring man is sweet, whether he eat little or

---

different points in the great sphere before him. Yet this verse falls in with one great object of the Book, which is to compose the minds of the servants of God to stillness and confidence under his inscrutable dispensations. Solomon supposes a wide extent of unjust oppression, not a village, town or city, but a province under perverting influence. This is truly a dark page in providence, which exercises the patience and faith of the saints (Ps. 73:12f; Jer. 12:1), stumbles the ill instructed, and opens wide the caviler's mouth.

There is no cause to marvel at the matter, as if it were unexpected, to allow hard thoughts of God, to complain of his dispensations, or to be weary of his service. God does not look on as an unconcerned spectator. If He "keeps silence," his forbearance is not forgetfulness. He is only waiting, as in his dealings with the chosen nation, his own best and fittest time for their deliverance (Exo. 3:7ff). Messiah's kingdom is brightened with the sunbeam: "He shall deliver the needy when he crieth; the poor also, and him that hath no helper" (Ps. 72:12ff).

5:9. The word "moreover" connects this statement, though somewhat obscurely, with the preceding. There is a level, where the rich and poor meet together (Prov. 22:2). The curse upon the ground is so far mitigated that while "bread" is still "eaten in the sweat of the face" (Gen. 3:17) there is profit, directly or indirectly, for all. The king himself is served by the field. He is more dependent upon the

laborer than the laborer is on him. He has more need of the laborer's strength than the laborer has of his royal crown. Humility, therefore, is the lesson for the rich, contentment for the poor. All of us may be reminded of the important truth, with its daily responsibilities, that all are members of one body, parts of one great whole.

5:10–12. The tempter may paint a brilliant prospect of happiness. But fact and experience prove that he who loves silver or any worldly abundance will be satisfied neither with the possession nor with the increase. The appetite is created, not satisfied. The vanity of this disease is coveting what does not satisfy when we have it. Hunger is satisfied with meat, and thirst with drink. But hunger or thirst for this world's wealth is as unsatisfied at the end as at the beginning. This is also vanity.

Nor is it to be forgotten that an increase of goods is followed with a corresponding increase of consumers. Solomon's expensive establishment kept pace with his increasing treasures (1 Ki. 4:22–26). In all similar cases, the multitude of retainers increases. A certain appearance must be maintained.

Even in the common comforts of life, is not the balance often in favor of the poor? Having little to lose they have but little fear of losing. Their sleep is therefore the natural fruit of weariness without care, whereas the abundance of the rich is often a sleeping weight. When the last thoughts are of the world and the heart centered there, carefulness is the

8507 art, n ms הַשֶּׁמֶשׁ hashshāmesh the sun	6484 n ms עֹשֶׁר ʿōsher riches	8490.155 v Qal pass ptc ms שָׁמוּר shāmûr having been kept	3937, 1196 prep, n mp, ps 3ms לִבְעָלָיו livʿālâv to its owners	3937, 7750 prep, n fs, ps 3ms לְרָעָתוֹ lerāʾāthô to his disaster	**14.** 6.111 cj, v Qal pf 3ms וְאָבַד weʾāvadh and they will be lost
6484 art, n ms הָעֹשֶׁר hāʿōsher the riches	2000 art, dem pron הַהוּא hahûʾ the those	904, 6275 prep, n ms בְּעִנְיַן beʿinyan in an occupation	7737 adj רָע rāʿ evil	3314.511 cj, v Hiphil pf 3ms וְהוֹלִיד wehôlîdh and he will father	1158 n ms בֵּן bēn a son 375 cj, sub וְאֵין weʾên but there is not
904, 3135 prep, n fs, ps 3ms בְּיָדוֹ beyādhô in his hand	4114 indef pron מְאוּמָה meʾûmāh something	**15.** 3626, 866 prep, rel part כַּאֲשֶׁר kaʾăsher just as	3428.111 v Qal pf 3ms יָצָא yātsāʾ he came out	4623, 1027 prep, n fs מִבֶּטֶן mibbeṭen from the womb of	525 n fs, ps 3ms אִמּוֹ ʾimmô his mother 6414 adj עָרוֹם ʿārôm naked
8178.121 v Qal impf 3ms יָשׁוּב yāshûv he will return	3937, 2050.141 prep, v Qal inf con לָלֶכֶת lālekheth to go	3626, 8054, 971.111 prep, rel part, v Qal pf 3ms כְּשֶׁבָּא keshebbāʾ like that he came	4114 cj, indef pron וּמְאוּמָה ûmeʾûmāh but something	3940, 5558.121 neg part, v Qal impf 3ms לֹא־יִשָּׂא lōʾ-yissāʾ he will not carry	
904, 6221 prep, n ms, ps 3ms בַּעֲמָלוֹ vaʿămālô because of his toil	8054, 2050.521 rel part, v Hiphil impf 3ms שֶׁיֹּלֵךְ sheyōlēkh which he will cause to go	904, 3135 prep, n fs, ps 3ms בְּיָדוֹ beyādhô in his hand	**16.** 1612, 2173 cj, cj, dem pron וְגַם־זֹה wegham-zōh and also this	7750 n fs רָעָה rāʿāh an evil	
2571.153 v Qal act ptc fs חוֹלָה chôlāh being weak	3725, 6202 adj, prep כָּל־עֻמַּת kol-ʿummath all corresponding to	8054, 971.111 rel part, v Qal pf 3ms שֶׁבָּא shebbāʾ how he came	3772 adv כֵּן kēn so	2050.121 v Qal impf 3ms יֵלֵךְ yēlēkh he will go	4242, 3620 cj, intrg, n ms וּמַה־יִּתְרוֹן ûmah-yithrôn and what profit
3937 prep, ps 3ms לוֹ lô to him	8054, 6218.121 rel part, v Qal impf 3ms שֶׁיַּעֲמֹל sheyaʿămōl that he toils	3937, 7593 prep, art, n fs לָרוּחַ lārûach to the wind	**17.** 1612 cj גַּם gam also	3725, 3219 adj, n mp, ps 3ms כָּל־יָמָיו kol-yāmâv all his days	904, 2932 prep, art, n ms בַּחֹשֶׁךְ bachōshekh in the darkness
404.121 v Qal impf 3ms יֹאכֵל yōʾkhēl he will eat	3832.111 cj, v Qal pf 3ms וְכָעַס wekhāʿas and he is vexed	7528.542 v Hiphil inf abs הַרְבֵּה harbēh making abundant	2582 cj, n ms, ps 3ms וְחָלְיוֹ wechāleyô and his suffering	7397 cj, n ms וָקֶצֶף wāqātseph and anger	**18.** 2079 intrj הִנֵּה hinnēh behold

much: ... if he has little food or much, *BB* ... Full belly or empty, sound is the cottar's sleep, *Knox* ... Those who work hard sleep in peace; it is not important if they eat little or much, *NCV.*

but the abundance of the rich will not suffer him to sleep: ... rich person's stomach is too full to let him sleep, *Beck* ... to him who is full, sleep will not come, *BB* ... the excess of the rich does not allow him to sleep, *Fenton* ... rich people worry about their wealth and cannot sleep, *NCV.*

13. There is a sore evil which I have seen under the sun, namely, riches kept for the owners thereof to their hurt: ... wealth was hoarded by its owner at great cost to himself, *Anchor* ... wealth retained by the owner to his own hurt, *Berkeley* ... wealth kept by the owner to be his downfall, *BB* ... wealth kept to the injury of its possessor, *Fenton.*

14. But those riches perish by evil travail: ... I saw destruction of his wealth by an evil chance, *BB* ... that wealth perishing by an unfortunate accident, *Fenton* … that wealth was lost in an unfortunate enterprise, *Goodspeed* … By cruel misadventure they are lost, *Knox*.

and he begetteth a son, and there is nothing in his hand: … became the father of a son, without a thing in his hand, *Goodspeed* … a son is born to him, and he has nothing to leave him, *JB* … to the son he has begotten nothing he leaves but poverty, *Knox* … the man has nothing to leave to his son, *Moffatt*.

15. As he came forth of his mother's womb, naked shall he return to go as he came: … as he came, so must he go, *JB* … Naked he came, when he left his mother's womb, and naked still death finds him, *Knox* … Naked he came from his mother's womb, and naked he must return, *Moffatt* … he goes just as he came, *NAB*.

and shall take nothing of his labour, which he may carry away in his hand: … nothing to show for all his long endeavour, *Knox* … he has nothing to take with him, *Moffatt* … when they die they leave with nothing, *NCV*.

16. And this also is a sore evil, that in all points as he came, so shall he go: … exactly as a man is born, thus will he die, *NASB* … They leave just as they came, *NCV* … As a man comes, so he departs, *NIV*.

and what profit hath he that hath laboured for the wind?: … what is the advantage to him, *NASB* … what do they gain from chasing the wind?, *NCV* … what does he gain, since he toils for the wind?, *NIV*.

17. All his days also he eateth in darkness, and he hath much sorrow and wrath with his sickness: … in darkness, in constant vexation, misery and anger?, *Anchor* … in darkness, and hath much vexation, and sickness, and irritation, *Darby* … All his days are in the dark, and he has much sorrow, pain, disease, and trouble, *BB* … in darkness, and much anxiety, sickness, and vexation, *Fenton*.

18. Behold that which I have seen: it is good and comely for one to eat and to drink, and to enjoy the good of all his labour that he taketh under the sun all the days of his life, which God giveth him: … what is satisfying and suitable is to eat and drink and enjoy oneself in all one's struggle, *Anchor* … good, yes, excellent, is to eat and drink and enjoy good things with all your hard work, *Beck* … it is good and fair for a man to take meat and drink and to have joy in all his work, *BB* … one should eat and drink and get enjoyment out of all his toil, *Goodspeed*.

for it is his portion: … that is what one gets out of it, *Anchor* … that is your lot, *Beck* … that is his reward, *BB* … this is the lot of humanity, *JB*.

---

atmosphere of the day and hurried restlessness often the weariness of the night. Thus are sleepless nights connected with anxious days.

5:13–17. Another illustration of the utter vanity of riches. This profound Book discloses many humbling secrets. Is the man repining about his hard lot and ready to envy his more wealthy neighbor? Let him study here the lesson set before him and return with a contented and thankful heart, "Thank God! I have blessings with less care, temptation, and disappointment."

Riches centered in selfish aggrandizement are kept for the owners thereof to their hurt. And grievous indeed is the hurt. Such strong temptations to pride, vainglory, love of the world, forgetfulness of God! They are always a temptation. So often a rise in the world is declension or apostasy from God. It is only when they are consecrated to God and laid out in the service of our fellow creatures that they become a blessing.

Here, however, the fortune which the miser had heaped up has perished by some kind of evil travail. There is nothing in his hand. He leaves his child a beggar, and he returns to his mother's womb naked as he came forth (Job 1:21; 1 Tim.

6:7). The miser's present course is indeed a sore evil. All his profit of pouring out his heart upon the world will be found at last to have been only laboring for the wind (Hos. 8:7; 12:1).

5:18–20. A bright vision comes before the wise man, in contrast with the frowning cloud just before. Solomon shows us the reality of happiness even in a world of sin and sorrow. "All things are ours," "things present" as well as "things to come" (1 Cor. 3:22). And good and comely is the privilege of connecting our present blessings with the enjoyment of God.

Is this the picture of mere worldly happiness, as if we might plead against overstrictness and in favor of more indulgence? We think not. The law of discipleship in the Old and New Testament is substantially the same—self-denial, taking up the cross. Solomon only insists that the true servant of God is really the happiest of men, that "God giveth us richly all things to enjoy" (1 Tim. 6:17). This is the gift of God, every day of our life a new gift, specially to be employed for his glory and in his service.

It is most important to set out Christian liberty while we inculcate Christian mortification. We must be careful not to give unworthy views of the real hap-

866, 7495.111	603	3005	866, 3413	3937, 404.141, 3937, 8685.141	3937, 7495.141
rel part, v Qal pf 1cs	pers pron	adj	rel part, adj	prep, v Qal inf con, cj, prep, v Qal inf con	cj, prep, v Qal inf con
אֲשֶׁר־רָאִיתִי	אָנִי	טוֹב	אֲשֶׁר־יָפֶה	לֶאֱכֹל־וְלִשְׁתּוֹת	וְלִרְאוֹת
ʼăsher-rāʼîthî	ʼānî	tôv	ʼăsher-yāpheh	leʼekhōl-welishtôth	welirʼôth
what I have seen	I	good	that beautiful	to eat and to drink	and to see

3009B	904, 3725, 6219	8054, 6218.121	8809, 8507	4709
adj	prep, adj, n ms, ps 3ms	rel part, v Qal impf 3ms	prep, art, n ms	n ms
טוֹבָה	בְּכָל־עֲמָלוֹ	שֶׁיַּעֲמֹל	תַּחַת־הַשֶּׁמֶשׁ	מִסְפַּר
tôvāh	bekhol-ʻămālô	sheyaʻămōl	tachath-hashshemesh	mispar
good	because of all his toil	which he toils	under the sun	the number of

3219, 2522	866, 5598.111, 3937	435	3706, 2000	2610	1612
n mp, n mp, ps 3ms	rel part, v Qal pf 3ms, prep, ps 3ms	art, n mp	cj, pers pron	n ms, ps 3ms	19. cj
יְמֵי־חַיָּיו	אֲשֶׁר־נָתַן־לוֹ	הָאֱלֹהִים	כִּי־הוּא	חֶלְקוֹ	גַּם
yemê-chayyāw	ʼăsher-nāthan-lô	hāʼĕlōhîm	kî-hûʼ	chelqô	gam
the days of his lifetime	which He has given to him	God	because it	his portion	also

3725, 119	866	5598.111, 3937	435	6484	5420
adj, art, n ms	rel pron	v Qal pf 3ms, prep, ps 3ms	art, n mp	n ms	cj, n mp
כָּל־הָאָדָם	אֲשֶׁר	נָתַן־לוֹ	הָאֱלֹהִים	עֹשֶׁר	וּנְכָסִים
kol-hāʼādhām	ʼăsher	nāthan-lô	hāʼĕlōhîm	ʻōsher	ûnekhāsîm
every man	whom	He has given to him	God	riches	and treasures

8375.511	3937, 404.141	4623	3937, 5558.141	881, 2610
cj, v Hiphil pf 3ms, ps 3ms	prep, v Qal inf con	prep, ps 3ms	cj, prep, v Qal inf con	do, n ms, ps 3ms
וְהִשְׁלִיטוֹ	לֶאֱכֹל	מִמֶּנּוּ	וְלָשֵׂאת	אֶת־חֶלְקוֹ
wehishlîṭô	leʼĕkhōl	mimmennû	welāsēʼth	ʼeth-chelqô
and He will empower him	to eat	from them	and to bear	his portion

3937, 7975.141	904, 6219	2173	5164	435	2026	3706	3940
cj, prep, v Qal inf con	prep, n ms, ps 3ms	dem pron	n fs	n mp	pers pron	cj	neg part
וְלִשְׂמֹחַ	בַּעֲמָלוֹ	זֹה	מַתַּת	אֱלֹהִים	הִיא	כִּי	20. לֹא
welismōach	baʻămālô	zōh	mattath	ʼĕlōhîm	hîʼ	kî	lōʼ
and to be glad	in his toil	this	a gift from	God	it	because	not

7528.542	2226.121	881, 3219	2522	3706	435	6257.551
v Hiphil inf abs	v Qal impf 3ms	do, n mp	n mp, ps 3ms	cj	art, n mp	v Hiphil ptc ms
הַרְבֵּה	יִזְכֹּר	אֶת־יְמֵי	חַיָּיו	כִּי	הָאֱלֹהִים	מַעֲנֶה
harbēh	yizkōr	ʼeth-yemê	chayyāw	kî	hāʼĕlōhîm	maʻăneh
making abundant	he will remember	the days of	his life	because	God	causing to reply

904, 7977	3949	3552	7750	866	7495.115	8809	8507
prep, n fs	n ms, ps 3ms	6:1 sub	n fs	rel part	v Qal pf 1cs	prep	art, n ms
בְּשִׂמְחַת	לִבּוֹ	יֵשׁ	רָעָה	אֲשֶׁר	רָאִיתִי	תַּחַת	הַשֶּׁמֶשׁ
besimchath	libbô	yēsh	rāʼāh	ʼăsher	rāʼîthî	tachath	hashshāmesh
with the gladness of	his heart	there is	an evil	which	I have seen	under	the sun

7521	2026	6142, 119	382	866	5598.121, 3937	435	6484
cj, adj	pers pron	prep, art, n ms	n ms	rel pron	v Qal impf 3ms, prep, ps 3ms	art, n mp	n ms
וְרַבָּה	הִיא	עַל־הָאָדָם	אִישׁ	אֲשֶׁר	יִתֶּן־לוֹ	הָאֱלֹהִים	עֹשֶׁר
werabbāh	hîʼ	ʻal-hāʼādhām	ʼîsh	ʼăsher	yitten-lô	hāʼĕlōhîm	ʻōsher
and great	it	upon men	a man	whom	He does give to him	God	riches

2.

5420	3638	375	2742	3937, 5497	4623, 3725
cj, n mp	cj, n ms	cj, sub, ps 3ms	adj	prep, n fs, ps 3ms	prep, n ms
וּנְכָסִים	וְכָבוֹד	וְאֵינֶנּוּ	חָסֵר	לְנַפְשׁוֹ	מִכֹּל
ûnekhāsîm	wekhāvôdh	weʼênennû	chāsēr	lenaphshô	mikkōl
and treasures	and honor	and it is not to him	lacking	to his soul	from all

866, 181.721	3940, 8375.521	435	3937, 404.141	4623
rel part, v Hithpael impf 3ms	cj, neg part, v Hiphil impf 3ms, ps 3ms	art, n mp	prep, v Qal inf con	prep, ps 3ms
אֲשֶׁר־יִתְאַוֶּה	וְלֹא־יַשְׁלִיטֶנּוּ	הָאֱלֹהִים	לֶאֱכֹל	מִמֶּנּוּ
'ăsher-yith'awweh	welō'-yashlîṭennû	hā'ĕlōhîm	le'ĕkhōl	mimmennû
that he desires	but He does not empower him	God	to eat	from it

3706	382	5425	404.121	2172	1961	2582	7737	2000
cj	n ms	adj	v Qal impf 3ms, ps 3ms	dem pron	n ms	cj, n ms	adj	pers pron
כִּי	אִישׁ	נָכְרִי	יֹאכְלֶנּוּ	זֶה	הֶבֶל	וָחֳלִי	רָע	הוּא
kî	'îsh	nākherî	yō'khelennû	zeh	hevel	wāchālî	rā'	hû'
rather	a man	foreign	he will eat it	this	a vanity	and suffering	evil	it

19. Every man also to whom God hath given riches and wealth, and hath given him power to eat thereof, and to take his portion, and to rejoice in his labour; this is the gift of God: … he has a bonus from God, *Anchor* … this is given by God, *BB* … God gives some people the ability to, *NCV.*

20. For he shall not much remember the days of his life: … will not brood over the shortness of his life, *Anchor* … shall not often think of the brevity of his life, *Berkeley* … will not give much thought to the days of his life, *BB* … such a person will hardly notice the passing of time, *JB.*

because God answereth him in the joy of his heart: … when God keeps his mind occupied with happy thoughts, *Anchor* … God keeps his heart occupied in gladness, *Berkeley* … God lets him be taken up with the joy of his heart, *BB* … God is giving him his heart's delight, *Moffatt.*

6:1. There is an evil which I have seen under the sun, and it is common among men: … which bears heavily on men, *Anchor* … and it is frequent among, *Darby* … it is hard on men, *BB* … it is prevalent among, *NASB.*

2. A man to whom God hath given riches, wealth, and honour, so that he wanteth nothing for his soul of all that he desireth, yet God giveth him not power to eat thereof: … does not give him the power to have joy of it, *BB* … is unable to enjoy it, *Moffatt* … does not grant him power to partake of them, *NAB* … does not let them enjoy such things, *NCV.*

but a stranger eateth it: … a strange man takes it, *BB* … an outsider gets the good of it, *Moffatt* … a foreigner enjoys them, *NASB* … a foreigner consumes it, *NKJV.*

this is vanity, and it is an evil disease: … a sore misfortune, *Moffatt*

… a dire plague, *NAB* … is useless and very wrong, *NCV* … is emptiness and a grave disorder, *NEB.*

3. If a man beget an hundred children, and live many years, so that the days of his years be many, and his soul be not filled with good: … but does not find happiness, *Anchor* … if he isn't satisfied with good things, *Beck* … but his soul takes no pleasure in good, *BB* … but his life is not filled with pleasantness, *Fenton.*

and also that he have no burial: … doesn't even get buried, *Beck* … he is not honoured at his death, *BB* … when he also comes not to have a tomb, *Fenton.*

I say, that an untimely birth is better than he: … a stillborn child is better off than he, *Anchor* … better that such a one, I say, be born dead, *Beck* … a birth before its time is better than he, *BB* … I say an abortion is preferable to him, *Fenton.*

---

piness to be found in the world. We have seen that riches well nigh shut us out of heaven (Matt. 19:23) and that the love of them "drown men in destruction and perdition (1 Tim. 6:9f). Must we not then cast them away? The Preacher gives the due balance. They are not essentially evil. As we have said, the evil is in their abuse, in their love, not in their possession.

6:1–2. This evidently continues the last chapter. Covetousness is again before us. The man, like Solomon himself, wanted nothing for his soul of all that he desired thereof. But here was the contrast, and the case was common among men. The gifts of God abounded to overflowing, but here God gave not the power to eat thereof. Sickness, affliction or worldly disappointment restrained the blessing. It

seems to have been a judicial infliction. He did not use the gifts of his bountiful Father for their rightful purpose. Most justly, therefore, he is deprived of their blessing. The gifts of God are blessed indeed to us when we own them to be his property! But never let us forget the responsibility which they bring with them. We all have our responsibilities. And we are happy just in the proportion that we acknowledge them. Selfishness blasts the harvest. We might as well look for it from the seed corn laid up in the granary instead of being cast into the ground. Our real happiness, therefore, is the thankful improvement of God's own gifts, acknowledging his prerogative to give the power of enjoyment, no less than the blessing to be enjoyed.

3.

Strong's	Parsing	Hebrew	Translit.	English
524, 3314.521	cj, v Hiphil impf 3ms	אִם־יוֹלִיד	'im-yôlîdh	if he will father
382	n ms	אִישׁ	'îsh	a man
4109	num	מֵאָה	mē'āh	one hundred
8523	cj, n fp	וְשָׁנִים	weshānîm	and years
7521	adj	רַבּוֹת	rabbôth	many
2513.121	v Qal impf 3ms	יִחְיֶה	yichăyeh	and he will live
7521	cj, adj	וְרַב	werav	and many

Strong's	Parsing	Hebrew	Translit.	English
8054, 2030.126	rel part, v Qal impf 3mp	שֶׁיִּהְיוּ	sheyihyû	that they will be
3219, 8523	n mp, n fp, ps 3ms	יְמֵי־שָׁנָיו	yemê-shānāv	the days of his years
5497	cj, n fs, ps 3ms	וְנַפְשׁוֹ	wenaphshô	but his soul
3940, 7881.122	neg part, v Qal impf 3fs	לֹא־תִשְׂבַּע	lō'-thisba'	it is not satisfied
4623, 3009B	prep, art, n fs	מִן־הַטּוֹבָה	min-haṭṭôvāh	from the goodness

Strong's	Parsing	Hebrew	Translit.	English
1612, 7185	cj, cj, n fs	וְגַם־קְבוּרָה	wegham-qevûrāh	and also a burial
940, 2030.112	neg part, v Qal pf 3fs	לֹא־הָיְתָה	lō'-hāyethāh	it is not
3937	prep, ps 3ms	לוֹ	lô	to him
569.115	v Qal pf 1cs	אָמַרְתִּי	'āmartî	I will say
3005	adj	טוֹב	ṭôv	better
4623	prep, ps 3ms	מִמֶּנּוּ	mimmennû	than it
5491	art, n ms	הַנָּפֶל	hannāphel	the miscarriage

4.

Strong's	Parsing	Hebrew	Translit.	English
3706, 1961	cj, prep, art, n ms	כִּי־בַהֶבֶל	kî-vahevel	because into the vanity
971.111	v Qal pf 3ms	בָּא	bā'	he will come
904, 2932	cj, prep, art, n ms	וּבַחֹשֶׁךְ	ûvachōshekh	then into the darkness
2050.121	v Qal impf 3ms	יֵלֵךְ	yēlēkh	he will go

5.

Strong's	Parsing	Hebrew	Translit.	English
904, 2932	cj, prep, art, n ms	וּבַחֹשֶׁךְ	ûvachōshekh	and with the darkness
8428	n ms, ps 3ms	שְׁמוֹ	shemô	his name
3803.421	cj, v Pual impf 3ms	יְכֻסֶּה	yekhusseh	it will be covered
1612, 8507	cj, n ms	גַּם־שֶׁמֶשׁ	gam-shemesh	also the sun
3940, 7495.111	neg part, v Qal pf 3ms	לֹא־רָאָה	lō'-rā'āh	it has not seen
3940	cj, neg part	וְלֹא	welō'	and not

6.

Strong's	Parsing	Hebrew	Translit.	English
3156.111	v Qal pf 3ms	יָדָע	yādhā'	it has known
5369	n fs	נַחַת	nachath	rest
3937, 2172	prep, dem pron	לָזֶה	lāzeh	to this one
4623, 2172	prep, dem pron	מִזֶּה	mizzeh	more than to that one
437	cj, cj	וְאִלּוּ	we'illû	and if
2513.111	v Qal pf 3ms	חָיָה	chāyāh	he will live
512	num	אֶלֶף	'eleph	one thousand

Strong's	Parsing	Hebrew	Translit.	English
8523	n fp	שָׁנִים	shānîm	years
6718	n fd	פַּעֲמַיִם	pa'ămayim	two times
3009B	cj, n fs	וְטוֹבָה	weṭôvāh	yet goodness
3940	neg part	לֹא	lō'	not
7495.111	v Qal pf 3ms	רָאָה	rā'āh	he will see
1950B, 3940	intrg part, neg part	הֲלֹא	hălō'	is not
420, 4887	prep, n ms	אֶל־מָקוֹם	'el-māqôm	to a place
259	num	אֶחָד	'echādh	one

7.

Strong's	Parsing	Hebrew	Translit.	English
3725	art, n ms	הַכֹּל	hakkōl	everyone
2050.151	v Qal act ptc ms	הוֹלֵךְ	hôlēkh	going
3725, 6221	adj, n ms	כָּל־עֲמַל	kol-'ămal	all the toil of
119	art, n ms	הָאָדָם	hā'ādhām	the man
3937, 6552	prep, n ms, ps 3ms	לְפִיהוּ	lephîhû	for his mouth
1612, 5497	cj, cj, art, n fs	וְגַם־הַנֶּפֶשׁ	wegham-hannephesh	yet also the soul
3940	neg part	לֹא	lō'	not

8.

Strong's	Parsing	Hebrew	Translit.	English
4527.222	v Niphal impf 3fs	תִּמָּלֵא	thimmālē'	it is full
3706	cj	כִּי	kî	because
4242, 3252	intrg, n ms	מַה־יוֹתֵר	mah-yôthēr	what the remainder
3937, 2550	prep, art, n ms	לֶחָכָם	lechākhām	to the wise
4623, 3809	prep, art, n ms	מִן־הַכְּסִיל	min-hakkesîl	more than the fool

9.

Strong's	Parsing	Hebrew	Translit.	English
4242, 3937, 6270	intrg, prep, n ms	מַה־לֶּעָנִי	mah-le'ānî	what to the afflicted
3156.151	v Qal act ptc ms	יוֹדֵעַ	yôdhēa'	one who knows
3937, 2050.141	prep, v Qal inf con	לַהֲלֹךְ	lahlōkh	to walk
5224	prep	נֶגֶד	neghedh	before
2522	art, n mp	הַחַיִּים	hachayyim	the living
3005	adj	טוֹב	ṭôv	better
4920	n ms	מַרְאֵה	mar'ēh	the sight of

4. For he cometh in with vanity: … In wind it came, *BB* … In futility it came, *JB* … A baby born dead is useless, *NCV* … Its coming is an empty thing, *NEB*.

and departeth in darkness: … to the dark it will go, *BB* … goes into obscurity, *NASB* … It returns to darkness, *NCV*.

and his name shall be covered with darkness: … his name is wrapped in darkness!, *Fenton* … in darkness will its name be buried, *JB* … its name is enveloped in darkness, *NAB* … its name is covered in obscurity, *NASB* … without even a name, *NCV*.

5. Moreover he hath not seen the sun, nor known any thing: … though it never saw the sun nor knew anything, *Anchor* … saw not the sun, and it had no knowledge, *BB* … has never so much as seen or known the sun, *JB* … That baby never saw the sun and never knew anything, *NCV*.

this hath more rest than the other: … it rests more peacefully, *Anchor* … it is better with this than with the other, *BB* … rests better than him!, *Fenton* … will rest more easily, *JB*.

6. Yea, though he live a thousand years twice told, yet hath he seen no good: … without seeing prosperity, *Beck* … but experiences no enjoyment, *Berkeley* … and has not experienced pleasure!, *Fenton* … would never have known the good things of life, *JB*.

do not all go to one place?: … does not everyone have the same destination?, *Anchor* … are not the two going to the same place?, *BB* … Do we not all reach the same goal at last?, *Knox* … are not both alike bound for the same end?, *Moffatt*.

7. All the labour of man is for his mouth: … toils on to satisfy his hunger, *Moffatt* … People work just to feed themselves, *NCV* … end of all man's toil is but to fill his belly, *NEB, REB*.

and yet the appetite is not filled: … his wants are never satisfied, *Anchor* … the longing is not satisfied, *Berkeley* … his wants are never met, *Moffatt* … yet his desire is not fulfilled, *NAB*.

8. For what hath the wise more than the fool?: … How then is a wise man better off than a fool?, *Anchor* … What advantage does a wise man have over a fool, *Beck* … Is wise man more to be envied than fool?, *Knox* … fares no better than, *Moffatt*.

what hath the poor, that knoweth to walk before the living?: … what advantage has a poor man who knows how to walk before the living?, *Beck* … what has the poor man by walking wisely before the living?, *BB* … what of the pauper who knows how to behave in society?, *JB* … a poor man who lives uprightly, *Moffatt*.

9. Better is the sight of the eyes than the wandering of the desire: …

6:3–6. In the case here supposed, two of nature's fondest desires are alluded to: a quiver full of children and the days of many years. Yet if the soul is not filled with good, nothing would be of avail for our happiness. As a proof of the ill esteem in which he is held, his life may end with obloquy, no respect paid the miser at his burial, his death unhonored, unlamented. Sordid accumulation is a dark cloud upon his name to the last. The Preacher decides without hesitation upon this case. Better not to have been born at all—or if born, to have died at the birth—to have gone at once from the womb to the grave.

"I say, then," concludes the wise man, "that an untimely birth is better than he. He cometh in with vanity," seeming to have been born to no purpose. He leaves no trace or remembrance behind. His name is covered with darkness and he is immediately forgotten. His pleasures are momentary. Surely it is not life but enjoyment that gives value to existence and makes the vital difference. Life, though a thousand years twice told, without seeing good is only protracted misery. The longest inhabitant of earth, as well as he that has not seen the sun, do not all go to one place?

But may we not look at this picture on a higher level? All hangs upon this point: the soul, the whole man, filled with good. And what good is there that will fill the man? Only when as a sinner he finds a reconciled God in Christ, his way to God, his peace with God. Never was a more refreshing truth than from one who found the witness and seal of it in contact with heathen misery.

6:7–8. The labor of man is ordinarily for his mouth, for the support of life. Such is the ordinance of God, the curse of the fall, "In the sweat of thy face shalt thou eat bread" (Gen. 3:19). If the curse be removed, the cross remains. Man can do no more by his labor than satisfy his bodily wants. "He that laboureth, laboureth for himself; for his mouth craveth it of him" (Prov. 16:26).

Yet with all our labor the appetite is not filled. The same natural cravings return from day to day. Worldly desires are no less unsatisfied. The covetous man—the more he has, the more he wants. Strange delusion to suppose that more of this world would bring increase of happiness!

The last clause is obscure. But a careful consideration of the statement will bring out a satisfac-

7593	7758	1961	1612, 2172	4623, 2050.141, 5497	6084
n fs	cj, *n fs*	n ms	cj, dem pron	prep, v Qal inf con, n fs	n fd
רוּחַ	וּרְעוּת	הֶבֶל	גַּם־זֶה	מֵהֲלָךְ־נָפֶשׁ	עֵינַיִם
rûach	ûreʿûth	hevel	gam-zeh	mēhelákh-nápheš	ʿênayim
wind	and a striving for	a vanity	also this	than the proceeding of the soul	eyes

10.

866, 2000	3156.255	8428	7410.211	3647	4242, 8054, 2030.111
rel part, pers pron	cj, v Niphal ptc ms	n ms, ps 3ms	v Niphal pf 3ms	adv	intrg, rel part, v Qal pf 3ms
אֲשֶׁר־הוּא	וְנוֹדָע	שְׁמוֹ	נִקְרָא	כְּבָר	מַה־שֶּׁהָיָה
ʾăšer-hûʾ	wenôdhāʿ	shemô	niqŏrāʾ	kevār	mah-shehāyāh
what he	and being known	its name	it has been called	already	what that it has been

3706	4623	8054, 8959	6196	3937, 1833.141	3940, 3310.121	119
cj	prep, ps 3ms	rel pron, art, adj	prep	prep, v Qal inf con	cj, neg part, v Qal impf 3ms	n ms
11. כִּי	מִמֶּנּוּ	שֶׁהַתַּקִּיף	עִם	לָדִין	וְלֹא־יוּכַל	אָדָם
kî	mimmennû	shehattaqqîph	ʿim	lādhîn	welō-yûkhal	ʾādhām
because	than he	who is stronger	with	to judge	and he is not able	a man

3937, 119	4242, 3252	1961	7528.552	7528.542	3552, 1745
prep, art, n ms	intrg, n ms	n ms	v Hiphil ptc mp	v Hiphil inf abs	sub, n mp
לָאָדָם	מַה־יֹּתֵר	הָבֶל	מַרְבִּים	הַרְבֵּה	יֵשׁ־דְּבָרִים
lāʾādhām	mah-yōthēr	hāvel	marbîm	harbēh	yēsh-devārîm
to the man	what the remainder	a vanity	what increases	making abundant	there are words

12.

3706	4449, 3156.151	4242, 3005	3937, 119	904, 2522	4709
cj	intrg, v Qal act ptc ms	intrg, adj	prep, art, n ms	prep, art, n mp	*n ms*
כִּי	מִי־יוֹדֵעַ	מַה־טּוֹב	לָאָדָם	בַּחַיִּים	מִסְפַּר
kî	mî-yôdhēaʿ	mah-ṭôv	lāʾādhām	bachayyîm	mispar
because	who one who knows	what is good	for humankind	among the living	the number of

3219, 2522	1961	6449.121	3626, 7009	866
n mp, n mp	n ms, ps 3ms	cj, v Qal impf 3ms, ps 3mp	prep, art, n ms	cj
יְמֵי־חַיֵּי	הֶבְלוֹ	וְיַעֲשֵׂם	כַּצֵּל	אֲשֶׁר
yemê-chayyê	hevlô	weyaʿăśēm	katstsēl	ʾăšer
the days of the life of	his vanity	and He will make them	like the shadow	because

4449, 5222.521	3937, 119	4242, 2030.121	313	8809	8507	3005
intrg, v Hiphil impf 3ms	prep, art, n ms	intrg, v Qal impf 3ms	prep, ps 3ms	prep	art, n ms	adj
מִי־יַגִּיד	לָאָדָם	מַה־יִּהְיֶה	אַחֲרָיו	תַּחַת	הַשֶּׁמֶשׁ	**7:1** טוֹב
mî-yaggîd	lāʾādhām	mah-yihyeh	ʾachărâv	tachath	hashshāmesh	ṭôv
who will explain	to humankind	what will be	after him	under	the sun	a good

what you can see than what you can imagine, *Anchor* ... the object seen than the sting of desire, *JB* ... Better aim at what lies in view than hanker after dreams, *Knox* ... a joy at hand than wants that roam abroad, *Moffatt*.

this is also vanity and vexation of spirit: ... is futility and a grasping of the wind, *Anchor* ... is to no purpose and a desire for wind, *BB* ... all is frustration, and labour lost, *Knox* ... is useless—like chasing the wind, *NCV*.

10. That which hath been is named already: ... Whatever is was named long ago, *Beck* ... has been named before, *BB* ... What has been is already defined, *JB* ... Whatever happens has been determined long ago, *Moffatt*.

and it is known that it is man: ... its destiny was known, *Beck* ... of what man is there is knowledge, *BB* ... what man is has been known, *Goodspeed* ... we know what people are, *JB*.

neither may he contend with him that is mightier than he: ... Man cannot dispute with what is stronger, *Anchor* ... A human being can't struggle with One mightier, *Beck*.

11. Seeing there be many things that increase vanity: ... many sayings that multiply vanity, *NAB* ... many words which increase futility, *NASB* ... The more you say, the more useless it is, *NCV* ... The more words one uses the greater is the emptiness of it all, *NEB*.

what is man the better?: ... what profit is there for a man?, *NAB* ... What then is the advantage to a man?, *NASB* ... What good does it do?, *NCV* ... how does that profit anyone?, *NIV*.

12. For who knoweth what is good for man in this life: ... what is man's good, *Anchor* ... who knows what is best, *Fenton*.

all the days of his vain life which he spendeth as a shadow?: ... which pass like a shadow?, *Anchor* ... which he goes through like a shade?,

BB ... their short life passes like a shadow, *NCV*.

for who can tell a man what shall be after him under the sun?: ... who will say what is to be after him, *BB* ... who can inform man what will be after him, *Fenton* ... Who can tell anyone what will happen after him, *JB* ... Who can tell them what the future will bring?, *NCV*.

7:1. A good name is better than precious ointment: ... more pleasant than costly perfume, *Beck* ... better than oil of great price, *BB* ... better than sweet perfume, *Fenton* ... than costly oil, *JB*.

and the day of death than the day of one's birth: ... the day of one's death is more important than the day of one's birth, *Anchor* ... is more pleasant than the day you're born,

---

tory meaning. The wise man has nothing more than the fool; similarly, the poor, who know to walk before the living, do not have any advantage above their more simple neighbors. Both provide for themselves by the fruit of their labor. In fact, man's external condition in natural satisfaction is far more equalized than appears on the surface. Each has his station and his work. Happy indeed are they who labor in dependence upon God, Who alone can bless their work. And thrice blessed are they, who are laboring for eternity, and who yet receive the reward of their labor as the free gift of their divine Master (cf. John 6:27).

6:9. The sight of the eyes is the reality before us. The wandering of the desire is the longing pursuit of some unattainable object never reached. The fruitless search only ends in vanity and vexation of spirit. Better therefore to enjoy what we have in possession, than to be roving up and down in anxious weariness. For what can be more wretched, than when the false pictures of the world palm themselves upon us for realities, when the shadows begin to pass away, and there is no substance to supply their place!

6:10. The Preacher is here reviewing the result of his long and extensive inquiry. That which has been, the whole of what can be obtained from all sources (i.e. wisdom—pleasure, honor, riches), has been already named. All have opened before us, as so many shades of vanity.

His religion is self-wrought, and man is its center. Whatever it be, it never brings him close to God. Therefore, it always leaves him short of peace with God. What is wanting is the teaching of humility.

A being thus fraught with infirmity and corruption, a very worm in utter weakness and helplessness, cannot contend with his Maker, Who is infinitely mightier than he (Isa. 14:9).

6:11. Let us look at the point to be demonstrated. No fruit of happiness can be found in this world's vanity. The several parts have been brought out before us, and the many things have been proved to increase, instead of removing, the vanity. Past, present and future—all partake of the same vanity.

The question, therefore, is clearly decided, but is man the better, in regard to his true happiness, for any of them? No. Every form of happiness is but a phantom. He is, therefore, no better for having more opportunities than others to follow such shadows (1:2f).

A sickening prospect, if this world be our all! We may well then ask, "Who knows what is good for a man?" Indeed, what we think is good may be evil, and what we think is evil may be good. Thus, we run a hazard in making our own choices. O LORD, save us from the foolish exchange of eternity for trifles. While the future is clouded in darkness, and no man can tell me what will be after me, let me lie passive in your hand, and be active in your present work, and all will be peace. Whatever be, let it be your choice for me; not mine for myself.

7:1. A good name is a substantial good; it brightens a man's life and embalms his memory (cf. Ps. 112:6; Prov. 10:7). Solomon could form a just estimate of this good, because he had known both its possession and its loss. Elsewhere, he compares it with "great riches," finding the name to bring more inward joy. Here, he weighs it against precious ointment—a valuable treasure.

Though the day of a birth was certainly joyous (John 16:21), the day of death will be infinitely better. Is not the day that will deliver us from sin and sorrow far better than the day that brought us into them? Does not every returning birthday rejoice the heart with the remembrance—a year nearer home? The conflict then will end forever! The term of exile from the LORD then finished! (2 Cor. 5:6ff). How complete will be the consciousness—"To die is gain! To depart, and to be with Christ is far better"

8428	4623, 8467	3005	3219	4323	4623, 3219	3314.241
n ms	prep, n ms	adj	cj, n ms	art, n ms	prep, n ms	v Niphal inf con, ps 3ms
שֵׁם	מִשֶּׁמֶן	טוֹב	וְיוֹם	הַמָּוֶת	מִיּוֹם	הִוָּלְדוֹ
shēm	mishshemen	ṭôv	wᵉyôm	hammāweth	mîyôm	hiwwālᵉdhô
a name	than olive oil	better	and the day of	the death	than the day of	his being born

3005	3937, 2050.141	420, 1041, 60	4623, 2050.141	420, 1041	5136
2. adj	prep, v Qal inf con	prep, n ms, n ms	prep, v Qal inf con	prep, n ms	n ms
טוֹב	לָלֶכֶת	אֶל־בֵּית־אֵבֶל	מִלֶּכֶת	אֶל־בֵּית	מִשְׁתֶּה
ṭôv	lālekheth	'el-bêth-'ēvel	millekheth	'el-bêth	mishteh
'better	to walk	into the house of mourning	than to go	to the house of	a feast

904, 866	2000	5677	3725, 119	2508	5598.121	420, 3949
prep, rel part	pers pron	n ms	adj, art, n ms	cj, art, n ms	v Qal impf 3ms	prep, n ms, ps 3ms
בַּאֲשֶׁר	הוּא	סוֹף	כָּל־הָאָדָם	וְהַחַי	יִתֵּן	אֶל־לִבּוֹ
ba'asher	hû'	sôph	kol-hā'ādhām	wᵉhachay	yittēn	'el-libbô
where	it	the end of	all men	and the living	he will set	to his heart

3005	3833	4623, 7926	3706, 904, 7741	6686	3296.121	3949
3. adj	n ms	prep, n ms	cj, prep, n ms	n mp	v Qal impf 3ms	n ms
טוֹב	כַּעַס	מִשְּׂחֹק	כִּי־בְרֹעַ	פָּנִים	יִיטַב	לֵב
ṭôv	ka'as	missᵉchōq	kî-vᵉrōa'	pānîm	yîṭav	lēv
better	vexation	than laughter	because with the grief of	the face	it goes well	the heart

3949	2550	904, 1041	60	3949	3809	904, 1041
4. n ms	n mp	prep, n ms	n ms	cj, n ms	n mp	prep, n ms
לֵב	חֲכָמִים	בְּבֵית	אֵבֶל	וְלֵב	כְּסִילִים	בְּבֵית
lēv	chăkhāmîm	bᵉvêth	'ēvel	wᵉlēv	kᵉsîlîm	bᵉvêth
the heart of	the wise	in the house of	mourning	but the heart of	fools	in the house of

7977	3005	3937, 8471.141	1648	2550	4623, 382	8471.151	8302
n fs	5. adj	prep, v Qal inf con	n fs	n ms	prep, n ms	v Qal act ptc ms	n ms
שִׂמְחָה	טוֹב	לִשְׁמֹעַ	גַּעֲרַת	חָכָם	מֵאִישׁ	שֹׁמֵעַ	שִׁיר
simchāh	ṭôv	lishmōa'	ga'ărath	chākhām	mē'îsh	shōmēa'	shîr
rejoicing	better	to listen to	the rebuke of	the wise	than a man	hearing	the song of

3809	3706	3626, 7249	5708	8809	5707	3772	7926	3809
n mp	6. cj	prep, n ms	art, n mp	prep	art, n ms	adv	n ms	art, n ms
כְּסִילִים	כִּי	כְּקוֹל	הַסִּירִים	תַּחַת	הַסִּיר	כֵּן	שְׂחֹק	הַכְּסִיל
kᵉsîlîm	kî	khᵉqôl	hassîrîm	tachath	hassîr	kēn	sᵉchōq	hakkᵉsîl
fools	because	like the sound of	the thorns	under	the pot	so	the laughter of	the fool

Beck ... day of death is better than the day of birth, *Moffatt, NCV.*

2. It is better to go to the house of mourning, than to go to the house of feasting: ... to go to a funeral than to a banquet, *Beck* ... to go to the house of weeping, than to the house of feasting, *BB* ... to go to a funeral than to a party, *NCV.*

for that is the end of all men: ... how all men end, *Anchor* ... where everybody ends up, *Beck* ... is the destiny of all men, *Berkeley* ... to this end everyone comes, *JB* ... We

all must die, *NCV* ... to be mourned is the lot of every man, *NEB.*

and the living will lay it to his heart: ... takes it to heart, *Anchor* ... should keep that in mind, *Moffatt* ... should think about this, *NCV.*

3. Sorrow is better than laughter: ... Better is grief than laughter, *Anchor* ... Vexation is better than, *Darby* ... Sorrow is better than joy, *BB* ... Grief is better than gaiety, *Moffatt.*

for by the sadness of the countenance the heart is made better: ...

it clouds the face but it improves the mind, *Anchor* ... a sad face makes a merry heart, *Beck* ... by the facial sadness the heart is made glad, *Berkeley* ... when the face is sad the mind gets better, *BB.*

4. The heart of the wise is in the house of mourning: ... the thoughts of the wise, *Anchor* ... the mind of the wise, *Goodspeed, NASB* ... A wise person thinks about death, *NCV.*

but the heart of fools is in the house of mirth: ... the thoughts of fools to the place of amusement,

Anchor ... the mind of fools, *Goodspeed, NASB* ... a fool thinks only about having a good time, *NCV.*

5. It is better to hear the rebuke of the wise: ... to listen to the sharp criticism, *Beck* ... to hear the reproof, *Berkeley* ... to take note of the protest, *BB* ... attend to the reprimand, *JB.*

than for a man to hear the song of fools: ... than to fools singing your praise, *Beck* ... than listen to a song sung by a fool, *JB* ... than hear thy praises sung by fools, *Knox* ... than to be praised by a fool, *NCV.*

6. For as the crackling of thorns under a pot: ... Loud but not long the thorns crackle, *Knox* ... like net-tles crackling under kettles, *Moffatt* ... as the noise of thorns, *Young.*

so is the laughter of the fool: ... is the loud laughter of, *Anchor* ... is the cackle of, *Moffatt.*

this also is vanity: ... frustration, *Knox* ... is vain, *Moffatt* ... is futility, *NASB* ... Both are useless, *NCV.*

(Phil. 1:21, 23). Born an heir of trouble (Job 5:7), crowned an heir of glory! Who can doubt but the coronation day must be the better day—the day of unspeakable and everlasting joy!

7:2. A heap of paradoxes are rising before us, like the beatitudes which preface the Sermon on the Mount. But the paradoxes of the Bible open out valuable truths. These are the words of sober wisdom. Thousands of Christian mourners—all who are chastened as sons—have responded and borne testimony to their truth. Because our heavenly Father accompanies even his most severe punishment with whispers of love, his children almost dread the removal of the discipline—lest they should also lose so rich a blessing. This is not the judgment of the world, though. They do not love to be brought into contact with realities, or to be reminded of the coming "days of darkness" (11:8). Indeed, there is an unwelcome message to their conscience—Are you ready to meet this solemn, hastening season? The wise man does not say that it is sweeter, but that it is better to go to the house of mourning.

The value of the house of mourning is in the lesson it teaches. Here is the end of all men. What better lesson can there be? If anything will set the thoughtless to think, this will be it. It is what all must expect—what all must arrive at—"going the way of all the earth" (Josh. 23:14; cf. Heb. 9:27). It is the grand design of the house of feasting to destroy recollection, but the house of mourning makes the last scene palpable. It is the divine ordinance to bring the living to thoughtfulness; far gone must they be, if they do not lay it to bears, and fasten it there.

7:3–4. Sorrow is better than laughter. So valuable, so needful is it, that we doubt whether it be safe to be without sorrow, till we are without sin. The house of mourning is the wise man's school. Here we are disciplined to lessons of inestimable value. We obtain the knowledge of that dark mystery—our own hearts.

Often when our sky is bright, we forget that the clouds may quickly form. Here the sight of sorrow brings us to a right recollection, and we can bless our God, since He is leading us through a wilderness—not a paradise. We seem to be bereaved. But the main matter is untouched. Enough is left for a song in the house of our pilgrimage (Ps. 119:54). If we look at the medicine, we take it from Him as exactly fitted to our case. It is weighed out by his own hand. We see how the different ingredients "work together" (not the sweet alone without the bitter) "for good" (Rom. 8:28). If we complain of the cross as a fainting burden, we will carry it to Him. Cannot He Who appointed, support us under it, and carry us through it?

But no wonder, that with such lessons to be learned, and such consolations to be enjoyed, the heart of the wise should be in the house of mourning. Although we could go to "the house of mirth," our hearts can never rest there. The world can never be our home—its resources are too poor for our wants.

7:5. All of us are offensive in some way (Jam. 3:2) thus, none of us are above the need of rebuke. However, we do not all value rebuke; indeed, it is often hard to receive it from another, even "when our heart condemns us." Let me then bring home this probing point. Are the "faithful wounds of a friend" welcome to us? Do we heartily admit that his "open rebuke is better than secret love" (Prov. 27:5f)—yea, an exercise of true Christian love? (Ps. 141:5).

7:6. The laughter of the fool is nothing but the crackling of thorns under a pot—a mere blaze for the moment (Pss. 58:9; 118:12). Whether it be the intoxication of the drunkard, the foolishness of the trifler, the nonsense which amuses by its wit or folly, it only brings out more fully the conviction. This is also vanity. Indeed, what other fruit could be found in pleasure pursued, possessed, enjoyed, without God? Let the joy be admitted. But how short-lived! Nothing left to reflect on! Solemn is the warning from a voice

1612, 2172	1961		3706	6480	2054.321	2550	6.321
cj, cj, dem pron	n ms		cj	art, n ms	v Poel impf 3ms	n ms	cj, v Piel impf 3ms
וְגַם־זֶה	הָבֶל	**7.**	כִּי	הָעֹשֶׁק	יְהוֹלֵל	חָכָם	וִיאַבֵּד
w^{e}gham-zeh	hāvel		kî	hā'ōsheq	y^{e}hôlēl	chākhām	wî'abbēdh
and also this	a vanity		indeed	the extortion	it causes to be insane	the wise	and it destroys

881, 3949	5152		3005	321	1745	4623, 7519	3005	774, 7593
do, n ms	n fs		adj	*n fs*	n ms	prep, n fs, ps 3ms	adj	adj, n fs
אֶת־לֵב	מַתָּנָה	**8.**	טוֹב	אַחֲרִית	דָּבָר	מֵרֵאשִׁיתוֹ	טוֹב	אֶרֶךְ־רוּחַ
'eth-lēv	mattānāh		ṭôv	'achărîth	dāvār	mērē'shîthô	ṭôv	'erekh-rûach
the heart	a gift		better	the end of	a thing	than its beginning	better	a long spirit

4623, 1392, 7593		414, 963.323	904, 7593	3937, 3832.141	3706	3833
prep, adj, n fs		adv, v Piel juss 2ms	prep, n fs, ps 2ms	prep, v Qal inf con	cj	n ms
מִגְּבַהּ־רוּחַ	**9.**	אַל־תְּבַהֵל	בְּרוּחֲךָ	לִכְעוֹס	כִּי	כַעַס
migg^{e}vahh-rûach		'al-t^{e}vahēl	b^{e}rûchăkhā	likh'ôs̱	kî	kha'as̱
than a haughty spirit		do not hasten	in your spirit	to be angry	because	anger

904, 2536	3809	5299.121		414, 569.123	4242	2030.111
prep, *n ms*	n mp	v Qal impf 3ms		adv, v Qal juss 2ms	intrg	v Qal pf 3ms
בְּחֵיק	כְּסִילִים	יָנוּחַ	**10.**	אַל־תֹּאמַר	מֶה	הָיָה
b^{e}chêq	k^{e}s̱îlîm	yānûach		'al-tō'mar	meh	hāyāh
in the bosom of	fools	it will come to rest		do not say	why	is it

8054, 3219	7518	2030.116	3005	4623, 431	3706	3940	4623, 2551
rel part, art, n mp	art, adj	v Qal pf 3cp	adj	prep, dem pron	cj	neg part	prep, n fs
שֶׁהַיָּמִים	הָרִאשֹׁנִים	הָיוּ	טוֹבִים	מֵאֵלֶּה	כִּי	לֹא	מֵחָכְמָה
shehayyāmîm	hāri'shōnîm	hāyû	ṭôvîm	mē'ēlleh	kî	lō'	mēchokhmāh
that the days	the former	they were	better	than these	because	not	from wisdom

8068.113	6142, 2172		3009B	2551	6196, 5338	3252
v Qal pf 2ms	prep, dem pron		adj	n fs	prep, n fs	cj, n ms
שָׁאַלְתָּ	עַל־זֶה	**11.**	טוֹבָה	חָכְמָה	עִם־נַחֲלָה	וְיֹתֵר
shā'altā	'al-zeh		ṭôvāh	chokhmāh	'im-nachălāh	w^{e}yōthēr
you have asked	about this		good	wisdom	with an inheritance	and a remainder

7. Surely oppression maketh a wise man mad: ... can turn [even] a wise man into a fool, *Anchor* ... extortion maketh the wise man foolish, *ASV* ... A wise man oppressing others becomes a fool, *Beck* ... The wise are troubled by the ways of the cruel, *BB*.

and a gift destroyeth the heart: ... take away his courage, *Anchor* ... a bribe destroyeth the understanding, *ASV* ... a bribe corrupts the mind, *Beck* ... the giving of money, *BB*.

8. Better is the end of a thing than the beginning thereof: ... is the completion of a thing than its beginning, *Berkeley* ... end of a thing is better than its start, *BB* ... is the end of speech than its beginning, *NAB, Douay* ... better to finish something than to start it, *NCV*.

and the patient in spirit is better than the proud in spirit: ... better is the patient one than the haughty one, *Berkeley* ... a gentle spirit is better than pride, *BB* ... better patience than ambition, *JB*.

9. Be not hasty in thy spirit to be angry: ... Do not be easily upset, *Anchor* ... not hasty in your spirit to be offended, *Berkeley* ... not quick to let your spirit be angry, *BB* ... Do not be too easily exasperated, *JB*.

for anger resteth in the bosom of fools: ... is typical of fools, *Anchor* ... resentment abides in, *Berkeley* ... wrath is in the heart of, *BB* ... exasperation dwells in the heart of, *JB*.

10. Say not thou, What is the cause that the former days were better than these?: ... not ask why the past was better than the present, *JB* ... Never ask why the old times were better than ours, *Knox* ... Don't ask, "Why was life better in the 'good old days'?", *NCV*.

for thou dost not inquire wisely concerning this: ... is not a question prompted by wisdom, *JB* ... a fool's question, *Knox* ... is not wise to ask such questions, *NCV, NIV* ... is not from wisdom that you ask, *NRSV*.

11. Wisdom is good with an inheritance: ... is good to have wisdom as well as, *Anchor* ... is as good as an inheritance, *ASV* ... enhances an inheritance, *Beck* ... is as beneficial as a legacy, *Berkeley*.

of love. "Woe unto you that laugh now! for ye shall mourn and weep" (Luke 6:25).

7:7–8. The wise man bids us notice his special emphasis—"Indeed." Often he dwells on the evils of oppression (3:16; 4:1; 5:8). Oppression may be either the active power of inflicting suffering, or the passive enduring of it. The latter would seem to be the more natural meaning, wrong cruelly inflicted, the misery of being beaten down by tyranny. In the oppressor himself it is an ebullition of selfishness (Ps. 73:8)—a galling chain to his victims—sometimes making even a wise man mad (Exo. 5:21). More than once it has thrown the man of God off his sober balance and hurried him into a state nearly allied to madness.

However, evil falls back upon the oppressor himself. One selfish principle naturally begets another. The act of oppression is often traced to the gift tendered as the price of the oppression, destroying one's heart, blotting out every principle of moral integrity, rendering one callous to suffering and deaf to the claims of justice (Prov. 17:23). There was a good reason for the Mosaic veto: restraining the influence of gifts (Exo. 23:8; Deut. 16:19). There is indeed peril on both sides. Tyranny forces irrational conduct; bribery lack of feeling. The standard of the Bible is the only security. "He that ruleth over men must be just—ruling in the fear of God" (2 Sam. 23:3).

The first clause is not indeed a universal maxim. Sometimes the ending is far worse than the beginning. Yet it often holds good. Solomon had already given an example (v. 1). In the instance just referred to (cp. also Prov. 20:21), the oppressor may appear to have the advantage at first, but the end may bring him low. The ordinary trials of the Christian life are grievous in the beginning, but fruitful in the end.

The second clause of v. 7 naturally contrasts patience with pride. Pride is the source of impatience, as humility is the principle of gentleness and endurance. Our patience harmonizes with the will of God, ministering to our comfort, as pride adds to our trouble. Every way therefore better is the patient in spirit than the proud in spirit.

7:9. A most important rule! So deeply affecting our happiness, and not less the beauty and consistency of our Christian profession. It is indeed possible to conceive of being angry, and not to sin (Eph. 4:26). Anger is a holy passion in the bosom of Yahweh (Nah. 1:2). It was displayed in the pure humanity of the divine Savior (Mark 3:5), and it was the intense sensibility of sorrow in the man of God when he witnessed the debasing idolatry of the chosen nation (Exo. 32:19). And yet it would be most dangerous to presume upon this rare purity, when in the infinite majority of cases, it is the ebullition of pride, selfishness and folly.

The impulse of anger forbidden here is hastiness. A quick word, even if only a trifle, is a rude extinguisher for the moment! It is a sudden gust that puts all holy feelings to flight! Unfortunately, even in the church of God this damper to spirituality is felt. The sad influence of this hasty spirit is deeply to be deprecated. We must lift "up holy hands without wrath" (1 Tim. 2:8).

Often does Solomon graphically mark this evil in his practical code. "He that is soon angry dealeth foolishly" (Prov. 14:17). Commonly, he contrasts it with its opposite grace, "He that is slow to wrath is of great understanding; but he that is hasty of spirit exalteth folly. A wrathful man stirreth up strife; but he that is slow to anger appeaseth strife. He that is slow to anger is better than he that taketh a city" (Prov. 14:29; 15:18; 16:32). The Apostolic rule is to the same purport, and of universal application. "Let every man be slow to speak, slow to wrath" (Jam. 1:19).

7:10. Impatience often produces a querulous spirit. We should remember this; indeed, we know the former days only by report. Present days are a felt reality, and pressure naturally induces us to believe that former days were better than these.

The rebuke is evidently directed against that dissatisfied spirit, which puts aside our present blessings, exaggerates our evils and reflects upon the government of God as full of inequalities, and upon his providence, in having cast us in such evil times.

7:11–12. Wisdom is better than an inheritance, and is profitable unto mankind. The proof is manifest. For—not only does it provide a shadow from many temporal evils, but specially it gives life to them that have it. Money is indeed a shadow. It surrounds with friends, protects from foes (cf. Prov. 19:4; 10:19) and secures many external blessings. Thus "the rich man's wealth is his strong city. The ransom of a man's life are his riches" (Prov. 10:15; 13:8). But they profit not in the day of wrath (Prov. 10:2).

Since the advantage of this true wisdom is so vast, let the diligence in seeking it be proportioned. If

12.

Strong's	Parsing	Hebrew	Translit.	English
3937, 7495.152	prep, v Qal act ptc mp	לְרֹאֵי	lerō'ê	to those who see
8507	art, n ms	הַשֶּׁמֶשׁ	hashshāmesh	the sun
3706	cj	כִּי	kî	because
904, 7009	prep, n ms	בְּצֵל	betsēl	in the shadow of
2551	art, n fs	הַחָכְמָה	hachokhmāh	the wisdom
904, 7009	prep, n ms	בְּצֵל	betsēl	in the shadow of
3826B	art, n ms	הַכָּסֶף	hakkāseph	the silver
3620	cj, n ms	וְיִתְרוֹן	weyithrōn	and the profit of
1907	n fs	דַּעַת	da'ath	knowledge
2551	art, n fs	הַחָכְמָה	hachokhmāh	the wisdom
2513.322	v Piel impf 3fs	תְּחַיֶּה	techayyeh	it keeps alive
1196	n mp, ps 3fs	בְּעָלֶיהָ	ve'ālêāh	its owners

13.

Strong's	Parsing	Hebrew	Translit.	English
7495.131	v Qal impv 2ms	רְאֵה	re'ēh	see
881, 4801	do, n ms	אֶת־מַעֲשֵׂה	'eth-ma'ăsēh	the work of
435	art, n mp	הָאֱלֹהִים	hā'ĕlōhîm	God
3706	cj	כִּי	kî	because
4449	intrg	מִי	mî	who
3310.121	v Qal impf 3ms	יוּכַל	yûkhal	is he able
3937, 8963.341	prep, v Piel inf con	לְתַקֵּן	lethaqqēn	to make straight
881	do	אֵת	'ēth	[do]
866	rel part	אֲשֶׁר	'āsher	what

14.

Strong's	Parsing	Hebrew	Translit.	English
6003.311	v Piel pf 3ms, ps 3ms	עִוְּתוֹ	'iwwethô	He has made it crooked
904, 3219	prep, n ms	בְּיוֹם	beyôm	on the day of
3009B	adj	טוֹבָה	tôvāh	good
2030.131	v Qal impv 2ms	הֱיֵה	hĕyēh	be
904, 3005	prep, adj	בְטוֹב	vetôv	with good
904, 3219	cj, prep, n ms	וּבְיוֹם	ûveyôm	and in the day of
7750	n fs	רָעָה	rā'āh	evil
7495.131	v Qal impv 2ms	רְאֵה	re'ēh	see
1612	cj	גַּם	gam	also
881, 2172	do, dem pron	אֶת־זֶה	'eth-zeh	this
3937, 6202, 2172	prep, prep, dem pron	לְעֻמַּת־זֶה	le'ummath-zeh	for beside this
6449.111	v Qal pf 3ms	עָשָׂה	'āsāh	He has done
435	art, n mp	הָאֱלֹהִים	hā'ĕlōhîm	God
6142, 1750	prep, n fs	עַל־דִּבְרַת	'al-divrath	concerning the manner of
8054, 3940	rel part, neg part	שֶׁלֹּא	shellō'	that not
4834.121	v Qal impf 3ms	יִמְצָא	yimtsā'	he will find
119	art, n ms	הָאָדָם	hā'ādhām	humankind
313	prep, ps 3ms	אַחֲרָיו	'achărâv	after him
4114	indef pron	מְאוּמָה	me'ûmāh	something

15.

Strong's	Parsing	Hebrew	Translit.	English
881, 3725	do, art, n ms	אֶת־הַכֹּל	'eth-hakkōl	everything
7495.115	v Qal pf 1cs	רָאִיתִי	rā'îthî	I have seen
904, 3219	prep, n mp	בִּימֵי	bîmê	in the days of
1961	n ms, ps 1cs	הֶבְלִי	hevlî	my vanity
3552	sub	יֵשׁ	yēsh	there is
6926	n ms	צַדִּיק	tsaddîq	a righteous man
6.151	v Qal act ptc ms	אֹבֵד	'ōvēdh	perishing

and by it there is profit to them that see the sun: ... it is an advantage to men while they live, *Anchor* ... is useful to those, *Fenton* ... more advantage it shall bring thee than all the rest, *Knox* ... is gain to those, *KJVII*.

12. For wisdom is a defence, and money is a defence: ... the shelter of wisdom is like the shelter of wealth, *Anchor* ... protects us as money protects us, *Beck* ... keeps a man from danger even as money does, *BB* ... is like money: they both help, *NCV*.

but the excellency of knowledge is, that wisdom giveth life to them that have it: ... with the added advantage of knowing that wisdom gives life to its possessors, *Anchor* ... value of knowledge is that wisdom gives life to its owner, *BB* ... advantage of knowledge is that wisdom preserves the life of its owner, *Goodspeed* ... knowledge does more good than money, it safeguards a man's life, *Moffatt*.

13. Consider the work of God: ... God's creation, *JB* ... Mark well God's doings, *Knox* ... Ponder the doings, *Moffatt* ... Look at what God has done, *NCV*.

for who can make that straight, which he hath made crooked?: ... can straighten what God has bent?, *JB* ... who can straighten what he twists?, *Moffatt*.

14. In the day of prosperity be joyful: ... Be pleased when things go well, *Anchor* ... Be happy when you're prosperous, *Beck* ... enjoy life, *Berkeley* ... When things are going well, enjoy yourself, *JB*.

but in the day of adversity consider: ... when they go badly, look out!, *Anchor* ... when bad times come realize, *Beck* ... in the day of evil take thought, *BB* ... when they are going badly, consider this, *JB*.

God also hath set the one over against the other: ... arranged that one should correspond to the other, *Anchor* ... made the one side by side with the other, *ASV* ... that God made the one as well as the other, *Beck* ... made both this and that, *Fenton*.

to the end that man should find nothing after him: ... so that man

may never know what lies ahead, *Anchor* ... to prevent man from finding out what will happen next, *Beck* ... no man can discover anything about events after himself!, *Fenton* ... so that we should take nothing for granted, *JB*.

15. All things have I seen in the days of my vanity: ... observed all this in my unhappy days, *Fenton* ... have seen all sorts of things in my empty life, *Goodspeed* ... In my days of baffled enquiry, *Knox* ... All manner of things have I seen in my fleeting life, *Moffatt*.

there is a just man that perisheth in his righteousness: ... sometimes a good man perished by his goodness, *Fenton* ... have seen pious men ruined for all their piety, *Knox* ... good man perishing by his very goodness, *Moffatt* ... have seen good people die in spite of their goodness, *NCV*.

and there is a wicked man that prolongeth his life in his wickedness: ... sometimes a bad man is preserved by his crimes!, *Fenton* ... evil-doers live long in all their wickedness, *Knox* ... the evil man flourishing upon his evil, *Moffatt* ... evil people live a long time in spite of their evil, *NCV*.

---

it is worth seeking at all, it is worth seeking first. And if it is not sought first, it will not be sought at all.

7:13. "The works of the LORD are great, sought out of all them that have pleasure therein. His work is honourable and glorious" (Ps. 111:2f). Such is the Psalmist's commendation. Who will not respond to it? Solomon here places the work of Providence before us and bids us consider it. And truly a most interesting and enriching study it is.

There is indeed no want of conformity to his own divine standard. Yet there are many things crooked in man's eye, because they cross his own will, thwarting his own imaginary happiness. Man's will goes one way—God's dispensation another. In every part of his course, man must expect to meet with God's crook, and hard is it to bear, till the spirit is thoroughly tamed to bear it.

Therefore, it is profitable to carefully ponder how God deals with humanity. Let us command our judgment and reason to stand by, that we may with reverence, submission and faith, consider the work of God. The vision in his own time will speak for itself. We can see light and order above, when all seems confusion below. Meanwhile let us mark his hand, rest and stay upon his will and carefully gather up all the instruction of his discipline. When the whole work will be complete, every particle will be seen to have fallen into its own proper place. Only then will everything appear to be whole, every way worthy of God—the eternal manifestation of his glory.

7:14. Christians should consider the work of God, for it is there that they find their refuge and rest. God's rule states, "In the day of prosperity be joyful." It does not become us to walk before our

Father with a wrinkled brow, doubting, desponding. Rather, we should give Him his just right in an affectionate and delighting confidence.

And yet if we be joyful, must we not rejoice with trembling (Ps. 2:11)? Is it not a day of prosperity, a time of special temptation? How hard to maintain an honorable walk and the enjoyment of Christian privilege in the atmosphere of ease! Wise indeed therefore is the appointment that makes the day of prosperity to be not our entire lot. It is hard to hold a full cup steady. There is a valuable balance of the day of adversity, equally of divine appointment.

Thus the brightest prosperity is found in nature's darkest adversity. We all know how the vicissitudes of the natural seasons, set over against each other, conduce to the healthiness of the atmosphere. Not less necessary is a measure and proportion of each of these seasons to maintain the Christian temperament in healthful vigor. Either without the other would be defective in operation.

Surely then, God has so wisely disposed these changes, and so accurately appointed their several proportions, that a man will find nothing after him—nothing superfluous, defective or irregular. If a man should take upon himself to review the work after him, and conceive that a greater or less degree of prosperity or adversity would have been better—or that either would have sufficed without the balance of the other—he only stands before us in all the folly and presumption of fancying himself to be wiser than God. What God has done, He has done best.

7:15. Solomon was a man of vast observation. His whole life indeed at best was made up of days of vanity—how much more his time of apostasy from God. Yet he had employed it in making an extensive

The following interlinear text is presented in Hebrew reading order (right to left).

Verse 16

Strong's	Parsing	Hebrew	Transliteration	English
414, 2030.123	adv, v Qal juss 2ms	אַל־תְּהִי	'al-tᵉhî	do not be
904, 7750	prep, n fs, ps 3ms	בְּרָעָתוֹ	bᵉrā'āthô	in his evil
773.551	v Hiphil ptc ms	מַאֲרִיךְ	ma'ărîkh	lengthening
7857	n ms	רָשָׁע	rāshā'	a wicked man
3552	cj, sub	וְיֵשׁ	wᵉyēsh	and is there
904, 6928	prep, n ms, ps 3ms	בְּצִדְקוֹ	bᵉtsidhqô	in his righteousness
6926	adj	צַדִּיק	tsaddîq	righteous
7528.542	v Hiphil inf abs	הַרְבֵּה	harbēh	making abundant
414, 2549.723	cj, adv, v Hithpael juss 2ms	וְאַל־תִּתְחַכַּם	wᵉ'al-tithchakkam	and do not show yourself to be wise
3252	n ms	יוֹתֵר	yôthēr	a remainder
4066	intrg	לָמָּה	lāmmāh	why

Verse 17

Strong's	Parsing	Hebrew	Transliteration	English
4066	intrg	לָמָּה	lāmmāh	why
5722	adj	סָכָל	sākhāl	foolish
414, 2030.123	cj, adv, v Qal juss 2ms	וְאַל־תְּהִי	wᵉ'al-tᵉhî	and do not be
7528.542	v Hiphil inf abs	הַרְבֵּה	harbēh	making abundant
414, 7855.123	adv, v Qal juss 2ms	אַל־תִּרְשַׁע	'al-tirsha'	do not act wickedly
8460.723	v Hithpoel impf 2ms	תִּשּׁוֹמֵם	tishshômēm	will you devastate

Verse 18

Strong's	Parsing	Hebrew	Transliteration	English
904, 2172	prep, dem pron	בָּזֶה	bāzeh	on this
270.123	v Qal impf 2ms	תֶּאֱחֹז	te'ĕchōz	you will seize
866	rel part	אֲשֶׁר	'ăsher	that
3005	adj	טוֹב	tôv	better
6496	n fs, ps 2ms	עִתֶּךָ	'ittekhā	your time
904, 3940	prep, neg part	בְּלֹא	bᵉlō'	when not
4322.123	v Qal impf 2ms	תָּמוּת	thāmûth	will you die
435	n mp	אֱלֹהִים	'ĕlōhîm	God
3706, 3486.152	cj, v Qal act ptc ms	כִּי־יָרֵא	kî-yᵉrē'	because the one who fears
881, 3135	do, n fs, ps 2ms	אֶת־יָדֶךָ	'eth-yādhekhā	your hand
414, 5299.523	adv, v Hiphil juss 2ms	אַל־תַּנַּח	'al-tannach	do not cause to rest
1612, 4623, 2172	cj, cj, prep, dem pron	וְגַם־מִזֶּה	wᵉgham-mizzeh	and also of that

Verse 19

Strong's	Parsing	Hebrew	Transliteration	English
4623, 6463	prep, num	מֵעֲשָׂרָה	mē'ăsārāh	than ten
3937, 2550	prep, art, n ms	לְחָכָם	lechākhām	to the wise
6022.122	v Qal impf 3fs	תָּעֹז	tā'ōz	it is stronger
2551	art, n fs	הַחָכְמָה	hachokhmāh	the wisdom
881, 3725	do, n ms, ps 3mp	אֶת־כֻּלָּם	'eth-kullām	all of them
3428.121	v Qal juss 3ms	יֵצֵא	yētsē'	he will come out of

Verse 20

Strong's	Parsing	Hebrew	Transliteration	English
904, 800	prep, art, n fs	בָּאָרֶץ	bā'ărets	on the earth
6926	adj	צַדִּיק	tsaddîq	righteous
375	sub	אֵין	'ên	there is not
119	n ms	אָדָם	'ādhām	a man
3706	cj	כִּי	kî	indeed
904, 6111	prep, art, n fs	בָּעִיר	bā'îr	in the city
2030.116	v Qal pf 3cp	הָיוּ	hāyû	they are
866	rel part	אֲשֶׁר	'ăsher	which
8384	n mp	שַׁלִּיטִים	shallîṭîm	rulers

Verse 21

Strong's	Parsing	Hebrew	Transliteration	English
866	rel part	אֲשֶׁר	'ăsher	which
3937, 3725, 1745	prep, adj, art, n mp	לְכָל־הַדְּבָרִים	lᵉkhol-haddᵉvārîm	to all the things
1612	cj	גַּם	gam	also
2490.121	v Qal impf 3ms	יֶחֱטָא	yechĕṭā'	he will sin
3940	cj, neg part	וְלֹא	wᵉlō'	and not
6449.121, 3005	v Qal impf 3ms, n ms	יַעֲשֶׂה־טוֹב	ya'ăseh-ṭôv	he will do good
866	rel pron	אֲשֶׁר	'ăsher	who

---

16. Be not righteous over much: ... do not set too much store by piety, *Knox* ... Be not over-good, *Moffatt* ... Be not just to excess, *NAB* ... Don't be too right, *NCV*.

neither make thyself over wise: ... nor play the wise man to excess, *Knox* ... be not over-wise, *Moffatt* ... don't be too wise, *NCV*.

why shouldest thou destroy thyself?: ... if thou wouldst not be bewildered over thy lot, *Knox* ... why expose yourself to trouble?, *Moffatt* ... lest you be ruined, *NAB, Douay* ... Why make yourself a laughing-stock?, *NEB*.

17. Be not over much wicked: ... Do not be very wicked [either], *Anchor* ... not abound in wickedness, *Berkeley* ... not be wicked to excess, *JB* ... plunge not deep in evil-doing, *Knox* ... Do not do much wrong, *KJVII*.

neither be thou foolish: ... nor play the fool, *Berkeley* ... folly eschew, *Knox* ... neither become thou foolish, *Rotherham*.

why shouldest thou die before thy time?: ... Why come to your end before your time?, *BB* ... why should you kill yourself before your time?, *Fenton* ... else thou shalt perish before thy time, *Knox.*

18. It is good that thou shouldest take hold of this: ... best to grasp one thing, *Anchor* ... good to hold on to the one, *Beck* ... to take this in your hand, *BB* ... To piety thou must needs cling, *Knox.*

yea, also from this withdraw not thine hand: ... and not let go the other, *Anchor* ... yet live by that other caution too, *Knox* ... yet not avoid the other, *Moffatt* ... and not to let that one go, *NAB.*

for he that feareth God shall come forth of them all: ... who fears God will consider both sides, *Anchor* ... the fear of God makes both ways successful, *Beck* ... he who has the fear of God will be free of the two, *BB* ... whoever reverences GOD will escape from all, *Fenton.*

19. Wisdom strengtheneth the wise more than ten mighty men which are in the city: ... is a surer ally than ten city magistrates, *Knox* ... is a stronghold to the wise man more than ten rulers, *MAST* ... is better protection for the wise than a dozen wardens, *Moffatt* ... is a better defense for the wise man than would be ten princes, *NAB.*

20. For there is not a just man upon earth: ... not a single good man, *Moffatt* ... no man on earth so just, *NAB* ... not a righteous man, *NASB* ... not a good person, *NCV.*

that doeth good, and sinneth not: ... whose good deeds are without some sin, *Moffatt* ... as to do good and never sin, *NAB* ... who continu-

survey of the world before him. Often has he mentioned the sight before his eyes (e.g., 4:1–4; 5:8).

Where is the servant of God who would exchange the most abject poverty for the highest prosperity of the wicked? If the just man perisheth, "he shall enter into peace" (Isa. 57:1f). If the wicked prolongs his days, continuing in sin, surely the very sight of him excites not our envy, but our deepest compassion. We can only tremble, lest this prolongation should be the righteous and merciful God enduring him with much long-suffering as a vessel of wrath, fitted for destruction (Rom. 9:22).

7:16–18. The two strange things that had fallen under Solomon's observation, the righteous perishing in his righteousness and the wicked escaping with impunity, suggested double cautions. On the one side, the externally righteous need to be guarded against a false religion; even the upright against a false display of true religion. On the other, the wicked, escaping for a time, should not presume upon continued security.

To whom, and to what, does the admonition apply? It does not warn us against true righteousness, but it is a wholesome caution against the vain affectation of it. Every right principle has its counterfeit. That which in sobriety is righteousness often carries its name beyond the true boundary. Religion is made to consist mainly in externals. Christian duties are pressed beyond their due proportion, interfering with immediate obligations and making sins where God has not made them.

But we are warned against another extreme. Neither make yourself appear overly wise—a wholesome practical rule! Avoid all affectation or high pretensions to superior wisdom. Guard against that opinionative confidence which seems to lay down the law, and critically finds fault with every judgment differing from its own.

We have valuable cautions against all extremes. It is good indeed to take hold of this. Lay it up in your heart as a certain truth that the fear of the LORD is the keeping of his children, sustaining them against the deadly influence of the fear of man. Learn to be truly righteous.

7:19–20. Solomon never seems to have wearied in his commendation of wisdom. He had just pronounced it to be better than riches (vv. 11f). Now he prefers it to strength, as the principle of Christian courage, energizing the whole soul. This wisdom is evidently identified with the fear of the LORD, which had just been pronounced to be an effective cover from unscriptural extremes. There was therefore good reason to take hold of it. It has more strength than mere physical courage, more than ten mighty men in defending the city.

We have indeed good reason to cherish this upholding principle. For there is not a just man upon the earth who does not sin, and therefore who does not need the strength of this divine wisdom in his spiritual conflicts and temptations.

We must not overlook this humbling testimony to the universal and total corruption of the whole race of man. This important statement lies at the foundation of all right views of truth. Though just men are made perfect in heaven (Heb. 12:23), on earth just men do indeed perform good acts, but still sin.

7:21–22. "Also" seems to point to an admonition suggested by the statement just given of man's universal corruption. Even the just man in his

1744.326	414, 5598.123	3949	866	3940, 8471.123	881, 5860
v Piel impf 3mp	adv, v Qal juss 2ms	n ms, ps 2ms	cj	neg part, v Qal impf 2ms	do, n ms, ps 2ms
יְדַבְּרוּ	אַל־תִּתֵּן	לִבֶּךָ	אֲשֶׁר	לֹא־תִשְׁמַע	אֶת־עַבְדְּךָ
yᵉdhabbērû	'al-tittēn	libbekhā	'ăsher	lō'-thishma'	'eth-'avdᵉkhā
they speak	do not set on	your heart	because	you will not hear	your servant

7327.351	**22.** 3706	1612, 6718	7521	3156.111	3949	866	1612, 879
v Piel ptc ms, ps 2ms	cj	cj, n fp	adj	v Qal pf 3ms	n ms, ps 2ms	rel part	cj, pers pron
מְקַלֶלְךָ	כִּי	גַם־פְּעָמִים	רַבּוֹת	יָדַע	לִבֶּךָ	אֲשֶׁר	גַם־אַתְּ
mᵉqalᵉlekhā	kî	gam-pᵉ'āmîm	rabbôth	yādha'	libbekhā	'ăsher	gam-'atte
cursing you	because	also times	many	it knows	your heart	that	also you

7327.313	311	**23.** 3725, 2173	5441.315	904, 2551	569.115
v Piel pf 2ms	adj	adj, dem pron	v Piel pf 1cs	prep, art, n fs	v Qal pf 1cs
קִלַּלְתָּ	אֲחֵרִים	כָּל־זֹה	נִסִּיתִי	בַחָכְמָה	אָמַרְתִּי
qillaltā	'ăchērîm	kol-zōh	nissîthî	vachokhmāh	'āmartî
you have cursed	others	all this	I tested	with the wisdom	I said

2549.125	2026	7632	4623	**24.** 7632	4242, 8054, 2030.111	6233
v Qal juss 1cs	cj, pers pron	adj	prep, ps 1cs	adj	intrg, rel part, v Qal pf 3ms	cj, adj
אֶחְכָּמָה	וְהִיא	רְחוֹקָה	מִמֶּנִּי	רָחוֹק	מַה־שֶּׁהָיָה	וְעָמֹק
'echkākāmāh	wᵉhî'	rᵉchôqāh	mimmenî	rāchôq	mah-shehāyāh	wᵉ'āmōq
let me become wise	but it	far away	from me	far	what that it has been	and deep

6233	4449	4834.121	**25.** 5621.115	603	3949	3937, 3156.141
adj	intrg	cj, v Qal impf 3ms, ps 3ms	v Qal pf 1cs	pers pron	cj, n ms, ps 1cs	prep, v Qal inf con
עָמֹק	מִי	יִמְצָאֶנּוּ	סַבּוֹתִי	אֲנִי	וְלִבִּי	לָדַעַת
'āmōq	mî	yimtsā'ennû	sabbôthî	'ănî	wᵉlibbî	lādha'ath
deep	who	will he find it	I turned around	I	and my heart	to know

3937, 8780.141	1272.341	2551	2918	3937, 3156.141	7856
cj, prep, v Qal inf con	cj, v Piel inf con	n fs	cj, n ms	cj, prep, v Qal inf con	n ms
וְלָתוּר	וּבַקֵּשׁ	חָכְמָה	וְחֶשְׁבּוֹן	וְלָדַעַת	רֶשַׁע
wᵉlāthûr	ûvaqqēsh	chokhmāh	wᵉcheshbôn	wᵉlādha'ath	resha'
and to investigate	and to seek	wisdom	and a reckoning	and to know	the wickedness of

3815	5724	2014	**26.** 4834.151	603	4914	4623, 4323
n ms	cj, art, n fs	n fp	cj, v Qal act ptc ms	pers pron	adj	prep, n ms
כֶּסֶל	וְהַסִּכְלוּת	הוֹלֵלוֹת	וּמוֹצֵא	אֲנִי	מַר	מִמָּוֶת
kesel	wᵉhassikhlûth	hôlēlôth	ûmôtse'	'ănî	mar	mimmāweth
folly	and the foolishness of	follies	and finding	I	more bitter	than death

881, 828	866, 2026	4848	2870	3949	626	3135
do, art, n fs	rel part, pers pron	n mp	cj, n mp	n ms, ps 3fs	n mp	n fd, ps 3fs
אֶת־הָאִשָּׁה	אֲשֶׁר־הִיא	מְצוֹדִים	וַחֲרָמִים	לִבָּהּ	אֲסוּרִים	יָדֶיהָ
'eth-hā'ishshāh	'ăsher-hî'	mᵉtsôdhîm	wachărāmîm	libbāhh	'ăsûrîm	yādhêāh
the woman	who she	traps	and nets	her heart	bonds	her hands

ally does good and who never sins, *NASB* ... that he can do right always and never do wrong, *NEB*.

21. Also take no heed unto all words that are spoken: ... do not take seriously all words, *NASB* ... Don't listen to everything people say, *NCV* ... do not pay attention to everything men say, *NEB*.

lest thou hear thy servant curse thee: ... speaking ill of you, *NAB* ... you might hear your servant insulting you, *NCV* ... or you may hear your servant disparage you, *NEB* ... lest thou hear thine own servant reviling thee!, *Rotherham*.

22. For oftentimes also thine own heart knoweth that thou thyself

likewise hast cursed others: ... you yourself have reviled others, *Anchor* ... how frequently others have been cursed by you, *BB* ... you have abused others, *JB* ... conscience will tell thee how often thou too has spoken ill of others,

23. All this have I proved by wisdom: ... tested by wisdom,

Goodspeed … Thanks to wisdom, I have found all this to be true, *JB* … I have tested by means of wisdom, *Moffatt* … I probed in wisdom, *NAB*.

I said, I will be wise: … resolved to be wise, *JB* … Wisdom, cried I, I must have, *Knox* … I thought to become wise, *Moffatt* … I will acquire wisdom, *NAB*.

but it was far from me: … was beyond my reach!, *JB* … yet all the while she withdrew from me, *Knox* … wisdom remained out of reach, *Moffatt* … it was too hard for me, *NCV*.

24. That which is far off, and exceeding deep, who can find it out?: … no one can lay hands upon the heart of things, *Moffatt* … Who can discover it?, *NASB* … is too hard for anyone to understand, *NCV* … deeper than man can fathom, *NEB*.

25. I applied mine heart to know, and to search, and to seek out wisdom, and the reason of things: … I sought and pursued wisdom and reason, *NAB, Douay* … to seek wisdom and an explanation, *NASB* … tried very hard to find wisdom, to find some meaning for everything, *NCV* … set my mind to inquire and search for wisdom and for the reason in things, *NEB* … turned my mind to understand, to investigate and to search out wisdom and the scheme of things, *NIV*.

and to know the wickedness of folly: … wickedness is foolish, *Douay* … it is foolish to be evil, *NCV* … it is folly to be wicked, *NEB* … to understand the stupidity of wickedness, *NIV*.

even of foolishness and madness: … folly is madness, *Douay* … it is crazy to act like a fool, *NCV* … and madness to act like a fool, *NEB*.

26. And I find more bitter than death the woman, whose heart is snares and nets: … was my experience with woman, whose thoughts are traps and snares, *Anchor* … whose heart is full of tricks and nets, *BB* … a woman who has craft and vices in her heart, *Fenton* … some women are worse than death and are as dangerous as traps, *NCV*.

and her hands as bands: … whose hands are chains, *Anchor* … snares in her hands, *Fenton* … her arms are chains, *JB* … whose clasp is a chain, *Moffatt*.

whoso pleaseth God shall escape from her: … by God's favor one may escape her, *Anchor* … If you're pleasing to God, you'll escape her, *Beck* … with whom God is pleased will get free from her, *BB* … man who is pleasing to God eludes her, *JB*.

---

frailty, much more the careless and ungodly, may offend in word (Jam. 3:2). The wise counsel therefore to avoid the vexation of this evil world is not to resent. Do not pay attention to all words that are spoken, because some words are spoken unadvisedly or in passion. They were not intended for us, and we have no right to hear them.

Few of us can plead "Not Guilty" to the indictment of evil-speaking. If we recall our conversation at the end of the day, how many breaches of the law of love! how seldom are our words free from that which we should not like to have repeated!

7:23–25. The Preacher turns again to his own history. He had first exercised his wisdom in intellectual research. Here he soon found his bottom. Notwithstanding all his advantages of a comprehensive understanding, all his extensive and multifarious resources, when he said he would be wise, it was far from him. He was always opening some new vein in the golden mine. Yet even his powerful mind was made to feel its limits, and to cry out—Who can find it out? "Such knowledge is too wonderful for me; it is high, I cannot attain unto it" (Ps. 139:6).

Heavenly wisdom teaches the same lesson, only with a deeper and more practical impression. Our highest knowledge is but a mere atom when compared with the unsearchable extent of our ignorance. The more we know of God, the more we are humbled in the sense of our ignorance.

Solomon's disappointment could not be attributed to any lack of heart in his object. Nothing could exceed his untiring pursuit. He heaps word upon word to attempt some adequate conception of the intensity of his ardor.

But his interest was mainly fixed in knowing the wickedness of folly, especially of that sin which bears upon it the peculiar stamp of folly (Gen. 34:7), even deserving the name of madness. For what is man living for his own lusts, but the picture of man having lost his understanding? (Hos. 4:11). But in this unhallowed track, he plunged himself into perilous hazard. Far better (as our first parents found too late) to know nothing of evil, than to learn it experimentally. Far better would it have been for Solomon to have known foolishness and madness by observation, by the records of conscience, by the testimony of the word, than by the terrible personal experiment. Who has not need of the prayer—"Keep your servant also from presumptuous sins?" (Ps. 19:13). Practical godliness is the keeping of the soul: "He that is begotten of God keepeth himself, and that wicked one toucheth him not" (1 John 5:18).

7:26. We have had many striking pictures of the vanity of the world and its utter insufficiency for

3004.151	3937, 6686	435	4561.221	4623	2490.151
v Qal act ptc ms	prep, n mp	art, n mp	v Niphal impf 3ms	prep, ps 3fs	cj, v Qal act ptc ms
טוֹב	לִפְנֵי	הָאֱלֹהִים	יִמָּלֵט	מִמֶּנָּה	וְחוֹטֵא
ṭôv	liphnê	hā'ĕlōhîm	yimmālēṭ	mimmennāh	wᵉchôṭē'
the one acting with goodness	before	God	he will escape	from her	but the sinner

4058.221	904	**27.** 7495.131	2172	4834.115	569.112	7237
v Niphal impf 3ms	prep, ps 3fs	v Qal impv 2ms	dem pron	v Qal pf 1cs	v Qal pf 3fs	n ms
יִלָּכֵד	בָּהּ	רְאֵה	זֶה	מָצָאתִי	אָמְרָה	קֹהֶלֶת
yillākhedh	bāhh	rᵉ'ēh	zeh	mātsā'thî	'āmᵉrāh	qōheleth
he will be captured	by her	see	this	I have found	it says	the preacher

259	3937, 259	3937, 4834.141	2918	**28.** 866	5968, 1272.312	5497	3940
num	prep, num	prep, v Qal inf con	n ms	rel part	adv, v Piel pf 3fs	n fs, ps 1cs	cj, neg part
אַחַת	לְאַחַת	לִמְצֹא	חֶשְׁבּוֹן	אֲשֶׁר	עוֹד־בִּקְשָׁה	נַפְשִׁי	וְלֹא
'achath	lᵉ'achath	limtsō'	cheshbôn	'ăsher	'ōdh-biqŏshāh	naphshî	wᵉlō'
one	to one	to find	a reckoning	which	still it will seek	my soul	but not

4834.115	119	259	4623, 512	4834.115	828	904, 3725, 431
v Qal pf 1cs	n ms	num	prep, num	v Qal pf 1cs	cj, n fs	prep, adj, dem pron
מָצָאתִי	אָדָם	אֶחָד	מֵאֶלֶף	מָצָאתִי	וְאִשָּׁה	בְּכָל־אֵלֶּה
mātsā'thî	'ādhām	'echādh	mē'eleph	mātsā'thî	wᵉ'ishshāh	vᵉkhol-'ēlleh
I have found	a man	one	among one thousand	I have found	but a woman	among all these

3940	4834.115	**29.** 3937, 940	7495.131, 2172	4834.115	866	6449.111
neg part	v Qal pf 1cs	prep, n ms	v Qal impv 2ms, dem pron	v Qal pf 1cs	rel part	v Qal pf 3ms
לֹא	מָצָאתִי	לְבַד	רְאֵה־זֶה	מָצָאתִי	אֲשֶׁר	עָשָׂה
lō'	mātsā'thî	lᵉvadh	rᵉ'ēh-zeh	mātsā'thî	'ăsher	'āsāh
not	I have found	besides	see this	I have found	that	He made

435	881, 119	3596	2065	1272.316	2920	7521	**8:1** 4449
art, n mp	do, art, n ms	adj	cj, pers pron	v Piel pf 3cp	n mp	adj	intrg
הָאֱלֹהִים	אֶת־הָאָדָם	יָשָׁר	וְהֵמָּה	בִקֵּשׁוּ	חִשְּׁבֹנוֹת	רַבִּים	מִי
hā'ĕlōhîm	'eth-hā'ādhām	yāshār	wᵉhēmmāh	viqŏshû	chishshᵉvōnôth	rabbîm	mî
God	the man	upright	but they	they have sought	devices	many	who

but the sinner shall be taken by her: ... whomever he disapproves will be caught by her, *Anchor* ... if you sin, she'll catch you, *Beck* ... the sinner will be ensnared by her, *Berkeley* ... is captured by her, *JB*.

27. Behold, this have I found, saith the preacher: ... is what I think, *JB* ... I have discovered this, *NASB* ... This is what I learned, *NCV*.

counting one by one, to find out the account: ... examined one thing after another to draw some conclusion, *JB* ... adding one thing to another that I might discover the answer, *NAB* ... added all these things together to find some meaning for everything, *NCV*.

28. Which yet my soul seeketh, but I find not: ... after searching long without finding anything, *Anchor* ... what I search for again and again I can't find, *Beck* ... What my heart sought continually, that I did not find, *Berkeley* ... I am still looking for, although unsuccessfully, *JB*.

one man among a thousand have I found; but a woman among all those have I not found: ... but not one woman in all these did I find [to be wise], *Anchor* ... I found one man who had it, but in all these I didn't find a woman, *Beck* ... one man in a thousand, I may find, but a woman better than other women—never, *JB* ... one true man in a thousand, but never a true woman!, *Moffatt*.

29. Lo, this only have I found, that God hath made man upright: ... has created man straightforward, *JB* ... man's nature was simple enough when God made him, *Knox* ... made the race of men upright, *Moffatt* ... made people good, *NCV*.

but they have sought out many inventions: ... and human artifices are human inventions, *JB* ... these endless questions are of his own devising, *Knox* ... many a cunning wile have they contrived, *Moffatt* ... have found all kinds of ways to be bad, *NCV*.

8:1. Who is as the wise man?: ... can compare with, *Anchor* ... is like, *Beck* ... Who compares with the sage?, *JB* ... No one is like the wise person, *NCV*.

and who knoweth the interpretation of a thing?: ... Who else understands what things mean?, *Anchor* ...

our happiness. We are now turning over to another page to see the vileness of sin, its certain tendency to our misery and ruin. Solomon had often drawn this graphic picture for the warning of others. Here he describes the apparatus of a fowler as the picture of the heart of the unprincipled woman. Mark the mighty power of the temptation! Such a multitude of devices! Such consummate skill in the application of them! the spell of enchantment chaining her deluded victims with irresistible influence!

What then is the escape from this extreme peril? Man's highest moral sense, all his strength of resolution, is absolutely powerless. The sovereign grace of God is omnipotent. Prayer brings this secure cover and spreads it over those who, like Joseph in similar temptation (Gen. 39:9f), are good before Him. But the sinner will be taken by her (Prov. 2:19; 22:14). We read of the bitterness of death (1 Sam. 15:32) and of an even worse bitterness: "The end of a strange woman is bitter as wormwood, and her steps take hold on hell" (Prov. 5:4f). The bitterness of hell is incurable: death may be honorable when one dies for a good cause and goes to the grave in peace. Such a one is lamented, desired, with the sweet savor of a holy life, and many good works to follow him, but for a man to putrefy alive, under the plague of impure lust in the bosom of a harlot, is a bitterness beyond that of death. This act not only separates the soul from the body, but separates both from God.

7:27–28. The word "behold" marks the sad testimony he is about to give. Conceive him looking at the multitude of his courtiers standing before him, counting one by one, trying to determine how many faithful and true; his soul is seeking, but not finding. Yet the unhappy result is that he could find only one faithful man among a thousand, and not even one godly woman! What a contrast to his father's house and court! "Mine eyes," said the man of God, "are upon the faithful in the land, that they may dwell with me" (Ps. 101:6).

We cannot suppose that Solomon's judgment of women was a universal sweeping condemnation. He had no difficulty finding female virtue in its own legitimate sphere—indeed, he had given many testimonies of the virtue of women. But here his view was evidently confined to the walls of his own harem (cf. 1 Ki. 11:3). And among the thousand strange women (1 Ki. 5:1) dwelling in that crowded seraglio he himself was living in the open breach of God's law (1 Ki. 5:10), in the gross vio-

lation of marriage purity, casting away all the domestic happiness of endeared affection and undivided love. How could he expect to find "the virtuous woman," whom he so beautifully portrays—"her price far above rubies?" Here he only informs us that, looking where he had no warrant to find the jewel, the result was unmingled disappointment. And such will always be the fruit of sin. Child of God! Be thankful for the bitterness of the draught from the "broken cistern," as the weaning discipline, that turns your heart back to your God.

7:29. This is a most important verse. It opens up to us a hidden mystery, man's original sinless created state and his awful apostasy from it—how God made man and how man unmade himself. All he has found are streams of wickedness that were beyond the ken of his sight. But he saw enough to trace the direful Fall as the fountainhead of corruption.

Such was man—made upright. Yet "being in honor, he abideth not. How is the gold become dim, and the most fine gold changed!" (Ps. 49:12; Lam. 4:1). How different from the holy creature which came out of his Maker's hands.

The wicked have sought out many inventions to fall away from God. For example, man's discontent with the happiness which God has provided for him—this was their first invention. Hence they fancied a higher perfection than that in which man had been confirmed, thus yielding to follow the new way, which Satan and his deceived heart had placed before them, despising their Creator's law, suspecting his truth, nay, even aspiring to share his sovereignty. This first invention was the parent of the many, all marked by the same falsehood, folly and impiety, all flowing out of the bottomless depths of the heart alienated from God, full of windings and turnings, "turning every one to his own way" (Isa. 53:6). All sin is only a form of self-love, instead of the love of God. The many inventions take the throne in turn.

8:1. Two things Solomon had desired to seek out—wisdom and folly (7:25). The latter he had known to his cost, and most faithfully has he described it. He now turns to the former—Who is as the wise man? There is no one to be set by him, however splendidly endowed, rich, noble or learned. "Wisdom is the principal thing" (Prov. 4:7), worth all the pains of prayer and diligence to gain and to hold fast.

But it is the practical quality that we chiefly regard—to know the interpretation of a thing. In the

3626, 2550	4449	3156.151	6842	1745	2551	119
prep, art, n ms	cj, intrg	v Qal act ptc ms	n ms	n ms	n fs	n ms
כְּהֶחָכָם	וּמִי	יוֹדֵעַ	פֵּשֶׁר	דָּבָר	חָכְמַת	אָדָם
kᵉhechākhām	ûmî	yōdhēa'	pēsher	dāvār	chokhmath	'ādhām
like the wise	and who	one who knows	an interpretation of	a matter	the wisdom of	a man

213.522	6686	6010	6686	8521.421	603
v Hiphil impf 3fs	n mp, ps 3ms	cj, n ms	n mp, ps 3ms	v Pual impf 3ms	**2.** pers pron
תָּאִיר	פָּנָיו	וְעֹז	פָּנָיו	יְשֻׁנֶּא	אֲנִי
tā'îr	pānâv	wᵉ'ōz	pānâv	yᵉshunne'	'ănî
it causes to shine	his face	and the strength of	his face	it is changed	I

6552, 4567	8490.131	6142	1750	8095	435
n ms, n ms	v Qal impv 2ms	cj, prep	n fs	n fs	n mp
פִּי־מֶלֶךְ	שְׁמוֹר	וְעַל	דִּבְרַת	שְׁבוּעַת	אֱלֹהִים
pî-melekh	shᵉmôr	wᵉ'al	divrath	shᵉvû'ath	'ĕlōhîm
the mouth of the king	keep	and concerning	the manner of	the oath of	God

414, 963.223	4623, 6686	2050.123	414, 6198.123	904, 1745	7737
adv, v Niphal juss 2ms	prep, n mp, ps 3ms	v Qal impf 2ms	adv, v Qal juss 2ms	prep, n ms	adj
3. אַל־תִּבָּהֵל	מִפָּנָיו	תֵּלֵךְ	אַל־תַּעֲמֹד	בְּדָבָר	רָע
'al-tibbāhēl	mippānâv	tēlēkh	'al-ta'āmōdh	bᵉdhāvār	rā'
do not be dismayed	before him	you will go	do not stand	when the matter	evil

3706	3725, 866	2759.121	6449.121	904, 866	1745, 4567
cj	adj, rel part	v Qal impf 3ms	v Qal impf 3ms	prep, rel part	n ms, n ms
כִּי	כָּל־אֲשֶׁר	יַחְפֹּץ	יַעֲשֶׂה	**4.** בַּאֲשֶׁר	דְּבַר־מֶלֶךְ
kî	kol-'ăsher	yachpōts	ya'ăseh	ba'ăsher	dᵉvar-melekh
because	all that	he is pleased with	he will do	where	the word of the king

8378	4449	569.121, 3937	4242, 6449.123	8490.151
n ms	cj, intrg	v Qal impf 3ms, prep, ps 3ms	intrg, v Qal impf 2ms	**5.** v Qal act ptc ms
שִׁלְטוֹן	וּמִי	יֹאמַר־לוֹ	מַה־תַּעֲשֶׂה	שׁוֹמֵר
shiltôn	ûmî	yō'mar-lô	mah-ta'ăseh	shômēr
supremacy	and who	he will say to him	what are you doing	the one who keeps

4851	3940	3156.121	1745	7737	6496	5122
n fs	neg part	v Qal impf 3ms	n ms	adj	cj, n fs	cj, n ms
מִצְוָה	לֹא	יֵדַע	דָּבָר	רָע	וְעֵת	וּמִשְׁפָּט
mitswāh	lō'	yēdha'	dāvār	rā'	wᵉ'ēth	ûmishpāt
a commandment	not	he will experience	a thing	evil	both the time	and the judgment

3156.121	3949	2550	3706	3937, 3725, 2761	3552	6496	5122
v Qal impf 3ms	n ms	n ms	cj	prep, adj, n ms	sub	n fs	cj, n ms
יֵדַע	לֵב	חָכָם	**6.** כִּי	לְכָל־חֵפֶץ	יֵשׁ	עֵת	וּמִשְׁפָּט
yēdha'	lēv	chākhām	kî	lᵉkhol-chēphets	yēsh	'ēth	ûmishpāt
it will know	the heart of	the wise	because	for every desire	there is	a time	and a judgment

knows how to explain things?, *Beck* ... who knows the true meaning of things?, *Berkeley* ... who knoweth the explanation of things?, *Darby*.

a man's wisdom maketh his face to shine: ... lights up his face, *Anchor* ... brightens his face, *Berkeley* ... illumines his face, *Goodspeed* ... brings happiness, *NCV*.

and the boldness of his face shall be changed: ... the hardness of his countenance is transformed, *Anchor* ... changes his grim look, *Beck* ... the crudeness of his face becomes refined, *Berkeley* ... his hard face will be changed, *BB*.

2. I counsel thee to keep the king's commandment: ... Be willing to

do what the king orders, *Beck* ... Obey the king, *Moffatt* ... Observe the precept of the king, *NAB* ... Do as the king commands, *NEB*.

and that in regard of the oath of God: ... because of the divine promise, *JB* ... for you swore him loyalty before God, *Moffatt* ... in view of your oath to God, *NAB* ...

because you made a promise to God, *NCV*.

3. Be not hasty to go out of his sight: ... not hurry from his presence in agitation, *Anchor* ... Rebel not rashly against him, *Moffatt* ... not hasty to withdraw from the king, *NAB, Douay* ... Don't be too quick to leave the king, *NCV*.

stand not in an evil thing: ... nor hesitate to go when the errand is distasteful, *Anchor* ... persist not in an evil thing, *ASV* ... do not mess with contrary matters, *Berkeley* ... not fixed in an evil design, *BB*.

for he doeth whatsoever pleaseth him: ... he does as he pleases,

Anchor ... though he does anything he likes, *Beck* ... does whatsoever he will, *Goodspeed* ... will do as he likes in any case, *JB*.

4. Where the word of a king is, there is power: ... the king's word is supreme, *Moffatt* ... his word is sovereign, *NAB* ... the word of the king is authoritative, *NASB* ... What the king says is law, *NCV*.

and who may say unto him, What doest thou?: ... none dare ask him what he means, *Moffatt* ... no one tells him what to do, *NCV* ... Who can question what he does?, *NEB* ... who can call in question what he does?, *REB*.

5. Whoso keepeth the commandment shall feel no evil thing: ... who obeys will avoid trouble, *Anchor* ... will experience no harm, *Berkeley* ... will be safe, *NCV*.

and a wise man's heart discerneth both time and judgment: ... the wise mind will know when and how to act, *Anchor* ... if you're wise, you will know when and how to do things, *Beck* ... has knowledge of time and of decision, *BB* ... knows the proper time and procedure, *NASB* ... wise person does the right thing at the right time, *NCV*.

6. Because to every purpose there is time and judgment: ... there is a time of judgment coming, *Moffatt* ...

---

field of science, the gifts of wisdom and interpretation are distinct. Many a man may see clearly through his own optics, but he has no talent to remove the cloud that obstructs his brother's vision.

Thus wisdom, here so highly commended, has no practical influence as a mere intellectual quality. But as a heavenly principle, it makes the face to shine from intercourse with a brighter world.

8:2. Having commended wisdom in its bright shining beauty, the Preacher now enforces some of its practical rules. Loyalty is a component part of Christian obedience (Tit. 3:1). The command, "Render unto Caesar the things that are Caesar's," stands upon the same ground as, "Unto God the things that are God's" (Matt. 22:21). The preacher speaks with authority—I counsel you to keep the king's commandment. This obedience has respect to the oath of God.

Yet no earthly sovereign can claim the right of absolute obedience. The service of man must ever be subordinated to the supreme claims of the service of God. To God, the oath of allegiance is bound indissolubly. Soul and body are alike the purchase of the Son of God (1 Cor. 6:19f; Ps. 119:106). Where therefore man's command is contrary, we must show respectful but unflinching determination.

8:3–5. These wise and important rules have a special reference to despotic power. The standing daily before the kings (cf. 1 Ki. 10:8; Est. 1:14) was the mark of obedient readiness. Hastiness therefore to go out of his sight would be an insolent or disrespectful taking offense, seeming to fling off all alle-

giance. Where the word of a king is, there is power. The autocrat—whether he be good or bad—whether he be a Solomon (1 Ki. 2:29–46) or a Herod (Matt. 14:9f), is without control. He does whatever pleases him, and who will say to him, "What are you doing?"

But we speak not only of the courtiers or the immediate attendants of the earthly sovereign. Who of us does not lie under a primary obligation to the "King of kings?" It is an honorable "happiness" (cp. 1 Ki. 10:8) to stand continually before Him, yet great carefulness and reverence is required!

This path of keeping the commandment will preserve us from feeling evil. Every command bears the stamp of infinite tenderness and love. Not one is supernumerary. Yet our course must not be one command standing upon the ruins of another, but the exercise of godly wisdom—just where the Lord has marked out our path, there to lay ourselves out for Him.

Too often in the ordinary course we encumber the path with difficulties of our own framing. Sincere Christians are not always wise. The husbandman never fails to discern the time. He never mistakes the season for the plow, the seed-time and the harvest. But in "God's husbandry" (1 Cor. 3:9), how few seem to discern the value of the season, how much good timing, whether in saying or doing, adds to beauty and effect! (Prov. 15:23; 25:11).

8:6–7. All concerning us is determined in the counsels of God, and all in judgment. The time is the best time, because it is God's time. It is a solemn thought to us all, most precious to the

3156.151 v Qal act ptc ms יֹדֵעַ yōdhēa' knowing	3706, 375 cj, sub, ps 3ms כִּי־אֵינֶנּוּ kî-'ênennû because there is not to him	**7.**	6142 prep, ps 3ms עָלָיו 'ālâv upon him	7521 adj רַבָּה rabbāh much	119 art, n ms הָאָדָם hā'ādhām humankind	3706, 7750 cj, n fs כִּי־רָעַת kî-rā'ath when the trouble of

3937 prep, ps 3ms לוֹ lô to him	5222.521 v Hiphil impf 3ms יַגִּיד yaggîdh he will tell	4449 intrg מִי mî who	2030.121 v Qal impf 3ms יִהְיֶה yihyeh it will be	3626, 866 prep, rel part כַּאֲשֶׁר ka'ăsher like what	3706 cj כִּי kî because	4242, 8054, 2030.121 intrg, rel part, v Qal impf 3ms מַה־שֶּׁיִּהְיֶה mah-sheyihyeh what that it will be

8.	375 sub אֵין 'ên there is not	119 n ms אָדָם 'ādhām a man	8384 n ms שַׁלִּיט shallît a ruler	904, 7593 prep, art, n fs בָּרוּחַ bārûach over the spirit	3937, 3727.141 prep, v Qal inf con לִכְלוֹא likhlô' to hold back	881, 7593 do, art, n fs אֶת־הָרוּחַ 'eth-hārûach the spirit	375 cj, sub וְאֵין we'ên and there is not

8378 n ms שִׁלְטוֹן shiltôn supremacy	904, 3219 prep, n ms בְּיוֹם beyôm with the day of	4323 art, n ms הַמָּוֶת hammāweth the death	375 cj, sub וְאֵין we'ên and there is not	5097 n fs מִשְׁלַחַת mishlachath a discharge	904, 4560 prep, art, n fs בַּמִּלְחָמָה bammilchāmāh in the battle

3940, 4561.321 cj, neg part, v Piel impf 3ms וְלֹא־יְמַלֵּט welō'-yemallēt and it will not allow to escape	7856 n ms רֶשַׁע resha' wickedness	881, 1196 do, n mp, ps 3ms אֶת־בְּעָלָיו 'eth-be'ālâv its owners	**9.**	881, 3725, 2172 do, adj, dem pron אֶת־כָּל־זֶה 'eth-kol-zeh all this	7495.115 v Qal pf 1cs רָאִיתִי rā'îthî I have seen

5598.142 cj, v Qal inf abs וְנָתוֹן wenāthôn and setting on	881, 3949 do, n ms, ps 1cs אֶת־לִבִּי 'eth-libbî my heart	3937, 3725, 4801 prep, adj, n ms לְכָל־מַעֲשֶׂה lekhol-ma'ăseh every deed	866 rel part אֲשֶׁר 'ăsher that	6449.211 v Niphil pf 3ms נַעֲשָׂה na'ăsāh it is done	8809 prep תַּחַת tachath under	8507 art, n ms הַשָּׁמֶשׁ hashshāmesh the sun	6496 n fs עֵת 'ēth a time

866 rel part אֲשֶׁר 'ăsher which	8375.111 v Qal pf 3ms שָׁלַט shālat he will tyrannize	119 art, n ms הָאָדָם hā'ādhām the man	904, 119 prep, n ms בְּאָדָם be'ādhām against a man	3937, 7737 prep, n ms לְרַע lera' for disaster	3937 prep, ps 3ms לוֹ lô to him	**10.** 904, 3772 cj, prep, adv וּבְכֵן ûvekhēn and when thus

7495.115 v Qal pf 1cs רָאִיתִי rā'îthî I saw	7857 n mp רְשָׁעִים reshā'îm the wicked	7196.155 v Qal pass ptc ms קְבֻרִים qǒvurîm having been buried	971.116 cj, v Qal pf 3cp וָבָאוּ wāvā'û that they had entered	4623, 4887 cj, prep, n ms וּמִמְּקוֹם ûmimmeqôm but from the place	7202 adj קָדוֹשׁ qādhôsh holy

there is a time and a judgment for everything, *NAB* … there is a proper time and procedure for every delight, *NASB* … is a right time and a right way for everything, *NCV*.

therefore the misery of man is great upon him: … though to-day men are being crushed under the king in misery, *Moffatt* … it is a great affliction for man, *NAB* … when a man's trouble is heavy upon him, *NASB* … yet people often have many troubles, *NCV*.

7. For he knoweth not that which shall be: … does not know what will happen, *Anchor* … People worry a lot because they don't know what the future will bring, *Beck* … No one is certain what is to be, *BB* … none of us know what will be, *Fenton*.

for who can tell him when it shall be?: … how it will happen [when it does]?, *Anchor* … how things will turn out?, *Beck* … as to what may happen, who can inform us?, *Fenton* … no one can tell them what will happen, *NCV*.

8. There is no man that hath power over the spirit to retain the spirit: ... can control the wind or hold it back, *Beck* ... can be master over the wind to restrain the wind, *Berkeley* ... has authority over the wind, to keep the wind, *BB* ... has power over the breath, to retain the breath, *Fenton.*

neither hath he power in the day of death: ... the day of one's death cannot be determined, *Anchor* ... nor can any man hold back the day of his death, *Beck* ... no one can prevail in the day of death, *Berkeley* ... no one hath control over the day of death, *Darby.*

and there is no discharge in that war: ... is no immunity in the battle, *Anchor* ... no furlough during battle, *Berkeley* ... In war no man's time is free, *BB* ... nor is there release in war, *Goodspeed.*

neither shall wickedness deliver those that are given to it: ... nor can wealth save its owner, *Anchor* ... wickedness will not set free the one who is guilty of it, *Beck* ... neither will wickedness liberate those who practice it, *Berkeley* ... evil will not keep the sinner safe, *BB.*

9. All this have I seen, and applied my heart unto every work that is done under the sun: ... having devoted my mind to all the work which is done, *Goodspeed* ... having carefully studied everything taking place, *JB* ... as I gave heed to all that befalls us, *Knox* ... as thoughtfully I pondered what goes on within this world, *Moffatt.*

there is a time wherein one man ruleth over another to his own hurt: ... has power over another to injure him, *Goodspeed* ... tyrannises over another to the former's detriment, *JB* ... rules over man to his undoing, *Knox* ... has exercised authority over another man to his hurt, *NASB.*

10. And so I saw the wicked buried: ... borne to their tombs, *Anchor* ... evil men put to rest, *BB* ... saw the funerals of evil people, *NCV* ... considered the lawless when buried, *Rotherham.*

who had come and gone from the place of the holy: ... taken even from the holy place, *BB* ... praised from the holy place, *Goodspeed* ... who used to go in and out from the holy place, *NASB* ... from the place of holiness, *NKJV.*

and they were forgotten in the city where they had so done: ... were forgotten in the city as having behaved like that, *Berkeley* ... were praised in the town because of what they had done, *BB* ... and lauded in the city where they had acted thus, *Goodspeed* ... are soon forgotten, *NASB.*

this is also vanity: ... is futility, *NASB* ... is useless, *NCV* ... is emptiness, *NEB* ... is meaningless, *NIV.*

Christian, that each of us has been in the mind of God from all eternity.

But how little does man conceive the responsibility of indifference to the purpose of God! The evil of this willful ignorance in the concerns of eternity is ruinous beyond all calculation. Let God's time of mercy be neglected, and great indeed will be the misery. The door once shut, is shut forever (Matt. 25:10; Luke 13:24–28).

Much of the future is far beyond the keenest and most sagacious eye. What or when it will be is our present exercise. But prayer and diligence will bring the light in God's fittest time. Meanwhile, this ignorance does not touch our security or cloud our confidence.

8:8. One event, specially stamped with uncertainty, but linked with the divine purpose, is "a time to die" (3:2). This most momentous event in man's history hangs upon the Almighty. Who can tell a man whom it will be? But the word once given—who has power over the spirit, to retain the spirit? Man, after all his mightiest efforts to make himself independent of God, cannot retain his spirit in its tabernacle prison a single moment beyond the time. Nay, he has no power at all in the day of death.

No truth is more certain—perhaps none more often repeated; yet none more practically forgotten. Men live as if they were never to die—as if they were exempted from the universal law. The wicked "strengtheneth himself in his wickedness" (Ps. 52:7). But he can neither outwit nor outbrave the enemy. Given to his wickedness, he will find that it is no deliverance for him. His "covenant with death and with hell will be disannulled." He "will be driven away in his wickedness" (Isa. 28:14–18; Prov. 14:32).

8:9–10. Solomon tells us, once and again, that his views were the result of his own careful observation. Often had he seen the rule of man perverted from its legitimate end, exercised to the hurt, not of the ruled only, but of the ruler raised up to a throne, only that his fall might be more tremendous (Exo. 9:16). Well may "the rich rejoice, in that he is made low" (Jam. 1:10).

But let us follow Solomon in his field of observation. Wickedness, so far from being a deliverance, becomes an occasion of hurt. The wicked may have come and gone in pomp and ceremony from the place of the holy. But the great leveler comes without respect of persons.

1961	1612, 2172	3772, 6449.116	866	904, 6111	8319.726	2050.326
n ms	cj, dem pron	adv, v Qal pf 3cp	rel part	prep, art, n fs	cj, v Hithpael impf 3mp	v Piel impf 3mp
הָבֶל	גַּם־זֶה	כֵּן־עָשׂוּ	אֲשֶׁר	בָעִיר	וְיִשְׁתַּכְּחוּ	יְהַלֵּכוּ
hável	gam-zeh	kēn-'āsû	'ǎsher	vā'îr	weyishtakkechû	yehallēkhû
a vanity	also this	so they had done	where	in the city	then they were forgotten	they walked

11.

4529	6142, 3772	4259	7750	4801	6851	375, 6449.211	866
adj	prep, adv	adv	art, n fs	n ms	n ms	sub, v Niphal pf 3ms	cj
מָלֵא	עַל־כֵּן	מְהֵרָה	הָרָעָה	מַעֲשֵׂה	פִתְגָם	אֵין־נַעֲשָׂה	אֲשֶׁר
mālē'	'al-kēn	mehērāh	hārā'āh	ma'ǎsēh	phithghām	'ên-na'ǎsāh	'ǎsher
full	therefore	quickly	the evil	the work of	a decree	it has not been executed	because

12.

866	7737	3937, 6449.141	904	1158, 119	3949
cj	n ms	prep, v Qal inf con	prep, ps 3mp	n mp, art, n ms	n ms
אֲשֶׁר	רָע	לַעֲשׂוֹת	בָּהֶם	בְּנֵי־הָאָדָם	לֵב
'ǎsher	rā'	la'ǎsôth	bāhem	benê-hā'ādhām	lēv
because	evil	to do	within them	the children of humankind	the heart of

1612, 3156.151	3706	3937	773.551	4109	7737	6449.151	2490.151
cj, v Qal act ptc ms	cj	prep, ps 3ms	cj, v Hiphil ptc ms	num	n ms	v Qal act ptc ms	v Qal act ptc ms
גַּם־יוֹדֵעַ	כִּי	לוֹ	וּמַאֲרִיךְ	מְאַת	רָע	עֹשֶׂה	חֹטֵא
gam-yôdhēa'	kî	lô	ûma'ǎrîkh	me'ath	rā'	'ōseh	chōte'
also knowing	yet	to him	and lengthening	one hundred	evil	doing	a sinner

3486.126	866	435	3937, 3486.152	2030.121, 3005	866	603
v Qal impf 3mp	rel pron	art, n mp	prep, v Qal act ptc mp	v Qal impf 3ms, adj	rel part	pers pron
יִירְאוּ	אֲשֶׁר	הָאֱלֹהִים	לְיִרְאֵי	יִהְיֶה־טוֹב	אֲשֶׁר	אָנִי
yîre'û	'ǎsher	hā'ělōhîm	leyir'ê	yihyeh-tôv	'ǎsher	'ānî
they will fear	who	God	to those who fear	it is good	that	I

13.

3940, 773.521	3937, 7857	3940, 2030.121	3005	4623, 3937, 6686
cj, neg part, v Hiphil impf 3ms	prep, art, n ms	neg part, v Qal impf 3ms	cj, adj	prep, prep, n mp, ps 3ms
וְלֹא־יַאֲרִיךְ	לָרָשָׁע	לֹא־יִהְיֶה	וְטוֹב	מִלְּפָנָיו
welō'-ya'ǎrîkh	lārāshā'	lō'-yihyeh	wetôv	millephānâv
and he will not lengthen	to the wicked	it will not be	but good	from before Him

435	4623, 3937, 6686	3486.151	375	866	3626, 7009	3219
n mp	prep, prep, n mp	v Qal act ptc ms	sub, ps 3ms	rel part	prep, art, n ms	n mp
אֱלֹהִים	מִלִּפְנֵי	יָרֵא	אֵינֶנּוּ	אֲשֶׁר	כַּצֵּל	יָמִים
'ělōhîm	milliphnê	yārē'	'ênennû	'ǎsher	katstsēl	yāmîm
God	from before	fearing	there is not to him	which	like the shadow	days

14.

866	6926	3552	866	6142, 800	6449.211	866	3552, 1961
rel pron	n mp	sub	rel part	prep, art, n fs	v Niphil pf 3ms	rel part	sub, n ms
אֲשֶׁר	צַדִּיקִים	יֵשׁ	אֲשֶׁר	עַל־הָאָרֶץ	נַעֲשָׂה	אֲשֶׁר	יֵשׁ־הֶבֶל
'ǎsher	tsaddîqîm	yēsh	'ǎsher	'al-hā'ārets	na'ǎsāh	'ǎsher	yesh-hevel
whom	the righteous	there are	that	on the earth	it is done	which	there is a vanity

11. Because sentence against an evil work is not executed speedily: ... a sentence against a crime isn't quickly carried out, *Beck* ... punishment for an evil work comes not quickly, *BB* ... when quick punishment is not inflicted upon crime, *Fenton* ... the sentence on the evildoer is not carried out on the instant, *JB*.

therefore the heart of the sons of men is fully set in them to do evil: ... that is why man's mind is filled with thoughts of doing evil, *Anchor* ... men are encouraged to do wrong, *Beck* ... minds of the sons of men are fully determined to do evil, *Goodspeed* ... hearts are full of desire to do wrong, *JB*.

12. Though a sinner do evil an hundred times, and his days be prolonged: ... his life is long, *BB* ... and still continues living, *Goodspeed* ... lives on, *JB* ... though the sinner presume on the divine patience that has borne with a hundred misdeeds, *Knox*.

yet surely I know that it shall be well with them that fear God,

which fear before him: ... those who go in fear of God and are in fear before him, *BB* ... those who reverence GOD,—who fear before Him, *Fenton* ... who fear God, who are in awe before him, *Goodspeed* ... there is good in store for people who fear God, because they fear him, *JB*.

13. But it shall not be well with the wicked, neither shall he prolong his days, which are as a shadow: ... he cannot thrive, *Moffatt* ... will not be well for the evil man and he will not lengthen his days, *NASB* ... will not go well for evil people, *NCV* ... good is not to the wicked, and he doth not prolong days, *Young*.

because he feareth not before God: ... Reckless of God's frown, *Knox* ... for his lack of reverence toward God, *NAB, Douay* ... they do not honor God, *NCV* ... he standeth not in awe before God, *Rotherham*.

14. There is a vanity which is done upon the earth: ... there are anom-alies in life, *Anchor* ... something being done on earth that makes no sense, *Beck* ... is a fruitlessness that happens, *Berkeley* ... a thing which is to no purpose, *BB*.

that there be just men, unto whom it happeneth according to the work of the wicked: ... to whom what happens should happen to the wicked, *Anchor* ... righteous persons suffer for what the wicked do, *Beck* ... good men to whom is given the same punishment as those who are

---

8:11. Wondrous are the dispensations of divine mercy! But not less wondrous is the wickedness of man in turning all this world of mercy into an occasion of deeper sin. The LORD delays sending punishment in order to bring mercy, but wicked people mistake God's grace as a license to commit sin.

As to the bold and presumptuous sinner—if he expected the thunderbolt to fall upon his head in the very act of sin, would he not turn pale at the thought? But because sentence is not speedily executed, he goes on secure, because he goes unpunished.

But because sentence is not speedily executed, it is not the less sure for the delay. The scoffer asked in contempt, "Where is the promise of his coming?" But the promise will come in God's time, and sweep them away (Luke 17:26–29; 2 Pet. 3:3–6). And yet the wickedness of man abuses the long suffering of God, as an occasion of more desperate rebellion. Indeed, "after his hardness and impenitent heart, he treasureth up unto himself wrath against the day of wrath and revelation of the righteous judgment of God" (Rom. 2:4f). Never let it be supposed that God's patience is the proof that He thinks lightly of sin.

8:12–13. The sinner's heart is so fully set to do evil, that he may do it an hundred times. Instead of the thunderbolt of vengeance, his days may be prolonged. He may even grow bolder than ever in sin. He may be exalted in outward prosperity, while the children of God are crushed in affliction. The sanctuary expounds the difficulty and solves the apparent contradiction. The end shows all to be infallibly right. At the great day, there will be a clear discernment between the righteous and the wicked.

It may often seem to be ill with the godly, and well with the sinner. We see Joseph in the pit (Gen. 37:24), Job in the ashes (Job 2:8), Lazarus at the rich man's gate (Luke 16:20f). We may see Haman in power (Est. 3:1), the foolish in prosperity (Ps. 73:3). But the statement on both sides stands firm. "Many indeed are the afflictions of the righteous" (Ps. 34:19). But "you hast given them the heritage of those that fear your name" (Ps. 61:5).

In summation, the child of God at his worst is still well in his soul: the servant of sin at his best will not be well, because his soul does not prosper. Each lives for the present life under the blessing or curse of God. Each will reap the full harvest of their principles throughout eternity. Balance the whole, and who can for a moment doubt on which side lies the well, on which side the ill? The ill of the godly, whatever that may be, is but for a moment; and his well is for eternity. The contrast is dark beyond expression. The ungodly grasps at happiness and embraces vanity. He cannot prolong his days at his will. His shadow passes away, and all his portion is dark despair.

8:14–15. We have another picture of vanity doubly marked. The all wise and righteous Governor of the world never forgets the vitally important distinction between the righteous and the wicked. But He is not pleased to make it the standard of his providential dispensation (9:1f). It often therefore happens as if the just were punished, and the wicked rewarded. It would seem as if the righteous "had cleansed his heart in vain" (Ps. 73:13). This may justly be called a vanity, not as reflecting upon the government of God in permitting them, but because the instruments are the fruit of man's corruption, and the display is that of the utterly unsatisfactory state of earthly things. But, be it remembered, we only see the surface view. There are depths in providence far beyond our vision. In his own time and way, the LORD will bring perfect order out of seeming confusion and astonish us with the manifestation of his glory.

7857	3552	7857	3626, 4801	420	5236.551
n mp	cj, sub	art, n mp	prep, n ms	prep, ps 3mp	v Hiphil ptc ms
רְשָׁעִים	וְיֵשׁ	הָרְשָׁעִים	כְּמַעֲשֵׂה	אֲלֵהֶם	מַגִּיעַ
rᵉshā'îm	wᵉyēsh	hārᵉshā'îm	kᵉma'ăsēh	'ălēhem	maggîa'
the wicked	and there are	the wicked	according to the deeds of	to them	causing harm

569.115	6926	3626, 4801	420	8054, 5236.551
v Qal pf 1cs	art, n mp	prep, n ms	prep, ps 3mp	rel pron, v Hiphil ptc ms
אָמַרְתִּי	הַצַּדִּיקִים	כְּמַעֲשֵׂה	אֲלֵהֶם	שֶׁמַּגִּיעַ
'āmartî	hatstsaddîqîm	kᵉma'ăsēh	'ălēhem	shemmaggîa'
I said	the righteous	according to the deeds of	to them	who causing harm

15.

375, 3005	866	881, 7977	603	8099.315	1961	8054, 1612, 2172
sub, adj	cj	do, art, n fs	pers pron	cj, v Piel pf 1cs	n ms	rel part, cj, dem pron
אֵין־טוֹב	אֲשֶׁר	אֶת־הַשִּׂמְחָה	אֲנִי	וְשִׁבַּחְתִּי	הָבֶל	שֶׁגַּם־זֶה
'ên-ṭôv	'ăsher	'eth-hassimchāh	'ănî	wᵉshibbachtî	hāvel	sheggam-zeh
there is not good	because	enjoyment	I	and I extolled	a vanity	that also this

3937, 7975.141	3937, 8685.141	524, 3937, 404.141	3706	8507	8809	3937, 119
cj, prep, v Qal inf con	cj, prep, v Qal inf con	cj, prep, v Qal inf con	cj	art, n ms	prep	prep, art, n ms
וְלִשְׂמוֹחַ	וְלִשְׁתּוֹת	אִם־לֶאֱכוֹל	כִּי	הַשֶּׁמֶשׁ	תַּחַת	לָאָדָם
wᵉlismôach	wᵉlishtôth	'im-le'ĕkhôl	kî	hashshemesh	tachath	lā'ādhām
and to be glad	and to drink	only to eat	except	the sun	under	to humankind

2522	3219	904, 6221	4004.121	2000
n mp, ps 3ms	n mp	prep, n ms, ps 3ms	v Qal impf 3ms, ps 3ms	cj, pers pron
חַיָּיו	יְמֵי	בַּעֲמָלוֹ	יִלְוֶנּוּ	וְהוּא
chayyâv	yᵉmê	va'ămālô	yilwennû	wᵉhû'
his life	the days of	in his toil	it will accompany him	and it

16.

5598.115	3626, 866	8507	8809	435	866, 5598.111, 3937
v Qal pf 1cs	prep, rel part	art, n ms	prep	art, n mp	rel part, v Qal pf 3ms, prep, ps 3ms
נָתַתִּי	כַּאֲשֶׁר	הַשֶּׁמֶשׁ	תַּחַת	הָאֱלֹהִים	אֲשֶׁר־נָתַן־לוֹ
nāthattî	ka'ăsher	hashshāmesh	tachath	hā'ĕlōhîm	'ăsher-nāthan-lô
I set	when	the sun	under	God	that He has given to him

6449.211	866	881, 6275	3937, 7495.141	2551	3937, 3156.141	881, 3949
v Niphil pf 3ms	rel part	do, art, n ms	cj, prep, v Qal inf con	n fs	prep, v Qal inf con	do, n ms, ps 1cs
נַעֲשָׂה	אֲשֶׁר	אֶת־הָעִנְיָן	וְלִרְאוֹת	חָכְמָה	לָדַעַת	אֶת־לִבִּי
na'ăsāh	'ăsher	'eth-hā'inyān	wᵉlir'ôth	chokhmāh	lādha'ath	'eth-libbî
they are done	that	the occupations	and to see	wisdom	to know	my heart

6142, 800	3706	1612	904, 3219	904, 4050	8517	904, 6084	375
prep, art, n fs	cj	cj	prep, art, n ms	cj, prep, art, n ms	n fs	prep, n fd, ps 3ms	sub, ps 3ms
עַל־הָאָרֶץ	כִּי	גַּם	בַּיּוֹם	וּבַלַּיְלָה	שֵׁנָה	בְּעֵינָיו	אֵינֶנּוּ
'al-hā'ārets	kî	gham	bayyôm	ûvallaylāh	shēnāh	bᵉ'ênâv	'ênennû
on the earth	that	also	in the day	and in the night	sleep	in his eyes	there is not to him

17.

7495.151	7495.115	881, 3725, 4801	435	3706	3940	3310.121	119
v Qal act ptc ms	v Qal pf 1cs	do, adj, n ms	art, n mp	cj	neg part	v Qal impf 3ms	art, n ms
רָאֹה	וְרָאִיתִי	אֶת־כָּל־מַעֲשֵׂה	הָאֱלֹהִים	כִּי	לֹא	יוּכַל	הָאָדָם
rō'eh	wᵉrā'îthî	'eth-kol-ma'ăsēh	hā'ĕlōhîm	kî	lō	yûkhal	hā'ādhām
seeing	and I saw	all the works of	God	that	not	he is able	humankind

3937, 4834.141	881, 4801	866	6449.211	8809, 8507	904, 8340	866
prep, v Qal inf con	do, art, n ms	rel part	v Niphil pf 3ms	prep, art, n fs	prep, rel part	cj
לִמְצוֹא	אֶת־הַמַּעֲשֶׂה	אֲשֶׁר	נַעֲשָׂה	תַּחַת־הַשֶּׁמֶשׁ	בְּשֶׁל	אֲשֶׁר
limtsô	'eth-hamma'ăseh	'ăsher	na'ăsāh	thachath-hashshemesh	bᵉshel	'ăsher
to find	the deeds	that	they are done	under the sun	in that	because

evil, *BB* ... are good men who are treated as if they had done like the wicked, *Fenton.*

again, there be wicked men, to whom it happeneth according to the work of the righteous: ... to whom what happens should happen to the just, *Anchor* ... some wicked persons get what the righteous deserve, *Beck* ... are evil men who get the reward of the good, *BB* ... are wicked who are treated as though they had done like the good, *Fenton.*

I said that this also is vanity: ... such a thing makes no sense, *Anchor* ... this also is futility, *Berkeley* ... is to no purpose, *BB.*

15. Then I commended mirth: ... cheerfulness, *Fenton* ... I praise joy, *JB* ... I praised gladness, *KJVII* ... I praise pleasure, *Moffatt.*

because a man hath no better thing under the sun, than to eat, and to drink, and to be merry: ... than to eat and drink, and be glad, *Fenton* ... since human happiness lies only in eating and drinking and in taking pleasure, *JB* ... best thing for man is to eat and drink and enjoy himself, *Moffatt* ... nothing good for man under the sun except eating and drinking and mirth, *NAB.*

for that shall abide with him of his labour the days of his life, which God giveth him under the sun: ... and be at rest from his toil in the days of life, *Fenton* ... this comes from what someone achieves during the days of life, *JB* ... and to keep this up as he toils right through the life God gives him, *Moffatt* ... is the accompaniment of his toil, *NAB.*

16. When I applied mine heart to know wisdom: ... I set my mind to acquire wisdom, *Anchor* ... I concentrated on knowing wisdom, *Beck* ... I devoted my mind to the knowledge of wisdom, *Goodspeed* ... I gave my mind to the study of wisdom, *Moffatt.*

and to see the business that is done upon the earth: ... to observe the activity, *Anchor* ... seeing the work that is done, *Beck* ... to study all the busy life of the world, *Moffatt* ... to observe what is done, *NAB.*

(for also there is that neither day nor night seeth sleep with his eyes:): ... for day and night it never sleeps, *Anchor* ... a man may even do without sleep day and night, *Beck* ... for both day and night his eyes see no sleep, *Goodspeed* ... for day and night our eyes enjoy no rest, *JB.*

17. Then I beheld all the work of God, that a man cannot find out the work that is done under the sun: ... cannot discover what it is that is going on, *Anchor* ... realized that a man can't find out the meaning of all the work God requires, *Beck* ... not possible for a man to discover the whole of the result, *Fenton* ... cannot get to the bottom of everything taking place, *JB.*

Leave yourself with God, and be at peace. Let this living faith preserve you from that brooding discontent, which seems to throw a cloud upon the goodness of your most gracious God (2:24; 3:12; 5:18; 1 Tim. 4:3ff). Never suppose that the overflow of temporal enjoyments can form the chief good. Enjoy the gifts of God, whatever portion of them be allotted to you, as the stream from the fountain of his special interest in you (Gen. 33:5). This enjoyment can never be in unholy sensualism or unrestrained indulgence, but with that Christian mirth as in the bright era of the Church (Acts 2:46). Let this be our abiding portion all the days of our life, every new day bringing a fresh gift of God for his service and glory. Whatever we may lose, the grand interest is secured.

8:16–17. All the efforts of diligence fail to enlighten: "How unsearchable are his judgments, and his ways past finding out" (Rom. 11:33).

We open our Bibles, and the doctrines instantly press upon us with difficulties. But to cavil is rebellion. If we reject one doctrine for its difficulties, we may as well reject another, standing as they all do upon the same testimony. God makes no mistakes. But "he gives not account of any of his matters" (Job 33:13). It is no more unnatural that some of the doctrines of revelation should overwhelm our understanding, than that the sun in full blaze should overpower our sight. Yet if the mind is shaken, the heart is upheld in energy.

Clearly, revelation was not proposed to indulge curiosity, but to provide a remedy for man's blindness and misery. If it be viewed with a merely speculative eye, we marvel not, that it should stir up hard thoughts of God. That man is obviously treated, and ever has been treated since Adam's fall, as a creature under punishment none can deny. Does this not strongly prove a sure, though mysterious connection with Adam's sin, charged upon his children to the end?

But to turn to one field of inquiry—the business that is done upon the earth. To obtain a clear and satisfying view of the whole framework of the divine government—to search into the reason of the administration, and out of all the seeming incongruities to bring out one work of beauty, order and completeness—all this is labor and travail. Labor and wisdom, the two grand instruments of discovery, even in their combined exercise, both leave us in darkness. We can only pray for humility to

6219.121	**119**	**3937, 1272.341**	**3940**	**4834.121**	**1612**	**524, 569.121**
v Qal impf 3ms	art, n ms	prep, v Piel inf con	cj, neg part	v Qal impf 3ms	cj, cj	cj, v Qal impf 3ms
יַעֲמֹל	הָאָדָם	לְבַקֵּשׁ	וְלֹא	יִמְצָא	וְגַם	אִם־יֹאמַר
ya'ămōl	hā'ādhām	levaqqēsh	welō'	yimtsā'	wegham	'im-yō'mar
he will toil	the man	to seek	and not	he will find	and also	if he will say

2550	**3937, 3156.141**	**3940**	**3310.121**	**3937, 4834.141**		**3706**	**881, 3725, 2172**
art, n ms	prep, v Qal inf con	neg part	v Qal impf 3ms	prep, v Qal inf con		cj	do, *adj*, dem pron
הֶחָכָם	לָדַעַת	לֹא	יוּכַל	לִמְצֹא	**9:1**	כִּי	אֶת־כָּל־זֶה
hechākhām	lādha'ath	lō'	yûkhal	limtsō'		kî	'eth-kol-zeh
the wise	to know	not	he will be able	to find		because	all this

5598.115	**420, 3949**	**3937, 987B.141**	**881, 3725, 2172**	**866**	**6926**	**2550**
v Qal pf 1cs	prep, n ms, ps 1cs	cj, prep, v Qal inf con	do, *adj*, dem pron	rel part	art, n mp	cj, art, n mp
נָתַתִּי	אֶל־לִבִּי	וְלָבוּר	אֶת־כָּל־זֶה	אֲשֶׁר	הַצַּדִּיקִים	וְהַחֲכָמִים
nāthattî	'el-libbî	welāvûr	'eth-kol-zeh	'ăsher	hatstsaddîqîm	wehachăkhāmîm
I set	to my heart	and to explain	all this	that	the righteous	and the wise

5860	**904, 3135**	**435**	**1612, 157**	**1612, 7985**	**375**	**3156.151**
cj, n mp, ps 3mp	prep, *n fs*	art, n mp	cj, n fs	cj, n fs	*sub*	v Qal act ptc ms
וַעֲבָדֵיהֶם	בְּיַד	הָאֱלֹהִים	גַּם־אַהֲבָה	גַּם־שִׂנְאָה	אֵין	יוֹדֵעַ
wa'ăvādhêhem	beyadh	hā'ĕlōhîm	gam-'ahvāh	gham-sin'āh	'ên	yôdhēa'
and their slaves	by the hand of	God	both love	and hate	there is not	one who knows

119	**3725**	**3937, 6686**		**3725**	**3626, 866**	**3937, 3725**	**4907**
art, n ms	art, n ms	prep, n mp, ps 3mp		art, n ms	prep, rel part	prep, art, n ms	n ms
הָאָדָם	הַכֹּל	לִפְנֵיהֶם	**2.**	הַכֹּל	כַּאֲשֶׁר	לַכֹּל	מִקְרֶה
hā'ādhām	hakkōl	liphnêhem		hakkōl	ka'ăsher	lakkōl	miqōreh
humankind	everything	before them		everything	just as	to everyone	a happening

259	**3937, 6926**	**3937, 7857**	**3937, 3005**	**3937, 2999**	**3937, 3042**
num	prep, art, n ms	cj, prep, art, n ms	prep, art, adj	cj, prep, art, adj	cj, prep, art, adj
אֶחָד	לַצַּדִּיק	וְלָרָשָׁע	לַטּוֹב	וְלַטָּהוֹר	וְלַטָּמֵא
'echādh	latstsaddîq	welārāshā'	lattôv	welattāhôr	welattāmē'
one	to the righteous	and to the wicked	to the good	and to the clean	and to the unclean

3937, 2319.151	**3937, 866**	**375**	**2159.151**	**3626, 3005**
cj, prep, art, v Qal act ptc ms	cj, prep, rel pron	sub, ps 3ms	v Qal act ptc ms	prep, art, adj
וְלַזֹּבֵחַ	וְלַאֲשֶׁר	אֵינֶנּוּ	זֹבֵחַ	כַּטּוֹב
welazzōvēach	wela'ăsher	'ênennû	zōvēach	kattôv
and to the one who sacrifices	and to who	there is not to him	sacrificing	like the good

3626, 2490.151	**8123.255**	**3626, 866**	**8095**	**3486.151**		**2172**
prep, art, v Qal act ptc ms	art, v Niphal ptc ms	prep, rel part	n fs	v Qal act ptc ms		dem pron
כַּחֹטֶא	הַנִּשְׁבָּע	כַּאֲשֶׁר	שְׁבוּעָה	יָרֵא	**3.**	זֶה
kachōte'	hanishbā'	ka'ăsher	shevû'āh	yārē'		zeh
so the sinner	and the one who swears	just as	an oath	fearing		this

7737	**904, 3725**	**866, 6449.211**	**8809**	**8507**	**3706, 4907**	**259**	**3937, 3725**	**1612**
adj	prep, n ms	rel part, v Niphal pf 3ms	prep	art, n ms	cj, n ms	num	prep, art, n ms	cj, cj
רָע	בְּכֹל	אֲשֶׁר־נַעֲשָׂה	תַּחַת	הַשֶּׁמֶשׁ	כִּי־מִקְרֶה	אֶחָד	לַכֹּל	וְגַם
rā'	bekhōl	'ăsher-na'ăsāh	tachath	hashshemesh	kî-miqōreh	'echādh	lakkōl	wegham
evil	in all	that it is done	under	the sun	that a fate	one	to everyone	and also

3949	**1158, 119**	**4527.111, 7737**	**2014**	**904, 3949**
n ms	*n mp*, art, n ms	v Qal pf 3ms, n ms	cj, n fp	prep, n ms, ps 3mp
לֵב	בְּנֵי־הָאָדָם	מָלֵא־רָע	וְהוֹלֵלוֹת	בִּלְבָבָם
lēv	benê-hā'ādhām	mālē'-rā'	wehôlēlôth	bilvāvām
the heart of	the children of humankind	it is full of evil	and folly	in their hearts

because though a man labour to seek it out, yet he shall not find it: ... however hard he may search he will not find out, *Anchor* ... man may search hard for it without finding it, *Beck* ... you may wear yourself out in the search, but you will never find it, *JB* ... the more a man labours to read that riddle, the less he finds out, *Knox.*

yea further; though a wise man think to know it, yet shall he not be able to find it: ... says he knows, he cannot discover it all, *Anchor* ... claims to know it, he isn't able to discover its meaning, *Beck* ... thinks that he is on the point of knowing it, he will be unable to find it, *Goodspeed* ... Not even a sage can get to the bottom of it, even if he says that he has done so, *JB.*

9:1. For all this I considered in my heart even to declare all this: ... thought about all I had observed, *Anchor* ... thought about all this and came to understand, *Beck* ... All this I took to heart and clearly understood, *Berkeley* ... applied myself to all this and experienced all this to be so, *JB.*

that the righteous, and the wise, and their works, are in the hand of God: ... just and wise men and what they do are in God's power, *Anchor* ... every task of theirs is in God's keeping, *Knox* ... God controls good people and wise people and what they do, *NCV* ... their deeds are in the hand of God, *NRSV.*

no man knoweth either love or hatred by all that is before them: ... whether he will favor them or not, no one knows, *Anchor* ... whether they are loved or hated, people do not know what will confront them, *Beck* ... nor can any tell whether they have earned his love, or his displeasure!, *Knox* ... no man knows whether love or hate awaits him, *NIV.*

2. All things come alike to all: ... Anything may happen to anybody, *Beck* ... are alike for all, *Berkeley* ... for all of us is reserved a common fate, *JB.*

there is one event to the righteous, and to the wicked: ... the same chance befalls the innocent and the guilty, *Anchor* ... same thing hap-

pens to you whether you're righteous or wicked, *Beck* ... one fortune for the righteous and for the wicked, *Berkeley* ... for the upright and for the wicked, *JB.*

to the good and to the clean, and to the unclean: ... the good and the bad, the [ritually] clean and the unclean, *Anchor* ... clean or unclean, *Beck* ... the good and the pure and to the impure, *Berkeley* ... whether we are ritually pure or not, *JB.*

to him that sacrificeth, and to him that sacrificeth not: ... one who brings a sacrifice and the one who does not, *Anchor* ... whether you sacrifice or don't, *Beck.*

as is the good, so is the sinner: ... is with the virtuous, so it is with the sinner, *Anchor* ... good person is treated like a sinner, *Beck* ... As fares the good, so the sinner, *Berkeley* ... the same for the good and for the sinner, *JB.*

and he that sweareth, as he that feareth an oath: ... as with the one who swears, so with him who is

believe that whatever is done, however contrary to our apprehensions, is both wise and righteous.

Are we then to refrain from searching into the works of God? Far from it. We are encouraged "to seek them out" (Ps. 111:2). A spiritual understanding of the "loving-kindness of the LORD" will be to us an enriching harvest (Ps. 107:43).

The "secret things," as "belonging to the LORD our God," will still remain "secret." But "the things that are revealed" will be the precious portion for "us and for our children," for all the purposes of godly obedience.

9:1–2. The mysteries of providence still pressed heavily upon Solomon's mind. Proud man would bring the God of heaven and earth to his bar. His humble child is taught the infinite distance between the creature and God. He therefore bows before Him, and hears the voice out of the cloud, "Be still, and know that I am God" (Ps. 46:10). He could not find out all the work of God (Ecc. 8:17). But his search brought out many valuable discoveries. The security of God's people was a bright and precious

truth. He considered in his heart to declare all this, that the righteous and the wise are in the hand of God. We are spared no trials however severe, but nothing touches our foundation. We are in his hand.

And yet all things come alike to all. There is one event to the righteous on the one side and to the wicked on the other side. The same providential dispensations belong to both. If Abraham was rich, so was Haman (Gen. 13:2; Est. 5:11). If Ahab was slain in battle, so was Josiah (1 Ki. 22:34; 2 Ki. 23:29). The LORD's outward dispensation proved, therefore, neither his love nor his hatred.

9:3. Solomon is here continuing his subject. He seems to consider that in some view it is an evil, that all things come alike to all. Not that he reflects upon this appointment of God, as if it were evil in itself. But it is evil in its consequence and abuse as it were of no account, whether men were righteous or wicked, since there is one event to all.

Sad, indeed, is the consciousness that this is a spiritual world within, where all is distorted and contradictory, and where the unhappy victims of the

4.

1013.221	866	3706, 4449	420, 4322.152	313	904, 2522
v Niphal impf 3ms	rel pron	cj, intrg	prep, art, v Qal act ptc mp	cj, prep, ps 3ms	prep, n mp, ps 3mp
יִבָּחֵר	אֲשֶׁר	כִּי־מִי	אֶל־הַמֵּתִים	וְאַחֲרָיו	בְּחַיֵּיהֶם
yibbāchēr	'ăsher	kî-mî	'el-hammēthîm	we'achărâv	bechayyêhem
he is chosen	whom	because who	to the dead	and after it	during their lifetime

4623, 765	3005	2000	2508	3706, 3937, 3732	1023	3552	3725, 2522	420
prep, art, n ms	adj	pers pron	n ms	cj, prep, n ms	n ms	sub	adj, art, n mp	prep
מִן־הָאַרְיֵה	טוֹב	הוּא	חַי	כִּי־לְכֶלֶב	בִּטָּחוֹן	יֵשׁ	כָּל־הַחַיִּים	אֶל
min-hā'aryēh	ṭôv	hû'	chay	kî-lekhelev	biṭṭāchôn	yēsh	kol-hachayyîm	'el
than the lion	better	it	living	because to a dog	trust	is there	all the living	to

5.

4322.152	8054, 4322.126	3156.152	2522	3706	4322.151
cj, art, v Qal act ptc mp	rel part, v Qal impf 3mp	v Qal act ptc mp	art, n mp	cj	art, v Qal act ptc ms
וְהַמֵּתִים	שֶׁיָּמֻתוּ	יוֹדְעִים	הַחַיִּים	כִּי	הַמֵּת
wehammēthîm	shêyāmuthû	yôdh'îm	hachayyîm	kî	hammēth
but the dead	that they will die	knowing	the living	because	the dead one

3706	7964	3937	375, 5968	4114	3156.152	375
cj	n ms	prep, ps 3mp	cj, sub, adv	indef pron	v Qal act ptc mp	sub, ps 3mp
כִּי	שָׂכָר	לָהֶם	וְאֵין־עוֹד	מְאוּמָה	יוֹדְעִים	אֵינָם
kî	sākhār	lāhem	we'ên-'ôdh	me'ûmāh	yôdh'îm	'ênām
because	a reward	to them	and there is not still	something	knowing	there is not to them

6.

1612, 7352	1612, 7985	1612	157	1612	2228	8319.211
cj, n fs, ps 3mp	cj, n fs, ps 3mp	cj	n fs, ps 3mp	cj	n ms, ps 3mp	v Niphal pf 3ms
גַּם־קִנְאָתָם	גַּם־שִׂנְאָתָם	גַּם	אַהֲבָתָם	גַּם	זִכְרָם	נִשְׁכָּח
gam-qin'āthām	gam-sin'āthām	gam	'ahvāthām	gam	zikhrām	nishkach
and their jealousy	and their hatred	both	their love	both	the memory of them	it has been forgotten

904, 3725	3937, 5986	5968	375, 3937	2610	6.112	3647
prep, n ms	prep, n ms	adv	sub, prep, ps 2mp	cj, n ms	v Qal pf 3fs	adv
בְּכֹל	לְעוֹלָם	עוֹד	אֵין־לָהֶם	וְחֵלֶק	אָבָדָה	כְּבָר
bekhōl	le'ôlām	'ôdh	'ên-lāhem	wechēleq	'āvādhāh	kevār
in all	unto eternity	anymore	there is not to them	and a portion	it has perished	already

7.

4035	904, 7977	404.131	2050.131	8507	8809	866, 6449.211
n ms, ps 2ms	prep, n fs	v Qal impv 2ms	v Qal impv 2ms	art, n ms	prep	rel part, v Niphal pf 3ms
לַחְמֶךָ	בְּשִׂמְחָה	אֱכֹל	לֵךְ	הַשָּׁמֶשׁ	תַּחַת	אֲשֶׁר־נַעֲשָׂה
lachmekhā	besimchāh	'ĕkhōl	lēkh	hashshāmesh	tachath	'ăsher-na'ăsāh
your bread	with gladness	eat	go	the sun	under	that it is done

435	7813.111	3647	3706	3302	904, 3949, 3005	8685.131
art, n mp	v Qal pf 3ms	adv	cj	n ms, ps 2ms	prep, n ms, adj	cj, v Qal impv 2ms
הָאֱלֹהִים	רָצָה	כְּבָר	כִּי	יֵינֶךָ	בְלֶב־טוֹב	וּשְׁתֵה
hā'ĕlōhîm	rātsāh	khevār	kî	yênekhā	velev-ṭôv	ûshethēh
God	He favors	already	because	your wine	with a merry heart	and drink

afraid to swear, *Anchor* … one who swears an oath like the one who is afraid of taking an oath, *Beck* … as the one swearing so the one who reveres an oath, *Berkeley* … for someone who takes a vow, as for someone who fears to do so, *JB*.

3. This is an evil among all things that are done under the sun: … is another evil among those occurring, *JB* … nothing does more hurt, *Knox* … is no evil like this in the world, *Moffatt* … Among all the things that happen under the sun, this is the worst, *NAB, Douay*.

that there is one event unto all: … same fate for everyone, *JB* … this equality of fortunes, *Knox* … that things turn out the same for all, *NAB, Douay* … What happens to one happens to all, *NCV*.

yea, also the heart of the sons of men is full of evil: … is full of wickedness, *JB* … what wonder if men's hearts, while yet they live, are full of malice and defiance?, *Knox* … it makes men seethe with evil aims,

Moffatt ... Hence the minds of men are filled with evil, *NAB, Douay.*

and madness is in their heart while they live: ... folly lurks in our hearts throughout our lives, *JB* ... and mad desires during their life, *Moffatt* ... insanity is in their hearts throughout their lives, *NASB* ... minds are full of evil and foolish thoughts while they live, *NCV.*

and after that they go to the dead: ... their [only] future is to die, *Anchor* ... afterward there is their death, *Berkeley* ... until we end among, *JB* ... then they join the dead, *Moffatt.*

4. For to him that is joined to all the living there is hope: ... while one is among the living, *Anchor* ... for someone still linked to the rest of the living, *JB* ... one still alive has something to live for, *Moffatt.*

for a living dog is better than a dead lion: ... better be a live dog than a dead lion, *JB* ... (even a live dog is better than a dead lion),

Moffatt ... a live dog is better off than a dead lion, *NAB, Douay.*

5. For the living know that they shall die: ... at least know that they will die, *Anchor* ... are conscious that death will come to them, *BB* ... are at least aware that they are going to die, *JB.*

but the dead know not any thing: ... nothing at all, *Anchor* ... are not conscious of anything, *BB.*

neither have they any more a reward: ... no longer have any compensation, *Anchor* ... is no more reward for them, *Beck* ... they have no more fame, *Fenton* ... No more wages for them, *JB.*

for the memory of them is forgotten: ... when their memory has perished, *Anchor* ... they are forgotten, *Beck* ... the remembrance of them is forgotten!, *Fenton* ... every trace of them has vanished away, *Knox.*

6. Also their love, and their hatred, and their envy, is now perished: ...

Their love, their hate, their ardor have completely vanished, *Anchor* ... Their loving, hating, and envying is gone now, *Beck* ... their love, yes, their hatred, even their jealousy have long since vanished, *Berkeley* ... their former loves, and hatreds, and ambitions perish, *Fenton.*

neither have they any more a portion for ever in any thing that is done under the sun: ... no part forevermore in all that happens, *Anchor* ... never again will they have a part in anything done, *Beck* ... no longer do they have a share in all that is taking place, *Berkeley* ... have no more possession, for ever, in all that they accomplished, *Fenton.*

7. Go thy way, eat thy bread with joy: ... take your bread with joy, *BB* ... Eat your food with pleasure, *Fenton* ... eat thy bread with a stout heart, *Knox* ... eat your bread in happiness, *NASB.*

and drink thy wine with a merry heart: ... with a glad heart, *BB* ... with a happy mind, *Goodspeed* ... to

delusion are so depraved that they cannot understand their own depravity. Such a world of evil! If we only knew it, would we trifle with sin? It is impossible for the sinner to be more dangerously mad than he is, except by growing into greater wickedness.

9:4–6. Solomon had before taken an opposite view. He had praised the dead, which were already dead, more than the living, which were yet alive. Here, however, he praises the high advantage of life above death. It is awful indeed to see the state of the living, their hearts full of evil, even to madness. But while there is life, while we are joined to all the living, there is hope.

Another ground for this preference is that the living know that they will die, hence, therefore, the time and opportunity, perhaps also the desire, to make preparation. There is time to fix our interest in heaven, to live upon the real substantials of godliness and to look upon this world's glare with sober dignity, as utterly beneath "the high calling of God in Christ Jesus." All of this world is passing away. The glory and great end of life is that eternal life, which makes it "gain to die" (Phil. 1:21).

On the other hand, the dead do not know anything. They have no further knowledge of anything here on earth. They have no further reward of their worldly labor. The memory of them is soon forgotten. The love, hatred and envy, which they bare to others and others to them, is now perished—so far as connected with this world. Whatever might have been their portion on earth, they have it no longer.

9:7–9. Some striking pictures of vanity have been before us. Here is God's bright remedy. Go your way. Enjoy your mercies while you have them. The charge of melancholy is a libel upon religion. The man that is an heir to "a lively hope, anchored within the veil" (1 Pet. 1:3; Heb. 6:19), what ground does he have for melancholy? We find him greatly rejoicing, even in the midst of heaviness (1 Pet. 1:6).

Eat your bread and drink your wine with a merry heart. Temporal blessings are doubly sweet, as coming from Him. He is exalted to bestow them, and we are invited to receive them.

Solomon's directions are for a joyous religion. We must not forget the "time to mourn" (3:4) nor the moderation needed in our times of rejoicing

8467	3968	933	2030.126	904, 3725, 6496	881, 4801
cj, n ms	adj	n mp, ps 2ms	v Qal juss 3mp	prep, adj, n fs	do, n mp, ps 2ms
וְשֶׁמֶן	לְבָנִים	בְגָדֶיךָ	יִהְיוּ	בְּכָל־עֵת **8.**	אֶת־מַעֲשֶׂיךָ
weshemen	levānîm	veghādhêkhā	yihyû	bekhol-'ēth	'eth-ma'ăsêkhā
and the olive oil	white	your garments	may they be	during all times	your deeds

866, 154.113	6196, 828	2522	7495.131	414, 2741.121	6142, 7513
rel pron, v Qal pf 2ms	prep, n fs	n mp	v Qal impv 2ms	adv, v Qal juss 3ms	prep, n ms, ps 2ms
אֲשֶׁר־אָהַבְתָּ	עִם־אִשָּׁה	חַיִּים	רְאֵה **9.**	אַל־יֶחְסָר	עַל־רֹאשֶׁךָ
'āsher-'āhavtā	'im-'ishshāh	chayyîm	re'ēh	'al-yechāsār	'al-rō'shekhā
whom you love	with a wife	life	see	may it not be lacking	on your head

3725	8507	8809	5598.111, 3937	866	1961	2522	3725, 3219
adj	art, n ms	prep	v Qal pf 3ms, prep, ps 2ms	rel part	n ms, ps 2ms	n mp	adj, n mp
כֹּל	הַשֶּׁמֶשׁ	תַּחַת	נָתַן־לְךָ	אֲשֶׁר	הֶבְלֶךָ	חַיֵּי	כָּל־יְמֵי
kōl	hashshemesh	tachath	nāthan-lekhā	'āsher	hevlekhā	chayyê	kol-yemê
all	the sun	under	He has given to you	which	your vanity	the life of	all the days of

904, 6221	904, 2522	2610	2000	3706	1961	3219
cj, prep, n ms, ps 2ms	prep, art, n mp	n ms, ps 2ms	pers pron	cj	n ms, ps 2ms	n mp
וּבַעֲמָלְךָ	בַּחַיִּים	חֶלְקְךָ	הוּא	כִּי	הֶבְלֶךָ	יְמֵי
ûva'ămālekhā	bachayyîm	chelqōkhā	hû'	kî	hevlekhā	yemê
and by your toil	among the living	your portion	it	because	your vanity	the days of

3135	4834.122	866	3725	8507	8809	6221	866, 887
n fs, ps 2ms	v Qal impf 3fs	rel part	adj	art, n ms	prep	n ms	rel part, pers pron
יָדְךָ	תִּמְצָא	אֲשֶׁר	כֹּל **10.**	הַשָּׁמֶשׁ	תַּחַת	עָמֵל	אֲשֶׁר־אַתָּה
yādhekhā	timtsā'	'āsher	kōl	hashshāmesh	tachath	'āmēl	'āsher-'attāh
your hand	it will find	that	all	the sun	under	a laborer	which you

2918	4801	375	3706	6449.131	904, 3699	3937, 6449.141
cj, n ms	n ms	sub	cj	v Qal impv 2ms	prep, n ms, ps 2ms	prep, v Qal inf con
וְחֶשְׁבּוֹן	מַעֲשֶׂה	אֵין	כִּי	עֲשֵׂה	בְּכֹחֶךָ	לַעֲשׂוֹת
wecheshbôn	ma'ăseh	'ên	kî	'ăsēh	bekhōchākhā	la'ăsôth
or a reckoning	a deed	there is not	because	do	with your strength	to do

8178.115	8427	2050.151	887	866	904, 8061	2551	1907
v Qal pf 1cs	adv	v Qal act ptc ms	pers pron	rel part	prep, pn	cj, n fs	cj, n fs
שָׁבְתִּי **11.**	שָׁמָּה	הֹלֵךְ	אַתָּה	אֲשֶׁר	בִּשְׁאוֹל	וְחָכְמָה	וְדַעַת
shavtî	shāmmāh	hōlēkh	'attāh	'āsher	bish'ôl	wechokhmāh	wedha'ath
I turned again	to there	going	you	which	in Sheol	or wisdom	or knowledge

3937, 1399	3940	4955	3937, 7316	3940	3706	8809, 8507	7495.142
prep, adj	cj, neg part	art, n ms	prep, art, adj	neg part	cj	prep, art, n fs	cj, v Qal inf abs
לַגִּבֹּרִים	וְלֹא	הַמֵּרוֹץ	לַקַּלִּים	לֹא	כִּי	תַּחַת־הַשֶּׁמֶשׁ	וְרָאֹה
laggibbōrîm	welō'	hammērôts	laqqallîm	lō'	kî	thachath-hashshemesh	werā'ōh
to the mighty	and not	the race	to the swift	not	that	under the sun	and seeing

---

thy contenting, *Knox* ... with a cheer-ful heart, *NASB*.

for God now accepteth thy works: ... taken pleasure in, *BB* ... is well pleased by your doing so, *Fenton* ... has already accepted your deeds, *Goodspeed* ... has already approved your actions, *JB*.

8. Let thy garments be always white: ... your clothes be white all the time, *NASB* ... Put on nice clothes, *NCV* ... Always be clothed in white, *NIV*.

and let thy head lack no ointment: ... let not oil be lacking on your head, *NASB* ... spare not the perfume for your head, *Douay* ... make your-self look good, *NCV* ... always anoint your head with oil, *NIV*.

9. Live joyfully with the wife whom thou lovest all the days of the life of thy vanity: ... with the woman you love all the fleeting days of your life, *Anchor* ... with the woman of your love all the days of your foolish life, *BB* ... Spend your life with the woman you love, all the days of futile life, *JB* ... See life with the wife whom thou hast loved, all the days of the life of thy vanity, *Young*.

which he hath given thee under the sun, all the days of thy vanity: ... that God grants you, *Anchor* ... has allotted you, *Beck* ... your allotted span here under the sun, empty as they are, *NEB*.

for that is thy portion in this life, and in thy labour which thou takest under the sun: ... is your compensation while you live and toil, *Anchor* ... is what you get in life for the hard work, *Beck* ... is your part in life and in your work, *BB* ... is your

lot in life and in the effort you expend, *JB*.

10. Whatsoever thy hand findeth to do, do it with thy might: ... with your full strength, *Anchor* ... with all your power, *BB* ... Whatever lies in thy power, do while do it thou canst, *Knox* ... Throw yourself into any pursuit that may appeal to you, *Moffatt*.

for there is no work, nor device, nor knowledge, nor wisdom, in the grave, whither thou goest: ... no doing or reckoning or knowing or understanding in Sheol, *Anchor* ... no work or planning, knowledge or skill, *Beck* ... no work or substance or knowledge or wisdom in Sheol,

Goodspeed ... neither achievement, nor planning, nor science, nor wisdom in Sheol, *JB*.

11. I returned, and saw under the sun, that the race is not to the swift: ... is not won by the speediest, *JB* ... is not won by the swift, *Moffatt*.

nor the battle to the strong: ... nor the battle by the champions, *JB* ... nor battles by the brave, *Moffatt* ... nor the battle by the valiant, *NAB* ... the battle is not to the warriors, *NASB*.

neither yet bread to the wise, nor yet riches to men of understanding: ... not the wise who get food, nor the intelligent wealth, *JB* ... nor

(1 Cor. 7:30), nor the profit of seasons of humiliation and restraint (Dan. 10:2f). Yet we should remember our obligation to shine, to exhibit our white garments of praise, and use the fragrant ointment (S.S. 1:3; John 12:3), as the customary mark of festive occasions. Nor should this be the rule for particular times or peculiar circumstances. Let your garments always be white—a rule in the true spirit of the precept, which involves both our duty and our privilege. "Rejoice evermore" (1 Thess. 5:16). In our deepest sorrow, our ground for rejoicing is the same.

Solomon could not have laid down his last rule of happiness without a poignant pang in the recollection of his own awful violation of it. Live joyfully with the wife whom you lovest—a single, undivided love so contrary to the unrestrained lust, which had been his appetite and indulgence. Here is a special freeness of delight and liberty of love, yet under the godly restraint of honor and sobriety (Gen. 26:8; Prov. 5:19).

9:10. We now have a rule: to stimulate the glow of vital energy. There are works to be done, difficulties to be overcome, talents to be traded with, the whole might to be engaged. Every moment brings its own responsibility. And the rule for the discharge of this responsibility is, "Whatsoever your hand finds to do, do it with your might." Obviously, some limitation is implied. That which occasion calls for (Judg. 9:33), in the path of duty and of providence, is the thing to be done. The active exercise of the hands as the instrument of the work will bring a fruitful result.

The main sphere for this important and invaluable rule is the work for eternity—the "working out of our own salvation" (Phil. 2:12). The purchase price binds us to the work under the most constraining obligation (1 Cor. 6:20). We cease to be our own from the first moment that we are bound to Him.

But look at our great Exemplar Who says, "I must work the works of him that sent me while it is day." Here was doing with his might, the motive also was the same. "The night cometh, when no man can work" (John 9:4). There is no work, nor device, nor knowledge, nor wisdom in a grave. Here the highest glory of earth concludes. You are traveling to the end. Every moment brings you nearer. And when you come to the grave, there is no work there. We cannot do our undone duties there. All power is withered and gone.

9:11. Solomon is now returning to another view of the matter, which caused him perplexity. It is natural indeed to believe that the race would be to the swift and the battle to the strong, that prudent wisdom would obtain a competent provision, and that courtly skill would be the way to favor. But it is not always so.

There is, indeed, an adaptation of these means to the end and a tendency to work the proposed end. But with all men's practiced and persevering efforts, the issue is with God: "Time and chance happens unto them all." Not that there is anything fortuitous or unforeseen but something that we cannot see that balances against seeming probabilities, some occurrence which providence casts in the way,

6484	3937, 1032.256	3940	1612	4035	3937, 2550	3940	1612	4560
n ms	prep, art, v Niphal ptc mp	neg part	cj, cj	n ms	prep, art, n mp	neg part	cj, cj	art, n fs
עֹשֶׁר	לַנְּבֹנִים	לֹא	וְגַם	לֶחֶם	לַחֲכָמִים	לֹא	וְגַם	הַמִּלְחָמָה
'ōsher	lannĕvōnîm	lō'	wĕgham	lechem	lachăkhāmîm	lō'	wĕgham	hammilchāmāh
riches	to the discerning	not	and also	food	to the wise	not	and also	the battle

7424.121	6535	3706, 6496	2682	3937, 3156.152	3940	1612
v Qal impf 3ms	cj, n ms	cj, n fs	n ms	prep, v Qal act ptc mp	neg part	cj, cj
יִקְרֶה	וָפֶגַע	כִּי־עֵת	חֵן	לַיֹּדְעִים	לֹא	וְגַם
yiqŏreh	wāphegha'	kî-'ēth	chēn	layyōdhĕ'îm	lō'	wĕgham
it will happen to	and a chance	rather a time	favor	to those who know	not	and also

12.

3626, 1759	881, 6496	119	3940, 3156.121	1612	3706	881, 3725
prep, art, n mp	do, n fs, ps 3ms	art, n ms	neg part, v Qal impf 3ms	cj	cj	do, n ms, ps 3mp
כַּדָּגִים	אֶת־עִתּוֹ	הָאָדָם	לֹא־יֵדַע	גַם	כִּי	אֶת־כֻּלָּם
kaddāghîm	'eth-'ittô	hā'ādhām	lō'-yēdha'	gam	kî	'eth-kullām
like the fish	his time	the man	he will not know	also	because	all of them

904, 6583	270.158	3626, 7109	7737	904, 4850	8054, 270.256
prep, art, n ms	art, v Qal pass ptc fp	cj, prep, art, n fp	adj	prep, n fs	rel part, v Niphal ptc mp
בַּפָּח	הָאֲחֻזוֹת	וְכַצִּפֳּרִים	רָעָה	בִּמְצוֹדָה	שֶׁנֶּאֱחָזִים
bappāch	hā'ăchuzôth	wĕkhatstsippŏrîm	rā'āh	bimtsôdhāh	shenne'ĕchāzîm
in the snare	those being caught	or like the birds	evil	in a net	which being caught

3626, 8054, 5489.122	7737	3937, 6496	119	1158	3483.456	3626
prep, rel part, v Qal impf 3fs	adj	prep, n fs	art, n ms	n mp	v Pual ptc mp	prep, ps 3mp
כְּשֶׁתִּפּוֹל	רָעָה	לְעֵת	הָאָדָם	בְּנֵי	יוּקָשִׁים	כָּהֶם
kĕshettippôl	rā'āh	lĕ'ēth	hā'ādhām	bĕnê	yûqāshîm	kāhēm
when it will fall	evil	at a time	humankind	the children of	being ensnared	like them

13.

1448	8507	8809	2551	7495.115	1612, 2173	6849	6142
cj, adj	art, n ms	prep	n fs	v Qal pf 1cs	cj, dem pron	adv	prep, ps 3mp
וּגְדוֹלָה	הַשָּׁמֶשׁ	תַּחַת	חָכְמָה	רָאִיתִי	גַם־זֹה	פִּתְאֹם	עֲלֵיהֶם
ûghĕdhôlāh	hashshāmesh	tachath	chokhmāh	rā'îthî	gam-zōh	pith'ōm	'ălêhem
and great	the sun	under	wisdom	I have seen	also this	suddenly	upon them

14.

971.111, 431	8507	4746	904	596	7278	6111	420	2026
cj, v Qal pf 3ms, prep, ps 3fs		sub	prep, ps 3fs	cj, n mp	adj	n fs	prep, ps 1cs	pers pron
וּבָא־אֵלֶיהָ		מְעָט	בָּהּ	וַאֲנָשִׁים	קְטַנָּה	עִיר	אֵלַי	הִיא
ûvā'-'ēlêāh		me'āt	bāhh	wa'ănāshîm	qŏtannāh	'îr	'ēlay	hî'
and he came to it		a few	in it	and men	insignificant	a city	to me	it

1448	4848	6142	1161.111	881	5621.111	1448	4567
adj	n mp	prep, ps 3fs	cj, v Qal pf 3ms	do, ps 3fs	cj, v Qal pf 3ms	adj	n ms
גְדֹלִים	מְצוֹדִים	עָלֶיהָ	וּבָנָה	אֹתָהּ	וְסָבַב	גָּדוֹל	מֶלֶךְ
gĕdhōlîm	mĕtsôdhîm	'ālêāh	ûvānāh	'ōthāhh	wĕsāvav	gādhôl	melekh
great	siege works	against it	and he built	it	and he surrounded	great	a king

15.

881, 6111	4561.311, 2000	2550	4693	382	904	4834.111
do, art, n fs	cj, v Piel pf 3ms, pers pron	adj	adj	n ms	prep, ps 3fs	cj, v Qal pf 3ms
אֶת־הָעִיר	וּמִלַּט־הוּא	חָכָם	מִסְכֵּן	אִישׁ	בָהּ	וּמָצָא
'eth-hā'îr	ûmillat-hû'	chākhām	miskēn	'îsh	vāhh	ûmātsā'
the city	and he he rescued	wise	needy	a man	in it	but someone found

2000	4693	881, 382	2226.111	3940	119	904, 2551
art, dem pron	art, adj	do, art, n ms	v Qal pf 3ms	neg part	cj, n ms	prep, n fs, ps 3ms
הַהוּא	הַמִּסְכֵּן	אֶת־הָאִישׁ	זָכַר	לֹא	וְאָדָם	בְּחָכְמָתוֹ
hahû'	hammiskēn	'eth-hā'îsh	zākhar	lō'	wĕ'ādhām	bĕchokhmāthô
the that	the needy	the man	they will remember	not	but humankind	by his wisdom

bread by the wise, nor wealth by the clever, *Moffatt* ... nor a livelihood by the wise, nor riches by the shrewd, *NAB* ... neither is bread to the wise, nor wealth to the discerning, *NASB*.

nor yet favour to men of skill: ... nor the learned favour, *JB* ... nor honour by the learned, *Moffatt* ... by the experts, *NAB* ... to men of ability, *NASB*.

but time and chance happeneth to them all: ... chance and mischance befall, *JB* ... death and misfortune, *Moffatt* ... a time of calamity comes to all alike, *NAB* ... time and chance overtake them all, *NASB*.

12. For man also knoweth not his time: ... no more knows his own time, *NAB* ... No one knows what will happen next, *NCV* ... when his hour will come, *NEB, NIV* ... no one can anticipate the time of disaster, *NRSV*.

as the fishes that are taken in an evil net: ... like fish caught in an accursed net, *Anchor* ... than fish taken in the fatal net, *NAB* ... caught in a treacherous net, *NASB* ... caught in the destroying net, *REB*.

and as the birds that are caught in the snare: ... seized in a snare, *Berkeley* ... taken by deceit, *BB* ... trapped in the snare, *NAB* ... like little birds which were caught in a trap, *Rotherham*.

so are the sons of men snared in an evil time, when it falleth suddenly upon them: ... that drops upon them suddenly, *Moffatt* ... are caught when the evil time falls suddenly, *NAB* ... are trapped by evil when it suddenly falls, *NCV* ... are trapped when bad times come suddenly, *NEB*.

13. This wisdom have I seen also under the sun: ... which I have observed, *Anchor* ... have seen this bit of wisdom, *Beck* ... observed this result of intelligence, *Fenton* ... another example of the wisdom I have acquired, *JB*.

and it seemed great unto me: ... struck me as significant, *Anchor* ... made a deep impression on me, *Beck, Berkeley* ... was astonishing to me!, *Fenton* ... strikes me as important, *JB*.

14. There was a little city, and few men within it: ... a small town, with only a few inhabitants, *JB* ... a small town with only a few people in it, *NCV* ... small town with few inhabitants, *NEB*.

and there came a great king against it, and besieged it, and built great bulwarks against it: ... mighty king made war on it, laying siege to it and building great siegeworks round it, *JB* ... attacked it, he invested it, and built great siegeworks round it, *Moffatt* ... surrounded it and threw up great siegeworks about it, *NAB*.

15. Now there was found in it a poor wise man: ... a man who was poor but wise, *Anchor* ... a poor person possessing intelligence was found there, *Fenton* ... in that town a poverty-stricken sage, *JB*.

and he by his wisdom delivered the city: ... kept the town safe, *BB* ... rescued the town by his intelligence, *Fenton* ... saved it by his skill, *Moffatt* ... used his wisdom to save his town, *NCV*.

yet no man remembered that same poor man: ... this poor man afterwards, *JB* ... not a soul remembered that poor man!, *Moffatt* ... later on, everyone forgot about him, *NCV*.

16. Then said I, Wisdom is better than strength: ... better than might!, *Anchor* ... more effective than brute force, *JB* ... has the better of valour, *Knox*.

nevertheless the poor man's wisdom is despised: ... is not respected, *BB* ... is not valued, *JB* ... goes for nothing, *Knox* ... wins no honour or deference for him, *Moffatt* ... people forgot about the poor man's wisdom, *NCV*.

and his words are not heard: ... went unheeded, *Anchor* ... nobody listens to what he says, *Beck* ... are not considered, *Berkeley* ... stopped listening to what he said, *NCV*.

---

which determines success with a decisive effect upon our lot in life. We do not see the direction, and, therefore, we cannot clearly judge. But all things fall into the place infallibly ordained by God.

9:12. Time and chance happen to all alike and where they are least expected. For man knoweth not his time (8:7). This is true of success or failure, either of which depends not upon man's effort but upon God's supreme will. The illustrations limit the reference to the ungodly and show the ignorance of the time to be man's ruin for eternity—as the fishes taken in an evil net or the birds caught in a snare.

9:13–15. This incident, illustrating the power of wisdom, passed under Solomon's own eye. He saw it under the sun. And though others might have passed it by, it seemed great to him—perhaps the more so, as being overclouded with poverty. Here was a great king against a little city, a besieging army building great bulwarks against it when there were only a few men within it. The danger appeared to be imminent and the destruction certain. Yet at the moment of extremity, one poor wise man by his wisdom delivered the city. We might have expected the highest rewards for this poor wise man. Yet we are told that no man remembered him. When he had wrought the deliverance, no man looked after him. He sank into forgetfulness. His wisdom was despised, and his words were not heard.

4693 art, n ms	2551 cj, n fs	4623, 1400 prep, n fs	2551 n fs	3009B adj	603 pers pron	569.115 cj, v Qal pf 1cs
הַמִּסְכֵּן	וְחָכְמַת	מִגְּבוּרָה	חָכְמָה	טוֹבָה	אָנִי	**16.** וְאָמַרְתִּי
hammiskēn	wechokhmath	miggevûrāh	chokhmāh	tôvāh	'ānî	we'āmartî
the needy	and wisdom of	than might	wisdom	better	I	and I said

2550 n mp	1745 n mp	8471.256 v Niphal ptc mp	375 sub, ps 3mp	1745 cj, n mp, ps 3ms	995.157 v Qal pass ptc fs
חֲכָמִים	**17.** דִּבְרֵי	נִשְׁמָעִים	אֵינָם	וּדְבָרָיו	בְּזוּיָה
chăkhāmîm	divrê	nishmā'îm	'ênām	ûdhevārâv	bezûyāh
the wise	the words of	being listened to	they are not	and his words	being despised

3009B adj	904, 3809 prep, art, n mp	5090.151 v Qal act ptc ms	4623, 2285 prep, n fs	8471.256 v Niphal ptc mp	904, 5369 prep, n fs
18. טוֹבָה	בַּכְּסִילִים	מוֹשֵׁל	מִזַּעֲקַת	נִשְׁמָעִים	בְּנַחַת
tôvāh	bakkesîlîm	môshēl	mizza'ăqath	nishmā'îm	benachath
better	among fools	a ruler	than the outcry of	they are more heard	in calmness

3009B adj	6.321 v Piel impf 3ms	259 num	2490.151 cj, v Qal act ptc ms	7417 n ms	4623, 3747 prep, n mp	2551 n fs
טוֹבָה	יְאַבֵּד	אֶחָד	וְחוֹטֶא	קְרָב	מִכְּלֵי	חָכְמָה
tôvāh	ye'abbēdh	'echādh	wechôte'	qerāv	mikkelê	chokhmāh
good	he will destroy	one	but a sinner	battle	than the weapons of	wisdom

5218.521 v Hiphil impf 3ms	919.521 v Hiphil impf 3ms	4323 n ms	2155 n mp	7528.542 v Hiphil inf abs
יַבִּיעַ	יַבְאִישׁ	מָוֶת	**10:1** זְבוּבֵי	הַרְבֵּה
yabbîa'	yav'îsh	māweth	zevûvê	harbēh
they cause to pour out	they cause to stink	death	flies of	making abundant

4746 sub	5724 n fs	4623, 3632 prep, n ms	4623, 2551 prep, n fs	3479 adj	7836.151 v Qal act ptc ms	8467 n ms
מְעָט	סִכְלוּת	מִכָּבוֹד	מֵחָכְמָה	יָקָר	רוֹקֵחַ	שֶׁמֶן
me'āt	sikhlûth	mikkāvôdh	mēchokhmāh	yāqār	rôqēach	shemen
a little	folly	than honor	than wisdom	more precious	the perfumer	the olive oil of

3937, 7972 prep, n ms, ps 3ms	3809 n ms	3949 cj, n ms	3937, 3332 prep, n fs, ps 3ms	2550 n ms	3949 n ms
לִשְׂמֹאלוֹ	כְּסִיל	וְלֵב	לִימִינוֹ	חָכָם	**2.** לֵב
lismō'lô	kesîl	welēv	lîmînô	chākhām	lēv
to his left	the foolish	but the heart of	to his right	the wise	the heart of

569.111 cj, v Qal pf 3ms	2742 adj	3949 n ms, ps 3ms	2050.151 v Qal act ptc ms	3626, 8054, 5723 prep, rel part, art, n ms	1612, 904, 1932 cj, cj, prep, art, n ms
וְאָמַר	חָסֵר	לִבּוֹ	הֹלֵךְ	כְּשֶׁהַסָּכָל	**3.** וְגַם־בַּדֶּרֶךְ
we'āmar	chāsēr	libbô	hōlēkh	keshehassākhāl	wegham-badderekh
but he will say	lacking	his heart	walking	when the fool	and also on the way

---

17. The words of wise men are heard in quiet: ... quiet words of wise men are to be heeded, *Anchor* ... What wise persons say quietly is heard, *Beck* ... which come quietly, *BB* ... calm words of the wise make themselves heard, *JB*.

more than the cry of him that ruleth among fools: ... rather than the shouting of a king of fools, *Anchor* ... the yelling of a ruler among, *Beck* ... shouting rules among fools!, *Fenton* ... above the shouts of someone commanding an army of, *JB*.

18. Wisdom is better than weapons of war: ... instruments of war, *BB* ... Arms cannot match wisdom, *Knox* ... than weapons of conflict, *Young*.

but one sinner destroyeth much good: ... rogue can ruin a great deal of, *Anchor* ... one error, *Beck* ... one blunder destroys much success!, *Fenton* ... a single sin undoes a deal of good, *JB*.

10:1. Dead flies cause the ointment of the apothecary to send forth a stinking savour: ... make a bottle of perfume stink, *Anchor* … make a perfumer's oil stink and ferment, *Beck* … putrefy the perfumer's ointment, *Berkeley* … make the oil of the perfumer give out an evil smell, *BB*.

so doth a little folly him that is in reputation for wisdom and honour: … A small folly may outweigh wisdom [and] honor, *Anchor* … a little foolishness outweighs wisdom and honor, *Beck* … outweighs an abundance of wisdom, *Berkeley* … annuls great wisdom, *Goodspeed*.

2. A wise man's heart is at his right hand: … goes in the right direction, *BB* … mind makes for his success, *Goodspeed* … leads him aright, *JB* … sense will keep him right, *Moffatt*.

but a fool's heart at his left: … in the wrong, *BB* … mind makes for his failure, *Goodspeed* … leads him astray, *JB* … mind leads him wrong, *Moffatt*.

3. Yea also, when he that is a fool walketh by the way, his wisdom faileth him: … he has no wit, *JB* … shows lack of sense, *Moffatt* … in his lack of understanding, *NAB* … his sense is lacking, *NASB*.

and he saith to every one that he is a fool: … everyone remarks, 'How

---

9:16. What is the application to ourselves that makes it practical truth? Learn to estimate men by their wisdom and godliness, not by their outward show. Value wisdom as the gift of God. The more we feel our need of the gift, the more stimulating must be our earnest pleading for the continued supply. The wise man learned from this history that it was better than strength, inasmuch as one poor wise man in the city showed himself stronger than a large army without. And it is most encouraging to see great results from apparently feeble means, which the world knew nothing of, and which, if they did know, they would only despise.

Learn also to prepare for disappointment. Work for the best interests of your fellow creatures but not for their approbation or reward. Let not their praise be our motive. Many may obtain what they do not deserve or what justly belongs to us. But there is no ground to be disheartened by failure. If we miss the worldly favor and seem to be forgotten, the time is at hand when "the honor that cometh from God only" will be found to be the substantial and unfading reward.

9:17–18. The words of the wise man had just been spoken of as slighted and not remembered. Here, however, considerable weight is ascribed to them. Though the case of the foregoing verse is of frequent occurrence, exceptions may be found. The words of the wise, spoken in quiet and unobtrusiveness, may be little thought of at the time and yet may command attention when circumstances bring them out.

The contrast drawn from the history of the wise man is vivid. Not only is wisdom better than strength, but better than weapons of war—strength made ready and armed for the exigency. And yet, if we see that one wise man, though poor and unhonored, can do much good, sad indeed is the conviction forced upon us from the contrary side. One sinner destroys much good.

10:1. The accident here referred to might often happen. Where flies and winged insects of all kinds abounded, one or more falling in might spoil the apothecary's ointment. Solomon drew many of his illustrations from common life. And his quick discernment made a ready application of the incident to set out and enforce a moral principle. The lesson that he draws from it is that as the dead fly, though only a little creature, gives an ill savor to the most costly ointment, so even a small measure of folly mars a fair reputation for wisdom and honor. He had just before mentioned the awful fact that "one sinner destroyeth much good." The apostle, as we have seen, makes a similar statement of the wide-spreading plague even of a small measure of evil. "A little leaven leaveneth the whole lump" (1 Cor. 5:6).

But it is not only the shame of gross sins that injures purity. A little folly is enough to produce immense mischief. The minor morals of the Christian code require strict attention. Take care that the Christian life is wholly Christianized in outward points. The neglect of serving the LORD in little things excites revolt.

10:2–3. This is a proverbial rather than a literal maxim. We have had it in substance before. "The wise man's eyes are in his head; but the fool walketh in darkness" (2:14). Here it contrasts the wise man's ready prudence and circumspection with the fool's rashness and want of thoughtfulness. The right hand is more ready for exercise than the left, and therefore illustrates the better advantage that the wise man makes of his resources.

For want, however, of sound discipline, we lose the power of mastering the mind. Frivolous minds continue amusing themselves with listlessness and creating for themselves fictions of fancy, yielding

4.

3937, 3725	5722	2000	524, 7593	5090.151	6148.122	6142
prep, n ms	adj	pers pron	cj, *n ms*	art, v Qal act ptc ms	v Qal impf 3fs	prep, ps 2ms
לְכֹל	סָכָל	הוּא	אִם־רוּחַ	הַמּוֹשֵׁל	תַּעֲלֶה	עָלֶיךָ
lakkōl	sākhāl	hū'	'im-rûach	hammôshēl	ta'ăleh	'ālêkhā
to everyone	foolish	he	if the spirit of	the ruler	it goes up	against you

5.

4887	414, 5299.523	3706	4995	5299.521	2491	1448	3552
n ms, ps 2ms	adv, v Hiphil juss 2ms	cj	n ms	v Hiphil impf 3ms	n mp	adj	sub
מְקוֹמְךָ	אַל־תַּנַּח	כִּי	מַרְפֵּא	יַנִּיחַ	חֲטָאִים	גְּדוֹלִים	יֵשׁ
meqômkhā	'al-tannach	kî	marpē'	yanîach	chătā'îm	gedhôlîm	yēsh
your place	do not leave	because	calm	it causes to rest	sins	great	there is

7750	7495.115	8809	8507	3626, 8145	8054, 3428.153	4623, 3937, 6686
n ms	v Qal pf 1cs	prep	art, n ms	prep, n fs	rel part, v Qal act ptc fs	prep, prep, *n mp*
רָעָה	רָאִיתִי	תַּחַת	הַשָּׁמֶשׁ	כִּשְׁגָגָה	שֶׁיֹּצָא	מִלִּפְנֵי
rā'āh	rā'îthî	tachath	hashshāmesh	kishghāghāh	shêyōtsā'	milliphnê
an evil	I have seen	under	the sun	like an inadvertent sin	that going out	from before

6.

8384	5598.211	5723	904, 4953	7521	6474	904, 8586
art, adj	v Niphal pf 3ms	art, n ms	prep, art, n mp	adj	cj, adj	prep, art, n ms
הַשַּׁלִּיט	נִתַּן	הַסֶּכֶל	בַּמְּרוֹמִים	רַבִּים	וַעֲשִׁירִים	בַּשֵּׁפֶל
hashshallît	nittan	hassekhel	bammeromîm	rabbîm	wa'ăshîrîm	bashshēphel
the ruler	it has been placed	the folly	in the heights	many	and riches	in the low places

7.

3553.126	7495.115	5860	6142, 5670	8015	2050.152	3626, 5860
v Qal impf 3mp	v Qal pf 1cs	n mp	prep, n mp	cj, n mp	v Qal act ptc mp	prep, n mp
יֵשְׁבוּ	רָאִיתִי	עֲבָדִים	עַל־סוּסִים	וְשָׂרִים	הֹלְכִים	כַּעֲבָדִים
yēshēvû	rā'îthî	'ăvādhîm	'al-sûsîm	wesārîm	hōlekhîm	ka'ăvādhîm
they will sit	I have seen	slaves	on horses	and officials	walking	like slaves

8.

6142, 800	2763.151	1508	904	5489.121	6805.151
prep, art, n fs	v Qal act ptc ms	n ms	prep, ps 3ms	v Qal impf 3ms	cj, v Qal act ptc ms
עַל־הָאָרֶץ	חֹפֵר	גּוּמָץ	בּוֹ	יִפּוֹל	וּפֹרֵץ
'al-hā'ārets	chōphēr	gûmmāts	bô	yippôl	ûphōrēts
on the ground	the digger	a pit	in it	he will fall	and the one breaking through

9.

1474	5574.121	5357	5450.551	63	6321.221
n ms	v Qal impf 3ms, ps 3ms	n ms	v Hiphil ptc ms	n fp	v Niphal impf 3ms
גָּדֵר	יִשְּׁכֶנּוּ	נָחָשׁ	מַסִּיעַ	אֲבָנִים	יֵעָצֵב
gādhēr	yishshekhennû	nāchāsh	massîa'	'ăvānîm	yē'ātsēv
a fence	it will bite him	a serpent	the one who quarries	stones	he will be hurt

---

silly he is!', *JB* ... he calls everyone a fool, *Moffatt* ... he calls everything foolish, *NAB* ... demonstrates to everyone that he is a fool, *NASB*.

4. If the spirit of the ruler rise up against thee: ... anger of the ruler burst upon, *NAB* ... temper rises against you, *NASB* ... is angry with you, *NCV* ... anger of the ruler flares up at you, *REB*.

leave not thy place: ... forsake not your place, *NAB* ... abandon your position, *NASB* ... Don't leave your job, *NCV* ... resign your post, *NEB*.

for yielding pacifieth great offences: ... mildness abates great offenses, *NAB* ... composure allays great offenses, *NASB* ... Remaining calm solves great problems, *NCV* ... submission makes amends for great mistakes, *NEB*.

5. There is an evil which I have seen under the sun: ... an amiss-ness I have seen, *Berkeley* ... a wrong I have seen, *Fenton* ... a source of trouble I have marked, *Knox* ... something else wrong that happens, *NCV*.

as an error which proceedeth from the ruler: ... seems like a mistake attributable to, *Anchor* ... an error often made by, *Beck* ... the sort of misjudgement to which rulers are prone, *JB*.

6. Folly is set in great dignity: ... Fools come to the top, *Knox* ... fools often get high posts from him, *Moffatt* ... Fools are given important positions, *NCV* ... the fool given high office, *NEB*.

and the rich sit in low place: ... down go rank and riches, *Knox* ...

while the noble have a lowly seat, *Moffatt* ... gifted people are given lower ones, *NCV* ... the great and the rich in humble posts, *NEB*.

7. I have seen servants upon horses: ... slaves mounted on horses, *Anchor* ... slaves you will see riding on horseback, *Knox*.

and princes walking as servants upon the earth: ... aristocrats walking on foot like slaves, *Anchor* ... rulers walking on the earth as servants, *BB* ... going afoot at their bri-dle-rein, *Knox* ... plodding afoot like slaves, *Moffatt*.

8. He that diggeth a pit shall fall into it: ... who makes a hole for others will himself go into it, *BB* ... Fall into pit thou shalt not, if thou dig none, *Knox*.

and whoso breaketh an hedge, a serpent shall bite him: ... who breaks down a wall may be bitten by a snake, *Anchor* ... who makes a hole through a wall the bite of a snake will be a punishment, *BB* ... breaks a fence, a snake may sting him!, *Fenton* ... who undermines a wall gets bitten by a snake, *JB*.

9. Whoso removeth stones shall be hurt therewith: ... who dislodges stones may be hurt, *Anchor* ... If you quarry stones, you may get hurt, *Beck* ... who gets out stones from the earth will be damaged by them, *BB*.

and he that cleaveth wood shall be endangered thereby: ... he must take care who would chop down trees, *Anchor* ... if you split wood, you may

---

no solid advantage. Intellectual power, sometimes of a high order, is wasted in this desultory occupation, without any one practical result.

A thorough keeping of the heart with God is our best security, living upon truths, not upon notions; seeking grace for our souls; substituting the spiritual for the sensuous; connecting excited feelings with pure, simple doctrines. If we have found the satisfying sweetness of our doctrine, we will not readily give it up. Doing so is a fearful peril. If our Bible is degraded to a commonplace book, we will lose the keen appetite for its contents. The dread of error will be less felt, and with it will fade away the love of truth.

10:4. Here loyalty is inculcated. This rule has been given before. The faithful adviser may be constrained to give unpalatable counsel, and the spirit of the ruler may rise up against him. Still let him not hastily leave his place. Generally speaking, the rule of patience is wisdom. Although good sense, Christian patience is rarely to be found. Surely, the subject, like the soldier, should hold the place assigned to him, even if it affords much trial. Let him not throw up his commission, but rather restrain all impatient or disloyal thoughts.

The triumph over the spirit is a far higher glory than an earthly victory. A triumph over ourselves is more glorious than a victory over others (Prov. 16:32). The vehement impulse seems to show that we think more of ourselves than of our cause. Yet this yielding must never arise from cowardice, from a mean-spirited fear of losing the favor of man. Where conscience is concerned, the true-hearted man must at once leave his place, whatever be the consequence. In an upright course, fear not the face of man, while not forgetting man. Yet where conscience is not concerned, nothing is to be gained by the display of an unbending spirit.

10:5–7. Solomon followed up his exhortation to loyalty by noticing a common occasion of disloyalty that is misgovernment. He had often alluded to this disorder as a national evil, especially when men have been raised, or have risen, to a high elevation. The records of all ages, particularly of our own, show men raised from the people to the highest honor in the state. The evil here noted is the misplacing of men, folly set in great dignity. This is an error which proceeds from the ruler. The responsibility lies at his door to fix the fittest men in the places which most need them, doing nothing either by partiality or by prejudice. A matter of much evil and grief is the capricious advancement of despicable upstarts—power placed in unworthy hands, great interests entrusted to men of low life, who have neither will nor wisdom to discharge their trust rightly.

The evil is greatly increased when the high stations of the Church are bestowed upon unworthy men, passing over men of God, who are sound in doctrine and upright in heart. How will a man behave himself in his high responsibility? None but those who are divinely furnished can stand the trial and glorify God in it.

10:8–9. These four pithy illustrations obviously point to one and the same end. Evil will fall upon the heads of its own authors. He that digs the pit may fall into it himself. As the breaking of an old hedge might hazard a serpent's bite, so the attempt to root up ancient fences of government may be an undoing project. The removal of stones from a building may bring them upon the head of the guilty. Even the splitting of wood may be a work of

10.

904	1260.151	6320	5725.221	904	524, 7233.311
prep, ps 3mp	v Qal act ptc ms	n mp	v Niphal impf 3ms	prep, ps 3mp	cj, v Piel pf 3ms
בָּהֶם	בּוֹקֵעַ	עֵצִים	יְסַכֵּן	בָּם	אִם־קֵהָה
bāhem	bôqēa'	'ētsîm	yissākhen	bām	'im-qēhāh
by them	the one who splits	wood	he will be endangered	by them	if he makes blunt

1298	2000	3940, 6686	7327.311	2524
art, n ms	cj, pers pron	neg part, n mp	v Pilpal pf 3ms	cj, n mp
הַבַּרְזֶל	וְהוּא	לֹא־פָנִים	קִלְקַל	וַחֲיָלִים
habbarzel	wehû'	lō'-phānîm	qilqal	wachăyālîm
the iron	and it	no edges	he will considered ruined	and double strength

11.

1428.321	3620	3916.541	2551	524, 5574.121
v Piel impf 3ms	cj, n ms	v Hiphil inf con	n fs	cj, v Qal impf 3ms
יְגַבֵּר	וְיִתְרוֹן	הַכְשֵׁיר	חָכְמָה	אִם־יִשֹּׁךְ
yeghabbēr	weyithrôn	hakhshêr	chokhmāh	'im-yishshōkh
he will cause to prevail	but an advantage	to cause to succeed	wisdom	if it bites

5357	904, 3940, 4043	375	3620	3937, 1196	4098
art, n ms	prep, neg part, n ms	cj, sub	n ms	prep, n ms	art, n ms
הַנָּחָשׁ	בְּלוֹא־לָחַשׁ	וְאֵין	יִתְרוֹן	לְבַעַל	הַלָּשׁוֹן
hannāchāsh	belô'-lāchash	we'ên	yithrôn	leva'al	hallāshôn
the serpent	when not a charming	then there is not	a profit	to the owner of	the tongue

12.

1745	6552, 2550	2682	8004	3809	1142.322
n mp	n ms, n ms	n ms	cj, n fp	n ms	v Piel impf 3fs, ps 3ms
דִּבְרֵי	פִּי־חָכָם	חֵן	וְשִׂפְתוֹת	כְּסִיל	תְּבַלְּעֶנּוּ
divrê	phî-chākhām	chēn	wesiphthôth	kesîl	tevalle'ennû
the words of	the mouth of the wise	favor	but the lips of	the foolish	they will consume him

13.

8795	1745, 6552	5724	321	6552	2014
n fs	n mp, n ms, ps 3ms	n fs	cj, n fs	n ms, ps 3ms	n fs
תְּחִלַּת	דִּבְרֵי־פִיהוּ	סִכְלוּת	וְאַחֲרִית	פִּיהוּ	הוֹלֵלוּת
techillath	divrê-phîhû	sikhlûth	we'achărîth	pîhû	hôlēlûth
the beginning of	the words of his mouth	foolishness	and the end of	his mouth	folly

14.

7737	5723	7528.521	1745	3940, 3156.121	119
adj	cj, art, n ms	v Hiphil impf 3ms	n mp	neg part v Qal impf 3ms	art, n ms
רָעָה	וְהַסָּכָל	יַרְבֶּה	דְּבָרִים	לֹא־יֵדַע	הָאָדָם
rā'āh	wehassākhāl	yarbeh	dhevārîm	lō'-yēda'	hā'ādhām
evil	and the fool	he will multiply	words	he does not know	the man

4242, 8054, 2030.121	866	2030.121	4623, 313	4449	5222.521	3937
intrg, rel part, v Qal impf 3ms	cj, rel part	v Qal impf 3ms	prep, prep, ps 3ms	intrg	v Hiphil impf 3ms	prep, ps 3ms
מַה־שֶּׁיִּהְיֶה	וַאֲשֶׁר	יִהְיֶה	מֵאַחֲרָיו	מִי	יַגִּיד	לוֹ
mah-sheyihyeh	wa'ăsher	yihyeh	mē'achărâv	mî	yaggîd	lô
what that it will be	and what	it will be	after him	who	he will tell	to him

be injured, *Beck* ... in the cutting of wood there is danger, *BB* ... he who chops wood takes a risk, *JB*.

10. If the iron be blunt, and he do not whet the edge: ... for want of sharpening, the blade is blunt, *JB* ... Blunt tool that has grown dull from long disuse, *Knox* ... axe is blunt and its edge unwhetted, *Moffatt* ... the iron becomes dull, though at first he made easy progress, *NAB*.

then must he put to more strength: ... you have to work twice as hard, *JB* ... shall cost thee pains a many, *Knox* ... more strength must be put into the blow, *Moffatt* ... he must increase his efforts, *NAB*.

but wisdom is profitable to direct: ... if thou hadst been wise sooner, thou shouldst have toiled less, *Knox* ... successful skill comes from shrewd sense, *Moffatt* ... the craftsman has the advantage of his skill, *NAB*.

11. Surely the serpent will bite without enchantment: ... stings without a charmer, *Fenton* ... bites before it is charmed, *Moffatt* ... a snake bites the tamer before it is tamed, *NCV* ... may bite when it is not charmed, *NKJV*.

and a babbler is no better: ... what good is the tamer?, *NCV* ... The babbler is no different, *NKJV* ... the snake-charmer loses his fee, *REB* ... there is no advantage in a charmer, *RSV*.

12. The words of a wise man's mouth are gracious: ... has a winning way, *Beck* ... are sweet to all,

BB ... words of a wise mouth profit, *Fenton* ... sayings of a sage give pleasure, *JB*.

but the lips of a fool will swallow up himself: ... devour him, *Anchor* ... what a fool says destroys him, *Beck* ... engulf him, *Berkeley* ... what a fool says procures his own ruin, *JB*.

13. The beginning of the words of his mouth is foolishness: ... words have their origin in stupidity, *JB* ... his preface idle talk, *Knox* ... words are folly from the start, *Moffatt* ...

fool begins by saying foolish things, *NCV*.

and the end of his talk is mischievous madness: ... in treacherous folly, *JB* ... his conclusion madness, *Knox* ... they end in mad mischief, *Moffatt* ... ends by saying crazy and wicked things, *NCV*.

14. A fool also is full of words: ... prates on and on, *Moffatt* ... multiplieth words, *MRB* ... talks too much, *NCV* ... talks on and on, *NEB* ... talks at great length, *REB*.

---

personal danger. It is far more easy to blame than to mend; to pull down the house, than to build it up again. Yet such is the power of self-delusion. If the mysterious finger could show the handwriting upon the wall—onward men will go—so natural and easy is the downward path!

10:10. Whatever be the object of the man in cleaving the wood, he cannot work effectively with blunted tools. If, therefore, he does not whet his hatchet's edge, he must put forth more strength. Still he delivers only heavy, ineffectual blows. Thus unskillful and indolent workmen often increase their difficulties due to the lack of hearty exertion. In working for God, our materials are rough. Feeble, indeed, are our efforts to split the knotty wood. The stubborn will resists, and there is no apparent result.

The secret of this bluntness is that we have not whetted the edge, that prayer has been let down, that faith has been in slumbering exercise, that the lust of the world has been indulged, and heavenly prospects clouded. Yet we must not cast away the enfeebled weapon.

After all, the grand cause of failure is that we do not go straight to God for the strength of omnipotence to be "made perfect in weakness" (2 Cor. 12:9).

There will indeed be perplexities to the end, but wisdom, "the wisdom that is from above," is profitable to direct. It puts us in the right way of working. It sets before us the best objects and the most fitting occasions. The want of this practical wisdom has hindered much good and induced much injury to the great end. "If any of you lack wisdom, let him ask of God, that gives to all men

liberally, and upbraideth not; and it will be given him" (Jam. 1:5).

10:11. Scripture elsewhere alludes to man's power in enchanting the serpent, but without enchantment surely the serpent will bite. It is his nature (v. 8). The babbler is no better. It is as much his nature to babble, and quite as dangerous, as for the serpent to bite. He is all tongue. Well indeed is this tongue described as an "unruly evil, full of deadly poison!" (Jam. 3:8).

The evil here more distinctly in view is breach of confidence. So baneful is its influence that it is hardly safe to trust in a friend, or to put confidence in a guide. No other sin tends more to banish the divine Comforter from our houses and from our hearts. What proof can there be of grace in the heart, if there be not a bridle on the tongue?

10:12–15. Again we have the contrast drawn out between wisdom and folly—between that which comes from God and the flowing stream of our corrupt nature.

How valuable is the art of enchanting our tongues, bringing them under wholesome discipline, so that they may pacify and instruct. True, heavenly wisdom pervades the entire new man, as folly pervades every faculty of the old man. The words therefore of the wise man's mouth are gracious. Thus it was with our divine Master. When this Incarnate Wisdom was manifested, it is no wonder that they were awed "at the can we marvel, that they wondered "at the gracious words, which proceeded out of his mouth" (Luke 4:22).

Here is wisdom in its solid influence. Now mark the contrast of folly. The lips of the fool swallow up himself. Adonijah's self-willed proclamation was his

15.

6219	3809	3129.322	866	3940, 3156.111	3937, 2050.141
n ms	art, n mp	v Piel impf 3fs, ps 3ms	rel part	neg part, v Qal pf 3ms	prep, v Qal inf con
עֲמַל	הַכְּסִילִים	תְּיַגְּעֶנּוּ	אֲשֶׁר	לֹא־יָדַע	לָלֶכֶת
'āmal	hakkesîlîm	teyagge'ennû	'ăsher	lō'-yādha'	lālekheth
the toil of	the foolish	it will weary him	that	he does not know	to go

16.

420, 6111	341, 3937	800	8054, 4567	5470	8015	904, 1269
prep, n fs	intrj, prep, ps 2fs	n fs	rel pron, n ms, ps 2fs	n ms	cj, n mp, ps 2fs	prep, art, n ms
אֶל־עִיר	אִי־לָךְ	אֶרֶץ	שֶׁמַּלְכֵּךְ	נַעַר	וְשָׂרַיִךְ	בַּבֹּקֶר
'el-'îr	'î-lākh	'erets	shemmalkēkh	nā'ar	wesārayikh	babbōqer
to a city	woe to you	O land	whom your king	a youth	and your officials	in the morning

17.

404.126	869	800	8054, 4567	1158, 2814	8015
v Qal impf 3mp	n mp, ps 2fs	n fs	rel pron, n ms, ps 2fs	n ms, n mp	cj, n mp, ps 2fs
יֹאכֵלוּ	אַשְׁרֵיךְ	אֶרֶץ	שֶׁמַּלְכֵּךְ	בֶּן־חוֹרִים	וְשָׂרַיִךְ
yō'khēlû	'ashrēkh	'erets	shemmalkēkh	ben-chôrîm	wesārayikh
they eat	blessed you	O land	whom your king	a son of leaders	and your officials

18.

904, 6496	404.126	904, 1400	3940	904, 8689	904, 6342
prep, art, n fs	v Qal impf 3mp	prep, n fs	cj, neg part	prep, art, n ms	prep, n fd
בָּעֵת	יֹאכֵלוּ	בִּגְבוּרָה	וְלֹא	בַשְּׁתִי	בַּעֲצַלְתַּיִם
bā'ēth	yō'khēlû	bighvûrāh	welō'	vashshethî	ba'ătsaltayim
at the time	they will eat	with strength	and not	with revelry	because of slothfulness

4493.221	4908	904, 8591	3135	1872.121	1041
v Niphal impf 3ms	art, n ms	cj, prep, n fs	n fd	v Qal impf 3ms	art, n ms
יִמַּךְ	הַמְּקָרֶה	וּבְשִׁפְלוּת	יָדַיִם	יִדְלֹף	הַבַּיִת
yimmakh	hammeqāreh	ûveshiphlûth	yādhayim	yidhlōph	habbāyith
it will sag	the beam	and because of the lowering of	hands	it will leak	the house

19.

3937, 7926	6449.152	4035	3302	7975.321	2522	3826B
prep, n ms	v Qal act ptc mp	n ms	cj, n ms	v Piel impf 3ms	n mp	cj, art, n ms
לִשְׂחוֹק	עֹשִׂים	לֶחֶם	וְיַיִן	יְשַׂמַּח	חַיִּים	וְהַכֶּסֶף
lischôq	'ōsîm	lechem	weyayin	yesammach	chayyîm	wehakkeseph
for laughter	making	bread	and wine	it will make glad	life	and the silver

a man cannot tell what shall be: ... what is to come, *NAB* ... what will happen, *NASB* ... No one knows the future, *NCV* ... no man knows what is coming, *NEB*.

and what shall be after him, who can tell him?: ... no one can tell what will happen after death, *NCV* ... who can tell him what will come after that?, *NEB* ... who can tell anyone what the future holds?, *NRSV*.

15. The labour of the foolish wearieth every one of them: ... exertions so exhaust him, *Anchor* ... fool wears himself out with hard work, *Beck* ... efforts of a fool weary him, *Berkeley* ... endeavours of fools exhaust them, *Fenton*.

because he knoweth not how to go to the city: ... he cannot find his way to town, *Anchor* ... doesn't even know the way, *Beck* ... has no knowledge of the way, *BB* ... cannot even find his own way into town, *JB*.

16. Woe to thee, O land, when thy king is a child: ... is a boy, *Goodspeed* ... with a lad for king, *JB* ... that has young blood on the throne, *Knox* ... is a mere boy, *Moffatt*.

and thy princes eat in the morning!: ... nobles are drunk in the morning!, *Fenton* ... feast in the morning!, *Goodspeed* ... whose court sits feasting till daybreak!, *Knox* ... revel in the morning!, *Moffatt*.

17. Blessed art thou, O land, when thy king is the son of nobles: ... is of true princely breed, *Knox* ... is a free man, *MAST* ... is nobly born, *Moffatt* ... comes from a good family, *NCV*.

and thy princes eat in due season: ... feast when feast should be, *Knox* ... revel at right hours, *Moffatt* ... dine at the right time, *NAB* ... eat only at mealtime, *NCV*.

for strength, and not for drunkenness!: ... to comfort their hearts, not all in revelry, *Knox* ... stalwart men, not sots!, *Moffatt* ... (for vigor and not in drinking bouts), *NAB* ... with self-control, and not as drunkards, *NEB*.

18. By much slothfulness the building decayeth: ... Because of indolence the roof beams sag, *Anchor* ...

the roof sinketh in, *ASV* ... Laziness makes the roof collapse, *Beck* ... Through continual neglect the ceiling sinks, *Berkeley.*

and through idleness of the hands the house droppeth through: ... a lazy man has a leaky house, *Anchor* ... the house leaketh, *ASV* ... taking it easy makes the house leak, *Beck* ...

because of slack hands the house leaks, *Berkeley.*

19. A feast is made for laughter: ... banquet for enjoyment, *Berkeley* ... With mirth they make bread, *Goodspeed* ... We give parties to enjoy ourselves, *JB* ... Food will cheer thee, *Knox.*

and wine maketh merry: ... cheers the living, *Berkeley* ... makes glad the heart, *BB* ... gladdens life, *Goodspeed.*

but money answereth all things: ... money has to bring about everything, *Berkeley* ... by the one and the other money is wasted, *BB* ... is useful for all things!, *Fenton* ... has an answer for everything, *JB.*

---

own ruin (1 Ki. 1:5; 2:25). Rehoboam's foolishness, giving grievous instead of gracious words to his people, made his "own tongue to fall upon [himself]" (1 Ki. 12:1–19; cf. Ps. 64:8). Wisdom guides the nearest way to our own security (Prov. 10:9), but folly the surest road to our own ruin.

The next distinctive feature in the portrait of the fool is his torrent of words. He talks from first to last in the circle of folly, talking on at random, determined to have the last word, although at the end it is the same as at the beginning.

In fact, it is generally found that those who have the most discourse have the least knowledge. Words are too often the substitute for thinking, rather than the medium of thought. In the use of them, men think they know their own wisdom. But how few comparatively know their own foolishness! The fool passing from his words to his daily business—his labor wearies every one connected with him. Impertinently busy, without any object, yet so extreme is his ignorance upon the most ordinary matters that it is as if he knew not the plainest track, how to go to the city, close at hand.

10:16–17. Solomon's code of morals comes out with greater point and brightness, the more it is examined. This Book of Ecclesiastes is truly a handbook of morals for all ranks and classes of society—not among the least important is the rank of the great and noble of the earth. Kings and rulers, like Solomon, were far from being exempted from the common laws of men merely because of their rank. Rather, Solomon warns them against sins which might have seemed to belong only to the lowest and most degraded of their people. In point of fact, the higher the rank, the more aggravated the sin. Solomon particularly reproves the sin of intemperance here, which is not only ruinous to the prince, but brings a curse upon the nation.

Solomon had naturally learned to connect the personal character of the monarch with the prosperity of the land. Indeed, a child monarch, as Josiah,

and others, may be a national blessing. But when the king is a child in understanding, then woe unto you, O land (1 Ki. 3:7).

In contrast with the woe of a childish monarch, is the blessing of a king—the son of nobles. And as before, it was the child, not in years, but in qualities; so he now speaks of a king noble not in blood, but in wisdom and godliness. The completeness of the blessing is that when the king reigns in righteousness, the princes, following his example, will "rule in judgment" (Isa. 32:1). The contrast is marked in well-disciplined exercise. They did not eat in the morning in unrestrained indulgence, but in due season, in moderation, for strength, and not for drunkenness.

10:18. Luxury and intemperance give ready occasion to much slothfulness. They are naturally linked together: "The drunkard and the glutton will come to poverty: and drowsiness will clothe a man with rags" (Prov. 23:21). The ruler and princes, given up to sensual indulgence, will slumber in the affairs of the state. The commonwealth therefore will be like a building decaying for want of proper support, a house slipping through, not weather-proof, for the idle want of exterior to keep it in repair.

Want of family discipline issues in the same result. When evils, apparently trifling, are allowed, the tendency to decay becomes more and more visible. Indeed everywhere the neglect of present effort hastens on the ruinous crisis. Public institutions and laws, however permanent they may seem to be, need continual and active review. Otherwise, abuses creep in, like moss on an old building or a gap in the wall. In the former example, though the moss is scarcely observable, it gradually widens with threatening prospect.

10:19. Many are the resources of laughter and merriment, but money brings a wider range of influence. It not only answers the pleasure, the feasting and wine, but all things, which the craving appetite of man can desire. In itself it is a blessing, contributing largely to our temporal comfort. If we

Ecclesiastes 10:20–11:3

20.

414, 7327.323	4567	904, 4234	1612	881, 3725	6257.121
adv, v Piel juss 2ms	n ms	prep, n ms, ps 2ms	cj	do, art, n ms	v Qal impf 3ms
אַל־תְּקַלֵּל	מֶלֶךְ	בְּמַדָּעֲךָ	גַּם	אֶת־הַכֹּל	יַעֲנֶה
'al-teqallēl	melekh	bemaddā'ăkhā	gam	'eth-hakkōl	ya'ăneh
do not curse	a king	because of your experience	also	everything	it will answer

8452	5991	3706	6474	414, 7327.323	5085	904, 2410
art, n md	n ms	cj	n ms	adv, v Piel juss 2ms	n ms, ps 2ms	cj, prep, n mp
הַשָּׁמַיִם	עוֹף	כִּי	עָשִׁיר	אַל־תְּקַלֵּל	מִשְׁכָּבְךָ	וּבְחַדְרֵי
hashshāmayim	'ôph	kî	'āshîr	'al-teqallēl	mishkāvekhā	ûvechadhrê
the heavens	the bird of	because	the rich	do not curse	your bed	and in inner rooms of

1745	5222.521	3796	1196	881, 7249	2050.521
n ms	v Hiphil impf 3ms	art, n fd	cj, n ms	do, art, n ms	v Hiphil impf 3ms
דָּבָר	יַגֵּיד	הַכְּנָפַיִם	וּבַעַל	אֶת־הַקּוֹל	יוֹלִיךְ
dāvār	yaggêdh	hakkenāphayim	ûva'al	'eth-haqqôl	yôlîkh
a word	it will tell	the wings	and the owner of	the voice	it will cause to go

11:1

3706, 904, 7524	4448	6142, 6686	4035	8365.331
cj, prep, n ms	art, n mp	prep, n mp	n ms, ps 2ms	v Piel impv 2ms
כִּי־בְרֹב	הַמָּיִם	עַל־פְּנֵי	לַחְמְךָ	שַׁלַּח
kî-verōv	hammāyim	'al-penê	lachmekhā	shallach
because with the abundance of	the water	upon the surface of	your bread	send out

2.

3940	3706	3937, 8470	1612, cj	3937, 8124	5598.131, 2610	4834.123	3219
neg part	cj	prep, num	cj, cj	prep, num	v Qal impv 2ms, n ms	v Qal impf 2ms, ps 3ms	art, n mp
לֹא	כִּי	לִשְׁמוֹנָה	וְגַם	לְשִׁבְעָה	תֶּן־חֵלֶק	תִּמְצָאֶנּוּ	הַיָּמִים
lō'	kî	lishmônāh	wegham	leshiv'āh	ten-chēleq	timtsā'ennû	hayyāmîm
not	because	to eight	or even	to seven	give a portion	you will find it	the days

3.

1700	5854	524, 4527.226	6142, 800	7750	4242, 2030.121	3156.123
n ms	art, n mp	cj, v Niphal impf 3mp	prep, art, n fs	n fs	intrg, v Qal impf 3ms	v Qal impf 2ms
גֶּשֶׁם	הֶעָבִים	אִם־יִמָּלְאוּ	עַל־הָאָרֶץ	רָעָה	מַה־יִּהְיֶה	תֵּדַע
geshem	he'āvîm	'im-yimmāle'û	'al-hā'ārets	rā'āh	mah-yihyeh	thēdha'
rain	the clouds	if they are full of	on the earth	an evil	what will be	you will know

904, 7103	524	904, 1924	6320	524, 5489.121	7671.526	6142, 800
prep, art, n fs	cj, cj	prep, art, n ms	n ms	cj, cj, v Qal impf 3ms	v Hiphil impf 3mp	prep, art, n fs
בַּצָּפוֹן	וְאִם	בַּדָּרוֹם	עֵץ	וְאִם־יִפּוֹל	יָרִיקוּ	עַל־הָאָרֶץ
batstsāphôn	we'im	baddārôm	'ēts	we'im-yippôl	yārîqû	'al-hā'ārets
in the north	or if	in the south	a tree	and if it does fall	they will pour out	upon the earth

---

20. Curse not the king, no not in thy thought: ... no treasonable thought, *Knox* ... do not make light of the king, *NAB* ... make fun of the king, *NCV*.

and curse not the rich in thy bed-chamber: ... no ill word even in, *Knox* ... revile the rich, *NAB* ... make fun of rich people, *NCV*.

for a bird of the air shall carry the voice: ... may carry the news, *Beck* ... will catch the echoes of it, *Knox* ... may carry the sound, *Moffatt* ... might carry your words, *NCV*.

and that which hath wings shall tell the matter: ... fly off to betray thy secret, *Knox* ... may betray the secret, *Moffatt* ... may tell what you say, *NAB* ... winged creature will make the matter known, *NASB*.

11:1. Cast thy bread upon the waters: ... Ship your grain on the water, *Beck* ... Put your bread on the face of, *BB* ... Trust your goods far and wide at sea, *Moffatt* ... Invest what you have, *NCV*.

for thou shalt find it after many days: ... you will get a return, *Beck* ... after a long time it will come back to you, *BB* ... eventually you will recover it, *JB* ... till you get good returns after a while, *Moffatt*.

2. Give a portion to seven, and also to eight: ... Offer a share to seven or eight people, *JB* ... Take shares in several ventures, *Moffatt* ... Make seven or eight portions, *NAB* ... Invest what you have in several different businesses, *NCV*.

for thou knowest not what evil shall be upon the earth: ... can never tell what disaster may occur,

JB ... what will go wrong in this world, *Moffatt* ... what misfortune may come, *NAB* ... what disasters might happen, *NCV*.

... will pour rain on, *Anchor* ... they send it down on, *BB* ... they will shed it on, *JB* ... the rain comes, where the clouds gather, *Knox*.

place where the tree falleth, there it shall be: ... where it falls, there it remains, *Anchor* ... will lie where it fell, *Beck* ... in whatever place it comes down, there it will be, *BB* ... where the stick falls it lies, *Moffatt*.

3. If the clouds be full of rain, they empty themselves upon the earth:

and if the tree fall toward the south, or toward the north, in the

---

despise it, we must be content to live without many of the ordinary indulgences of life.

And yet this universal empire of money involves many limitations: it cannot give health, happiness or immortality; it cannot provide the principles of moral excellence; it cannot give peace of conscience or furnish a ransom for the soul. Yet with all these reserves, as an instrument of commerce, it answers all things. The man who has it lacks nothing that the world can give.

The real sphere of the usefulness of money is the object and use of it; when we hold it as stewards, the two great ends are combined in one—the glory of God, and the good of our fellow creatures.

10:20. The advice given here seems to be a caution against speaking lightly of the faults of rulers. Do not assume that you can criticize with impunity. Kings and nobles, especially in despotic governments, supply the need of just laws by spies, who do their work too surely to admit of escape, reporting to their rulers expressions they have overheard that may be the ground of treasonable accusation. If the thought that the eye and the ear of God were always open to our most secret thoughts, we should often be kept from speaking what, if discovered, might bring us into trouble.

If the thought of disloyalty against the king be forbidden, much more against the Great King. He does not want a bird of the air to carry the voice. "I know the things that come into your mind, every one of them" (Ezek. 11:5). All is heard and noted with infallible clearness and certainty. Learn then the lesson to "kiss the Son" (Ps. 2:12) with reverential affection. And say not—"We will not have this man to reign over us" (Luke 19:14). How powerless the case against a fellow-creature! God may in a moment interpose and nullify it. How much more powerless the curse of our thought against him! But oh! his curse against us—the handwriting upon the wall—the harbinger of unspeakable eternal ruin!

11:1. Precept and promise are linked together: faith in the promise gives life to the precept. Though there will be many trials in the work of God, there can be no disappointment. "All the promises of

God," those of the Old, no less than of the New Testament, are "in [Christ Jesus] yea, and in him are Amen" (2 Cor. 1:20). Divine faithfulness is therefore their security. The labor wrought out, the seed sown, will assuredly bring its own harvest.

The figure here is that of bread, or rather bread-corn cast upon the face of the waters, apparently wasted and perished, yet found after many days. It might be asked, "Of what use can it be to cast it away? And how vain the hope of finding it again!" It might seem to be the business of a senseless fool, a waste and unwarranted destruction of the "precious seed." The inundation of the Nile illustrates the figure. The time for sowing the seed is just when the waters are going down, leaving a loamy bed, in which the seed apparently lost is deposited, and produces a most luxuriant harvest.

11:2. Here Solomon adds another motive to beneficence. Every day is an opportunity. How long it may last, who can tell? "As we have therefore opportunity, let us do good" (Gal. 6:10), not giving it to one or two, or even to seven, as if we might stop there, but also to eight. The allusion may be to the Jewish custom of distributing portions on festive occasions.

But a strange reason is given for this energy of love. You do not know evil will be on the earth. "Therefore," says the selfist, "I may want my money for myself. Times may alter. An evil day may be at hand. I must be prudent, and restrain. It is best to save while I can."

11:3. Solomon abounds in happy illustrations. Here he pictures the sun exhaling its watery vapors from the earth, not to retain, but to discharge them, that they may break as clouds upon the earth again. And is not the man of God the cloud full of rain, blessed, as a child of Abraham, that he may be made a blessing? (Gen. 12:2). The blessing will not be lost. There is good security for the return of well-principled benevolence. Where it has been dispensed, there let it be looked for.

Let me ask then, what blessing am I bringing to my fellow creatures? Does my profession attract and recommend my principles? Are those around me enriched by my gifts and graces? Are they benefited

3940 neg part	7593 n fs	8490.151 v Qal act ptc ms		2008.121 v Qal impf 3ms	8427 adv	6320 art, n ms	8054, 5489.121 rel part, v Qal impf 3ms	4887 n ms
לֹא	רוּחַ	שֹׁמֵר	**4.**	יְהוּא	שָׁם	הָעֵץ	שֶׁיִּפּוֹל	מְקוֹם
lō'	rûcha	shōmēr		yehû'	shām	hā'ēts	sheyippôl	meqôm
not	wind	the one who observes		it will be	there	the tree	where it falls	the place

3626, 866 prep, rel part	7403.121 v Qal impf 3ms	3940 neg part	904, 5854 prep, art, n mp	7495.151 cj, v Qal act ptc ms	2319.121 v Qal impf 3ms
5. כַּאֲשֶׁר	יִקְצוֹר	לֹא	בֶעָבִים	וְרֹאֶה	יִזְרָע
ka'ăsher	yiqtsôr	lō'	ve'āvîm	werō'eh	yizrā'
just as	he will harvest	not	into the clouds	and the one who looks	he will sow

904, 1027 prep, n fs	3626, 6344 prep, n fp	7593 art, n fs	4242, 1932 intrg, n ms	3156.151 v Qal act ptc ms	375 sub, ps 2ms
בַּבֶּטֶן	כַּעֲצָמִים	הָרוּחַ	מַה־דֶּרֶךְ	יוֹדֵעַ	אֵינְךָ
baveten	ka'ătsāmîm	hārûach	mah-derekh	yôdhēa'	'ênekhā
in the womb	like the bones	the wind	what the way of	knowing	there is not to you

6449.121 v Qal impf 3ms	866 rel pron	435 art, n mp	881, 4801 do, n ms	3156.123 v Qal impf 2ms	3940 neg part	3722 adv	4529 art, adj
יַעֲשֶׂה	אֲשֶׁר	הָאֱלֹהִים	אֶת־מַעֲשֵׂה	תֵּדַע	לֹא	כָּכָה	הַמְּלֵאָה
ya'ăseh	'ăsher	hā'ĕlōhîm	'eth-ma'ăsēh	thēdha'	lō'	kākhāh	hammelē'āh
He makes	who	God	the work of	you will know	not	so	the full

3937, 6394 cj, prep, art, n ms	881, 2320 do, n ms, ps 2ms	2319.131 v Qal impv 2ms	904, 1269 prep, art, n ms		881, 3725 do, art, n ms
וְלָעֶרֶב	אֶת־זַרְעֶךָ	זְרַע	בַּבֹּקֶר	**6.**	אֶת־הַכֹּל
welā'erev	'eth-zar'ekhā	zera'	babbōqer		'eth-hakkōl
and toward the evening	your seed	sow	in the morning		everything

2172 dem pron	338 intrg	3156.151 v Qal act ptc ms	375 sub, ps 2ms	3706 cj	3135 n fs, ps 2ms	414, 5299.523 adv, v Hiphil juss 2ms
זֶה	אֵי	יוֹדֵעַ	אֵינְךָ	כִּי	יָדֶךָ	אַל־תַּנַּח
zeh	'ê	yôdhē'	'ênekhā	kî	yādhekhā	'al-tannach
this	where	knowing	there is not to you	because	your hand	do not cause to rest

3005 adj	3626, 259 prep, num	524, 8530 cj, cj, num, ps 3mp	173, 2172 intrg, dem pron	1950B, 2172 intrg part, dem pron	3916.121 v Qal impf 3ms
טוֹבִים	כְּאֶחָד	וְאִם־שְׁנֵיהֶם	אוֹ־זֶה	הֲזֶה	יִכְשָׁר
tôvîm	ke'echādh	we'im-shenêhem	'ô-zeh	hăzeh	yikhshār
good	like one	or whether the two of them	or that	will this	it will succeed

5142 cj, adj	214 art, n ms	3005 cj, adj	3937, 6084 prep, art, n fd	3937, 7495.141 prep, v Qal inf con	881, 8507 do, art, n fs		3706 cj
7. וּמָתוֹק	הָאוֹר	וְטוֹב	לָעֵינַיִם	לִרְאוֹת	אֶת־הַשֶּׁמֶשׁ	**8.**	כִּי
ûmāthôq	hā'ôr	wetôv	la'ênayim	lir'ôth	'eth-hashshāmesh		kî
and sweet	the light	and good	to the eyes	to see	the sun		because

4. He that observeth the wind shall not sow: ... whose eye is on, *Moffatt* ... who pays heed to, *NAB* ... who watches, *NASB* ... Those who wait for perfect weather, *NCV*.

and he that regardeth the clouds shall not reap: ... who studies clouds will never reap, *Moffatt* ... who watches, *NAB* ... looks at, *NASB* ... who look at every cloud will never harvest, *NCV*.

5. As thou knowest not what is the way of the spirit: ... how the spirit enters, *Anchor* ... how the spirit comes, *Beck* ... how the wind blows, *Berkeley* ... no more knowledge of the course of the wind, *Fenton*.

nor how the bones do grow in the womb of her that is with child: ... the body grows in a pregnant womb, *Beck* ... how the embryo develops in the womb of a pregnant woman, *Berkeley* ... the growth of the bones in the body of, *BB* ... the bones of the embryo in the belly of the pregnant, *Fenton*.

even so thou knowest not the works of God who maketh all: ... how God works in everything he does, *Anchor* ... God's work who makes everything, *Beck* ... have no knowledge of, *BB* ... know not the action of GOD, who produces everything!, *Fenton*.

6. In the morning sow thy seed, and in the evening withhold not thine hand: ... until evening, do not cease from labour, *JB* ... let evening find thee still at work, *Knox* ... stay not your hand till evening, *Moffatt*.

for thou knowest not whether shall prosper, either this or that: ... which will succeed, *JB* ... which sowing shall speed better, *Knox* ... what shall be blessed, *KJVII* ... if this or that shall prosper, *Moffatt*.

or whether they both shall be alike good: ... which of the two is the better, *JB* ... whether both shall thrive to thy profit, *Knox* ... be fruitful in the same way, *KJVII* ... shall have success, *Moffatt*.

7. Truly the light is sweet: ... Sweet is the light of life, *Moffatt* ... Sunshine is sweet, *NCV* ... light of day is sweet, *REB*.

and a pleasant thing it is for the eyes to behold the sun: ... it is good for the eyes to see, *NASB* ... it is good

---

by my prayers and good service? The power to do good flows from the willingness to do it. The very breathing of the heart is the principle of love. Let me not wait for the call of importunity, but hasten at once into the sphere of practical work. Splendid services are not always required, but acts of kindness to the weakest and meanest of his people, worked out in the true spirit of love to himself (Matt. 25:40).

11:4. Solomon still seems to have in his eye the dispensing of charity. And he is led to remark how trifling hindrances damp its glow and restrain its exercise. The man who is constantly observing the wind and thinking how every gust will blow away his seed will never sow. Nor will he, who in feebleness of purpose regards the clouds, ever reap. Just so, little objections of doubt as to the fitness of objects, under the feigned name of prudence, occupy the mind, and the season of opportunity passes away.

This expressive figure describes a large class of Christian professors of the same "doubtful mind" (Luke 12:29) forming presences against the present season of doing good and putting off duty to a more fitting time. This is the man who would not sow in wind or rain, lest his seed should be blown away, and his harvest lost. Whereas by yielding to present discouragements, he never does his business to good purpose and really loses his harvest. "The sluggard will not plow by reason of the cold; therefore will he beg in harvest, and have nothing" (Prov. 20:4). Mark the present call to duty: the opportunity of good is put into our hands now, and we should not let future contingencies frame an excuse for delay of service.

11:5. Another humbling and valuable recollection of human ignorance! Man prides himself upon what he knows, or fancies he knows. Much more reason has he to be humbled for the far wider extent of his ignorance. He does not see the harvest from the distribution of his charity. But his ignorance does not disprove the fact. How little does he know of the things before his eyes! How ignorant are we of our own being! So "fearfully and wonderfully made!" so "curiously wrought!" (Ps. 139:12ff).

If, then, we cannot know Him in his ordinary works of nature, in his works near home, much less can we know the works of God, who makes all. Truly he "doeth great things and unsearchable; marvelous things without number" (Job 5:9).

And ought not this sense of ignorance to furnish a convincing reply to many things that are called objections to revelation? We should indeed be prepared to expect difficulties, nor should we forget our own nature, by insisting upon a view of things to our beclouded reason wholly free from difficulty. If we do not have complete evidence according to our measure, should we not be thankful for any measure that may be vouchsafed instead of rejecting the guidance of the lesser light, because it was not the sun itself? Knowledge of God's works is valuable, just so far as it is connected with a sense of our own ignorance, and an earnest application for divine teaching and practical obedience.

11:6. The seed sown upon the prepared soil promises a rich harvest: "Sow to yourselves," says Hosea, "in righteousness; reap in mercy" (Hos. 10:12). The morning and evening work mark the diligence—"instant in season, out of season" (2 Tim. 4:2). The active exercise of charity seems to be the lesson primarily inculcated. The uncertainty as to particular results instead of bringing doubts and difficulties, quickens to diligence. The morning and evening imply also the continuousness of the exercise. Charity is too often a fitful impulse, rather than the daily habit. It must not be confined to alms giving, which is the mere external work.

11:7–8. Solomon, drawing to the close of his discourse, brings us nearer to eternity and presses

524, 8523	7528.542	2513.121	119	904, 3725	7975.121
cj, n fp	v Hiphil inf abs	v Qal impf 3ms	art, n ms	prep, adj, ps 3mp	v Qal juss 3ms
אִם־שָׁנִים	הַרְבֵּה	יִחְיֶה	הָאָדָם	בְּכֻלָּם	יִשְׂמָח
'im-shānîm	harbēh	yichăyeh	hā'ādhām	bekhullām	yismach
if years	making abundant	he will live	the man	during all of them	may he be glad

2226.121	881, 3219	2932	3706, 7528.542	2030.126
cj, v Qal juss 3ms	do, n mp	art, n ms	cj, v Hiphil inf abs	v Qal impf 3mp
וְיִזְכֹּר	אֶת־יְמֵי	הַחֹשֶׁךְ	כִּי־הַרְבֵּה	יִהְיוּ
weyizkōr	'eth-yemê	hachōshekh	kî-harbēh	yihyû
and may he remember	the days of	the darkness	because causing to be abundant	they will be

3725, 8054, 971.111	1961	**9.** 7975.131	1005	904, 1006
adj, rel part, v Qal pf 3ms	n ms	v Qal impv 2ms	n ms	prep, n fp, ps 2ms
כָּל־שֶׁבָּא	הֶבֶל	שְׂמַח	בָּחוּר	בְּיַלְדוּתֶיךָ
kol-shebbā'	hāvel	semach	bāchûr	beyaldhûthêkha
all that it will come	a vanity	be glad	O young man	during your youth

3296.521	3949	904, 3219	904, 1006	2050.331
cj, v Hiphil juss 3ms, ps 2ms	n ms, ps 2ms	prep, n mp	n fp, ps 2ms	cj, v Piel impv 2ms
וִיטִיבְךָ	לִבְּךָ	בִּימֵי	בְּחוּרוֹתֶךָ	וְהַלֵּךְ
wîtîvekha	libbekha	bîmê	vechûrôthekha	wehallēkh
and may it please you	your heart	in the days of	your youth	and walk incessantly

904, 1932	3949	904, 4920	6084	3156.131	3706
prep, n mp	n ms, ps 2ms	cj, prep, n mp	n fd, ps 2ms	cj, v Qal impv 2ms	cj
בְּדַרְכֵי	לִבְּךָ	וּבְמַרְאֵי	עֵינֶיךָ	וְדַע	כִּי
bedharkê	libbekha	ûvemar'ê	'ênêkha	wedhā'	kî
in the ways of	your heart	and in the sight of	your eyes	and know	that

6142, 3725, 431	971.521	435	904, 5122	**10.** 5681.531
prep, adj, dem pron	v Hiphil impf 3ms, ps 2ms	art, n mp	prep, art, n ms	cj, v Hiphil impv 2ms
עַל־כָּל־אֵלֶּה	יְבִיאֲךָ	הָאֱלֹהִים	בַּמִּשְׁפָּט	וְהָסֵר
'al-kol-'ēlleh	yevî'ăkha	hā'ĕlōhîm	bammishpāṭ	wehāsēr
concerning all these	He will bring you	God	into the judgment	and remove

3833	4623, 3949	5882.531	7750	4623, 1340	3706, 3317
n ms	prep, n ms, ps 2ms	cj, v Hiphil impv 2ms	n fs	prep, n ms, ps 2ms	cj, art, n fs
כַּעַס	מִלִּבֶּךָ	וְהַעֲבֵר	רָעָה	מִבְּשָׂרֶךָ	כִּי־הַיַּלְדוּת
ka'as	millibbekha	weha'ăvēr	rā'āh	mibbesārekha	kî-hayyaldhûth
vexation	from your heart	and cause to pass on	evil	from your body	because the youth

8267	1961	**12:1** 2226.131	881, 1282.152	904, 3219
cj, art, n fs	n ms	cj, v Qal impv 2ms	do, v Qal act ptc mp, ps 2ms	prep, n mp
וְהַשַּׁחֲרוּת	הֶבֶל	וּזְכֹר	אֶת־בּוֹרְאֶיךָ	בִּימֵי
wehashshachărûth	hāvel	ûzăkhōr	'eth-bôr'ekha	bîmê
and the dawn of life	a vanity	and remember	your Creator	in the days of

---

to see the light of day, *NCV* … it pleases the eyes to see the sun, *NIV*.

8. But if a man live many years, and rejoice in them all: … let him be happy in them all, *Anchor* … he should enjoy all of them, *Beck* … and he has joy in all his years, *BB* … People ought to enjoy every day of their lives, *NCV*.

yet let him remember the days of darkness; for they shall be many: … remembering that the days of darkness will be many, *Anchor* … there will be many dark days, *Beck* … keep in mind the dark days, because they will be great in number, *BB* … remember this: You will be dead a long time, *NCV*.

All that cometh is vanity: … what lies ahead is oblivion, *Anchor* … is nothingness, *Berkeley* … is to no purpose, *BB* … futility awaits you, *JB*.

9. Rejoice, O young man, in thy youth: … Be happy, young man, while you are young, *Anchor* … Enjoy yourself, *Beck* … Take pleasure, *Berkeley* … Have joy, *BB*.

and let thy heart cheer thee in the days of thy youth: ... revel in the days of your vigor, *Anchor* ... while you're still young and vigorous, *Beck* ... let your heart be glad in the days of your strength, *BB* ... let your mind be glad in the days of your vigor, *Goodspeed*.

and walk in the ways of thine heart: ... go where your thoughts incline you, *Anchor* ... follow the prompting and desire of, *JB* ... follow where thought leads, *Knox* ... follow your heart's desire, *Moffatt*.

and in the sight of thine eyes: ... do what your eyes fancy, *Anchor* ... in the desire of your eyes, *BB* ... all that attracts you, *Moffatt* ... whatever you want to do, *NCV*.

but know thou, that for all these things God will bring thee into judgment: ... call you to account, *Anchor* ... make you give an account, *Beck* ... be your judge, *BB* ... judge you for everything you do, *NCV*.

10. Therefore remove sorrow from thy heart: ... Ward off grief, *NAB* ... remove vexation from, *NASB* ...

Don't worry, *NCV* ... Banish discontent, *NEB*.

and put away evil from thy flesh: ... trouble from your presence, *NAB* ... pain from your body, *NASB* ... forget the troubles, *NCV* ... shake off the troubles of the body, *NEB*.

for childhood and youth are vanity: ... dawn of youth is fleeting, *NAB* ... prime of life are fleeting, *NASB* ... useless, *NCV* ... mere emptiness, *NEB*.

12:1. Remember now thy Creator in the days of thy youth: ... Think

---

closely the matter of preparation for it. Present comfort is indeed admitted, "Truly light is sweet: and a pleasant thing it is to the eyes to behold the sun." His rising is the most magnificent spectacle in the creation. Thus to enjoy the light of the sun, our present earthly comfort, is sweet to those whose hearts center in earth, how much more to those, who by Solomon's rules have obtained wisdom to be delivered from the vanity and vexation so deeply connected with the best of this world's blessings.

While the sun shines upon the earthly horizon, the evil days are put to a distance. We can scarcely admit the possibility of a change of scene. We exclude the prospect of dark days as an unwelcome intruder. The young revel in their pleasure as if it would never end. But oh! the folly, the presumption of creatures born for an eternal existence, and to whom the present life is but the preparation time for a never-ending one, and to whom death is but the door of eternity, so willfully shutting their eyes to this near approach—determining to live for this life only, and to let eternity take its chance!

But whatever be the sweetness of the present prosperity—though we live many years, and, comparatively speaking, rejoice in them all—yet remember what is beyond! To the man of God, indeed, all is light, whatever his outward days may be. But the case here supposed, at least mainly so, is one who finds all his good things here, and looks for nothing beyond, who has never put forth one hearty effort upon his soul's salvation. Days of darkness, at least towards the close of life, must be calculated upon.

11:9–10. It is not natural for the young man to think of the many days of darkness. There is indeed a becoming grace in the liveliness of youth, and

most readily would we show him all the over-flowing pleasures, which the Bible fully allows and which the last judgment will not condemn. And, indeed, we cannot doubt, but the exhortation to joy and cheerfulness would be most cordially welcome, if Solomon's meaning did not speak too clearly in the opposite direction, giving an apparent license, only to ground upon it a most solemn admonition.

Obviously, therefore, the wise man is referring to excessive indulgence. The pleasures of sin, not of godliness, are described by the walk after the way of our heart and the sight of our eyes.

If, then, unlawful gratification be the subject, the exhortation to rejoice and be cheerful in it cannot be intended—but emphatically the very contrary. It is in truth the language, not unusual in Scripture, of deep, solemn, cutting irony.

While, indeed, man "turned every one to his own way" (Isa. 53:6), the honey of indulgence passes away, but the sting remains behind. Whether it be physical or intellectual happiness, if it be sought as an end, there must be vanity. The unwelcome thought forces itself, notwithstanding all the smothering of conviction. There is judgment to come. For all these things, for all the sins and vanities of your youth that are now so grateful to our senses.

What, then, is the present way of escape? Separate yourself from sin, ere sin bind you to hell. Remove sorrow and evil from you. They are both linked together. Evil brings sorrow both to body and soul. Let there be an instant tearing away from besetting indulgences.

12:1. This earnest and affectionate exhortation continues the preceding chapter. Solomon had

Row 1

5236.516	7750	3219	3940, 971.126	866	5912	1006
cj, v Hiphil pf 3cp	art, n fs	n mp	neg part, v Qal impf 3mp	rel part	adv	n fp, ps 2ms
וְהִגִּיעוּ	הָרָעָה	יְמֵי	לֹא־יָבֹאוּ	אֲשֶׁר	עַד	בְּחוּרֹתֶיךָ
wehiggî'û	hārā'āh	yemê	lō-yāvō'û	'āsher	'adh	bechûrōthêkhā
and they will come near	the evil	the days of	they do not come	that	until	your youth

Row 2 (2.)

866	5912	2761	904	375, 3937	569.123	866	8523
rel part	adv	n ms	prep, ps 3mp	sub, prep, ps 1cs	v Qal impf 2ms	rel part	n fp
אֲשֶׁר	עַד **2.**	חֵפֶץ	בָּהֶם	אֵין־לִי	תֹּאמַר	אֲשֶׁר	שָׁנִים
'āsher	'adh	chêphets	vāhem	'ên-lî	tō'mar	'āsher	shānîm
that	until	delight	in them	there is not to me	you will say	which	years

Row 3

3676	3507	214	8507	3940, 2931.122
cj, art, n mp	cj, art, n ms	cj, art, n ms	art, n fs	neg part, v Qal impf 3fs
וְהַכּוֹכָבִים	וְהַיָּרֵחַ	וְהָאוֹר	הַשֶּׁמֶשׁ	לֹא־תֶחְשַׁךְ
wehakkôkhāvîm	wehayyārēach	wehā'ôr	hashshemesh	lō-thechăshakh
and the stars	and the moon	and the light	the sun	it does not become dark

Row 4 (3.)

8054, 2194.126	904, 3219	1703	313	5854	8178.116
rel part, v Qal impf 3mp	prep, art, n ms	art, n ms	adv	art, n mp	cj, v Qal pf 3cp
שֶׁיָּזֻעוּ	בַּיּוֹם **3.**	הַגָּשֶׁם	אַחַר	הֶעָבִים	וְשָׁבוּ
shêyāzu'û	bayyôm	haggāshem	'achar	he'āvîm	weshāvû
when they will tremble	on the day	the rain	after	the clouds	and they have returned

Row 5

2524	596	6003.716	1041	8490.152
art, n ms	n mp	v Hithpael pf 3cp	art, n ms	v Qal act ptc mp
הֶחָיִל	אַנְשֵׁי	וְהִתְעַוְּתוּ	הַבַּיִת	שֹׁמְרֵי
hechāyil	'anshê	wehith'awwethû	habbayith	shōmerê
the strength	the men of	and they have become bent over	the household	the watchmen of

Row 6

4745.316	3706	3023.154	1025.116
v Piel pf 3cp	cj	art, v Qal act ptc fp	cj, v Qal pf 3cp
מִעֵטוּ	כִּי	הַטֹּחֲנוֹת	וּבָטְלוּ
mi'ētû	kî	hattōchănôth	ûvātelû
they have been made few	that	the women who grind	and they have ceased

Row 7 (4.)

5646.416	904, 724	7495.154	2931.116
cj, v Pual pf 3cp	prep, art, n fp	art, v Qal act ptc fp	cj, v Qal pf 3cp
וְסֻגְּרוּ **4.**	בָּאֲרֻבּוֹת	הָרֹאוֹת	וְחָשְׁכוּ
wesuggerû	bā'ărubbôth	hārō'ôth	wechāshekhû
and they have been shut	through the windows	the women who look	and they have dimmed

Row 8

7251.121	3024	7249	904, 8584.141	904, 8226	1878
cj, v Qal impf 3ms	art, n fs	n ms	prep, v Qal inf con	prep, art, n ms	n fd
וְיָקוּם	הַטַּחֲנָה	קוֹל	בִּשְׁפַל	בַּשּׁוּק	דְּלָתַיִם
weyāqûm	hattachănāh	qôl	bishphal	bashshûq	dhelāthayim
and someone rises	the grinding	the sound of	when becoming low	on the street	the doors

Row 9 (5.)

1612	8302	3725, 1351	8249.226	7109	3937, 7249
cj	art, n ms	adj, n fp	cj, v Niphal impf 3mp	art, n fs	prep, n ms
גַּם **5.**	הַשִּׁיר	כָּל־בְּנוֹת	וְיִשַּׁחוּ	הַצִּפּוֹר	לְקוֹל
gam	hashshîr	kol-benôth	weyishshachû	hatstsippôr	leqôl
also	the song	all the daughters of	then they are brought low	the bird	at the sound of

Row 10

8614	5525.521	904, 1932	2957	3486.126	4623, 1393
art, n ms	cj, v Hiphil impf 3ms	prep, art, n ms	cj, n mp	v Qal impf 3mp	prep, adj
הַשָּׁקֵד	וְיָנֵאץ	בַּדֶּרֶךְ	וְחַתְחַתִּים	יִרָאוּ	מִגָּבֹהַּ
hashshāqēdh	weyānē'ts	badderekh	wechathchattîm	yirā'û	miggāvōahh
the almond tree	and it will blossom	on the road	and the terrors	they are afraid	from high

of, *Beck* … Be mindful of, *Berkeley* … Let your mind be turned to, *BB* … Do not forget thy Maker, *Knox*.

while the evil days come not: … days of trouble have not come yet, *Anchor* … before the troubling days come, *Berkeley* … Ere sorrow's days come, *Fenton* … before the bad days come, *JB*.

nor the years draw nigh, when thou shalt say, I have no pleasure in them: … catch up with you, *Beck* … and the years are far away when you will say, *BB* … and the years full of grief, *Fenton* … before the years come which, you will say, give you no pleasure, *JB*.

2. While the sun, or the light, or the moon, or the stars, be not darkened: … When you get old, the light from the sun, moon, and stars will grow dark, *NCV* … before the sun and the light of day give place to darkness, before the moon and the stars grow dim, *NEB*.

nor the clouds return after the rain: … and the clouds cumulate after the rain, *Berkeley* … the rain clouds will never seem to go away, *NCV* … and the clouds return with the rain, *NRSV*.

3. In the day when the keepers of the house shall tremble: … the palace guardians will, *Anchor* … guardians of the house will, *Beck* … watchers of the house, *Berkeley* … are shaking for fear, *BB*.

and the strong men shall bow themselves: … powerful men will stoop, *Anchor* … strong men are bent, *Berkeley* … strong men are bent double, *JB*.

and the grinders cease because they are few: … grinding women will cease work because, *Anchor* … the grinders will stop because, *Beck* … women who were crushing the grain are at rest because their number is small, *BB* … women, one by one, quit grinding, *JB*.

and those that look out of the windows be darkened: … they will find it dark who look out from the lattices, *Anchor* … will not see light, *Beck* … are unable to see, *BB* … find their sight growing dim, *JB*.

4. And the doors shall be shut in the streets, when the sound of the grinding is low: … As the sound of the mill becomes, *Anchor* … is subdued, *Darby* … fades away, *JB* … you will barely hear the millstone grinding grain, *NCV*.

and he shall rise up at the voice of the bird: … voice of the birds will be silenced, *Anchor* … will awaken when the birds begin singing, *Beck* … one rises at the voice of a bird, *Berkeley* … the first cry of a bird wakes you up, *JB*.

and all the daughters of music shall be brought low: … all who sing songs will be hushed, *Anchor* … but their melodies will be muffled, *Beck* … all the notes of song sink

warned the young man by emphatic irony against those passions and pleasures to which his slippery age is most addicted. Now for the grand object set before him—your Creator.

This remembrance of God, though our paramount duty, is far from being our nature and habit. Is not forgetfulness of God our course, keeping Him out of mind like the heathen, "not liking to retain God in [our] knowledge?" (Rom. 1:28). Alas! do we not naturally make every effort to shrink from Him? The heart too plainly witnesses to this revolt.

The remembrance of our Creator is in connection with every godly exercise. Does a day ever pass in the willful neglect of the Bible without serious loss? Do we not suffer seriously in our own souls by giving too little time, too little heart, to secret prayer? Wherever God can be found, let us be in the act and energy of seeking him.

12:2. These evil days are yet further described, a mental gloom, as if, like Job, we were going "mourning without the sun" (Job 30:29), or as if the lesser luminaries were eclipsed, as in the Apostle's voyage, "when neither sun, nor stars, in many days appeared; and all hope that we should be saved was taken away" (Acts 27:20). Another

feature of the desolation the clouds not returning after the rain, the end of one trouble, the beginning of another.

Decayed of sense and weakened of physical energy is the general picture of old age. Cheerless indeed it is without religion, earthly comforts withering like the plants in the desert, nothing to supply their place, leaving one world with no hope or joy for another. And is this time of darkness the season to begin the service of God, which asks for man's energy in his best estate?

Let us look then at what resources we have to meet this last stage of life. No sun can dispel the clouds and sorrows of old age, but Christ, Who is the Son of Righteousness. They roll along the stormy sky. Let every intermission of the trouble bring in solemn, active preparation for the last great storm, storing the heart with such remembrance of our Creator, as may be a stay, when all is sinking around us. The presence of the chief good will sweep away threatening evil. The gray head, if found in the way of righteousness, is indeed a crown of glory (Prov. 16:31).

12:3–6. The last verse is a prelude to this elegant and figurative picture of old age. Criticism has

5628.721	2376	6815.522	34	3706, 2050.151
cj, v Hithpael impf 3ms	art, n ms	cj, v Hiphil impf 3fs	art, n fs	cj, v Qal act ptc ms
וְיִסְתַּבֵּל	הֶחָגָב	וְתָפֵר	הָאֲבִיּוֹנָה	כִּי־הֹלֵךְ
weyistabbēl	hechāghāv	wethāphēr	hā'ăvîyōnāh	kî-hōlēkh
and it will stuff itself	the grasshopper	and it is made ineffective	the caperberry	because going

119	420, 1041	5986	5621.116	904, 8226	5792.152
art, n ms	prep, n ms	n ms, ps 3ms	cj, v Qal pf 3cp	prep, art, n ms	art, v Qal act ptc mp
הָאָדָם	אֶל־בֵּית	עוֹלָמוֹ	וְסָבְבוּ	בַּשּׁוּק	הַסֹּפְדִים
hā'ādhām	'el-bêth	'ôlāmô	wesāvevû	vashshûq	hassōphedhîm
the man	to the house of	his eternity	and they will go around	in the street	the lamenters

6.

5912	866	3940, 7651.121	2346	3826B	7827.122	1583	2174
adv	rel part	neg part, v Qal impf 3ms	n ms	art, n ms	cj, v Qal impf 3fs	n fs	art, n ms
עַד	אֲשֶׁר	לֹא־יִרְחַק	חֶבֶל	הַכֶּסֶף	וְתָרֻץ	גֻּלַּת	הַזָּהָב
'adh	'ăsher	lō'-yirchaq	chevel	hakkeseph	wethāruts	gullath	hazzāhāv
until	that	it will not separate	the cord of	the silver	or it is smashed	the bowl of	the gold

8132.222	3656	6142, 4141	7827.211	1574	420, 988
cj, v Niphal impf 3fs	n fs	prep, art, n ms	cj, v Niphal pf 3ms	art, n ms	prep, art, n ms
וְתִשָּׁבֶר	כַּד	עַל־הַמַּבּוּעַ	וְנָרֹץ	הַגַּלְגַּל	אֶל־הַבּוֹר
wethishshāvēr	kadh	'al-hammabbûa'	wenārōts	haggalgal	'el-habbôr
or it is broken	the jar	on the spring	and it is smashed	the wheel	to the cistern

7.

8178.121	6312	6142, 800	3626, 8054, 2030.111	7593	8178.122
cj, v Qal juss 3ms	art, n ms	prep, art, n fs	prep, rel part, v Qal pf 3ms	cj, art, n fs	v Qal impf 3fs
וְיָשֹׁב	הֶעָפָר	עַל־הָאָרֶץ	כְּשֶׁהָיָה	וְהָרוּחַ	תָּשׁוּב
weyāshōv	he'āphār	'al-hā'ārets	keshehāyāh	wehārûach	tāshûv
and may it return	the dust	upon the earth	just as it was	and the spirit	it will return

---

low, *Goodspeed* ... when all the singing has stopped, *JB*.

5. Also when they shall be afraid of that which is high: ... men will grow afraid of a height, *Anchor* ... you will also be afraid of steep places, *Beck* ... going uphill is an ordeal, *JB* ... old age fears a height, *Moffatt*.

and fears shall be in the way: ... terrors will lurk on the road, *Anchor* ... dangers along the road, *Beck* ... you are frightened at every step you take, *JB*.

and the almond tree shall flourish: ... will blossom, *Anchor* ... the tree is white with flower, *BB* ... is in flower, *JB* ... when his hair is almond white, *Moffatt*.

and the grasshopper shall be a burden: ... the locust be weighed down, *Anchor* ... will drag itself along, *Beck* ... the locust is burdensome, *Goodspeed* ... he drags his limbs along, *Moffatt*.

and desire shall fail: ... desire is at an end, *BB* ... the spirit flags and fades, *Moffatt* ... Your appetite will be gone, *NCV* ... desire no longer is stirred, *NIV*.

because man goeth to his long home: ... on the way to his long-lasting home, *Anchor* ... to his everlasting home, *ASV* ... goes to his eternal home, *Berkeley* ... goes to his last resting-place, *BB*.

and the mourners go about the streets: ... gather in the street, *Anchor* ... those who are sorrowing are in, *BB* ... people will go to your funeral, *NCV* ... the wailers shall go round in, *Rotherham*.

6. Or ever the silver cord be loosed: ... be cut, *Anchor* ... is snapped, *Beck* ... is severed, *Berkeley* ... the silver thread snaps, *JB*.

or the golden bowl be broken: ... shattered, *Berkeley* ... is cracked, *JB* ... yonder golden skein unrav-

elled, *Knox* ... golden lamp drops broken, *Moffatt*.

or the pitcher be broken at the fountain: ... shattered at the spring, *Anchor* ... is smashed over the spring, *Beck* ... bucket by the fountain be shivered, *Rotherham*.

or the wheel broken at the cistern: ... the water wheel broken, *Anchor* ... is shattered, *Beck* ... the pulley broken at the well-head, *JB* ... wheel lost in the well, *Knox*.

7. Then shall the dust return to the earth as it was: ... [man's] dust will return to the earth, *Anchor* ... Man goes to the earth that he was, *Fenton* ... You will turn back into the dust of the earth again, *NCV*.

and the spirit shall return unto God who gave it: ... the breath of life will return, *Anchor* ... his Soul will return to, *Fenton* ... the life-breath returns, *Douay*.

wasted much useless ingenuity in its explanation. The more common interpretation, apart from one or two doubtful points, is mainly satisfactory. Solomon had before given a general view. He now enters into particulars, the succession of pains and discomfort, which usually belong to this period of life. Such a picture of infirmity sometimes sinks almost to the level of mere animal existence. Yet upon this feeble stay are often borne the vast concerns of eternity. That which ought to be filling the most vigorous energy of life is delayed to the last stage of an enfeebled habit.

The figure is that of a house hastening to ruin. The keepers of the house evidently represent the hands and arms hanging down in tremulous weakness "in age" (HED #5986), the time when our strength fails. The strong men bowing picture the legs and thighs—before so robust, now beginning to bend under a burden hitherto carried with vigor (Isa. 35:3). In the grinders, we see the teeth performing the millstone work for our food, cutting the meat and breaking it into small pieces. Yet even here, when the grinders are few, the masticating labor makes the meals a daily drudgery. Still more grievous is the trial, when they that look out of the windows are darkened, a very common affliction, when the eyes looking through the socket are dim, so that they cannot see, or see only indistinctly. The doors are shut in the streets. The opening for the mutual communion is barred up—and though unnatural effort may partially open the door, yet it is a poor compensation for the easy-flowing pleasures of younger and brighter days. The door of speech as well as of hearing is shut up. The sound of the grinding is low. The loss of the teeth affects the speech. Early wakefulness is another trial. He rises up at the noise of the bird, not "going forth to his work and to his labor" (Ps. 104:23), but in feeble weariness. All the daughters of music will be brought low. The lungs, the voice, the ear, the organs employed in the production or enjoyment of it will be brought low.

The picture proceeds, parking the feebleness of the feet. They will be afraid of that which is high. Every ascent, which in earlier days they had bounded with youthful elasticity, becomes a trouble. They have lost their enterprise. The fears of stumbling in the way are a matter of apprehension. "The hoary head" is like an almond tree, covered with its snow-white blossoms. So extreme is the feebleness, that, proverbially speaking, the grasshopper, even in its lightest hop, is a burden. Even the desire for the world of pleasure, in which Solomon had attempted to find or to make a center of rest disappears (ch. 2). "The earthly house of tabernacle" is falling to pieces. The inhabitant is on the brink of his long home, and the mourners go about the streets. The Jewish custom of public or hired mourners was probably referred to, a mercenary, because unnatural sorrow, a burden indeed to our secrecies and sympathies.

The imagery of the next verse, beautiful as it is, presents some difficulties in the interpretation. It evidently describes the loosing of the inexplicable bond of union between the body and soul. We have seen the gradual wasting, and now we have come to the final struggle, the extinction of the vital principle. The figure appears to be that of drawing water from the well. Here is the cord (called silver, and the bowl, gold for preciousness), the bowl or bucket, the pitcher and a wheel. As, when these are broken, we can draw water no more; so when the vital parts are decayed, there is no hope to draw life into the cistern of the body. Here then is the moment of death. Then will the dust return.

12:7. Here is the end of our earthly history, all the vessels broken up and man in the stillness of death. The body ultimately returns to its original material: "The Lord God formed man of the dust of the ground" (Gen. 2:7). Poor, mean material! Yet till sin came into the world, resulting in immortality. Sin brought the sentence of death, "Dust you are; and unto dust will you return" (Gen. 3:19). This sentence stands in full force. "You take away their breath, they die, and return to their dust. His breath goes forth; he returns to his earth" (Pss. 104:29; 146:4).

Yet it returns to the earth, not to waste or to be scattered and lost. There will be a reunion, for happiness or for misery, and that for eternity. But the spirit, who can tell what it is, and what is its destiny? God gave it, when he "breathed into his nostrils the breath of life, and man became a living soul" (Gen. 2:7; cp. Job 33:4).

What then is the end of all? Each part of man returns to his original source: his body to the earth as it was, and the spirit to God of whom it is, and who gave it. And where now is the spirit found? In unconscious slumber of the grave? Far from it. It returns to God, its home where it came to "the Father of spirits," Who claims it for himself. The body sleeps as the earnest of awaking again. But the soul is in conscious immortality.

7237	569.111	1961	1961	5598.111	866	420, 435
art, n ms	v Qal pf 3ms	n mp	n ms	v Qal pf 3ms, ps 3fs	rel pron	prep, art, n mp
הַקּוֹהֶלֶת	אָמַר	הֲבָלִים	הֲבֵל	**8.** נְתָנָהּ	אֲשֶׁר	אֶל־הָאֱלֹהִים
haqqôheleth	'āmar	heⱱālîm	heⱱēl	nethānāhh	'ăsher	'el-hā'ĕlōhîm
the preacher	he has said	the vanities	a vanity of	He gave it	Who	to God

5968	2550	7237	8054, 2030.111	3252	1961	3725
adv	n ms	n ms	rel pron, v Qal pf 3ms	cj, n ms	n ms	art, n ms
עוֹד	חָכָם	קֹהֶלֶת	שֶׁהָיָה	וְיֹתֵר **9.**	הֲבֵל	הַכֹּל
'ôdh	chākhām	qōheleth	shehāyāh	weyōthēr	hāⱱel	hakkōl
still	a wise man	the preacher	who he was	and the remainder	a vanity	everything

8963.311	2811.311	237.311	881, 6194	4064.311, 1907
v Piel pf 3ms	cj, v Piel pf 3ms	cj, v Piel pf 3ms	do, art, n ms	v Piel pf 3ms, n fs
תִּקֵּן	וְחִקֵּר	וְאִזֵּן	אֶת־הָעָם	לִמַּד־דָּעַת
tiqqēn	wechiqqēr	we'izzēn	'eth-hā'ām	limmadh-dā'ath
he unraveled	and he completely searched	and he intently listened	the people	he taught knowledge

1745, 2761	3937, 4834.141	7237	1272.311	7528.542	5091
n mp, n ms	prep, v Qal inf con	n ms	v Piel pf 3ms	v Hiphil inf abs	n mp
דִּבְרֵי־חֵפֶץ	לִמְצֹא	קֹהֶלֶת	בִּקֵּשׁ **10.**	הַרְבֵּה	מְשָׁלִים
divrê-chēphets	limtsō'	qōheleth	biqqēsh	harbēh	meshālîm
words of pleasure	to find	the preacher	he sought	making abundant	proverbs

2550	1745	583	1745	3598	3918.155
n mp	n mp	n fs	n mp	n ms	cj, v Qal pass ptc ms
חֲכָמִים	דִּבְרֵי	אֱמֶת **11.**	דִּבְרֵי	יֹשֶׁר	וְכָתוּב
chākhāmîm	divrê	'ĕmeth	divrê	yōsher	wekhāthûv
the wise	the words of	truth	the words of	uprightness	and what was written

5598.216	641	1196	5378.156	3626, 5033	3626, 1921
v Niphal pf 3cp	n fp	n mp	v Qal pass ptc mp	cj, prep, n fp	prep, art, n fp
נִתְּנוּ	אֲסֻפּוֹת	בַּעֲלֵי	נְטוּעִים	וּכְמַשְׂמְרוֹת	כַּדָּרְבֹנוֹת
nittenû	'ăsuppôth	ba'ălê	netû'îm	ûkhemasmerôth	kaddārebōnôth
they were given	a collection	the owners of	having been driven in	and like nails	like the goads

2178.231	1158	4623, 2065	3252	259	4623, 7749.151
v Niphal impv 2ms	n ms, ps 1cs	prep, dem pron	cj, n ms	num	prep, v Qal act ptc ms
הִזָּהֵר	בְּנִי	מֵהֵמָּה	וְיֹתֵר **12.**	אֶחָד	מֵרֹעֶה
hizzāhēr	benî	mēhēmmāh	weyōthēr	'echādh	mērō'eh
be warned	my son	from these	and the remainder	one	from a shepherd

---

8. Vanity of vanities, saith the preacher: ... Futility of futilities, *Berkeley* ... All things are to no purpose, *BB* ... Sheer futility, *JB* ... Everything is useless!, *NCV*.

all is vanity: ... all is futile, *Berkeley* ... is to no purpose, *BB* ... everything is futile, *JB* ... everything is useless, *NCV*.

9. And moreover, because the preacher was wise: ... In addition to becoming a wise man himself, *Anchor* ... Besides being a sage, *JB*

... Abundant wisdom the Spokesman had, *Knox* ... The more wise the Speaker became, *Moffatt*.

he still taught the people knowledge: ... instructed the people in what he had learned, *Anchor* ... taught the people his knowledge, *Beck* ... taught the people what he himself knew, *JB* ... the more he taught the people knowledge, *Moffatt*.

yea, he gave good heed: ... pondering and examining, *Anchor* ... thought it over carefully, *Beck* ...

weighing and searching out, *Berkeley* ... having weighed, *JB* ... very carefully thought about, *NCV*.

and sought out, and set in order many proverbs: ... composition of many wise sayings, *Anchor* ... arranged it in many proverbs, *Beck* ... he made many proverbs, *Berkeley* ... studied and emended many proverbs, *JB*.

10. The preacher sought to find out acceptable words: ... tried to find felicitous language, *Anchor* ...

delightful words, *Beck* ... words which were pleasing, *BB* ... took pains to write in an attractive style, *JB*.

and that which was written was upright, even words of truth: ... honestly to express the truth, *Anchor* ... to write correctly the reliable words of truth, *Berkeley* ... writing was in words upright and true, *BB* ... wrote accurately truthful conclusions, *Fenton*.

11. The words of the wise are as goads: ... like spurs, *Berkeley* ... pointed, *BB* ... discourses of philosophers are like pegs, and stakes, *Fenton*.

and as nails fastened by the masters of assemblies: ... driven home with a mallet, *Anchor* ... driven home like spikes, *Berkeley* ... together are like nails fixed with a hammer, *BB* ... like nails driven with a sledge, *Goodspeed*.

which are given from one shepherd: ... provided by one, *Berkeley* ... by one guide, *BB* ... by one teacher, *Goodspeed* ... all echoing one shepherd's voice, *Knox*.

12. And further, by these, my son, be admonished: ... be warned, *Anchor* ... take note of this, *BB* ... you must realise, *JB* ... avoid anything beyond the scriptures of wisdom, *Moffatt*.

In this sure confidence of waking consciousness did the divine Savior yield his returning spirit into his Father's hands (Luke 23:46). In the same confidence did he receive the spirit of his first martyr falling asleep in Him (Acts 7:59f).

12:8. The Preacher (so he calls himself three times in vv. 8–10) has now concluded his subject. He had begun with this statement as his text (1:2). The whole Book may be considered the material and substance of his sermon, worked out with a large variety of illustrations and proofs. He is now shutting up his discourse, and how can he do it so impressively, as by leaving his text as his last word of demonstration? O what vanity has God written upon all things under the sun! He has made our happiness to depend—not on the uncertain connections of this life, but upon his own most blessed self—a portion that never fails.

12:9. Before the Preacher concludes, he adds a few words concerning himself, calculated to give weight and authority to his sentence. His wisdom was the special gift of God (cf. 1 Ki. 3:5–12), a special talent for his people. Now, therefore, the more wise he was, the more ready was he still to teach the people knowledge. Physical science in all its diversified branches might have formed the matter of his teaching. But this was not his main object. That which attracted the royal stranger's interest was "his wisdom concerning the name of the LORD," the knowledge and service of God. To this he applied himself under divine inspiration with unwearied energy.

12:10. Here was his wisdom—seeking to find out acceptable words! Think of the great moment belonging to them, of the great care to seek and find them out, like the pearls in the ocean. They were not men-pleasing words, not flattering words of vanity.

But let us look to it in our familiar Christian intercourse. Oh! we have great need of unceasing godly exercise. Be sure that the words of truth, not

of man's wisdom, are the weapons for conviction. Do not let Christian accommodation descend to rational contrivance. Zeal for the souls of our fellowmen must be "according to knowledge," holy simplicity and uprightness: not coloring, but truth; not disputing, but leaving upon the conscience the plain testimony. To live near to God while we are walking before men is a divine reality.

12:11. What are these words of the wise? They are no light words. They cannot be the maxims of human wisdom, because—unlike these multifarious tossings—they are given from one Source. They are his words, and they come from Him. They are not partly inspired, and therefore only partly the Word of God. But it is the Shepherd breathing his own mind into the mind of his several penmen, thus preserving the revelation contained therein and bringing out for our repose an unfaltering testimony and an infallible appeal.

Solomon illustrates the power of the words of the wise by goads, so needful to urge on the sluggish oxen in their forward pace, turning neither to the right hand nor to the left. And who of us does not need the goad? Slumbering as we are in cold formality—hearing the word, as if we heard it not—what a mercy is it to feel the piercing point of the goad, experimentally to know the "Scripture as profitable for reproof" (2 Tim. 3:16).

The nails also form the Shepherd's furniture to fasten his tent to the ground, and to make the sheepfold thoroughly secure not less are they needed by us. The smart of the goad is felt, yet it is slight and transient! We want the fastening impression, the nails driven home to the conscience, a steady divine influence fixing our hearts in the ways and service of God.

12:12. One more last word, before the Preacher sums up, addressing the reader as his own son and pouring out to him the yearnings of an affectionate

3990	7377	375	7528.542	5809	6449.141
cj, n ms	n ms	sub	v Hiphil inf abs	n mp	v Qal inf con
וְלָהַג	קֵץ	אֵין	הַרְבֵּה	סְפָרִים	עֲשׂוֹת
welahagh	qēts	'ên	harbēh	sephārîm	'ăsôth
and to studying	a limit	there is not	causing to be abundant	books	the making of

3725	1745	5677	1340	3132	7528.542
art, n ms	n ms	n ms	n ms	n fs	v Hiphil inf abs
הַכֹּל	דָּבָר	סוֹף	בָּשָׂר	יְגִעַת	הַרְבֵּה
hakkōl	dāvār	sôph	bāsār	yeghi'ath	harbēh
everything	the matter	the end of	the body	weariness of	causing to be abundant

13.

8490.131	881, 4851	3486.131	881, 435	8471.211
v Qal impv 2ms	cj, do, n fp, ps 3ms	v Qal impv 2ms	do, art, n mp	v Niphal pf 3ms
שְׁמוֹר	וְאֶת־מִצְוֹתָיו	יְרָא	אֶת־הָאֱלֹהִים	נִשְׁמָע
shemôr	we'eth-mitswôthâv	yerā'	'eth-hā'ĕlōhîm	nishmā'
keep	and his commandments	fear	God	it has been listened to

14.

971.521	435	881, 3725, 4801	3706	3725, 119	3706, 2172
v Hiphil impf 3ms	art, n mp	do, adj, n ms	cj	adj, art, n ms	cj, dem pron
יָבִא	הָאֱלֹהִים	אֶת־כָּל־מַעֲשֶׂה	כִּי	כָּל־הָאָדָם	כִּי־זֶה
yāvi'	hā'ĕlōhîm	'eth-kol-ma'ăseh	kî	kol-hā'ādhām	kî-zeh
He will bring	God	all deeds	because	all of humankind	because this

524, 7737	524, 3005	3725, 6180.255	6142	904, 5122
cj, cj, adj	cj, adj	adj, v Niphal ptc ms	prep	prep, n ms
וְאִם־רָע	אִם־טוֹב	כָּל־נֶעְלָם	עַל	בְּמִשְׁפָּט
we'im-rā'	'im-tôv	kol-ne'ălām	'al	vemishpāt
of whether evil	whether good	all which is hidden	on account of	into judgment

of making many books there is no end: ... book learning is an endless occupation, *Anchor* ... writing books involves endless hard work, *JB* ... there is no end to the buying of books, *Moffatt* ... People are always writing books, *NCV*.

and much study is a weariness of the flesh: ... is exhausting, *Anchor* ... wears you out physically, *Beck* ... from overmuch study nature rebels, *Knox* ... excessive devotion to books is wearying to the body, *NASB*.

13. Let us hear the conclusion of the whole matter: ... To sum up the whole matter, *JB* ... To sum it all up, in conclusion, *Moffatt* ... The last word, when all is heard, *Douay* ... everything has been heard, so I give my final advice, *NCV*.

Fear God, and keep his commandments: ... Reverence God, and observe his laws, *Anchor* ... Stand in awe of God, obey his orders, *Moffatt* ... Honor God and obey, *NCV*.

for this is the whole duty of man: ... this concerns all mankind, *Goodspeed* ... that is the duty of everyone, *JB* ... is the whole meaning of man, *Knox* ... that is everything for every man, *Moffatt*.

14. For God shall bring every work into judgment: ... will judge every deed, *Anchor* ... will call all our deeds to judgement, *JB* ... No act of thine but God will bring it under his scrutiny, *Knox* ... will have every single thing before him, *Moffatt*.

with every secret thing: ... according to its hidden intentions, *Anchor* ... even everything hidden, *Berkeley* ... with regard to everything concealed, *Goodspeed* ... with all its hidden qualities, *NAB, Douay*.

whether it be good, or whether it be evil: ... be it good or bad, *JB* ... and pronounce it good or evil, *Knox* ... to decide whether it is good or evil, *Moffatt*.

---

heart. The mass of books accumulating is the best comment upon this verse. How many of them are utterly worthless! How small a proportion even of what is valuable can he read by one man! How many, written with much labor, are, probably, never read at all!

12:13. Here is the nail, which the great Master and Prophet of his Church would fasten as in a sure place. The Preacher summons us, and summons himself with us, to hear the conclusion of the whole matter. Two short sentences sum up the whole: fear God, and keep his commandments. The sentences are in their right order. The fear of God is the hidden principle of obedience, not of nature's growth. It is the work of the Spirit in the heart of the regenerate. It is the covenant promise, securing the faithfulness of the children of God (Jer. 32:40).

The keeping of the commandments, at least in the case of the disciples of the LORD, primarily regards the great commandment "to believe in the name of his Son Jesus Christ." The gospel, therefore, is not obscured, even when the terms of it are not expressly given, so that, rightly understood, we fully identify the free grace and spiritual obedience of the gospel with the more legal exhortation to fear God, and keep his commandments.

12:14. The Book naturally ends with the winding up of our eventful history, the eternal destiny of every child of man.

How solemn the stamp that it will give to the conclusion of the matter, the blessedness of the fear and service of God! The day will unmask all. All things, now so inexplicable, will be made plain. Solomon had propounded many dark sayings in this Book—many things which he could not comprehend. All these "hidden things of darkness" will be fully brought to light (1 Cor. 4:5), when the LORD, the righteous Judge, will bring every work to judgment, and good and evil will be separated forever.

The brighter displays of the gospel revelation bring the Judge before us in all his glorious and unspeakable majesty. God is the Judge in the person of the divine Mediator (John 5:22; Acts 10:42; 17:31). The Great White throne is raised up. The Judge of the world sits thereon. "Before his face the earth and the heaven flee away, and no place is found for them." The dead, small and great, stand before God. The books are opened; and another book is opened, which is the book of life. The dead are judged out of those things, which are written in the books according to their works (Rev. 20:11f).

Every work will be found there at that day. What a stimulus to self-denying consecration is the thought of the stewardship with which we are invested, the account to be given of it, and the awful guilt of having wasted our LORD's goods in the indolent delusion that they were our own! (Luke 16:1f). Whatever refinement may be mixed with selfish indulgence, it will be found to have carried with it a mass of neglected personal responsibility. The day will declare it, when conviction and repentance will have been too late. Hypocrisy will be disclosed, sincerity will be rewarded, because nothing is hidden from Him. All other things are vain. But it is not vain to fear the LORD: they that do good will have their works follow them to heaven; and they that have done evil will have their works hunt and pursue them to hell.

THE BOOK OF

SONG OF SONGS

Expanded Interlinear
Various Versions
Verse-by-Verse Commentary

THE BOOK OF
SONG OF SONGS שִׁיר הַשִּׁירִים

1:1	8302 n ms שִׁיר shîr the song of	8302 art, n mp הַשִּׁירִים hashshîrîm the songs	866 rel part אֲשֶׁר 'ăsher which	3937, 8406 prep, pn לִשְׁלֹמֹה lishlōmōh of Solomon	**2.**	5583.121 v Qal juss 3ms, ps 1cs יִשָּׁקֵנִי yishshāqēnî may he kiss me	4623, 5573 prep, n fp מִנְּשִׁיקוֹת minneshîqôth of the kisses of

6552 n ms, ps 3ms פִּיהוּ pîhû his mouth	3706, 3005 cj, adj כִּי־טוֹבִים kî-ṭôvîm because better	1782 n mp, ps 2ms דֹּדֶיךָ dōdhêkhā your loving	4623, 3302 prep, n ms מִיָּיִן mîyāyin than wine	**3.**	3937, 7666 prep, n ms לְרֵיחַ lereâch as the scent of	8467 n mp, ps 2ms שְׁמָנֶיךָ shemānêkhā your oils	3005 adj טוֹבִים ṭôvîm good	8467 n ms שֶׁמֶן shemen oil

7671.622 v Hophal impf 3fs תּוּרַק tûraq it will be poured out	8428 n ms, ps 2ms שְׁמֶךָ shemekhā your name	6142, 3772 prep, adv עַל־כֵּן 'al-kēn therefore	6183 n fp עֲלָמוֹת 'ălāmôth the young women	154.116 v Qal pf 3cp, ps 2ms אֲהֵבוּךָ 'ăhēvûkhā they have loved you

1:1. The song of songs, which is Solomon's: ... I will sing the song of all songs, *NEB* ... The Sublime Song of Solomon, *Anchor*.

2. Let him kiss me with the kisses of his mouth: for thy love is better than wine: ... that he may smother me with kisses, *NEB* ... sweeter is your love than wine, *Anchor* ... Wine cannot ravish the senses like that embrace, *Knox*.

3. Because of the savour of thy good ointments thy name is as ointment poured forth, therefore do the virgins love thee: ... Your breath is a charming perfume!, *Fenton* ... fragrant is the scent of your anointing oils, *REB* ... The smell of your perfume is pleasant, *NCV* ... Your name spoken is a spreading perfume—that is why the maidens love you, *Douay* ... Your oils have a pleasing fragrance, Your name is like purified oil, *NASB* ... Turaq oil is your name. Therefore girls love you, *Anchor*.

4. Draw me, we will run after thee: ... Lead me away!, *NKJV* ... Draw me after you, let us make haste, *NRSV* ... Take me away with you— let us hurry!, *NIV* ... Take me to you, and we will go after you, *BB* ... Entice me!—I'll run after you!, *Fenton*.

the king hath brought me into his chambers: ... takes me into his rooms, *NCV* ... inner rooms, *Beck* ... to his home, *Fenton*.

we will be glad and rejoice in thee: ... We rejoice and delight in you, *NIV* ... exult and joy in you, *Anchor* ... are glad and happy for you, *Beck* ... let us thrill with delight, *Moffatt*.

*I*t is safe to say that no other Book in the Bible has aroused more controversy or bewilderment than this amazing production composed by Solomon, the son of David. In ancient times, it was treated with a great deal of diffidence, for it seemed at first to be devoid of theology. It is written as a tale of a torrid love affair between young Solomon and a young lady who some speculate to be from Shunem (cf. 1 Ki. 1:3; 2:22), located near Mt. Gilboa. Her personal name is nowhere spelled out, but she obviously had been raised in a home dominated by brothers who had little consideration for her status as a girl less suited to the rigors of viticulture and sheepherding that would normally be assigned to a teenaged boy. She found herself dark skinned from much labor under a hot sun, much to her regret. Quite naturally, she explained this to her young lover, Prince Solomon, with whom she had attained a warm friendship in their rural setting in Shunem. Apparently, he owned some pastureland adjacent to hers and thus they had become close friends.

Interestingly enough, Song of Songs begins in medias res, as it were, rather than furnishing some sort of introduction such as would normally be expected. Obviously, we have here a vivid memoir of their falling in love and their sheer delight in being with one another in a setting of relative privacy. And yet, the locus of these opening lines sug-

gests that she was sharing this romance with someone in the vicinity of Jerusalem, where there were
other young ladies with whom she shared these rec-
ollections. Their response in v. 4 seems to have been
both cordial and admiring.

But the question arises as to who these "daughters of Jerusalem" might have been as they responded
with interest to her yearning for Solomon's growing
affection. Were they members of a royal harem? What
were they doing in the court grounds of the capital
city? And what point in Solomon's career is indicated
in this remarkable Book? One thing which seems
abundantly clear is that Solomon had no governmental responsibilities as yet. While it is true that he is
referred to as "king" (HED #4567) in 1:4, 12; 3:9, 11
and 7:5, it should be noted that Biblical Hebrew had
no specific term for "crown prince" in the sense of
royal status as heir apparent for the throne. They had
a term for "prince" (namely rō'sh; HED #7513), but
it was used of a tribal head, one who furnished leadership to each of the twelve tribes.

However, nowhere is Solomon spoken of as a
mere prince. Since he was born to David and
Bathsheba, chosen by the decree of God himself as
David's successor and given the special title of
Jedidiah ("Beloved of Yahweh"), there could not be
any doubt as to who would be David's successor, so
far as God was concerned. (Cf. 2 Sam. 12:24f.) The
only title, therefore, which could clearly indicate this
was melekh, "king," in the sense of crown prince.
Naturally enough, the older sons of David, such as
Amnon, Absalom or Adonijah, would have made
every effort to take over David's throne upon his
decease, for they supposed that the principle of pri-
mogeniture should be adhered to in Israel, as was
usual in the ancient Near East (to say nothing of the
practice in the later kingdoms of Europe and
England). But God had decreed otherwise, and in the
final days of David's career, he had to reconfirm
God's choice of Solomon as his successor (cf. 1 Ki.
1:32–50). In this connection, it is well to note that the
appointment of a crown prince was occasionally followed by the later successors of the Davidic dynasty.
A familiar example is Jehoram, who was appointed
number two king by his father, Jehoshaphat. So also
Uzziah, who was appointed the crown prince by King
Jotham (750–731 B.C.); likewise Ahaz was intended
to be the successor to Jotham (744–715 B.C.), even
though he was not the oldest son.

In Solomon's case, at this early stage of his
career, he was obviously not yet particularly involved

in any specific duties of government, even though he
had his headquarters in the Jerusalem area.
Therefore, upon occasion, he would figure promi-
nently in public celebrations and palatial luxury. Yet
it cannot be said that he was preoccupied with mere
entertainment and self-indulgence during his youth,
even though no learned professors or teaching scholars were specifically listed for him. It was by his own
preference that he mastered such an amazing amount
of knowledge during his college or university years.
First Kings 4:29–34 makes it clear that he was the
most amazing polymath in all of recorded history:
"God gave Solomon wisdom and a breadth of understanding as measureless as the sand of the
seashore." First Kings 5:30f states, "And Solomon's
wisdom surpassed the wisdom of all the sons of the
East and all the wisdom of Egypt. For he was wiser
than all men, even than Ethan the Ezrahite, or
Heman or Calcol or Darda, the sons of Manol; and
his fame was known in all the surrounding nations."
It is a fair assumption that Solomon studied all of
their written works, even those which dated back to
times prior to the conquest of Jebusite Jerusalem
before it fell to the bold assault of General Joab and
his "mighty men." Quite possibly, some of this wisdom literature dated back even to the time of
Melchizedek, before the city was occupied by the
Jebusites. But at any rate, it is clear that Solomon
immersed himself in the records and wisdom literature of the Sumerians, the Babylonians and the rich
literature of the Egyptians. Most of these works have
perished in the course of time, but fortunately, a portion at least of the 3000 proverbs referred to in 4:32
found a canonical status in the Book of Proverbs.

But a deep involvement in philosophy and
proverbial literature only whetted Solomon's
appetite for natural science as well. His absorption
with trees and bushes is indicated in 4:33, and in all
likelihood he went on to compose exhaustive reports
of extensive groves and arboretums that flourished
so notably during the periods of generous rainfall
with which Israel was then blessed. After his
achievements in forestry, he directed his attention to
zoology, with particular research in animal life,
including even the various species of birds, along
with the various species of freshwater and saltwater
fish. Presumably, he contributed many volumes for
the royal library in Jerusalem.

1:1–4. The Roman poet Horace commends
Homer's technique in the *Iliad* by which he immediately captured the interest of the reader (or hearer) by

4.

5082.131	313	7608.120	971.511	4567	2410
v Qal impv 2ms, ps 1cs	prep, ps 2ms	v Qal juss 1cp	v Hiphil pf 3ms, ps 1cs	art, n ms	n mp, ps 3ms
מָשְׁכֵנִי	אַחֲרֶיךָ	נָרוּצָה	הֱבִיאַנִי	הַמֶּלֶךְ	חֲדָרָיו
māshekhēnî	'achărêkhā	nārûtsāh	hěvî'anî	hammelekh	chădhārâv
draw me	after you	let us hurry	he has brought me into	the king	his inner rooms

1559.120	7975.120	904	2226.520	1782	4623, 3302
v Qal juss 1cp	cj, v Qal juss 1cp	prep, ps 2fs	v Hiphil juss 1cp	n mp, ps 2ms	prep, n ms
נָגִילָה	וְנִשְׂמְחָה	בָּךְ	נַזְכִּירָה	דֹּדֶיךָ	מִיַּיִן
nāghîlāh	wenismechāh	bākh	nazkîrāh	dhōdhêkhā	mîyayin
let us rejoice	and let us be glad	in you	and let us recall	your love	more than wine

5.

4478	154.116	8265	603	5173	1351	3503
n mp	v Qal pf 3cp, ps 2ms	adj	pers pron	cj, adj	n fp	pn
מֵישָׁרִים	אֲהֵבוּךָ	שְׁחוֹרָה	אֲנִי	וְנָאוָה	בְּנוֹת	יְרוּשָׁלָם
mêshārîm	'ăhēvûkhā	shechôrāh	'ănî	wenā'wāh	benôth	yerûshālām
uprightness	they have loved you	black	I	and beautiful	O daughters of	Jerusalem

6.

3626, 164	7223	3626, 3523	8406	414, 7495.128	8054, 603
prep, n mp	pn	prep, n fp	pn	adv, v Qal juss 2mp, ps 1cs	cj, pers pron
כְּאָהֳלֵי	קֵדָר	כִּירִיעוֹת	שְׁלֹמֹה	אַל־תִּרְאוּנִי	שֶׁאֲנִי
ke'āhelēy	qēdhār	kîrî'ôth	shelōmōh	'al-tir'ûnî	she'ănî
like the tents of	Kedar	like the curtains of	Solomon	do not look at me	because I

8268	8054, 8241.112	8507	1158	525
adj	cj, v Qal pf 3fs, ps 1cs	art, n fs	n mp	n fs, ps 1cs
שְׁחַרְחֹרֶת	שֶׁשְּׁזָפָתְנִי	הַשֶּׁמֶשׁ	בְּנֵי	אִמִּי
shecharchōreth	sheshshezāphathnî	hashshāmesh	benê	'immî
dark complected	because it has tanned me	the sun	the sons of	my mother

5351.316, 904	7947.116	5386.153	881, 3884	3884
v Piel pf 3cp, prep, ps 1cs	v Qal pf 3cp, ps 1cs	v Qal act ptc fs	do, art, n mp	n ms, ps 1cs
נִחֲרוּ־בִי	שָׂמֻנִי	נֹטֵרָה	אֶת־הַכְּרָמִים	כַּרְמִי
nichărû-vî	sāmunî	nōtērāh	'eth-hakkerāmîm	karmî
they were angry with me	they appointed me	a keeper	the vineyards	my vineyard

7.

8054, 3937	3940	5386.115	5222.531	3937	8054, 154.112	5497
rel part, prep, ps 1cs	neg part	v Qal pf 1cs	v Hiphil impv 2ms	prep, ps 1cs	rel pron, v Qal pf 3fs	n fs, ps 1cs
שֶׁלִּי	לֹא	נָטָרְתִּי	הַגִּידָה	לִי	שֶׁאָהֲבָה	נַפְשִׁי
shellî	lō'	nātāretî	haggîdhāh	lî	she'āhevāh	naphshî
which to me	not	I have kept	tell	to me	whom it loves	my soul

353	7749.123	353	7547.523	904, 6937	8054, 4066
intrg	v Qal impf 2ms	intrg	v Hiphil impf 2ms	prep, art, n mp	cj, intrg
אֵיכָה	תִרְעֶה	אֵיכָה	תַּרְבִּיץ	בַּצָּהֳרָיִם	שַׁלָּמָה
'êkhāh	thir'eh	'êkhāh	tarbîts	batstsāherāyim	shallāmāh
where	you will pasture	where	you will cause to lie down	during the noontime	because why

---

we will remember thy love more than wine: the upright love thee: ... We mention thy loves more, *Young* ... mention thy caresses beyond wine, Sincerely they love thee, *Rotherham* ... let us praise your love ... and your caresses more than any song, *NEB*.

5. I am black, but comely, O ye daughters of Jerusalem: ... I am black and beautiful, *NRSV* ... Dark of skin, and yet I have beauty, *Knox*.

as the tents of Kedar, as the curtains of Solomon: ... as the curtains of Salma, *Douay* ... Like the tents of Qedar, Like the pavilions of Salmah, *Anchor* ... Like pavilions of Kedar, Like Solomon's tents, *Fenton* ... like the hangings of Solomon, *Goodspeed*.

6. Look not upon me, because I am black, because the sun hath looked upon me: ... Fear me not, because I am very dark, *Young* ... Look not upon me, because I am swarthy, *ASV* ... Stare not at me that I am swart, *Anchor* ... Do not look askance at me ... the scorching sun has tanned me, *Berkeley* ... Take no note of this Ethiop colour, *Knox*.

my mother's children were angry with me: ... mother's sons were incensed against me, *ASV* ... The sons of my mother were cruel to me, *Fenton* ... my mother's son has burned me, *Goodspeed*.

they made me the keeper of the vineyards; but mine own vineyard have I not kept: ... they sent me to watch over the vineyards; so I did not watch over my own vineyard, *NEB* ... They made me a vineyard guard, *Anchor* ... So my own Vineyard I

never could guard!, *Fenton* ... but I did not look after the vineyard of my charms, *Moffatt*.

7. Tell me, O thou whom my soul loveth, where thou feedest, where thou makest thy flock to rest at noon: ... Where thou delightest, Where thou liest down at noon, *Young* ... Tell me, my true love, where is now thy pasture-ground, where now is thy restingplace under the noon's heat?, *Knox*.

for why should I be as one that turneth aside by the flocks of thy companions?: ... that I may not be left picking lice as I sit among your companions' herds, *REB*, *NEB* ... Why should I look for you near your friend's sheep, like a woman who wears a veil?, *NCV* ... why have I to be as one wandering by the flocks of your friends?, *BB* ... Why should I go wandering alone, With my flock not alongside of yours?, *Fenton*.

---

plunging into the heart of the story, rather than starting the account from its earliest beginnings. The epic begins *in medias res*, the challenge between Achilles and Agememnon after the ten-year siege of Troy has been conducted for a period of years. In a certain sense, this is true of the initial chapter of Song of Songs, which opens the account of the beautiful love affair between the prince and the charming young lady he met on a farm in Shunem. Rather than relating how they first got to know each other, Solomon commences with her first visit to Jerusalem and the splendors of David's palace grounds.

Quite clearly, she had already become completely enamored of the handsome young favorite of the royal family. They had already gotten to the kissing stage in their personal relationship, and she felt almost intoxicated by his heady perfume. She was completely aware of the deep admiration the young ladies of Jerusalem felt toward this brilliant young scion of the royal house, who was not only the most eligible of all of the bachelors in Israel in view of his high standing in the kingdom, but had shown unparalleled scholarship in his mastery of foreign languages and every brand of science (cf. 1 Ki. 4:30–34). No one could compare with him in his breadth of understanding as exhibited in the Book of Proverbs. His readiness to search out the highest possible attainments that money could buy, aided by the finest of experts in the building of the holy Temple and the royal palaces of breath-taking grandeur—these he was free to pursue without distraction of governmental duties such as would devolve upon him at the later stage of his career. King David himself would necessarily be deeply involved in planning for the erection of his great audience hall on Mt. Moriah. He would be directing the living quarters for his harem and for accommodation of his staff employees and various

agents and functionaries involved in diplomatic service. He would have been deeply involved in the procurement of cedars of Lebanon and other materials required for the holy Temple which his son would erect after his father's decease.

As for the Shulammite maiden herself, now deeply in love with her peerless lover, she could think of nothing else but the joy of his loving embrace and the thrill of his costly perfume: "Take me away with you," she urged, after she had seen the luxury of his palace. He happily obliged her and showed her the full display of his living quarters.

1:5–7. But if it was privacy she longed for, this was hardly possible in the presence of the Jerusalem singers who were flocking around them. From the standpoint of the Shulammite, it would be far more appropriate to leave the Jerusalem scene and return to the setting scene where they had first fallen in love with each other. In Shunem, they could center their attention wholly on each other, without the distraction of Jerusalem onlookers. She felt it was time to slip away from public view and renew the joy of being alone together with their flocks up north. There she will not have to cover her face with a veil, as would be expected in the suburban scene. (Verse 7 uses a homonym of the verb 'āṭāh [HED #6057], the homonym of another verb which means "make a sudden dash." The German Bible renders it *herumlaufen* or "run around"; but Gesenius-Buhl translates it as *verhullen*, "cover or veil over.") The NIV renders it: "Why should I be like a veiled woman." Quite naturally, the Shulammite would have preferred to enjoy the informality of her father's farm, where the two lovers could dress as they pleased. Solomon gladly concurred with her suggestion to slip away from Jerusalem and care for their young goats and livestock, who first brought them together in love.

8.

2030.125	3626, 6057.153	6142	5953	2358	524, 3940	3156.124
v Qal impf 1cs	prep, v Qal act ptc fs	prep	n mp	n mp, ps 2ms	cj, neg part	v Qal impf 2fs
אֶהְיֶה	כְּעֹטְיָה	עַל	עֶדְרֵי	חֲבֵרֶיךָ	אִם־לֹא	תֵּדְעִי
'ehyeh	ke'ōṭeyāh	'al	'edhrêy	chăvērêkhā	'im-lō'	thēdhe'î
will I be	like wrapping	beside	the flocks of	your companions	if not	you know

3937	3413	904, 5571	3428.132, 3937	904, 6357
prep, ps 2fs	art, adj	prep, art, n fp	v Qal impv 2fs, prep, ps 2fs	prep, n mp
לָךְ	הַיָּפָה	בַּנָּשִׁים	צְאִי־לָךְ	בְּעִקְבֵי
lākh	hayyāphāh	bannāshîm	tse'î-lākh	be'iqŏvêy
to you	O beautiful one	among the women	go out for yourself	in the hoofprints of

6887	7749.132	881, 1459	6142	5088	7749.152
art, n fs	cj, v Qal impv 2fs	do, n fp, ps 2fs	prep	n mp	art, v Qal act ptc mp
הַצֹּאן	וּרְעִי	אֶת־גְּדִיֹּתַיִךְ	עַל	מִשְׁכְּנוֹת	הָרֹעִים
hatstsō'n	ûre'î	'eth-gedhîyōthayikh	'al	mishkenôth	hārō'îm
the flocks	and pasture	your young goats	beside	the dwelling places of	the shepherds

9.

3937, 5671	904, 7681	6799	1880.315	7761
prep, n fs, ps 1cs	prep, n mp	pn	v Piel pf 1cs, ps 2fs	n fs, ps 1cs
לְסֻסָתִי	בְּרִכְבֵי	פַּרְעֹה	דִּמִּיתִיךְ	רַעְיָתִי
lesusāthî	berikhvê	phar'ōh	dimmîthîkh	ra'ăyāthî
to my mare	with the chariots of	Pharaoh	I have compared you	my woman friend

10.

5171.116	4029	904, 8781	6939	904, 2838
v Qal pf 3cp	n mp, ps 2fs	prep, art, n mp	n ms, ps 2fs	prep, art, n mp
נָאווּ	לְחָיַיִךְ	בַּתֹּרִים	צַוָּארֵךְ	בַּחֲרוּזִים
nā'wû	lechāyayikh	battōrîm	tsawwā'rēkh	bachărûzîm
they are lovely	your cheeks	with the ornaments	your neck	with the necklaces

11.

8781	2174	6449.120, 3937	6196	5534	3826B
n mp	n ms	v Qal impf 1cp, prep, ps 2fs	prep	n fp	art, n ms
תּוֹרֵי	זָהָב	נַעֲשֶׂה־לָּךְ	עִם	נְקֻדּוֹת	הַכָּסֶף
tôrēy	zāhāv	na'ăseh-lākh	'im	nequddôth	hakkāseph
ornaments of	gold	we will make for you	with	beads of	the silver

12.

5912, 8054, 4567
adv, rel part, art, n ms
עַד־שֶׁהַמֶּלֶךְ
'adh-shehammelekh
when that the king

904, 4672	5556	5598.111	7666	7154	4915	1782
prep, adv, ps 3ms	n ms, ps 1cs	v Qal pf 3ms	n ms, ps 3ms	n ms	art, n ms	n ms, ps 1cs
בִּמְסִבּוֹ	נִרְדִּי	נָתַן	רֵיחוֹ	צְרוֹר	הַמֹּר	דּוֹדִי
bimsibbô	nirdî	nāthan	rêchô	tserôr	hammōr	dôdhî
on all around him	my spikenard	it has given	its fragrance	a bag of	the myrrh	my beloved

13. (with "a bag of")

14.

3937	1033	8157	4053.121	838	3852	1782
prep, ps 1cs	prep	n md, ps 1cs	v Qal impf 3ms	n ms	art, n ms	n ms, ps 1cs
לִי	בֵּין	שָׁדַי	יָלִין	אֶשְׁכֹּל	הַכֹּפֶר	דּוֹדִי
lî	bên	shādhay	yālîn	'eshkōl	hakkōpher	dôdhî
to me	between	my breasts	he will spend the night	a cluster of	the henna	my beloved

15.

3937	904, 3884	6086	6086	2079	3413	7761	2079
prep, ps 1cs	prep, n mp	pn	pn	intrj, ps 2fs	adj	n fs, ps 1cs	intrj, ps 2fs
לִי	בְּכַרְמֵי	עֵין	גֶּדִי	הִנָּךְ	יָפָה	רַעְיָתִי	הִנָּךְ
lî	bekharmê	'ên	gedhî	hinnākh	yāphāh	ra'ăyāthî	hinnākh
to me	in the vineyards of	En	Gedi	behold you	beautiful	my beloved	behold you

16.

3413	6084	3225	2079	3413	1782	652	5456	652, 6446
adj	n fd, ps 2fs	n fp	intrj, ps 2ms	adj	n ms, ps 1cs	cj	adj	cj, n fs, ps 1cp
יָפָה	עֵינַיִךְ	יוֹנִים	הִנְּךָ	יָפֶה	דּוֹדִי	אַף	נָעִים	אַף־עַרְשֵׂנוּ
yāphāh	'ênayikh	yônîm	hinnekhā	yāpheh	dhōdhî	'aph	nā'îm	'aph-'arsēnû
beautiful	your eyes	doves	behold you	beautiful	my beloved	truly	pleasant	truly our couch

8. If thou know not, O thou fairest among women, go thy way forth by the footsteps of the flock, and feed thy kids beside the shepherds' tents: ... If you do not know, O most beautiful among women, follow the tracks of the flock and pasture the young ones near the shepherds' camps, *Douay* ... Follow the sheep tracks, And graze your kids Close to, *Anchor* ... And pasture thy kids by the huts of, *Rotherham* ... beside the shepherds' booths, *Darby*.

9. I have compared thee, O my love, to a company of horses in Pharaoh's chariots: ... To my joyous one in chariots of Pharaoh, I have compared thee, my friend, *Young* ... My darling, you are like a mare among the king's stallions, *NCV* ... compared you, my love, To my filly among, *NKJV* ... To a steed, *ASV* ... My dear, I think you're like a mare harnessed to, *Beck*.

10. Thy cheeks are comely with rows of jewels, thy neck with chains of gold: ... Your cheeks are lovely between plaited tresses, your neck with its jewelled chains, *NEB* ... cheeks are beautiful with earrings, *NIV* ... made charming with ringlets, With corals your neck!, *Fenton* ... lovely in pendants, your neck in jewels, *Douay* ... Soft as doves are thy cheeks, thy neck smooth as coral, *Knox* ... Your cheeks adorned with bangles, Your neck with beads, *Anchor*.

11. We will make thee borders of gold with studs of silver: ... We will make you braided plaits of gold set with beads of silver, *NEB* ... gold earrings with silver hooks, *NCV* ... Garlands of gold we do make for thee, *Young* ... I will make for you girdles of gold, With silver for clasps!, *Fenton*.

12. While the king sitteth at his table: ... the king is seated, *BB* ... By the time the king is in his circle, *Rotherham* ... While the king was on his couch, *NRSV*.

my spikenard sendeth forth the smell thereof: ... The smell of my perfume spreads out to the king on his couch, *NC* ... my spices send out their perfume, *BB* ... his nard gave forth its fragrance, *Goodspeed*.

13. A bundle of myrrh is my wellbeloved unto me; he shall lie all night betwixt my breasts: ... My lover is for me a sachet of myrrh to rest in my bosom, *Douay, NAB* ... Between my breasts he lodges, *Anchor* ... He shall pass the night between my breasts, *Darby*.

14. My beloved is unto me as a cluster of camphire in the vineyards of En-gedi: ... is for me a spray of henna blossom, *REB* ... a cluster of henna-flowers, *ASV* ... A cluster of cypress is my love to me, *Anchor* ... My dove, you're a cluster of roses, In En-gedi's gardens!, *Fenton*.

15. Behold, thou art fair, my love; behold, thou art fair; thou hast doves' eyes: ... Oh, you are beautiful, my love, so beautiful!, *Beck* ... how fair with dove-like eyes!, *Moffatt* ... Thine eyes are as doves, *ASV*.

16. Behold, thou art fair, my beloved, yea, pleasant: ... How beautiful you are, my love, and how handsome!, *REB* ... How handsome you are, my lover! Oh, how charming!, *NIV* ... and how you delight me!, *JB*.

also our bed is green: ... bed is the grass, *NCV* ... Yea! our couch is covered with leaves, *Rotherham* ... shaded with branches, *NEB* ... Our couch, too, is verdant, *Douay* ... leafy couch is luxuriant, *Berkeley* ... is fresh, *Beck*.

17. The beams of our house are cedar, and our rafters of fir: ... Our bower's beams are cedars, Our rafters cypresses, *Anchor* ... fir-tree boughs, And the Cypress our screen!, *Fenton* ... rafters are pine, *NRSV*.

1:8–11. To this the young prince agreed, encouraging her to enjoy the delightful setting of the grape fields and flocks with which their romance began. He eloquently renewed his deep admiration, acclaiming her as his own beautiful treasure, whom he would adore in the privacy of fields of Shunem. He ardently acclaimed her as his precious treasure, far beyond the artificial adornments worn by the stylish city girls of Jerusalem. He found her a paragon of true beauty and charm entirely apart from the ostentatious adornments of silver and gold. Such jewelry would come along in time, of course, but what captivated her royal lover was her natural loveliness and spontaneous affection.

1:12–17. The remainder of the chapter portrays a delightful private luncheon at which the young prince poured out his admiration for her without stint, comparing her to the fragrance of the henna blossoms of the vineyards of En-Gedi by the Dead Sea. Here he alludes to himself as melekh (HED #4567), or "king," but in view of his complete freedom of governmental responsibility, the term here should be understood merely as "crown prince." Yet he cast himself before her as his adored fiancee, who enchanted him with her peerless beauty and charm: "Your eyes are like doves," he tells her. And she, for her part, poured out her unbounded admiration for his handsome perfection and irresistible charm. The fragrance of the cedar

17.

2352	603	2:1	1294	7633	753	1041	7264	17.	7776
n fs	pers pron		n mp	n ms, ps 1cp	n mp	n mp, ps 1cp	n fp		adj
חֲבַצֶּלֶת	אֲנִי		בְּרוֹתִים	רַחִיטֵנוּ	אֲרָזִים	בָּתֵּינוּ	קֹרוֹת		רַעֲנָנָה
chăvatstseleth	'ănî		berôthîm	rachîtênû	'ărāzîm	bāttênû	qôrôth		ra'ănānāh
a crocus of	I		cypresses	our rafters	cedars	our houses	the beams of		luxurious

8642	8236	2.	6231	3626, 8236	1033	2431	3772	7761	1033
art, pn	n fs		art, n mp	prep, n fs	prep	art, n mp	adv	n fs, ps 1cs	prep
הַשָּׁרוֹן	שׁוֹשַׁנַּת		הָעֲמָקִים	כְּשׁוֹשַׁנָּה	בֵּין	הַחוֹחִים	כֵּן	רַעְיָתִי	בֵּין
hashshārôn	shôshannath		hā'ămāqîm	keshôshannāh	bên	hachôchîm	kēn	ra'āyāthî	bên
the Sharon	a lily of		the valleys	like a lily	between	the thorns	so	my beloved	between

1351	3.	3626, 8931	904, 6320	3402	3772	1782	1033
art, n fp		prep, n ms	prep, n mp	art, n ms	adv	n ms, ps 1cs	prep
הַבָּנוֹת		כְּתַפּוּחַ	בַּעֲצֵי	הַיַּעַר	כֵּן	דּוֹדִי	בֵּין
habbānôth		kethappûach	ba'ătsê	hayya'ar	kēn	dôdhî	bên
the daughters		like an apple tree	among the trees of	the forest	so	my beloved	between

1158	904, 7009	2629.315	3553.115	6780	5142
art, n mp	prep, n ms, ps 3ms	v Piel pf 1cs	cj, v Qal pf 1cs	cj, n ms, ps 3ms	adj
הַבָּנִים	בְּצִלּוֹ	חִמַּדְתִּי	וְיָשַׁבְתִּי	וּפִרְיוֹ	מָתוֹק
habbānîm	betsillô	chimmadhtî	weyāshavtî	ûphiryô	māthôq
the sons	in his shadow	I have taken pleasure	and I sat	and his fruit	sweet

3937, 2541	4.	971.511	420, 1041	3302	1764	6142	157
prep, n ms, ps 1cs		v Hiphil pf 3ms, ps 1cs	prep, n ms	art, n ms	cj, n ms, ps 3ms	prep, ps 1cs	n fs
לְחִכִּי		הֱבִיאַנִי	אֶל־בֵּית	הַיַּיִן	וְדִגְלוֹ	עָלַי	אַהֲבָה
lechikkî		hĕvî'anî	'el-bêth	hayyāyin	wedhighlô	'ālay	'ahvāh
to my palate		he has brought me	to the house of	the wine	and his banner	over me	love

5.	5759.333	904, 836	7790.333	904, 8931
	v Piel impv 2mp, ps 1cs	prep, art, n fp	v Piel impv 2mp, ps 1cs	prep, art, n mp
	סַמְּכוּנִי	בָּאֲשִׁישׁוֹת	רַפְּדוּנִי	בַּתַּפּוּחִים
	sammekhûnî	bā'ăshîshôth	rappedhûnî	battappûchîm
	provide for me	with the raisin cakes	spread out for me	with the apples

3706, 2571.153	157	603	6.	7972	8809	3937, 7513	3332
cj, v Qal act ptc fs	n fs	pers pron		n ms, ps 3ms	prep	prep, n ms, ps 1cs	cj, n fs, ps 3ms
כִּי־חוֹלַת	אַהֲבָה	אֲנִי		שְׂמֹאלוֹ	תַּחַת	לְרֹאשִׁי	וִימִינוֹ
kî-chôlath	'ahvāh	'ănî		semō'lô	tachath	lerō'shî	wîmînô
because being sick	love	I		his left hand	beneath	my head	and his right hand

2354.322	7.	8123.515	881	1351	3503
v Piel impf 3fs, ps 1cs		v Hiphil pf 1cs	do, ps 2mp	n fp	pn
תְּחַבְּקֵנִי		הִשְׁבַּעְתִּי	אֶתְכֶם	בְּנוֹת	יְרוּשָׁלַם
techabbeqênî		hishba'ättî	'ethkhem	benôth	yerûshālam
it will embrace me		I will cause to swear	you	O daughters of	Jerusalem

904, 6895	173	904, 359	7898	524, 5996.528
prep, n fp	cj	prep, n fp	art, n ms	cj, v Hiphil impf 2mp
בִּצְבָאוֹת	אוֹ	בְּאַיְלוֹת	הַשָּׂדֶה	אִם־תָּעִירוּ
bitsvā'ôth	'ô	be'aylôth	hassādheh	'im-tā'îrû
by the female gazelles	or	by the female deer of	the field	if you will arouse

524, 5996.328	881, 157	5912	8054, 2759.122	8.	7249	1782
cj, cj, v Polel impf 2mp	do, art, n fs	adv	rel part, v Qal impf 3fs		n ms	n ms, ps 1cs
וְאִם־תְּעוֹרְרוּ	אֶת־הָאַהֲבָה	עַד	שֶׁתֶּחְפָּץ		קוֹל	דּוֹדִי
we'im-te'ôrerû	'eth-hā'ahvāh	'adh	shettechăppāts		qôl	dôdhî
or if you will awaken	the love	until	that it desires		the voice of	my beloved

2079, 2172	971.111	1860.351	6142, 2098	7376.351	6142, 1421
intrj, dem pron	v Qal pf 3ms	v Piel ptc ms	prep, art, n mp	v Piel ptc ms	prep, art, n fp
הִנֵּה־זֶה	בָּא	מְדַלֵּג	עַל־הֶהָרִים	מְקַפֵּץ	עַל־הַגְּבָעוֹת
hinnēh-zeh	bā'	mᵉdhallēgh	'al-hehārîm	mᵉqappēts	'al-haggᵉvā'ôth
behold this one	he will come	leaping	on the mountains	jumping	on the hills

9.	1880.151	1782	3937, 6906	173	3937, 6314	358	2079, 2172
	v Qal act ptc ms	n ms, ps 1cs	prep, n ms	cj	prep, n ms	art, n mp	intrj, dem pron
	דּוֹמֶה	דּוֹדִי	לִצְבִי	אוֹ	לְעֹפֶר	הָאַיָּלִים	הִנֵּה־זֶה
	dômeh	dhôdhî	litsvî	'ô	lᵉ'ōpher	hā'ayyālîm	hinnēh-zeh
	being like	my beloved	a gazelle	or	a fawn of	the male deer	behold this one

2:1. I am the rose of Sharon: ... The meadow-saffron of Sharon, *Rotherham* ... I am an asphodel, *NEB* ... in the Plain of Sharon, *NCV* ... flower of Saron, *Douay* ... crocus of the plain, *Anchor* ... narcissus, *Darby*.

and the lily of the valleys: ... a lily growing in, *REB* ... lotus, *Anchor* ... a hyacinth, *Goodspeed*.

2. As the lily among thorns, so is my love among the daughters: ... Like a lotus among brambles, *Anchor* ... Like a hyacinth among thistles, *Goodspeed* ... As the lily-flower among the thorns of the waste, *BB* ... among brambles, so is my love among maidens, *RSV*.

3. As the apple tree among the trees of the wood, so is my beloved among the sons: ... Like an apricot-tree, *NEB* ... As a citron among trees of the forest, *Young* ... is my lover among the young men, *NIV*.

I sat down under his shadow with great delight, and his fruit was sweet to my taste: ... I enjoy sitting in his shadow, *NCV* ... In his shade I delighted, and sat down, *Young* ... In his delightful shade I sit, *JB* ... I delight to rest in his shadow, *NAB*.

4. He brought me to the banqueting house and his banner over me was love: ... Hee brought mee into the wine cellar, *Geneva* ... into the house of wine, *Rotherham* ... taken me into the wine-garden and given me loving glances, *REB* ... his intention toward me was love, *NRSV* ... brought to his bower, And his banner above, *Fenton*.

5. Stay me with flagons: ... Sustain me with raisin-cakes, *Rotherham* ... with raisins, *NRSV* ... grape-cakes, *Young* ... with dainties, *Berkeley* ... Make me strong with wine-cakes, *BB*.

comfort me with apples: ... Brace me with, *Anchor* ... refresh me, *RSV* ... revive me, *REB* ... he revived me with apricots, *NEB*.

for I am sick of love: ... faint with love, *REB, NRSV* ... lovesick, *NKJV* ... overcome with love, *BB* ... I was weak with love, *Beck*.

6. His left hand is under my head, and his right hand doth embrace me: ... His left arm pillows my head, his right arm is round me, *REB* ... right arm holds me tight, *NCV* ... right hand be clasped within mine!, *Fenton*.

7. I charge you, O ye daughters of Jerusalem, by the roes, and by the hinds of the field: ... I make you promise solemnly, *Beck* ... I adjure you, ... by the gazelles, *RSV* ... gazelles or hinds of the steppe, *Anchor*.

that ye stir not up, nor awake my love, till he please: ... wake not nor arouse the dear love until she please!, *Rotherham* ... Do not rouse her, do not disturb my love until she is ready, *NEB* ... not to awaken or excite my feelings of love until it is ready, *NCV* ... neither incite nor excite Love until it is eager, *Anchor*.

8. The voice of my beloved! behold, he cometh leaping upon the mountains, skipping upon the hills: ... Listen! My lover! Look! Here he comes, leaping across the mountains, bounding over the hills, *NIV* ... See, he comes dancing on the mountains, stepping quickly on the hills, *BB*.

9. My beloved is like a roe or a young hart: ... My love resembles a

beams of their trysting place lent a perfect setting for their joyous fellowship.

2:1–7. Oddly enough, the closing lines of ch. 1 merge into a delightful self-appreciation on the part of the bride herself. Thrilled with the ecstatic endearment of her lover, she reveled in his adoration of her without any shade of modest reserve. All alone without any onlookers, she picked up, as it were, the infatuation of her wooer whose boundless adoration of her made her sense the gorgeous color

and ravishing fragrance of the rose garden in which they were resting—completely elated as she was in sensing his unbounded admiration and infatuation for her even as they enjoyed the delicious apples just fallen from the trees whose shade they sought.

2:8–14. Quite abruptly, the scene shifts back to a return to the palace grounds in Jerusalem, where they attended a delightful banquet in company with the rest of the elite at a bountiful feast being served near the palace grounds. Proudly, the prince escorted

Song of Songs 2:10–16

6198.151 v Qal act ptc ms עוֹמֵד 'ômēdh standing	313 prep אַחַר 'achar behind	3926 n ms, ps 1cp כָּתְלֵנוּ kāthelēnû our wall	8148.551 v Hiphil ptc ms מַשְׁגִּיחַ mashgîach gazing	4623, 2574 prep, art, n fp מִן־הַחַלֹּנוֹת min-hachăllōnôth from the windows	6957.551 v Hiphil ptc ms מֵצִיץ mētsîts peering through
4623, 2867 prep, art, n mp מִן־הַחֲרַכִּים min-hachărakkîm from the lattice	**10.** 6257.111 v Qal pf 3ms עָנָה 'ānāh he answered	1782 n ms, ps 1cs דּוֹדִי dhôdhî my beloved	569.111 cj, v Qal pf 3ms וְאָמַר we'āmar and he said	3937 prep, ps 1cs לִי lî to me	7251.132 v Qal impv 2fs קוּמִי qûmî get up
3937 prep, ps 2fs לָךְ lākh for yourself					
7761 n fs, ps 1cs רַעְיָתִי ra'ăyāthî my beloved	3413 adj, ps 1cs יָפָתִי yāphāthî my beautiful	2050.132, 3937 cj, v Qal impv 2fs, prep, ps 2fs וּלְכִי־לָךְ ûlăkhî-lākh and come for yourself	**11.** 3706, 2079 cj, intrj כִּי־הִנֵּה kî-hinnēh because behold	5843 art, n ms הַסְּתָו hassāthāv the winter	
5882.111 v Qal pf 3ms עָבָר 'āvār it has passed on	1703 art, n ms הַגֶּשֶׁם haggeshem the rain	2599.111 v Qal pf 3ms חָלַף chālaph it has passed away	2050.111 v Qal pf 3ms הָלַךְ hālakh it has gone	3937 prep, ps 3ms לוֹ lô for itself	**12.** 5524 art, n mp הַנִּצָּנִים hanitstsānîm the flowers
7495.216 v Niphal pf 3cp נִרְאוּ nir'û they have appeared	904, 800 prep, art, n fs בָּאָרֶץ vā'ārets in the land	6496 n ms עֵת 'ēth the time of	2243 art, n ms הַזָּמִיר hazzāmîr the pruning	5236.511 v Hiphil pf 3ms הִגִּיעַ higgîa' it has caused to arrive	7249 cj, n ms וְקוֹל weqôl and the sound of
8782 art, n fs הַתּוֹר hattôr the turtledove	8471.211 v Niphal pf 3ms נִשְׁמַע nishma' it has been heard	904, 800 prep, n fs, ps 1cp בְּאַרְצֵנוּ be'artsēnû in our land	**13.** 8711 art, n fs הַתְּאֵנָה hatte'ēnāh the fig tree	2691.112 v Qal pf 3fs חָנְטָה chānetāh it has become ripe	
6532 n fp, ps 3fs פַגֶּיהָ phaggêāh it unripened fruit	1655 cj, art, n fp וְהַגְּפָנִים wehaggephānîm and the vines	5758 n ms סְמָדַר semādhar blossom	5598.116 v Qal pf 3cp נָתְנוּ nāthenû they have given	7666 n ms רֵיחַ rêach a fragrance	7251.132 v Qal impv 2fs קוּמִי qûmî get up
2030.132 v Qal impv 2fs לְכִי lekhî come					
7761 n fs, ps 1cs רַעְיָתִי ra'ăyāthî my beloved	3413 adj, ps 1cs יָפָתִי yāphāthî my beautiful	2050.132, 3937 cj, v Qal impv 2fs, prep, ps 2fs וּלְכִי־לָךְ ûlăkhî-lākh and come for yourself	**14.** 3225 n fs, ps 1cs יוֹנָתִי yônāthî O my dove	904, 2380 prep, n mp בְּחַגְוֵי bechaghwê in the clefts of	5748 art, n ms הַסֶּלַע hassela' the rock
904, 5848 prep, n ms בְּסֵתֶר besēther under the cover of	4238 art, n fs הַמַּדְרֵגָה hammadhrēghāh the cavity	7495.532 v Hiphil impv 2fs, ps 1cs הַרְאִינִי har'înî allow me to see	881, 4920 do, n mp, ps 2fs אֶת־מַרְאַיִךְ 'eth-mar'ayikh your appearance	8471.532 v Hiphil impv 2fs, ps 1cs הַשְׁמִיעִינִי hashmî'înî allow me to hear	
881, 7249 do, n ms, ps 2fs אֶת־קוֹלֵךְ 'eth-qôlēkh your voice	3706, 7249 cj, n ms, ps 2fs כִּי־קוֹלֵךְ kî-qôlēkh because your voice	6388 adj עָרֵב 'ārēv pleasant	4920 cj, n mp, ps 2fs וּמַרְאֵיךְ ûmar'êkh and your appearance	5173 adj נָאוֶה nā'weh beautiful	

15.

270.133, 3937	8217	8217	7277	2341.352	3884
v Qal impv 2mp, prep, ps 1cp	n mp	n mp	adj	v Piel ptc mp	n mp
אֶחֱזוּ־לָנוּ	שׁוּעָלִים	שׁוּעָלִים	קְטַנִּים	מְחַבְּלִים	כְּרָמִים
'echĕzû-lānû	shū'ālîm	shū'ālîm	qōṭanîm	mᵉchabbᵉlîm	kᵉrāmîm
catch for us	foxes	foxes	small	ruining	vineyards

16.

3884	5758	1782	3937	603	3937	7749.151
cj, n mp, ps 1cp	n ms	n ms, ps 1cs	prep, ps 1cs	cj, pers pron	prep, ps 3ms	art, v Qal act ptc ms
וּכְרָמֵינוּ	סְמָדַר	דּוֹדִי	לִי	וַאֲנִי	לוֹ	הָרֹעֶה
ûkherāmênû	sᵉmādhar	dôdhî	lî	wa'ănî	lô	hārō'eh
and our vineyards	blossom	my beloved	to me	and I	to him	the shepherd

buck, *Anchor* … My lover is like a gazelle, Or a fawn of the groves!, *Fenton* … or a young stag, *RSV* … or a young wild goat, *NEB*.

behold, he standeth behind our wall, he looketh forth at the windows, showing himself through the lattice: … gazing in at the windows, looking through, *RSV* … Look, he stands … peeking through the windows, looking through the blinds, *NCV* … letting himself be seen through the spaces, *BB* … Look! he is hiding behind our wall, To the window he peeps! Thro' the flowers spread over, *Fenton*.

10. My beloved spake, and said unto me, Rise up, my love, my fair one, and come away: … Get up, my darling; let's go away, my beautiful one, *NCV* … My beloved sings, and he calls to me, *Berkeley* … Let me wander, sweet, with you, *Fenton*.

11. For, lo, the winter is past, the rain is over and gone: … the season of rain, *Berkeley*.

12. The flowers appear on the earth: … Blossoms appear through all the land, *NCV* … in the countryside, *REB* … the time of pruning the vines has come, *Douay*.

the time of the singing of birds is come: … the spring-song, *Rotherham* … the season of birdsong, *REB* … the season of singing has come, *NIV* … the ringdove's note is heard, *Moffatt*.

and the voice of the turtle is heard in our land: … the voice of the dove is sounding, *BB* … the turtledove, *RSV* … and turtle-dove's cooing, *REB*.

13. The fig tree putteth forth her green figs, and the vines with the tender grape give a good smell: … The fig tree forms its early fruit, *NIV* … melloweth her winter figs, *Darby* … the figs are ripening red, *Moffatt* … and the vines are in blossom; they give forth fragrance, *RSV*.

Arise, my love, my fair one, and come away: … Get up from your bed, my beautiful one, and come away, *BB* … Rise up, my darling, *REB*.

14. O my dove, that art in the clefts of the rock: … In the retreats of the crag, *Rotherham* … My beloved is like a dove hiding in the cracks of the rock, *NCV*.

in the secret places of the stairs: … In the covert of the precipice, *Darby* … In the hiding-place of the terrace, *Rotherham* … or in crannies on the terraced hillside, *REB* … in the secret recesses of the cliff, *Douay* … In a precipice hid!, *Fenton*.

let me see thy countenance, let me hear thy voice; for sweet is thy voice, and thy countenance is comely: … let me see your face and hear your voice; for your voice is sweet, your face is lovely, *REB* … Your voice is sweet, and you look lovely, *Beck* … Allow me to listen to your coos, *Fenton*.

15. Take us the foxes, the little foxes, that spoil the vines: for our vines have tender grapes: … Catch the jackals for us, the little jackals, the despoilers of vineyards, for our vineyards are full of blossom, *REB*

his sweetheart to a place of honor. Having just awoken from his nap at the farm, he came running to join her; with great exuberance he aroused her from her rest, and they reveled in the spring beauty of the sunlit glens around them with their beautiful flowers and melodious song of the birds from the branches above them. Already, the fig trees were showing forth their new fruit, and the vineyards were bulging with their fragrant grapes as the lovers went about to inspect them. A beautiful spring had dawned upon them and banished the chill of winter and all its discomforts. What a delightful change they saw and

heard about them as they listened to the chirping birds in the cliffs beside them! But to her admiring lover, she was more lovely to hear and more thrilling to behold than any beauty of nature that confronted them as they traversed the scene before them.

2:15–17. Verse 15 reverts very briefly to the Shulammite's older brothers, who seemed to accompany them as they proceeded through the adjacent fields. They expressed real annoyance at the little foxes who had impaired or consumed the new grapes which were destined for the production of wine. But the only response of the bride herself was

415

904, 8236	17.	5912	8054, 6558.121	3219	5308.116	7020
prep, art, n fp		adv	rel part, v Qal impf 3ms	art, n ms	cj, v Qal pf 3cp	art, n mp
בַּשּׁוֹשַׁנִּים		עַד	שֶׁיָּפוּחַ	הַיּוֹם	וְנָסוּ	הַצְּלָלִים
bashshôshanîm		'adh	shêyāphûach	hayyôm	wenāsû	hatstselālîm
among the lilies		until	that it blows	the day	and they will flee	the shadows

5621.131	1880.131, 3937	1782	3937, 6906	173	3937, 6314	358
v Qal impv 2ms	v Qal impv 2ms, prep, ps 2ms	n ms, ps 1cs	prep, n ms	cj	prep, *n ms*	art, n mp
סֹב	דְּמֵה־לְךָ	דוֹדִי	לִצְבִי	אוֹ	לְעֹפֶר	הָאַיָּלִים
sōv	demēh-lekhā	dhôdhî	litsvî	'ô	le'ōpher	hā'ayyālîm
go around	be like for yourself	O my beloved	a gazelle	or	a fawn of	the male deer

6142, 2098	1366	3:1	6142, 5085	904, 4050	1272.315	881
prep, *n mp*	pn		prep, n ms, ps 1cs	prep, art, n mp	v Piel pf 1cs	do
עַל־הָרֵי	בָתֶר		עַל־מִשְׁכָּבִי	בַּלֵּילוֹת	בִּקַּשְׁתִּי	אֵת
'al-hārê	vāther		'al-mishkāvî	ballêlôth	biqqashtî	'ēth
on the mountains of	Bether		on my bed	during the nights	I sought	

8054, 154.112	5497	1272.315	3940	4834.115	2.	7251.125	5167
rel pron, v Qal pf 3fs	n fs, ps 1cs	v Piel pf 1cs, ps 3ms	cj, neg part	v Qal pf 1cs, ps 3ms		v Qal juss 1cs	part
שֶׁאָהֲבָה	נַפְשִׁי	בִּקַּשְׁתִּיו	וְלֹא	מְצָאתִיו		אָקוּמָה	נָּא
she'āhevāh	naphshî	biqqashtîw	welō'	metsā'thîw		'āqûmāh	nā'
whom it loves	my soul	I sought him	but not	I found him		let me rise up	please

5621.325	904, 6111	904, 8226	904, 7624	1272.325	881
cj, v Poel juss 1cs	prep, art, n fs	prep, art, n mp	cj, prep, art, n fp	v Piel juss 1cs	do
וַאֲסוֹבְבָה	בָעִיר	בַּשְּׁוָקִים	וּבָרְחֹבוֹת	אֲבַקְשָׁה	אֵת
wa'ăsôvevāh	vā'îr	bashshewāqîm	ûvārechōvôth	'ăvaqōshāh	'ēth
and let me go about	in the city	in the streets	and in the squares	let me seek	

8054, 154.112	5497	1272.315	3940	4834.115	3.	4834.116
rel pron, v Qal pf 3fs	n fs, ps 1cs	v Piel pf 1cs, ps 3ms	cj, neg part	v Qal pf 1cs, ps 3ms		v Qal pf 3cp, ps 1cs
שֶׁאָהֲבָה	נַפְשִׁי	בִּקַּשְׁתִּיו	וְלֹא	מְצָאתִיו		מְצָאוּנִי
she'āhevāh	naphshî	biqqashtîw	welō'	metsā'thîw		metsā'ûnî
whom it loves	my soul	I sought him	but not	I found him		they found me

8490.152	5621.152	904, 6111	881	8054, 154.112	5497	7495.117
art, v Qal act ptc mp	art, v Qal act ptc mp	prep, art, n fs	do	rel pron, v Qal pf 3fs	n fs, ps 1cs	v Qal pf 2mp
הַשֹּׁמְרִים	הַסֹּבְבִים	בָּעִיר	אֵת	שֶׁאָהֲבָה	נַפְשִׁי	רְאִיתֶם
hashshōmerîm	hassōvevîm	bā'îr	'ēth	she'āhevāh	naphshî	re'îthem
the watchmen	those going about	in the city		whom it loves	my soul	you have seen

4.	3626, 4746	8054, 5882.115	4623	5912	8054, 4834.115	881	8054, 154.112
	prep, sub	rel part, v Qal pf 1cs	prep, ps 3mp	adv	rel part, v Qal pf 1cs	do	rel pron, v Qal pf 3fs
	כִּמְעַט	שֶׁעָבַרְתִּי	מֵהֶם	עַד	שֶׁמָּצָאתִי	אֵת	שֶׁאָהֲבָה
	kim'at	she'āvartî	mēhem	'adh	shemmātsā'thî	'ēth	she'āhevāh
	like a moment	that I passed on	from them	until	that I found		whom it loves

5497	270.115	3940	7791.525	5912, 971.515
n fs, ps 1cs	v Qal pf 1cs, ps 3ms	cj, neg part	v Hiphil impf 1cs, ps 3ms	adv, rel part, v Hiphil pf 1cs, ps 3ms
נַפְשִׁי	אֲחַזְתִּיו	וְלֹא	אַרְפֶּנּוּ	עַד־שֶׁהֲבֵיאתִיו
naphshî	'ăchaztîw	welō'	'arpennû	'adh-shehvê'thîw
my soul	I held him	and not	I would allow him to desist	until that I brought him

420, 1041	525	420, 2410	2106.153
prep, *n ms*	n fs, ps 1cs	cj, prep, *n ms*	v Qal act ptc fs, ps 1cs
אֶל־בֵּית	אִמִּי	וְאֶל־חֶדֶר	הוֹרָתִי
'el-bêth	'immî	we'el-chedher	hôrāthî
to the house of	my mother	and to the inner room of	she who conceived me

... Let us hunt little foxes together, The bad foxes, who spoil our grapes, *Fenton* ... that make havoc of the vineyards, for our vineyards are in fruit, *JB* ... And our vines are all blossom!, *Rotherham*.

16. My beloved is mine, and I am his: ... My lover belongs to me and I to him, *Douay, NAB*.

he feedeth among the lilies: ... He that pastureth among lilies!, *Rotherham* ... he delights in the, *NEB* ... pastures his flock among, *RSV* ... he takes his food among the flowers, *BB* ... who is pasturing his flock among the hyacinths, *Goodspeed*.

17. Until the day break, and the shadows flee away: ... While the day brings a cooling breeze, *Beck* ... day is cool and the shadows are dispersing, *NEB* ... day dawns and the shadows disappear, *NCV* ... day breathes cool and the shadows lengthen, *Douay* ... Till the evening comes, and the sky slowly becomes dark, *BB*.

turn, my beloved, and be thou like a roe or a young hart upon the mountains of Bether: ... be like a gazelle, or a young stag upon rugged moun-

tains, *RSV* ... Gambol, ... upon the craggy mountains, *Goodspeed* ... and play ... on my perfumed slopes!, *Moffatt* ... on the hills where aromatic spices grow, *REB* ... on the hills where cinnamon grows, *NEB* ... On the mountains of separation!, *Young*.

3:1. By night on my bed I sought him whom my soul loveth: I sought him, but I found him not: ... On my bed I dreamt of him tonight, *Fenton* ... On my couch by night, *Young* ... I sought the man who is my sweetheart, *JB* ... Night after night in bed I dreamed I sought my beloved, and sought him in vain, *Moffatt* ... In the night watches, as I lay abed, I searched for my heart's love, and searched in vain, *Knox* ... I called him, but he did not answer, *Berkeley*.

2. I will rise now, and go about the city in the streets, and in the broad ways I will seek him whom my soul loveth: ... Now to stir abroad, and traverse the city, searching every alley-way and street for him I love so tenderly!, *Knox* ... go the rounds of the city through streets and squares, seeking my true love, *REB* ... by the streets, and by the open places,

Geneva ... in the streets and crossings I will seek, *NAB*.

I sought him, but I found him not: ... I have called him but he has not answered, *NEB* ... I looked for him but couldn't find him, *Beck*.

3. The watchmen that go about the city found me: to whom I said, Saw ye him whom my soul loveth?: ... The sentinels found me, as they went about in the city, *NRSV* ... came upon me, as they made their rounds of the city. 'Have you seen my true love?' I asked them, *REB* ... The guards found me They who patrol the city. Have you seen the one I love?, *Anchor* ... Have you seen my sweetheart?, *JB*.

4. It was but a little that I passed from them, but I found him whom my soul loveth: ... Soon after I parted from them I found the beloved of my life!, *Fenton* ... Scarcely had I left them when I found him, *Berkeley*.

I held him, and would not let him go, until I had brought him into my mother's house, and into the chamber of her that conceived me: ... till I should bring him to the home of my

the joy of walking with her lover as he admired and cherished the beauty of the gorgeous lilies that lined their path. Leaving the disgruntled brothers behind her, she encouraged him to enjoy to the full the new-grown verdure and run through the rural paradise like a young stag or gazelle. (The reference to the hill of Bether is unique in Scripture, and we have no clue as to its location [v. 17].) And then he added that they could climb up to the rocky cliffs on higher ground and play a sort of peekaboo from the caves above, where she could lift her lovely voice in song with all of the special effects that these caverns made possible.

3:1–3. This passage describes her feverish search for her dearly beloved during those hours of darkness which normally would be avoided. This young lady was caught up in a passionate desire to find where her lover was spending the night. She could hardly bear to be without him, and so she left her sleeping quarters and plunged through the dark-

ness, even though no prudent lass should hazard the manifold dangers and risks involved. It is difficult to assume that any intelligent woman would even think of such temerity when guarded by no armed warrior at her side. So reckless an adventure can hardly be set forth as an actual occurrence, no matter how intense was her desire. For this reason, it has been suggested that the Shulammite was in the grip of a romantic imagination which enraptured her in a feverish dream. The NASB footnote may be correct in labeling this episode as a mere dream. It would seem most unlikely that such a paragon of beauty, completely without armor or sword, could ever have made it through without scathe.

3:4–5. Yet it must be admitted that her success in finding her lover during the murky darkness of a great city seems to have been her actual experience. Her plaintive appeal to the night police seems to have resulted in her meeting up with her prince after all and joining him for the rest of the evening. "I

5.

173	904, 6895	3503	1351	881	8123.515
cj	prep, n fp	pn	n fp	do, ps 2mp	v Hiphil pf 1cs
אוֹ	בִּצְבָאוֹת	יְרוּשָׁלַם	בְּנוֹת	אֶתְכֶם	הִשְׁבַּעְתִּי
'ô	bitsvā'ôth	yerûshālam	benôth	'ethkhem	hishba'ättî
or	by the female gazelles	Jerusalem	O daughters of	you	I will cause to swear

5912	881, 157	524, 5996.328	524, 5996.528	7898	904, 359
adv	do, art, n fs	cj, cj, v Polel impf 2mp	cj, v Hiphil impf 2mp	art, n ms	prep, n fp
עַד	אֶת־הָאַהֲבָה	וְאִם־תְּעוֹרְרוּ	אִם־תָּעִירוּ	הַשָּׂדֶה	בְּאַיְלוֹת
'adh	'eth-hā'ahvāh	we'im-te'ôrerû	'im-tā'îrû	hassādheh	be'aylôth
until	the love	or if you will awaken	if you will arouse	the field	by the female deer of

6.

6476	3626, 8820	4623, 4198	6148.153	2148	4449	8054, 2759.122
n ms	prep, n fp	prep, art, n ms	v Qal act ptc fs	dem pron	intrg	rel part, v Qal impf 3fs
עָשָׁן	כְּתִימְרוֹת	מִן־הַמִּדְבָּר	עֹלָה	זֹאת	מִי	שֶׁתְּחַפָּץ
'āshān	kethîmerôth	min-hammidhbār	'ōlāh	zō'th	mî	shettechăppāts
smoke	like columns of	from the wilderness	coming up	this one	who	that it desires

76	4623, 3725	3972	4915	7281.457
n fs	prep, n ms	cj, n fs	n ms	v Pual ptc fs
אַבְקַת	מִכֹּל	וּלְבוֹנָה	מוֹר	מְקֻטֶּרֶת
'avqath	mikkōl	ûlăvônāh	môr	mequttereth
perfumed powder of	among all	and frankincense	myrrh	having been sent up in smoke with

7.

3937	5623	1399	8666	8054, 3937, 8406	4433	2079	7691.151
prep, ps 3fs	adv	n mp	num	rel part, prep, pn	n fs, ps 3ms	intrj	v Qal act ptc ms
לָהּ	סָבִיב	גִּבֹּרִים	שִׁשִּׁים	שֶׁלִּשְׁלֹמֹה	מִטָּתוֹ	הִנֵּה	רֹכֵל
lāhh	sāvîv	gibbōrîm	shishshîm	shellishlōmōh	mittāthô	hinnēh	rōkhēl
to it	all around	warriors	sixty	of Solomon	the bed	behold	a trader

8.

4064.456	2820	270.156	3725	3547	4623, 1399
v Pual ptc mp	n fs	v Qal pass ptc mp	adj, ps 3mp	pn	prep, n mp
מְלֻמְּדֵי	חֶרֶב	אֲחֻזֵי	כֻּלָּם	יִשְׂרָאֵל	מִגִּבֹּרֵי
melummedhê	cherev	'ăchuzê	kulām	yisrā'ēl	miggibbōrê
having being trained in	a sword	girded with	all of them	Israel	from the warriors of

9.

687	904, 4050	4623, 6586	6142, 3525	2820	382	4560
n ms	prep, art, n mp	prep, n ms	prep, n fs, ps 3ms	n fs, ps 3ms	n ms	n fs
אַפִּרְיוֹן	בַּלֵּילוֹת	מִפַּחַד	עַל־יְרֵכוֹ	חַרְבּוֹ	אִישׁ	מִלְחָמָה
'appiryôn	ballêlôth	mippachadh	'al-yerēkhô	charbô	'îsh	milchāmāh
a palanquin	in the night	from the alarm	on his thigh	his sword	each	war

10.

6204	3976	4623, 6320	8406	4567	3937	6449.111
n mp, ps 3ms	art, pn	prep, n mp	pn	art, n ms	prep, ps 3ms	v Qal pf 3ms
עַמּוּדָיו	הַלְּבָנוֹן	מֵעֲצֵי	שְׁלֹמֹה	הַמֶּלֶךְ	לוֹ	עָשָׂה
'ammûdhāv	hallevānôn	mē'ătsê	shelōmōh	hammelekh	lô	'āsāh
its posts	the Lebanon	from the trees of	Solomon	the king	for himself	he has made

7821.155	8761	736	4980	2174	7798	3826B	6449.111
v Qal pass ptc ms	n ms, ps 3ms	n ms	n ms, ps 3ms	n ms	n fs, ps 3ms	n ms	v Qal pf 3ms
רָצוּף	תּוֹכוֹ	אַרְגָּמָן	מֶרְכָּבוֹ	זָהָב	רְפִידָתוֹ	כֶּסֶף	עָשָׂה
rātsûph	tôkhô	'argāmān	merkāvô	zāhāv	refîdhāthô	kheseph	'āsāh
upholstered	its interior	purple cloth	its seat	gold	its back	silver	he has made

11.

157	4623, 1351	3503	3428.134	7495.134	1351	6995
n fs	prep, n fp	pn	v Qal impv 2fp	cj, v Qal impv 2fp	n fp	pn
אַהֲבָה	מִבְּנוֹת	יְרוּשָׁלָם	צְאֶינָה	וּרְאֶינָה	בְּנוֹת	צִיּוֹן
'ahvāh	mibbenôth	yerûshālām	tse'ênāh	ûre'ênāh	benôth	tsîyôn
love	from the daughters of	Jerusalem	go out	and look	O daughters of	Zion

mother, to the room of my parent, *NAB* … I held him fast in my embrace and brought him to, *Moffatt* … I took him by the hands, and did not let him go, *BB*.

5. I charge you, O ye daughters of Jerusalem, by the roes, and by the hinds of the field: … Daughters of Jerusalem, I make you promise, *Beck* … I adjure you, … by the gazelles or the wild does, *NRSV* … or hinds of the steppe, *Anchor*.

that ye stir not up, nor awake my love, till he please: … wake not nor arouse the dear love until she please, *Rotherham* … Do not rouse her, do not disturb my love until she is ready, *NEB* … neither incite or excite Love until it is eager, *Anchor* … not to awaken or excite my feelings of love until it is ready, *NCV* … that you will not interrupt our love, *Good News*.

6. Who is this that cometh out of the wilderness like pillars of smoke, perfumed with myrrh and frankincense: … What is this coming up from the desert like columns of smoke, *Berkeley* … up from the meadows, Like columns of smoke from the burn-ing of myrrh?, *Fenton* … ascending from the steppe, … Redolent with myrrh and incense, *Anchor* … Like palm-trees of smoke, *Young* … erect as a column, *Knox* … breathing of myrrh and frankincense, *JB*.

with all powders of the merchant?: … With incense and sweets from afar?, *Fenton* … from all the pow-dered spices that merchants bring?, *NEB* … All the pedlar's powders?, *Anchor* … and with the perfume of every exotic dust?, *NAB* … with every scent to be bought?, *Moffatt*.

7. Behold his bed, which is Solomon's; threescore valiant men are about it, of the valiant of Israel: … Why, that is Solomon's chariot, With sixty brave warriors around!, *Fenton* … Look! It is Solomon carried in his state litter, *REB* … it is the traveling couch, *NASB* … carriage, escorted by sixty warriors, the noblest of Israel, *NIV* … warriors are around it from among the heroes of, *Berkeley*.

8. They all hold swords, being expert in war: … They all handle the sword, *MAST* … all skilled with the sword and trained to do combat, *Berkeley* … skilled swordsmen, all expert in handling arms, *REB*.

every man hath his sword upon his thigh because of fear in the night: … each with his sword at his thigh, against alarms by night, *RSV* … ready at his side to ward off the demon of the night, *NEB* … sword upon his hip, against danger, *Goodspeed*.

9. King Solomon made himself a chariot of the wood of Lebanon: … A palanquin King Solomon made himself, Of the trees, *Rotherham* … a palace of the trees, *Geneva* … a sedan chair From the timber, *NASB* … a carriage of wood, *NAB*.

10. He made the pillars thereof of silver, the bottom thereof of gold, the covering of it of purple, the midst thereof being paved with love, for the daughters of Jerusalem: … Its pillars of silver are made, And its panels of gold! And its cushions are purple! Its carpet is broi-dered with lace, Made by Jerusalem's girls!, *Fenton* … Its uprights were made of silver, its headrest of gold; its seat was of purple stuff, its lining of

found him whom my soul loves; I held on to him and would not let him go." Yet this is followed by the statement that she had brought him into her mother's house, "into the room of her who conceived me." Clearly, this Shulammite girl had a monogamous relationship with her royal lover, a thrilling and total commitment, including not only the marriage bond itself, but also a real commitment to her mother—perhaps even to the unappreciative brothers who had been less than kind to their lovely younger sister.

Verse 5 seems to indicate that they were still in Jerusalem, and she put her love to bed, at the same time admonishing the Jerusalem choristers to keep quiet and enable him to enjoy a full sleep after a busy day in the big city. She even cautioned the tame gazelles to avoid disturbing his rest with unnecessary disturbance during the night.

3:6–11. At this point, a triumphant wedding parade was announced by way of preparation for the marriage of the prince to his sweetheart from the north. Whether this was to take place in the Jerusalem quarters belonging to Solomon is not altogether clear. The women's choral group was on hand, rejoicing as the prince sat in his sedan chair, surrounded by an armed honor guard consisting of sixty legionnaires. They constituted his safety and sang his praise. No hostile coup d'etat could be launched against the heir apparent of David's throne, even though he might well have chosen some foreign queen who would have added prestige to the throne of Israel. Later, however, he was des-tined to enter into a cordial alliance with the mighty kingdom of Egypt when Solomon's amazing exper-tise in every field of knowledge greatly intrigued the queen of Sheba. She actually took the step of going up to Jerusalem in order to question him and ascertain whether he really possessed the amazing knowledge which surpassed any scholarship which Egypt could display. Her visit with him resulted in a profound admiration for his wisdom and doubtless established a cordial relationship with the Hebrew king. But there is absolutely no evidence in the

Strong's	Parsing	Hebrew	Transliteration	English
904, 3219	prep, n ms	בְּיוֹם	beyôm	on the day of
525	n fs, ps 3ms	אִמּוֹ	'immô	his mother
8054, 6064.312, 3937	rel part, v Piel pf 3fs, prep, ps 3ms	שֶׁעִטְּרָה־לּוֹ	she'itterāh-lô	which she has crowned him
904, 6065	prep, art, n fs	בָּעֲטָרָה	bā'ătārāh	at the diadem
8406	pn	שְׁלֹמֹה	shelōmōh	Solomon
904, 4567	prep, art, n ms	בַּמֶּלֶךְ	bammelekh	at the king

4:1

Strong's	Parsing	Hebrew	Transliteration	English
7761	n fs, ps 1cs	רַעְיָתִי	ra'ăyāthî	my beloved
3413	adj	יָפָה	yāphāh	beautiful
2079	intrj, ps 2fs	הִנָּךְ	hinnākh	behold you
3949	n ms, ps 3ms	לִבּוֹ	libbô	his heart
7977	n fs	שִׂמְחַת	simchath	the gladness of
904, 3219	cj, prep, n ms	וּבְיוֹם	ûveyôm	and on the day of
2969	n fs, ps 3ms	חֲתֻנָּתוֹ	chăthunnāthô	his wedding

Strong's	Parsing	Hebrew	Transliteration	English
3626, 5953	prep, n ms	כְּעֵדֶר	ke'ēdher	like a flock of
7998	n ms, ps 2fs	שַׂעְרֵךְ	sa'ărēkh	your hair
3937, 7046	prep, n fs, ps 2fs	לְצַמָּתֵךְ	letsammāthēkh	your veil
4623, 1185	prep, prep	מִבַּעַד	mibba'adh	from behind
3225	n fp	יוֹנִים	yônîm	doves
6084	n fd, ps 2fs	עֵינַיִךְ	'ênayikh	your eyes
3413	adj	יָפָה	yāphāh	beautiful
2079	intrj, ps 2fs	הִנָּךְ	hinnākh	behold you

2.

Strong's	Parsing	Hebrew	Transliteration	English
3626, 5953	prep, n ms	כְּעֵדֶר	ke'ēdher	like a flock of
8514	n fd, ps 2fs	שִׁנַּיִךְ	shinnayikh	your teeth
1609	pn	גִּלְעָד	gil'ādh	Gilead
4623, 2098	prep, n ms	מֵהַר	mēhar	from the hills of
8054, 1611.116	rel part, v Qal pf 3cp	שֶׁגָּלְשׁוּ	sheggāleshû	which they have come down
6008	art, n fp	הָעִזִּים	hā'izzîm	the goats

Strong's	Parsing	Hebrew	Transliteration	English
8054, 3725	rel part, n ms, ps 3mp	שֶׁכֻּלָּם	shekkullām	which all of them
4623, 7650	prep, art, n fs	מִן־הָרַחְצָה	min-hārachtsāh	from the washing
8054, 6148.116	rel part, v Qal pf 3cp	שֶׁעָלוּ	she'ālû	which they have come up
7378.158	art, v Qal pass ptc fp	הַקְּצוּבוֹת	haqqetsûvôth	those have been shorn

3.

Strong's	Parsing	Hebrew	Transliteration	English
8004	n fp, ps 2fs	שִׂפְתֹתַיִךְ	siphthōthayikh	your lips
8528	art, adj	הַשָּׁנִי	hashshānî	the scarlet
3626, 2432	prep, n ms	כְּחוּט	kechût	like the thread of
904	prep, ps 3mp	בָּהֶם	bāhem	among them
375	sub	אֵין	'ên	there is not
8316	cj, adj	וְשַׁכֻּלָה	weshakkulāh	and bereft
8709.554	v Hiphil ptc fp	מַתְאִימוֹת	math'îmôth	bearing twins

Strong's	Parsing	Hebrew	Transliteration	English
3937, 7046	prep, n fs, ps 2fs	לְצַמָּתֵךְ	letsammāthēkh	your veil
4623, 1185	prep, prep	מִבַּעַד	mibba'adh	from behind
7834	n fs, ps 2fs	רַקָּתֵךְ	raqqāthēkh	your temple
7705	art, n ms	הָרִמּוֹן	hārimmôn	the pomegranate
3626, 6644	prep, n fs	כְּפֶלַח	kephelach	like a slice of
5173	adj	נָאוֶה	nā'weh	beautiful
4199	cj, n mp, ps 2fs	וּמִדְבָּרֵךְ	ûmidhbārēkh	and your mouth

4.

Strong's	Parsing	Hebrew	Transliteration	English
512	num	אֶלֶף	'eleph	one thousand
3937, 8860	prep, n fp	לְתַלְפִּיּוֹת	lethalpîyôth	for stacks of stones
1161.155	v Qal pass ptc ms	בָּנוּי	bānûy	having been built
6939	n ms, ps 2fs	צַוָּארֵךְ	tsawwā'rēkh	your neck
1784	pn	דָּוִיד	dāwîdh	David
3626, 4166	prep, n ms	כְּמִגְדַּל	kemiggedhal	like the tower of

5.

Strong's	Parsing	Hebrew	Transliteration	English
8530	num	שְׁנֵי	shenê	the two of
1399	art, n mp	הַגִּבּוֹרִים	haggibbôrîm	the warriors
8377	n mp	שִׁלְטֵי	shiltê	the shields of
3725	n ms	כֹּל	kōl	all
6142	prep, ps 3ms	עָלָיו	'ālâv	on it
8847.155	v Qal pass ptc ms	תָּלוּי	tālûy	having been hung
4182	art, n ms	הַמָּגֵן	hammāghēn	the shields

Strong's	Parsing	Hebrew	Transliteration	English
904, 8236	prep, art, n mp	בַּשּׁוֹשַׁנִּים	bashshôshanîm	among the lilies
7749.152	art, v Qal act ptc mp	הָרֹעִים	hārō'îm	those grazing
6909	n fs	צְבִיָּה	tsevîyāh	a female gazelle
8751	n mp	תְּאוֹמֵי	te'ômê	twins of
6314	n mp	עֳפָרִים	'ăphārîm	fawns
3626, 8530	prep, num	כִּשְׁנֵי	kishnê	like two
8157	n md, ps 2fs	שָׁדַיִךְ	shādhayikh	your breasts

leather, *REB* ... the posts made of silver, the canopy of gold, the seat of purple; the centre is inlaid with ebony, *JB* ... its framework inlaid with ivory, *NAB* ... within are pictured tales of love, for your pleasure, maidens of Jerusalem, *Knox*.

11. Go forth, O ye daughters of Zion, and behold king Solomon with the crown wherewith his mother crowned him in the day of his espousals, and in the day of the gladness of his heart: ... Come out, you daughters of Zion, to look At King Solomon wearing the wreath That his mother had woven for him, For the day he was wed,—For the day of the joy of his heart, *Fenton* ... Daughters of Zion, come and see King Solomon, wearing the diadem with which his mother crowned him on his wedding day, on the day of his heart's joy, *JB*.

4:1. Behold, thou art fair, my love; behold, thou art fair; thou hast doves' eyes within thy locks: ... How beautiful you are, my dearest, how beautiful! Your eyes are doves behind your veil, *REB* ... Eyes soft as dove's eyes, half-seen behind thy veil, *Knox* ... you have doves' eyes within your locks, *KJVII*.

thy hair is as a flock of goats, that appear from mount Gilead: ... hair that clusters thick as the flocks of goats, when they come home from the Galaad hills, *Knox* ... Dark streams your hair like goats a-down the slopes of Gilead, *Moffatt* ... which are reclining on the sides of Mount Gilead, *Rotherham*.

2. Thy teeth are like a flock of sheep that are even shorn, which came up from the washing: ... Your teeth are white like newly sheared sheep just coming from their bath, *NCV* ... a flocke of sheepe in good order, *Geneva* ... ewes ready for shearing, *Goodspeed* ... which have come up fresh from the dipping, *NEB*.

whereof every one bear twins, and none is barren among them: ... Each has its twin; not one of them is alone, *NIV* ... all of them big with twins, none of them thin and barren, *Douay* ... each ewe has twins and none has cast a lamb, *NEB* ... They are in pairs, not one of them is missing, *Berkeley* ... And not one among them has lost her young, *NASB*.

3. Thy lips are like a thread of scarlet, and thy speech is comely: ... Like a scarlet fillet your lips, *Anchor* ... a crimson thread, and when you talk, your mouth is lovely, *Beck* ... a line of scarlet, guardians of that sweet utterance, *Knox* ... your mouth so delicious, *Moffatt* ... and your words enchanting, *JB*.

thy temples are like a piece of a pomegranate within thy locks: ... Your cheeks, behind your veil, are halves of pomegranate, *JB* ... Like a pomegranate slice your brow, *Anchor* ... your parted lips behind your veil are like a pomegranate cut open, *NEB, REB* ... Your cheeks are love-apples concealed by your veil, *Fenton*.

4. Thy neck is like the tower of David builded for an armoury: ... like David's tower girt with battlements, *Douay, NAB* ... made for a store-house of arms, *BB* ... built with elegance, *NIV* ... built with rows of stones, *NCV* ... built with encircling courses, *REB*.

Scripture indicating that she had marital relations with him, despite the later traditions that arose in certain Arabic traditions, especially those related by Josephus (*Antiquities*, II:x:2), which made out the birth of a son by Solomon and the queen—a tradition embraced by the Ethiopians as the origin of their own royal line. Perhaps it should be added that the territory of Sheba was located in the south of the Arabian Peninsula and hardly constituted a part of the kingdom of Egypt as such. (So much for the queen of Sheba!)

The final verse of ch. 3 urged the young maidens to give all honor and glory to their mighty crown prince as he celebrated the wedding to his lovely fiancee from the north.

4:1–3. It is fair to assume that this chapter records some of the highlights of their honeymoon in the region of Shunem and even further north in the land of Lebanon (cf. v. 8). All of the noise and glamor of Jerusalem had been left behind, and they were bent on just being by themselves and the deep satisfaction of thrilling and soul-satisfying fellowship rather than the distracting confusion of the capital city. They were now free to revel in the attractiveness and charm which they expressed to each other with mutual infatuation. As he reveled in her total perfection, he exclaimed, "How beautiful you are, my darling!" Again, the young bridegroom compared her, as his treasure, to the eyes of doves and then admired the dark goat's hair which crowned her head. He then compared her lovely teeth to a flock of newly shorn sheep, with every matching tooth in place. Then he marveled her lips as a perfect scarlet in color and lovely in shape. As he continued his enraptured survey of her face, he admired the perfect color of her forehead, comparing it to pomegranates (which leaves it a bit uncertain as to the exact hue, since pomegranates bear white, yellow and bright red in their fruit).

4:4–5. Most original is his description of her neck itself, comparing it to the tower of David (concerning which we have no specific information), which must have been exceptionally shapely with its perfect smoothness, serving as a repository

6.

5912	8054, 6558.121	3219	5308.116	7020	2050.125	3937
adv	rel part, v Qal impf 3ms	art, n ms	cj, v Qal pf 3cp	art, n mp	v Qal impf 1cs	prep, ps 1cs
עַד	שֶׁיָּפוּחַ	הַיּוֹם	וְנָסוּ	הַצְּלָלִים	אֵלֶךְ	לִי
'adh	sheyyāphûach	hayyôm	wenāsû	hatstselālîm	'ēlekh	lî
until	that it blows	the day	then they will flee	the shadows	I will go	for myself

420, 2098	4915	420, 1421	3972	**7.** 3725	3413
prep, n ms	art, n ms	cj, prep, n fs	art, n fs	n ms, ps 2fs	adj
אֶל־הַר	הַמּוֹר	וְאֶל־גִּבְעַת	הַלְּבוֹנָה	כֻּלָּךְ	יָפָה
'el-har	hammôr	we'el-giv'ath	hallevônāh	kullākh	yāphāh
to the mountain of	the myrrh	and to the hill of	the frankincense	all of you	beautiful

7761	4113	375	904	**8.** 882	4623, 3976	3738	882
n fs, ps 1cs	cj, n ms	sub	prep, ps 2fs	prep, ps 1cs	prep, pn	n fs	prep, ps 1cs
רַעְיָתִי	וּמוּם	אֵין	בָּךְ	אִתִּי	מִלְּבָנוֹן	כַּלָּה	אִתִּי
ra'äyāthî	ûmûm	'ên	bākh	'ittî	millevānôn	kallāh	'ittî
my beloved	and a blemish	there is not	on you	with me	from Lebanon	a bride	with me

4623, 3976	971.124	8227.124	4623, 7513	556	4623, 7513	7987
prep, pn	v Qal impf 2fs	v Qal impf 2fs	prepl, n ms	pn	prepl, n ms	pn
מִלְּבָנוֹן	תָּבוֹאִי	תָּשׁוּרִי	מֵרֹאשׁ	אֲמָנָה	מֵרֹאשׁ	שְׂנִיר
millevānôn	tāvô'î	tāshûrî	mērō'sh	'āmānāh	mērō'sh	senîr
from Lebanon	you will come	you will gaze	from the top of	Amana	from the top of	Senir

2874	4779	761	4623, 2121	5432
cj, pn	prep, n fp	n mp	prep, n mp	n mp
וְחֶרְמוֹן	מִמְּעֹנוֹת	אֲרָיוֹת	מֵהַרְרֵי	נְמֵרִים
wechermôn	mimme'ōnôth	'ărāyôth	mēharerê	nemērîm
and Hermon	from the dwelling places of	the lions	from the mountains of	leopards

9.

3955.314	269	3738	3955.314	904, 259	4623, 6084
v Piel pf 2fs, ps 1cs	n fs, ps 1cs	n fs	v Piel pf 2fs, ps 1cs	prep, num	prep, n md, ps 2fs
לִבַּבְתִּנִי	אֲחֹתִי	כַּלָּה	לִבַּבְתִּנִי	בְּאַחַד	מֵעֵינַיִךְ
libbavtinî	'ăchōthî	khallāh	libbavtinî	be'achadh	mē'ênayikh
you have captivated me	my sister	a bride	you have captivated me	with one of	from your eyes

904, 259	6291	4623, 6968	**10.** 4242, 3412.116	1782	269	3738
prep, num	n ms	prep, n mp, ps 2fs	intrg, v Qal pf 3cp	n mp, ps 2fs	n fs, ps 1cs	n fs
בְּאַחַד	עֲנָק	מִצַּוְּרֹנָיִךְ	מַה־יָּפוּ	דֹּדַיִךְ	אֲחֹתִי	כַּלָּה
be'achadh	'ānāq	mitstsawwerōnāyikh	mah-yāphû	dhōdhayikh	'ăchōthî	khallāh
with one	necklace	from your necklaces	how it is beautiful	your love	my sister	a bride

4242, 3004.116	1782	4623, 3302	7666	8467	4623, 3725, 1336
intrg, v Qal pf 3cp	n mp, ps 2fs	prep, n ms	cj, n ms	n mp, ps 2fs	prep, adj, n mp
מַה־טֹּבוּ	דֹּדַיִךְ	מִיַּיִן	וְרֵיחַ	שְׁמָנַיִךְ	מִכָּל־בְּשָׂמִים
mah-tōvû	dhōdhayikh	mîyayin	werêach	shemānayikh	mikkol-besāmîm
how they are better	your love	than wine	and the fragrance of	your oils	from all the spices

11.

5499	5382.127	8004	3738	1756	2560	8809	4098
n ms	v Qal impf 3fp	n fp, ps 2fs	n fs	n ms	cj, n ms	prep	n fs, ps 2fs
נֹפֶת	תִּטֹּפְנָה	שִׂפְתוֹתַיִךְ	כַּלָּה	דְּבַשׁ	וְחָלָב	תַּחַת	לְשׁוֹנֵךְ
nōpheth	tittōphenāh	siphthôthayikh	kallāh	devash	wechālāv	tachath	leshônēkh
fresh honey	they drip	your lips	a bride	honey	and milk	beneath	your tongue

7666	7969	3626, 7666	3976	**12.** 1629
cj, n ms	n fp, ps 2fs	prep, n ms	pn	n ms
וְרֵיחַ	שַׂלְמֹתַיִךְ	כְּרֵיחַ	לְבָנוֹן	גַּן
werêach	salmōthayikh	kerêach	levānôn	gan
and the fragrance of	your clothing	like the fragrance of	Lebanon	a garden

whereon there hang a thousand bucklers, all shields of mighty men: ... A thousand shields hang on its walls; each shield belongs to a strong soldier, *NCV* ... hung round with a thousand targes, all armour of heroes, *Moffatt* ... A thousand shields hung thereon, All the equipment of heroes, *Rotherham*.

5. Thy two breasts are like two young roes that are twins, which feed among the lilies: ... two fawns, twins of a gazelle, that pasture among the hyacinths, *Goodspeed* ... graceful thy breasts as two fawns that feed, *Knox* ... twins of a roe, *MRB* ... Browsing on the lotus, *Anchor*.

6. Until the day break, and the shadows flee away, I will get me to the mountain of myrrh, and to the hill of frankincense: ... Until the day breathes its evening coolness and the shadows lengthen and disappear, *Berkeley* ... At the cool of the day when the shadows extend, *Fenton* ... till the cool of the dawn, ... I will hie

me to your scented slopes, your fragrant charms, *Moffatt*.

7. Thou art all fair, my love; there is no spot in thee: ... My darling, everything about you is beautiful, and there is nothing at all wrong with you, *NCV* ... You are wholly beautiful, my beloved, and without a blemish, *JB* ... You are beautiful, my dearest, beautiful without a flaw, *REB*.

8. Come with me from Lebanon, my spouse, with me from Lebanon: ... Venture forth from Lebanon, and come to me, my bride, my queen that shall be!, *Knox* ... Come from Lebanon, my promised bride, come from Lebanon, come on your way, *JB*.

look from the top of Amana, from the top of Shenir and Hermon, from the lions' dens, from the mountains of the leopards: ... Hurry down from the summit of Amana, *REB* ... Depart from the peak of Amana, from the peak of Senir and, *NRSV* ... the top of anti-lebanon,

... from where lions dwell, from the mountains where panthers roam, *Beck* ... from the lions' lairs, and the hills the leopards haunt, *NEB*.

9. Thou hast ravished my heart, my sister, my spouse; thou hast ravished my heart with one of thine eyes, with one chain of thy neck: ... What a wound thou hast made, my bride, my true love, what a wound thou hast made in this heart of mine!, *Knox* ... You have made my heart beat faster, my sister, my bride; You have made my heart beat faster with a single glance of your eyes, With a single strand of your necklace, *NASB* ... with a turn of your neck!, *Moffatt* ... You enbolden my heart, My Darling, my Perfect!, *Fenton*.

10. How fair is thy love, my sister, my spouse!: ... Your love is so sweet, my sister, my bride, *NCV* ... How sweet your caresses, my bride, my own, *Moffatt* ... What spells lie in your love, ... my promised bride!, *JB* ... How beautiful are your

---

of beautiful shields, no less than a thousand in number. Next, the infatuated lover compared her bosoms to a pair of newborn gazelle fawns browsing among the white lilies.

4:6–7. Apparently, the evening had by now overtaken them and there was less to gaze at until the next morning arrives. And so he chose a well-favored hill to the north where the fragrance of myrrh might waft over them as they lay themselves to rest until the next morning light. Thus, he summed up her captivating beauty by paying her one more admiring compliment before they bed down together. To him she seemed absolutely flawless!

4:8. Verse 8 seems to imply that on the following day they hiked together all the way to the hills of Lebanon, an area which was then evidently in subjection to David's authority at this period. The royal couple then climbed the hill of Amana in the Anti-Lebanon Range and also Mt. Senir, which belonged to the same range. It is quite remarkable to read of a honeymoon like this one, especially in view of the political importance of young Solomon. But he was undoubtedly quite careful to conceal his real identity as the two of them hiked over the truly beautiful terrain of the north. Wild animals roamed there as well,

such as lions and leopards, though no mention is made of savage attacks. The summit of Mt. Hermon was no small feat to reach, for it was (and is) the loftiest eminence in that whole area of Lebanon and Palestine. Interestingly enough, the long-term irrigation of Israel is largely dependent upon the amount of snow that covers its peak even today.

4:9. The young couple found nothing but delight as they traveled from one scenic site to another. Despite whether figurative language, through it all, her lover never tired of her company. In fact, though they would travel the furthermost regions of the land, his desire to be with her only increased. He exclaimed, "You have stolen my heart, my sister and my bride!" Not only did she maintain her sweetness and poise, but she made him even more deeply in love than before. He could hardly find words to adequately express his complete joy in her captivating charm which had totally enraptured his heart under the impact of a single glance from her enchanting gaze.

4:10–16. At this point, Solomon launches into the lengthiest panegyric of the entire Book: (1) Her love is more intoxicating than wine; (2) the enchantment of her perfume makes her irresistible

(reading right-to-left)

Strong's	Parsing	Hebrew	Translit.	English
4754	n ms	מַעְיָן	ma'ăyān	a place of springs
5457.155	v Qal pass ptc ms	נָעוּל	nā'ûl	having been locked
1570	n ms	גַּל	gal	a spring
3738	n fs	כַּלָּה	khallāh	a bride
269	n fs, ps 1cs	אֲחֹתִי	'ăchōthî	my sister
5457.155	v Qal pass ptc ms	נָעוּל	nā'ûl	having been locked

13.

Strong's	Parsing	Hebrew	Translit.	English
4162	n mp	מְגָדִים	meghādhîm	fruit harvests
6780	n ms	פְּרִי	perî	fruit of
6196	prep	עִם	'im	with
7705	n mp	רִמּוֹנִים	rimmônîm	pomegranates
6758	n ms	פַּרְדֵּס	pardēs	an orchard of
8367	n mp, ps 2fs	שְׁלָחַיִךְ	shelāchayikh	your shoots
2964.155	v Qal pass ptc ms	חָתוּם	chāthûm	having been sealed

14.

Strong's	Parsing	Hebrew	Translit.	English
3725, 6320	adj, n mp	כָּל־עֲצֵי	kol-'ătsê	all the trees of
6196	prep	עִם	'im	with
7360	cj, n ms	וְקִנָּמוֹן	weqinnāmôn	and cinnamon
7354	n ms	קָנֶה	qāneh	calamus
3880	cj, n ms	וְכַרְכֹּם	wekharkōm	and saffron
5556	n ms	נֵרְדְּ	nērd	spikenard
6196, 5556	prep, n mp	עִם־נְרָדִים	'im-nerādhîm	with spikenard
3852	n mp	כְּפָרִים	kephārîm	henna

15.

Strong's	Parsing	Hebrew	Translit.	English
908	n fs	בְּאֵר	be'ēr	a well of
1629	n mp	גַּנִּים	ganîm	gardens
4754	n ms	מַעְיָן	ma'ăyān	a spring of
1336	n mp	בְשָׂמִים	vesāmîm	spices
3725, 7513	adj, n mp	כָּל־רָאשֵׁי	kol-rā'shê	all the best of
6196	prep	עִם	'im	with
167	cj, n mp	וַאֲהָלוֹת	wa'ăhālôth	and aloes
4915	n ms	מֹר	mōr	myrrh
3972	n fs	לְבוֹנָה	levônāh	frankincense

16.

Strong's	Parsing	Hebrew	Translit.	English
971.132	cj, v Qal impv 2fs	וּבוֹאִי	ûvô'î	and come
7103	n ms	צָפוֹן	tsāphôn	O north wind
5996.132	v Qal impv 2fs	עוּרִי	'ûrî	wake up
4623, 3976	prep, pn	מִן־לְבָנוֹן	min-levānôn	from Lebanon
5320.152	cj, v Qal act ptc mp	וְנֹזְלִים	wenōzelîm	and flowing
2522	adj	חַיִּים	chayyîm	living
4448	n md	מַיִם	mayim	water

Strong's	Parsing	Hebrew	Translit.	English
1782	n ms, ps 1cs	דוֹדִי	dhôdhî	my beloved
971.121	v Qal juss 3ms	יָבֹא	yāvō'	may he come
1336	n mp, ps 3ms	בְשָׂמָיו	vesāmâv	its balsam oils
5320.126	v Qal juss 3mp	יִזְּלוּ	yizzelû	may they flow
1629	n ms, ps 1cs	גַנִּי	ghannî	my garden
6558.532	v Hiphil impv 2fs	הָפִיחִי	hāphîchî	blow
8816	n fs	תֵימָן	thêmān	O south wind

5:1

Strong's	Parsing	Hebrew	Translit.	English
3937, 1629	prep, n ms, ps 1cs	לְגַנִּי	leghanî	to my garden
971.115	v Qal pf 1cs	בָּאתִי	bā'thî	I have come
4162	n mp, ps 3ms	מְגָדָיו	meghādhâv	his fruit harvests
6780	n ms	פְּרִי	perî	the fruit of
404.121	cj, v Qal juss 3ms	וְיֹאכַל	weyō'khal	that he may eat
3937, 1629	prep, n ms, ps 3ms	לְגַנּוֹ	leghannô	to his garden

Strong's	Parsing	Hebrew	Translit.	English
3403	n ms, ps 1cs	יַעְרִי	ya'rî	my honeycomb
404.115	v Qal pf 1cs	אָכַלְתִּי	'ākhaltî	I have eaten
6196, 1336	prep, n ms, ps 1cs	עִם־בְּשָׂמִי	'im-besāmî	with my balsam oil
4915	n ms, ps 1cs	מוֹרִי	môrî	my myrrh
741.115	v Qal pf 1cs	אָרִיתִי	'ārîthî	I have gathered
3738	n fs	כַּלָּה	khallāh	a bride
269	n fs, ps 1cs	אֲחֹתִי	'ăchōthî	my sister

Strong's	Parsing	Hebrew	Translit.	English
8685.133	v Qal impv 2mp	שְׁתוּ	shethû	drink
7739	n mp	רֵעִים	rē'îm	O friends
404.133	v Qal impv 2mp	אִכְלוּ	'ikhlû	eat
6196, 2560	prep, n ms, ps 1cs	עִם־חֲלָבִי	'im-chălāvî	with my milk
3302	n ms, ps 1cs	יֵינִי	yênî	my wine
8685.115	v Qal pf 1cs	שָׁתִיתִי	shāthîthî	I have drunk
6196, 1756	prep, n ms, ps 1cs	עִם־דִּבְשִׁי	'im-divshî	with my honey

2.

Strong's	Parsing	Hebrew	Translit.	English
7249	n ms	קוֹל	qôl	the voice of
5996.151	v Qal act ptc ms	עֵר	'ēr	being awake
3949	cj, n ms, ps 1cs	וְלִבִּי	welibbî	but my heart
3585	adj	יְשֵׁנָה	yeshēnāh	sleeping
603	pers pron	אֲנִי	'ănî	I
1782	n mp	דּוֹדִים	dôdhîm	O beloved ones
8335.133	cj, v Qal impv 2mp	וְשִׁכְרוּ	weshikhrû	and become drunk

breasts, *REB* ... How wonderful have been thy loves, *Young.*

how much better is thy love than wine! and the smell of thine ointments than all spices!: ... How much better are your breasts than wine, and the fragrance of your oil, *Beck* ... the fragrance of your ointments than all kinds of perfume!, *Goodspeed.*

11. Thy lips, O my spouse, drop as the honeycomb: honey and milk are under thy tongue; and the smell of thy garments is like the smell of Lebanon: ... Your lips drip honey, my bride, and sweetmeats and milk are under your tongue; and the fragrance of your garments is the fragrance, *Douay* ... As for your lips, my bride, they distil sweetness, *Goodspeed* ... Your lips distil odours, my Perfect, Honey and butter are under your tongue!, *Fenton* ... honey-sweet thy tongue, and soft as milk; the perfume of thy garments is very incense, *Knox* ... syrup and milk are under your tongue, and your dress has the scent, *NEB.*

12. A garden inclosed is my sister, my spouse; a spring shut up, a fountain sealed: ... A garden walled-in is my sister, my bride; a garden shut up, a spring of water stopped, *BB* ... A garden locked ... a spring sealed up, *NASB.*

13. Thy plants are an orchard of pomegranates, with pleasant fruits; camphire, with spikenard: ... Your groove a pomegranate grove With fruits delectable, *Anchor* ... Thy shoots are a park of pomegranates, with precious fruits, *MAST* ... Your two cheeks are an orchard of pomegranates, an orchard full of rare fruits, *NEB* ... The produce of the garden is pomegranates; with all the best fruits; henna and spikenard, *BB* ... What wealth of grace is here! Well-ordered rows of pomegranates, tree of cypress and tuft of nard, *Knox.*

14. Spikenard and saffron; calamus and cinnamon, with all trees of frankincense; myrrh and aloes, with all the chief spices: ... nard and crocus, ... with all kinds of incense trees, *Beck* ... with myrrh and with eaglewood, all the best spices!, *Moffatt* ... Nard and saffron, sweet cane and cinnamon, With all woods of frankincense, *Rotherham* ... or any rarest perfume, *Knox.*

15. A fountain of gardens, a well of living waters, and streams from Lebanon: ... You are a garden fountain, a well of water flowing fresh, *Douay, NAB* ... A garden fountain, A well of living water, Cascading, *Anchor* ... The fountain in my garden is a spring of running water pouring down, *NEB.*

16. Awake, O north wind; and come, thou south; blow upon my garden, that the spices thereof may flow out. Let my beloved come into his garden, and eat his pleasant fruits: ... breathe on my garden to waft out the perfume!, *Moffatt* ... that its fragrance may be wafted abroad, *NRSV* ... Let my lover enter the garden and eat its best fruits, *NCV.*

5:1. I am come into my garden, my sister, my spouse: ... Come in, my love, to my Garden, *Fenton* ... Into his garden, then, let my true love come, and taste his fruit, *Knox.*

I have gathered my myrrh with my spice; I have eaten my honeycomb with my honey; I have drunk my wine with my milk: ... to take my myrrh with my spice; my wax with my honey, *BB* ... I eat my honey and my sweetmeats, *Douay* ... eaten the honey of my thicket, *Rotherham* ... eaten my honey and my syrup, *NEB.*

eat, O friends; drink, yea, drink abundantly, O beloved: ... Take meat, O friends; take wine, yes, be overcome with love, *BB* ... and be drunk with love, *NRSV* ... Come, dearest, eat of my butter, Come, drink and be drunken with, *Fenton* ... Drink and imbibe deeply, O lovers, *NASB.*

2. I sleep, but my heart waketh: ... I slept, but my mind was alert,

to him; (3) her lips are sweeter than any honeycomb; (4) the aroma of her body is more captivating than the cedars of Lebanon; (5) she is like a well-watered garden; (6) her seductive spell fills him like the orchards of pomegranates along with henna, nard and saffron; (7) her body is wreathed with the heady fragrance of incense, myrrh, aloes and all the finest of spices; (8) she is like a garden fountain of water like that which rolls down from Mt. Lebanon itself. Surely, the young prince had surpassed the finest efforts of the most gifted of poets. He then tapers off with an appeal to the winds from the north and the south to blow over this enchanted garden of love. It is not quite certain which of them spoke the final verse, but it is more likely to have been her invitation to her swain than the other way around.

5:1. The first verse of this chapter opens with a repeated invitation for the two lovers to make love together, exchanging their kisses and embraces as entrancing as the sweetness of myrrh, spice, honey, wine and milk. But by this time, they exchanged the most ardent wishes of love, cheering them both to drink their cup of joy to the very full.

5:2–4. Quite unexpectedly, v. 2 records an unhappy experience that somewhat marred their relationship through a temporary misunderstanding. Apparently, the young lady, herself just a bit exhausted by the strenuous mountain hike which they had just finished, sank into a deep sleep in her little cottage in the environs of Jerusalem. She must have relished this opportunity to have a welcome rest. But what she had not reckoned on was the

Song of Songs 5:3–7

1782	1909.151	6858.132, 3937	269	7761	3225
n ms, ps 1cs	v Qal act ptc ms	v Qal impv 2fs, prep, ps 1cs	n fs, ps 1cs	n fs, ps 1cs	n fs, ps 1cs
דּוֹדִי	דּוֹפֵק	פִּתְחִי־לִי	אֲחֹתִי	רַעְיָתִי	יוֹנָתִי
dôdhî	dhōphēq	pithchî-lî	'ăchōthî	ra'ăyāthî	yônāthî
my beloved	knocking	open to me	my sister	my beloved	my dove

8866	8054, 7513	4527.211, 3030	7261	7732	4050
adj, ps 1cs	cj, n ms, ps 1cs	v Niphal pf 3ms, n ms	n fp, ps 1cs	n mp	n ms
תַּמָּתִי	שֶׁרֹּאשִׁי	נִמְלָא־טָל	קְוֻצּוֹתַי	רְסִיסֵי	לַיְלָה
thammāthî	sherrō'shî	nimlā'-ṭāl	qǒwwutsṣôthay	resîsê	lāyelāh
my perfect one	because my head	it has been filled with dew	my locks	the dewdrops of	night

3.

6838.115	881, 3930	355	3980.125	7647.115	881, 7559
v Qal pf 1cs	do, n fs, ps 1cs	intrg	v Qal impf 1cs, ps 3fs	v Qal pf 1cs	do, n fd, ps 1cs
פָּשַׁטְתִּי	אֶת־כֻּתָּנְתִּי	אֵיכָכָה	אֶלְבָּשֶׁנָּה	רָחַצְתִּי	אֶת־רַגְלַי
pāshaṭtî	'eth-kuttānettî	'êkhākhāh	'elbāshennāh	rāchatstî	'eth-raghlay
I have taken off	my long garment	how	will I put it on	I have bathed	my feet

4.

355	3047.325	1782	8365.111	3135	4623, 2815
intrg	v Piel impf 1cs, ps 3mp	n ms, ps 1cs	v Qal pf 3ms	n fs, ps 3ms	prep, art, n ms
אֵיכָכָה	אֲטַנְּפֵם	דּוֹדִי	שָׁלַח	יָדוֹ	מִן־הַחֹר
'êkhākhāh	'ăṭannephēm	dôdhî	shālach	yādhô	min-hachōr
how	will I soil them	my beloved	he put forth	his hand	from the hole

5.

4753	2064.116	6142	7257.115	603	3937, 6858.141
cj, n mp, ps 1cs	v Qal pf 3cp	prep, ps 3ms	v Qal pf 1cs	pers pron	prep, v Qal inf con
וּמֵעַי	הָמוּ	עָלָיו	קַמְתִּי	אֲנִי	לִפְתֹּחַ
ûmē'ay	hāmû	'ālâv	qamtî	'ānî	liphtōach
and my inward parts	they were in tumult	because of him	I got up	I	to open

3937, 1782	3135	5382.116, 4915	697	4915	5882.151
prep, n ms, ps 1cs	cj, n fd, ps 1cs	v Qal pf 3cp, n ms	cj, n fp, ps 1cs	n ms	v Qal act ptc ms
לְדוֹדִי	וְיָדַי	נָטְפוּ־מוֹר	וְאֶצְבְּעֹתַי	מוֹר	עֹבֵר
ledhôdhî	weyādhay	nāṭephû-mōr	we'etsbe'ōthay	môr	'ōvēr
for my beloved	and my hands	they dripped with myrrh	and my fingers	myrrh	passing through

6.

6142	3834	4662	6858.115	603	3937, 1782	1782
prep	n fp	art, n ms	v Qal pf 1cs	pers pron	prep, n ms, ps 1cs	cj, n ms, ps 1cs
עַל	כַּפּוֹת	הַמַּנְעוּל	פָּתַחְתִּי	אֲנִי	לְדוֹדִי	וְדוֹדִי
'al	kappôth	hamman'ûl	pāthachtî	'ānî	ledhôdhî	wedhôdhî
upon	the handles of	the bolt	I opened	I	for my beloved	but my beloved

2665.111	5882.111	5497	3428.112	904, 1744.341
v Qal pf 3ms	v Qal pf 3ms	n fs, ps 1cs	v Qal pf 3fs	prep, v Piel inf con, ps 3ms
חָמַק	עָבָר	נַפְשִׁי	יָצְאָה	בְּדַבְּרוֹ
chāmaq	'āvār	naphshî	yātse'āh	vedhabberô
he had gone away	he had passed on	my soul	it has gone out	when his speaking

1272.315	3940	4834.115	7410.115	3940	6257.111
v Piel pf 1cs, ps 3ms	cj, neg part	v Qal pf 1cs, ps 3ms	v Qal pf 1cs, ps 3ms	cj, neg part	v Qal pf 3ms, ps 1cs
בִּקַּשְׁתִּיהוּ	וְלֹא	מְצָאתִיהוּ	קְרָאתִיו	וְלֹא	עָנָנִי
biqqashtîhû	welō'	metsā'thîhû	qǒrā'thîw	welō'	'ānānî
I sought for him	but not	I found him	I called him	but not	he answered me

7.

4834.116	8490.152	5621.152	904, 6111	5409.516
v Qal pf 3cp, ps 1cs	art, v Qal act ptc mp	art, v Qal act ptc mp	prep, art, n fs	v Hiphil pf 3cp, ps 1cs
מְצָאֻנִי	הַשֹּׁמְרִים	הַסֹּבְבִים	בָּעִיר	הִכּוּנִי
metsā'unî	hashshōmerîm	hassōvevîm	bā'îr	hikkûnî
they found me	the watchmen	those going about	in the city	they struck me

Anchor ... I was sleeping, but my heart kept vigil, *Douay*.

it is the voice of my beloved that knocketh, saying, Open to me, my sister, my love, my dove, my undefiled: ... I dreamed—ah! there is my darling knocking!, *Moffatt* ... A knock on the door, and then my true love's voice; Let me in, my true love, so gentle, my bride, so pure!, *Knox* ... Open, my Darling, ... my Most Perfect!, *Fenton*.

for my head is filled with dew, and my locks with the drops of the night: ... wet with dew, *RSV* ... drenched with dew, My locks with the night mist, *Anchor* ... See, how bedewed is this head of mine, how the night rains have drenched my hair!, *Knox*.

3. I have put off my coat; how shall I put it on? I have washed my feet; how shall I defile them?: ... I have removed my tunic, *Anchor* ... put off my clothing!—Why dress me again?, *Fenton* ... taken off my dress, How can I put it on again?, *NASB* ... my garments; why should I put them on again?, *Goodspeed* ... washed my feet, how should I pollute them?, *Darby*.

4. My beloved put in his hand by the hole of the door, and my bow-els were moved for him: ... his hand on the door, and my heart was moved, *BB* ... hand to the latch, and my heart was thrilled within me, *RSV* ... thrust in his hand at the window, *Rotherham* ... my heart grew desirous of him, *Berkeley* ... And my breast sighs for him!, *Fenton* ... I trembled to the core of my being, *JB*.

5. I rose up to open to my beloved; and my hands dropped with myrrh, and my fingers with sweetsmelling myrrh, upon the handles of the lock: ... myrrh ran off my hands, pure myrrh off my fingers, *JB* ... And my fingers gave off their perfume On the key of the lock, *Fenton* ... and my fingers dropping myrrh and on the handles of the bar, *Berkeley* ... with liquid myrrh, upon the handles of the bolt, *NRSV*.

6. I opened to my beloved; but my beloved had withdrawn himself, and was gone: ... beloved withdrew—he passed on, *Young* ... had turned and gone, *RSV*.

my soul failed when he spake: ... my soul was feeble when his back was turned on me, *BB* ... My soul sank at his flight, *Anchor* ... My heart stopped, *LIVB* ... I almost died when he turned away, *Beck*.

I sought him, but I could not find him; I called him, but he gave me no answer: ... I went after him, but I did not come near him; I said his name, *BB* ... My soul ran to find, it sought to speak to him, But it found him not! I called!—But he did not reply!, *Fenton*.

7. The watchmen that went about the city found me, they smote me, they wounded me; the keepers of the walls took away my veil from me: ... Making their rounds in the city the sentinels found me; they beat me, they wounded me, they took away my mantle, those sentinels of the walls, *NRSV* ... they gave me blows and wounds, *BB* ... they beat me, they wounded me, they took away my mantle, *RSV* ... The guardsmen ... took away my shawl from me, *NASB*.

8. I charge you, O daughters of Jerusalem, if ye find my beloved, that ye tell him, that I am sick of love: ... I adjure you. ... If ye find my beloved, What will ye tell him? That I am love-sick, *MAST* ... maidens of Jerusalem, fall you in with the man I long for, give him this news of me, that I pine away with love, *Knox* ... That I am overcome with, *BB* ... That I am afflicted for love!, *Fenton*.

---

undiminished enthusiasm with which her lover yearned for renewed fellowship. Quite naturally, she had locked the door to her little lodge, and it took her lover no little effort to gain her attention. He called to her from the window (such as it was) and pleaded with her to let him in. However, she decided to make suitable preparation before consorting with her man, and so she protested to him through the window (probably a mere shutter which prevented seeing him face to face). Even though she was aware that he was impatiently eager to be admitted through her locked door, she preferred to give her hair a bit of combing and perfume and also a bit of washing for her dusty feet. This, of course, resulted in quite a bit of delay, as she primped her hair and got herself looking and smelling the way

any bride should. She explained the reason for this delay as she responded to his call and saw him fumbling at the latch of her window without success.

5:5–6. As soon as she could finish her minimal preparations for admitting him entrance through her door at last, she discovered to her dismay that he had been quite grieved at being put off and had given up on entering. He could not wait for her any more and he was deeply grieved. She unlocked her door and looked around for him in vain. She kept calling him by name, but there was no answer.

5:7. Altogether panicked, she ran down toward the city, looking everywhere she might locate him in the early morning dusk. But to make matters worse, the night watchmen thought of her as some kind of a nightwalker and they confiscated her mantle.

the walls	the watchmen of	from on me	my shawl	they carried away	they wounded me
הַחֹמוֹת	שֹׁמְרֵי	מֵעָלַי	אֶת־רְדִידִי	נָשְׂאוּ	פְּצָעוּנִי
hachōmôth	shōmᵉrê	mēʿālay	ʾeth-rᵉdhîdhî	nāsᵉʾû	pᵉtsāʿûnî
art, n fp	v Qal act ptc mp	prep, prep, ps 1cs	do, n ms, ps 1cs	v Qal pf 3cp	v Qal pf 3cp, ps 1cs
2440	8490.152	4623, 6142	881, 7577	5558.116	6728.116

8.

my beloved	if you find	Jerusalem	O daughters of	you	I will cause to swear
אֶת־דּוֹדִי	אִם־תִּמְצְאוּ	יְרוּשָׁלָם	בְּנוֹת	אֶתְכֶם	הִשְׁבַּעְתִּי
ʾeth-dôdhî	ʾim-timtsᵉʾû	yᵉrûshālām	bᵉnôth	ʾethkhem	hishbaʿtî
do, n ms, ps 1cs	cj, v Qal impf 2mp	pn	n fp	do, ps 2mp	v Hiphil pf 1cs
881, 1782	524, 4834.128	3503	1351	881	8123.515

9.

what your beloved	I	love	that being sick with	to him	how will you tell
מַה־דּוֹדֵךְ	אָנִי	אַהֲבָה	שֶׁחוֹלַת	לוֹ	מַה־תַּגִּידוּ
mah-dôdhēkh	ʾānî	ʾahvāh	shechôlath	lô	mah-taggîdhû
intrg, n ms, ps 2fs	pers pron	n fs	rel part, v Qal act ptc fs	prep, ps 3ms	intrg, v Hiphil impf 2mp
4242, 1782	603	157	8054, 2571.153	3937	4242, 5222.528

more than a beloved	what your beloved	among the women	O beautiful one	more than a beloved
מִדּוֹד	מַה־דּוֹדֵךְ	בַּנָּשִׁים	הַיָּפָה	מִדּוֹד
middôdh	mah-dôdhēkh	bannāshîm	hayyāphāh	middôdh
prep, n ms	intrg, n ms, ps 2fs	prep, art, n fp	art, adj	prep, n ms
4623, 1782	4242, 1782	904, 5571	3413	4623, 1782

10.

and red	gleaming	my beloved	you have caused us to swear	that thus
וְאָדוֹם	צַח	דּוֹדִי	הִשְׁבַּעְתָּנוּ	שֶׁכָּכָה
wᵉʾādhôm	tsach	dôdhî	hishbaʿtānû	shekkākhāh
cj, adj	adj	n ms, ps 1cs	v Hiphil pf 2ms, ps 1cp	rel part, adv
121	6970	1782	8123.513	8054, 3722

11.

pure gold	fine gold of	his head	than ten thousand	having been distinguished more
פָּז	כֶּתֶם	רֹאשׁוֹ	מֵרְבָבָה	דָּגוּל
pāz	kethem	rōʾshô	mērᵉvāvāh	dāghûl
n ms	n ms	n ms, ps 3ms	prep, num	v Qal pass ptc ms
6580	3929	7513	4623, 7526	1763.155

12.

like doves	his eyes	like the raven	black	something flowing	his locks
כְּיוֹנִים	עֵינָיו	כָּעֹרֵב	שְׁחֹרוֹת	תַּלְתַּלִּים	קְוֻצּוֹתָיו
kᵉyônîm	ʿênâv	kāʿōrēv	shechōrôth	taltallîm	qᵉwutstsôthâv
prep, n fp	n fd, ps 3ms	prep, art, n ms	adj	n mp	n fp, ps 3ms
3626, 3225	6084	3626, 6397	8265	8864	7261

13.

his cheeks	on a setting	being set	in the milk	being bathed	water	beside springs of
לְחָיָו	עַל־מִלֵּאת	יֹשְׁבוֹת	בֶּחָלָב	רֹחֲצוֹת	מַיִם	עַל־אֲפִיקֵי
lᵉchāyāw	ʿal-millēʾth	yōshᵉvôth	bechālāv	rōchᵃtsôth	māyim	ʿal-ʾăphîqê
n mp, ps 3ms	prep, n fs	v Qal act ptc fp	prep, art, n ms	v Qal act ptc fp	n mp	prep, n mp
4029	6142, 4539	3553.154	904, 2560	7647.154	4448	6142, 665

dripping	lilies	his lips	spices	towers of	the spices	like the garden bed of
נֹטְפוֹת	שׁוֹשַׁנִּים	שִׂפְתוֹתָיו	מֶרְקָחִים	מִגְדְּלוֹת	הַבֹּשֶׂם	כַּעֲרוּגַת
nōtᵉphôth	shôshanîm	siphthôthâv	merqāchîm	mighdᵉlôth	habbōsem	kaʿărûghath
v Qal act ptc fp	n mp	n fp, ps 3ms	n mp	n fp	art, n ms	prep, n fs
5382.154	8236	8004	5003	4166	1336	3626, 6410

14.

with the jewel	having been set	gold	cylinders of	his hands	passing through	myrrh
בַּתַּרְשִׁישׁ	מְמֻלָּאִים	זָהָב	גְּלִילֵי	יָדָיו	עֹבֵר	מוֹר
battarshîsh	mᵉmullāʾîm	zāhāv	gᵉlîlê	yādhâv	ʿōvēr	môr
prep, art, n ms	v Pual ptc mp	n ms	n mp	n fd, ps 3ms	v Qal act ptc ms	n ms
904, 8997	4527.456	2174	1591	3135	5882.151	4915

4753	6488	8514	6190.457	5800	**15.** 8225	6204
n mp, ps 3ms	*n ms*	n fs	*v Pual ptc fs*	n mp	n fp, ps 3ms	*n mp*
מֵעָיו	עֶשֶׁת	שֵׁן	מְעֻלֶּפֶת	סַפִּירִים	שׁוֹקָיו	עַמּוּדֵי
mē'âv	'esheth	shēn	me'ullepheth	sappîrîm	shôqâv	'ammûdhê
his midsection	a plate of	ivory	having been covered with	sapphires	his thighs	pillars of

8667	3354.456	6142, 132, 6580	4920	3626, 3976	1013.155
n ms	v Pual ptc mp	prep, *n mp*, n ms	n ms, ps 3ms	prep, art, pn	v Qal pass ptc ms
שֵׁשׁ	מְיֻסָּדִים	עַל־אַדְנֵי־פָז	מַרְאֵהוּ	כַּלְּבָנוֹן	בָּחוּר
shēsh	meyussādhîm	'al-'adhnê-phāz	mar'ēhû	kallevānôn	bāchûr
alabaster	having been set	on bases of gold	his appearance	like the Lebanon	those chosen

9. What is thy beloved more than another beloved, O thou fairest among women? what is thy beloved more than another beloved, that thou dost so charge us?: ... What is your lover but a lover, O most beautiful of women? What is your lover but a lover, that you do so adjure us?, *Goodspeed* ... Nay, but tell us, ... how shall we know this sweetheart of thine from another's? Why is he loved beyond all else, that thou art so urgent with us?, *Knox* ... That you put us on oath?, *Fenton*.

10. My beloved is white and ruddy, the chiefest among ten thousand: ... My lover is fair and ruddy, *Berkeley* ... loved one is white and red, *BB* ... healthy and tan, *NCV* ... clear and ruddy, Conspicuous above a myriad!, *Young* ... all radiant and ruddy, distinguished, *NRSV* ... dazzling and ... Outstanding among ten thousand, *NASB*.

11. His head is as the most fine gold: ... most delicate gold, *BB* ... dazzles like the purest gold, *Knox*.

his locks are bushy, and black as a raven: ... locks are wavy, *Berkeley* ... luxuriant, *Anchor* ... like clusters of dates, *NASB* ... palm branches, *Goodspeed* ... are palm fronds, *NAB*.

12. His eyes are as the eyes of doves by the rivers of waters, washed with milk, and fitly set: ... like doves by waterducts, Splashing in milky spray, Sitting by brimming pools, *Anchor* ... gentle as doves by the brook-side, only these are bathed in milk, eyes full of repose, *Knox* ... doves by springs of water. They seem to be bathed in cream and are set like jewels, *NCV* ... Bathing in milk, set as gems in a ring, *Rotherham* ... Bathed in milk, and reposed in their setting, *NASB*.

13. His cheeks are as a bed of spices, as sweet flowers: ... a bed of balsam, Banks of sweet-scented herbs, *NASB* ... raised bed of balsam, Growing plants of perfume, *Rotherham* ... towers of perfumes, *Young* ... exhaling perfumes, *Goodspeed* ... with ripening aromatic herbs, *NAB*.

his lips like lilies, dropping sweet-smelling myrrh: ... His lips lotuses, Dripping liquid myrrh, *Anchor* ... hyacinths, dropping flowing myrrh, *Goodspeed* ... lips are red blossoms; they drip choice myrrh, *NAB* ... diffusing perfume, *Fenton*.

14. His hands are as gold rings set with the beryl: his belly is as bright ivory overlaid with sapphires: ... hands are rods of gold, set with gilded stones, *Berkeley* ... fingers are golden tapers tipped with topaz pink, *Moffatt* ... hands are rods of gold, studded with Tarshish-stones, *Goodspeed* ... arms are rods of gold adorned with chrysolites, *Douay* ... heart bright ivory, covered with sapphires, *Young* ... belly a plaque of ivory overlaid with lapis lazuli, *NEB*.

15. His legs are as pillars of marble, set upon sockets of fine gold: his countenance is as Lebanon, excellent as the cedars: ... pillars of stone on a base of delicate gold; his looks are as Lebanon, beautiful as the cedar-tree, *BB* ... aspect is like Lebanon, *MRB* ... stature is like

5:8–16. But before long, she came across some of the Jerusalem singers and begged them to tell her if they had seen the prince anywhere around. Apparently, none of them recognized her as the wife of the prince. But after attempting to identify herself to them, they asked her to describe the man she was looking for. In v. 9, they ask her to describe carefully what he looked like (she probably felt it unwise to blurt out who he was in view of her disheveled costume) and tried to describe her lover in such a way as to pick up a clue as to where they might have noticed him in the semi-darkness of the suburbs of Jerusalem. Surely, they would have recalled him in his majestic person and fine costume, and his beautiful locks adorned by a golden helmet surmounting his dark hair. Surely, if they had seen him, they would have noticed him quite clearly, such a striking Adonis as he was with his beautiful eyes and teeth and the gold rings. How could these young ladies fail to notice and marvel at this handsome young hero whose form was like that of a model fashioned by a peerless artist? She added that his legs were perfectly formed and the impact of his appearance was like a cedar of Lebanon. This glorious depiction

3626, 753 prep, art, n mp	16.	2541 n ms, ps 3ms	4619 n mp	3725 cj, n ms, ps 3ms	4398 n mp	2172 dem pron	1782 n ms, ps 1cs
כָּאֲרָזִים		חִכּוֹ	מַמְתַקִּים	וְכֻלּוֹ	מַחֲמַדִּים	זֶה	דּוֹדִי
kā'ărāzîm		chikkô	mamthaqqîm	wekhullô	machămaddîm	zeh	dhôdhî
like the cedars		his palate	sweetnesses	and all of him	pleasantries	this one	my beloved

2172 cj, dem pron	7739 n ms, ps 1cs	1351 n fp	3503 pn	6:1	590 intrg	2050.111 v Qal pf 3ms	1782 n ms, ps 2fs
וְזֶה	רֵעִי	בְּנוֹת	יְרוּשָׁלָם		אָנָה	הָלַךְ	דּוֹדֵךְ
wezeh	rē'î	benôth	yerûshālām		'ānāh	hālakh	dôdhēkh
and this one	my friend	O daughters of	Jerusalem		where	has he gone	your beloved

3413 art, adj	904, 5571 prep, art, n fp	590 intrg	6680.111 v Qal pf 3ms	1782 n ms, ps 2fs
הַיָּפָה	בַּנָּשִׁים	אָנָה	פָּנָה	דּוֹדֵךְ
hayyāphāh	bannāshîm	'ānāh	pānāh	dhôdhēkh
O beautiful one	among the women	where	has he turned	your beloved

1272.320 cj, v Piel juss 1cp, ps 3ms	6196 prep, ps 2fs	2.	1782 n ms, ps 1cs	3495.111 v Qal pf 3ms	3937, 1629 prep, n ms, ps 3ms
וּנְבַקְשֶׁנּוּ	עִמָּךְ		דּוֹדִי	יָרַד	לְגַנּוֹ
ûnevaqŏshennû	'immākh		dôdhî	yāradh	leghannô
that we may search for him	with you		my beloved	he has gone down	to his garden

3937, 6410 prep, n fp	1336 art, n ms	3937, 7749.141 prep, v Qal inf con	904, 1629 prep, art, n mp	3937, 4092.141 cj, prep, v Qal inf con	8236 n mp
לַעֲרוּגוֹת	הַבֹּשֶׂם	לִרְעוֹת	בַּגַּנִּים	וְלִלְקֹט	שׁוֹשַׁנִים
la'ărûghôth	habbōsem	lir'ôth	bagganîm	welilqōṭ	shôshanîm
to the garden bed of	the spice	to pasture	in the gardens	and to gather	lilies

3.	603 pers pron	3937, 1782 prep, n ms, ps 1cs	1782 cj, n ms, ps 1cs	3937 prep, ps 1cs	7749.151 art, v Qal act ptc ms	904, 8236 prep, art, n mp
	אֲנִי	לְדוֹדִי	וְדוֹדִי	לִי	הָרֹעֶה	בַּשּׁוֹשַׁנִים
	'ănî	ledhôdhî	wedhôdhî	lî	hārō'eh	bashshôshanîm
	I	to my beloved	and my beloved	to me	the shepherd	among the lilies

4.	3413 adj	879 pers pron	7761 n fs, ps 1cs	3626, 8995 prep, pn	5173 adj	3626, 3503 prep, pn	371 adj
	יָפָה	אַתְּ	רַעְיָתִי	כְּתִרְצָה	נָאוָה	כִּירוּשָׁלָם	אֲיֻמָּה
	yāphāh	'atte	ra'yāthî	kethirtsāh	nā'wāh	kîrûshālām	'ăyummāh
	beautiful	you	my beloved	like Tirzah	beautiful	like Jerusalem	breathtaking

3626, 1763.258 prep, art, v Niphal ptc fp	5.	5621.532 v Hiphil impv 2fs	6084 n md, ps 2fs	4623, 5224 prep, prep, ps 1cs	8054, 2062 cj, pers pron
כַּנִּדְגָּלוֹת		הָסֵבִּי	עֵינַיִךְ	מִנֶּגְדִּי	שֶׁהֵם
kanidhgālôth		hāsbî	'ênayikh	minneghdî	shehēm
like the raised standards		turn away	your eyes	from before me	because they

Lebanon, as striking as the cedars, *Berkeley* … Erect his stature as Lebanon itself, noble as Lebanon cedar, *Knox* … Imposing as the, *NAB*.

16. His mouth is most sweet: yea, he is altogether lovely: … mouth is sweetness—and all of him desirable, *Young* … His conversation is sweetness itself, he is altogether lovable, *JB*

… sweet to kiss, and I desire him very much, *NCV* … whispers are sweetness itself, wholly desirable, *NEB*.

This is my beloved, and this is my friend, O daughters of Jerusalem: … Such is my lover, and such is my friend, *Berkeley* … This is my love, this my mate, O Jerusalem girls, *Anchor*.

6:1. Whither is thy beloved gone, O thou fairest among women? whither is thy beloved turned aside? that we may seek him with thee: … Where has he hidden himself?, *Berkeley* … Where wanders your lover? We will seek him with you!, *Fenton* … O rarest of beautiful women, where has your loved one gone? We will help you find him, *LIVB*.

2. My beloved is gone down into his garden, to the beds of spices, to feed in the gardens, and to gather lilies: ... to his field, To the sweet smelling hedge-rows, To the pastures enclosed, and is gathering, *Fenton* ... to the beds where balsam grows, to delight in the gardens, and to pick, *REB* ... To the balsam beds, To browse in the gardens, To pluck lotuses, *Anchor* ... To pasture his flock in the gardens, and gather hyacinths, *Goodspeed* ... to take food in the gardens, *BB*.

3. I am my beloved's, and my beloved is mine: he feedeth among the lilies: ... I am for my loved one, and my loved one is for me; he takes food among, *BB* ... I am my lover's,—my lover is mine!—He strolls amongst, *Fenton* ... He who feeds on the lotus, *Anchor* ... who pastures his flock among the hyacinths, *Goodspeed*.

4. Thou art beautiful, O my love, as Tirzah, comely as Jerusalem, terrible as an army with banners: ... My darling charms me like delight; Like Jerusalem's prospect;—I tremble like flags!, *Fenton* ... Lovely as Jerusalem, Awesome as an army, *NKJV* ... enchanting as Jerusalem, formidable as an army!, *JB* ... captivating as an army with, *Berkeley*.

5. Turn away thine eyes from me, for they have overcome me: ... Avert your eyes from me, For they drive me wild, *Anchor* ... for they disturb me, *RSV* ... they have confused me, *NASB* ... they take me by assault!, *JB* ... they excite me too much, *NCV*.

thy hair is as a flock of goats that appear from Gilead: ... Your hair, as it falls across your face, is like a flock of goats frisking down the slopes of Gilead, *LIVB* ... which take their rest on the side of Gilead, *BB* ... Going down from, *NKJV* ... that lie along the side of, *MRB*.

---

of his heroic perfection serves as a response corresponding to Solomon's rapturous description of her as his sweetheart in ch. 4. "Such is the magnificent hero whom I adore," is the bride's final contribution to describing her dearly beloved.

6:1–4. Unfortunately enough, the Shulammite lass failed to stir up any recollection of her superman, even though the Jerusalem choristers had been stirred up and were eager to locate him—both for her sake and for their own curiosity as well. They were perfectly eager to join with her in search of this paragon of lordly beauty. It might seem a bit strange that none of the girls noticed him somewhere in the milling throng outside of the city itself. They may have concluded that it could not have been Solomon himself, since he was so well-known and universally admired. But whether any other distinguished figure was visiting Jerusalem at this time, these singers would be more than eager to join the prince wherever he might be. Recognizing the Shulammite's striking beauty ("O thou fairest among women"), they were happy to scout out everywhere in all of Jerusalem. This entourage of search-partners came upon him very soon, for the bride had discovered where he had gone. It was to his own cherished garden plot where he had stayed for a while until the morning sun would make it easy for him to get together with his precious bride. Of course, what a suitable place for him to rest, in the midst of his spice gardens and lilies and his favorite lambs that fed there.

To his wife's relief, he had evidently recovered from his disappointment at her cottage and there was no mention of it whatever. On the contrary, he burst out with rapturous joy, comparing her perfect countenance to the capital city of Tirzah and of Jerusalem as well. It would seldom occur to a modern admirer to compare a beautiful woman to a beautiful city, but we have already encountered the same kind of admiration in some of his earlier speeches. Few modern lovers would feel overjoyed at seeing their lady love come upon them like a military regiment. But Tirzah was, at that time, a beautifully located community up on the hills located to the west of the Jordan River, eleven miles northwest of Nablus. Greatly admired though it was, Tirzah was later cruelly ravaged by King Omri of Israel around 800 B.C., when he finally defeated a rival king named Zimri. It should be added that Tirzah never really recovered from Omri's devastation. But it should also be noted that the earlier prominence of Tirzah in this Book furnishes decisive proof in favor of the Solomonic period as the time when Song of Songs was composed. This serves to discredit the skepticism of those scholars who would argue for a much later date than the time of Solomon (v. 4).

6:5–7. It should be understood, however, that Solomon was thinking more particularly of the emotional impression his sweetheart made upon him as he saw her coming down to renew fellowship with him after the unhappy episode of the night just past. He found himself just as infatuated with her as ever before. The impact of her peerless dark eyes, the captivating richness of her beautiful tresses overwhelmed him all over again. Likewise, he admired her perfect white teeth which resembled a flock of freshly bathed white sheep—not a tooth

7580.516	7998	3626, 5953	6008	8054, 1611.116
v Hiphil pf 3cp, ps 1cs	n ms, ps 2fs	prep, n ms	art, n fp	rel part, v Qal pf 3cp
הִרְהִיבֻנִי	שַׂעְרֵךְ	כְּעֵדֶר	הָעִזִּים	שֶׁגָּלְשׁוּ
hirhîvunî	sa'ărēkh	ke'ēdher	hā'izzîm	sheggāleshû
they confound me	your hair	like a flock of	the goats	which they have come down

4623, 1609	**6.** 8514	3626, 5953	7636	8054, 6148.116
prep, art, pn	n fd, ps 2fs	prep, n ms	art, n fp	rel part, v Qal pf 3cp
מִן־הַגִּלְעָד	שִׁנַּיִךְ	כְּעֵדֶר	הָרְחֵלִים	שֶׁעָלוּ
min-haggil'ādh	shinnayikh	ke'ēdher	hārechēlîm	she'ālû
from the Gilead	your teeth	like a flock of	the ewe lambs	which they have come up

4623, 7650	8054, 3725	8709.554	8316	375	904
prep, art, n fs	rel part, n ms, ps 3mp	v Hiphil ptc fp	cj, adj	sub	prep, ps 3mp
מִן־הָרַחְצָה	שֶׁכֻּלָּם	מַתְאִימוֹת	וְשַׁכֻּלָה	אֵין	בָּהֶם
min-hārachtsāh	shekkullām	math'îmôth	weshakkulāh	'ên	bāhem
from the washing	which all of them	bearing twins	and bereft	there is not	among them

7. 3626, 6644	7705	7834	4623, 1185	3937, 7046	**8.** 8666	2065
prep, n fs	art, n ms	n fs, ps 2fs	prep, prep	prep, n fs, ps 2fs	num	pers pron
כְּפֶלַח	הָרִמּוֹן	רַקָּתֵךְ	מִבַּעַד	לְצַמָּתֵךְ	שִׁשִּׁים	הֵמָּה
kephelach	hārimmôn	raqqāthēkh	mibba'adh	letsammāthēkh	shishshîm	hēmmāh
like a slice of	the pomegranate	your temple	from behind	your veil	sixty	they

4573	8470	6637	6183	375	4709	**9.** 259	2026
n fp	cj, num	n fp	cj, n fp	sub	n ms	num	pers pron
מְלָכוֹת	וּשְׁמֹנִים	פִּילַגְשִׁים	וַעֲלָמוֹת	אֵין	מִסְפָּר	אַחַת	הִיא
melākhôth	ûshemōnîm	pîlaghshîm	wa'ălāmôth	'ên	mispār	'achath	hî'
queens	and eighty	concubines	and young women	there is not	a number	one	she

3225	8866	259	2026	3937, 525	1276	2026
n fs, ps 1cs	adj, ps 1cs	num	pers pron	prep, n fs, ps 3fs	adj	pers pron
יוֹנָתִי	תַמָּתִי	אַחַת	הִיא	לְאִמָּהּ	בָּרָה	הִיא
yônāthî	thammāthî	'achath	hî'	le'immāh	bārāh	hî'
my dove	my perfect one	one	she	of her mother	flawless	she

3937, 3314.153	7495.116	1351	861.326	4573
prep, v Qal act ptc fs, ps 3fs	v Qal pf 3cp, ps 3fs	n fp	cj, v Piel impf 3mp, ps 3fs	n fp
לְיוֹלַדְתָּהּ	רָאוּהָ	בָּנוֹת	וַיְאַשְּׁרוּהָ	מְלָכוֹת
leyôladhtāh	rā'ûhā	vānôth	way'ashsherûhā	melākhôth
of the one who bore her	they saw her	daughters	and they declared her blessed	queens

6637	2054.326	**10.** 4449, 2148	8625.257	3765, 8266
cj, n fp	cj, v Piel impf 3mp, ps 3fs	intrg, dem pron	art, v Niphal ptc fs	cj, n ms
וּפִילַגְשִׁים	וַיְהַלְלוּהָ	מִי־זֹאת	הַנִּשְׁקָפָה	כְּמוֹ־שָׁחַר
ûphîlaghshîm	wayhalelûāh	mî-zō'th	hanishqāphāh	kemô-shāchar
and concubines	and they praised her	who this one	the one looking down	like a dawn

3413	3626, 3970	1276	3626, 2636	371	3626, 1763.158
adj	prep, art, n fs	adj	prep, art, n fs	adj	prep, art, v Niphal ptc fp
יָפָה	כַלְּבָנָה	בָּרָה	כַּחַמָּה	אֲיֻמָּה	כַּנִּדְגָּלוֹת
yāphāh	khallevānāh	bārāh	kachammāh	'ăyummāh	kanidhgālôth
beautiful	like the moon	flawless	like the sun	breathtaking	like the raised standards

11. 420, 1634	90	3495.115	3937, 7495.141	904, 3	5337
prep, n fs	n ms	v Qal pf 1cs	prep, v Qal inf con	prep, n mp	art, n ms
אֶל־גִּנַּת	אֱגוֹז	יָרַדְתִּי	לִרְאוֹת	בְּאִבֵּי	הַנָּחַל
'el-ginnath	'ĕghôz	yāradhtî	lir'ôth	be'ibbê	hannāchal
to the orchard of	nut trees	I went down	to look	on the green sprouts of	the valley

6. Thy teeth are as a flock of sheep which go up from the washing: … teeth white as ewes fresh from the washing, *Knox* … as a row of the lambs, That have come up from, *Young*.

whereof every one beareth twins, and there is not one barren among them: … each is paired, not one of them is missing, *Berkeley* … Because all of them are forming twins, And a bereaved one is not among them, *Young* … All of which bear twins, And not one among them has lost her young, *NASB* … Each has its twin, not one of them is alone, *NIV*.

7. As a piece of a pomegranate are thy temples within thy locks: … As the halves of a pomegranate, so are your cheeks behind your veil, *Berkeley* … Your cheeks under your veil, are love-apples!, *Fenton* … thy cheeks shew through their veil rosy as skin of pomegranate!, *Knox* … Your parted lips behind your veil are like a pomegranate cut open, *REB*.

8. There are threescore queens, and fourscore concubines, and virgins without number: … There are sixty queens, and eighty servant-wives, and young girls without number, *BB* … There may be sixty Queens, with their seventy attendants, And maids without number, *Fenton* … princesses, four score concubines, and young women past counting, *REB* … and harem daughters beyond number, *Berkeley*.

9. My dove, my undefiled is but one; she is the only one of her mother, she is the choice one of her that bare her: … One there is beyond compare; for me, none so gentle, none so pure! Only once her mother travailed; she would have no darling but this, *Knox* … She is her mother's only daughter, the brightest of the one who gave her birth, *NCV* … She is the pure one of her that bare her, *MRB* … she is kind to the one who gave her birth, *Beck*.

The daughters saw her, and blessed her; yea, the queens and the concubines, and they praised her: … The maidens saw her and called her happy, *RSV* … The daughters saw her and declared her fortunate, the queens and concubines, and they sang her praises, *Douay* … Girls have seen her and proclaimed her blessed, *JB* … The young women saw her and called her happy; the queens and the slave women also praised her, *NCV*.

10. Who is she that looketh forth as the morning, fair as the moon, clear as the sun, and terrible as an army with banners?: … Who is this that bursts out like the Dawn? And fair as the silvery Moon?—Like the Sun on a fluttering flag?, *Fenton* … breaks forth like the dawn, as beautiful as the moon, As bright as the sun, as august as the most distinguished?, *Goodspeed* … She is as pretty as the moon, as bright as the sun, as wonderful as an army flying flags, *NCV* … majestic as the starry heavens?, *REB*.

11. I went down into the garden of nuts to see the fruits of the valley, and to see whether the vine flourished, and the pomegranates budded: … I went down to the orchard of nut trees To see the blossoms of the valley, To see whether the vine had budded Or the pomegranates had bloomed, *NASB* … I came down to the nut garden to look at the fresh growth, *Douay* … to see the fresh

missing! And her lovely temples bore the loveliness of a peeled pomegranate.

6:8–11. At this point, we come to a very unexpected disclosure of the existence of an enormous harem right there in Jerusalem. There were no less than sixty queens, eighty concubines and an unspecified number of "virgins." Whether he and she were still alone together in Solomon's garden is not quite clear. The statement he reported regarding their attitude of approval toward the Shulammite is somewhat unexpected, for they had actually had an opportunity to look her over and decide whether she would measure up to the standards of the royal palace. "The daughters saw her and called her blessed." Obviously, they had decided to welcome her as a perfectly qualified member of the harem. This might very likely have marred the relationship so far as she was concerned. How could there have been such a large collection of queens even before Solomon got to be the king of all Israel? To be sure, it is stated that eventually he acquired 700 wives and 300 concubines (1 Ki. 11:3), who influenced him to pay homage to the false gods of the Near East, even to the extent of building a "high place" for Chemosh of the Moabites. Consequently, he encountered the stern disfavor of Yahweh. The result was that Israel later split up into two kingdoms rather than one (1 Ki. 11:4–13). Even though he tried to introduce the Shulammite into the main harem, the glow of romance was seriously impaired and ended up in disillusionment so far as she was concerned (vv. 8f). Yet, he still attempted to maintain the love affair with her and granted her a high status in the society of the sixty queens, who apparently felt no serious jealousy toward this farm girl from the north. They seem to have concurred with him in regard to her physical beauty and charm and even came to admire her for her unique loveliness and gentle modesty (v. 10).

The next utterance apparently came from the harem queens, who were deeply impressed by her firm and queenly poise as she descended to inspect

3937, 7495.141	1950B, 6775.112	1655	5525.516	7705	3940
prep, v Qal inf con	intrg part, v Qal pf 3fs	art, n fs	v Hiphil pf 3cp	art, n mp	**12.** neg part
לִרְאוֹת	הֲפָרְחָה	הַגֶּפֶן	הֵנֵצוּ	הָרִמֹּנִים	לֹא
lir'ôth	hăphārechāh	haggephen	hēnētsû	hārimmōnîm	lō'
to see	has it budded	the vine	had they blossomed	the pomegranates	not

3156.115	5497	7947.112	4980	6194, 5259	8178.132
v Qal pf 1cs	n fs, ps 1cs	v Qal pf 3fs, ps 1cs	n fp	n ms, ps 1cs, n ms	**13.** v Qal impv 2fs
יָדַעְתִּי	נַפְשִׁי	שָׂמַתְנִי	מַרְכְּבוֹת	עַמִּי־נָדִיב	שׁוּבִי
yādha'ättî	naphshî	sāmathnî	markevôth	'ammî-nādhîv	shûvî
I knew	my soul	it had set me	chariots	my people noblemen	return

8178.132	8203	8178.132	8178.132	2463.120, 904
v Qal impv 2fs	art, pn	v Qal impv 2fs	v Qal impv 2fs	cj, v Qal juss 1cp, prep, ps 2fs
שׁוּבִי	הַשּׁוּלַמִּית	שׁוּבִי	שׁוּבִי	וְנֶחֱזֶה־בָּךְ
shûvî	hashshûlammîth	shûvî	shûvî	wenechĕzeh-bākh
return	the Shulammite	return	return	that we may look on you

4242, 2463.128	904, 8203	3626, 4383	4402
intrg, v Qal impf 2mp	prep, art, pn	prep, n fs	art, n fd
מַה־תֶּחֱזוּ	בַּשּׁוּלַמִּית	כִּמְחֹלַת	הַמַּחֲנָיִם
mah-techĕzû	bashshûlammîth	kimchōlath	hammachănāyim
what will you look at	on the Shulammite	like the round formation of	the two encampments

	4242, 3412.116	6718	904, 5458	1351, 5259	2644
7:1	intrg, v Qal pf 3cp	n fp, ps 2fs	prep, art, n fp	n fs, n ms	n mp
	מַה־יָּפוּ	פְעָמַיִךְ	בַּנְּעָלִים	בַּת־נָדִיב	חַמּוּקֵי
	mah-yāphû	phe'āmayikh	banne'ālîm	bath-nādhîv	chammûqê
	how they are beautiful	your feet	in the sandals	O daughter of a nobleman	the curvatures of

3525	3765	2559	4801	3135	554	8634
n fd, ps 2fs	prep	n mp	n ms	n fd	n ms	**2.** n ms, ps 2fs
יְרֵכַיִךְ	כְּמוֹ	חַלָּאִים	מַעֲשֵׂה	יְדֵי	אָמָּן	שָׁרְרֵךְ
yerēkhayikh	kemô	chălā'îm	ma'ăsēh	yedhê	'āmmān	shārerēkh
your thighs	like	ornaments	the work of	the hands of	a master craftsman	your navel

98	5653	414, 2741.121	4327	1027	6431	2498
n ms	art, n ms	adv, v Qal juss 3ms	art, n ms	n fs, ps 2fs	n fs	n fp
אַגַּן	הַסַּהַר	אַל־יֶחְסַר	הַמָּזֶג	בִּטְנֵךְ	עֲרֵמַת	חִטִּים
'aggan	hassahar	'al-yechăsar	hammāzegh	bitnēkh	'ărēmath	chittîm
a goblet of	the roundness	may it not lack	the mixed wine	your belly	a heap of	wheat

5657.157	904, 8236	8530	8530	8157	3626, 8530	6314	8751
v Qal pass ptc fs	prep, art, n mp	**3.**	num	n md, ps 2fs	prep, num	n mp	n mp
סוּגָה	בַּשּׁוֹשַׁנִּים		שְׁנֵי	שָׁדַיִךְ	כִּשְׁנֵי	עֳפָרִים	תָּאֳמֵי
sûghāh	bashshôshanîm		shenê	shādhayikh	kishnê	'ăphārîm	tā'ămê
having been edged	with the lilies		the two of	your breasts	like two	fawns	twins of

6909	6939	3626, 4166	8514	6084	1320	904, 2919
n fs	**4.** n ms, ps 2fs	prep, n ms	art, n fs	n fd, ps 2fs	n fp	prep, pn
צְבִיָּה	צַוָּארֵךְ	כְּמִגְדַּל	הַשֵּׁן	עֵינַיִךְ	בְּרֵכוֹת	בְּחֶשְׁבּוֹן
tsevîyāh	tsawwā'rēkh	kemighdal	hashshēn	'ênayikh	berēkhôth	becheshbôn
a female gazelle	your neck	like a tower of	the ivory	your eyes	pools	in Heshbon

6142, 8554	1366B	653	3626, 4166	3976	7099.151
prep, n ms	pn	n ms, ps 2fs	prep, n ms	art, pn	v Qal act ptc ms
עַל־שַׁעַר	בַּת־רַבִּים	אַפֵּךְ	כְּמִגְדַּל	הַלְּבָנוֹן	צוֹפֶה
'al-sha'ar	bath-rabbîm	'appēkh	kemighdal	hallevānôn	tsôpheh
beside the gate of	Bath-Rabbim	your nose	like a tower of	the Lebanon	keeping watch over

shoots in the valley, to see if the vines were budding and the pomegranate trees in flower, *JB* ... I went down to a garden of nut-trees to look at the rushes by the stream, *NEB*.

12. Or ever I was aware, my soul made me like the chariots of Amminadib: ... I am trembling; you have made me as eager for love as a chariot driver is for battle, *Good News* ... I was not aware my longing had made me like the chariots of my noble people, *Beck* ... Before I knew it, my heart had made me the blessed one of my kinswomen, *NAB* ... I did not know myself; she made me feel more than a prince reigning over the myriads of his people, *NEB*.

13. Return, return, O Shulamite; return, return, that we may look upon thee: ... Why offended?—Return to me! ... Let me see you!, *Fenton* ... Come back, maid of Sulam, come back; let us feast our eyes on thee, *Knox* ... that we may gaze at you!, *NASB*.

What will ye see in the Shulamite? As it were the company of two armies: ... How will you gaze on Shulamite in the Dance of the two Camps?, *Anchor* ... What do you see in Shulammith? As the chorus of 'Mahanaim', *Young* ... Why should you look at that sulker, More than at a Mahanami Dancer?, *Fenton* ... Why are you looking at the girl from Shulam, dancing between two lines of dancers?, *JB* ... We would see her in the sword-dance, *Moffatt*.

7:1. How beautiful are thy feet with shoes, O prince's daughter!: ... How beautiful are your feet in sandals, O maiden of queenly form!, *Berkeley* ... How fine your steps are in your slippers! Smart girl!, *Fenton* ... How beautiful are thy goings with shoes, *Geneva* ... How beautiful are thy steps in sandals, *Mast* ... Ah, princely maid, how dainty are the steps of thy sandalled feet!, *Knox*.

the joints of thy thighs are like jewels, the work of the hands of a cunning workman: ... Your curvy thighs like ornaments Crafted by artist hands, *Anchor* ... The turnings of thy sides are as ornaments, Work of the hands of an artificer, *Young* ... The edge of your skirts is like lace,—And made by the hand of the skilful!, *Fenton* ... The curve of your thighs is like the curve of a necklace, work of a master hand, *JB*.

2. Thy navel is like a round goblet, which wanteth not liquor: ... a rounded bowl in which mingled wine is never lacking, *Berkeley* ... Your vulva a rounded crater; May it never lack punch!, *Anchor* ... Your belt is a bowl not deficient in drink, *Fenton*.

thy belly is like an heap of wheat set about with lilies: ... Your stomach is a store of grain with lilies round it, and in the middle a round cup full of wine, *BB* ... a mound of wheat Hedged with lotuses, *Anchor* ... Is your waist a field of ripe corn, and encircled with lilies?, *Fenton*.

3. Thy two breasts are like two young roes that are twins: ... two fawns, twins of a gazelle, *RSV* ... twins of a roe, *MRB*.

4. Thy neck is as a tower of ivory; thine eyes like the fishpools in Heshbon, by the gate of Bath-rabbim: ... Thy neck rising proudly like a tower, but all of ivory; deep, deep thy eyes, like those pools at Hesebon, under Beth-rabbim Gate, *Knox* ... Your neck is stately ... your eyes as

---

a garden of nuts trees to see how far they had developed. Every step she took reflected a firm and imposing poise and showed her manifesting something of the quiet glory of the sun and the moon as she strode firmly down to the path to see how the grapes and pomegranates were doing.

6:12–13. But as she was inspecting the new growth, she apparently found herself surrounded by some charioteers from her native town, who urged her to come back home once more. They begged her to go back to her home and the neighbors of her native home, hoping she would brighten her home grounds with her return. They all had been missing her! Yet, it is just possible that the chariots sent to fetch her may have been sent by the harem, rather than from Shunem. Yet the reference to the performing of the traditional dance may point rather to the warm welcome of her fellow citizens, who would dance to the tune of Mahanaim ("Two Armies") with her.

7:1–3. This chapter seems to fit in with a return visit to the Jerusalem harem rather than to a group of fellow villagers at home. The flattering expressions of admiration and delight seemed to be more courtly in their wedding than one would expect to hear in some outlying community. The heroine was ardently greeted and admired in language of the young Solomon and his eloquent followers, hailing her as having a royal standing. But the outspoken admiration of her body and waist sound very much like the estimation of Solomon himself as he rejoiced in her beautifully rounded thighs shaped like ornamental goblets and her slenderly molded waist adorned with white lilies. Her perfectly shaped breasts received praise with full candor, rather than being noted with silent pleasure as would be customary today.

7:4–5. Interestingly enough, the enthusiastic praise by ladies of the harem serves to emulate what young Solomon had spoken when they were alone

5.

7513	1863	3626, 3888	6142	7513		1894	6686
n ms, ps 2fs	cj, n fs	prep, art, pn	prep, ps 2fs	n ms, ps 2fs	**5.**	pn	n mp
רֹאשֵׁךְ	וְדַלַּת	כַּכַּרְמֶל	עָלַיִךְ	רֹאשֵׁךְ		דַּמֶּשֶׂק	פְּנֵי
rō'shēkh	wedhallath	kakkarmel	'ālayikh	rō'shēkh		dhammāseq	penê
your head	and the flowing of	like the Carmel	upon you	your head		Damascus	the surface of

6.

4242, 3412.114	904, 7584	646.155	4567	3626, 736
intrg, v Qal pf 2fs	prep, art, n mp	v Qal pass ptc ms	n ms	prep, art, n ms
מַה־יָּפִית	בָּרְהָטִים	אָסוּר	מֶלֶךְ	כָּאַרְגָּמָן
mah-yāphîth	bārehātîm	'āsûr	melekh	kā'argāmān
how are you beautiful	by the courses	is imprisoned	a king	like the purple cloth

7.

1880.112	7253	2148	904, 8921	157	4242, 5459.114
v Qal pf 3fs	n fs, ps 2fs	dem pron	prep, art, n mp	n fs	cj, intrg, v Qal pf 2fs
דָּמְתָה	קוֹמָתֵךְ	זֹאת	בַּתַּעֲנוּגִים	אַהֲבָה	וּמַה־נָּעַמְתְּ
dāmethāh	qômāthēkh	zō'th	batta'ănûghîm	'ahvāh	ûmah-nā'amt
it is like	your height	this	among the delights	O love	and how are you pleasant

8.

904, 8887	6148.125	569.115	3937, 838	8157	3937, 8887
prep, n ms	v Qal juss 1cs	v Qal pf 1cs	prep, n mp	cj, n md, ps 2fs	prep, n ms
בְתָמָר	אֶעֱלֶה	אָמַרְתִּי	לְאַשְׁכֹּלוֹת	וְשָׁדַיִךְ	לְתָמָר
vethāmār	'e'ĕleh	'āmartî	le'ashkōlôth	weshādhayikh	lethāmār
in the palm tree	let me go up	I said	clusters	and your breasts	a date-palm tree

3626, 838	8157	2030.126, 5167	904, 5773	270.125
prep, n mp	n md, ps 2fs	cj, v Qal juss 3mp, part	prep, n mp, ps 3ms	v Qal juss 1cs
כְּאַשְׁכְּלוֹת	שָׁדַיִךְ	וְיִהְיוּ־נָא	בְּסַנְסִנָּיו	אֹחֲזָה
ke'eshkelôth	shādhayikh	weyihyû-nā'	besanesinnâv	'ōchăzāh
like the clusters of	your breasts	and may they be please	on its clusters of dates	let me take hold

9.

3626, 3302	2541	3626, 8931	653	7666	1655
prep, n ms	cj, n ms, ps 2fs	prep, art, n mp	n ms, ps 2fs	cj, n ms	art, n fs
כְּיֵּן	וְחִכֵּךְ	כַּתַּפּוּחִים	אַפֵּךְ	וְרֵיחַ	הַגֶּפֶן
keyên	wechikkēkh	kattappûchîm	'appēkh	werêach	haggephen
like the wine	and your palate	like the apples	your nose	and the fragrance of	the vine

3585	8004	1729.151	3937, 4478	3937, 1782	2050.151	3009B
adj	n fd	v Qal act ptc ms	prep, n mp	prep, n ms, ps 1cs	v Qal act ptc ms	art, adj
יְשֵׁנִים	שִׂפְתֵי	דּוֹבֵב	לְמֵישָׁרִים	לְדוֹדִי	הוֹלֵךְ	הַטּוֹב
yeshēnîm	siphthê	dôvēv	lemêshārîm	ledhôdhî	hôlēkh	hattôv
the sleeping	the lips of	dripping on	of straightness	for my beloved	proceeding	the good

10. 11.

1782	2050.131		9010	6142	3937, 1782	603	
n ms, ps 1cs	v Qal impv 2ms	**11.**	n fs, ps 3ms	cj, prep, ps 1cs	prep, n ms, ps 1cs	pers pron	**10.**
דוֹדִי	לְכָה		תְּשׁוּקָתוֹ	וְעָלַי	לְדוֹדִי	אֲנִי	
dhôdhî	lekhāh		teshûqāthô	we'ālay	ledhôdhî	'ănî	
my beloved	come		his longing	and concerning me	to my beloved	I	

12.

8326.520	904, 3849	4053.120	7898	3428.120
v Hiphil juss 1cp	prep, art, n mp	v Qal juss 1cp	art, n ms	v Qal juss 1cp
נַשְׁכִּימָה	בַּכְּפָרִים	נָלִינָה	הַשָּׂדֶה	נֵצֵא
nashkîmāh	bakkepārîm	nālînāh	hassādheh	nētsē'
let us rise early	in the villages	let us spend the night	the field	let us go out to

5758	6858.311	1655	6775.112	524	7495.120	3937, 3884
art, n ms	v Piel pf 3ms	art, n fs	v Qal pf 3fs	cj	v Qal juss 1cp	prep, art, n mp
הַסְּמָדַר	פִּתַּח	הַגֶּפֶן	פָּרְחָה	אִם	נִרְאֶה	לַכְּרָמִים
hassemādhar	pittach	haggephen	pārechāh	'im	nir'eh	lakkerāmîm
the blossom	it has opened	the vine	it has budded	whether	let us see	to the vineyards

limpid pools, *LIVB* … Your eyes the pools in Heshbon By the gate of Bat-Rabbim, *Anchor*.

thy nose is as the tower of Lebanon which looketh toward Damascus: … Thy face as a tower of Lebanon looking to, *Young* … Your nose is shapely like the tower of Lebanon overlooking, *LIVB*.

5. Thine head upon thee is like Carmel, and the hair of thine head like purple; the king is held in the galleries: … And the tresses hanging from your head are like purple drapes, your flowing locks could captivate a king, *Beck* … your flowing locks are lustrous black, tresses braided with ribbons, *REB* … Your hair is like royal tapestry, *NIV* … The king is captivated by your tresses, *NASB* … The king is fettered by [thy] ringlets!, *Darby*.

6. How fair and how pleasant art thou, O love, for delights!: … How beautiful and how sweet you are, *BB* … How fair and pleasant you are, O loved one, delectable maiden!, *NRSV* … Why are you so charming and pleasant?—I love her, involved in delights, *Fenton* … My love, with all your charms!, *NASB*.

7. This thy stature is like to a palm tree, and thy breasts to clusters of grapes: … Your very figure is like a palm tree, *NAB* … You are tall like a palm tree, and your breasts are like

its bunches of fruit, *NCV* … its fruit-clusters your breasts, *JB*.

8. I said, I will go up to the palm tree, I will take hold of the boughs thereof: … What thought should I have but to reach the tree's top, and gather its fruit?, *Knox* … I have decided, 'I shall climb the palm tree, I shall seize its clusters of dates!', *JB* … I declare I could climb up that Palm,—I would hang by its thorns, *Fenton* … take hold of its fruit stalks, *NASB* … Oh then let thy breasts I pray thee be like vine-clusters, *Rotherham*.

now also thy breasts shall be as clusters of the vine, and the smell of thy nose like apples: … the fragrance of your breath as of apples, *Berkeley* … scent of your vulva like apples, *Anchor* … smell of thy breath, *ASV* … of thy countenance, *Mast* … and your breath like apricots, *Beck* … fragrance of thy face as citrons, *Young*.

9. And the roof of thy mouth like the best wine for my beloved, that goeth down sweetly, causing the lips of those that are asleep to speak: … And your mind like the beautiful wine, That comes to the truly in love, And moistens their lips in their sleep!, *Fenton* … The wine goes down smoothly for my beloved, Moving gently the lips of sleepers, *NKJV* … And your palate like finest wine, flowing pleasantly into my mouth, stirring my lips and teeth, *Goodspeed* … mouth soft to my love's caress as

good wine is soft to the palate, as food to lips and teeth, *Knox* … and your palate like sweet wine. Flowing down the throat of my love, as it runs on the lips of those who sleep, *JB*.

10. I am my beloved's, and his desire is toward me: … and on me is his desire, *Young* … I belong to my lover and for me he yearns, *Douay* … My true love, I am all his; and who but I the longing of his heart?, *Knox*.

11. Come, my beloved, let us go forth into the field; let us lodge in the villages: … Come with me, my true love; for us the country ways, the cottage roof for shelter, *Knox* … let's go out into the country and spend the night in the fields, *NCV* … spend the night among the villages, *Douay* … let us take rest among the cypress-trees, *BB* … lie among the henna-bushes, *NEB*.

12. Let us get up early to the vineyards; let us see if the vine flourish, whether the tender grape appear, and the pomegranates bud forth: there will I give thee my loves: … go out early to the vine-gardens; let us see if the vine is in bud, if it has put out its young fruit, and the pomegranate is in flower, *BB* … and see whether the vines have budded, whether the grape blossoms have opened and the pomegranates are in bloom, *RSV* … Can watch the Vines blossom,—The flowers unfolding, Or the bright peaches flourish,

---

together. He praised her neck as an ivory tower. He likened her sparkling eyes to the pools of Heshbon and her nose was like that of the tower of Lebanon (in shape rather than size) as it faces Damascus off toward the east. Her lovely head was shaped like Mt. Carmel, that handsome promontory overlooking Ake or Acre, which was later named Haifa. This site later acquired great prominence as the scene of the dramatic contest between the prophet Elijah and the prophets of Baal, in which the pagan priests were totally unsuccessful in calling down fire from God out of heaven. This compelled the wicked King Ahab to acknowledge Yahweh as the only true God in heaven. But even in David's time, this landmark

was noted for its luscious grape clusters. It is quite possible that the Shulammite's hair was tinted, as if it had been colored with purple, much to the admiration of her prince.

7:6–13. At this juncture, the young man felt moved to express his deep admiration for her irresistible charm of appearance and speech. He likened her to a tall and stately palm tree, laden with luscious clusters of dates, and suggestive of the perfection of her bosoms. The very breath she breathed bore the aroma of apples. Her perfect mouth and lips affected him like choice wine as it gently heightened the emotions of those to whom she spoke. To these terms of passionate admiration she granted an allusion to the

5525.516	7705	8427	5598.125	881, 1782	3937
v Hiphil pf 3cp	art, n mp	adv	v Qal impf 1cs	do, n mp, ps 1cs	prep, ps 2fs
הֵנֵצוּ	הָרִמּוֹנִים	שָׁם	אֶתֵּן	אֶת־דּוֹדַי	לָךְ
hēnētsû	hārimmônîm	shām	'ettēn	'eth-dōdhay	lākh
they have blossomed	the pomegranates	there	I will give	my beloved	to you

13.	1786	5598.116, 7666	6142, 6860	3725, 4162	2413
	art, n mp	v Qal pf 3cp, n ms	cj, prep, n mp, ps 1cp	adj, n mp	adj
	הַדּוּדָאִים	נָתְנוּ־רֵיחַ	וְעַל־פְּתָחֵינוּ	כָּל־מְגָדִים	חֲדָשִׁים
	haddûdhā'îm	nāthenû-rêach	we'al-pethāchênû	kol-meghādhîm	chădhāshîm
	the mandrakes	they have given a fragrance	and above our doors	all fruit harvests	new

1612, 3584	1782	7121.115	3937	**8:1**	4449	5598.121	3626, 250
cj, adj	n ms, ps 1cs	v Qal pf 1cs	prep, ps 2fs		intrg	v Qal impf 3ms, ps 2ms	prep, n ms
גַּם־יְשָׁנִים	דּוֹדִי	צָפַנְתִּי	לָךְ		מִי	יִתֶּנְךָ	כְּאָח
gam-yeshānîm	dōdhî	tsāphantî	lākh		mî	yittenkhā	ke'āch
also old	my beloved	I have stored	for you		who	will he allow you	like a brother

3937	3352.151	8157	525	4834.125	904, 2445
prep, ps 1cs	v Qal act ptc ms	n mp	n fs, ps 1cs	v Qal impf 1cs, ps 2ms	prep, art, n ms
לִי	יוֹנֵק	שְׁדֵי	אִמִּי	אֶמְצָאֲךָ	בַּחוּץ
lî	yônēq	shedhê	'immî	'emtsā'ăkhā	vachûts
to me	nursing	the breasts of	my mother	I would find you	in the street

5583.125	1612	3940, 972.126	3937	**2.**	5268.125
v Qal impf 1cs, ps 2ms	cj	neg part, v Qal impf 3mp	prep, ps 1cs		v Qal impf 1cs, ps 2ms
אֶשָּׁקְךָ	גַּם	לֹא־יָבוּזוּ	לִי		אֶנְהָגְךָ
'eshshāqōkhā	gam	lō'-yāvûzû	lî		'enhāghekhā
I would kiss you	also	they would not despise	me		I would lead you

971.525	420, 1041	525	4064.322	8615.525
v Hiphil impf 1cs, ps 2ms	prep, n ms	n fs, ps 1cs	v Piel impf 3fs, ps 1cs	v Hiphil impf 1cs, ps 2ms
אֲבִיאֲךָ	אֶל־בֵּית	אִמִּי	תְּלַמְּדֵנִי	אַשְׁקְךָ
'ăvî'ăkhā	'el-bêth	'immî	telammedhēnî	'ashqōkhā
I would bring you	to the house of	my mother	she would teach me	I would give you drink

4623, 3302	7837	4623, 6302	7705	**3.**	7972	8809	7513
prep, n ms	n ms	prep, n ms	n ms, ps 1cs		n ms, ps 3ms	prep	n ms, ps 1cs
מִיַּיִן	הָרֶקַח	מֵעָסִיס	רִמֹּנִי		שְׂמֹאלוֹ	תַּחַת	רֹאשִׁי
mîyayin	hāreqach	mē'ăsîs	rimmōnî		semō'lô	tachath	rō'shî
from the wine of	the spice	from the juice of	my pomegranate		his left hand	beneath	my head

3332	2354.322	**4.**	8123.515	881	1351
cj, n fs, ps 3ms	v Piel impf 3fs, ps 1cs		v Hiphil pf 1cs	do, ps 2mp	n fp
וִימִינוֹ	תְּחַבְּקֵנִי		הִשְׁבַּעְתִּי	אֶתְכֶם	בְּנוֹת
wîmînô	techabbeqēnî		hishba'ātî	'ethkhem	benôth
and his right hand	it would embrace me		I will cause to swear	you	O daughters of

3503	4242, 5996.528	4242, 5996.328	881, 157	5912
pn	intrg, v Hiphil impf 2mp	cj, intrg, v Polel impf 2mp	do, art, n fs	adv
יְרוּשָׁלָם	מַה־תָּעִירוּ	וּמַה־תְּעֹרְרוּ	אֶת־הָאַהֲבָה	עַד
yerûshālām	mah-tā'îrû	ûmah-te'ōrerû	'eth-hā'ahvāh	'adh
Jerusalem	why will you arouse	indeed why will you strongly arouse	the love	until

8054, 2759.122	**5.**	4449	2148	6148.153	4623, 4198	7805.753
rel part, v Qal impf 3fs		intrg	dem pron	v Qal act ptc fs	prep, art, n ms	v Hithpael ptc fs
שֶׁתֶּחְפָּץ		מִי	זֹאת	עֹלָה	מִן־הַמִּדְבָּר	מִתְרַפֶּקֶת
shettechpāts		mî	zō'th	'ōlāh	min-hammidhbār	mithrappeqeth
that it desires		who	this one	coming up	from the wilderness	leaning

Fenton ... Then I shall give you the gift of my love, *JB*.

13. The mandrakes give a smell, and at our gates are all manner of pleasant fruits, new and old, which I have laid up for thee, O my beloved: ... The Love-apples give out their scent, And over our doors are new flowers, And the old ones, my love, that I treasured for you!, *Fenton* ... love's apples yielding their scent, and the fruitage of all my charms, *Moffatt* ... Both fresh and mellowed fruits, my lover, I have kept in store for you, *NAB* ... The love apples give out a fragrance, *Beck* ... the most exquisite fruits are at our doors, *JB*.

8:1. O that thou wert as my brother, that sucked the breasts of my mother!: ... I wish you were like my brother who fed, *NCV* ... who took milk from my mother's breasts!, *BB*.

when I should find thee without, I would kiss thee; yea, I should not be despised: ... When I met in the street I could kiss you,—And they could cry shame if I did!, *Fenton* ... Then if I met you out of doors, I could kiss you without people thinking ill of me, *JB*.

2. I would lead thee, and bring thee into my mother's house, who would instruct me: I would cause thee to drink of spiced wine of the juice of my pomegranate: ... I would take you by the hand into my mother's house, and she would be my teacher, *BB* ... She would tell me to serve you with grapes, And to mingle the pomegranate's spice!, *Fenton* ... To my mother's house I will lead thee, my captive; there thou shalt teach me my lessons, and I will give thee spiced wine to drink, fresh brewed from my pomegranates, *Knox*.

3. His left hand should be under my head, and his right hand should embrace me: ... His left should be clasped round my head, And his right hand be folded in mine!, *Fenton* ... His left hand pillows my head; his right hand, even now, ready to embrace me!, *Knox*.

4. I charge you, O daughters of Jerusalem, that ye stir not up, nor awake my love, until he please: ... I want you to swear, ... Do not arouse or awaken my love, Until she pleases, *NASB* ... I adjure you, ... by the gazelles and hinds of the field, *Douay* ... That you neither incite nor excite Love until it is eager, *Anchor*.

5. Who is this that cometh up from the wilderness, leaning upon her beloved?: ... Who is she coming up from the Pasture, With her Guardian Companion?, *Fenton* ... up from the waste places, resting on her loved one?, *BB* ... ascending from the steppe, Leaning on her lover?, *Anchor* ... this that makes her way up by the desert road, all gaily clad, leaning upon the arm of her true love?, *Knox*.

I raised thee up under the apple tree: there thy mother brought thee forth: there she brought thee forth that bare thee: ... Under the apricot tree I aroused you, *Beck* ... Under the citron-tree I have waked thee, There did thy mother pledge thee, There she gave a pledge that bare thee, *Young* ... Under the apple tree I awakened you, where your mother was in travail with you, where she that bore you was in travail, *Goodspeed* ... there your mother conceived you, there she who was in labor gave you birth, *NIV*.

6. Set me as a seal upon thine heart, as a seal upon thine arm: ... a signet on your heart, As a signet on your arm, *Anchor* ... Hold me close to thy heart, close as locket or bracelet fits, *Knox* ... like a reminder bracelet on your arm, *Beck*.

delightful times they recently had together. Whether ladies of the harem were at hand as she reaffirmed her commitment to the king and acknowledged his infatuation with her, she clearly affirmed that she belonged to her royal lover, and by way of rekindling their special relationship together, entirely apart from the ladies of the official harem. Right now was the right season for just the two of them to leave the city and check up on the progress of the grape arbors and the pomegranates which furnished a fitting scene for their loving fellowship. In v. 13, she refers to the mandrakes (HED #1786) which were reputed as the source of an effective love potion for those seeking such. Still, other fruits were by this time ready for tasting, some of which she had already gathered for them to enjoy together in their favorite bowers. Obviously, she was here doing her best to keep their romance going, even though a large harem may expect his attention as well.

8:1–5. With amazing persistence the Shulammite did her very best to keep their special relationship unimpaired, despite the distractions of harem and palace. At this point, she resorted to a somewhat different approach than ever before. She conjured up a more tender and personal affection toward him as if he might feel of himself as if he had been part of her home in Shunem, where her mother might have fed him as a baby at her breast. She envisioned the role of an affectionate sister, committed to furnishing him with wholesome food and drink and sleeping together as partners in the same crib. She would even wish to have been on hand when her own mother would have given him birth after her pangs were over.

6142, 1782	8809	8931	5996.315	8427	2341.312
prep, n ms, ps 3fs	prep	art, n ms	v Polel pf 1cs, ps 2ms	adv	v Piel pf 3fs, ps 2ms
עַל־דּוֹדָהּ	תַּחַת	הַתַּפּוּחַ	עוֹרַרְתִּיךָ	שָׁמָּה	חִבְּלַתְךָ
'al-dôdhāhh	tachath	hattappûach	'ôrartîkhā	shāmmāh	chibbelathkhā
on her beloved	beneath	the apple tree	I awakened you	there	she travailed with you

525	8427	2341.312	3314.112	6. 7947.131	3626, 2460
n fs, ps 2ms	adv	v Piel pf 3fs	v Qal pf 3fs, ps 2ms	v Qal impv 2ms, ps 1cs	prep, art, n ms
אִמֶּךָ	שָׁמָּה	חִבְּלָה	יְלָדַתְךָ	שִׂימֵנִי	כַּחוֹתָם
'immekhā	shāmmāh	chibbelāh	yelādhathkhā	sîmēnî	khachôthām
your mother	there	she travailed	she gave birth to you	set me	like the seal

6142, 3949	3626, 2460	6142, 2307	3706, 6006	3626, 4323	157	7482
prep, n ms, ps 2ms	prep, art, n ms	prep, n fs, ps 2ms	cj, adj	prep, art, n ms	n fs	adj
עַל־לִבֶּךָ	כַּחוֹתָם	עַל־זְרוֹעֶךָ	כִּי־עַזָּה	כַּמָּוֶת	אַהֲבָה	קָשָׁה
'al-libbekhā	kachôthām	'al-zerô'ekhā	ki-'azzāh	khammāweth	'ahvāh	qāshāh
upon your heart	like the seal	on your arm	because strong	like the death	love	hard

3626, 8061	7352	7859	7859	813	8354	7. 4448	7521	3940
prep, n fs	n fs	n mp, ps 3fs	n mp	n fs	n fs	n md	adj	neg part
כִּשְׁאוֹל	קִנְאָה	רְשָׁפֶיהָ	רִשְׁפֵי	אֵשׁ	שַׁלְהֶבֶתְיָה	מַיִם	רַבִּים	לֹא
khish'ôl	qin'āh	reshāphêāh	rishpê	'ēsh	shalhevethyāh	mayim	rabbîm	lō'
like the grave	jealousy	its flames	flames of	fire	a flame from Yah	waters	many	not

3310.126	3937, 3637.341	881, 157	5282	3940	8278.126
v Qal impf 3mp	prep, v Piel inf con	do, art, n fs	cj, n mp	neg part	v Qal impf 3mp, ps 3fs
יוּכְלוּ	לְכַבּוֹת	אֶת־הָאַהֲבָה	וּנְהָרוֹת	לֹא	יִשְׁטְפוּהָ
yûkhlû	lekhabbôth	'eth-hā'ahvāh	ûnehārôth	lō'	yishtephûāh
they are able	to extinguish	the love	and floods	not	they can flow over it

524, 5598.121	382	881, 3725, 2019	1041	904, 157	972.142
cj, v Qal impf 3ms	n ms	do, adj, n ms	n ms, ps 3ms	prep, art, n fs	v Qal inf abs
אִם־יִתֵּן	אִישׁ	אֶת־כָּל־הוֹן	בֵּיתוֹ	בָּאַהֲבָה	בּוֹז
'im-yittēn	'îsh	'eth-kol-hôn	bêthô	bā'ahvāh	bôz
if he apportioned	a man	all the wealth of	his household	with the love	being despised

972.126	3937	8. 269	3937	7278	8157
v Qal impf 3mp	prep, ps 3ms	n fs	prep, ps 1cp	adj	cj, n md
יְבֻזוּ	לוֹ	אָחוֹת	לָנוּ	קְטַנָּה	וְשָׁדַיִם
yāvûzû	lô	'āchôth	lānû	qotannāh	weshādhayim
it would be completely despised	to him	a sister	to us	young	and breasts

375	3937	4242, 6449.120	3937, 269	904, 3219
sub	prep, ps 3fs	intrg, v Qal impf 1cp	prep, n fs, ps 1cp	prep, art, n ms
אֵין	לָהּ	מַה־נַּעֲשֶׂה	לַאֲחוֹתֵנוּ	בַּיּוֹם
'ên	lāhh	mah-na'ăseh	la'ăchôthēnû	bayyôm
there is not	to her	what shall we do	for our sister	on the day

8054, 1744.421, 904	9. 524, 2440	2026	1161.120	6142	3029
rel part, v Pual impf 3ms, prep, ps 3fs	cj, n fs	pers pron	v Qal impf 1cp	prep, ps 3fs	n fs
שֶׁיְּדֻבַּר־בָּהּ	אִם־חוֹמָה	הִיא	נִבְנֶה	עָלֶיהָ	טִירַת
sheyyedhubbar-bāhh	'im-chômāh	hî	nivneh	'āleāh	tîrath
which it will be spoken about her	if a wall	she	we will build	upon her	a battlement of

3826B	524, 1878	2026	6961.120	6142	4008	753	10. 603	2440
n ms	cj, cj, n fs	pers pron	v Qal impf 1cp	prep, ps 3fs	n ms	n ms	pers pron	n fs
כָּסֶף	וְאִם־דֶּלֶת	הִיא	נָצוּר	עָלֶיהָ	לוּחַ	אֶרֶז	אֲנִי	חוֹמָה
kāseph	we'im-deleth	hî	nātsûr	'āleāh	lûach	'ārez	'ănî	chômāh
silver	and if a door	she	we will barricade	upon her	planks of	cedar	I	a wall

for love is strong as death; jealousy is cruel as the grave: ... as mighty as death, as strong as Sheol, *Goodspeed* ... for stern as death is love, relentless as the nether world is devotion, *Douay* ... passion as relentless as Sheol, *JB* ... Jealousy is as severe as Sheol, *NASB*.

the coals thereof are coals of fire, which hath a most vehement flame: ... Its flashes are flashes of fire, The very flame of the LORD, *NASB* ... As for passion, its bolts are bolts of fire, furious flames, *Goodspeed* ... violent are its flames, *BB*.

7. Many waters cannot quench love, neither can the floods drown it: ... No torrents can sweep it away, *Anchor* ... Nor will rivers overflow it, *NASB* ... Deep waters cannot quench love, nor floods sweep it away, *Douay* ... Even much water cannot put out the flame of love, *NCV*.

if a man would give all the substance of his house for love, it would utterly be contemned: ... If a man should offer for love all the wealth of his house, it would be scornfully refused, *Berkeley* ... If one give all the wealth of his house for love, Treading down—they tread upon it, *Young* ... Were one to offer all he owns to purchase love, he would be roundly mocked, *Douay*.

8. We have a little sister, and she hath no breasts: ... Our sister is little and she has no breasts as yet, *Douay* ... A little sister we have, still unripe for the love of man, *Knox* ... We have a young sister, and her breasts are not yet grown, *NIV*.

what shall we do for our sister in the day when she shall be spoken for?: ... with our sister when she is asked in marriage?, *REB* ... At the time when her growth is complete?, *Fenton* ... when her courtship begins?, *Douay*.

9. If she be a wall, we will build upon her a palace of silver: ... If she is as hard as a wall We will build on her turrets of silver, *Fenton* ... If she is a rampart, on the crest we shall build a battlement of silver, *JB* ... make on her a strong base of silver, *BB* ... build on her a silver buttress, *Anchor* ... build by her a palace, *Young*.

and if she be a door, we will inclose her with boards of cedar: ... But if a swing-door,—Will deck her with panels of cedar!, *Fenton* ... barricade her with planks, *NASB* ... reinforce it with a cedar plank, *Douay* ... yield she as a door yields, we have cedar boards to fasten her, *Knox*.

10. I am a wall, and my breasts like towers: ... impregnable this breast as a fortress, *Knox* ... breasts represent its towers, *JB*.

then was I in his eyes as one that found favour: ... as one to whom

8:6. In v. 6, she speaks earnestly of a very special relationship, more intimate than even the normal commitment of two young lovers who have to grow in grace and understanding as over the years they get to know each other more profoundly. This would weld them together even more closely than possible when they took their marriage vows. But what she longed for even went beyond the tender relation of siblings brought up together in a home where deepest commitment is involved. Verse 6 eloquently expresses a deep yearning for a truly perfect interpersonal commitment beyond anything that even Solomon could conceive.

She then went on to state that a true seal upon her heart established a binding power as strong as death itself. Her commitment to her beloved was total and beyond alienation. If it was really Solomon who recorded this account of their relationship together, he surely could never have forgotten this all-consuming tenderness and devotion surpassing anything he had ever experienced during his later years. But surprisingly enough, she warned him that out of that love there could arise a cruel jealousy in the face of betrayal and treachery. And she added that woe would ensue from the lover betrayed, and even the flame of God's wrath would overtake the heartless wretch who would turn his back upon his loving spouse.

8:7. On the other hand, when love is real and totally sincere, there is no power of flood or hardship that can result in abandonment of self-dedication to the other person involved. No adversity, no pressure could possibly make that kind of a lover abandon the one beloved.

8:8–9. The final portion of this Song of Songs quite unexpectedly brings in a visit of the older brothers from that family in Shunem. It may possibly date from an earlier stage in the life of this amazing girl from whom her family members formerly expected rather little. They noted that her breasts were a bit slow in development, which meant that she would not be likely to attract the interest of marriageable young men in the immediate future. They really did not know what to do with her. What could they do for her during her teenage years? Maybe they should keep her in seclusion until she developed more comeliness and charm.

8:10–13. Yet as it afterward turned out, they did not need to worry that much about her. It so happened that a very important young man had acquired

8157	3626, 4166	226	2030.115	904, 6084	3626, 4834.153	8361
cj, n md, ps 1cs	prep, art, n fp	adv	v Qal pf 1cs	prep, n fd, ps 3ms	prep, v Qal act ptc fs	n ms
וְשָׁדַי	כַּמִּגְדָּלוֹת	אָז	הָיִיתִי	בְעֵינָיו	כְּמוֹצֵאת	שָׁלוֹם
weshādhay	kammighdālôth	'āz	hāyîthî	ve'ênâv	kemôts'ēth	shālôm
and my breasts	like the towers	then	I was	in his eyes	like the one finding	peace

3884	2030.111	3937, 8406	904, 1202	1202	5598.111	881, 3884
n ms	v Qal pf 3ms	prep, pn	prep, pn	pn	v Qal pf 3ms	do, art, n ms
כֶּרֶם	הָיָה	לִשְׁלֹמֹה	בְּבַעַל	הָמוֹן	נָתַן	אֶת־הַכֶּרֶם
kerem	hāyāh	lishlōmōh	beva'al	hāmôn	nāthan	'eth-hakkerem
a vineyard	it was	to Solomon	at Baal	Hamon	he gave	the vineyard

11.

3937, 5386.152	382	971.521	904, 6780	512	3826B	3884
prep, v Qal act ptc mp	n ms	v Hiphil impf 3ms	prep, n ms, ps 3ms	num	n ms	n ms, ps 1cs
לַנֹּטְרִים	אִישׁ	יָבִא	בְּפִרְיוֹ	אֶלֶף	כֶּסֶף	כַּרְמִי
lannōterîm	'îsh	yāvi'	bephiryô	'eleph	kāseph	karmî
to the keepers	each	he brought	with its fruit	one thousand	silver	my vineyard

12.

8054, 3937	3937, 6686	512	3937	8406	4109
rel part, prep, ps 1cs	prep, n mp, ps 1cs	art, num	prep, ps 2ms	pn	cj, num
שֶׁלִּי	לְפָנָי	הָאֶלֶף	לְךָ	שְׁלֹמֹה	וּמָאתַיִם
shellî	lephānāy	hā'eleph	lekha	shelōmōh	ûmā'thayim
which to me	before me	the one thousand	to you	O Solomon	and two hundred

3937, 5386.152	881, 6780	3553.153	904, 1629	2358	7477.552
prep, v Qal act ptc mp	do, n ms, ps 3ms	art, v Qal act ptc fs	prep, art, n mp	n mp	v Hiphil ptc mp
לְנֹטְרִים	אֶת־פִּרְיוֹ	הַיּוֹשֶׁבֶת	בַּגַּנִּים	חֲבֵרִים	מַקְשִׁיבִים
lenōterîm	'eth-piryô	hayyôsheveth	bagganîm	chăvērîm	maqōshivîm
to the keepers	its fruit	O dweller	in the gardens	companions	being attentive

13.

3937, 7249	8471.532	1300.131	1782	1880.131, 3937
prep, n ms, ps 2fs	v Hiphil impv 2fs, ps 1cs	v Qal impv 2ms	n ms, ps 1cs	cj, v Qal impv 2ms, prep, ps 2ms
לְקוֹלֵךְ	הַשְׁמִיעִינִי	בְּרַח	דּוֹדִי	וּדְמֵה־לְךָ
leqôlēkh	hashmî'înî	berach	dôdhî	ûdhemēh-lekhā
to your voice	cause me to hear	flee	my beloved	and make yourself resemble

14.

3937, 6906	173	3937, 6314	358	6142	2098	1336
prep, n ms	cj	prep, n ms	art, n mp	prep	n mp	n mp
לִצְבִי	אוֹ	לְעֹפֶר	הָאַיָּלִים	עַל	הָרֵי	בְשָׂמִים
litsvî	'ô	le'ōpher	hā'ayyālîm	'al	hārê	vesāmîm
a gazelle	or	a fawn of	the male deer	upon	the mountains of	spices

good chance had come, *BB* ... Thus have I become in his eyes As one producing peace, *Anchor* ... and the man who claimed me found in me a bringer of content, *Knox* ... As he looked at me, I became a happy woman, *Beck*.

11. Solomon had a vineyard at Baal-hamon; he let out the vineyard unto keepers; every one for the fruit thereof was to bring a thousand pieces of silver: ... he let out his vineyard to tenants. Each was to bring for its fruit a thousand shekels, *NIV* ... rented the vineyards for others to tend, and everyone who rented had to pay twenty-five pounds of silver for the fruit, *NCV* ... For its fruit one would have to pay, *Douay*.

12. My vineyard, which is mine, is before me: ... My farm is myself,— to be plain, *Fenton* ... my own, lies before me, *Berkeley* ... at my own disposal, *Douay*.

thou, O Solomon, must have a thousand, and those that keep the fruit thereof two hundred: ... The thousand is yours, O Solomon, and two hundred each to those keeping the fruit, *Berkeley* ... For you, Solomon,—there is the thousand;— To the tenants two hundred for rents!, *Fenton*.

13. Thou that dwellest in the gardens, the companions hearken to thy voice: cause me to hear it: ... You who have your resting-place in the gardens, the friends give ear to your voice; make me give ear to it, *BB* ... O you who sit in the gardens, My companions are listening for your voice—Let me hear it!, *NASB* ... O garden-dweller, my friends are listening, *Douay* ... O girl who lives in my garden, while my companions are listening, let me hear your voice, *Beck*.

14. Make haste, my beloved, and be thou like to a roe or to a young **hart upon the mountains of spices:** ... Bolt, my love, Be like a buck, Or a young stag, On the spice mountains, *Anchor* ... Come away, my lover, and be like a gazelle ... on the spice-laden mountains, *NIV* ... Come into the open, my beloved, and show yourself ... on the spice-bearing mountains, *REB*.

a piece of property right next to the old family farm. There he began to develop a fine grade orchard at Baal-Hamon, which was of no ordinary size. In fact, it grew so verdantly that this young man from Jerusalem could sell his harvest for no less than a thousand shekels. Naturally enough, the nice young lady became acquainted with this nice young man (who probably did not reveal to anyone his true identity), and he was recognized as having the best vineyard in all of Shunem. The buying public here referred to as "the companions" (HED #2358, meaning "friends" or "comrades") may very well have been all the more attracted to this vineyard because of the sprightly young lass that helped him harvest and sell his crop. In such a setting, romance is apt to develop, and then even marriage itself!

8:14. The very last verse of this remarkable passage closes with a word of encouragement and good cheer to her employer and friend, perhaps at the end of market hours: "Go for it now and run your way up to the heights like a young deer or a red deer," as they enjoy the hilltops and glens through which they love to make sport. This is the last portion of the narrative of this amazing young woman. She is forever committed to Solomon and desires that their companionship continue in its fervency.

PROVERBS OVERVIEW

Background

Outline

Summary

Overview

BACKGROUND

Authorship

According to its title and subtitles, the Book of Proverbs is the work of Solomon (1:1; 10:1; 25:1), son of David, third king of Israel (ca. 970–930 B.C.). Hezekiah's men did not write the proverbs (25:1); they copied them into the Book. Although some interpret Agur (30:1) and Lemuel (31:1) as Solomonic pen names in order to maintain Solomonic authorship, this is not necessary.

The Critical Consensus. With the naturalistic attack upon the Bible known as historical criticism, the significance of the titles was reinterpreted, based on three assumptions. The first was that the Bible is a purely human work, "inspired" only as any great work of literature or art is called inspired. The second assumption is that all biblical documents were written long after the dates claimed by the text, and long after the events that they purport to describe. (This was especially true for the Pentateuch, according to the theory, but has been applied to nearly every biblical Book.) For the Book of Proverbs, this meant that the descriptions of Solomon's wisdom (1 Ki. 3; 4; 10) were written long after his reign and exaggerated in order to glorify David's son. Solomon may have been wise, according to the theory, but his greatest contribution to wisdom in Israel was a stable government that promoted the growth of a society with the leisure to pursue such learned discourse.

The third assumption is that literary forms develop from simple to complex. Applied to the Book of Proverbs, this means that proverbs began as one-line sayings (e.g., 22:28), which came to be combined into the couplets found mainly in Prov. 10:1–22:16 and 25:1–29:27. Individual proverbs were then clustered around a common theme (cf. 25:1–7; 26:23–28), and, finally, extended poems were composed (cf. Prov. 1:2–9:18; 23:29–35; 24:30–34; 27:23–27; 30:1–33; 31:10–31).

According to the theory, the original collection, Prov. 10:1–22:16, was probably pre-exilic, and may even include some Solomonic sayings. At some point, a smaller collection, adapted from an Egyptian document called "The Wisdom of Amenemope" was added (22:17–24:22), and then another collection of "sayings of wise" (24:23–34),

a later "Solomonic" collection (25:1–29:27) and three short works (Agur [ch. 30], Lemuel's mother [31:1–9] and the song of the virtuous wife [31:10–31]) were appended. There is little agreement among the theory's proponents about the sequence of these additions, although those critics who assume that acrostics (poems in which each line begins with the next letter of the alphabet) were "advanced" and therefore late conclude that Prov. 31:10–31 was probably the latest.

The longer poems, Prov. 1:2–9:18, are said to have been composed long after the Jews had returned from exile (538–36 B.C.). The main reason for this late date is Wisdom's description as a person in these chapters. According to the theory, personification of an abstract entity was unknown in the ancient Near East until brought there by the Greeks when Alexander conquered the Persian Empire (334–26 B.C.). These poems were prefixed to the collection in order to give it an explicitly theological basis. The title (1:1) was then added in order to lend the entire work the authority of Solomon, based on his reputation for wisdom. This is the standard explanation of the development of the Book of Proverbs.

The theories further attempt to discern the actual place of origin and use of the proverbs. A common opinion today is that various proverbs originated in the family, at court or in the schools of the wise and thus reflect the unique concerns of each. They were used in schools, where "the wise" prepared young men of upper-class background for their positions of leadership in Israel. There is, however, no biblical evidence for such schools in Israel (although we know that they existed in, e.g., Mesopotamia), and we know very little about how proverbs originated (cf. 1 Sam. 10:10ff; 19:24).

The Ancient Near Eastern Evidence. This description of the Book's origins is based on literary theory, not on any available biblical or ancient Near Eastern evidence. Kenneth A. Kitchen studied all of the available ancient Near Eastern "instruction" materials, which are roughly comparable to Proverbs. He found short, one-line sayings and longer poems in texts from before and after Solomon. He also found that the instructional documents had two basic outlines. One consists of a simple title followed by a list of sayings (cf. Prov. 25:1–29:27; 30:1–33; 31:1–9). The other includes a title (cf. Prov. 1:1) followed by a more or less extensive prologue (cf. Prov. 1:2–9:18). This is followed in turn by one or more sets of subtitles and proverbs (cf. Prov. 10:1–24:22; 24:23–34). Both types were used in Egypt and Mesopotamia before and after Solomon.

The evidence does not support the standard theory of the literary development of Proverbs outlined above. Neither the length of the individual proverb or poem, nor the overall form of an instructional document enables us to assign it even a relative date. Thus, since the external and internal evidence are consistent with each other, the biblical titles and subtitles remain our best evidence for the Book's origin and date.

In addition to these literary findings, we now know that abstract qualities such as wisdom were personified long before the time of Solomon and that acrostics (e.g., Prov. 31:10–31) were also in use by the time of his reign.

Proverbs and Amenemope. Another issue related to the Book's composition is its literary relationship to other ancient Near Eastern documents, especially those from Egypt. Since 1923, when an ancient Egyptian document called the "Wisdom of Amenemope" was first published, scholars have debated to what degree, if any, this document may be related to Prov. 22:17–23:22. Some interpret this section of Proverbs as an adaptation of Amenemope, or vice versa. Others argue that both descend from an unknown original, while still others claim that there is no definable relationship, that both documents merely reflect the common concerns of ancient Near Eastern wisdom.

The pieces of evidence that underlie this discussion include both language and content. The word "also" in Prov. 24:23 leads us to expect a previous group of "words of the wise." Prov. 22:17 is the nearest occurrence of the phrase "the words of the wise" (its only other occurrence is in Prov. 1:6), where it is the direct object of the verb "hear," not a title. The Septuagint puts "to the words of the wise" at the head of the verse as the indirect object of "incline [your ear]," and adds "my words" as the object of "hear" (cf. NRSV). Some scholars therefore say that the Septuagint reflects the original Hebrew text in which this phrase was the title of the section, and that the Hebrew should therefore be corrected to reflect this, explicitly marking 22:17 as the beginning of a separate document. There is,

however, no need to change the Hebrew text, especially since this involves a twofold modification: moving the phrase "the words of the wise" to the beginning of the verse and supplying another object for "incline your ear" (NRSV adds "my words").

Secondly, the format or style of the sayings changes from couplets that are largely observations or conclusions (Prov. 10:1–22:16, with a few exceptions) to sets of four or more lines, most of which entail a command or prohibition and a motivating explanation (e.g., 22:22f; 23:1ff, 17–21). Stylistic groupings typify the entire Book, e.g., longer poems, such as chs. 1–9; largely antithetical sayings, such as chs. 10–15; 28–29; and emblematic proverbs, such as chs. 25–26. The style of the basic units of 22:17–24:22 is also found in other chapters (e.g., 20:13, 19, 22; 25:6f, 8ff; 26:4f, 25; 27:1f, 10f, 23f; 28:21; 30:32f). Since the pattern of the Book follows group sayings stylistically, there does not seem to be any need to posit a separate (i.e., foreign) source.

If the masoretic reading of the word at the end of 22:20 (Hebrew shilshôm; "formerly"; HED #8425) is followed, then the "thirty [sayings]" (NIV, NRSV) parallel the thirty "houses" (sections) of Amenemope. (This word is rendered "excellent things" by NASB, NKJV.) If the word shilshôm is changed to read "thirty," the lack of a noun is anomalous. Hebrew omits the noun modified by a numeral only with units of measure, weight or time, and only when these are clear from the context. The NIV and NRSV add the word "sayings," but no suggested division of Prov. 22:17–24:22 into thirty sayings has garnered general agreement. (Most divide or combine sayings that would not be so affected apart from a search for thirty sections.) This inability is all the more striking given the lack of a noun, which would have specified what thirty referred to. If shilshôm is correct, it provides a good parallel with "today" (v. 19b), but this occurrence is anomalous; in the rest of its biblical occurrences it is always part of a compound saying. The other word (temôl, "yesterday," "recently," "formerly"; HED #8873) is not in this verse. This is a difficult problem, but even if the reading "thirty" could be proven, which seems unlikely, this would not prove that these verses depend upon Amenemope.

Fourth, the two documents share some topics and metaphors (e.g., money "flying away" [23:5], the "trap" [22:25]). Although the two documents

Overview

share many topics, the parallels are vague and general, shared with other biblical passages and ancient Near Eastern instructional texts in general, and seem to reflect the general concerns of life rather than a common literary history. Even where the ideas or images are similar, they are rarely identical; neither are they necessarily used in the same way (e.g., in Amenemope 9.11.17–18 the "trap" is the words of the wicked, whereas in Prov. 22:25 it is the angry man's way of life). On the other hand, both documents have the same purpose: "to know how to return an answer to him who said it, and to direct a report to one who has sent him, in order to guide him to the ways of life" (Amenemope, Introduction, 1:5–7; cf. Prov. 22:21). Once again, however, given the generally similar purpose of Proverbs and the ancient Near Eastern instructional material (to prepare young men for their lives in positions of prominence and leadership), this is not surprising.

Finally, the documents are organized differently, so that passages addressing similar themes are in different order, and each document lacks passages found in the other. In conclusion, we cannot prove any relationship between them beyond their general participation in the concerns of ancient Near Eastern wisdom, but neither can we disprove the possibility of a literary relationship.

This discussion also bears on the nature of 22:17–24:22 as an independent (i.e., non-Solomonic) collection, since this identification is based largely on the assumption that these verses reflect Amenemope. Although Solomon may have incorporated a smaller document into his original work, there is no good reason to assume that these are not Solomon's own proverbs (see comments below on 24:23).

Conclusion on Origins. A reasonable explanation of the Book's development is that Solomon created Prov. 1–24 as a unified literary composition. He specifically ascribed 24:23–34 to others by saying that "these are also sayings of the wise" (24:23), thus including himself among the wise. He may have included the sayings of Agur (ch. 30) and Lemuel's mother (31:1–9) as appendices to his work, or merely testified to their value. About two centuries later, Hezekiah's servants incorporated more Solomonic sayings into the Book (chs. 25–29). Perhaps because they did not want to divide the explicitly Solomonic materials, they inserted this

material between Solomon's original work (1:1–24:34) and the appendices (now 30:1–33; 31:1–9). Or perhaps they included the last two chapters as material under the Solomonic seal, appending them to the entire collection (again, in order to maintain the unity of the Solomonic material).

Proverbs 31:10–31 may be part of Solomon's original work, part of the words of Lemuel's mother or an independent poem appended at some unknown date (the Septuagint inserts Prov. 25–29 between 31:9 and 31:10, yielding the order 31:1–9; chs. 25–29; 31:10–31). As the commentary shows, however, it nicely (and perhaps necessarily) complements the message of the entire Book, balancing the portraits of Wisdom and Folly in chs. 1–9 and illustrating wisdom's effect on a woman and her household.

A further conclusion regards their actual origin. Individual statements are based on observation (24:30–34), but their authority is ultimately divine (2:5f; 3:1–12). The genius of the creator of a proverb is the ability to note the common element between individual and apparently disparate circumstances (cf. 30:15–33). This is the same ability that enables the poet to discover the metaphors that create the meaning of so many of the proverbs. They do not come, however, merely as well-intentioned advice, but as the Word of God, designed to bless and encourage his people and to warn the wicked, calling them to repentance.

The Meaning of Solomonic Authorship. What does it mean to call this Book "the proverbs of Solomon" (1:1)? It may mean that Solomon created or composed all of these sayings. In response to his prayer for wisdom to judge Israel justly and truthfully (1 Ki. 3:9), God made him wise so "that no one like you has gone before you, nor shall anyone like you come after you" (1 Ki. 3:12). According to the historical account of his reign (1 Ki. 4:32f), he "spoke 3000 proverbs and 1005 songs." The Book of Proverbs thus preserves only a few of his sayings.

It is also possible that "the proverbs of Solomon" does not mean authorship in the modern sense, but rather refers to Solomonic authority. That is, he composed some proverbs himself, and some that he heard from others he judged worthy of inclusion in his collection (e.g., Prov. 30–31). Those who were considered "wise" would visit Jerusalem in order to test their wisdom against his (1 Ki. 4:34; 10:1–13), which may explain how he heard the sayings of Agur and of Lemuel's mother (see the commentary on 30:1).

The Book of Proverbs is thus called Solomon's because he composed it, incorporating true wisdom wherever he found it, his own and that of others, including non-Israelites. He may therefore have been as much a compiler or editor as an "author." This does not impugn his authority or the inspiration of the contents of the Book of Proverbs, since every part of the process by which each portion of Scripture came to be written was under the control of God.

This view of the Solomonic composition of Prov. 1–24 thus means that these chapters, at least, were conceived as a literary unit. This unity implies that:

•Prov. 1–24 must be approached as an intentional whole, not interpreted as though they were originally separate compositions that happen to be juxtaposed because some later editor thought that they fit together in this way;

•Prov. 1–9 are the foreword or introduction to the rest of the Book and are vital to its proper interpretation and use, providing the theological and moral framework within which its counsel is to be read, and showing the consequences of receiving or rejecting that advice;

•Prov. 1–9 are not originally independent poems, but have been intentionally arranged in order to emphasize the main points of the value and importance of wisdom for life, and to stir the young and naive to seek and obey the wisdom contained in the rest of the Book;

•Prov. 10–24 were intended to be read in light of the theological foundation of the first nine chapters, which rescues them from being interpreted as merely self-interested advice;

•Prov. 2:1–8, which refers to the divine origin of the contents of the Book, is a programmatic statement for the entire Book, placing Wisdom's authority on the same level as that of the prophets who spoke for the LORD.

Wisdom in the Ancient Near East

The Book of Proverbs arose, not in a vacuum, but within an ancient Near Eastern literary tradition often called "instruction" literature. These texts, found in Egypt and Mesopotamia (i.e., on both sides of Israel), are written by fathers for their sons in order to prepare them for successful lives in the upper echelons of court and society. Many of their sayings have parallels in Proverbs (see on Amenemope, above), but they also contain a number of sayings that are more crude than anything found, or even implied, in Scripture.

They are primarily pragmatic, aimed in general at teaching young men how to advance in rank and position, rather than how to avoid death and please the LORD (or their gods). That there are similarities should not be surprising, since most of the major issues of life are common to all peoples—domestic and political relationships, honesty, integrity and justice, to name a few. The fundamental difference, however, is that Proverbs explicitly builds its advice upon the moral and theological foundation provided by the first nine chapters.

Wisdom in the Bible

Proverbs and similar sayings occur throughout the Bible, which provides examples of how these types of sayings were developed and used. They range from "Like Nimrod, a mighty hunter before the LORD" (Gen. 10:9) to Samson's riddle (Judg. 14:12–18). Proverbs were coined in response to unusual circumstances, such as "Is Saul also among the prophets?" (1 Sam. 10:12; cf. 19:24), as well as handed down from "the ancients." "Out of the wicked comes forth wickedness" (1 Sam. 24:13).

Both Jeremiah (in Jerusalem) and Ezekiel (in Babylon) quoted "the fathers eat sour grapes, but the children's teeth are set on edge" (Jer. 31:29; Ezek. 18:2), and Ezekiel cites, as another proverb, "Like mother, like daughter" (Ezek. 16:44; lit. "Her mother [is] her daughter") in condemning Judah.

The prophetic warning that a person or place would be made a proverb or byword (Jer. 24:9; Ezek. 14:8) is illuminated by "Go now to my place which was in Shiloh, … and see what I did to it" (Jer. 7:12, 14; cf. 26:6, 9). Shiloh and its temple were probably destroyed by the Philistines after Israel's defeat at Aphek (1 Sam. 4:10). Although it is not recorded elsewhere in Scripture, "Go to Shiloh" could thus have become a saying that meant "Be warned."

Just as the wisdom of Solomon was celebrated (1 Ki. 3:3–28; 4:29–34; 10:1–13), other Israelite individuals and even towns were known for their wisdom

Overview

(2 Sam. 14:2; 15:31; 20:15–18). Some, such as Ahithophel, became royal officials due to the value of their counsel (2 Sam. 15:31, 34; 16:20–17:4, 23).

In addition to these references, the gospels and the epistle of James are dense with sayings typical of a proverbial approach to wisdom. Although most of these probably originated with Jesus (e.g., "Give Caesar's what is Caesar's, and God what is God's" [Mark 12:17]), some were already familiar to his listeners (e.g., "Do you not say, 'Yet three months and then the harvest?'" [John 4:35]); many have since become proverbial (e.g., "The last shall be first, and the first last" [Matt. 20:16]), although they are often quoted without regard for their original meaning.

Wisdom and Israel's Covenant

Although the word "covenant" occurs only once in Proverbs (2:17, which refers to the strange woman's [marital] covenant), the covenantal concept is not lacking. Its place is taken by the word tôrāh (traditionally "law," better "teaching," "guidance" or "instruction"), which identifies the teacher's words with the Covenant. Many proverbs identify moral standards based squarely on the Covenant and the Decalogue, as well as on specific regulations of covenantal law. The proverbs can thus be grouped according to the commandments (cf. the discussion of "Topical Index," above).

Further, although the Book of Proverbs seems curiously aloof from the rest of the Bible, not mentioning any particulars of Israel's history or religious practice (except for a few references to sacrifice), its focus on obedience lies squarely within the community of ancient Israel and assumes this knowledge of its readers. It does this by assuming Israel's covenantal background, preferring Yahweh (traditionally "the LORD," which occurs eighty-seven times), which is God's covenantal name, to Elohim ("God," which occurs only six times, twice in parallel to Yahweh). Much like the prophets, who rarely invoke the Covenant by name, Proverbs builds upon it, applying its many requirements to daily life. The Book of Deuteronomy often sheds light on the proverbs and itself equates obedience to the Covenant with wisdom (Deut. 4:5–8).

Solomon's Audience

The Original Readers. The Book of Proverbs was probably addressed to young men from rela-

tively wealthy backgrounds (cf. the commentary on 22:6). This is suggested by the description of the virtuous wife (31:10–31), who had such trappings of wealth as servants, property and businesses, as well as by the many references to contact with the king (e.g., 16:12–15; 25:1–7). An original audience of upper-class youths would also explain the Book's emphasis on justice (see "Justice" in the topical index), since they were the ones who would be responsible for justice in the land. Since leadership was largely hereditary in Israel, the sons of leaders would themselves tend to become leaders in their turn. There would have been little purpose in addressing these concerns so frequently in the proverbs unless their counsel could be applied to situations in which they would eventually find themselves.

Nor do the constant agricultural images mean that the Book is addressed primarily to farmers as opposed to members of the upper or ruling class. Ancient Israel's economy was largely agrarian, and most of the population, including the upper levels of society, would have been involved in or concerned with agriculture in some way. Even if they were not living or working on the land (if they were, e.g., chariot-traders or merchants), they would have been well acquainted with the requirements and processes of farming (e.g., 20:8, 26), as well as with the ebb and flow of the agricultural calendar (e.g, 10:5). The image of the shepherd was also a common metaphor of kingship, in both Israel (especially the prophets, e.g., Ezek. 34, which contrasts wicked shepherds with the LORD, Israel's true shepherd) and the ancient Near East in general (cf. the commentary on 27:23–27).

Proverbs and Modern Readers. Despite its original purpose, the Book of Proverbs remains highly applicable to modern readers, even though few will be political or social leaders or live under a Yahwistic monarchy.

One virtue of proverbs is their breadth of application. For example, a verse that addresses relationship to the king can be applied to any relationship that entails authority or responsibility, such as an employer or supervisor. In the same way, proverbs that mention parents, brothers, friends or neighbors can be applied to nearly any relationship; the closer the relationship, the stronger the effect of one individual's behavior on the other person.

Relationships (whether they are marital, legal, political, familial or friendship) lie at the center of most people's lives. These social ties lie also at the center of many of the proverbs, which show how the attitude toward righteousness and wisdom determines a person's behavior toward others. Those who reject wisdom pursue sins that destroy community (e.g., 10:6, 11; 11:11; 16:28; 17:9; 19:28; 26:20–28), whereas the wise (i.e., those who submit to wisdom's counsel) seek to heal relationships and encourage those around them (e.g., 12:18; 13:17; 16:24; 25:13, 25).

Overview

OUTLINE

The Internal Outline. Proverbs may be outlined according to its headings and subheadings, which divide it into four main sections:

Content and Genre. Although any outline of the Book's subject or content dies the death of a thousand qualifications, it is possible to distinguish some general patterns. The tendency of the proverbs to address the same themes again and again, however, means that an outline by subject would be a tapestry, not an arrow.

TOPICAL INDEX

One sign of wisdom is the ability to apply the right proverb to a situation (cf. 24:11; 26:4f). This is only possible for those who know which proverbs are potentially applicable, which implies complete knowledge of all the proverbs. One way to do this is to memorize the entire Book!

Another approach is to compile an index that groups the proverbs which address a particular theme or topic; an index helps find all the verses related to that topic. Because interpretations of individual verses and labels for topics vary, indices vary from person to person. Since your index will be for your use, choose topics and sub-topics that help you find what you want, and constantly reassess your assignments of verses, as well as your list of topics. (Other indices, published in commentaries or as separate books, will help.)

Most verses can be assigned to more than one topic. Proverbs 31:4–7, for example, could be listed under "kingship," "drunkenness" or "justice." The challenge is to discover which topic is most central to each verse. Proverbs 10:1, for example, could be listed under several headings, namely "children and parents," "the effect of children's behavior on their parents" or "wisdom and folly (sub-topic: their effect on others)." The first is probably too broad, since it will encompass all of the verses that address the parent-child relationship, including parents' need to discipline children, children's attitudes and behaviors toward their parents and references to "my son." On the other hand, to list Prov. 10:1 under "the effect of children's behavior on their parents" may be to assign it too narrow a topic, since there will be only a few other verses on this topic (e.g., 23:15f, 24f). The best way to start might be to collect all the verses that fit under the broadest topic and then subdivide that topic (or reassign verses) as you continue to study the Book.

The first two topics listed above for 10:1 also face the disadvantage of being based on the occur-rence of particular words, such as "father" or "mother." A topical index should reflect the content of each verse, not just its words (a topical index is thus not a concordance, although a concordance would help when beginning to create a topical index). Proverbs often address topics obliquely, or figuratively, so that verses that refer to, for example, familial relationships are often used to address larger, or different, concerns. Proverbs 10:1, for example, describes how children's choices affect their parents' well-being. So while it is true that parents are immediately, and most poignantly, affected by the behavior of their children, after-marriage decisions primarily affect marriage partners.

The proverbs thus often use the rubric of the family to illustrate how decisions affect others (family, friends, neighbors, co-workers, employers, etc.). A person's father and mother are the first figures of authority in life and the first people whom children seek to please, as well as being a relationship with which most can identify. (Fewer people would be able to identify immediately with proverbs expressed in terms of the relationship between a master and a slave, or a king and his courtiers; although there are quite a few of these, their application must be "teased out" from the particular [and foreign] to the universal.)

A complete index will include topics, sub-topics and cross-references. For example, "Advice" or "Counsel" (depending on your translation) would fit under "Speech" (a very common topic) and might include cross-references to "Offering Advice" or "Responding to Advice."

The proverbs can also be grouped under the Ten Commandments (Exo. 20:1–17; Deut. 5:6–21) or their logic (below) or form (e.g., "Better than").

This brief index certainly does not exhaust the range of topics addressed by the proverbs. It is intended to encourage you to create your own as you continue to study the Book of Proverbs. The actual labels that you use will probably depend on your translation, as well as on where you find the focus of each verse.

TOPICAL INDEX

Overview

SUMMARY

The fundamental theme of Proverbs is that wisdom, a humble and obedient attitude, is the source of life. To neglect or reject it is to choose death (8:32–35). This is reflected in wisdom's foil (folly), which is scornful rejection of and rebellion against the instructions of wisdom (1:7). To obey (i.e., to seek wisdom) is to discover God himself and to find life (2:5; 8:35), so that wisdom is also identified as the fear of the LORD. To be foolish, on the other hand (i.e., to rebel by rejecting wisdom's instruction and guidance), is to love death (8:36).

Proverbs 1–9. The introduction or prologue (chs. 1–9) lays the theological foundation for the proverbs found in the rest of the Book (chs. 10–31). These chapters portray wisdom as desirable because of its many benefits (e.g., 3:2, 4, 6b, 8, 10, 14–18; 8:10f, 15–21), and especially because it preserves life (1:33; 2:21; 3:2, 16, 18, 22; 4:4, 10, 13, 22; 8:35; 9:6, 11). Wisdom is able to offer these benefits because it is integral to the way in which the world was created (3:19f; 8:22–31), but mainly because of its divine origin (2:6; 8:22).

The repeated warning of the opening chapters, on the other hand, is that the sinful behaviors that characterize folly (whether violence, sexual immorality, laziness, etc.) lead inevitably to death (1:18f, 32; 2:18f, 22; 5:5f, 23; 6:32; 7:26f; 8:36; 9:18). Furthermore, wisdom protects its students from all of these dangers, as well as others.

The first nine chapters thus contrast two paths or ways of life. The way of wisdom (which is obedience) describes a life lived in the fear of the LORD (1:7; 9:10), that is, a life bent on obeying his counsel (3:5f). The way of folly (which is rebellion) is intent only upon its own desires and standards, and deliberately rejects the ways and counsel of wisdom (1:7; 9:7f). Wisdom leads to blessing (i.e., the knowledge of God and life), while folly leads only to death (8:32–36).

The contrast between these ways is fundamental to the Book of Proverbs. It represents an absolute difference between a person's natural condition, which is naive and foolish (22:15), and the condition of those who seek to obey God (1:7). Just as roads that lead to separate destinations diverge, the foolish become more foolish (26:12), and the wise grow in wisdom (1:5; 21:11; 25:12; 27:17). Also,

like roads or paths, both conditions are fluid, in that a person is, at every moment, turning toward one or the other (19:27).

It may be popular to say that there is some of each (good and bad, wisdom and folly, righteousness and wickedness) in everyone, but that is not the view of Proverbs. Everyone is either wise or foolish; there is no middle ground. This apparent reductionism actually reflects the profound truth that every life is traveling toward either life or death, and inches along its path one thought, deed and word at a time. The call of Proverbs is to turn from folly to wisdom, from death to life (9:4ff). Proverbs thus resembles the gospel and epistles of John, who consistently describes life as a series of choices between polar opposites, with no intermediate ground.

Proverbs 10–31. The rest of the Book illustrates this contrast in many different areas of life, ranging from self-control (e.g., the words, emotions and work ethic) to personal and corporate relationships (e.g., friendship, business and justice). This contrast dominates chs. 10–15 and 28–29, in which antithetical proverbs are especially frequent, often contrasting wisdom and folly under the rubric of righteousness and wickedness. The individual proverbs thus provide many pointed applications of the general principle of the prologue, and do so both to provide counsel in a particular area of life (e.g., the risk of marrying a fool; 11:22; 21:9, 19; 25:24), and, by their multiple interwoven themes, to create a fine grid of wise choices that enables each student to extend the principles of wisdom into other areas of life.

The Book closes with a poem that returns to its beginning, portraying a virtuous wife in order to illustrate wisdom in daily life (cf. 31:30). She thus embodies the prologue's figure of Wisdom, stands in contrast to Folly, and incarnates the counsel of the body of the Book (10:1–31:9).

Wisdom. The chief characteristic of those who are in a positive relationship with the LORD is wisdom. "Righteousness" and "wisdom" are thus nearly interchangeable in Proverbs when they describe human attitudes or behavior. Righteousness is not an abstract concept, however, but is based on a commitment to the LORD's covenant, which in turn reflects the individual's relationship to the LORD himself. That attitude, called the "fear of the LORD," is the internal submission of the heart so that one obeys the word of God (see comments on 3:5f). No amount of ritual or external religious activity pleases God if the heart is rebellious (15:8, 29). On the other hand, to fear the LORD is to obey Him (1:7) by fleeing evil (e.g., 3:7; 8:13; 14:27; 16:6; 23:17) and pursuing instead the wisdom that leads to life (9:10; 10:27; 14:26f; 19:23; 22:4).

The standard is thus identical to that found throughout Scripture (cf., Deut. 6:5; 1 Sam. 15:22; Isa. 1:11–15; Jer. 7:22f; Hos. 6:4–7; Mic. 6:6ff; Mark 12:32f) and no different than that which lies at the heart of the gospel itself, which requires turning to God (e.g., 1 Thess. 1:9). Although Proverbs may appear to teach a form of salvation by works (earning God's approval), it is more useful to think of the Book as anticipating the emphases of such later writings as the epistle of James (esp. Jas. 2:8, 14–26) and the teachings of Jesus (e.g., Matt. 6:14f; 25:14–46); these describe the behaviors that characterize a righteous life.

Wisdom is thus the outworking of a heart of obedience, a heart which has settled beforehand its commitment to the LORD's ways, and not its own (3:5f). Although the word translated "wisdom" can refer to "skill" (cf. Exo. 31:6; 35:25f, 35; 36:1f), in Proverbs it does not mean merely "clever" or "resourceful," as though these were natural qualities that characterize the astute. The wise are humble and quick to seek advice because they know their limitations. They are also gracious, because they understand that every person is a special creation of God. The wise speak carefully since they know the power of words, and value justice, righteousness, loyalty and truth—the standards of the God who stands behind the Covenant. Obedience is thus the heartbeat of wisdom, and yields a joyful life.

A special aspect of wisdom is its personification in Prov. 1–9 (esp. 1:20–33; 8:1–35; 9:1ff). Wisdom claims attributes and abilities that belong to God alone. For example, wisdom gives wealth and honor (8:18–21), guides and protects individuals (2:12–22; 3:23–26) and reigns over kings (8:15f). Most of all, wisdom is the source of life (2:21; 3:16, 18; 4:13; 8:35; 9:11). It is not, however, these characteristics which are most striking, because in every case the pronouns could be translated as "it" (the verbs and adjectives are feminine because the word translated wisdom is feminine gender; "she" is the translators' choice), so that "wisdom" could be understood abstractly.

Far more important are the passages which describe Wisdom (the capital "W" seems more appropriate here) as standing, calling, inviting, rebuking (e.g., 2:20–33), and a participant in creation (3:19f; 8:22–31). These last two references are especially important, because in the first, wisdom is an attribute of God, whereas in the second, Wisdom is just as clearly portrayed as separate from Him. Christians through the centuries have been quick to identify this person with Christ, the second Person of the Godhead, just as several major Christological passages (John 1:1–14; Col. 1:15–20; Heb. 1:1–4) seem to reflect Prov. 8:22–31 (cf. also 1 Cor. 1:24, 30; Col. 2:3).

Any theory about plurality with reference to God, however, would sink upon striking the adamant monotheism of the Covenant. We should probably, therefore, understand these descriptions of Wisdom as hinting at a backdrop that was Christ, but that the backdrop would remain dark until the light of the Incarnation.

Folly. A better translation of the word normally rendered "fool" might be "rebel," and for "folly" read "rebellion" (cf. 1:7; 9:18). Since the English "fool" and its derivatives connote silliness or stupidity, these are not helpful renderings of the biblical terms, but are misleading. Although the commentary uses the traditional terms ("fool," "folly," etc.), the point of the Book is that a fool is anyone who rejects the offer of wisdom (the gift of God that leads to life) by refusing to submit to the instruction of God. Fools prefer to follow their own "understanding" (cf. 3:5b), which is really no wisdom at all and which leads only to death.

Because they reject the authority of God and his covenant, fools cannot profit from wisdom (17:16; 26:7, 9) or correction (17:10; 27:22). Their delight is wickedness (10:23), unlike the wise, who rejoice to grow in wisdom and understanding (10:23; 15:21). The result of foolish behavior is destruction and death (1:32; 2:22; 8:36). Wisdom is priceless (3:13ff), and it offers rich rewards, especially life (3:16ff; 8:35; 9:6, 10f). Folly promises "pleasure" (9:17) but actually delivers the grave (9:18).

Folly is expressed in many ways, primarily in its attitude toward God and his standards, but then, inevitably, in its interaction with others. Despising those around them, especially when they are righteous (i.e., wise), the arrogant view others as tools which they can manipulate to accomplish their own ends. Preferring their own understanding, and the sound of their own thoughts (18:1), they are isolated, and they reject the advice and counsel that would help them succeed (12:15; 18:2). They use words as weapons, neither regarding their power (12:18) nor caring that they destroy others thereby (6:12–19; 11:13; 29:5).

Although folly is manifold and varied, at heart it is quite simple. It is against anyone and anything that might turn it away from its chosen course, even though that course leads to difficulty (e.g., 15:19; 22:3) and, ultimately, death (e.g., 14:11f).

Finally, the Book of Proverbs holds out no hope for fools. Having rejected wisdom in their hearts, they cannot acquire the insight they need (1:24–32), as though wisdom were merely the skill to avoid disaster. Even verses which might seem to imply that fools can change actually use the fool as a foil (26:12; 29:20) to show the utter hopelessness of the arrogant and hasty. Fools cannot, and will not, be separated from their folly (15:21; 26:11; 27:22). In fact, to attempt to "convert" a fool is a hopeless and thankless task (9:7f; 23:9), which will only frustrate and may even endanger the one who tries (19:19; 26:4; 29:9).

The Person of God in Proverbs. The portrayal of God in Proverbs is of a rather distant figure, who created (3:19f; 20:12; 21:1) and judges (5:21; 15:3, 11; 16:2; 17:3; 21:2) all things, rendering to each according to his words, deeds and motives (3:32; 8:35; 10:3, 29; 11:20; 12:2; 15:25, 29; 16:5, 7). He is also the universal Sovereign (16:4; 21:1, 30f) Who controls everything from the throw of the dice (16:33) to a person's words (16:1) and steps (16:9; 20:24). At the same time, He guards (3:26; 10:29) and blesses (2:6; 10:22) all who trust (3:5f; 22:19), honor (3:9f) and obey (1:7; 3:7f) Him—those who are his friends (3:32). Even his discipline is that of a loving Father (3:11f), Who desires the best possible life for his children (10:22).

In addition to these explicit statements is the implication that since a wise life pleases the LORD, his standards (as revealed in Proverbs) reveal his nature. For example, those attitudes and actions that He hates or despises—hypocrisy (15:8; 21:27; 28:9, dishonesty (3:32; 11:1; 12:22; 20:23), violence (6:16–19), wickedness (11:20; 15:9, 26), pride (16:5), injustice (17:15)—are also condemned by the Covenant, explicitly or implicitly.

The consistent condemnation of anger, for example, reveals not only that human rage does not yield the righteous life required by God (Jas. 1:20; cf. Ps. 4:4; Eph. 4:28), but also that frustrated rage does not characterize the LORD. Since humans were created to be like Him (Gen. 1:26ff), it should not characterize their hearts or relationships either.

The "Commonalities" of Life. Proverbs 30:15–31 demonstrate the true genius of the wise, noting similarities between disparate objects or situations. The ability to discern order within random experience, to abstract principles common to various settings is the mark of the wise. It is also the basis of the truth content of a proverb.

Not everyone who befriends an angry person becomes angry (cf. 22:24f), nor does wise counsel guarantee success (cf. 21:30f; 24:5f). Still these consequences are common enough that the discerning individual notices the relationship and says, "Look before you leap." Observing other situations, however, the wise also say, "He who hesitates is lost." (In Proverbs, the former is always the better course of action!) This generalization may reflect a shared quality that is intrinsic to the situations (e.g., 30:15b–16, 21ff, 24–28, 29ff), or it may characterize a common response, either the observer's (30:18f) or the LORD's (6:16–19). The ability to abstract a general principle from experience or observation and then to synthesize that principle into a few words is an outstanding characteristic of wisdom (cf. 24:30–34).

Understanding Proverbs

In one sense, a commentary on Proverbs circumvents the purpose of the Book, which is to help students grow morally and intellectually (1:2–6). Students of the proverbs will gain the greatest benefit from them by studying them first, before looking at the comments or suggestions of others. This section of the Overview outlines an approach to the proverbs.

Apart from its title and sub-titles, Proverbs is an entirely poetic Book, and therefore needs to be approached as poetry. Although biblical poetry lacks the rhythm and rhyme that we associate with poetry in English, its characteristics are obvious as soon as we pay attention to how it communicates its

Overview

message. These characteristics are often called parallelism, imagery and terseness (density).

Although their terseness is visible in the original text, most proverbs contain ten or fewer words in Hebrew. Terseness, per se, is not an aspect that needs to be interpreted, since it is common to all proverbial literature (cf. English proverbs, which usually have four to six words: "A rolling stone gathers no moss"; "Look before you leap").

This method of studying a proverb for preaching or teaching is listed as a series of steps, but these often overlap. The process is not, therefore, linear, but more like a spiral, gradually focusing on the central meaning of the text. If we understand the verse aright, however, the result of each step will be consonant with and reinforce the others.

Read the verse in several translations. This is necessary because of the enormous amount of interpretation underlying even the most "literal" translation into English, and translators often paraphrase, expand, explain or otherwise interpose themselves between you and the text. The proverbs are extremely short texts, often of only five to ten words, several of which are fairly uncommon. Their syntax is often complicated by their brevity, so that determining whether a given word is subject or object, predicate or substantive (especially participles), is often difficult.

Parallelism. Describe the relationship between the lines of the verse (the basic relationship is often called "parallelism"), and answer the question. "Which element lies at the heart of this relationship?" There are two basic relationships between lines: lines that are contrasting and lines that are complementary. The former are called "antithetical," since they use antonyms to create the contrast; the latter are called "synonymous," since they use synonyms. Here are two examples:

A wise son makes a father glad,
 a foolish son is his mother's grief (10:1).
Pride before destruction,
 and a haughty spirit before stumbling (16:18).

The first is antithetical (note the contrast between "wise" and "foolish" and between "glad" and "grief"). The second is synonymous, as the pairs "pride/haughty spirit" and "destruction/stumbling" show.

A subtype of synonymous parallelism is the emblematic proverb, in which one line presents a picture (the "emblem"), and the other explains what the picture means:

Cold water to the thirsty;
 so is good news from a distant land (25:25).

These proverbs, which are fairly common in Proverbs 25–27 (and which could be called "miniature parables" [cf. Matt. 13:45]), consists of a single comparison that impels us to ask what the picture and emblem have in common after we are sure that we understand what the image portrays. "Double" and "triple" emblems have two or three pictures, all of which illustrate the point made in the second line (e.g., 26:1ff).

We must first ask what the emblems describe (for which a Bible dictionary or encyclopedia is often necessary), then what they have in common, and finally how the "caption" relates to their common element. A few emblematic parallelisms include a third line that explains the common element that is the main point of the comparison:

Like the cold of snow in harvest
 is a faithful messenger to those who send him,
 for he refreshes his masters (25:13).

Even though the proverb makes the point of comparison explicit, we still need to be sure that we understand, in this case, the weather patterns of Israel (what was the weather like in harvest? could they expect snow?) in order to appreciate the nature and depth of refreshment that a faithful messenger affords.

Trying to determine how the lines are related is one way to encourage ourselves to pay close attention to the meaning of each line, as well as to the meaning of the lines as they were written. Unlike proverbs in English, biblical proverbs are not one-liners; they make their point by using paired statements. As an exercise, it is often helpful to try to reduce a proverb to a single statement, but we must remember that the biblical poets did not make their points in this way and be careful that we do not obscure or override their artistry. For example, in 11:23:

The desire of the righteous is only good,
  but the hope of the wicked is wrath.

The subtle distinction between "desire" and "hope" does not contrast two different emotions, one apportioned to each type of person. Instead, together they reflect the truth that we hope for what we desire. This leads us in turn to evaluate hopes and dreams, since they reveal the true nature of the hearts.

Logic. A proverb's logic is how it makes its point. This step is tied so closely to the preceding that to do one is often to do the other. Some proverbs, for example, identify a person who acts in one way as actually doing something quite different:

He also who is slack in his work,
  is a brother to a destructive person (18:9).

Another type commands a particular action or attitude, and then explains its importance:

Do not speak in a fool's ears,
  for he despises the wisdom of your words (23:9).

Yet another type says that one thing is better than another, and explains why:

Better a little with the fear of the Lord,
  than great treasure and turmoil with it (15:16).

Some proverbs progress from cause to effect (21:21), or vice versa (21:25):

Whoever pursues righteousness and loyalty
  finds life, righteousness, and honor (21:21).
The sluggard's desire puts him to death
  because his hands refuse to work (21:25).

Identifying the proverb's logic helps us see how the poet made his point and also provides a check for our understanding of the parallelism.

Imagery. Many proverbs describe things that are literally impossible. For example, wine can neither make fun of anyone, nor get into fights, yet Solomon says:

Wine is a mocker, strong drink is a brawler,
Whoever goes astray by them is not wise (20:1).

We need to ask what wine and strong drink have in common with mocking and fighting. What enables the poet to make this statement, which sounds absurd if we take it literally? The first step in interpreting an image is to determine what the poet was actually describing. In interpreting 20:26, for example, we need to ask what winnowing was, who did it, and why, as well as what the wheel was used for:

A wise king winnows the wicked,
  and turns the wheel over them (20:26).

Once we understand the picture that the poet was drawing (the reality that his image points to), we can ask what common trait or quality he saw, and points out, by using this image.

Although there are technical terms for images, labels are not as important as understanding what enabled the poet to compare two things, or to substitute one for another. There are the two main types of images: those that name both halves of the comparison (e.g., "wine" and "mocker") and those that substitute one thing for something else:

The way of the sluggard is like a hedge of thorns,
  but the path of the upright is a road (15:19).

Both comparisons also entail a substitution ("way" and "path" are substitutes for "life"). The substitution communicates his meaning because life, like a path, has a beginning and end, and involves many choices.

Since the proverbs were written against an Iron Age, agrarian and monarchical background, the proper interpretation of some figures will require more or less research (usually a multi-volume Bible encyclopedia will suffice). The genius of poetry (to point out what we often see but don't realize) demands that we work at understanding the figures in order to see along with the poet.

Context. Outside the extended poems (Prov. 1–9; 23:29–35; 24:30–34; etc.), the immediate context of a proverb (the preceding and following verses) is rarely as important as it is in other parts of Scripture, although there are some small topical clusters (e.g., 16:1ff, which discusses God's sovereignty; cf. also 16:9, 25, 33). The real context of a proverb consists of all the other proverbs that touch on the same topic (see "Topical Index" above), which need to be considered in interpreting a verse.

Application. When we understand a proverb, we should have a reasonably good idea of its advice. There are two complementary approaches to their application: (1) The most obvious is that every proverb explicitly or implicitly contrasts wisdom and folly, commends the former and warns us against the latter. This "behavior" can refer to acts, attitudes or emotions. The first step of applying a proverb is to determine how it contrasts wisdom and folly (or comparable terms, such as "righteousness" and "wickedness")—specifically, which aspect of life it addresses and what it says about it. (2) Another aspect of applying a proverb is to think about it externally (as it applies to those around us) and internally (as it applies to us). Proverbs 10:1, for example, seems tautological (i.e., too obvious for words). This verse, however, records an observation that has implications for many aspects of life.

First, we can *extend* its observation. Seeing how someone's choices and decisions affect others enables us to consider our relationship with that person, since we may be affected by his or her decisions, just as, for example, his parents are. This is a form of "decompression"—drawing out the story that underlies the proverb.

We can also *reverse* its observation, so that our parents' opinion of us may be a good guide to our trustworthiness as a friend, counselor or business partner.

We can also apply it *internally*—which kind of son or daughter do we want to be to our parents? what kind of friend to others? which do we want our children to become? what can we do to work toward delighting others, rather than grieving them? does Proverbs have any further advice on this topic?

This also entails imagining future circumstances that parallel, or are analogous to, the type of situations that called forth the proverb. How will we act, think, speak in like circumstances? Just as we "decompress" its stories to understand the proverb, so we project its story into the future of our own lives so that it can guide our behavior.

We must also consider each proverb in light of Who God is and what He requires, lest we allow Proverbs to yield only pious advice. At least part of the reason that wisdom is so closely identified as an attribute of God in Prov. 1–9, is so we will consider Who God is and what He is like as we seek to obey what we find in this Book. Every proverb can, therefore, be linked, negatively and positively, to the LORD's person and works. Like the steps of uncovering and projecting the proverb's stories, this too can be narrated within the scope, or against the backdrop, of redemptive history. Considering Prov. 10:1, the character of God is such that He never grieves or disappoints those who are his, that He will never act foolishly or carelessly, and that those who know and love Him will come to rejoice fully in Him. Because God is like this, and we are to be like Him, we too should ask Him to make us this kind of person, and strive then to be such.

Notes on Translation

Poetic texts are notoriously difficult to translate, often because the original language is more compressed, more picturesque and apparently less explicit than prose. Many topics could be addressed in discussing translation, but some seem especially helpful in approaching the Book of Proverbs.

"He who." As the grammatical analysis shows, the form translated "he who" is usually a masculine singular participle. Although generally translated as "he who," this is the Hebrew equivalent of "whoever," "anyone who," "the person (or the one) who." Even when the participle must refer to a male because of the context, the proverb can still be applied to anyone who reads. Consider this proverb:

> Better to live in the wilderness
> than with an argumentative and
> troublesome wife (21:19).

While clearly addressed to men, both men and women need to consider a person's character before discovering that they would have been better off on the roof (21:9; 25:24) or in the wilderness (21:19) than married to that person, just as character is more important than appearance (11:22).

Some modern translations, moreover, are explicitly "gender neutral." They may avoid "he who" by, for example, pluralizing subjects and objects. The following renderings of Prov. 28:26 illustrate the difference:

Those who trust in their own wits are fools;
   but those who walk in wisdom come through
   safely (NRSV).
He who trusts in himself is a fool,
   but he who closes his eyes to them
   receives many curses (NIV).

Both translations accurately reflect the meaning of the Hebrew text. Hundreds of plural referents, however, seem to dull the edge of specificity created by the singular "he who" and "whoever."

The difficulty of applying this policy consistently is revealed even in "gender neutral" translations such as NRSV. Although it consistently renders the proverbs in the plural, the references to adultery in the early chapters all warn men against women (cf. the next topic, below):

So is he who sleeps with his neighbor's wife;
   no one who touches her will go unpunished
   (6:29; NRSV)

rather than, for example:

So is anyone who sleeps with another's spouse;
   no one who touches that person will
   go unpunished.

The clumsiness of the second rendering illustrates the difficulty of representing a culturally conditioned original accurately, and with an eye (and ear) to the culture for which the version is being made.

"Strange Women" and "Adulteresses." There are several references to prostitutes in Proverbs (e.g., 6:26; 29:3; 7:10 uses "prostitute" in a simile). Other passages refer to "strange" or "foreign" women (Prov. 2:16–19; 5:3–14, 20; 6:24–35; 7:1–27). Many translations, however, render these texts with the word "adulteress." Compare the following translations of, for example, Prov. 5:20. The first is a "traditional" rendering, the second is "gender neutral," and the third is my own:

For why should you, my son, be enraptured
   by an *immoral woman*,
And be embraced in the arms of a *seductress*?
   (NKJV)

Why should you be intoxicated, my son,
   by *another woman*,
and embrace the bosom of an *adulteress*?
   (NRSV)

For why should you, my son, be intoxicated by
   a *strange woman*
and embrace the bosom of a *foreign woman*?

These statements warn against any sexual activity outside marriage, contrasting a "stranger" or "foreigner" with a person's spouse (as NRSV's rendering of the first line correctly implies). They are not warnings against a particular type of woman who is somehow prone to sexual immorality. Nor are these references cryptic warnings against cultic prostitution (as some commentators suggest), although their exhortations to chastity have the effect of forbidding participation in the sexual rituals that were part of some Canaanite worship.

"Soul." The word often translated "soul" (nephesh; HED #5497) is one way in which Biblical Hebrew refers to a person and often functions as a reflexive pronoun, such as English "myself" or "yourself." Moreover, there is little evidence that the Israelites thought of the soul as an entity separate from the physical body (Ecc. 3:21, which is making a different point, uses the word rûach [HED #7593 "spirit," "breath," "wind"]). Proverbs 6:32, for example, is rendered correctly by NASB (and most other translations):

Whoever commits adultery with a woman
   lacks sense;
He who would destroy *himself* ["his soul"]
   does it (6:32; NASB).

Few versions deal consistently with this issue, using "soul" in some places and a reflexive pronoun in others. It is thus important to consider the referent of the word nephesh in each context.

Verbal Conjugations. The verbal conjugations (sometimes called "tenses") are far less significant in biblical poetry than in prose, and the parallelism between lines encouraged the poets to vary the form of the verb. Because they are intended to apply to as many situations as possible, proverbs are usually rendered in the present or future. (For example, English proverbs may be timeless, e.g., "Different strokes for different folks," or present tense, e.g., "A stitch in time saves nine." This is called a global or gnomic present, i.e., "universal" or "concerned with wisdom," respectively.) Putting a proverb in the past tense changes it into a historical statement, so that it is no longer proverbial, e.g., "A stitch in time saved nine." Proverbs can also be translated using the future tense, since the future can express potential or tendency:

You see a man skilled in his work:
He *will* not *stand* before average men—
he *will stand* before kings (22:29).

The decision to translate a particular proverb as present or future may reflect a translation's philosophy or an attempt to distinguish in translation the different verbal conjugations of Hebrew, or there may be other reasons, such as variety of expression. There are very few verses in which the Hebrew conjugation has explicitly temporal meaning, so that different conjugations are often translated with the same English tense.

Conjunctions. Although Hebrew has a number of conjunctions, wᵉ (HED #2134) is by far the most frequent. Its meaning depends entirely upon the context, which helps accomplish the "mental" or "intellectual" purpose of the Book by forcing the reader to think about how the lines joined by the conjunction are related.

If the two lines are contrasting (see "Parallelism"), it is often translated "but"; when they are complementary, it is translated "and." In these two verses, the second lines are identical; the translation of the wᵉ is determined by the content of the first line.

The wise of heart accept commands,
   but a babbling fool will be thrown down (10:8).
Whoever winks the eye causes trouble,
   and a babbling fool will be thrown down (10:10).

The second line usually lacks a conjunction, thus encouraging the reader to determine their relationship by their content. Translators often add one in order to make the proverb read more smoothly, as in:

The first to plead his cause seems just,

Until another comes and examines him (18:17; NASB).

The [original] italics show that the adverb was added by the translators or editors). This represents the meaning of the text; its specificity, however, relieves the reader of the need to reflect on the relationship between these lines, which is, after all, one of the benefits of studying proverbs.

Translators tend to be especially "helpful" in emblematic proverbs, adding such modifiers as "like," "as," and "so." Compare, for example, these two renditions of Prov. 25:14:

Clouds and wind without rain;
A man who boasts of a false gift.
Like clouds and wind without rain
   is a man who boasts of his gifts falsely (NASB).

Both represent the sense of the Hebrew text. The second, however, obviates some of the need for reflection on why the poet constructed these lines in this way, i.e., how these lines are related.

The Ambiguity of Word Order. English sentences depend on word order to identify the parts of the sentence. For example, to change "the man ate the apple" into "the apple ate the man" changes the meaning, even though all of the words are identical. Other languages, such as German, Latin or Greek, use endings (called "inflections") that show each word's syntactical function. Because the words' endings indicate their function, word order is more "free" than in English (although inflected languages usually have rules governing some aspects of word order).

Biblical Hebrew is not inflected, but it does not depend on word order as heavily as English (especially in poetry). Since the predicate of many proverbial lines is a participle, which may function as a noun, a verb or an adjective, the syntax of some lines cannot be fixed absolutely. Proverbs 20:26, for example, could be translated as either of these:

A wise king winnows the wicked,
   and rolls the wheel over them, (or)

Whoever winnows the wicked is a wise king,
   and he rolls the wheel over them.

The difference is slight, but real. The former answers the question *"what* does a wise king *do?"*; the latter, *"who is* a wise king?" This particular text does not require us to prefer one translation over another, but we need to be aware that some differences between translations reflect different interpretations of the structure of the line.

Proverbial Ambiguity. Because words have ranges of meaning, because some words occur infrequently in Biblical Hebrew, because of the vagaries of poetic syntax, and because some function words, such as conjunctions and other particles have several meanings (e.g., kî [HED #3706] and can be translated "because," "that," "when," "but,"

etc.), some proverbs are ambiguous. For example, translating kî in Prov. 19:18 as "while" or "because" affects our understanding of the first line of the verse: "Discipline your son *while/because* there is hope" (see the commentary).

The commentary thus often suggests more than one interpretation for a verse. This is sometimes due to ignorance (words or images are sometimes not well understood) and sometimes because the words are multifaceted (e.g., kî, above). Most of the latter cases are probably intentionally ambiguous, written that way in order to encourage students to ponder the implications of each potential meaning.

ECCLESIASTES OVERVIEW

Background

Outline

Summary

Overview

BACKGROUND

The wisdom of Ecclesiastes is a necessary facet of the Old Testament. In bold style the author deals with the fundamental tensions present in our lives. He teaches the vanity of human behavior uninformed by the fear of God. Refusing to avoid the difficult questions of life, he invites the reader into an intimate discussion of the struggles of his life.

Ecclesiastes' Place in Wisdom Literature

Ecclesiastes is one of a group of books known as wisdom literature; other books include Job and Proverbs. In these books, wisdom is seen as the ability to apply the observed laws of the created universe. The wise man is responsible for observing and communicating these laws to the next generation. In contrast, a fool disregards and/or disdains wisdom. The goal of wisdom is more than just success in life or obtaining a good name. Ultimately, in biblical wisdom literature, contrasted with wisdom literature from surrounding cultures, the wise man is a man who pleases and fears Yahweh.

Title

The Hebrew title, Qoheleth (HED #7237), has the form of a feminine singular Qal active participle. Hebrew often uses the feminine gender to name an office, function or title. Qoheleth is treated as a masculine, probably pointing to an office filled by a male. Thus, it is most likely that Qoheleth is not a proper name. Besides these seven occurrences of this form, it occurs nowhere else in the Bible. Most know Qoheleth by the title given it in the Septuagint, Ecclesiastes (not to be confused with the apocryphal Ecclesiasticus). When translated, Ecclesiastes means "preacher." "Qoheleth" is related to qāhal (HED #7234) meaning "assembly" or "convocation."

Author

In the writings of most of the church fathers and most Jewish tradition, Solomon has been recognized as the author, or Qoheleth. The first words of the Book announce "the son of David, king in Jerusalem," very much like the first words of Proverbs, "The proverbs of Solomon the son of David, king of Israel." So also in 1:12, "king over Israel in Jerusalem." Other allusions pointing to great wisdom (1:16), various accomplishments, and great wealth (2:4-8) resonate with the biblical descriptions of Solomon. However, opposition to Solomonic authorship also has a long history. Questions about his authorship were first raised in the Talmud. Later Luther argued very strongly that Solomon's sayings were compiled by scholars. Since Solomon's name is not explicitly mentioned, there is room for different interpretations. Some see King Hezekiah as the author. Hezekiah was also a rich king who accomplished much (2 Chr. 29:1–32:33). Furthermore, he is associated with the preservation of wisdom (Pro. 25:1).

Date & Location

Not surprisingly, issues of date and location are tied to the issue of authorship. If Solomon is the author, Ecclesiastes was probably written around the tenth century in Palestine, surely in Jerusalem. Hezekiah ruled during the eighth century. Those who see in Ecclesiastes the work of a compiler exercise much more liberty in fixing a date and location. Reasonably, Gleason Archer argues for the work to have been done in the tenth century at Palestine.

Important Themes

Vanity. "All is vanity" (Ecc. 1:2). "Vanity" has remained the most frequent translation of hevel (HED #196). Today "vanity" is more easily understood as "conceit," instead of "futility." The Hebrew word has a basic meaning of "breath" or "vapor." In Ecclesiastes, hevel has negative connotations, futile or worthless. It could be translated "absurd" or "nonsense" (CEV). Hevel is used to describe labor and the products of labor (2:11), enjoyment of pleasures (2:1), death of fool and wise alike (2:15), search for wealth (5:10), and the lack of immediate retribution (8:10).

In seven of over twenty-five occurrences of hevel, qōheleth emphasizes and clarifies the absurdity of life through the phrase that should probably be translated "a chasing after wind" (1:14; 2:11, 17, 26; 4:4, 16; 6:9). The author gives a mental image of the absurd.

Retribution. The author denounces as absurd the unjust treatment of the wicked and the righteous. "There is something else meaningless that occurs on earth: righteous men who get what the wicked deserve, and wicked men who get what the righteous deserve" (Ecc. 8:14). The main passages that comment on the principle of retribution or justice are 3:16–22, 8:10–14, 7:15ff, and 9:1–6.

Qoheleth believes that the wicked and the righteous will be treated justly at God's command. "God shall judge the righteous and the wicked: for there is a time there for every purpose and for every work" (3:17). However, Qoheleth does not believe that this principle can be used to predict or describe someone's situation in life. He has observed the wicked being treated as the righteous and the righteous as the wicked.

Fear of God. The fear of God should be one of the distinguishing characteristics for the Christian seeking wisdom. Qoheleth would agree with the Psalmist (111:10) in linking the fear of the LORD and wisdom. For Qoheleth, the fear of God is derived from a firm belief in God's sovereignty (3:14). Fear, sometimes reverence, is an appropriate response by a person confronted by the incomprehensibility and mystery of God's actions (8:17).

Ecclesiastes uses the verb yārē' (HED #3486) to communicate the concept of fearing God. The epilogue crowns the message of Ecclesiastes: "Fear God and keep his commandments" (12:13). These injunctions are reminiscient of similar commands in Deuteronomy (5:29; 6:2; 8:6; 13:4). "This is the whole duty of man," (12:13). Just as we should, the writer looks to these commands for meaning in his life.

Overview

OUTLINE

SUMMARY

Ecclesiastes should not be viewed as a collection of unconnected wisdom sayings. Neither should a strict logical structure be forced on this book. Instead, there is a loose structure that points to an over-arching theme. The fear of God is the answer to the inability of man-centered wisdom to rise above observations of the absurd.

The Preacher announces his identity as "the son of David, king in Jerusalem" (1:1). The prologue is used to announce the major theme of the book. (1:2–11) Two repeated phrases are found here, "vanity of vanities," and "nothing new under the sun." The author then discusses his search for meaning, the results, and his answers. He hoped in wisdom (1:12–18; 2:12–16). He looked to pleasures, both physical and aesthetic (2:1–11). He also tried to achieve meaning through toil and production of wealth (2:17–23). He found that none of these completely satisfied his desire for fulfillment. But, he did derive some wisdom from his pursuits. The wise man is satisfied with the life he has been given. He enjoys those things that can be enjoyed (2:24ff). After all, God has allotted certain experiences to certain people (3:1–8). But that allotment is a mystery, we must fear God (3:9–15). He was very sure of God's judgment, that it was true (3:16–22).

God's judgment is not always apparent. Qoheleth observed many troubles, or evils in his life. He observed those who were oppressed without hope of help or aid (4:1ff). He saw the problems that resulted from envy of neighbors (4:4ff). He saw the one who was trapped by his desire for wealth. Sadly, this one is alone; no one would inherit the fruit of his labors (4:7–12). The author writes about the lack of fulfillment found in advancement (4:13–16). He also notes the troubles that worshippers of God get into when they speak hastily, as fools (5:1–7). At the end of this section he briefly returns to evil of political injustice (5:8, 9). Qoheleth sees all of the pain and trouble that results from actions not informed by a fear of God. He explains that neither wealth (5:10–6:9) nor man (6:10ff) is able to alleviate these problems. But instead he points out that troubles or frustrations are not always to be avoided (7:1–14). Excess, however, will lead to further destruction. Moderation is a key (7:15–22). He closes this section by reminding and enforcing the lessons learned by wisdom (7:23–29).

The next four chapters deal with the wise man's way to wisdom. A wise man accepts authority for God is over all authority (8:1–9). A wise man lives as if the judgment were immediate, but trusts God's timing (8:10–17). A wise man enjoys the gifts of God even though he knows his destiny is death (9:1–12). Qoheleth points out that even though wisdom is more powerful than strength, its memory is easily lost (9:13–17) and its work easily negated (9:18–10:20). Ecclesiastes closes this section by thinking about how present behavior effects the future, when the future is altered by behavior (11:1–10). He also reminds his readers that since they will be old one day they should include that consideration in their present actions (12:1–8). The author's final injunction "Fear God and keep his commandments," is the captsone for Ecclesiastes (12:8–14).

SONG OF SONGS OVERVIEW

Background

Outline

Summary

Overview

BACKGROUND

A Short Survey of Critical Understanding of Song of Songs

The unique character of the Song of Songs has aroused much diverse understanding of its purpose and meaning for the life of Bible students. It was only natural to speculate at length about the inclusion of a Book in the Holy Bible which never even mentions the name of God. How could this be a truly inspired Book in the Hebrew canon when it teaches nothing which is truly theological? The internal data of the text furnishes clear evidence that the production is about Solomon, if not directly composed by him for publication. It is a document allowed for profit or encouragement for the people of God as they seek to serve Him and proclaim his unique power as LORD of all creation—why the complete absence of doctrinal teaching? The answer has to be found in a careful appreciation of what it does teach for the guidance of God's people.

The answer to this problem is best discovered by the rich beauty of the kingdom of God, Who made the Promised Land in the days of David and Solomon a virtual paradise of beauty and joy. In his steadfast care, the loving Father of mankind has provided all that we need as his covenant people. In a period of abundant rainfall, verdant slopes of lush growth (as is obvious from the way their pleasure spots are described) must have furnished a special abundance such as Israel had never known before, or since. The royal prince and the village lass were chosen as ideal exemplars of romantic and thrilling love. Even though some disappointments and frustrations occurred in their courtship, the privilege of full-blown ecstasy was granted to them both. We serve a God Who loves us and watches over us according to his infinite love and care. Human love is meant to be received with deepest gratitude. However, the scriptural record also assures that the real purpose is not to enjoy a problem-free career down here on earth. God's real purpose is for us to run well the race that He has set before us, looking unto Him, the Author of our salvation and our highest possible joy.

After these general observations, it is appropriate to give a brief survey of the various approaches adopted by Bible scholars who have dealt with this amazing little Book in its relationship to the other sixty-five Books of holy Scripture.

Gustave Oehler (in the Zondervan publication translated at Yale in 1983) speaks of Song of Songs as an exaltation of conjugal love and a noble commitment between two young people who fell in love with each other when they were on a farm in Shunem. Young Solomon took her down to Jerusalem, to the Jordan and to Lebanon, and even gave her a highly festive wedding down in the capital city. Despite episodes of confusion or misunderstanding, and the occasional contact with a harem located in the Jerusalem area, the most striking pronouncement with which the final chapter affirms the sanctity of romantic love is in v. 8: "For love is as strong as death, its jealousy unyielding as the grave."

R. K. Harrison (*Introduction to the Old Testament*, p. 486) defines the Hebrew title of the Book as "The best or most excellent of songs." He does not seem averse to dating it to the time of Solomon himself when the kingdom of Israel dominated Lebanon, Trans-jordan and the Sinai to the south. The amazing variety of animals, exotic trees, plants and fish of the streams suggests an outstanding polymath. (Lebanon supplied the wood for his chariot, adorned with silver and gold, and upholstered with rich purple.) Hermon is referred to in 4:8, Tirzah in 6:4, Damascus in 7:4. The author was quite familiar with the entire area of Syria-Palestine and the Lebanon range as far as En-Gedi. Six times Solomon is referred to by name (1:3; 3:7, 9, 11; 8:11f) and the immense wealth available for any vehicle or structure that suits his fancy is apparent. Even though it has been questioned whether Solomon actually spoke the statements he seems to have made, there is little ground for doubting that he expressed himself the way he does here.

Turning now to the other commentators, we find Heinrich Ewald endeavoring to supply a rival contestant for the Shulammite's heart and hand. Ultimately, the unnamed rival lover clouded in mystery, manages to win out over the crown prince himself. One may be quite justified in doubting that an unnamed personage ever could have won out over the crown prince of Israel. Amazingly enough, S. R. Driver finally settled for this alternative, understanding that young Solomon took her to Jerusalem from her rustic home. Thus Solomon learned to love her deeply with an affection that far transcended simple admiration of her merely physical assets; he came to appreciate her beauty of soul.

Heinrich Ewald felt that there must have been a second lover who never is named in the narrative, but who tried to rescue her from the polygamist atmosphere which the prince could offer her, far less appropriate than the setting of the Jerusalem harem. His dealings with her are set forth in those chapters where he treated her with gentle and courtly deference. Needless to say, it is hard to see how the real hero in this triangle could have remained completely anonymous. Furthermore, the dialogues of the last chapter seem to leave the Shulammite very definitely committed to her royal suitor—who, after all, had given her a very sumptuous public wedding in Jerusalem itself.

J. G. Wetzstein felt that Song of Songs was not to be considered a historical account of anything that truly transpired in the life of Solomon or his sylvan bride. Rather, it was a folk series of wedding songs of the sort preserved in the so-called *wasfs* or flattering ditties, perpetrated in the Syrian traditions and intended to embellish the festive nature of these happy occasions—a tradition surviving from many centuries. Strangely enough, however, there is absolutely no evidence that the Israelites ever followed this custom at any of their own celebrations. They can be attested only for the Syrian tradition. Moreover, there is not the slightest resemblance between the *wasfs* and the beautiful diction of these two lovers who came to know each other so long before, even when Tirzah was still the leading city in Palestine.

R. K. Harrison has shown real discernment in pointing out how skillfully the author of Song of Songs steered a middle course between prurient sexuality and a respect for the grandeur and nobility of the deeply enamored couple. He points out the remarkable combination between a sincere spirituality and the radiant linking together of two wholesome young people. It serves to highlight the glory of romance between those who came from far different social backgrounds, and yet were welded into a love match of peculiar tenderness.

The Mishna (Yadaim iii, 5) indicates that very earnest contention had arisen by the time of the Council of Jamnia in A.D. 95. Rabbi Judah was firmly in favor of its canonicity, even though Rabbi Joze voted in the negative. However, Rabbi Ben Joseph Akiba, one of the leading authorities in the study of the Mishna, firmly defended the canonicity of Song of Songs against its detractors, explaining that it was entirely allegorical and therefore was rich in meaning and personal edification. In fact, he declared this powerful dictum: "In the whole world there is nothing to equal the day in which the Song of Songs was given to Israel. All the Writings are holy, but the Song of Songs is the holy of holies." Unfortunately for him, the Roman government forbade the study or teaching of the Hebrew Bible after the rebellion of Bar Kochba. This failed to silence him in the pursuit of Bible teaching, and as a result he was put to death in A.D. 135. In later centuries, this cruel repression was finally abandoned after the triumph of Constantine the Great in A.D. 312, at the Battle of the Milvian Bridge. Later, in 325, he convened a comprehensive synod at Nicaea that established Christianity as the official religion of the Roman Empire. He passed away in 337, but not before establishing a departure from the norm. The official shift from paganism to the Christian religion proved to be conclusive from the Council of Nicaea in the following centuries. The entire Roman Empire was oriented to the once-detested religion of Greco-Roman idolatry. The Jewish faith retained the loyalty of the Hebrew race, and to a certain extent, this adherence to the Old Testament alone since all of Christendom acknowledged the authority of the older Testament. There were, however, persecutions from time to time when their intransigence seriously interfered with government policy. They continued to be tolerated by the Christian community most of the time.

But so far as the Song of Songs was concerned, both Jewish and Roman believers settled largely on the allegorical or symbolic basis.

Saadia Ben Joseph, a learned authority on the Hebrew Bible, is reputed to have come to the conclusion (ca. A.D. 940) that Song of Songs really requires a key to determine its teaching, and unfortunately that key has been lost. Still the Mishna and the Talmud tended to deal with it as a testimony of the graciousness of God as the divine Lover of Israel, which is favored with his steadfast mercies.

To the Christian experts, the Shulammite was a symbol of the church of Christ, an interpretation suggested by John 3:29; Eph. 5:22f; and Rev. 18:23.

475

Overview

As for Hippolytus of Rome, he concurred with the symbolic approach in regard to Solomon and his bride. Origen, Jerome, Augustine and Cocceius interpreted it as prophetic of the triumph of the Reformation. Ambrose and a few other scholars tended to identify the bride as the Virgin Mary. Luther understood Song of Songs as more or less symbolic of the Solomonic kingdom as such.

Rashi and Ibn Ezra understood the special presence of the LORD as it reposed between the cherubim in the Ark of the Covenant. As for Bernard of Clairvaux (1090–1153), he preached no less than eighty-six sermons on the first two chapters only and discovered what he determined to be a reference to Christ's crucifixion. Yet he went on to state quite categorically that there is not the slightest hint that allegory is being used anywhere in the lyrics of the Song of Songs as liturgical terms.

As for Franz Delitzsch, he saw two main characteristics: one portraying Solomon as wooing a country maid in Shunem and their visits to the wild life of northern Israel (cf. S.S. 6:13). Quite in contrast, Solomon also entices her to the courtly life of Jerusalem. In both settings, he found himself increasingly infatuated with this amazing country girl who completely won his heart.

In the most favored interpretation of the Song of Songs in the last fifty years or so, there seems to be a strong preference for understanding it as a clear account of an actual love affair between the young prince and his lovely neighbor in Shunem. To this writer, this seems to be the best way to interpret it if we maintain a consistent attitude toward our Bible study in general. We are to read this Book as we read any other Book in the Bible. It has an important lesson to teach us, and that is the glory and worthiness of romantic love. This, too, is a gracious and ennobling gift from God. Yet this is not to say that some godly men and women are truly chosen by the LORD to serve Him and our society, loving Jesus and his transforming grace, even though marriage is not in God's plan for their lives. The most glorious of the New Testament soulwinners, like Paul and John, achieved God's highest and best, even without the temporal blessing of godly spouses.

OUTLINE

Overview

SUMMARY

The Song of Songs of Solomon

In order to understand the function of the remarkable collection of poems that compose this unique Book, it is helpful to examine the amazing capabilities of the gifted son of King David, as described in 1 Ki. 4. There we are told that the LORD granted to this handsome young prince an unparalleled mental ability as a student of natural history and a connoisseur of the scholarly productions of all the surrounding nations (v. 29). (The wisdom literature of Phoenicia, Babylon, Egypt, and perhaps even India, may be found in Proverbs and Ecclesiastes.) His curiosity led him to careful study of various types of birds, animals and fish. First Kings 4:33 states, "And he spoke of trees, from the cedar that is in Lebanon, even to the hyssop that grows in the wall; he spoke also of animals and birds and creeping things and fish." Obviously, his observations were committed to writing, quite as voluminous as the enormous literature produced in Egypt and Babylon and Phoenicia and Syria. Presumably, he acquainted himself with all of those foreign publications that appealed to him, and he must have made voluminous contributions to the royal library in the palaces on Mt. Moriah. All of these documents, however, were later consigned to the flames when the troops of Nebuchadnezzar destroyed the entire city of Jerusalem in 587 and 586 B.C.

What bearing, then, does this diverse scholarship have upon the authorship of the Song of Songs? It simply demonstrates that the gifted young prince, even before his father died, became a phenomenal connoisseur of the literature of Egypt and the Middle East. He especially cultivated the genre of love poetry. Regrettably, there has been a very low survival rate of the great literature of ancient times, mostly because of the perishable materials upon which this genre would be recorded. Clay tablets and stone stelae would hardly be suitable for romantic poetry; the only exceptions of surviving literature from the Solomonic age would be those Egyptian compositions recorded on papyrus and preserved in the tombs of mummies interred in the zero humidity of the west bank. (These appear on pp. 467f in *Ancient Near Eastern Texts,* 3rd edition, published by Princeton University Press.)

It would have been only natural for a young prince held in high favor by his doting father, King David, to take vacations from Jerusalem to the various provinces or tribes of the kingdom of the twelve tribes. His curiosity drove him to familiarize himself with the various species of birds, beasts and trees that were to be found in the hills and valleys of his father's realm. He especially prized the vineyards and olive groves of the hillsides, as they were surrounded by banks of beautiful flowers. The grazing fields of the cattle and sheep brought him great pleasure during the warm, moist seasons of the year. Apparently, one of his favorite haunts was the fertile terrain near Shunem in the territory of the tribe of Issachar. There he took notice of a lovely young maiden (whose personal name is not given), employed by her older brothers in tending the family vineyards. There her face and arms took on a rich tan—for which she later felt it necessary to apologize as a deeply tanned outdoor laborer, in contrast with the creamy white skin of fashionable ladies of Jerusalem.

Distinctive Features of the Tale of Romance

1. This is the only Book in the Bible which makes no specific mention of God. We might expect some definite references to the gracious leading of the LORD in this narrative of the thrilling love affair between the prince and the country lass who captured his heart in the delightful paradise of the flourishing estate in Shunem in which she had been raised. The romance is soon enhanced by her visits down to the royal palace and grounds of Jerusalem, where they were surrounded by the luxurious appointments of the City of David and the glories of the Temple and palaces of Mt. Moriah.

2. Quite clearly this romance took place before Solomon had become deeply involved in governmental duties. As crown prince, he already is referred to as melekh (HED #4567) or "king," but certainly not as a crowned sovereign over the Israelite Empire, which at that time extended from the Sinai peninsula to the banks of the Euphrates. The term melekh was the only one suitable at that time for a crown prince designate. The normal term for "prince" in Biblical Hebrew was either rō'sh (HED #7513) or nāsî' (HED #5562). But rō'sh was used only of army captains or tribal leaders; nāsî'

478

referred to an army commander. Therefore, the only title available for a crown prince was melekh, as one set apart as the chosen successor to the crown. Despite the fact that he had not been officially presented to Israel as David's successor, 1 Chr. 22:9f makes it clear that Solomon was quite early appointed by God to serve as David's heir. The older sons of David had already lost their lives before David passed on, except for Adonijah (who made an attempt to seize the throne right after David died, but was successfully outmaneuvered by Zadok, Nathan and Benaiah, according to 1 Ki. 1:45–49). This took place some time later than the courtship of the Shulammite. But it was not until then that the young melekh designate became the melekh as enthroned sovereign.

3. The romance between Solomon and the Shulammite did not conform at all to the normal practice in the Israelite tradition. Usually, the father of the male lover would negotiate with the father of the bride-to-be first, before the solemnizing of the marriage compact and the days of feasting that would normally follow. But this romance was a spontaneous infatuation that began on Solomon's summer vacation, where he simply fell in love with a charming young teenager who responded to him with deepest admiration and devotion. Nowhere else in Scripture do we have such a delightful illustration of spontaneous affection between two loving hearts. This was a special blessing from the LORD and should be appreciated as such.

4. The constant shift in location of the action as between Shunem and Jerusalem seems to be rather bewildering. The very first chapter seems to place the lovers in the palace grounds of Jerusalem. The "daughters of Jerusalem" are in conversation with the country lass from the north (1:5ff) as she relates to them the hardships imposed upon her while tending the livestock and the vineyards of her father's estate. Thus she tries to explain the deep, rich tan she has developed in the out-of-doors (for proper young ladies were not supposed to get dark skinned in those days). A little further on in this chapter, she responds gratefully to the perfume and myrrh provided to her by her royal lover (1:12f), much to his delight. Further on, in 2:1–7, she is ushered into the royal dining hall, and over the festive table flutters a "banner of love" ("his banner over me is love"). This, incidentally, is the most frequently quoted

passage from Song of Songs, for it readily lends itself to a spiritual application, symbolic of the banner of God's love over his redeemed. It is a meaningful display of his yearning compassion for our fallen human race.

The latter part of ch. 2 (vv. 10–17) presents a setting in the flowering, fruit-bearing beauty of her father's farm. In ch. 3, the setting is clearly back in Jerusalem, whereas in ch. 4 it is shifted back to Shunem. Chapter 5 seems to present a wooded setting in the neighborhood of Jerusalem, and the sweet young lover pours out terms of utmost admiration for her beloved, surpassing anything that has been said before. This she does in the presence of the "daughters of Jerusalem," continuing into the first three verses of ch. 6. From v. 4 onward, however, Solomon responds with complete adulation for her beauty and charm, surpassing any other damsel in all the kingdom.

5. The identity of the "daughters of Jerusalem" seems at first to be confusing. In view of Solomon's later acquisition of many wives and concubines, it would be natural to speculate that this group of attractive young women might be the earliest installment of his harem. The term "daughters of Jerusalem" can hardly be so understood. Nowhere is a husband's mate referred to as the daughter of a city, rather than of a specific father or family, so far as the Bible is concerned. It is obvious from the friendly relationship between the Shulammite and this group of performers that there is no sexual relationship between the young prince and this choral group of singers. As early as the time of Moses, when the Israelites had made a safe crossing of the Red Sea, there was a considerable number of ladies who joined with Miriam in exalting the LORD for his marvelous deliverance from the Egyptian charioteers, who proclaimed "Sing to Yahweh, for He is highly exalted; the horse and his rider He has hurled into the sea" (Exo. 15:21). In all probability, the Israelites appreciated the role of gifted young women as choral entertainers at their banquets and celebrations, as recorded in their inscriptions and art work. In the time of King Saul and young David, we read of the victorious chants of the women who called out to David after his victory over Goliath and his fellow Philistines: "Saul has slain his thousands, and David his ten thousands." It seems obvious from these examples that

Overview

young people's choruses were trained and enlisted as celebrants at times of national victory and success. It is altogether likely that during a period of successive military triumphs in David's career, there would be a large number of young women enlisted and trained to participate in the praise of God in connection with these triumphs over the enemy—particularly so after the abortive effort of Absalom to overthrow his father and assume supreme power in Israel. This would explain the presence and cordial participation of this choral group as "the daughters of Jerusalem."

6. Bible students have indulged in much debate concerning the factuality of this love affair between Solomon and the lovely young woman from Shunem. Since God is not expressly mentioned in Song of Songs, there has been a good deal of speculation about the possibility of allegory being hidden in this remarkable narrative. From post-apostolic times, there has been an effort to interpret Solomon as a symbol of Christ, and the Shulammite as a representative of the Church. Rabbi Aqiba in the first century A.D. identified the Shulammite as a type of national Israel. This was confirmed by Saadia, Rashi and Ibn Ezra in later centuries—so also some of the Christian interpreters, who, of course, understood the bride as the Christian Church rather than Israel. The earliest known identification was that of Hippolytus (A.D. 200). Following him were Gregory of Nyssa, Ambrose of Milan and his famous disciple, St. Augustine, along with St. Jerome and St. Ambrose. It was Origen, back in the third century, who composed no less than ten volumes of allegorical interpretation for the Song of Songs. Martin Luther felt that the allegorists were hardly correct, but he did see in Song of Songs a sort of encomium of the peace and secure position of Israel under the rule of David and Solomon.

There are many defenders of an allegorical interpretation for Song of Songs even today, including those who are convinced that without bringing in some sort of typology, the Book would have no place in the Bible whatever. Therefore, we should see in the figure of Solomon a type of the Lord Jesus, and in the Shulammite, the Church (or, within Jewish circles, Adonai and Israel). This approach was deemed necessary according to the allegorists and dramatists, if the Song of Songs were to be considered as a real part in the Holy Bible. This concern is certainly of prime importance, but it runs into the danger of imposing upon this masterpiece a symbology which is hardly to be proved. Is this then to be held as a unique exception in the biblical canon, that what is apparently narrated as an historical episode in Solomon's life never really took place? Is this admissible as consonant with our commitment to the total trustworthiness of the Bible and the Bible alone (*sola Scriptura*)? Despite the impressive scholarship of such leading scholars in biblical interpretation down through the ages (beginning with Rabbi Aqiba, Ibn Ezra, Origen, Jerome, Bernard and Calvin), there seems to be insufficient evidence to warrant manipulating the record of this Book as if it were intended to teach what it does not actually say.

It is, therefore, safe to say that what we have in Song of Songs is a cordial recognition of the great blessing of spontaneous, romantic love. Above and beyond the customary formalities of parent-arranged marriage contracts, God may bestow upon his covenant children the thrill of a deep emotion, or even an infatuation, as a bestowment of his grace. It would seem that well before young Solomon became involved in dynastic union with a queen of Egypt or any royalty from other nations in contact with the Hebrew Empire, this crown prince was led into a wholesome and exalting union with a lovely, warmhearted and deeply affectionate young lady from the countryside in Issachar. While the text does not actually record that she really did unite with her royal lover in marriage, it is a fair inference that she became his wife, perhaps even his first wife. It would not have been until later years that he built up his enormous harem in the pursuit of international influence and prestige.

APPENDICES

Explanation of Grammar

Translations of the Various Versions

*Books of the Old and New Testaments
and the Apocrypha*

How the Old Testament Came to Us

Manuscripts

Appendices

APPENDIX A

Explanation of Grammar

Explanation of Verb Stems

There are basically seven verb stems in the Hebrew language. Verbs are either active or passive, and they deal with past, present or future actions or conditions. The mood of the verb relates the general meaning, but context—the relationships of words within the literary unit—always determines the final meaning.

This volume uses a verb numbering system formatted to give (1) the word number; (2) the mood; (3) the tense; and (4) the person, gender and number. The first number is to the left of the decimal point, and the last three numbers are to the right of the decimal point. Following is a brief explanation of the numbers that occur to the right of the decimal point.

Mood (first position)

1. *Qal*—simple active verb stem. The Qal mood accounts for most of the verbs in the Old Testament. Qal usually indicates an action of the subject (*he told*). It can also indicate the state of the subject (*he was old*).

2. *Niphal*—the simple passive or reflexive counterpart of the Qal stem. Used passively, Niphal means the action of the verb is received by the subject (*he was told,* or, *it was told*). Although rare, Niphal is sometimes used reflexively, meaning that the subject performs the action of the verb upon himself or herself (*he realized*). The reflexive meaning is usually expressed using the Hithpael.

3. *Piel*—the intensive active or causative stem. The most common use of the Piel is as intensification of the action of the verb (*he often told,* or, *he fully explained*). It sometimes, however, is used in a causative sense like the Hiphil (*he caused to learn/he taught*).

4. *Pual*—the intensive passive counterpart of the Piel stem (*he was often told,* or, *he was completely informed,* or, *it was fully explained*).

5. *Hiphil*—the causative active counterpart of the Qal stem (*he caused to tell*). Sometimes it is used in a declarative sense (*he declared guilty*). Some Hiphil verbs are closer to the meaning of the simple active use of the Qal stem (*he destroyed*). Finally, some Hiphil verbs do not fit any of these categories, and they must be understood by their context.

6. *Hophal*—the causative passive counterpart of the Hiphil stem (*he was caused to tell*).

7. *Hithpael*—reflexive action (*he realized*). However, some Hithpael verbs are translated in a simple active sense like the Qal stem (*he prayed*), since the one performing the action is not transferring that action to anyone or anything else.

Tense (second position)

1. *Perfect.* The Hebrew perfect may be translated as a simple completed action (*he walked* to the store). It may also be translated as a *past perfect*, which is an action completed prior to a point of reference in past time (she gave money as *she had promised*). The perfect is translated in the present tense when the verb concerns the subject's attitude, experience, perception or

state of being (*you are old,* or, *I love you*). It may also represent action that is viewed as completed as soon as it was mentioned (*I anoint you* as king over Israel, 2 Ki. 9:3).

When this tense is used in promises, prophecies and threats, it commonly means that the action of the verb is certain and imminent (A star *will come* out of Jacob, Num. 24:17). Since this use is common in the prophetic writings, it is usually called the *prophetic perfect*. It is usually translated into English as either a present or future tense verb.

Finally, when the perfect occurs with the vav conjunctive prefixed, it is usually translated in the future tense (*I will lie down* with my fathers, Gen. 47:30).

2. *Imperfect.* This tense indicates an incomplete action or state. Perhaps the most common use of the imperfect is to describe a simple action in future time (*he will reign* over you). The imperfect is also used to express habitual or customary actions in the past, present or future (And so *he did* year by year, 1 Sam. 1:7; A son *honors* his father, Mal. 1:6; The LORD *will reign* forever and ever, Exo. 15:18). The imperfect frequently expresses contingency, and English modal auxiliaries such as *may, can, shall, might, could, should, would* and *perhaps* are used with the verb (Who is the LORD that I *should obey* his voice?, Exo. 5:2).

The modal use of the imperfect is common after the particles אֵיךְ (how) and אוּלַי (perhaps), and the interrogatives מַה (what), מִי (who) and לָמָה (why). Two other uses of the imperfect are the *jussive* and *cohortative*.

The jussive expresses a desire for action from a third person subject (I pray *let* the king *remember* the LORD your God, 2 Sam. 14:11;

May the LORD *lift up* his countenance unto you, Num. 6:26). The cohortative expresses the speaker's desire or intention to act, so it occurs only in the first person singular and plural (*let me pass* through the roadblock, *let us draw near* to God).

3. *Imperative.* This tense occurs only in the second person singular and plural. The main use of the imperative is in direct commands (*Separate yourself* from me, Gen. 13:9). The imperative can also grant permission (*Go up,* and *bury* your father, according as he made you swear, Gen. 50:6). It may also disclose a request (*Give* them, I pray, a talent of silver, 2 Ki. 5:22).

Imperatives may convey a wish (*May you be* the mother of thousands of millions, Gen. 24:60).

Imperatives are even used sarcastically (Come to Bethel and *transgress*, Amos 4:4).

Some uses of the imperative, however, do not carry the ordinary force of meaning. Sometimes it emphatically and vividly communicates a promise or prediction (And in the third year *sow* and *reap*, *plant* vineyards and *eat* the fruits thereof, 2 Ki. 19:29).

4. *Infinitive.* The infinitive occurs in either the absolute or the construct state. Infinitives express the idea of a verb, but they are not limited by person, gender and number.

The infinitive absolute is used in several ways. It most often stands before a finite verb of the same root to intensify the certainty or force of the verbal idea (You shall *surely* die, Gen. 2:17). It also functions as a verbal noun (*slaying* cattle and *killing* sheep, Isa. 22:13; It is not good *to eat* much honey, Prov. 25:27).

Appendices

The infinitive absolute sometimes occurs after an imperative (Kill me *at once*, Num. 11:15; Listen *diligently* to me, Isa. 55:2). It may also occur after a verb to show continuance or repetition (*Keep on* hearing but do not understand, Isa. 6:9; and it went *here and there*, Gen. 8:7). Frequently, it is used in place of an imperative (*Remember[ing]* the Sabbath day, Exo. 20:8). Sometimes it is used in place of a finite verb (and he *made* him ruler over all the land of Egypt, Gen. 41:43).

The infinitive construct also has several uses. It may function as the object or subject of a sentence (I know not how *to go out* or *come in*, 1 Ki. 3:7; *to obey* is better than sacrifice, 1 Sam. 15:22). However, it most often occurs after the subject to express purpose (he turned aside *to see*, Exo. 3:4). The infinitive construct may also occur after a finite verb to express a gerundial meaning (The people sin against the LORD *by eating* blood, 1 Sam. 14:33). Moreover, it is frequently used in temporal clauses (*When you eat* from it, you shall surely die, Gen. 2:17).

5. *Participle.* This tense in the Hebrew does not indicate person, but it does indicate gender and number. It may be either masculine or feminine, and either singular or plural. Participles may also occur in either the active or passive voice. However, only the Qal stem has both active and passive participles. Verbal tense is not indicated by the Hebrew participle, so it must be inferred from the context, whether it is *past*, *present* or *future* tense. Uses of the participle include the following.

Since it is a verbal noun, a participle may indicate a continuous activity or state (I saw also the LORD *sitting* upon a throne, Isa. 6:1). Participles may also be used as attributive or predicative adjectives. As an attributive adjective, it follows the noun it modifies, and it agrees with the noun in gender, number and definiteness (blessed is *he who comes* in the name of the LORD, Ps. 118:26; the glory of the LORD was like a *devouring* fire, Exo. 24:17).

As a predicative adjective, the participle follows the noun it modifies and agrees with the noun in gender and number, but it never has the definite article (the man is *standing*, the women are *standing*). When the noun is indefinite, the participle may be attributive or predicative, so context must determine the correct translation. Participles are also used as substantives (one who climbs, *climber*; one who works, *worker*; one who loves, *lover*).

Person, Gender, and Number (third position)

Person—whether the verb is *first person* (I, we), *second person* (you) or *third person* (he, she, it, they).

Gender—whether the verb is *masculine, feminine* or *common*.

Number—whether the verb is *singular* or *plural* (Infinitives are only indicated as construct or absolute. Participles are indicated as active or passive, masculine or feminine and singular or plural).

Verb Identification Chart

Following is the verb identification chart used in this volume, for the three digits following the decimal of every verb. This pattern follows the usual verb chart found in Hebrew grammars.

First numeral after decimal:

1. Qal
2. Niphal
3. Piel
4. Pual
5. Hiphil
6. Hophal
7. Hithpael

Second numeral after decimal:

1. Perfect
2. Imperfect
3. Imperative
4. Infinitive
5. Participle

Third numeral after decimal:

Perfect	Imperfect	Imperative	Infinitive	Participle
1. 3ms	3ms	2ms	construct	active ms
2. 3fs	3fs	2fs	absolute	active mp
3. 2ms	2ms	2mp		active fs
4. 2fs	2fs	2fp		active fp
5. 1cs	1cs			passive ms
6. 3cp	3mp			passive mp
7. 2mp	3fp			passive fs
8. 2fp	2mp			passive fp
9. 1cp	2fp			
0.	1cp			

Grammatical Abbreviations*:

abs=absolute; act=active; adj=adjective; adv=adverb; art=article; c=common (neither masculine, nor feminine); cj=conjunction; con=construct (genitival); d=dual; dem pron=demonstrative pronoun; do=direct object; f=feminine; impf=imperfect; impv=imperative; inf=infinitive; intrg=interrogative; intrg part=interrogative particle; intrj=interjection; juss=jussive (optative); m=masculine; n=noun; neg part=negative particle; num=number; p=plural; part=particle; pass=passive; pers pron=personal pronoun; pf=perfect; pn=proper noun; prep=preposition; ps=pronominal suffix; ptc=participle; rel part=relative particle; rel pron=relative pronoun; s=singular; sub=substantive; v=verb; 1=1st person; 2=2nd person; 3=3rd person.

*construct relationships are shown by italicizing.

485

Appendices

APPENDIX B

Translations of the Various Versions

In order to provide the reader with a sample representation of many versions of the Old Testament, the following versions are compared with the King James Version. These versions are used as much as needed to illustrate various shades of meaning and main differences among the translations. All of the material could not be included. Rather, the best representation of the thirty-seven versions listed below has been used.

Abbreviation:	Translation:
Anchor	Anchor Bible Commentaries
ASV	American Standard Version
BB	Dutton's Basic Bible
Beck	An American Translation
Berkeley	Berkeley's Version in Modern English
CEV	Contemporary English Version
Darby	Darby's The Holy Scripture
Douay	The Douay Version
Fenton	Fenton's Holy Bible
Geneva	Geneva Bible
Good News	Good News, The Bible in Today's English
Goodspeed	The Bible, An American Translation by Edgar Goodspeed
GW	God's Word
JB	The Jerusalem Bible
KJVII	King James Version II
Knox	The Holy Bible
LIVB	Living Bible
MAST	The Holy Scriptures According to the Masoretic Text
MLB	Modern Language Bible
Moffatt	A New Translation of the Bible
MRB	The Modern Readers Bible
NAB	New American Bible
NASB	New American Standard Bible
NCV	New Century Version
NEB	New English Bible
NIV	New International Version
NKJV	New King James Version
NLT	The New Living Translation
NRSV	New Revised Standard Version
Phillips	The Old Testament in Modern English
REB	Revised English Bible
Rotherham	Rotherham's Emphasized Bible
RSV	Revised Standard Version
Torah	A New Translation of the Holy Scriptures According to the Traditional Hebrew Text
Tyndale	Tyndale's Old Testament
WEB	The Webster Bible (1833)
Young	Young's Literal Translation

APPENDIX C

Books of the Old and New Testaments and the Apocrypha

Old Testament

Genesis
Exodus
Leviticus
Numbers
Deuteronomy
Joshua
Judges
Ruth
1 Samuel
2 Samuel
1 Kings
2 Kings
1 Chronicles
2 Chronicles
Ezra
Nehemiah
Esther
Job
Psalms
Proverbs
Ecclesiastes
Song of Songs
Isaiah
Jeremiah
Lamentations
Ezekiel
Daniel
Hosea
Joel
Amos
Obadiah
Jonah
Micah
Nahum
Habakkuk
Zephaniah
Haggai
Zechariah
Malachi

New Testament

Matthew
Mark
Luke
John
Acts
Romans
1 Corinthians
2 Corinthians
Galatians
Ephesians
Philippians
Colossians
1 Thessalonians
2 Thessalonians
1 Timothy
2 Timothy
Titus
Philemon
Hebrews
James
1 Peter
2 Peter
1 John
2 John
3 John
Jude
Revelation

Books of the Apocrypha

1 & 2 Esdras
Tobit
Judith
Additions to Esther
Wisdom of Solomon
Ecclesiasticus of the Wisdom of Jesus Son of Sirach
Baruch
Prayer of Azariah and the Song of the Three Holy Children
Susanna
Bel and the Dragon
The Prayer of Manasses
Maccabees 1–4

Appendices

APPENDIX D

How the Old Testament Came to Us

The Hebrew canon was written over a period of about 1000 years (1450–400 B.C.). These books were considered inspired and therefore canonical from the time they were written. The word *canon* means a "straight edge," "rod" or "ruler." It came to mean "the rule" or "the standard" of divine inspiration and authority. The only true test of canonicity is the testimony of God regarding the authority of his own Word.

Protestants and Jews have always agreed to a standard 39 books of the Old Testament as canonical, although the Jews have divided them differently to form 22, 24 or 36 books. The Roman Catholic Church, since the Council of Trent in A.D. 1546, also accepts seven books of the Apocrypha (Tobit, Judith, Wisdom, Ecclesiasticus, Baruch, 1 and 2 Maccabees, and some additions to the books of Esther and Daniel) as canonical.

We no longer have access to the infallible original manuscripts (called "the autographs") of the Hebrew Scriptures. The earliest manuscripts in some cases are a thousand years removed from the original writing. However, they constitute our primary authority as to the inspired Word of God, and all copies and orthodox translations are dependent upon the best and earliest Hebrew and Aramaic manuscripts. We must review all written evidence upon which our modern editions of the Hebrew Bible are based and have some knowledge of the wide range of evidence with which Old Testament textual criticism deals.

Hebrew texts take priority in value, since God's revelation came first to Israel in the Hebrew tongue. Moreover, in the instances where very early manuscripts have been found, divine guidance is evident in the extreme accuracy of the copies.

Liberal scholars consider only the human side of the equation, thereby rejecting inspiration. From a nearly spiritually dead European church came the school of theology which developed a theory on the development of the Biblical text known as Documentary Hypothesis. Due, in particular, to the development of deistic philosophy and evolutionary science, the stage was set for literary and redaction criticism of the Bible and the rejection of the supernatural.

As a precursor, however, the humanistic philosophies developed during the Age of Enlightenment made their way into the churches of Europe, sadly producing a spiritual deadness. Consequently, every area of academics was affected, producing an antireligious stupefaction upon the milieu of the scholarly world.

With regard to the Pentateuch, the most famous of these theories is known as JEDP. Julius Wellhausen is perhaps the most famous proponent of this theory publishing his version in the 1800s.

The Documentary Hypothesis method of document analysis was used on the works of Homer, Horace and Shakespeare, as well as on works purported to have been written by them. However, it was eventually used only to attack the validity and reliability of the Bible. The "J" document is titled as such because of the use of *Yahweh* (sometimes called Jehovah), and the "E" document is titled as such because of the use of *Elohim* for God. Whether God's name or title is used, it is speculated, determines whether that section of the first Books of the Pentateuch is from the "J" or the "E" document. It is theorized that if the entire Pentateuch were written by one person, only one name would be used for God. The dozens of etymological unifying elements threaded throughout the Pentateuch are simply ignored. The "D" document is considered a *deuteronomic work*, and the "P" document is considered primarily a *priestly editorial*. Dates of these documents are set at 950 B.C. for J, 850 B.C. for E, 625 B.C. for D and 450 B.C. for P. The first five Books of the Bible, known for millennia as the Books of Moses, are viewed by JEDP theorists as four documents written over hundreds of years instead of one document written by Moses, as the Bible itself claims.

The major assumptions of the Documentary Hypothesis are (1) the guideline of divine names (Yahweh and Elohim) as evidence of diverse authorship; (2) the origin of J, E and P as separate documents, written at different periods of time; (3) the separate origin of E as distinct from J and compared prior to J; and (4) the origin of D in the reign of Josiah (621 B.C.). As referred to above, the essential purpose of the JEDP theory was to discount the miraculous and the prophetical. However, with the discovery of the Dead Sea Scrolls, this theory has been thoroughly disproven to the point that no Bible scholar who understands the Bible to be inspired can possibly subscribe to such a theory.

With regard to Isaiah, two or three separate writers are usually proposed; but theories range all the way up to nine. Once again, the so-called stylistic differences noted are merely a pretext for discounting the miraculous and the prophetical.

The Dead Sea Scrolls have clearly pointed to the unity of the Old Testament, particularly with regard to the Pentateuch and Isaiah. Moreover, the unity of each Book defends the miracles and prophecies of the Bible as genuine and thoroughly accurate.

Appendices

APPENDIX E

Manuscripts

The Masoretic Text

The Masoretic Text (MT) was developed A.D. 500–950, and it gave the final form to the Old Testament. It preserved in writing the oral tradition (*masorah*) concerning correct vowels and accents, and the number of occurrences of rare words of unusual spellings.

Vowel Pointing of YHWH

Due to Jewish fears of bringing upon themselves possible retribution for breaking the third commandment, they began refusing to pronounce the divine name. This began in Nehemiah's time. It became the normal practice to substitute the title "Lord" (*adonai*) for the name Yahweh when reading aloud. The Masoretes, to indicate this replacement, inserted the vowels from *Adonai* under the consonants of YaHWeH, resulting in the word YeHoWaH, which came to be pronounced as *Jehovah*. Scholars of the Renaissance period misunderstood the purpose of this vowel pointing and began pronouncing the name as *Jehovah*, rather than pronouncing the name *Yahweh* or the title *Adonai*. This erroneous pronunciation became so common that many are still generally unwilling to accept the more correct pronunciation, Yahweh.

Qere Kethib

The terms are used to refer to textual variants that are understood, though not written. The word *qere* means "what is read," and the word *kethib* means "what is written." (Hence, "read

for what is written.") One classic example of a *qere kethib* is mentioned in the preceding paragraph. Although the text has *written* Yahweh, Adonai is *read,* the hearers understanding what was meant by the reader. *Qere kethibs* were marginal notes written to the side of the manuscript.

The Masoretes

The Masoretes deserve much credit for their painstaking care in preserving the consonantal text that was entrusted to them. They devoted greater attention to accurately preserving the Hebrew Scriptures than has ever been given to any ancient literature in human history. They left the consonantal text exactly as it was given to them, refusing to make even the most obvious corrections. The work of the Masoretes has preserved for us a text which essentially duplicates the text considered authoritative at the time of Christ. Moreover, the Qumran evidence is that we have a Hebrew text with a true record of God's revelation.

The Major Codices

1. British Museum Oriental 4445—a copy of the Pentateuch consonantal text (A.D. 850), vowel points added one century later, most of Genesis and Deuteronomy missing.

2. Codex Cairensus (C)—former prophets and latter prophets, copied by Aaron ben Asher (A.D. 895).

3. Leningrad MS—latter prophets (A.D. 916).

4. Leningrad MS B-19A—entire Old Testament, contains Ben Asher Masoretic Text (A.D. 1010), faithful copy of A.D. 980 MS (since lost), basis for Kittel's *Biblia Hebraica* (3rd edition and subsequent editions).

5. Samaritan Pentateuch—earliest MSS of this version is still in Nablus, withheld by Samaritan sectarians from publication, about 6,000 variants from MT (mostly spelling differences), contains biased sectarian insertions, no MS of the Samaritan Pentateuch known to be older than tenth century A.D.

6. Bologna Edition of the Psalter—A.D. 1477.

7. Soncino Edition of the Old Testament—(vowel-pointed) A.D. 1488.

8. Second Bomberg Edition of the Old Testament—(A.D. 1525–26) printed under the patronage of Daniel Bomberg, became basis for all modern editions up to 1929; contains text of Jacob ben Chayim, with Masorah and Rabbinical notes.

The Qumran Manuscripts

The Qumran manuscripts, or Dead Sea Scrolls, were discovered in a series of caves near the canyon of Wadi Qumran, along the northwest coast of the Dead Sea.

Technical identification of these documents consists of: (1) a number specifying which of the caves was the scene of the discovery of the document, (2) an abbreviation of the name of the book itself and (3) a superscript letter indicating the order in which the manuscript came to light, as opposed to other copies of the same book.

Thus, the famous Dead Sea Scroll of Isaiah is labeled 1 QIsa, meaning that it was the first discovered, or most important, manuscript of Isaiah found in Cave 1 at Wadi Qumran. This particular discovery severely damaged any theories of multiple authorship. The following is a list of the most important finds at Wadi Qumran.

1. Dead Sea Scroll of Isaiah (1QIsa)—(150-100 B.C.) entire sixty-six chapters, same family of MS as MT.

2. Habakkuk Commentary (1QpHb)—(100-50 B.C.) chapters one and two only, with commentary notes between verses; commentary is usually concerned with how each verse is fulfilled in recent (Hasmonean) history and current events.

3. Hebrew University Isaiah Scroll (1QIsb)—(copied ca. 50 B.C.) substantial portions of chapters 41–66, closer to MT than 1QIsa is.

4. 1Q Leviticus fragments—(fourth or second century B.C.) a few verses each of chapters 19–22, written in paleo-Hebrew script.

5. 4Q Deuteronomy-B—32:41–43, written in hemistichs as poetry, not as prose, no date suggested.

6. 4Q Samuel-A—1 Samuel 1, 2, twenty-seven fragments (first century B.C.).

7. 4Q Samuel-B—1 Samuel 16, 19, 21, 23 (225 B.C. or earlier).

8. 4Q Jeremiah-A (no date suggested).

9. 4Q XII-A (XII signifies a MS of the minor prophets)—(third century B.C.) cursive script.

10. 4Q Qoha—(second century B.C.) cursive text of Ecclesiastes, derived from a source that is at least third century B.C. or earlier.

11. 4Q Exodus—a fragment of chapter 1.

12. 4Q Exodus—portions of chapters 7, 29, 30, 32 (and perhaps others), written in paleo-Hebrew script.

Appendices

13. 4Q Numbers—written in square Hebrew with Samaritan type expansions (after 27:33 there is an insert derived from Deuteronomy 3:21).

14. 4Q Deuteronomy-A—chapter 32 (Song of Moses).

15. 11Q Psalms—a manuscript of Psalms from cave 11, copied in formal bookhand style of the Herodian period, the bottom third of each page has been lost, thirty-three Psalms are preserved with fragments containing portions of four others, Psalms represented are 93, 101–103, 105, 109, 118, 119, 121–130, 132–146, 148–150, and 151 from the LXX.

16. Nash Papyrus—(100–50 B.C.) contains the Decalogue and the Shema (Exo. 20:1–17 and Deut. 6:4–9), purchased by W. L. Nash from an Egyptian antique dealer.

The Aramaic Targums

The word Targum means "interpretation," and these documents became necessary because the Hebrew people lost touch with their ancestral Hebrew during the Babylonian exile and Persian empire period. First there was a need for an interpreter in the synagogue services, and later the interpretations were written down. However, there is no evidence of a written Targum until about A.D. 200. Because their primary purpose was for interpretation, they have limited value for textual criticism. Following is a list of several targums:

1. The Targum of Onkelos on the Torah—(ca. third century A.D.) produced by Jewish scholars in Babylon. Traditionally assigned to a certain Onkelos, supposedly a native of Pontus. It is not quoted by extant Palestinian sources earlier than A.D. 1000.

2. The Targum of Jonathan ben Uzziel on the Prophets section (i.e., Joshua–Kings, Isaiah–Malachi)—(fourth century A.D.) composed in Babylonian circles. Far more free in its rendering of the Hebrew text than in Onkelos.

3. The Targum of Pseudo-Jonathan on the Torah—(ca. A.D. 650) a mixture of Onkelos and Midrashic materials.

4. The Jerusalem Targum on the Torah—(ca. A.D. 700).

The Septuagint (LXX)

This is the Greek translation of the Hebrew Old Testament. It was translated for Greek-speaking Jews who knew no Hebrew. It is called the LXX because it was said to have been translated by seventy, or more accurately seventy-two, Jewish scholars. This was the common Bible of New Testament times, and it is quoted frequently in the New Testament. However, Matthew and the author of Hebrews follow a text that is closer to the MT. We must remember that the Septuagint is a translation of inspired Scripture, not the original or even a copy of the original. As such, it is subject to error as is any other translation.

It should also be noted, however, that the translators of the Septuagint were highly skilled to translate an accurate Greek Old Testament that could be depended upon by the New Testament writers for quotations and by early Christians for use. When all of the Greek manuscripts are compared with the Hebrew manuscripts, a rather high degree of textual certainty exists in spite of some difficulties.

Bibliography

Aharoni, Yohanan. *The Archeology of the Land of Israel: From the Pre-historic Beginnings to the End of the First Temple Period.* Translated by Anson F. Rainey. Philadelphia: The Westminster Press, 1982.

Aharoni, Yohanan. *The Land of the Bible: A Historical Geography*, rev. Philadelphia: The Westminster Press, 1979.

Aharoni, Yohanan, Michael Avi-yonah, Anson F. Rainey, and Ze'ev Safrai. *The Macmillan Bible Atlas*, rev. 3rd ed. New York: Macmillan Publishing Co., 1993.

Albright, W. F. "Chronology," Bulletin of the American Schools of Oriental Research, 100 (1945), 16–22.

Allis, Oswald T. *The Old Testament: Its Claims and its Critics.* Philadelphia: Presbyterian and Reformed Publishing Company, 1972.

Amerding, Carl E. *The Old Testament and Criticism.* Grand Rapids, MI: William B. Eerdmans Publishing Company, 1984.

Archer, Gleason L. *Encyclopedia of Bible Difficulties.* Grand Rapids, MI: Zondervan Publishing House, 1982.

Archer, Gleason L. *A Survey of Old Testament Introduction*, rev. ed. Chicago: Moody Press, 1994.

Barker, Kenneth, gen. ed. *The NIV Study Bible: New International Version.* Grand Rapids, MI: Zondervan Bible Publishers, 1985.

Beitzel, Barry J. *The Moody Atlas of Bible Lands.* Chicago: Moody Press, 1985.

Blaikie, D. D. *The Expositor's Bible. 2 Samuel.* New York: A. C. Armstrong & Son, 1890. [Adapted for 2 Samuel Commentary.]

Blaiklock, Edward M. and R. H. Harrison, eds. *The New International Dictionary of Biblical Archeology.* Grand Rapids, MI: Zondervan Publishing House, 1983.

Bridges, Charles. *A Commentary on Ecclesiastes.* Great Britain: Billing & Sons Ltd., Worcester, 1860. [Adapted for Ecclesiastes Commentary.]

Bromiley, Geoffrey W., ed. *The International Standard Bible Encyclopedia,* 4 vols. Grand Rapids, MI: William B. Eerdmans Publishing Company, 1979.

Brown, Francis, S.R. Driver, Charles A. Briggs. *The New Brown-Driver-Briggs-Gesenius Hebrew and English Lexicon.* Peabody, MA: Hendrickson Publishers, 1979.

Cook, F. C., ed. *The Bible Commentary,* 10 vols. Grand Rapids: MI: Baker Book House, 1981. Reprinted from the edition published by Charles Scribner's Sons, New York, 1871–1881 under the title, *The Holy Bible ... with an Explanatory and Critical Commentary ....*

Craigie, Peter C. *Ugarit and the Old Testament*. Grand Rapids, MI: William B. Eerdmans Publishing Company, 1985.

Davis, John D. *The Westminster Dictionary of the Bible*, rev. by Henry Snyder Gehman. Philadelphia: The Westminster Press, 1944.

Dillard, Raymond B. *An Introduction to the Old Testament*. Grand Rapids, MI: Zondervan Publishing House, 1994.

Douglas, J. D., ed. *New Bible Dictionary*. 2d Edition. Wheaton, IL: Tyndale House Publishers, Inc., 1973.

Eissfedlt, Otto. *The Old Testament, an Introduction*. Translated by Ackroyd. New York: Harper, 1965.

Even-Shoshan, Abraham, ed. *A New Concordance of the Old Testament Using the Hebrew and Aramaic Text*. Grand Rapids, MI: Baker Book House, 1990.

Finegan, Jack. *Light from the Ancient Past: The Archaeological Background of Judaism and Christianity*, 2nd ed. Princeton: Princeton University Press, 1959.

Freedman, David N. *Pottery, Poetry, and Prophecy*. Winona Lake, IN: Eisenbrauns, 1980.

Freedman, Noel David, ed. *The Anchor Bible Dictionary*, 6 vols. New York: Doubleday, 1992.

Gaebelein, Frank E., gen. ed. *The Expositor's Bible Commentary*, 12 vols. John H. Sailhamer, Walter C. Kaiser, Jr., R. Laird Harris, Ronald B. Allen. Grand Rapids, MI: Zondervan Publishing House, 1990.

Gottwald, Norman K. *The Hebrew Bible—a Socio-Literary Introduction*. Philadelphia: Fortress Press, 1985.

Harris, R. Laird. *Inspiration and Canonicity of the Bible*. Grand Rapids, MI: Zondervan Publishing House, 1957.

Harris, R. Laird, Gleason L. Archer, Jr. and Bruce K. Waltke, eds. *Theological Wordbook of the Old Testament*, 2 vols. Chicago: Moody Press, 1980.

Harrison, R. K., B. K. Waltke, D. Guthrie, G. D. Fee. *Biblical Criticism: Historical, Literary and Textual*. Grand Rapids, MI: Zondervan Publishing House, 1980.

Harrison, R. K. *Old Testament Times*. Grand Rapids, MI: William B. Eerdmans Publishing Company, 1970.

Holladay, William L. *A Concise Hebrew and Aramaic Lexicon of the Old Testament*. Grand Rapids, MI: William B. Eerdmans Publishing Company, 1971.

Horton, Stanley M., ed. *Systematic Theology*. Springfield, MO: Logion Press, 1994.

Bibliography

Humphreys, W. Lee. *Crisis and Story: An Introduction to the Old Testament*. Mountain View, CA: Mayfield Publishing Co., 1990.

Howard, David M., Jr. *An Introduction to the Old Testament Historical Books*. Chicago: Moody Press, Inc., 1993.

Jennings, F. C. *Studies in Isaiah*. Neptune, NJ: Loizeaux Brothers, 1935, 1970.

Johns, Alger F. *A Short Grammar of Biblical Aramaic*. Berrien Springs, MI: Andrews University Press, 1963.

Kaiser, Walter C., Jr. *Toward an Old Testament Theology*. Grand Rapids, MI: Acadamie Books, 1978.

Kautzch, E. and A. E. Cowley, eds. *Gesenius' Hebrew Grammar*. Oxford: Clarendon Press, 1910.

Keil, C. F. and F. Delitzsch. *Commentary on the Old Testament*. Translated by James Martin. Peabody, MA: Hendrickson Publishers, 1989.

Keller, Werner. *The Bible as History*, 2nd rev. ed. Translated by William Neil and B. H. Rasmussen. New York: Bantam Books, 1982.

Kelley, Page H. *Biblical Hebrew: An Introductory Grammar*. Grand Rapids, MI: William B. Eerdmans Publishing Company, 1992.

Kitchen, K. A. *The Bible in its World: The Bible and Archaeology Today*. Exeter: Paternoster Press, 1977.

Koehler, Ludwig and Walter Baumgartner. *The Hebrew and Aramaic Lexicon of the Old Testament*, 4 vols. Leiden, Netherlands: E. J. Brill, 1994.

Lasor, William Sanford, David Allan Hubbard, Frederic William Bush. *Old Testament Survey: The Message, Form, and Background of The Old Testament*. Grand Rapids, MI: William B. Eerdmans Publishing Company, 1992.

LaSor, William, David Allan Hubbard, and Frederic William Bush. *Old Testament Survey: The Message, Form, and Background of The Old Testament*. 2nd ed. Grand Rapids, MI: William B. Eerdmans Publishing Co., 1996.

Leupold, H. C. *Exposition of The Psalms*. Grand Rapids, MI: Baker Book House, 1969.

Lewis, C. S. *Reflections on the Psalms*. London: Geoffrey Bles, 1958.

Luckenbill, D. D. *Ancient Records of Assyria and Babylonia*, 2 vols. Chicago: The University of Chicago Press, 1926–1927.

Martens, Elmer A. *God's Design: A Focus on Old Testament Theology*. Grand Rapids, MI: Baker Book House, 1986.

Mays, James L. *Psalms*. (Interpretation). Louisville: John Knox Press, 1994.

Merrill, Eugene H. *An Historical Survey of the Old Testament.* Nutley, NJ: The Craig Press, 1966.

Merrill, Eugene H. *Kingdom of Priests: A History of Old Testament Israel.* Grand Rapids, MI: Baker Book House, 1996.

Miller, J. Maxwell and John H. Hayes. *A History of Ancient Israel and Judah.* Philadelphia: The Westminster Press, 1986.

New Interpreter's Bible. Nashville, TN: Abingdon Press, 1994.

Owens, John Joseph. *Analytical Key to the Old Testament*, 4 vols. Grand Rapids, MI: Baker Book House, 1990.

Payne, J. Barton. *The Theology of the Older Testament.* Grand Rapids, MI: Academie Books, 1962.

Petersen, David L., Kent Harold Richards. *Interpreting Hebrew Poetry.* Minneapolis: Fortress Press, 1992.

Pfeiffer, Charles F., ed. *Baker's Bible Atlas.* Grand Rapids, MI: Baker Book House, 1961.

Pfeiffer, Charles F. *Old Testament History.* Grand Rapids, MI: Baker Book House, 1987.

Pfeiffer, Charles F., Howard F. Vos, and John Rea, eds. *Wycliffe Bible Encyclopedia*, 2 vols. Chicago: Moody Press, 1975.

Pritchard, James B., ed. *The Ancient Near East: An Anthology of Texts and Pictures*, vol. 1. Princeton: Princeton University Press, 1973.

Purkiser, W. T., ed. *Exploring the Old Testament.* Kansas City, MO: Beacon Hill Press, 1955.

Rahlfs, Alfred, ed. *Septuaginta.* Stuttgart, Germany: Deutsche Bibelgesellschaft Stuttgart, 1935.

Rogerson, John and Philip Davies. *The Old Testament World.* Englewood Cliffs, NJ: Prentice-Hall, 1989.

Schoville, Keith N. *Biblical Archaeology in Focus.* Grand Rapids, MI: Baker Book House, 1982.

Schultz, Samuel J. *The Old Testament Speaks.* New York: Harper & Brothers, Publishers, 1960.

Seow, Choon Leong. *A Grammar for Biblical Hebrew.* Nashville, TN: Abingdon Press, 1987.

Shanks, Hershel, ed. Ancient Israel: *A Short History from Abraham to the Roman Destruction of the Temple.* Englewood Cliffs, NJ: Prentice-Hall, 1988.

Smith, George Adam. *The Historical Geography of the Holy Land.* London: Hodder and Stoughton, 1931.

Soulen, Richard N. *Handbook of Biblical Criticism.* Atlanta: John Knox Press, 1978.

Bibliography

Stuart, Douglas K. *Studies in early Hebrew meter.* Missoula, MT: Scholars Press, 1976.

Tyndale Old Testament Commentary, Downers Grove, IL: InterVarsity, 1925–.

Van Der Woude, A. S., ed. *The World of the Old Testament.* Translated by Sierd Woudstra. Grand Rapids, MI: William B. Eerdmans Publishing Company, 1989.

Waltke, Bruce K. and M. O'Connor. *An Introduction to Biblical Hebrew Syntax.* Winona Lake, IN: Eisenbrauns, 1990.

Watts, John D. W. *The Word Biblical Commentary on the Old Testament,* 34 vols. Waco, TX: Word Books, 1987.

Watts, J. Wash. *Old Testament Teaching.* Nashville, TN: Broadman Press, 1967.

Whiston, William, trans. *The Works of Josephus.* Peabody, MA: Hendrickson Publishers, Inc., 1995.

White, Wilbert Webster. *Studies in Old Testament Characters.* New York: The Biblical Seminary in New York, 1931.

Yonge, C. D., trans. *The Works of Philo.* Peabody, MA: Hendrickson Publishers, Inc.,1993.